The Federal Government Deficit as a Percentage of GDP, 1970 I-1992 IV

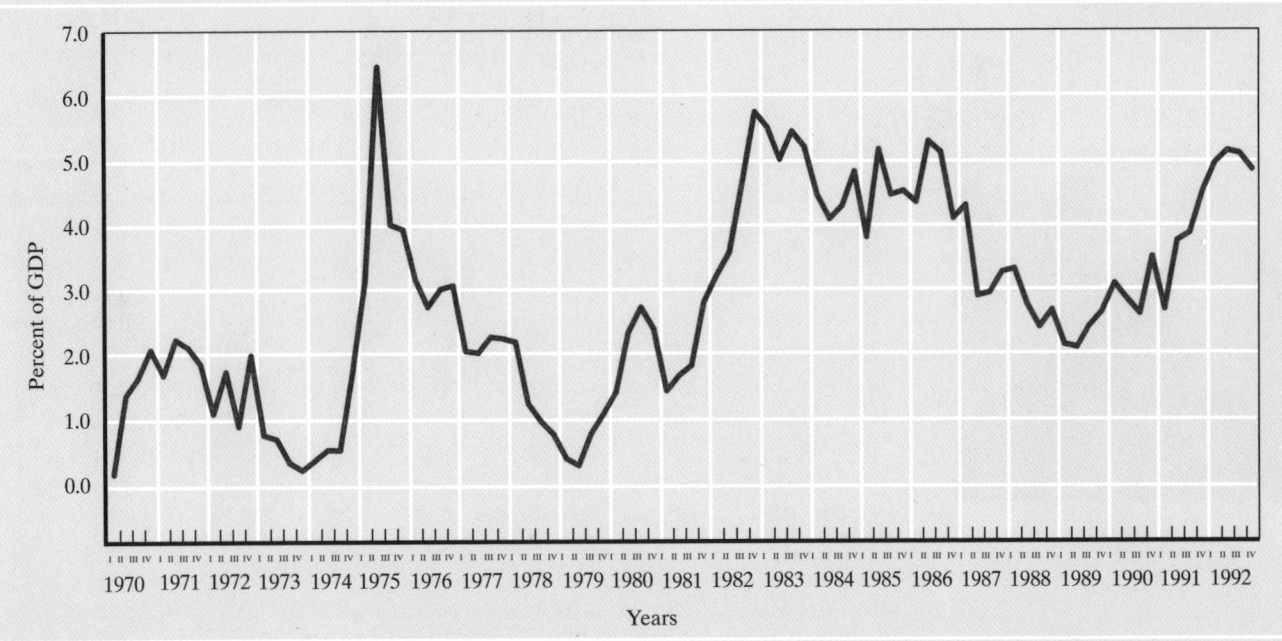

The Federal Government Debt as a Percentage of GDP, 1970 I-1992 IV

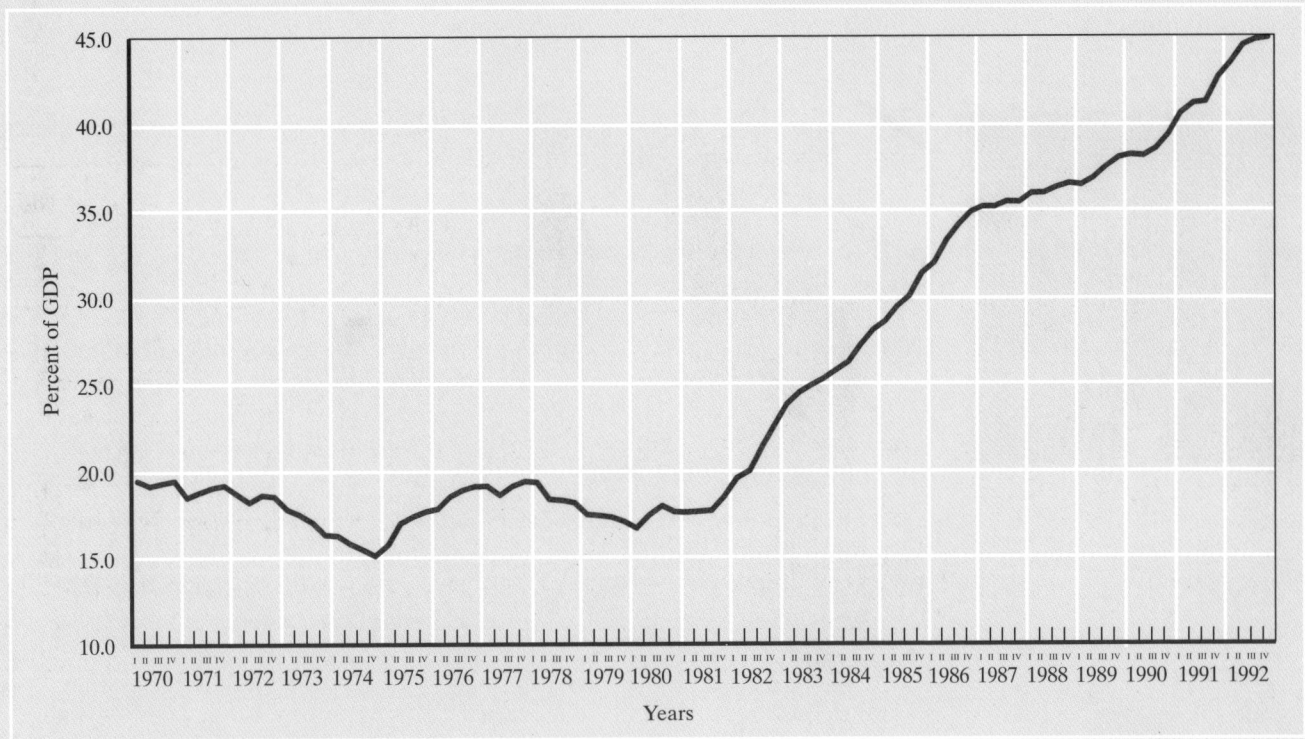

About the Authors

Karl E. Case is the Marion Butler McLean Professor in the History of Ideas and Professor of Economics at Wellesley College. He also lectures on Economics and Tax Policy in the International Tax Program at Harvard Law School and is a Visiting Scholar at the Federal Reserve Bank of Boston. He received his B.A. from Miami University in 1968, spent three years in the army, and received his M.A. and Ph.D. from Harvard University. In 1980 and 1981 he was a Liberal Arts Fellow in Law and Economics at Harvard Law School.

Professor Case's research has been in the areas of public finance, taxation, and housing. He is the author or coauthor of four other books, including *Economics and Tax Policy* and *Property Taxation: The Need for Reform*, as well as numerous articles in professional journals.

For the past 16 years, he has taught at Wellesley, where he was Department Chair from 1982 to 1985. Before coming to Wellesley, he spent two years as Head Tutor (director of undergraduate studies) at Harvard, where he won the Allyn Young Teaching Prize. He has been a member of the AEA's Committee on Economic Education and was Associate Editor of the *Journal of Economic Education*, responsible for the section on innovations in teaching. He teaches at least one section of the principles course every year.

Ray C. Fair is Professor of Economics at Yale University. He is a member of the Cowles Foundation at Yale, a Research Associate of the National Bureau of Economic Research, and a Fellow of the Econometric Society. He received a B.A. in economics from Fresno State College in 1964 and a Ph.D. in economics from M.I.T. in 1968. He taught at Princeton University from 1968 to 1974 and has been at Yale since 1974.

Professor Fair's research has primarily been in the areas of macroeconomics and econometrics, with particular emphasis on macroeconometric model building. He is the author of five other books, including *Specification, Estimation, and Analysis of Macroeconometric Models* (Harvard Press, 1984), and numerous journal articles.

Professor Fair has taught introductory and intermediate economics at Yale. He has also taught graduate courses in macroeconomic theory and macroeconometrics.

Third Edition

PRINCIPLES OF
ECONOMICS

Third Edition

PRINCIPLES OF ECONOMICS

Karl E. Case
Wellesley College

Ray C. Fair
Yale University

Prentice Hall, Inc., Englewood Cliffs, New Jersey 07632

Case, Karl E.
    Principles of Economics / Karl E. Case, Ray C. Fair — 3rd ed.
    p. cm.
    Includes bibliographical references and index.
    ISBN 0-13-095886-7
    1. Economics. I. Fair, Ray C. II. Title.
HB171.5.C3123 1994   93-22584
330—dc20   CIP

Acquisitions Editor: *J. Stephen Dietrich*
Development Manager: *Steven Rigolosi*
Development Editors: *Bob Nirkind* and *Barbara Brooks*
Production Editor: *Mary Cavaliere*
Supplements Development Editors: *David Shea* and *O'Donnell and Associates*
Marketing Manager: *Patti Arneson*
Advertising: *Lori Cowen* and *Ann Marie Dunn*
Art Director: *Patricia Woszczyk*
Interior Design: *Lorraine Mullaney*
Page Layout: *Kerry Reardon* and *John Jordan*
Cover Design: *Patricia Woszczyk*
Cover Illustration: *Theo Rudnak*
Prepress and manufacturing buyers: *Trudy Pisciotti* and *Patrice Fraccio*
Editorial assistants: *Liz Becker* and *Renée Pelletier*
Photo research: *Barbara Scott* and *Melinda Reo*
Editor-in-Chief: *Valerie Ashton*
Managing Editors, Production: *Frances Russello* and *Joyce Turner*

This book was published electronically at the Prentice Hall facility in Englewood Cliffs, NJ.

Photo credits follow index.

 © 1994, 1992, 1989
    by Prentice-Hall, Inc.
    A Paramount Communications Company
    Englewood Cliffs, New Jersey 07632

Printed in the United States of America
10 9 8 7 6 5 4 3

ISBN   0-13-095886-7

Prentice Hall International (UK) Limited, *London.*
Prentice Hall of Australia Pty. Limited, *Sydney*
Prentice Hall Canada Inc., *Toronto*
Prentice Hall Hispanoamericana, S.A., *Mexico*
Prentice Hall of India Private Limited, *New Delhi*
Prentice Hall of Japan, Inc., *Tokyo*
Simon & Schuster Asia Pte. Ltd., *Singapore*
Editora Prentice Hall do Brasil, Ltda., *Rio de Janeiro*

Brief
Table of Contents

v

INTERNATIONAL ECONOMICS 871

Contents

MACROECONOMICS 527

PART FIVE Concepts and Problems in Macroeconomics 529

Preface

With the twenty-first century only a few years away, the pace of economic events in the United States and abroad continues to accelerate. The world has changed significantly since the publication of the second edition of *Principles of Economics* in 1992. The United States elected a new President and has a new tax code. The recession of 1990–1991 turned into a painfully slow recovery. The Soviet Union ceased to exist, dissolving into 15 independent states. Yeltsin's Russia is struggling to transform a socialist system into a market-based economy. After years of stagnation, China has begun to experience rapid growth and inflation. The oil fires in Kuwait are out, and the dramatic events of the Persian Gulf War are almost forgotten as the world struggles with suffering in places like Bosnia and Somalia.

Because events have changed the economic landscape so rapidly, we decided to revise *Principles of Economics* after two years, rather than the usual three. The third edition features many all-new and updated examples relevant to the students of the 1990s. Revising after two years also allowed us to take into account the federal government's reindexation of the national income data from base year 1982 to 1987 and to focus on GDP rather than GNP.

In addition, we continued to receive feedback from colleagues and users of the text. To date, more than 70,000 students and professors have used *Principles of Economics*. In the third edition, we have made every effort to be responsive to our readers' suggestions while maintaining the book's basic focus and pedagogical organization. We have moved material on international trade and comparative advantage to the introductory chapters and have continued to integrate global examples throughout the text. We have worked hard to provide current applications of theory while cutting extraneous material and shortening the text's basic coverage. (The third edition is more than 100 pages shorter then the second edition.) We have also added new problem sets to each chapter and 10 new case studies. The result, we hope, is a principles book that will set the standard for today's students.

THE PLAN OF THE THIRD EDITION

Despite major revisions and new features, the themes of the third edition are the same themes of the first two editions. The purpose of this book is to introduce the discipline of economics and to provide a basic understanding of how economies function. This requires a blend of economic theory, institutional material, and real-world applications. We have tried to maintain a reasonable balance between these ingredients in every chapter in this book. Like the first two editions, the third edition also attempts to present a number of theoretical views in an evenhanded way.

While we have chosen to present microeconomics first, we have designed the text so that professors may proceed directly to macroeconomics after teaching the five introductory chapters.

Microeconomics

Market research and comments from users of the second edition convinced us that the organization of the microeconomic material is pedagogically sound. For this reason, we have not altered the presentation drastically.

The organization of the microeconomic material continues to reflect our belief that the best way to understand how market economies operate—and the best way to understand basic economic theory—is to work through the perfectly competitive model first, including discussions of output *and* input markets and the connections between them, before turning to noncompetitive market structures. When students understand how a simple competitive system works, they can start thinking about how the pieces of the economy "fit together." We think this is a better approach to teaching economics than some of the more traditional approaches, which encourage students to think of economics as a series of disconnected alternative market models.

Doing competition first also allows students to see the power of the market system. It is impossible to discuss the things that markets do well until students have seen how a simple system determines the allocation of resources. This is our purpose in Chapters 6–11. Chapter 12 remains a pivotal chapter that links the world of perfect competition with the imperfect world of noncompetitive markets, externalities, imperfect information, and poverty, all of which we discuss in Chapters 13–17. In Chapters 18–20 students use everything they've learned in Chapters 6–17 to take a closer look at some of the fields of applied microeconomics (the economics of taxation, labor economics, and urban and regional economics).

Macroeconomics

Although we have made a number of changes to the content of the macroeconomic material, we remain committed to the view that it is a mistake simply to throw aggregate demand and supply curves at students in the first few chapters of a principles book. Aggregate demand and supply curves are very complex theoretical constructs—indeed, we encountered debates regarding the aggregate supply curve everywhere we turned. To understand the AS and AD curves, one needs to know about the functioning of the goods market, the money market, and the labor market. The logic behind the simple demand curve is simply wrong when applied to the relationship between aggregate demand and the price level. Similarly, the logic behind the simple supply curve is wrong when applied to the relationship between aggregate supply and the price level.

Part of teaching economics is teaching economic reasoning. Our discipline is built around deductive logic. Once we teach students a pattern of logic, we want and expect them to apply it to new circumstances. When they apply the logic of a simple demand curve or simple supply curve to the aggregate demand or aggregate supply curve, the logic does not fit. We believe the best way to teach the reasoning embodied in the aggregate demand and aggregate supply curves without creating serious confusion is to build up to them carefully.

ORGANIZATION   As in the second edition, the macroeconomic section begins with three introductory chapters (21–23) that introduce students to macroeconomic tools, national income accounting, and inflation and unemployment. These chapters are

followed by two chapters that present the basic functioning of the goods market (Chapters 24 and 25) and two chapters that present the basic functioning of the money market (Chapters 26 and 27). It is in these chapters that students are introduced to the concepts of fiscal and monetary policy. These four chapters are followed by a chapter that brings the two markets together. This chapter, Chapter 28, does in essence a very simplified version of IS/LM analysis verbally. (The IS and LM curves are included in an appendix to Chapter 28 for those instructors who are interested in teaching them.)

Given the groundwork that has been laid in Chapter 28, Chapter 29 proceeds directly to derive the aggregate demand curve and then the aggregate supply curve. The two curves are then put together to determine the aggregate price level and to discuss the various theories of inflation.

Following the development of the AD and AS curves, we turn to a more detailed look at the labor market in Chapter 30 and discuss various theories of unemployment. By the end of Chapter 30, students have put the goods market, the money market, and the labor market together, and they have analyzed inflation, unemployment, and monetary and fiscal policy. Chapter 31 uses the material learned earlier to analyze a number of current macroeconomic issues, including the budget deficit and the defeat of President Bush in 1992.

In Chapter 32, we take a closer look at the behavior of households and firms in the macroeconomy, and in Chapter 33 we use the material in Chapter 32 to analyze further macroeconomic issues. Chapters 32 and 33 have been grouped into an optional part that can be skipped without losing the flow of the material. We close the macro section of the book by looking at some current debates in macroeconomics (Chapter 34) and economic growth (Chapter 35).

CONTENT   In preparing the third edition, we have maintained the two innovations we introduced in the second edition. The first of these is the treatment of aggregate supply. Clearly, there is strong disagreement among economists and across economics textbooks on the exact nature of the aggregate supply curve. All economists agree that if input prices rise at the same rate as output prices, the aggregate supply curve is vertical; firms have no incentive to change output if their costs and revenues change at the same rate. For the AS curve to have a positive slope in the short run, input prices must either be constant or there must be some lag in their adjustment.

Some textbooks assume that input prices are constant when the overall price level changes, essentially treating the aggregate supply curve as if it were the sum of individual market supply curves. This assumption of constant input prices is obviously unrealistic, and in the second edition we changed our description of the short-run *AS* curve to one that assumes some lag in input price adjustment when the overall price level changes. In addition, we clarified and expanded our description of the long-run aggregate supply curve, incorporating the concept of potential GDP.

Second, we continue to distinguish between inflation (a change in the overall price level) and *sustained* inflation (an increase in the overall price level that continues for some period of time). There can be confusion in students' minds as to what inflation is and whether or not it is a purely monetary phenomenon, and we think that this distinction helps to clarify our discussions.

HIGHLIGHTS OF THE THIRD EDITION

Recent Data, Examples, Events, and Topics

Every chart, table, and graph in the book has been revised with the most recent data available. The national income data now focus on GDP rather than GNP, and all data have been revised to base year 1987. In addition, we have integrated topics that have generated a great deal of attention over the last few years—the economics of information, environmental economics, the recession of 1990–1991, the national debt, the defeat of President Bush in 1992, the economics of health care reform, the provisions of the new tax law, and the recent experiences of Russia and Poland, to name just a few.

Increased Coverage of Global Material

We have increased our coverage of international material in several ways. First, we have moved a discussion of comparative advantage and international trade from Chapter 36 to Chapter 2. (We do maintain a chapter on international trade in the International Economics section of the book as well.) Second, we have added many new "Global Perspective" boxes throughout the text. These boxes are designed to illustrate economic logic with global examples and to emphasize today's global economy. Third, we introduce imports and exports into the simple goods market model early in macroeconomics. We do, however, continue to believe that a complete treatment of open-market macroeconomics should not be taught until students have mastered the logic of a simple closed macroeconomy. For this reason, we have chosen to place the "open economy macro" chapter in International Economics, the final section of the book. Finally, we have attempted to integrate international examples directly into the text whenever appropriate. All international examples are marked by a globe icon in the book's table of contents.

Optional Chapters

We have tried to keep uppermost in our minds that time is always tight in a principles course. For this reason, we have made sure that certain chapters can be skipped without losing the flow of the material. In microeconomics, Chapter 11 (on the capital market) can be skipped because Chapter 10 (on input markets in general) covers the basics of the capital market. Similarly, the "topics" chapters in Part Four can be skipped if time is short.

In macroeconomics, Chapters 32–35 are optional. The chapters in the international section, with the exception of Chapter 37, can be taught at any time that the instructor feels is appropriate.

Student Learning Aids

Each chapter begins with a brief overview of what the student has learned in the previous chapter and ends with a brief "look ahead" to the following chapter. To help students study, key terms have been printed in boldface and glossed to the margins. Each chapter ends with a point-by-point summary of the chapter, a list of review terms and concepts (cross-referenced to text page), and a problem set.

Because many believe that economics must be relevant to be interesting, we have created two types of boxes for the third edition. *Global Perspective* boxes provide economic examples from around the world. *Issues and Applications* boxes focus on current events and debates in economics and apply the theory learned in the text to real-world events and situations.

In addition, we have set the major principles of economics off from the text in such a way as to highlight their importance. These highlights flow logically from the preceding text and into the text that follows. Students can use these as a way of reviewing the key points in each chapter to prepare for exams.

Problem Sets

Each chapter and appendix ends with a problem set that asks students to think about what they've learned in the chapter. These problems are not simple memorization questions. Rather, they ask students to perform graphical analysis or to apply economics to a real-world situation or policy decision. Approximately 40% of the problems are new to the third edition. The answers to these problems, as well as additional problem sets, are available in the Instructor's Manual.

Case Studies

The end-of-part case studies introduced in the second edition proved to be quite popular. The third edition features 10 new case studies on topics ranging from the black market for ivory to industrial policy. Each case study is accompanied by a video and questions for analytical thinking. The cases are not simply additional problems, and they are not simple extensions of the text material. They are meant to be applications of some of the *ideas* that the part was designed to teach and are designed to foster critical thinking and "thinking like an economist." They might be used as assignments or for class discussion.

THE TEACHING/LEARNING PACKAGE

Each component of the teaching and learning package has been carefully crafted to ensure that the principles of economics course is a rewarding experience for both instructors and students. All of the supplements have been rewritten for the third edition. In addition, several innovative new supplements are available. To see a sample chapter from each of the ancillaries, ask your sales representative for a Case/Fair supplements sampler.

Study Guides

Two comprehensive study guides, one for microeconomics and one for macroeconomics, have been prepared by Professor Thomas Beveridge of North Carolina State University. These study aids reinforce the textbook and provide students with additional applications and exercises. Each chapter in the study guides corresponds to a chapter in the textbook and contains the following features:

- *Learning Objectives with Summaries and Practice Questions.* A list of learning goals for the chapter, along with a brief summary of the material, helpful study hints, practice questions with solutions, and page references to the text.
- *Tips and Learning Suggestions.* Suggestions to help students grasp the material better and to make more of their study time. This section also points out common errors or potential sources of confusion that arise as students attempt to learn economic principles.
- *Matching Vocabulary.* A brief review of the chapter's important vocabulary.
- *Exercises and Problem Sets.* The tools of graphic analysis are extremely important in the study of economics. This portion of the study guide requires the use of graphic analysis to solve economic problems. It also presents real-world situations and asks students to apply economic theory to their own experiences.
- *True/False and Multiple-Choice Questions.* A series of questions designed to test students' grasp of the material and to help them prepare for exams.
- *Short-Answer and Discussion Questions.* Analytical questions that ask students to think more deeply about economic theory and issues.
- *Solutions.* Complete solutions—not just answers—to all questions in the study guide, complete with page references to the textbook.

Annotated Instructor's Editions with Data Update Request Card

Two instructor's editions have been prepared for the third edition. The AIE for *Principles of Microeconomics* has been prepared by Professor Dereka Rushbrook of Ripon College. The AIE for *Principles of*

Macroeconomics has been prepared by Professor Michael R. Donihue of Colby College. Both are special printings of the text that include marginal annotations divided into seven categories:

- *Theory Applied*
- *Global Example*
- *Suggested Outside Reading*
- *Teaching Note*
- *Student Misconception*
- *For Discussion*
- *FYI*

Both AIEs also include an ABC News video icon to indicate the availability of a video clip on the topic discussed in the text. In addition, the AIEs include a reply card that allows professors to receive free semiannual data updates from the authors and Prentice Hall.

Instructor's Manuals

Two innovative instructor's manuals, both by Professor Marc Lieberman of Vassar College, are available, one for *Principles of Microeconomics* and one for *Principles of Macroeconomics*. The instructor's manuals are the key integrative supplement in the teaching and learning package and have been designed with the *teaching* of economics in mind. Each chapter in the instructor's manuals corresponds to a chapter in the student text and includes suggestions for integrating all of the elements of the teaching/learning package into the classroom. The manuals also include a summary of chapter coverage; lecture suggestions with graphs; additional applications; additional problem sets with solutions; and answers to all end-of-chapter text questions. The manuals have been designed so that instructors can easily xerox and distribute the relevant material in the manual.

Test Item File

A revised, expanded, and comprehensive test bank of approximately 4,500 short-answer/essay, multiple-choice, true/false, and problem set questions has been prepared by Professor Teresa Riley of Youngstown State University. The questions are divided into three levels of difficulty—easy, moderate, and difficult—and

are page-referenced to the text. Problem sets (a series of questions based on a graph or scenario) can contain all three levels. Also included are challenging questions that require students to undertake several steps of reasoning, or to work backwards from effect to cause. A test item file is available for both *Principles of Microeconomics* and *Principles of Macroeconomics*.

New Prentice Hall Test Manager 2.0

The test item file is designed for use with the new version of the Prentice Hall Test Manager, a computerized package that allows users to custom design, save, and generate classroom tests. Available in both 3.5" and 5.25" IBM versions, the test manager also permits professors to edit and add or delete questions from the test item file, to edit existing graphics and create new graphics, and to export files to various word processing programs, including WordPerfect and Microsoft Word. Graphics capability ensures that all graphs included in the test item file can be printed next to the appropriate questions.

For those with limited access to computers or secretarial support, Prentice Hall's Telephone Testing Service allows professors to order customized tests by calling a toll-free telephone number a few days before the test is to be administered. Additional information about the various forms of testing service can be obtained from your Prentice Hall sales representative.

Transparency Resource Package, Transparency Masters, and Electronic Transparencies

There are more than 300 graphs and charts in the combined *Principles of Economics text*. All of these are available as transparency masters. The Transparency Resource Package, prepared by Professor Rhona Free of Eastern Connecticut State University, also includes reproductions of key text graphs on full-color 8 1/2" × 11" acetates for classroom use. In addition, more than 70 sets of additional data (not found in the textbook) and summary diagrams are included as full-color transparencies. These data are drawn from a variety of public and private sources and can be used to supplement lectures or stimulate classroom discussions. The time-series data are also available in electronic format.

A Transparency Resource Package is available for both *Principles of Microeconomics* and *Principles of Macroeconomics*. The package is provided in a three-ring binder, with the transparencies appearing on the right page and their accompanying lecture notes on the left page.

ABC/Prentice Hall Video Library for *Principles of Economics*

ABC News and Prentice Hall have combined their experience in academic publishing and global reporting to provide a comprehensive video ancillary to the third edition. The library contains 35 news clips from the ABC News programs *Nightline*, *World News Tonight*, *Business World*, and *On Business*. Each of the clips has been chosen to illustrate or supplement a specific discussion in the text. The ABC News icon appears in the margin of the Annotated Instructor's Edition to indicate the availability of a video. All the videos are timely or timeless, and many can be used at different points in the course.

ABC News/Prentice Hall Video Guide

A guide for professors providing suggestions for integrating the ABC/PH Video Library into the classroom. In addition to a brief summary and the running time of each clip, the guide (prepared by Professor Steven Tomlinson of the University of Texas at Austin) includes teaching notes, in-class exercises, handouts, and transparency masters that tie the news analysis to economic analysis. The Video Guide is an ideal companion to the Instructor's Manuals.

The *New York Times* "Contemporary View" Program

The *New York Times* and Prentice Hall are sponsoring "Themes of the Times": a program designed to enhance student access to current information of relevance in the classroom.

Through this program, the core subject matter provided in the text is supplemented by a collection of time-sensitive articles from one of the world's most distinguished newspapers, The *New York Times*. These articles demonstrate the vital, ongoing connections between what is learned in the classroom and what is happening in the world around us.

A series of discussion questions to accompany the articles is also available. A new edition of the mini-newspaper is available semiannually. To enjoy the wealth of information of The *New York Times* daily, a reduced subscription rate is available in deliverable areas. For information, call toll-free: 1-800-631-1222.

Software for *Principles of Economics*

Developed for use with the third edition by Professor Julia Friedman of Macalester College and Professor Ray Whitman of the University of the District of Columbia, the Prentice Hall *Principles of Economics* software provides graphical simulations for 16 micro and macro topics. The software allows students to manipulate data and graphs, while the accompanying documentation provides the same data sets and graphs with a series of questions and problems. The package offers professors the opportunity to use a computer package in the classroom and students the opportunity to learn the basics of the most popular spreadsheet programs on the market. A demo disk is included with the supplements sampler; ask your sales representative for a copy.

ACKNOWLEDGMENTS

We are grateful to many people for help on the third edition. As was the case for the second edition, we are most grateful to Steven Rigolosi, Managing Editor of Development for Business and Economics at Prentice Hall, for overseeing the entire project. The quality of the book owes much to his wise guidance. Bob Nirkind and Barbara Brooks were the development editors for this edition, and they made numerous improvements chapter by chapter. Steven Deng proofread the entire manuscript in pages. We also owe much to Stephen Dietrich, Executive Editor for Economics at Prentice Hall, for his help and enthusiasm. He put together a terrific team for the teaching and learning package and worked tirelessly to ensure that everything fits together.

We are greatly indebted to the supplements team for their help in preparing the teaching/learning package that accompanies the text. Specifically, we would like to thank Tom Beveridge, Marc Lieberman, Steve Tomlinson, Teri Riley, Rhona Free, Julia Friedman,

Ray Whitman, Dereka Rushbrook, and Michael Donihue. We'd also like to thank David Shea at Prentice Hall and Carrie O'Donnell of O'Donnell and Associates for their help in managing the development of the supplements. We have benefited enormously from working with this dedicated team of professionals.

For his much-appreciated input into *Principles of Microeconomics*, we'd like to thank Richard DuBoff of Bryn Mawr. And for keeping us aware of the student's perspective, we are grateful to Melissa Lam.

A great deal of credit also goes to the many "behind-the-scenes" people at Prentice Hall who helped us prepare the third edition. We'd like to thank Mary Cavaliere, our production editor (who took over the project at a critical stage of production); Barbara Scott, photo researcher, for her first-class photos; Lorraine Mullaney for her interior design; Pat Wosczyk for cover design and Theo Rudnak for the cover illustration; Deirdre Cavanaugh, market research analyst, for her suggestions and input into the revision; Carol Carter, director of marketing; Lori Cowen and Ann Marie Dunn, advertising manager and copywriter, for their creative flair; John Jordan and Kerry Reardon for rising to the challenge of electronic page composition; and Liz Becker and Renée Pelletier editorial assistants, who helped us in innumerable ways. Special thanks go to Patti Arneson, Senior Marketing Manager, for her devotion to the project through the last two editions.

Last, but not least, the following individuals were of immense help in reviewing all or part of this book and the teaching/learning package in various stages of development:

Lew Abernathy, University of North Texas ■ Jack Adams, University of Maryland ■ Doulas Agbetsiafa, Indiana University at South Bend ■ Sam Alapati, Rutgers University ■ Polly Allen, University of Connecticut ■ Stuart Allen, University of North Carolina at Greensboro ■ Jim Angresano, Hampton-Sydney College ■ Kenneth S. Arakelian, University of Rhode Island ■ Harvey Arnold, Indian River Community College ■ Nick Apergis, Fordham University ■ Kidane Asmeron, Pennsylvania State University ■ James Aylesworth, Lakeland Community College ■ Kari Battaglia, University of North Texas ■ Daniel K. Benjamin, Clemson University ■ William T. Bogart, Case Western Reserve University ■ Bruce Bolnick, Northeastern University ■ G. E. Breger, University of South Carolina ■ Dennis Brennan, William Rainey Harper Junior College ■ David Buffum, College of the Holy Cross ■ Lindsay Caulkins, John Carroll University ■ Atreya Chakraborty, Boston College ■ Harold Christensen, Centenary College ■ Daniel Christiansen, Albion College ■ Samuel Kim-Liang Chuah, Walla Walla College ■ David Colander, Middlebury College ■ Daniel Condon, University of Illinois at Chicago; Moraine Valley Community College ■ David

Cowen, University of Texas at Austin ■ Ronald Crowe, University of Central Florida ■ Michael Donihue, Colby College ■ Robert Driskill, Ohio State University ■ Richard B. DuBoff, Bryn Mawr College ■ Gary Dymski, University of Southern California ■ Jay Egger, Towson State University ■ Noel J. J. Farley, Bryn Mawr College ■ Mosin Farminesh, Temple University ■ Dan Feaster, Miami University of Ohio ■ Susan Feiner, Virginia Commonwealth University ■ Getachew Felleke, Albright College ■ Lois Fenske, South Puget Sound Community College ■ William Field, DePauw University ■ Bill Foeller, State University of New York at Fredonia ■ Roger Nils Folsom, San Jose State University ■ Sean Fraley, College of Mount Saint Joseph ■ N. Galloro, Chabot College ■ Tom Gausman, Northern Illinois University, DeKalb ■ Shirley J. Gedeon, University of Vermont ■ Gary Gigliotti, Rutgers University ■ Lynn Gillette, Texas A&M University ■ Sarah L. Glavin, Boston College ■ Devra Golbe, Hunter College ■ Roger Goldberg, Ohio Northern University ■ Douglas Greenley, Moorhead State University ■ Lisa M. Grobar, California State University at Long Beach ■ Benjamin Gutierrez, Indiana University at Bloomington ■ A. R. Gutowsky, California State University at Sacramento ■ David R. Hakes, University of Missouri at St. Louis ■ Stephen Happel, Arizona State University ■ Mitchell Harwitz, State University of New York at Buffalo ■ David Hoaas, Centenary College ■ Harry Holzer, Michigan State University ■ Bobbie Horn, University of Tulsa ■ John Horowitz, Ball State University ■ Janet Hunt, University of Georgia ■ Fred Inaba, Washington State University ■ Richard Inman, Boston College ■ Shirley Johnson, Vassar College ■ Farhoud Kafi, Babson College ■ R. Kallen, Roosevelt University ■ Arthur E. Kartman, San Diego State University ■ Hirshel Kasper, Oberlin College ■ Bruce Kaufman, Georgia State University ■ Dominique Khactu, The University of North Dakota ■ Phillip King, San Francisco State University ■ Barbara Kneeshaw, Wayne County Community College ■ Barry Kotlove, Elmira College ■ David Kraybill, University of Georgia at Athens ■ Rosung Kwak, University of Texas at Austin ■ Melissa Lam, Wellesley College ■ Jim Lee, Fort Hays State University ■ Judy Lee, Leeward Community College ■ Gary Lemon, DePauw University ■ Alan Leonard, Northern Illinois University ■ George Lieu, Tuskegee University ■ Stephen E. Lile, Western Kentucky University ■ Jane Lillydahl, University of Colorado at Boulder ■ Al Link, University of North Carolina at Greensboro ■ Robert Litro, U.S. Air Force Academy, Wallingford, CT ■ Burl F. Long, University of Florida ■ Gerald Lynch, Purdue University ■ Karla Lynch, University of North Texas ■ Michael Magura, University of Toledo ■ Don Maxwell, Central State University ■ Nan Maxwell, California State University at Hayward ■ J. Harold McClure, Jr., Villanova University ■ Rick McIntyre, University of Rhode Island ■ K. Mehtaboin, College of St. Rose ■ Shahruz Mohtadi, Suffolk University ■ Joe L. Moore, Arkansas Technical University ■ Robert Moore, Occidental College ■ Doug Morgan, University of California at Santa Barbara ■ Norma C. Morgan, Curry College ■ John Murphy, North Shore Community College, Massachusetts ■ Veena Nayak, State University of New York at Buffalo ■ Randy Nelson, Colby College ■ David Nickerson, University of British Columbia ■ Rachel Nugent, Pacific Lutheran

University ■ Akorlie A. Nyatepe-Coo, University of Wisconsin at LaCrosse ■ Norman P. Obst, Michigan State University ■ William C. O'Connor, Western Montana College ■ Kent Olson, Oklahoma State University ■ Carl Parker, Fort Hays State University ■ Spirog Patton, Neumann College ■ Tony Pizelo, Spokane Community College ■ Michael Rendich, Westchester Community College ■ Lynn Rittenoure, University of Tulsa ■ David C. Rose, University of Missouri at St. Louis ■ Richard Rosenberg, Pennsylvania State University ■ Mark Rush, University of Florida at Gainesville ■ Dereka Rushbrook, Ripon College ■ David L. Schaffer, Haverford College ■ Gary Sellers, University of Akron ■ Jean Shackleford, Bucknell University ■ Linda Shaffer, California State University at Fresno ■ Geoff Shepherd, University of Massachusetts at Amherst ■ Bih-Hay Sheu, University of Texas at Austin ■ Alden Shiers, California Polytechnic State University ■ Sue Skeath, Wellesley College ■ Paula Smith, Central State University, Oklahoma ■ John Solow, University of Iowa at Iowa City ■ Dusan Stojanovic, Washington University, St. Louis ■ Ernst W. Stromsdorfer,

Washington State University ■ Michael Taussig, Rutgers University ■ Timothy Taylor, Stanford University ■ Sister Beth Anne Tercek, SND, Notre Dame College of Ohio ■ Jack Trierweler, Northern State University ■ Brian M. Trinque, University of Texas at Austin ■ Ann Velenchik, Wellesley College ■ Chris Waller, Indiana University at Bloomington ■ Walter Wessels, North Carolina State University ■ Joan Whalen-Ayyappan, DeVry Institute of Technology ■ Robert Whaples, Wake Forest University ■ Leonard A. White, University of Arkansas ■ Abera Zeyege, Ball State University ■ James Ziliak, Indiana University at Bloomington

We welcome comments about the third edition. Please write to us care of Economics Editor, Prentice Hall, Englewood Cliffs, NJ 07632.

Karl E. Case
Ray C. Fair

INTERNATIONALIZE YOUR EDUCATION!

Join International Business Seminars on an Overseas Adventure

EARN COLLEGE CREDIT ■ GAIN INTERNATIONAL EXPERTISE

INTERACT WITH TOP-LEVEL EXECUTIVES ■ VISIT THE WORLD'S GREATEST CITIES

May 30, 1994 - June 23, 1994

VISIT ORGANIZATIONS SUCH AS: Procter & Gamble Italia, NATO, The European Parliament, Elektra Breganz, Philip Morris, Allianz Insurance, Deutsche Aerospace, Digital Equipment, Coca-Cola, G.E. International, Ernst & Young, Esso Italiana, Guccio Gucci, Targetti Lighting, University of Innsbruck, and British Banks Association.

Prentice Hall International Business Scholarship 1994

Prentice Hall and International Business Seminars have joined forces to create a scholarship for students to study and travel in Europe in the summer of 1994. We believe that in today's global business envi-

ronment students should be exposed to as many different cultures as possible. Although many campuses reflect diversity in both their students and faculty, nothing can replace the educational value of learning about a continent, country, or city firsthand.

Each professor may sponsor one student to apply for the scholarship.

You can receive more information on the PH Business Scholarship and/or additional travel programs with International Business Seminars by contacting your local Prentice Hall representative or International Business Seminars, P.O. Box 30279, Mesa, Arizona 85275—telephone: (602) 830-0901; fax: (602) 924-0527.

INTRODUCTION

PART ONE

Introduction to Economics

Simply stated, _**economics**_ is the study of how societies choose to allocate scarce resources among competing uses. Many of the decisions we make are economic decisions, and many of our interactions with others are influenced by economic institutions. To understand society, you must have a basic knowledge of economics. You cannot hope to understand the rapid pace of world events, including the difficulties facing the independent republics of the former Soviet Union, without an understanding of how economic systems function.

As you begin your study of economics, keep in mind that economics will teach you a new way of looking at the world. In some cases, you will find that the topics we discuss are completely unfamiliar to you. But most of the time you will be looking at things that you already know about from a different perspective. You will discover, for example, that the complex decisions of huge multinational corporations are based on some of the same principles that guide everyday choices like whether to take a day off or to stay up late studying.

1 The Scope and Method of Economics

The study of economics should begin with a sense of wonder. Pause for a moment and consider a typical day in your life. For breakfast you might have bread made in a local bakery with flour produced in Minnesota from wheat grown in Kansas and bacon from pigs raised in Ohio packaged in plastic made in New Jersey. You spill coffee from Colombia on your shirt made in Texas from textiles shipped from South Carolina.

After class you drive with a friend in a Japanese car on an interstate highway system that took 20 years and billions of dollars worth of resources to build. You stop for gasoline refined in Louisiana from Saudi Arabian crude oil brought to the United States on a supertanker that took three years to build at a shipyard in Maine.

At night you call your brother in Mexico City. The call travels over newly laid fiber-optic cable to a powerful antenna that sends it to a transponder on one of over 1,000 communications satellites orbiting the earth.

You use or consume tens of thousands of things, both tangible and intangible, every day: buildings, the music of a rock band, the compact disc it is recorded on, telephone services, staples, paper, toothpaste, tweezers, soap, a digital watch, fire protection, antacid tablets, beer, banks, electricity, eggs, insurance, football fields, computers, buses, rugs, subways, health services, sidewalks, and so forth. Somebody made all these things. Somebody decided to organize men and women and materials to produce them and distribute them. Thousands of decisions went into their completion. Somehow they got to you.

One hundred twenty million people in the United States—almost half the total population—work at hundreds of thousands of different kinds of jobs producing nearly six trillion dollars worth of goods and services every year. Some cannot find work; some choose not to work for pay. Some are rich; others are poor.

The United States imports $60 billion worth of petroleum and petroleum products each year and exports $37 billion worth of food. High-rise office buildings go up in central cities. Condominiums and homes are built in the suburbs. In other places homes are abandoned and boarded up.

Some countries are wealthy. Others are impoverished. Some are growing. Some are stagnating. Some businesses are doing well. Others are going bankrupt.

At any moment in time every society faces constraints imposed by nature and by previous generations. Some societies are handsomely endowed by nature with fertile land, water, sunshine, and natural resources. Others have deserts and few mineral resources. Some societies receive much from previous generations—art, music, technical knowledge, beautiful buildings, and productive factories. Others are left with overgrazed, eroded land, cities leveled by war, or polluted natural environments. *All* societies face limits.

Economics is the study of how individuals and societies choose to use the scarce resources that nature and previous generations have provided. The key word in this definition is "choose." Economics is a behavioral science. In large measure it is the study of how people make choices. The choices that people make, when added up, translate into societal choices.

> **economics** The study of how individuals and societies choose to use the scarce resources that nature and previous generations have provided.

The purpose of this chapter and the next is to elaborate on this definition and to introduce the subject matter of economics. What is produced? How is it produced? Who gets it? Why? Is the result good or bad? Can it be improved?

WHY STUDY ECONOMICS? YES

There are four main reasons to study economics: to learn a way of thinking, to understand society, to understand global affairs, and to be an informed voter.

To Learn a Way of Thinking

Probably the most important reason for studying economics is to learn a particular way of thinking. A good way to introduce economics is to review three of its most fundamental concepts—*opportunity cost, marginalism,* and *efficient markets.* If your study of economics is successful, you will find yourself using these concepts every day in making decisions, both on economic matters and on matters that have nothing to do with economics.

Yes

OPPORTUNITY COST What happens in an economy is the outcome of thousands of individual decisions. Households must decide how to divide up their incomes over all the goods and services available in the marketplace. Individuals must decide whether to work or not to work, whether to go to school, and how much to save. Businesses must decide what to produce, how much to produce, how much to charge, and where to locate. It is not surprising that economic analysis focuses on the process of decision making.

Nearly all decisions involve trade-offs. There are advantages and disadvantages, costs and benefits, associated with every action and every choice. A key concept that recurs again and again in analyzing the decision-making process is the notion of *opportunity cost*. The full "cost" of making a specific choice includes what we give up by not making the alternative choice. That which we forgo, or give up, when we make a choice or a decision is called the **opportunity cost** of that decision.

The concept applies to individuals, businesses, and entire societies. The opportunity cost of going to a movie is the value of the other things you could have done with the same money and time. If you decide to take time off in lieu of working, the opportunity cost of your leisure is the pay that you would have earned had you worked. Part of the cost of a college education is the income you could have earned by working full time instead of going to school. If a firm purchases a new piece of modern equipment for $3000, it does so because it expects that equipment to generate more profit. There is an opportunity cost, however, since that $3000 could have been deposited in an interest-earning account. To a society, the opportunity cost of using resources for military hardware is the value of the private/civilian goods that could have been produced with the same resources.

The reason that opportunity costs arise is that resources are *scarce*. Scarce simply means *limited*. Consider one of our most important resources—time. There are only 24 hours in a day, and we must live our lives under this constraint. Many things in life are scarce, and much of economics is concerned with behavior in the face of *scarcity*. People are forced to make choices in the face of scarcity. If your neighbor mows his lawn today, he won't have time to take his children to the zoo, and this is an opportunity cost of mowing the lawn.

MARGINALISM AND SUNK COSTS A second key concept used in analyzing choices is the notion of *marginalism*. In weighing the costs and benefits of a decision, it is important to weigh only the costs and benefits that are contingent upon the decision. Suppose, for example, that you lived in New Orleans and that you were weighing the costs and benefits of visiting your mother in Iowa. If business required that you travel to Kansas City, the cost of visiting Mom would be only the additional, or *marginal,* time and money cost of getting to Iowa from Kansas City.

Consider the cost of producing this book. Assume that 10,000 copies are produced. The total cost of producing the copies includes the cost of the authors' time in writing the book, the cost of editing, the cost of making the plates for printing, and the cost of the paper and ink. If the total cost were $600,000, then the average cost of one copy would be $60, which is simply $600,000 divided by 10,000.

Although average cost is an important concept, a book publisher must know more than simply the average cost of a book. For example, suppose a second printing is being debated. That is, should another 10,000 copies be produced? In deciding whether to proceed, the costs of writing, editing, making plates, and so forth are irrelevant. Why? Because they have already been incurred—they are *sunk costs.* **Sunk costs** are costs that cannot be avoided, regardless of what is done in the future, because they have already been incurred. All that matters are the costs associated with the additional, or *marginal,* books to be printed. Technically, as you will see later in the book, *marginal cost* is the cost of producing one more unit of output.

There are numerous examples in which the concept of marginal cost is useful. For an airplane that is about to take off with empty seats, the marginal cost of an extra passenger is essentially zero; the total cost of the trip is essentially unchanged by the addition of an extra passenger. Thus, setting aside a few seats to be sold at

opportunity cost That which we forgo, or give up, when we make a choice or a decision.

sunk costs Costs that cannot be avoided, regardless of what is done in the future, because they have already been incurred.

big discounts can be profitable even if the fare for those seats is far below the average cost per seat of making the trip. As long as it succeeds in filling seats that would otherwise have been empty, it is a profitable thing to do—marginal revenue is greater than marginal cost.

no

EFFICIENT MARKETS—NO FREE LUNCH Suppose you are driving on a highway with three lanes going in your direction and you come upon a toll plaza with six toll booths. Three toll booths are straight ahead in the three lanes of traffic, and the three other booths are off to the right. Which lane should you choose? It is usually the case that the wait time is approximately the same no matter what you do. There are usually enough people searching for the shortest line so as to make all the lines about the same length. If one line is much shorter than the others, cars will quickly move into it until the lines are equalized. There are usually enough drivers searching for the fastest line to equalize the average wait time.

As you will see later, the term *profit* in economics has a very precise meaning. Economists, however, often loosely refer to "good deals" or profitable ventures with no risk as *profit opportunities*. Using the term loosely, a profit opportunity exists at the toll booths if one line is shorter than the others. The general view of economics is that profit opportunities are rare. At any one time there are many people searching for such opportunities, and as a consequence few exist. At toll booths it is seldom the case that one line is substantially shorter than the others. Markets like this, where any profit opportunities are eliminated almost instantaneously, are said to be **efficient markets.** (We discuss *markets, the institutions through which buyers and sellers interact and engage in exchange, in detail in Chapter 2.)

The common language way of expressing the efficient markets hypothesis is "there's no such thing as a free lunch." How should you react when a stockbroker calls up with a hot tip on the stock market? With skepticism. There are thousands of individuals each day looking for hot tips in the market, and if a particular tip about a stock is valid there will be an immediate rush to buy the stock, which will quickly drive its price up. By the time the tip gets to your broker and then to you, the profit opportunity that arose from the tip (assuming that there was one) likely has disappeared. Similar arguments can be made for bond markets and commodity markets, where there are many "experts" who take quick advantage of any news that affects prices.

This economists' view that there are very limited profit opportunities around can, of course, be carried too far. There is a story about two people walking along, one an economist and one not. The noneconomist sees a twenty dollar bill on the sidewalk and says, "There's a twenty dollar bill on the sidewalk." The economist replies, "That is not possible. If there were, somebody would already have picked it up."

There are clearly times when profit opportunities exist. Someone has to be first to get the news, and some people have quicker insights than others. Nevertheless, news travels fast, and there are thousands of people with quick insights. The general view that profit opportunities are rare is close to the mark.

efficient market A market in which profit opportunities are eliminated almost instantaneously.

market An institution through which buyers and sellers interact and engage in exchange.

To Understand Society

Another reason for studying economics is to understand society better. You cannot hope to understand how a society functions without a basic knowledge of its economy, and you cannot understand a society's economy without knowing its economic history. Clearly, past and present economic decisions have an enormous influence on the character of life in a society. The current state of the physical environment, the level of material well-being, and the nature and number of jobs are all products of the economic system.

To get a sense of the ways in which economic decisions have shaped our environment, imagine that you are looking out of a window on the top floor of a high-rise office building in any large city. The workday is about to begin. All around you are other tall glass and steel buildings full of workers. In the distance you see the smoke of factories. Looking down, you see thousands of commuters pouring off trains and buses, and cars backed up on freeway exit ramps. You see trucks carrying goods from one place to another. You also see the face of urban poverty: Just beyond the freeway is a large public housing project and, beyond that, burned-out and boarded-up buildings.

What you see before you is the product of millions of economic decisions made over hundreds of years. People at some point decided to spend time and money building those buildings and factories. Somebody cleared the land, laid the tracks, built the roads, and produced the cars and buses.

Not only have economic decisions shaped the physical environment, they have determined the character of society as well. At no time has the impact of economic change on the character of a society been more evident than in England during the late eighteenth and early nineteenth centuries, a period that we now call the

Industrial Revolution. Increases in the productivity of agriculture, new manufacturing technologies, and the development of more efficient forms of transportation led to a massive movement of the British population from the countryside to the city. At the beginning of the eighteenth century, approximately two out of three people in Great Britain were engaged in agriculture. By 1812, only one in three remained in agriculture, and by 1900 the figure was fewer than one in ten. People jammed into overcrowded cities and worked long hours in factories. The world had changed completely in two centuries—a period that, in the run of history, was nothing more than the blink of an eye.

It is not surprising that the discipline of economics began to take shape during this period. Social critics and philosophers looked around them and knew that their philosophies must expand to accommodate the changes. Adam Smith's *Wealth of Nations* appeared in 1776. It was followed by the writings of David Ricardo, Karl Marx, Thomas Malthus, and others. Each tried to make sense out of what was happening. Who was building the factories? Why? What determined the level of wages paid to workers or the price of food? What would happen in the future, and what *should* happen? The people who asked these questions were the first economists.

Similar changes continue to affect the character of life today. As late as 1950, approximately one out of six people in the United States lived on farms. In 1990, the figure was a little over one in fifty-five. The tremendous productivity of modern corporate farms using new agricultural technologies, combined with the very high borrowing costs of the early 1980s, made survival on small, less efficient family farms very difficult. Thousands of farmers went bankrupt, defaulted on loans, and lost their farms at auctions.

The plight of small farmers across the United States has important political and social dimensions. But at its roots it is an economic problem: The price paid for agricultural products today does not cover what it costs many farmers to produce them. They lose money and are forced out of business. Why? What determines the price of corn? Of wheat? What determines the interest rates that farmers must pay on loans to buy equipment and seed?

The study of economics is an essential part of the study of society.

Industrial Revolution The period in England during the late eighteenth and early nineteenth centuries in which new manufacturing technologies and improved transportation gave rise to the modern factory system and a massive movement of the population from the countryside to the cities.

To Understand Global Affairs

A third reason for studying economics is to understand global affairs. News headlines are filled with economic stories: a potential trade war between the United States and the European Community (the EC), the struggle to prevent further collapse of the economies of Eastern Europe and the former Soviet Union, starvation and poverty in Africa.

All countries are part of a world economy, and understanding international relations begins with a basic knowledge of the economic links among countries. The recent deterioration of the real estate market in Japan may, for example, have important consequences for the U.S. stock market and U.S. export industries. In Vietnam, normalization of relations with the United States could lead to investment by U.S. firms, thus creating jobs and raising wages in Vietnam. Currently, an important discussion between the United States and China focuses on the U.S. granting of "most favored nation" trading status to that country.

Another important issue in today's world is the widening gap between rich nations and poor nations. In 1993 world population was about 5.4 billion. Of that number, 4.1 billion lived in less-developed countries and 1.3 billion lived in more-developed countries. The 75% of the world's population that lives in the less-developed countries receives less than 20% of the world's income. In dozens of countries, per capita income is a few hundred dollars a year.

In recent years, these issues have played a significant role in the Middle East. Although Iraq's invasion of Kuwait in August, 1990 had a great deal to do with Iraq's desire to control world oil production and prices, issues of relative wealth and poverty were also involved. Kuwait, a tiny country located on the Persian Gulf, had the highest per capita income in the world in 1990. At the same time, much of the rest of the Arab world lived in poverty. This huge gap between the rich and poor led to a good deal of popular support among Arabs for the Iraqi invasion.

> An understanding of economics is essential to an understanding of global affairs.

To Be an Informed Voter

A knowledge of economics is essential to be an informed voter. During the last 25 years, the U.S. economy has been on a roller coaster. In 1973–1974, the Organization of Petroleum Exporting Countries (OPEC) stopped shipping oil to the United States and at the same time succeeded in raising the price of crude oil by 400 percent. Simultaneously, a sequence of events in the world food market drove food prices up by 25 percent. By mid-1974, prices in the United States were rising across the board at a very rapid rate. Partially as a result of government policy to fight runaway inflation, the economy went into a recession in 1975. (An *inflation* is an increase in the overall price level in the economy.) The recession succeeded in slowing price increases, but in the process millions found themselves unemployed and there was a great deal of economic hardship.

From 1979 through 1983, it happened all over again. Prices rose rapidly, the government reacted with more policies designed to stop prices from rising, and the United States ended up with an even worse recession in 1982. By the end of that year, 10.8% of the work force was unemployed. Then, in mid-1990—after almost eight years of strong economic performance—the U.S. economy went into another recession. During the third and fourth quarters of 1990 and the first quarter of 1991, gross domestic product (GDP)—a measure of the total output (production) of the U.S. economy—fell, and unemployment again increased sharply.

The recession of 1990–1991 was followed by a very slow recovery, which became the key issue in the 1992 presidential election. Exit polls on election day, November 3, 1992, showed that the number one issue on people's minds was the economy. Indeed, the three presidential debates among former President Bush, H. Ross Perot, and President Clinton focused on the candidates' positions on economic issues. Among the questions discussed: How should the country deal with the huge deficits and massive government debt run up over the last decade? Is there anything that the federal government can do to stimulate the U.S. economy and to create new jobs with good wages? What should be done about runaway health costs and the lack of universal health insurance? Should the United States sign the North American Free Trade Agreement with Mexico and Canada? Should the United States send foreign aid to the Russian Republic and other countries of the former Soviet Union to help them revive their economies?

> When we participate in the political process, we are voting on issues that require a basic understanding of economics.

THE SCOPE OF ECONOMICS

Most students taking economics for the first time are surprised by the breadth of what they study. Some think that economics will teach them about the stock market or what to do with their money. Others think that economics deals exclusively with problems like inflation and unemployment. In fact, it deals with all these subjects, but they are pieces of a much larger puzzle.

Economics has deep roots in, and close ties to, social philosophy. An issue of great importance to philosophers, for example, is distributional justice. Why are some people rich and others poor, and whatever the answer, is this fair? A number of nineteenth century social philosophers wrestled with these questions, and out of their musings economics as a separate discipline was born.

The easiest way to get a feel for the breadth and depth of what you will be studying is to explore briefly the way economics is organized. First of all, there are two major divisions of economics: microeconomics and macroeconomics.

Microeconomics and Macroeconomics

microeconomics The branch of economics that examines the functioning of individual industries and the behavior of individual decision-making units, that is, business firms and households.

Microeconomics deals with the functioning of individual industries and the behavior of individual economic decision-making units: single business firms and households. Microeconomics explores the decisions that individual businesses and consumers make. The choices of firms about what to produce and how much to charge and the choices of households about what to buy and how much of it to buy help to explain why the economy produces the things it does.

Another big question that microeconomics addresses is who gets the things that are produced. Wealthy households get more output than do poor households, and the forces that determine this distribution of output are the province of microeconomics. Why do we have poverty? Who is poor? Why do some jobs pay more than others? Why do teachers or plumbers or baseball pitchers get paid what they do?

Think again about all the things you consume in a day, and then think back to that view out over a big city. Somebody decided to build those factories. Somebody decided to construct the roads, build the housing, produce the cars, knit the T-shirts, and smoke the bacon. Why? What is going on in all those buildings? It is easy to see that understanding individual micro decisions is very important to any understanding of your society.

Macroeconomics looks at the economy as a whole. Instead of trying to understand what determines the output of a single firm or industry or the consumption patterns of a single household or group of households, macroeconomics examines the factors that determine national output, or national product. Microeconomics is concerned with *household* income; macroeconomics deals with *national* income.

While microeconomics focuses on individual product prices and relative prices, macroeconomics looks at the price level and how quickly (or slowly) it is rising (or falling). Microeconomics questions how many people will be hired (or fired) this year in a particular industry or in a certain geographical area, and the factors that determine how much labor a firm or industry will hire. Macroeconomics deals with *aggregate* employment and unemployment: how many jobs exist in the economy as a whole, and how many people who are willing to work will not be able to find work.

To summarize:

macroeconomics The branch of economics that examines the economic behavior of aggregates—income, employment, output, and so on—on a national scale.

> Microeconomics looks at the individual unit—the household, the firm, the industry. It sees and examines the "trees." Macroeconomics looks at the whole, the aggregate. It sees and analyzes the "forest."

Table 1.1 summarizes these divisions and some of the subjects with which they are concerned.

TABLE 1.1
Examples of Microeconomic and Macroeconomic Concerns

DIVISION OF ECONOMICS	PRODUCTION	PRICES	INCOME	EMPLOYMENT
Microeconomics	*Production/Output in Individual Industries and Businesses* How much steel How much office space How many cars	*Price of Individual Goods and Services* Price of medical care Price of gasoline Food prices Apartment rents	*Distribution of Income and Wealth* Wages in the auto industry Minimum wage Executive salaries Poverty	*Employment by Individual Businesses and Industries* Jobs in the steel industry Number of employees in a firm Number of accountants Number of doctors
Macroeconomics	*National Production/Output* Total industrial output Gross domestic product Growth of output Decline during recessions	*Aggregate Price Level* Consumer prices Producer prices Rate of inflation	*National Income* Total wages and salaries Total corporate profits	*Employment and Unemployment in the Economy* Total number of jobs Unemployment rate Discouraged workers

The Diversity of Economics

Individual economists focus their research and study in many diverse areas. Many of these specialized fields are reflected in the advanced courses offered at most colleges and universities. Some are concerned with economic history or the history of economic thought. Others focus on international economics or growth in less-developed countries. Still others study the economics of cities (urban economics) or the relationship between economics and law. (See the Issues and Applications box entitled "The Fields of Economics" for more details.)

Economists also differ in the emphasis they place on theory. Some economists specialize in developing new theories, while others spend their time testing the theories of others. Some economists hope to expand the frontiers of knowledge, while others are more interested in applying what is already known to the formulation of public policies.

As you begin your study of economics, look through your school's course catalogue and talk to the faculty about their interests. You will discover that economics encompasses a broad range of inquiry and is linked to many other disciplines.

THE METHOD OF ECONOMICS

positive economics An approach to economics that seeks to understand behavior and the operation of systems without making judgments. It describes what exists and how it works.

normative economics An approach to economics that analyzes outcomes of economic behavior, evaluates them as good or bad, and may prescribe preferred courses of action.

Economics asks and attempts to answer two kinds of questions, positive and normative. **Positive economics** attempts to understand behavior and the operation of economic systems *without making judgments* about whether the outcomes are good or bad. It strives to describe what exists and how it works. What determines the wage rate for unskilled workers? What would happen if we abolished the corporate income tax? Who would benefit? Who would lose? The answers to such questions are the subject of positive economics.

Normative economics, on the other hand, looks at the outcomes of economic behavior and asks if they are good or bad and whether the outcomes can be made better. Normative economics involves judgments and prescriptions for preferred courses of action. Should the government be involved in regulating the price of gasoline? Should the income tax be changed to reduce or increase the burden on upper income families? Should AT&T have been broken up into a set of smaller companies? Should we protect the automobile industry from foreign competition? Should the savings and loan industry be regulated? Normative economics is often called *policy economics*.

Of course most normative questions involve positive questions. To know whether the government *should* take a particular action, we must know first if it *can* and second what the consequences are likely to be. (For example, if AT&T is broken up, will there be more competition and lower prices?)

Some claim that positive, value-free economic analysis is impossible. They argue that analysts come to problems with biases that cannot help but influence their work. Furthermore, even in choosing what questions to ask or what problems to analyze, economists are influenced by political, ideological, and moral views.

While this argument has some merit, it is nevertheless important to distinguish between analyses that attempt to be positive and those that are intentionally and explicitly normative. Economists who ask explicitly normative questions should be forced to specify their grounds for judging one outcome superior to another.

THE FIELDS OF ECONOMICS

A good way to convey the diversity of economics is to describe some of its major fields of study and the issues that economists address.

- *Industrial organization* looks carefully at the structure and performance of industries and firms within an economy. How do businesses compete? Who gains and who loses?
- *Urban and regional economics* studies the spatial arrangement of economic activity. Why do we have cities? Why are manufacturing firms locating farther and farther from the center of urban areas? What leads to abandonment and decline in some neighborhoods?
- *Econometrics* applies statistical techniques and data to economic problems in an effort to test hypotheses and theoretical models. Most schools require economics majors to take at least one course in statistics or econometrics.
- *Comparative economic systems* examines the ways alternative economic systems function. What are the advantages and disadvantages of different systems? How do capitalist economies differ from socialist economies? What is the best way to convert the planned economies of the former Soviet Union to a market system?
- *Economic development* focuses on the problems of poor countries. What can be done to promote development in these nations? Important concerns of development economists usually include population growth and control, provision for basic needs, and strategies for international trade.

- *Labor economics* deals with the factors that determine wage rates, employment, and unemployment. How do people decide whether to work, how much to work, and at what kind of job? Why and how do people get training? Why are some skills in plentiful supply while others are scarce? What determines the number of jobs in a particular industry or in the economy as a whole? How have the roles of unions and management changed in recent years?
- *International economics* studies trade flows among countries and international financial institutions. What are the advantages and disadvantages for a country that allows its citizens to buy and sell freely in world markets? Should countries impose restrictions on imports to protect their own industries? What determines exchange rates? Can they be manipulated? Why is the dollar strong or weak?
- *Public economics* examines the role of government in the economy. What are the economic functions of government, and what should they be? How should the government finance the services that it provides? What effects do taxes have? What kinds of government programs should confront the problems of poverty, unemployment, and air and water pollution?
- *Economic history* traces the development of the modern economy. What economic and political events and scientific advances caused the Industrial Revolution that began in eighteenth century Great Britain? What explains the tremendous growth and progress of post–World War II Japan? What

Specialists in all fields of economics attended President Clinton's Economic Summit in Little Rock, Arkansas in 1992. Pictured from left to right are Vice President Al Gore, President Clinton, and Marian Wright Edelman of the Children's Defense Fund.

was the Great Depression of the 1930s all about?

- *Law and economics* analyzes the economic function of legal rules and institutions. How does the law change the behavior of individuals and businesses? Do different liability rules make accidents and injuries more, or less, likely? What are the economic costs of crime?
- *The history of economic thought,* which is grounded in philosophy, studies the development of economic ideas and theories over time, from Adam Smith in the eighteenth century to the works of economists such as Thomas Malthus, Karl Marx, John Stuart Mill, Jeremy Bentham, Stanley Jevons, Leon Walras, Alfred Marshall, John R. Hicks, and John Maynard Keynes. Because economic theory is constantly developing and changing, studying the history of ideas helps give meaning to modern theory and puts it in perspective.

What does it mean to be better? The criteria for such evaluations must be clearly spelled out and thoroughly understood for conclusions to have meaning.

Positive economics is often divided into descriptive economics and economic theory. **Descriptive economics** is simply the compilation of data that describe phenomena and facts. Examples of such data appear in the *Statistical Abstract of the United States,* a large volume of data published by the Department of Commerce every year that describes many features of the U.S. economy.

Where do all these data come from? The Census Bureau produces an enormous amount of raw data every year, as do the Bureau of Labor Statistics, the Bureau of Economic Analysis, and nongovernment agencies such as the University of Michigan Survey Research Center. One important study now published annually is the *Survey of Consumer Expenditure,* which asks individual households to keep careful records of all their expenditures over a long period of time. Another is the *National Longitudinal Survey of Labor Force Behavior,* conducted over many years by the Center for Human Resource Development at Ohio State University.

Economic theory attempts to generalize about data and interpret them. An **economic theory** is a statement or set of related statements about cause and effect, action and reaction. One of the first theories you will encounter in this text is the *law of demand,* which was most clearly stated by Alfred Marshall in 1890: When the price of a product rises, people tend to buy less of it; when the price of a product falls, they tend to buy more.

The process of observing regular patterns from raw data and drawing generalizations from them is called **inductive reasoning.** In all sciences, theories begin with inductive reasoning and observed regularities. For example, Aristotle believed that the speed at which objects fall toward the earth depends on their size as well as their weight. But in a series of experiments carried out between 1589 and 1591, Galileo was able to show that bodies of very different sizes seemed to fall at approximately the same speed when dropped from the Leaning Tower of Pisa. Over a century later, Galileo's data led Sir Isaac Newton to formulate the theory of gravity, which eventually became the basis of Albert Einstein's work.

Social scientists, including economists, study human behavior. They develop and test theories of how human beings, institutions, and societies behave. The behavior of human beings is by its nature not as regular or predictable as the behavior of electrons, molecules, or planets, but there are patterns, regularities, and tendencies.

Theories do not always arise out of formal numerical data. All of us have been collecting observations of people's behavior and their responses to economic stimuli for most of our lives. We may have observed our parents' reaction to a sudden increase— or decrease—in income or to the loss of a job or the acquisition of a new one. We have all seen people standing in line waiting for a bargain. And, of course, our own actions and reactions are another important source of data. When we read a theory about behavior that is inconsistent with our own experience, we question it.

Theories and Models

In many disciplines, including physics, chemistry, meteorology, political science, and economics, theorists build formal models of behavior. **A model** is a formal statement of a theory. It is usually a mathematical statement of a presumed relationship between two or more variables.

A variable is a measure that can change from time to time or from observation to observation. Income is a variable—it has different values for different people, and different values for the same person at different times. The rental price of a

---

descriptive economics The compilation of data that describe phenomena and facts.

economic theory A statement or set of related statements about cause and effect, action and reaction, in economic life.

inductive reasoning The process of observing regular patterns from raw data and drawing generalizations from them.

model A formal statement of a theory. Usually a mathematical statement of a relationship between two or more variables.

variable A measure that can change from time to time or from observation to observation.

movie on a videocassette is a variable; it has different values at different stores and at different times. There are countless other examples.

Because all models simplify reality by stripping part of it away, they are abstractions. Critics of economics often point to abstraction as a weakness. Most economists, however, see abstraction as a real strength.

The easiest way to see how abstraction can be helpful is to think of a map. A map, like a model, is a substitute for the real thing. It is a representation of reality that is simplified and also abstract. A city or state appears on a piece of paper as a series of lines and colors. The amount of reality that the map maker can strip away before the map loses something essential depends upon what it is going to be used for. If I want to drive from St. Louis to Phoenix, I need to know only the major interstate highways and roads. I lose absolutely nothing and gain clarity by cutting out the local streets and roads. If, on the other hand, I need to get around in Phoenix, I may need to see every street and alley.

Most maps are two-dimensional representations of a three-dimensional world; they show where roads and highways go but do not show hills and valleys along the way. Trail maps for hikers, however, have "contour lines" that represent changes in elevation. When you are in a car, changes in elevation matter very little; they would make a map needlessly complex and much more difficult to read. But if you are on foot carrying a 60-pound pack, a knowledge of elevation is crucial.

Like maps, economic models are abstractions that strip away detail to expose only those aspects of behavior that are important to the question being asked. The principle that irrelevant detail should be cut away is called the principle of **Ockham's razor** after the fourteenth century philosopher William of Ockham.

Ockham's razor The principle that irrelevant detail should be cut away.

But be careful. Although abstraction is a powerful tool for exposing and analyzing specific aspects of behavior, it is possible to oversimplify. Economic models and the theories that give rise to them strip away a good deal of social and political reality to get at underlying concepts. When an economic theory is used to help formulate actual government or institutional policy, political and social reality must often be reintroduced if the policy is to have a chance of working.

The key here is that the appropriate amount of simplification and abstraction depends upon the use to which the model will be put. To return to the map example: You don't want to walk around San Francisco with a map made for drivers—there are too many very steep hills!

ALL ELSE EQUAL: *ceteris paribus* It is almost always true that whatever you want to explain with a model depends on more than one factor. Suppose, for example, that you want to explain the total number of miles driven by owners of automobiles in the United States. The number of miles driven will change from year to year or month to month; it is a variable. The issue, if we want to understand and explain changes that occur, is what factors cause those changes.

Obviously, many things might have an impact on total miles driven. First of all, more or fewer people may be driving. This, in turn, can be affected by changes in the driving age, by population growth, or by changes in state laws. Other factors might include the price of gasoline, the household's income, the number and age of children in the household, the distance from home to work, the location of shopping facilities, and the availability and quality of public transport. When any of these variables change, the members of the household may drive more or less. If changes in any of these variables affect large numbers of households across the country, the total number of miles driven will change.

Very often we need to isolate or separate out these effects. For example, suppose that we want to know the impact on driving of a higher tax on gasoline. This change would raise the price of gasoline at the pump, but would not, at least in the short run, affect income, work place location, number of children, and so forth.

To isolate the impact of one single factor, we use the device of **ceteris paribus,** or "**all else equal.**" We ask: What is the impact of a change in gasoline price on driving behavior, *ceteris paribus,* or assuming that nothing else changes? If gasoline prices rise by 10%, how much less driving will there be, assuming no simultaneous change in anything else—that is, assuming that income, number of children, population, laws, and so on all remain constant?

ceteris paribus Literally, "all else equal." Used to analyze the relationship between two variables while the values of other variables are held unchanged.

> Using the device of *ceteris paribus* is one part of the process of abstraction. In formulating economic theory, the concept helps us simplify reality in order to focus on the relationships that we are interested in. We can then think about the relationship between two variables by simply assuming that all else is equal.

EXPRESSING MODELS IN WORDS, GRAPHS, AND EQUATIONS Consider the following statements. "Lower airline ticket prices cause people to fly more frequently." "Higher interest rates slow the rate of home sales." "When firms produce more output, employment increases." "Higher oil prices lead to more exploration for oil and higher levels of production in Texas." "Higher gasoline prices cause people to drive less and to buy more fuel efficient cars." "When the U.S. dollar falls in value against the value of foreign currencies, firms that export products produced in the United States find their sales increasing."

Each of these statements expresses a relationship between two variables that can be quantified. In each case there is a stimulus and a response, a cause and an effect. In each case, the effect depends on decisions made by people. Quantitative relationships can be expressed in a variety of ways. Sometimes words are sufficient to express the essence of a theory, but often it is necessary to be more specific about the nature of a relationship or about the magnitude of a response. The most common method of expressing the quantitative relationship between two variables is *graphing* that relationship on a two-dimensional plane. In fact, we will use graphical analysis extensively in Chapter 2 and beyond. Because it is essential that you be familiar with the basics of graphing, a careful review of graphing techniques is presented in the appendix to this chapter.

Quantitative relationships between variables can also be presented through *equations.* For example, suppose we discovered that over time, U.S. households collectively spend, or consume, 90% of their income and save 10% of their income. We could then write:

$$C = .90Y \text{ and } S = .10Y$$

where C is consumption spending, Y is income, and S is saving. Writing explicit algebraic expressions like these helps us understand the nature of the underlying process of decision making. Understanding this process is what economics is all about.

CAUTIONS AND PITFALLS In formulating theories and models, economists are especially careful to avoid two pitfalls: the post hoc fallacy and the fallacy of composition.

The Post Hoc Fallacy Theories often make statements, or sets of statements, about *cause and effect*. It can be quite tempting to look at two events that happen in sequence and assume that the first caused the second to happen. Clearly, this is not always the case. This common error is called the **post hoc, ergo propter hoc** (or "after this, therefore because of this") fallacy.

post hoc, ergo propter hoc Literally, "after this (in time), therefore because of this." A common error made in thinking about causation: If Event A happens before Event B happens, it cannot be inferred that A caused B.

There are thousands of examples. The Toronto Blue Jays have won seven games in a row. Last night, I went to the game and they lost. I must have "jinxed" them. They lost *because* I went to the game.

Stock market analysts indulge in what is perhaps the most striking example of the post hoc fallacy in action. Every day the stock market goes up or down, and every day some analyst on some national news program singles out one or two of the day's events as the *cause* of some change in the market: "Today the Dow Jones industrial average rose five points on heavy trading; analysts say that the increase was due to progress at the arms negotiations in Geneva." Research has shown that daily changes in stock market averages are very largely random. While major news events, like President Clinton's election in 1992, clearly have a direct influence on certain stock prices, most daily changes cannot be directly linked to specific news stories.

Very closely related to the post hoc fallacy is the often erroneous link between correlation and causation. Two variables are said to be *correlated* if one variable changes when the other variable changes. But correlation does not imply causation. Cities that have high crime rates also have lots of automobiles, so there is a very high degree of correlation between number of cars and crime rates. Can we argue, then, that cars *cause* crime? No. The reason for the correlation between numbers of cars and crime may have nothing to do with cause and effect. Big cities have lots of people, lots of people have lots of cars, and therefore big cities have lots of cars. Big cities also have high crime rates for many reasons—crowding, poverty, anonymity, unequal distribution of wealth, and the ready availability of drugs, to mention only a few. But the presence of cars is not one of them.

This caution must also be viewed in reverse. Sometimes events that seem entirely unconnected actually *are* connected. In 1978 Governor Michael Dukakis of Massachusetts ran for reelection. Still young, attractive, and quite popular most of the time, Dukakis was nevertheless defeated in the Democratic primary that year. The weekend before, the Boston Red Sox, in the thick of the division championship race, had been badly beaten by the New York Yankees in four straight games. Some very respectable political analysts believe that hundreds of thousands of Boston sports fans vented their anger on the incumbent governor the following Tuesday.

The Fallacy of Composition To conclude that what is true for a part is necessarily true for the whole is to fall into the **fallacy of composition.** Often what holds for an individual does not hold for a group or for society as a whole. One classic example is that of the farmer who knows he will be better off if he produces more wheat. His income is essentially the number of bushels of wheat he produces multiplied by the price he gets per bushel. Individual farmers cannot control the market price of wheat; all they can control is the amount they produce. Thus, producing more means more income. But if *all* farmers produce more, the price of wheat falls and farmers may, in fact, be worse off.

fallacy of composition The belief that what is true for a part is necessarily true for the whole.

Suppose that a large group of cattle ranchers graze their cattle on the same range. To an individual rancher, more cattle and more grazing mean a higher income. But because its capacity is limited, the land can support only so many cattle. If every cattle rancher increased the number of cattle sent out to graze, the land would become overgrazed and barren, and everyone's income would fall. In short:

> Theories that seem to work well when applied to individuals or households often break down when they are applied to the whole.

TESTING THEORIES AND MODELS: EMPIRICAL ECONOMICS In science, a theory is rejected when it fails to explain what is observed or when another theory better explains what is observed. Prior to the sixteenth century almost everyone believed that the earth was the center of the universe and that the sun and stars rotated around it. The astronomer Ptolemy (127–151 A.D.) built a model that explained and predicted the movements of the heavenly bodies in a geocentric (earth-centered) universe. Early in the sixteenth century, however, the Polish astronomer Nicholas Copernicus found himself dissatisfied with the Ptolemaic model and proposed an alternative theory or model, placing the sun at the center of the known universe and relegating the earth to the status of one planet among many. The battle between the competing models was waged, at least in part, with data based on observations—actual measurements of the movements of the planets. The new model ultimately predicted much better than the old, and in time it came to be accepted.

In the seventeenth century, building on the works of Copernicus and others, Sir Isaac Newton constructed yet another body of theory that seemed to predict planetary motion with still more accuracy. Newtonian physics became the accepted body of theory, relied on for almost 300 years. Then Albert Einstein did his work. The theory of relativity replaced Newtonian physics because it predicted even better. Relativity was able to explain some things that earlier theories could not.

Economic theories are also confronted with new and often conflicting data from time to time. The collection and use of data to test economic theories is called **empirical economics.**

empirical economics The collection and use of data to test economic theories.

Numerous large data sets are available to facilitate economic research. For example, economists studying the labor market can now test behavioral theories against the actual working experiences of thousands of randomly selected people who have been surveyed continuously since the 1960s by economists at Ohio State University. Macroeconomists continuously monitoring and studying the behavior of the national economy pass thousands of items of data, collected by both government agencies and private companies, back and forth on floppy disks and over telephone lines. Housing market analysts analyze data tapes containing observations recorded in connection with millions of home sales.

One of the key problems in all scientific research is the need to isolate and measure the responsiveness of one variable to a change in another variable *ceteris paribus.* Physical scientists, such as physicists and geologists, can often impose the condition of *ceteris paribus* by conducting controlled experiments. They can, for example, measure the effect of one chemical on another while literally holding all else constant in an environment that they control completely. Social scientists, who study people, rarely have this luxury.

While controlled experiments are difficult in economics and other social sciences, they are not impossible. Researchers can isolate and measure the effect of one variable on another. There are a number of ways to do this. One way is to observe the behavior of groups of similar people under different circumstances. For example, suppose you wanted to estimate the effect of the tax rate reductions enacted by Congress in 1986 on the amount that households save, an important tax policy issue. Of course, you could look at household saving before and after the change. But who's to say that what you observe is not due to increases in income that occurred at the same time? To isolate the tax effect, you could look at a set of households whose income did not change. Sophisticated computer programs are now allowing economists to isolate variables more easily than ever before.

Economic Policy

Economic theory helps us understand how the world works, but the formulation of *economic policy* requires a second step. We must have objectives. What do we want to change? Why? What is good and what is bad about the way the system is operating? Can we make it better?

Such questions force us to be specific about the grounds for judging one outcome superior to another. What does it mean to be better? Four criteria are frequently applied in making these judgments:

Criteria for Judging Economic Outcomes:	1. Efficiency 2. Equity 3. Growth 4. Stability

EFFICIENCY In physics "efficiency" refers to the ratio of useful energy delivered by a system to the energy supplied to it. An efficient automobile engine, for example, is one that uses up a small amount of fuel per mile for a given level of power.

In economics, **efficiency** means *allocative efficiency*. An efficient economy is one that produces what people want and does so at the least possible cost. If the system allocates resources to the production of things that nobody wants, it is inefficient. When steel beams lie in the rain and rust because somebody fouled up a shipping schedule, this is inefficient. If a firm could produce its product using 25% less labor and energy without sacrificing quality, it too is inefficient.

To use the term more technically, an efficient change in the allocation of resources is one that at least potentially makes some people better off without making others worse off. The clearest example of an efficient change is a voluntary exchange. If you and I each want something that the other has and we agree to exchange, we are both better off, and no one loses. If a company reorganizes its production or adopts a new technology that enables it to produce more of its product with fewer resources, without sacrificing quality, this is an efficient change; at least potentially, the resources saved could be used to produce *more* of something.

Inefficiencies can arise in numerous ways. Sometimes they are caused by government regulations or tax laws that distort otherwise sound economic decisions. When only one firm exists in a market and competition is prohibited or nonexistent, the incentive for efficient allocation and innovation may be lost. If firms that cause environmental damage are in no way held accountable for their actions, the incentive to minimize those damages is lost, and the result is inefficient.

We shall deal with the concept of efficiency in much more detail later. For now, though, it is important to understand two things about it. First, it assumes that the ultimate purpose of an economic system is to produce what people want. When we say a change makes people better off, it is the people themselves who define what "better off" means. For example, by engaging in a voluntary exchange, you and I reveal that we are both better off afterwards than before. A voluntary exchange is efficient because it improves the well-being of the participants *as they themselves define it*.

Second, since most changes that can be made in an economy will leave some people better off and others worse off, we must have a way of comparing the gains and losses that may result from any given change. Most often we simply compare

efficiency In economics, allocative efficiency. An efficient economy is one that produces what people want and does so at the least possible cost.

their sizes in dollar terms. A change is at least potentially efficient if the value of the resulting gains exceeds the value of the resulting losses.

equity Fairness.

EQUITY While efficiency has a fairly precise definition that can be applied with some degree of rigor, **equity** ("fairness") lies in the eye of the beholder. Few people agree on what is fair and what is unfair. To many, fairness implies a more equal distribution of income and wealth. Fairness may imply alleviating poverty, but the extent to which poverty should be reduced is the subject of enormous disagreement. For thousands of years philosophers have wrestled with the principles of justice that should guide social decisions. They will probably wrestle with such questions for thousands of years to come.

Despite the impossibility of defining equity or fairness universally, public policy makers judge the fairness of economic outcomes all the time. Rent control laws were passed because some legislators thought that landlords treated low-income tenants unfairly. Certainly most social welfare programs are created in the name of equity.

GROWTH As the result of technological change, the building of machinery, and the acquisition of knowledge, societies learn to produce new things and to produce old things better. In the early days of the U.S. economy, it took nearly half the population to produce the required food supply. Today less than 2% of the country's population is engaged in agriculture.

economic growth An increase in the total output of an economy.

When we devise new and better ways of producing the things we use now and develop new products and services, the total amount of production in the economy increases. **Economic growth** is an increase in the total output of an economy. If output grows faster than the population, output per capita rises, and standards of living increase. Presumably, when an economy grows there is more of what people want. Rural and agrarian societies become modern industrial societies as a result of economic growth and rising per capita output.

Some policies discourage economic growth and others encourage it. Tax laws, for example, can be designed to encourage the development and application of new production techniques. Research and development in some societies are subsidized by the government. Building roads, highways, bridges, and transport systems in developing countries may speed up the process of economic growth. If businesses and wealthy people invest their wealth outside their country rather than in its own industries, growth in their home country may be slowed.

stability A condition in which output is steady or growing, with low inflation and full employment of resources.

STABILITY Economic **stability** refers to the condition in which national output is steady or growing, with low inflation and full employment of resources. An economy may at times be unstable. During the 1950s and 1960s, the U.S. economy experienced a long period of relatively steady growth, stable prices, and low unemployment. Between 1951 and 1969, consumer prices never rose more than 5% in a single year, and in only two years did the number of unemployed exceed 6% of the labor force. The decades of the 1970s and 1980s, however, were unstable. The United States experienced two periods of rapid price inflation (over 10%) and two periods of severe unemployment. In 1982, for example, 12 million people (10.8% of the work force) were looking for work. The beginning of the 1990s was another period of instability, with a recession occurring in 1990–1991. The causes of instability and the ways in which governments have attempted to stabilize the economy are the subject matter of macroeconomics.

An Invitation

This chapter is meant to prepare you for what is to come. The first part of the chapter invited you into an exciting discipline that deals with important issues and questions. You cannot begin to understand how a society functions without knowing something about its economic history and its economic system.

The second part of the chapter introduced, in a very rough way, the method of reasoning that economics requires and some of the tools that economics uses. We believe that learning to think in this very powerful way will help you better understand the world.

As you proceed, it is important that you keep track of what you've learned in earlier chapters. This book has a plan; it proceeds step by step, each section building on the last. It would be a good idea to read through the table of contents and glance through each chapter before you read it to be sure you understand where it fits in the big picture.

Summary

1. *Economics* is the study of how individuals and societies choose to use the scarce resources that nature and previous generations have provided.

Why Study Economics?

2. There are many reasons to study economics, including (a) to learn a way of thinking, (b) to understand society, (c) to understand global affairs, and (d) to be an informed voter.

3. All societies at all times face constraints imposed by nature and previous generations; resources are scarce.

4. That which we forgo when we make a choice or a decision is the *opportunity cost* of that decision.

5. Economics is a surprisingly broad discipline. It has deep roots in social philosophy and deals with important societal issues.

The Scope of Economics

6. *Microeconomics* deals with the functioning of individual markets and industries and with the behavior of individual decision-making units: firms and households.

7. *Macroeconomics* looks at the economy as a whole. It deals with national output, national income, the overall price level, and the general rate of inflation.

8. Economics is a broad and diverse discipline with many special fields of inquiry. These include economic history, international economics, and urban economics.

The Method of Economics

9. Economics asks and attempts to answer two kinds of questions: positive and normative. *Positive economics* attempts to understand behavior and the operation of economies without making judgments about whether the outcomes are good or bad. *Normative economics* looks at the results or outcomes of economic behavior and asks if they are good or bad and whether they can be improved.

10. Positive economics is often divided into two parts, descriptive economics and economic theory. *Descriptive economics* involves the compilation of data that accurately describe economic facts and events. *Economic theory* attempts to generalize and explain what is observed. It involves statements of cause and effect—of action and reaction.

11. An economic *model* is a formal statement of an economic theory. Models simplify and abstract from reality.

12. It is often useful to isolate the effects of one variable or another while holding "all else constant." This is the device of *ceteris paribus*.

13. Models and theories can be expressed in many ways. The most common ways are in words, in graphs, and in equations.

14. Because one event happens before another, the second event does not necessarily happen as a result of the first event. To assume that "after" implies "because" is to commit the fallacy of *post hoc, ergo propter hoc*.

15. The belief that what is true for a part is necessarily true for the whole is the *fallacy of composition*.

16. *Empirical economics* involves the collection and use of data to test economic theories. In principle, the best model is the one that yields the most accurate predictions.

17. To make policy, one must be careful to specify criteria for making judgments. Four specific criteria are used most often in economics: *efficiency, equity, growth,* and *stability*.

REVIEW TERMS AND CONCEPTS

ceteris paribus 16
descriptive economics 14
economic growth 20
economics 5
economic theory 14
efficiency 19
efficient markets 7
empirical economics 18

equity 20
fallacy of composition 17
inductive reasoning 14
Industrial Revolution 8
macroeconomics 11
market 7
microeconomics 10
model 14

normative economics 12
Ockham's razor 15
opportunity cost 6
positive economics 12
post hoc, ergo propter hoc 17
stability 20
sunk costs 6
variable 14

PROBLEM SET

1. One of the scarce resources that constrain our behavior is time. Each of us has only 24 hours in a day. How do you go about allocating your time in a given day among competing alternatives? How do you go about weighing the alternatives? Once you choose a most important use of time, why do you not spend all your time on it? Use the notion of opportunity cost in your answer.

2. Which of the following statements might be made by someone studying economics? Briefly explain your answer.
   a. A tax imposed on business firms' payrolls is likely to be shifted to workers in the form of lower wages.
   b. When one firm in an industry has too much power, the result is an inefficient allocation of resources.
   c. Higher-income households pay a smaller portion of their incomes in sales taxes than lower-income households do.
   d. Sales taxes are inequitable because they fall more heavily on the poor.

3. Describe one of the major economic issues facing the government of your city or your state. (*Hint:* You might look at a local newspaper. Most issues that make it into the paper will

have an impact on people's lives.) Who will be affected by the resolution of this issue? What alternative actions have been proposed? Who will be the winners? The losers?

4. Evidence suggests that the land in Kansas is best suited for wheat production and that the land in Ohio is best suited for corn production. Suppose that the Congress passes a law that forces all Ohio farmers to produce wheat and Kansas farmers to produce corn. Explain why such a law would be inefficient.

5. Suppose that a city is considering building a bridge across a river. The bridge will be paid for out of tax dollars, and the city gets its revenues from a sales tax imposed on things sold in the city. The bridge would provide more direct access for commuters and shoppers and would alleviate the huge traffic jam that occurs every morning at the bridge down the river. Who would gain if the bridge were built? Could those gains be measured? How? Who would be hurt? Could those costs be measured? How would you determine if it were efficient to build the bridge?

6. Define equity. How would you decide if building the bridge described in question 5 was fair/equitable?

APPENDIX TO CHAPTER 1
HOW TO READ AND UNDERSTAND GRAPHS

Economics is the most quantitative of the social sciences. If you flip through the pages of this or any other economics text, you will see countless tables and graphs. These tables and graphs serve a number of purposes. First, they illustrate important economic relationships. Second, they make difficult problems easier to understand and analyze.

Finally, patterns and regularities that may not be discernible in simple lists of numbers can often be seen when those numbers are laid out on a graph.

A **graph** is a two-dimensional representation of a set of numbers, or data. There are many ways that numbers can be illustrated by a graph.

TIME SERIES GRAPHS

It is often useful to see how a single measure or variable changes over time. One way to present this information is to plot the values of the variable on a graph, with each value corresponding to a different time period. A graph of this kind is called a **time series graph.** On a time series graph, time is measured along the horizontal scale and the variable being graphed is measured along the vertical scale. Figures 1A.1 and 1A.2 are time series graphs that present the total income in the U.S. economy for each year between 1975 and 1992.[1] These graphs are based on the data found in Table 1A.1. By displaying these data graphically, we can see clearly that (1) total personal disposable income has been increasing steadily since 1975, and (2) during certain periods, disposable income was increasing at a faster rate than during other periods.

Graphs must be read very carefully. For example, look at Figure 1A.2, which plots the same data that are plotted in Figure 1A.1. Because the values on the vertical axis in Figure 1A.2 start at $2300 billion rather than zero, and because the vertical scales are different, you may be led to believe that income is growing much more rapidly in Figure 1A.2 than in Figure 1A.1. This is not true, of course. The same variable is plotted in both graphs.

It is also important to think carefully about the variables that are being graphed. The income measure in Figures 1A.1 and 1A.2 is the total after-tax income of all households in the

---

[1]The measure of income presented in the graphs is disposable personal income. It is an approximation of the total personal income received by all households in the United States added together minus the taxes that they pay.

TABLE 1A.1
Total Disposable Income in the United States, 1975–1992 (in Billions of 1987 Dollars)

YEAR	TOTAL DISPOSABLE PERSONAL INCOME
1975	2355.4
1976	2440.9
1977	2512.6
1978	2638.4
1979	2710.1
1980	2733.6
1981	2795.8
1982	2820.4
1983	2893.6
1984	3080.1
1985	3162.1
1986	3261.9
1987	3289.6
1988	3404.3
1989	3464.9
1990	3516.5
1991	3509.0
1992	3585.1

Source: *Economic Report of the President*, 1993 and updates.

United States. If the number of households is increasing, *total* income can grow even if the incomes of individual households do not. In fact, this is exactly what has happened in the United States. A typical family's income has actually changed very little in real terms since 1975. You can see this clearly in Table 1A.2 and Figure 1A.3, which show that a typical family's income was about $33,000 in 1975 and about $35,000 in 1990—a very small change over 15 years.

FIGURE 1A.1
Total Disposable Personal Income in the United States: 1975–1992 (in Billions of 1987 Dollars)
(Source: *Economic Report of the President*, 1993 and updates.)

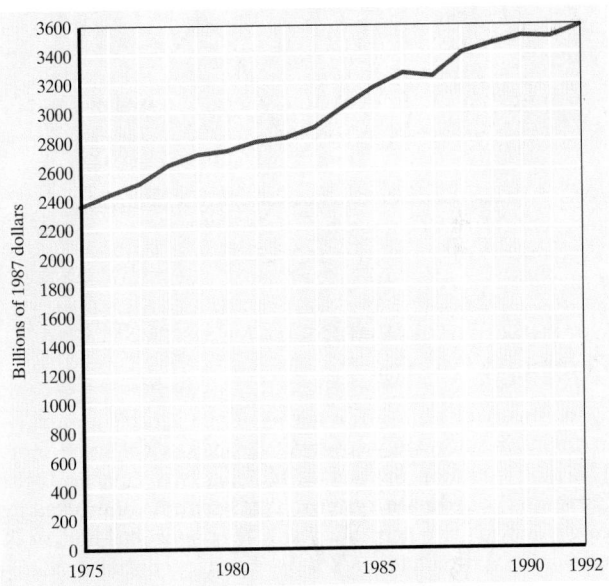

FIGURE 1A.2
Total Disposable Personal Income in the United States: 1975–1992 (in Billions of 1987 Dollars)
(Source: *Economic Report of the President*, 1993 and updates.)

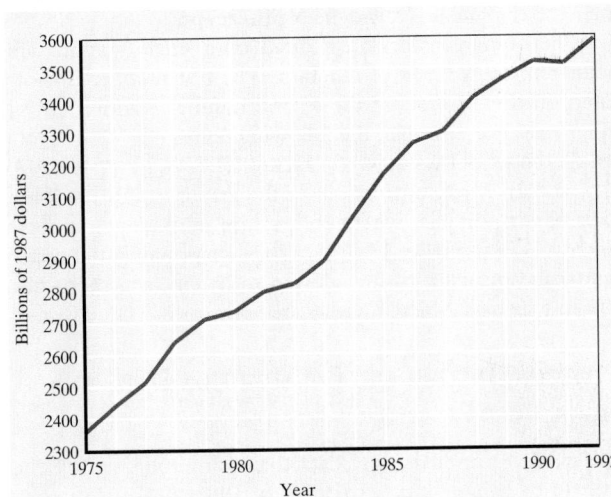

FIGURE 1A.3
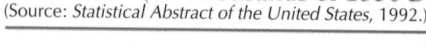
Median Family Income in the United States:
1975–1990 (in Thousands of 1990 Dollars)
(Source: *Statistical Abstract of the United States*, 1992.)

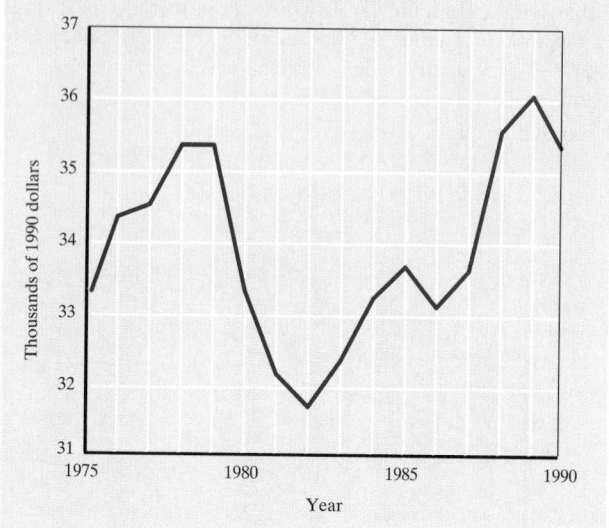

TABLE 1A.2
Median Family Income, 1975–1990 (in 1990 Dollars)

YEAR	MEDIAN FAMILY INCOME
1975	33,328
1976	34,359
1977	34,528
1978	35,361
1979	35,362
1980	33,346
1981	32,190
1982	31,738
1983	32,378
1984	33,251
1985	33,689
1986	35,129
1987	35,632
1988	35,565
1989	36,062
1990	35,353

Source: *Statistical Abstract of the United States*, 1992, p. 449.

GRAPHING TWO VARIABLES ON A CARTESIAN COORDINATE SYSTEM

More important than simple graphs of one variable are graphs that contain information on two variables at the same time. The most common method of graphing two variables is the **Cartesian coordinate system.** This system is constructed by simply drawing two perpendicular lines: a horizontal line, or **X axis**, and a vertical line, or **Y axis**. The axes contain measurement scales that intersect at 0 (zero). This point is called the **origin.** On the vertical scale, positive numbers lie above the horizontal axis (that is, above the origin) and negative numbers lie below it. On the horizontal scale, positive numbers lie to the right of the vertical axis (to the right of the origin) and negative numbers lie to the left of it. The point at which the graph intersects the *Y* axis is called the **Y-intercept.**

When two variables are plotted on a single graph, each point represents a *pair* of numbers. The first number is measured on the X axis and the second number is measured on the Y axis. For example, the following points (X, Y) are plotted on the set of axes drawn in Figure 1A.4: (4,2), (2, –1), (–3, 4), (–3, –2). Most, but not all, of the graphs in this book are plots of two variables where both values are positive numbers (such as [4,2] in Figure 1A.4). On these graphs, only the upper right-hand quadrant of the coordinate system (i.e., the quadrant in which all X and Y values are positive) will be drawn.

PLOTTING INCOME AND CONSUMPTION DATA FOR HOUSEHOLDS

Table 1A.3 presents some data that were collected by the Bureau of Labor Statistics (BLS). In 1986 the Bureau con-

ducted a survey of 5,000 households. Each household was asked to keep careful track of all its expenditures. The table shows average income and average spending for those households that were surveyed, ranked by income. For example, if you take only the top fifth (20%) of the households, their average income was $76,660, and their average spending was $55,411.

Figure 1A.5 presents the numbers from Table 1A.3 graphically using the Cartesian coordinate system. Along the horizontal scale, the X axis, we measure average income. Along the vertical scale, the Y axis, we measure average consumption spending. Each of the five pairs of numbers from the table is represented by a point on the graph. Since all numbers are positive numbers, we need to show only the upper right quadrant of the coordinate system.

To help you read this graph, we have drawn a dotted line connecting all the points where consumption and income would be equal. *This 45° line does not represent any data.* Rather, it represents the line along which all variables on the X axis correspond exactly to the variables on the Y axis (for example, [1,1], [2,2], [3.7,3.7], etc.). The heavy blue line traces out the BLS data; the dotted line is only to help you read the graph.

There are several things to look for when reading a graph. The first thing you should notice is whether the line slopes upward or downward as you move from left to right. This particular graph slopes upward, indicating that there seems to be a *positive relationship* between income and spending: The higher a household's income, the more

FIGURE 1A.4
A Cartesian Coordinate System

A Cartesian coordinate system is constructed by drawing two perpendicular lines; a vertical axis (the Y axis) and a horizontal axis (the X axis). Each axis is a measuring scale.

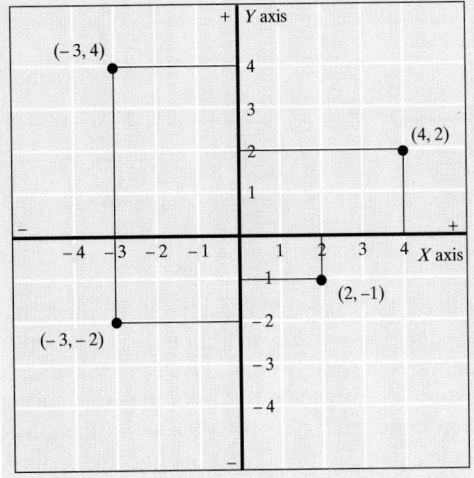

FIGURE 1A.5
Household Consumption and Income

A graph is a simple two-dimensional geometric representation of data. This graph displays the data from Table 1A.3. Along the horizontal scale (*X* axis), we measure household income. Along the vertical scale (*Y* axis), we measure household consumption. *Note:* At point *A*, consumption equals \$12,908 and income equals \$5,637; at point *B*, consumption equals \$17,924 and income equals \$14,115.

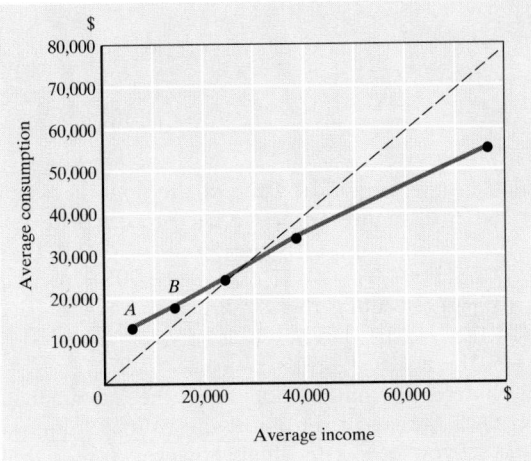

a household tends to consume. If we had graphed the percentage of each group receiving welfare payments along the Y axis, the line would presumably slope downward, indicating that welfare payments are lower at higher income levels. The income level/welfare payment relationship is thus a *negative* one.

SLOPE

The **slope** of a line or curve is a measure that indicates whether the relationship between the variables is positive or negative and how much of a response there is in *Y* (the

variable on the vertical axis) when *X* (the variable on the horizontal axis) changes. The slope of a line between two points is the change in the quantity being measured on the *Y* axis divided by the change in the quantity being measured on the *X* axis. We will normally use Δ (the Greek letter delta) to refer to a change in a variable. In Figure 1A.6, the slope of the line between points *A* and *B* is Δ*Y* divided by Δ*X*. Sometimes it's easy to remember slope as "the rise over the run," indicating the vertical change over the horizontal change.

TABLE 1A.3
Consumption Expenditures and Income, 1991*

	AVERAGE INCOME	AVERAGE CONSUMPTION EXPENDITURES
Bottom fifth	$ 5,637	$ 12,908
2nd fifth	14,115	17,924
3rd fifth	24,500	24,673
4th fifth	38,376	34,247
Top fifth	76,660	55,411

Source: *Statistical Abstract of the United States*, 1992, p. 442.

*Income and consumption data are for consumer units. Consumer units are defined as (1) all members of a particular household related by blood, marriage, adoption, or other legal arrangements, (2) a person living alone or sharing a household with others, but who is financially independent, or (3) two or more persons living together who pool their incomes.

To be precise, Δ*X* between two points on a graph is simply X_2 minus X_1, where X_2 is the *X* value for the second point and X_1 is the *X* value for the first point. Similarly, Δ*Y* is defined as Y_2 minus Y_1, where Y_2 is the *Y* value for the second point and Y_1 is the *Y* value for the first point. Slope, then, is equal to

$$\frac{\Delta Y}{\Delta X} = \frac{Y_2 - Y_1}{X_2 - X_1}.$$

As we move from *A* to *B* in Figure 1A.6a, both *X* and *Y* increase; the slope is thus a positive number. On the other hand, as we move from *A* to *B* in Figure 1A.6b, *X* increases [$(X_2 - X_1)$ is a positive number], but *Y* decreases [$(Y_2 - Y_1)$ is a negative number]. The slope in Figure 1A.6b is thus a negative number, since a negative number divided by a positive number gives a negative quotient.

FIGURE 1A.6

A Curve with a Positive Slope (a) and a Curve with a Negative Slope (b)

A *positive* slope indicates that increases in X are associated with increases in Y and that decreases in X are associated with decreases in Y. A *negative* slope indicates the opposite—when X increases, Y decreases and when X decreases, Y increases.

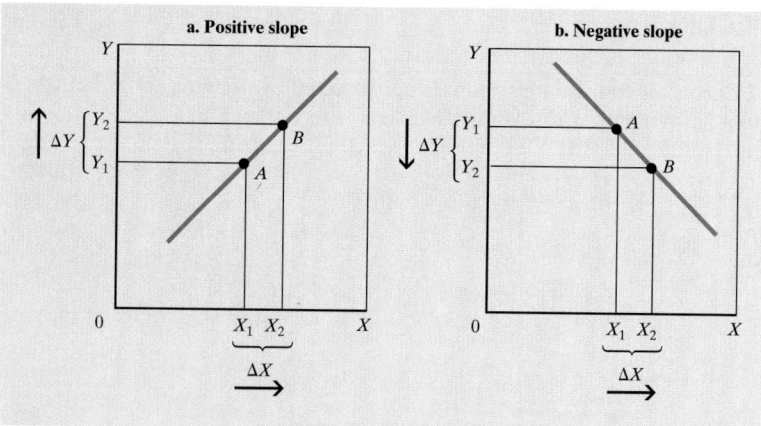

To calculate the numerical value of the slope between points A and B in Figure 1A.5, we need to calculate ΔY and ΔX. Since consumption is measured on the Y axis, ΔY is 5,016 [$(Y_2 - Y_1) = (17,924 - 12,908)$]. Since income is measured along the X axis, ΔX is 8,478 [$(X_2 - X_1) = (14,115 - 5,637)$]. The slope between A and B is $\Delta Y/\Delta X = 5,016/8,478 = +.592$.

Another interesting thing to note about the data graphed in Figure 1A.5 is that all the points lie roughly along a straight line. (If you look very closely, however, you can see that the slope declines as one moves from left to right; the curve becomes slightly less steep.) A straight line has a constant slope. That is, if you pick any two points along it and calculate the slope, you will always get the same number. A

horizontal line has a zero slope (ΔY is zero); a vertical line has an "infinite" slope, since ΔY is too big to be measured.

Unlike the slope of a straight line, the slope of a *curve* is continually changing. Consider, for example, the curves in Figure 1A.7. Figure 1A.7a shows a curve with a positive slope that decreases as you move from left to right. The easiest way to think about the concept of increasing or decreasing slope is to imagine what it is like walking up a hill from left to right. If the hill is steep (as it is in the first part of Figure 1A.7a), you are moving a lot in the Y direction for each step you take in the X direction. If the hill is less steep (as it is further along in Figure 1A.7a), you are moving less in the Y direction for every step you take in the X direction. Thus, when the hill is steep, slope

FIGURE 1A.7

Changing Slopes Along Curves

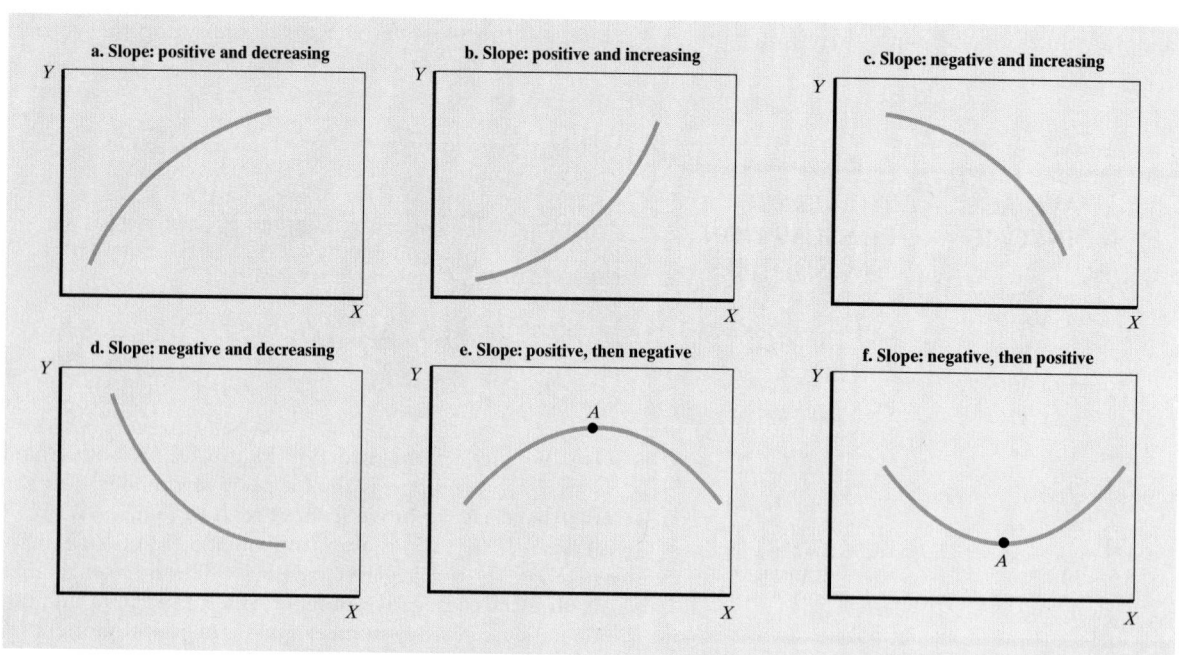

$(\Delta Y/\Delta X)$ is a larger number than it is when the hill is flatter. The curve in Figure 1A.7b has a positive slope, but its slope *increases* as you move from left to right.

The same analogy holds for curves that have a negative slope. Figure 1A.7c shows a curve with a negative slope that increases (in absolute value)[2] as you move from left to right. This time think about skiing down a hill. At first, the descent in Figure 1A.7c is gradual (low slope), but as you proceed down the hill (to the right), you descend more quickly (high slope). Figure 1A.7d shows a curve with a negative slope that *decreases* in absolute value as you move from left to right.

In Figure 1A.7e, the slope goes from positive to negative as X increases. In 1A.7f, the slope goes from negative to positive. At point A in both, the slope is zero. (Remember, slope is defined as $\Delta Y/\Delta X$. At point A, Y is not changing [$\Delta Y = 0$]. Therefore slope at point A is zero.)

SOME PRECAUTIONS

When you read a graph, it is important to think carefully about what the points in the space defined by the axes represent. Table 1A.4 and Figure 1A.8 present a graph of consumption and income that is very different from the one in Table 1A.3 and Figure 1A.5. First, each point in Figure 1A.8 represents a different year; in Figure 1A.5, each point represented a different group of households at the *same* point in time (1991). Second, the points in Figure 1A.8 represent *aggregate* consumption and income for the whole nation measured in *billions* of dollars; in Figure 1A.5, the points represented average *household* income and consumption measured in dollars.

---

[2]The *absolute value* of a number is its value disregarding its sign, that is, disregarding whether it is positive or negative: −7 is bigger in absolute value than −4; −9 is bigger in absolute value than +8.

FIGURE 1A.8

National Income and Consumption

It is important to think carefully about what is represented by points in the space defined by the axes of a graph. In this graph, we have income graphed with consumption, as was the case in Figure 1A.5, but here each observation point is national income and aggregate consumption in *different years*, measured in billions of dollars.

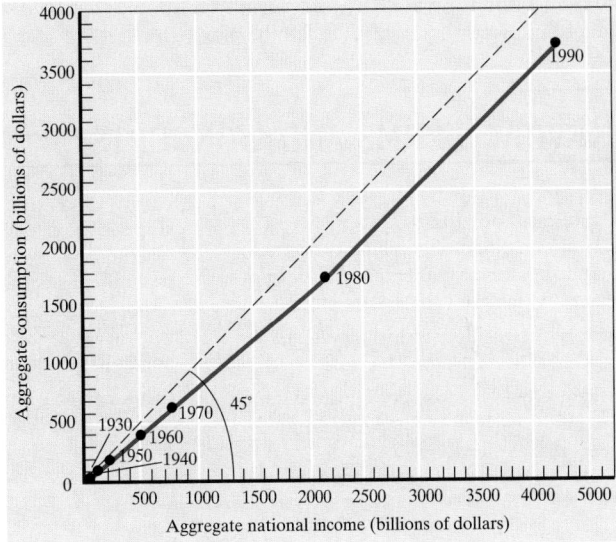

It is interesting to compare these two graphs. All points on the aggregate consumption curve in Figure 1A.8 lie below the 45-degree line, which means that aggregate consumption is always less than aggregate income. On the other hand, the graph of average household income and consumption in Figure 1A.5 crosses the 45-degree line, implying that for some households consumption is larger than income.

TABLE 1A.4

Aggregate Income and Consumption for the Entire United States, 1930–1990

	AGGREGATE NATIONAL INCOME (BILLIONS OF DOLLARS)	AGGREGATE CONSUMPTION (BILLIONS OF DOLLARS)
1930	73.8	69.9
1940	79.6	71.0
1950	239.8	192.1
1960	425.7	332.4
1970	833.5	646.5
1980	2198.2	1748.1
1990	4468.3	3748.4

Source: *Economic Report of the President*, 1993.

SUMMARY

1. A *graph* is a two-dimensional representation of a set of numbers, or data. A *time-series graph* illustrates how a single variable changes over time.

2. The most common method of graphing two variables on one graph is the *Cartesian coordinate system,* which includes an X (horizontal) *axis* and a Y (vertical) *axis*. The points at which the two axes intersect is called the *origin*. The point at which a graph intersects the Y axis is called the *Y-intercept.*

3. The *slope* of a line or curve indicates whether the relationship between the two variables graphed on a Cartesian coordinate system is positive or negative and how much of a response there is in Y (the variable on the vertical axis) when X (the variable on the horizontal axis) changes. The slope of a line between two points is the change in the quantity being measured on the Y axis divided by the change in the quantity being measured on the X axis.

REVIEW TERMS AND CONCEPTS

Cartesian coordinate system A common method of graphing two variables that makes use of two perpendicular lines against which the variables are plotted. 24

graph A two-dimensional representation of a set of numbers, or data. 22

origin On a Cartesian coordinate system, the point at which the horizontal and vertical axes intersect. 24

slope A measurement that indicates whether the relationship between variables is positive or negative and how much of a response there is in Y (the variable on the vertical axis) when X (the variable on the horizontal axis) changes. 26

times series graph A graph illustrating how a variable changes over time. 23

X axis On a Cartesian coordinate system, the horizontal line against which a variable is plotted. 24

Y axis On a Cartesian coordinate system, the vertical line against which a variable is plotted. 24

Y-intercept The point at which a graph intersects the Y axis. 24

PROBLEM SET

1. Graph each of the following sets of numbers. Draw a line through the points and calculate the slope of each line.

1		2		3		4		5		6	
X	Y	X	Y	X	Y	X	Y	X	Y	X	Y
1	5	1	25	0	0	0	40	0	0	0.1	100
2	10	2	20	10	10	10	30	10	10	0.2	75
3	15	3	15	20	20	20	20	20	20	0.3	50
4	20	4	10	30	30	30	10	30	10	0.4	25
5	25	5	5	40	40	40	0	40	0	0.5	0

2. For each of the following equations graph the line and calculate its slope.
   a. $P = 10 - 2q_D$ (Put q_D on the X-axis)
   b. $P = 100 - 4q_D$ (Put q_D on the X-axis)
   c. $P = 50 + 6q_S$ (Put q_S on the X-axis)
   d. $I = 10{,}000 - 500r$ (Put I on the X-axis)

3. For each of the graphs in Figure 1 below, say whether the curve has a positive or negative slope. Give an intuitive explanation for the slope of each curve.

FIGURE 1

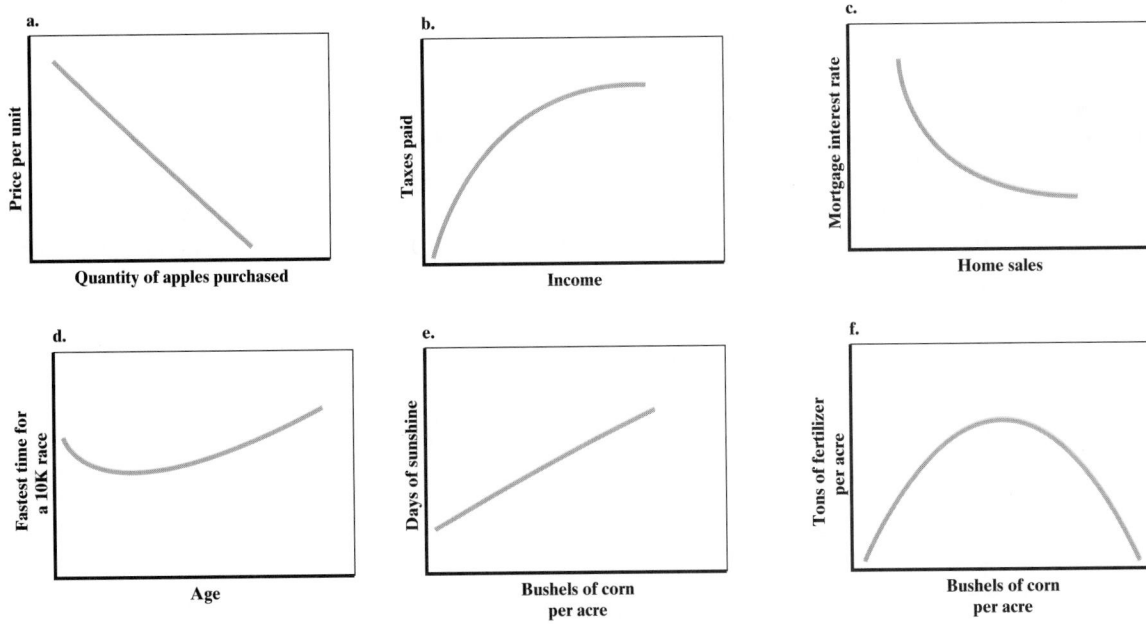

2 The Economic Problem: Scarcity and Choice

Chapter 1 began with a broad definition of economics. As you saw there, every society has some system or mechanism that transforms what nature and previous generations provide into useful form. Economics is the study of that process and its outcomes. Economists attempt to answer the questions: What gets produced? How is it produced? Who gets it? Why? Is it good or bad? Can it be improved?

This chapter explores these questions further. In a sense, this entire chapter *is* the definition of economics. It lays out the central problems addressed by the discipline and provides the framework that will guide you through the rest of the book.

Human wants are unlimited, but resources are not. Limited, or *scarce,* resources force individuals and societies to *choose.* The central function of any economy, no matter how simple or how complex, is to transform resources into useful form in accordance with those choices. The process by which this transformation takes place is called **production.**

The term **resources** is very broad. Some resources are the product of nature: land, wildlife, minerals, timber, energy, even the rain and the wind. At any given time, the resources, or **inputs,** available to a society also include those things that have been produced by previous generations, such as buildings and equipment. Things that are produced and then used to produce other valuable goods or services later on are called

production The process by which resources are transformed into useful forms.

resources or inputs Anything provided by nature or previous generations that can be used directly or indirectly to satisfy human wants.

capital resources, or simply **capital.** Buildings, machinery, equipment, tables, roads, bridges, desks, and so forth are part of the nation's *capital stock. Human resources*—labor, skills, and knowledge—are also an important part of a nation's resources.

Producers are those who take resources and transform them into usable products, or **outputs.** Private manufacturing firms purchase resources and produce products for the market. Governments do so as well. National defense, the justice system, police and fire protection, and sewer services are all examples of outputs produced by the government, which is sometimes called the *public sector.*

Individual households often produce products for themselves. A household that owns its own home is in essence using land and a structure (capital) to produce "housing services" that it consumes itself. The Boston Symphony Orchestra is no less a producer than General Motors. An orchestra takes capital resources–a building, musical instruments, lighting fixtures, musical scores, and so on–and combines them with land and highly skilled labor to produce performances.

capital Things that have already been produced that are in turn used to produce other goods and services.

producers Those people or groups of people, whether private or public, who transform resources into usable products, or output.

outputs Usable products.

Scarcity, Choice, and Opportunity Cost

In the second half of this chapter, we discuss the global economic landscape. To understand the different types of economic systems, it is important to understand the basic economic concepts of scarcity, choice, and opportunity cost.

The Three Basic Questions

All societies must answer **three basic questions:**

1. What will be produced?
2. How will it be produced?
3. Who will get what is produced?

three basic questions The questions that all societies must answer: (1) What will be produced? (2) How will it be produced? (3) Who will get what is produced?

Stated a slightly different way, the economic system must determine the *allocation of scarce resources* among producers, the *mix of output,* and the *distribution of that output* (see Figure 2.1).

FIGURE 2.1
The Economic Problem

All societies are endowed by nature and by previous generations with limited–or scarce–resources. Every society must decide how to use these inputs to satisfy human wants. Specifically, resources must be divided up among producers who transform them into useful things–*products* or *outputs*–that must then be divided up among households or members of society.

The three basic questions: 1. What will be produced?   2. How will it be produced?   3. Who will get what is produced?

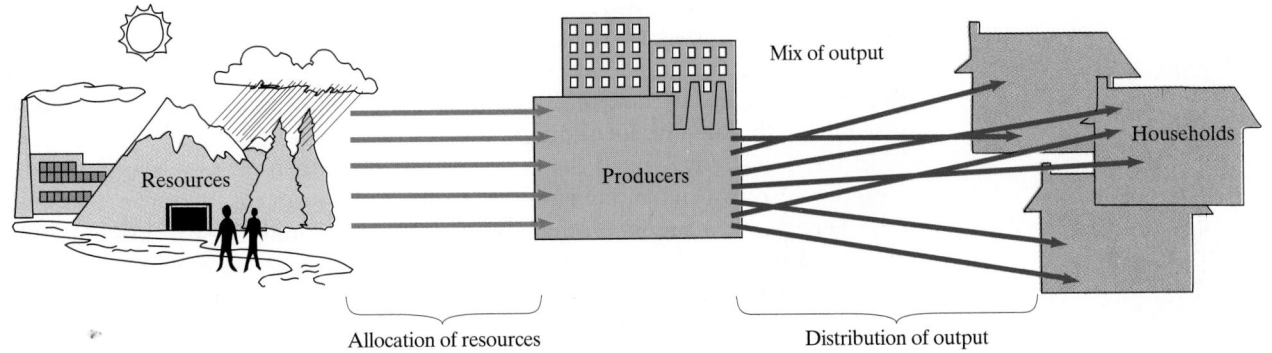

SCARCITY AND CHOICE IN A ONE-PERSON ECONOMY The simplest economy is one in which a single person lives alone on an island where no one has ever been before. Consider Bill, the survivor of a plane crash, who finds himself cast ashore in such a place. Here, individual and society are one; there is no distinction between social and private. *Nonetheless, nearly all of the basic decisions that characterize complex economies must be made.* That is, although Bill himself will get whatever he produces, he still must decide how to allocate the resources of the island, what to produce, and how and when to produce it.

First, Bill must decide *what* he wants to produce. Notice that the word *needs* does not appear here. Needs are absolute requirements, but beyond just enough water, basic nutrition, and shelter to survive, they are very difficult to define. What is an "absolute necessity" for one may not be for another. In any case, Bill must put his wants in some order of priority and make some choices.

Next he must look at the *possibilities.* What can he do to satisfy his wants, given the limits of the island? In every society, no matter how simple or complex, no matter how rich or poor, people are constrained in what they can do. In this society of one, Bill is constrained by time, his physical condition, his knowledge, his skills, and the resources and climate of the island.

Given that resources are limited, or scarce, Bill must decide *how* to use them best to satisfy his hierarchy of wants. Food would probably come close to the top of his list. Should he spend his time simply gathering fruits and berries? Should he hunt for game? Should he clear a field and plant seeds? The planting option involves more time than the other two. If Bill takes time away from gathering food today, he will have less to eat today, but he may have more to eat tomorrow.

Clearly, the answers to these questions depend on the character of the island, its climate, its flora and fauna (*are* there any fruits and berries?), the extent of his skills and knowledge (does he know anything about farming?), and his preferences (he may be a vegetarian).

OPPORTUNITY COST The concepts of *constrained choice* and *scarcity* are central to the discipline of economics. They can be applied when discussing the behavior of individuals like Bill and when analyzing the behavior of large groups of people in complex societies.

Given the scarcity of time and resources, Bill has less time to gather fruits and berries if he chooses to hunt—he trades more meat for less fruit. There is a trade-off between food and shelter, too. If Bill likes to be comfortable, he may work on building a nice place to live, but that may require giving up the food he might have produced. As we noted in Chapter 1, we call that which we forgo when we make a choice the **opportunity cost** of the choice.

opportunity cost That which we give up, or forgo, when we make a choice.

Bill may occasionally decide to rest, to lie on the beach and enjoy the sun. In one sense, that benefit is free—he doesn't have to pay for the privilege. In reality, however, it does have a cost, an opportunity cost. Lying in the sun means using time that otherwise could have been spent doing something else. The true cost of that leisure is the value to Bill of the other things he could have produced, but did not, during the time he spent on the beach.

In the 1960s, the United States decided to put a man on the moon. To do so required devoting enormous resources to the space program, resources that could have been used to produce other things. The opportunity cost of placing a man on the moon was the total value of all the other things that those resources could have produced. Among other possibilities, taxes might have been lower. That would have meant more income for all of us to spend on goods and services.

Those same resources could also have been used for medical research, for aid to education, to build a bridge, or to support the arts.

In making everyday decisions it is sometimes helpful to think about opportunity costs. Should I go to the dorm party or not? First, it costs $4 to get in. When I pay out money for anything, I give up the other things that I could have bought with that money. Second, it costs two or three hours. Clearly, time is a valuable commodity for a college student. I have exams next week and I need to study. I could go to a movie. I could go to another party. I could sleep. Just as Bill must weigh the value of sunning on the beach against more food or better housing, so I must weigh the value of the fun I may have at the dorm party against everything else I might otherwise do with the time and money.

SCARCITY AND CHOICE IN AN ECONOMY OF TWO OR MORE Now suppose that another survivor of the crash, Colleen, appears on the island. Now that Bill is not alone things are more complex, and some new decisions must be made. Bill's and Colleen's preferences about what things to produce are likely to be different. They will probably not have the same knowledge or skills. Perhaps Colleen is very good at tracking animals, while Bill has a knack for building things. How should they split the work that needs to be done? Once things are produced, they must decide how to divide them. How should their products be *distributed?*

The mechanism for answering these fundamental questions is clear when Bill alone is on the island. The "central plan" is his; he simply decides what he wants and what to do about it. The minute someone else appears, however, a number of decision-making arrangements immediately become possible. One or the other may take charge, in which case that person will decide for both of them. The two may agree to cooperate, with each having an equal say, and come up with a joint plan. Or they may agree to split the planning, as well as the production duties. Finally, they may go off to live alone at opposite ends of the island. Even if they live apart, however, they may take advantage of each other's presence by specializing and trading.

> Modern industrial societies must answer exactly the same questions that Colleen and Bill must answer, but the mechanics of larger economies are naturally more complex. Instead of two people living together, the United States has over 250 million. Still decisions must be made about what to produce, how to produce it, and who gets it.

SPECIALIZATION, EXCHANGE, AND COMPARATIVE ADVANTAGE The idea that members of society benefit by specializing in what they do best has a long history and is one of the most important and powerful ideas in all of economics. David Ricardo, a major nineteenth-century British economist, formalized the point precisely. According to Ricardo's **theory of comparative advantage,** specialization and free trade will benefit all trading parties, even when some are "absolutely" more efficient producers than others. Ricardo's basic point applies just as much to Colleen and Bill as it does to different nations.

To keep things simple, suppose that Colleen and Bill have only two tasks to accomplish each week: gathering food to eat and cutting logs to be used in constructing a house. If Colleen could cut more logs than Bill in one day, and Bill could gather more nuts and berries than Colleen could, specialization would clearly lead to more total production. Both Bill and Colleen would benefit if

theory of comparative advantage Ricardo's theory that specialization and free trade will benefit all trading parties, even those that may be absolutely more efficient producers.

TABLE 2.1
Comparative Advantage in a Two-Person Society

PRODUC-TION PER DAY	(1) FUEL (LOGS)	(2) FOOD (BUSHELS)
Colleen	10	10
Bill	4	8

Colleen only cuts logs and Bill only gathers nuts and berries. But suppose that Bill is slow and somewhat clumsy in his nut-gathering and that Colleen is better at both cutting logs *and* gathering food. Ricardo's point is that it still pays for them to specialize and exchange.

Suppose that Colleen can cut 10 logs per day and that Bill can cut only 4. Also suppose that Colleen can gather 10 bushels of food per day and that Bill can gather only 8. Assume also that Bill and Colleen value bushels of food and logs equally. How then can the two gain from specialization and exchange? Think of opportunity costs. When Colleen gives up a day of food production to work on the house, she cuts 10 logs and sacrifices 10 bushels of food. The opportunity cost of 10 logs is thus 10 bushels of food if Colleen switches from food to logs (see row 1 in Table 2.1). But because Bill can cut only 4 logs in a day, he has to work for 2 1/2 days to cut 10 logs. In 2 1/2 days, Bill could have produced 20 bushels of food (2 1/2 days × 8 bushels per day). The opportunity cost of 10 logs is thus *20* bushels of food if Bill switches from food to logs.

The point is clear. Even though Colleen is *absolutely* more efficient at food production than Bill, she should specialize in logs and let Bill specialize in food. This way, the maximum number of logs and bushels are produced. A person or a country is said to have a comparative advantage in producing a good or service if it is *relatively* more efficient than a trading partner at doing so. Colleen is relatively more efficient at log production because the opportunity cost of switching from food to logs is lower for her than it is for Bill.

Looking at the situation from the point of view of food production leads to exactly the same conclusion. Consider the opportunity cost of collecting 10 bushels of food. If Colleen shifted a day from log cutting to food production, 10 logs would be lost to gain 10 bushels of food. It would take Bill 1 1/4 days to produce 10 bushels of food, but since he is so bad at log cutting, the cost of his switching from log cutting to food production is only 5 logs (1 1/4 days × 4 logs per day). Thus, the opportunity cost of switching from logs to food for Bill is lower than it is for Colleen: Bill has a comparative advantage in food gathering. Thus, Bill and Colleen should specialize and exchange, with Colleen cutting logs and Bill gathering food.

The theory of comparative advantage shows that trade and specialization work to raise productivity. But specialization may also lead to the development of skills that enhance productivity even further. By specializing in log cutting, Colleen will get even stronger shoulders. By spending more time at gathering food, Bill will refine his food-finding skills. The same applies to countries that engage in international trade. A country that specializes in producing textiles will refine its skills in textile making, while a country that specializes in growing corn will increase its corn-growing skills.

The degree of specialization in modern industrial societies is breathtaking. Once again let your mind wander over the range of products and services available or under development today. As knowledge expands, specialization becomes a necessity. This is true not only for scientists and doctors, but also in every career from tree surgeon to divorce lawyers. Understanding specialization and trade will help you to explain much of what goes on in the world. It will also help you understand why today's economy is considered "global."

WEIGHING PRESENT AND EXPECTED FUTURE COSTS AND BENEFITS Very often we find ourselves weighing benefits available today against benefits available tomorrow. Here too the notion of opportunity cost is helpful.

While alone on the island, Bill had to choose between cultivating a field and just gathering wild nuts and berries. Gathering nuts and berries provides food now; gathering seeds and clearing a field for planting will yield food tomorrow, if all goes well. Using today's time to farm may well be worth the effort if doing so will yield more food than Bill would otherwise have in the future. By planting, Bill is trading present value for future values. Working to gather seeds and clear a field has an opportunity cost—the present leisure he might consume and the value of the berries he might gather if he did not work the field.

The simplest example of trading present for future benefits is the act of saving. When I put income aside today for use in the future, I give up some things that I could have had today in exchange for something tomorrow. The saver must weigh the value of what that income can buy today against what it might be expected to buy later. Since nothing is certain, some judgment about future events and expected values must be made. What are interest rates likely to be? What will my income be in ten years? How long am I likely to live?

We trade off present and future benefits in small ways all the time. If you decide to study rather than go to the dorm party, you are trading present fun for the expected future benefits of higher grades. If you decide to go outside on a very cold day and run five miles, you are trading discomfort in the present for being in better shape later on.

CAPITAL GOODS AND CONSUMER GOODS   A society trades present for expected future benefits when it devotes a portion of its resources to research and development or to investment in capital. As we said earlier, *capital* in its broadest definition is anything that is produced that will be used to produce other valuable goods or services over time.

Building capital means trading present benefits for future ones. Bill and Colleen might trade gathering berries or lying in the sun for cutting logs to build a nicer house in the future. In a modern society, resources used to produce capital goods could have been used to produce **consumer goods,** that is, goods for present consumption. Heavy industrial machinery does not directly satisfy the wants of anyone, but producing it requires resources that could instead have gone into producing food, clothing, toys, or golf clubs.

consumer goods Goods produced for present consumption.

Capital is everywhere. A road is capital. Once built, we can drive on it or transport goods and services over it for many years to come. The benefits of producing it will be realized over many years. A house is also capital. When it is built, the builder presumes that it will provide shelter and valuable services for a long time. Before a new manufacturing firm can start up, it must put some capital in place. The buildings, equipment, and inventories that it owns are its capital. As it contributes to the production process, this capital yields valuable services through time.

Capital need not be tangible. When you spend time and resources developing skills or getting an education, you are investing in human capital—your own human capital—that will continue to exist and yield benefits to you for years to come. A computer program produced by a software company may come on a tangible disk that costs 75¢ to make, but its true intangible value comes from the ideas embodied in the program itself, which will drive computers to do valuable tasks over time. It too is capital.

The process of using resources to produce new capital is called **investment.** (In everyday language, the term *investment* is often used to refer to the act of buying a share of stock or a bond, as in "I invested in some Treasury bonds." In economics,

investment The process of using resources to produce new capital.

however, investment always refers to the creation of capital: the purchase or putting in place of buildings, equipment, roads, houses, and the like.) A wise investment in capital is one that yields future benefits that are more valuable than the present cost. When you spend money for a house, for example, presumably you value its future benefits; that is, you expect to gain more from living in it than you would from the things you could buy today with the same money.

Capital is able to generate future benefits in excess of cost by increasing the *productivity of labor*. A person who has to dig a hole can dig a bigger hole with a shovel than without a shovel. A computer can do in several seconds what it took hundreds of bookkeepers hours to do 15 years ago. This increased productivity makes it less costly to produce products.

In Chapter 1 we talked about the enormous amount of capital–buildings, roads, factories, housing, cars, trucks, telephone lines, and so forth–that you might see from a window high in a skyscraper. Much of it was put in place by previous generations, yet it continues to provide valuable services today; it is part of this generation's endowment of resources. In order to build every building, every road, every factory, every house, every car or truck, society must forgo using resources to produce consumer goods today. To get an education, I pay tuition and put off joining the work force for awhile.

> Because resources are scarce, the opportunity cost of every investment in capital is forgone present consumption.

The Production Possibility Frontier

production possibility frontier (ppf) A graph that shows all the combinations of goods and services that can be produced if all of society's resources are used efficiently.

A simple graphical device called the **production possibility frontier (ppf)** illustrates the principle of constrained choice and scarcity. The ppf is a graph that shows all the combinations of goods and services that can be produced if all of society's resources are used efficiently. Figure 2.2 shows a ppf for a hypothetical economy.

FIGURE 2.2
Production Possibility Frontier

The production possibility frontier illustrates a number of economic concepts. One of the most important is *opportunity cost*. The opportunity cost of producing more capital goods is that fewer consumption goods can be produced. Moving from *E* to *F*, ΔK is the change in the number of capital goods; here it shows an increase. To produce more capital goods, resources must be transferred from the production of consumer goods. ΔC is the change in number of consumer goods; here it shows a decrease.

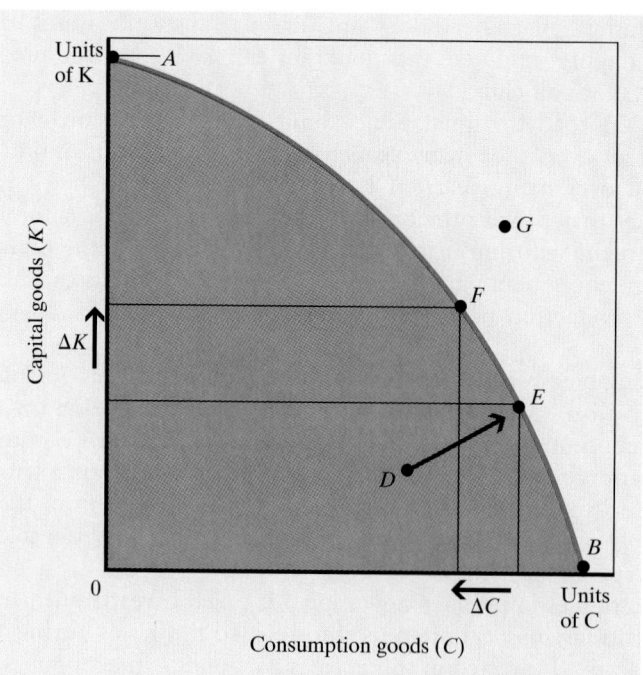

On the Y axis we measure the quantity of capital goods (K) produced, and on the X axis, the quantity of consumption goods (C). All points below and to the left of the curve (the shaded area) represent combinations of capital and consumption goods that are possible for the society given the resources available and existing technology. Points above and to the right of the curve, such as point G, represent combinations that cannot be reached. If an economy were to end up at point A on the graph, it would be producing no consumption goods at all; all resources would be used for the production of capital. On the other hand, if an economy were to end up at point B, it would be devoting all of its resources to the production of consumer goods and none of its resources to the formation of capital.

While all economies produce some of each kind of good, different economies emphasize different things. About 17% of gross output in the United States in 1991 was new capital. In Japan, capital accounted for 32% of gross output in 1991, while in Argentina the figure was only 9 percent. Japan is closer to point A on its ppf, Argentina closer to B, and the United States is somewhere in between.

Points that are actually on the production possibility frontier can be thought of as points of both full employment and production efficiency. Resources are not going unused, and there is no waste. Points that lie within the shaded area, but that are not on the frontier, represent either unemployment or production inefficiency. An economy producing at point D in Figure 2.2 can produce more capital goods and more consumption goods, for example, by moving to E. This is possible only if resources were initially not fully employed or if resources were not being used efficiently.

UNEMPLOYMENT   During the Great Depression of the 1930s, the U.S. economy experienced prolonged unemployment. Millions of workers who were willing to work found themselves without jobs. In 1933, 25% of the civilian labor force was unemployed. This figure stayed above 14% until 1940, when increased defense spending by the United States created millions of jobs. In 1975, and again in 1982, the economy experienced high levels of unemployment. In June of 1975, the unemployment rate went over 9% for the first time since the 1930s. In December of 1982, when the unemployment rate hit 10.8%, nearly 12 million were out looking for work.

In addition to the hardship that falls on the unemployed themselves, unemployment of labor means unemployment of capital. During the downturn of 1982, industrial plants were running at less than 69% of their total capacity. That meant that a considerable fraction of the nation's industrial capital was sitting idle and, in effect, being wasted. Clearly, when there is unemployment we are not producing all that we can.

Periods of unemployment correspond to points inside the production possibility frontier, points like D in Figure 2.2. Moving onto the frontier from a point like D means moving up and to the right, achieving full employment and increasing production of both capital goods and consumer goods.

INEFFICIENCY   Recall from Chapter 1 that an efficient economy is one that produces the things that people want at the least cost. Although production inefficiency occurs when a country is producing inside its production possibility frontier, an economy is also inefficient when it is producing at the wrong point on the ppf—that is, when it is producing a combination of goods and services that does not match the wants of its people.

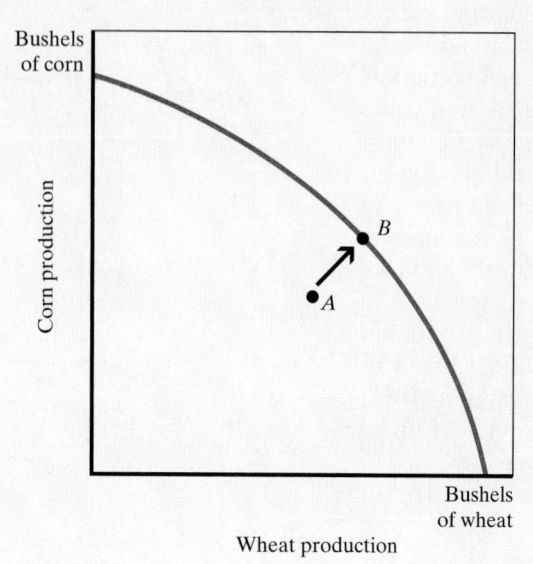

FIGURE 2.3
Inefficiency from Misallocation of Land in Farming

Society can end up inside its production possibility frontier at a point like A by using its resources inefficiently. If, for example, Ohio's climate and soil were best suited for corn production and those of Kansas were best suited for wheat production, a law that forces Kansas farmers to produce corn and Ohio farmers to produce wheat would result in less of both. In such a case, society might be at point A rather than point B.

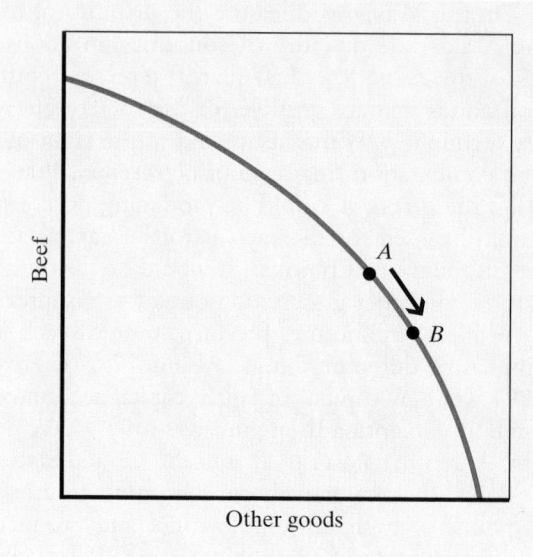

FIGURE 2.4
Inefficient Mix of Output Resulting from a Monopoly

Even if resources are combined efficiently in production, the result is inefficient if the economy is not producing the combination of goods and services that people want. This can occur if a monopoly controls an industry.

Certainly, a badly managed economy will not produce up to potential and will be inside the ppf. Suppose, for example, that the land and climate in Ohio are best suited for corn production and that the land and climate in Kansas are best suited for wheat production. If Congress passes a law forcing farmers in Ohio to plant 50% of their acreage in wheat and farmers in Kansas to plant 50% in corn, neither corn nor wheat production will be up to potential. The economy will be at a point like A in Figure 2.3–inside the production possibility frontier. Allowing each state to specialize in producing the crop that it produces best increases the production of both corn and wheat and moves the economy to a point like B in Figure 2.3.

In extreme cases, a wrong output mix is obvious. Suppose, for example, that a society uses all of its resources to produce beef efficiently, but that everyone in the society is a vegetarian. The result is a total waste of resources (assuming that the society cannot trade beef for vegetables with another society).

A wrong mix of output can be less obvious, however. Beef production is a highly competitive industry in the United States. Hundreds of thousands of farmers sell millions of cattle each year to hundreds of meat packing firms. Most grocery stores have plentiful stocks at reasonable prices because there are many suppliers competing for business.

Suppose that the government were to grant the sole right to produce beef (that is, a *monopoly*) to a single company. Even if all resources remained fully and efficiently employed, the monopoly would push the economy to a less desirable point on the ppf–that is, a point at which beef is underproduced and other goods are overproduced, a point such as *B* instead of *A* in Figure 2.4. In the absence of the monopoly, the society can move back to point *A*, which more closely matches the preferences of its people.

NEGATIVE SLOPE AND OPPORTUNITY COST As we've seen, points that lie on the production possibility frontier represent points of full employment and efficiency of production. But society can choose only one point on the curve. Because a society's choices are constrained by available resources and existing technology, when those resources are fully and efficiently employed it can produce more capital goods only by reducing production of consumption goods.

Recall that the slope of a curve between two points can be measured by dividing the change between the points on the *Y* axis (ΔY) by the change between the points on the *X* axis (ΔX). (Review the appendix to Chapter 1.) Moving from point *E* to point *F* in Figure 2.2 involves increasing capital production by ΔK units and decreasing production of consumption goods by ΔC units. Capital production increases (ΔK is a positive number) and consumption goods production decreases (ΔC is a negative number). Thus the value of the slope of a ppf, $\Delta K/\Delta C$, is a negative number.

The value of the slope of a society's production possibility frontier is called its **marginal rate of transformation (MRT).** The MRT is the number of units of capital goods you can get by giving up one unit of consumer goods. If in moving from *E* to *F* in Figure 2.2 we gain 100 units of capital goods and give up 50 units of consumer goods, the marginal rate of transformation would be -2. How do we arrive at this figure? Remember

marginal rate of transformation (MRT) The value of the slope of the production possibilities frontier. The number of units of one kind of good you can get by giving up one unit of another kind of good.

$$MRT = \text{slope of ppf} = \frac{\Delta Y}{\Delta X} = \frac{+100}{-50} = -2$$

We can transform consumer goods into capital goods at a rate of 2 to 1–two units of capital goods for every one unit of consumer goods.

A valuable feature of the production possibility frontier is that it forces you to think of opportunity cost. If we want more consumer goods, the cost is a sacrifice of capital goods.

> The marginal rate of transformation is thus actually a way of stating the opportunity cost. If the marginal rate of transformation of capital goods into consumption goods is currently -2, the opportunity cost of a unit of consumption goods is the two units of capital goods that must be forgone.

THE LAW OF INCREASING OPPORTUNITY COSTS We have noted that the slope of the ppf indicates the trade-off that a society faces between two goods that it produces. We can learn something further about the shape of the frontier and the terms of this trade-off. Let us look at the trade-off between corn and wheat production in Kansas and Ohio. In a recent year Kansas and Ohio together produced 510 million bushels of corn and 380 million bushels of wheat. Table 2.2

TABLE 2.2
Production Possibility
Schedule for Total Wheat
and Corn Production in
Ohio and Kansas

POINT ON PPF	TOTAL CORN PRODUCTION (MILLIONS OF BUSHELS PER YEAR)	TOTAL WHEAT PRODUCTION (MILLIONS OF BUSHELS PER YEAR)
A	700	100
B	650	200
C	510	380
D	400	500
E	300	550

presents these two numbers plus some hypothetical combinations of corn and wheat production that might exist for Kansas and Ohio together. Figure 2.5 graphs the data from Table 2.2.

Now suppose that the demand for corn dramatically increases. If this happens, farmers would probably shift some of their acreage from wheat production to corn production. Such a shift is represented by a move from point *C* up and to the left along the ppf toward points *A* and *B* in Figure 2.5. As this happens, it becomes more and more difficult to produce additional corn. The best land for corn production was presumably in corn, and the best land for wheat production in wheat. As we try to produce more and more corn, the land is less and less well suited to that crop. And as we take more and more land out of wheat production, we will be taking increasingly better wheat-producing land. All of this is to say that the opportunity cost of more corn, measured in terms of wheat, increases.

Moving from *E* to *D*, we can get 100 million bushels of corn (400 - 300) by sacrificing only 50 million bushels of wheat (550 - 500)—that is, we get two bushels of corn for every bushel of wheat. However, when we are already taxing the ability of the land to produce corn, it becomes more difficult to produce more corn, and the opportunity cost goes up. Moving from *B* to *A*, we

FIGURE 2.5
Corn and Wheat Production
in Ohio and Kansas

The ppf illustrates that the opportunity cost of corn production increases as we shift resources from wheat production to corn production. Moving from *E* to *D*, we get an additional 100 million bushels of corn at a cost of 50 million bushels of wheat. Moving from *B* to *A*, we get only 50 million bushels of corn at a cost of 100 million bushels of wheat. The cost *per bushel* of corn–measured in lost or forgone wheat–has increased four times.

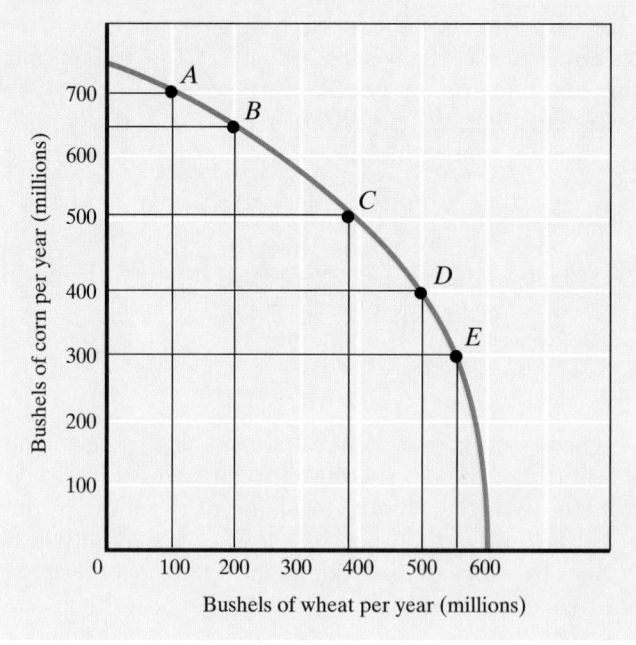

can get only 50 million bushels of corn (700 - 650) by sacrificing 100 million bushels of wheat (200 - 100). For every bushel of wheat, we now get only half a bushel of corn. On the other hand, if the demand for *wheat* were to increase substantially and we were to move down and to the right along the production possibility frontier, it would become increasingly difficult to produce wheat, and the opportunity cost of wheat, in terms of corn, would rise.

It is important to remember that the ppf represents choices available within the constraints imposed by the current state of agricultural technology. In the long run, technology may improve, and when that happens we have *growth.*

ECONOMIC GROWTH   **Economic growth** is characterized by an increase in the total output of an economy. It occurs when a society acquires new resources or when society learns to produce more with existing resources. New resources may mean a larger labor force or an increased capital stock. The production and use of new machinery and equipment (capital) increases the productivity of workers. Improved productivity also comes from technological change and *innovation,* the discovery and application of new, efficient techniques of production.

economic growth An increase in the total output of an economy. It occurs when a society acquires new resources or when it learns to produce more using existing resources.

The last 30 years have seen dramatic increases in the productivity of U.S. agriculture. Based on data compiled by the Department of Agriculture, Table 2.3 shows that yield per acre in corn production has quadrupled since the late 1930s, while the labor required to produce it has dropped dramatically. Productivity in wheat production has also increased, at only a slightly less remarkable rate: Output per acre has tripled, while labor requirements are down nearly 90 percent. These increases are the result of more efficient farming techniques, more and better capital (tractors, combines, and other equipment), and advances in scientific knowledge and technological change (hybrid seeds, fertilizers, and so forth). As you can see in Figure 2.6, increases such as these shift the ppf up and to the right.

Sources of Growth and the Dilemma of the Poor Countries   Economic growth arises from many sources, the two most important of which, over the years, have been the accumulation of capital and technological advances. For poor countries, capital is essential; they must build the communication networks and transportation systems necessary to develop industries that function efficiently. They also need capital goods to develop their agricultural sectors.

TABLE 2.3
Increasing Productivity in Corn and Wheat Production in the United States, 1935–1990

	CORN		WHEAT	
	YIELD PER ACRE (BUSHELS)	LABOR HOURS PER 100 BUSHELS	YIELD PER ACRE (BUSHELS)	LABOR HOURS PER 100 BUSHELS
1935–1939	26.1	108	13.2	67
1945–1949	36.1	53	16.9	34
1955–1959	48.7	20	22.3	17
1965–1969	78.5	7	27.5	11
1975–1979	95.3	4	31.3	9
1981–1985	107.2	3	36.9	7
1985–1990	112.8	NA*	38.0	NA

Source: U.S. Department of Agriculture, Economic Research Service, *Agricultural Statistics,* 1992.

*Data no longer available.

FIGURE 2.6
Economic Growth Shifts the ppf Up and to the Right

Productivity increases have enhanced the ability of the United States to produce both corn and wheat. As Table 2.3 shows, productivity increases were more dramatic for corn than for wheat. The shifts in the ppf were thus not parallel.

Note: The ppf also shifts if the amount of land or labor in corn and wheat production changes. Although we emphasize productivity increases here, the actual shifts between years were in part due to land and labor changes.

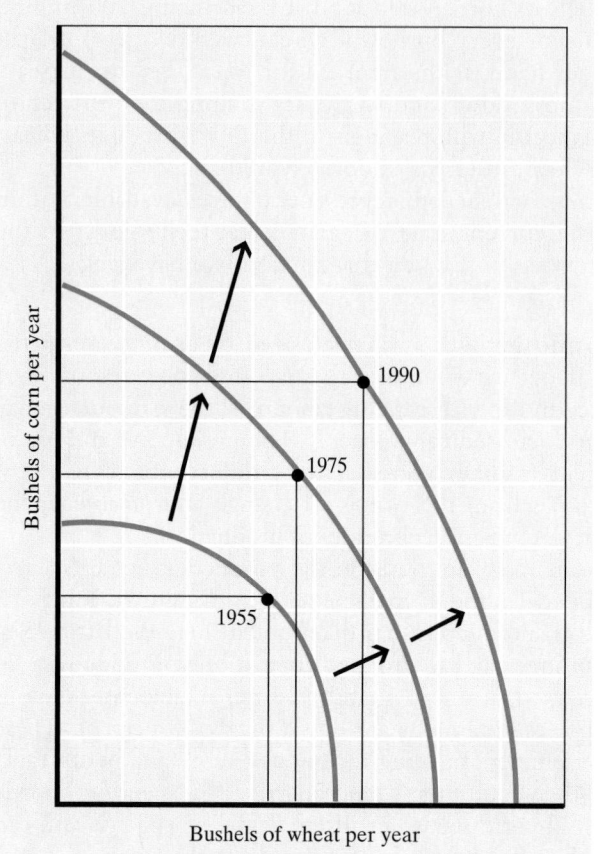

Recall that capital goods are produced only at a sacrifice of consumption goods. The same can be said for technological advances. Technological advances come from research and development that uses resources, and thus it too must be paid for. The resources used to produce capital goods–to build a road, a tractor, or a manufacturing plant–*and* to develop new technologies could have been used to produce consumption goods.

When a large part of a country's population is very poor, taking resources out of the production of consumption goods such as food and clothing is very difficult. In addition, in some countries those wealthy enough to invest in domestic industries may choose instead to invest abroad because of political turmoil at home. As a result, it often falls to the governments of poor countries to generate revenues for capital production and research out of tax collections.

All these factors have contributed to the growing gap between rich and poor nations. Figure 2.7 graphs the result, using production possibility frontiers. On the left, the rich country devotes a larger portion of its production to capital, while the poor country produces mostly consumption goods. On the right, you see the result: The ppf of the rich country shifts up and out farther and faster.

Although it exists only as an abstraction, the production possibility frontier illustrates a number of very important concepts that we shall use throughout the rest of this book: scarcity, unemployment, inefficiency, opportunity cost, the law of increasing opportunity cost, and economic growth.

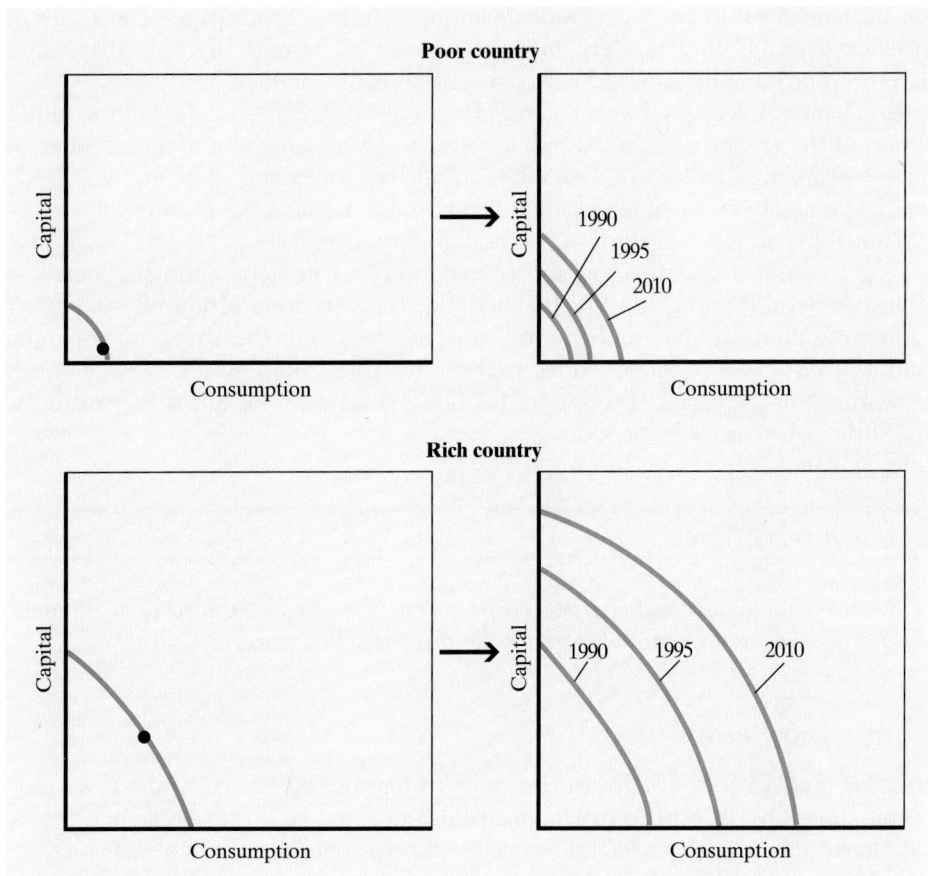

FIGURE 2.7
Capital Goods and Growth in
Poor and Rich Countries

Rich countries find it easier to
devote resources to the production of capital than poor countries do. But the more resources
that flow into capital production,
the faster the rate of economic
growth. Thus the gap between
poor and rich countries has
grown over time.

The Economic Problem

Recall that the three basic questions facing all economic systems are (1) What will
be produced? (2) How will it be produced? (3) Who will get it?

When Bill was alone on the island, the mechanism for answering these questions was simple: He thought about his own wants and preferences, looked at the
constraints and limits imposed by the resources of the island and his own skills and
time, and made his decisions. As he set about his work, he allocated available
resources quite simply, more or less by dividing up his available time. Distribution
of the output was irrelevant. Because Bill was the society, he got it all.

Introducing even one more person into the economy—in this case,
Colleen—changed all that. With Colleen on the island, resource allocation involves
deciding not only how each person spends time but also who does what. Labor
must be allocated to the various tasks. And now there are two sets of wants and
preferences. And even after two people decide what to produce, they have to
decide how to divide it. If Bill and Colleen go off on their own and form two
completely separate self-sufficient economies, there will be lost potential. Clearly,
two people can do many more things together than one person can do alone. They
may use their comparative advantages in different skills to specialize. Cooperation
and coordination may give rise to gains that would otherwise not be possible.

When a society consists of millions of people, the problem of coordination and
cooperation becomes enormous, but so does the potential for gain. In large, complex economies, specialization can go wild, with people working in jobs as differ-

ent in their detail as an impressionist painting is from a blank page. The range of products available in a modern industrial society is beyond anything that could have been imagined a hundred years ago, and so is the range of jobs.

In Chapter 1 we asked you to consider a typical day in your life and to think about all the things that you use or consume. Think now about the number of people that were involved in designing, producing, packaging, shipping, wholesaling, and retailing every single product that you use. Look at the food in the cafeteria line, for example, and think about how it got where it is.

The amount of coordination and cooperation in a modern industrial society is almost impossible to imagine. Yet something seems to drive economic systems, if sometimes clumsily and inefficiently, toward producing the things that people want. Given scarce resources, how, exactly, do large, complex societies go about answering the three basic economic questions? This is the **economic problem,** and this is what this text is about.

economic problem Given scarce resources, how exactly do large, complex societies go about answering the three basic economic questions?

ECONOMIC SYSTEMS

Now that you understand the economic problem, we can explore how different economic systems go about answering the three basic questions.

Command Economies

In some modern societies government plays a big role in answering the basic economic questions. In **command economies,** a central authority or agency generally draws up a plan that establishes what will be produced and when, sets production goals, and makes rules for distribution. Planners in command economies use complex computer programs to determine the materials, labor, and energy inputs required to produce a variety of output targets. The final output targets are then set with an eye toward the same constraint that the single manager of a one-person economy faces–limited resources. Centrally determined income policies then establish how much compensation workers and managers are to receive for their labors.

command economy An economy in which a central authority or agency draws up a plan that establishes what will be produced and when, sets production goals, and makes rules for distribution.

Even in "pure" planned economies, people do exercise some choice. Commodities are sold at prices set by the government, and to the extent that they are able to pay those prices people are free to buy what is available. Sometimes more is demanded than is produced; sometimes goods are left on the shelves. These signals are used in the next plan to adjust output targets.

It is an understatement to say that over the last decade, the planned economies have not fared well. In fact, the planned economies of Eastern Europe and the former Soviet Union–including the Russian Republic–have almost completely collapsed. (Another former command economy, that of Poland, is doing slightly better. For more details, see the Global Perspective box titled "What's Next for Eastern Europe and the Russian Republic?".) China remains committed to many of the principles of a planned economy, but reforms have moved it sharply away from pure central planning.

Laissez-Faire Economies: The Free Market

laissez-faire economy Literally from the French: "allow [them] to do." An economy in which individual people and firms pursue their own self-interests without any central direction or regulation.

At the opposite end of the spectrum from the command economy is the **laissez-faire economy.** The term *laissez faire,* which, translated literally from French, means "allow [them] to do," implies a complete lack of government involvement

WHAT'S NEXT FOR EASTERN EUROPE AND THE RUSSIAN REPUBLIC?

In the late 1980s the command economies of Eastern Europe collapsed like a string of dominoes. The process began when the Berlin Wall, which had separated the communist East from the capitalist West for nearly 30 years, was torn down in November, 1989. Finally, in 1991, the once mighty Soviet Union disintegrated, ending 75 years of communism and nearly half a century of cold war with the West.

What lies ahead for the economies of the newly independent countries of the former Soviet Union and for the economies of the other Eastern European nations? One fear is that complete economic collapse will lead to chaos and ethnic warfare, and the events of 1992 and 1993 in Bosnia and Serbia attest to this danger. There is, however, one country where the transition from central planning and government control to the free market is beginning to show some signs of working: Poland.

An economic success story is taking shape in Poland, three years after the country became the first in Eastern Europe to risk the rigors of "shock therapy."

Industrial production, which declined a precipitous 39 percent in 1990 and 1991, is on the rise, and Poland is on track this year to become the first among former Communist nations to record annual economic growth.

Although inflation is still 40 percent and the unemployment rate is 13.5 percent, Western analysts see encouraging evidence

that centrally planned economies, which once tilted toward arms, steel and other heavy industries, can be reshaped without social upheaval.

The recovery is being fueled both by the expanding private sector and, surprisingly, by state-owned companies that have managed to shift exports quickly from the East Bloc to the West.

Poland's exports have soared since 1988, to $14 billion from $8 billion, with 80 percent of this year's sales heading West. The major exporters remain under state ownership, although many are to be privatized in the coming year ....

Polish policy makers were supported in 1990 by an overwhelming public consensus for radical change, and have been encouraged since then to stay the course by an explosion of pent-up entrepreneurial spirit and by a relatively productive agricultural sector that was already largely in private hands ....

"I think they've made it," said Jeffrey Sachs, the Harvard economist who helped shape Poland's economic program .... "They have definitely turned the corner. The panic is over. The reforms are secure."

While the modest short-term growth is welcome, economists like Mr. Sachs are most excited by the long-term changes underlying the numbers.

The "shock therapy" described in the article refers to rapid decontrol of prices and privatization of government enterprises. Would such a policy lead to similar results in the Russian Republic, which is currently experiencing severe difficulties? Professor Sachs believes strongly that

As the Polish economy has moved toward a free market, it has encouraged businesspeople to enter the import and export industries. As a result, import/export seminars and trade fairs have become quite common in the once-Socialist country.

this "shock therapy" is the only approach that will help Russia get on its feet economically. Other economists are skeptical, pointing to the fact that Poland had many more capitalist institutions and markets already in place than Russia currently does. What will become of the Russian economy? Only time will tell.

Source: Stephen Engelberg, "21 Months of 'Shock Therapy' Resuscitates Polish Economy," *The New York Times*, December 17, 1992, p. 1.

in the economy. In this type of economy, individual people and firms pursue their own self-interest without any central direction or regulation; the sum total of millions of individual decisions ultimately determines all basic economic outcomes. The central institution through which a laissez-faire system answers the basic questions is the **market,** a term that is used in economics to signify an institution through which buyers and sellers interact and engage in exchange.

The interactions between buyers and sellers in any market range from simple to complex. Early explorers of the North American Midwest who wished to

market The institution through which buyers and sellers interact and engage in exchange.

exchange with Native Americans did so simply by bringing their goods to a central place and trading them. Today suppliers and demanders interact through market institutions that are much more complex. Consider the Federal Funds market, for example. Banks must keep a specific percentage of their deposits on hand as a "reserve" for anyone who wants to make withdrawals. Any money beyond this can be lent out or put to work earning interest. Among the many ways that banks with extra reserves do this is to seek out other banks in need of cash in the Federal Funds market. The banks never communicate directly, and no money ever really moves, because all communications and transactions are done electronically through a desk in New York. Nonetheless, buyers and sellers exchange in this market.

Even more traditional shopping now takes place electronically. A jewelry maker in Maine may sell gold necklaces to a buyer through the Home Shopping Network that shows the product on television—customers call in orders and pay with a credit card. Ultimately, funds are transferred through a complicated chain of financial transactions. The result is that a buyer in Oakland, California, buys a necklace from an unseen jewelry producer in Maine and pays for it out of income made by working as an account executive for an advertising firm that specializes in marketing toothpaste. In short:

> Some markets are simple and others are complex, but they all involve buyers and sellers engaging in exchange. The behavior of buyers and sellers in a laissez-faire economy determines what gets produced, how it is produced, and who gets it.

The following chapters explore market systems in great depth. A quick preview is worthwhile here, however.

CONSUMER SOVEREIGNTY In a free, unregulated market, goods and services are produced and sold only if the supplier can make a profit. In simple terms, making a profit means selling goods or services for more than it costs to produce them. Clearly, you can't make a profit unless someone wants the product that you are selling. This logic leads to the notion of **consumer sovereignty:** The mix of output found in any free market system is dictated ultimately by the tastes and preferences of consumers who "vote" by buying or not buying. Businesses rise and fall in response to consumer demands; no central directive or plan is necessary.

In a free market economy, producers may be small or large. One person who hand paints eggshells may start to sell them as a business; a woman who has been showing her poodle may start handling other people's dogs in the show ring. On a larger scale, a group of furniture designers may put together a large portfolio of sketches, several million dollars, and start a bigger business. At the extreme are huge corporations like IBM, General Motors, and Exxon, each of which sells tens of billions of dollars worth of products every year.

INDIVIDUAL PRODUCTION DECISIONS Under a free market system, individual producers must also figure out how to organize and coordinate the actual production of their products or services. The owner of a small shoe repair shop must buy the equipment and tools that she needs, hang signs, and set prices by herself. In a big corporation, so many people are involved in planning the production process that in many ways corporate planning resembles the planning in a command economy. Whether the firms are large or small, however, production decisions are made by separate private organizations acting in what they perceive to be their own interests.

consumer sovereignty The idea that consumers ultimately dictate what will be produced (or not produced) by choosing what to purchase (and what not to purchase).

Decision making that is structured in this way, proponents of free market systems argue, leads to more efficient production. If a producer produces inefficiently, competitors will come along, fight for the business, and eventually take it away. Thus in a free market economy, competition forces producers to use efficient techniques of production. It is competition, then, that ultimately dictates how outputs are produced.

DISTRIBUTION OF OUTPUT   In a free market system, the distribution of output—who gets what—is also determined in a decentralized way. The amount that any one household gets depends on its income and wealth. *Income* is the amount that a household earns each year. It comes in a number of forms: wages, salaries, interest, dividends, and the like. *Wealth* is the amount that households have accumulated out of past income through saving or inheritance.

To the extent that income comes from working for a wage, it is at least in part determined by individual choice. You will work for the wages available in the market only if these wages (and the things they can buy) are sufficient to compensate you for what you give up by working. If you don't work your leisure certainly has a value. You may also discover that you can increase your income by getting more education or training. You *can't* increase your income, however, if you acquire a skill that no one wants.

Although your income determines how much of society's output you can buy and consume, not all income comes from working. Individuals may also earn income by owning all or part of a business for which they do not work. Those who risk their wealth by buying shares in companies or by lending it out to be used for business investments earn a return on their wealth. Returns may come directly, as profit, or indirectly, as interest or dividends on stock. (We discuss these options in detail in Chapter 3.) In a free market economy, people make independent decisions about what to do with their wealth.

> In sum: In a free market system, then, the basic economic questions are answered without the help of a central government plan or directives. This is what the "free" in free market means—the system is left to operate on its own, with no outside interference. Individuals pursuing their own self-interest will go into business and produce the products and services that people want; others will decide whether to acquire skills or not, whether to work or not, and whether to buy, sell, invest, or save the income that they earn.

PRICE THEORY   The basic coordinating mechanism in a free market system is price. A **price** is the amount that a product sells for per unit, and it reflects what society is willing to pay. Prices of inputs—labor, land, capital—determine how much it costs to produce a product. Prices of various kinds of labor, or *wage rates,* determine the rewards for working in different jobs and professions. Many of the independent decisions made in a market economy involve the weighing of prices and costs, so it is not surprising that much of economic theory focuses on the factors that influence and determine prices. This is why microeconomic theory is often simply called *price theory.*

price The amount that a product sells for per unit. It reflects what society is willing to pay.

Mixed Systems, Markets, and Governments

The differences between command economies and laissez-faire economies in their pure forms are enormous. But in fact these pure forms do not exist in the world; all real systems are in some sense "mixed." That is, individual enterprise exists and independent choice is exercised even in economies in which the government plays the major role.

Conversely, no market economies exist without government involvement and government regulation. The United States has basically a free market economy, but government purchases accounted for about 19% of its total production in 1992. The government directly employs about 17% of all workers, and taxes are about a third of the total income of the economy. The government also redistributes income by means of taxation and social welfare expenditures, and it regulates many economic activities.

One of the major themes in this book, and indeed in economics, is the tension between the advantages of free, unregulated markets and the need for government involvement in the economy. Advocates of free markets argue that they work best when left to themselves. They produce only what people want; without buyers, sellers go out of business. Competition forces firms to adopt efficient production techniques. Wage differentials lead people to acquire needed skills. Competition also leads to innovation in both production techniques and products. The result is quality and variety. But market systems have problems too.

> Even staunch defenders of the free enterprise system recognize that market systems are not perfect. First, they do not always produce what people want at lowest cost—there are inefficiencies. Second, rewards (income) may be unevenly distributed, and some groups may be left out. Third, periods of unemployment and inflation recur with some regularity.

Many people point to these problems as reasons for government involvement. Indeed, for some problems government involvement may be the only solution. But government decisions are made by people who presumably, like the rest of us, act in their own self-interest. While governments may indeed be called upon to improve the functioning of the economy, there is no guarantee that they will do so. Just as markets may fail to produce an allocation of resources that is perfectly efficient and fair, governments may fail to improve matters.

public, or social, goods Goods and services whose benefits are social, or collective.

INEFFICIENCIES Free markets may not produce all the goods that people want and are willing to pay for. There are some goods and services whose benefits are social, or *collective,* such as national defense, open park areas, a justice system, and police protection. These are called **public,** or **social, goods.** The fact that the benefits of such goods are collective presents the private market with a problem: Once a public good is produced, everyone gets to enjoy its benefits, whether they have paid for it or not. If police protection lowers a city's crime rate, all citizens of that city are safer.

How, then, can a private business firm make a profit "selling" such a service to individual consumers? In most cases, it cannot. A private firm selling an automobile won't give it to you unless you pay for it. A producer of a public good doesn't have that option. Thus, if there is a public good that citizens decide they want, they must collectively arrange for its production. Traditionally, societies have funded public goods through governments, which are granted taxing authority.

Government intervention may also be necessary because private decision makers in search of profits can make bad decisions from society's point of view. The market system provides an incentive to produce a product if, and only if, people are willing to pay more for it than the cost of the resources needed to produce it. This works to society's advantage as long as the resource costs reflect the *full* cost to society of producing the product. For example, if the environment is damaged during the production process and producers do not factor in these costs, profit-producing activities may not balance out to society's advantage. Governments involve themselves in free markets to make sure that decision makers consider all the benefits and costs of their decisions. That is why we have the Environmental Protection Agency and similar agencies.

Markets work best when they are competitive. Recall that competition forces producers to choose the most efficient methods of production. Inefficient producers are driven out of business by the forces of competition. Competition also leads to innovation and new products. Sometimes, however, powerful firms in free markets can gain control of their markets and block competition. A firm that gains control of a market may stifle innovation, charge higher prices than necessary, and cause a general misallocation of resources. Since the turn of the century, noncompetitive behavior has been illegal in the United States.

REDISTRIBUTION OF INCOME Governments may also get involved in a basically free market system because the final distribution of income (and thus of output) is considered inequitable. Free market systems are based on the principle of individual self-interest and enterprise: Our rewards are supposed to be commensurate with how well we compete. But some people are not well equipped to compete—some are physically unable to work, some are mentally unable to hold a job. Whatever the cause, thousands of people find that they cannot get along economically. Sometimes this is their fault, and sometimes it is not. In all cases, however, society must decide what, if anything, to do about it.

Every government redistributes income to a certain extent. In the United States, welfare, unemployment compensation, and a host of other programs have been designed to assist people who are poor or are temporarily without work.

Income redistribution is a subject of endless debate. Some claim that taxes on the rich and programs for the poor destroy the incentives that the market provides for hard work, enterprise, and risk taking. Others argue that because many of the poor, particularly children, are in the position they are in through no fault of their own, cuts in income redistribution programs are cruel and unfair.

STABILIZATION Macroeconomics explores the causes and consequences of unemployment and price inflation. In market economies, the level of unemployment is not planned, and prices are set freely by the forces of supply and demand. But governments can, through taxing and spending policies and by regulating the banking system, exert some stabilizing influence over prices and over the general level of output and employment. Like income redistribution, the desirability and the character of government involvement in the macroeconomy are hotly debated.

LOOKING AHEAD

This chapter has described the economic problem in broad terms. We have outlined the questions that all economic systems must answer. We also discussed very broadly the two kinds of economic systems and some of the advantages and disadvantages of each. In the next chapter we turn from the general to the specific. There we discuss in some detail the institutions of U.S. capitalism: how the private sector is organized, what the government actually does, and how the international sector operates. Chapters 4 and 5 then begin the task of analyzing the way market systems work.

SUMMARY

1. Every society has some system or mechanism for transforming what nature and previous generations have provided into useful form. Economics is the study of that process and its outcomes.

2. *Producers* are those who take resources and transform them into usable products, or *outputs*. Private firms, households, and governments all produce something.

Scarcity, Choice, and Opportunity Cost

3. All societies must answer *three basic questions:* What will be produced? How will it be produced? Who will get what is produced? These three questions make up the *economic problem.*

4. One person alone on an island must make the same basic decisions that complex societies make. When society consists of more than one person, questions of distribution, cooperation, and specialization arise.

5. Even if one individual or nation is absolutely more efficient at producing goods than another, all parties will gain if they specialize in producing goods in which they have a *comparative advantage.*

6. Because resources are scarce relative to human wants in all societies, using resources to produce one good or service implies *not* using them to produce something else. This concept of *opportunity cost* is central to an understanding of economics.

7. Using resources to produce *capital* that will in turn produce benefits in the future implies *not* using those resources to produce consumer goods in the present.

8. A *production possibility frontier* (ppf) is a graph that shows all of the combinations of goods and services that can be produced if all of society's resources are used efficiently. The production possibility frontier illustrates a number of important economic concepts: scarcity, unemployment, inefficiency, increasing opportunity cost, and economic growth.

9. The *marginal rate of transformation (MRT)* is the value of the slope of the production possibilities frontier. The MRT represents opportunity cost: the sacrifice in one type of good necessary to produce more of another type of good.

10. *Economic growth* occurs when society produces more, either by acquiring more resources or by learning to produce more with existing resources. Improved productivity may come from additional capital, or from the discovery and application of new, more efficient, techniques of production.

11. In large complex societies, the potential gains from cooperation and specialization are enormous, but so are the problems.

Economic Systems

12. In some modern societies, government plays a big role in answering the three basic questions. In *command economies,* a central authority generally draws up a plan that determines what will be produced, how it will be produced, and who will get it.

13. A *laissez-faire economy* is one in which individuals independently pursuing their own self-interest, without any central direction or regulation, ultimately determine all basic economic outcomes.

14. A *market* is an institution through which buyers and sellers interact and engage in exchange. Some markets involve simple face-to-face exchange; others involve a complex series of transactions, often over great distance or electronically.

15. There are no purely planned economies and no pure laissez-faire economies; all economies are mixed. Individual enterprise, independent choice, and relatively free markets exist in centrally planned economies, and there is significant government involvement in market economies such as that of the United States.

16. One of the great debates in economics revolves around the tension between the advantages of free, unregulated markets and the need for government involvement in the economy. Free markets produce what people want, and competition forces firms to adopt efficient production techniques. The need for government intervention arises because free markets are characterized by an unequal distribution of income and experience regular periods of inflation and unemployment.

REVIEW TERMS AND CONCEPTS

PROBLEM SET

1. Kristen and Anna live in the beach town of Santa Monica. They own a small business in which they make wristbands and potholders and sell them to people on the beach. The price of a wristband is $1, and the price of a potholder is $1. Kristen can make 15 wristbands per hour, but only 3 potholders. Anna is a bit slower and can make only 12 wristbands or 2 potholders in an hour.

OUTPUT PER HOUR		
	KRISTEN	ANNA
Wristbands	15	12
Potholders	3	2

a. For Kristen, what is the opportunity cost of a potholder? For Anna? Who has a comparative advantage in the production of potholders? Explain.

b. Who has a comparative advantage in the production of wristbands? Explain.

c. Assume that Kristen works 20 hours per week in the business. If Kristen were in business on her own, graph the possible combinations of potholders and wristbands that she could produce in a week. Do the same for Anna.

d. If Kristen devoted half of her time (10 out of 20 hours) to wristbands and half of her time to potholders, how many of each would she produce in a week? If Anna did the same thing, how many of each would she produce? How many wristbands and potholders would be produced in total?

e. Suppose that Anna spent all 20 hours of her time on wristbands and Kristen spent 17 hours on potholders and 3 hours on wristbands. How many of each would be produced?

2. Define capital. What distinguishes land from capital? Is a tree capital?

3. Studying economics instead of going to town and partying is like building a boat instead of lying on the beach. Explain this statement carefully using the concepts of capital and opportunity cost.

4. Suppose that a simple society has an economy with only one resource, labor. Labor can be used to produce only two commodities–X, a necessity good (food), and Y, a luxury good (music and merriment). Suppose that the labor force consists of 100 workers. One laborer can produce either at a rate of five units of necessity per month (by hunting and gathering) or at a rate of 10 units of luxury per month (by writing songs, playing the guitar, dancing, and so on).

a. On a graph, draw the economy's production possibility frontier. Where does the ppf intersect the Y axis? Where does it intersect the X axis? What meaning do those points have?

b. What is the marginal rate of transformation?

c. Suppose the economy ended up producing at a point *inside* the ppf. Give at least two reasons why this could occur. What could be done to move the economy to a point *on* the ppf?

d. Suppose you succeeded in lifting your economy to a point on its ppf. What point would you choose? How might your small society decide the point at which it wanted to be?

e. Once you have chosen a point on the ppf, you still need to decide how your society's product will be divided up. If you were a dictator, how would you decide? What would happen if you left product distribution to the "free market"?

3

The Structure of the U.S. Economy: The Private, Public, and International Sectors

The previous chapter described the economic problem. All societies are endowed by nature and by previous generations with scarce resources. These resources are combined and transformed by a process called "production" into goods and services that are demanded by the members of society. At the end of Chapter 2, we briefly described the economic systems that exist in the world today.

This chapter describes the basic institutional structure of the U.S. economy in more detail. Because most production is undertaken by private individuals and organizations, we first look at the private sector. The **private sector** is made up of independently owned firms that exist to make a profit, nonprofit organizations, and individual households. It includes Chrysler Corporation, Occidental College, the Catholic Church, soybean farms in Iowa, the corner drug store, and the baby-sitter down the street. The private sector is defined by independent ownership and control. In essence, it includes all the decision-making units within the economy that are not part of the government.

Next, we turn to a discussion of the public sector. The **public sector** is the government and its agencies at all levels—federal, state, and local. Government employees—tax assessors, public school teachers, post office workers, colonels in

private sector Includes all independently owned profit-making firms, nonprofit organizations, and households; all the decision-making units in the economy that are not part of the government.

public sector Includes all agencies at all levels of government—federal, state, and local.

the army, and the President—work in the public sector. Just as the Ford Motor Company uses land, labor, and capital to produce automobiles, the public sector uses land, labor, and capital to produce public goods and services such as police and fire protection, education, and national defense. The public sector in the United States also produces some things that are simultaneously produced by the private sector. The post office provides overnight express-mail service that competes directly with similar services provided by private firms such as Federal Express and United Parcel Service. The University of Michigan, part of the public sector, directly competes for "buyers" of its "product" with private sector colleges and universities such as Northwestern and Colorado College.

Finally, we provide a brief introduction to the **international sector** and discuss the importance of imports and exports to the U.S.. economy. From any one country's perspective, the international sector consists of the economies of the rest of the world. The U.S. economy has, over the last several decades, become increasingly influenced by events abroad. The collapse of real estate values in Tokyo, the elimination of farm subsidies in France, the decline in Russian oil production, and other global events all have important implications for the functioning of the U.S. economy. In a very real sense there is only one economy: the world economy.

international sector From any one country's perspective, the economies of the rest of the world.

Recall the distinction drawn in Chapter 1 between descriptive economics and economic theory, and then notice what this chapter is not. We do not analyze behavior in this chapter. Here we describe institutions only as they exist. We also try very hard to avoid any normative distinctions. We do not talk about proper or improper roles of government in the economy, for example, or the things that governments might do to make the economy more efficient or fair.

In Chapter 4, we begin to analyze behavior. Before we begin the analysis in Chapter 4, however, it is important to have some sense of the institutional landscape. One purpose for studying economics is to understand the world and what people actually do. This chapter provides some important facts that describe the realities of the U.S. economy.

THE PRIVATE SECTOR: BUSINESS AND INDUSTRIAL ORGANIZATION IN THE UNITED STATES

How is business organized in the United States? Let us see first how the law permits *individual firms* to be organized. Then we can talk about the different ways that *industries* are structured. An individual firm's behavior depends on both its own legal structure and its relationship to other firms in its industry.

The Legal Organization of Firms

Most private sector activity takes place within business firms that exist to make a profit. Some other private sector organizations that exist for reasons other than profit—clubs, cooperatives, and nonprofit organizations, for example—do produce goods or services. Because these organizations represent a small fraction of private sector activity, however, we focus here on profit-making firms.

A business set up to make profits may be organized in one of three basic legal forms: (1) a *proprietorship*, (2) a *partnership*, or (3) a *corporation*. A single business may pass through more than one of these forms of organization during its development.

proprietorship A form of business organization in which a person simply sets up to provide goods or services at a profit. In a proprietorship, the proprietor, or owner, is the firm. The assets and liabilities of the firm are the owner's assets and liabilities.

THE PROPRIETORSHIP The least complex and most common form a business can take is the simple **proprietorship.** There is no legal process involved in starting a proprietorship. You simply start operating. You must, however, keep records of revenues and costs and pay personal income taxes on your profit.

A professor who does consulting on the side, for example, receives fees and has costs (computer expenses, research materials, and so forth). This consulting business is a proprietorship, even though the proprietor is the only employee and the business is very limited. A large restaurant that employs hundreds of people may also be a proprietorship if it is owned by a single person. Most doctors and lawyers in private practice report their incomes and expenses as proprietors.

In a proprietorship, one person owns the firm. In a sense, that person *is* the firm. If the firm owes money, the proprietor owes the money; if the firm earns a profit, the proprietor earns a profit. There is no limit to the proprietor's responsibility; if the business gets into financial trouble, the proprietor alone is liable. That is, if a business does poorly or ends up in debt, those debts are the proprietor's personal responsibility. There is no wall of protection between a proprietor and her business, as we will see there is between corporations and their owners.

The Internal Revenue Service estimates that there are over 13.5 million proprietorships in the United States. That is one for every 15 adults in the country. Needless to say, most of these proprietorships are small; while they make up over 70% of all businesses, they account for only about 6% of total sales (see Table 3.1).

partnership A form of business organization in which there is more than one proprietor. The owners are responsible jointly and separately for the firm's obligations.

THE PARTNERSHIP A **partnership** is a proprietorship with more than one proprietor. When two or more people agree to share the responsibility for a business, they form a partnership. While no formal legal process is required to start this kind of business, most partnerships are based on agreements, signed by all the partners, that detail who pays what part of the costs and how profits shall be divided. Because profits from partnerships are taxable, accurate records of receipts and expenditures must be kept and each party's profits must be reported to the IRS.

In a partnership, as in a proprietorship, there is no limit to the liability of the owners (that is, the partners) for the debts of the firm. But with a partnership it can be worse because each partner is both jointly and separately liable for all the debts of the partnership. If you own one third of a partnership that goes out of business with a debt of $300,000, you owe your creditors $100,000, and so does each of your partners. But if your partners skip town, you owe the entire $300,000.

Just under 9% of all firms in the United States are partnerships, and they account for only 4.2% of total sales (see again Table 3.1).

corporation A form of business organization resting on a legal charter that establishes the corporation as an entity separate from its owners. Owners hold shares and are liable for the firm's debts only up to the limit of their investment, or share in the firm.

THE CORPORATION A **corporation** is a formally established legal entity that exists separately from those who establish it and those who own it. To establish

TABLE 3.1
Number of Firms and Sales by Type of Business, 1988

	NUMBER OF FIRMS (THOUSANDS)	PERCENT OF TOTAL FIRMS	TOTAL SALES ($ BILLIONS)	PERCENT OF TOTAL SALES
Proprietorships	13,679	72.4	672	6.1
Partnerships	1,654	8.7	464	4.2
Corporations	3,563	18.9	9,804	89.7
Total	18,896	100.0	10,940	100.0

Source: Statistical Abstract of the United States, 1992, p. 520.

	BILLIONS OF DOLLARS	PERCENT OF BEFORE-TAX PROFIT
Profits before tax	372.3	100.0
Minus profits tax liability	- 140.5	- 37.7
Profits after tax	231.8	62.3
Minus dividends paid	- 149.3	- 40.1
Undistributed profits	82.5	22.2

Source: U.S. Department of Commerce, Bureau of Economic Analysis.

TABLE 3.2
The Distribution of Corporate Profits in 1992

a corporation, a corporate charter must be obtained from a state government. In most states this is quite easily accomplished. A lawyer simply fills out the appropriate paper work and files it with the right state agency, along with certain fees. When a corporation is formed, **shares of stock** (certificates of partial ownership) are issued and either sold or assigned. A corporation is owned by its shareholders, who are in a sense partners in the success or failure of the firm. Shareholders differ from simple partners, however, in two important ways: First, the liability of shareholders is limited to the amount they paid for the stock. If the company goes out of business or bankrupt, the shareholders may lose what they have invested, but no more than that. They are *not* liable for the debts of the corporation beyond the amount they invested. Second, the federal government and all but four states levy special taxes on corporations. It does not levy special taxes on proprietors and partners.

> **share of stock** A certificate of partial ownership of a corporation that entitles the holder to a portion of the corporation's profits.

The federal corporate income tax is a tax on the **net income,** or profits, of corporations. The tax is 15% of net income on the first $50,000, but it rises to 25% for taxable income between $50,000 and $75,000 and to 34% after income exceeds $75,000. (In 1993, as part of President Clinton's deficit reduction package, the top rate was raised to 35% on taxable net income over $10 million.) Actually, 99% of all corporate net income is taxed at the 34% rate.[1] In essence, this means that tax is paid twice on corporate net income: once by the corporation when it pays tax on its profits, and again by the shareholders when they pay personal income tax on their **dividends,** that is, the share of profits they receive from the corporation.

> **net income** The profits of a firm.

The special privilege granted to corporations limiting their liability is often called a *franchise*. Some view the corporate tax as a payment to the government in exchange for this grant of limited liability status. In New York State, the state corporation tax is actually called the franchise tax.

> **dividends** The portion of a corporation's profits that the firm pays out each period to shareholders. Also called "distributed profits."

Corporate net income is usually divided into three pieces. Some of it, of course, is paid to federal and state governments in the form of *taxes*. Some of it is paid out to shareholders as *dividends* (sometimes called *distributed profits*). And some of it usually stays within the corporation to be used for the purchase of capital assets. This part of corporate profits is called **retained earnings,** or *undistributed profits.*

In 1992, corporations in the United States earned total profits of $372.3 billion. Out of this, $140.5 billion in taxes were paid, leaving $231.8 billion in after-tax profits. Of this amount, $149.3 billion was paid out to shareholders and the rest, $82.5 billion, was retained. In percentage terms, taxes accounted for 37.7%, while shareholders directly received 40.1% of total profits (see Table 3.2).

> **retained earnings** The profits that a corporation keeps, usually for the purchase of capital assets. Also called "undistributed profits."

Turning again to Table 3.1, in 1988 there were 3.563 million corporations, just under 20% of all firms. But these 3.563 million firms accounted for about 90% of total sales. Needless to say, many corporations are very large. Each year *Fortune*

---

[1] *Statistical Abstract of the United States, 1992,* and authors' estimate.

magazine publishes a list of the 500 largest industrial corporations in the United States. Topping the *Fortune* 500 in 1992 was General Motors. GM's total sales in 1991 were nearly $110 billion. The company employed over 750,000 people that year!

The internal organization of a firm, whether it is a proprietorship, a partnership, or a corporation, affects its behavior and the behavior of potential investors. For example, because they are protected by the limited liability status of a corporation, potential investors may be more likely to back high-risk but potentially high-payoff ventures.

While the internal structure of a firm is important, it is less important to an understanding of a firm's behavior than is the organization of the industry or the market in which the firm competes. For example, whether it is a proprietorship or a corporation, a firm with little or no competition is likely to behave differently from a firm facing stiff competition from many rivals. With this in mind, we now expand our focus from the individual firm to the industry that encompasses many firms.

The Organization of Industries

industry All the firms that produce a similar product. The boundaries of a "product" can be drawn very widely—"agricultural products"— less widely—"dairy products"—or very narrowly—"cheese." The term *industry* can be used interchangeably with the term *market*.

market organization The way an industry is structured. Structure is defined by how many firms there are in an industry, whether products are differentiated or are virtually the same, whether or not firms in the industry can control prices or wages, and whether or not competing firms can enter and leave the industry freely.

The term **industry** is used loosely to refer to groups of firms that produce similar products. Industries can be defined narrowly or broadly, depending on the issue being discussed. For example, a company that produces and packages cheese is a part of the cheese industry, the dairy products industry, the food products industry, and the agricultural products industry.[2]

Whether we define industries broadly or narrowly, how firms within any industry behave depends on how that industry is organized. When we speak of **market organization** we refer to the way an industry is structured: how many firms there are in an industry, whether products are virtually the same or differentiated, whether or not firms in the industry can control prices or wages, whether or not competing firms can freely enter and leave the industry, and so forth. The kind of industry—or *market*—in which a firm operates determines, in large part, how it will behave.

In the discussion that follows, we analyze industries as if their structures fit their definitions precisely. In reality, however, industries are not always easy to categorize. Some industries have some characteristics generally associated with one form of organization and other characteristics associated with a different form of organization. Nonetheless, these categories provide a useful and convenient framework for thinking about the organization of industries in the U.S. economy.

perfect competition An industry structure (or market organization) in which there are many firms, each small relative to the industry, producing virtually identical products and in which no firm is large enough to have any control over prices. In perfectly competitive industries, new competitors can freely enter and exit the market.

PERFECT COMPETITION At one end of the market-organization spectrum is the competitive industry in which many relatively small firms produce nearly identical products. **Perfect competition** is a very precisely defined form of industry structure. (The word *perfect* here does not refer to virtue. It simply means "total," or "complete.") In a perfectly competitive industry, *no single firm has any control over prices*. That is, no single firm is large enough to affect the market price of its product or the prices of the inputs that it buys. This crucial observation follows from two characteristics of competitive industries. First, a competitive industry is com-

---

[2] The U.S. Department of Commerce has devised a code system, the Standard Industrial Classification (S.I.C.) System, which defines industries at various levels of detail.

posed of many firms, each small relative to the size of the industry. Second, every firm in a perfectly competitive industry produces exactly the same product; the output of one firm cannot be distinguished from the output of the others. Products in a perfectly competitive industry are said to be **homogeneous.**

These characteristics limit the decisions open to competitive firms and simplify the analysis of competitive behavior. Because all firms in a perfectly competitive industry produce virtually identical products, and because each firm is small relative to the market, perfectly competitive firms have no control over the prices at which they sell their output. Taking prices as a given, then, each firm can decide only how much output to produce and how to produce it.

Consider agriculture, the classic example of a perfectly competitive industry. A wheat farmer in Kansas has absolutely no control over the price of wheat. Prices are determined not by the individual farmers but rather by the interaction of many suppliers and many demanders. The only decisions left to the wheat farmer are how much wheat to plant and when and how to produce the crop.

Another mark of perfectly competitive industries is ease of entry. *Ease of entry* means that new firms can easily enter a market and compete for profits. No barriers exist to prevent new firms from competing. New firms can, and do, frequently enter such industries in search of profits, while others go out of business when they suffer losses. For example, during the 1970s copier technology improved dramatically. The quality of copy machines made by Xerox and other firms improved while their cost declined sharply. As the costs of producing copier machines and the price of copy services declined, the demand for copy services among college students increased. To meet this demand, copy services quickly sprang up around most colleges and universities in the United States. Because the capital required to enter the industry (basically, a copy machine) was relatively low and the potential profits were high, a great many new firms were attracted to the industry.

When a firm *exits* an industry, it simply stops producing a product. Sometimes an exiting firm goes out of business altogether. During the last ten years, for example, thousands of small farmers have gone out of business, sold off their assets, paid what bills they could, and disappeared.

To summarize:

> Perfectly competitive industries are made up of many firms, each small relative to the size of the total market. In these industries, individual firms do not distinguish or differentiate their products from those of their competitors. Product prices are determined by market forces and are virtually unaffected by decisions of any single firm. Entry into and exit from the market are relatively easy.

MONOPOLY At the other end of the spectrum is **monopoly,** a market or industry in which only one firm produces a product for which there are no close substitutes.

When there is only one firm in a market, that firm sets the price of its product. This does not mean, however, that monopolies can set any price they please. Even monopolies face the constraint of the market. Even if a firm produces a good that everyone likes, the firm gains nothing if it charges a price so high that no one buys it. The price a monopolist chooses determines the quantity it will be able to sell. Thus, even a monopolist is subject to discipline imposed by the market.

For a monopoly to remain a monopoly, it must find some way to keep other firms from entering its market and competing for profits. Often governments erect these **barriers to entry** themselves. Sometimes they grant an exclusive license to one producer. In Taiwan, for example, the national government licensed only one

homogeneous products
Undifferentiated outputs: products that are identical to, or indistinguishable from, one another.

monopoly An industry structure (or market organization) in which there is only one large firm that produces a product for which there are no close substitutes. Monopolists can set prices but are subject to market discipline. For a monopoly to continue to exist, something must prevent potential competitors from entering the industry and competing for profits.

barrier to entry Something that prevents new firms from entering and competing in an industry.

company to produce beer and excluded beer imports until 1987. In the United States, public utilities—electric power and gas companies, for example, most of which are privately owned—have traditionally been shielded by the government from competition. For many years the American Telephone and Telegraph Company was essentially the exclusive producer of telephone services, both local and long distance. However, dramatic changes in the telecommunications industry in the last few years, including the break-up of AT&T by the courts in 1983, have made that market much more competitive.

A private company may also hold a monopoly by virtue of a patent. The Polaroid Corporation, for instance, was the only producer of instant cameras for many years because it developed and patented the technology.

In sum:

> A monopoly is a one-firm industry that produces a product for which there are no close substitutes. Such a firm can set price, but its pricing behavior is constrained by its market: It can sell a product only if people are willing to buy it. A monopolist is protected from competition by barriers to entry.

monopolistic competition An industry structure (or market organization) in which many firms compete, producing similar but slightly differentiated products. There are close substitutes for the product of any given firm. Monopolistic competitors have some control over price. Price and quality competition follow from product differentiation. Entry and exit are relatively easy, and success invites new competitors.

MONOPOLISTIC COMPETITION Somewhere between monopoly and competition, but much closer to competition, is a very common hybrid market organization called **monopolistic competition.** In a monopolistically competitive industry, many firms compete for essentially the same customers, but each firm produces a slightly different product. If these firms can *differentiate* their products successfully, they establish a *brand loyalty* that allows them to enjoy the benefits of a monopoly. Procter & Gamble is the only producer of Ivory Soap—it "monopolizes" the market for Ivory—but the soap business is still very competitive because many close substitutes are available. Prentice Hall is the only company that can sell this book, but there are many other economics texts.

While individual firms in perfectly competitive markets have no control over price, monopolistic competitors do exercise some price-setting power. That control is quite limited, however, because of the many close substitutes available. Monopolistically competitive firms are thus subject to a great deal of "market discipline."

A good example of monopolistic competition can be found in the music industry. Every rock band has a unique style; each has its own name. Entry is relatively inexpensive; all you need are musicians, instruments, amplifiers, and a P.A. system. Thinking of each band as a small firm, management differentiates the product in an attempt to compete, and the competition is fierce. Very successful rock bands are more like monopolies, however; there are no "close" substitutes for Red Hot Chili Peppers, U2, or the Rolling Stones.

In monopolistically competitive industries, there is both *price and quality competition*. Firms often enter these industries because they have an idea for a new product that represents a slight variation or improvement on an old one. Perhaps the purest example of a monopolistically competitive market is the restaurant industry. Every major city in the world contains hundreds and hundreds of restaurants, each producing a slightly differentiated product in a highly competitive way. The cosmetics and clothing industries are also monopolistically competitive. Firms in such industries must decide on output, price, and quality of product.

Free, or at least relatively easy, entry and exit characterize monopolistic competition. When a firm enjoys success in one of its product lines, its profits invite new firms to come into its market with new brands or similar styles. Many new restaurants are born every year and many unsuccessful ones quietly expire.

To summarize:

> Monopolistically competitive firms contain large numbers of relatively small firms. Unlike firms in perfectly competitive industries, firms in monopolistically competitive industries differentiate their products. Individual firms produce unique products and thus, despite their small size, exercise some control over price. Entry and exit are relatively easy.

OLIGOPOLY An industry in which there are only a small number of firms is called an **oligopoly.** The automobile industry in the United States, for example, has only three major U.S. competitors and a few smaller ones. A total of seven firms produce 100% of all the primary copper produced in the United States, and four large firms control 89% of the breakfast cereal industry. Except for the fact that each contains only a few competitors, however, oligopolistic industries have little in common. In some, products are highly differentiated (automobiles and cereal, for example); in others, they are not (the steel industry, for example). In some, the industry is dominated by one very large firm; in others, the participating firms are of roughly equal size and have roughly equal power.

Oligopolies behave somewhat unpredictably. In markets where two or three large rivals compete head-on, the competing firms often execute strategies that anticipate counterstrategies. In setting price, for example, one firm must take into account how its competitors in the oligopoly are likely to react. One firm's action usually triggers a reaction from another, which in turn triggers still another reaction, and so on. The strategies and counterstrategies employed by these firms determine who gets the sales. As a result, oligopolies are characterized by a great deal of uncertainty, and it is difficult to generalize about their behavior.

Entry into an oligopolistic industry is usually possible, but difficult. Because firms in oligopolies are generally large, a large initial investment is usually required to break in.

In sum:

> Oligopolies are industries with a few large firms, but beyond that it is hard to generalize. In some oligopolies, firms differentiate their products; in others, they do not. Individual firms do exercise control over prices and generally behave "strategically" with respect to one another.

oligopoly An industry structure (or market organization) with a small number of (usually) large firms producing products that range from highly differentiated (automobiles) to standardized (copper). In general, entry of new firms into an oligopolistic industry is difficult but possible.

The four main kinds of market organization in the United States are summarized in Figure 3.1.

	Number of firms	Products differentiated or homogeneous	Firms have price-setting power	Free entry	Distinguishing characteristics	Examples
Perfect competition	Many	Homogeneous	No	Yes	Price competition only	Wheat farmer Textile firm
Monopolistic competition	Many	Differentiated	Yes, but limited	Yes	Price and quality competition	Restaurants Music industry
Oligopoly	Few	Either	Yes	Limited	Strategic behavior	Breakfast cereal Primary copper
Monopoly	One	A single, unique product	Yes	No	Still constrained by market demand	Public utility Beer in Taiwan

FIGURE 3.1
Characteristics of Different Market Organizations

How Competitive Is the U.S. Economy?

In an article published in the early 1980s, William G. Shepherd provides some evidence on the extent of competition in the U.S. economy.[3] Shepherd defines four market types that correspond roughly to the categories we have just defined: (1) pure monopolies, (2) industries with dominant firms, (3) tight oligopolies, and (4) effectively competitive industries.

In Shepherd's classification scheme, monopolies are just as we described them. One firm accounts for 100% (or nearly 100%) of an industry's total sales. No close substitutes for its product exist and entry to the market is blocked. Industries with dominant firms are near-monopolies. In such industries, the dominant firm accounts for 50% to 90% of total industry sales, no close rivals exist, and entry to the market is difficult. Tight oligopolies are industries in which the top four firms account for over 60% of total sales and in which entry barriers are high. Finally, Shepherd lumps everything else together in the "effectively competitive" category.

The classification "effectively competitive" signifies more than just perfect competition. It also includes all of what we described as monopolistic competition. In Shepherd's "effectively competitive" group, the top four firms control less than 40% of the market, and entry barriers are low.

Table 3.3 shows what happened, according to Shepherd's estimates, to the level of competition in the U.S. economy between 1939 and 1980. Pure monopolies, a category that includes most public utilities and some patented goods, accounted for only 2.5% of total national income in 1980, down from 6.2% in 1939. In fact, purely monopolistic and dominant-firm industries together accounted for just a little over 5% of national income in 1980. On the other hand, 76.7% of national income originates in sectors that Shepherd classifies as effectively competitive, up from 52.4% in 1939. The estimates indicate that the percentage of national income originating in tight oligopolies has been cut in half since 1958.

The U.S. economy has apparently become significantly more competitive over the years. A number of factors may have contributed to this change. Without going into detail here, these factors include increased competition from imports, deregulation (particularly in the trucking, airline, and telecommunications industries), and enforcement of antimonopoly laws.

Structural Change Since 1970

Table 3.4 gives a breakdown of national income by major product type or industry. These data point to a number of important changes. First, the percent of total national income accounted for by manufacturing has been continuously shrinking

[3]William G. Shepherd, "Causes of Increased Competition in the U.S. Economy, 1939–1980," *Review of Economics and Statistics* LXIV (November 1982), 613–626.

TABLE 3.3

Trends in Competition in the U.S. Economy 1939–1980: Percentage Share of National Income by Industry Category

	1939	1958	1980
Pure monopoly	6.2	3.1	2.5
Dominant firm	5.0	5.0	2.8
Tight oligopoly	36.4	35.6	18.0
Effectively competitive firm	<u>52.4</u>	<u>56.3</u>	<u>76.7</u>
Total	100.0	100.0	100.0

Source: William G. Shepherd, "Causes of Increased Competition in the U.S. Economy, 1939–1980," *Review of Economics and Statistics* LXIV (November 1982), 613–626.

	1970	1980	1990
Agriculture, forestry, fisheries	3.1	2.7	2.3
Mining and construction	6.7	7.5	6.0
Manufacturing	25.8	23.5	18.2
Transportation	3.8	3.8	3.2
Communications and utilities	3.9	4.0	4.2
Wholesale and retail trade	15.3	14.7	14.3
Finance, insurance, real estate	11.5	12.3	14.6
Services	13.1	15.1	21.7
Government	15.9	14.2	14.6
Other	.9	2.1	.9
Total	100.0	100.0	100.0

TABLE 3.4
Percentage Share of National Income by Major Sector, 1970, 1980, and 1990

Sources: *Statistical Abstract of the United States, 1987,* Table 704, and U.S. Department of Commerce, *Survey of Current Business* (Feb. 1991). 1980 figures do not add to exactly 100 due to rounding.

for 20 years. In 1970 more than a quarter of U.S. national income originated in the manufacturing sector. The decline since then has been due in part to increased competition from abroad: Americans buy a tremendous number of products, including automobiles, textiles, televisions, VCR's, cameras, and machine tools, from Korea, Japan, and Taiwan. One of the biggest-selling new manufactured items in the United States today is the fax machine. But even though the fax machine was invented in the United States, not a single machine is currently manufactured in this country. By 1990, the portion of total U.S. income originating in the manufacturing sector had dropped to only 18.2%, less than one fifth of national income.

The fastest growing sector of the U.S. economy has been the service sector. Americans eat at restaurants, stay at hotels, and consume recreation, entertainment, and personal services at a far greater rate than ever before. The other sector that seems to have grown between 1970 and 1990 is finance, insurance, and real estate. There are increasing numbers of people working for banks, financial services companies, stockbrokers, and the like.

One frequently voiced concern is that "good" jobs are being lost and replaced by "bad" ones. Manufacturing in the United States is a high-wage sector. Most people who work in plants receive substantial hourly wages. As manufacturing has declined, though, more and more jobs have opened up in the expanding service sector, where hourly wages are low relative to those in manufacturing.

While some people are deeply concerned over this structural change in the U.S. economy, others see it as a natural consequence of continued economic growth and progress. Looking again at Table 3.4, notice that the first category, "agriculture, forestry, and fisheries," is also declining in relative importance. As recently as 1870, agriculture accounted for 22% of national income. But as farmers learned more and more productive farming methods, the need for farm labor declined, and so did food prices. With lower food prices, people could spend their incomes on other things—manufactured goods and services. Because agriculture needed fewer workers, labor was available to be employed in the new expanding sectors. Thus as the U.S. economy grew and developed, some sectors, such as agriculture, shrank in relative importance and others, such as manufacturing and services, grew in relative importance.

Modern economies are in a continuous state of change. Resources are always moving. Literally thousands of new firms are started every year, and old, tired firms—not to mention young, inefficient ones—go out of business every day. Some firms grow rapidly in size, while others shrink. In the process, the basic industrial structure changes. In a very real sense, the purpose of this book is to help you understand this process. Why are new firms formed? Why do others go out of business? Why are some sectors expanding while others are contracting?

THE PUBLIC SECTOR: TAXES AND GOVERNMENT SPENDING IN THE UNITED STATES

Thus far we have talked only about the sets of decisions facing small, independent, private firms. But this is only part of the story. While the U.S. economy is basically a market economy, it also has a public sector that plays a major role in determining the allocation of resources, the mix of output, and the distribution of rewards. To understand the workings of any economic system, it is necessary to understand the role of government—the public sector. Government in the United States operates on three different levels—federal, state, and local. Each of these levels has assumed a different set of functions and responsibilities over the years, and although there is some overlap, each level derives its main revenues from different sources. How big is this public sector? What does it spend its money on, and where does it get its money?

The Size of the Public Sector

gross domestic product (GDP)
The total value of all goods and services produced by a national economy within a given time period.

The **gross domestic product,** or **GDP,** is the total value of all goods and services produced in the economy in a given period of time, say, a year.[4] The concept of GDP is used extensively in macroeconomics. Here it is enough to say that the GDP is used as a measure of the total annual "output" of a nation. As you can see from Figure 3.2, public expenditure at all levels, as a percentage of GDP, increased from 18.4% 1940 to 33.4% in 1990. The federal portion of total expenditures increased more rapidly, more than doubling since 1940, while the state and local share only grew from 8.4% of GDP to 10.3% in the same period.[5]

---

[4]A more complete definition of GDP is "the market value of all *final* goods and services produced within a given period of time by factors of production located within a country." Otherwise, U.S.-produced tires when resold on U.S.-produced cars would be counted twice.

[5]Federal grants to state and local governments are included as a federal expenditure rather than a state and local expenditure because they are paid for out of federal tax revenues. Federal grants in 1990 amounted to $132.3 billion. Including this figure with state and local expenditures would push state and local expenditures to 12.7% of GDP in 1990.

FIGURE 3.2
Total Government Expenditure as a Percentage of GDP, 1940–1990

Total government expenditures grew from 18.4% of GDP in 1940 to 33.4% in 1990. While the share of state and local governments grew less than two percentage points, the federal share more than doubled.
(*Source: Economic Report of the President*, 1991, 1993. Grants to states and localities included in federal.)

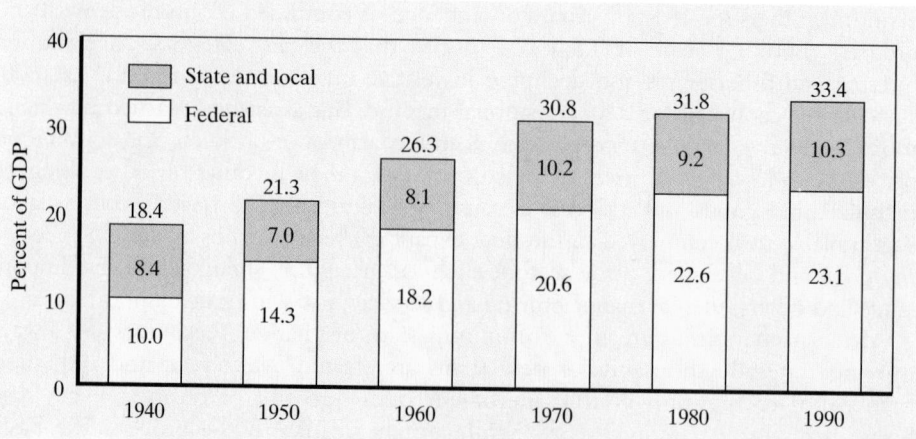

Government spending can be broken into three major categories: *purchases of goods and services, transfer payments to households,* and *interest payments.* **Purchases of goods and services** make up that portion of national output that government actually uses, or "consumes," directly. They include the airplanes purchased from McDonnell Douglas by the air force, the new Senate office building (in the year that it was built), and the paper, books, and pens produced by private companies that are used by government employees. This category also includes the wages and salaries paid for the services of government employees.

Table 3.5 shows that government purchases of goods and services have not increased as dramatically as total government expenditures has. In fact, government purchases of goods and services (the sum of both defense and nondefense purchases) have stayed at roughly the same percentage of GDP (about 20%) for the last 30 years.

Transfer payments are cash payments made directly to households for which no current services are received—social security benefits, unemployment compensation payments, welfare payments, and so forth. **Interest payments** are also cash payments, but they are paid to those who own government bonds. Taken together, transfer payments and interest payments account for nearly the entire increase in government expenditure between 1960 and 1980. During the 1980s, transfer payments stopped growing as a percentage of GDP.

The increase in the size of the social security system accounts for much of the increase in transfer payments. Social security is a self-financing system in which benefits are paid out of taxes contributed by workers and their employers. Some have argued that because workers who have contributed will ultimately be entitled to benefits, the system should be separated from other federal receipts and expenditures for accounting purposes, but this has not been done so far.

As Table 3.5 shows, interest payments in 1990 almost doubled as a percentage of GDP over the 1980 level. This is because of the huge deficits run up during the early 1980s. When the government spends more than it taxes, it must borrow. It does so by issuing bonds, and it must pay interest on the bonds.

government purchases of goods and services A category of government spending that includes the portion of national output that the government uses, or "consumes," directly—F14s for the navy, memo pads for the FBI, salaries for government employees.

government transfer payments Cash payments made by the government directly to households for which no current services are received. They include social security benefits, unemployment compensation, and welfare payments.

government interest payments Cash payments made by the government to those who own government bonds.

GOVERNMENT EXPENDITURE AS A PERCENTAGE OF GDP	1940	1950	1960	1970	1980	1990
Total	18.4	21.3	26.3	30.8	31.8	33.4
Purchases of goods and services, nondefense	11.9	8.5	10.6	13.4	13.5	13.2
Purchases of goods and services, defense	2.2	5.0	8.8	7.6	5.3	5.7
Transfer payments	2.7	6.2	5.7	8.3	11.7	12.3
Interest payments (net)	1.2	1.5	1.3	1.2	1.2	2.2
Subsidies	0.4	0.0	0.0	0.3	0.2	0.0

GOVERNMENT EMPLOYMENT AS A PERCENTAGE OF TOTAL EMPLOYMENT (EXCLUDING MILITARY) IN THE ECONOMY	1950	1960	1970	1980	1990
Total	13.3	15.4	17.7	18.0	16.6
Federal	4.2	4.2	3.8	3.2	2.8
State and local	9.1	11.2	13.9	14.8	13.8

Source: Economic Report of the President, 1991, 1993.

TABLE 3.5

The Size of the Public Sector, 1940–1990

Total government expenditure has grown as a percentage of GDP, but government purchases of goods and services, that part of the national output "consumed" by the government, has grown little since 1960. Government employment fell as a percent of the total between 1970 and 1990.

Another way to look at the relative size of the public sector is to look at government employment as a percentage of total employment (see again Table 3.5). In 1990 federal government civilian employment was only 2.8% of total employment. In addition, federal civilian employment as a percentage of total employment in the United States has fallen steadily since 1950, and it is actually lower now than it was in 1950. State and local government employment grew steadily as a fraction of total employment in the economy through 1980. Since 1980, however, it has dropped back to about the 1970 level. Total government employment in 1990 was 16.6% of total employment in the economy, down from 18.0% in 1980.

How big is the public sector in the United States relative to the public sectors in other countries? Good statistics on employment and spending are not easy to find, but Figure 3.3 presents some international comparisons based on taxes collected. The figure shows total national and local taxes as a percentage of gross domestic product (GDP).

In 1975, U.S. federal, state, and local taxes amounted to 29.6% of GDP. This placed the United States in a tie for tenth place among the 19 countries in the comparison. Between 1975 and 1989, taxes as a percentage of GDP increased in all 19 countries. The smallest increase was registered in the United States, where taxes as a percentage of GDP remained virtually constant. As of 1989, only Turkey among the group of more developed countries had lower taxes as a percentage of GDP than the United States.

Government Expenditures

The detailed breakdown of the federal budget for fiscal year 1991 in Table 3.6 shows that the top six categories account for over 82% of the total. National defense and social security alone account for about 40% of federal spending. Table

FIGURE 3.3

Taxes as a Percentage of Gross Domestic Product, 1975 and 1989

Source: *Statistical Abstract of the United States*, 1992, pp. 318–319.

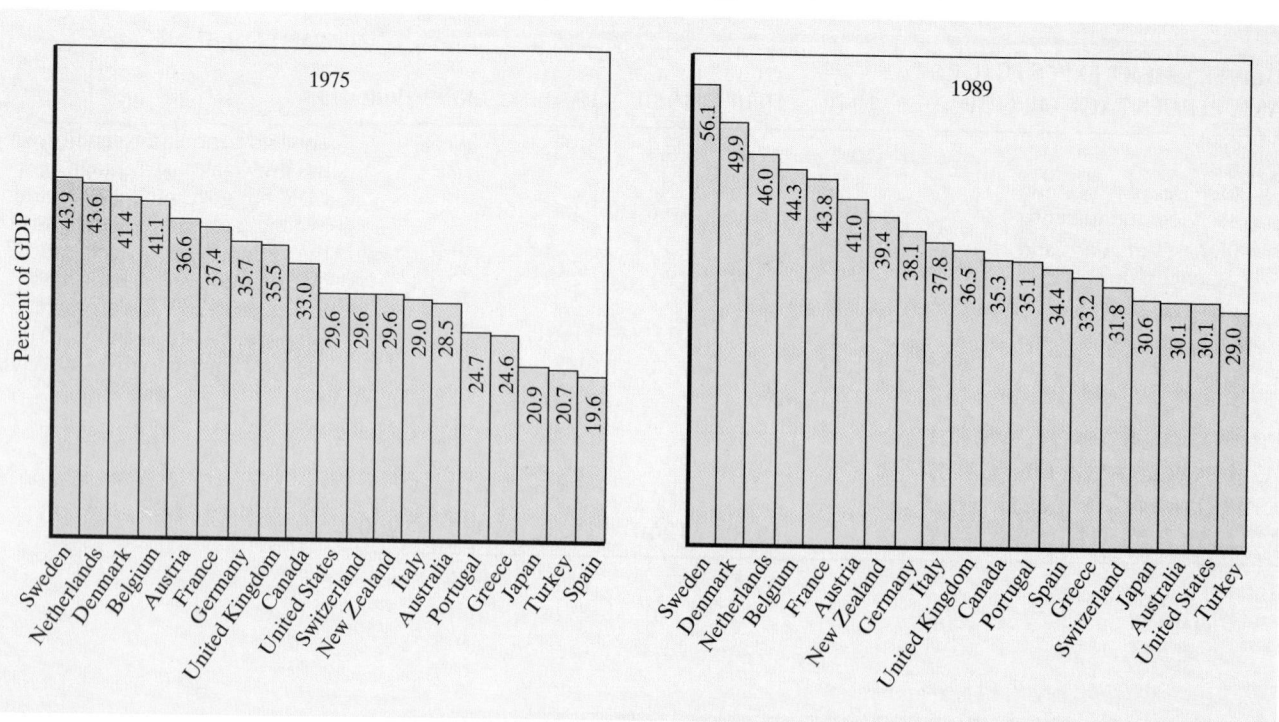

TABLE 3.6
Federal Expenditures by Function 1991

	BILLIONS OF DOLLARS	PERCENTAGE OF TOTAL
National defense	273.3	20.7
Social security	269.0	20.3
Net interest	194.5	14.7
Income security	170.8	12.9
Medicare	104.5	7.9
Commerce and housing credit	75.6	5.7
Health	71.2	5.4
Education, training, employment	42.8	3.2
Veterans benefits	31.3	2.4
Transportation	31.1	2.4
International affairs	15.9	1.2
Agriculture	15.2	1.1
Science, space, and technology	16.1	1.2
Natural resources environment	18.6	1.4
Administration of justice	12.3	0.9
General governments	11.7	0.9
Community and regional development	6.8	0.5
Miscellaneous and offsetting receipts	- 37.7	- 2.8
Total	1323.0	100.0

Source: Statistical Abstract of the United States, 1992, pp. 318–319.

TABLE 3.7
Federal Expenditures by Function: Percentage Shares of Total Compared for 1982 and 1992

	1982	1992	CHANGE IN SHARE
National defense	24.9	21.6	- 3.3
Social Security	20.9	20.4	- 0.5
Net interest	11.4	14.2	+ 2.8
Income security	14.4	14.2	- 0.2
Medicare	6.3	8.5	+ 2.2
Health	3.7	6.6	+ 2.9
International affairs	1.6	1.3	- 0.3
All other	16.8	13.2	- 3.6
Total	100.0	100.0	

Source: U.S. Dept. of Commerce, Economic Indicators, 1992.

3.7 compares the same categories for 1982 and 1992. With the end of the Cold War, expenditures for national defense have been shrinking. Expenditures for Medicare, health, and net interest have been growing. The crisis in health care costs that was such an important issue in the 1992 presidential election is evident in these numbers. Medicare and health care expenditures taken together rose from 10% of the budget in 1982 to 15% of the budget in 1992. (For more on this topic, see the Issues and Applications box on page 67 titled "Health Care: The Issue of the 1990s.") Interest paid by the government to bondholders (net interest) has risen sharply since 1982 because the amount of outstanding debt on which interest must be paid has increased sharply.

TABLE 3.8
State and Local
Expenditures by Function

	BILLIONS OF DOLLARS, 1990	PERCENTAGE OF TOTAL, 1990	PERCENTAGE OF TOTAL, 1975
Education	288.1	34.7	38.2
Public welfare	107.3	12.9	11.8
Health and hospitals	74.6	9.0	8.2
Highways	61.1	7.3	9.8
Interest on debt	58.9	7.1	3.8
Police and fire	43.6	5.2	5.2
General administration	39.1	4.7	3.8
Other*	158.8	19.1	19.2
Total	831.5	100.0	100.0

*Includes parks, sanitation, and housing, among other areas.
Source: Statistical Abstract of the United States, 1992, p. 284.

Table 3.8 shows state and local government spending by category in 1990. In that year, 34.7% of all state and local spending went for education, mostly public elementary and secondary education, although all states spend money on higher education as well. Since 1975, education and highways have contracted as a portion of the total budget, while interest on debt, general administration, and health and hospitals have assumed a larger share. The overall distribution of state and local government spending across functions during the 15 years did not change very much, however.

Sources of Government Revenue

A breakdown of the sources of federal tax revenues appears in Table 3.9. Until 1991, the biggest single source of revenue for the federal government was the *individual income tax,* which accounted for 46.3% of total revenues in 1980. That figure dropped to 40.8% by 1992. Federal income tax is withheld from most people's pay each week by their employers, who send it to the Internal Revenue Service. Self-employed people are responsible for sending in their own estimated taxes four times each year. Each year we must add up our total income, subtract the items that we are allowed to exclude or deduct, and figure out the total tax that we should have paid for the previous year. If we owe more than we paid, we must send the difference to the IRS by April 15. If we paid more than we owe, we get a refund.

TABLE 3.9
Federal Receipts by Source,
1980 and 1992

	1980		1992	
	BILLIONS OF DOLLARS	PERCENT	BILLIONS OF DOLLARS	PERCENT
Individual income taxes	256.2	46.3	474.1	40.8
Social insurance taxes	186.8	33.8	489.7	42.2
Corporation income taxes	70.3	12.7	115.3	9.9
Indirect business taxes	39.6	7.2	81.5	7.0
Total	553.0	100.0	1160.6	100.0

Source: U.S. Department of Commerce, Bureau of Economic Analysis.

HEALTH CARE: THE ISSUE OF THE 1990S

No issue received more attention during the 1992 presidential campaign than health care reform. The health care sector in the United States is huge and growing. In 1960, total expenditures on health care in the United States amounted to only $27.1 billion, or just over 5% of GDP. By 1992, those figures had risen to over $800 billion and more than 14% of GDP. A study by the U.S. Office of Management and Budget projects that an incredible 18% of GDP will be spent on health care by the year 2000. No other country in the world spends more than 10% of its GDP on health care.

Health care is part of the private sector and part of the public sector. Some doctors work in private practice, some in private for-profit hospitals, and others in hospitals run by federal, state, and local governments. In 1990 alone, federal, state, and local governments spent $268.6 billion, or 40.3% of their total spending, on health care.

Most government health care spending is done through two programs: Medicaid and Medicare. Medicaid provided benefits to 25 million poor people in 1990 at a cost of $65 billion. The vast majority of people on Medicaid are eligible by virtue of being recipients of Aid to Families with Dependent Children (AFDC). Medicare provided benefits to 34 million elderly and disabled persons in 1990. These people are eligible regardless of income level. The total Medicare budget in 1990 was $109 billion. Medicare benefits are paid out of a trust fund administered by the Social Security Administration and funded by a special payroll tax paid by all workers in the United States.

In 1990, 212 million of the 246 million Americans were covered by either a government program or by private health insurance. Thirty-four million were not covered at all.

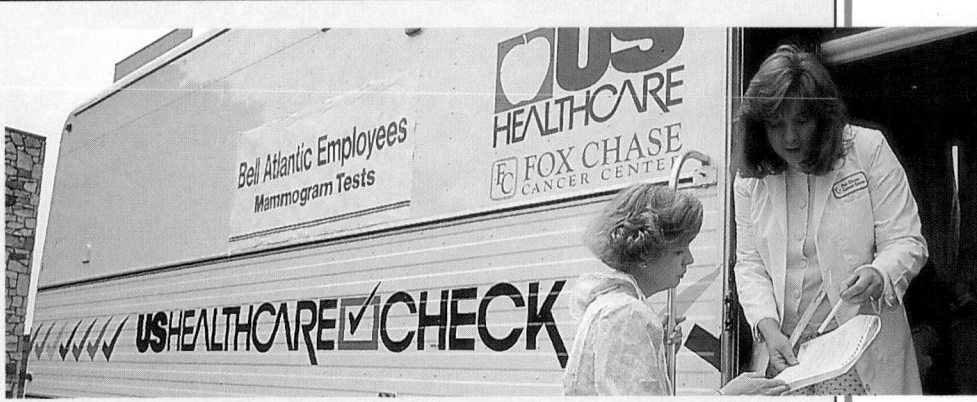

The largest and most successful HMO in the United States is U.S. Healthcare, which delivers medical care to more than 1.2 million people in six East Coast states.

Costs: High and Rising

Health insurance is very expensive. Employers who provide health insurance spent over $3000 per worker in 1991. General Motors alone spent $3.4 billion, or over $900 per car manufactured.

There are a number of reasons why costs are so high. First, the average age of Americans is increasing. A large population "bubble" referred to as the "baby boom generation" is now entering middle age, and health care costs rise with age. Second, people are living longer, which increases the need for expensive long-term nursing home care. Third, incredible technological advances have brought with them expensive new diagnostic equipment, medicines, and treatments such as organ transplants, genetically engineered drugs, magnetic resonance imaging, and heart by-pass surgery. Fourth, because most people are covered by insurance, consumers of health care have an incentive to "overconsume." Finally, malpractice suits have led to huge damage awards and very high malpractice insurance costs for doctors and others in the health care business.

Proposals for Reform

A number of developed countries, including Canada, Great Britain, and Germany, have national health care systems that provide coverage to all. At the same time, these countries manage to spend a far smaller portion of their GDP's on health care. How do they do it?

In addition to cost controls, most successful national systems use some type of rationing to hold down costs. The idea is that certain types of costly procedures simply will not be provided to all who need them. For example, a person who is very likely to die soon will most likely not receive a costly organ transplant that may prolong life for only a few months. The state of Oregon took a step in this direction in 1991, when it passed a law limiting the access of Medicaid recipients to more than 120 specific procedures deemed too costly. Needless to say, the law was controversial.

Another potential solution is the move toward universal enrollment in *health maintenance organizations* (*HMO's*). HMO's receive a fixed annual fee for each enrollee. Thus, they have an incentive to be more efficient in prescribing procedures, treatments, and medication.

Social insurance taxes are levied at a flat rate on wages and salaries up to a maximum amount. Because these taxes are figured as a percentage of wages and salaries and are levied on both employers and employees, they are also known as **payroll taxes.** Although the rules have become increasingly complex in recent years, for most people the payroll tax is levied at a flat rate of 7.65% on employees and another 7.65% on employers. Self-employed persons pay between 12.8% and 14.2% depending on their income.

Social insurance taxes go into one of several trust funds that pay social security cash and health benefits to retirees, the disabled, and the survivors of workers who paid into the system. Social insurance taxes on payrolls also fund the unemployment compensation system. The unemployment tax is paid by employers at a rate of 6.2% on the first $7000 of the wages of each covered employee although rates and limits vary by state.

Payroll taxes now account for a much larger portion of federal revenues than they have in the past. In 1992, they brought in 42.2% of total federal revenues, up from 33.8% twelve years earlier. In 1965, they brought in only 19% of total revenues. The tax rate has been increased steadily because of worries about the future solvency of the system. A huge number of people will reach retirement age soon after the year 2000. At the same time, the labor force will be smaller. Because the tax rate required to support the increasing number of elderly then would be intolerable, the rate was sharply increased during the 1970s. It continues to increase now, in order to generate a surplus in the social security trust funds that should prevent the collapse of the system in the future.

Corporate income taxes are levied on the net income of corporations only, not on the profits of other forms of business organization, such as proprietorships or partnerships, which are taxed directly as ordinary personal income to the owners. While payroll taxes have been increasing as a share of total tax revenues, corporate income taxes have had their ups and downs. In 1960, they accounted for nearly 25% of federal revenues. Table 3.9 shows that they accounted for 12.7% in 1980 and only 9.9% in 1992. Big cuts came in 1981 when Congress enacted the Economic Recovery Tax Act, designed to stimulate business investment. The Tax Reform Act of 1986 sharply reduced personal income taxes and partly offset the lost revenues by increasing the corporation tax.

All other tax revenues—indirect business taxes—make up only about 7% of the federal total. The main types of indirect business taxes at the federal level are **excise taxes**. These are taxes on specific commodities like cigarettes, alcoholic beverages, gasoline, tires and tubes, telephone service.

The sources of state and local revenues in 1992 appear in Table 3.10. Sales taxes, levied primarily by states, account for 30.2% of the total. Property taxes, which account for 27.2% of the total, are levied primarily by local governments (such as counties, cities, and towns) on the estimated, or "assessed," value of commercial, industrial, and residential property. Personal income taxes account for 23% of state and local revenues, while social insurance taxes account for 9.6% and corporate taxes account for 3.8 percent.

THE INTERNATIONAL SECTOR: IMPORTS AND EXPORTS IN THE UNITED STATES

One of the great economic lessons of the 1970s and 1980s was that all economies, regardless of their size, depend to some extent on other economies and are affected by events outside their borders. Ask anyone in Iowa about the

TABLE 3.10
State and Local Tax
Receipts, 1992

	BILLIONS OF DOLLARS	PERCENT OF TOTAL TAXES
Sales taxes	200.8	30.2
Property taxes	180.5	27.2
Personal income taxes	153.2	23.0
Social insurance taxes	63.7	9.6
Corporate taxes	25.2	3.8
Other	41.4	6.2
Total	664.8	100.0

Source: U.S. Department of Commerce, Bureau of Economic Analysis.

impact of foreign trade on farm prices and therefore on the well-being of American farmers. Or ask steel workers in Pittsburgh and Youngstown about the effect of cheap German and Japanese steel on the economies of those towns. One of the biggest issues in the 1992 presidential election campaign was the North American Free Trade Agreement (NAFTA) signed by President Bush in December, 1992. The purpose of NAFTA is to reduce trade barriers between the United States, Canada, and Mexico.

The United States economy is by no means "closed." Thousands of transactions between the United States and virtually every country in the world take place daily. In 1991 the United States sold $40.1 billion in agricultural products to the rest of the world and bought over $50 billion in petroleum products from other countries. Overall, the United States imported $620.4 billion worth of goods and services in 1991, 11.0% of its GDP.

The growth of the international sector of the U.S. economy is a relatively recent phenomenon. Prior to 1970, imports and exports of goods and services accounted for a relatively small and stable fraction of U.S. GDP. Table 3.11 on page 70 shows imports and exports for selected years since 1929. In all but a few years between 1929 and 1970, imports accounted for only 4% to 6% of GDP. During the Depression and immediately following World War II, the figure dropped below 4%, but never rose above 6 percent.

Beginning in 1970, however, the volume of international trade increased significantly. Imports and exports doubled as a percentage of GDP by the end of the 1970s. Imports reached more than 11% by 1980. Exports dropped to 7.6% in 1985 and 1986, but rebounded to over 10% by 1990. Imports have held steady at around 11% of GDP since 1987.

THE COMPOSITION OF U.S. TRADE   Table 3.12 on page 71 lists the types of merchandise imported and exported in 1992. Perhaps the most surprising thing about this merchandise is its tremendous diversity.

The largest category—about 40% of U.S. exports and one-quarter of its imports—is capital goods except automotive, a very broad category that includes many specialized and diverse products. The second most important category of U.S. exports is industrial supplies and materials—$105.3 billion in 1992. In third and fourth places are consumer goods except automotive and automobiles.

Prior to 1970, imports of petroleum and petroleum products never amounted to more than $3 billion annually and were never more than 10% of total imports. The rapid increase in oil prices in 1973–1974 changed all this.

TABLE 3.11

U.S. Imports and Exports of Goods and Services, 1929–1992

	EXPORTS OF GOODS AND SERVICES		IMPORTS OF GOODS AND SERVICES	
	BILLIONS OF DOLLARS	PERCENTAGE OF GDP	BILLIONS OF DOLLARS	PERCENTAGE OF GDP
1929	7.1	6.8	5.9	5.7
1933	2.4	4.3	2.1	3.8
1945	7.4	3.5	7.9	3.7
1955	21.1	5.5	18.1	4.5
1960	25.3	5.0	22.8	4.5
1965	35.4	5.3	31.5	4.7
1970	57.0	5.8	55.8	5.7
1974	124.3	8.9	127.5	9.1
1976	148.9	8.8	151.1	9.0
1978	186.1	8.6	212.3	9.8
1980	279.2	10.6	293.9	11.1
1981	303.0	10.2	317.7	10.7
1982	282.6	9.0	303.2	9.7
1983	276.7	8.3	328.1	9.9
1984	302.4	8.2	405.1	11.0
1985	302.1	7.6	417.6	10.5
1986	319.2	7.6	451.7	10.7
1987	364.0	8.2	507.1	11.4
1988	444.2	9.2	552.2	11.5
1989	508.0	9.7	587.7	11.2
1990	557.0	10.1	625.9	11.3
1991	598.2	10.5	620.0	10.9
1992	636.3	10.7	666.7	11.2

Source: Economic Report of the President, 1993 and updates.

Table 3.13 chronicles the rise and fall of crude petroleum as a major import. By 1980 crude oil accounted for more than one-quarter of total imports. But in the early 1980s the United States began to cut its consumption of petroleum. By 1987, petroleum and natural gas accounted for only 7.6% of total imports. With the 1990 invasion of Kuwait, oil prices rose and the dollar volume of imports jumped back to over 10% of the total.

Two other important categories of imports that have received a great deal of attention because of their impact on major U.S. industries are automobiles and iron and steel. In 1992 imports of automobiles and parts totaled $90.8 billion.

FROM INSTITUTIONS TO THEORY

This chapter has sketched the institutional structure of the U.S. economy. As we turn to economic theory, both positive and normative, you should reflect on the basic realities of economic life in the United States presented here. Why is the service sector expanding and the manufacturing sector contracting? Why is the public sector as large as it is? What economic functions does it perform? What determines the level of imports and exports? What effects do cheap foreign products have on the U.S. economy?

EXPORTS	BILLIONS OF DOLLARS	PERCENTAGE OF TOTAL
Agricultural products	44.4	10.0
Nonagricultural products	400.4	90.0
Total	444.8	100.0
Food, feeds, and beverages	40.6	9.1
Industrial supplies and materials	105.3	23.7
Capital goods except automotive (machinery, aircraft, etc.)	176.8	39.7
Automobiles, vehicles, parts, and engines	47.2	10.6
Consumer goods except automotive	50.4	11.3
All other	24.5	5.5
Total	444.8	100.0

IMPORTS	BILLIONS OF DOLLARS	PERCENTAGE OF TOTAL
Petroleum and petroleum products	51.0	9.4
Nonpetroleum products	493.1	91.6
Total	544.1	100.0
Food, feeds, and beverages	28.0	5.1
Industrial supplies and materials	133.3	24.5
Capital goods except automotive (machinery, aircraft, etc.)	134.0	24.6
Automobiles, vehicles, parts, and engines	90.8	16.7
Consumer goods except automotive	122.8	22.6
All other	35.4	6.5
Total	544.1	100.0

Source: U.S. Department of Commerce, Bureau of Economic Analysis.

TABLE 3.12
Major Categories of Merchandise Imports and Exports by the United States, 1992

	BILLIONS OF DOLLARS	PERCENTAGE OF TOTAL IMPORTS
1970	1.4	3.6
1974	16.5	16.5
1975	19.3	20.0
1978	32.1	18.6
1979	46.1	21.9
1980	65.7	26.8
1981	61.9	23.7
1982	45.9	18.8
1983	36.8	14.3
1984	36.5	11.2
1985*	35.9	10.4
1986*	24.5	6.6
1987*	30.8	7.6
1988*	29.6	6.8
1989*	38.8	8.3
1990*	48.9	10.0
1991*	42.4	8.9

Source: Statistical Abstract of the United States, 1981, 1987, 1990, 1992. *Figures for 1985–1991 include natural gas.

TABLE 3.13
U.S. Imports of Crude Petroleum, 1970–1991

One of the most important questions in economics concerns the relative merits of public sector involvement in the economy. Should the government be involved in the economy, or should the market be left to its own devices? Before we can confront these and other important issues, we need to establish a theoretical framework. Our study of the economy and its operation begins in Chapter 4 with the behavior of suppliers and demanders in private markets.

SUMMARY

1. The *private sector* is made up of privately owned firms that exist to make a profit, nonprofit organizations, and individual households. The *public sector* is the government and its agencies at all levels—federal, state, and local. The *international sector* is the global economy.

The Private Sector: Business and Industrial Organization in the United States

2. A *proprietorship* is a firm with a single owner. A *partnership* has two or more owners. Proprietors and partners are fully liable for all the debts of the business. A *corporation* is a formally established legal entity that limits the liability of its owners. The owners are not responsible for the debts of the firm beyond what they invest.

3. The term *industry* is used loosely to refer to groups of firms that produce similar products. Industries can be broadly or narrowly defined. A company that produces cheese belongs to the cheese industry, the dairy industry, the food products industry, and the agricultural products industry.

4. In *perfect competition,* no single firm has any control over prices. This follows from two characteristics of this industry structure: (1) Perfectly competitive industries are composed of many firms, each small relative to the size of the industry, and (2) each firm in a perfectly competitive industry produces exactly the same product—that is, products are *homogeneous.*

5. A *monopoly* is a *market organization,* or industry structure, in which there is only one firm producing a product for which there are no close substitutes. To remain a monopoly in a profitable industry, a firm must be able to block the entry of competing firms.

6. *Monopolistic competition* is an industry structure in which many firms compete, but in which each firm produces a slightly different product. Although each firm's product is unique, however, there are many close substitutes. Entry and exit into monopolistically competitive industries are relatively easy.

7. An *oligopoly* is an industry with a small number of firms. In general, entry of new firms into an oligopolistic industry is difficult but possible.

The Public Sector: Taxes and Government Spending in the United States

8. Public expenditures at all levels increased from 18.4% of GDP in 1940 to 33.4% in 1990. The federal portion of total expenditures grew more rapidly than the state and local portions, more than doubling since 1940.

9. Other measures of the size of the public sector have not increased as rapidly. Government employment increased slightly from 15.4% of total employment in 1960 to 16.6% in 1990.

10. National defense and social security account for over 40% of federal spending. The top four categories of state and local spending are education, public welfare, health and hospitals, and highways.

11. Individual income taxes and social insurance taxes together accounted for over 80% of federal revenues in 1992. Over the last quarter century, social insurance taxes have increased dramatically as a portion of total federal revenues. Sales taxes and property taxes accounted for about 57% of state and local revenues in 1992.

The International Sector: Imports and Exports in the United States

12. Thousands of transactions between the United States and virtually every other country in the world take place daily. This has led to the increased importance of the international sector in the United States economy. In 1992, the United States imported $666.7 billion worth of goods and services, 11.2% of its GDP.

REVIEW TERMS AND CONCEPTS

barrier to entry   57

corporate income tax   68

corporation   54

dividends   55

excise tax   69

government interest payments   63

government purchases of goods and
    services   62

government transfer payments   63

gross domestic product (GDP)   62

homogeneous products   57

industry   56

international sector   53

market organization   56

monopolistic competition   58

monopoly   57

net income   55

oligopoly   59

partnership   54

perfect competition   56

private sector   52

proprietorship   54

public sector   52

retained earnings   55

shares of stock   55

social insurance,
    or payroll, tax   68

PROBLEM SET

1. The federal budget was a major issue during the presidential campaign of 1992. What changes in the budget, if any, has President Clinton proposed since assuming the presidency in January, 1993?

2. The latest data on the federal budget and on international trade in this chapter are for 1992. What events during 1993 had an impact on federal receipts and expenditures? On the volume of imports and exports?

3. The chapter contains conflicting evidence on whether the public sector has expanded relative to the rest of the economy in the last 10 to 20 years. Discuss.

4. What are the differences between a proprietorship and a corporation? If you were going to start a small business, which form of organization would you choose? What are the advantages and disadvantages of the two forms of organization?

5. "Most firms are corporations, but they account for a relatively small portion of total output in the United States."

Do you agree or disagree with this statement? Explain your answer.

6. In 1991 shareholders directly received only 44.1% of total corporate profits. What happened to the rest?

7. Perfectly competitive industries are made up of large numbers of firms, each small relative to the size of the industry and each producing homogeneous products. What does this imply about an individual firm's ability to influence price? Explain your answer.

8. How is a monopolistically competitive industry like a monopoly? In what ways is it like a perfectly competitive industry?

9. How is it possible for government spending to increase as a percentage of GDP while taxes and government employment are both decreasing?

10. Why does the federal government seem to be spending much more on interest payments now than it was a decade ago? Explain.

4

Demand, Supply, and Market Equilibrium

Chapters 1 and 2 introduced the discipline, methodology, and subject matter of economics. Chapter 3 described the institutional landscape of the U.S. economy—its private, public, and international sectors. We now begin the task of analyzing how a market economy actually works. This chapter and the next present an overview of the way individual markets work. They introduce some of the concepts that are needed to understand microeconomics.

As we proceed to define terms and make assumptions, it is important to keep in mind what we are doing. In Chapter 1 we were very careful to explain what economic theory attempts to do. Theories are abstract representations of reality, like a map that represents a city. We believe that the models presented here will help you understand the workings of the economy just as a map helps you get where you want to go in a city. But just as a map presents one view of the world, so too does any given theory of the economy. Alternatives exist to the theory that we present. We believe, however, that the theory presented here, while abstract, is useful in gaining an understanding of how the economy works.

In the simple island society discussed in Chapter 2, the economic problem was solved directly. Colleen and Bill allocated their time and used the resources of the island to satisfy their wants. Bill might be a farmer, Colleen a hunter and carpenter. He might be a civil engineer, she a doctor. Exchange occurred, but complex markets were not necessary.

In societies of many people, however, production must satisfy wide-ranging tastes and preferences. Producers therefore *specialize*. Farmers produce more food than they can eat in order to sell it to buy manufactured goods. Physicians are paid for specialized services, as are attorneys, construction workers, and editors. When there is specialization, there must be exchange, and exchange takes place in markets.

This chapter begins to explore the basic forces at work in market systems. The purpose of our discussion is to explain how the individual decisions of households and firms together, without any central planning or direction, answer the three basic questions: What will be produced, how will it be produced, and for whom will it be produced? We begin with some definitions.

FIRMS AND HOUSEHOLDS: THE BASIC DECISION-MAKING UNITS

Throughout this book, we discuss and analyze the behavior of two fundamental decision-making units: *firms*—the primary producing units in an economy—and *households*—the consuming units in an economy. Both are made up of people performing different functions and playing different roles. In essence, then, what we are developing is a theory of human behavior.

A **firm** exists when a person or a group of people decides to produce a product or products by transforming *inputs* (that is, resources in the broadest sense) into *outputs* (the products that are sold in the market). Some firms produce goods, others produce services. Some are large, some are small, and some are in between. But all firms exist to transform resources into things that people want. The Boston Symphony Orchestra takes labor, land, a building, musically talented people, electricity, and other inputs and combines them to produce concerts. The production process can be extremely complicated. The first flutist in the orchestra, for example, uses training, talent, previous performance experience, a score, an instrument, the conductor's interpretation, and her own feelings about the music to produce just one contribution to an overall performance.

Most firms exist to make a profit for their owners, but some do not. Columbia University, for example, fits the description of a firm: It takes inputs in the form of labor, land, skills, books, and buildings and produces a service that we call education. Although it sells that service for a price, it does not *exist* to make a profit, but rather to provide education of the highest quality possible at the most reasonable cost possible.

Still, most firms exist to make a profit. They engage in production because they can sell their product for more than it costs to produce it. The analysis of firm behavior that follows rests on the assumption that *firms make decisions in order to maximize profits.*

An **entrepreneur** is one who organizes, manages, and assumes the risks of a firm. It is the entrepreneur who takes a new idea or a new product and turns it into a successful business. All firms have implicit in them some element of entrepreneurship. When a new firm is created, whether a proprietorship, a partnership, or a corporation, someone must organize the new firm, arrange financing, hire employees, and take risks. That person is an entrepreneur. Sometimes existing companies introduce new products, and sometimes new firms develop or improve

firm An organization that transforms resources (inputs) into products (outputs). Firms are the primary producing units in a market economy.

entrepreneur A person who organizes, manages, and assumes the risks of a firm, taking a new idea or a new product and turning it into a successful business.

on an old idea, but at the root of it all is entrepreneurship, which some see as the core idea of the free enterprise system.

At the root of the debate about the potential of free enterprise in formerly socialist Eastern Europe is the question of entrepreneurship. Does an entrepreneurial spirit exist in that part of the world? If not, can it be developed? Without it the free enterprise system breaks down.

The consuming units in an economy are **households.** A household may consist of any number of people: a single person living alone, a married couple with four children, or 15 unrelated people sharing a house. Household decisions are presumably based on the individual tastes and preferences of the consuming unit. The household buys what it wants and can afford. In a large, heterogeneous, and open society such as the United States, wildly different tastes find expression in the marketplace. A six-block walk in any direction on any street in Manhattan or a drive from the Chicago Loop south into rural Illinois should be enough to convince anyone that it is difficult to generalize about what people like and do not like.

Even though households have wide-ranging preferences, they also have some things in common. All—even the very rich—have ultimately limited incomes, and all must pay in some way for the things they consume. While households may have some control over their incomes—they can work more or less—they are also constrained by the availability of jobs, current wages, their own abilities, and their accumulated and inherited wealth (or lack thereof).

INPUT MARKETS AND OUTPUT MARKETS

Households and firms interact in two basic kinds of markets: product, or output, markets and input, or resource, markets. Goods and services that are intended for use by households are exchanged in **product**, or **output**, **markets**. In output markets, competing firms *supply* and households *demand*.

In order to produce goods and services, firms must buy resources in **input**, or **resource**, **markets**. Firms buy inputs from households, which supply these inputs. When a firm decides how much to produce (supply) in output markets, it must simultaneously decide how much of each input it needs to produce the desired level of output. To produce automobiles, Chrysler Corporation must use many inputs, including tires, steel, complicated machinery, and many different kinds of skilled labor.

Figure 4.1 shows the circular flow of economic activity through a simple market economy. Note that the flow is clockwise, reflecting the direction of activity in input and output markets. For example, final goods and services flow from firms to households through output markets. Labor services flow from households to firms through input markets. Payment (most often in money form) for goods and services flows in a counterclockwise direction.

In input markets, households *supply* resources. Most households earn their incomes by working—they supply their labor in the **labor market** to firms that demand labor and pay workers for their time and skills. Households may also loan their accumulated or inherited savings to firms for interest or exchange those savings for claims to future profits, as when a household buys shares of stock in a corporation. In the **capital market**, households supply the funds that firms use to buy capital goods in exchange for interest or claims to future profits. Households may also supply land or other real property in exchange for rent in the **land market**.

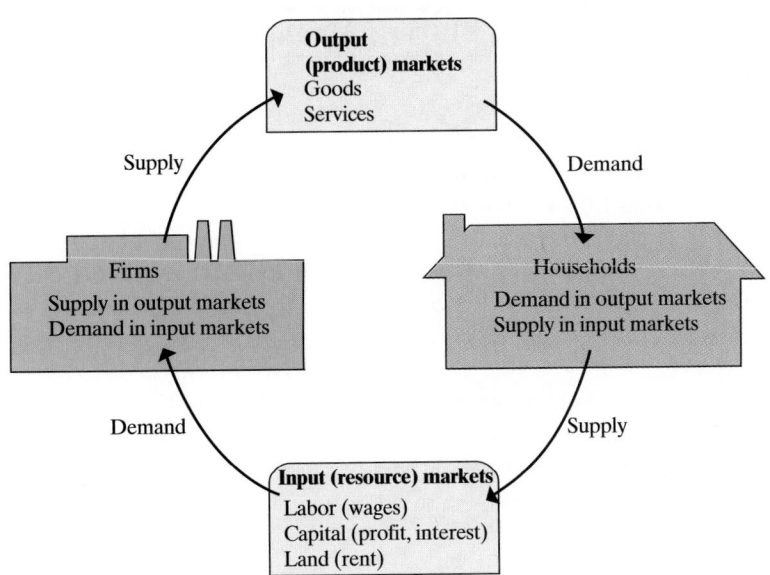

FIGURE 4.1
The Circular Flow of
Economic Activity

Diagrams like this one show the "circular flow" of economic activity, hence the name "circular flow diagram." Here, goods and services flow clockwise: Labor services supplied by households flow to firms, and final goods and services produced by firms flow to households. Money (not pictured here) flows in the opposite (counterclockwise) direction: Payment for goods and services flows from households to firms, and payment for labor services flows from firms to households.

Inputs into the production process are also called **factors of production.** Land, labor, and capital are the three key factors of production. Throughout this text, we use the terms "input" and "factor of production" interchangeably. Thus, input markets and factor markets mean the same thing.

Early economics texts included entrepreneurship as a type of input, just like land, labor, and capital. Treating entrepreneurship as a separate factor of production has fallen out of favor, however, partially because it is unmeasurable. Most economists today implicitly assume that it is in plentiful supply. That is, if profit opportunities exist, it is likely that entrepreneurs will crop up to take advantage of them. This assumption has turned out to be a good predictor of actual economic behavior and performance.

The supply of inputs and their prices ultimately determine the income of households. The amount of income earned by a household thus depends on the decisions it makes concerning the supply of inputs. Whether to stay in school, how much and what kind of training to get, whether to start a business, how many hours to work, whether to work at all, and how to invest savings are all household decisions that affect income.

As you can see, then:

> Input and output markets are connected through the behavior of both firms and households. Firms determine the quantities and character of outputs produced and the types and quantities of inputs demanded. Households determine the types and quantities of products demanded and the quantities and types of inputs supplied.[1]

factors of production The inputs into the production process. Land, labor, and capital are the three key factors of production.

---

[1] Our description of markets begins with the behavior of firms and households. Modern orthodox economic theory essentially combines two distinct but closely related theories of behavior. The "theory of household behavior," or "consumer behavior," has its roots in the works of nineteenth-century utilitarians such as Jeremy Bentham, William Jevons, Carl Menger, Leon Walras, Vilfredo Pareto, and F. Y. Edgeworth. The "theory of the firm" developed out of the earlier classical political economy of Adam Smith, David Ricardo, and Thomas Malthus. In 1890 Alfred Marshall published the first of many editions of his *Principles of Economics*. That volume pulled together the main themes of both the classical economists and the utilitarians into what is now called "neoclassical economics." While there have been many changes over the years, the basic structure of the model that we build can be found in Marshall's work.

DEMAND IN PRODUCT/OUTPUT MARKETS

In real life, households make many decisions at the same time. To see how the forces of demand and supply work, however, let us focus first on the amount of a single product that an individual household decides to consume within some given period of time, such as a month or a year.

> As we might expect, a household's decision about what quantity of a particular output, or product, to demand depends upon a number of factors:
> - The *price of the product* in question.
> - The *income available* to the household.
> - The *amount of accumulated wealth* of the household.
> - The *prices of other products* available to the household.
> - The *tastes or preferences* of the household.
> - The *expectations* of the household about future income, wealth, and prices.

Important ✗

quantity demanded The amount (number of units) of a product that a household would buy in a given period if it could buy all it wanted at the current market price.

Quantity demanded is the amount (number of units) of a product that a household would buy in a given period *if it could buy all it wanted at the current market price.*

It is important to see demand as distinct from supply. Of course, the amount of a product that households finally purchase depends on the amount of product actually available in the market. But the quantity demanded at any moment may exceed or fall short of the quantity supplied. These differences between the quantity demanded and the quantity supplied are very important. The phrase "*if it could buy all it wanted*" is critical because it allows for the possibility that quantity supplied and quantity demanded may be unequal.

Our analysis of demand and supply is leading up to a theory of how market prices are determined. Prices are determined by interaction between demanders and suppliers. To understand this interaction, we first need to know how product prices influence the behavior of suppliers and demanders *separately*. We therefore begin our discussion of output markets by focusing exclusively on this relationship.

CHANGES IN QUANTITY DEMANDED VERSUS CHANGES IN DEMAND The most important relationship in individual markets is that between market price and quantity demanded. For this reason, we will begin our discussion by analyzing the likely response of households to changes in price using the device of *ceteris paribus,* or "all else equal." That is, we will attempt to derive a relationship between the quantity demanded of a good per time period and its own price, holding income, wealth, other prices, tastes, and expectations constant.

It is very important to distinguish between price changes, which affect the quantity of a good demanded, and changes in other factors (such as income), which change the entire relationship between price and quantity. For example, if a family begins earning a higher income, it might buy more of a good at every possible price. To be sure that we distinguish between changes in price and other changes that affect demand, we will throughout the rest of the text be very precise about terminology. Specifically, changes in the *price* of a product affect the *quantity demanded* per period. Changes in *any other factor,* such as income or preferences, affect *demand.* Thus we say that an increase in the *price* of Coca-Cola, is likely to cause a decrease in the *quantity of Coca-Cola demanded.* Similarly, we say that an increase in *income* is likely to cause an increase in the *demand* for most goods.

Price and Quantity Demanded: The Law of Demand

A **demand schedule** shows the quantities of a product that a household would be willing to buy at different prices. Table 4.1 presents a hypothetical demand schedule for Anna, a student who went off to college to study economics while her boyfriend went to art school. If telephone calls were free (a price of zero), Anna would call her boyfriend every day, or 30 times a month. At a price of $.50 per call, she makes 25 calls a month. When the price hits $3.50, she cuts back to seven calls a month. This same information presented graphically is called a **demand curve.** Anna's demand curve is presented in Figure 4.2.[2]

DEMAND CURVES SLOPE DOWNWARD Our data show that at lower prices, Anna calls her boyfriend more frequently; at higher prices, she calls less frequently. There is thus a *negative, or inverse, relationship between quantity demanded and price.* When price rises, quantity demanded falls, and when price falls, quantity demanded rises. The slope of a demand curve, then, is always negative.[3] This negative relationship between price and quantity demanded is often referred to as the **law of demand,** a term first used by economist Alfred Marshall in his 1890 textbook.

Many people are put off by the abstractness of demand curves. Of course, we don't actually draw our own demand curves for products. When we want to make

demand schedule A table showing how much of a given product households would be willing to buy at different prices.

demand curve A graph illustrating how much of a given product a household would be willing to buy at different prices.

law of demand The negative relationship between price and quantity demanded: As price rises, quantity demanded decreases, and as price falls, quantity demanded increases.

TABLE 4.1
Anna's Demand Schedule for Telephone Calls

PRICE (PER CALL)	QUANTITY DEMANDED (CALLS PER MONTH)
$ 0	30
.50	25
3.50	7
7.00	3
10.00	1
15.00	0

---

[2]Drawing a smooth curve, as we do in Figure 4.2, suggests that Anna can make a quarter of a phone call or half of a phone call. For example, according to the graph, at a price of $12 per call, Anna would make half a call and at $8 per call, about a call and a half. While fractional purchases are for goods that are *divisible,* such as phone calls—you might talk for one minute instead of two minutes—and products sold by weight, they are impossible for large purchases, such as automobiles. We use the term *lumpy* to describe goods that cannot be divided. You would not draw a smooth, downward sloping curve of a household's demand for automobiles, for example, because there might be only one (or at most two) points, and any points in between would be meaningless. Whenever we draw a smooth demand curve, we are assuming divisibility.

[3]Recall from the Chapter 1 appendix that the slope of a line equals $\Delta Y/\Delta X$. In this case, the slope is the change in price (ΔP) divided by the change in quantity demanded (ΔQ_d). For example if ΔP is positive (a price increase) then ΔQ_d will be negative (a decrease in quantity demanded). A positive number divided by a negative number yields a negative number.

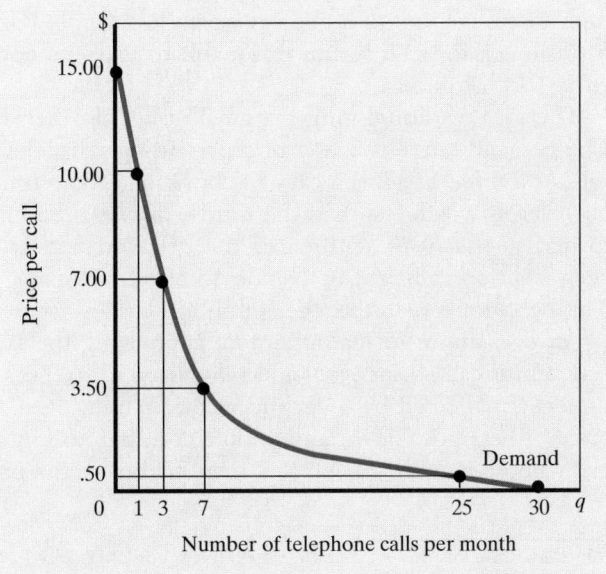

FIGURE 4.2
Anna's Demand Curve

The relationship between price and quantity demanded presented graphically is called a *demand curve.* Demand curves have a negative slope, indicating that lower prices cause quantity demanded to increase.

a purchase, we usually face only a single price, and how much we would buy at other prices is irrelevant. But demand curves help analysts understand the kind of behavior that households are *likely* to exhibit if they are actually faced with a higher or lower price. We know, for example, that if the price of a good rises enough, the quantity demanded must ultimately drop to zero. The demand curve is thus a tool that helps us explain economic behavior and predict reactions to possible price changes.

Marshall's definition of a social "law" captures the idea:

> The term "law" means nothing more than a general proposition or statement of tendencies, more or less certain, more or less definite...a *social law* is a statement of social tendencies; that is, that a certain course of action may be expected from the members of a social group under certain conditions.[4]

It seems reasonable to expect that consumers will demand more of a product at a lower price and less of it at a higher price. Households must divide their incomes over a wide range of goods and services. If the price of a pound of beef rises while income and the prices of all other products remain the same, the household must sacrifice more of something else in order to buy each pound of beef. If I spend $4.50 for a pound of prime beef, I am sacrificing the other things that I might have bought with that $4.50. If prime beef were to jump to $7 per pound, while chicken breasts remained at $1.99 (remember *ceteris paribus*—we are holding all else constant), I would have to give up more chicken and/or other items in order to buy that pound of beef. So I would probably eat more chicken and less beef. Anna calls her boyfriend three times when phone calls cost $7 each. A fourth call would mean sacrificing $7 worth of other purchases. At a price of $3.50, however, the opportunity cost of each call is lower, and she calls more frequently.

Another explanation behind the fact that demand curves are very likely to slope downward rests on the notion of *utility*. Economists use utility as a measure of happiness or satisfaction. Presumably we consume goods and services because they give us utility. But as we consume more of a product within a given period of time, it is likely that each additional unit consumed will yield successively less satisfaction. The utility I gain from a second ice cream cone is likely to be less than the utility I gained from the first; the third is worth even less, and so forth. This *law of diminishing marginal utility* is an important concept in microeconomics. If each successive unit of a good is worth less to me, I am not going to be willing to pay as much for it. It is thus reasonable to expect a downward slope in the demand curve for that good.

The idea of diminishing marginal utility also helps to explain Anna's behavior. The demand curve is a way of representing what she is willing to pay per phone call. At a price of $7, she calls her boyfriend three times per month. A fourth call, however, is worth less than the third—that is, the fourth call is worth less than $7 to her, so she stops at three. If the price were only $3.50, however, she would keep right on calling. But even at $3.50, she would stop at seven calls per month. This behavior reveals that the eighth call has less value to Anna than the seventh.

An even more formal argument supporting the law of demand involves what economists call *income effects* and *substitution effects*. Let's consider the ways that consumers are affected by a decline in price, using beef again as our example. If the price of beef goes down and people continue to buy the exact same quantities of every good, including beef, that they did before the price of beef fell, *they will have*

---

[4]Alfred Marshall, *Principles of Economics,* 8th ed. (New York: Macmillan, 1948), p. 33. (The first edition was published in 1890.)

money left over. They are better off and can afford more of all goods, including beef. This is called the **income effect** of a price decline.

At the same time, the price decline implies that beef is cheaper relative to other goods, including potential substitutes. A decline in the price of beef means that it is more attractive relative to chicken. Stated another way, the real cost of a unit of beef is what you must sacrifice in order to consume it. If the price of beef falls relative to the price of other goods, consumption of a unit of beef now requires a smaller sacrifice of other goods. Thus, when the price of beef falls, consumers tend to substitute it for other goods. This is called the **substitution effect** of a price decline.

Returning to our original example, consider Anna's response to an increase in price from $3.50 to $7 per telephone call. First, these calls to her boyfriend are now more expensive relative to alternative ways of communicating, such as writing letters. Thus, she is likely to substitute letter writing and call less frequently (substitution effect). Second, she is worse off overall because of the higher price. If she calls the same number of times at the higher price, she will have less income to spend on other things. Her income will no longer buy everything that it did before, and she must cut something. One of the things she is likely to cut is telephone calls (income effect).

In sum:

> It is reasonable to expect quantity demanded to fall when price rises, *ceteris paribus,* and to expect quantity demanded to rise when price falls, *ceteris paribus.* Demand curves therefore have a negative slope.

OTHER PROPERTIES OF DEMAND CURVES Two additional things are notable about Anna's demand curve. First, it intersects the *Y,* or price, axis. This means that there is a price above which no calls will be made. In this case, Anna simply stops calling when the price reaches $15 per call.

> As long as households have limited incomes and wealth, all demand curves will intersect the price axis. For any commodity, there is always a price above which a household will not, or cannot, pay. Even if the good or service is very important, all households are ultimately "constrained," or limited, by income and wealth.

Second, Anna's demand curve intersects the *X,* or quantity, axis. Even at a zero price, there is a limit to the number of phone calls Anna will make. If telephone calls were free, she would call 30 times a month, but not more.

> That demand curves intersect the quantity axis is a matter of common sense. Demands for most goods are limited, if only by time, even at a zero price.

Other Determinants of Household Demand

Of the many factors likely to influence a household's demand for a specific product, we have considered only the price of the product itself. Other determining factors include household income and wealth, the prices of other goods, and, of course, tastes and preferences.

INCOME AND WEALTH Before we proceed, we need to define two terms that are often confused, *income* and *wealth.* A household's **income** is the sum of all the

income The sum of all a household's wages, salaries, profits, interest payments, rents, and other forms of earnings in a given period of time. It is a flow measure.

wages, salaries, profits, interest payments, rents, and other forms of earnings received by the household *in a given period of time.* Income is thus a *flow* measure: We must specify a time period for it—income *per month* or *per year.* You can spend or consume more or less than your income in any given period. If you consume less than the amount of your income, you save. In order to consume more than your income in a period, you must either borrow or draw on savings accumulated from previous periods.

wealth, or net worth The total value of what a household owns minus what it owes. It is a stock measure.

Wealth is the total value of what a household owns less what it owes. Another word for wealth is **net worth**—the amount a household would have left if it sold off all its possessions and paid off all its debts. Wealth is a *stock* measure: It is measured at a given moment, or point, in time. If, in a given period, you spend less than your income, you save; the amount that you save is added to your wealth. Saving is the flow that affects the stock of wealth. When you spend more than your income, you *dissave*—you reduce your wealth.

Clearly, households with higher incomes and higher accumulated savings or inherited wealth can afford to buy more things. In general, then, we would expect higher demand at higher levels of income/wealth and lower demand at lower levels of income/wealth. Goods for which this relationship holds true are called **normal goods.**

normal goods Goods for which demand goes up when income is higher and for which demand goes down when income is lower.

But generalization in economics can be hazardous. Sometimes demand for a good falls when household income rises. Consider, for example, the various qualities of meat available. When a household's income rises, it is likely to buy higher quality meats—its demand for filet mignon is likely to rise—but its demand for lower quality meats—chuck steak, for example—is likely to fall. Transportation is another example. At higher incomes, people can afford to fly. People who can afford to fly are less likely to take the bus long distances. Thus higher income may reduce the number of times someone takes a bus. Goods for which demand falls when income rises are called **inferior goods.**

inferior goods Goods for which demand falls when income rises.

PRICES OF OTHER GOODS AND SERVICES No consumer decides in isolation on the amount of any one commodity to buy. Rather, each decision is part of a larger set of decisions that are made simultaneously. Obviously, households must apportion their incomes over many different goods and services. As a result, the price of any one good can and does affect the demand for other goods.

This is most obviously the case when goods are substitutes for each other. To return to our lonesome first-year student: If the price of a telephone call rises to $10, Anna will call her boyfriend only once a month. But of course she can get in touch with him in other ways. Presumably she substitutes some other, less costly, form of communication, such as writing more letters.

Consider another example: There is currently much discussion about the relative merits of cars produced in the United States and cars produced in Japan. Recently, U.S. consumers have faced a sharp rise in the price of Japanese cars. As a result, we would expect to see consumers substitute American-made cars for Japanese-made cars. The demand for U.S. cars should rise and the quantity of Japanese cars demanded should fall.

substitutes Goods that can serve as replacements for one another; when the price of one increases, demand for the other goes up.

When an *increase* in the price of one good causes demand for another good to *increase* (a positive relationship), we say that the goods are **substitutes.** A *fall* in the price of a good causes a *decline* in demand for its substitutes. Substitutes are goods that can serve as replacements for one another.

perfect substitutes Identical products.

To be substitutes, two products need not be identical. Identical products are called **perfect substitutes.** Japanese cars are not identical to American cars. Nonetheless, all have four wheels, are capable of carrying people, and run on gasoline. Thus, significant changes in the price of one country's cars can be expected to influence demand for the other country's cars. Compact discs are substitutes for records and tapes, restaurant meals are substitutes for meals eaten at home, and flying from New York to Washington is a substitute for taking the train.

Often, two products "go together"—that is, they complement each other. Our lonesome letter writer, for example, will find her demand for stamps and stationery rising as she writes more letters. Bacon and eggs are **complementary goods,** as are cars and gasoline, and cameras and film. During a price war among the airlines in the summer of 1992 when travel became less expensive, the demand for taxi service to and from airports and for luggage increased across the country. When two goods are complements, a *decrease* in the price of one results in *increase* in demand for the other, and vice versa.

complements, complementary goods Goods that "go together"; a decrease in the price of one results in an increase in demand for the other, and vice versa.

Because any one good may have many potential substitutes and complements at the same time, a single price change may affect a household's demands for many goods simultaneously; the demand for some of these products may rise while the demand for others may fall. In the last few years, for example, it has become quite inexpensive to rent videotapes. With the decrease in rental prices, the demand for videocassette recorders/players (VCRs) has increased dramatically. At the same time, however, fewer people are going to see movies at the theater. Clearly, videotapes and video players are complements. Movies at home and movies in the theater are substitutes.

TASTES AND PREFERENCES   Income, wealth, and the prices of things available are the three factors that determine the combinations of things that a household is *able* to buy. You know that you cannot afford to rent an apartment at $1200 per month if your monthly income is only $400. But within these constraints, you are more or less free to choose what to buy. Your final choice depends upon your individual tastes and preferences.

Changes in preferences can and do manifest themselves in market behavior. As the medical consequences of smoking have become more and more clear, for example, more and more people have stopped smoking. As a result, the demand for cigarettes has dropped significantly. Fifteen years ago the major big-city marathons drew only a few hundred runners. Now tens of thousands enter and run. The demand for running shoes, running suits, stopwatches, and other running items has greatly increased.

Within the constraints of prices and incomes, it is preference that shapes the demand curve. But it is difficult to generalize about tastes and preferences. First of all, they are volatile: Five years ago, more people smoked cigarettes, fewer people had VCRs, and very few teenaged boys had pierced ears. Second, they are idiosyncratic: Some people like to talk on the telephone, while others prefer the written word; some people prefer dogs, while others are crazy about cats; some people like chicken wings, while others prefer legs. The diversity of individual demands is almost infinite.

EXPECTATIONS   What you decide to buy today certainly depends on today's prices and your current income and wealth. But you also have expectations about what your position will be in the future. You may have expectations about future changes in prices, too, and these may affect your decisions today.

Examples of the ways in which expectations affect demand abound. When people buy a house or a car, they often must borrow part of the purchase price and pay it back over a number of years. In deciding what kind of house or car to buy, they presumably must think about their income today, as well as what their income is likely to be in the future.

As another example, consider a student in her final year of medical school living on a scholarship of $10,000. Compare her with another person earning $5 an hour at a full-time job, with no expectation of a significant change in income in the future. The two have virtually identical incomes. But even if they had the same tastes, the medical student is likely to demand different things, simply because she expects a major increase in income later on.

Increasingly, economic theory has come to recognize the importance of expectations. We will devote a good deal of time to discussing how expectations affect more than just demand. For the time being, however, it is important to understand that demand depends on more than just *current* incomes, prices, and tastes.

Shift of Demand versus Movement along a Demand Curve

Recall that a demand curve shows the relationship between quantity demanded and the price of a good. Such demand curves are derived while holding income, tastes, and other prices constant. If this condition of *ceteris paribus* were relaxed, however, we would have to derive an entirely new relationship between price and quantity.

Let us return once again to Anna (Table 4.1 and Figure 4.2). Suppose that when we derived the demand schedule in Table 4.1, Anna had a part-time job that paid $200 per month. Now suppose that her parents inherit some money and begin sending her an additional $200 per month. Assuming that she keeps her job, Anna's income is now $400 per month.[5]

With her higher income, Anna would probably call her boyfriend more frequently, regardless of the price of a call. Table 4.2 and Figure 4.3 present Anna's original-income schedule (D_1) and increased-income demand schedule (D_2). At $.50 per call, the frequency of her calls (or the quantity she demands) increases from 25 to 33 calls per month; at $3.50 per call, frequency increases from 7 to 18 calls per month; at $10 per call, frequency increases from one to seven calls per month.[6]

---

[5]The income from home may affect the amount of time Anna spends working. In the extreme, she may quit her job and her income will remain at $200. In essence, she would be spending the entire $200 on leisure. Here we assume that she keeps the job and that her income is higher. The point is that since labor supply decisions affect income, they are closely tied to output demand decisions. In a sense, they are made simultaneously.

TABLE 4.2
Shift of Anna's Demand Schedule Due to Increase in Income

PRICE (PER CALL)	SCHEDULE D$_1$ QUANTITY DEMANDED (CALLS PER MONTH AT AN INCOME OF $200 PER MONTH)	SCHEDULE D$_2$ QUANTITY DEMANDED (CALLS PER MONTH AT AN INCOME OF $400 PER MONTH)
$ 0	30	35
.50	25	33
3.50	7	18
7.00	3	12
10.00	1	7
15.00	0	2

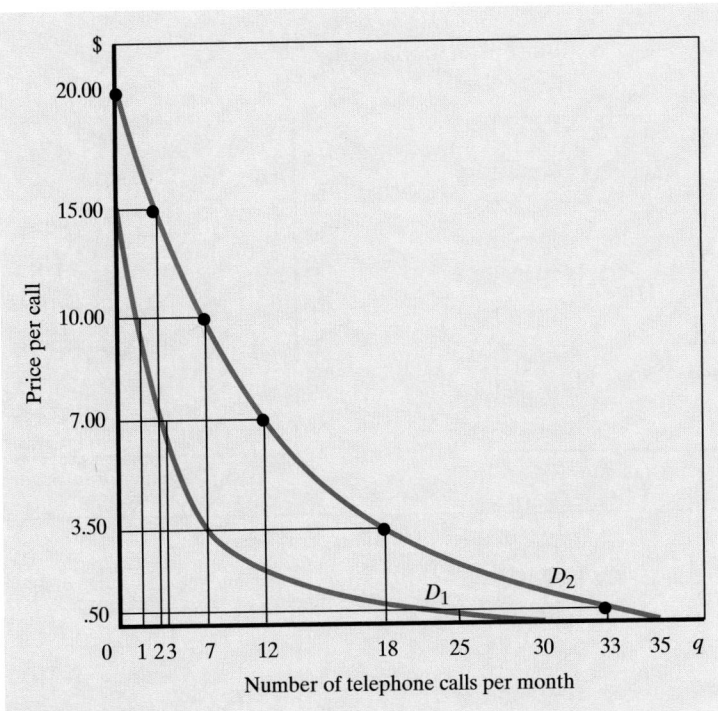

FIGURE 4.3
Shift of a Demand Curve
Following a Rise in Income

When the price of a good changes, we move *along* the demand curve for that good. When any other factor that influences demand changes (income, tastes, etc.), the relationship between price and quantity is different; there is a *shift* of the demand curve, in this case from D_1 to D_2.

The conditions that were in place at the time the original demand curve was derived have now changed. In other words, a factor that affects Anna's demand for telephone calls (in this case, her income) has changed, and there is now a new relationship between price and quantity demanded. Such a change is referred to as a **shift of the demand curve.**

It is very important to distinguish between a *change in quantity demanded*—that is, some movement *along* a demand curve—and a *shift of demand*. Demand schedules and demand curves show the relationship between the price of a good or service and the quantity demanded per period, *ceteris paribus*. If price changes, quantity demanded will change—this is a **movement along the demand curve.** When any of the other factors that influence demand change, however, a new relationship between price and quantity demanded is established—this is a *shift of the demand curve*. The result, then, is a *new* demand curve. Changes in income, preferences, or prices of other goods cause the demand curve to shift:

shift of a demand curve The change that takes place in a demand curve when a new relationship between quantity demanded of a good and the price of that good is brought about by a change in the original conditions.

movement along a demand curve What happens when a change in price causes quantity demanded to change.

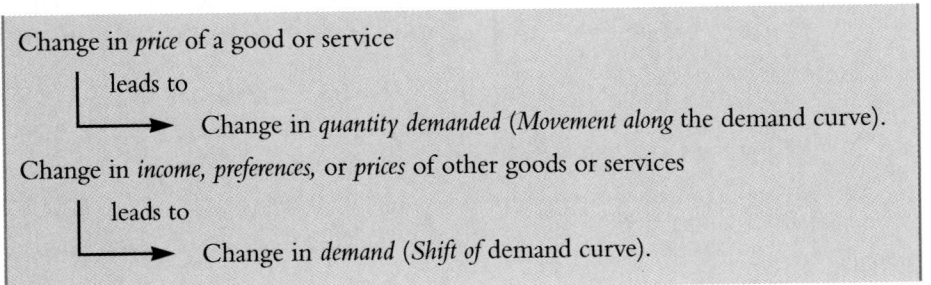

Change in *price* of a good or service

└─ leads to
      → Change in *quantity demanded* (*Movement along* the demand curve).

Change in *income, preferences,* or *prices* of other goods or services

└─ leads to
      → Change in *demand* (*Shift of* demand curve).

---

[6]Note in Figure 4.3 that even if calls are free, Anna's income matters; at zero price, her demand increases. With a higher income, she may visit her boyfriend more, for example, and more visits might mean more phone calls to organize and plan.

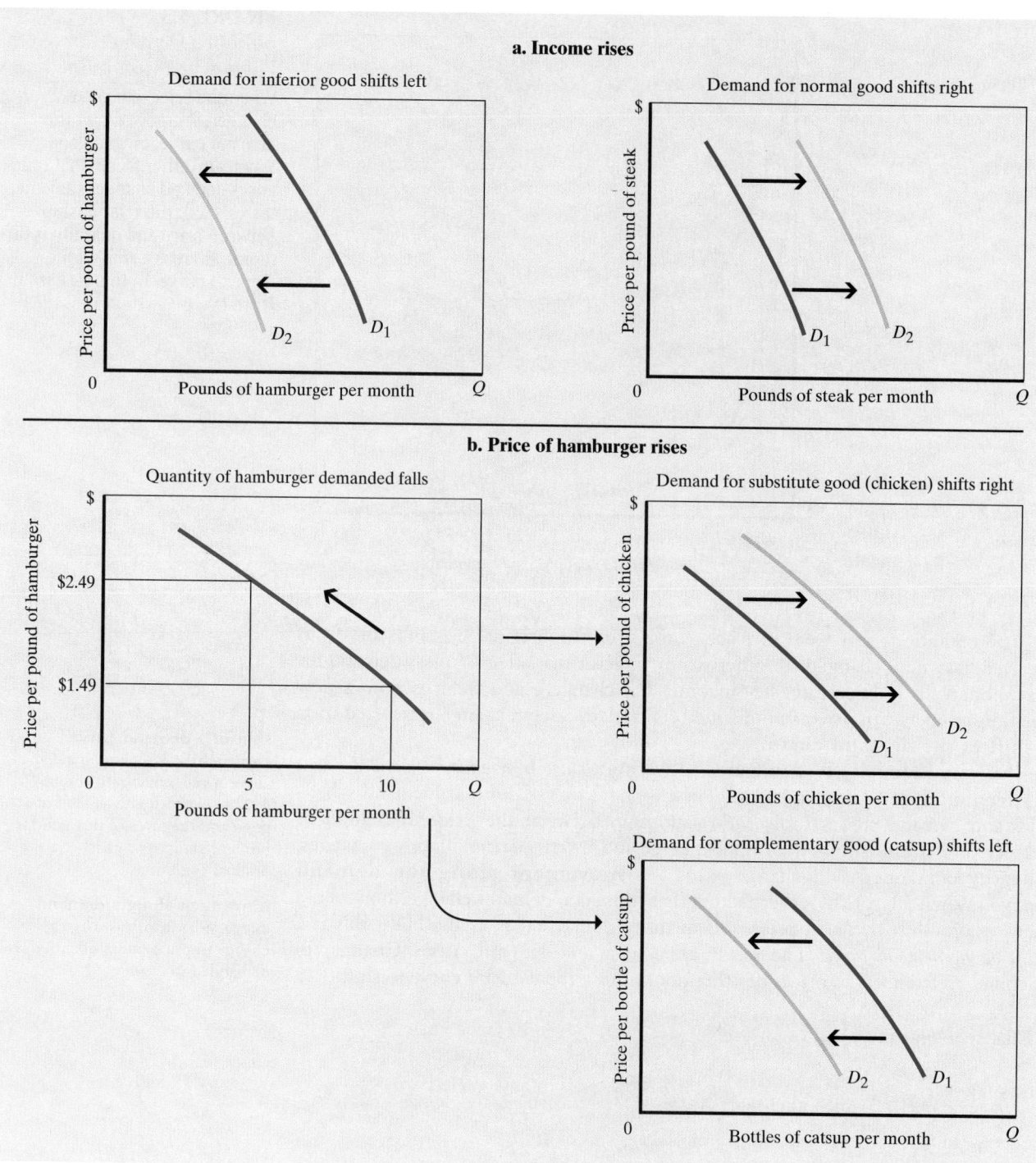

FIGURE 4.4

Shifts versus Movement along a Demand Curve

a. When income increases, the demand for inferior goods *shifts down* (to the left) and the demand for normal goods *shifts up* (to the right). b. If the price of hamburger rises, the quantity of hamburger demanded declines—a movement along the demand curve. The same price would shift the demand for chicken (a substitute for hamburger) up (to the right) and the demand for catsup (a complement to hamburger) down (to the left).

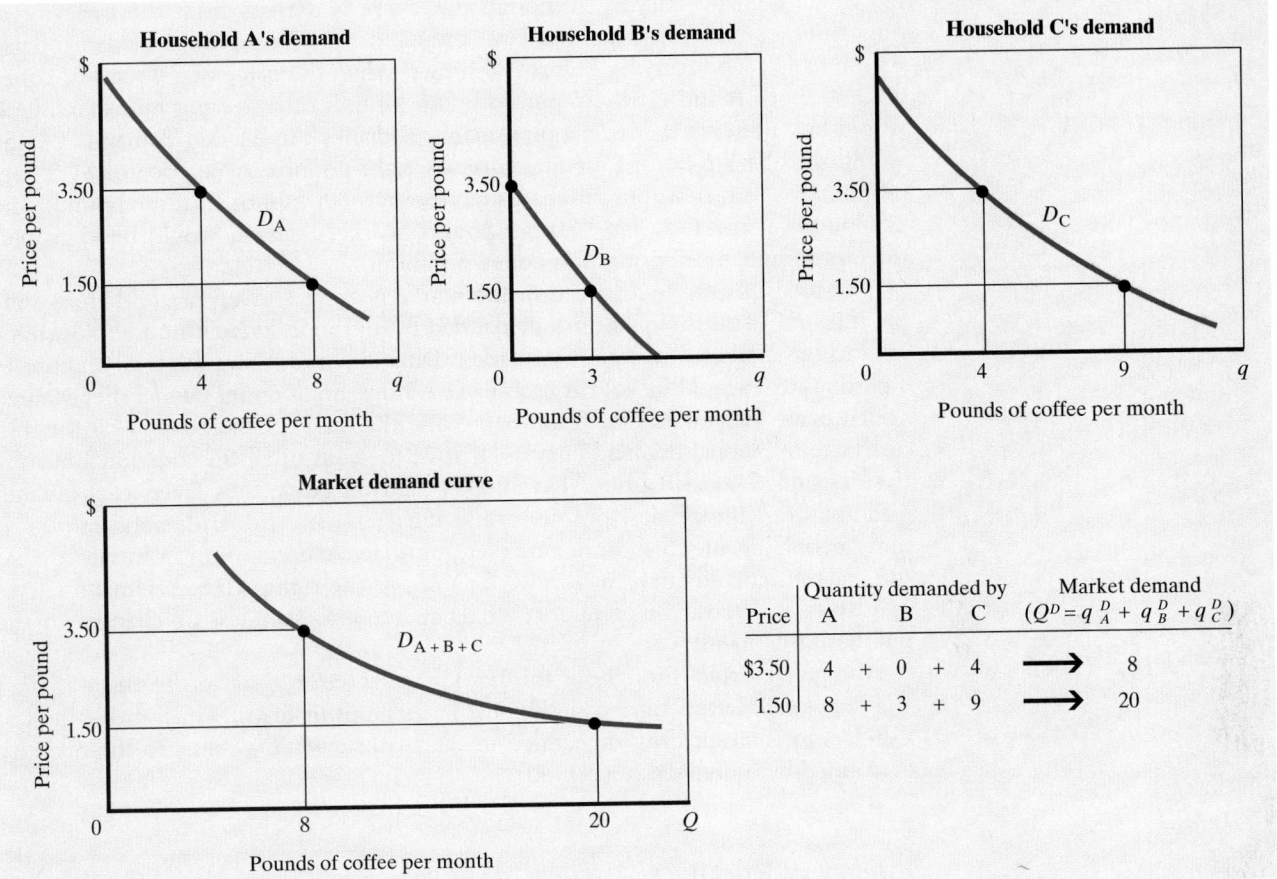

FIGURE 4.5

Deriving Market Demand from Individual Demand Curves

Total demand in the marketplace is simply the sum of the demands of all the households shopping in a particular market. It is the sum of all the individual demand curves added horizontally—that is, the sum of all the individual quantities demanded at each price.

Figure 4.4 illustrates this point. In Figure 4.4a, an increase in household income causes demand for hamburger (an inferior good) to decline, or shift to the left. (Remember that quantity is measured on the horizontal axis, so a decrease means a move to the left.) Demand for steak (a normal good), on the other hand, increases, or shifts to the right, when income rises.

In Figure 4.4b, an increase in the price of hamburger causes a household to buy less hamburger each month. In other words, the higher price causes the *quantity demanded* to decline. This change represents a movement *along* the demand curve for hamburger. In place of hamburger, the household buys more chicken. The household's demand for chicken (a substitute for hamburger) rises—the demand curve shifts to the right. At the same time, the demand for catsup (a good that complements hamburger) declines—its demand curve shifts to the left.

From Household Demand to Market Demand

Market demand is simply the sum of all the quantities of a good or service demanded per period by all the households buying in the market for that good or service. Figure 4.5 shows the derivation of a market demand curve from three

market demand The sum of all the quantities of a good or service demanded per period by all the households buying in the market for that good or service.

individual demand curves. (Although this curve is derived from the behavior of only three people, most markets have thousands or even millions of demanders.) As the table accompanying Figure 4.5 shows, when the price of a pound of coffee is $3.50, both A and C would purchase four pounds of coffee per month, while B would buy none; at that price, presumably, B drinks tea. Market demand at $3.50 would thus be a total of four plus four, or eight pounds. At a price of $1.50 per pound, however, A would purchase eight pounds per month, B three pounds, and C nine pounds. Thus, at $1.50 per pound, market demand would be eight plus three plus nine, or 20 pounds of coffee per month.

The total quantity demanded in the marketplace at a given price, then, is simply the sum of all the quantities demanded by all the individual households shopping in the market *at that price.* A market demand curve shows the total amount of a product that would be sold at each price if households could buy all they wanted at that price. As you can see from Figure 4.5, the market demand curve is the sum of all the individual demand curves—that is, the sum of all the individual quantities demanded at each price. The market demand curve thus takes its shape and position from the shapes, positions, and *number* of individual demand curves. If more people decide to shop in a market, more demand curves must be added, and the market demand curve will move, or shift, to the right. Market demand curves may shift as a result of preference changes, income changes, or changes in the number of demanders.

As a general rule throughout this book, capital letters refer to the entire market and lower case letters refer to individual households or firms. Thus, in Figure 4.5, Q refers to total quantity demanded in the market, while q refers to the quantity demanded by individual households.

SUPPLY IN PRODUCT/OUTPUT MARKETS

In addition to dealing with households' demands for outputs, microeconomic theory also deals with the behavior of business firms, which supply in output markets and demand in input markets (see again Figure 4.1). Firms engage in production, and we assume that they do so for profit. Profit, you will recall, is the difference between revenues and costs. Successful firms make profits because they are able to sell their products for more than it costs to produce them.

Supply decisions can thus be expected to depend upon profit potential. Because profit is the simple difference between revenues and costs, supply is likely to react to changes in revenues and changes in costs of production. The amount of revenue that a firm earns depends on the price of its product in the market and on how much it sells. Costs of production depend on many factors, the most important of which are (1) the kinds of inputs needed to produce the product, (2) the amount of each input required, and (3) the prices of inputs.

The supply decision is just one of several decisions that firms make in order to maximize profit. There are usually a number of ways to produce any given product. A golf course can be built by hundreds of workers with shovels and grass seed or by a few workers with heavy earth-moving equipment and sod blankets. Hamburgers can be individually fried by a short-order cook or grilled by the hundreds on a mechanized moving grill. Firms must choose the production technique most appropriate to their products and projected levels of production. The "appropriate" method of production is the one that minimizes cost, thus maximizing profit.

Which production technique is best, in turn, depends on the prices of inputs. Where labor is cheap and machinery is expensive and difficult to transport, firms are likely to choose techniques that use a great deal of labor. Where machines are available and labor is scarce or expensive, they are likely to choose more capital-intensive methods. Obviously, the technique ultimately chosen determines input requirements. Thus, by choosing an output supply target and the most appropriate technology, firms determine which inputs to demand.

To summarize:

> Assuming that its objective is to maximize profits, a firm's decision about what quantity of output, or product, to supply is likely to depend on
> 1. The price of the good or service
> 2. The cost of producing the product, which in turn depends on
>   - The prices of required inputs (labor, capital, and land), and
>   - The technologies that can be used to produce the product
> 3. The prices of related products.

With the caution that no single decision exists in a vacuum, then, let us begin our examination of firm behavior by focusing on the output supply decision and the relationship between quantity supplied and output price, *ceteris paribus*.

Price and Quantity Supplied: The Law of Supply

Quantity supplied is the amount of a particular product that a firm would be willing and able to offer for sale at a particular price during a given time period. A **supply schedule** shows how much of a product a firm will supply at alternative prices. Table 4.3 itemizes the quantities of soybeans that an individual farmer such as Clarence Brown might supply at various prices. If the market paid only $1 a bushel for soybeans, Brown would not supply any soybeans. For one thing, it costs more than $1 to produce a bushel of soybeans; for another, Brown can use his land more profitably to produce something else. At $1.75 per bushel, however, at least some soybean production takes place on Brown's farm, and a price increase from $1.75 to $2.25 per bushel causes the quantity supplied by Brown to increase from 10,000 to 20,000 bushels per year. The higher price may justify shifting land from wheat to soybean production or putting previously fallow land into soybeans. Or it may lead to more intensive farming of land already in soybeans, using expensive fertilizer or equipment which was not cost-justified at the lower price.

In general, then, we can reasonably expect an increase in market price to lead to an increase in quantity supplied. In other words, there is a positive relationship between the quantity of a good supplied and price. This statement is sometimes referred to as the **law of supply.**

The information in a supply schedule presented graphically is called a **supply curve.** Supply curves slope upward. The upward, or positive, slope of Brown's curve in Figure 4.6 on the next page, for example, reflects this positive relationship between price and quantity supplied.

Note in Brown's supply schedule, however, that when price rises above $4 to $5, quantity supplied no longer increases. Often the ability of an individual firm to respond to an increase in price is limited, or constrained, by its existing scale of operations, or capacity, in the short run. For example, Brown's ability to produce more soybeans depends upon the size of his farm, the fertility of his soil, and the types of equipment he has. The fact that output stays constant at 45,000 bushels per year suggests that he is running up against the limits imposed by the size of his farm and his existing technology.

TABLE 4.3
Clarence Brown's Supply Schedule for Soybeans

PRICE (PER BUSHEL)	QUANTITY SUPPLIED (BUSHELS PER YEAR)
$1.00	0
1.75	10,000
2.25	20,000
3.00	30,000
4.00	45,000
5.00	45,000

quantity supplied The amount of a particular product that a firm would be willing and able to offer for sale at a particular price during a given time period.

supply schedule A table showing how much of a product firms will supply at different prices.

law of supply The positive relationship between price and quantity of a good supplied: An increase in market price will lead to an increase in quantity supplied, and a decrease in market price will lead to a decrease in quantity supplied.

supply curve A graph illustrating how much of a product a firm will supply at different prices.

FIGURE 4.6

Clarence Brown's Individual Supply Curve

A producer will supply more when the price of output is higher. The slope of a supply curve is positive.

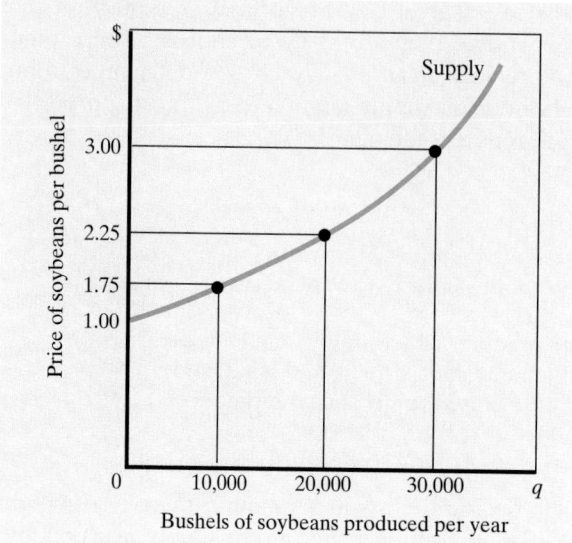

In the longer run, however, Brown may acquire more land, or technology may change, allowing for more soybean production. The terms *short run* and *long run* have very precise meanings in economics and will be discussed in detail later. Here it is important only to understand that time plays a critical role in supply decisions. When prices change, firms' immediate response may be different from what they are able to do after a month or a year; short-run and long-run supply curves are often different.

Other Determinants of Firm Supply

Of the factors listed above that are likely to affect the quantity of output produced by a given firm, we have thus far discussed only the price of output. Other factors that affect supply include the cost of producing the product and the prices of related products.

THE COST OF PRODUCTION Regardless of the price that a firm can command for its product, price must exceed the cost of producing the output for the firm to make a profit. Thus, the supply decision is likely to change in response to changes in the cost of production. Cost of production, in turn, depends on a number of factors, including the available technologies and the price of the inputs (labor, land, capital, energy, and so forth) that the firm needs.

Technological change can have an enormous impact on the cost of production over time. Consider agriculture. The introduction of fertilizers, the development of complex farm machinery, and, more recently, the use of bioengineering to increase the yield of individual crops have all powerfully affected the cost of producing agricultural commodities. Farm productivity in the United States has been increasing dramatically for decades. Yield per acre of corn production has quadrupled since the late 1930s, and the amount of labor required to produce 100 bushels of corn has fallen from 108 hours in the late 1930s to 20 hours in the late 1950s to less than three hours today.

When a technological advance lowers the cost of production, output is likely to increase. When yield per acre increases, individual farmers can and do produce more. The output of the Ford Motor Company increased substantially after the introduction of assembly line techniques. The production of electronic calculators, and later personal computers, boomed with the development of inexpensive techniques to produce microprocessors.

Cost of production is also affected directly by the price of the factors of production. During the summer of 1990, world oil prices jumped dramatically after Iraq's invasion of Kuwait. Increased oil prices raised the cost of production in many industries. Cab drivers faced higher gasoline prices, airlines faced higher fuel costs, and manufacturers faced higher costs of heating their plants. As a result, cabs probably spent less time driving around looking for fares, marginally profitable air routes were shut down, and some manufacturing plants stopped running extra shifts. The moral of this story: Increases in input prices raise costs of production and are likely to reduce supply.

THE PRICES OF RELATED PRODUCTS Firms often react to changes in the prices of related products. For example, if land can be used for either corn or soybean production, an increase in soybean prices may cause individual farmers to shift acreage out of corn production and into soybeans. Thus, an increase in soybean prices actually affects the amount of corn supplied.

Similarly, if beef prices rise, producers may respond by raising more cattle. But leather comes from cowhide. Thus, an increase in beef prices may actually increase the supply of leather.

Shift of Supply versus Movement along a Supply Curve

A supply curve shows the relationship between the quantity of a good or service supplied by a firm and the price brought by that good or service in the market. Higher prices are likely to lead to an increase in quantity supplied, *ceteris paribus*. Remember: The supply curve is derived holding everything constant except price. When the price of a product changes *ceteris paribus*, a change in the quantity supplied follows—that is, a movement along the supply curve takes place. But, as you have seen, supply decisions are also influenced by factors other than price. New relationships between price and quantity supplied come about when factors other than price change, and the result is a *shift* of the supply curve. When factors other than price cause supply curves to shift, we say that there has been a *change in supply*.

Recall that the cost of production depends upon the price of inputs and the technologies of production available. Now suppose that a major breakthrough in the production of soybeans has occurred: Genetic engineering has produced a superstrain of disease- and pest-resistant seed. Such a technological change would enable individual farmers to supply more soybeans at *any* market price. Table 4.4

TABLE 4.4
Shift of Supply Schedule for Soybeans Following Development of a New Disease-Resistant Seed Strain

PRICE (PER BUSHEL)	SCHEDULE S₁ QUANTITY SUPPLIED (BUSHELS PER YEAR USING OLD SEED)	SCHEDULE S₂ QUANTITY SUPPLIED (BUSHELS PER YEAR USING NEW SEED)
$1.00	0	5,000
1.75	10,000	23,000
2.25	20,000	33,000
3.00	30,000	40,000
4.00	45,000	54,000
5.00	45,000	54,000

and Figure 4.7 describe this change. At $3 a bushel, farmers would have produced 30,000 bushels from the old seed (schedule S_1 in Table 4.4); with the lower cost of production and higher yield resulting from the new seed, they produce 40,000 bushels (schedule S_2 in Table 4.4). At $1.75 per bushel, they would have produced 10,000 bushels from the old seed, but with the lower costs and higher yields, output rises to 23,000 bushels.

Increases in input prices may also cause supply curves to shift. We have already mentioned the increase in oil prices that occurred in 1990. Since fertilizers are made in part from petrochemicals and in part from tractors that run on gasoline, Brown, the farmer, would have faced higher costs in 1990 than he did in 1989. Such increases in cost of production shift the supply curve back to the left—that is, less is produced at any given market price. If Brown's soybean supply curve shifted far enough to the left, it would intersect the price axis at a higher point, meaning that it would take a higher market price to induce Brown to produce any soybeans at all.

As with demand, it is very important to distinguish between *movements along* supply curves (changes in quantity supplied) and *shifts in* supply curves (changes in supply):

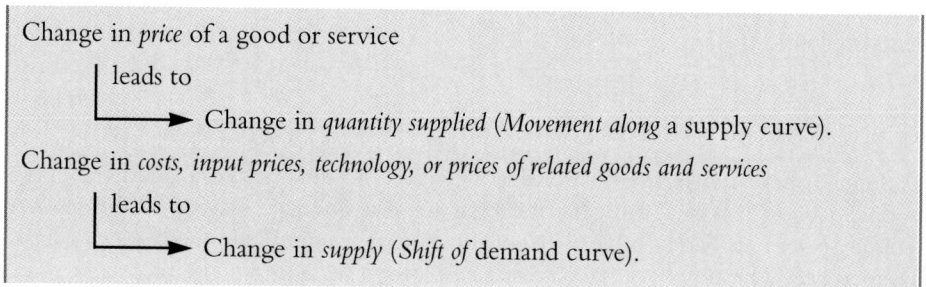

Change in *price* of a good or service

   | leads to

   └────────▶ Change in *quantity supplied* (*Movement along* a supply curve).

Change in *costs, input prices, technology, or prices of related goods and services*

   | leads to

   └────────▶ Change in *supply* (*Shift of* demand curve).

FIGURE 4.7

Shift of Supply Curve for Soybeans Following Development of a New Seed Strain

When the price of an output changes, we move *along* the supply curve for that product; the quantity supplied rises or falls. When any other factor affecting supply changes, the supply curve *shifts* up or down.

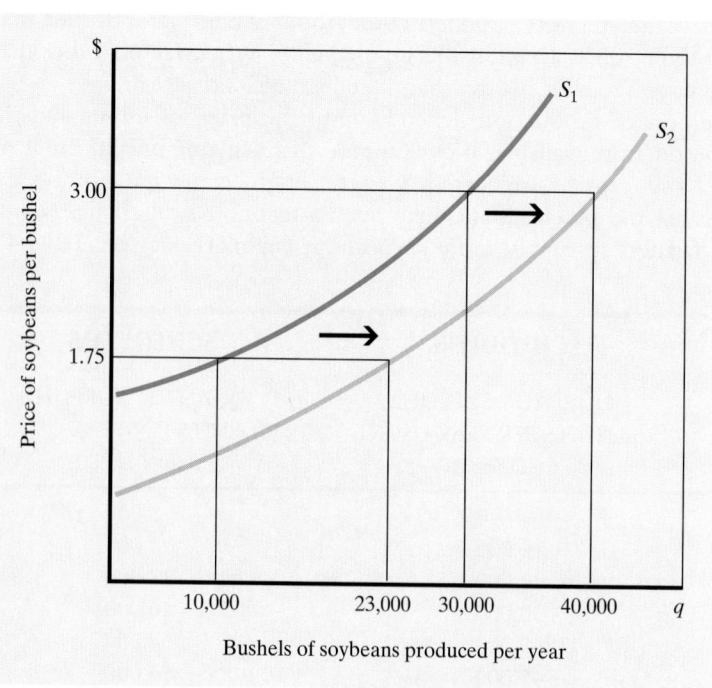

From Individual Firm Supply to Market Supply

Market supply is determined in the same fashion as market demand. It is simply the sum of all that is supplied each period by all producers of a single product. Figure 4.8 derives a market supply curve from the supply curves of three individual firms. (In a market with more firms, total market supply would be the sum of the amounts produced by each of the firms in that market.) As the table accompanying Figure 4.8 shows, at a price of $3 farm A supplies 30,000 bushels of soybeans, farm B supplies 10,000 bushels, and farm C supplies 25,000 bushels. At this price, the total amount supplied in the market is 30,000 plus 10,000 plus 25,000, or 65,000 bushels. At a price of $1.75, however, the total amount supplied is only 25,000 bushels (10,000 plus 5,000 plus 10,000). The market supply curve is thus the simple addition of the individual supply curves of all the firms in a particular market—that is, the sum of all the individual quantities supplied at each price.

market supply The sum of all that is supplied each period by all producers of a single product.

FIGURE 4.8
Deriving Market Supply from Individual Firm Supply Curves

Total supply in the marketplace is the sum of all the amounts supplied by all the firms selling in the market; it is the sum of all the individual quantities supplied at each price.

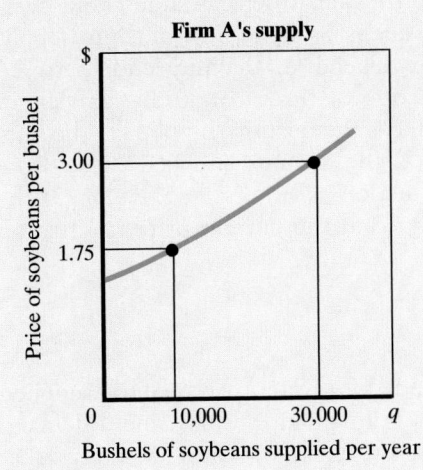

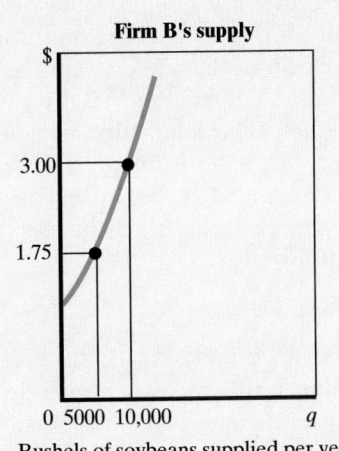

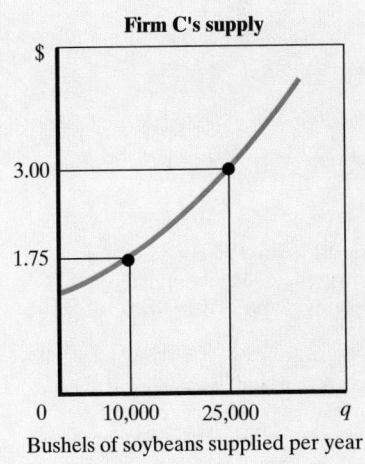

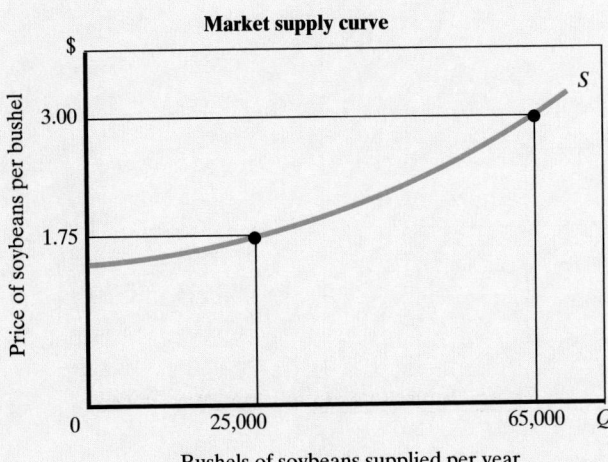

Price	Quantity supplied by			Market supply $(Q^S = q_A^S + q_B^S + q_C^S)$
	A	B	C	
$3.00	30,000 +	10,000 +	25,000	⟶ 65,000
1.75	10,000 +	5,000 +	10,000	⟶ 25,000

The position and shape of the market supply curve depends upon the positions and shapes of the individual firms' supply curves from which it is derived. But it also depends on the number of firms that produce in that market. If firms that produce for a particular market are earning high profits, other firms may be tempted to go into that business. When the technology to produce computers for home use became available, literally hundreds of new firms got into the act. The popularity and profitability of professional football has three times led to the formation of new leagues. When new firms enter an industry, the supply curve shifts to the right. When firms go out of business, or "exit" the market, the supply curve shifts to the left.

So far we have identified a number of factors that influence the amount that households demand and firms supply in product, or output, markets. The discussion has emphasized the role of market price as a determinant both of quantity demanded and of quantity supplied. We are now ready to see how supply and demand in the market interact to determine the final market price.

✳ MARKET EQUILIBRIUM

We have been very careful in our discussions thus far to separate household decisions about how much to demand from firm decisions about how much to supply. The operation of the market, however, clearly depends on the interaction between suppliers and demanders. At any moment, one of three conditions prevails in every market: (1) the quantity demanded exceeds the quantity supplied at the current price, a situation called *excess demand;* (2) the quantity supplied exceeds the quantity demanded at the current price, a situation called *excess supply;* or (3) the quantity supplied equals the quantity demanded at the current price, a situation called **equilibrium.**

equilibrium The condition that exists when quantity supplied and quantity demanded are equal.

excess demand The condition that exists when quantity demanded exceeds quantity supplied at the current price.

Excess Demand

Excess demand exists when quantity demanded is greater than quantity supplied at the current price. Figure 4.9, which plots both a supply curve and a demand curve on the same graph, illustrates such a situation. As you can see, market

FIGURE 4.9

Excess Demand

At a price of $1.75 per bushel, quantity demanded exceeds quantity supplied. When *excess demand* arises, there is a tendency for price to rise. As price rises from $1.75 to $2.50, quantity demanded falls from 50,000 to 35,000 and quantity supplied rises from 25,000 to 35,000. When quantity demanded equals quantity supplied, excess demand is eliminated and the market is in equilibrium.

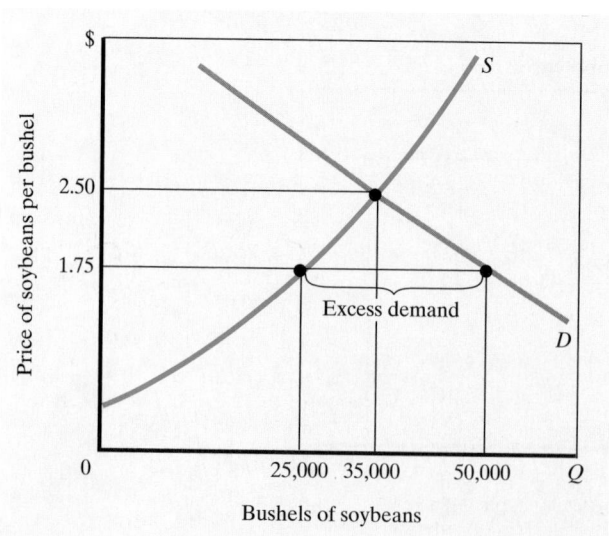

demand at $1.75 per bushel (50,000 bushels) exceeds the amount that farmers are currently producing (25,000 bushels).

When excess demand occurs in an unregulated market, there is a tendency for price to rise as demanders compete against each other for the limited supply. The adjustment mechanisms may differ, but the outcome is always the same. For example, consider the mechanism of an auction. In an auction, items are sold directly to the highest bidder. When the auctioneer starts the bidding at a low price, many people bid for the item. At first there is excess demand: Quantity demanded exceeds quantity supplied. As would-be buyers offer higher and higher prices, bidders drop out, until the one who offers the most ends up with the item being auctioned. Price rises until quantity demanded and quantity supplied are equal.

At a price of $1.75 (see Figure 4.9 again), farmers produce soybeans at a rate of 25,000 bushels per year, but at that price the demand is for 50,000 bushels. Most farm products are sold to local dealers who in turn sell large quantities in major market centers, where bidding would push prices up if quantity demanded exceeded quantity supplied. As price rises above $1.75, two things happen: (1) the quantity demanded falls as buyers drop out of the market and perhaps choose a substitute, and (2) the quantity supplied increases as farmers find themselves receiving a higher price for their product and shift additional acres into soybean production.[7]

This process continues until the excess demand is eliminated. In Figure 4.9, this occurs at $2.50, where quantity demanded has fallen from 50,000 to 35,000 bushels per year and quantity supplied has increased from 25,000 to 35,000 bushels per year. When quantity demanded and quantity supplied are equal and there is no further bidding, the process has achieved an equilibrium, a situation in which there is no natural tendency for further adjustment. Graphically, the point of equilibrium is the point at which the supply curve and the demand curve intersect.

The process through which excess demand leads to higher prices is different in different markets. Consider the market for houses in the hypothetical town of Boomville with a population of 25,000 people, most of whom live in single-family homes. Normally about 75 homes are sold in the Boomville market each year. But last year, a major business opened a plant in town, creating 1,500 new jobs that pay good wages. This attracted new residents to the area, and real estate agents now have more buyers than there are properties for sale. Quantity demanded now exceeds quantity supplied. In other words, there is excess demand.

Auctions are not unheard of in the housing market, but they are rare. This market usually works more subtly, but the outcome is the same. Properties are sold very quickly and housing prices begin to rise. Boomville sellers soon learn that there are more buyers than usual, however, and they begin to "hold out" for higher offers. As prices for houses in Boomville rise, quantity demanded eventually drops off and quantity supplied increases. Quantity supplied increases in at least two ways: (1) Encouraged by the high prices, builders begin constructing new houses, and (2) some people, attracted by the higher prices their homes will fetch, put their houses on the market. Discouraged by higher prices, however, some potential buyers (demanders) may begin to look for housing in neighboring towns and settle on commuting. Eventually, equilibrium will be reestablished, with the quantity of houses demanded just equal to the quantity of houses supplied.

---

[7]Once farmers have produced in any given season, they cannot change their minds and produce more, of course. When we derived Clarence Brown's supply schedule in Table 4.3, we imagined him reacting to prices that existed at the time he decided how much land to plant in soybeans. In Figure 4.9, the upward slope shows that higher prices justify shifting land from other crops. Final price may not be determined until final production figures are in. For our purposes here, however, we have ignored this timing problem. Perhaps the best way to think about it is that demand and supply are *flows*, or *rates*, of production—that is, we are talking about the number of bushels produced *per production period*. Adjustments in the rate of production may take place over a number of production periods.

While the mechanics of price adjustment in the housing market differ from the mechanics of an auction, the outcome is exactly the same:

> When quantity demanded exceeds quantity supplied, price tends to rise. When the price in a market rises, quantity demanded falls and quantity supplied rises until an equilibrium is reached at which quantity demanded and quantity supplied are equal.

This process is called *price rationing*. When excess demand exists, some people will be satisfied and some will not. When the market operates without interference, price increases will distribute what is available to those who are willing and able to pay the most. As long as there is a way for buyers and sellers to interact, those who are willing to pay more will make that fact known somehow. (The nature of the price system as a rationing device is discussed in great detail in Chapter 5.)

Excess Supply

excess supply The condition that exists when quantity supplied exceeds quantity demanded at the current price.

Excess supply exists when the quantity supplied exceeds the quantity demanded at the current price. As with excess demand, the mechanics of price adjustment in the face of excess supply can differ from market to market. When there is a surplus of a particular product, that product remains unsold. If automobile dealers find themselves with unsold cars in the fall when the new models are coming in, for example, you can expect to see price cuts. Sometimes dealers offer discounts to encourage buyers; sometimes buyers themselves simply offer less than the price initially asked. In any event, products do no one any good sitting in dealers' lots or on warehouse shelves. The auction metaphor introduced earlier can also be applied here: If the initial asking price is too high, no one bids, and the auctioneer tries a lower price. In 1989, when stores found themselves with large inventories and weak sales at Christmas, most retailers held big sales a week or two before the holiday. Quantities supplied exceeded quantities demanded at the current prices, so stores cut prices.

Across the state from Boomville is Bustville, where last year a manufacturer of drugs shut down its operations and 1,500 people found themselves out of work. With no other prospects for work, many residents decided to pack up and move. They put their houses up for sale, but there were few buyers. The result was an excess supply of houses: The quantity of houses supplied exceeded the quantity demanded at the current prices.

As houses sit unsold on the market for months, sellers start to cut their asking prices. Potential buyers begin offering considerably less than sellers are asking. As prices fall, two things are likely to happen. First, the low housing prices may attract new buyers. People who might have bought in a neighboring town see that there are housing bargains to be had in Bustville, and quantity demanded rises in response to price decline. Second, some of those who put their houses on the market may be discouraged by the lower prices and decide to stay in Bustville. Developers are certainly not likely to be building new housing in town. Lower prices thus lead to a decline in quantity supplied as potential sellers pull their houses from the market. This was exactly the situation in New England and California in the early 1990s.

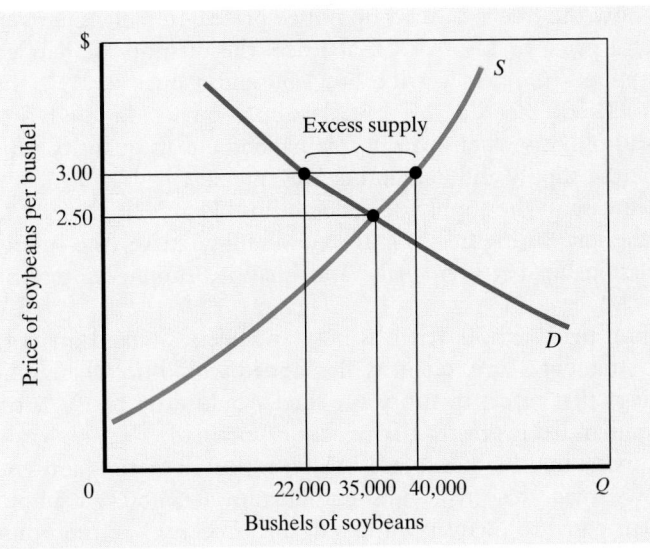

FIGURE 4.10
Excess Supply

At a price of $3, quantity supplied exceeds quantity demanded by 18,000 bushels. This excess supply will cause price to fall.

Figure 4.10 illustrates another excess supply situation. At a price of $3 per bushel, farmers are supplying soybeans at a rate of 40,000 bushels per year, but buyers demand only 22,000. With 18,000 (40,000 minus 22,000) bushels of soybeans going unsold, the market price falls. As price falls from $3 to $2.50, quantity supplied decreases from 40,000 bushels per year to 35,000. The lower price causes quantity demanded to rise from 22,000 to 35,000. At $2.50, quantity demanded and quantity supplied are equal. For the data shown here, then, $2.50 and 35,000 bushels are the equilibrium price and quantity.

During 1985 and 1986, crude oil production worldwide exceeded the quantity demanded, and prices fell significantly as competing producer countries tried to maintain their share of world markets. Although the mechanism by which price is adjusted is different for automobiles, housing, soybeans, and crude oil, the outcome is the same:

> When quantity supplied exceeds quantity demanded at the current price, the price tends to fall. When price falls, quantity supplied is likely to decrease and quantity demanded is likely to increase until an equilibrium price is reached where quantity supplied and quantity demanded are equal.

Changes in Equilibrium

When supply and demand curves shift, the equilibrium price and quantity change. The following example will help to illustrate this point.

South America is a major producer of coffee beans. A cold snap there can reduce the coffee harvest enough to affect the world price of coffee beans. In the mid-1970s, a major freeze hit several South American countries and drove up the price of coffee in U.S. grocery stores from around $1.50 a pound to $4.50 a pound.

Figure 4.11 illustrates how the freeze pushed up coffee prices. Initially, the market was in equilibrium at a price of $1.50. At that price, the quantity demanded was equal to quantity supplied (Q_1^*). At a price of $1.50 and a quantity Q_1^*, the demand curve (labeled D) intersected the initial supply curve (labeled S_1). (Remember that equilibrium exists when quantity demanded equals quantity supplied—the point at which the supply and demand curves intersect.)

The freeze caused a decrease in the supply of coffee beans. That is, it caused the supply curve to shift to the left. In Figure 4.11, the new supply curve (the supply curve that shows the relationship between price and quantity supplied after the freeze) is labeled S_2.

At the initial equilibrium price, $1.50, there is now an excess demand for coffee. If the price were to remain at $1.50, quantity demanded would not change; it would remain at Q_1^*. But at that price, quantity supplied would drop to Q_S. At a price of $1.50, quantity demanded is greater than quantity supplied.

When excess demand exists in a market, price can be expected to rise, and rise it did. As the figure shows, price rose to a new equilibrium at $4.50. At $4.50, quantity demanded is again equal to quantity supplied, this time at Q_2^*—the point at which the new supply curve (S_2) intersects the demand curve.

Notice that as the price of coffee rose from $1.50 to $4.50, two things happened. First, the quantity demanded declined (a movement along the demand curve) as people shifted to substitutes such as tea and hot cocoa. Second, the quantity supplied began to rise, but within the limits imposed by the damage from the freeze.[8] That is, the quantity supplied increased in response to the higher price *along* the new supply curve, which lies to the left of the old supply curve. The final result was a higher price ($4.50), a smaller quantity finally exchanged in the market (Q_2^*), and coffee bought only by those willing to pay $4.50 per pound.

---

[8] It might also be that some countries or areas with high costs of production, previously unprofitable, come into production and ship to the world market at the higher price.

FIGURE 4.11

The Coffee Market: A Shift of Supply and Subsequent Price Adjustment

Before the freeze, the coffee market was in equilibrium at a price of $1.50. At that price, quantity demanded equaled quantity supplied. The freeze shifted the supply curve to the left (from S_1 to S_2), increasing equilibrium price to $4.50.

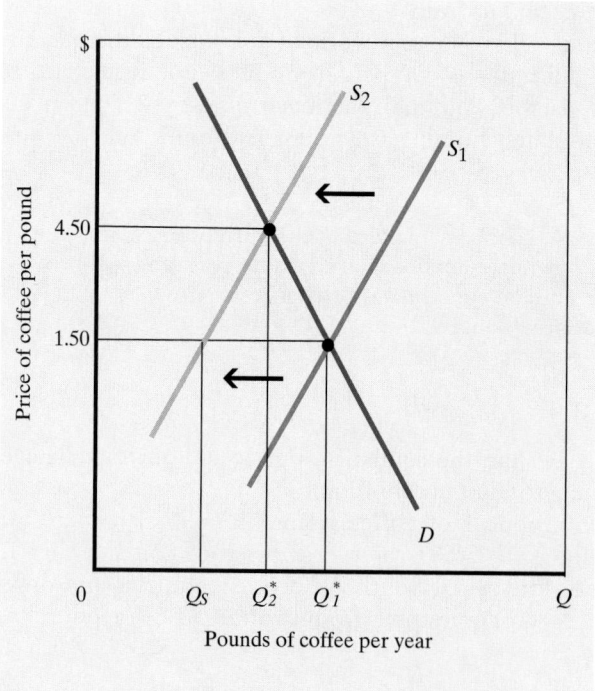

Figure 4.12 presents ten examples of supply and demand shifts and the resulting changes in equilibrium price and quantity. Be sure to go through each graph carefully and ensure that you understand each.

FIGURE 4.12
Examples of Supply and Demand Shifts for Product X

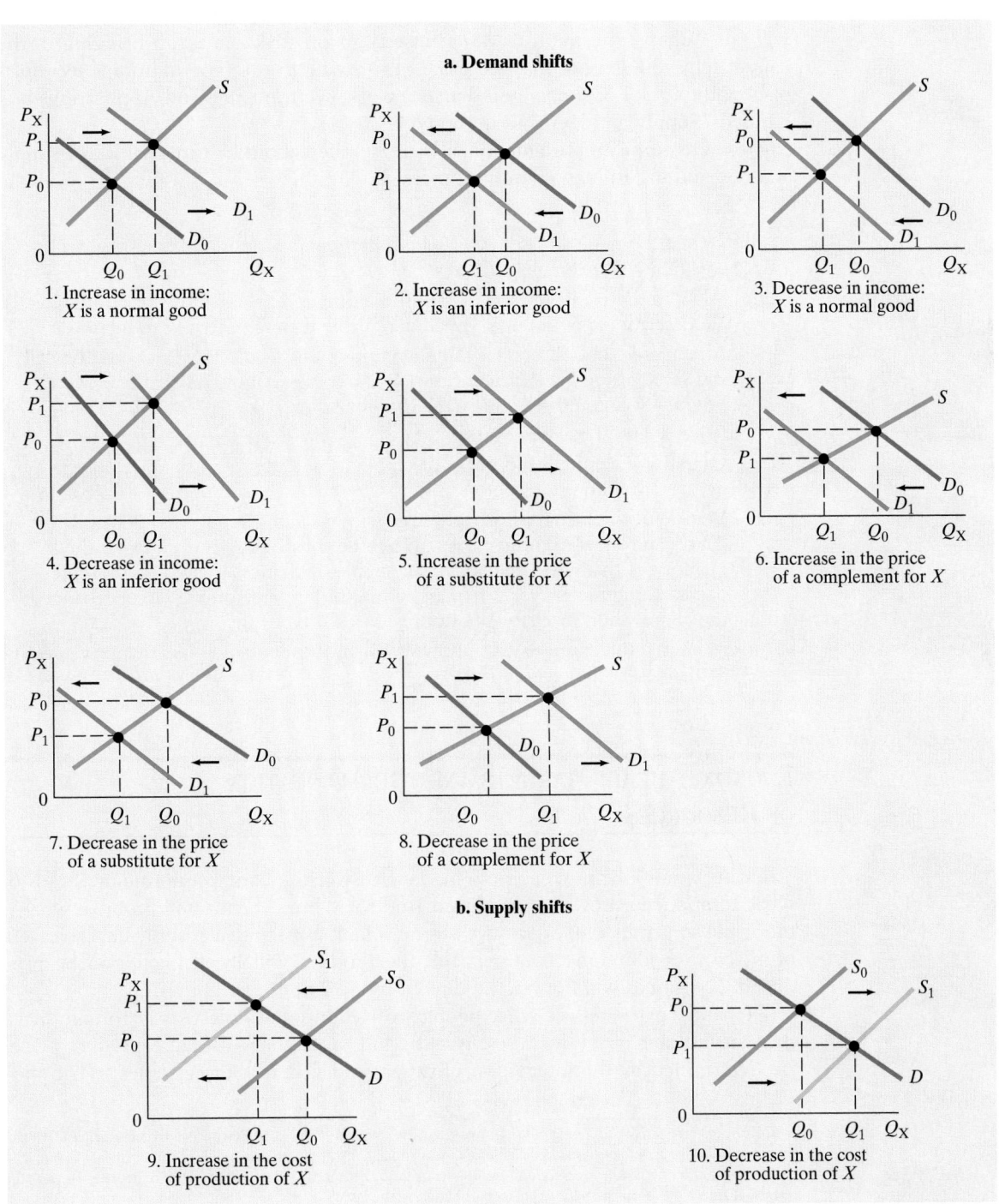

a. Demand shifts

1. Increase in income:
   X is a normal good

2. Increase in income:
   X is an inferior good

3. Decrease in income:
   X is a normal good

4. Decrease in income:
   X is an inferior good

5. Increase in the price
   of a substitute for X

6. Increase in the price
   of a complement for X

7. Decrease in the price
   of a substitute for X

8. Decrease in the price
   of a complement for X

b. Supply shifts

9. Increase in the cost
   of production of X

10. Decrease in the cost
   of production of X

DEMAND AND SUPPLY IN PRODUCT MARKETS: A REVIEW

As you continue your study of economics, you will discover that it is a discipline full of controversy and debate. There is, however, little disagreement about the basic way that the forces of supply and demand operate in free markets. If you hear that a freeze in Florida has destroyed a good portion of the citrus crop, you can bet that the price of oranges will rise.[9] If you read that the weather in the Midwest has been good and a record corn crop is expected, you can bet that corn prices will fall. When fishermen in Massachusetts go on strike and stop bringing in the daily catch, you can bet that the price of fish will go up. (For additional examples of how the forces of supply and demand work, see the Issues and Applications box entitled "Supply and Demand in the News.")

Here are some important points to remember about the mechanics of supply and demand in product, or output, markets:

1. Demand is determined by household preferences, household income, and wealth, prices, and expectations.
2. Supply is determined by costs of production and prices. Costs of production are determined by input prices and available technologies of production.
3. A demand curve shows how much a household would buy if it could buy all it wanted at the given price. A supply curve shows how much a firm would produce if it could sell all it wanted at the given price.
4. Price is always price per unit.
5. Quantity demanded and quantity supplied are always per time period, that is, per day, per month, or per year.
6. Be careful to distinguish between movements along supply and demand curves and shifts of those curves. When the price of a good changes, the quantity of that good demanded, or supplied, changes—that is, a movement occurs along the curve. When any of the other determining factors change, the curves shift, or change position.
7. Market equilibrium exists only when quantity supplied equals quantity demanded at the current price.

LOOKING AHEAD: MARKETS AND THE ALLOCATION OF RESOURCES

You can already begin to see how markets answer the basic economic questions of what is produced, how it is produced, and for whom. Firms will produce what is profitable to produce. If a product can be sold at a price that is sufficient to leave a profit after production costs are paid, the product will in all likelihood be produced. Resources will flow in the direction of profit opportunities.

Demand curves reflect what people are willing and able to pay for products; they are influenced by incomes, wealth, and preferences. Because product prices are determined by the interaction of supply and demand, prices reflect what peo-

---

[9] In economics you have to think twice, however, even about a "safe" bet. If you bet that the price of frozen orange juice will rise after a freeze, you will lose your money. It turns out that much of the crop that is damaged by a freeze can be used, but for only one thing—to make frozen orange juice. Thus, a freeze actually *increases* the supply of frozen juice on the national market. Following the last two hard freezes in Florida, the price of oranges shot up, but the price of orange juice fell sharply!

ISSUES AND APPLICATIONS
SUPPLY AND DEMAND IN THE NEWS

The basic forces of supply and demand are at work throughout the world, as the following news articles illustrate. As an exercise, draw and label demand and supply diagrams for each situation.

1. An increase in demand, a decrease in supply, and a rise in prices after a natural disaster (*New York Times,* August 30, 1992):

With supplies of ice, basic foods and building materials scarce and many restaurants and gas stations still closed in the aftermath of Hurricane Andrew, state officials said today that complaints of price gouging were pouring in.

"There are people charging $5 for a bag of ice that normally costs $1," said Bob Butterworth, Florida's Attorney General. "They are charging $125 for a motel room that was $35 before the storm. Plywood has doubled in price."

By midday Saturday, the Attorney General's office and the Department of Agriculture and Consumer Services had received nearly 2,500 complaints. Callers reported tuna fish at $8 a can, $15 for a gallon of water, gasoline selling at $2 a gallon, candy bars priced at $4, and $200 chain saws going for $900.

2. A decrease in demand and a decline in the price of a luxury good (fine French wines), resulting in a downward shift in demand for a substitute and a downward shift in demand for an input (labor):

During the early 1990s, many countries experienced economic hard times. The United States recovered from the recession of 1990/91 very slowly. Germany found it more difficult to absorb the former East Germany than it had expected. In Japan, real estate values fell, and economic growth slowed sharply. The Middle East and Eastern Europe had even more severe problems. As a result, incomes fell in many parts of the world, and demand for many

products declined (shifted to the left).

Among the hardest hit products were luxury goods. One of the great luxuries in the world is fine French wine. According to a front-page *Wall Street Journal* article on October 20, 1992, "For most fine French wines, sales growth is evaporating, surpluses are ballooning and prices are plummeting." Liquor stores across the United States reported large inventories of unsold wines and sharply falling prices. In 1992, Chateau Talbot, a top French winery, sold 800,000 bottles of fine wine on the market at 30% to 40% below the price of the same wine a year earlier. U.S. winemakers also felt the decline in demand. As French wines fell in price, the demand for U.S. wine, a substitute for French wine, fell as well.

The decline in prices pushed many marginal wine producers out of business, and many vineyards in France were forced to lay off workers. One large French producer fired 40% of his winery's staff. (Recall the circular flow diagram, Figure 4.1. Firms that sell output also demand labor. The demand for labor depends on the profitability of those firms.)

3. A decrease in world supply causing prices to rise (*New York Times,* October 21, 1992):

Coffee...prices surged yesterday on the Coffee, Sugar and Cocoa Exchange in New York as Brazilian producers continued to withhold their crop from the market.

"There is a discrepancy between high internal prices and world prices that does not make it worthwhile for Brazilian producers to sell," said Sandra Kaul, an analyst with Shearson Lehman Brothers Inc., adding that Brazil is the only producer with fresh supplies of coffee.

4. A decrease in supply, an increase in price, and perhaps a decline in the quantity demanded (*New York Times,* June 14, 1990):

A farm worker in Campinas, Brazil uses an ancient technique to sift coffee beans. In 1992, Brazilian coffee growers caused a decrease in the world supply of coffee when they withheld their crop from the market.

For the first time in almost 10 years, the wholesale price of cocaine is rising sharply in New York and other American cities, suggesting that extensive law-enforcement efforts in this country and Latin America may finally be reducing the availability of the drug, Federal officials and independent drug experts say.

In New York and Los Angeles, wholesale cocaine prices have jumped by more than 40 percent since December....

Federal officials and other drug experts have been closely following cocaine prices since late last summer when Colombia declared war on drug traffickers and President Bush announced an intensified anti-drug campaign....

Prices in Miami, one of the principal hubs for importing, jumped several thousand dollars in September, a month after Colombian police and soldiers went into action.

Source: Joseph B. Treaster, "Price Gouging Is Widely Cited in Storm Region," *New York Times,* August 30, 1992; "Coffee Surges in New York As Brazilians Hold Off Crop," *New York Times,* October 21, 1992; Cocaine Prices Rise, and Police Efforts May Be Responsible," *New York Times,* June 14, 1990.

ple are willing to pay. If people's preferences or incomes change, resources will be allocated differently. Consider, for example, an increase in demand—a shift in the market demand curve. Beginning at an equilibrium, households simply begin buying more. At the equilibrium price, quantity demanded becomes greater than quantity supplied. When there is excess demand, prices will rise, and higher prices mean higher profits for firms in the industry. Higher profits, in turn, provide existing firms with an incentive to expand and new firms with an incentive to enter the industry. Thus, the decisions of independent private firms responding to prices and profit opportunities determine *what* will be produced. No central direction is necessary.

Firms in business to make a profit have a good reason to choose the best available technology—lower costs mean higher profits. Thus, individual firms determine *how* to produce their products, again with no central direction.

Adam Smith saw this self-regulating feature of markets more than 200 years ago:

> Every individual…by pursuing his own interest…promotes that of society. He is led…by an invisible hand to promote an end which was no part of his intention.[10]

The term Smith coined, the "invisible hand," has passed into common parlance and is still used by economists today to refer to the self-regulation of markets.

So far we have barely touched on the question of distribution—*who* gets what is produced? But part of the answer can be seen in the simple supply and demand diagrams. When a good is in short supply, price rises. As it does, those who are willing and able to continue buying do so; others stop buying. Willingness and ability to pay depend on preferences, income, and wealth, which are in part determined in input markets. Wage rates, for example, affect how much workers can earn.

The next chapter begins with a more detailed discussion of these topics. How, exactly, is the final allocation of resources (the mix of output and the distribution of output) determined in a market system?

---

[10]Adam Smith, *The Wealth of Nations*, p. 456.

SUMMARY

1. In societies with many people, production must satisfy wide-ranging tastes and preferences, and producers must therefore specialize.

Firms and Households: The Basic Decision-Making Units

2. A *firm* exists when a person or a group of people decides to produce a product or products by transforming resources, or *inputs*, into *outputs*—the products that are sold in the market. Firms are the primary producing units in a market economy.

3. We assume firms make decisions to maximize profits.

Input Markets and Output Markets

4. *Households* and firms interact in two basic kinds of markets: *product, or output, markets* and *input, or resource, markets*. Goods and services intended for use by households are exchanged in output markets. In output markets, competing firms supply and competing households demand. In input markets, competing firms demand and competing households supply.

5. Ultimately, firms determine the quantities and character of outputs produced, the types and quantities of inputs demanded, and the technologies used in production. Households determine the types and quantities of products demanded and the types and quantities of inputs supplied.

Demand in Product/Output Markets

6. Quantity demanded by an individual household is likely to depend upon (1) income, (2) wealth, (3) the price of the product, (4) the prices of other products, (5) tastes and preferences, and (6) expectations about the future.

7. For an individual household, quantity demanded is the amount of a product that it would buy in a given period if it could buy all it wanted at the current price.

8. A *demand schedule* shows the quantities of a product that a household would buy at different prices. The same information presented graphically is called a *demand curve*.

9. The *law of demand* states that there is a negative relationship between price and quantity demanded: As price rises, quantity demanded decreases, and vice versa. Demand curves slope downward.

10. All demand curves eventually intersect the price axis because there is always a price above which a household cannot, or will not, pay. All demand curves also eventually intersect the quantity axis because demand for most goods is limited, if only by time, even at a zero price.

11. When an increase in income causes demand for a good to rise, that good is a *normal good*. When an increase in income causes demand for a good to fall, that good is an *inferior good*.

12. If a rise in the price of good X causes demand for good Y to increase, the goods are *substitutes*. If a rise in the price of X causes demand for Y to fall, the goods are *complements*.

13. Market demand is simply the sum of all the quantities of a good or service demanded per period by all the households buying in the market for that good or service. It is the sum of all the individual quantities demanded at each price.

Supply in Product/Output Markets

14. Quantity supplied by a firm depends on (1) the price of the good or service, (2) the cost of producing the product, which includes the prices of required inputs and the technologies that can be used to produce the product, and (3) the prices of related products.

15. Market supply is the sum of all that is supplied each period by all producers of a single product. It is the sum of all the individual quantities supplied at each price.

16. It is very important to distinguish between *movements* along demand and supply curves and *shifts* of demand and supply curves. The demand curve shows the relationship between price and quantity demanded. The supply curve shows the relationship between price and quantity supplied. A change in price is a movement along the curve. Changes in tastes, income, wealth, expectations, or prices of other goods and services cause demand curves to shift; changes in costs, input prices, technology, or prices of related goods and services cause supply curves to shift.

Market Equilibrium

17. When quantity demanded exceeds quantity supplied at the current price, excess demand exists and the price tends to rise. When prices in a market rise, quantity demanded falls and quantity supplied rises until an equilibrium is reached at which quantity supplied and quantity demanded are equal.

18. When quantity supplied exceeds quantity demanded at the current price, excess supply exists and the price tends to fall. When price falls, quantity supplied decreases and quantity demanded increases until an equilibrium price is reached where quantity supplied and quantity demanded are equal.

REVIEW TERMS AND CONCEPTS

PROBLEM SET

1. Illustrate the following with supply and demand curves:

a. Between 1992 and 1993, employment and income in California fell, creating a decline in the demand for housing and lowering home prices.

b. In 1992, the U.S. dollar fell in value on foreign currency markets. One result was that U.S. exports looked less expensive to foreign buyers. As a result, the demand for U.S.-produced wheat increased.

c. Before economic reforms were implemented in Poland, the price of meat was held substantially below equilibrium by law. When reforms were implemented, prices rose dramatically, the quantity demanded fell, and the quantity supplied rose.

d. Suppose that the government imposes a regulation that sharply decreases the number of trees available for lumber production in the United States to protect two endangered species. Illustrate the effects on the lumber market and on the housing market.

2. There has been a great debate among housing policy analysts over the best way to increase the number of housing units available to low-income households. One strategy is to provide people with housing "vouchers," paid for by the government, that can be used to "rent" housing supplied by the private market. A second strategy is to have the government subsidize housing suppliers or simply to build public housing.

a. Illustrate both supply- and demand-side strategies using supply and demand curves. Which strategy will result in higher rents?

b. Critics of housing vouchers (the demand-side strategy) argue that because the supply of housing to low-income households is limited and will not respond at all to higher rents, demand vouchers will serve only to drive up rents and make landlords better off. Illustrate their point with supply and demand curves.

3. In August of 1991, the Boston Red Sox were battling it out with the Toronto Blue Jays for first place in the American League East. On August 2, the Red Sox played the Blue Jays in Boston. All tickets to the Blue Jays game were sold out a month in advance, and many people who wanted to get tickets could not. The following week the Sox traveled to Ohio to play the Cleveland Indians (a team in last place). The Cleveland game broke records for low attendance. In fact, only 1,600 went to that game in a stadium that seats 80,000! Fenway Park in Boston holds 36,000 people. Cleveland Stadium holds 80,000. Assume for simplicity that tickets to all regular season games are priced at $10.

a. Draw supply and demand curves for tickets to each of the two games. Draw one graph for each game. (*Hint:* Supply is fixed. It does not change with price.)

b. Is there a pricing policy that would have filled the ball park for the Cleveland game?

c. The price system was not allowed to work to ration the Blue Jays tickets. How do you know? How do you suppose the tickets were rationed?

d. Suppose that the Cleveland game had actually attracted 30,000 fans. Redraw the graph of the Cleveland game. Does your answer to b. change? If the Indians adopted such a strategy, would it bring in more or less revenue?

4. The U.S. government administers two programs that affect the market for cigarettes. Media campaigns and labeling requirements are aimed at making the public aware of the health dangers of cigarettes. At the same time, the Department of Agriculture maintains a program of price supports for tobacco. Under this program, the supported price is above the market equilibrium price, and the government limits the amount of land that can be devoted to tobacco production. Are these two programs at odds with respect to the goal of reducing cigarette consumption? Explain carefully. As a part of your answer, illustrate graphically the effects of both policies on the market for cigarettes.

5. In 1999, a rare disease hits the U.S. cattle herd, causing a 20% decrease in U.S. beef production. As a result chicken prices rise. Illustrate this situation with supply and demand curves (draw diagrams for both markets).

6. Consider the market for pizza. Suppose that the market demand for pizza is given by the equation $Q_d = 300 - 20P_d$ and the market supply for pizza is given by the equation $Q_s = 20P_s - 100$, where Q_d = quantity demanded, Q_s = quantity supplied, P_d = price consumers pay (per pizza), and P_s = price producers receive (per pizza).

a. Graph the supply and demand schedules for pizza using $5 through $15 as the values of P_d and P_s.

b. In equilibrium, how many pizzas would be sold and at what price?

c. What would happen if suppliers set the price of pizza at $15? Explain the market adjustment process.

d. Suppose that the price of hamburgers, a substitute for pizza, doubles. Assume that this leads to a doubling of the demand for pizza (that is, at each price consumers demand twice as much pizza as before). Write the equation for the new market demand for pizza.

e. Find the new equilibrium price and quantity of pizza.

The Price System, Supply and Demand, and Elasticity

5

THE PRICE SYSTEM: RATIONING AND
ALLOCATING RESOURCES
 Price Rationing
 Constraints on the Market and Alternative
  Rationing Mechanisms
 Prices and the Allocation of Resources

SUPPLY AND DEMAND ANALYSIS:
 AN OIL IMPORT FEE

ELASTICITY
 Price Elasticity of Demand
 Calculating Elasticities
 The Determinants of Demand Elasticity
 Other Important Elasticities

LOOKING AHEAD

Every society has a system of institutions that determines what is produced, how it is produced, and to whom it is distributed. Although in some societies these decisions are made centrally, through planning agencies or by government directive, in every society many decisions are made in a decentralized way, through the operation of markets.

Markets exist in all societies, and Chapter 4 provided a bare-bones description of how markets operate. The first half of this chapter reflects briefly on the outcomes of supply and demand in market operation. The second half of the chapter introduces the important concept of elasticity. An understanding of the basic functioning of markets is essential to the study of both microeconomics and macroeconomics.

THE PRICE SYSTEM: RATIONING AND ALLOCATING RESOURCES

The market system, also referred to as the price system, performs two important and closely related functions in a society with unregulated markets. First, it provides an automatic mechanism for distributing scarce goods and services. That is, it serves as a **price rationing** device for allocating goods and services to con-

price rationing The process by which the market system allocates goods and services to consumers when quantity demanded exceeds quantity supplied.

sumers when the quantity demanded exceeds the quantity supplied. Second, the price system ultimately determines both the allocation of resources among producers and the final mix of outputs.

✳Price Rationing

Consider first the simple process by which the price system eliminates excess demand. Figure 5.1 shows hypothetical supply and demand curves for lobsters caught off the coast of New England.

Lobsters are considered a delicacy. They are served in the finest restaurants, and people cook them at home on special occasions. Maine produces most of the lobster catch in the United States, and anyone who drives up the Maine coast cannot avoid the hundreds of restaurants selling lobster rolls, steamed lobster, and baked stuffed lobster.

As Figure 5.1 shows, the equilibrium price of live New England lobsters was $3.23 per pound in 1993. At this price, lobster boats brought in lobsters at a rate of 45 million pounds per year—an amount that was just enough to satisfy demand.

Market equilibrium existed at $3.23 per pound, because at that price quantity demanded was equal to quantity supplied. (Remember that equilibrium occurs at the point where the supply and demand curves intersect. In Figure 5.1, this occurs at point C.)

Now suppose that in 1994 the waters off a section of the Maine coast become contaminated with a poisonous parasite. As a result, the Department of Agriculture is forced to close 20,000 square miles of the most productive lobstering areas. Even though many of the lobster boats shift their trapping activities to other waters, there is a sharp reduction in the quantity of lobster supplied. The supply curve shifts to the left, from S_{1993} to S_{1994}. This shift in the supply curve creates a situation of excess demand at $3.23. At that price, the quantity demanded is 45 million pounds and the quantity supplied is 22 million pounds (Q_S). Quantity demanded exceeds quantity supplied by 23 million pounds (45 million minus 22 million).

FIGURE 5.1
The Market for Lobsters

Suppose that in 1994, 20,000 square miles of lobstering waters off the coast of Maine are closed. The supply curve shifts to the left. Before the waters are closed, the lobster market is in equilibrium at $P_1 = \$3.23$ and at $Q_1^* = 45$ million pounds. The decreased supply of lobster leads to higher prices, and a new equilibrium is reached at $P_2 = \$4.50$ and $Q_2^* = 35$ million pounds. If the price had not changed, the lobster catch would have dropped to 22 million pounds (Q_S). When the price rises to $4.50, the quantity demanded drops, moving from point C to point B along the demand curve (D). At the same time, the quantity supplied increases, moving from point A to point B along the supply curve (S_{1994}).

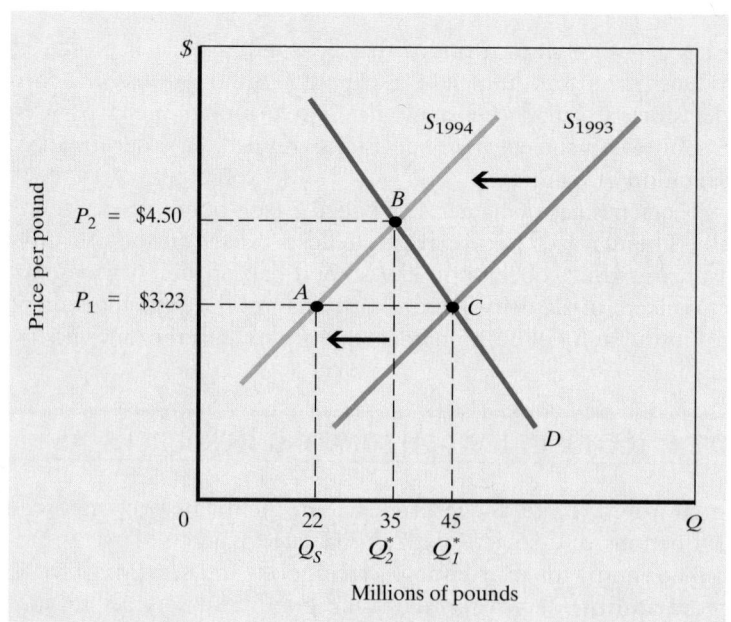

The reduced supply causes the price of lobster to rise sharply. As the price rises, the available supply is "rationed." Who gets it? Those who are willing and able to pay the most.

You can see the market's price rationing function clearly in Figure 5.1. As the price rises from \$3.23 (P_1), the quantity demanded declines along the demand curve, moving from point C (45 million pounds) toward point B (35 million pounds). The higher prices mean that restaurants must charge much more for lobster rolls and stuffed lobsters. As a result, many people simply decide to stop buying lobster or order it less frequently when they dine out. Some restaurants drop it from the menu entirely, and some shoppers at the fish counter turn to substitutes such as swordfish and salmon.

As the price rises, lobster trappers (suppliers) also change their behavior. They stay out longer and put out more traps than they did when the price was \$3.23 per pound. Quantity supplied increases from 22 million pounds (Q_S) to 35 million pounds (Q_2^*). This increase in price brings about a movement along the 1994 supply curve from point A to point B.

Finally, a new equilibrium is established at a price of \$4.50 per pound (P_2) and a total output of 35 million pounds (Q_2^*). At the new equilibrium, total production is 35 million pounds per year, and the market has determined who gets the lobsters. *The lower total supply is rationed to those who are willing and able to pay the higher price.*

This idea of "willingness to pay" is central to the distribution of available supply, and willingness depends on both desire (preferences) and income/wealth. Willingness to pay does not necessarily mean that only the very rich will continue to buy lobsters when the price increases, however. Lower-income people may continue to buy some lobster, but they will have to be willing to sacrifice more of other goods in order to do so.

In sum:

> The adjustment of price is the rationing mechanism in free markets. Price rationing means that whenever there is a need to *ration* a good—that is, when excess demand exists—in a free market, the price of the good will rise until the market clears.

There is some price that will clear any market you can think of. Consider the market for a famous painting such as van Gogh's *Portrait of Dr. Gachet.* Figure 5.2

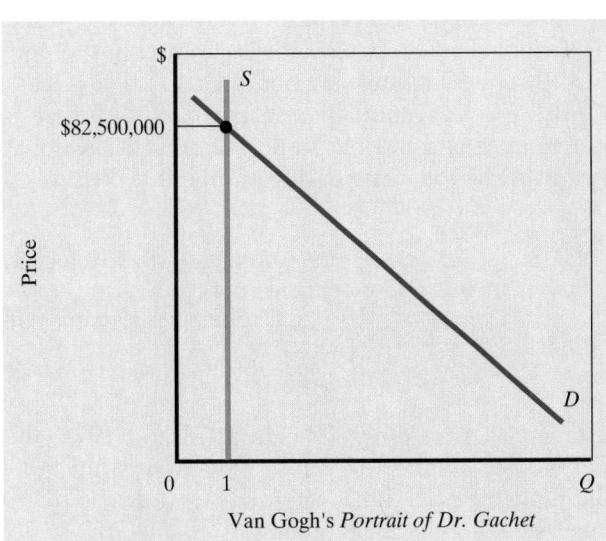

Van Gogh's *Portrait of Dr. Gachet*

FIGURE 5.2

Market for a Rare Painting

There is some price that will clear any market, even if supply is strictly limited. In an auction for a unique painting, the price (bid) will rise to eliminate excess demand until there is only one bidder willing to purchase the single available painting.

illustrates the operation of such a market. At a low price, there would be an enormous excess demand for such an important painting. The price would be bid up until there was only one remaining demander. The demander who gets the painting would be the one who is willing and able to pay the most. Presumably, that price would be very high. In fact, van Gogh's *Portrait of Dr. Gachet* sold for $82.5 million in 1990. If the product is in strictly scarce supply, as a single painting is, its price is said to be *demand determined;* that is, its price is determined solely and exclusively by the amount that the highest bidder, or highest bidders, are willing to pay. (For another example of price rationing, see the Issues and Applications box entitled "Price Rationing: The Drought of 1988.")

One might interpret the statement that "there is some price that will clear any market" to mean "everything has its price." That is not exactly what it means. Suppose you own a small silver bracelet that has been in your family for many generations. It is quite possible that you wouldn't sell it for *any* amount of money. Does this mean that the market is not working, or that quantity supplied and quantity demanded are not equal? Not at all. It means simply that *you* are the highest bidder. By turning down all bids, you are setting your own price, revealing that the bracelet is worth more to you than to those who bid on it. To keep the bracelet, you must be willing to forgo what anybody offers for it.

Constraints on the Market and Alternative Rationing Mechanisms

On occasion, both governments and private firms decide to use some mechanism other than the market system to ration an item for which there is excess demand at the current price. Policies designed to stop price rationing are commonly justified in a number of ways.

The rationale most often used is "fairness." It is not "fair" to let landlords charge high rents, not "fair" for oil companies to run up the price of gasoline, not "fair" for insurance companies to charge enormous premiums, and so on. After all, the argument goes, we have no choice but to pay—housing and insurance are necessary, and one needs gasoline to get to work. While it is not precisely true that price rationing allocates goods and services solely on the basis of income and wealth, income and wealth do constrain willingness to pay. Why should all the gasoline or all the tickets to the World Series go just to the rich? it is asked.

Various schemes to keep price from rising to equilibrium are based on several perceptions of injustice, among them (1) that price-gouging monopolists are bad, (2) that income is unfairly distributed, and (3) that some items are necessities, and everyone should be able to buy them at a "reasonable" price. Regardless of the rationale, the following examples should make two things clear:

1. Attempts to bypass price rationing in the market and to use alternative rationing devices are much more difficult and costly than they would seem at first glance.
2. Very often, such attempts distribute costs and benefits among households in unintended ways.

OIL, GASOLINE, AND OPEC In 1973 and 1974, the Organization of Petroleum Exporting Countries (OPEC) imposed an embargo on shipments of crude oil to the United States. What followed was a drastic reduction in the quantity of gasoline available at local gas pumps.

PRICE RATIONING: THE DROUGHT OF 1988

Figures A and B illustrate the situation that existed in the U.S. markets for corn and wheat in 1987 and 1988. In 1987, total corn production in the United States was 7.072 billion bushels, and market price averaged $1.94 per bushel. Wheat production in 1987 was 2.107 billion bushels and market price averaged $2.57 per bushel.

The spring and summer of 1988 brought a severe heat wave and drought to most of the United States. The severe weather had a significant impact on both corn and wheat production and shifted the supply curve to the left, from S_{1987} to S_{1988}. At the old price of $1.94, the quantity of corn demanded (7.072 billion bushels in 1987) was much greater than the quantity supplied in 1988. As a result, the price of corn rose sharply as demanders bid for available supplies. Equilibrium was finally reached at a price of $2.60 per bushel.

Notice in Figure A that as the price of corn rose from $1.94 to $2.60, the quantity demanded declined. The higher price reduced the quantity demanded along the demand curve from point A to point B. Clearly, less corn was available, and the available corn (only 4.921 billion bushels) ultimately was purchased by those who were willing to pay the most for it.

What were the effects of this increase in price and decrease in quantity supplied? Corn is used for a variety of purposes in the United States. A substantial portion of it is used to feed livestock and poultry, some is used in food production (corn flakes, canned corn, and so forth), and some of it is exported. Because of the higher prices, some of those who used corn in 1987 were not able to use it in 1988. Many chicken and hog farmers sold off their stocks rather than pay higher feed prices.

Similar events took place in the wheat market, which is illustrated in Figure B. In 1987, wheat production in the United States was 2.107 billion

bushels, and its average price that year was $2.57. In 1988, supply dropped (the supply curve shifted to the left) as a result of the drought, creating excess demand (quantity demanded was greater than quantity supplied). The excess demand caused the price to be bid up to $3.70 before the market returned to equilibrium.

As you can see in Figure B, the higher price resulted in a decline in the quantity demanded, or a movement along the demand curve from point C to point D. As with corn, less wheat was available (final 1988 output was 1.811 billion bushels), and what was produced had to be divided among those who wanted it.

Who ended up with the available wheat? Once again, those buyers who were willing to pay the higher price. Price continued to rise until the market reached equilibrium. Only when the quantity demanded fell until it was equal to the quantity supplied did price stop rising.

FIGURE A
Supply, Demand, and Prices in the Market for U.S. Corn, 1987–1988
Source: U.S. Department of Agriculture, *Crop Reports*.

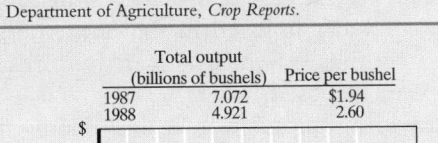

	Total output (billions of bushels)	Price per bushel
1987	7.072	$1.94
1988	4.921	2.60

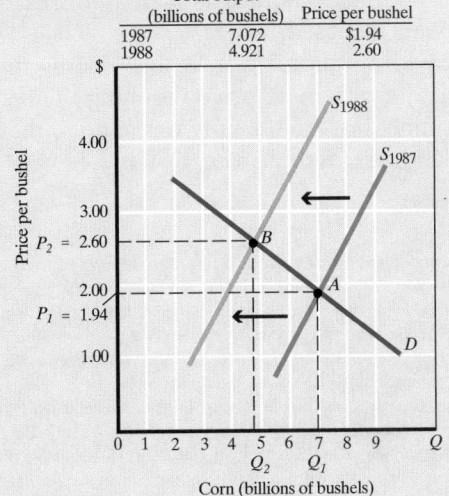

Corn (billions of bushels)

FIGURE B
Supply, Demand, and Prices in the Market for U.S. Wheat, 1987–1988
Source: U.S. Department of Agriculture, *Crop Production*, annual.

	Total output (billions of bushels)	Price per bushel
1987	2.107	$2.57
1988	1.811	3.70

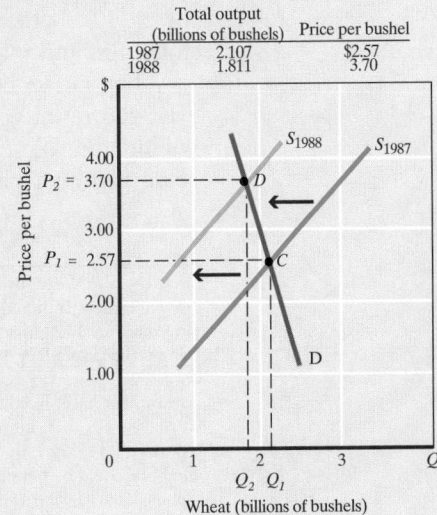

Wheat (billions of bushels)

price ceiling A maximum price that sellers may charge for a good, usually set by government.

Had the market system been allowed to operate, refined gasoline prices would have increased dramatically until quantity supplied was equal to quantity demanded. Those who were willing and able to pay a very high price would have been the ones to get the gasoline. But the government decided that rationing gasoline to only those who were willing and able to pay the most was unfair, and Congress imposed a **price ceiling,** or maximum price, of 57¢ per gallon of leaded regular gasoline. That price ceiling was intended to keep gasoline "affordable," but it also perpetuated the shortage. At the restricted price, quantity demanded remained greater than quantity supplied, and the available gasoline had to be divided up somehow among all potential demanders.

You can see the effects of the price ceiling by looking carefully at Figure 5.3. If the price had been set by the interaction of supply and demand, it would have increased to approximately $1.50 per gallon. Instead, Congress made it illegal to sell gasoline for more than 57¢ per gallon. At that price, quantity demanded (Q_D) exceeded quantity supplied (Q_S). The difference between Q_S and Q_D was the total shortage. Since the price system was not allowed to function, an alternative rationing system had to be found to distribute the Q_S gallons of gasoline.

queuing A nonprice rationing mechanism that uses waiting in line as a means of distributing goods and services.

Several devices were tried. The most common of all nonprice rationing systems is **queuing,** a term that simply means waiting in line. During 1974 very long lines began to appear at gas stations, starting as early as 5 A.M. Often people waited for hours to purchase gasoline. Under this system, gasoline went to those who were willing to pay the most, but the sacrifice was measured in hours and aggravation, rather than in dollars.[1]

favored customers Those who receive special treatment from dealers during shortages.

A second nonprice rationing device used during the gasoline shortage was that of **favored customers.** Many gas station owners decided not to sell gasoline to the general public at all but to reserve their scarce supplies for friends and favored customers. Not surprisingly, many customers tried to become "favored" by offering side payments to gas station owners. Owners also charged high prices for service. By doing so, they increased the real price of gasoline but hid it in service overcharges to get around the ceiling.

ration coupons Tickets or coupons that entitle individual persons to purchase a certain amount of a given product per month.

Yet another method of dividing up available supply is the use of **ration coupons.** It was suggested in both 1974 and 1979 that families be given ration tickets, or coupons, that would entitle them to purchase a certain number of gallons of gasoline each month; that way, everyone would get the same amount, regardless of income. Such a system was employed in the United States during the 1940s, when wartime price ceilings on meat, sugar, butter, tires, nylon stockings, and many other items were imposed.

When ration coupons are used with no prohibition against trading them, however, the result is almost identical to a system of price rationing. Those who are willing and able to pay the most simply buy up the coupons and use them to purchase gasoline, chocolate, fresh eggs, or anything else that is sold at a restricted

---

[1]You can also show formally that the result is inefficient—that there is a resulting net loss of total value to society. First, there is the cost of waiting in line. As you will see in great detail later on, time has a value. With price rationing, no one has to wait in line and the value of that time is saved. Second, there may be additional lost value if the gasoline ends up in the hands of someone who places a lower value on it than someone else who gets no gas. Suppose, for example, that the market price of gasoline if unconstrained would rise to $2, but that the government has it fixed at $1. There will be long lines to get gas. Imagine that to motorist A, ten gallons of gas is worth $35 but that she fails to get it because her time is too valuable to wait in line. To motorist B, ten gallons is worth only $15, but his time is worth much less, so he gets the gas. Clearly, in the end, A could pay B for the gas and both could be better off. If A pays B $30 for the gas, A is $5 better off and B is $15 better off. In addition, A doesn't have to wait in line. Thus, the allocation that results from nonprice rationing involves a net loss of value. Such losses are called *dead weight losses*.

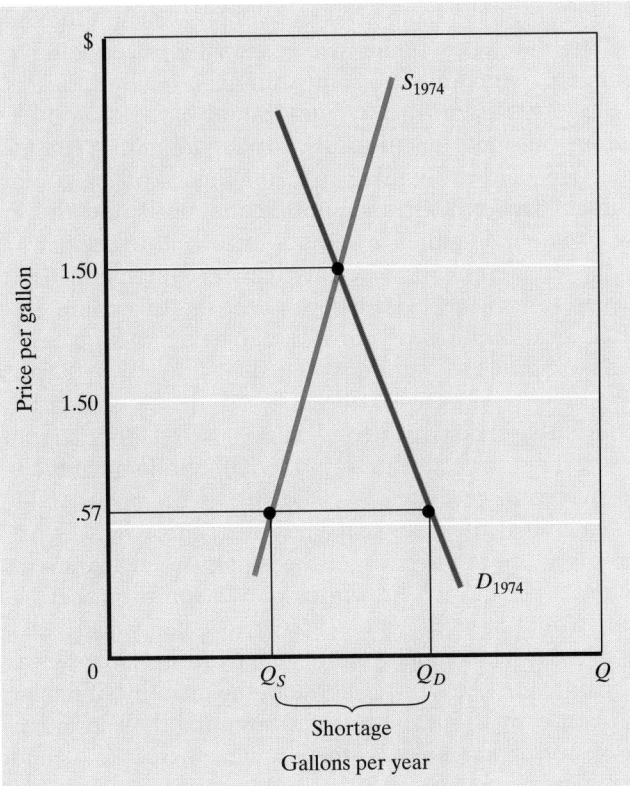

FIGURE 5.3

Shortage Created by a Price Ceiling of 57¢ per Gallon of Leaded Gasoline in 1974

In 1974, a ceiling price of 57¢ per gallon of leaded regular gasoline was imposed. If the price had instead been set by the interaction of supply and demand, it would have increased to approximately $1.50 per gallon. At 57¢ per gallon, the quantity demanded (Q_D) exceeded the quantity supplied (Q_S). Since the price system was not allowed to function, an alternative rationing system had to be found to distribute the Q_S gallons of gasoline.

price.[2] This means that the price of the restricted good will effectively rise to the market-clearing price. For instance, suppose that you decide not to sell your ration coupon. You are then forgoing what you would have received by selling the coupon. Thus the "real" price of the good you purchase will be higher (if only in opportunity cost) than the restricted price. Even when trading coupons is declared illegal, it is virtually impossible to stop black markets from developing. In a **black market,** illegal trading takes place at market-determined prices. (See the Issues and Applications box entitled "Tickets? Supply Meets Demand on the Sidewalk.")

black market A market in which illegal trading takes place at market-determined prices.

SUPER BOWL XX, 1986 Important sporting events such as the World Cup for soccer and the Super Bowl for U.S. football are held in stadiums that have finite seating capacities. In most cases many, many fans, far more than can fit into the largest stadium, want to attend those events, even at high ticket prices. A classic example was Super Bowl XX, in which the Chicago Bears played the New England Patriots at the Super Dome in New Orleans on January 26, 1986. Neither team had ever been in a Super Bowl, and the fans in both Chicago and Boston were very enthusiastic.

The Super Dome contains just over 73,000 seats, and for the Super Bowl, the National Football League had to decide how to divide up those seats and how much to charge for them. If the NFL's only objective had been to maximize current revenues from ticket sales, it could have put them up for sale in Boston and Chicago at a very high price.

---

[2]Of course, if you are assigned a number of tickets, and you sell them, you are better off than you would be with price rationing. Ration tickets thus serve as a way of redistributing income.

The NFL had other objectives, however. One important one was fairness. Selling the tickets at the market-clearing price would have brought cries of "price gouging." According to some estimates, if all the tickets had been put on the market at $400 each, the stadium would have sold out. (As it happened, individual tickets did trade on the black market for over $1000.) But at $400 a ticket, only the rich or those willing to make big sacrifices could go to the game. The less affluent fans who had supported the Bears and the Patriots through many lean years would be either frozen out or forced to sacrifice a lot to purchase a ticket.

In an attempt to solve the "fairness" problem, the NFL issued about half the tickets (a total of 36,000) to each of the two teams to distribute to their fans at a fixed price ceiling ($\bar{P}$) of $75 per ticket, a high but not ridiculous price. (The remaining tickets were distributed in other ways.) Figure 5.4 illustrates the situation. The supply curve, labeled S, is simply a vertical line to show that the quantity of available tickets was fixed at 36,000; quantity supplied was not determined by price. The curve labeled D is a hypothetical demand curve. If the NFL had wanted to maximize revenues, it could have set a price of $400 and sold all the tickets. (Remember, the market is in equilibrium when $Q_D = Q_S$ at a given price. This occurs at the intersection of the supply and demand curves—in this case, at a price of $400 per ticket.) At a price of $75, on the other hand, approximately 225,000 fans would have bought tickets if that many had been available. Just as with the gasoline price ceiling, a shortage existed because the quantity of tickets demanded (225,000, or Q_D) was greater than the quantity of tickets supplied (36,000, or Q_S).

As it turned out, both teams rewarded their loyal fans: Super Bowl tickets went to season ticket holders. In Chicago, there was a random, lottery-type drawing, even among the season ticket holders. Initially, then, the market did not play a big role in setting the price of Super Bowl tickets. The NFL and the two teams involved distributed the tickets at a price far below equilibrium, using what they felt was a more fair system. Then the fun began. On January 16, the *Boston Globe*

FIGURE 5.4

The Market for Tickets to Super Bowl XX

The supply curve, labeled S, is a vertical line that shows that the quantity of available Super Bowl tickets was fixed at 36,000; quantity supplied was not determined by price. The curve labeled D is a hypothetical demand curve. If the NFL had wanted to maximize revenues, it could have set a price of $400 and sold all the tickets. At a price of $75, approximately 225,000 fans would have bought tickets if that many had been available. A shortage of Super Bowl tickets existed because quantity demanded was greater than quantity supplied at the given price.

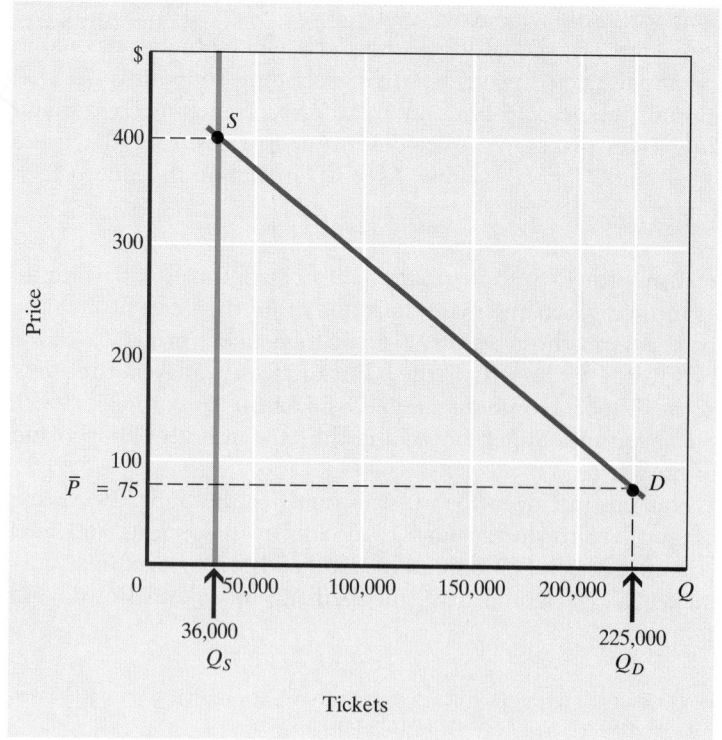

TICKETS? SUPPLY MEETS DEMAND ON THE SIDEWALK

Whenever a limit is placed on price, there is the opportunity for profit. "Scalpers" make their living by obtaining tickets (either by standing in line or by buying them from those willing to sell) and then reselling those tickets to those willing to pay more. In most states, scalping is illegal. The point of restricting prices, whether done by private promoters or the government, is to make the tickets available at affordable prices. Remember, however, that if that price is set below equilibrium, some nonprice rationing mechanism—such as standing in line, a lottery, or favored customers—must be used to distribute the tickets.

Is scalping good or bad for society? The fact that it is illegal might suggest that it is bad. But as the following article from the *New York Times* suggests, most economists do not. Think carefully about the arguments presented. What side are you on?

Ticket scalping has been very good to Kevin Thomas, and he makes no apologies. He sees himself as a classic American entrepreneur: a high-school dropout from the Bronx who taught himself a trade, works seven nights a week, earns $40,000 a year, and at age 26 has $75,000 in savings, all by providing a public service outside New York's theaters and sports arenas.

He has just one complaint. "I've been busted about 30 times in the last year," he said one recent evening, just after making $280 at a Knicks game. "You learn to deal with it—I give the cops a fake name, and I pay the fines when I have to, but I don't think it's fair. I look at scalping like working as a stockbroker, buying low and selling

high. If people are willing to pay me the money, what kind of problem is that?"

It is a significant problem to public officials in New York and New Jersey, who are cracking down on street scalpers like Mr. Thomas and on licensed ticket brokers. Undercover officers are enforcing new restrictions on reselling tickets at marked-up prices, and the attorneys general of the two states are pressing well-publicized cases against more than a dozen ticket brokers.

But economists tend to see scalping from Mr. Thomas's perspective. To them, the governments' crusade makes about as much sense as the old campaigns by Communist authorities against "profiteering." Economists argue that the restrictions inconvenience the public, reduce the audience for cultural and sports events, waste the police's time, deprive New York City of tens of millions of dollars of tax revenue, and actually drive up the cost of many tickets.

Economists see another illustration of [this] lesson at the Museum of Modern Art, where people wait in line for up to two hours to buy tickets for the Matisse exhibit. But there is an alternative on the sidewalk: scalpers who evade the police have been selling the $12.50 tickets to the show at prices ranging from $20 to $50.

"You don't have to put a very high value on your time to pay $10 or $15 to avoid standing in line for two hours for a Matisse ticket," said Richard H. Thaler, an economist at Cornell University. "Some people think it's fairer to make everyone stand in the line, but that forces everyone to engage in a totally unproductive activity, and it discriminates in favor of people who have the most free time. Scalping gives other people a chance, too. I can see no justification for outlawing it."

Source: John Tierney, "Tickets? Supply Meets Demand on the Sidewalk," *New York Times*, December 26, 1992.

The prices paid in the black market for tickets to the Super Bowl seem to get higher and higher every year. Tickets to Super Bowl XXVII in 1993 were reportedly sold for as much as $5,000 each.

ran dozens of advertisements that read: "Super Bowl Tickets wanted: Top $$$$ Paid in Cash...call 24 hours." Within a very short time, a national market had been established, and those who were willing and able to pay the top dollar were communicating their desires to those who were lucky enough to have the tickets. Price offers ranged from $500 to $1000 *per ticket!* Many of the offers came from travel agents, who resold the tickets at even higher prices.

Now consider the people who got to buy their tickets for $75. The moment the market appeared, the price of those tickets went up. Going to the game now meant giving up over $500—the opportunity cost of the ticket. Even though they didn't have to reach in their pockets and pull out the $500, the outcome was exactly the same as if each ticket holder had been awarded enough cash to buy a ticket at its market price less $75. That is, the real price of the ticket was $500 − $75 = $425, which is approximately what the price of Super Bowl tickets would have been had the market been allowed to function freely.

The above examples describe the nature of the price rationing system and suggest some alternatives to it. There is a problem with these alternatives, though:

> No matter how good the intentions of private organizations and governments are, it is very difficult to prevent the price system from operating and to stop willingness to pay from asserting itself. Every time an alternative is tried, the price system seems to sneak in the back door. With favored customers and black markets, the final distribution may be even more unfair than that which would result from simple price rationing.

Prices and the Allocation of Resources

Thinking of the market system as a mechanism for allocating scarce goods and services among competing demanders reveals much about its nature. But the market determines much more than just the distribution of final outputs. It also determines what gets produced and how resources are allocated among competing uses.

Consider a change in consumer preferences that leads to an increase, or shift, in demand for a specific good or service. During the 1970s, for example, people began going to restaurants much more frequently than before. Researchers think that this trend, which continues today, is partially the result of social changes such as a dramatic rise in the number of two-earner families and partially the result of rising incomes. The market responded to this change in demand by shifting resources, both capital and labor, into more and better restaurants.

With the increase in demand, the price of eating out rose, and the restaurant business became more profitable. The higher profits attracted new businesses and provided old restaurants with an incentive to expand. As new capital, seeking profits, flowed into the restaurant business, so too did labor. New restaurants need chefs. Chefs need training, and the higher wages that came with increased demand provided an incentive for them to get it. In response to the increase in demand for training, new cooking schools opened up and existing schools began to offer courses in the culinary arts.

This story could run on and on, but the point is clear:

> Price changes resulting from shifts of demand in output markets cause profits to rise and fall. Profits attract capital; losses lead to disinvestment. Higher wages attract labor and encourage workers to acquire skills. At the core of the system, supply, demand, and prices in input and output markets determine the allocation of resources and the ultimate combinations of things produced.

SUPPLY AND DEMAND ANALYSIS: AN OIL IMPORT FEE

The basic logic of supply and demand is a powerful tool of analysis. As an extended example of the power of this logic, we will consider a recent proposal to impose a tax on imported oil. The idea of raising the federal gasoline tax was hotly debated during the 1992 presidential race, with H. Ross Perot arguing strongly for such a tax. Many economists, however, believe that a fee on *imported* crude oil, which is used to produce gasoline, would have better effects on the economy than would a gasoline tax.

Consider the facts. Between 1985 and 1989, the United States increased its dependence on oil imports. In 1985, total crude oil consumption in the United States was 12.2 million barrels per day. Of that amount, domestic production accounted for about 9.0 million barrels per day (74%), while imports accounted for about 3.2 million barrels per day (26%). At that time, the world price of crude oil averaged $24 per barrel, down from a high of $31.77 per barrel in 1981.

By 1988, the price of a barrel of crude oil on world markets had dropped to an average of $12.57. These lower import prices led to lower gasoline prices and heating oil prices, which in turn led to an increase in the quantity of oil demanded. At the same time, the availability of cheap imported oil drove marginal domestic producers out of the market and actually reduced the amount of oil produced in the United States.

The results of the price decreases in foreign oil can be seen in the numbers for 1989. In 1989, the total U.S. demand for crude oil was 13.6 million barrels per day. Of that amount, only 7.7 million barrels (57%) were produced in the United States, a reduction of 14% from 1985 levels. In the same year, imports accounted for 5.9 million barrels per day (43% of the total), an increase of 84%.

This heavy dependence on foreign oil sources left the United States vulnerable to the price shock that followed the Iraqi invasion of Kuwait in August of 1990. In 1988, oil from Iraq and Kuwait accounted for 8.3% of total U.S. imports. In the months following the invasion, the world price of crude shot up to $40 per barrel.

But even before the Iraqi crisis, many economists and some politicians had recommended a stiff oil import fee (or tax) that would, it was argued, reduce U.S. dependence on foreign oil by (1) reducing overall consumption (and helping to reduce air pollution), and (2) increasing domestic production. But would such a tax accomplish its goals?

Simple supply and demand analysis makes the arguments of these import fee proponents easier to understand. The two diagrams in Figure 5.5 show the world market for crude oil and the U.S. market for crude oil in 1989. World production was about 56 million barrels per day in 1989, and the average world price was about $18. These amounts are shown as the equilibrium price and quantity in Figure 5.5a.

Figure 5.5b shows the U.S. market. Assume that the United States can buy all the oil that it wants at the world price of $18. This means that domestic producers cannot get away with charging any more than $18 per barrel. (Why would anyone pay more than $18 for a barrel of U.S.-produced oil when they can get as much foreign oil as they want for $18 per barrel?) The curve labeled $Supply_{US}$ shows the amount that domestic suppliers will produce at each price level. At a price of $18, domestic production is 7.7 million barrels (q_{US}). Stated somewhat differently, U.S. producers will produce at point A on the supply curve. As mentioned earlier, in 1989 the total quantity of oil demanded in the United States was 13.6 million barrels per day. This can also be seen in Figure 5.5b. At a price of $18, the quantity demanded is point C on the demand curve.

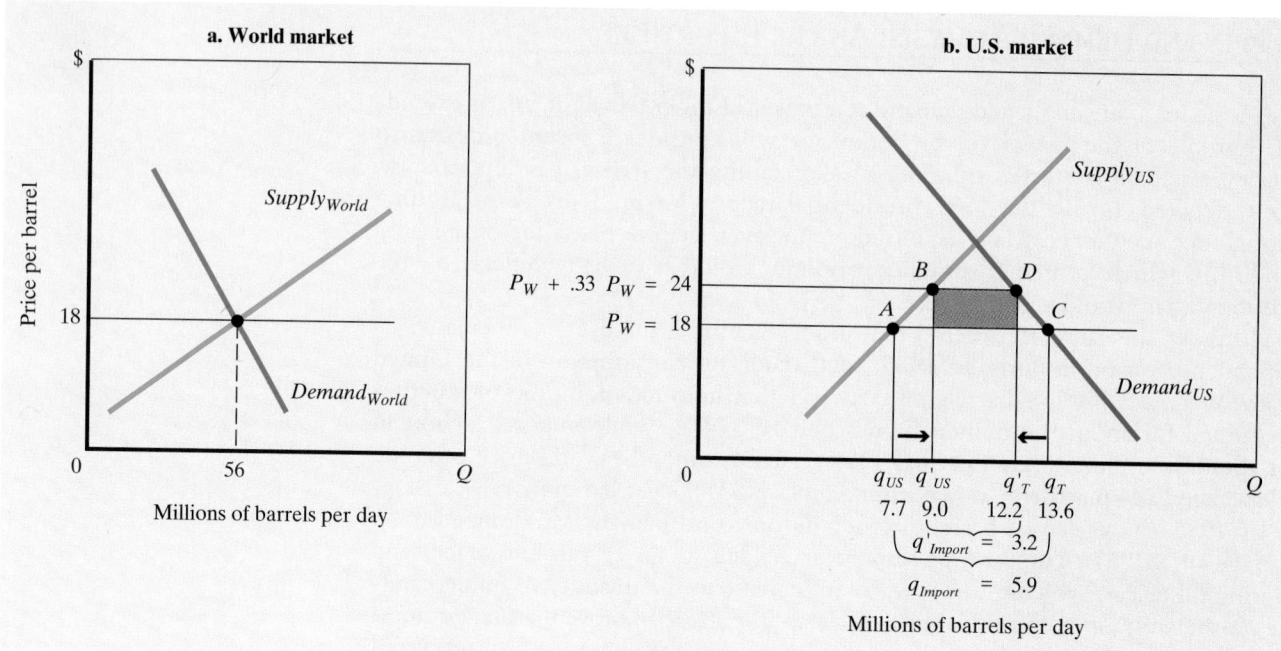

FIGURE 5.5

The World and U.S. Markets for Crude Petroleum, 1989

At a world price of $18, domestic production is 7.7 million barrels (q_{US}) and the total quantity of oil demanded in the United States is 13.6 million barrels per day (q_T). The difference is total imports (q_{Import} = 5.9 million barrels per day). If the government levies a tax of 33% on imports, the price of imported oil rises to $24. The quantity demanded falls to q'_T, or 12.2 million barrels per day. At the same time, the quantity supplied by domestic producers increases to q'_{US} (9.0 million barrels per day) and the quantity of imports falls to 3.2 million barrels per day (12.2 – 9.0). Tax revenue is equal to the shaded area in Figure 5.5b.

The difference between the total quantity demanded (q_T = 13.6 million barrels per day) and domestic production (q_{US} = 7.7 million barrels per day) is total imports (q_{Import} = 5.9 million barrels per day).

Now suppose that the government levies a tax of 33% on imported oil. Since the import price is $18 ($P_W$), a tax of $6 (or .33 × $18) per barrel means that importers of oil in the United States will pay a total of $24 per barrel ($18 + $6).

Figure 5.5b shows the result of the tax. First, the higher price leads to a reduction in the quantity of oil demanded. The quantity demanded drops to 12.2 million barrels per day (q'_T), which is just about equal to the quantity demanded in 1985. This is a movement *along* the demand curve from point C to point D. At the same time, the quantity supplied by domestic producers increases to 9.0 million barrels per day (q'_{US}), which is just about equal to total domestic production in 1985. With an increase in domestic quantity supplied and a decrease in domestic quantity demanded, imports (q'_{Import}) decrease to 3.2 million barrels per day (12.2 – 9.0).

The tax also generates revenues for the federal government. The total tax revenue collected is equal to the tax per barrel ($6) times the number of imported barrels. Since the quantity imported is 3.2 million barrels per day, total revenue is $6 × 3.2 million, or $19.2 million *per day*. This amount is equal to about $7 billion per year ($19.2 per day × 365 days per year) and is represented by the shaded area in the diagram.

What does all of this mean? In the final analysis, an oil import fee would (1) increase domestic production, and (2) reduce overall consumption. This would in turn help with the problem of air pollution and simultaneously reduce U.S. dependence on foreign oil. In addition, it would help to reduce the U.S. government's budget deficit, which is now running over two hundred billion dollars per year.

ELASTICITY

The principles of supply and demand enable us to make certain predictions about how households and firms are likely to behave in both national and international markets. When the price of a good rises, for example, households are likely to purchase less of it, and firms are likely to supply more of it. When costs of production fall, firms are likely to supply more—supply will increase, or shift to the right. When the price of a good falls, households are likely to buy fewer substitutes—demand for substitutes is likely to decrease, or shift to the left.

The size, or magnitude, of these reactions can be very important. You have already seen that during the oil embargo of the early 1970s, the Organization of Petroleum Exporting Countries (OPEC) succeeded in increasing the price of crude oil substantially. This raised revenues to the oil producing countries, and so we might expect this strategy to work for everyone. But if the banana exporting countries, which we will call OBEC, had done the same thing, the strategy would not have worked.

Why? Suppose the banana exporting countries decide to cut production by 30% in order to drive up the world price of bananas. At first, when the quantity of bananas supplied declines, the quantity demanded is greater than the quantity supplied and the world price rises. The issue for OBEC, however, is *how much* the world price will rise. That is, how much will people be willing to pay in order to continue consuming bananas? Unless the percentage increase in price is greater than the percentage decrease in output, the OBEC countries will lose revenues. In fact, the news is not good. There are many reasonable substitutes for bananas. As the price of bananas rises, people simply eat fewer bananas and eat more pineapples or oranges. Many people are simply not willing to pay a higher price for bananas. The quantity of bananas demanded declines 30%—to the new quantity supplied—after only a modest price rise, and OBEC fails in its mission.

The quantity of oil demanded is not nearly as responsive to a change in price as is the quantity of bananas demanded because no substitutes for oil are readily available. When the price of crude oil went up in the early 1970s, 130 million motor vehicles, getting an average of 12 miles per gallon and consuming over 100 billion gallons of gasoline each year, were on the road in the United States. Millions of homes were heated with oil, and industry ran on equipment that used petroleum products. When OPEC cut production, price rose sharply. Quantity demanded fell, but nonetheless the price increased over 400 percent. What makes the cases of OPEC and OBEC different is the magnitude of the response in the quantity demanded to a change of price.

The importance of actual measurement can hardly be overstated. Without the ability to measure and predict how much people are likely to respond to economic changes, all the economic theory in the world would be of little help to policy makers. In fact, most of the research being done in economics today involves the collection and analysis of quantitative data that "measures" behavior. This is a dramatic change in the discipline of economics that has taken place only in the last 30 years.

Economists commonly measure responsiveness using the concept of **elasticity.** Elasticity is a general concept that can be used to quantify the response in one variable when another variable changes. If some variable, *A,* changes in response to changes in another variable, *B,* the elasticity of *A* with respect to *B* is equal to the percentage change in *A* divided by the percentage change in *B;* that is,

$$\text{The Elasticity of } A \text{ with Respect to } B = \frac{\% \Delta A}{\% \Delta B}$$

We may speak of the elasticity of demand or supply with respect to price, of the elasticity of investment with respect to the interest rate, or of the elasticity of tax payments with respect to income. We begin with a discussion of price elasticity of demand.

Price Elasticity of Demand

You have already been exposed to the law of demand. Recall that, when prices rise, quantity demanded can be expected to decline, *ceteris paribus,* and when prices fall, quantity demanded can be expected to rise. The normal negative relationship between price and quantity demanded is reflected in the downward slope of demand curves.

SLOPE AND ELASTICITY   The slope of a demand curve may in a rough way reveal the responsiveness of the quantity demanded to price changes, but slope can be quite misleading. In fact, it is not a good formal measure of responsiveness.

Consider the two identical demand curves in Figure 5.6. The only difference between the two is that quantity demanded is measured in pounds in the graph on the left and in ounces in the graph on the right. When we calculate the numerical value of each slope, however, we get very different answers. The curve on the left has a slope of −1/5, and the curve on the right has a slope of −1/80, yet they represent the *exact same behavior.* If we had changed dollars to cents on the *Y* axis, the

FIGURE 5.6

Slope Is Not a Useful Measure of Responsiveness of Demand

Changing the unit of measure from pounds to ounces changes the measured slope of the demand curve dramatically. But the behavior of buyers in the two diagrams is identical. Since slope depends on the unit of measure on both *X* and *Y* axes, it is a poor measure of "responsiveness."

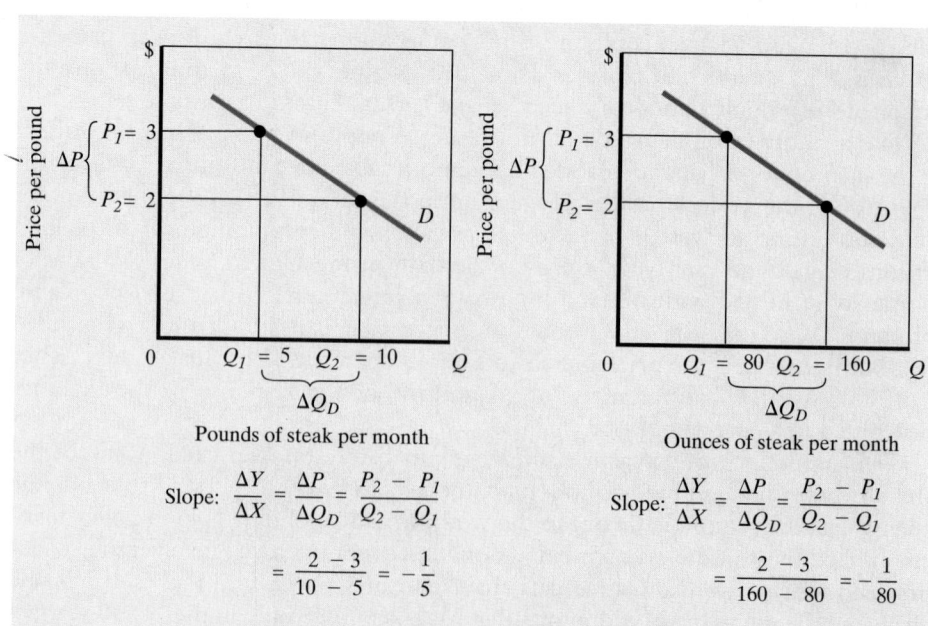

TABLE 5.1
Hypothetical Demand Elasticities for Four Products

PRODUCT	% Δ PRICE	% Δ QUANTITY DEMANDED	ELASTICITY ($\% \Delta Q_D \div \% \Delta P$)	
Insulin	+10%	0%	0	Perfectly inelastic
Basic telephone service	+10%	−1%	−.1	Inelastic
Beef	+10%	−10%	−1.0	Unitarily elastic
Bananas	+10%	−30%	−3.0	Elastic

two slopes would be −20 and −1.25 respectively. (Review the Appendix to Chapter 1 if you don't understand how these numbers are calculated.)

The problem is that the numerical value of the slope of a line or curve depends on the units used to measure the variables on the axes. To correct this problem, we convert the changes in price and quantity to percentages. The price increase in Figure 5.6 leads to a decline of five pounds, or 80 ounces, in the quantity of steak demanded—a decline of 50% from the initial 10 pounds, or 160 ounces, whether we measure it in pounds or ounces.

We define **price elasticity of demand,** then, simply as the ratio of the percentage change in quantity demanded to the percentage change in price. Stated mathematically:

$$\text{Price Elasticity of Demand} = \frac{\% \text{ Change in Quantity Demanded}}{\% \text{ Change in Price}} = \frac{\% \Delta Q_D}{\% \Delta P}$$

price elasticity of demand The ratio of the percentage change in quantity demanded to the percentage change in price.

Percentage changes should always carry the sign (plus or minus) of the change—positive changes, or increases, take a (+); negative changes, or decreases, take a (−). The law of demand implies that price elasticity of demand is nearly always a negative number: Price increases (+) will lead to decreases in quantity demanded (−), and vice versa. Thus, the numerator and denominator should have opposite signs, resulting in a negative ratio.

Table 5.1 gives the hypothetical responses of demanders to a 10% price increase in four markets. Insulin is absolutely necessary to an insulin-dependent diabetic, and the quantity demanded is unlikely to respond to an increase in price. When the quantity demanded does not respond at all to a price change, the percentage change in quantity demanded is zero, and the elasticity is zero. In this case, we say that the demand for insulin is **perfectly inelastic.** Figure 5.7a illustrates the per-

perfectly inelastic demand Demand in which quantity demanded does not respond at all to a change in price.

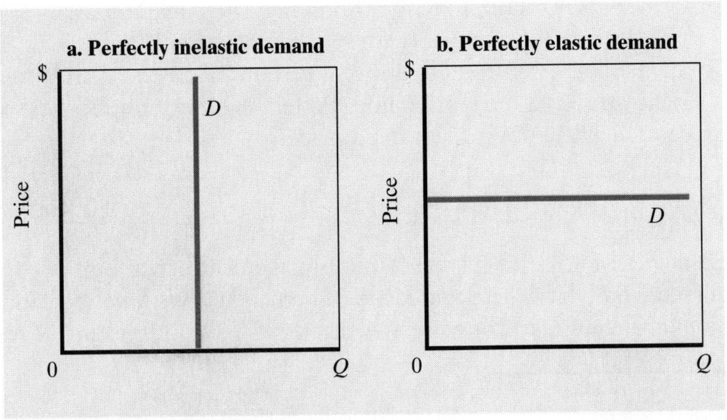

FIGURE 5.7
Perfectly Elastic and Perfectly Inelastic Demand Curves

Figure 5.7a shows a perfectly inelastic demand curve. Price elasticity of demand is zero. Quantity demanded is fixed; it does not change at all when price changes. Figure 5.7b shows a perfectly elastic demand curve. A tiny price increase drives the quantity demanded to zero. In essence, perfectly elastic demand implies that individual producers can sell all they want at the going market price.

a. Perfectly inelastic demand

b. Perfectly elastic demand

fectly inelastic demand for insulin. Because quantity demanded does not change *at all* when price changes, the demand curve is simply a vertical line.

Unlike insulin, basic telephone service is generally considered a necessity, but not an absolute necessity. If a 10% increase in telephone rates results in a 1% decline in the quantity of service demanded, demand elasticity is −.1 (−1 ÷ 10).

When the percentage change in quantity demanded is smaller in absolute size than the percentage change in price, then elasticity is less than one in absolute size.[3] When a product has an elasticity between zero and minus (negative) one, we say that demand is **inelastic.** The demand for basic telephone service is inelastic at −.1. Stated more simply, inelastic demand means that there is some responsiveness of demand, but not a great deal, to a change in price.

A warning: You must be very careful about signs. Because it is generally understood that demand elasticities are negative (demand curves have a negative slope), they are often reported and discussed without the negative sign. For example, a technical paper might report that the price elasticity of demand for housing "appears to be inelastic, or less than one (.6)." What the writer means is that the estimated elasticity is −.6, which is between zero and minus one. Its absolute value is less than one.

Returning to Table 5.1, we see that a 10% increase in beef prices drives down the quantity of beef demanded by 10 percent. Demand elasticity is thus −1 (−10 ÷ 10). When the percentage change in quantity of product demanded is the same as the percentage change in price, we say that the demand for that product has **unitary elasticity.** The numerical value of a unitarily elastic product is always minus one (−1). As Table 5.1 shows, the demand for beef has unitary elasticity.

When the percentage decrease in quantity demanded is larger than the percentage increase in price in absolute size, we say that demand is **elastic.** The demand for bananas, for example, is likely to be quite elastic because there are many substitutes for bananas (other fruits, for instance). If a 10% increase in the price of bananas leads to a 30% decrease in the quantity of bananas demanded, the price elasticity of demand for bananas is −3.0 (−30 ÷ 10). (For another example of the elasticity of demand, see the Issues and Applications box entitled "Elasticity and Tax Revenues: Gasoline Taxes in the Nation's Capital.")

Finally, if a small increase in the price of a product causes the quantity demanded to drop immediately to zero, demand for that product is said to be **perfectly elastic.** Suppose, for example, that you produce a product that can be sold only at a predetermined, fixed price. If you charged even one penny more, no one would buy your product because people would simply buy from another producer who hadn't raised the price. This is very close to reality for domestic oil producers, who cannot charge more than the world price for crude oil (see again Figure 5.5), and for farmers, who cannot charge more than the current market price for their crops.

A perfectly elastic demand curve is illustrated in Figure 5.7b. Because the quantity demanded drops to zero above a certain price, the demand curve for a perfectly elastic good is a horizontal line. Perfect elasticity implies that individual producers can sell all they want at a fixed price.

Calculating Elasticities

Elasticities must be calculated cautiously. Return for a moment to the demand curves in Figure 5.6. That these two identical demand curves have dramatically different slopes should be enough to convince you that slope is a poor measure of responsiveness.

---

inelastic demand Demand that responds somewhat, but not a great deal, to changes in price. Inelastic demand always has a numerical value between zero and minus one.

unitary elasticity A demand relationship in which the percentage change in quantity of a product demanded is the same as the percentage change in price (a demand elasticity of −1).

elastic demand Elastic demand describes a demand relationship in which the percentage change in quantity demanded is larger in absolute value than the percentage change in price.

perfectly elastic demand Demand in which quantity demanded drops to zero at the slightest increase in price.

[3]The term "absolute size" or "absolute value" means ignoring the sign. The absolute value of −4 is 4; the absolute value of −3.8 is greater than the absolute value of 2.

ELASTICITY AND TAX REVENUES: GASOLINE TAXES IN THE NATION'S CAPITAL

In analyzing the effects of an excise tax, the concept of elasticity is very important. The elasticity of demand for the taxed product in part determines the total amount of tax that the government will ultimately collect, and it determines whether producers or consumers ultimately bear the burden of the tax.

Unless tax administrators and fiscal planners consider the potential reactions of those affected by a tax, they may be in for a surprise. Perhaps the classic example of bad planning involved the efforts of Washington, DC, to raise revenues in 1980.

In that year, Washington was faced with a huge fiscal deficit. The city needed to raise revenues quickly. As part of a tax increase package, Mayor Marion Barry proposed a new 6% gasoline tax. The tax went into effect on August 6, 1980. It was imposed on top of an existing ten-cents-per-gallon tax, and it had the effect of raising the price of gasoline about eight additional cents per gallon.

This was the second highest local gasoline tax in the nation (second to Chicago). It pushed the price of unleaded gasoline in the District to between $1.32 and $1.35 per gallon, while in nearby Maryland the same gasoline sold for $1.25. While city officials predicted some drop in sales, they expected to raise a substantial amount of revenue with the tax.

As you will see later in the chapter, the elasticity of demand for any good depends upon the ease with which consumers can substitute other

When Washington, D.C. officials imposed a 6% tax on gasoline sold in the nation's capital, they failed to take elasticity of demand into account. The goal was increased revenue; the result was decreased revenue.

goods for the taxed good. Anybody in Washington who lived near a border had an easily accessible, non-taxed, perfect substitute available for DC gasoline; they merely had to drive across the border and buy their gas in Maryland or Virginia. Those who commuted into the city only had to remember to fill up before they came to town. The result was catastrophic for the district.

By the end of the first month, gasoline sales in DC had fallen 27.5 percent! Since the tax raised prices by 6%, the elasticity of demand was over 4.0. The city had predicted revenues of $960,000 in the first month, but actual revenues were just $750,000.

While data are hard to come by, one survey claims that by October sales had dropped by 40% and 242 workers had been laid off by gasoline stations in the District. While no hard data exist on the number of gasoline stations that closed as a result, it is clear that some did.

On Monday, November 24, Mayor Barry admitted defeat, and the tax was officially lifted on December 1 of the same year. It had been in effect less than four months.

The story of the District's gasoline tax is extreme, but it highlights problems that governments have in trying to forecast the amount of revenue that they will collect.

The concept of elasticity circumvents the measurement problem posed by the graphs in Figure 5.6 by converting the changes in price and quantity into percentage changes. Recall that elasticity of demand is the *percentage* change in quantity divided by the *percentage* change in price.

CALCULATING PERCENTAGE CHANGES   Because we need to know percentage changes to calculate elasticity, let's begin our example by calculating the percentage change in quantity demanded. Figure 5.6a shows that the quantity of steak demanded increases from five pounds (Q_1) to ten pounds (Q_2) when price drops from \$3 to \$2 per pound. Thus, the change in quantity demanded (ΔQ_D) is equal to $Q_2 - Q_1$, or five pounds.

To convert this change into a percentage change, we must decide on a *base* against which to calculate the percentage. It is often convenient to use the initial value of quantity demanded as the base—that is, to calculate the change as a percentage of the initial value of quantity demanded (Q_1).

To calculate percentage change in quantity demanded using the initial value as the base, the following formula is used:

$$\% \text{ Change in } Q_D = \frac{\Delta Q_D}{Q_1} \times 100 = \frac{Q_2 - Q_1}{Q_1} \times 100.$$

In Figure 5.6, $Q_2 = 10$ and $Q_1 = 5$. Thus:

$$\% \text{ Change in } Q_D = \frac{10 - 5}{5} \times 100 = \frac{5}{5} \times 100 = 100\%.$$

Expressing this equation verbally, we can say that an increase in quantity demanded from five pounds to ten pounds is a 100% increase from five pounds. Note that you arrive at exactly the same result if you use the diagram in Figure 5.6b. An increase from Q_1 (80 ounces) to Q_2 (160 ounces) is a 100% increase. (Use the foregoing equation to verify that this is true.)

We can calculate the percentage change in price in a similar way. Once again, let's use the initial value of P (that is, P_1) as the base for calculating the percentage. Using P_1 as the base, the formula for calculating the percentage change in P is simply:

$$\% \text{ Change in } P = \frac{\Delta P}{P_1} \times 100 = \frac{P_2 - P_1}{P_1} \times 100.$$

In Figure 5.6a, P_2 equals 2, and P_1 equals 3. Thus, the change in P, or ΔP, is a negative number: $P_2 - P_1 = 2 - 3 = -1$. This is true because the change is a decrease in price. Plugging the values of P_1 and P_2 into the equation above, we get:

$$\% \text{ Change in } P = \frac{2 - 3}{3} \times 100 = \frac{-1}{3} \times 100 = 33.3\%.$$

In other words, decreasing price from \$3 to \$2 is a 33.3% decline.

ELASTICITY IS A RATIO OF PERCENTAGES   Once all the changes in quantity demanded and price have been converted into percentages, calculating elasticity is a matter of simple division. Recall that the formal definition of elasticity is:

$$\text{Price Elasticity of Demand} = \frac{\% \text{ Change in Quantity Demanded}}{\% \text{ Change in Price}}.$$

If demand is elastic, the ratio of percentage change in quantity demanded to percentage change in price will have an absolute value greater than one. If demand is inelastic, the ratio will have an absolute value less than one. If the two percentages are exactly equal, so that a given percentage change in price causes an equal percentage change in quantity demanded, elasticity is equal to minus one; this is unitary elasticity.

Substituting the percentages calculated above, we see that a 33.3% decrease in price (−33.3%) leads to a 100% increase in quantity demanded; thus:

$$\text{Price Elasticity of Demand} = \frac{+100\%}{-33.3\%} = -3.0.$$

According to these calculations, the demand for steak is elastic.

A MORE PRECISE WAY OF CALCULATING PERCENTAGES: THE MIDPOINT FORMULA
Although simple, the use of the initial values of P and Q as the bases for calculating percentage changes can be misleading. Let's return to the example of demand for steak in Figure 5.6a, where we have a change in quantity demanded (ΔQ_D) of five pounds. Using the initial value Q_1 as the base, we calculated that this change represents a 100% increase over the base. Now suppose that the price of steak rises back to $3, causing the quantity demanded to drop back to five pounds. How much of a percentage decrease in quantity demanded is this? We now have $Q_1 = 10$ and $Q_2 = 5$. Using the same formula we used above, we get:

$$\% \text{ Change in Quantity Demand} = \frac{\Delta Q_D}{Q_1} \times 100 = \frac{Q_2 - Q_1}{Q_1} \times 100 =$$
$$\frac{5 - 10}{10} \times 100 = -50\%.$$

Thus, an increase from five pounds to ten pounds is a 100% increase (since the initial value used is 5), while a decrease from ten pounds to five pounds is only a 50% decrease (since the initial value used is 10). This does not make much sense because in both cases we are calculating elasticity on the same interval on the demand curve. Changing "direction" of the calculation should not change the elasticity.

To describe percentage changes more accurately, a simple convention has been adopted. Instead of using the initial values of Q and P as the bases for calculating percentages, we use the *midpoint* as the base. That is, we use the value halfway between P_1 and P_2 for the base in calculating the percentage change in price, and the value halfway between Q_1 and Q_2 as the base for calculating percentage change in quantity demanded.

Thus, the **midpoint formula** for calculating the percentage change in quantity demanded becomes:

$$\% \text{ Change in } Q_D = \frac{\Delta Q_D}{(Q_1 + Q_2)/2} \times 100 = \frac{Q_2 - Q_1}{(Q_1 + Q_2)/2} \times 100.$$

Substituting the numbers from Figure 5.6a we get:

$$\% \text{ Change in } Q_D = \frac{10 - 5}{(10 + 5)/2} \times 100 = \frac{5}{7.5} \times 100 = 66.6\%.$$

Using the point halfway between P_1 and P_2 as the base for calculating the percentage change in price, we get:

$$\% \text{ Change in } P = \frac{\Delta P}{(P_1 + P_2)/2} \times 100 = \frac{P_2 - P_1}{(P_1 + P_2)/2} \times 100.$$

midpoint formula A more precise way of calculating percentages using the value halfway between P_1 and P_2 for the base in calculating the percentage change in price, and the value halfway between Q_1 and Q_2 as the base for calculating the percentage change in quantity demanded.

Substituting the numbers from Figure 5.6a yields:

$$\% \text{ Change in } P = \frac{2-3}{(2+3)/2} \times 100 = \frac{-1}{2.5} \times 100 = -40.0\%.$$

We can thus say that a change from a quantity of 5 to a quantity of 10 is a +66.6% change using the midpoint formula, and a change in price from \$3 to \$2 is a −40% change using the midpoint formula.

Using these percentages to calculate elasticity yields:

$$\text{Price Elasticity of Demand} = \frac{\% \Delta Q_D}{\% \Delta P} = \frac{66.6\%}{-40.0\%} = -1.67.$$

Using the midpoint formula in this case gives a lower demand elasticity, but the demand remains elastic because the percentage change in Q_D is still greater than the percentage change in P in absolute size.

The calculations based on the midpoint approach are summarized in Table 5.2.

ELASTICITY CHANGES ALONG A STRAIGHT-LINE DEMAND CURVE An interesting and important point is that elasticity changes from point to point along a demand curve even if the slope of that demand curve does not change—that is, even along a straight-line demand curve. Indeed, the differences in elasticity along a demand curve can be quite large.

Consider the demand schedule shown in Table 5.3 and the demand curve in Figure 5.8. Herb works about 20 days per month in a downtown San Francisco office tower. On the top floor of the building is a nice dining room. If lunch in the dining room costs \$10, Herb would eat there only twice a month. If the price of lunch falls to \$9, he would eat there twice as often, or four times a month. (Herb would bring his lunch to work on other days.) If lunch were only a dollar, he would eat there 20 times a month.

TABLE 5.2
Calculating Price Elasticity

FIRST, CALCULATE PERCENTAGE CHANGE IN QUANTITY DEMANDED:

$$\% \text{ Change in } Q_D = \frac{\Delta Q_D}{(Q_1 + Q_2)/2} \times 100 = \frac{Q_2 - Q_1}{(Q_1 + Q_2)/2} \times 100$$

Substituting the numbers from Figure 5.6:

$$\% \text{ Change in } Q_D = \frac{10-5}{(10+5)/2} \times 100 = \frac{5}{7.5} \times 100 = 66.6\%$$

NEXT, CALCULATE PERCENTAGE CHANGE IN PRICE:

$$\% \text{ Change in } P = \frac{\Delta P}{(P_1 + P_2)/2} \times 100 = \frac{P_2 - P_1}{(P_1 + P_2)/2} \times 100$$

Substituting the numbers from Figure 5.6:

$$\% \text{ Change in } P = \frac{2-3}{(2+3)/2} \times 100 = \frac{-1}{2.5} \times 100 = -40.0\%$$

PRICE ELASTICITY COMPARES THE PERCENTAGE CHANGE IN QUANTITY DEMANDED AND THE PERCENTAGE CHANGE IN PRICE:

$$\frac{\% \Delta Q_D}{\% \Delta P} = \frac{66.6\%}{-40.0\%} = -1.67 = \text{PRICE ELASTICITY OF DEMAND}$$

Let's calculate price elasticity of demand between points A and B on the demand curve in Figure 5.8. Moving from A to B, the price of a lunch drops from $10 to $9 (a decrease of $1) and the number of dining room lunches that Herb eats per month increases from two to four (an increase of two). We will use the midpoint approach.

First, we calculate the percentage change in quantity demanded:

$$\%\Delta Q_D = \frac{\Delta Q_D}{\left(Q_1 + Q_2\right)/2} \times 100 = \frac{Q_2 - Q_1}{\left(Q_1 + Q_2\right)/2} \times 100.$$

Substituting the numbers from Figure 5.8, we get:

$$\%\Delta Q_D = \frac{4-2}{\left(4+2\right)/2} \times 100 = \frac{2}{3} \times 100 = 66.7\%.$$

Next, we calculate the percentage change in price:

$$\%\Delta P = \frac{\Delta P}{\left(P_1 + P_2\right)/2} \times 100 = \frac{P_2 - P_1}{\left(P_1 + P_2\right)/2} \times 100.$$

Substituting the numbers from Figure 5.8:

$$\%\Delta P = \frac{9-10}{\left(9+10\right)/2} \times 100 = \frac{-1}{9.5} \times 100 = -10.5\%.$$

Finally, we calculate elasticity by comparing the two ratios as:

$$\text{Elasticity of Demand} = \frac{\%\Delta Q_D}{\%\Delta P} = \frac{66.7\%}{-10.5\%} = -6.4.$$

The percentage change in quantity demanded is 6.4 times larger than the percentage change in price. In other words, Herb's demand between points A and B is quite responsive; his demand between points A and B is elastic.

TABLE 5.3
Demand Schedule for Office Dining Room Lunches

PRICE (PER LUNCH)	QUANTITY DEMANDED (LUNCHES PER MONTH)
$11.00	0
10.00	2
9.00	4
8.00	6
7.00	8
6.00	10
5.00	12
4.00	14
3.00	16
2.00	18
1.00	20
0	22

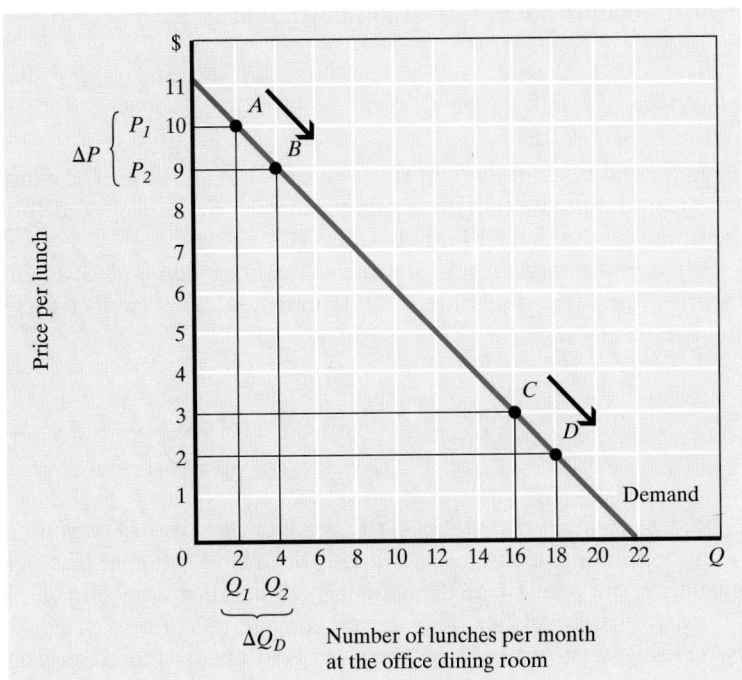

FIGURE 5.8
Demand for Lunch at the Office Dining Room

To calculate elasticity, we convert the changes ΔQ_D and ΔP into percentage changes. Between points A and B, demand is quite elastic at −6.4. Between points C and D, demand is quite inelastic at −0.294.

Now consider a different movement along the same demand curve in Figure 5.8. Moving from point C to point D, the graph indicates that at a price of $3, Herb eats in the office dining room 16 times per month; if the price drops to $2, he eats there 18 times per month. These changes expressed in numerical terms are exactly the same as the price and quantity changes between points A and B in the figure—price falls $1, and quantity demanded increases by two meals. Expressed in percentage terms, however, these changes are very different.

Using the midpoints as the base, the $1 price decline is only a 10.5% reduction when price is up around $9.50. The same $1 price decline is a 40% reduction when price is down around $2.50. The two-meal increase in quantity demanded is a 66.7% increase when Herb averages only two and a half meals per month, but it is only an 11.8% increase when he averages 17 meals per month. The elasticity of demand between points C and D is thus 11.8% divided by –40%, or –.294. (Work these numbers out for yourself by using the midpoint formula.)

The percentage changes between A and B are very different from those between C and D, and so are the elasticities. Herb's demand is quite elastic (–6.4) between points A and B; a 10.5% reduction in price caused a 66.7% increase in quantity. But his demand is inelastic (–.294) between points C and D; a 40% decrease in price caused only an 11.8% increase in quantity.

ELASTICITY AND TOTAL REVENUE We have seen that OPEC was successful in the early 1970s in increasing its revenues by restricting supply and pushing up the market price of crude oil. On the other hand, we argued that a similar strategy by OBEC, the Organization of Banana Exporting Countries, would probably fail. The reason that OBEC would be likely to fail where OPEC succeeded, we said, was that the quantity of oil demanded is not as responsive to a change in price as is the quantity of bananas demanded. In other words, the demand for oil is more inelastic than is the demand for bananas.

We can now use the more formal definition of elasticity to make our argument of why OPEC would succeed and OBEC would fail more precise. In any market, $P \times Q$ is total revenue (TR) received by producers:

$$TR = P \times Q$$

OPEC's total revenue is the price per barrel of oil times the number of barrels its participant countries sell. To wheat producers, total revenue is the price per bushel (P) times the number of bushels sold (Q).

When price increases in a market, quantity demanded declines. When price declines, quantity demanded (Q_D) increases. The two factors move in opposite directions:

Effects of Price Changes on Quantity Demanded:	$P \uparrow \rightarrow Q_D \downarrow$ and $P \downarrow \rightarrow Q_D \uparrow$.

Because total revenue (TR) is the product of P and Q, whether TR rises or falls in response to a price increase depends on which is bigger, the percentage increase in price or the percentage decrease in quantity. If the percentage decrease in quantity demanded is smaller than the percentage increase in price, total revenue will rise. This is what occurs when demand is inelastic. (Recall that *inelastic* means that the percentage change in quantity demanded is less than the percentage change in price.) In this case, the percentage price rise simply outweighs the percentage quantity decline, and $P \times Q$ (*TR*) rises:

> Effect of Price Increase on a Product with Inelastic Demand: $\uparrow P \times Q_D \downarrow = TR \uparrow$.

If, on the other hand, the percentage decline in quantity demanded following a price increase is larger than the percentage increase in price, total revenue will fall. This occurs when demand is elastic. (Recall that *elastic* means that the percentage change in quantity demanded is greater than the percentage change in price.) The percentage price increase is outweighed by the percentage quantity decline:

> Effect of Price Increase on a Product with Elastic Demand: $\uparrow P \times Q_D \Downarrow = TR \downarrow$.

The opposite is true for a price cut. When demand is elastic (that is, when $\%\Delta Q_D > \%\Delta P$), a cut in price increases total revenues:

> Effect of Price Cut on a Product with Elastic Demand: $\downarrow P \times Q_D \uparrow = TR \uparrow$.

When demand is inelastic (that is, when $\%\Delta Q_D < \%\Delta P$), a cut in price reduces total revenues:

> Effect of Price Cut on a Product with Inelastic Demand: $\Downarrow P \times Q_D \uparrow = TR \downarrow$.

Review the logic of these equations to make sure you understand the reasoning thoroughly. Table 5.4 also summarizes the relationship between total revenue and elasticity.

With this knowledge, we can now easily see why the OPEC cartel was so effective. The demand for oil is inelastic. Restricting the quantity of oil available led to a huge increase in the price of oil—the percentage increase in the price of oil was larger in absolute value than the percentage decrease in the quantity of oil demanded. Hence, OPEC's total revenues went up. On the other hand, an OBEC

TABLE 5.4

Changes in Total Revenues in Response to Price Change

Note: Total revenue equals $P \times Q$. P equals price; Q equals quantity sold; Q_D equals quantity demanded.

	VALUE OF E_D*			
	ELASTIC $(E_D > 1)$ $\%\Delta Q_D > \%\Delta P$	UNITARILY ELASTIC $(E_D = 1)$ $\%\Delta Q_D = \%\Delta P$	INELASTIC $(1 > E_D > 0)$ $\%\Delta Q_D < \%\Delta P$	PERFECTLY INELASTIC $(E_D = 0)$ $\Delta Q_D = 0$
Effect of a fall in P on total revenue ($P \times Q$)	Increase	Constant	Decrease	Fall in ($P \times Q$) is proportional to fall in P
Effect of a rise in P on total revenue ($P \times Q$)	Decrease	Constant	Increase	Rise in ($P \times Q$) is proportional to rise in P

*Where E_D = absolute value of demand elasticity.

cartel would not be effective because the demand for bananas is elastic. A small increase in the price of bananas results in a large decrease in the quantity of bananas demanded and thus causes total revenues to fall.

The Determinants of Demand Elasticity

Elasticity of demand is a way of measuring quantitatively the responsiveness of consumers' demand to changes in price. As a measure of behavior, it can be applied to individual households or to market demand as a whole. I love peaches and I would hate to give them up. My demand for peaches is therefore inelastic. But not everyone is crazy about peaches, and, in fact, the market demand for peaches is relatively elastic. Because no two people have exactly the same preferences, reactions to price changes will be different for different people, and this makes generalizations hazardous. Nonetheless, a few principles do seem to hold.

AVAILABILITY OF SUBSTITUTES   Perhaps the most obvious factor affecting demand elasticity is the availability of substitutes. When substitute products are easily obtained, the quantity demanded is likely to respond quite readily to changes in price. Consider a number of farm stands lined up along a country road. If every stand sells fresh corn of roughly the same quality, Mom's Green Thumb will find it very difficult to charge a price much higher than the competition charges because a nearly perfect substitute is available just down the road. The demand for Mom's corn is thus likely to be very elastic: An increase in price will lead to a rapid decline in the quantity demanded of Mom's corn.

When substitutes are not readily available, demand is likely to be less elastic. In Table 5.1, we considered two products that have no readily available substitutes, local telephone service and insulin for diabetics, and there are many others. Demand for these products is likely to be quite inelastic.

THE IMPORTANCE OF BEING UNIMPORTANT   When an item represents a relatively small part of our total budget, we tend to pay little attention to its price. For example, if I pick up a pack of mints once in a while when I go to the supermarket, I might not even notice an increase in price from $.25 to $.35, yet that is a 40% increase in price. In cases such as these, we are not likely to respond very much to changes in price, and demand is likely to be inelastic.

THE TIME DIMENSION   When the oil producing nations cut output and succeeded in pushing up the price of crude oil in the early 1970s, few substitutes were immediately available. Demand was relatively inelastic, and prices rose substantially. During the last 20 years, however, we have had time to adjust our behavior in response to the higher price, and the quantity demanded has fallen dramatically. Automobiles manufactured today get more miles per gallon, and some drivers have cut down on their driving. Millions have insulated their homes, most have turned down their thermostats, and some have explored alternative energy sources.

All this illustrates a very important point:

> The elasticity of demand in the short run may be very different from the elasticity of demand in the long run. In the longer run, demand is likely to become more elastic, or responsive, simply because households make adjustments over time and producers develop substitute goods.

Other Important Elasticities

So far we have been discussing price elasticity of demand, which measures the responsiveness of quantity demanded to changes in price. However, as we noted earlier, elasticity is a perfectly general concept. If B causes a change in A and we can measure the change in both, we can calculate the elasticity of A with respect to B. Let us look briefly at three other important types of elasticity: (1) income elasticity of demand, (2) cross-price elasticity, and (3) elasticity of supply.

INCOME ELASTICITY OF DEMAND **Income elasticity of demand,** which measures the responsiveness of demand with respect to changes in income, is defined as:

$$\text{Income Elasticity of Demand} = \frac{\%\ \text{Change in Quantity Demanded}}{\%\ \text{Change in Income}} = \frac{\%\Delta Q_D}{\%\Delta I}$$

> **income elasticity of demand** Measures the responsiveness of demand with respect to changes in income.

Calculating and measuring income elasticities are important for many reasons. Government policy makers spend a great deal of time and money weighing the relative merits of different policies. During the 1970s, for example, the Department of Housing and Urban Development (HUD) conducted a huge experiment in four cities to estimate the income elasticity of housing demand. In the "housing allowance demand experiment," low-income families received housing vouchers over an extended period of time, and researchers watched their housing consumption for several years. Most estimates, including the ones from the HUD study, put the income elasticity of housing demand between .5 and .8. That is, a 10% increase in income can be expected to raise the quantity of housing demanded by a household by 5 to 8 percent.

Recall from Chapter 4 that consumption of **normal goods** rises as income increases. We can now say more formally that income elasticity for normal goods is *positive*. Because an increase in income leads to an increase in demand and a decrease in income leads to a decrease in demand, both numerator and denominator of the elasticity formula have the same sign. The quotient is therefore positive. For **inferior goods,** income elasticity is *negative*. Because an increase in income leads to a decrease in the demand for an inferior good and a decrease in income leads to an increase in demand, the numerator and denominator of the elasticity formula have opposite signs. The quotient is therefore negative. For a third category of goods, **luxury goods,** income elasticity is positive and greater than one—that is, demand goes up *faster* than income as income rises, and the percentage change in demand is larger than the percentage change in income.

> **normal goods** Goods for which income elasticity is positive. Demand for normal goods rises when income rises and decreases when income decreases.

> **inferior goods** Goods for which income elasticity is negative. Demand for inferior goods rises when income decreases and decreases when income rises.

> **luxury goods** Goods for which income elasticity is positive and greater than one.

CROSS-PRICE ELASTICITY OF DEMAND **Cross-price elasticity of demand,** which measures the response of quantity of one good demanded to a change in the price of another good, is defined as:

> **cross-price elasticity of demand** A measure of the response in the quantity of one good demanded to a change in the price of another good.

$$\text{Cross - Price Elasticity of Demand} = \frac{\%\ \text{Change in Quantity of } Y \text{ Demanded}}{\%\ \text{Change in Price of } X}$$

$$= \frac{\%\Delta Q_Y^D}{\%\Delta P_X}$$

Like income elasticity, cross-price elasticity can be either positive or negative. A *positive* cross-price elasticity indicates that an increase in the price of X causes the demand for Y to rise. This implies that the goods are **substitutes.** If cross-price

> **substitutes** Goods for which an increase in the price of one increases the demand for the other; goods for which cross-price elasticity is positive.

complements Goods for which an increase in the price of one decreases the demand for the other; goods for which cross-price elasticity is negative.

elasticity of supply A measure of the response of quantity of a good supplied to a change in price of that good. Likely to be positive in output markets.

elasticity of labor supply A measure of the response of labor supplied to a change in the price of labor. Can be positive or negative.

elasticity turns out to be *negative,* an increase in the price of X causes a decrease in the demand for Y. This implies that the goods are **complements.**

ELASTICITY OF SUPPLY **Elasticity of supply,** which measures the response of quantity of a good supplied to a change in price of that good, is defined as:

$$\text{Elasticity of Supply} = \frac{\text{\% Change in Quantity Supplied}}{\text{\% Change in Price}} = \frac{\%\Delta Q^S}{\%\Delta P}.$$

In output markets, the elasticity of supply is likely to be a positive number—that is, a higher price leads to an increase in the quantity supplied, *ceteris paribus.* (Recall our discussion of upward-sloping supply curves in this chapter and the last.)

In input markets, however, some interesting problems crop up. Perhaps the most studied elasticity of all is the **elasticity of labor supply,** which measures the response of labor supplied to a change in the price of labor. Economists have examined household labor supply responses to such government programs as welfare, social security, the income tax system, need-based student aid, and unemployment insurance, among others.

In simple terms, the elasticity of labor supply is defined as:

$$\text{Elasticity of Labor Supply} = \frac{\text{\% Change in Quantity of Labor Supplied}}{\text{\% Change in the Wage Rate}}$$

$$= \frac{\%\Delta L^S}{\%\Delta W}.$$

It seems reasonable at first glance to assume that an increase in wages increases the quantity of labor supplied. That would imply an upward-sloping supply curve and a positive labor supply elasticity. But this is not necessarily so. An increase in wages makes workers better off: They can work the same amount and have higher incomes. One of the things that they might like to "buy" with that higher income is more leisure time. "Buying" leisure simply means working fewer hours, and the "price" of leisure is the lost wages. Thus it is quite possible that an increase in wages to some groups will lead to a reduction in the quantity of labor supplied. If this happens, the labor supply curve will have a negative slope.

LOOKING AHEAD

We have now examined the basic forces of supply and demand, discussed the nature of the market/price system, and introduced the concept of elasticity. These basic concepts will serve as building blocks for what comes next. Whether you are studying microeconomics or macroeconomics, you will be studying the function of markets and the behavior of market participants in more detail in the following chapters.

Since the concepts presented in the first five chapters are so important to your understanding of what is to come, this might be a good point for a brief review of Part One.

SUMMARY

The Price System: Rationing and Allocating Resources

1. In a market economy, the market system (or price system) serves two functions. It determines the allocation of resources among producers and the final mix of outputs. It also distributes goods and services on the basis of willingness and ability to pay. In this sense, it serves as a *price rationing* device.

2. Governments, as well as private firms, sometimes decide not to use the market system for rationing an item for which there is an excess demand at current prices. If price is not allowed to rise to equilibrium, other mechanisms must be found. Examples of nonprice rationing systems include *queuing, favored customers, ration coupons,* and lotteries. The most common rationale for policies or practices designed to avoid price rationing is "fairness."

3. Attempts to bypass the market and use alternative nonprice rationing devices are much more difficult and costly than it would seem at first glance. Schemes that open up opportunities for favored customers, *black markets,* and side payments often end up less "fair" than the free market.

Supply and Demand Analysis: An Oil Import Fee

4. The basic logic of supply and demand is a powerful tool for analysis. For example, supply and demand analysis shows that an oil import tax will reduce quantity demanded, increase domestic production, and generate revenues for the government.

Elasticity

5. *Elasticity* is a perfectly general measure of responsiveness that can be used to quantify many different relationships. If one variable, *A,* changes in response to changes in another variable, *B,* the elasticity of *A* with respect to *B* is equal to the percentage change in *A* divided by the percentage change in *B.*

6. The slope of a demand curve is an inadequate measure of responsiveness, because its value depends on the units of measurement used. For this reason, elasticities are calculated using percentages.

7. *Price elasticity of demand* is the ratio of the percentage change in quantity demanded of a good to the percentage change in price of that good. *Perfectly inelastic* demand is demand whose quantity demanded does not respond at all to changes in price; its numerical value is zero. *Inelastic* demand is demand whose quantity demanded responds somewhat, but not a great deal, to changes in price; its numerical value is between zero and negative one. *Elastic* demand is demand in which the percentage change in quantity demanded is larger in absolute value than the percentage change in price. *Unitary elasticity* of demand describes a relationship in which the percentage change in the quantity of a product demanded is the same as the percentage change in price; unitary elasticity has a numerical value of negative 1. *Perfectly elastic* demand describes a relationship in which a small increase in the price of a product causes the quantity demanded for that product to drop to zero.

8. Elasticity changes from point to point along a straight-line demand curve.

9. If demand is elastic, a price increase will reduce the quantity demanded by a larger percentage than the percentage increase in price, and total revenue ($P \times Q$) will fall. If demand is inelastic, a price increase will increase total revenue.

10. If demand is elastic, a price cut will cause quantity demanded to increase by a greater percentage than the percentage decrease in price, and total revenue will rise. If demand is inelastic, a price cut will cause quantity demanded to increase by a smaller percentage than the percentage decrease in price, and total revenue will fall.

11. The elasticity of demand depends on (1) the availability of substitutes, (2) the importance of the item in individual budgets, and (3) the time frame in question.

12. There are several important elasticities. *Income elasticity of demand* measures the responsiveness of the quantity demanded with respect to changes in income. *Cross-price elasticity of demand* measures the response of quantity of one good demanded to a change in the price of another good. *Elasticity of supply* measures the response of quantity of a good supplied to a change in the price of that good. The *elasticity of labor supply* measures the response of the quantity of labor supplied to a change in the price of labor.

REVIEW TERMS AND CONCEPTS

PROBLEM SET

1. Illustrate the following with supply and/or demand curves:
   a. A perfectly elastic demand curve.
   b. A labor supply curve along which elasticity of labor supply is positive.
   c. The effect of an increase in income on the price of a normal good.
   d. The effect of an increase in income on the price of an inferior good.
   e. A situation of excess labor supply (unemployment) caused by a "minimum wage" law.
   f. The effect of a sharp increase in heating oil prices on the demand for insulation material.

2. The box on page 113 makes the argument that scalping, which is illegal in most states, may in fact serve a useful function. Do you agree or disagree? Write an essay explaining your answer.

3. A sporting goods store has estimated the demand curve for Brand A running shoes as a function of price. Use the following diagram to answer the questions below:

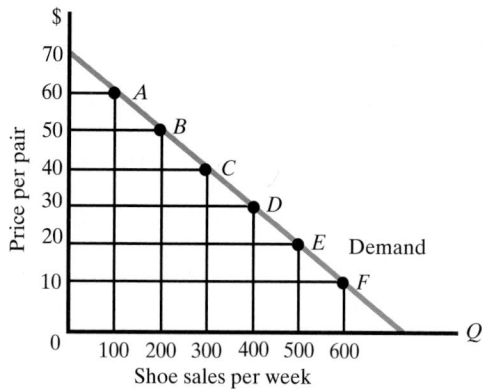

a. Calculate demand elasticity using the midpoint formula between points A and B, between points C and D, and between points E and F.
b. If the store currently charges a price of $50, then increases it by $10, what happens to total revenue from

shoe sales (P × Q)? Repeat the exercise for initial prices of $30 and $10.
c. Explain why the answers to a. can be used to predict the answers to b.

4. For the past ten years the price of natural gas sold in interstate commerce has been regulated by the federal government. In 1983 the regulated price was thought to be substantially below equilibrium.
   a. Illustrate the situation with supply and demand curves.
   b. If prices had been held at their 1983 levels for a long time, how would we have known that they were not at an equilibrium? What evidence would you have looked for?
   c. Those in favor of deregulation argued that deregulation would increase the supply of natural gas. How could deregulation increase the supply of natural gas?
   d. Those in favor of maintaining the regulations argued that the supply of natural gas is very inelastic. If supply is very inelastic, and thus will not respond to high prices, what will happen if price is deregulated? (*Hint:* Draw another graph.)

5. Taxicab fares in most cities are regulated. Several years ago, taxicab drivers in Boston obtained permission to raise their fares 10%, and they anticipated that revenues would increase by about 10% as a result. They were disappointed, however. When the commissioner granted the 10% increase, revenues increased by only about 5 percent.
   What can you infer about the elasticity of demand for taxicab rides? What were taxicab drivers assuming about the elasticity of demand?

6. Studies have fixed the short-run price elasticity of demand for gasoline at the pump at 0.20. Suppose that continued difficulties in the Persian Gulf lead to a sudden cutoff of crude oil supplies. As a result, U.S. supplies of refined gasoline drop 10 percent.
   a. If gasoline was selling for $1.40 per gallon before the cutoff, how much of a price increase would you expect to see in the coming months?
   b. Suppose that the government imposes a price ceiling on gas at $1.40 per gallon. How would the relationship between consumers and gas station owners change?

THE IVORY MARKET

To many people, elephants are synonymous with Africa and the struggle to save endangered wildlife. These "whales of the land" are the focus of numerous fund-raising efforts to save them. Between 1979 and 1989, the number of African elephants fell from approximately 1.2 million to 600,000.

But there is another side to the story. Elephants inflict damage on the continent's natives, both human (over 500 Zimbabweans were killed by elephants in the 1980s) and animal (through habitat destruction of woodlands as they have been pushed into smaller ranges). Though troublesome elephants have been killed by government officials or farmers protecting their crops, the primary reason for the reduction in the number of elephants has been ivory poaching.

In 1989, a pound of ivory sold for about $140. With an average tusk size of 13 pounds, a dead elephant represented a yield of close to $3600 at a time that the average annual wage in Kenya was $1000. In Kenya alone, the elephant population fell from 167,000 in 1973 to 16,000 in 1989, although it has since risen to 26,000. This reversal can be attributed partly to a hard-line program against poaching (including a shoot-to-kill policy against poachers) and partly to an international ban on trade in ivory signed in January 1990, by the Convention of International Trade in Endangered Species (CITES). The price of ivory immediately sank to $5 a pound after the ban. The Kenyan government publicly burned a 12-ton pile of ivory valued at over $3 million (pre-ban). The number of elephants killed for ivory in Kenya dropped to less than 50 a year. However, this apparently effective policy has not been without controversy—especially in countries like

A herd of elephants in Zimbabwe, which has an aggressive elephant-management policy.

South Africa and Zimbabwe.

During the 1980s, South Africa's national parks board earned $14 million and Zimbabwe earned more than $13 million from the sale of elephant products, mostly ivory. Zimbabwe has an aggressive management policy that incorporates the rural population (whose annual family income is about $200) into the conservation effort. "Ownership" of the elephants and the revenue they generate has led communities to set aside land for elephants to reduce the likelihood that crop-damaging elephants will be killed. The result: Elephant herds in southern Africa have been increasing. In 1992, this program generated approximately $2 million for participating communities. At the same time, the villages stockpiled $1.6 million (at pre-ban prices) worth of ivory—but saw all this wealth disintegrate when the ban took effect.

These experiences have led to different responses to the ivory ban. East African countries (whose elephant

herds have been thinning) have generally been supportive, fearing that poaching could decimate elephant herds—which are a primary tourist attraction. Southern African nations fear that the ban will limit the revenues that elephants might generate, reducing funds for conservation and the incentives of those who live with the elephant to protect it.

QUESTIONS FOR ANALYTICAL THINKING:

1. Draw a supply and demand graph to illustrate the effect of the international ban on trade in ivory on the market. Can you think of any other ways to achieve the same outcome (that is, protection of African elephants)?

2. Under CITES, countries may trade in banned products if they sign a bilateral treaty. Zimbabwe and Japan have considered signing such an agreement for ivory.

How might this affect the market for ivory in other African nations?

3. An international ban on trade in rhino horn was signed in 1977. Nevertheless, the horns are still readily available in many countries (at almost $1000 a pound), and the black rhino population has declined from 40,000 to less than 2,000 over the past 20 years. Can you think of any reason the ban might work for ivory but not rhino horn, as is apparently the case? You might want to consider the fact that rhino horn is in different parts of the world variously considered a traditional medicine for reducing fevers, an aphrodisiac, and the only acceptable dagger handle Ivory serves primarily decorative purposes.

4. Consider the factors that affect the supply of (live) elephants and the supply of ivory/elephant meat. How do these interact in the short run? The long run? To what extent is the supply elastic or inelastic? Use a production possibilities frontier to represent this problem.

MICROECONOMICS

PART TWO

Foundations of Microeconomics: Consumers and Firms

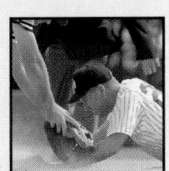

In Part One, we introduced a few of the key concepts in economics. Now it's time to go beyond the basics. In this part, we take a closer look at the behavior of households and firms, the two primary decision-making units in the economy. To do so, we will build a model of a simple, but complete, economic system.

The material in Part Two is greatly simplified and sometimes abstract. It is important to remember as you proceed, however, that these abstractions help to explain the basic market forces that operate in real economies.

Some of the important questions we'll explore in Chapters 6 through 12 are:

- What lies behind the simple supply and demand curves described in Part One? (Chapters 6–8)
- What determines when an industry will expand and when it can be expected to contract? (Chapter 9)
- How do labor markets determine what jobs are available, who will fill them, and what wages will be? (Chapter 10)
- What roles do the stock market, the bond market, and the banking system play in determining what goods and services will be available to consumers? (Chapter 11)
- How does investment in capital increase the productivity of labor and raise wages? (Chapter 11)
- How well do perfectly competitive markets perform? (Chapter 12)
- Is there a role for government in a market economy? (Chapter 12)

6

Household Behavior and Consumer Choice

Now that we have discussed the basic forces of supply and demand, we can go behind the supply and demand curves and explore the underlying behavior of the two fundamental decision-making units in the economy, households and firms.

Figure 6.1 presents a diagram of a simple competitive economy. The figure is an expanded version of the circular flow diagram first presented in Figure 4.1. It is designed to guide you through Part Two of this book. You will see the "big picture" much more clearly if you follow this diagram closely as you work your way through the next six chapters. (For your convenience, the diagram will be repeated several times in the next few chapters.) Figure 6.2 shows where the material that is about to be discussed in each chapter fits into the diagram.

Recall that households and firms interact in two kinds of markets: output (product) markets, shown at the top of Figure 6.1, and input (factor) markets, shown at the bottom. Households *demand* outputs and *supply* inputs. In contrast, firms *supply* outputs and *demand* inputs. This chapter explores the behavior of households, focusing first on household demand for outputs and then on household supply in labor and capital markets.

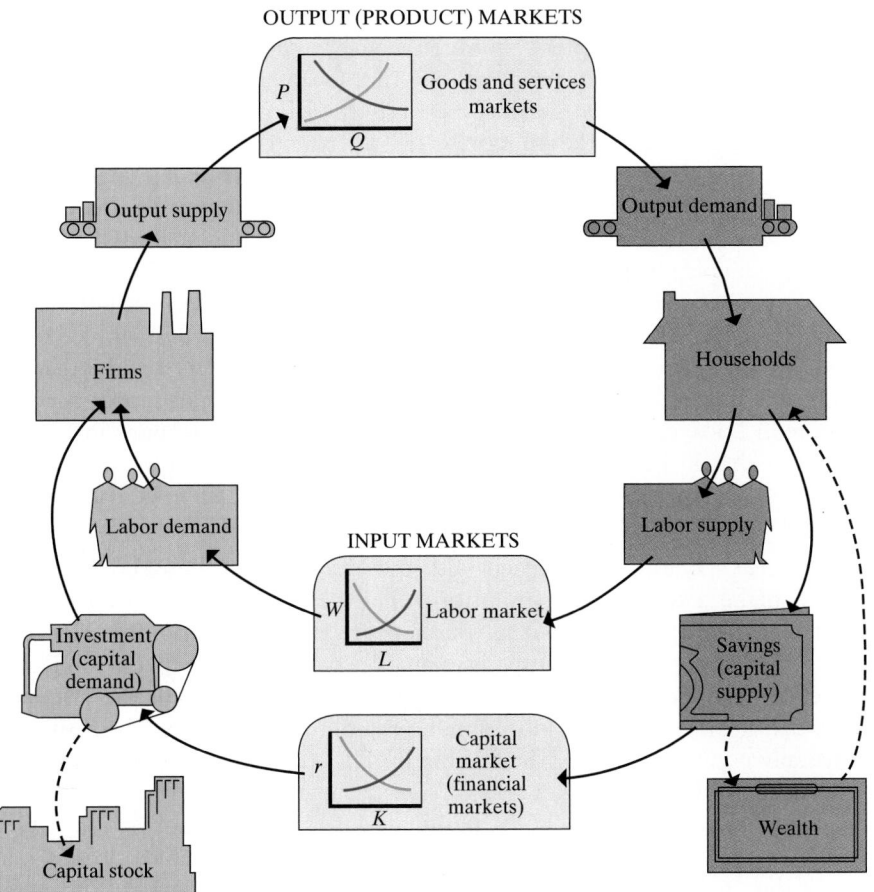

OUTPUT (PRODUCT) MARKETS

Goods and services markets

Output supply

Output demand

Firms

Households

Labor demand

INPUT MARKETS

Labor supply

Labor market

Investment (capital demand)

Savings (capital supply)

Capital market (financial markets)

Wealth

Capital stock

FIGURE 6.1
Firm and Household Decisions

Households demand in output markets and supply labor and capital in input markets. To simplify our analysis, we have not included the government and international sectors in this circular flow diagram. These topics will be discussed in detail later.

FIGURE 6.2
Understanding the Microeconomy and the Role of Government

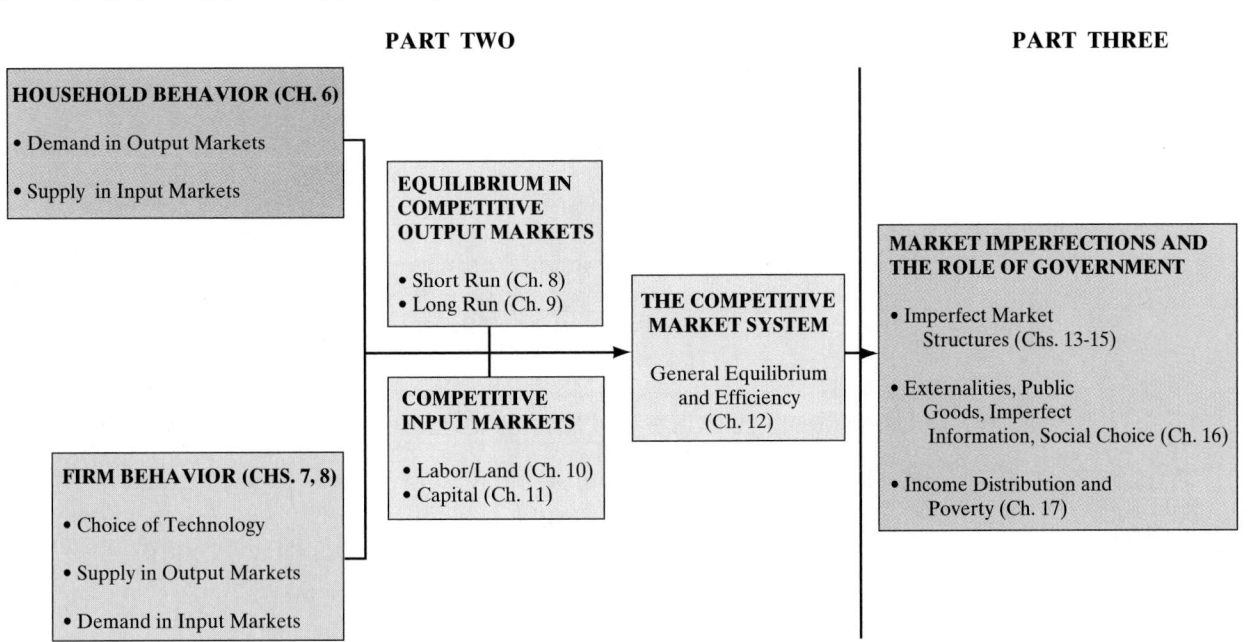

PART TWO

PART THREE

HOUSEHOLD BEHAVIOR (CH. 6)

• Demand in Output Markets

• Supply in Input Markets

EQUILIBRIUM IN COMPETITIVE OUTPUT MARKETS

• Short Run (Ch. 8)
• Long Run (Ch. 9)

THE COMPETITIVE MARKET SYSTEM

General Equilibrium and Efficiency (Ch. 12)

MARKET IMPERFECTIONS AND THE ROLE OF GOVERNMENT

• Imperfect Market Structures (Chs. 13-15)

• Externalities, Public Goods, Imperfect Information, Social Choice (Ch. 16)

• Income Distribution and Poverty (Ch. 17)

FIRM BEHAVIOR (CHS. 7, 8)

• Choice of Technology

• Supply in Output Markets

• Demand in Input Markets

COMPETITIVE INPUT MARKETS

• Labor/Land (Ch. 10)
• Capital (Ch. 11)

The remaining chapters in Part Two focus on firms and the interaction between firms and households. Chapters 7 through 9 analyze the behavior of firms in output markets in both the short run and the long run. Chapter 10 focuses on the behavior of firms in input markets in general, especially the labor and land markets. Chapter 11 discusses the capital market in more detail. Chapter 12 puts all the pieces together and analyzes the functioning of a complete market system. Following Chapter 12, Part Three of the book relaxes many assumptions and begins to analyze market imperfections and the potential for and pitfalls of government involvement in the economy. The plan for Chapters 6 through 17 is outlined in Figure 6.2.

Throughout this book, all diagrams that describe the behavior of households are drawn or highlighted in *blue*. All diagrams that describe the behavior of firms are drawn or highlighted in *red*. (You may have noticed in Chapters 4 and 5 that household output demand curves were always blue, while firm output supply curves were always red.) Look carefully at the small supply and demand diagrams in Figure 6.1, and notice that in both the labor and capital markets, the supply curves are blue. This is because labor and capital are supplied by households. The demand curves for labor and capital are red because firms demand these inputs for production.

ASSUMPTIONS   Before we proceed with our discussion of household choice, we need to make a few basic assumptions. The key assumption that we make in Chapters 6 through 12 is that all markets are *perfectly competitive*. Recall from Chapter 3 that a perfectly competitive market is one in which no single firm is large enough to have any control over the price of its products or the prices of the inputs that it buys. Similarly, no single household in a perfectly competitive market has any control over the prices of the products that it buys or the prices of the inputs (labor and capital) that it sells.

We also assume that households and firms possess all the information they need to make market choices. Specifically, we assume that households possess knowledge of the qualities and prices of everything available in the market. Firms know all that there is to know about wage rates, capital costs, and output prices. This is often referred to as the assumption of **perfect knowledge.**

perfect knowledge The assumption that households possess a knowledge of the qualities and prices of everything available in the market and that firms have all available information regarding input prices and qualities.

By the end of Chapter 12 we will have a complete picture of an economy, but it will be based on this set of fairly restrictive assumptions. At first, this may seem unrealistic to you. Keep the following in mind, however:

> Much of the economic analysis in the chapters that follow applies to all forms of market structure. Indeed, much of the power of economic reasoning is that it is quite general. When we turn to imperfect markets in Part Three, we will discover that much of the decision-making logic described in Chapters 6 through 12 for both households and firms applies there as well. Since monopolists, oligopolists, monopolistic competitors, and perfect competitors share the objective of maximizing profits, it should not be surprising that their behavior is in many ways similar. We focus here on perfect competition because many of these basic principles are easier to learn in the simplest of cases first.

HOUSEHOLD CHOICE IN OUTPUT MARKETS

As Figure 6.1 shows, every household must make three basic decisions:

1. How much of each output to demand;
2. How much labor to supply; and
3. How much to spend today and how much to save for the future.[1]

---
[1] As you will see in Chapters 10 and 11, this decision is of primary importance in the capital market.

These decisions are represented by the blue curves in each of the markets' supply and demand diagrams.

As we begin our fairly lengthy look at demand in output markets, you must keep in mind that the choices underlying the demand curve are only part of the larger household-choice problem. Closely related decisions about how much to work and how much to save are equally important and must, in a sense, be made simultaneously.

The Determinants of Household Demand

As we saw in Chapter 4,

> Several factors influence the quantity of a given good or service demanded by a single household:
>
> ■ The price of the product
> ■ The income available to the household
> ■ The amount of accumulated wealth of the household
> ■ The prices of other products available to the household
> ■ The tastes and preferences of the household, and
> ■ Expectations about future income, wealth, and prices.

Demand schedules and demand curves express the relationship between quantity demanded and price, *ceteris paribus;* changes in income, in other prices, or in preferences *shift* demand curves to the left or right. We refer to these shifts as "changes in demand." But the interrelationship among these variables is more complex than the simple exposition in Chapter 4 might lead you to believe.

The Budget Constraint

Before we examine the household choice process, we need to discuss exactly what choices are open or not open to households. If you look carefully at the list of items that influence household demand, you will see that the first four actually *define* the set of options available. In other words:

> Information on a household's income and wealth and information on product prices make it possible to distinguish those combinations of goods and services that are affordable from those that are not.[2]

Income, wealth, and prices thus define what we call a household's **budget constraint.** The budget constraint facing any household results primarily from limits imposed externally by one or more markets. In competitive markets, for example, households cannot control prices; they must buy goods and services at market-determined prices. A household has some control over its income: Its members can choose to work or not, and they can sometimes decide how many hours to work and how many jobs to hold. But there are constraints in the labor market, too. The amount that household members are paid is limited by current market wage rates; whether they can get a job is determined by the availability of jobs.

budget constraint The limits imposed on household choices by income, wealth, and product prices.

---

[2]Remember that we drew the distinction between income and wealth in Chapter 4. *Income* is the sum of a household's earnings within a given period; it is a flow variable. *Wealth,* on the other hand, is a stock variable; briefly, it is what a household owns minus what it owes at a given point in time.

While income does in fact depend, at least in part, on the choices that households make, for the time being we will treat it as a given. As we discuss consumer choice in output markets, it helps at first to treat income as a simple limit, or constraint. Later on we will relax this assumption and explore labor supply choices in more detail.

The income, wealth, and price constraints that surround the exercise of choice are best illustrated with an example. Consider Barbara, a recent graduate of a Midwestern university, who takes a job as an account manager at a public relations firm. Let's assume that she receives a salary of $1000 per month (after taxes), and that she has no wealth and no credit. Barbara's monthly expenditures are limited to her flow of income. Table 6.1 summarizes some of the choices open to her.

A careful search of the housing market reveals four vacant apartments. The least expensive is a one-room studio with a small kitchenette that rents for $400 per month, including utilities. If she lived there, Barbara could afford to spend $250 per month on food and still have $350 left over for other things.

About four blocks away is a one-bedroom apartment with wall-to-wall carpeting and a larger kitchen. It has much more space, but it is 50% more expensive: The rent is $600, including utilities. If Barbara took this apartment, she might cut her food expenditures by $50 per month and have only $200 per month left for everything else.

In the same building as the one-bedroom apartment is an identical unit, but it is on the top floor of the building and has a balcony facing west toward the sunset. The balcony and view add $100 to the monthly rent. To live there, Barbara would be left with only $300 to split between food and other expenses.

Just because she was curious, Barbara took a look at a townhouse in the suburbs that was renting for $1000 per month. Obviously, unless she could get along without eating or doing anything else that costs money, she could not afford it. The combination of the townhouse and any amount of food is outside her budget constraint.

Notice that we have used the information that we have on income and prices to identify different combinations of housing, food, and other items that are available to a single-person household with an income of $1000 per month. We have said nothing about the process of choosing. Rather, we have carved out what is called a **choice set** or **opportunity set,** the set of options that is defined and limited by Barbara's budget constraint.

choice set, or opportunity set
The set of options that is defined and limited by a budget constraint.

PREFERENCES, TASTES, TRADE-OFFS, AND OPPORTUNITY COST So far, we have discussed only the limits facing consumers. We have identified the combinations of goods and services that are available and those that are not. Within the constraints imposed by limited incomes and fixed prices, however, households are free to choose what they will buy and what they will not buy. Their ultimate choices are governed by their individual preferences and tastes.

It will help you to think of the household-choice process as a process of allocating income over a large number of available goods and services. A household's final demand for any single product is just one of many outcomes that result from

TABLE 6.1
Possible Budget Choices of a Person Earning $1000 per Month After Taxes

BUNDLE	MONTHLY RENT	FOOD	OTHER EXPENSES	TOTAL	AVAILABLE
A	$400	$250	$350	$1000	Yes
B	$600	$200	$200	$1000	Yes
C	$700	$150	$150	$1000	Yes
D	$1000	$100	$100	$1200	No

the decision-making process. Think, for example, of a demand curve that shows a household's reaction to a drop in the price of air travel. There are certain periods every year when people travel less frequently. During these periods, special fares flood the market and many people decide to take trips that they otherwise would not have taken. The decision to travel, however, is a decision not to do or buy something else. If I live in Florida and decide to spend $229 to visit my mother in Nashville, that is $229 that I will not be spending on new clothes, dinners at a restaurant, or a new set of tires.

As you can see, then, a change in the price of a single good changes the constraints within which households choose, and this may change the entire allocation–demand for some goods and services may rise while demand for others may fall. A complicated set of trade-offs lies behind the shape and position of a household's demand curve for a single good. Whenever a household makes a choice, it is really weighing the good or service it chooses against *all* the other things that the same money could buy.

Consider again our young account manager and her options as listed in Table 6.1. Her choice of an apartment from among the three alternatives that lie within her budget constraint depends on her own tastes and preferences. She must make a personal, subjective judgment about the relative values that she places on housing, food, and other things. If she hates to cook, likes to eat at restaurants, and goes out three nights a week, she will probably trade off some housing for dinners out and money to spend on clothes and other things. She will probably rent the studio for $400. But she may love to spend long evenings at home reading, listening to classical music, and sipping wine while watching the sunset. In that case, she will probably trade off some restaurant meals, evenings out, and travel expenses for the added comfort of the larger apartment with the balcony and the view.

Thinking of constraints in this way highlights a very important point:

> As long as a household faces a limited budget–and all households ultimately do–the real cost of any good or service is the value of the other goods and services that could have been purchased with the same amount of money. The real cost of a good or service is its opportunity cost, and opportunity cost is determined by relative prices and income.

THE BUDGET CONSTRAINT MORE FORMALLY   Consider a household with no wealth and a known income (I). Assume that the household purchases only two goods, X and Y. In addition, assume that X and Y sell for known prices, P_X and P_Y. The budget constraint here is quite simple: The household may choose any combination of X and Y as long as the total amount spent on the two does not exceed income. We can write the constraint more formally:

$$P_X \cdot X + P_Y \cdot Y \leq I$$

where X is the number of units of good X, and Y is the number of units of good Y. The total amount spent on X (P_X times X) plus the total amount spent on Y (P_Y times Y) must be less than or equal to ($\leq$) income (I).

This same budget constraint is illustrated graphically in Figure 6.3. In the diagram, each point represents a combination of X and Y. Point A, for example, represents X_A units of X and Y_A units of Y. The budget constraint itself, line segment DE, shows all the combinations of X and Y that the household could buy if it spent *all* its income. If the household chose point D, it would be spending *all* its income on Y and buying no X at all. If it did, the number of units of Y it could buy would be I/P_Y (I divided by the price of Y). If your allowance is $1 a week,

FIGURE 6.3

Budget Constraint and Opportunity Set for a Household Consuming Only Two Goods

A household's budget constraint separates those combinations of goods and services that are available, given its limited income, from those that are not. Along a budget constraint, a household spends all its income; below the budget constraint, the household does not spend all its income. Those combinations that are available make up the household's opportunity set.

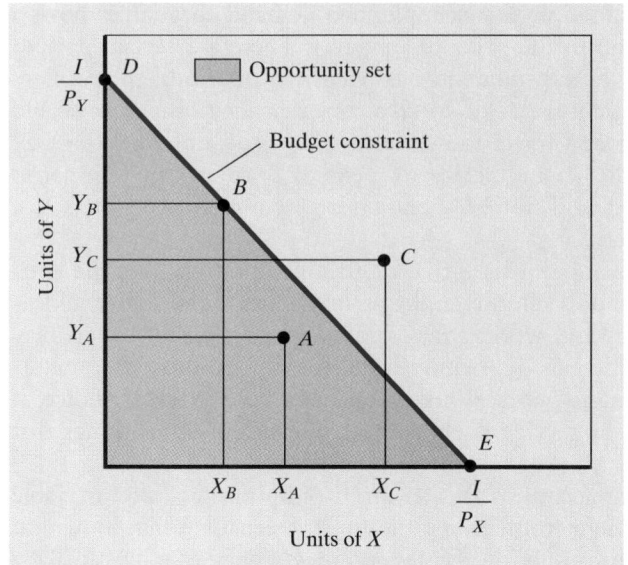

gum costs $.25 a pack, and you spend your entire allowance on gum, you can buy four packs ($1 divided by $.25). If the household spent its entire income on X and nothing on Y, the total amount of X it could buy would be I/P_X (indicated by point E in Figure 6.3).

All points on or below and to the left of the budget constraint, DE, are *available options*. Together, these points make up the opportunity set. It is represented by the shaded area in the figure. Point A is available, but at that point the household does not spend its entire income.[3] Point C is not available because it represents a particular combination of X and Y (X_C and Y_C) that cannot be purchased with an income of I. The household's problem is to pick one of the points in the shaded area—a choice that depends on its own unique tastes and preferences.

Figure 6.4 illustrates the effect of an increase in the price of X on the household's budget constraint. The point where the constraint DE intersects the X axis (which, you recall, measures the number of units of good X that would be purchased if the household spent its entire income on X) moves in to the left. If the price of gum went up to $.50, you could buy only 2 packs with your dollar allowance instead of 4. The only point on the old budget constraint that remains the same on the new one is point D on the Y axis. At that point, the household buys no X, so an increase in the price of X has no effect.

This shift, or *swivel*, in its budget constraint presents the household with an entirely new choice set, and presumably the household will pick an entirely new bundle of options. The opportunity set is smaller, which means that the household has fewer options.

Figure 6.4 thus illustrates a very important point. We said earlier that when the price of a single good such as X changes, more than just the quantity of good X demanded is affected. The household is now faced with an entirely new problem—the opportunity set has changed. Opportunity sets get bigger when prices fall and smaller when prices rise. The opportunities open to the account manager, as described in Table 6.1, are reduced if rents rise. On the other hand, if you visit

---

[3]Saving can be thought of in a number of ways. The two-dimensional world of X and Y is a representation of a multidimensional world. One dimension that is left out is time. Saving is the way we use income earned today to buy goods in the future. For now, we assume that households consume all their income and thus choose a point that lies on the budget constraint.

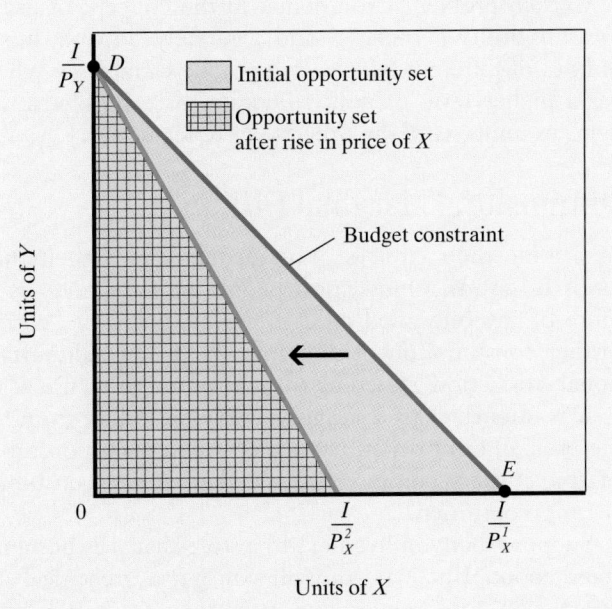

FIGURE 6.4
The Effect of an Increase in the Price of X on a Household's Budget Constraint

When the price of a good increases, the budget constraint swivels, reducing the opportunities available and limiting choice.

your mother in Nashville frequently, and you fly to get there, a decline in air fares increases, or opens up, opportunities–not just opportunities to fly more, but also to buy other goods and services as well.

To summarize:

> The budget constraint is defined by income, wealth, and prices. Within those limits, households are free to choose, and the household's ultimate choice depends on its own likes and dislikes.

The range of goods and services available in a modern society is as vast as consumer tastes are variable, and this makes any generalization about the household choice process hazardous. Nonetheless, the theory of household behavior that follows is an attempt to derive some logical propositions about the way households make choices.

THE BASIS OF CHOICE: UTILITY

You have seen that individual tastes and preferences ultimately determine the decisions that households make within the constraints imposed by the market. Somehow, from the millions of things that are available, each of us manages to sort out a set of goods and services to buy. When we make our choices, we make specific judgments about the relative worth of things that are very different.

During the nineteenth century, this notion of the subjective weighing of values was formalized into a concept called utility. Whether one item is preferable to another depends upon how much **utility,** or satisfaction, it yields relative to its alternatives. What is it that enables us to decide on the relative worth of a new puppy or a stereo? A trip to the mountains or a weekend in New York City? Working or not working? As we make our choices, we are effectively weighing the utilities we would receive from all the possible available goods.

utility The basis of choice. The satisfaction, or reward, a product yields relative to its alternatives.

Certain problems are implicit in the concept of utility. First, it is impossible to measure utility completely and accurately. Second, it is impossible to compare the utilities of different people—that is, one cannot say whether person A or person B has a higher level of utility. Despite these problems, however, the idea of utility helps us understand the process of choice better.

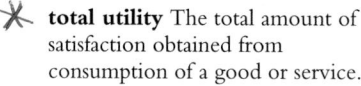

Diminishing Marginal Utility

In making their choices, most people spread their incomes over many different kinds of goods. One reason people prefer variety is that consuming more and more of any one good reduces the marginal, or "extra," satisfaction we get from further consumption of the same good. Formally, **marginal utility** is the additional satisfaction gained by the consumption or use of *one more* unit of something.

It is important to distinguish marginal utility from total utility. **Total utility** is the total amount of satisfaction obtained from consumption of a good or service. Marginal utility comes only from the *last unit* consumed; total utility comes from *all* units consumed.

Suppose that you live next to a store that sells homemade ice cream that you are crazy about. But even though you get a great deal of pleasure from eating ice cream, you don't spend your entire income on it. The first cone of the day tastes heavenly. The second is merely delicious. The third is still very good, but it's clear that the glow is fading. Why? Because the more of any one good we consume in a given period, the less satisfaction, or utility, we get out of each additional, or marginal, unit. In 1890 Alfred Marshall called this "familiar and fundamental tendency of human nature" the **law of diminishing marginal utility.**[4]

Consider this simple example. Frank loves country music, and a country band is playing seven nights a week at a club near his house. Table 6.2 shows how the utility he derives from the band might change as he goes to the club more and more frequently. The first visit generates 12 "utils," or units of utility. If Frank goes again another night he enjoys it, but not quite as much as the first night. The second night by itself yields 10 additional utils. *Marginal utility* is 10, while the *total utility* derived from two nights at the club is 22. Three nights per week at the club provide 28 total utils; the marginal utility of the third night is 6, since total utility rose from 22 to 28. Figure 6.5 graphs total and marginal utility using the data in Table 6.2. Total utility increases up through Frank's fifth trip to the club, but levels off on the sixth night. Marginal utility, which has declined from the beginning, is now at zero.

Allocating Income to Maximize Utility

How many times in one week would Frank go to the club? The answer depends on three things: Frank's income, the price of admission to the club, and the alternatives available. If the price of admission were zero and no alternatives existed, he would probably go to the club five nights a week. (Remember, the sixth does not increase his utility, so why should he bother to go?) But Frank is also a basketball fan. His city has many good high school and college teams, and he can go to games six nights a week if he wants to.

Let us say for now that admission to both the country music club and the basketball games is free—that is, there is no price/income constraint. There is a time constraint, however, because there are only seven nights in a week. Table 6.3 lists Frank's total and marginal utilities from attending basketball games and going to country music clubs. From column 3 of the table we can conclude

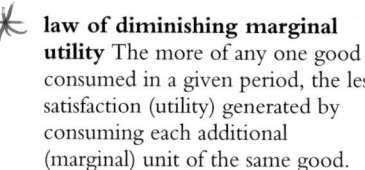

marginal utility The additional satisfaction gained by the consumption or use of *one more* unit of something.

total utility The total amount of satisfaction obtained from consumption of a good or service.

law of diminishing marginal utility The more of any one good consumed in a given period, the less satisfaction (utility) generated by consuming each additional (marginal) unit of the same good.

TABLE 6.2
Total Utility and Marginal Utility of Trips to the Club per Week

TRIPS TO CLUB	TOTAL UTILITY	MARGINAL UTILITY
1	12	12
2	22	10
3	28	6
4	32	4
5	34	2
6	34	0

[4]Alfred Marshall, *Principles of Economics,* 8th ed. (New York: Macmillan, 1948), p. 93 (1st ed., 1890).

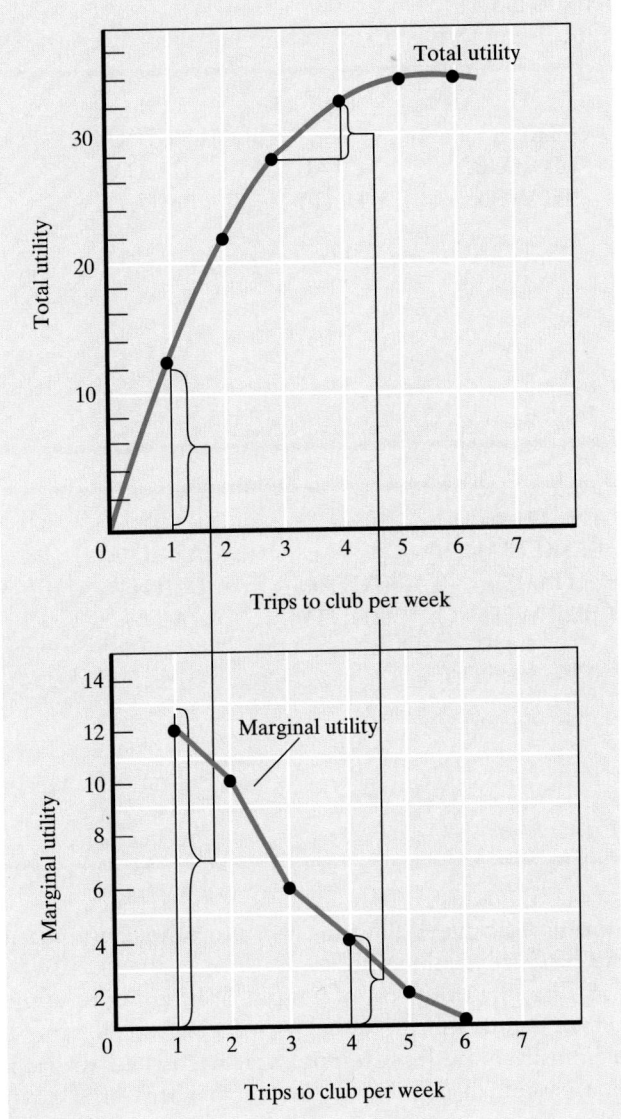

FIGURE 6.5

Graphs of Frank's Total and Marginal Utility

Marginal utility is the additional utility gained by consuming one additional unit of a commodity–in this case trips to the club. As long as a good yields positive marginal utility, total utility will increase with output. When marginal utility is zero, total utility stops rising.

that on the first night Frank will go to a basketball game. The game is worth far more to him (21 utils) than a trip to the club (12 utils).

On the second night, Frank's decision is not so easy. As he has been to one basketball game this week, the second is worth less (12 utils as compared to 21). In fact, it is worth so much less that he is indifferent to whether he goes to the game or the club. So he splits the next two nights: One night he sees ball game number two (12 utils), the other he spends at the club (12 utils). At this point, Frank has been to two ball games and spent one night at the club. Where will Frank go on evening four? To the club again, because the marginal utility from a second trip to the club (10 utils) is greater than the marginal utility from attending a third basketball game (9 utils).

Frank is splitting his time among the two activities in order to maximize total utility. At each successive step, he chooses the activity that yields the most marginal utility. Continuing with this logic, you can see that spending three nights at the club and four nights watching basketball produces total utility of

TABLE 6.3
Allocation of Fixed Expenditure per Week between Two Alternatives

(1) TRIPS TO CLUB PER WEEK	(2) TOTAL UTILITY	(3) MARGINAL UTILITY (MU_X)	(4) PRICE (P_X)	(5) $\dfrac{MU_X}{P_X}$
1	12	12	$3.00	4.0
2	22	10	3.00	3.3
3	28	6	3.00	2.0
4	32	4	3.00	1.3
5	34	2	3.00	0.7
6	34	0	3.00	0

(1) BASKETBALL GAMES PER WEEK	(2) TOTAL UTILITY	(3) MARGINAL UTILITY (MU_Y)	(4) PRICE (P_Y)	(5) $\dfrac{MU_Y}{P_Y}$
1	21	21	$6.00	3.5
2	33	12	6.00	2.0
3	42	9	6.00	1.5
4	48	6	6.00	1.0
5	51	3	6.00	.5
6	51	0	6.00	0

76 utils each week (28 plus 48). No other combination of games and club trips can produce as much utility.

So far, the only cost of a night of listening to country music is a forgone basketball game, and the only cost of a basketball game is a forgone night of country music. Now let's suppose that it costs $3 to get into the club and $6 to go to a basketball game. Suppose further that after paying rent and taking care of other necessary expenses Frank has only $21 left over to spend on entertainment. Typically, consumers allocate limited incomes, or *budgets,* over a large set of goods and services. Here we have a limited income ($21) being allocated over only two goods, but the principle is the same. Income ($21) and prices ($3 and $6) define Frank's budget constraint. Within that constraint, Frank chooses in order to maximize utility.

Because the two activities now cost different amounts, we need to find the *marginal utility per dollar* spent on each activity. If Frank is to spend his money on the combination of activities lying within his budget constraint that gives him the most total utility, each night he must choose the activity that gives him the *most utility per dollar spent.* As you can see from column 5 in Table 6.3, Frank gets 4 utils per dollar on the first night he goes to the club (12 utils ÷ $3 = 4 utils per dollar). On night two he goes to a game and gets 3.5 utils per dollar (21 utils ÷ $6 = 3.5 utils per dollar). On night three it's back to the club. Then what happens? When all is said and done–work this out for yourself–Frank ends up going to two games and spending three nights at the club. No other combination of activities that $21 will buy yields more utility.

The Utility-Maximizing Rule

In general, a utility-maximizing consumer spreads out his or her expenditures until the following condition holds:

$$\text{Utility - Maximizing Rule} : \frac{MU_X}{P_X} = \frac{MU_Y}{P_Y} \text{ for all pairs of goods.}$$

where MU_X is the marginal utility derived from the last unit of X consumed, MU_Y is the marginal utility derived from the last unit of Y consumed, P_X is the price per unit of X, and P_Y is the price per unit of Y.

To see why this utility-maximizing rule is true, think for a moment about what would happen if it were *not* true. For example, suppose MU_X/P_X were greater than MU_Y/P_Y; that is, suppose that a consumer purchased a bundle of goods such that the marginal utility from the last dollar spent on X were greater than the marginal utility from the last dollar spent on Y. This would mean that the consumer could increase her or his utility by spending a dollar less on Y and a dollar more on X. But as a consumer shifts to buying more X and less Y, she runs into diminishing marginal utility. Buying more units of X *decreases* the marginal utility derived from consuming additional units of X. As a result, the marginal utility of another dollar spent on X, MU_X/P_X, falls. Now *less* is being spent on Y and that means its marginal utility *increases*. This process continues until $MU_X/P_X = MU_Y/P_Y$. When this condition holds, there is no way for the consumer to increase his or her utility by changing the bundle of goods purchased.

You can see how the utility-maximizing rule works in Frank's choice between country music and basketball. At each stage, Frank chooses the activity that gives him the most utility per dollar. If he goes to a game, the utility he will derive from the next game–marginal utility–falls. If he goes to the club, the utility he will derive from his next visit falls, and so forth.

Another way of looking at this condition is as follows:

$$\text{Utility - Maximizing Rule} : \frac{MU_X}{MU_Y} = \frac{P_X}{P_Y} \text{ for all pairs of goods.}$$

This is simply another way of writing $MU_X/P_X = MU_Y/P_Y$. All we have done is to multiply both sides by P_X and divide both sides by MU_Y.

The ratio of the marginal utility of X to the marginal utility of Y is called the **marginal rate of substitution (MRS).** The marginal rate of substitution is the rate at which a household is willing to give up Y to get an additional unit of X. When MU_X/MU_Y is equal to four, for example, one additional unit of X is four times more valuable than one additional unit of Y. In other words, I would be willing to trade four units of Y for one additional unit of X. The price ratio, P_X/P_Y, tells me the rate at which the market allows me to trade off X for Y. When P_X/P_Y is equal to five, for example, one unit of X sells for five times more than one unit of Y–that is, if I gave up one unit of X, I could buy five units of Y.

If MU_X/MU_Y were four and P_X/P_Y were five, I would, in fact, buy more Y. I lose no utility if I trade one unit of X for *four* units of Y, but the market will get me *five* units of Y if I forgo buying one unit of X. Thus, I gain utility if I consume less X and more Y. The opposite would occur if MU_X/MU_Y were greater than the price ratio. But consuming more Y lowers MU_Y, and buying less X raises MU_X.

marginal rate of substitution (MRS) The rate at which a person is willing to substitute Y for X; it is the number of units of Y a person is willing to give up in exchange for a unit of X. More formally, it is the ratio of the marginal utility derived from consuming good X to the marginal utility derived from consuming good Y.

That pushes the ratio MU_X/MU_Y, the marginal rate of substitution, toward the price ratio. When they are equal, no further adjustment will increase utility.[5]

Diminishing Marginal Utility and Downward-Sloping Demand

The concept of diminishing marginal utility offers us one reason why people spread their incomes over a variety of goods and services rather than spending them all on one or two items. It also leads us to conclude that demand curves slope downward.

If a demand curve shows how much of a product will be purchased either by a single household or by all households in the market at each price, it also tells us about willingness to pay. In private markets, we have to pay for what we want to get it. Consumption is contingent upon payment. This means that we are forced to reveal through our behavior how much each good is worth to us. More formally, we must reveal the value that we place on the utility gained from consuming a marginal unit of a good.

You can see this by looking carefully at the household demand curve in Figure 6.6. As we move to the right along the X axis, the quantity of X that the household consumes per period is increasing and marginal utility is decreasing. As long as the utility gained from additional consumption of the good exceeds its price, consumption will continue. At a price of P_X^1, the household buys q_X^1 units of good X. This means that up to q_X^1 (to the left of point A), the value of the marginal utility gained from each unit of X is *greater* than P_X^1. Beyond q_X^1 (to the right of point A), however, the value of the marginal utility gained from additional units of X is *less* than P_X^1. Thus, consumption stops at q_X^1. In other words, if at a price of P_X^1 a household chooses to buy q_X^1 units of good X, it must be that q_X^1 is the utility-maximizing choice at P_X^1. Otherwise, the household would have chosen a different quantity to buy.

If the price drops to P_X^2, the household will consume more. It will buy X as long as the value of the marginal utility gained from additional units is greater than P_X^2, a lower value than P_X^2. Moving from point A to point B, the household is buying units that were not worth buying (in utility terms) at a price of P_X^1, but which are worth buying at a price of P_X^2.

---

[5]This condition is an important one. As long as it holds for all consumers, it can be shown that the distribution of final output is *efficient*—that is, there are no trades that can be made to make both parties better off. This matter is discussed in detail in Chapter 12.

FIGURE 6.6

Diminishing Marginal Utility and Downward-Sloping Demand

Up to q_X^1 (to the left of point A), the value of the marginal utility gained from each unit of X is greater than P_X^1. Above q_X^1 (to the right of point A), the value of the marginal utility gained from additional units of X is less than P_X^1. In moving from point A to point B, the household is buying units that were *not* worth buying (in utility terms) at a price of P_X^1, but which *are* worth buying at a price of P_X^1. Because marginal utility declines, more will be purchased at lower prices.

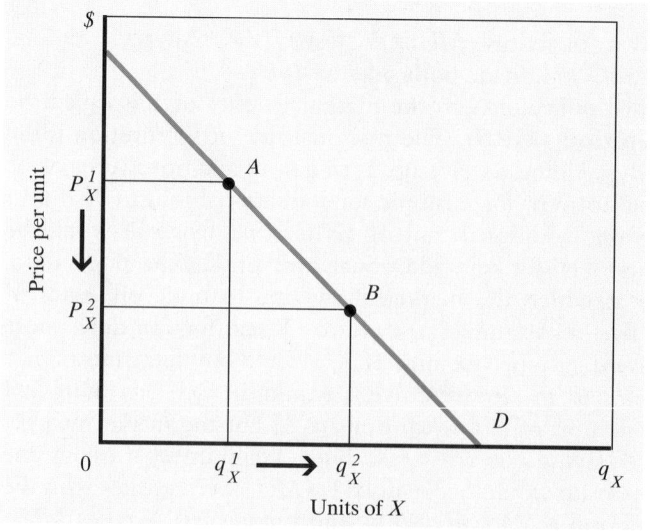

It follows, then, that as long as marginal utility diminishes with additional consumption of a good, the quantity demanded will increase when the price of that good falls, *ceteris paribus*. Goods that simply did not provide enough utility to warrant purchase at the higher prices *do* provide enough utility to warrant their purchase at the lower prices. The law of diminishing marginal utility thus leads us to conclude that demand curves always slope downward to the right.

The concept of utility as we have discussed it here is abstract. It may seem artificial, first because utility cannot be measured, and second because comparisons cannot be made between individuals. While the idea of utility is, we believe, a helpful way of thinking about the choice process, there is an explanation for downward-sloping demand curves that does not rely on the concept of utility or the assumption of diminishing marginal utility. This explanation centers on income and substitution effects.

INCOME AND SUBSTITUTION EFFECTS

Another way of thinking about household choices avoids any direct use of the concept of utility. It also leads us to the conclusion that a negative, or downward-sloping, relationship is very likely to exist between quantity demanded and price.

Keeping in mind that consumers face constrained choices, consider the probable response of a household to a decline in the price of some heavily used product, *ceteris paribus*. How might a household currently consuming many goods be likely to respond to a fall in the price of one of those goods if its income, its preferences, and all other prices remained unchanged? Clearly, the household would face a new budget constraint, and its final choice of all goods and services might change. A decline in the price of gasoline, for example, may affect not only how much gasoline you purchase but also the kind of car you buy, when and how much you travel, where you go, and, not so directly, how many movies you see this month and how many projects around the house you get done.

THE INCOME EFFECT Price changes affect households in two ways. First, if we assume that households confine their choices to products that improve their well-being, then a decline in the price of any product, *ceteris paribus*, makes the household unequivocally better off. In other words, if a household continues to buy the exact same amount of every good and service after the price decrease, it will have income left over. That extra income may be spent on the product whose price has declined, hereafter called good *X*, or on other products. The change in consumption of *X* due to this improvement in well-being is called the **income effect of a price change.**

Suppose that I live in Florida and that three times a year I fly to Nashville to visit my mother. Suppose further that last year a round-trip ticket to Nashville cost $229. This year, however, increased competition among the airlines has led one airline to offer round-trip tickets to Nashville for $129. Assuming that the price remains at $129 all year, I am better off this year than I was last year. I can now fly home exactly the same number of times, and I will have spent $300 less for airline tickets than I did last year. Now that I'm better off, I have additional opportunities. I could fly home a fourth time this year, leaving $171 ($300 minus $129) to spend on other things, or I could fly home the same number of times (three) and spend all of the extra $300 on other things.

FIGURE 6.7

The Effects of a Decrease in Price on Quantity Demanded

At prices P_X^1 and P_Y^1, this household consumes q_X^1 units of good X (point A on the initial opportunity set). If the price of X falls to P_X^2, *ceteris paribus* (holding income, I, and the price of Y, P_Y, constant), the budget constraint swivels out to the right, increasing the opportunities for the household to buy more X and more Y. If the household moves from point A to point B, it has chosen to buy more of both X and Y. The demand curve in Figure 6.7b shows the quantity of X demanded as a function of the price of X.

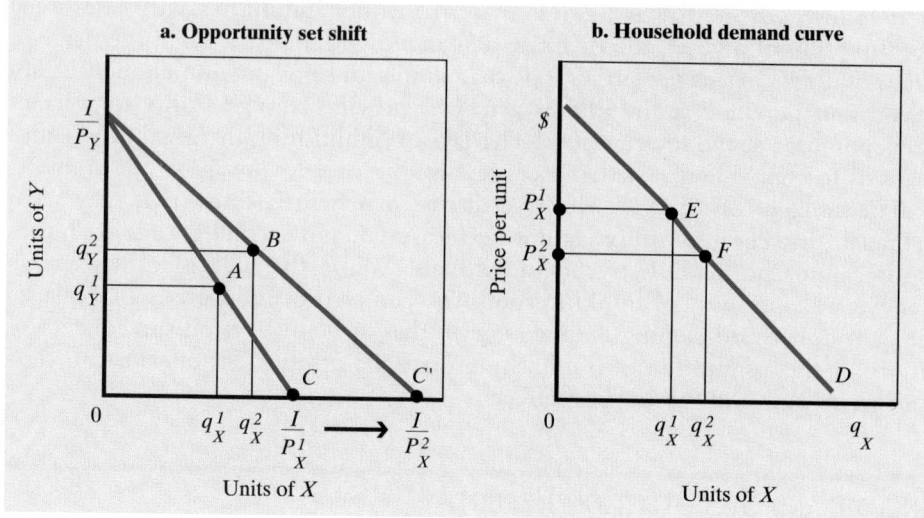

The income effect of this price change is illustrated in Figure 6.7. Figure 6.7a shows how a household's budget constraint is affected by a decrease in the price of a good, X. Assuming that income (I) and the price of Y (P_Y) remain constant, a drop in the price of X from P_X^1 to P_X^2 swivels the budget constraint to the right. Recall that the point where the budget constraint crosses the X axis (point C in the original budget constraint) is the total amount of X that the household could buy if it spent all of its income on X. This amount is equal to I divided by the price of X (I/P_X^1). When the price of X decreases from P_X^1 to P_X^2, the total amount of X that the household could buy if it spent all its income on X increases from I/P_X^1 to I/P_X^2.

Assume that the household decided initially to buy q_X^1 units of X and q_Y^1 units of Y (point A on the initial budget constraint). After the price change, the consumption opportunities facing the household are expanded; the opportunity set is larger. Just as I can buy more trips home and other things when the price of a round-trip ticket to Nashville drops, the household can buy more X, more Y, or more of both when the price of X falls. If the household decides to buy more of both X *and* Y, it might choose a point like point B on the expanded budget constraint.

Figure 6.7a contains enough information for us to graph two points on our household's demand curve for X. When the price of X was P_X^1, the quantity of X demanded was q_X^1; when the price of X dropped to P_X^2, the quantity of X demanded rose to q_X^2. Figure 6.7 plots the two points on the household demand curve.

THE SUBSTITUTION EFFECT The fact that a price decline leaves households better off is only part of the story. When the price of a product falls, that product also becomes *relatively* cheaper. That is, it becomes more attractive relative to potential substitutes. A fall in the price of a product, X, might cause a household to shift its purchasing pattern away from substitutes toward X. This shift is called the **substitution effect of a price change.**

Earlier, we made the point that the "real" cost or price of a good is what one must sacrifice in order to consume it. This opportunity cost is determined by relative prices.

To see why this is so, consider again the choice that I face when a round-trip ticket to Nashville costs $229. Each trip that I take requires a sacrifice of $229 worth of other goods and services. When the price drops to $129, the opportunity cost of a ticket has dropped by $100. In other words, after the price decline, I have to sacrifice only $129 (rather than $229) worth of other goods and services to visit Mom.

To clarify the distinction between the income and substitution effects in your mind, imagine how I would be affected if two things happened to me simultaneously. First, the price of round-trip air travel between Florida and Nashville drops from $229 to $129. Second, my income is reduced by $300. I am now faced with new relative prices, but–assuming I flew home three times last year–I am no better off than I was before the price of a ticket declined. The decrease in the price of air travel has exactly offset my decrease in income.

Despite the fact that I am no better off than I was, I am still likely to take more trips home. Why? Because the opportunity cost of a trip home is now lower, *ceteris paribus* (that is, assuming no change in the prices of other goods and services). A trip to Nashville now requires a sacrifice of only $129 worth of other goods and services, not the $229 worth that it did before. Thus, I will substitute away from other goods toward trips to see my mother.

Everything works in the opposite direction when a price rises, *ceteris paribus*. A price increase makes households worse off. If income and other prices don't change, spending the same amount of money buys less, and households will be forced to buy less. They may purchase less X or cut spending on other things. This is the income effect. In addition, when the price of a product rises, that item becomes more expensive relative to potential substitutes, and the household is likely to substitute other goods for it. This is the substitution effect. (For another example of the income and substitution effects, see the Issues and Applications box entitled "The Tax Laws and the Income and Substitution Effects.")

What do the income and substitution effects tell us about the demand curve? Quite simply:

> Both the income and substitution effects imply a negative relationship between price and quantity demanded–in other words, downward-sloping demand. When the price of something falls, *ceteris paribus,* we are better off, and we are likely to buy more of that good and other goods (income effect). And because lower price also means "less expensive relative to substitutes," we are likely to buy more of the good (substitution effect). When the price of something rises, we are worse off, and we will buy less of it (income effect); higher price also means "more expensive relative to substitutes," and we are likely to buy less of it and more of other goods (substitution effect).[6]

---

[6]Careful thought should convince you that for some goods the income and substitution effects work in opposite directions. As you recall, when our income rises, we may buy less of some goods. In Chapter 4, we called such goods *inferior goods*.

When the price of an inferior good rises, it is, like any other good, more expensive relative to substitutes, and we are likely to buy less of it as we replace it with lower-priced substitutes. However, the price increase leaves us worse off, and when we are worse off we increase our demand for inferior goods. Thus, the income effect could lead us to buy more of the good, partially offsetting the substitution effect.

Even if a good is "very inferior," demand curves will slope downward as long as the substitution effect is larger than the income effect. But it is possible, at least in theory, for the income effect to be larger. In such a case, a price increase would actually lead to an increase in quantity demanded. This possibility was pointed out by Alfred Marshall in *Principles of Economics*. Marshall attributes the notion of an upward-sloping demand curve to Sir Robert Giffen, and for this reason the notion is often referred to as *Giffen's paradox*. Fortunately or unfortunately, no one has ever demonstrated that a Giffen good has ever existed.

THE TAX LAWS AND THE INCOME AND SUBSTITUTION EFFECTS

After Hurricane Andrew hit Florida in 1992, the Thomas J. Lipton Company donated $50,000 to help rebuild the state. Increased tax rates may bring about decreased charitable giving as a result of the substitution effect.

Charitable contributions are an important source of revenue for the nonprofit sector. In 1990, individuals in the United States contributed about $102 billion to such tax-exempt nonprofit organizations as museums, churches, and colleges.

Charitable contributions are afforded special treatment in the U.S. tax code. Individuals, families, and corporations are permitted to deduct their contributions to most nonprofit organizations from their taxable income. Thus, for every dollar donated to such an organization, there is a tax saving. Changes in the tax laws during the 1980s were not favorable to charitable giving, however. A recent paper by Charles Clotfelter examines the effects of the revised tax laws on charitable contributions in the 1980s. To understand how taxes affect charitable giving, the *income* and *substitution effects* are critical.

How Taxes Can Affect Behavior

Almost everyone must file a tax return each year. Filers are permitted to take either a standard deduction of a specified amount or to "itemize."

The expenditures that can be deducted include charitable contributions.

When deductions are itemized, the amount of tax saving from a deduction depends on the taxpayer's tax rate bracket. Before the 1981 Economic Recovery Tax Act, the highest tax bracket was 70 percent. This meant that if someone in that bracket donated $1000 to the Red Cross, the net cost of that gift to the donor was only $300. Why? Because a tax rate of 70% meant that deducting a gift of $1000 from taxable income saved the donor $700 in taxes.

In 1981, the highest tax rate was reduced to 50 percent. Worried nonprofit organizations were quick to point out that this tax cut increased the "cost" of giving substantially. When the top tax rate decreased from 70% to 50%, the net cost of the $1000 gift rose from $300 to $500—an increase of 66.7 percent!

The Tax Reform Act of 1986 reduced the rate affecting the highest-income households even further, from 50% to 38.5 percent. Thus, the net cost of the $1000 contribution rose from $300 before 1981, to $500 between 1981 and 1986, to $615 in 1987.

The Predicted Effects

How might we expect households to respond to the lower tax rates? First, because tax rates were decreased, households had more disposable income after the cuts. Assuming that charitable giving is a normal good, this income effect should lead to more giving. But giving to charity is now more expensive relative to other goods. The opportunity cost of a $1000 donation before 1981 was $300; in 1986 it was $500. This substitution effect, which should lead to fewer charitable contributions, is what the nonprofit sector worried about.

What Really Happened?

Clotfelter found that the overall effects of lower tax rates on charitable giving were relatively small over the period he studied but were generally in line with what theory would predict. For example, he found the largest reductions in giving among the highest-income households facing the highest tax brackets. These people had the largest substitution effects. On the other hand, nonitemizers (i.e., those who took the standard deduction) actually increased their giving somewhat. This result is exactly what theory would predict. Those who do not itemize their deductions do not receive any tax benefits from giving to charity. Thus, for those who took the standard deduction, the tax cut had an income effect but no substitution effect. We would expect a strong income effect that is not accompanied by an offsetting substitution effect to lead to increased charitable donations, and this is exactly what happened.

Source: Based on Charles T. Clotfelter, "The Impact of Tax Reform on Charitable Giving: A 1989 Perspective," the Office of Tax Policy Research, Working Paper Series, Working Paper No. 90-7, School of Business Administration, University of Michigan (Ann Arbor), December 1, 1989.

CONSUMER SURPLUS

The argument, made several times already, that the market forces us to reveal a great deal about our personal preferences is an extremely important one, and it bears repeating at least once more here. If you are free to choose within the constraints imposed by prices and your income and you decide to buy, say, a cheeseburger for $2.50, you have "revealed" that a cheeseburger is worth at least $2.50 to you.

A simple market demand curve such as the one in Figure 6.8a illustrates this point quite clearly. At the current market price of P_X^1, consumers will purchase Q_X^1. There is only one price in the market, and the demand curve tells us how much of X households would buy if they could purchase all they wanted at the posted price. Anyone who values a unit of X higher than P_X^1 will buy it; anyone who does not value it that highly will not.

Some people, however, value X at more than P_X^1. As Figure 6.8a shows, even if the price were at P_X^2, someone would still buy one unit of the good. If that person were able to buy the good at a price of P_X^1, she would earn what is called a **consumer surplus.** Consumer surplus is the difference between the maximum amount a person is willing to pay for a good and its current market price.

The second unit of X in Figure 6.8a is valued at more than the market price as well, although the consumer surplus gained is slightly less. Point B on the simple market demand curve shows the maximum amount that someone would be willing to pay for the second unit of output. The consumer surplus earned by that person is equal to the shaded area between B and the price, P_X^1. Similarly, for the third unit of X, maximum willingness to pay is given by point C; consumer surplus is a bit lower than it is at points A and B, but it is still significant.

The total value of the consumer surplus suggested by the data in Figure 6.8a is roughly equal to the area of the shaded triangle in Figure 6.8b. To understand why this is so, think about offering X to consumers at successively lower prices. If the good were actually sold at a price P_X^1, those near point A on the demand curve would get a large surplus; those at point B would get a smaller surplus. Those at point E would get none.

consumer surplus The difference between the maximum amount a person is willing to pay for a good and its current market price.

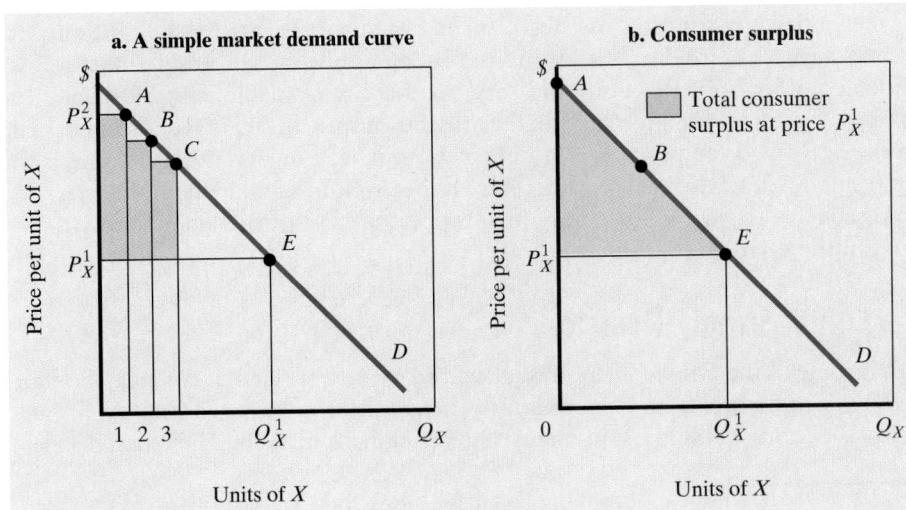

FIGURE 6.8

Market Demand, Revealed Preference, and Consumer Surplus

If a good is produced and sold at a price P_X^1, all those who value the good at less than P_X^1 will not buy it, and all those who value it at more than P_X^1, will buy it. Even at a price of P_X^2, one unit of X would be sold (point A on the demand curve in Figure 6.8a). The difference between the maximum amount that a person is willing to pay for a good and its current market price is the person's consumer surplus. The total consumer surplus suggested by the data in Figure 6.8a is represented by the shaded area in Figure 6.8b.

The idea of consumer surplus helps to explain an old paradox that dates back to Plato. Adam Smith wrote about it in 1776:

> The things which have the greatest value in use have frequently little or no value in exchange; and on the contrary, those which have the greatest value in exchange have frequently little or no value in use. Nothing is more useful than water: but it will purchase scarce any thing; scarce anything can be had in exchange for it. A diamond, on the contrary, has scarce any value in use; but a very great quantity of other goods may frequently be had in exchange for it.[7]

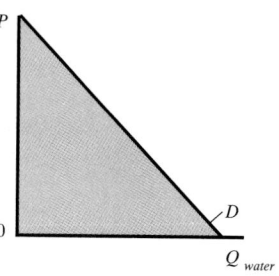

Although diamonds have arguably more than "scarce any value in use" today, Smith's **diamond/water paradox** is still instructive, at least where water is concerned.

The low price of water owes much to the fact that it is in plentiful supply. Each of us enjoys an enormous consumer surplus when we consume nearly free water. We tend to take water for granted, but imagine what would happen to its price if there were simply not enough for everyone. If water were in very short supply, it would command a high price indeed. Although water has enormous use value, it commands only a low price because it is so plentiful. Thus, we all enjoy a very significant consumer surplus. As the figure in the margin shows, at a price of zero, the "value" of water is the entire shaded area.

Although utility is not directly observable or measurable, behavior certainly is. By observing behavior in response to price changes over time or by observing demand at different locations where people face different prices, economists can actually estimate and plot demand curves. Governments often use such analyses to decide whether to go ahead with plans to build a new power plant, road, or bridge.

Consumer surplus measurement is a key element in **cost-benefit analysis,** the formal technique by which the benefits of a public project are weighed against its costs. To decide whether to build a new electrical power plant, we need to know the value, to consumers, of the electricity that it will produce. Just as the value of water to consumers is not just its price times the quantity that people consume, the value of electricity generated is not just the price of electricity times the quantity the new plant will produce. The total value that should be weighed against the costs of the plant includes the consumer surplus that electricity users will enjoy if the plant is built.

HOUSEHOLD CHOICE IN INPUT MARKETS

So far, we have focused on the decision-making process that lies behind output demand curves. Households with limited incomes allocate those incomes across various combinations of goods and services that are available and affordable. In looking at the factors affecting choices in the output market, we assumed that income was fixed, or given. We noted at the outset, however, that income is in fact partially determined by choices that households make in input markets (look back at Figure 6.1). We now turn to a discussion of the labor supply decision and the saving decision.

The Labor Supply Decision

Most income in the United States is wage and salary income paid in compensation for labor. Household members supply labor in exchange for wages or salaries. As in output markets, households face constrained choices in input markets. They must decide

---

[7]Adam Smith, *The Wealth of Nations*, Modern Library Edition (New York: Random House, 1937), p. 28 (1st ed., 1776). The cheapness of water is referred to by Plato in *Euthydem.*, 304B.

1. whether to work,
2. how much to work, and
3. what kind of a job to work at.

In essence, household members must decide how much labor to supply. The choices they make are limited by

1. the availability of jobs,
2. market wage rates, and
3. the skills of the household.

As with decisions in output markets, the labor supply decision involves a set of trade-offs. There are basically two alternatives to working for a wage: (1) not working, and (2) unpaid work. If I don't work, I sacrifice income for the benefits of staying at home and reading, watching TV, going swimming, or sleeping. Another option is to work and produce, but not for a money wage. In this case, I sacrifice money income for the benefits of growing my own food in my garden, bringing up my children, or taking care of my house.

As with the trade-offs in output markets, my final choice depends on how I value the alternatives available. If I work, I earn a wage that I can use to buy things. Thus, the trade-off is between the value of the goods and services I can buy in the market with the wages I earn working versus the value of things I can produce at home–home-grown food, manageable children, clean clothes, and so on–or the value I place on leisure. (This choice is illustrated in Figure 6.9.) In general, then:

> The wage rate can be thought of as the price–or the opportunity cost–of either the benefits of unpaid work or of leisure.

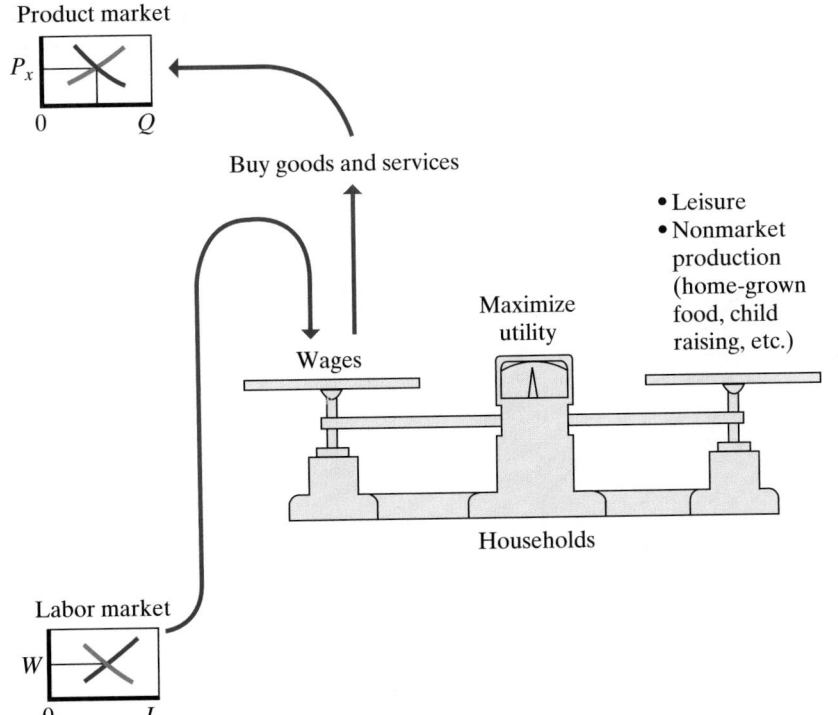

FIGURE 6.9
The Trade-off Facing Households

The decision to enter the work force involves a trade-off between wages (and the goods and services that wages will buy) on the one hand, and leisure and the value of nonmarket production on the other. The opportunity cost of one hour of leisure is W, the wage rate per hour.

The Price of Leisure

Adding the labor supply decision to a household's choices in output markets is almost like adding another good to that household's opportunity set. In our analysis in the early part of this chapter, households had to allocate a limited budget across a set of goods and services. Now they must choose among goods, services, and *leisure*.

When we add leisure to the picture, however, we do so with one important difference. Trading off one good for another involves buying less of one and more of another, so households simply reallocate *money* from one good to the other. "Buying" more leisure, however, means reallocating *time* between work and non-work activities.

If we assume that jobs are available, that households have the option of part-time work, that households receive no nonwage income (such as interest, dividends, or gifts from family members), and that there are no taxes, we can draw the budget constraint facing a typical household. Figure 6.10 shows the new opportunity set that includes leisure. The quantity of leisure consumed appears on the X axis; on the Y axis is the amount of daily income. Assuming that the primary motive for working is to obtain the things that wages will buy, we can think of the Y axis as a measure of all other goods. Since there is no nonwage income, the only way to get goods and services is by working to earn wages.

If I decide to use all my time for leisure activities, I will earn no income and consume no other goods, the situation indicated by point A on the budget constraint. If I decide to work every hour of the day and night for a wage of W per hour, I will earn $24W$ per day and be at point B on the budget constraint. If I take a regular job and work eight hours per day, I will earn $8W$ per day and consume 16 hours of leisure, point C on the budget constraint. For each hour of leisure that I decide to consume, I give up W. In other words, W is the *price of leisure* (see Figure 6.10).

Conditions in the labor market determine the budget constraints and final opportunity sets that face households. The availability of jobs and the wage rates of those jobs determine the final combinations of goods and services that a household can afford. The final choice within these constraints depends on the unique tastes and preferences of each household. Some people place very little value on leisure, while others place a high value on things like playing tennis or lying on the beach—but everyone needs to put food on the table.

FIGURE 6.10
The Labor-Leisure Choice

By plotting income on the Y axis and hours of leisure on the X axis, the graph shows all combinations of daily income and leisure available to someone who can choose how many hours to work at wage rate W. If he chose not to work, he would consume 24 hours of leisure and earn no income. If he worked all the time, he would earn $24W$ per day and have no leisure at all. The budget constraint is a straight line with a constant slope of $-W$. For every additional unit of leisure consumed, income drops by W.

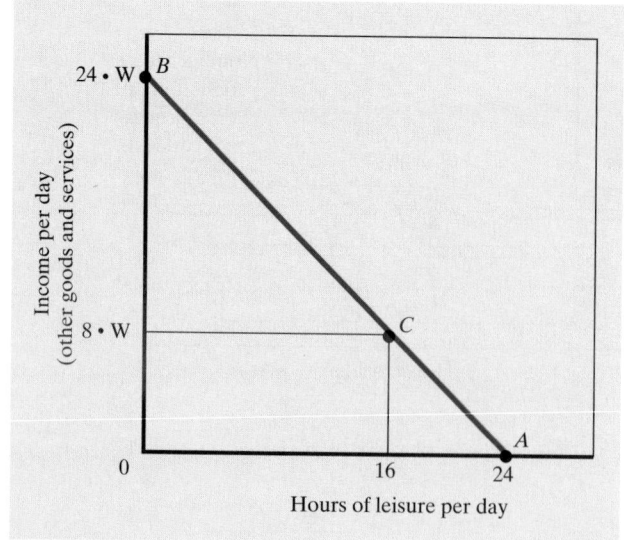

Income and Substitution Effects of a Wage Change

A **labor supply curve** shows the quantity of labor supplied as a function of the wage rate. The shape of the labor supply curve depends on how households react to changes in the wage rate.

Consider an increase in wages. First of all, an increase in wages makes households better off; if they work the same number of hours—that is, if they supply the same amount of labor—they will earn higher incomes and be able to buy more goods and services. But they can also buy more leisure. If leisure is a normal good (that is, a good for which demand increases as income increases), an increase in income will lead to a higher demand for leisure and a lower labor supply. This is the *income effect of a wage increase.*

There is also, however, a potential *substitution effect of a wage increase.* A higher wage rate means that leisure is more expensive. If you think of the wage rate as the price of leisure, each individual hour of leisure consumed at a higher wage costs more in forgone wages. As a result, we would expect households to substitute other goods for leisure. This means working more, or a lower demand for leisure and a higher labor supply.

Note that in the labor market the income and substitution effects work in *opposite* directions when leisure is a normal good. The income effect of a wage increase implies buying more leisure and working less; the substitution effect implies buying less leisure and working more. Whether households will supply more labor overall or less labor overall when wages rise depends, then, on the relative strength of both the income and the substitution effects.

If the substitution effect is greater than the income effect, the wage increase will increase labor supply. This suggests that the labor supply curve slopes upward, or has a positive slope, like the one in Figure 6.11a. If the income effect outweighs the substitution effect, however, a higher wage will lead to added consumption of leisure, and labor supply will decrease. This implies that the labor supply curve "bends back," as the one in Figure 6.11b does.

During the early years of the Industrial Revolution in late eighteenth-century Great Britain, the textile industry operated under what was called the "putting-out" system. Spinning and weaving were done in small cottages to supplement the family farm income, hence the term "cottage industry." During that period, wages and household incomes rose considerably. Some economic historians claim that this higher income actually led many households to take more leisure and work fewer hours; the empirical evidence suggests a backward-bending labor supply curve.

Just as income and substitution effects helped us understand household choices in output markets, they now help us understand household choices in input markets. The point here is simple:

> When leisure is added to the choice set, the line between input and output market decisions becomes blurred. In fact, households decide simultaneously how much of each good to consume and how much leisure to consume.

LABOR SUPPLY AND TAXES In recent years much has been written about the effect of taxes on the incentive to work. Because taxes take some of what we earn, the argument goes, people work less, and some may even decide to stay out of the labor force altogether. If we reduce tax rates, the argument continues, people will work harder, more people will work, and the economy will be more productive. Using the language of economics, the question here is: How do tax rates affect the supply of labor?

labor supply curve A diagram that shows the quantity of labor supplied as a function of the wage rate. Its shape depends on how households react to changes in the wage rate.

FIGURE 6.11
Two Labor Supply Curves

If we think of leisure as a normal good, an increase in wages that increases income may lead via the income effect to more leisure and less work. When the income effect outweighs the substitution effect, the result may be a "backward-bending" labor supply curve: lower labor supply at higher wages.

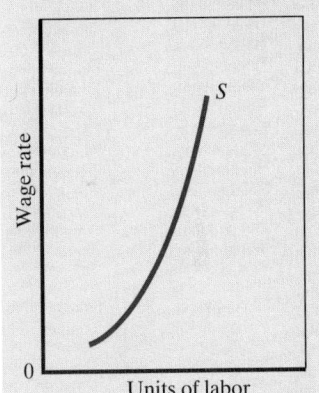

a. Substitution effect dominates

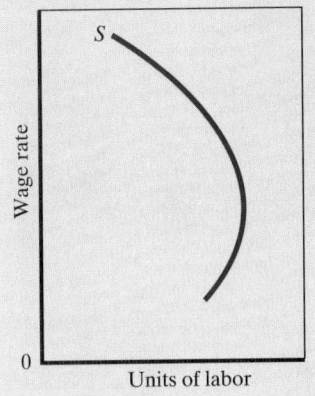

b. Income effect dominates

Let's first look to theory for an answer. Jennifer does freelance drafting, working mostly on illustrations and graphics for books and magazines. Suppose she works for $10 per hour and pays 20% of what she earns in taxes. If she works 50 hours per week, she makes $500 and pays taxes of $100, taking home $400. At these tax and wage rates, each hour of leisure "costs" Jennifer $8. If she works an extra hour, she makes $10, of which $2 goes to taxes. Eight dollars, then, is both Jennifer's after-tax wage and the price of one hour of leisure.

Now suppose the tax rate is suddenly reduced to 10 percent. Will Jennifer work more? As you can guess, the answer to this question depends on the size of the income and substitution effects. In this case, the two effects work in opposite directions. First, the tax cut means that Jennifer's after-tax wage rate is higher. By working an additional hour, she now takes home $9 instead of just $8. This means that the price, or opportunity cost, of an added hour of leisure is higher. When the relative price of a good—in this case leisure—rises, households will substitute other goods for it. This substitution effect should push Jennifer in the direction of working more hours.

But things are not this simple. Jennifer is also better off now. By working 50 hours, she still earns $500 before tax, but she now takes home $450 instead of $400. She may decide to "spend" some of this added "income" on leisure. This income effect should push Jennifer in the direction of working less. It is clear, then, that:

> Whether a tax rate cut increases or decreases the overall supply of labor depends on the relative size of the income and substitution effects.

Many empirical studies have tried to estimate the actual effect of taxes on labor supply. The available evidence suggests that, in general, the substitution effect is somewhat larger—that is, that tax cuts should indeed lead to a larger labor supply. The elasticity, or responsiveness, of labor supply for most groups seems, however, to be fairly low—that is, inelastic. (This subject is explored in much more detail in Chapter 19.)

Saving and Borrowing: Present Versus Future Consumption

We began this chapter by looking behind the demand curve to examine the way households allocate a fixed income over a large number of available goods and services. We then pointed out that, at least in part, choices made by households determine income levels. Within the constraints imposed by the market, households decide whether to work and how much to work.

So far, however, we have talked about only the current period—the allocation of current income among alternative uses and the work/leisure choice today. But households can also (1) use present income to finance future spending—they can *save*—or (2) use future income to finance present spending—they can *borrow*.

When a household decides not to spend part of its current income but rather to save it, it is using current income to finance future consumption. That future consumption may come in three years, when you use your savings to buy a car; in ten years, when you sell stock to put a deposit on a house; or in 45 years, when you retire and begin to receive money from your pension plan. On the other hand, most people cannot finance large purchases—a house or condominium, for example—out of current income and savings. They almost always borrow money and sign a mortgage. When a household borrows, it is, in essence, financing a current purchase with future income. It pays back the loan out of future income.

Even in simple economies such as the two-person, desert-island economy of Colleen and Bill (see Chapter 2), people must make decisions about *present versus future consumption*. Colleen and Bill had a number of options: They could (1) produce goods for today's consumption by hunting and gathering, (2) consume leisure by sleeping on the beach, or (3) work on projects to enhance future consumption opportunities. Building a house or a boat over a five-year period is trading present for future consumption.

When a household saves, it usually puts the money into something that will generate a flow of interest or profit. There is no sense in putting money under your mattress when you can make it work in so many ways: savings accounts, money market funds, common stocks, corporate bonds, and so forth–many of which are virtually risk free. When you put your money in any of these places, you are actually lending it out, and the borrower pays you a fee for its use. This fee usually takes the form of *interest*.

Business firms borrow most often to finance capital investment projects. The amount of capital investment in an economy is constrained in the long run by the saving rate of that economy.[8] You can think of household *saving,* then, as the economy's supply of capital. Look back at Figure 6.1. When a firm borrows to finance a capital acquisition, it is almost as if households have supplied the capital for the fee we call interest.

Just as changes in wage rates affect household behavior in the labor market, so do changes in interest rates affect household behavior in capital markets. When interest rates change, they affect both the cost of borrowing *and* the return to saving. Higher interest rates mean that borrowing is more expensive–required monthly payments on a newly purchased house or car will be higher. But higher interest rates also mean that saving will earn a higher return: $1000 invested in a 5% savings account or bond yields $50 per year, but if rates rise to 10%, the annual interest rises to $100.

But what impact do interest rates have on saving behavior? As with the effect of wage changes on labor supply behavior, the effect of changes in interest rates on saving behavior can best be understood in terms of income and substitution effects. Suppose, for example, that I have been saving for a number of years for retirement. Will an increase in interest rates lead to an increase or a decrease in my saving? The answer is not obvious. First, because each dollar saved will earn a higher rate of return, the "price" of spending today in terms of forgone future spending is higher. That is, each dollar that I spend today (instead of saving) costs me more in terms of future consumption because my saving will now earn a higher return. On this score I will be led to save *more,* and this is the substitution effect at work.

But note that I will also earn more on all the saving that I have done to date, and in this sense I am better off. I will not need to save as much for retirement or future consumption as I did before. Consequently, I will be led to save *less,* and this is the income effect at work. The final impact of a change in interest rates depends on the relative size of the income and substitution effects. The hypothetical saving function in Figure 6.12 shows saving increasing as the interest rate rises. If you think carefully about it, the shape of the curve in the figure

---

[8]Here we are looking at a country as if it were isolated from the rest of the world—as if it were a closed economy. Very often, however, capital investment is financed by funds loaned or provided by foreign citizens or governments. For example, in recent years a substantial amount of Japanese savings has found its way into the United States to buy stocks, bonds, and other financial instruments. In part, these flows finance capital investment. Also, the United States and other countries that contribute funds to the World Bank and the International Monetary Fund have provided billions in outright grants and loans to help developing countries produce capital.

FIGURE 6.12
Saving as a Function of the Interest Rate

The interest rate determines the trade-off between present and future consumption. Higher interest rates mean that a dollar saved now buys more future consumption. Thus, higher interest rates encourage saving. But higher interest rates also mean that savers will earn more on saving from earlier years, reducing the need to save. The final effect depends on the relative strength of these substitution and income effects.

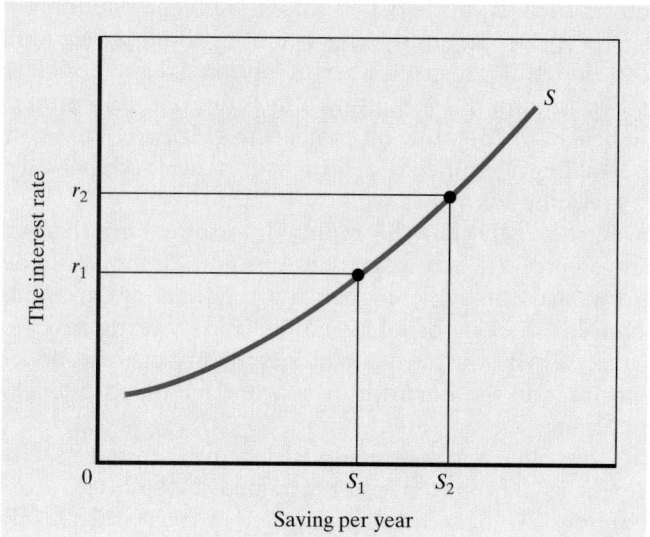

financial capital market The complex set of institutions in which suppliers of capital (households that save) and the demand for capital (business firms wanting to invest) interact.

assumes that the substitution effect is larger than the income effect. Most of the empirical evidence suggests that this is so.

Saving and investment decisions involve a huge and complex set of institutions, the **financial capital market,** in which the suppliers of capital (households that save) and the demand for capital (business firms that want to invest) interact. We treat capital markets in detail in Chapter 11.

A QUICK REVIEW: HOUSEHOLDS IN OUTPUT AND INPUT MARKETS

In probing the behavior of households in both input and output markets, we went behind the household output demand curve, using the simplifying assumption that income was fixed and given, in order to examine the nature of constrained choice. Income, wealth, and prices set the limits, or *constraints,* within which households must make their choices in output markets. Within those limits, households make their choices on the basis of personal tastes and preferences.

The notion of *utility* helps to explain the process of choice. The law of *diminishing marginal utility* partly explains why people seem to spread their incomes over many different goods and services and why demand curves have a negative slope. Another important explanation behind the negative relationship between price and quantity demanded lies in *income effects* and *substitution effects.*

As we turned to input markets, we relaxed the assumption that income was fixed and given. In the labor market, households are forced to weigh the value of leisure against the value of goods and services that can be bought with wage income. Once again, we found household preferences for goods and leisure operating within a set of constraints imposed by the market. Households also face the problem of allocating income and consumption over more than one period of time. They can finance spending in the future with today's income by saving and earning interest, or they can spend tomorrow's income today by borrowing.

We now have a rough sketch of the factors that determine *output demand* and *input supply.* (You can review these in Figure 6.1.) In the next three chapters, we turn to firm behavior and explore in detail the factors that affect *output supply* and *input demand.*

SUMMARY

Household Choice in Output Markets

1. In perfectly competitive markets, prices are determined by the forces of supply and demand, and no single household or firm has any control over them. The assumption of a perfectly competitive market underlies all of our discussions through Chapter 12. Much of what we say in these chapters, however, can be generalized to the other forms of market structure. We also assume that households possess *perfect knowledge* of product prices, product availability, product quality, and wage rates.

2. Every household must make three basic decisions: (1) how much of each product, or output, to demand, (2) how much labor to supply, and (3) how much to spend today and how much to save for the future.

3. Income, wealth, and prices define a household's *budget constraint*. The budget constraint separates those combinations of goods and services that are available from those that are not. All the points below and to the left of a graph of a household's budget constraint make up its *choice set,* or *opportunity set.*

4. It is best to think of the household choice problem as one of allocating income over a large number of goods and services. A change in the price of one good may change the entire allocation. Demand for some goods may rise while demand for others may fall.

5. As long as a household faces a limited income, the *real* cost of any single good or service is the value of the *other* goods and services that could have been purchased with the same amount of money.

6. Within the constraints of prices, income, and wealth, household decisions ultimately depend on preferences–likes, dislikes, and tastes.

The Basis of Choice: Utility

7. The idea of subjective weighing of values was formalized in the nineteenth century into the concept of *utility:* Whether one item is preferable to another depends on how much utility, or satisfaction, it yields relative to its alternatives.

8. The *law of diminishing marginal utility* says that the more of any good we consume in a given period of time, the less satisfaction, or utility, we get out of each additional, or marginal, unit of that good.

9. Households allocate income among goods and services in order to maximize utility. This implies choosing activities that yield the highest marginal utility per dollar. In a two-good world,

households will choose so as to equate the marginal utility per dollar spent on *X* with the marginal utility per dollar spent on *Y.* This is the *utility-maximizing rule.*

Income and Subsitution Effects

10. The fact that demand curves slope downward, or have a negative slope, can be explained in two ways: (1) Marginal utility for all goods diminishes, and (2) for most goods both the *income and substitution effects* of a price decline lead to more consumption of the good.

Consumer Surplus

11. When any good is sold at a fixed price, households must "reveal" whether that good is worth the price being asked. For many people who buy in a given market, the product is worth more than its current price. Those people receive a *consumer surplus.*

Household Choice in Input Markets

12. In the labor market, a trade-off exists between the value of the goods and services that can be bought in the market or produced at home and the value that one places on leisure. The opportunity cost of paid work is leisure and unpaid work. The wage rate is the price, or opportunity cost, of either the benefits of unpaid work or of leisure.

13. The income and substitution effects of a change in the wage rate work in opposite directions. Higher wages mean that (1) leisure is more expensive (likely response: people work *more*–substitution effect), and (2) more income is earned in a given number of hours so some time may be spent on leisure (likely response: people work *less*–income effect).

14. The effect of a tax cut on labor supply cannot be predicted from theory alone. Whether a cut in the tax rate increases or decreases the overall supply of labor depends on the relative size of the income and substitution effects.

15. In addition to deciding how to allocate its present income among goods and services, a household may also decide to save or borrow. When a household decides to save part of its current income, it is using current income to finance future spending. When a household borrows, it finances current purchases with future income.

16. A change in interest rates has a positive effect on saving if the substitution effect dominates the income effect, and a negative effect if the income effect dominates the substitution effect.

REVIEW TERMS AND CONCEPTS

$$\frac{MU_X}{P_X} = \frac{MU_Y}{P_Y} \text{ for all pairs of goods}$$

$$\text{or } \frac{MU_X}{MU_Y} = \frac{P_X}{P_Y} \text{ for all pairs of goods}$$

PROBLEM SET

1. Sketch the following budget constraints:

	P_X	P_Y	INCOME
a.	$20	$50	$1000
b.	$40	$50	$1000
c.	$20	$100	$1000
d.	$20	$50	$2000
e.	$.25	$.25	$7.00
f.	$.25	$.50	$7.00
g.	$.50	$.25	$7.00

2. On January 1, Professor Smith made a resolution to lose some weight and save some money. He decided that he would strictly budget $100 for lunches each month. For lunch he has only two choices: the faculty club, where the price of a lunch is $5, and Alice's Restaurant, where the price of a lunch is $10. Every day that he doesn't eat lunch, he runs five miles.

    a. Assuming that Professor Smith spends the entire $100 each month at either Alice's or the club, sketch his budget constraint. Show actual numbers on the axes.

    b. Last month Professor Smith chose to eat at the club 10 times and at Alice's 5 times. Does this choice fit within his budget constraint?

    c. Last month, Alice ran a half-price lunch special all month. All lunches were reduced to $5. Show the effect on Professor Smith's budget constraint.

    d. During the sale, Professor Smith continued to eat at Alice's only 5 times, but ate at the club 15 times. This implies that Alice's meals are "inferior goods." Explain why. (*Hint:* Use income and substitution effects.)

3. Reform of the U.S. welfare system has been a goal of many administrations, including President Clinton's. The major thrust of welfare reform proposals over the last two decades has been to restore the incentive to work. Because welfare programs are for low-income families, those who earn income lose their eligibility for welfare. This acts as a stiff "tax" on working.

    In 1981, President Reagan proposed and the Congress approved significant cuts in welfare expenditures. Cutting benefits would make living on welfare less attractive, it was argued, and lead to an expansion of the labor supply. But the way the welfare changes were enacted led to a second effect. Before the cuts, a welfare recipient's benefits were reduced by $.50 for every dollar he or she earned. For example, someone who earned $200 per month would lose $100 in

welfare benefits; thus, his or her final income would rise by only $100. After the cuts, the implicit tax rate went up to 80%: Benefits were reduced by $.80 for every dollar earned. For example, after the cuts, a person earning $200 would lose $160 in benefits. This meant that final income would rise by only $40.

    Using the income and substitution effects, explain how the Reagan cuts could lead to either an increase or a decrease in labor supply.

4. Sketch the income/leisure budget constraint facing a person with

    a. a 24-hour endowment of time daily,

    b. $50 in property income per day (received regardless of work effort),

    c. a job that requires a minimum of eight hours of work per day and that pays a wage of $10 per hour, plus time-and-a-half for all work over eight hours (1.5 × $10), and

    d. no other work opportunities.

    Note: All these should be embodied in a *single* income/leisure budget constraint.

5. For each of the following events, consider how you might react. What things might you consume more of? What things might you consume less of? Would you work more or less? Would you increase or decrease your saving? Are your responses consistent with the discussion of household behavior in this chapter?

    a. Tuition at your college is cut 25 percent.

    b. You receive an award that pays you $300 per month for the next five years.

    c. The price of food doubles (if you are on a meal plan, assume that your board charges double).

    d. A new business opens up nearby offering part-time jobs at $20 per hour.

6. Assume that as a result of two recent hijackings and bombings, peoples' desire to fly diminishes significantly. Describe and graph (using supply and demand curves) how you might expect the air travel market to react. What might happen to the price of airline tickets? Explain consumers' reactions to any price changes in terms of income and substitution effects.

7. Is it possible for a unit of a good to have a negative marginal utility? Can you think of an example? How would consumption of this unit affect total utility? Why would it make no sense to knowingly purchase a good with negative utility?

APPENDIX TO CHAPTER 6
INDIFFERENCE CURVES

Early in this chapter, you saw how a consumer choosing between two goods is constrained by the prices of those goods and by his or her income. This appendix returns to that example and analyzes the process of choice more formally. (Before we proceed, review carefully the text under the heading "The Budget Constraint More Formally.")

ASSUMPTIONS

We base the following analysis on four assumptions:

1. We assume that this analysis is restricted to goods that yield positive marginal utility, or, more simply, that "more is better." One way to justify this assumption is to say that if more of something actually makes you worse off, you can simply throw it away at no cost. This is the assumption of free disposal.

2. We assume diminishing marginal rate of substitution. That is, as more of X and less of Y is consumed, MU_X/MU_Y declines. As you consume more of X and less of Y, the rate at which you are willing to substitute X for Y declines–X becomes less valuable in terms of units of Y, or Y becomes more valuable in terms of X. This is almost, but not precisely, equivalent to assuming diminishing marginal utility.

3. We assume that consumers have the ability to choose among the combinations of goods and services available. Confronted with the choice between two alternative combinations of goods and services, A and B, a consumer will respond in one of three ways: (1) She prefers A over B, (2) she prefers B over A, or (3) she is indifferent between A and B.

4. We assume that consumer choices are consistent with a simple postulate of rationality. If a consumer shows that he prefers A to B and subsequently shows that he prefers B to a third alternative, C, he should prefer A to C if confronted with a choice between the two.

Deriving Indifference Curves

If we accept these four assumptions, we can construct a "map" of a consumer's preferences. These preference maps are made up of indifference curves. An **indifference curve** is a set of points, each point representing a combination of goods X and Y, all of which yield the same total utility.

Figure 6A.1 shows how we might go about deriving an indifference curve for a hypothetical consumer. Each

FIGURE 6A.1
An Indifference Curve

An indifference curve is a set of points, each representing a combination of some amount of X and some amount of Y, that all yield the same amount of total utility. The consumer depicted here is indifferent between bundles A and B, B and C, and A and C.

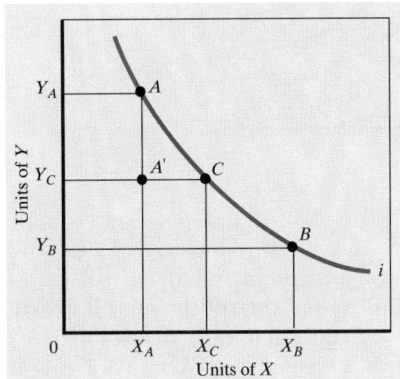

point in the diagram represents some amount of X and some amount of Y. Point A in the diagram, for example, represents X_A units of X and Y_A units of Y. Now suppose that we take some amount of Y away from our hypothetical consumer, moving him to A'. At A' he has the same amount of X–that is, X_A units–but less Y; he now has only Y_C units of Y. Since "more is better," our consumer is unequivocally worse off at A' than he was at A.

To compensate for the loss of Y, we now begin giving our consumer some more X. If we give him just a little, he will still be worse off than he was at A; if we give him lots of X, he will be better off. But there must be some quantity of X that will just compensate for the loss of Y. By giving him that amount, we will have put together a bundle, Y_C and X_C, which yields the exact same total utility as bundle A. If confronted with a choice between bundles A and C, our consumer will say "Either one; I don't care." In other words, he is *indifferent* between A and C. When confronted with a choice between bundles C and B (which represents X_B and Y_B units of X and Y), he is also indifferent. The points along the curve labeled i in Figure 6A.1 represent all the combinations of X and Y that yield the same total utility to our consumer. That curve is thus an indifference curve.

Obviously, each consumer has a whole set of indifference curves. Return for a moment to Figure 6A.1. Starting at point A again, imagine that we give the con-

FIGURE 6A.2
A Preference Map: A Family of Indifference Curves

Each consumer has a unique family of indifference curves called a preference map. Higher indifference curves represent higher levels of total utility.

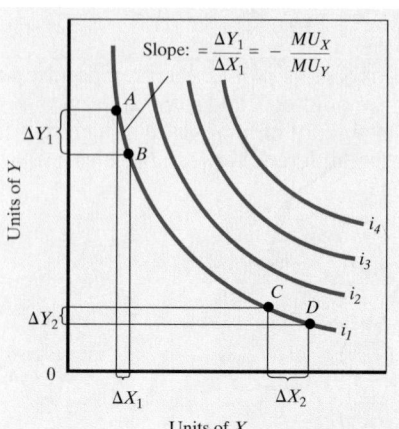

To understand the convex shape, compare the segment of curve i_1 between A and B with the segment of the same curve between C and D. Moving from A to B, the consumer is willing to give up a substantial amount of Y to get a small amount of X. (Remember that total utility is constant along an indifference curve; the consumer is therefore indifferent between A and B.) Moving from C to D, however, the consumer is willing to give up only a small amount of Y to get more X.

This changing trade-off makes complete sense when you remember the law of diminishing marginal utility. Notice that between A and B, a lot of Y is consumed, and the marginal utility derived from a unit of Y is likely to be small. At the same time, though, only a little bit of X is being consumed, so the marginal utility derived from consuming a unit of X is likely to be high.

Suppose, for example, that X is pizza and Y is soda. Near A and B, a thirsty, hungry football player who has ten sodas in front of him but only one slice of pizza will trade several sodas for another slice. Down around C and D, however, he has 20 slices of pizza and only a single soda. Now he will trade several slices of pizza to get an additional soda.

We can show how the trade-off changes more formally by deriving an expression for the slope of an indifference curve. Let's look at the arc (i.e., the section of the curve) between A and B. We know that in moving from A to B, total utility remains constant. That means that the utility lost as a result of consuming less Y must be matched by the utility gained from consuming more X. We can approximate the loss of utility by multiplying the marginal utility of Y (MU_Y) by the number of units by which consumption of Y is curtailed (ΔY). Similarly, we can approximate the utility gained from consuming more X by multiplying the marginal utility of X (MU_X) by the number of additional units of X consumed (ΔX). Remember, since the consumer is indifferent between points A and B, total utility is the same at both points. Thus, these two must be equal in magnitude—that is, the gain in utility from consuming more X must equal the loss in utility from consuming less Y. Since ΔY is a negative number (because consumption of Y decreases from A to B), it follows that:

$$MU_X \bullet \Delta X = -(MU_Y \bullet \Delta Y).$$

If we divide both sides by MU_Y and by ΔX, we obtain:

$$\Delta Y / \Delta X = -\left(\frac{MU_X}{MU_Y}\right).$$

Recall that the slope of any line is calculated by dividing the change in Y (ΔY) by the change in X (ΔX). This leads us to conclude that:

> The slope of an indifference curve is the ratio of the marginal utility of X to the marginal utility of Y, and it is negative.

sumer a tiny bit more X *and* a tiny bit more Y. Because more is better, we know that the new bundle will yield a higher level of total utility, and the consumer will be better off. Now, just as we constructed the first indifference curve, we can construct a second one. What we get is an indifference curve that parallels the first, but that is *higher* and to the *right* of it. Because utility along an indifference curve is constant at all points, every point along the new curve represents a higher level of total utility than every point along the first.

Figure 6A.2 shows a set of four indifference curves. The curve labeled i_4 represents the combinations of X and Y that yield the highest level of total utility among the four. Many other indifference curves exist between those shown on the diagram; in fact, their number is infinite. Notice that as you move up and to the right, utility increases.

The shapes of the indifference curves depend upon the preferences of the consumer, and the whole set of indifference curves is called a **preference map**. Each consumer has a unique preference map.

Properties of Indifference Curves

The indifference curves shown in Figure 6A.2 are drawn bowing in toward the origin, or zero point, on the axes. In other words, the absolute value of the slope of the indifference curves decreases, or the curves get flatter, as we move to the right. Thus, we say that indifference curves are convex toward the origin. This shape follows directly from the assumption of diminishing marginal rate of substitution and makes sense if you remember the law of diminishing marginal utility.

Now let's return to our pizza (X) and soda (Y) example. As we move down from the $A:B$ area to the $C:D$ area, our football player is consuming less soda and more pizza. The marginal utility of pizza (MU_X) is falling and the marginal utility of soda (MU_Y) is rising. That means that MU_X/MU_Y is falling, and the absolute value of the slope of the indifference curve is declining. And, indeed, it does get flatter.

Consumer Choice

As you recall, demand depends upon income, the prices of goods and services, and preferences or tastes. We are now ready to see how preferences as embodied in indifference curves interact with budget constraints to determine how the final quantities of X and Y will be chosen.

In Figure 6A.3, a set of indifference curves is superimposed on a consumer's budget constraint. Recall that the budget constraint separates those combinations of X and Y that are available to our consumer from those that are not. The constraint simply shows those combinations that can be purchased with an income of I at prices P_X and P_Y. The budget constraint crosses the X axis at I/P_X, or the number of units of X that can be purchased with I if nothing is spent on Y. Similarly, the budget constraint crosses the Y axis at I/P_Y, or the number of units of Y that can be purchased with an income of I if nothing is spent on X. The shaded area is the consumer's opportunity set. The slope of a budget constraint is $-P_X/P_Y$.

Consumers will choose from among available combinations of X and Y the one that maximizes utility. In graphic terms, the consumer will move along the budget constraint until he or she is on the highest possible indifference curve. Utility rises by moving from points such as A or C (which lie on i_1) toward B (which lies on i_2). Any movement away from point B moves the consumer to a lower indifference curve—a lower level of utility. In this case, utility is maximized when our consumer buys X^* units of X and Y^* units of Y. At point B, the budget constraint is just tangent to (that is, just touches) indifference curve i_2.

> As long as indifference curves are convex to the origin, utility maximization will take place at that point at which the indifference curve is just tangent to the budget constraint.

The tangency condition has important implications. Where two curves are tangent, they have the same slope, which implies that the slope of the indifference curve is exactly equal to the slope of the budget constraint at the point of tangency:

$$-\frac{MU_X}{MU_Y} = -\frac{P_X}{P_Y}.$$

$$\underbrace{\quad}_{\text{slope of indifference curve}} = \underbrace{\quad}_{\text{slope of budget constraint}}$$

FIGURE 6A.3
Consumer Utility-Maximizing Equilibrium

Consumers will choose that combination of X and Y that maximizes total utility. Graphically, the consumer will move along the budget constraint until the highest possible indifference curve is reached. At that point, the budget constraint and the indifference curve are tangent. This occurs at X* and Y* (point B).

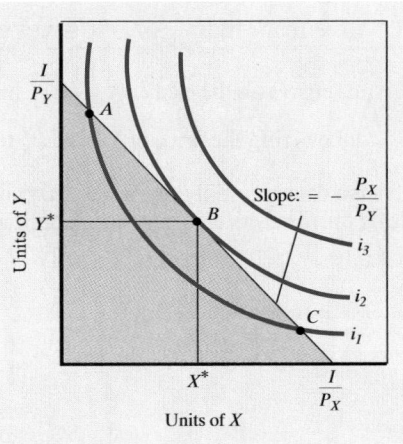

By multiplying both sides by MU_Y and dividing both sides by P_Y, we can rewrite this utility-maximizing rule as:

$$\frac{MU_X}{P_X} = \frac{MU_Y}{P_Y}.$$

This is the same rule derived in our earlier discussion without using indifference curves. We can describe this rule intuitively by saying that consumers maximize their total utility by equating the marginal utility per dollar spent on X with the marginal utility per dollar spent on Y. If this rule did not hold, utility could be increased by shifting money from one good to the other.

DERIVING A DEMAND CURVE FROM INDIFFERENCE CURVES AND BUDGET CONSTRAINTS

We now turn to the task of deriving a simple demand curve from indifference curves and budget constraints. A demand curve shows the quantity of a single good, X in this case, that a consumer will demand at various prices. To derive the demand curve, we need to confront our consumer with several alternative prices for X while keeping other prices, income, and preferences constant.

Figure 6A.4 shows the derivation. We begin with price P_X^1. At that price, the utility-maximizing point is A, where the consumer demands X_1 units of X. Therefore, in the right-hand diagram, we plot P_X^1 against X_1. This is the first point on our demand curve.

Now we lower the price of X to P_X^2. Lowering the price expands the opportunity set, and the budget constraint shifts to the right. Because the price of X has fallen, if our consumer spends all of his income on X, he can buy more of it. He is also better off, since he can move to a higher indifference curve. The new utility-maximizing point is B, where the consumer demands X_2 units of X. Because the consumer demands X_2 units of X at a price of P_X^2 we plot P_X^2 against X_2 in the right-hand diagram. A second price cut to P_X^3 moves our consumer to point C, where he demands X_3 units of X, and so on. Thus, we see how the demand curve can be derived from a consumer's preference map and budget constraint.

FIGURE 6A.4
Deriving a Demand Curve from Indifference Curves and a Budget Constraint

In Figure 6A.4, indifference curves are labeled i_1, i_2, and i_3; budget constraints are shown by the three diagonal lines from $\dfrac{I}{P_Y}$ to $\dfrac{I}{P_X^1}$, $\dfrac{I}{P_X^2}$, and $\dfrac{I}{P_X^3}$. Lowering the price of X from P_X^1 to P_X^2 and then to P_X^3 shifts the budget constraint to the right. At each price there is a different utility-maximizing combination of X and Y. Utility is maximized at point A on i_1, point B on i_2, and point C on i_3. Plotting the three prices against the quantities of X chosen results in a standard downward-sloping demand curve.

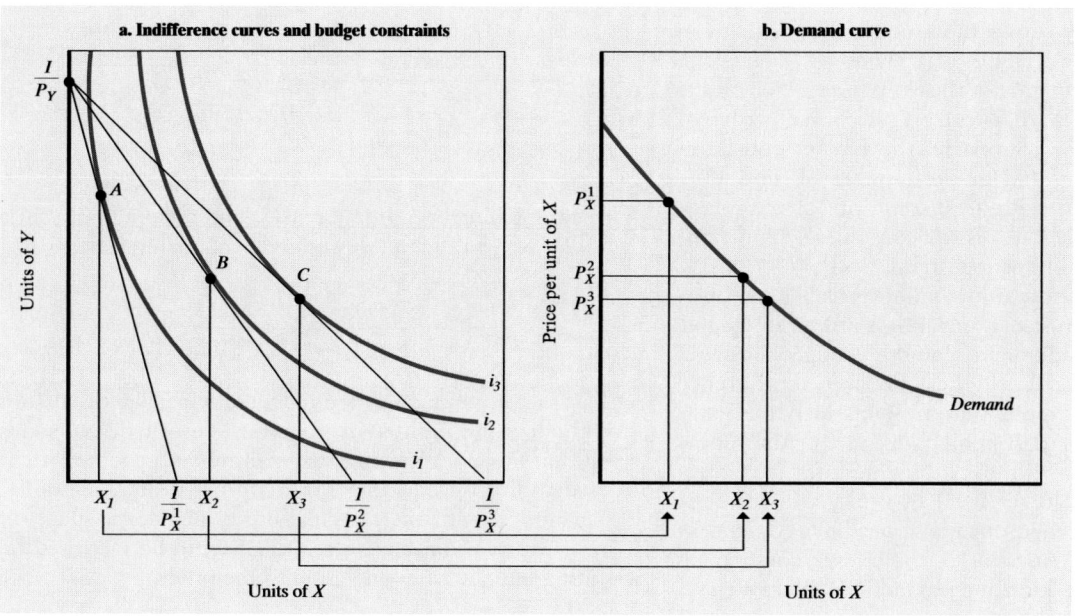

SUMMARY

1. An *indifference curve* is a set of points, each point representing a combination of goods X and Y, all of which yield the same total utility. A particular consumer's set of indifference curves is called a *preference map*.

2. The slope of an indifference curve is the ratio of the marginal utility of X to the marginal utility of Y, and it is negative.

3. As long as indifference curves are convex to the origin, utility maximization will take place at that point at which the indifference curve is just tangent to (that is, just touches) the budget constraint. The utility-maximizing rule can also be written as $MU_X/P_X = MU_Y/P_Y$.

Review Terms and Concepts

indifference curve A set of points, each point representing a combination of goods X and Y, all of which yield the same total utility.   165

preference map A consumer's set of indifference curves.   166

Problem Set

1. Which of the four assumptions that were made at the beginning of the appendix are violated by the indifference curves in Figure 1? Explain.

2. Assume that a household receives a weekly income of $100. If Figure 2 represents that household's choices as the price of X changes, plot three points on the household's demand curve.

3. If Ann's marginal rate of substitution of Y for X is 5 (that is, $MU_X/MU_Y = 5$), the price of X is $9.00, and the price of Y is $2.00, she is spending too much of her income on Y. Do you agree or disagree? Explain your answer using a graph.

4. Assume that Jim is a rational consumer who consumes only two goods, apples (A) and nuts (N). Assume that his marginal rate of substitution of apples for nuts is given by the following formula:

$$MRS = MU_N/MU_A = A/N$$

That is, Jim's MRS is simply equal to the ratio of the number of apples consumed to the number of nuts consumed.

a. Assume that Jim's income is $100, the price of nuts is $5, and the price of apples is $10. What quantities of apples and nuts will he consume?

b. Find two additional points on his demand curve for nuts ($P_N = 10 and $P_N = 2).

c. Sketch one of the equilibrium points on an indifference curve graph.

FIGURE 1

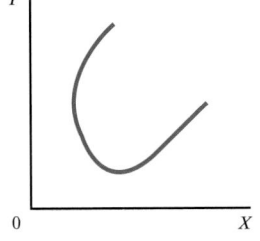
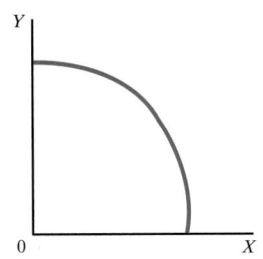

FIGURE 2

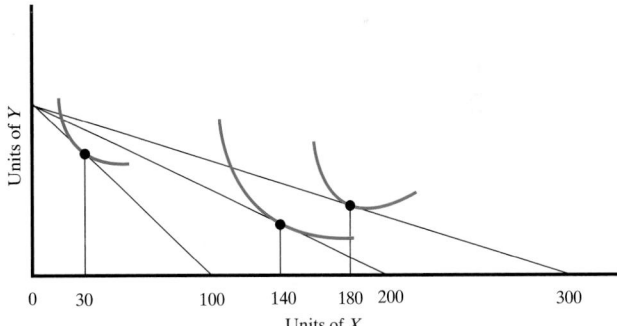

7

The Behavior of Profit-Maximizing Firms and the Production Process

In Chapter 6, we took a brief look at the household decisions that lie behind supply and demand curves. We spent some time discussing household choices: how much to work and how to choose among the wide range of goods and services available in the market within the constraints of prices and income. We also identified some of the influences on household demand in output markets, as well as some of the influences on household supply behavior in input markets.

We now turn to the other side of the system and examine the behavior of firms. Business firms purchase inputs in order to produce and sell outputs. In other words, they *demand* factors of production in input markets and *supply* goods and services in output markets. Figure 7.1 repeats the now familiar circular flow diagram you first encountered in Chapter 6. Here in Chapter 7 we look inside the firm at the production process that actually transforms inputs into outputs. Chapters 8 and 9 use information on input prices and production technology to derive cost curves, from which we derive firms' output supply curves. In Chapters 10 and 11, we discuss input markets (specifically, labor, land, and capital markets)

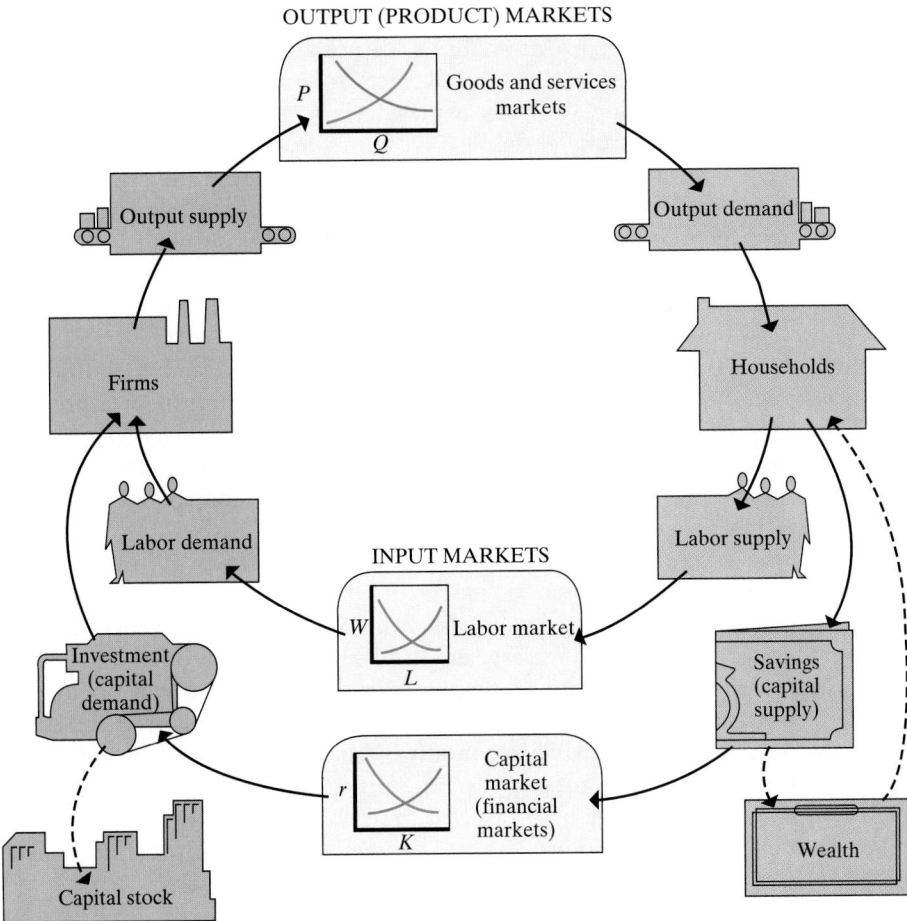

OUTPUT (PRODUCT) MARKETS

Goods and services markets

Output supply

Output demand

Firms

Households

Labor demand

INPUT MARKETS

Labor supply

Labor market

Investment (capital demand)

Savings (capital supply)

Capital market (financial markets)

Wealth

Capital stock

FIGURE 7.1
Firm and Household Decisions

Firms supply output and demand labor and capital in input markets. This chapter and the next four chapters focus on the left side of this diagram—everything that is highlighted in red.

and derive firms' input demand curves. Chapter 12 puts all the pieces of the system together and analyzes how the system as a whole functions. In Chapters 13 through 17, we relax some of our assumptions—including the assumption of perfect competition—and examine the role of government in a market economy.

> While Chapters 7 through 12 describe the behavior of perfectly competitive firms, much of what we say in these chapters applies to firms that are not perfectly competitive as well. For example, when we turn to monopoly in Chapter 13, we will be describing firms that are similar to competitive firms in many ways. All firms, whether competitive or not, demand inputs, engage in production, and produce outputs. All firms have an incentive to maximize profits and thus to minimize costs.

Central to our analysis is the process of **production,** the process by which inputs are combined, transformed, and turned into outputs. Firms vary in size and internal organization, but they all take inputs and transform them into things for which there is some demand. An independent accountant, for example, combines labor, paper, telephone service, time, learning and a personal computer to provide help to confused taxpayers. A rock band combines talent, energy, instruments, costumes, amplifiers, lighting, and labor to produce music. An automobile plant uses steel, labor, plastic, electricity, machines and countless other inputs to produce cars. Before we begin our discussion of the production process, however, we need to clarify some of the assumptions on which our analysis is based.

production The process by which inputs are combined, transformed, and turned into outputs.

PRODUCTION IS NOT LIMITED TO FIRMS While our discussions in the next several chapters focus on profit-making business firms, it is important to understand that production and productive activity are not confined to private business firms. Households also engage in transforming factors of production (labor, capital, energy, natural resources, etc.) into useful things. When I work in my garden, I am combining land, labor, fertilizer, seeds, and tools (capital) into the vegetables I eat and the flowers I enjoy. The child-rearing activities of parents transform their young into productive human beings. The government also combines land, labor, and capital to produce public services for which demand exists—national defense, police and fire protection, and education, to name a few.

Private business firms are set apart from other producers, such as households and government, by their purpose. A **firm** exists when a person or a group of people decides to produce a good or service to meet a perceived demand. In most cases, firms exist to make a profit. They engage in production (that is, they transform inputs into outputs) because they can sell their products for more than it costs to produce them.

Even among firms that exist to make a profit, however, there are many important differences. A firm's behavior is likely to depend upon how it is organized internally and upon its relationship to the firms with which it competes. How many competitors are there? How large are they? How do they compete?

In Chapter 3 we discussed the different ways that businesses can organize—as proprietorships, as partnerships, or as corporations. We also discussed the different forms of industry in the U.S. economy—perfect competition, monopolistic competition, oligopoly, and monopoly. Before we finish with microeconomics, we will analyze the behavior of all four of these industry types. But it is logical to start with the simplest. Thus, the next three chapters will deal exclusively with the behavior of firms in perfectly competitive industries.

PERFECT COMPETITION As you learned in Chapter 3, **perfect competition** exists in an industry that contains many relatively small firms producing identical products. The most important characteristic of a perfectly competitive industry is that no single firm has any control over prices. In other words, an individual firm cannot affect the market price of its product or of the inputs that it buys. This important characteristic follows from two assumptions. First, a competitive industry is composed of many firms, each small relative to the size of the industry. Second, every firm in a perfectly competitive industry produces **homogeneous products,** which means that the output of one firm cannot be distinguished from the output of the others.

These assumptions limit the decisions open to competitive firms and simplify the analysis of competitive behavior. Firms in perfectly competitive industries do not differentiate their products, nor do they make decisions about price. Rather, each firm takes prices as given—that is, as determined in the market by the laws of supply and demand—and decides only how much to produce and how to produce it.

The idea that competitive firms are "price takers" is central to our discussion. Of course, we do not mean by this that firms cannot affix price tags to their merchandise; all firms have this ability. We simply mean that—given the availability of perfect substitutes—any product priced over the market price will not be sold. Thus, to sell any goods, competitive firms must adhere to the market price.

These assumptions also imply that the demand for the product of a competitive firm is *perfectly elastic*. Take, for example, the Ohio corn farmer whose situ-

firm An organization that comes into being when a person or a group of people decides to produce a good or service to meet a perceived demand. Most firms exist to make a profit.

perfect competition An industry structure (or market organization) in which there are many firms, each small relative to the industry, producing virtually identical products and in which no firm is large enough to have any control over prices. In perfectly competitive industries, new competitors can freely enter and exit the market.

homogeneous products Undifferentiated products; products that are identical to, or indistinguishable from, one another.

ation is shown in Figure 7.2. The left side of the diagram represents the current conditions in the market. Corn is currently selling for $2.45 per bushel.[1] The right side of the diagram shows the demand for corn as the farmer sees it. If she were to raise her price, she would sell no corn at all; because there are perfect substitutes available, the quantity demanded of her corn would drop to zero. To lower her price would be silly because she can sell all she wants at the current price. (Remember, each farmer's production is very small relative to the entire corn market.)

In perfect competition we also assume that firms can freely enter and exit the industry. The assumption of **free entry** implies that if firms in an industry are earning high profits, new firms that seek to do the same thing are likely to spring up. There are no barriers that prevent a new firm from competing. Fast food restaurants are quick to spring up when a new shopping center opens, and new gas stations appear when a housing development or a new highway is built. Where profit opportunities present themselves, we assume that firms will enter and compete for them.

free entry The condition that exists when there are no barriers to prevent new firms from competing for profits in a profitable industry.

Free exit is possible when firms can simply stop producing their product and leave a market. Firms incur no additional costs by exiting the industry, hence the term *"free exit."* In the 1950s, for example, two major industries in the Northeast were textiles and furniture. As time went on and conditions changed, fewer and fewer of those firms remained in business. Generally speaking, a firm closes down because it is suffering losses or because profits are insufficient. New England tex-

free exit The condition that exists when firms can simply stop producing their product and leave a market. Firms incur no additional costs by exiting the industry; hence the term *"free exit."*

[1]Recall that capital letters refer to the entire market and lower case letters refer to representative firms. For example, in Figure 7.2, Q refers to industry output and q refers to a representative firm's output. Similarly, the market demand curve is labeled D and the demand curve facing the firm is labeled d.

FIGURE 7.2

Demand Facing a Single Firm in a Perfectly Competitive Market

In perfectly competitive industries, each firm is small relative to the size of the industry. In addition, the products of one firm cannot be distinguished from the products of others. It follows, therefore, that individual firms have no control over market prices. Figure 7.2b shows that if a representative firm in a perfectly competitive market raises the price of its output above $2.45, the quantity demanded of *that firm's* output will drop to zero. Each firm faces a perfectly elastic demand curve, d.

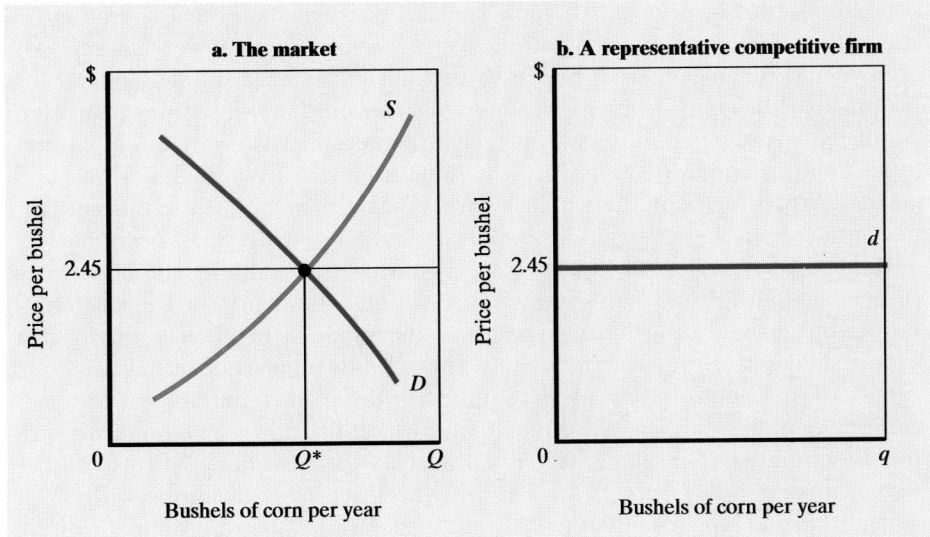

tile and furniture producers found themselves facing increasing foreign competition, as well as lower production costs in the southern United States. While some firms packed up and moved, others simply left the business altogether.

As you saw in Chapter 3, the best examples of perfect competition are probably found in agriculture. In that industry, products are absolutely homogeneous—it is impossible to distinguish one farmer's wheat from another's—and prices are set by the forces of supply and demand in a huge national market.

THE BEHAVIOR OF PROFIT-MAXIMIZING FIRMS

All types of firms must make several basic decisions to achieve what we assume to be their primary objective—maximum profits. Perfectly competitive firms have three basic decisions to make. Actually, *all* firms must make these three decisions, but (as we will see later) noncompetitive firms have other decisions to make as well. The three basic decisions are:

1. How much output to supply (quantity of product);
2. How to produce that output (what production technique to use); and
3. How much of each input to demand.

The first and last choices are linked by the second choice. Once a firm has decided how much to produce, the choice of a production method determines the firm's input requirements. If a sweater company decides to produce 5,000 sweaters this month, it knows how many production workers it will need, how much electricity it will use, how much raw yarn to purchase, and how many sewing machines to run. A grower who sets out to produce and ship 3,000 bushels of apples knows how many pickers to hire, how many baskets to have on hand, and so forth.

Similarly, given a technique of production, any set of input quantities determines the amount of output that can be produced. Certainly the number of machines and workers employed in a sweater mill determines how many sweaters can be produced, and the number of trees and pickers determines the number of bushels of apples a grower can ship.

Changing the *technology* of production will change the relationship between input and output quantities. An apple orchard that uses expensive equipment to raise pickers up into the trees will harvest more fruit with fewer workers in a given period of time than an orchard in which pickers use simple ladders. It is also possible that two different technologies can produce the same quantity of output. For example, a fully computerized textile mill with only a few workers running the machines may produce the same number of sweaters as a mill with no sophisticated machines but many workers. The firm would then presumably choose the technology that minimizes its costs for a given level of output.

Remember as we proceed that we are discussing and analyzing the behavior of *perfectly competitive* firms. Thus, we will say nothing about price-setting behavior, product quality and other characteristics of the product, or choices that lead to product differentiation. In perfect competition, both input and output prices are beyond a firm's control—they are determined in the market and are not the decisions of any individual firm. And remember that all firms in a given industry produce the same exact product. When we analyze the behavior of firms in other kinds of markets (in Chapters 13 and 14), the three basic decisions will be expanded to include the setting of prices and the determination of product quality.

Profits and Economic Costs

As noted earlier, we assume that firms are in business to make a profit and that the behavior of firms is guided by the goal of maximizing profits. But what is profit? In simplest terms, **profit** is the difference between total revenues and total costs:

> Profit = Total Revenue (*TR*) – Total Cost (*TC*).

Revenues are simply receipts from the sale of the product. **Total revenue (TR)** is equal to the number of units produced and sold *(q)* times the price received per unit *(P)*. *Costs,* however, are more complicated. In economics, the definition of costs includes more than simple out-of-pocket costs. **Economic costs** are the *full* costs of production and include (1) a normal rate of return, and (2) the opportunity cost of each factor of production.

NORMAL RATE OF RETURN   When someone decides to start a firm, he or she must commit resources. To operate a manufacturing firm, you need a plant and some equipment. To start a restaurant, you need to buy grills, ovens, tables, chairs, and so forth. In other words, you must invest in capital. Such investment requires resources that stay tied up in the firm as long as it operates. Even firms that have been around a long time must continue to invest. Plant and equipment wear out and must be replaced. Firms that decide to expand must put new capital in place. This is as true of proprietorships, where the resources come directly from the proprietor, as it is of corporations, where the resources needed to make investments come from shareholders.

Whenever resources are used to invest in a business, there is an opportunity cost. Instead of opening a candy store, I could put my funds into an alternative use such as a certificate of deposit or a government bond and earn interest. Instead of using its retained earnings to build a new plant, a firm could simply earn interest on those savings by doing likewise.

Why, then, do firms put their funds into the business rather than into the bank or into some other alternative use? When people decide to invest resources in a business, we assume that the decision is based on the expectation of profit. But a firm isn't profitable in a meaningful sense unless it earns more for its investors than what they forgo by not buying a bond or a certificate of deposit. Using resources to invest in a firm thus has an opportunity cost.

A **normal rate of profit** (also called a **normal rate of return**) is the rate that is just sufficient to keep owners or investors satisfied. From the standpoint of a manager, the normal rate of return is the opportunity cost of investment—that is, the "actual" cost of capital. In other words, it is the rate of profit just equal to the profit rate the firm could make by investing its resources elsewhere. If the rate of return were to fall below normal, it would be difficult or impossible for managers to raise resources needed to purchase new capital. Owners of the firm would be receiving profits that were lower than they could receive elsewhere in the economy.

If the firm has fairly steady revenues and the future looks secure, the normal profit rate should be very close to the interest rate on risk-free government bonds. I certainly won't keep investors interested in my firm if I don't pay them a rate of return at least as high as they can get from a risk-free government or corporate bond. If my firm is rock solid and the economy is steady, I may not have to pay a much higher rate. But if my firm is in a very speculative industry

profit The difference between total revenues and total costs.

revenue, or total revenue Receipts from the sale of a product. $P \times q$.

economic costs The full costs of production including (1) a normal rate of return on investment, and (2) the opportunity cost of each factor of production.

normal rate of profit, or normal rate of return A rate of profit that is just sufficient to keep owners and investors satisfied; for relatively risk-free firms it should be nearly the same as the interest rate on risk-free government bonds.

and the future of the economy is shaky, I may have to pay substantially more to keep my shareholders happy. In exchange for taking such a risk, they will expect a higher return.

A normal profit rate is added as part of costs in calculating the full economic costs of a business enterprise. Suppose, for example, that I am running a firm in a relatively safe industry where a 15% return on investment is considered normal. That is, if you were a shareholder in my firm and you owned $1000 worth of stock, you would expect to earn a profit of at least $150 per year on your investment. If the total asset value of my firm were $100,000, the annual economic costs of running my firm would include $15,000 ($100,000 × .15) of normal return. We add a normal return as a cost because it represents the opportunity cost of capital in this industry. After all, owners could always sell out and put their money in certificates of deposit or bonds.

economic profits, or excess profits Profits over and above the normal rate of return on investment; anything greater than the normal opportunity cost of capital.

Adding a normal profit rate to costs means that when a firm earns exactly a normal rate of return or profit, it actually earns zero economic profits. **Economic profits,** or **excess profits** as they are sometimes called, are profits over and above normal. In other words, profits are considered economic profits only if they are greater than the opportunity cost of investing in the industry.

When a firm earns *positive* economic profits, it is earning profit at a rate more than sufficient to retain the interest of investors. In fact, economic profits are likely to attract new firms into an industry and cause existing firms to expand.

When a firm suffers *negative* economic profits—that is, when it incurs economic losses—it is earning at a rate below that required to keep investors happy. Such economic losses may or may not be losses as an accountant would measure them. Even if I earn a positive profit of 10% on my assets, I am earning below normal profits, or economic losses, if a normal return for my industry is 15 percent. In this case, I have a net economic loss of 5% per year, and my investors will be looking to bail out. Economic losses may cause some firms to exit the industry; others will contract in size. Certainly new investment will not flow into such an industry.

OPPORTUNITY COSTS OF ALL INPUTS   Economic costs include the opportunity costs of all inputs, not just out-of-pocket costs. If you open a restaurant and work 40 hours a week helping to run it, the cost of running the restaurant includes the cost of your time, even if you do not pay yourself a formal wage. (If you don't pay yourself a wage, your time does not show up on the restaurant's books.) If you could be earning $15 per hour working full-time at a local factory, the opportunity cost of your time helping to run the restaurant is $600 per week (40 hours × $15). In analyzing costs, it is important to include both direct out-of-pocket costs *and* opportunity costs.

Short-Run versus Long-Run Decisions

The decisions made by a firm—how much to produce, how to produce it, and what inputs to demand—all take time into account. If a firm decides that it wants to double or triple its output, it may need time to arrange financing, hire architects and contractors, and build a new plant. Planning for a major expansion can take years. In the meantime, the firm must decide how much to produce within the constraint of its existing plant. If a firm decides that it wants to get out of a particular business, it may take time to arrange an orderly exit. There may be contract obligations to fulfill, equipment to sell, and so forth. Once again, the firm must decide what to do in the meantime.

A firm's immediate response to a change in the economic environment may also differ from its response over time. During the mid-1980s, for example, land and housing prices in New England and in the New York/New Jersey area boomed. The median price of an existing single-family home in the New York City metropolitan area jumped from $89,000 in 1983 to $192,000 in early 1988. Contractors who were in business in 1983 found themselves with an increasing demand for new homes and excellent profit potential. Developers and contractors were initially constrained, however. Building homes requires specialized equipment, skilled labor, and expensive materials, all of which were limited in supply. At first, developers could only continue to build approximately the same number of homes that they had been building all along.

But as the boom continued, two things happened that allowed more new homes to be built. Attracted by extraordinary profits, new firms entered the construction business, and existing firms expanded their operations. Many firms bought specialized equipment, hired construction workers, and set about building more homes and condominiums.

In 1989 and 1990, the boom ended as housing demand and prices began to decline. Many construction firms found themselves with excess equipment, office space, and workers. While workers could be laid off without much notice, selling equipment and reducing the scale of operations took longer. For many, the end of the boom meant significant losses or, at best, below-normal profits. For others, the only choice was getting out of the industry; many went bankrupt. These were all long-term adjustments that took place over the course of several years.

Because the character of immediate response differs from long-run adjustment, it is useful to define two time periods: the short run and the long run. Two assumptions define the **short run:** (1) a fixed scale (or a fixed factor of production—that is, fixed inputs) and (2) no entry into or exit from the industry. First, the short run is defined as that period during which existing firms have some *fixed factor of production*—that is, during which some factor locks them into their current scale of operations. Second, new firms cannot enter, and existing firms cannot exit, an industry in the short run. Firms may curtail operations, but they are still locked into some costs, even though they may be in the process of going out of business.

Just which factor or factors of production are fixed in the short run differs from industry to industry. For a manufacturing firm, the size of the actual physical plant is often the greatest limitation. A factory is built with a given production rate in mind. While that rate can be increased, output cannot increase beyond a certain limit in the short run. For a private physician, the limit may be her own capacity to see patients; the day has only so many hours. In the long run, she may invite others to join her practice and expand, but for now, in the short run, she *is* the firm, and her capacity is the firm's capacity. For a farmer, the fixed factor may be land. The capacity of a small farm is limited by the number of acres being cultivated.

In the **long run,** there are no fixed factors of production. Firms can plan for any output level they find desirable. They can double or triple output, for example. In addition, new firms can start up operations (enter the industry), and existing firms can go out of business (exit the industry).

No hard-and-fast rule specifies how long the short run is. The point is simply that firms make two basic kinds of decisions: those that govern the day-to-day operations of the firm and those that involve longer-term strategic planning. Sometimes major decisions can be implemented in weeks; often, however, the process takes years.

short run The period of time for which two conditions hold: The firm is operating under a fixed scale (fixed factor) of production and firms can neither enter nor exit an industry.

long run That period of time for which there are no fixed factors of production. Firms can increase or decrease scale of operation, and new firms can enter and existing firms can exit the industry.

✳ The Basis of Decisions: Market Prices of Output, Available Technology, and Input Prices

As we said earlier, the three fundamental decisions of firms are made with the objective of maximizing profits. Since profits equal total revenues minus total costs, each firm needs to know how much it costs to produce its product and how much its product can be sold for.

To know how much it costs to produce a good or service, I need to know something about the production techniques that are available and about the prices of the inputs required. To estimate how much it will cost me to operate a gas station, for instance, I need to know what equipment I need, how many workers, what kind of a building, and so forth. I also need to know the going wage rates for mechanics and unskilled laborers, the cost of gas pumps, interest rates, rents per square foot of land on high-traffic corners, and the wholesale price of gasoline. And, of course, I need to know how much I can sell gasoline and repair services for.

In the language of economics, I need to know three things:

The Bases of Decision Making:	1.	The market price of output;
	2.	The techniques of production that are available; and
	3.	The prices of inputs.

Output price determines potential revenues. The techniques available tell me how much of each input I need, and input prices tell me how much they will cost.

Together, the available production techniques, and the prices of inputs determine costs.

The rest of this chapter and the whole next chapter focus on *costs* of production. We begin at the heart of the firm, with the process of production itself. Faced with a set of input prices, firms must decide on the best, or optimal, method of production. The **optimal method of production** is the one that minimizes cost. With cost determined and the market price of output known, a firm will make a final judgment about the quantity of its product to produce and the quantity of each input to demand.

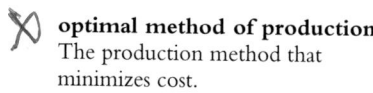

optimal method of production The production method that minimizes cost.

✳ THE PRODUCTION PROCESS

Recall that *production* is the process through which inputs are combined and transformed into outputs. **Production technology** relates inputs to outputs. Specific quantities of inputs are needed to produce any given service or good. Just as a loaf of bread requires certain amounts of water, flour, and yeast, some kneading and patting, as well as an oven, gas, or electricity, so a trip from downtown New York to Newark, New Jersey, can be produced with a taxicab, 45 minutes of a driver's labor, some gasoline, and so forth.

Most outputs can be produced in more than one way–that is, by using a number of different techniques. You can tear down an old building and clear a lot to create a park in several ways, for example. Five hundred men and women with small hammers could descend upon it and carry the pieces away by hand; this would be a **labor-intensive technology.** The same park could be produced by two people with a wrecking crane, a steam shovel, a backhoe, and a dump truck; this would be a **capital-intensive technology.** Similarly, different inputs can be combined to trans-

production technology The relationship between inputs and outputs.

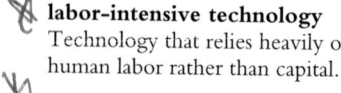

labor-intensive technology Technology that relies heavily on human labor rather than capital.

capital-intensive technology Technology that relies heavily on capital rather than human labor.

port people from Oakland to San Francisco. The Bay Area Rapid Transit (BART) carries thousands of people simultaneously under San Francisco Bay and uses a massive amount of capital relative to labor. Cab rides to San Francisco require much more labor relative to capital; a driver is needed for every couple of passengers.

An insurance company needs office space to produce its product, but office space can be assembled in a variety of ways. In suburban locations, office parks are often spacious, with trees and grass and buildings of two or three stories. In central cities, offices are stacked on top of one another in glass towers. Thus in central cities, a small amount of land is combined with a great deal of capital to produce insurance services. In suburban office parks, the same services are produced with more land and less capital.

In choosing the most appropriate technology, firms choose the one that minimizes the cost of production. For a firm in an economy with a plentiful supply of inexpensive labor but not much capital, the optimal method of production will involve labor-intensive techniques. In contrast, firms in an economy with high wages and high labor costs have an incentive to "substitute" away from labor and to use more capital-intensive, or labor-saving, techniques. Suburban office parks use more land and have more open space in part because land in the suburbs is more plentiful and less expensive than land in the middle of a big city. Spreading out is cheaper than building a high-rise office tower.

Production Functions: Total Product, Marginal Product, and Average Product

The relationship between inputs and outputs (that is, the technology of production) expressed numerically or mathematically is called a **production function (or total product function).** A production function shows units of total product as a function of units of inputs.

production function or (total product (TP) function) A mathematical or numerical expression of a relationship between inputs and outputs. It shows units of total product as a function of units of inputs.

Imagine, for example, a small sandwich shop. All the sandwiches made in the shop are grilled, and the shop owns only one grill, which can accommodate only two people comfortably. As columns 1 and 2 of Table 7.1 show, one person working alone can produce only 10 sandwiches per hour. He has to answer the phone, wait on customers, keep the tables clean, and so on. The second worker can stay at the grill full time and not worry about anything except making sandwiches. She can produce 15 sandwiches per hour. A third person trying to use the grill produces crowding, but, with careful use of space, more sandwiches can be produced. The third worker adds 10 sandwiches per hour. Note that the added output from hiring a third worker is less because of the capital constraint, *not* because the third worker is somehow less efficient or hard working. We assume that all workers are equally capable.

TABLE 7.1
Production Function

(1) LABOR UNITS (L) (EMPLOYEES)	(2) TOTAL PRODUCT (TP) (SANDWICHES PER HOUR)	(3) MARGINAL PRODUCT OF LABOR (MP_L) ($\Delta TP/\Delta L$)	(4) AVERAGE PRODUCT OF LABOR (AP_L) (TP/L)
0	0	–	–
1	10	10	10.0
2	25	15	12.5
3	35	10	11.7
4	40	5	10.0
5	42	2	8.4
6	42	0	7.0

The fourth and fifth workers can work at the grill only while the first three are putting the pickles, onions, and wrapping on the sandwiches they have made. But then the first three must wait to get back to the grill. Worker four adds a net of 5 sandwiches per hour to the total, and worker five adds just 2. Adding a sixth worker adds no output at all: The current maximum capacity of the shop is 42 sandwiches per hour.

Figure 7.3a graphs the total product data from Table 7.1.

marginal product (MP) The additional output that can be produced by adding one more unit of a specific input *ceteris paribus*.

MARGINAL PRODUCT AND THE LAW OF DIMINISHING RETURNS **Marginal product (MP)** is the additional output that can be produced by hiring one more unit of a specific input, holding all other inputs constant. As column 3 of Table 7.1 shows, the marginal product of the first unit of labor in the sandwich shop is 10 sandwiches; the marginal product of the second is 15; the third, 10; and so forth. The marginal product of the sixth worker is 0.

Figure 7.3b graphs the marginal product of labor curve from the data in Table 7.1. Geometrically, the marginal product curve represents a graph of the slope of the production function. Because slope equals the change in Y divided by the change in X, the slope of a production function is the change in total product (q, which is measured on the Y axis in Figure 7.3a) divided by the change in labor inputs (L, which is measured on the X-axis in Figure 7.3a). The slope of the production function is thus the additional output per additional unit of labor, or the *marginal product of labor (MP_L)* :

$$\text{Slope of Production Function} = \frac{\Delta q}{\Delta L} = MP_L.$$

FIGURE 7.3
Production Function for Sandwiches

A *production function* is a mathematical representation of the relationship between inputs and outputs. In Figure 7.3a, total product (sandwiches) is graphed as a function of labor inputs. The *marginal product* of labor is the additional output that one additional unit of labor produces. Figure 7.3b shows that the marginal product of the second unit of labor at the sandwich shop is 15 units of output; the marginal product of the fourth unit of labor is 5 units of output. The slope of a production function is the marginal product of labor (MP_L).

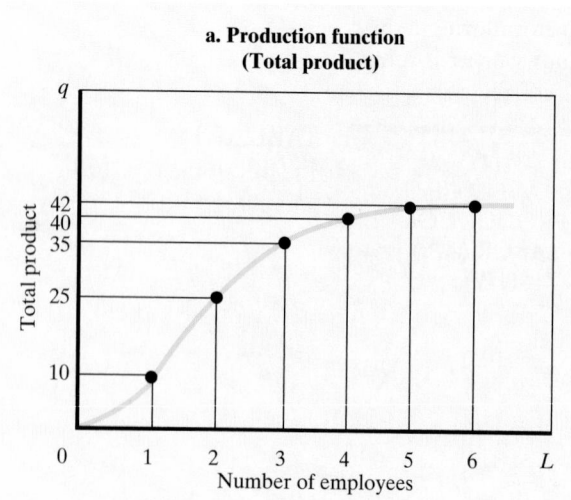

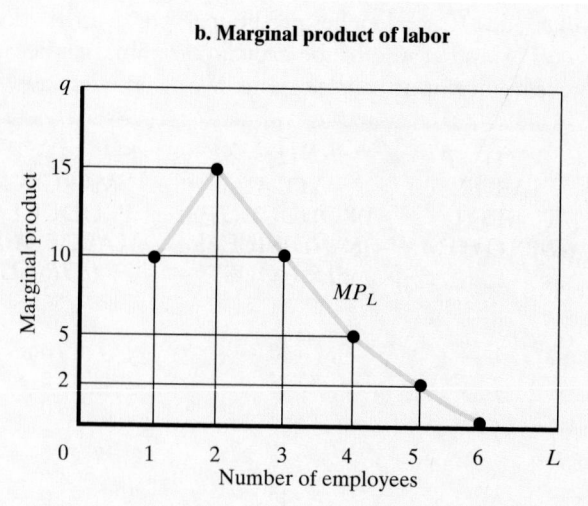

The **law of diminishing returns** states that *after a certain point, when additional units of a variable input are added to fixed inputs* (in this case, the building and grill), *the marginal product of the variable input declines.* The British economist David Ricardo first formulated the law of diminishing returns on the basis of his observations of agriculture in nineteenth-century England. Within a given area of land, he noted, successive "doses" of labor and capital yielded smaller and smaller increases in crop output. The law of diminishing returns is true in agriculture because the same land must be farmed more intensively to produce more product. In manufacturing, diminishing returns set in when a firm begins to strain the capacity of its existing plant.

At our sandwich shop, diminishing returns set in when the third worker is added. The marginal product of the second worker is actually higher than the first. The first worker takes care of the phone and the tables, which frees the second worker to concentrate exclusively on sandwich making. But from that point on, the grill gets crowded.

Diminishing returns characterize many productive activities. Consider, for example, an independent accountant who works primarily for private citizens preparing their tax returns. As he adds more and more clients, he must work later and later into the evening. An hour spent working at 1 A.M. after a long day is likely to be less productive than an hour spent working at 10 A.M. Here the fixed factor of production is the accountant himself. Ultimately, the capacity of his mind and body limit his production, much like the walls of a plant limit production in a factory.

Diminishing returns, or *diminishing marginal product,* begin to show up when more and more units of a variable input are added to a fixed input, such as scale of plant. Recall that we defined the short run as that period in which some fixed factor of production constrains the firm. It follows then, that:

> Diminishing returns always apply in the short run, and in the short run every firm will face diminishing returns. This means that every firm finds it progressively more difficult to increase its output as it approaches capacity production.

MARGINAL PRODUCT VERSUS AVERAGE PRODUCT   **Average product (AP)** is the average amount produced by each unit of a variable factor. At our sandwich shop with one grill, that variable factor is labor. In Table 7.1, you saw that the first two workers together produce 25 sandwiches per hour. Their average product is therefore 12.5 (25 ÷ 2). The third worker adds only 10 sandwiches per hour to the total. These 10 sandwiches are the *marginal* product of labor. (Recall that marginal product is the product of only the last unit of labor.) The *average product* of the first three units of labor, however, is 11.7 (the average of 10, 15, and 10). Stated in equation form, the marginal product of labor (MP_L) is the change in total output (Δq) divided by the change in labor (ΔL). The average product of labor (AP_L) is the *total* output (q) divided by total units of labor (L):

$$MP_L = \frac{\Delta q}{\Delta L}; \; AP_L = \frac{q}{L}.$$

Average product "follows" marginal product, but it does not change as quickly. If marginal product is above average, the average rises; if marginal product is below average, the average falls. Suppose, for example, that you have had six exams and that your average is 86. If you score 75 on the next exam, your average score will *fall,* but not all the way to 75. In fact, it will fall only to 84.4. If, on the other hand, you score a 95, your average will rise to 87.3. As columns 3 and 4 of Table

law of diminishing returns When additional units of a variable input are added to fixed inputs after a certain point, the marginal product of the variable input declines.

average product (AP) The average amount produced by each unit of a variable factor.

7.1 show, marginal product at the sandwich shop declines continuously after the third worker is hired. Average product also decreases, but more slowly.

Figure 7.4 shows a typical production function and the marginal and average product curves derived from it. The marginal product curve is a graph of the slope of the total product curve—that is, of the production function. Average product and marginal product start out equal. As marginal product climbs, the graph of average product follows it, but more slowly, up to L_1 (point A).

Notice that marginal product starts out increasing. (Remember that it did so in the sandwich shop as well.) Most production processes are designed to be run well by more than one worker. Take an assembly line, for example. To work efficiently, an assembly line needs a worker at every station; it's a cooperative process. The marginal product of the first workers is low or zero. But as workers are added, the process starts to run and marginal product rises.

At point A (L_1 units of labor), marginal product begins to fall. Because every plant has a finite capacity, efforts to increase production will always run into the limits of that capacity. At point B (L_2 units of labor), marginal product has fallen

FIGURE 7.4

Typical Production Function

Marginal and average product curves can be derived from total product curves. The marginal product of labor is defined as $\Delta q/\Delta L$; thus, it is the slope of the total product curve. Average product follows marginal product; it rises when marginal product is above it and falls when marginal product is below it.

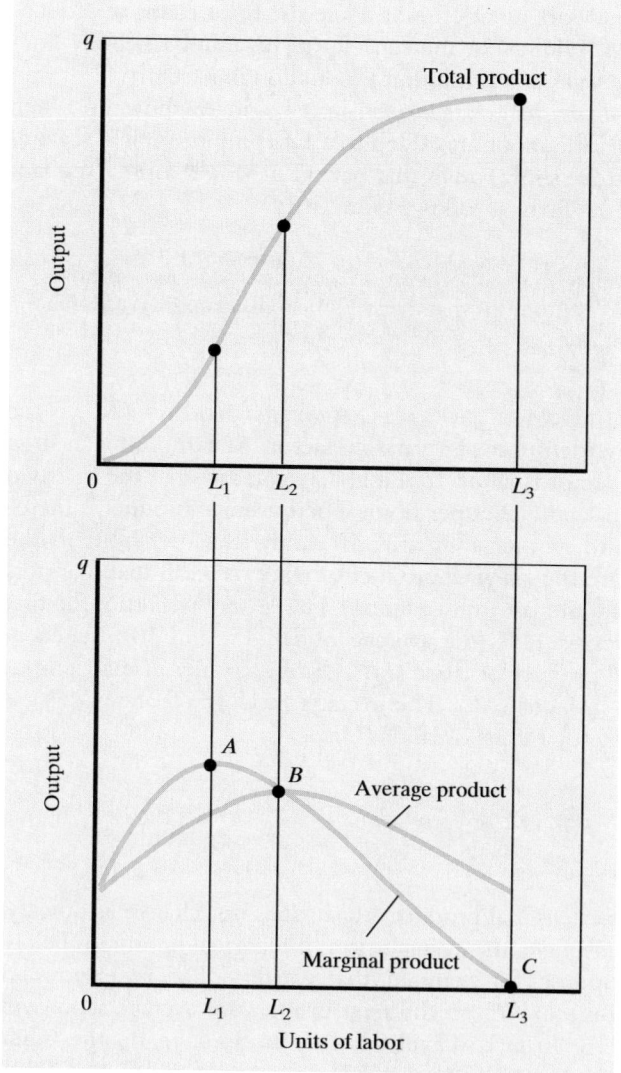

to equal the average product, which has been increasing. Between point B and point C (between L_2 and L_3 units of labor), marginal product falls below average product, and thus average product begins to follow it *down*. Average product is at its maximum at point B, where it is equal to marginal product.

At L_3 units of labor, the total product curve is flat–that is, it has a zero slope. At this point, more labor yields no more output, and marginal product is zero–the assembly line has no more positions, the grill is jammed, and the accountant is so tired that she can't see another client.[2] (If you have trouble understanding the relationships among the three curves in Figure 7.4, review the calculations in Table 7.1 and review the appendix on graphing in Chapter 1.)

Production Functions with Two Variable Factors of Production

So far we have considered production functions with only one variable factor of production. But inputs work together in production. In general, additional capital increases the productivity of labor. Because capital–buildings, machines, and so on–is of no use without people to operate it, we say that capital and labor are *complementary inputs*.

A simple example will clarify this point. Consider again the sandwich shop. If the demand for sandwiches began to exceed the capacity of the shop to produce them, the shop's owner might decide to expand capacity. This would mean opening up more space and purchasing more capital in the form of a new grill.

A second grill would essentially double the productive capacity of the shop. Table 7.2 shows the effect of a new grill on the marginal product of labor in the shop. With only one grill, the first worker produces 10 sandwiches per hour and the second produces 15. Diminishing returns set in with the third worker, who can crank out only 10 sandwiches. Returns continue to diminish with the fourth worker, who can make only 5 sandwiches. But with two grills, diminishing returns don't set in until there are two workers at *each* grill. The third and fourth workers produce 15 sandwiches each per hour. Remember, employee one is handling the phone and the tables, so employees two, three, and four can go full speed on the grills.

With two grills, the fifth worker is the one that begins to crowd. The fifth worker is the third sandwich maker on the first grill; she can produce only 10 sandwiches an hour. The sixth worker is the third worker on the second grill; he can also produce 10 sandwiches an hour. It is not until seven people are working

---

[2] In theory the total product curve could turn downward beyond L_3. This would imply that more workers would actually get in the way and that output would *fall*. If this were to happen, marginal product would actually be negative or beyond L_3.

UNITS OF LABOR	ONE GRILL		TWO GRILLS	
	TOTAL PRODUCT	MARGINAL PRODUCT	TOTAL PRODUCT	MARGINAL PRODUCT
0	0	0	0	0
1	10	10	10	10
2	25	15	25	15
3	35	10	40	15
4	40	5	55	15
5	42	2	65	10
6	42	0	75	10
7	42	0	80	5

TABLE 7.2
Marginal Product of Labor in Sandwich Production with Two Grills

FIGURE 7.5

Shift of a Marginal Product of Labor Curve Resulting from an Increase in Capital

When more capital is added in the form of a new grill, the productivity of labor is enhanced. The added capital shifts the marginal product of labor curve to the right. (Although Table 7.2 provides data on the marginal product of only seven workers, you should be able to figure out the MP_L of the eighth and ninth workers when there are two grills.)

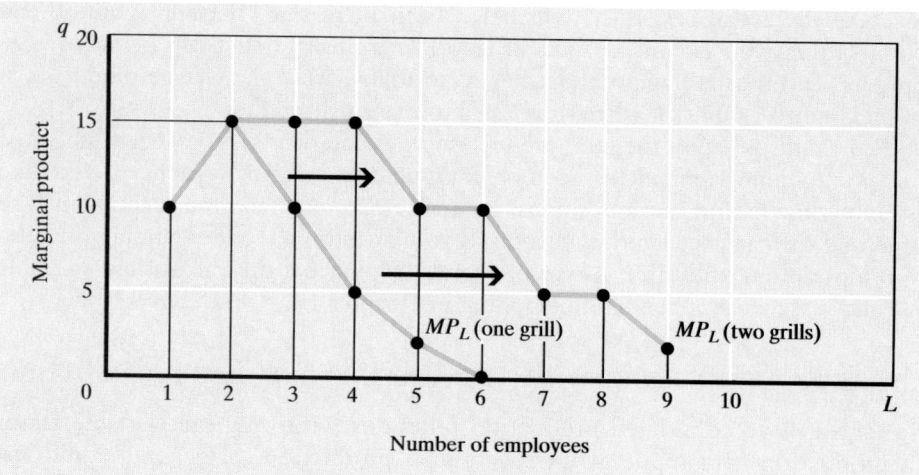

on the grills that marginal product drops to 5. (Look back at Table 7.2.) The productivity of labor has been enhanced by adding capital to the production process.

Figure 7.5 shows graphically how the increase in capital enhances the productivity of labor and shifts the marginal product curve to the right. This simple relationship lies at the heart of worries about productivity at the national and international levels. Building new, modern plants and equipment enhances a nation's productivity. Since the 1950s, for example, Japan has accumulated capital (i.e., built plant and equipment) faster than any other country in the world. The result is a very high average quantity of output per worker in Japan.

CHOICE OF TECHNOLOGY

As our sandwich shop example shows, inputs (factors of production) are complementary. Capital enhances the productivity of labor. Workers in the sandwich shop are more productive when they are not crowded on a single grill. Similarly, labor enhances the productivity of capital. When more workers are hired at a plant that is operating at 50% of capacity, previously idle machines suddenly become productive.

But inputs can also be substituted for one another. If labor becomes expensive, firms can adopt labor-saving technologies; that is, they can substitute capital for labor. Assembly lines can be automated by replacing human beings with machines. (See the Issues and Applications box entitled "Substitution of Capital for Labor: Robotics.") If capital becomes relatively expensive, firms can substitute labor for capital. In short, most goods and services can be produced in a number of ways, using alternative technologies. One of the key decisions that all firms must make is which technology to use.

Consider the choices available to the diaper manufacturer in Table 7.3. Five dif-

TABLE 7.3

Inputs Required to Produce 100 Diapers Using Alternative Technologies

TECHNOLOGY	UNITS OF CAPITAL (K)	UNITS OF LABOR (L)
A	2	10
B	3	6
C	4	4
D	6	3
E	10	2

SUBSTITUTION OF CAPITAL FOR LABOR: ROBOTICS

The ultimate substitution of capital for labor is robotics. Twenty years ago robots were confined to the world of science fiction. Today, robots are everywhere in industry. *The Statistical Abstract of the United States* provides data on the number of robots produced in the United States to perform such tasks as welding, soldering, machine-tool loading and unloading, assembly of components, painting, gluing, sealing, and so forth. The Japanese have used robots extensively in automobile production for years. In 1989, U.S. companies reported shipping over 2,000 complete robots and over $250 million in sales of robot accessories and components.

The following excerpt describes some of the ways that robots (capital) have been substituted for labor:

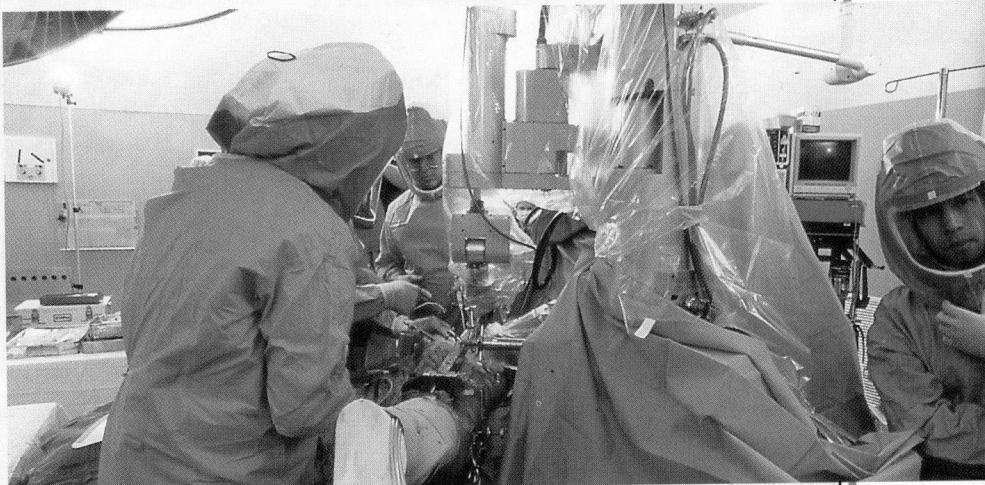

Robots have increased productivity not only in manufacturing industries but also in service industries. Transition Research's Helpmate robot, now in use at several hospitals, can carry patient's food trays and operate elevators.

The 1990's have seen sales rise to record levels for industrial robots that can efficiently paint, weld, seal, assemble and package a wide variety of goods, often with a precision humans cannot duplicate or under conditions they cannot endure. And new applications are springing up in other sectors: for instance, service robots that can tirelessly perform tasks like polishing supermarket floors or delivering patients' meals in hospitals....

[In addition,] improved robotic controls, better sensors and vastly superior machine-vision systems are allowing robots to be used successfully for tasks too mundane, tedious or dangerous for people to perform.

Robots have also proved indispensable, for example, in nuclear power plants. "We use them in remote inspection, tank cleaning, looking inside pipes and retrieval of loose parts," said Harry Roman, robotics and artificial intelligence manager for the Public Service Electric and Gas Company of New Jersey. "Our next target is repairs...."

Transitions Research's Helpmate robot, now in use at Danbury Hospital, can carry patients' food trays from the third-floor dietary department to the 12th-floor nursing unit—traversing several corridors and operating an elevator without human intervention—and speak to the receiving nurse or attendant: "Please unload compartment one. Press the green button...." Four Helpmates are currently being used in the field, at Danbury Hospital and elsewhere...."

Integrated Surgical Systems Inc. of Sacramento, Calif., is currently seeking clearance from the Food and Drug Administration to begin human clinical trials using a robot to remove hip bones for replacement by titanium implants.

The robot, which is programmed with the dimensions and exact location intended for the implant, carries out the surgery under the watchful eye of a doctor who can stop the process from a nearby computer monitor. The robot is capable of making cuts so precise that the gaps between the replacement and the remaining bone are 50 microns, about half the width of a human hair and one-twentieth the smallest average gap in surgery performed by humans, according to Dr. Howard Paul, Integrated Surgical's chief executive.

Source: Barnaby J. Feder, "Robotics Comes Back to Reality," *New York Times*, April 29, 1992.

ferent techniques of producing 100 diapers are available. Technology *A* is the most labor intensive, requiring ten hours of labor and two units of capital to produce 100 diapers. (You can think of units of capital as machine hours.) Technology *E* is the most capital intensive, requiring only two hours of labor but ten hours of machine time.

To choose a production technique, the firm must look to input markets to find out the current market prices of labor and capital. What is the wage rate (P_L), and what is the cost per hour of capital (P_K)?

Suppose that labor and capital are both available at a price of $1 per unit. Column 4 of Table 7.4 presents the calculations required to determine which technology is the best. The winner is technology *C*. Assuming that the firm's objective is to maximize profits, it will choose the least-cost technology. Using technology *C*, the firm can produce 100 diapers for $8. All four of the other technologies produce 100 diapers at a higher cost.

Now suppose that the wage rate (P_L) were to rise sharply, from $1 to $5. You might guess that this increase would lead the firm to substitute labor-saving capital for workers, and you'd be right. As column 5 of Table 7.4 shows, the increase in the wage rate means that technology *E* is now the cost-minimizing choice for the firm. Using ten units of capital and only two units of labor, the firm can produce 100 diapers for $20. All other technologies are now more costly.

To summarize:

> Two things determine the cost of production: (1) the technologies that are available, and (2) input prices. Profit-maximizing firms will choose the technology that minimizes the cost of production given current market input prices.

So far, we have looked only at a *single* level of output. That is, we have determined how much it will cost to produce 100 diapers using the best available technology when P_K = $1 or $5 and P_L = $1. But the best technique for producing 1,000 diapers or 10,000 diapers may be entirely different. The next chapter explores the relationship between cost and the level of output in some detail. One of our main objectives in that chapter will be to determine the amount that a competitive firm will choose to supply during a given time period.

TABLE 7.4
Cost-Minimizing Choice Among Alternative Technologies (100 Diapers)

TECHNOLOGY	UNITS OF CAPITAL (*K*)	UNITS OF LABOR (*L*)	COST = ($L \times P_L$) + ($K \times P_K$) IF P_L = $1, P_K = $1	IF P_L = $5 P_K = $1
A	2	10	$12	$52
B	3	6	$9	$33
C	4	4	$8	$24
D	6	3	$9	$21
E	10	2	$12	$20

SUMMARY

1. Firms vary in size and internal organization, but they all take *inputs* and transform them into *outputs* through a process called *production*.

2. In perfect competition, no single firm has any control over prices. This follows from two assumptions: (1) that perfectly competitive industries are composed of many firms, each small relative to the size of the industry, and (2) that each firm in a perfectly competitive industry produces *homogeneous products*.

3. The demand curve facing a competitive firm is perfectly elastic. If a single firm raises its price above the market price, it will sell nothing. Because it can sell all it produces at the market price, a firm has no incentive to reduce price.

The Behavior of Profit-Maximizing Firms

4. Profit-maximizing firms in all industries must make three choices: (1) how much output to supply, (2) how to produce that output, and (3) how much of each input to demand.

5. Profit equals *total revenue* minus total cost. *Economic cost* includes (1) a normal return, or profit, to the owners, and (2) the opportunity cost (rather than the money cost) of each factor of production and out-of-pocket cost.

6. A *normal rate of return* to capital is included in economic cost because tying up resources in the capital stock of a firm has an opportunity cost. If you start a business or buy a share of

stock in a corporation, you do so because you expect a profit. Investors will not invest their money in a business unless they are guaranteed a rate of return similar to or above the rate they can obtain by purchasing risk-free government bonds.

7. *Economic profits* are profits over and above a normal rate of return. A firm earning zero economic profits is a firm earning just exactly a normal rate of return. A firm does not show economic profits unless it is earning above a normal return for its owners. A firm actually earning a profit as an accountant measures it is suffering a loss from the perspective of economics if the profit rate is below normal.

8. Two assumptions define the *short run*: (1) a fixed scale or, more specifically, a fixed factor of production, and (2) no entry to or exit from the industry. In the *long run,* firms can choose any scale of operations they want, and new firms can enter and leave the industry.

9. To make decisions, firms need to know three things: (1) the market price of their output, (2) the techniques of production that are available, and (3) the price of inputs.

The Production Process

10. Production is the process through which inputs are combined and transformed into outputs. The relationship between inputs and outputs (that is, the *technology of production*) expressed numerically or mathematically is called a *production function,* or *total product function.*

11. The *marginal product* of a variable input is the additional product that an added unit of that input will produce if all other inputs are held constant. The *law of diminishing returns* states that when additional units of a variable input are added to fixed inputs after a certain point, the marginal product of the variable input will decline.

12. *Average product* is the average amount of product produced by each unit of a variable factor. If marginal product is above average product, the average product rises; if marginal product is below average product, the average product falls.

13. Capital and labor are at the same time complementary and substitutable inputs. Capital enhances the productivity of labor, but it can also be substituted for labor.

Choice of Technology

14. One of the key decisions that all firms must make is which technology to use. Profit-maximizing firms will choose that combination of inputs that minimizes costs and therefore maximizes profits.

REVIEW TERMS AND CONCEPTS

Equations:
profit = total revenue – total cost
marginal product of labor: $MP_L = \dfrac{\Delta q}{\Delta L}$

average product of labor: $AP_L = \dfrac{q}{L}$

PROBLEM SET

1. The graph below gives the current situation in the perfectly competitive market for corn in Iowa.

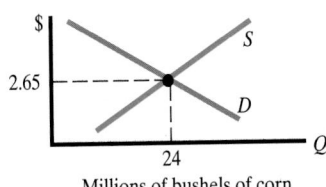

Millions of bushels of corn

a. Graph the demand curve facing a single representative corn farmer in Iowa.

b. Explain the shape of the demand curve carefully. What specific assumptions lie behind its shape?

2. Ted Baxter runs a small newspaper company in southern Oregon. The paper has been in business for 25 years. The total value of the firm's capital stock is $1,000,000, which Ted owns outright. This year the firm earned a total of $250,000 after out-of-pocket expenses. Without taking the opportunity cost of capital into account, this means that Ted is earning a 25% return on his capital. Suppose that risk-free bonds are currently paying a rate of 10% to those who buy them.

a. What is meant by the "opportunity cost of capital"?

b. Explain why opportunity costs are "real" costs even though they do not involve out-of-pocket expenses.

c. What is the opportunity cost of Ted's capital?

d. How much economic profit is Ted earning?

3. The following table gives total output or total product as a function of labor units used:

L	q = TP
0	0
1	5
2	9
3	12
4	14
5	15

a. Define diminishing returns.

b. Does the table indicate a situation of diminishing returns? Explain your answer.

4. The following graph shows total product, or total output, as a function of labor units used:

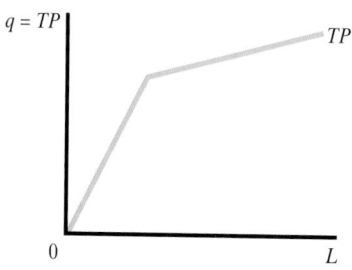

Graph the marginal product function and the average product function. Explain their shapes.

5. Suppose that wimps can be produced using two different production techniques, A and B. The following table provides the total input requirements for each of five different total output levels:

Tech.	Q = 1 K	Q = 1 L	Q = 2 K	Q = 2 L	Q = 3 K	Q = 3 L	Q = 4 K	Q = 4 L	Q = 5 K	Q = 5 L
A	2	5	1	10	5	14	6	18	8	20
B	5	2	8	3	11	4	14	5	16	6

a. Assuming that the price of labor (P_L) is $1 and the price of capital (P_K) is $2, calculate the total cost of production for each of the five levels of output using the optimal (least-cost) technology at each level.

b. How many labor hours (units of labor) would be employed at each level of output? How many machine hours (units of capital)?

c. Graph total cost of production as a function of output. (Put cost on the Y-axis and output, Q, on the X-axis.)

d. Repeat a. through c. under the assumption that the price of labor (P_L) rises from $1 to $3 while the price of capital (P_K) remains at $2.

APPENDIX TO CHAPTER 7

FROM TECHNOLOGY AND FACTOR PRICES TO COST: ISOQUANTS AND ISOCOSTS

This chapter has shown that the cost structure facing a firm depends on two key pieces of information: (1) input (factor) prices, and (2) technology. This appendix presents a more formal analysis of technology and factor prices and their relationship to cost.

A NEW LOOK AT TECHNOLOGY: ISOQUANTS

Table 7A.1 is expanded from Table 7.3 to show the various combinations of capital (K) and labor (L) that can be used to produce three different levels of output. For example, 100 units of X can be produced with two units of capital and ten units of labor, or with three units of K and six units of L, or with four units of K and four units of L, and so forth. Similarly, 150 units of X can be produced with three units of K and ten units of L, or with four units of K and seven units of L, and so forth.

TABLE 7A.1
Alternative Combinations of Capital (K) and Labor (L) Required to Produce 50, 100, and 150 Units of Output

	$q_x = 50$ K	$q_x = 50$ L	$q_x = 100$ K	$q_x = 100$ L	$q_x = 150$ K	$q_x = 150$ L
A	1	8	2	10	3	10
B	2	5	3	6	4	7
C	3	3	4	4	5	5
D	5	2	6	3	7	4
E	8	1	10	2	10	3

A graph that shows all the combinations of capital and labor that can be used to produce a given amount of output is called an **isoquant**. Figure 7A.1 graphs three isoquants, one each for $q_x = 50$, $q_x = 100$, and $q_x = 150$, based on the data in Table 7A.1. Notice that all the points on the graph have been connected, indicating that there are an infinite number of combinations of labor and capital that can produce each level of output. For example, 100 units of output can also be produced with 3.50 units of labor and 4.75 units of capital. (Verify that this point is on the isoquant labeled $q_x = 100$.)

Figure 7A.1 shows only three isoquants, but there are many more not shown. For example, there are separate isoquants for $q_x = 101$, $q_x = 102$, and so on. If we assume that producing fractions of a unit of output is possible, there must be an isoquant for $q_x = 134.57$, for $q_x = 124.82$, and so on. One could imagine an infinite number of isoquants in Figure 7A.1. The higher the level of output, the farther up and to the right the isoquant will lie.

Figure 7A.2 derives the slope of an isoquant. Because points A and B are both on the $q_x = 100$ isoquant, the two points represent two different combinations of K and L that can be used to produce 100 units of output. In moving from point A to point B along the curve, less capital is employed but more labor is used. An approximation of the amount of output lost by using less capital is ΔK times the marginal product of capital (MP_K). Recall that the marginal product of capital is the number of units of output produced by a single marginal unit of capital. Thus, $\Delta K \cdot MP_K$ is the total output lost by using less capital.

But for output to remain constant (as it must, because A and B are on the same isoquant), the loss of output from using less capital must be exactly matched by the added output produced by using more labor. This amount can be approximated by ΔL times the marginal product of labor (MP_L). Since the two must be equal, it follows that:

$$\Delta K \cdot MP_K = -\Delta L \cdot MP_L.[1]$$

If we then divide both sides of this equation by ΔL and then by MP_K, we arrive at the following expression for the slope of the isoquant:

> Slope of Isoquant : $\dfrac{\Delta K}{\Delta L} = -\dfrac{MP_L}{MP_K}$.

The ratio of MP_L to MP_K is called the **marginal rate of technical substitution**. It is the rate at which a firm can substitute capital for labor and hold output constant.

Factor Prices and Input Combinations: Isocosts

A graph that shows all the combinations of capital and labor that are available for a given total cost is called an **isocost line**. (Recall that total cost includes opportunity costs and a normal rate of return.) Just as there are an infinite number of isoquants (one for every possible level of output), there are an infinite number of isocost lines, one for every possible level of total cost.

---

[1] We need to add the negative sign to ΔL because in moving from point A to point B, ΔK is a negative number and ΔL is a positive number. The minus sign is needed to balance the equation.

FIGURE 7A.1

Isoquants Showing All Combinations of Capital and Labor That Can Be Used to Produce 50, 100, and 150 Units of Output

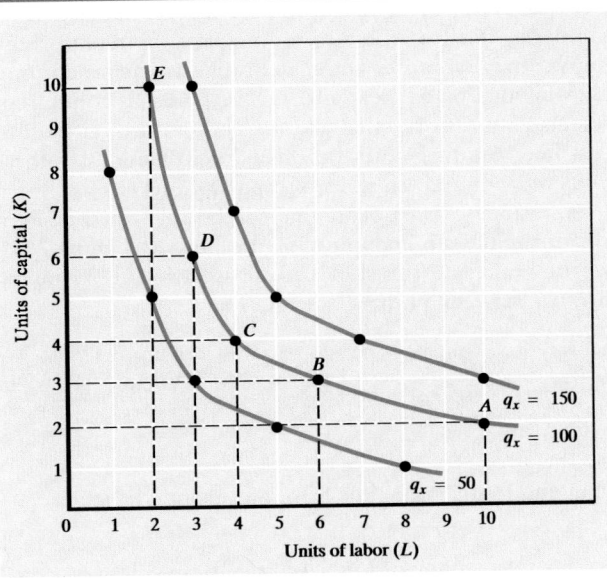

FIGURE 7A.2

The Slope of an Isoquant Is Equal to the Ratio of MP_L to MP_K

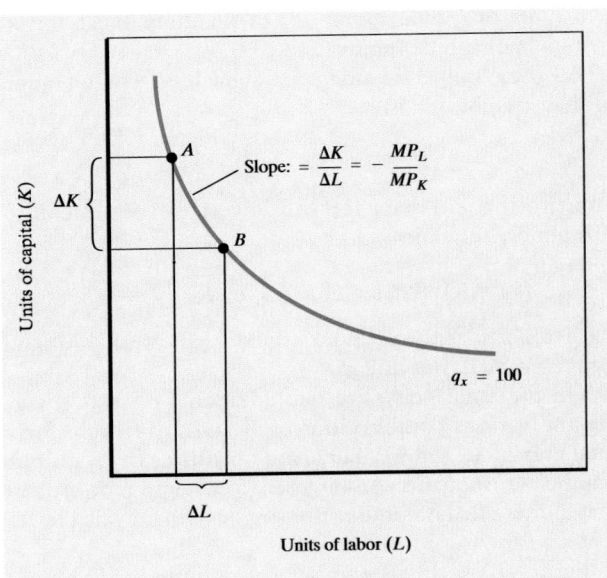

FIGURE 7A.3

Isocost Lines Showing the Combinations of Capital and Labor Available for $5, $6, and $7

An isocost line shows all the combinations of capital and labor that are available for a given total cost.

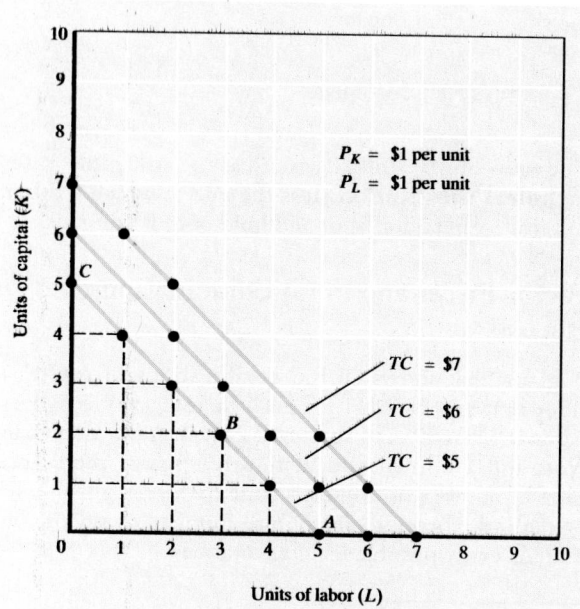

FIGURE 7A.4

Isocost Line Showing All Combinations of Capital and Labor Available for $25

One way to draw an isocost line is to determine the endpoints of that line and draw a line connecting them.

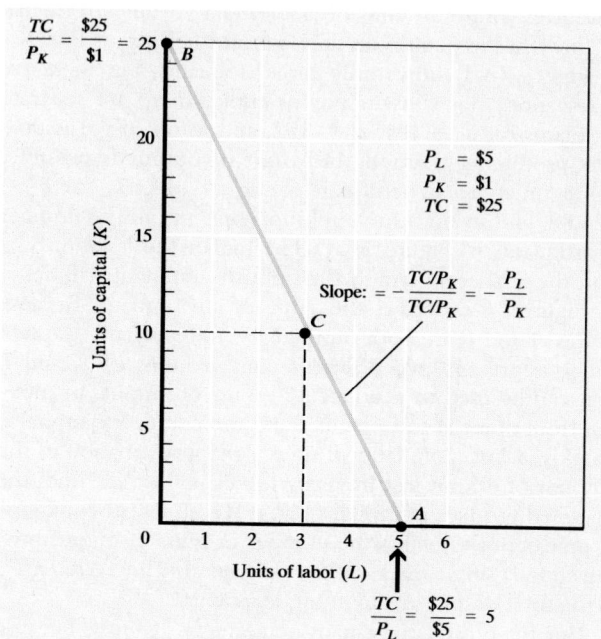

Figure 7A.3 shows three simple isocost lines assuming that the price of labor (P_L) is $1 per unit and that the price of capital (P_K) is $1 per unit. The lowest isocost line shows all the combinations of K and L that can be purchased for $5. For example, $5 will buy five units of labor and no capital (point A), or three units of labor and two units of capital (point B), or no units of labor and five units of capital (point C).

All these points lie along a straight line. The equation of that straight line is:

$$(P_K \cdot K) + (P_L \cdot L) = TC.$$

Substituting our data for the lowest isocost line into this general equation, we get:

$$(\$1 \cdot K) + (\$1 \cdot L) = \$5, \text{ or } K + L = 5.$$

Remember that the X and Y scales are units of labor and units of capital, not dollars.

On the same graph are two additional isocosts showing the various combinations of K and L available for a total cost of $6 and $7. These are only three of an infinite number of isoquants. At any total cost, there is an isocost that shows all the combinations of K and L available for that amount.

Figure 7A.4 shows another isocost line. This isocost assumes a different set of factor prices, $P_L = \$5$ and $P_K =$

$1. The diagram shows all the combinations of K and L that can be bought for $25. One way to draw the line is to determine the endpoints. For example, if the entire $25 were spent on labor, how much labor could be purchased? The answer is, of course, five units ($25 divided by $5 per unit). Thus, point A, which represents five units of labor and no capital, is on the isocost line. Similarly, if all of the $25 were spent on capital, how much capital could be purchased? The answer is 25 units ($25 divided by $1 per unit). Thus, point B, which represents 25 units of capital and no labor, is also on the isocost line. Another point on this particular isocost is three units of labor and ten units of capital, point C.

The slope of an isocost line can be calculated easily if you first find the endpoints of the line. In Figure 7A.4, we can calculate the slope of the isocost line by taking $\Delta K/\Delta L$ between points B and A. Thus,

$$\text{Slope of Isocost Line}: \frac{\Delta K}{\Delta L} = -\frac{TC/P_K}{TC/P_L} = -\frac{P_L}{P_K}.$$

Plugging in the endpoints from our example, we get:

$$\text{Slope of Line } AB = -\frac{\$5}{\$1} = -5.$$

FIGURE 7A.5

Finding the Least-Cost Combination of Capital and Labor to Produce 50 Units of Output

Profit-maximizing firms will minimize costs by producing their chosen level of output with the technology represented by the point at which the isoquant is tangent to an isocost line. Here, the cost-minimizing technology–three units of capital and three units of labor–is represented by point A.

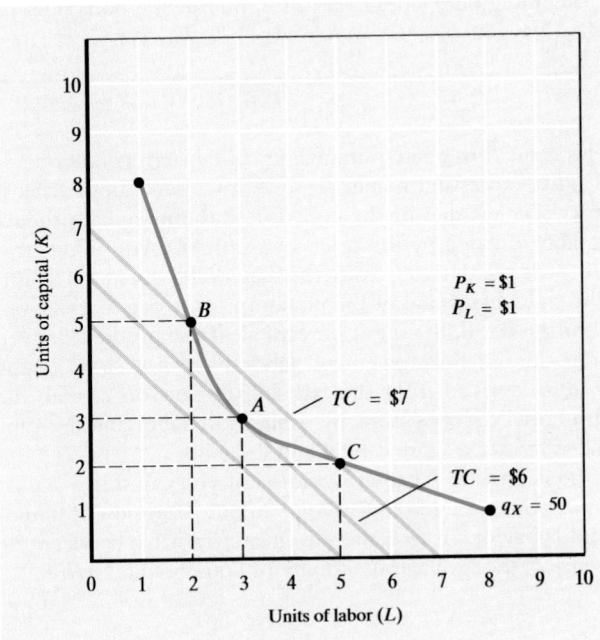

FIGURE 7A.6

Minimizing Cost of Production for $q_X = 50$, $q_X = 100$, and $q_X = 150$

Plotting a series of cost-minimizing combinations of inputs–shown in this graph as points A, B, and C–on a separate graph results in a *cost curve* like the one shown in Figure 7A.7.

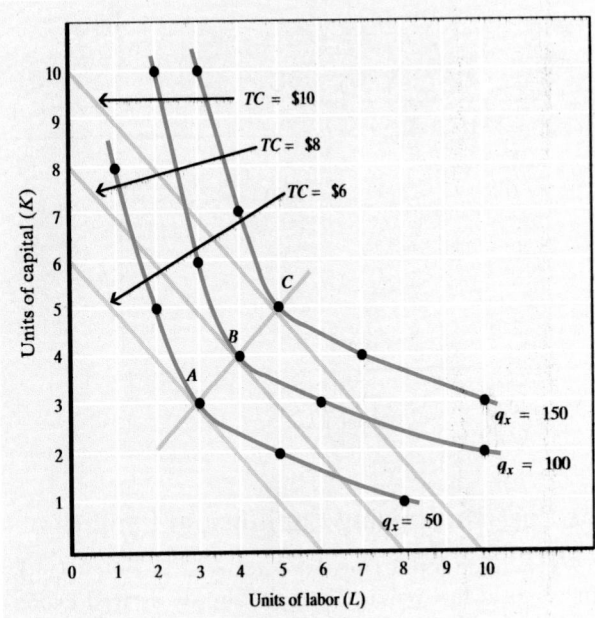

Finding the Least-Cost Technology with Isoquants and Isocosts

Figure 7A.5 superimposes the isoquant for $q_x = 50$ on the isocost lines in Figure 7A.3, which assume that $P_K = \$1$ and $P_L = \$1$. The question now becomes one of choosing among the combinations of K and L that can be used to produce 50 units of output. Recall that each point on the isoquant (labeled $q_x = 50$ in Figure 7A.5) represents a different technology–a different combination of K and L.

We assume that our firm is a competitive, profit-maximizing firm that will choose that particular combination that minimizes cost. Because every point on the isoquant lies on some particular isocost line, we can determine the total cost for each combination along the isoquant. For example, point B (five units of capital and two units of labor) lies along the isocost for a total cost of $7. Notice that five units of capital and two units of labor cost a total of $7. (Remember, $P_K = \$1$ and $P_L = \$1$.) But the same amount of output (50 units) can be produced at lower cost. Specifically, by using three units of labor and three units of capital (point A), total cost is reduced to

$6. *No other combination of K and L along isoquant $q_x = 50$ is on a lower isocost line.* In seeking to maximize profits, then,

> The firm will choose the combination of inputs that is least costly. The least costly way to produce any given level of output is indicated by the point of tangency between an isocost line and the isoquant corresponding to that level of output.[2]

In Figure 7A.5, the least-cost technology of producing 50 units of output is represented by point A, the point at which the $q_x = 50$ isoquant is just tangent to (that is, just touches) the isocost line.

Figure 7A.6 adds the other two isoquants from Figure 7A.1 to Figure 7A.5. Assuming that $P_K = \$1$ and $P_L = \$1$, the firm will move along each of the three isoquants until it finds the least-cost combination of K and L that can be used to produce that particular level of output. The result is plotted in Figure 7A.7. The minimum cost of producing 50 units of X is $6; the minimum cost of producing 100 units of X is $8; and the minimum cost of producing 150 units of X is $10.

---

[2]This assumes that the isoquants are continuous and convex (bowed) toward the origin.

FIGURE 7A.7

A Cost Curve Shows the *Minimum* Cost of Producing Each Level of Output

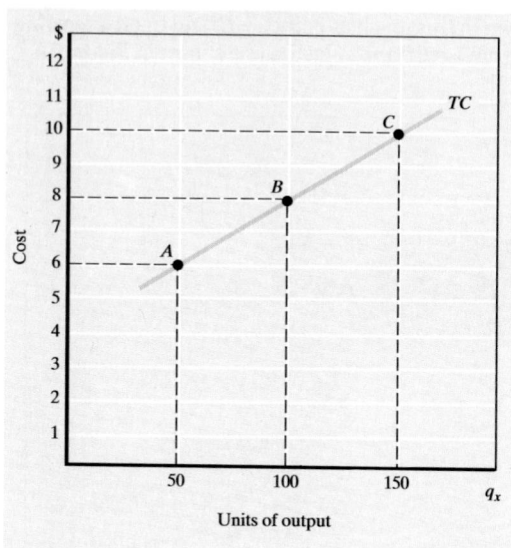

Units of output

The Cost-Minimizing Equilibrium Condition

When a line is just tangent to a curve, the two have the same slope at that point. (We have already derived expressions for the slope of an isocost and the slope of an iso-quant.) At each point of tangency (such as at points *A*, *B*, and *C* in Figure 7A.6), then, the following must be true:

$$\text{Slope of Isoquant} = -\frac{MP_L}{MP_K} = \text{Slope of Isocost} = -\frac{P_L}{P_K}.$$

Thus:

$$\frac{MP_L}{MP_K} = \frac{P_L}{P_K}$$

Dividing both sides by P_L and multiplying both sides by MP_K, we get:

$$\frac{MP_L}{P_L} = \frac{MP_K}{P_K}.$$

This is the firm's cost-minimizing equilibrium condition.

This expression makes sense if you think about what it says. The left side of the equation is the marginal product of labor divided by the price of a unit of labor. Thus, it is the product derived from the last dollar spent on labor. The right-hand side of the equation is the product derived from the last dollar spent on capital. If the product derived from the last dollar spent on labor were not equal to the product derived from the last dollar spent on capital, the firm could decrease costs by using more labor and less capital or by using more capital and less labor.

Look back to Chapter 6 and see if you can find a similar expression and some similar logic in our discussion of household behavior. In fact, there is great symmetry between the theory of the firm and the theory of household behavior.

SUMMARY

1. An *isoquant* is a graph that shows all the combinations of capital and labor that can be used to produce a given amount of output. The slope of an isoquant is equal to $-MP_L/MP_K$. The ratio of MP_L to MP_K is the *marginal rate of technical substitution*. It is the rate at which a firm can substitute capital for labor and hold output constant.

2. An *isocost line* is a graph that shows all the combinations of capital and labor that are available for a given total cost. The slope of an isocost line is equal to $-P_L/P_K$.

3. The least-cost method of producing a given amount of output is found graphically at the point at which an isocost line is just tangent to (that is, just touches) the isoquant corresponding to that level of production. The firm's cost-minimizing equilibrium condition is $MP_L/P_L = MP_K/P_K$.

REVIEW TERMS AND CONCEPTS

isocost line A graph that shows all the combinations of capital and labor available for a given total cost   189

isoquant A graph that shows all the combinations of capital and labor that can be used to produce a given amount of output.   189

marginal rate of technical substitution The rate at which a firm can substitute capital for labor and hold output constant.   189

Equations:

$$\text{slope of isoquant}: \frac{\Delta K}{\Delta L} = -\frac{MP_L}{MP_K}$$

$$\text{slope of isocost line}: \frac{\Delta K}{\Delta L} = -\frac{TC/P_K}{TC/P_L} = -\frac{P_L}{P_K}$$

PROBLEM SET

1. Assume that $MP_L = 5$ and $MP_K = 10$. Assume also that $P_L = \$2$ and $P_K = \$5$. This implies that the firm should substitute capital for labor. Explain why.

2. In the isoquant/isocost diagram (Figure 1), suppose that the firm is producing 1,000 units of output at point A using 100 units of labor and 200 units of capital. As an outside consultant, what actions would you suggest to management to improve profits? What would you recommend if the firm were operating at point B, using 100 units of capital and 200 units of labor?

3. Using the information from the isoquant/isocost diagram (Figure 2), and assuming that $P_L = P_K = \$2$, complete Table 1.

FIGURE 1

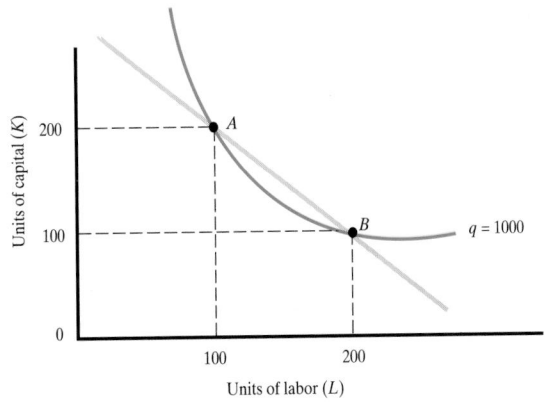

FIGURE 2

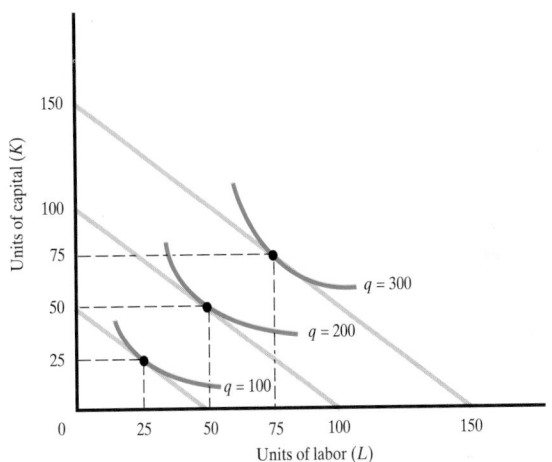

TABLE 1

OUTPUT UNITS	TOTAL COST OF OUTPUT	UNITS OF LABOR DEMANDED	UNITS OF CAPITAL DEMANDED
100			
200			
300			

8 Short-Run Costs and Output Decisions

This chapter continues our examination of the decisions that firms make in their quest for profits. You have seen that firms in perfectly competitive industries make three very specific decisions (see Figure 8.1). These decisions are:

1. How much output to supply;
2. How to produce that output (that is, which production technique to use); and
3. What quantity of each input to demand.

Remember though that *all* types of firms make these decisions, not just those in perfectly competitive industries. We continue to use perfectly competitive firms as a teaching device, but much of the material in this chapter applies to firms in noncompetitive industries as well.

We have assumed so far that firms are in business to earn profits and that they make choices in order to maximize those profits. (Remember that *profit* is the difference between revenues and costs.) Because firms in perfectly competitive markets are *price-takers* in both input and output markets, many decisions depend upon prices over which firms have no control. Like households, firms also face market constraints.

FIGURE 8.1

Decisions Facing Firms

DECISIONS	are based on	INFORMATION
1. The quantity of output to *supply*		1. The price of output
2. How to produce that output (which technique to use)		2. Techniques of production available*
3. The quantity of each input to *demand*		3. The price of inputs*
		*determines production costs

In the last chapter, we focused on the production process. This chapter focuses on *costs* of production. To calculate costs, a firm must know two things: the quantity and combination of inputs it needs to produce its product and how much those inputs cost. As we begin to examine how technology and input prices determine costs, we focus first on input markets. By the end of the chapter, we will have enough information to figure out how much of its product a firm is likely to supply (that is, how much output to produce) at each possible price. In other words, we will have derived the supply curve of a competitive firm in the short run.

Take a moment and look back at the circular flow diagram, Figure 7.1. There you can see exactly where we are in our study of the competitive market system. The goal of this chapter is to look behind the supply curve in output markets. It is important to understand, however, that producing output implies demanding inputs at the same time. You can also see in Figure 7.1 two of the information sources used by firms in their output supply and input demand decisions: Firms look to output markets for the price of output and to input markets for the prices of capital and labor.

COSTS IN THE SHORT RUN

Our emphasis in this chapter is on costs *in the short run only*. Recall that the short run is that period during which two conditions hold: (1) Existing firms face limits imposed by some fixed factor of production, and (2) new firms cannot enter, and existing firms cannot exit, an industry.

In the short run, all firms (competitive and noncompetitive) have costs that they must bear regardless of their output. Some costs, in fact, must be paid even if the firm stops producing (that is, even if output is zero). These kinds of costs are called **fixed costs,** and the important thing to remember about them is that firms can do nothing in the short run to avoid them or to change them. In the long run, a firm has no fixed costs, because it can expand, contract, or exit the industry.

Firms do have certain costs in the short run that depend on the level of output they have chosen. These kinds of costs are called **variable costs.** Fixed costs and variable costs together make up **total costs:**

$$TC = TFC + TVC,$$

where TC denotes total costs, TFC denotes total fixed costs, and TVC denotes total variable costs.

fixed cost Any cost that a firm bears in the short run that does not depend on its level of output. These costs are incurred even if the firm is producing nothing. There are no fixed costs in the long run.

variable cost Any cost that a firm bears that depends on the level of production chosen.

total costs Fixed costs plus variable costs.

Fixed Costs

In discussing fixed costs, we must distinguish between total fixed costs and average fixed costs.

TOTAL FIXED COST (TFC) Total fixed cost is sometimes referred to as *overhead*. If you operate a factory, you must heat the building to keep the pipes from freezing in the winter. Even if no production is taking place, you may have to keep the roof from leaking, pay a guard to protect the building from vandals, and make payments on a long-term lease. There may also be insurance premiums, taxes, and city fees to pay, as well as contract obligations to workers.

Fixed costs represent a larger portion of total costs for some firms than for others. Electric companies, for instance, maintain generating plants, thousands of miles of distribution wires, poles, transformers, and so forth. Usually, such plants are financed by issuing bonds to the public (that is, by borrowing). The interest that must be paid on these bonds represents a substantial part of the utilities' operating cost and is a fixed cost in the short run, no matter how much, if any, electricity is being produced.

For the purposes of our discussion in this chapter, we will assume that firms use only two inputs: labor and capital.[1] Recall that capital is both produced and yields services over time in the production of other goods and services. It is the plant and equipment of a manufacturing firm; the computers, desks, chairs, doors, and walls of a law office; and the boat that Bill and Colleen built on their desert island. It is sometimes assumed that capital is a fixed input in the short run and that labor is the only variable input. To be a bit more realistic, however, we will assume that capital has both a fixed *and* a variable component. After all, some capital can be purchased in the short run.

Consider a small consulting firm that employs several economists, research assistants, and secretaries. It rents space in an office building and has a five-year lease. The rent it pays on the office space can be thought of as a fixed cost in the short run. The monthly electric and heating bills are also essentially fixed (although the amounts may vary slightly from month to month). So are the salaries of the basic administrative staff. Payments on some capital equipment—a large copying machine, for instance, and the main word processing system—can also be thought of as fixed.

The same firm also has costs that vary with output. When there is a lot of work, the firm hires more employees at both the professional and research assistant level. The capital used by the consulting firm may also vary, even in the short run. Payments on the computer system do not change, but the firm may rent additional computer time when necessary. It can buy additional personal computers, word processing terminals, or databases quickly, if need be. It must pay for the copy machine, but the machine costs more when it is running than when it is not.

Total fixed costs (TFC) are those costs that do not change with output, even if output is zero. Column 2 of Table 8.1 presents data on the fixed costs of a hypothetical firm. Fixed costs are $1000 at all levels of output. Figure 8.2a shows total fixed costs as a function of output. Since *TFC* does not change with output, the graph is simply a straight horizontal line at $1000. The important thing to remember here is that:

> Firms have no control over fixed costs in the short run. For this reason, fixed costs are sometimes called **sunk costs.**

TABLE 8.1
Short-Run Fixed Cost (Total and Average) of a Hypothetical Firm

(1) q	(2) TFC	(3) AFC (TFC/q)
0	$1000	$ —
1	1000	1000
2	1000	500
3	1000	333
4	1000	250
5	1000	200

total fixed costs (TFC), or overhead The total of all costs that do not change with output, even if output is zero.

sunk costs Another name for fixed costs in the short run because firms have no choice but to pay them.

---
[1]While this may seem unrealistic, virtually everything that we will say about firms using these two factors can easily be generalized to firms that use many factors of production.

AVERAGE FIXED COST (AFC) **Average fixed cost (AFC)** is total fixed cost (*TFC*) divided by the number of units of output (*q*):

$$AFC = \frac{TFC}{q}.$$

For example, if the firm in Figure 8.2 produced three units of output, average fixed costs would be $333 ($1000 divided by three). If the same firm produced five units of output, average fixed cost would be $200 ($1000 divided by five). *Average fixed cost falls as output rises,* because the same total is being spread over, or divided by, a larger number of units (see column 3 of Table 8.1). This phenomenon is sometimes called **spreading overhead.**

Graphs of average fixed cost, like that in Figure 8.2b (which presents the average fixed cost data from Table 8.1), are downward–sloping curves. Notice that *AFC* approaches zero as the quantity of output increases. If output were 100,000 units, average fixed cost would equal only one cent per unit in our example ($1,000 ÷ 100,000 = $.01). Of course, *AFC* never actually reaches zero.

Variable Costs

Variable costs can be classified into three categories: total variable cost, marginal cost, and average variable cost.

TOTAL VARIABLE COST (TVC) **Total variable costs (TVC)** are those costs that depend on, or vary with, the level of output in the short run. To produce more output, a firm uses more inputs. The cost of additional output depends directly on the additional inputs that are required and how much they cost.

FIGURE 8.2
Short-Run Fixed Cost (Total and Average) of a Hypothetical Firm

Average fixed cost is simply total fixed cost divided by the quantity of output. As output increases, average fixed cost declines because we are dividing a fixed number ($1000) by a larger and larger quantity.

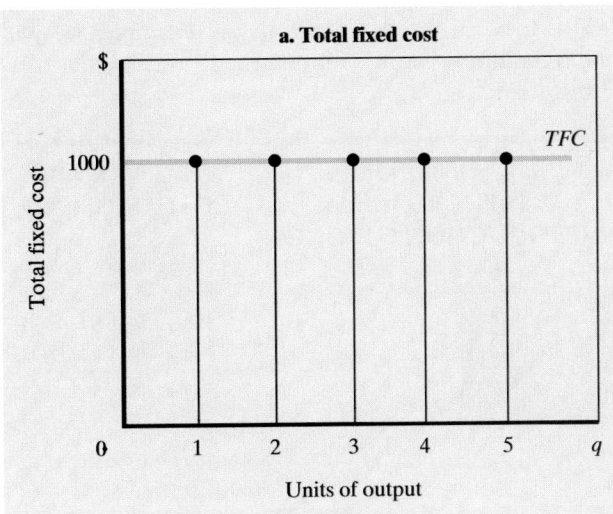
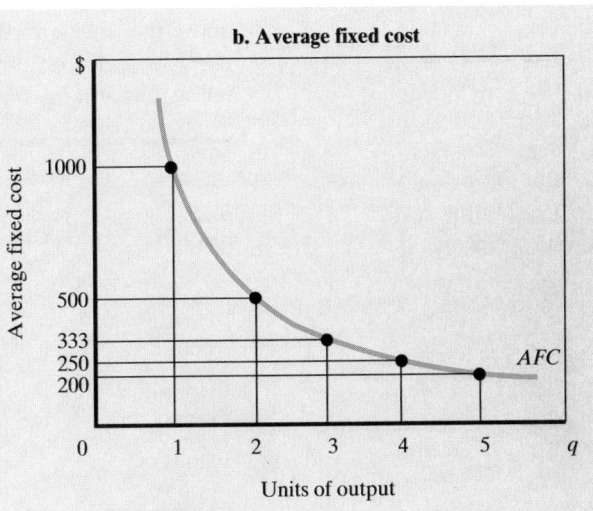

As you saw in Chapter 7, input requirements are determined by technology. Firms generally have a number of production techniques available to them, and the option they choose is assumed to be the one that produces the desired level of output at the least cost. To find out which technology involves the least cost, a firm must compare the total variable costs of producing that level of output using different production techniques.

This is as true of small businesses as it is of large manufacturing firms. Suppose, for example, that you are a small farmer. A certain amount of work has to be done to plant and harvest your 120 acres. You can get this work done in a number of ways. You might hire four farmhands and divide up the tasks, or you might buy several pieces of complex farm machinery (capital) and do the work single-handedly. Clearly, your final choice depends on a number of things. What machinery is available? What does it do? Will it work on small fields such as yours? How much will it cost to buy each piece of equipment? What wage will you have to pay farm hands? How many will you need to get the job done? If machinery is expensive and labor is cheap, you will probably choose the labor-intensive technology. If farm labor is expensive and the local farm equipment dealer is going out of business, you might get a good deal on some machinery and choose the capital-intensive method.

Having compared the costs of alternative production techniques, the firm may be influenced in its choice by the current *scale of its operation*. Remember, in the short run a firm is locked into a *fixed* scale of operations. A firm currently producing on a small scale may find that a labor-intensive technique is the least costly, whether or not labor is comparatively expensive; the same firm producing on a larger scale might find a capital-intensive technique less costly.

total variable cost curve A graph that shows the relationship between total variable cost and the level of a firm's output.

The **total variable cost curve** is a graph that shows the relationship between total variable cost and the level of a firm's output (q). At any given level of output, total variable cost depends on (1) the techniques of production that are available, and (2) the prices of the inputs required by each technology. To examine this relationship in more detail, let us look at some production figures for some hypothetical items called "frumps."

Table 8.2 presents an analysis that might lie behind three points on the total variable cost curve of a typical frump firm. In this case, there are two production techniques available, one somewhat more capital-intensive than the other. We will assume that the price of labor is $1 per unit and the price of capital is $2 per unit. For the purposes of this example, we focus on *variable capital*—that is, on capital that can be changed in the short run. In practice, some capital (such as buildings and large, specialized machines) is fixed in the short run. In our example, we will use K to denote variable capital. Remember, however, that the firm has other capital, capital that is fixed in the short run.

TABLE 8.2
Derivation of Total Variable
Cost Schedule from
Technology and Factor Prices

PRODUCE	USING TECHNIQUE	UNITS OF INPUT REQUIRED (PRODUCTION FUNCTION) K	L	TOTAL VARIABLE COST ASSUMING $P_K = \$2, P_L = \$1$ $TVC = K \cdot P_K + L \cdot P_L$
1 Unit of output	A	4	4	$(4 \times \$2) + (4 \times \$1) = \$12$
	B	2	6	$(2 \times \$2) + (6 \times \$1) = \boxed{\$10}$
2 Units of output	A	7	6	$(7 \times \$2) + (6 \times \$1) = \$20$
	B	4	10	$(4 \times \$2) + (10 \times \$1) = \boxed{\$18}$
3 Units of output	A	9	6	$(9 \times \$2) + (6 \times \$1) = \boxed{\$24}$
	B	6	14	$(6 \times \$2) + (14 \times \$1) = \$26$

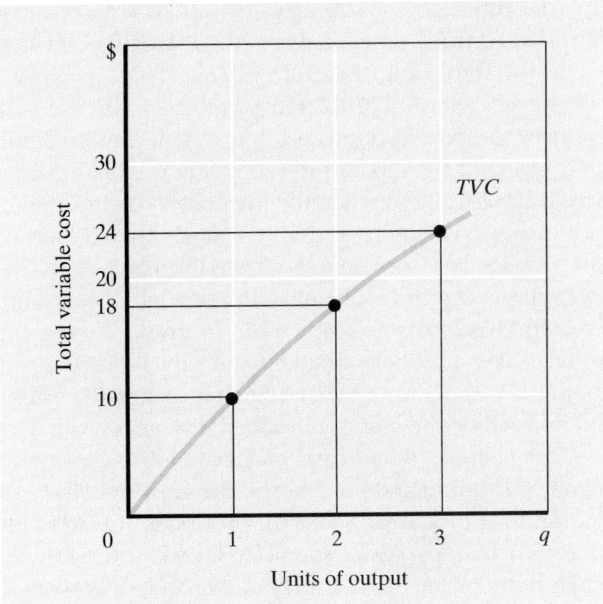

FIGURE 8.3
Total Variable Cost Curve

In Table 8.2, total variable cost is derived from production requirements and input prices. A total variable cost curve expresses the relationship between *TVC* and total output.

Analysis reveals that to produce one unit of output, the labor-intensive technique is least costly. Technique *A* requires four units of both capital and labor, which would cost a total of $12. Technique *B* requires six units of labor but only two units of capital for a total cost of only $10. To maximize profits, the firm would use technique *B* to produce one frump. The total variable cost of producing one unit of output would thus be $10.

The relatively labor-intensive technique *B* is also the best method of production for two units of output. Using *B,* the firm can produce two frumps for $18. If the firm decides to produce three frumps, however, technique *A* is the cheaper. Using the least-cost technology (*A*), the total variable cost of production is $24. The firm will use nine units of capital at $2 each and six units of labor at $1 each.

Figure 8.3 graphs the relationship between variable costs and output based on the data in Table 8.2, assuming the firm chooses, for each output, the least-cost technology.

The important point to remember here is that:

> The total variable cost curve embodies information about both factor, or input, prices and technology. It shows the cost of production using the best available technique at each output level, given current factor prices.

MARGINAL COST (MC)   The most important of all cost concepts is that of **marginal cost (MC),** the increase in total cost that results from the production of one more unit of output. Let us say, for example, that a firm is producing 1,000 units of output and decides to raise output to 1,001. Producing the extra unit raises costs, and the increase (that is, the cost of producing the 1,001st unit) is the marginal cost. Focusing on the "margin" is one way of looking at variable costs: Marginal costs reflect variable costs because they vary when output changes. Fixed costs do not change when output changes.

Table 8.3 shows how marginal cost is derived from total variable cost by simple subtraction. The total variable cost of producing the first frump is $10. Raising production from one unit to two units increases total variable cost from $10 to

TABLE 8.3
Derivation of Marginal Cost from Total Variable Cost

Units of output (frumps)	Total variable costs ($)	Marginal costs ($)
0	0	—
1	10	10
2	18	8
3	24	6

marginal cost (MC) The increase in total cost that results from producing one more unit of output.

$18; the difference is the *marginal cost* of the second unit, or $8. Raising output from two to three units increases total variable cost from $18 to $24. The marginal cost of the third unit, therefore, is $6.

Table 8.4 shows that marginal cost is simply the cost of the additional inputs, or resources, needed to produce the marginal unit of output. You saw in Table 8.2 that the least expensive method of producing one frump or two frumps was technique *B.* Here is what happens when the firm raises output from one unit to two units: To produce one unit of output, it uses technique *B,* two units of capital at $2 per unit and six units of labor at $1 per unit. Total variable cost is $10. To produce two units of output, technique *B* requires four units of capital (at $2 per unit) and ten units of labor (at $1 per unit). Total variable cost is $18. To produce the second unit, therefore, our frump producer uses two units of additional capital (at $2 each) and four units of additional labor (at $1 each), for a total additional cost of $8. Thus, the marginal cost of the second unit is $8—the cost of the added resources needed to produce it.

What happens when total output goes up by one more unit, from two to three frumps? To produce three frumps, the firm switches to technique *A,* which requires nine units of capital (at $2 each), more than twice as much capital as it took to produce two frumps. Why spend so much more on variable capital? Because this expenditure means that the firm can cut down on the amount of labor it uses. Producing two frumps required ten units of labor (at $1 each); producing three frumps requires only six. Although increasing output from two frumps to three requires the firm to spend an additional $10 on capital (five additional units at $2 each), it also means that it can cut back on labor, using four fewer units (at $1 each) and saving the firm $4. The marginal cost of the third unit is thus $6 ($10 − $4).

In reality, firms generally do not hire less labor when output rises. When firms in the real world expand, they normally use more capital and hire more labor, as our firm does in moving from one unit of output to two. Still, this example should drive home two points: (1) that costs at any level of output depend on technology *and* factor prices, and (2) that the technology appropriate at one level of production may not be appropriate at other levels of production.

TABLE 8.4
Derivation of Marginal Cost from Total Variable Cost, Technology, and Factor Prices

While the easiest way to derive marginal cost is to look at total variable cost and subtract, don't lose sight of the fact that when a firm increases its output level, it hires or demands more inputs. *Marginal cost* measures the *additional* cost of inputs required to produce each successive unit of output.

OUTPUT	LEAST-COST TECHNOLOGY	INPUT REQUIREMENTS		TOTAL VARIABLE COSTS ASSUMING $P_K = \$2$, $P_L = \$1$ $TVC = K \cdot P_K + L \cdot P_L$	
		K	*L*		
Unit 1	B	2	6	$(2 \times \$2) + (6 \times \$1) =$	$10
Unit 2	B	4	10	$(4 \times \$2) + (10 \times \$1) =$	$18
	Additional inputs needed	+2	+4		
	× Price of inputs	× $2	× $1		
	Marginal cost of unit 2	$4	$4		$8 = MC
Unit 2	B	4	10	$(4 \times \$2) + (10 \times \$1) =$	$18
Unit 3	A	9	6	$(9 \times \$2) + (6 \times \$1) =$	$24
	Additional inputs needed	+5	−4		
	× Price of inputs	× $2	× $1		
	Marginal cost of unit 3	$10	−$4		$6 = MC

THE SHAPE OF THE MARGINAL COST CURVE IN THE SHORT RUN The assumption of a fixed factor of production in the short run means that a firm is stuck at its current scale of operation (in our example, the size of the plant). As a firm tries to increase its output, it will eventually find itself trapped by that scale. Thus, our definition of the short run also implies that *marginal cost eventually rises with output.* The firm can hire more labor and use more materials—that is, it can add variable inputs—but diminishing returns eventually set in.

Recall the sandwich shop, with one grill and too many workers trying to prepare sandwiches on it, from Chapter 7. With a fixed grill capacity, more laborers could make more sandwiches, but the marginal product of each successive cook declined as more people tried to use the grill. If each additional unit of labor adds less and less to total output, it follows that it requires more labor to produce each additional unit of output. Thus, each additional unit of output costs more to produce. In other words, *diminishing returns, or decreasing marginal product, implies increasing marginal cost* (see Figure 8.4).

Recall too the accountant who makes a living by helping people file their tax returns. He has an office in his home and works alone. His fixed factor of production is his own time: There are only so many hours in a day, and he has only so much stamina. In the long run, he may decide to hire and train an associate, but in the meantime (the short run) he has to decide how much to produce, and that decision is constrained by his current scale of operations. The fact that he has no trained associate and that each day contains only 24 hours constrains the number of clients that he can take on. The biggest component of the accountant's cost is time. When he works, he gives up leisure and other things that he could do with his time. With more and more clients, he works later and later into the night; as he does so, he becomes less and less productive, and his hours become more and more valuable for sleep and relaxation. In other words, the marginal cost of doing each successive tax return rises.

To reiterate:

> In the short run, every firm is constrained by some fixed input that leads to diminishing returns to variable inputs and limits its capacity to produce. As a firm approaches that capacity, it becomes increasingly costly to produce successively higher levels of output. Marginal costs ultimately increase with output in the short run.

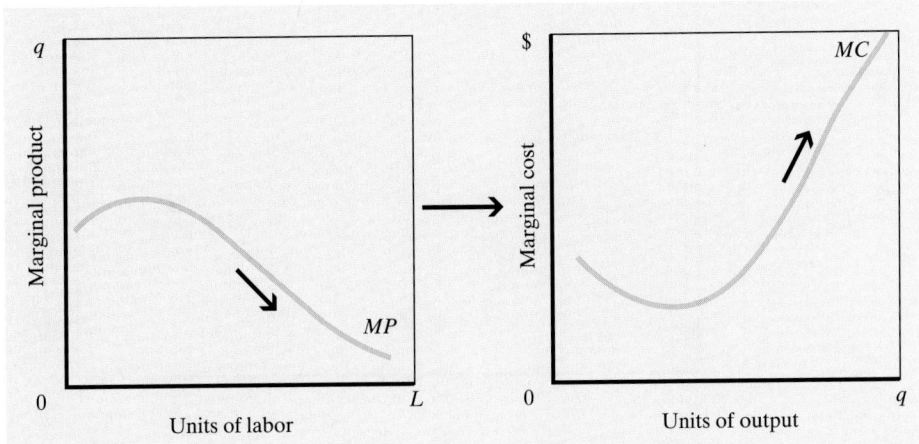

FIGURE 8.4
Declining Marginal Product Implies That Marginal Cost Will Eventually Rise with Output

In the short run, every firm is constrained by some fixed factor of production. Having a fixed input implies diminishing returns (declining marginal product) and a limited capacity to produce. As that limit is approached, marginal costs rise.

Figure 8.5 shows how the total variable cost curve and the marginal cost curve of a typical firm might look. The numbers shown for the first two units of output are those arrived at by the frump producer (see Figure 8.3). Notice first that the shape of the marginal cost curve is consistent with short-run diminishing returns. At first MC declines, but eventually the fixed factor of production begins to constrain the firm, and marginal cost rises. Up to 29 units of output, producing each successive unit of output costs slightly less than producing the one before. Beyond 29 units, however, the cost of each successive unit is greater than the one before.

Clearly, more output costs more in total than less output. Total variable costs (TVC), therefore, *always increase* when output increases. Even though the cost of each additional unit changes, *total* variable cost rises when output rises. Thus the *total* variable cost curve always has a positive slope.

The slope of the total variable cost curve varies, however. The slope of the curve reveals how quickly costs increase with output, and this relationship is reflected in marginal cost. Look carefully at the diagrams in Figure 8.5. The marginal cost of the first unit (MC_1) is $10. Going from zero to one unit of output increases total

FIGURE 8.5

Total Variable Cost and Marginal Cost for a Typical Firm

Total variable costs always increase with output. Marginal cost is the cost of producing each additional unit. Thus, the marginal cost curve shows how total variable cost changes with single unit increases in total output. When output rises from one to two units, cost goes from $10 to $18. The marginal cost of the second unit is therefore $8.

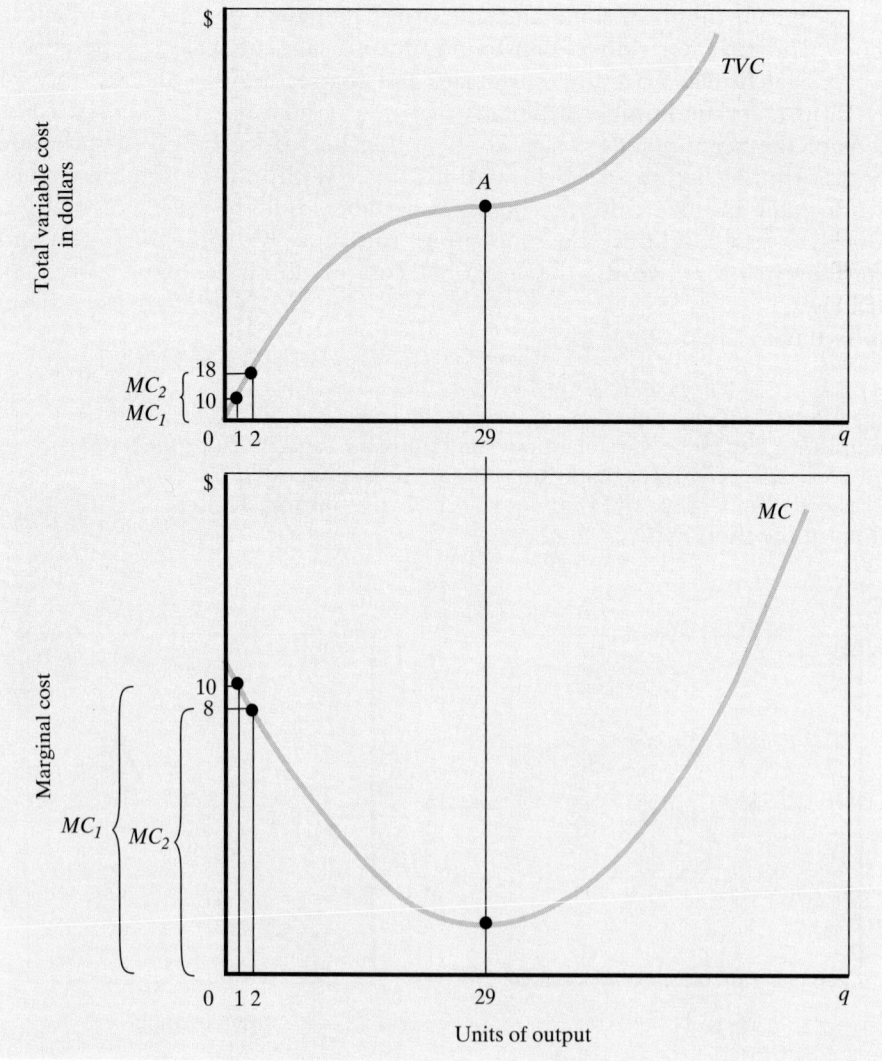

variable cost by $10, from zero to $10. The point on the total variable cost curve at two units is $18, but the cost of increasing production from one to two units—that is, the marginal cost of the second unit—is only $8 ($MC_2$).

Remember that the numerical value of the slope of a line is equal to the change in Y divided by the change in X; the slope of a total variable cost curve is thus the change in total variable cost divided by the change in output ($\Delta TVC/\Delta q$). Since marginal cost is by definition the change in total variable cost resulting from an increase in output of one unit ($\Delta q = 1$), *marginal cost actually is the slope of the total variable cost curve:*

$$\text{Slope of } TVC = \frac{\Delta TVC}{\Delta q} = \frac{\Delta TVC}{1} = \Delta TVC = MC.$$

Notice that up to 29 units, marginal cost decreases and the variable cost curve becomes flatter. The slope of the total variable cost curve is declining; that is, total variable cost increases, but at a *decreasing rate*. Beyond 29 units of output, marginal cost increases and the total variable cost curve gets steeper; total variable costs continue to increase, but at an *increasing rate*.

The point on the total variable cost curve at which a decreasing slope becomes an increasing slope is referred to as an *inflection point*. In Figure 8.5, the inflection point is found at point *A*. At that level of output, marginal cost stops declining and begins increasing.

AVERAGE VARIABLE COST (AVC)   A more complete picture of the costs of a hypothetical firm appears in Table 8.5. Column 2 shows total variable costs—derived from information on input prices and technology. Column 3 derives marginal cost by simple subtraction. For example, raising output from three units to four units increases variable costs from $24 to $32, making the marginal cost of the fourth unit $8 ($32 − $24). The marginal cost of the fifth unit is $10, the difference between $32 (*TVC*) for four units and $42 (*TVC*) for five units.

Average variable cost (AVC) is total variable cost divided by the number of units of output (*q*):

average variable cost (AVC) Total variable cost divided by the number of units of output.

$$AVC = \frac{TVC}{q}.$$

TABLE 8.5
Short-Run Costs of a Hypothetical Firm

(1) q	(2) TVC	(3) MC (ΔTVC)	(4) AVC (TVC/q)	(5) TFC	(6) TC ($TVC+TFC$)	(7) AFC (TFC/q)	(8) ATC (TC/q or $AFC+AVC$)
0	$ 0	$–	$—	$1000	$1000	$ —	$ —
1	10	10	10	1000	1010	1000	1010
2	18	8	9	1000	1018	500	509
3	24	6	8	1000	1024	333	341
4	32	8	8	1000	1032	250	258
5	42	10	8.4	1000	1042	200	208.4
—	—	—	—	—	—	—	—
—	—	—	—	—	—	—	—
500	8000	20	16	1000	9000	2	18

In Table 8.5, we calculate AVC in column 4 by dividing the numbers in column 2 (TVC) by the numbers in column 1 (q). For example, if the total variable cost of producing five units of output is $42, then the average variable cost is $42 divided by five units, or $8.40.

The important distinction to remember here is as follows:

> *Marginal cost* is the cost of *one additional unit*. *Average variable cost* is the average variable cost per unit of *all the units* being produced.

THE RELATIONSHIP BETWEEN AVERAGE VARIABLE COST AND MARGINAL COST
Average variable cost and marginal cost are related in a very specific way. When marginal cost is *below* average, average variable cost declines toward it. (Think again of the test score analogy introduced in Chapter 7. If you have an average score of 85 on three exams, and you then receive a 75, your average will fall.) In Table 8.5, the average variable cost of producing two units is $9 ($TVC/q = $18 \div 2$). The marginal cost of the third is $6, an amount lower than the marginal cost of the second unit. The average thus falls to $8 ($24 \div 3$).

Similarly, when marginal cost is *above* average variable cost, average variable cost increases toward it. If you had received a 95 on your last test instead of a 75, your average would have risen. In Table 8.5 the average variable cost of four units is $8. The marginal cost of the fifth unit is $10, and the average rises to $8.40. It follows, then, that:

> Average variable cost always moves toward marginal cost.

GRAPHING AVERAGE VARIABLE COSTS AND MARGINAL COSTS   The relationship between average variable cost and marginal cost can be illustrated graphically. Figure 8.6 duplicates the diagrams in Figure 8.5 but adds average variable cost. As the graphs show, average variable cost *follows* marginal cost, but lags behind because it is the average of all previous units.

The marginal cost of the first unit is the same as the average variable cost of producing just that unit, so marginal cost and average variable cost start together at point D. (If the reason for this is not clear to you, go back to Table 8.5 and review why for *one* unit $AVC = MC = 10.) Average variable costs from point D follow marginal cost down to point C. Marginal cost begins to rise at 29 units, but average cost does not begin to rise until marginal cost crosses it and *rises above it*. This occurs at 48 units, point C. It is always true that:

> Marginal cost intersects average variable cost at the lowest, or minimum, point of AVC.

Another example using test scores should help you to understand why this is so. Consider the following sequence of test scores: 95, 85, 92, 88. The average of these four is 90. Now suppose you get an 80 on your fifth test. This score will drag down your average to 88. Now suppose that you get an 85 on your sixth test. This score is higher than 80, but it's still *below* your 88 average. As a result, your average continues to fall (from 88 to 87.5), even though your marginal test score rose. But if instead of an 85 you get an 89—just one point over your average—you've turned your average around; it is now rising.

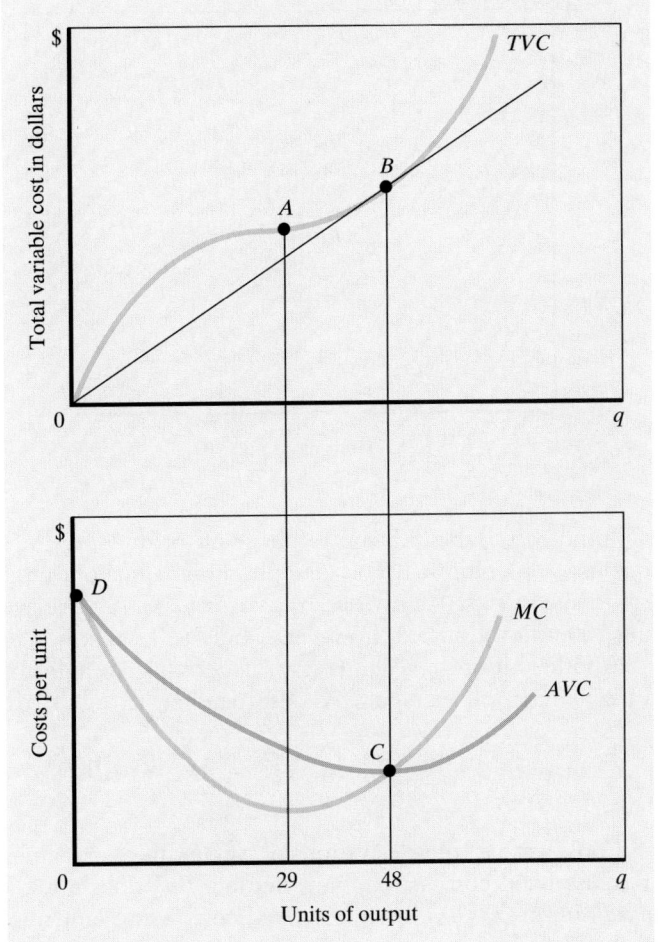

FIGURE 8.6
More Short-Run Costs

The relationship between marginal cost and average variable cost is important. When marginal cost is *below* average cost, average cost is declining. When marginal cost is *above* average cost, average cost is increasing. It follows that rising marginal cost will intersect average variable cost at the minimum point of *AVC*.

Total Costs

We are now ready to complete the cost picture by adding total fixed costs to total variable costs:

$$TC = TFC + TVC.$$

Total cost is graphed in Figure 8.7, where the same vertical distance (equal to *TFC*, which is constant) is simply added to *TVC* at every level of output. In Table 8.5 column 6 adds the total fixed cost of $1000 to total variable cost to arrive at total cost.

AVERAGE TOTAL COST (ATC) **Average total cost (ATC)** is total cost divided by the number of units of output *(q)*:

average total cost (ATC) Total cost divided by the number of units of output.

$$ATC = \frac{TC}{q}.$$

FIGURE 8.7
Total Cost Equals Total Fixed Cost Plus Total Variable Cost

Adding total fixed cost to total variable cost means adding the same amount of total fixed cost to every level of total variable cost. Thus, the total cost curve has the same shape as the total variable cost curve; it is simply higher by an amount equal to *TFC*.

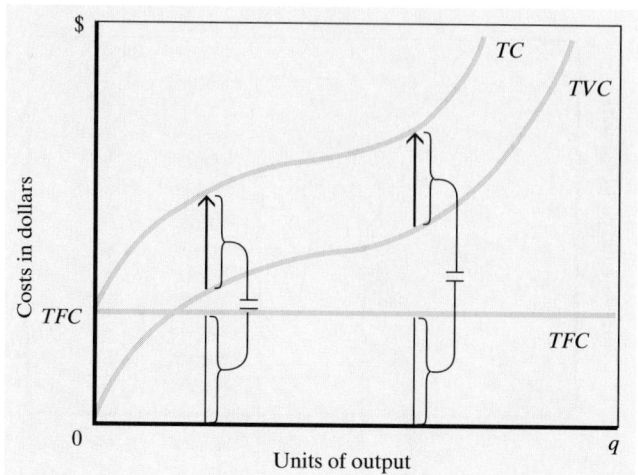

Column 8 in Table 8.5 shows the result of dividing the costs in column 6 by the quantities in column 1. For example, at five units of output, *total* cost is $1042; *average* total cost is $1042 divided by five, or $208.40. The average total cost of producing 500 units of output, however, is only $18—that is, $9000 divided by 500.

Another, more revealing, way of deriving average total cost is to add average variable cost and average fixed cost together:

$$ATC = AFC + AVC.$$

Look back at the derivation of average fixed cost in Table 8.1 and Figure 8.2. Because fixed cost is a constant number that does not change with output, *average fixed cost,* or *TFC/q,* is simply fixed cost (a constant number) divided by an ever-increasing number of units of output. This means that as output increases, average fixed cost declines steadily. If the output level is very high, average fixed cost is very small. The data used in Figure 8.2, where the *AFC* of two units of output is $500, and in Table 8.5, where the *AFC* drops to $200 at five units, show this clearly. If the firm goes on to produce 500 units of output, *AFC* declines to only $2 (see column 7 in Table 8.5).

We can also derive average total cost in a second way. The numbers in column 8 in Table 8.5 can be derived either by dividing total cost by the quantity of output *or* by summing *AVC* and *AFC* from columns 4 and 7 respectively. In other words, $ATC = AFC + AVC$.

Figure 8.8 derives average total cost graphically. The bottom part of the figure graphs the average fixed cost from Figure 8.2. The top part shows the declining average fixed cost added to average variable cost at each level of output. Because *AFC* gets smaller and smaller, *ATC* gets closer and closer to *AVC* as output increases, but the two lines never cross.

THE RELATIONSHIP BETWEEN AVERAGE TOTAL COST AND MARGINAL COST   The relationship between average *total* cost and marginal cost is exactly the same as the relationship between average *variable* cost and marginal cost. The average total cost curve follows the marginal cost curve, but lags behind because it is an average over all units of output. The average total cost curve lags behind the marginal cost curve even more than the average variable cost curve does, because the cost of

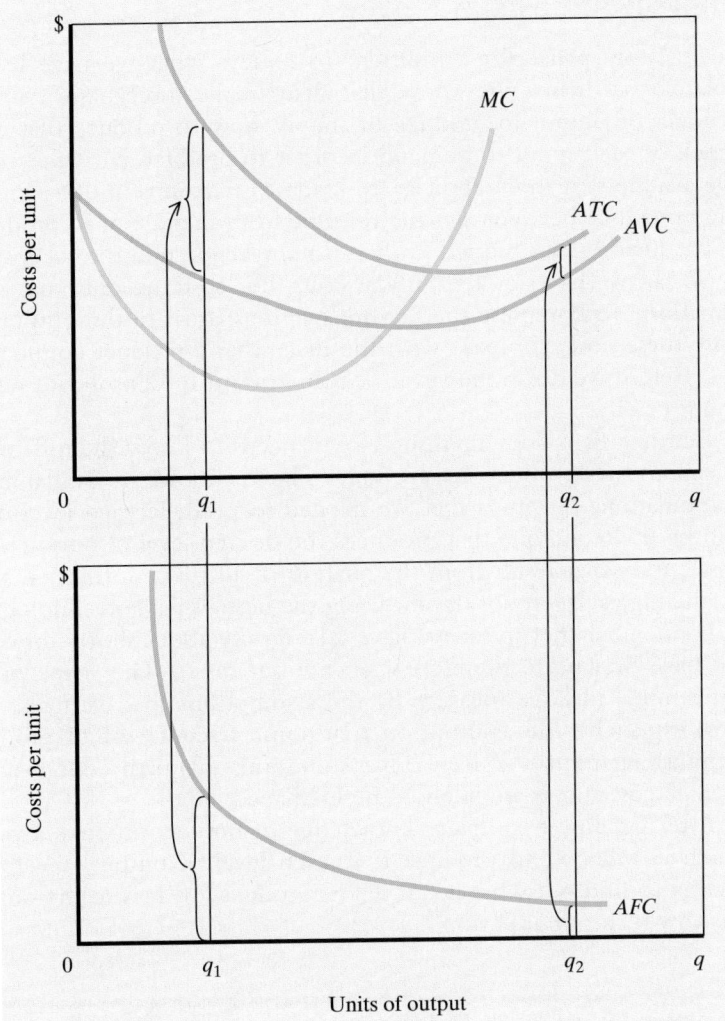

FIGURE 8.8

Average Total Cost =
Average Variable Cost +
Average Fixed Cost

To get average total cost, we add
average fixed and average variable
costs at all levels of output. Since
average fixed cost falls with output, an ever-declining amount is
added to *AVC*. Thus, *AVC* and *ATC*
get closer together as output
increases.

each added unit of production is now averaged not only with the variable cost of
all previous units produced, but with fixed costs as well.

Fixed costs equal $1000 and are incurred even when the output level is zero.
Thus, the first unit of output in the example in Table 8.5 costs $10 in variable cost
to produce. The second unit costs only $8 in variable cost to produce. The total
cost of two units is $1018; average total cost of the two is ($1010 + $8)/2, or
$509. The marginal cost of the third unit is only $6. The total cost of three units
is thus $1024, or $1018 + $6, and the average total cost of three units is ($1010 +
$8 + $6)/3, or $341.

As you saw with the test scores example, marginal cost is what drives changes in
average total cost:

If marginal cost is *below* average total cost, average total cost will *decline* toward
marginal cost; if marginal cost is *above* average total cost, average total cost will
increase. As a result, marginal cost intersects average *total* cost at *ATC*'s minimum
point, for the same reason that it intersects the average *variable* cost curve at its
minimum point.

Short-Run Costs: A Review

Let us now pause for a moment to review what we have learned about the behavior of firms. We know that firms make three basic choices: how much product or output to produce or supply, how to produce that output, and how much of each input to demand in order to produce what they intend to supply. We assume that these choices are made to maximize profits. Profits are equal to the difference between a firm's revenue from the sale of its product and the costs of producing that product: profit = total revenue minus total cost.

So far, we have looked only at costs, but costs are only one part of the profit equation. To complete the picture, we must turn to the output market and see how these costs compare with the price that a product commands in the market. Before we do so, however, it is important to consolidate what we have said about costs.

Before a firm does anything else, it needs to know the different methods that it can use to produce its product. The technologies available determine the combinations of inputs that are needed to produce each level of output. Firms choose the technique that produces the desired level of output at least cost. The cost curves that result from the analysis of all this information show the cost of producing each level of output using the best available technology.

Remember that so far we have talked only about short-run costs. The curves we have drawn are therefore *short-run cost curves*. The shape of these curves is determined in large measure by the assumptions that we make about the short run, especially the assumption that some fixed factor of production leads to diminishing returns. Given this assumption, marginal costs eventually rise, and average cost curves are likely to be U-shaped.

After gaining a complete knowledge of how to produce a product and how much it will cost to produce it at each level of output, the firm turns to the market to find out what it can sell its product for. It is to the output market that we now turn our attention.

OUTPUT DECISIONS: REVENUES, COSTS, AND PROFIT MAXIMIZATION

To calculate potential profits, firms must combine their cost analyses with information on potential revenues from sales. After all, if a firm can't sell its product for more than it costs to produce it, it won't be in business long. On the other hand, if the market gives the firm a price that is significantly greater than the cost it incurs to produce a unit of its product, the firm may have an incentive to expand output. Large profits might also attract new competitors to the market.

Let us now examine in detail how a firm goes about determining how much output to produce. For the sake of simplicity, we will continue to examine the decisions of a perfectly competitive firm. A perfectly competitive industry, you will recall, has many firms that are small relative to the size of the market. In such an environment, firms have no control over the market price of their products. Product price is determined by the interaction of many suppliers and many demanders.

Figure 8.9 shows a typical firm in a perfectly competitive industry. Price is determined in the market at P^*. The individual firm can charge any price that it wants for its product, but if it charges above P^*, the quantity demanded falls to zero, and the firm won't sell anything. Many other firms are producing exactly the same product, so why should consumers pay more than the going market price?

The firm could also sell its product for less than P^*, but there is no reason to do so. If the firm can sell all it wants to sell at the going market price of P^*, and we assume that it can, it would not be sensible to sell it for less.

All this implies that:

> In the short run a competitive firm faces a demand curve that is simply a horizontal line at the market equilibrium price. In other words, competitive firms face perfectly elastic demand in the short run.

In Figure 8.9, market equilibrium price is P^* and the firm's perfectly elastic demand curve is labeled d.

Total Revenue (TR) and Marginal Revenue (MR)

Profit is the difference between total revenue and total cost. **Total revenue** is the total amount that a firm takes in from the sale of its product. A perfectly competitive firm sells each unit of product for the same price, regardless of the output level it has chosen. Therefore, total revenue is simply the price per unit times the quantity of output that the firm decides to produce:

> **total revenue (TR)** The total amount that a firm takes in from the sale of its product: The price per unit times the quantity of output the firm decides to produce ($P \times q$).

$$\text{Total Revenue} = \text{Price} \times \text{Quantity}$$
$$TR = P \times q$$

Recall that price is assumed to be fixed in a competitive industry. Our firm is so small relative to the industry that changes in its output do not affect the market price. Thus, the only way a firm can affect the amount of revenue that it takes in is by adjusting output.

Marginal revenue (MR) is the added revenue that a firm takes in when it increases output by one additional unit. If a firm producing 10,521 units of output per month increases that output to 10,522 units per month, it will take in an additional amount of revenue each month. The revenue associated with the 10,522nd unit is simply the amount that the firm sells that one unit for. Thus, for a compet-

> **marginal revenue (MR)** The additional revenue that a firm takes in when it increases output by one additional unit. In perfect competition, P = MR.

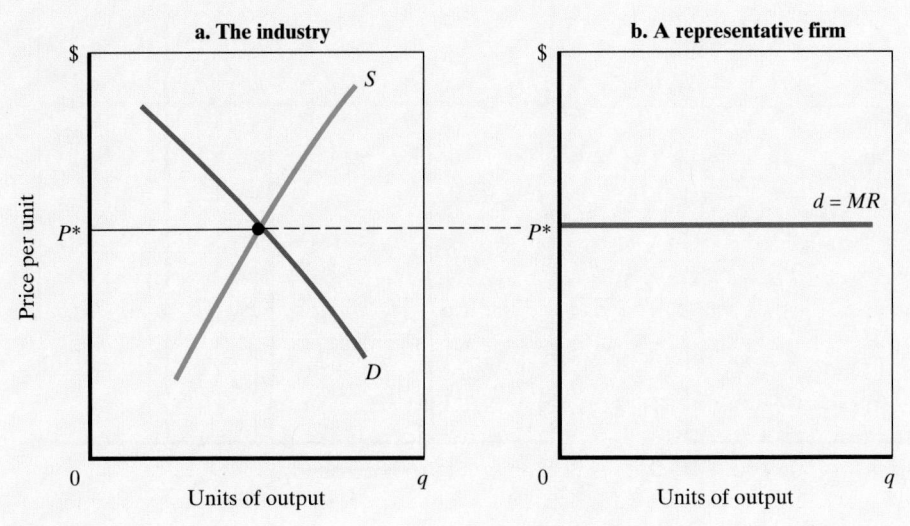

a. The industry   b. A representative firm

FIGURE 8.9
Demand Facing a Typical Firm in a Perfectly Competitive Market

Because perfectly competitive firms are very small relative to the market, they have no control over price. A firm can sell all it wants at the market price but would sell nothing if it charged a higher price. Thus, the demand curve facing a perfectly competitive firm is simply a horizontal line at the market equilibrium price, P^*.

itive firm, marginal revenue is simply equal to the current market price of each additional unit sold. In Figure 8.9, for example, the market price is P^*. Thus, if the representative firm raises its output from 10,521 units to 10,522 units, its revenue will increase by P^*.

A firm's *marginal revenue curve* is a curve that shows how much revenue the firm will gain by raising output by one unit at every level of output. The *marginal revenue curve and the demand curve facing a competitive firm are identical.* The horizontal line in Figure 8.9b can be thought of as both the demand curve facing the firm and its marginal revenue curve.

Comparing Costs and Revenues to Maximize Profit

The discussion in the next few paragraphs conveys one of the most important concepts in all of microeconomics. As we pursue our analysis, remember that we are working under two assumptions: (1) that the industry we are examining is perfectly competitive, and (2) that firms choose the level of output that yields the maximum, total profit.

THE PROFIT-MAXIMIZING LEVEL OF OUTPUT Look carefully at the diagrams in Figure 8.10. Once again we have the whole market, or industry, on the left and a single, typical small firm on the right. And again the current market price is P^*.

First, the firm observes market price (Figure 8.10a) and knows that it can sell all that it wants to for P^* per unit. Next, it must decide how much to produce. It might seem reasonable to pick the output level where marginal cost is at its minimum point—in this case, at q_1 in Figure 8.10b. After all, at that point the difference between marginal revenue and marginal cost is the greatest.

FIGURE 8.10

The Profit-Maximizing Level of Output for a Perfectly Competitive Firm

If price is above marginal cost, as it is at q_1 and q_2, profits can be increased by raising output; each additional unit increases revenues by more than it costs to produce the additional output. Beyond q^*, however, added output will reduce profits. At q_3, an additional unit of output costs more to produce than it will bring in revenue when sold on the market. Profit-maximizing output is thus q^*, the point at which $P^* = MC$.

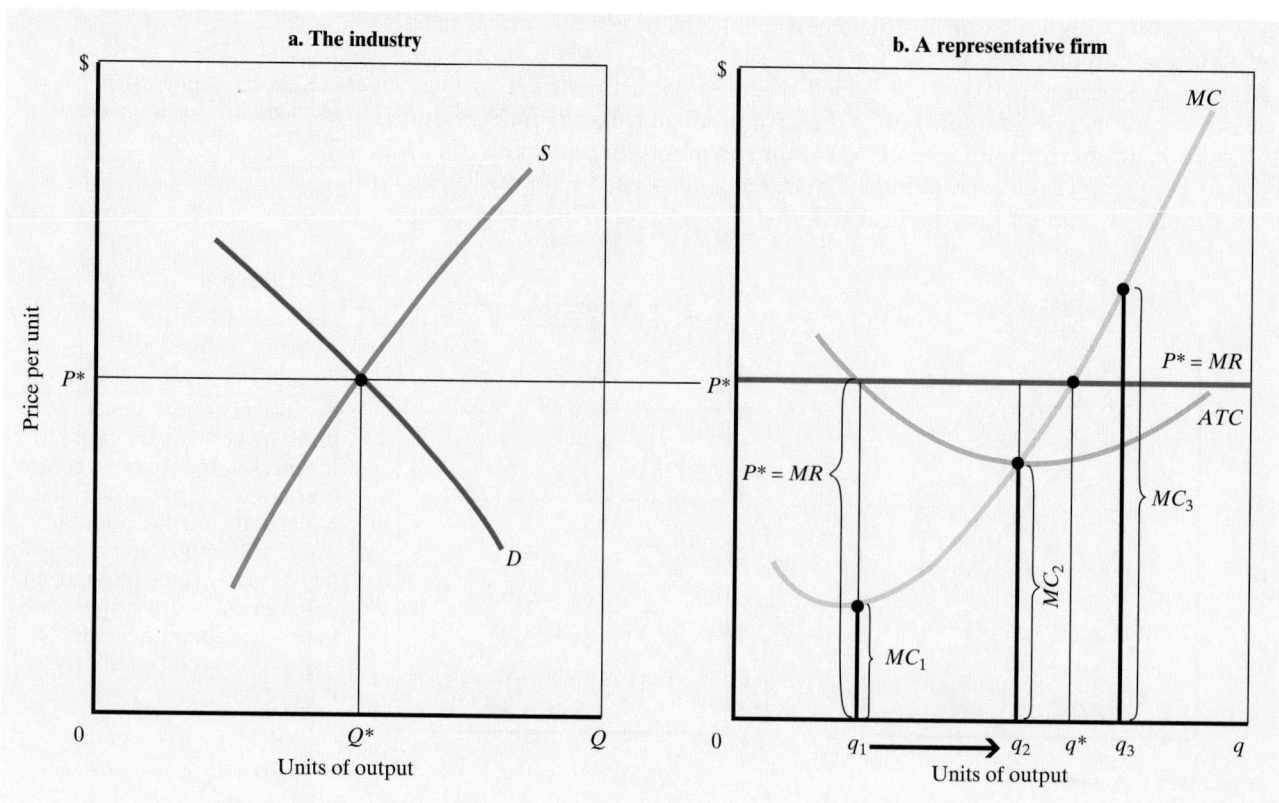

But remember that the firm wants to maximize the difference between *total* revenue and *total* cost, not that between *marginal* revenue and *marginal* cost. The marginal figures tell the firm only about the costs and revenues associated with a single unit of output. At q_1 marginal revenue is P^* and marginal cost is MC_1. As Figure 8.10b clearly shows, marginal revenue is *greater* than marginal cost at q_1. Think carefully about what this means. By increasing output during the next period by one more unit, the firm will take in more in additional revenue than it incurs in additional cost. Increasing output, then, means that total profits will rise because *the next unit adds marginal profit*. Clearly, a profit-maximizing firm would not stop producing at q_1. Instead, it would raise output.

So let us see what happens as the firm raises output to, say, q_2. At q_2, and at a price of P^*, average total cost is at a minimum but marginal revenue is still greater than marginal cost. Just as before, this means that the firm can earn higher profits by raising output even further. This leads us to conclude that:

> As long as marginal revenue is greater than marginal cost, even though the difference between the two may be getting smaller, added output means added profit. When marginal revenue exceeds marginal cost, the revenue gained by raising output one unit exceeds the cost incurred by doing so.

This logic eventually leads us to q^*. At an output of q^*, marginal cost increases to the point where it is equal to output price ($P^* = MR = MC$). If the firm were to produce *more* than q^* units, marginal cost would rise *above* marginal revenue, and profits would fall. At q_3 units of output, for example, marginal revenue is still P^*, but marginal cost has risen above P^* to MC_3. It does not pay for the firm to increase output if marginal cost is greater than marginal revenue, because any additional output above the point at which $P^* = MR = MC$ adds more to total cost than it adds to total revenue. Such additional output actually *reduces* profits.

The inevitable conclusion, then, is that:

> A profit-maximizing perfectly competitive firm will produce up to the point where the price of its output is just equal to short-run marginal cost—the point at which $P = MC$.[2]

Keep in mind, though, that all types of firms (not just those in perfectly competitive industries) are profit maximizers. Thus,

> The profit-maximizing output level for *all* firms is the output level where $MR = MC$.

(Make sure you understand why this is so.) In perfect competition, however, $MR = P$, as shown above. Hence, for perfectly competitive firms we can rewrite our profit-maximizing condition as $P = MC$.

A NUMERICAL EXAMPLE Table 8.6 presents some data for another hypothetical firm. Let's assume that the market has set a $20 unit price for the firm's product. Total revenue in column 6 is the simple product of $P \times q$ (the numbers in column 1 times $20). The table derives total, marginal, and average costs exactly as

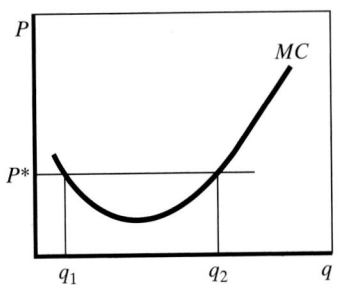

---

[2]To be very precise, it is possible for price to be equal to marginal cost at two points, one where marginal cost is declining and another where marginal cost is increasing (see graph to the right). Profit is maximized where marginal cost crosses price on its way *up* (q_2). The marginal costs of the first few units of production are high, because at such a low level of output the firm is not using its plant very efficiently. It would never make sense to produce at these low levels. In fact, to stop at the first point where $P = MC$ (q_1) would be to *minimize* profits. Can you figure out why?

TABLE 8.6
Profit Analysis for a Simple Firm

(1) q	(2) TFC	(3) TVC	(4) MC	(5) P = MR	(6) TR $(P \times q)$	(7) TC $(TFC + TVC)$	(8) PROFIT $(TR - TC)$
0	$10	$0	$—	$20	$0	$10	$–10
1	10	10	10	20	20	20	0
2	10	15	5	20	40	25	15
3	10	20	5	20	60	30	30
4	10	30	10	20	80	40	40
5	10	50	20	20	100	60	40
6	10	80	30	20	120	90	30

Table 8.5 did. Here, however, we have included revenues, and we can calculate the profit, which is shown in column 8.

Column 8 shows that a profit-maximizing firm would choose to produce either four or five of output. At each of those levels, profits are $40; at all other output levels, they are lower. Now let's see if "marginal" reasoning leads us to the same conclusion.

First, should the firm produce at all? If it produces nothing, it suffers losses equal to $10. If it increases output to one unit, marginal revenue is $20 (remember that it sells each unit for $20), and marginal cost is $10. Thus, it gains $10, just enough to cover fixed costs and break even. But that is better than a $10 loss.

Should the firm increase output to two units? The marginal revenue from the second unit is again $20, but the marginal cost is only $5. Thus, by producing the second unit the firm increases its profits by $15. The third unit adds the same amount to profits. Again, marginal revenue is $20 and marginal cost is $5, an increase in profit of $15, for a total profit of $30.

The fourth unit offers still more profit. Price is above marginal cost, which means that producing that fourth unit will increase profits. Price, or marginal revenue, is $20, and marginal cost is just $10. Thus, the fourth unit adds $10 to profit. At unit number five, however, diminishing returns push marginal cost up until it is just equal to price. The marginal revenue from producing the fifth unit, therefore, is just equal to the marginal cost incurred, and nothing is added to or subtracted from total profits.

At unit number six, marginal cost rises above price, and added production reduces profits. The marginal cost of the sixth unit is $30, but producing and selling it will bring in only $20, a reduction in total profit of $10. Clearly, the firm will not produce the sixth unit.

The profit-maximizing level of output is thus four or five units. The firm produces up to the point at which price and marginal cost are equal. (For an in-depth example of profit maximization see the Issues and Applications box entitled "Case Study in Marginal Analysis: An Ice Cream Store.")

The Short-Run Supply Curve

Consider how the typical firm described in Figure 8.10 would behave in response to an increase in price. In Figure 8.11a, assume that something happens that causes demand to increase (shift to the right), driving price from P_0 to P_1 and finally to P_2. When price is P_0, a profit-maximizing firm will choose output level q_0 in Figure 8.11b. To produce any less, or to raise output above that level, would lead to a lower level of profit. At P_1 the same firm would increase output to q_1, but it would stop there. Similarly, at P_2, the firm would raise output to q_2 units of output.

The MC curve in figure 8.11b relates price and quantity supplied. At any market price, the marginal cost curve shows the output level that maximizes profit. A curve that shows how much output a profit-maximizing firm will produce at

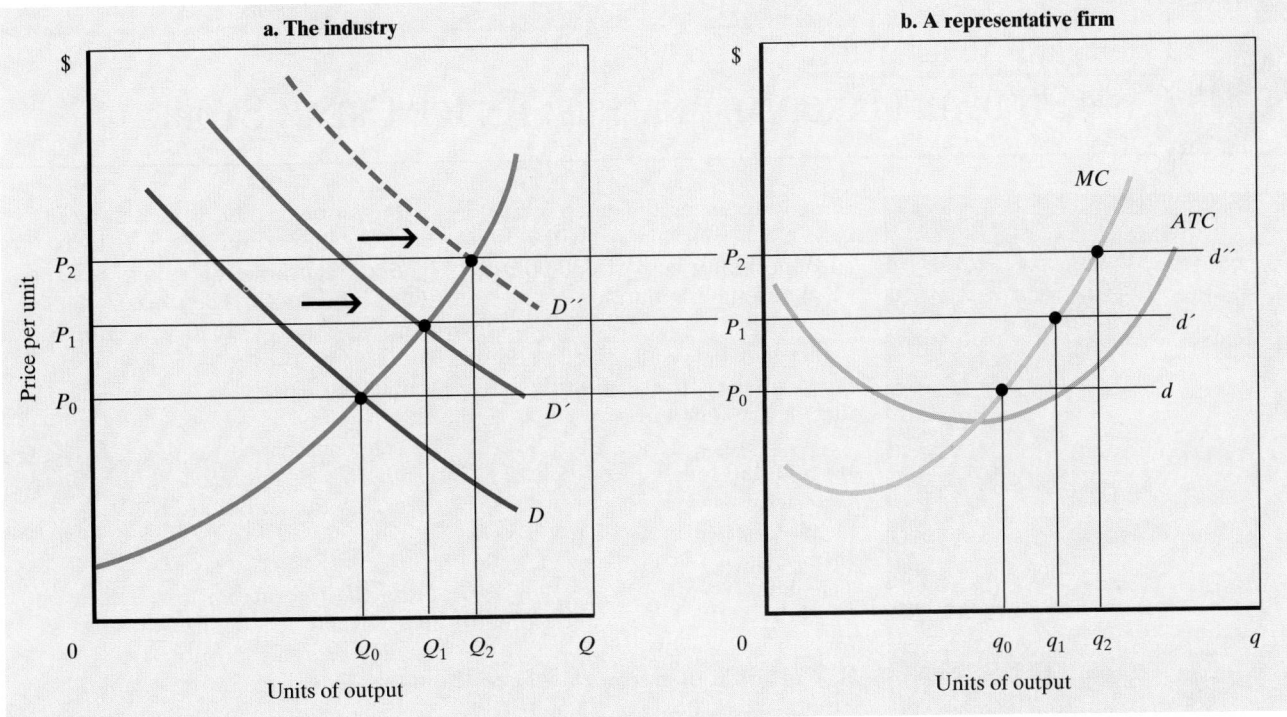

a. The industry

b. A representative firm

every price also fits the definition of a supply curve. (Review Chapter 4 if this point is not clear to you.) It therefore follows that:

> The marginal cost curve of a competitive firm is the firm's short-run supply curve.

As you will see, there is some price level below which the firm will shut down its operations and simply bear losses equal to fixed costs even if price is above marginal cost. This important point is discussed in the next chapter.

LOOKING AHEAD

At the beginning of this chapter we set out to combine information on technology, factor prices, and output prices to derive the supply curve of a competitive firm. We have now accomplished that goal.

Because marginal cost is such an important concept in microeconomics, you should carefully review any sections of this chapter that were unclear to you. Above all, keep in mind that the *marginal cost curve* carries information about both *input prices* and *technology*. The firm looks to output markets for information on potential revenues, and the current market price defines the firm's marginal revenue curve. The point where price (which is equal to marginal revenue in perfect competition) is just equal to marginal cost is the perfectly competitive firm's profit-maximizing level of output. Thus, the marginal cost curve *is* the perfectly competitive firm's supply curve in the short run.

In the next chapter, we turn to the long run. What happens when firms are free to choose their scale of operations without being limited by a fixed factor of production? Without diminishing returns that set in as a result of a fixed scale of production, what determines the shape of cost curves? What happens when new firms are able to enter industries in which profits are being earned? How do industries adjust when losses are being incurred? How does the structure of an industry evolve over long periods of time?

FIGURE 8.11
Marginal Cost Is the Supply Curve of a Perfectly Competitive Firm

At any market price* the marginal cost curve shows the output level that maximizes profit. Thus, the marginal cost curve of a perfectly competitive profit-maximizing firm is the firm's short-run supply curve.

*This is true except when price is so low that it pays a firm to shut down–a point that will be discussed in Chapter 9.

CASE STUDY IN MARGINAL ANALYSIS: AN ICE CREAM STORE

Marginal analysis is as important to the owner of a small ice cream store as it is to the managers of million-dollar manufacturing operations.

The following is a description of the decisions made in 1993 by the owner of a small ice-cream parlor in Ohio. After being in business for one year, this entrepreneur had to ask herself, should I stay in business?

The cost figures on which she based her decisions are presented below. These numbers are real, but they do not include one important item: the managerial labor provided by the owner. In her calculations,

the entrepreneur did not include a wage for herself, but we will assume an opportunity cost of $30,000 per year ($2500 per month).

Fixed Costs The fixed components of the store's monthly costs include the following:

Rent (1,150 square feet)	$2012.50
Electricity	325.00
Debt service (loan payment)	737.50
Maintenance	295.00
Telephone	65.00
Total	$3435.00

Not all of the items on this list are strictly fixed, however. Electricity costs, for example, would be slightly higher if the store produced more ice cream and stayed open longer, but the added cost would be minimal.

Variable Costs The ice-cream store's variable costs include two components: (1) behind-the-counter labor costs, and (2) the cost of making ice cream. The store employs high school students at a wage of $4.50 per hour. Including the employer's share of the social security tax (7.65% of wages), the gross cost of each hour of labor is $4.84 per hour. There are two employees working in the store at all times. The full cost of producing ice cream is $3.27 per gallon. Each gallon contains approximately 12 servings. Customers can add toppings free of charge, and the average cost of the toppings taken by a customer is about $.05:

Gross labor costs	$4.84/hour
Costs of producing one gallon of ice cream	
(12 servings per gallon)	$3.27
Average cost of added toppings per serving	$ .05

Revenues The store sells ice-cream cones, sundaes, and floats. The average price of a purchase at the store is $1.45. The store is open 8 hours per day, 26 days a month and serves an average of 240 customers per day:

Average purchase	$1.45
Days open per month	26
Average number of customers per day	240

From the information given above, it is possible to calculate the store's average monthly profit. Total revenue is equal to 240 customers × $1.45 per customer × 26 open days in an average month: TR = $9048 per month.

Profits The store sells 240 servings per day. Because there are 12 servings of ice cream per gallon, the store uses exactly 20 gallons per day (240 servings divided by 12). Total costs are $3.27 × 20, or $65.40, per day for ice cream and $12 per day for toppings (240 × $.05). The cost of variable labor is $4.84 × 8 hours × 2 workers, or $77.44 per day. Total variable costs are therefore $154.84 ($65.40 + $12.00 + $77.44) per day. Since the store is open 26 days a month, the total variable cost per month is $4025.84 ($154.84 × 26).

Adding fixed costs of $3435 to variable costs of $4025.84, we get total cost of operation of $7460.84 per month. Thus, the firm is averaging a profit of $1587.16 per month ($9048 − 7460.84). *But this is not an "economic profit" because we haven't accounted for the opportunity cost of the owner's time and efforts.* In fact, when we factor in an implicit wage of $2500 per month for the owner, we see that the store is suffering *losses* of $912.84 per month ($1587.16 − $2500).

Total Revenue (*TR*)	$9048.00
Total Fixed Cost (*TFC*)	3435.00
Total Variable Cost (*TVC*)	4025.84
Total Costs (*TC*)	7460.84
Total Profit (*TR* − *TC*)	1587.16
Adjustment for Implicit Wage	2500.00
Economic Profit	− 912.84

Should the entrepreneur stay in business? If she wants to make $2500 per month and she thinks that nothing about her business will change, she must shut down in the long run. But two things keep her going: (1) A decision to stay open longer, and (2) hope for more customers in the future.

Opening Longer Hours: Marginal Costs and Marginal Revenues—The store's normal hours of operation are noon until 8 P.M. On an experimental basis, the owner extends its hours until 11 P.M. for one month. The following table shows the average number of additional customers for each of the added hours:

Hour	Customers
8–9 P.M.	41
9–10 P.M.	20
10–11 P.M.	8

Assuming that the late customers spend an average of $1.45, we can calculate the marginal revenue and the marginal cost of staying open longer. The marginal cost of one serving of ice cream is $3.27 divided by 12 = $0.27 + .05 (for topping) = $0.32. (See table below.)

Marginal analysis tells us that the store should stay open for two additional hours. Each day that the store stays open from 8–9 P.M. it will make an added profit of $59.45 −$22.80, or $36.65. Staying open from 9–10 P.M. adds $29.00 −$16.08, or $12.92, to profit. Staying open the third hour, however, *decreases* profits because the marginal revenue generated by staying open from 10 to 11 P.M. is less than the marginal cost. The entrepreneur decides to stay open for two additional hours per day. This adds $49.57 ($36.65 + 12.92) to profits each day, a total of $1288.82 per month.

By adding the two hours, the store turns an economic loss of $912.84 per month into a $375.98 profit after accounting for the owner's implicit wage of $2500 per month.

The owner decides to stay in business. She now serves over 350 customers per day, and the price of a dish of ice cream has risen to $2.50 while costs have not changed very much. In 1993, she cleared a profit of nearly $10,000 per month!

Hour	Marginal Revenue (MR)	Marginal Cost (MC)		Added Profit per Hour (MR − MC)
8–9 P.M.	$1.45 × 41 = $59.45	Ice Cream: 0.32 × 41 =	$13.12	$36.65
		Labor: 2 × 4.84 =	9.68	
		Total	$22.80	
9–10 P.M.	$1.45 × 20 = $29.00	Ice Cream: 0.32 × 20 =	$6.40	$12.92
		Labor: 2 × 4.84 =	9.68	
		Total	$16.08	
10–11 P.M.	$1.45 × 8 = $11.69	Ice Cream: 0.32 × 8 =	$2.56	$−.55
		Labor: 2 × 4.84 =	9.68	
		Total	$12.24	

SUMMARY

1. Profit-maximizing firms make decisions in order to maximize profit (total revenue minus total cost).

2. To calculate production costs, firms must know two things: the quantity and combination of inputs they need to produce their product and how much those inputs cost.

Costs in the Short Run

3. *Fixed costs* are costs that do not change with the output of a firm. In the short run, firms cannot avoid them or change them, even if production is zero.

4. *Variable costs* are those that depend on, or vary with, the level of output chosen. Fixed costs plus variable costs equal *total costs* ($TC = TFC + TVC$).

5. *Average fixed cost* (AFC) is total fixed cost divided by the quantity of output. As output rises, average fixed cost declines steadily because the same total is being spread over a larger and larger quantity of output. This phenomenon is called *spreading overhead*.

6. Numerous combinations of inputs can be used to produce a given level of output. For a profit-maximizing firm, *total variable cost (TVC)* is the cost of the combination of inputs that produces each level of output at minimum cost.

7. *Marginal cost (MC)* is the increase in total cost that results from the production of one more unit of output. If a firm is producing 1,000 units, the additional cost of increasing output to 1,001 units is marginal cost. Marginal cost measures the cost of the additional inputs required to produce each successive unit of output.

8. In the short run, a firm is limited by a fixed factor of production, or a fixed scale of plant. As a firm increases output, it will eventually find itself trapped by that scale. Because of the fixed scale, marginal cost eventually rises with output.

9. Marginal cost is the slope of the total variable cost curve. The total variable cost curve always has a positive slope, because total costs always rise with output. But increasing marginal cost means that total costs ultimately rise at an increasing rate.

10. *Average variable cost (AVC)* is equal to total variable cost divided by the quantity of output.

11. When marginal cost is above average variable cost, average variable cost is *increasing*. When marginal cost is below average variable cost, average variable cost is *declining*. Marginal cost intersects average variable cost at AVC's minimum point.

12. *Average total cost (ATC)* is equal to total cost divided by the quantity of output. It is also equal to the sum of average variable cost and average fixed cost.

13. If marginal cost is below average total cost, average total cost will decline toward marginal cost. If marginal cost is above average total cost, average total cost will increase. Marginal cost intersects average total cost at ATC's minimum point.

Output Decisions: Revenues, Costs, and Profit Maximization

14. In the short run, a perfectly competitive firm faces a demand curve that is a horizontal line (in other words, perfectly elastic demand).

15. *Total revenue (TR)* is simply price times the quantity of output that a firm decides to produce and sell. *Marginal revenue (MR)* is the additional revenue that a firm takes in when it increases output by one unit.

16. For a perfectly competitive firm, marginal revenue is equal to the current market price of its product.

17. A profit-maximizing firm in a perfectly competitive industry will produce up to the point at which the price of its output is just equal to short-run marginal cost: $P = MC$. The more general profit-maximizing formula is $MR = MC$. ($P = MR$ in perfect competition.) The marginal cost curve of a perfectly competitive firm is the firm's short-run supply curve.

REVIEW TERMS AND CONCEPTS

average fixed cost (*AFC*)   197
average total cost (*ATC*)   205
average variable cost (*AVC*)   203
fixed cost   195
marginal cost (*MC*)   199
marginal revenue (*MR*)   209
spreading overhead   197
sunk costs   196
total cost (*TC*)   195

total fixed cost (*TFC*),
   or overhead   196
total revenue (*TR*)   209
total variable cost (*TVC*)   197
total variable cost curve   198
variable cost   195

Equations:
$TC = TFC + TVC$

$AFC = TFC/q$
slope of $TVC = MC$
$AVC = TVC/q$
$ATC = TC/q = AFC + AVC$
$TR = P \times q$
profit-maximizing level of output for all
   firms: $MR = MC$
profit-maximizing level of output for
   perfectly competitive firms: $P = MC$

PROBLEM SET

1. The following table gives capital and labor requirements for ten different levels of production:

q	K	L
0	0	0
1	2	5
2	4	9
3	6	12
4	8	15
5	10	19
6	12	24
7	14	30
8	16	37
9	18	45
10	20	54

a. Assuming that the price of labor (P_L) is \$5 per unit and the price of capital (P_K) is \$10 per unit, compute and graph the total variable cost curve, the marginal cost curve, and the average variable cost curve for the firm.
b. Do the curves have the shapes that you might expect? Explain.
c. Using the numbers here, explain the relationship between marginal cost and average variable cost.
d. Using the numbers here, explain the meaning of "marginal cost" in terms of additional inputs needed to produce a marginal unit of output.
e. If output price (P_X) was \$57, how many units of output would the firm produce? Explain.

2. Do you agree or disagree with each of the following statements? Explain your reasons.
a. If marginal cost is rising, average cost must also be rising.
b. A profit-maximizing firm must minimize cost. Thus firms will always produce the level of output at which average total cost is minimized.
c. Average fixed cost does not change as output changes.

3. A firm's cost curves are given by the following table:

q	TC	TFC	VC	AVC	ATC	MC
0	\$100	\$100				
1	130	100				
2	150	100				
3	160	100				
4	172	100				
5	185	100				
6	210	100				
7	240	100				
8	280	100				
9	330	100				
10	390	100				

a. Complete the table.
b. Graph AVC, ATC, and MC on the same graph. What is the relationship between the MC curve and ATC? Between MC and AVC?
c. Suppose that market price is \$30. How much will the firm produce in the short run? How much are total profits? Show them on the graph.
d. Suppose that market price is \$50. How much will the firm produce in the short run? What are total profits? Show them on the graph.
e. Suppose that market price is \$10. How much would the firm produce in the short run? What are total profits? Show them on the graph.

4. A 1993 Berkeley graduate inherited her mother's printing company. The capital stock of the firm consists of three machines of various vintages, all in excellent condition. All machines can be running at the same time:

	COST OF PRINTING AND BINDING PER BOOK	MAXIMUM TOTAL CAPACITY PER MONTH
Machine 1	\$1.00	100 books
Machine 2	\$2.00	200 books
Machine 3	\$3.00	500 books

a. Assume that "cost of printing and binding per book" includes *all* labor and materials, including the owner's own wages. Assume further that Mom signed a long-term contract (50 years) with a service company to keep the machines in good repair for a fixed fee of \$100 per month.
(1) Derive the marginal cost curve of the firm.
(2) Derive the total cost curve of the firm.
b. At $P = 2.50$, how many books would the company produce? What would total revenues be? Total costs? Total profits?

5. The following curve is a production function for a firm that uses just one variable factor of production, labor. It shows total output, or product, for every level of inputs:

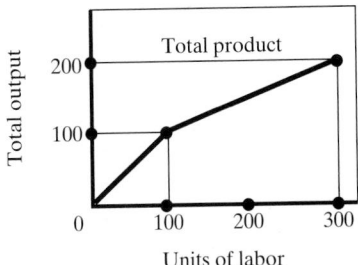

a. Derive and graph the marginal product curve.
b. Suppose that the wage rate is \$4. Derive and graph the marginal cost curve for the firm.
c. If output sells for \$6, what is the profit-maximizing level of output? How much labor will the firm hire?

9
Costs and Output Decisions in the Long Run

The last two chapters presented a theory of the behavior of profit-maximizing competitive firms in the short run. Recall that there are three fundamental decisions that all firms must make: (1) how much output to produce or supply, (2) how to produce that output, and (3) how much of each input to demand.

Firms use information on input prices, output prices, and technology to make the decisions that will lead to the most profit. Since profits equal revenues minus costs, firms must know how much their products will sell for and how much production will cost, using the most efficient technology.

In Chapter 8 we saw in detail how cost curves can be derived from production functions and input prices. Once a firm has a clear picture of its short–run costs, the price at which it sells its output determines the quantity of output that will maximize profit. Specifically, we saw that a profit-maximizing perfectly competitive firm will supply output up to the point that price (marginal revenue) equals marginal cost. The marginal cost curve of such a firm is thus the same thing as its supply curve.

In this chapter, we turn from the *short run* to the *long run*. The condition in which firms find themselves in the short run (Are they making profits? Are they incurring losses?) determines what is likely to happen in the long run. Remember that output (supply) decisions in the long run are less constrained than they are in the short run, for two reasons. First, in the long run, the firm has no fixed factor of production that confines its production to a given scale. Second, firms are free to enter industries in order to seek profits and to leave industries in order to avoid losses.

The long run has important implications for the shape of cost curves. As we saw, in the short run the assumption of a fixed factor of production, or scale of plant, eventually causes marginal cost to increase along with output. This is not the case in the long run, however. With no fixed scale, the shape of cost curves becomes more complex and less easy to generalize about. The shape of long-run cost curves has important implications for the way an industry's structure is likely to evolve over time. Later in this chapter we will discuss long-run costs in detail.

We begin our discussion of the long run by looking at firms in three short-run circumstances: (1) firms earning economic profits, (2) firms suffering economic losses but continuing to operate to reduce or minimize those losses, and (3) firms that find it in their interest to shut down and bear losses just equal to fixed costs. We then examine how these firms will alter their cost and production decisions in response to their short-run conditions.

Although we continue to focus on perfectly competitive firms, it should be stressed that *all* firms are subject to the spectrum of short-run profit or loss situations, regardless of market structure. Assuming perfect competition allows us to simplify our analysis and provides us with a strong background for understanding the discussions of imperfectly competitive behavior in later chapters.

SHORT-RUN CONDITIONS AND LONG-RUN DIRECTIONS

Before we begin our examination of firm behavior, let us review the concept of profit that we are using here. Recall that a normal rate of profit is included in costs as we measure them in economics. Thus, when we say that a firm is earning profits, we mean that it is earning a profit over and above a normal rate of return to capital. A "normal rate of return" is a profit rate that is just sufficient to keep current investors interested in the industry. Thus, when we speak of profits, we really mean "extranormal" profits. Sometimes, for emphasis, these extranormal profits are called *economic profits*.

When we use the term "profit," then, we are simply taking into account the opportunity cost of capital. By investing in a firm, its owners or lenders are forgoing what they could earn by investing elsewhere. This is why the normal rate of return must be at least equal to the interest rate on "safe" investments (government bonds, for example). Only when investors earn profits above the normal level are they earning economic profits. And only when they are earning economic profits are new investors likely to be attracted to the industry.

When we say that a firm is suffering *losses*, we mean that it is earning a profit rate for its investors that is below normal. Such a firm may be suffering losses as an accountant would measure them or simply be earning at a very low (that is, below normal) profit rate. Investors in a firm are not going to be happy if they earn a return of only 2% when they can get 6% in U.S. savings bonds. A firm that is **breaking even,** or earning zero economic profits, is one that is earning exactly a normal profit rate. New investors are not attracted, but current ones are not running away, either.

breaking even The situation in which a firm is earning exactly a normal profit rate.

With these facts in mind, then, we can say that for any firm one of three conditions holds at any given moment: (1) the firm is making economic profits, (2) the firm is suffering economic losses, or (3) the firm is just breaking even. Profitable firms will, of course, want to maximize their profits in the short run, while firms suffering losses will want to minimize those losses in the short run.

TABLE 9.1
Blue Velvet Car Wash:
Weekly Costs

TOTAL FIXED COSTS (TFC):

1. Normal return (profit) to investors	$1000
2. Other fixed costs (maintenance contract, heat, etc.)	1000
	$2000

TOTAL VARIABLE COSTS (TVC) (800 WASHES):

1. Labor	$1000
2. Materials	600
	$1600

TOTAL COSTS (TC = TFC + TVC) $3600

Total Revenue (TR) at $P = \$5$ ($800 \times \$5$)	**$4000**
Profit ($TR - TC$)	**$400**

Maximizing Profits

The best way to understand the behavior of a firm that is currently earning profits is by way of example.

EXAMPLE: THE BLUE VELVET CAR WASH When a firm earns revenues in excess of costs (including a normal profit rate), it is earning economic profits. Let us take as an example the Blue Velvet Car Wash. Suppose that investors have put up $500,000 to construct a building and purchase all the equipment required to wash cars. Let's also suppose that investors expect to earn a minimum return of 10% on their investment. If the money to set up the business were borrowed from the bank, the car wash owners would pay a 10% interest rate. In either case, the firm earns an economic profit only *after* it has paid its investors, or the bank, 10% of $500,000, or $50,000 every year. This normal profit of $50,000 is part of the firm's annual costs.

The car wash is open 50 weeks per year and is capable of washing up to 800 cars per week. Whether it is open and operating or not, the car wash has *fixed costs*. Those costs include $1000 per week to investors (that is, the $50,000 per year normal profit rate) and $1000 per week in other fixed costs (a basic maintenance contract on the equipment, a long-term lease, and so forth).

When the car wash is operating, there are also *variable costs*. Workers must be paid, and materials such as soap and wax must be purchased. The wage bill, let's say, is $1000 per week, and materials, electricity, and so forth run $600 if the car wash is run at full capacity. If the car wash is not in operation, there are no variable costs. Table 9.1 summarizes the costs of the Blue Velvet Car Wash.

This car wash business is quite competitive. There are many car washes of equal quality in the area, and they offer their service at $5. If Blue Velvet wants customers, it cannot charge a price for car washes above $5. (Recall the perfectly elastic demand curve facing perfectly competitive firms; review Chapter 8 if necessary.) If Blue Velvet washes 800 cars each week, it takes in revenues of $4000 from operating (800 cars × $5). Is this total revenue enough to make an economic profit?

The answer is yes. Revenues of $4000 are sufficient to cover both fixed costs of $2000 and variable costs of $1600, leaving an economic profit of $400 per week. If Blue Velvet shut down (that is, if it stopped operating the car wash), it would suffer losses equal to fixed costs of $2000. It is clearly in the firm's interest to continue operating.

GRAPHIC PRESENTATION Figure 9.1 graphs the performance of a firm that is earning economic profits in the short run. Figure 9.1a illustrates the industry, or the market, and Figure 9.1b illustrates a representative firm. At present, the market is clearing at a price of P^*. Thus, we assume that the individual firm can sell all it wants at P^*, but that it is constrained by its capacity; its marginal cost curve rises in the short run because of the assumption of a fixed factor. You already know that a perfectly competitive profit-maximizing firm produces up to the point that P^* equals marginal cost. As long as price (marginal revenue) exceeds marginal cost, firms can push up profits by increasing short-run output. The firm in the diagram, then, will produce, or supply, q^* units of output.

Both revenues and costs are shown graphically. *Total revenue* (TR) is simply the product of price and quantity ($P^* \times q^*$). On the diagram, total revenue is equal to the area of the rectangle P^*Aq^*0 (the area of a rectangle is equal to its length times its width).

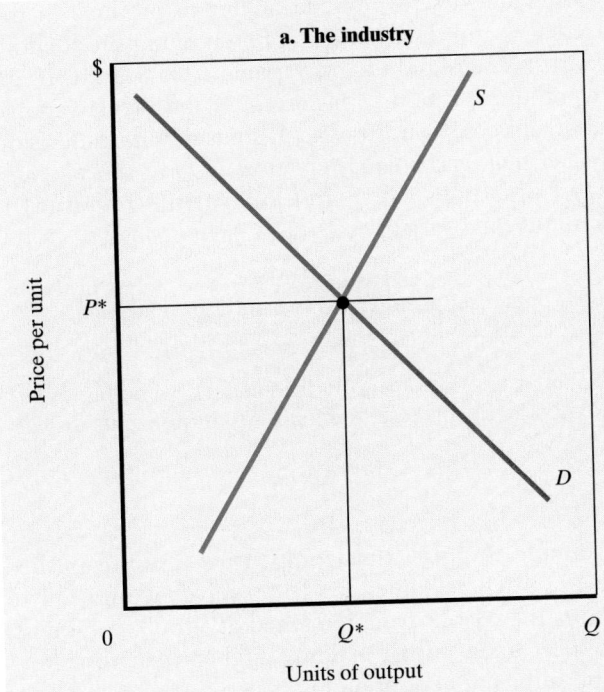

a. The industry

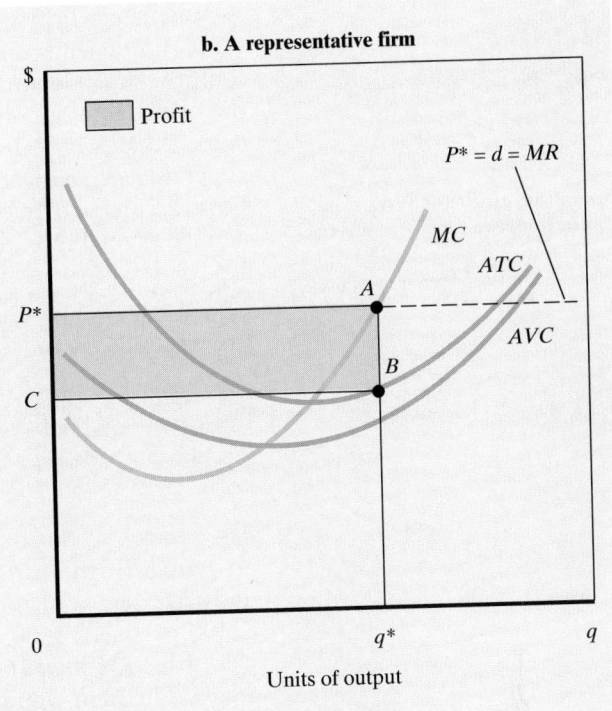

b. A representative firm

At output q^*, *average total cost is C;* numerically, it is equal to the length of line segment q^*B which is the same as $0C$. Since average total cost is derived by *dividing* total cost by q, we can get back to total cost by *multiplying* average total cost by q. That is,

$$ATC = \frac{TC}{q}$$

and

$$TC = ATC \times q.$$

Total cost (TC), then, is the area of rectangle CBq^*0. *Total economic profit* is simply the difference between total revenue (TR) and total cost (TC), and this is the area P^*ABC which is shaded pink in the diagram. This firm is earning positive economic profits.

As we will see later in the chapter, a firm that is earning economic profits in the short run and expects to continue to do so has an incentive to expand its scale of operation in the long run. Those profits also give new firms an incentive to enter and compete in the market.

Minimizing Losses

A firm that is not earning economic profit or breaking even is suffering a loss. Firms suffering losses fall into two categories: (1) those that find it advantageous to shut down operations immediately and bear losses equal to fixed costs, and (2) those that continue to operate in the short run to minimize their losses. The most important thing to remember here is that firms cannot exit the industry in the short run. The firm can shut down, but it cannot get rid of its fixed costs by going out of business. We assume that fixed costs must be paid in the short run no matter what the firm does.

FIGURE 9.1

Firm Earning Economic (Excess) Profits in the Short Run

A profit-maximizing perfectly competitive firm will produce up to the point where $P^* = MC$. At q^* total revenues are equal to $P^* Aq^*0$. Total costs are equal to ATC at q^* times q^*, or CBq^*0. Thus, profits ($TR - TC$) are equal to P^*ABC.

Whether a firm suffering losses decides to produce or not to produce in the short run depends on the advantages and disadvantages of continuing production. If a firm shuts down, it earns no revenues and has no variable costs to bear. If, on the other hand, it continues to produce, it both earns revenues and incurs variable costs. Because a firm must bear fixed costs *whether or not* it shuts down, its decision depends *solely on whether revenues from operating are sufficient to cover variable costs.* **Operating profit (or loss)** (sometimes called **net operating revenue**) is defined as total revenue (TR) minus total variable cost (TVC). In general:

> If revenues exceed variable costs, operating profit is positive and can be used to offset fixed costs and reduce losses, and it will pay the firm to keep operating.
>
> If revenues are smaller than variable costs, however, the firm suffers operating losses that push total losses above fixed costs. In this case, the firm can minimize its losses by shutting down.

operating profit (or loss) or **net operating revenue** Total revenue minus total variable cost $(TR - TVC)$. Also called net operating revenue.

PRODUCING AT A LOSS TO OFFSET FIXED COSTS: THE BLUE VELVET REVISITED To return to the car wash example, suppose that competitive pressure pushed the price per wash down to $3. Total revenues for Blue Velvet would fall to $2400 per week (800 cars × $3). If variable costs remained at $1600, total costs would be $3600 ($1600 + $2000 fixed costs), a figure higher than total revenues. The firm would then be suffering economic losses of $1200.

In the long run, Blue Velvet may want to go out of business, but in the short run it is stuck, and it must decide what to do.

The car wash has two options: operate or shut down. If it shuts down, it has no variable costs, but it also earns no revenues, and its losses will be equal to its fixed costs of $2000 (see Table 9.2, Case 1). If it decides to stay open (Case 2), it will make operating profits. Revenues will be $2400, more than sufficient to cover variable costs of $1600. By operating, the firm gains $800 per week operating profits that it can use to offset its fixed costs. By operating, then, the firm reduces its losses from $2000 to $1200.

TABLE 9.2
Decision to Shut Down Depends on Variable Costs and Revenues

CASE 1: SHUT DOWN		
Revenues $0	Fixed costs	$2000
	Variable costs	$0
	Total costs	$2000
Operating Profit*: $0		
Profit/loss**: -$2000		

Case 2: *P* = $3		
Revenues ($3 × 800) $2400	Fixed costs	$2000
	Variable costs	$1600
	Total costs	$3600
Operating Profit: $800		
Profit/loss: −$1200		

Case 3: *P* = $1.50		
Revenues: ($1.50 × 800) $1200	Fixed costs	$2000
	Variable costs	$1600
	Total costs	$3600
Operating Profit: −$400		
Profit/loss: −$2400		

*Operating profit = Total Revenue – Total Variable Costs.
**Profit = Total Revenue – Total Costs.

GRAPHIC PRESENTATION   Figure 9.2 graphs a firm suffering economic losses. The market price, set by the forces of supply and demand, is P^*. If the firm decides to operate, it will do best by producing up to the point where price (marginal revenue) is equal to marginal cost—in this case, at an output of q^* units.

Once again, total revenue (TR) is simply the product of price and quantity ($P^* \times q^*$), or the area of rectangle P^*Aq^*0. Average total cost is C, and it is equal to the length of q^*B and $0C$. Total cost is the product of average total cost and q^* ($ATC \times q^*$); on the graph, it is equal to the area of rectangle CBq^*0. Because total cost is greater than total revenue, the firm is suffering economic losses, shown on the graph by the area of rectangle $CBAP^*$.

Operating profit—the difference between total revenue and total *variable* cost—can also be identified. On the graph, total revenue is the area P^*Aq^*0. *Average variable cost at q^* is D, or the length of q^*E. Total variable cost is the product of average variable cost and q^* and is therefore equal to the area of rectangle DEq^*0. Profit on operation is thus the rectangle P^*AED.

Remember that average total cost is equal to average fixed cost plus average variable cost. This means that at every level of output average fixed cost is the difference between average total and average variable cost:

$$ATC = AFC + AVC$$
$$\text{or}$$
$$AFC = ATV - AVC.$$

In Figure 9.2, therefore, average fixed cost is equal to the length of BE (the difference between ATC and AVC at q^*). Since total fixed cost is simply average fixed cost times q^*, total fixed cost is equal to the area $CBED$. Thus, if the firm had shut down, its losses would be equal to $CBED$, the entire grey and pink shaded rectangle. By operating, the firm earns an operating profit equal to area P^*AED covering some fixed costs and reducing losses to $CBAP^*$.

FIGURE 9.2
Firm Suffering Economic Losses but Showing an Operating Profit in the Short Run

When price is sufficient to cover average variable costs, firms suffering short-run losses will continue to operate rather than shut down. Total revenues (P^*Aq^*0) cover variable costs (DEq^*0), leaving an operating profit of (P^*AED) to cover part of fixed costs and reduce losses.

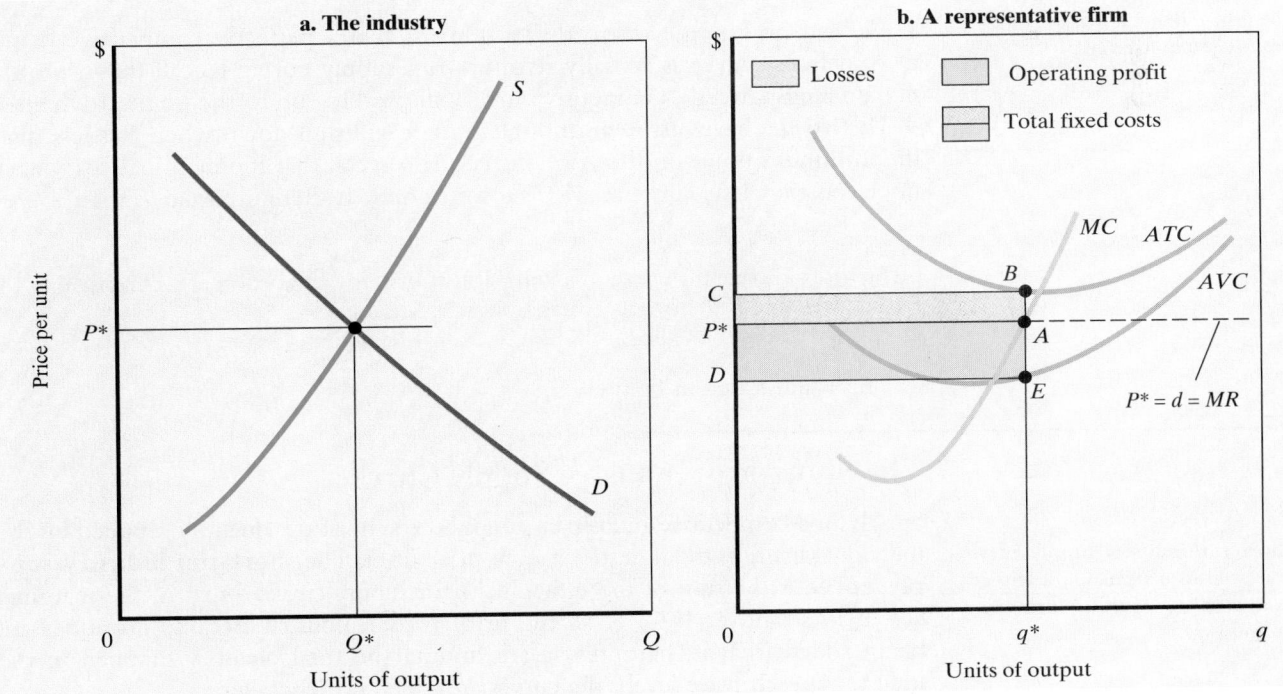

a. The industry

b. A representative firm

Units of output

Units of output

If we think only in averages, it seems logical that a firm in this position will continue to operate:

> As long as price (which is equal to average revenue per unit) is sufficient to cover average variable costs, the firm stands to gain by operating rather than by shutting down.

SHUTTING DOWN TO MINIMIZE LOSS   When revenues are insufficient to cover even variable costs, firms suffering losses find it advantageous to shut down, even in the short run.

Suppose, for example, that competition and the availability of sophisticated new machinery pushed the price of a car wash all the way down to $1.50. Washing 800 cars per week would then yield revenues of only $1200 (see Table 9.2, Case 3). With variable costs at $1600, operating would mean losing an additional $400 *over and above* fixed costs of $2000. This means that total losses would amount to $2400. Clearly, a profit-maximizing/loss-minimizing car wash would reduce its losses from $2400 to $2000 by shutting down, even in the short run.

From this example, we can generalize that:

> Any time that price (average revenue) is below the minimum point on the average variable cost curve, total revenue will be less than total variable cost, and operating profit will be negative (that is, there will be a loss on operation). In other words, when price is below all points on the average variable cost curve, the firm will suffer operating losses at any possible output level the firm could choose. When this is the case, the firm will stop producing ($q = 0$) and bear losses equal to fixed costs. This is why the bottom of the average variable cost curve is called the **shut-down point.** At all prices above it, the *MC* curve shows the profit-maximizing level of output. At all prices below it, optimal short-run output is zero.

shut-down point The lowest point on the average variable cost curve. When price falls below the minimum point on *AVC*, total revenue is insufficient to cover variable costs and the firm will shut down and bear losses equal to fixed costs.

We can now refine our earlier statement that a perfectly competitive firm's marginal cost curve is actually its short-run supply curve. Recall that a profit-maximizing perfectly competitive firm will produce up to the point at which $P = MC$. As we have just seen, though, a firm will shut down when P is less than the minimum point on the *AVC* curve. Also recall that the marginal cost curve intersects the *AVC* curve at *AVC*'s lowest point. It therefore follows that:

> The short-run supply curve of a competitive firm is that portion of its marginal cost curve that lies above its average variable cost curve.

This is illustrated in Figure 9.3.

The Short-Run Industry Supply Curve

short-run industry supply curve The sum of marginal cost curves (above *AVC*) of all the firms in an industry.

Supply in a competitive industry is simply the sum of the quantity supplied by the individual firms in the industry at each price level. The **short-run industry supply curve** is the sum of the individual firm supply curves—that is, the marginal cost curves (above *AVC*) of all the firms in the industry. Because quantities are being added (that is, because we are finding the total quantity supplied in the industry at each price level), the curves are added horizontally.

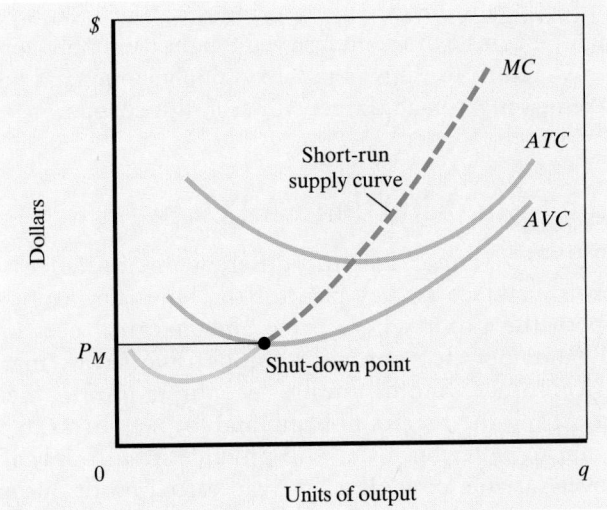

FIGURE 9.3
Short-Run Supply Curve of a
Perfectly Competitive Firm
At prices below average variable
cost, it pays a firm to shut down
rather than to continue operating. Thus, the short-run supply
curve of a competitive firm is the
part of its marginal cost curve
that lies *above* its average variable cost curve.

Figure 9.4 shows the supply curve for an industry with just three firms.[1] At a price of P_1, firm 1 produces 100 units, the output where $P = MC$. Firm 2 produces 200 units, and firm 3 produces 150 units. The total amount supplied on the market at P_1 is thus 450 (100 + 200 + 150). At a price of P_2, firm 1 produces 90 units, firm 2 produces 180 units, and firm 3 produces 120 units. At P_2, the industry thus supplies 390 units (90 + 180 + 120).

Two things can cause the industry supply curve to shift. In the short run, the industry supply curve shifts if something—an increase in the price of some input, for instance—shifts the marginal cost curves of all the individual firms simultaneously. For example, when the cost of producing components of home computers decreased, the marginal cost curves of all computer manufacturers shifted downward. Such a shift amounted to the same thing as an outward shift in their supply curves. Each firm was willing to supply more computers at each price level because computers were now cheaper to produce.

In the long run, an increase or decrease in the number of firms—and therefore in the number of individual firms' supply curves—shifts the total industry supply

FIGURE 9.4
The Industry Supply Curve
in the Short Run Is the
Horizontal Sum of the
Marginal Cost Curves
(above *AVC*) of all the Firms
in an Industry
If there are only three firms in the
industry, the industry supply
curve is simply the sum of all the
products supplied by the three
firms at each price. For example,
at P_1, firm 1 supplies 100 units,
firm 2 supplies 200 units, and firm
3 supplies 150 units, for a total
industry supply of 450.

---

[1]Perfectly competitive industries are assumed to have "many firms." Many is, of course, more than three. We use three firms here simply for the purposes of illustration.

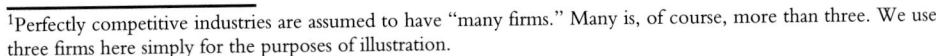

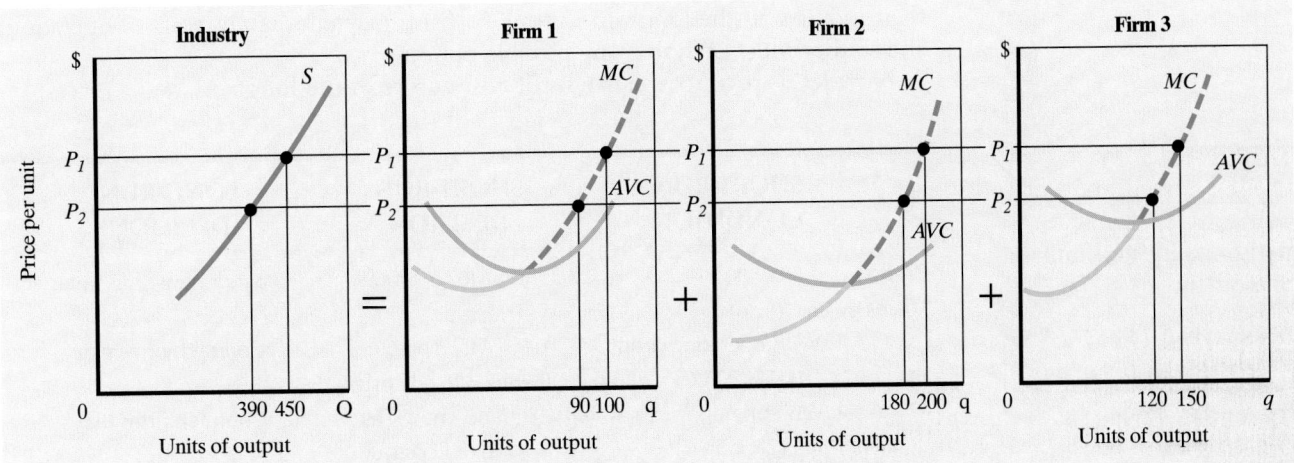

curve. If new firms enter the industry, the industry supply curve moves to the right; if firms exit the industry, the industry supply curve moves to the left.

We return to shifts in industry supply curves and discuss them further when we take up long-run adjustments later in this chapter.

Long-Run Directions: A Review

Table 9.3 summarizes the different circumstances that perfectly competitive firms may face as they plan for the long run. Profit-making firms will produce up to the point where price and marginal cost are equal in the short run. (Remember, for perfectly competitive firms, marginal revenue is equal to price.) Since "profit" means "economic profit," there is an incentive for firms to expand their scales of plant, and for new firms to enter in the long run.

Firms suffering losses will produce if, and only if, revenues are sufficient to cover variable costs. If a firm can earn a profit on operations, it can reduce the losses it would suffer if it shut down. Such firms, like profitable firms, will also produce up to the point where $P = MC$. If firms suffering losses cannot cover variable costs by operating, they will shut down and bear losses equal to fixed costs. Whether or not a firm that is suffering losses decides to shut down in the short run, it has an incentive to contract in the long run. The simple fact is that when firms are suffering economic losses, they will generally exit the industry in the long run.

In the short run, a firm's decision about how much to produce depends upon the market price of its product and the shapes of its cost curves. Remember that the short-run cost curves show costs that are determined by the *current* scale of plant. In the long run, however, firms have to choose among many *potential* scales of plant.

The long-run decisions of individual firms will depend on what their costs are likely to be at different scales of operation. Just as firms have to analyze different technologies to arrive at a cost structure in the short run, they must also compare their costs at different scales of plant in order to arrive at long-run costs. Perhaps a larger scale of operations will reduce production costs and provide an even greater incentive for a profit-making firm to expand. Or perhaps large firms will run into problems that constrain growth. The analysis of long-run possibilities is even more complex than the short-run analysis, because more things are variable—scale of plant is not fixed, for example, and there are no fixed costs because firms can exit their industry in the long run. In theory, firms may choose *any* scale of operation, and so they must analyze many possible options.

Now let us turn to an analysis of cost curves in the long run.

TABLE 9.3
Profits, Losses, and Perfectly Competitive Firms' Decisions in the Long and Short Run

	SHORT-RUN CONDITION	SHORT-RUN DECISION	LONG-RUN DECISION
Profits		$P = MC$: operate	Expand: new firms enter
Losses			
	1. With operating profit (TR ≥ TVC)	$P = MC$: operate (losses < fixed costs)	Contract: firms exit
	2. With operating losses (TR < TVC)	Shut down: losses = fixed costs	Contract: firms exit

LONG-RUN COSTS: ECONOMIES AND DISECONOMIES OF SCALE

As you already know, the shapes of short-run cost curves follow directly from the assumption of a fixed factor of production. As output increases beyond a certain point, the fixed factor, which we usually think of as fixed scale of plant, causes diminishing returns to other factors and thus increasing marginal costs. In the long run, however, there is no fixed factor of production. Firms can choose any scale of production. They can double or triple output or go out of business completely.

The shape of a firm's long-run average cost curve depends on how costs vary with scale of operations. For some firms, increased scale, or size, reduces costs; for others, increased scale leads to inefficiency and waste. When an increase in a firm's scale of production leads to lower average costs, we say there are **increasing returns to scale,** or **economies of scale.** When average costs do not change with the scale of production, we say that there are **constant returns to scale.** Finally, when an increase in a firm's scale of production leads to higher average costs, we say that there are **decreasing returns to scale,** or **diseconomies of scale.** Because these economies of scale are all found within the individual firm, they are considered *internal* economies of scale. Later in this chapter, we will talk about *external* economies of scale, which describe economies or diseconomies of scale on an industrywide basis.

> **increasing returns to scale, or economies of scale** An increase in scale of production leads to lower average costs per unit produced.
>
> **constant returns to scale** An increase in scale of production has no effect on average costs per unit produced.
>
> **decreasing returns to scale, or diseconomies of scale** An increase in a firm's scale of production leads to higher average costs per unit produced.

Increasing Returns to Scale

Technically, the phrase *increasing returns to scale* refers to the relationship between inputs and outputs. When we say that a production function exhibits increasing returns, we mean that a given percentage increase in the production of output requires a smaller percentage increase in the inputs. For example, if a firm were to double output, it would need less than twice as much of each input to produce that output. Stated the other way around, if a firm doubled or tripled inputs, it would more than double or triple output.

When firms can count on fixed input prices—that is, when the prices of inputs do not change with output levels—increasing returns to scale also means that as output rises, average cost of production falls. The term "economies of scale" refers directly to this reduction in cost per unit of output that follows from larger-scale production.

THE SOURCES OF ECONOMIES OF SCALE Most of the economies of scale that immediately come to mind are technological in nature. Automobile production, for example, would be much more costly per unit if a firm were to produce 100 cars per year by hand. Early in this century, Henry Ford introduced standardized production techniques that increased output volume, reduced costs per car, and made the automobile available to almost everyone.

Some economies of scale, however, do not result from technology but from sheer size. Very large companies, for instance, can buy inputs in volume at discounted prices. Large firms may also produce some of their own inputs at considerable savings. And they can certainly save in transport costs when items are shipped in bulk.

Economies of scale can be seen all around us. A bus that carries 100 people between Vancouver and Seattle uses less labor, capital, and gasoline than do 100 people driving 100 different automobiles. The cost per passenger (average cost) is lower on the bus. Roommates who share an apartment are taking advantage of economies of scale. Costs per person for heat, electricity, and space are lower when an apartment is shared than they would be if each person rented a separate apartment.

EXAMPLE: ECONOMIES OF SCALE IN EGG PRODUCTION Nowhere are economies of scale more visible than in agriculture. Consider the following example. A few years ago a major agribusiness moved into a small Ohio town and set up a huge egg-producing operation. The new firm, Chicken Little Egg Farms Inc., is completely mechanized. Complex machines feed the chickens and collect and box the eggs. Large refrigerated trucks transport the eggs all over the state daily. In the same town, some small farmers still own fewer than 200 chickens. These farmers collect the eggs, feed the chickens, clean the coops by hand, and deliver the eggs to county markets.

Table 9.4 presents some hypothetical cost data for Homer Jones's small operation and for Chicken Little Inc. Jones has his operation working well. He has several hundred chickens and spends about 15 hours per week feeding, collecting, delivering, and so forth. In the rest of his time he raises soybeans. We can value Jones's time at $8 per hour, because that is the wage he could earn working at a local manufacturing plant. When we add up all Jones's costs, including a rough estimate of the land and capital costs attributable to egg production, we arrive at $177 per week. Total production on the Jones farm runs about 200 dozen, or 2,400, eggs per week, which means that Jones's average cost comes out to $.074 per egg.

The costs of Chicken Little Inc. are much higher in total; weekly costs run over $30,000. A much higher percentage of costs are capital costs—the firm uses lots of sophisticated machinery that cost millions to put in place. Total output is 1.6 million eggs per week, and the product is shipped all over the Midwest. The comparatively huge scale of plant has driven average production costs all the way down to $.019 per egg.

While these numbers are hypothetical, you can see why small farmers in the United States are finding it difficult to compete with large-scale agribusiness concerns that can realize significant economies of scale. (For another example of economies of scale, see the Issues and Applications box entitled "Economies of Scale in the Brewing Industry.")

TABLE 9.4
Weekly Costs Showing Economies of Scale in Egg Production

JONES FARM	TOTAL WEEKLY COSTS
15 hours of labor (implicit value $8 per hour)	$120
Feed, other variable costs	25
Transport costs	15
Land and capital costs attributable to egg production	17
	$177
Total output	2400 eggs
Average cost	$.074 per egg

CHICKEN LITTLE EGG FARMS INC.	TOTAL WEEKLY COSTS
Labor	$5,128
Feed, other variable costs	4,115
Transport	2,431
Capital and land	19,230
	$30,904
Total output	1,600,000 eggs
Average cost	$.019 per egg

ECONOMIES OF SCALE IN THE BREWING INDUSTRY

Firms that face cost curves that decline with firm size have an incentive to grow. Firm size, in turn, determines the structure of the industry in the long run. If large-scale operations have significant cost advantages over small operations, one would expect to see a few large firms dominating the industry, rather than many small firms.

Over the years, economists have studied the cost structure of virtually every major industry using data gathered from individual firms. An excellent recent example is Victor Tremblay's work on the brewing industry, "Scale Economies, Technological Change, and Firm-Cost Asymmetries in the U.S. Brewing Industry."

From 1950 to 1983, the number of independent U.S. brewing companies decreased from 369 to 33, and the average size of firms in the industry grew dramatically. One possible reason for such a change, Tremblay hypothesized, is that economies of scale may have risen over the years, thus making survival possible for fewer and fewer firms.

To test his hypothesis, Tremblay put together a data set that contains observations on three national producers (Anheuser-Busch, Pabst, and Schlitz) and 19 regional producers for the period 1950 to 1978. From these data, he estimated short-run average cost functions and economies of scale for six different time periods. Tremblay's results suggest that significant scale economies do indeed exist in the brewing industry, and that they increased markedly over the period of the study.

The results tell an interesting story of the development of an industry:

Survival in brewing required that each

Empirical research has shown that significant economies of scale exist in the brewing industry. The result has been a decrease in the number of breweries and a dramatic increase in the average size of breweries.

firm build additional capacity and sell enough beer to take advantage of the rising scale economies. This competitive drive for greater production put downward pressure on beer prices and forced firms who were unable to exploit all economies of scale out of business. Thus, over 300 firms exited the industry, and concentration rose rapidly during this period.

Many factors may have caused economies of scale in brewing to increase during this time. At the plant level, faster packaging equipment and greater plant automation caused scale economies to rise. For example, modern canning lines fill 2,000 12-ounce cans per minute, whereas a typical high speed canning line operated at a rate of just 300 cans per minute in 1952....

Numerous innovations made large automated brewhouses less and less expensive to build and operate. For 1973, Keithahn ... found that plant construction costs per barrel of productive capacity declined by more than 35 percent for a plant with a 5.0 million barrel capacity compared to a 1.0 million barrel plant.

Furthermore, greater automation reduced labor expenses by reducing the number of workers needed to produce a given level of output. This is evident from the fact that the total number of production workers in brewing declined from a high of 64,800 in 1953 to just 29,500 in 1983, a period when annual production increased from 88.2 to 195.1 million barrels.

Multiplant scale economies, which developed in the late 1940s and early 1950s, were also an important determinant of optimal firm size in brewing. During this period, innovations in water treatment made it less costly to hold water (and therefore beer) quality constant across the country. This enabled brewers to decentralize their production operations while maintaining product homogeneity among different production facilities across the country. There were no multiplant producers in 1945, but most of the major brewers operated more than one plant by 1956.

Source: Victor Tremblay, "Scale Economies, Technological Change, and Firm-Cost Asymmetries in the U.S. Brewing Industry," *Quarterly Review of Economics and Business,* Summer 1987.

GRAPHIC PRESENTATION A firm's **long-run average cost curve (LRAC)** shows the different scales on which it can choose to operate in the long run. In other words, a firm's *LRAC* curve traces out the position of all its possible short-run curves, each corresponding to a different scale. It is the "envelope" of a series of short-run curves. At any time, the existing scale of plant determines the position and shape of the firm's short-run cost curve. But the firm must consider in its long-run strategic planning whether to build a plant of a *different* scale. The long-run average cost curve simply shows the positions of the different sets of short-run curves among which the firm must choose. In other words, the long-run average cost curve "wraps around" the set of all possible short-run curves like an envelope. (Later in this chapter, the Issues and Applications box entitled "The Long-Run Average Cost Curve: Flat or U-Shaped?" describes the debate on how the *LRAC* is constructed.)

Figure 9.5 shows short-run and long-run average cost curves for a firm that realizes economies of scale up to about 100,000 units of production and roughly constant returns to scale after that. The diagram shows three potential scales of operation, each with its own set of short-run cost curves. Each point on this *LRAC* curve represents the minimum cost at which the associated output level can be produced.

Once the firm chooses a scale on which to produce, it becomes locked into one set of cost curves in the short run. If the firm were to settle on Scale 1, it would not realize the major cost advantages of producing on a larger scale. By roughly doubling its scale of operations from 50,000 to 100,000 units (Scale 2), the firm reduces average costs per unit significantly.

Constant Returns to Scale

Technically, the term *constant returns* means that the quantitative relationship between input and output stays constant, or the same, when output is increased. If a firm doubles inputs, it doubles output; if it triples inputs, it triples output; and so forth. Furthermore, if input prices are fixed, constant returns implies that average cost of production does not change with scale. In other words, constant returns to scale means that the firm's long-run average cost curve remains flat.

The firm in Figure 9.5 exhibits roughly constant returns to scale between Scale 2

FIGURE 9.5

A Firm Exhibiting Economies of Scale

The long-run average cost curve of a firm shows the different scales on which the firm can choose to operate in the long run. Each scale of operation defines a different short run. Here we see a firm exhibiting economies of scale; moving from Scale 1 to Scale 3 reduces average cost.

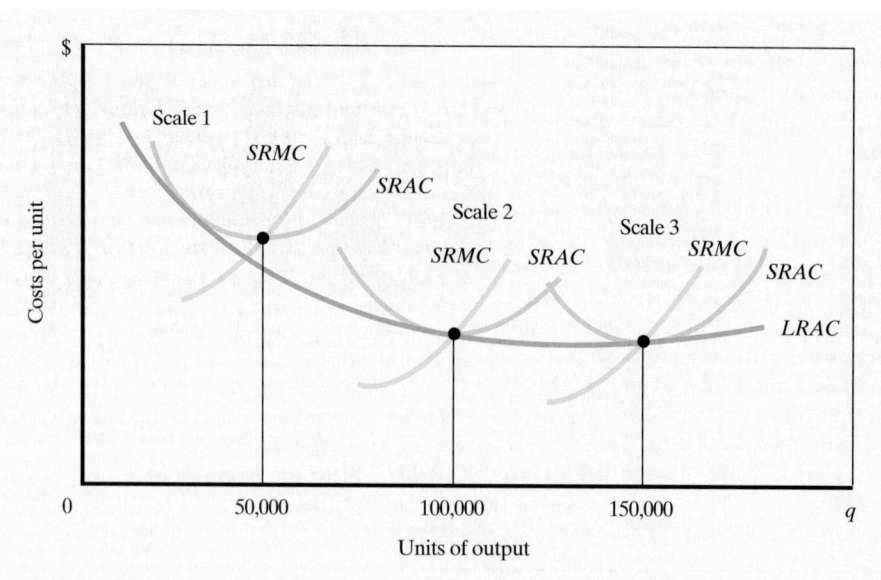

and Scale 3. The average cost of production is about the same in each. If the firm exhibited constant returns at higher levels, the *LRAC* would continue as a flat, straight line.

Economists have studied cost data extensively over the years to estimate the extent to which economies of scale exist. Evidence suggests that in most industries firms don't have to be gigantic to realize cost savings from scale economies. For example, automobile production is accomplished in thousands of separate assembly operations, each with its own economies of scale. Perhaps the best example of efficient production on a small scale is the manufacturing sector in Taiwan. Taiwan has enjoyed very rapid growth based on manufacturing firms that employ fewer than 100 workers!

One simple theoretical argument supports the empirical result that most industries seem to exhibit constant returns to scale (a flat *LRAC*) after some level of output. Competition always pushes firms to adopt the least-cost technology and scale. If cost advantages result with larger-scale operations, the firms that shift to that scale will drive the smaller, less efficient firms out of business. A firm that wants to grow when it has reached its "optimal" size can do so by building another identical plant. It thus seems logical to conclude that most firms face constant returns to scale *as long as* they can replicate their existing plants. Thus, when you look at developed industries, you can expect to see firms of different sizes operating with similar costs. These firms produce using roughly the same scale of plant, but larger firms simply have more plants.

Decreasing Returns to Scale

When average cost increases with scale of production, a firm faces *decreasing returns to scale,* or *diseconomies of scale.* The most often cited example of a diseconomy of scale is bureaucratic inefficiency. As size increases beyond a certain point, operations tend to become more difficult to manage. You can easily imagine what happens when a firm grows top-heavy with managers who have accumulated seniority and high salaries. The coordination function is more complex for larger firms than for smaller ones, and the chances that it will break down are greater.

A large firm is also more likely than a small firm to find itself facing problems with organized labor. Unions can demand higher wages and more benefits, go on strike, force firms to incur legal expenses, and take other actions that increase production costs. (This does not mean that unions are "bad," but rather that their activities often increase costs. A more detailed discussion of unions and labor appears in Chapter 19.)

Figure 9.6 describes a firm that exhibits both economies of scale and disec-

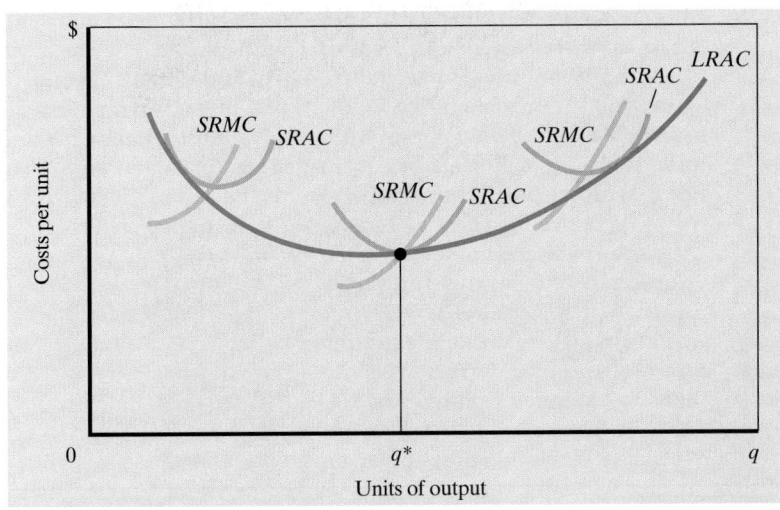

FIGURE 9.6

A Firm Exhibiting Economies and Diseconomies of Scale

Economies of scale push this firm's costs down to q^*. Beyond q^*, the firm experiences diseconomies of scale. q^* is the level of production at lowest average cost, using optimal scale.

THE LONG-RUN AVERAGE COST CURVE: FLAT OR U-SHAPED?

The long-run average cost curve has been a source of controversy in economics for many years. A long-run average cost curve was first drawn as the "envelope" of a series of short-run curves in a classic article written by Jacob Viner in 1931.* In preparing that article, Viner gave his draftsman the task of drawing the long-run curve through the minimum points of all the short-run average cost curves.

In a supplementary note written in 1950, Viner commented:

... the error in Chart IV is left uncorrected so that future teachers and students may share the pleasure of many of their predecessors of pointing out that if I had known what an envelope was, I would not have given my excellent draftsman the technically impossible and economically inappropriate task of drawing an AC curve which would pass through the lowest cost points of all the AC curves yet not rise above any AC curve at any point....†

While this story is an interesting part of the lore of economics, a more recent debate concentrates on the economic content of this controversy. In 1986, Professor Herbert Simon of Carnegie-Mellon University stated bluntly:

I think the textbooks are a scandal ... the most widely used textbooks use the old long-run and short-run cost curves to illustrate the theory of the firm.... [the U-shaped long-run cost curve] postulated that in the long run the size of the firm would increase to a scale associated with the minimum cost on the long-run curve. It was supposed to predict something about the size distribution of firms in the industry. It doesn't do that and there are other problems. Most serious is the fact that most empirical studies show the firm's cost curves not to be U-shaped, but in fact to slope down to the right and then level off, without a clearly defined minimum point.‡

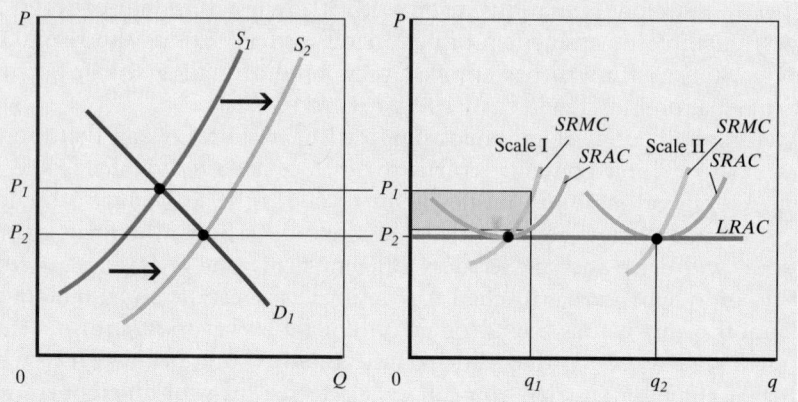

FIGURE 1

Long-Run Expansion in an Industry with Constant Returns to Scale

Professor Simon makes an important point. Suppose that we were to redraw Figure 9.7b with a flat long-run average cost curve. Figure 1 shows a firm earning short-run economic profits using Scale I, but there are no economies of scale to be realized.

Despite the lack of economies of scale, expansion of such an industry would likely take place in much the same way as we described in the text. First, existing firms have an incentive to expand. At current prices, a firm that doubles its scale would earn twice the economic profits even if cost did not fall with expansion. Of course, as long as economic profits persist, new firms have an incentive to enter the industry. Both of these events will shift the short-run industry supply curve to the right, from S_1 to S_2 and price will fall, from P_1 to P_2. Expansion and entry will stop only when price has fallen to $LRAC$. Only then will economic profits be eliminated. At equilibrium, $P = SRMC = SRAC = LRAC$.

This model does not predict the final firm size or the structure of the industry. When the long-run AC curve is U-shaped, firms stop expanding at the minimum point on $LRAC$ since further expansion means higher costs; thus, optimal firm size is determined technologically. If the $LRAC$ curve is flat, however, small firms and large firms have identical average costs.

If this is true, and it seems to be in many industries, the structure of the industry in the long run will depend on whether existing firms expand faster than new firms enter. If new firms enter quickly in response to profit opportunities, the industry will end up with large numbers of small firms. If, on the other hand, existing firms expand more rapidly than new firms enter, the industry may end up with only a few very large firms. There is thus an element of randomness in the way industries expand. In fact, most industries contain some large firms and some small firms, which is exactly what Simon's flat $LRAC$ model predicts.

*Jacob Viner, "Cost Curves and Supply Curves," *Zeitschrift fur Nationalokonomie*, vol. III (1-1931), pp. 23–46.

†George J. Stigler and Kenneth E. Boulding, eds., *AEA Readings in Price Theory*, vol. VI (Chicago. Richard D. Irwin, 1952), p. 227.

‡Interview with Herbert A. Simon, "The Failure of Armchair Economics," *Challenge*, November/December, 1986, pp. 23–24.

onomies of scale. Average costs decrease with scale of plant up to $q*$ and increase with scale after that. This long-run average cost curve looks very much like the short-run average cost curves we have examined in the last two chapters. But do not confuse the two:

> All short-run average cost curves are U-shaped, because we assume a fixed scale of plant that constrains production and drives marginal cost upward as a result of diminishing returns. In the long run, we make no such assumption; rather, we assume that scale of plant can be changed.

The shape of a firm's *long-run* average cost curve depends on how costs react to changes in scale. Some firms do see economies of scale, and their long-run average cost curves slope downward. Most firms seem to have flat long-run average cost curves. Still others encounter diseconomies, and their long-run average costs slope upward. Thus, the same firm can face diminishing returns—a short-run concept—and still have a long-run cost curve that exhibits economies of scale.

It is important to note that economic efficiency requires taking advantage of economies of scale (if they exist) and avoiding diseconomies of scale. The **optimal scale of plant** is the one that minimizes cost. In fact, we will see later in this chapter that competition forces firms to use the optimal scale.

optimal scale of plant The scale of plant that minimizes cost.

External Economies and Diseconomies

Sometimes average costs increase or decrease with the size of the *industry,* in addition to responding to changes in the size of the firm itself. When long-run average costs decrease as a result of industry growth, we say that there are **external economies.** When average costs increase as a result of industry growth, we say that there are **external diseconomies.** (Remember the distinction between external and internal economies: *internal* economies of scale are found within firms, while *external* economies occur on an industrywide basis.)

external economies and diseconomies When industry growth results in a decrease of long-run average costs, there are *external economies;* when industry growth results in an increase of long-run average costs, there are *external diseconomies.*

Consider, for example, the growth of the "high-tech" manufacturing industry in the United States. The 1970s saw a revolution of sorts concentrated around Boston, Massachusetts, and the "Silicon Valley," which lies in the peninsula south of San Francisco. So many new firms began to produce highly technical computer products that a new industry was born. Firms such as Digital Equipment Company, Prime, Wang Laboratories, Apple, Hewlett-Packard, and many others experienced very rapid rates of growth.

Before the high-tech boom, the Massachusetts economy had been stagnant, its unemployment rate the highest among the industrialized states. Many textile mills and shoe factories had gone out of business or moved their operations to the South or out of the United States altogether. As the new technology firms began to expand in the mid-1970s, they found a labor force that needed to be trained. In the infancy of the industry, the expanding firms bore virtually all the training costs themselves. As the industry grew and flourished, however, people began to acquire the necessary technical skills on their own in order to compete for the jobs. Private schools grew up all around Boston and San Jose (in the Silicon Valley) to train people for jobs in the high-tech field.

Once training costs were shifted from the firms to the employees, average cost of production in the industry fell. This decline in costs, which resulted from an external economy, was due to growth of the industry; it had nothing to do with cost advantages that any individual firm might have secured by producing on a larger scale.

YEAR	NEW HOUSING UNITS STARTED (MILLIONS)	PERCENTAGE INCREASE OVER PREVIOUS YEAR	PERCENTAGE CHANGE IN THE PRICE OF LUMBER PRODUCTS	PERCENTAGE CHANGE IN CONSUMER PRICES
1975	1.16	− 13.3	− 6.8	+ 9.1
1976	1.54	+ 32.8	+ 20.7	+ 5.8
1977	1.99	+ 29.2	+ 18.9	+ 6.5
1978	2.02	+ 1.5	+ 16.2	+ 7.7
1979	1.74	− 13.9	+ 9.9	+ 11.3

Sources: U.S. Bureau of the Census, *Construction Reports,* series C20; U.S. Bureau of Labor Statistics, *Producer Price Indexes,* annual.

TABLE 9.5
Construction Activity and the Price of Lumber Products, 1975–1979

Now let us consider construction, an industry made up of thousands of individual small firms. Recent decades have seen several construction booms during which the construction industry expanded. One of the biggest expansions took place between 1975 and 1979. Expansion, of course, affects the price of lumber and lumber products. Increases in construction activity cause the demand for lumber products to rise, and this price increase causes the cost of construction to shift upward for all construction firms.

Table 9.5 shows one indicator of construction activity: new housing units started. In 1976 and 1977, the industry grew very rapidly. In 1978, construction began on over two million new units of housing. This growth was accompanied by a very rapid increase in lumber prices as demand for lumber products ballooned. From 1975 to 1979, the price of lumber products increased over 83%, while prices in general increased only about 35 percent.

In the construction industry, a change in the scale of any individual firm's operations has no impact on the price of lumber, because no one firm has any control over the price. The increase in costs in the late 1970s resulted from expansion of the *industry* that led to an external diseconomy.

The concept of external economies and diseconomies is critical to the discussion of long-run industry adjustments that follows. As industries grow in response to profits or contract in response to losses, their costs of production can change.

LONG-RUN ADJUSTMENTS TO SHORT-RUN CONDITIONS

We began this chapter by discussing the different short-run positions in which firms may find themselves. Firms can be operating at a profit or suffering economic losses; they can be shut down or producing. We say that the *industry* is not in equilibrium if firms have an incentive to enter or exit in the long run. Thus, when firms are earning economic profits (profits above normal) or are suffering economic losses (profits below normal, or negative), the industry is not at an equilibrium, and firms will change their behavior. What they are likely to do depends in part on costs in the long run. This is why we spent a good deal of time discussing economies and diseconomies of scale.

We can now put these two ideas together and discuss the actual long-run adjustments that are likely to take place in response to short-run profits and losses.

Short-Run Profits: Expansion to Equilibrium

We begin our analysis of long-run adjustments with a perfectly competitive industry in which firms are earning economic profits. We assume that all firms in the industry are producing with the same technology of production, and that each firm has a long-run average cost curve that is U-shaped. A U-shaped long-run average cost curve implies that there are some economies of scale to be realized in the industry, and that all firms ultimately begin to run into diseconomies at some scale of operation.

Figure 9.7 shows a representative perfectly competitive firm initially producing at Scale 1. Market price is P_1, and firms are enjoying economic profits. Total revenue ($P_1 \times q_1 = P_1Aq_10$) exceeds total cost ([$SRAC$ at $q_1 \times q_1$] = CBq_10), and profit per period is equal to the shaded rectangle.

At this point, our representative firm has not realized all the economies of scale available to it. By expanding to Scale 2, it will reduce average costs significantly, and unless price drops it will increase profits. As long as firms are enjoying profits and economies of scale exist, firms will expand. Thus, we assume that the firm in Figure 9.7 shifts to Scale 2.

At the same time, the existence of economic profits will attract new entrants to the industry. Both the entrance of new firms and the expansion of existing firms have the same effect on the short-run industry supply curve (see Figure 9.7a). Both cause the short-run supply curve to shift to the right, from S to S'. Because the short-run industry supply curve is the sum of all the marginal cost curves (above the minimum point of AVC) of all the firms in the industry, it will shift to the right, for two reasons. First, since all firms in the industry are expanding to a larger scale, their individual short-run marginal cost curves shift to the right. Second, with new firms entering the industry, there are more firms and thus more marginal cost curves to add up.

As capital flows into the industry, the supply curve in Figure 9.7a shifts to the right and price falls. The question is, where will the process stop? In general:

> Firms will continue to expand as long as there are economies of scale to be realized, and new firms will continue to enter as long as economic profits are being earned.

FIGURE 9.7

Firms Expand in the Long Run When Increasing Returns to Scale Are Available

When there are economies of scale to be realized, firms have an incentive to expand. Thus firms will be pushed by competition to produce at their optimal scales. Price will be driven to the minimum point on the *LRAC* curve.

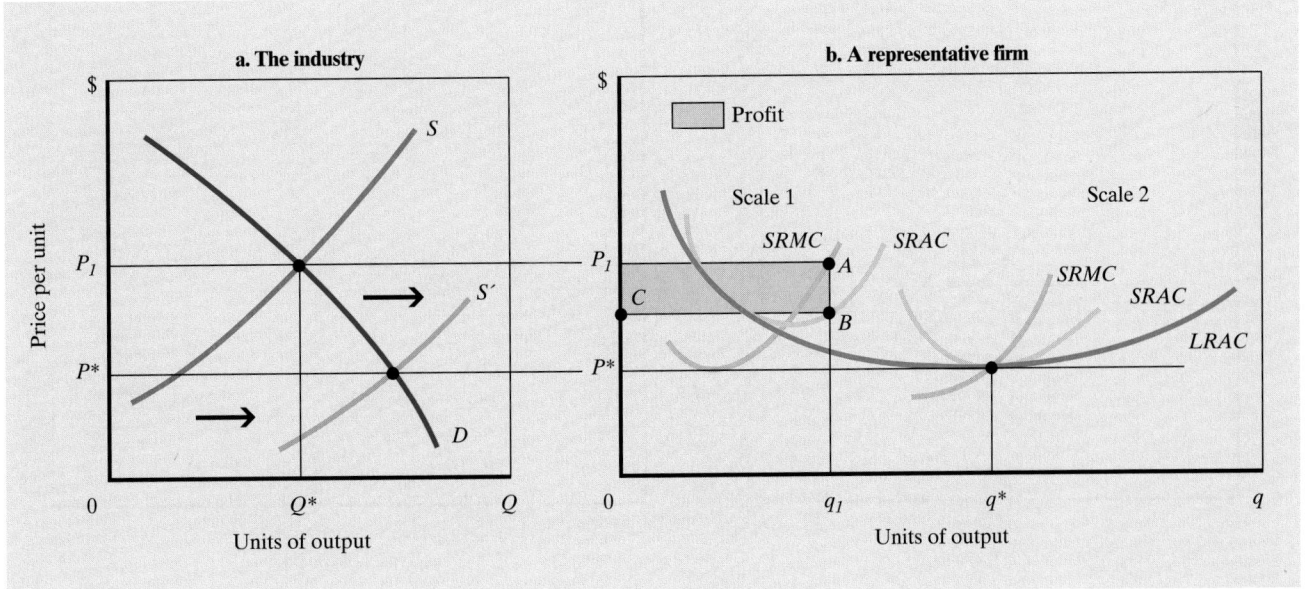

In Figure 9.7a, final equilibrium is achieved only when price falls to P^* and firms have exhausted all the economies of scale available in the industry. At P^*, no economic profits are being earned and none can be earned by changing the level of output.

Look carefully at the final equilibrium in Figure 9.7. Each firm will choose the scale of plant that produces its product at minimum long-run average cost. Competition drives firms to adopt not just the most efficient technology in the *short* run, but also the most efficient scale of operation in the *long* run.

In the long run, equilibrium price (P^*) is equal to long-run average cost, short-run marginal cost, and short-run average cost. Economic profits are driven to zero:

$$P^* = SRMC = SRAC = LRAC,$$

where $SRMC$ denotes short-run marginal cost, $SRAC$ denotes short-run average cost, and $LRAC$ denotes long-run average cost. No other price is an equilibrium. Any price above P^* means that there are profits to be made in the industry, and new firms will continue to enter. Any price below P^* means that firms are suffering economic losses, and firms will exit the industry. Only at P^* will economic profits be just equal to zero, and only at P^* will the industry be in equilibrium.

FIGURE 9.8

Long-Run Contraction and Exit in an Industry Suffering Short-Run Losses

When firms in an industry suffer losses, there is an incentive for them to exit. As firms exit, the supply curve shifts from S to S', driving price up to P^*. As price rises, losses are gradually eliminated and the industry returns to equilibrium.

Short-Run Losses: Contraction to Equilibrium

Firms that suffer short-run losses have an incentive to leave the industry in the long run, but cannot do so in the short run. As we have seen, some firms incurring losses will choose to shut down and bear losses equal to fixed costs. Others will continue to produce in the short run in an effort to minimize their losses.

Figure 9.8 depicts a firm that will continue to produce q_0 units of output in the short run, despite its losses. (We are assuming here that the firm is earning losses that are smaller than the firm's fixed costs.) With losses, the long-run picture will

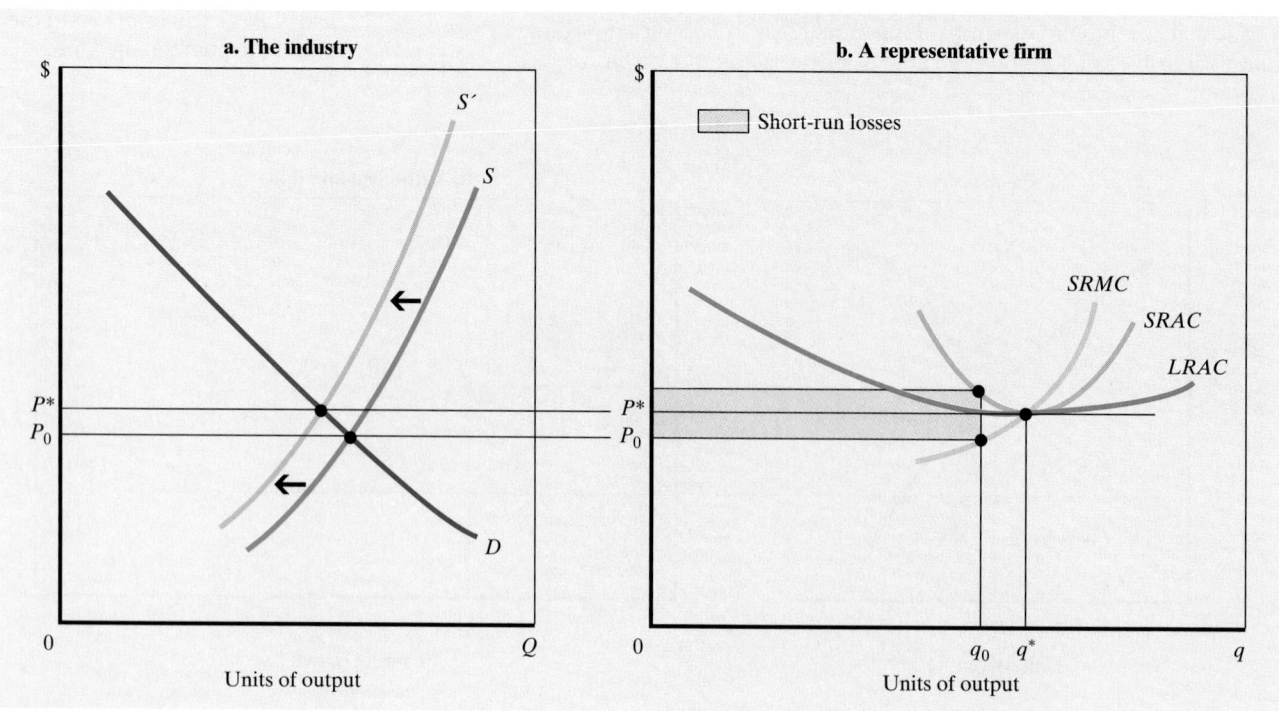

change. Firms have an incentive to get out of the industry, and as they exit the short-run supply curve of the industry shifts to the left. As it shifts, the equilibrium price rises.

Once again the question is: How long will this adjustment process continue? In general:

> As long as losses are being sustained in an industry, firms will shut down and leave the industry, thus reducing supply—shifting the supply curve to the left. As this happens, price rises. This gradual price rise reduces losses for firms remaining in the industry until those losses are ultimately eliminated.

In Figure 9.8, equilibrium occurs when price rises to P^*. At that point, remaining firms will maximize profits by producing q^* units of output. Price is just sufficient to cover average costs, and economic profits and losses are zero.

All of this leads us to conclude that:

> Whether we begin with an industry in which firms are earning profits or suffering losses, the final long-run competitive equilibrium condition is the same when we start with losses as it is when we start with profits:
>
> $$P = SRMC = SRAC = LRAC,$$
>
> and economic profits are zero. At this point, individual firms are operating at the most efficient scale of plant—that is, at the minimum point on their *LRAC* curve.

The Long-Run Adjustment Mechanism: Investment Flows Toward Profit Opportunities

The central idea in our discussion of entry, exit, expansion, and contraction is this:

> In efficient markets, investment capital flows toward profit opportunities. The actual process is complex and varies from industry to industry.

We talked about efficient markets in Chapter 1. The logic of efficient markets, you will recall, is that as profit opportunities develop they are quickly eliminated. To illustrate this point, we described driving up to a toll booth on a freeway and suggested that shorter-than-average lines are quickly eliminated as cars shift into them. So too are profits in competitive industries eliminated as new competing firms move into open slots, or perceived opportunities, in the industry.

In practice, the entry and exit of firms in response to profit opportunities usually involves the financial capital market. In capital markets, people are constantly looking for profits. When firms in an industry do well, capital is likely to flow into that industry in a variety of forms. Entrepreneurs start new firms, and firms producing entirely different products may join the competition in order to break into new markets. Several years ago, for example, the Gillette Company, a firm well known for making razors, shaving cream, and other home products, began making digital watches because it thought there was a profit to be made. Certainly companies in profitable lines of business have little trouble raising money for expansion projects.

When there is promise of extraordinary profits, investments are made and output expands. When firms end up suffering losses, firms contract, and some go out of business. It can take quite a while, however, for an industry to achieve **long-run competitive equilibrium,** the point at which $P = SRMC = SRAC = LRAC$ and economic profits are zero. In fact, because costs and tastes are in a constant state of flux, very few industries ever really get there. The economy is always changing. There are always some firms making profits and some firms suffering losses.

This, then, is a story about tendencies:

> Investment, in the form of new firms and expanding old firms, will, over time, tend to favor those industries in which profits are being made. At the same time, industries in which firms are suffering losses will gradually contract from disinvestment.

The Long-Run Industry Supply Curve

We now know what long-run competitive equilibrium means formally, and we have discussed briefly what long-run adjustment means in practice. To summarize:

> Long-run competitive equilibrium is achieved when entering firms responding to profits or exiting firms fleeing from losses drive price to a level that just covers long-run average costs. Economic profits are zero, and $P = LRAC = SRAC = SRMC$. At this point, individual firms are operating at the most efficient scale of plant—that is, at the minimum point on their $LRAC$ curve.

As we've said, long-run equilibrium is not easily achieved. But even if a firm or an industry does achieve long-run equilibrium, it will not remain at that point indefinitely. Economies are dynamic. As population and the stock of capital grow, and as preferences and technology change, some sectors will expand and some will contract. How do industries adjust to long-term changes?

When we defined and described economies and diseconomies earlier in this chapter, we discussed two very different types: *internal* and *external*. The extent of *internal* economies (or diseconomies) determines the shape of a firm's long-run average cost curve (*LRAC*). If a firm changes its scale and either expands or contracts in size, its average costs will increase, decrease, or stay the same *along* the *LRAC* curve. Recall that the *LRAC* curve shows the relationship between a firm's output (*q*) and average total cost (*ATC*). A firm enjoying internal *economies* will see costs decreasing as it expands its scale; a firm facing internal *diseconomies* will see costs increasing as it expands its scale.

But external economies and diseconomies have nothing to do with the size of *individual* firms in a competitive market. Since individual firms in perfectly competitive industries are very small relative to the market, other firms are affected only minimally when an individual firm changes its output or scale of operation. External economies and diseconomies arise from *industry* expansions; that is, they arise when many firms increase their output simultaneously or when new firms enter an industry. If industry expansion causes costs to increase (external diseconomies), the *LRAC* curves facing individual firms shift *upward;* costs increase regardless of the level of output finally chosen by the firm. Similarly, if industry expansion causes costs to decrease (external economies), the *LRAC* curves facing individual firms shift *downward;* costs decrease at all potential levels of output.

An example of an expanding industry facing external economies is illustrated in Figure 9.9. Initially, the industry and the representative firm are in long-run competitive equilibrium at the price P_1 determined by the intersection of the initial demand curve D_1 and the initial supply curve S_1. P_1 is the long-run equilibrium price; it intersects the initial long-run average cost curve ($LRAC_1$) at its minimum point. At this point, economic profits are zero.

Let us assume that as time passes, demand increases—that is, the demand curve shifts to the right from D_1 to D_2. This increase in demand will push price all the way to P_2. Without drawing the short-run cost curves, we know that economic profits now exist and that firms are likely to enter the industry to compete for them. In the absence of external economies or diseconomies, firms would enter the industry, shifting the supply curve to the right and driving price back to the bottom of the long-run average cost curve, where profits are zero. But the industry in Figure 9.9 enjoys external economies. As firms enter and the industry expands, costs decrease. And as the supply curve shifts to the right from S_1 toward S_2, the long-run average cost curve shifts downward to $LRAC_2$. Thus, to reach the new long-run equilibrium level of price and output, the supply curve must shift all the way to S_2. Only when the supply curve reaches S_2 is price driven down to the new equilibrium price of P_3, the minimum point on the *new* long-run average cost curve.

Presumably, further expansion would lead to even greater savings because the industry encounters external economies. The dashed line in Figure 9.9a, which traces out price and total output over time as the industry expands, is called the **long-run industry supply curve (LRIS).** When an industry enjoys external economies, its long-run supply curve slopes down. Such an industry is called a **decreasing-cost industry.**

long-run industry supply curve (LRIS) A graph that traces out price and total output over time as an industry expands.

decreasing-cost industry An industry that realizes external economies—that is, an industry in which average costs decrease as the industry grows. The long-run supply curve for such an industry has a negative slope.

FIGURE 9.9
A Decreasing-Cost Industry: External Economies

In a decreasing-cost industry, average cost declines as the industry expands. As demand expands from D_1 to D_2, price rises to P_2. As new firms enter and existing firms expand, supply shifts to S_2, driving price down. If costs decline as a result of the expansion to $LRAC_2$, the final price will be below P_1 at P_3. The long-run industry supply curve (LRIS) slopes downward in a decreasing-cost industry.

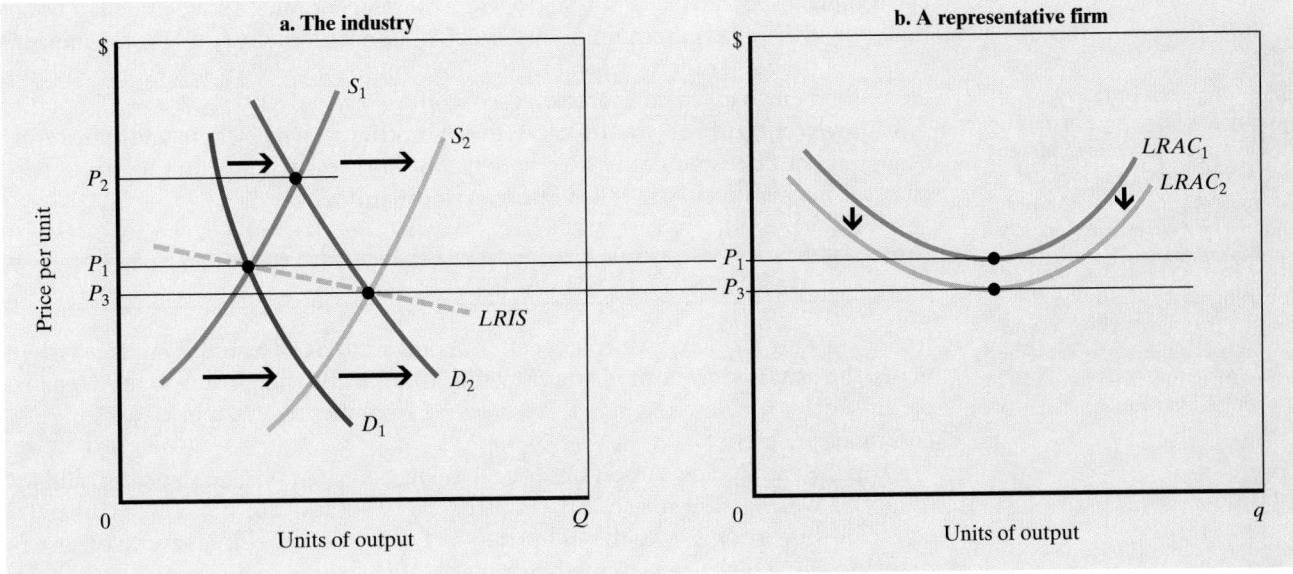

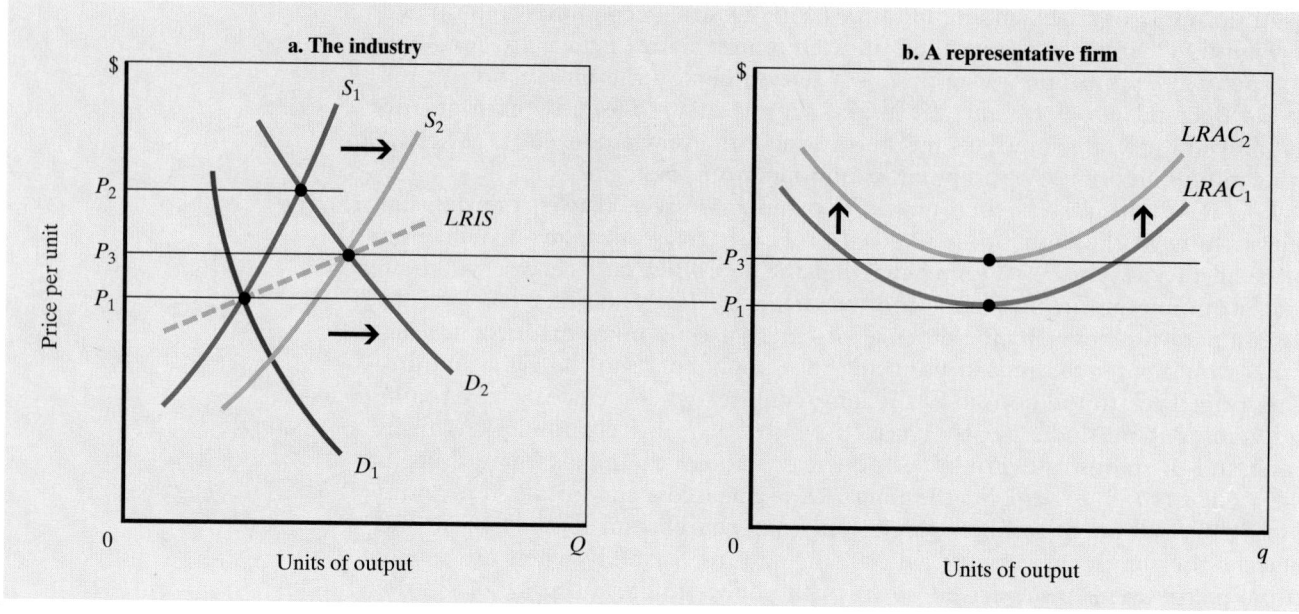

FIGURE 9.10

An Increasing-Cost Industry: External Diseconomies

In an increasing-cost industry, average cost increases as the industry expands. As demand shifts from D_1 to D_2, price rises from P_1 to P_2. As new firms enter and existing firms expand output, supply shifts from S_1 to S_2, driving price down. If long-run average costs rise as a result to $LRAC_2$, the final price will be P_3—above P_1. The long-run industry supply curve (*LRIS*) slopes up in an increasing-cost industry.

In Figure 9.10, we derive the long-run industry supply curve for an industry that faces *external diseconomies*. (These were suffered in the construction industry, you will recall, when increased house-building activity drove up lumber prices.) As demand expands from D_1 to D_2, price is driven up from P_1 to P_2. In response to the resulting higher profits, firms enter, shifting the short-run supply schedule to the right and driving price down. But this time, as the industry expands, the long-run average cost curve shifts up to $LRAC_2$ as a result of external diseconomies. Now, price has to fall back only to P_3 (the minimum point on $LRAC_2$), not all the way to P_1, to eliminate economic profits. This type of industry, whose long-run industry supply curve slopes up to the right, is called an **increasing-cost industry.**

It should not surprise you to know that industries in which there are no external economies or diseconomies of scale have flat, or horizontal, long-run industry supply curves. These industries are called **constant-cost industries.**

increasing-cost industry An industry that encounters external diseconomies—that is, an industry in which average costs increase as the industry grows. The long-run supply curve for such an industry has a positive slope.

constant-cost industry An industry that shows no economies or diseconomies of scale as the industry grows. Such industries have flat, or horizontal, long-run supply curves.

OUTPUT MARKETS: A FINAL WORD

In the last four chapters, we have been building a model of a simple market system under the assumption of perfect competition. Let us provide just one more example in order to review the actual response of a competitive system to a change in consumer preferences.

Over the past decade, Americans have developed a taste for wine in general and for California wines and "wine coolers" in particular. We know that household demand is constrained by income, wealth, and prices, and that income is, at least in part, determined by the choices that households make. Within these constraints, households choose, and, increasingly, they choose—or demand—wine. The demand curve for wine has shifted to the right, causing excess demand followed by an increase in price.

With higher prices, wine producers find themselves earning economic profits. *This increase in price and consequent rise in profits is the basic signal that leads to a reallocation of society's resources.* In the short run, wine producers are constrained by their current scales of operation. California has only a limited number of vineyards and only a limited amount of vat capacity, for example.

In the long run, however, one would expect to see resources flow in to compete for these economic profits, and this is exactly what happens. New firms enter the wine-producing business. New vines are planted and new vats and production equipment are purchased and put in place. Vineyard owners move into new states—Rhode Island, Texas, and Maryland—and established growers increase production. Overall, more wine is produced to meet the new consumer demand. At the same time, competition is forcing firms to operate using the most efficient technology available.

What starts as a shift in preferences thus ends up as a shift in resources. Land is reallocated and labor moves into wine production. All this is accomplished without any central planning or direction.

You have now seen what lies behind the demand curves and supply curves in competitive output markets. The next two chapters take up competitive *input* markets and complete the picture.

Summary

1. For any firm, one of three conditions holds at any given moment: (1) The firm is earning economic profits, (2) the firm is suffering losses, or (3) the firm is just breaking even—that is, earning a normal rate of return and zero economic profits.

Short-Run Conditions and Long-Run Directions

2. A firm that is earning economic profits in the short run and expects to continue to do so has an incentive to expand in the long run. Profits also provide an incentive for new firms to enter the industry.

3. In the *short run*, firms suffering losses are stuck in the industry. They can shut down operations ($q = 0$), but they must still bear fixed costs. In the long run, firms suffering losses can exit the industry.

4. A firm's decision about whether to shut down in the short run depends solely on whether its revenues from operating are sufficient to cover its variable costs. If revenues exceed variable costs, the *operating profits* can be used to pay some fixed costs and thus reduce losses.

5. Any time that price is below the minimum point on the average variable cost curve, total revenue will be less than total variable cost, operating profit will be negative, and the firm will shut down. The minimum point on the average variable cost curve (that is, the point where marginal cost and average variable cost intersect) is called the *shut-down point*. At all prices above it, the *MC* curve shows the profit-maximizing level of output. At all prices below it, optimal short-run output is zero.

6. The *short-run supply curve* of a firm in a perfectly competitive industry is the portion of its marginal cost curve that lies above its average variable cost curve.

7. Two things can cause the industry supply curve to shift: (1) in the short run, anything that causes marginal costs to change across the industry, such as an increase in the price of a particular input, and (2) in the long run, entry or exit of firms.

Long-Run Costs: Economies and Diseconomies of Scale

8. When an increase in a firm's scale of production leads to lower average costs, the firm exhibits *increasing returns to scale,* or *economies of scale.* When average costs do not change with the scale of production, the firm exhibits *constant returns to scale.* When an increase in a firm's scale of production leads to higher average costs, the firm exhibits *diseconomies of scale.*

9. A firm's *long-run average cost curve* (*LRAC*) shows the costs associated with different scales on which it can choose to operate in the long run.

10. When long-run average costs decrease as a result of industry growth, we say that the industry exhibits *external economies of scale.* When average costs increase as a result of industry growth, we say that the industry exhibits *external diseconomies of scale.*

Long-Run Adjustments to Short-Run Conditions

11. When short-run profits exist in an industry, firms will enter and existing firms will expand. These events cause the industry supply curve to shift to the right. When this happens, price falls and ultimately profits are eliminated.

12. When short-run losses are suffered in an industry, some firms exit and some firms reduce scale. These events cause the industry supply curve to shift to the left, raising price and eliminating losses.

13. *Long-run competitive equilibrium* is reached when $P = SRMC = SRAC = LRAC$ and economic profits are zero.

14. In efficient markets investment capital flows toward profit opportunities.

15. *The long-run industry supply curve (LRIS)* is a graph that traces out price and total output over time as an industry expands.

16. A *decreasing-cost industry* is one in which average costs fall as the industry expands. It exhibits external economies of scale, and its long-run industry supply curve slopes downward. An *increasing-cost industry* is one in which average costs rise as the industry expands. It exhibits external diseconomies of scale, and its long-run industry supply curve slopes upward. A *constant-cost industry* is one that shows no economies or diseconomies of scale as the industry grows. Its long-run industry supply curve is horizontal, or flat.

Review Terms and Concepts

breaking even   219
constant-cost industry   240
constant returns to scale   227
decreasing-cost industry   239
decreasing returns to scale, or diseconomies of scale   227
external economies and diseconomies   233
increasing-cost industry   240

increasing returns to scale, or economies of scale   227
long-run average cost curve (LRAC)   230
long-run competitive equilibrium   238
long-run industry supply curve (LRIS)   239
operating profit (or loss), or net operating revenue   222

optimal scale of plant   233
short-run industry supply curve   224
shut-down point   224

Equations:

$$ATC = AFC + AVC$$
$$AFC = ATC - AVC$$

Problem Set

1. Explain why it is possible that a firm with a production function that exhibits increasing returns to scale can run into diminishing returns at the same time.

2. For Cases A through F below, would you (1) operate or shut down in the short run and (2) expand your plant or exit the industry in the long run?

	A	B	C	D	E	F
Total revenue	1500	2000	2000	5000	5000	5000
Total cost	1500	1500	2500	6000	7000	4000
Total fixed cost	500	500	200	1500	1500	1500

3. The Smythe chicken farm outside of Little Rock, Arkansas, produces 25,000 chickens per month. Total cost of production at the Smythe farm is $28,000. Down the road are two other farms. The Faubus Farm produces 55,000 chickens a month and total cost is $50,050. Mega Farm produces 100,000 chickens per month at a total cost of $91,000. These data suggest that there are significant economies of scale in chicken production. Do you agree or disagree with this statement? Explain your answer.

4. Consider an industry that exhibits external diseconomies of scale in the long run. Suppose that over the next ten years demand for that industry's product increases rapidly. Describe in detail the adjustments likely to follow. Use diagrams in your answer.

5. A representative firm producing cloth is earning a short-run profit at a price of $10 per yard. Draw a supply and demand diagram showing equilibrium at this price. Assuming that the industry is a constant-cost industry, use the diagram to show the long-term adjustment of the industry and the firm as demand increases through time. Explain the adjustment mechanism.

6. Consider Adam, a baker of apple pies. To make one pie, Adam uses one hour of labor and one pound of apples. He bakes the pies in an oven that he leases for $100 per day. The hourly wage that Adam pays is $5, and each pound of apples costs $2. Assume that Adam has only one oven available, and that he can bake a maximum of 50 apple pies in one day.

a. What are Adam's fixed costs? Variable costs? Total costs? (Express these as a function of q, the number of apple pies.)

b. Determine and graph average variable cost, average fixed cost, average total cost, and marginal cost.

c. Suppose that the market for apple pies is perfectly competitive. Adam can therefore sell all the pies he wants in one day for $8 each. How many apple pies should Adam produce per day in the short run? What will his profits or losses be?

d. At a price of $8, how many pies should Adam produce in the long run? Explain your answer.

e. What is the minimum price necessary for Adam to operate in the short run? In the long run?

7. Do you agree or disagree with the following statements? Explain why in a sentence or two.

a. A firm will never sell its product for less than it costs to produce it.

b. If the short-run marginal cost curve is U-shaped, the long-run average cost curve is likely to be U-shaped as well.

c. Input prices are assumed to be fixed in deriving the long-run supply curve for a competitive industry.

Input Demand: The Labor and Land Markets

10

INPUT MARKETS
    Basic Concepts
    A Firm Using Only One Variable Factor of
        Production: Labor
    A Firm Employing Two Variable Factors of
        Production
    Land Markets and Pure Rent
    The Firm's Profit-Maximization Condition in
        Input Markets

INPUT DEMAND CURVES
    Shifts in Factor Demand Curves
    Elasticity of Demand in Input Markets

RESOURCE ALLOCATION AND THE MIX OF
   OUTPUT IN COMPETITIVE MARKETS

LOOKING AHEAD

As we have seen, all business firms must make three fundamental decisions: (1) how much to produce and supply in output markets; (2) how to produce that output, that is, which technology to use; and (3) how much of each input to demand. So far, our discussion of firm behavior has focused on the first two questions. In Chapters 7–9, we explained how profit-maximizing firms choose among alternative technologies and decide how much to supply in *output* markets.

We now turn to the behavior of firms in perfectly competitive *input* markets (highlighted in Figure 10.1), going behind input demand curves in much the same way that we went behind output supply curves in the previous two chapters. When we look behind input demand curves, we discover the exact same set of decisions that we saw when we analyzed output supply curves. In a very real sense, we have already talked about everything covered in this chapter. It is the *perspective* that is new.

The three main inputs are labor, land, and capital. Transactions in the labor and land markets are fairly straightforward. In the labor market, households sell labor directly to firms in exchange for wages. In the land market, landowners sell or rent land directly to others. The capital market is more complex, however. To

FIGURE 10.1

Firm and Household
Decisions

Firms and households interact in
both input and output markets.
This chapter highlights firm
choices in input markets.

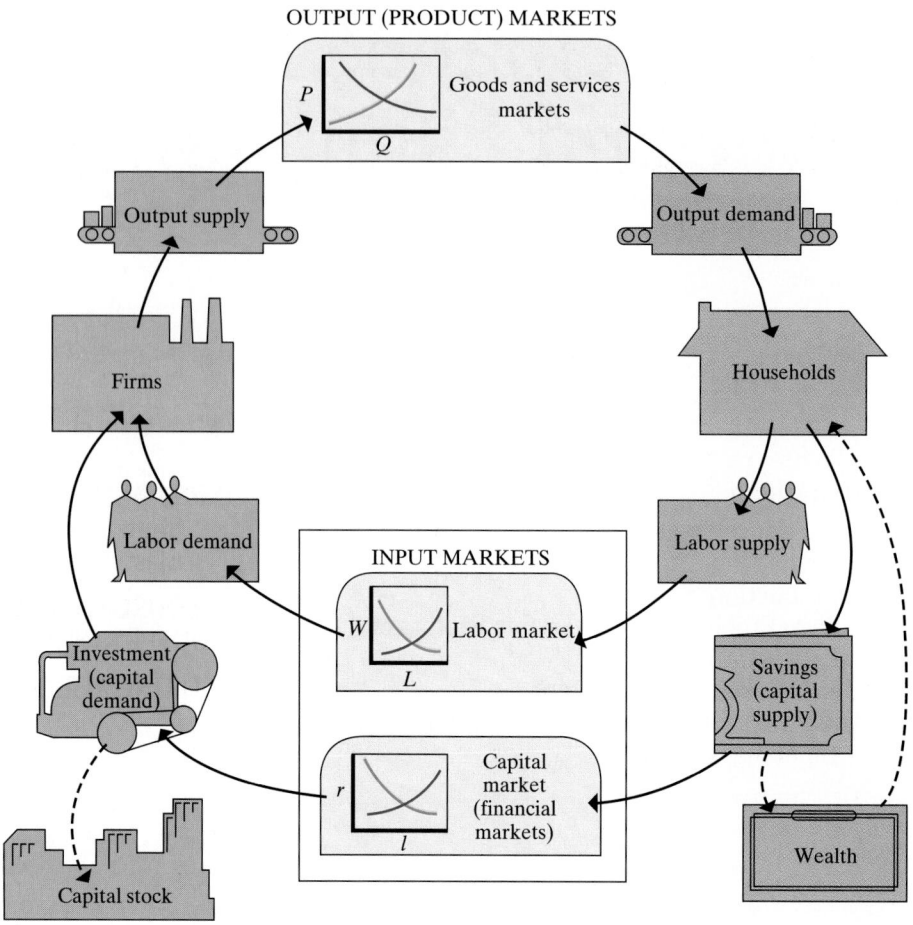

buy a capital asset—a machine, for example—a firm must use funds that it obtains
from households. The firm must then pay interest to the households for the use
of the funds. In a sense, then, households supply capital, just as they supply labor.
This chapter discusses input markets in general, while the next chapter focuses on
the capital market in some detail.

INPUT MARKETS

Before we begin our discussion of input markets, it will be helpful to establish
some basic concepts.

Basic Concepts

Four of the most important concepts in input markets are derived demand, complementary and substitutable inputs, diminishing returns, and marginal revenue product.

DEMAND FOR INPUTS: A *DERIVED DEMAND* A firm cannot make a profit unless there
is a demand for its product. Households must be willing to pay for the firm's output.
The quantity of output that a firm produces in both the long run and the short run
thus depends on the value that the market places on the firm's product. Because the

demand for inputs depends on the demand for outputs, input demand is really a **derived demand.** The key point you should take away from this chapter is that:

> The value of any input—labor, land, or capital—depends on how society values the things (outputs) that it produces. The price of any factor of production (input) in competitive markets depends on the value of its product.

derived demand The demand for resources (inputs) that is dependent on the demand for the outputs those resources can be used to produce.

The value attached to a product and the inputs needed to produce that product define the productivity of the inputs. Formally, the **productivity of an input** is the amount of output produced per unit of that input. When a large amount of output is produced per unit of an input, the input is said to be *highly productive.* When only a small amount of output is produced per unit of the input, the input is said to exhibit *low productivity.*

productivity of an input The amount of output produced per unit of the input.

Prices in competitive input markets depend on demand for inputs by firms, supply of inputs by households, and the interaction between the two. In the labor market, for example, households must decide whether to work and, if so, how much to work. In Chapter 6 we saw that the opportunity cost of working for a wage is either leisure or the value derived from unpaid labor—working in the garden, for instance, or raising children. In general, firms will demand workers as long as the value of what those workers produce exceeds what they must be paid. Households will supply labor as long as the wage they receive exceeds the value of leisure or the value that they derive from nonpaid work.

INPUTS: COMPLEMENTARY AND SUBSTITUTABLE   A major theme of this chapter is that inputs can be either **complementary** or **substitutable.** Two inputs used together may enhance, or complement, each other. A new machine that raises the productivity of labor may not be any good without someone to run it. Machines can also be substituted for labor, or—less often perhaps—labor can be substituted for machines.

complementary and substitutable inputs Factors of production that can be used together to enhance each other are *complementary inputs.* Factors of production that can be used in place of each other are *substitutable inputs.*

All this means that a firm's input demands are tightly linked to one another. An increase or decrease in wages naturally causes the demand for labor to change, but it may also have an effect on the demand for capital or land. If we are to understand the demand for inputs, therefore, we must understand the connections among labor, capital, and land.

DIMINISHING RETURNS   Recall that we defined the short run as that period during which some fixed factor of production limits a firm's capacity to expand. Under these conditions, the firm that decides to increase output will eventually encounter *diminishing returns.* Stated more formally, a fixed scale of plant means that the marginal product of variable inputs eventually declines. Recall also that **marginal product of labor (MP_L)** is the additional output that is produced if a firm hires one additional unit of labor. For example, if a firm pays for 400 hours of labor per week—10 workers working 40 hours each—and asks one worker to stay an extra hour, the product of the 401st hour is the *marginal product of labor* for that firm.

marginal product of labor (MP_L) The additional output produced by one additional unit of labor.

In Chapter 7, we talked at some length about declining marginal product at a sandwich shop. The first two columns of Table 10.1 reproduce some of the production data from that shop. You may remember that the shop has only one grill, at which only two or three people can work comfortably. In this example, the grill is the fixed factor of production in the short run and labor is the variable factor. The first worker can produce 10 sandwiches per hour, and the second can produce

(1) TOTAL LABOR UNITS (EMPLOYEES)	(2) TOTAL PRODUCT (SANDWICHES PER HOUR)	(3) MARGINAL PRODUCT OF LABOR (MP_L) (SANDWICHES PER HOUR)	(4) PRICE (P_X) (VALUE ADDED PER SANDWICH)*	(5) MARGINAL REVENUE PRODUCT ($MP_L \times P_X$) (PER HOUR)
0	0	—	—	—
1	10	10	$.50	$5.00
2	25	15	.50	7.50
3	35	10	.50	5.00
4	40	5	.50	2.50
5	42	2	.50	1.00
6	42	0	.50	0

*The "price" is essentially profit per sandwich; see discussion in text.

TABLE 10.1
Marginal Revenue Product per Hour of Labor in Sandwich Production (One Grill)

marginal revenue product
(MRP) The additional revenue a firm earns by employing one additional unit of input, *ceteris paribus*.

15 (see column 3 of Table 10.1). The second worker can produce more because the first is busy answering the phone and taking care of customers, as well as making sandwiches. After the second worker, however, marginal product declines; the third worker adds only 10 sandwiches per hour, because the grill gets crowded. The fourth worker can squeeze in quickly while the others are serving or wrapping, but adds only 5 additional sandwiches each hour, and so forth.[1]

In this case, the capacity of the grill ultimately limits output. To see how the firm might make a rational choice about how many workers to hire, we need to know more about the value of the firm's product and the cost of labor.

MARGINAL REVENUE PRODUCT   The **marginal revenue product (MRP)** of a variable input is the additional revenue a firm earns by employing one additional unit of that input, *ceteris paribus*. If labor is the variable factor, for example, hiring an additional unit will lead to added output (the marginal product of labor). The sale of that added output will yield revenue. Marginal revenue product is the revenue that is produced by selling the good or service that is produced by the marginal unit of labor. In a competitive firm, marginal revenue product is the value of a factor's marginal product.

Using labor as our variable factor, we can state this proposition more formally by saying that if MP_L is the marginal product of labor and P_X is the price of output, then the marginal revenue product of labor is:

$$MRP_L = MP_L \times P_X.$$

When calculating marginal revenue product, we need to be very precise about what is being produced. A sandwich shop, to be sure, sells sandwiches, but it does not produce the bread, meat, cheese, mustard, and mayo that go into the sandwiches. What the shop is producing is "sandwich cooking and assembly services." The shop is "adding value" to the meat, bread, and other ingredients by preparing and putting it all together in ready-to-eat form. With this in mind, let's assume that each finished sandwich in our shop sells for $.50 over and above the costs of its ingredients. Thus, the value of the service the shop is selling is $.50 per sandwich, and the only variable cost of providing that service is that of the labor used to put the sandwiches together. Thus, if X is the product of our shop, $P_X = \$.50$.

[1]As we said in Chapter 7, we assume that all workers are equally skilled and motivated. The third worker is no less hard working or skilled than the first two. Rather, the grill is getting crowded. Put another way, *the capital constraint is binding*.

Table 10.1, column 5, calculates the marginal revenue product of each worker if the shop charges $.50 per sandwich over and above the costs of its ingredients. The first worker produces 10 sandwiches per hour which, at $0.50 each, generates revenues of $5 per hour. The addition of a second worker yields $7.50 an hour in revenues. After the second worker, diminishing returns drive MRP_L down. The marginal revenue product of the third worker is $5 per hour; for the fourth worker, only $2.50, and so forth.

A Firm Using Only One Variable Factor of Production: Labor

Demand for an input depends on the marginal revenue product of that input and its unit cost, or price. The price of labor, for example, is the wage that is determined in the labor market. (At this point we are continuing to assume that the sandwich shop uses only one variable factor of production—labor. Remember that competitive firms are price-takers in both output and input markets. Such firms can hire all the labor they want to hire as long as they pay the market wage.) We can think of the hourly wage at the sandwich shop, then, as the marginal cost of a unit of labor.

All this implies that:

> A profit-maximizing firm will add inputs—in the case of labor, it will hire workers— as long as the marginal revenue product of that input exceeds its market price.

Look again at the figures for the sandwich shop in Table 10.1, column 5, and then suppose that the going wage for sandwich makers is $4 per hour. A profit-maximizing firm would hire three workers. The first worker would yield $5 per hour in revenues and the second would yield $7.50, but they would cost only $4 each per hour. The third worker would bring in $5 per hour, but still cost only $4 in marginal wages. The marginal product of the fourth worker ($2.50), however, would not bring in enough revenue to pay his salary. Total profit is thus maximized by hiring three workers.

Figure 10.2 presents this same information graphically. The labor market appears in Figure 10.2a; Figure 10.2b shows a single firm that employs workers. This firm, incidentally, does not represent just the firms in a single industry. Because firms in many different industries demand labor, the representative firm in Figure 10.2b represents any firm in any industry that uses labor.

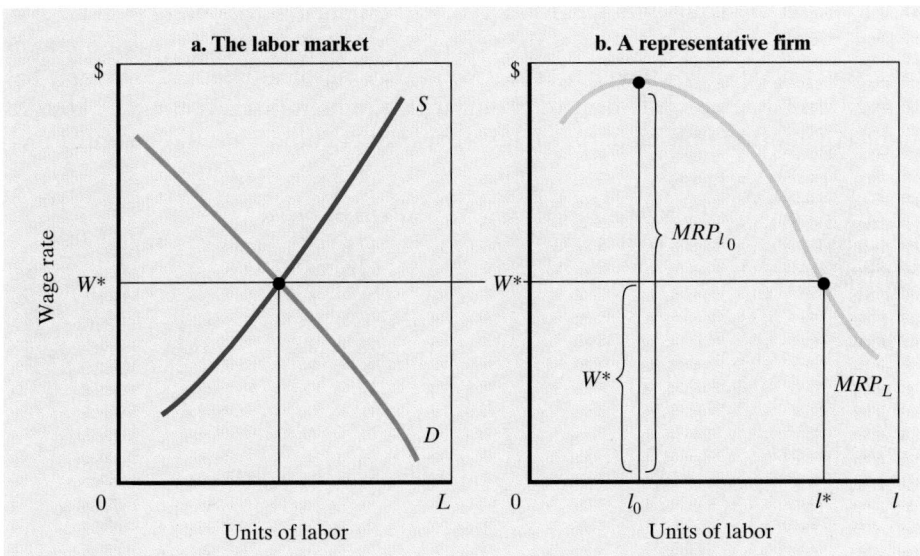

FIGURE 10.2
Marginal Revenue Product and Factor Demand for a Firm Using One Variable Input (Labor)

A competitive firm using only one variable factor of production will use that factor as long as its marginal revenue product exceeds its unit cost. A perfectly competitive firm will hire labor as long as MRP_L is greater than the going wage, W^*. The hypothetical firm will demand l^* units of labor.

The firm faces a market wage rate of W^*. We can think of this as the marginal cost of a unit of labor. (Note that we are now discussing the margin in units of *labor;* in previous chapters, we talked about marginal units of *output.*) Given W^*, how much labor would the firm demand?

One might think that l_0 units would be hired, the point at which the difference between marginal revenue product and wage rate is greatest. But the firm is interested in maximizing total profit, not marginal profit. At l_0, hiring one more unit of labor generates revenue equal to MRP_{l_0} at a cost of only W^*. Because MRP_L is greater than the cost of the input required to produce it, producing one more unit adds to profit. This will continue to be true as long as MRP_L remains above W^*, which is all the way to l^*. At that point, the wage rate is equal to the marginal revenue product of labor, or

$$W^* = MRP_L.$$

The firm will not demand labor beyond l^*, because the cost of hiring the *next* unit of labor after l^* would be greater than the value of what that unit produces. (Recall that the fourth sandwich maker can produce only an extra $2.50 an hour in sandwiches, while his salary is $4 per hour.)

Thus the curve in Figure 10.2b tells us how much labor a firm that uses only one variable factor of production will hire at each potential market wage rate. This description should sound familiar to you—it is, in fact, the description of a demand curve. Therefore we can now say that:

> When a firm uses only one variable factor of production, that factor's marginal revenue product curve is the firm's demand curve for that factor in the short run.

For another example of the relevance of marginal revenue product, see the Issues and Applications box entitled, "Millionaire Baseball Players and Their Marginal Revenue Product."

COMPARING MARGINAL REVENUE PRODUCT AND MARGINAL COST TO MAXIMIZE PROFITS   In Chapter 8, we saw that the marginal cost curve of a competitive firm is the same as its supply curve. That is, at any output price, the marginal cost curve determines how much output a profit-maximizing firm will produce. We came to this conclusion by comparing the marginal revenue that a firm would earn by producing one more unit of output with the marginal cost of producing that unit of output.

There is no difference between the reasoning in Chapter 8 and the reasoning in this chapter. The only difference is that what is being measured at the margin has changed. In Chapter 8, the firm was comparing the marginal revenues and costs of producing another unit of output. Here, the firm is comparing the marginal rev-

FIGURE 10.3

The Two Profit-Maximizing Conditions Are Simply Two Views of the Same Choice Process

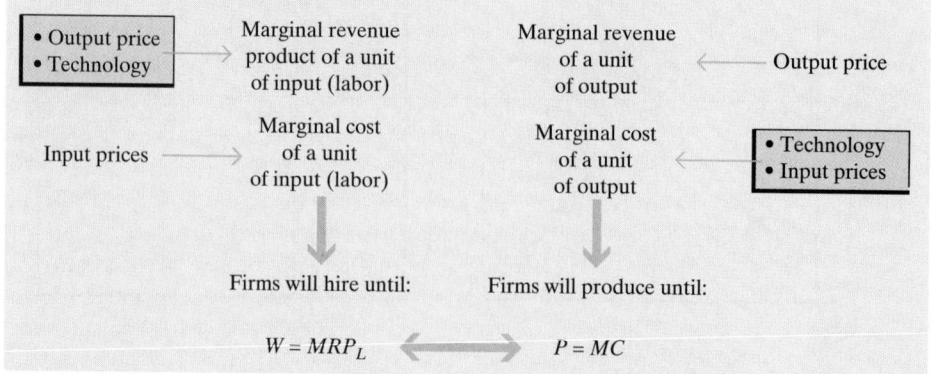

MILLIONAIRE BASEBALL PLAYERS AND THEIR MARGINAL REVENUE PRODUCT

Consider the following article which appeared in the *New York Times* on August 25, 1992:

Cal Ripken Jr., the Baltimore Orioles' remarkable shortstop, who hasn't missed a game in more than 10 years, signed the second most lucrative contract in baseball history yesterday, agreeing to a five-year deal for $30.5 million. The average annual value of $6.1 million is surpassed only by the $7.1 million average of Ryne Sandberg's contract extension that takes effect next year....

The Ripken contract bumps Bobby Bonilla's $5.8 million average with the Mets to third on the salary list. Jack Morris of Toronto, at $5,425,000 and Roger Clemens of Boston, at $5,380,250, round out the top five contract averages.*

How in the world could anyone be worth $6 million per year? Why would owners be willing to pay millions of dollars a year to a single player? As we've seen in this chapter, profit-maximizing employers will hire workers only as long as their marginal revenue product (MRP_L) is greater than or equal to their wage. Could it then be possible that Cal Ripken is "worth it"?

Gerald W. Scully, Professor of Management at the University of Texas at Dallas, has made a statistical estimate of the contribution that ballplayers made to the revenues of their teams during the 1980s. The results may surprise you:

"[In 1984]...an extra victory was worth $195,653. Now consider the effect on revenues of adding a hitter like Andre

The Baltimore Orioles' Cal Ripken Jr. recently signed a five-year contract for $30.5 million. Could it be that Ripken's marginal revenue product is greater than $6 million per year?

Dawson, the National League MVP of 1987, or a pitcher like Roger Clemens, the Cy Young Award winner in the American League in 1986. Dawson had a slugging average of .568 over 621 at bats. Chicago had a team slugging average of .432 over 5,583 at bats. Dawson contributed 11.1 percent of the at-bats and 0.63 of the team's slugging average. Given the relationship between slugging average and wins, those 63 points were conservatively worth 11 games. The marginal revenue [product] of those 11 games

was about $2.2 million. Roger Clemens posted a 24-4 record in Boston in 1986. Assuming that Clemens was the source of the margin of victory in those net 20 games, his performance was worth $3.9 million [in 1986].... By such economic standards such players are not overpaid."†

---

*"Ripken-Oriole Love Story Knotted by $30.5 million," New York Times, August 25, 1992.

†Gerald W. Scully, The Business of Major League Baseball (Chicago: University of Chicago Press, 1989), 155–156.

enues and costs of employing another unit of input. To see this similarity, look at Figure 10.3. (You may also find it helpful to compare Figure 10.2 with Figure 8.10). If the only variable factor of production is labor, the condition $W = MRP_L$ is the same condition as $P = MC$. The two statements say exactly the same thing.

In both cases, the firm is comparing the cost of production with potential revenues from the sale of product at the margin. In Chapter 8, the firm compared the price of output (P, which is equal to MR in perfect competition) directly with cost of production (MC), where cost was derived from information on factor prices and technology. (Review the derivation of cost curves if this is unclear.) Here, information on output price and technology is contained in the marginal revenue product curve, which is compared with information on input price to determine the optimal level of input to demand. This means that firms make *simultaneous* decisions about how much output to supply and how much of each input to demand.

The assumption of one variable factor of production makes the trade-off facing firms easy to see. Figure 10.4 shows that in essence firms weigh the value of labor as reflected in the market wage against the value of the product of labor as reflected in the price of output:

> Assuming that labor is the only variable input, if society values a good more than it costs firms to hire the workers to produce that good, the good will be produced. In general, the same logic also holds for more than one input. Firms weigh the value of outputs as reflected in output price against the value of inputs as reflected in marginal costs.

DERIVING INPUT DEMANDS   For the small sandwich shop, calculating the marginal product of a variable input (labor) and marginal revenue product was easy. Although it may be more complex, the decision process is essentially the same both for big corporations and for small proprietorships.

When an airline hires more flight attendants, for example, it increases the quality of its service to attract more passengers and thus sell more of its product. Flight attendants must be paid a wage, however. In deciding how many to hire, the firm must figure out how much new revenue the added flight attendants are likely to generate relative to their wages.

At the sandwich shop, diminishing returns set in at a certain point. The same holds true for an airplane. Once a sufficient number of attendants are on a plane, marginal additions add little to the quality of service, and the marginal product of each additional attendant diminishes. Like the grill, the airplane has a fixed physical capacity, and the addition of a variable factor beyond a certain level might even give rise to negative marginal product. Too many attendants could bother the passengers and make it difficult to get to the restrooms.

In making your own decisions, you too compare marginal gains with input costs in the presence of diminishing returns. Suppose you grow vegetables in your yard. You do this for a number of reasons. First, you save money at the grocery

FIGURE 10.4

The Trade-Off Facing Firms

Firms weigh the cost of labor as reflected in wage rates against the value of labor's marginal product. Assuming labor is the only variable factor of production, if society values a good more than it costs firms to hire the workers to produce that good, the good will be produced.

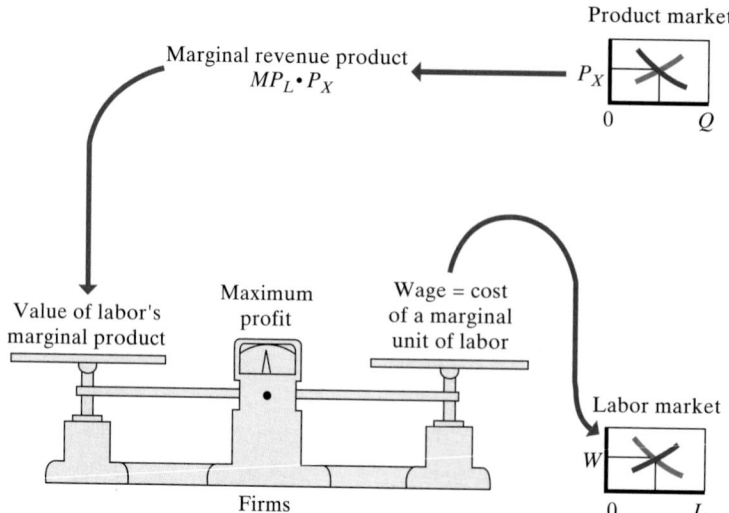

store—vegetables are an output with a measurable monetary value. Second, you can plant what you like, and the vegetables taste better fresh from the garden. Third, you simply like to work in the garden—you get sun, exercise, and fresh air.

Like the sandwich shop and the airline, you also face diminishing returns. You have only 625 square feet of garden to work with, and with land as a fixed factor in the short run, your marginal product will certainly decline. You can work all day every day, but your limited space will produce only so many string beans. The first few hours you spend each week watering, fertilizing, and dealing with major weed and bug infestations probably have a high marginal product. But after five or six hours, there is little else you can do to increase yield. Diminishing returns also apply to your sense of satisfaction. The farmers' markets are now full of cheap fresh produce that tastes nearly as good as yours. And once you have been out in the garden for a few hours, the hot sun and hard work start to lose their charm and the earth under your fingernails gives way to the less gritty pleasure of watching a baseball game on TV.

Although your gardening does not involve a salary (unlike the sandwich shop and the airline, which pay out wages), the labor you supply has a value that must be weighed, even if the cost of a unit of your labor is only the value you could derive by using that time doing something else, such as watching TV. When the returns from gardening diminish beyond a certain point, you must weigh the value of additional gardening time against leisure and the other options available to you.

It is as true for the sandwich shop as for you that less labor is likely to be employed as the cost of labor rises. If the competitive labor market pushed the daily wage to $6 per hour, the sandwich shop would hire only two workers instead of three (see Table 10.1). If you suddenly became very busy at school, your time would become more valuable and you would probably devote fewer hours to gardening.

A Firm Employing Two Variable Factors of Production

When a firm employs more than one variable factor of production, the analysis of input demand becomes more complicated, but the principles stay the same. We shall now consider a firm that employs variable capital (K) and labor (L) inputs, and thus faces factor prices P_K and P_L.[2] (Recall that *capital* refers to plant, equipment, and inventory used in production. We assume that some portion of the firm's capital stock is fixed in the short run, but that some of it is variable—for example, some machinery and equipment can be installed quickly.) Our analysis can be applied to any two factors of production and can easily be generalized to three or more. It can also be applied to the long run, when all factors of production are variable.

You have seen that inputs can be either complementary or substitutable. Land, labor, and capital are used *together* to produce outputs. The worker who uses a shovel digs a bigger hole than one with no shovel; add a steam shovel and that worker becomes even more productive. When an expanding firm adds to its stock of capital, it raises the productivity of its labor, and vice versa. Thus, each factor complements the other. At the same time, of course, land, labor, and capital can also be substituted for one another. If labor becomes expensive, some labor-saving technology may take its place.

In firms employing just one variable factor of production, a change in the price of that factor affects only the demand for the factor itself. When more than one factor can vary, however, we must consider the impact of a change in one factor price on the demand for other factors as well.

---

[2]The price of labor, P_L, is the same as the wage rate W. We will often use the term "P_L" instead of W to stress the symmetry between labor and capital.

TABLE 10.2
Response of a Firm to an Increasing Wage Rate

TECHNOLOGY	INPUT REQUIREMENTS PER UNIT OF OUTPUT		UNIT COST IF $P_L = \$1$ $P_K = \$1$ $(P_L \bullet L + P_K \bullet K)$	UNIT COST IF $P_L = \$2$ $P_K = \$1$ $(P_L \bullet L + P_K \bullet K)$
	K	**L**		
A (capital intensive)	10	5	$15	$20
B (labor intensive)	3	10	$13	$23

SUBSTITUTION AND OUTPUT EFFECTS OF A CHANGE IN FACTOR PRICE   Table 10.2 presents data on a hypothetical firm that employs variable capital and labor. Suppose that the firm faces a choice between two available technologies of production—technique A, which is capital intensive, and technique B, which is labor intensive. When the market price of labor is $1 per unit and the market price of capital is $1 per unit, the labor-intensive method of producing output is less costly. Each unit costs only $13 to produce using technique B, while the unit cost of production using technique A is $15. If the price of labor rises to $2, however, technique B is no longer less costly. Labor has become more expensive relative to capital. The unit cost rises to $23 for labor-intensive technique B, but to only $20 for capital-intensive technique A.

Table 10.3 shows the impact of such an increase in the price of labor on both capital and labor demand when a firm produces 100 units of output. When each input factor costs $1 per unit, the firm chooses technique B and demands 300 units of capital and 1,000 units of labor. Total variable cost is $1300. An increase in the price of labor to $2 causes the firm to switch from technique B to technique A. In doing so, it *substitutes* capital for labor. The amount of labor demanded drops from 1,000 to 500 units; the amount of capital demanded increases from 300 to 1,000 units, while total variable cost increases to $2,000.

The tendency of firms to substitute away from a factor whose price has risen and toward a factor whose price has fallen is called the **factor substitution effect.** The factor substitution effect is part of the reason that *input demand curves slope downward.* When an input, or factor of production, becomes less expensive, firms tend to substitute it for other factors and thus buy *more* of it. When a particular input becomes more expensive, however, firms tend to substitute other factors and buy *less* of it. When energy prices in the United States rose in 1990, for example, the country experienced a renewed emphasis on conservation. For some consumers, this meant the purchase of new insulation for their homes and smaller cars. Firms, as well as private citizens, tried to substitute capital for energy wherever they could.

factor substitution effect The tendency of firms to substitute away from a factor whose price has risen and toward a factor whose price has fallen.

TABLE 10.3
The Substitution Effect of an Increase in Wages on a Firm Producing 100 Units of Output

	TO PRODUCE 100 UNITS OF OUTPUT:		
	TOTAL CAPITAL DEMANDED	**TOTAL LABOR DEMANDED**	**TOTAL VARIABLE COST**
When $P_L = \$1$, $P_K = \$1$, firm uses technology B.	300	1000	$1300
When $P_L = \$2$, $P_K = \$1$, firm uses technology A.	1000	500	$2000

The firm described in Tables 10.2 and 10.3 continued to produce 100 units of output after the wage rate doubled. An *increase* in the price of a production factor, however, also means an increase in the costs of production and therefore an upward shift in the firm's cost curves. Notice that total variable cost increased from $1300 to $2000. When a firm faces higher costs, it is likely to produce less in the short run. If you recall that the supply curve of a perfectly competitive firm is the same thing as its marginal cost curve (above the minimum point of *AVC*), you can see that when the marginal cost curve shifts upward, quantity supplied declines, as shown in Figure 10.5. When a firm decides to cut output, its demand for all factors declines, including, of course, the factor whose price increased in the first place. This is called the **output effect of a factor price increase.**[3]

A *decrease* in the price of a factor of production, on the other hand, means lower costs of production and therefore a downward shift in the firm's cost curves. If their output price remains unchanged, firms will increase output. This, in turn, means that demand for all factors of production will increase. This is the **output effect of a factor price decrease.**

The output effect also helps explain why input demand curves slope downward. Output effects and substitution effects almost always work in the same direction.[4] Consider, for example, a decline in the wage rate. Lower wages mean that a firm will substitute labor for capital and other inputs. Stated somewhat differently, the factor substitution effect leads to an increase in demand for labor. Lower wages mean lower costs, and lower costs lead to more output. This increase in output means that the firm will hire more of all factors of production, including labor itself. This is the output effect of a factor price decrease. Notice that both effects lead to an increase in the demand for labor when the wage rate falls. Figure 10.6 summarizes these output and substitution effects.

---

[3]It is certainly possible that a cut in output involving a major switch in the optimal technique of production will *increase* the demand for some input factor. When this happens, the factor in demand is called an *inferior factor*. For purposes of our discussion, however, we will assume that increases in output increase the demand for all factors, and that decreases in production decrease the demand for all factors.

[4]In the rare case of an inferior factor, they work against each other. Can you figure out why?

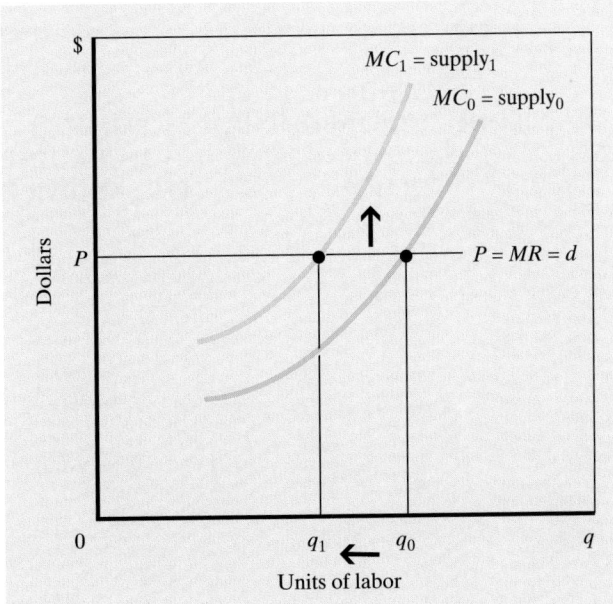

FIGURE 10.5
Decrease in Output from an Increase in Cost

Factor price increases raise the marginal cost of production at all output levels. Since a firm's marginal cost curve is also its supply curve, an increase in costs drives supply down. (Remember, perfectly competitive profit-maximizing firms produce at the point at which *P* [which is equal to *MR* in perfectly competitive firms] = *MC*.) Firms will produce less and as a result demand fewer inputs.

FIGURE 10.6

Summary of Output and Substitution Effects: Why Labor Demand Slopes Down

Input demand curves slope downward. When a factor price declines, firms tend to use more of it, and when a factor price increases, firms tend to use less of it. The actual change in quantity demanded is the sum of two effects: the output effect and the factor substitution effect.

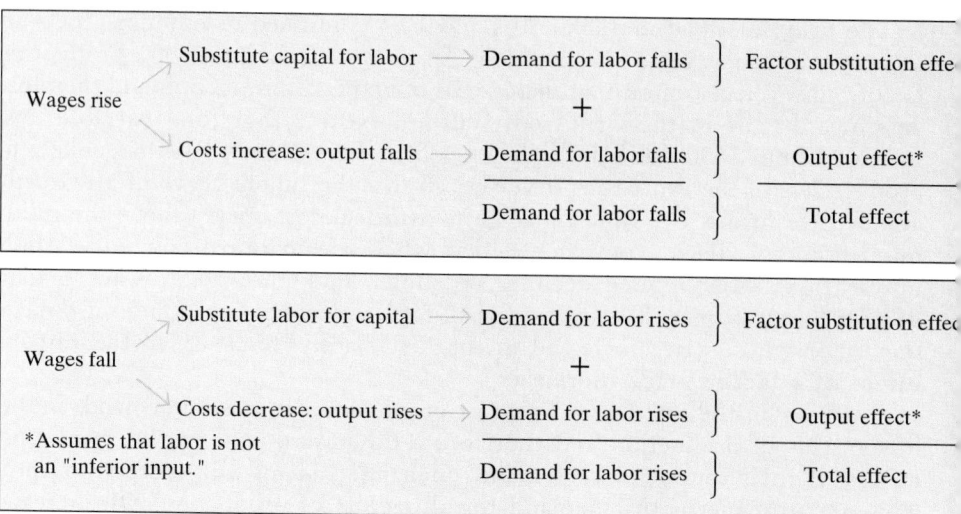

DERIVING AN INPUT DEMAND CURVE WHEN TWO FACTORS OF PRODUCTION ARE VARIABLE   Deriving a firm's input demand curve is more complicated when two factors of production are variable than it is when just one factor varies. Let's return to our example of the sandwich shop once again. Table 10.1 listed the shop's marginal product and marginal revenue product schedules, assuming a fixed grill capacity. If the market wage for sandwich makers were $4 per hour, the shop would hire three workers, each of whom would generate more than $4 per hour in revenues. Only if the market wage rate fell below $2.50 per hour and labor were the only variable factor of production would the firm increase the amount of labor demanded from three to four units. (The marginal revenue product of the fourth worker, $2.50 per hour, would then exceed the new market wage.)

But now let's assume that grill capacity is also variable in the short run.[5] Suppose that a decline in wages reduces cost enough to warrant an expansion. The purchase of a second grill will raise the productivity of labor and shift the

TABLE 10.4

Marginal Revenue Product per Hour of Labor in Sandwich Production (Two Grills)

[5]We continue to assume that we are in the short run and that the capacity of the shop is fixed. But within that fixed capacity, the firm must choose whether to install a new grill or not.

(1) TOTAL LABOR UNITS	(2) TOTAL PRODUCT (SANDWICHES PER HOUR)	(3) MARGINAL PRODUCT OF LABOR (MP_L) (SANDWICHES PER HOUR)	(4) PRICE (P_X) (VALUE ADDED PER SANDWICH)	(5) MARGINAL REVENUE PRODUCT ($MP_L \times P_X$) ($ PER HOUR)
0	—	—	—	—
1	10	10	$.50	$5.00
2	25	15	.50	7.50
3	40	15	.50	7.50
4	55	15	.50	7.50
5	65	10	.50	5.00
6	75	10	.50	5.00
7	80	5	.50	2.50
8	85	5	.50	2.50
9	87	2	.50	1.00
10	89	2	.50	1.00
11	89	0	.50	0

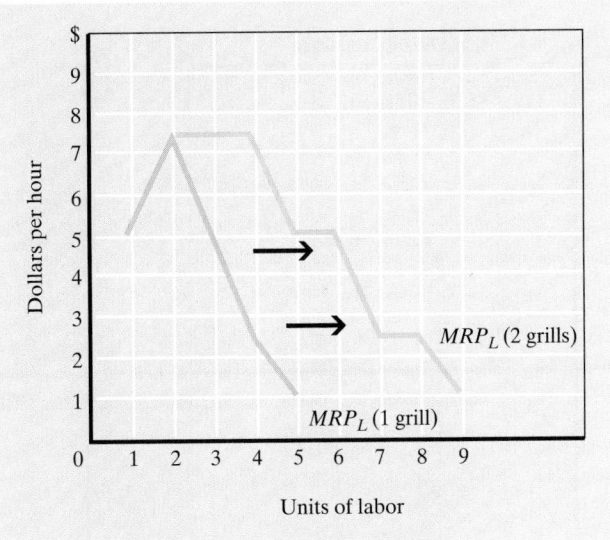

Expanding capacity by purchasing additional capital (a grill) increases the productivity of labor. The fifth worker added only $1 per hour to revenues with one grill. With two grills, the fifth worker brings in $5 per hour in revenue.

marginal revenue product curve out to the right. Earlier, when we discussed marginal revenue product as the additional revenue earned by hiring one additional unit of labor at the margin, *ceteris paribus,* we assumed that all other inputs (specifically, the grill capacity at the sandwich shop) remained constant. If we now change grill capacity, we get a new MRP_L schedule.

Consider the productivity of labor with two grills. Table 10.4 shows the marginal product and marginal revenue product of labor at a sandwich shop that has two grills. We know that two workers can fit comfortably at each grill. As column 3 shows, the first worker can produce 10 sandwiches per hour and the next three workers can each produce 15. When there was only one grill, the marginal product of the fifth worker was just 2 sandwiches (see Table 10.1), but when there is a second grill her productivity increases to 10 sandwiches. She is now the third worker on one of the grills (that is, the fifth or sixth worker hired).

Marginal revenue product also increases with the addition of a second grill. As column 5 of Table 10.4 shows, the MRP_L of the second, third, and fourth workers is now $7.50 per hour each. The fifth adds revenues of $5 per hour instead of just $1, and so on down the line. Figure 10.7 shows how the addition of new capital shifts the marginal revenue product curve of labor to the right. With the new grill in place, a wage rate of $4 per hour means that the shop can hire six workers instead of just three. The marginal revenue product of the sixth worker is $5 per hour, still above that worker's price of $4 per hour. The shop will draw the line at the seventh worker, whose MRP_L is only $2.50.

Figure 10.8 on the next page shows the typical response of a firm to a decline in the market wage. At the outset, the market is in equilibrium, with supply and demand equal at W_0 and the firm operating with a capital stock K_1. At the initial wage, the firm will hire as long as the marginal revenue product of labor exceeds the wage rate. The profit-maximizing level of labor demand is l_0 (the point at which $W_0 = MRP_L$).

Given these conditions, let us now assume that a sudden influx of "guest workers" from a neighboring region increases the supply of labor from S_0 to S_1 and drives down the wage rate in the labor market. The new lower wage, W_1, reduces the firm's costs. In response, the firm increases output and decides to purchase more variable capital. Just as the new grill did for the sandwich shop, the new capital increases the productivity of labor and shifts the marginal revenue product curve out to the right.

FIGURE 10.8
Factor Demand for a
Firm Employing Two
Variable Factors of
Production (Capital
and Labor)

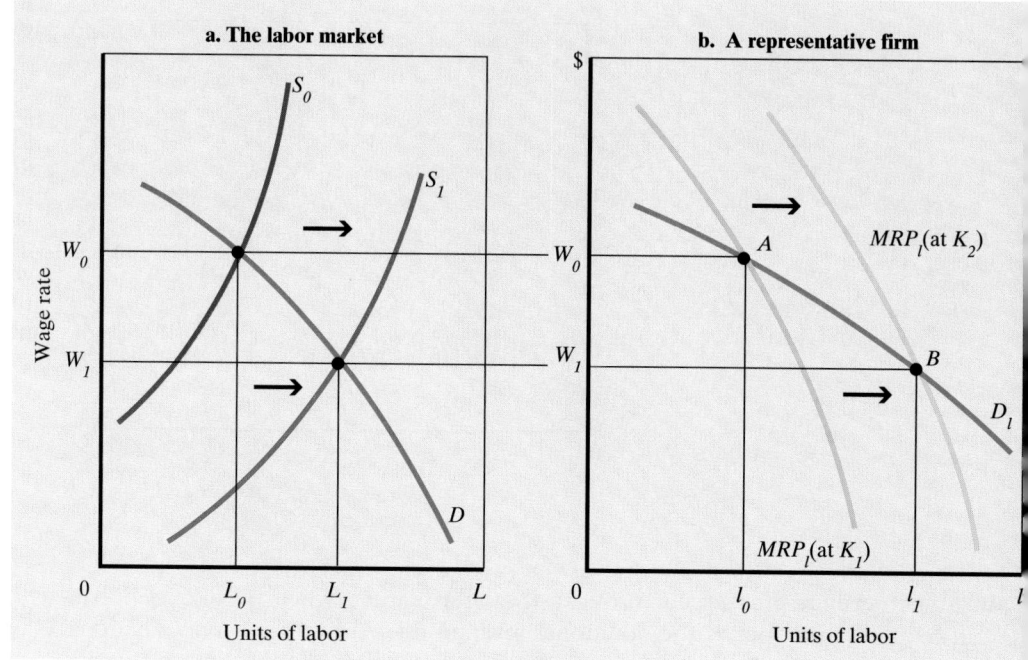

a. The labor market

b. A representative firm

The new marginal revenue product curve is labeled MRP_L (at K_2) in Figure 10.8b. With the new capital in place, the firm now hires labor up to l_1. At that point, the new wage is equal to the new MRP_L. At a wage of W_0, the quantity of labor demanded is l_0; at a wage of W_1, the quantity of labor demanded is l_1. Continuing with this logic, we can conclude that:

The demand-for-labor curve is the line connecting all points such as A and B in Figure 10.8b. A competitive profit-maximizing firm will hire labor until $W = MRP_L$.

This discussion is meant to illuminate two important points:

First, demand for any factor of production in a competitive industry depends upon its productivity and upon how its product is valued in the marketplace. Second, the productivity of any factor depends critically on the amount of other factors employed with it. The productivity of labor, for example, is enhanced when additional capital is used by a firm.

Land Markets and Pure Rent

Land, unlike labor and capital, has a special feature that we have not yet considered: It is in strictly fixed (perfectly inelastic) supply in total. The only real questions about land thus center around how much it is worth and to what use it will be put.

demand determined price The price of a good that is in fixed supply; it is determined exclusively by what firms and households are willing to pay for the good.

Because land is fixed in supply, we say that its price is **demand determined.** In other words, the price of land is determined exclusively by what households and firms are willing to pay for it. The return to any factor of production in fixed supply is called a **pure rent.**

pure rent The return to any factor of production that is in fixed supply.

Thinking of the price of land as demand determined can be confusing, however, because all land is not the same. Some land is clearly more valuable than other land. The value of a plot of land in an attractive part of Los Angeles near Beverly Hills is worth much more than the same size plot in the desert east of Los Angeles.

The price of an acre of prime Manhattan real estate is likely to be several hundred times that of an acre of land in a sleepy Wyoming town.

What lies behind these differences in land values? As with any other factor of production, land will presumably be sold or rented to the user who is willing to pay the most for it. The value of land to a potential user may depend upon the characteristics of the land itself or upon its location. For example, more fertile land should produce more farm products per acre and thus command a higher price than less fertile land. A piece of property located at the intersection of two highways may be of great value as a site for a gas station because of the amount of traffic that passes that intersection daily.

A numerical example may help to clarify our discussion. Consider the potential uses of a corner lot in a suburb of Kansas City. Alan wants to build a clothing store on the lot. He anticipates that he can earn economic profits of $10,000 per year there because of the land's excellent location. Bella, another person interested in buying the corner lot, believes that she can earn $35,000 per year in economic profit if she builds a drug store there. Clearly, Bella will be able to outbid Alan, and the landowner will sell (or rent) to the highest bidder.

Because location is often the key to profits, landowners are frequently able to "squeeze" their renters. One of the most popular locations in the Boston area, for example, is Harvard Square. There are dozens of restaurants in and around the square, and most of them are full most of the time. Despite this seeming success, most Harvard Square restaurant owners are not getting rich. Why? Because they must pay very high rents on the location of their restaurants. A substantial portion of each restaurant's revenues goes to rent the land that (by virtue of its scarcity) is the key to unlocking those same revenues.

Although Figure 10.9 shows that the supply of land is perfectly inelastic (a vertical line), the supply of land in a *given use* may not be perfectly inelastic or fixed. Think, for example, about farmland and land available for housing developments. As the population of a city grows, housing developers find themselves willing to pay more and more for land. As land becomes more valuable for development, some farmers sell out, and the supply of land available for development increases. This analysis would lead us to draw an upward-sloping sup-

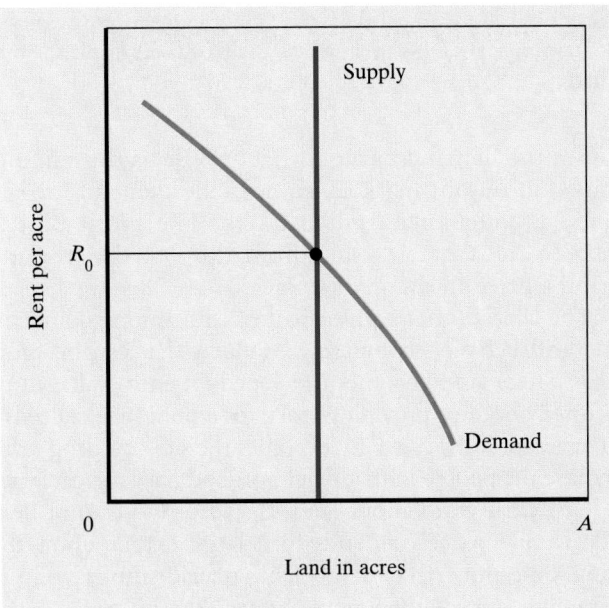

FIGURE 10.9
The Rent on Land Is Demand Determined

Because land in general (and each parcel in particular) is in fixed supply, its price is demand determined. Graphically, a fixed supply is represented by a vertical, perfectly inelastic, supply curve. Rent, R_0, depends exclusively on demand—what people are willing to pay.

ply curve (not a perfectly inelastic supply curve) for land in the land-for-development category.

Nonetheless, our major point—that land earns a pure rent—is still valid:

> The supply of land of a *given quality* at a *given location* is truly fixed in supply; its value is determined exclusively by the amount that the highest bidder is willing to pay for it. Since land cannot be reproduced, supply is perfectly inelastic.

RENT AND THE VALUE OF OUTPUT PRODUCED ON LAND   Because the price of land is demand determined, rent depends on what the potential users of the land are willing to pay for it. As we've seen, land will end up being used by whoever is willing to pay the most for it. But what determines willingness to pay? Let us now connect our discussion of land markets with our earlier discussions of factor markets in general.

As our example of two potential users bidding for a plot of land shows, the bids depend on the land's potential for profit. Alan's plan would generate $10,000 a year; Bella's would generate $35,000 a year. But these profits do not just materialize. Rather, they come from producing and selling an output that is valuable to households. Land in a popular downtown location is expensive because of what can be produced on it. Note that land is needed as an input into the production of nearly all goods and services. A restaurant located next to a popular theater can charge a premium price because it has a relatively captive clientele. Clearly, the restaurant must produce a quality product to stay in business, but the location alone provides a substantial profit opportunity.

It should come as no surprise to you that the demand for land follows the same rules as the demand for inputs in general. Recall that a profit-maximizing firm will employ an additional factor of production as long as its marginal revenue product exceeds its market price. For example, a profit-maximizing firm will hire labor as long as the revenue earned from selling labor's product is sufficient to cover the cost of hiring additional labor—which for perfectly competitive firms equals the wage rate, W. The same thing is true for land:

> A firm will pay for and use land as long as the revenue earned from selling the product produced on that land is sufficient to cover the price of the land. Stated in equation form, this means that the firm will use land up to the point at which $MRP_A = P_A$, where A is land (acres).

Just as the demand curve for labor reflects the value of labor's product as determined in output markets, so does the demand for land depend on the value of land's product in output markets. The profitability of the restaurant located next to the theater results from the fact that the meals produced there command a price in the marketplace.

The allocation of a given plot of land among competing uses thus depends on the trade-off between competing products that can be produced on that plot of land. Agricultural land becomes developed when its value in producing housing or manufactured goods or providing space for a mini mall exceeds its value in producing crops; a corner lot in Kansas City becomes the site of a drug store rather than a clothing store because the people in that neighborhood have a greater need for a drug store.

One final word about land: Because land cannot be moved physically, the value of any one parcel depends to a large extent upon the uses to which adjoining parcels are put. A factory belching acrid smoke will probably reduce the value of adjoining land, while a new highway that increases accessibility may enhance it.

The Firm's Profit-Maximization Condition in Input Markets

Thus far we have discussed the labor and land markets in some detail. Although we will put off a detailed discussion of capital until the next chapter, it is now possible to generalize about competitive demand for factors of production. As we've seen, every firm has an incentive to use variable inputs as long as the revenue generated by those inputs covers the costs of those inputs at the margin. More formally, firms will employ each input up to the point that its price equals its marginal revenue product. This condition holds for *all* factors at *all* levels of output:

Profit-Maximizing Condition for the Perfectly Competitive Firm:	$P_L = MRP_L = (MP_L \cdot P_X)$ $P_K = MRP_K = (MP_K \cdot P_X)$ $P_A = MRP_A = (MP_A \cdot P_X)$

where L is labor, K is capital, A is land (acres), X is output, and P_X is the price of that output.

When all these conditions are met, the firm will be using the optimal, or least costly, combination of inputs. Also, if all these conditions hold at the same time, it is possible to rewrite them in another way. Rewriting the first condition:

$$P_L = MRP_L$$
$$P_L = MP_L \times P_X.$$

By dividing both sides by PL and then by P_X, we get:

$$\frac{MP_L}{P_L} = \frac{1}{P_X}.$$

Similarly, $\dfrac{1}{P_X} = \dfrac{MP_K}{P_K}$ and $\dfrac{1}{P_X} = \dfrac{MP_A}{P_A}$. It therefore follows that

$$\frac{MP_L}{P_L} = \frac{MP_K}{P_K} = \frac{MP_A}{P_A}.$$

Your intuition tells you much the same thing that these equations do: The marginal product of the last dollar spent on capital must be equal to the marginal product of the last dollar spent on labor, which must be equal to the marginal product of the last dollar spent on land, and so forth. If this were not the case, the firm could produce more with less and reduce cost. Suppose, for example, that

$$\frac{MP_L}{P_L} > \frac{MP_K}{P_K}.$$

In this situation, the firm can produce more output by shifting dollars out of capital and into labor. Hiring more labor drives down the marginal product of labor, and using less capital increases the marginal product of capital. This means that the ratios come back to equality as the firm shifts out of capital and into labor.

So far we have used very general terms to discuss the nature of input demand by firms in competitive markets, where input prices and output prices are taken as given. The most important point here is that demand for a factor depends on the value that the market places on its marginal product.[6] The rest of this chapter explores the forces that determine the shapes and positions of input demand curves.

---

[6]If you worked through the appendix to Chapter 7, you saw this same condition derived graphically from an isocost/isoquant diagram. Note: $\dfrac{MP_L}{P_L} = \dfrac{MP_K}{P_K} \rightarrow \dfrac{MP_L}{MP_K} = \dfrac{P_L}{P_K}$

INPUT DEMAND CURVES

When we discussed supply and demand in Chapter 5, we spent a good deal of time talking about the factors that influence the responsiveness, or elasticity, of output demand curves. We have not talked about *input* demand curves in any detail, however, and we now need to say more about what lies behind them.

Shifts in Factor Demand Curves

Factor (input) demand curves are derived from information on technology (that is, production functions) and output price. A change in the demand for outputs, a change in the demand for complementary and substitutable inputs, changes in the prices of other inputs, and technological change can all cause factor demand curves to shift. These shifts in demand are important because they directly affect the allocation of resources among alternative uses, as well as the level and distribution of income.

THE DEMAND FOR OUTPUTS By now you know that a firm will demand an input as long as its marginal revenue product exceeds its market price. Marginal revenue product, which in perfect competition is equal to a factor's marginal product times the price of output, is the value of the factor's marginal product:

$$MRP_L = MP_L \times P_X.$$

The amount that a firm is willing to pay for a factor of production, then, depends directly on the value of the things that the firm produces. It follows that:

> If product demand increases, product price will rise and marginal revenue product (factor demand) will shift to the right. If product demand declines, product price will fall and marginal revenue product (factor demand) will shift to the left.

Go back and raise the price of sandwiches from $.50 to $1 in the sandwich shop example examined in Table 10.1 or Table 10.4 to see that this is so.

To the extent that any input is used intensively in the production of some product, changes in the demand for that product cause factor demand curves to shift and the prices of those inputs to change. Land prices are a good example. Thirty years ago, the area in Manhattan along the west side of Central Park from about 80th Street north was a run-down neighborhood full of abandoned houses. The value of land there was virtually zero. Landlords walked away from properties or sold them at very low prices because the demand for housing in that area was very low. The only prospective tenants were poor, and land used for housing of the poor has a low marginal revenue product because the output sells (or, in this case, rents) for low prices.

Then things changed. Manhattan's economy boomed, and many more people wanted to live on the Upper West Side. The building structures in that area were basically strong, and developers as well as "homesteaders" began to renovate them as early as the late 1960s. During the mid-1980s, this increased demand for housing caused rents to hit record levels. Some single-room apartments, for example, rented for as much as $1400 per month.

With the higher price of output (rent), input prices increased substantially. Small buildings on 80th Street and Central Park West sold for well over a million dollars, and the value of the land figures very importantly in these building prices. In essence, a shift in demand for an output (housing in the area) pushed up the marginal revenue product of land from zero to very high levels. Demand for housing in New York dropped in the 1990s, however, driving housing prices and land values lower. Once again, output demand determined the demand for an input (land) and affected its price.

THE DEMAND FOR COMPLEMENTARY AND SUBSTITUTABLE INPUTS In our discussion thus far, we have kept coming back to the fact that factors of production complement each other. The productivity of, and thus the demand for, any one factor of production depends upon the quality and quantity of the other factors with which it works. This was certainly the case at the sandwich shop, where the simple addition of the second grill raised the productivity of labor and shifted the shop's input demand curve up to the right.

The effect of capital accumulation on real wages is one of the most important themes in all of economics. In general:

> The production and use of capital enhances the productivity of labor, increases demand, and drives up wages.

Take as an example transportation. In a poor country like Bangladesh, one person with an ox cart can move a small load over bad roads very slowly. By contrast, the stock of capital used by workers in the transportation industry in the United States is enormous. A truck driver in the United States works with a substantial amount of capital. The typical 18-wheel tractor trailer, for example, is a piece of capital worth over $100,000. The roads themselves are capital that was put in place by the government. The amount of material that a single driver can now move between distant points in a short time is staggering relative to what it was just 20 years ago. This increase in productivity has resulted directly from the addition of new capital to the industry and is reflected in the wages and incomes of truck drivers.

The infusion of capital into an industry raises the productivity of other inputs in that industry. However, it may also serve as a substitute for labor and thus cause the demand for labor to fall. Nowhere has this been more evident than in agriculture, where the shift to modern capital-intensive methods of production has greatly enhanced the productivity of land but has substantially reduced the demand for labor. Table 10.5 shows the increases in productivity recorded for several agricultural outputs. As a result of these kinds of productivity increases, farm employment declined from just under 10 million in 1950 to 2.89 million in 1990.

CROP	1960–1974	1988–1990
Corn		
Yield per acre (bushels)	62.2	106.5
Labor hours per 100 bushels	11	3
Wheat		
Yield per acre (bushels)	25.2	35.4
Labor hours per 100 bushels	12	7
Potatoes		
Yield per acre (bushels)	195	288
Labor hours per short ton	5	3
Milk		
Milk per cow (hundreds of pounds)	75	143
Labor hours per hundredweight of milk	1.2	.2

Source: Department of Agriculture, Economic Research Service, *Agricultural Statistics* and authors' calculations.

TABLE 10.5
Increased Productivity and Reduced Demand for Labor in Agriculture, 1960–1990

THE PRICES OF OTHER INPUTS   When a firm has a choice among alternative technologies, the choice it makes will depend to some extent on relative input prices. You saw in Tables 10.2 and 10.3 that an increase in the price of labor substantially increased the demand for capital as the firm switched to a more capital-intensive production technique.

During the 1970s, the large increase in energy prices relative to prices of other factors of production had a number of effects on the demand for those other inputs. Insulation of new buildings, installation of more efficient heating plants, and similar efforts substantially raised the demand for capital as capital was substituted for energy in production. But it has also been argued that the energy crisis led to an increase in demand for labor. If capital and energy are complementary inputs—that is, if technologies that are capital intensive are also energy intensive—the argument goes, the higher energy prices tended to push firms away from capital-intensive techniques and toward more labor-intensive techniques.[7] A new highly automated technique, for example, might need fewer workers, but it would also require a vast amount of electricity to operate. High electricity prices could lead a firm to reject the new techniques and stick with an old, more labor-intensive, method of production.

technological change The introduction of new methods of production or new products intended to increase the productivity of existing inputs or to raise marginal products.

TECHNOLOGICAL CHANGE   Closely related to the impact of capital accumulation on factor demand is the potential impact of **technological change**—that is, the introduction of new methods of production or new products. A new technique of production is nearly always developed to reduce production costs. New technologies usually introduce ways to produce outputs with fewer inputs by increasing the productivity of existing inputs or by raising marginal products. Because marginal revenue product reflects productivity, increases in productivity directly shift input demand curves. If the marginal product of labor rises, for example, the demand for labor shifts to the right (increases).

Think for a moment about the dramatic impact of modern technology on the production of automobiles. Early in this century, the invention of assembly lines gave new meaning to the concept of mass production and raised the productivity of labor substantially. Today the word in automotive technology is robotics. Many of the tasks once performed along assembly lines by human workers are now handled by highly automated robots. These robots are clear substitutes for labor, but they also increase the productivity of those human beings remaining on the job. Robots are being introduced in industry at a rapid pace. A California company in 1992 received approval from the Food and Drug Administration to begin testing robots that do hip replacement surgery.

New products born of technological advance also influence factor demands. The computer age has made many skills obsolete, but it has created a demand for many more. In 1965, people who could repair expensive mechanical calculators were in demand. But as the price of calculators declined drastically, the demand for repair people dried up; today, when a calculator breaks, people simply throw it away and buy a new one. As for the descendant of the old calculator: In 1979, 279,000 personal computers were manufactured in the United States; in 1991, the figure was 7.1 million.[8] An enormous industry that did not even exist 15 years ago now employs thousands of people in thousands of companies producing software to make those machines work.

[7]This argument was made in a series of papers by Professor Dale Jorgenson of Harvard University.

[8]U.S. Department of Commerce, Bureau of the Census, *Statistical Abstract of the United States,* 1992, table 1273, p. 754.

In sum:

> Technological change can and does have a powerful influence on factor demands. As new products and new techniques of production are born, so are demands for new inputs and new skills. As old products become obsolete, so too do the labor skills and other inputs needed to produce them.

Elasticity of Demand in Input Markets

You will recall from Chapter 4 that a demand schedule, or demand curve, expresses the relationship between the price of an output or input and the quantity demanded, *ceteris paribus.* The shape of the demand curve expresses the way demand reacts to changes in price while all the other influences on it are held constant.

In the previous section, we explored how variables *other than the price of the factor itself* influence demand. In this section, we discuss the changes in quantity of a factor demanded that result from a change in the price of that factor. In general:

> Responsiveness, or elasticity, of input demand at the level of an individual firm depends on the magnitude of the substitution effects and output effects.

THE SIZE OF THE FACTOR SUBSTITUTION EFFECT   As you know, when the price of a factor of production rises, firms tend to substitute other factors for it. Conversely, when the price of a factor of production falls, firms tend to substitute it for other factors. The size of the factor substitution effect depends upon how easy it is to substitute one factor for another.

Substitution among factors is more difficult in some industries than in others. Consider two factors, land and capital, as they are used in two different kinds of industries, manufacturing and the large sector collectively called "finance, insurance, and real estate." In manufacturing, goods must move from station to station, often along an assembly line. The most efficient plan for most manufacturing firms is to have all production work done on the same level. This is essential for a firm producing bulky products like automobiles, which would be hard to move from level to level in a high-rise building during production. Finance, insurance, and real estate firms, on the other hand, provide services to businesses and households. The work is done on video display terminals (and, less frequently, on paper) in office buildings. The only things that need to be regularly moved from floor to floor are people, and this task is accomplished relatively easily.

When a firm builds a high-rise office tower, it is substituting capital for land. Office firms, which can conveniently be housed in high-rise office buildings, use less land and more capital by stacking up capital floor-by-floor in a building. Manufacturing firms find it more difficult to substitute capital for land and tend to be housed in single-story, sprawling plant facilities.

This observation goes a long way toward explaining why urban areas look the way they do. In city centers, land is scarce and expensive. The farther out from the center of the city one goes, the more land there is to develop and the lower is the price of land. Office firms that find it easy to substitute capital for land tend to locate in skyscrapers near the centers of cities. Manufacturing firms that find it difficult to substitute capital for land have in recent years been locating farther and farther out from the city.

The demand for land in manufacturing, then, is *inelastic,* because it is not easy to substitute capital for it. The demand for land in finance, insurance, and real estate, however, is quite *elastic,* because substitution possibilities are great.

THE SIZE OF THE OUTPUT EFFECT When the price of an input rises, costs increase; when the price of an input falls, costs decrease. Increasing costs tend to reduce output and thus reduce factor demand across the board. Decreasing costs increase total factor demand. Given these propositions, the size of the output effect that results from a change in a factor price depends on two things: (1) the relative intensity with which that factor is used, and (2) the elasticity of demand in the output market.

The effect of intensity of factor use is easy to see. If my firm uses little labor, a rise in wages does not have a large impact on my costs. Because they use more energy to heat their plants, firms in the North felt the rise in energy prices in 1990 much more than firms in the South and Southwest.

It is not as easy to understand why the elasticity of demand in *output* markets has anything to do with the size of the output effect, and thus the elasticity of demand, in factor markets. To shed some light on this, let us suppose that an increase in wages drives up costs for all firms in an industry by 25 percent. All of those firms then cut back on production, and the industry supply curve shifts left. As this shift occurs, the price of output rises. The shape of the demand curve will determine how much equilibrium output decreases and how high price will rise. If output demand is inelastic, the price of output will be pushed up quickly and firms will recover a large part of the cost increase in higher revenues. Thus, the output effect is small—output does not change very much. If output demand is elastic, however, the rise in price leads consumers to choose substitute products, and production drops off more. Thus, the output effect is large—in other words, output changes a great deal.

RESOURCE ALLOCATION AND THE MIX OF OUTPUT IN COMPETITIVE MARKETS

We now have a complete, but simplified, picture of household and firm decision making. (Review Figure 10.1 one more time to see how both households and firms interact in two arenas, output markets and input markets.) We have also examined some of the basic forces that determine the allocation of resources and the mix of output in perfectly competitive markets.

In this competitive environment, profit-maximizing firms make three fundamental decisions: (1) how much to produce and supply in output markets, (2) how to produce (which technology to use), and (3) how much of each input to demand. Chapters 7–9 looked at these three decisions from the perspective of the output market. We derived the supply curve of a competitive firm in the short run and discussed output market adjustment in the long run. Deriving cost curves, we learned, involves evaluating and choosing among alternative technologies. Finally, we saw how a firm's decision about how much product to supply in output markets implicitly determines input demands. Input demands, we argued, are also derived demands. That is, they are ultimately linked to the demand for output.

To show the connection between output and input markets, this chapter took these same three decisions and examined them from the perspective of input markets. Figure 10.10 shows just how close the connection between output and input decisions really is. Figure 10.10a presents the information on technology and input prices embodied in the marginal cost curve. Firms hire up to the point where output price

FIGURE 10.10
Short-Run Decisions of a
Perfectly Competitive Firm

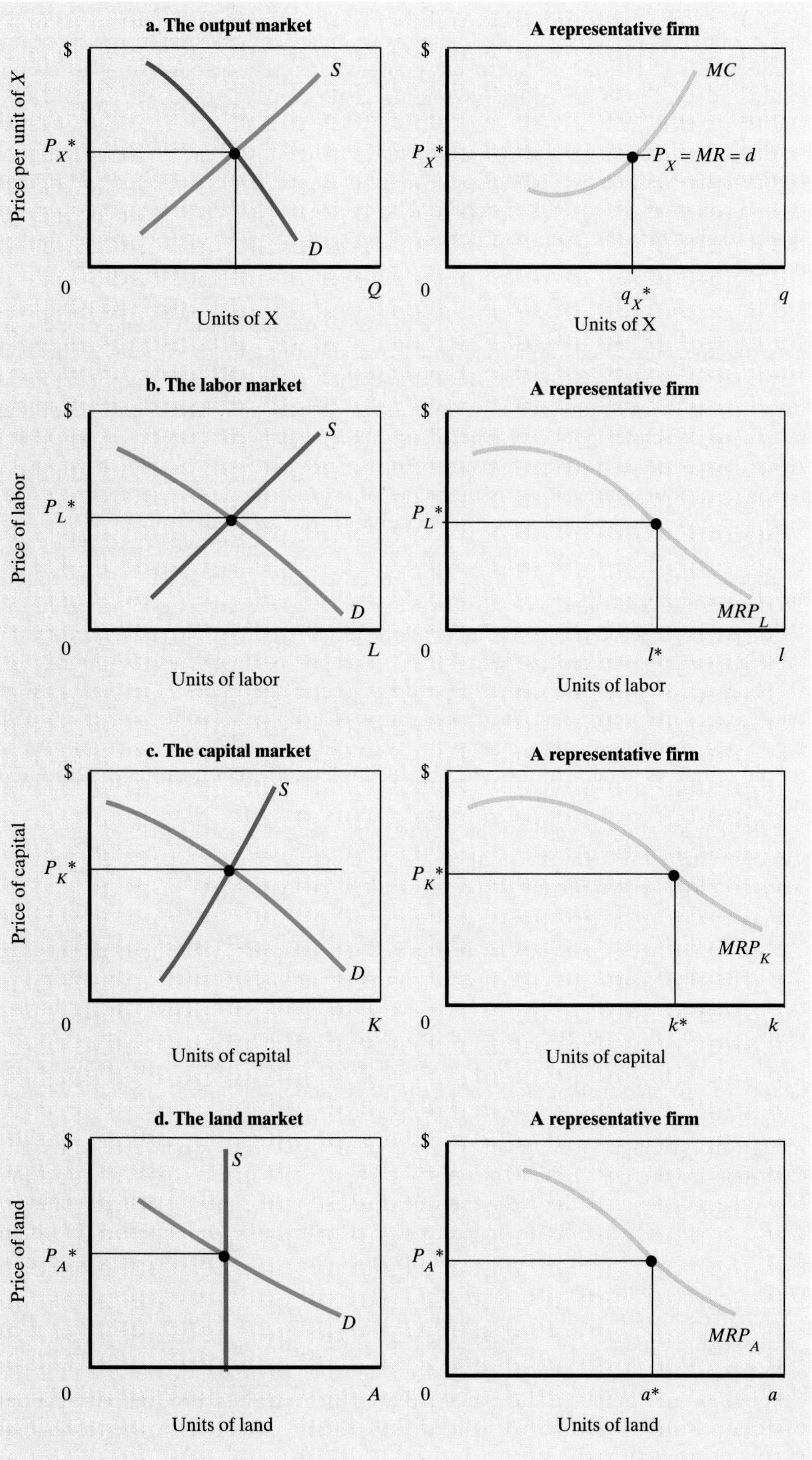

a. The output market

Price per unit of X

$

S

P_X^*

D

0

Units of X

Q

A representative firm

$

MC

P_X^* — $P_X = MR = d$

0

q_X^*

Units of X

q

b. The labor market

Price of labor

$

S

P_L^*

D

0

Units of labor

L

A representative firm

$

P_L^*

MRP_L

0

l^*

Units of labor

l

c. The capital market

Price of capital

$

S

P_K^*

D

0

Units of capital

K

A representative firm

$

P_K^*

MRP_K

0

k^*

Units of capital

k

d. The land market

Price of land

$

S

P_A^*

D

0

Units of land

A

A representative firm

$

P_A^*

MRP_A

0

a^*

Units of land

a

(that is, marginal revenue) is equal to marginal cost: $P_X^* = MC$. In Figures 10.10b, c, and d, output price and technological information are embodied in marginal revenue product curves. Firms hire up to the point where each factor's marginal revenue product is equal to its price (that is, marginal factor cost): $P_L^* = MRP_L$, $P_K^* = MRP_K$, and $P_A^* = MRP_A$.

The key is that k^*, l^*, and a^* must be fully consistent with q_X^*. That is, using the best available (least costly) technology, k^* units of capital, l^* units of labor, and a^* units of land will produce q_X^* units of output. The choice of q_X^* as the amount of output to *supply* implies that the firm must *demand* l^* units of labor, k^* units of capital, and a^* units of land.

TRADE-OFFS FACING FIRMS AND HOUSEHOLDS Looking at output and input markets together also sheds light on why firms and households choose as they do. Firms are in business to make a profit, and they must sell their output for more than it costs them to produce it. Output price reflects what households are willing to pay for consumer goods. *A firm will hire an input only if it can be used to produce a product that someone is willing to pay for.* Furthermore, a firm will hire an input, or factor of production, as long as the value of what it produces—its marginal revenue product—exceeds the price the firm has to pay for that factor.

Factor prices are determined by the interaction of supply and demand in input markets. A factor supply curve shows the prices required to attract the factor from its alternative use. The alternative to supplying labor, for example, is either leisure or unpaid work. The alternative to supplying financial resources for capital formation is present consumption. Because land is fixed in supply, its supply curve is vertical.

Thus, firms weigh the values of products against the values of resources. With their goal of maximizing profits, firms weigh what households reveal they are willing to pay in output markets against the wages that households require in order to supply resources. The firm provides the technology for transforming the resources into useful form.

Households also weigh the values of products supplied to the market against the values of the resources at their disposal. A household can consume leisure or it can work and use the income derived from work to buy goods.

THE DISTRIBUTION OF INCOME In the last few chapters, we have been focusing primarily on the firm. But throughout our study of microeconomics, we have also been building a theory that explains the distribution of income among households. We can now put the pieces of this puzzle together.

As we saw in this chapter, income is earned by households as payment for the factors of production that household members supply in input markets. Workers receive wages in exchange for their labor, owners of capital receive profits and interest in exchange for supplying capital (saving), and landowners receive rents in exchange for the use of their land (review Figure 10.1 if necessary). The incomes of workers depend on the wage rates determined in the market. The incomes of capital owners depend on the market price of capital (the amount households are paid for the use of their savings). And the incomes of landowners depend on the rental values of their land.

marginal productivity theory of income distribution At equilibrium, all factors of production end up receiving rewards determined by their productivity as measured by marginal revenue product.

If markets are competitive, the equilibrium price of each input is equal to its marginal revenue product ($W = MRP_L$, and so forth). In other words, at equilibrium, each factor ends up receiving rewards determined by its productivity as measured by marginal revenue product. This is referred to as the **marginal productivity theory of income distribution.** We will turn to a more complete analysis of income distribution in Chapter 17.

LOOKING AHEAD

We have now completed our discussion of competitive labor and land markets. (More on the labor market and labor unions can be found in Chapter 19.) The next chapter takes up the complexity of what we have been loosely calling the "capital market." There we discuss the relationship between the market for physical capital and financial capital markets and look at some of the ways that firms make investment decisions. Once we examine the nature of overall competitive equilibrium in Chapter 12, we can finally begin the process of relaxing some of the assumptions that have restricted the scope of our inquiry—most importantly, the assumption of perfect competition in input and output markets.

SUMMARY

1. The exact same set of decisions that lies behind output supply curves also lies behind input demand curves. It is only the perspective that is different.

Input Markets

2. Demand for inputs depends on demand for the outputs that they produce; input demand is thus a *derived demand*.

3. The value of any input depends on how society values the output that it produces. The price of any factor of production (input) depends on the value of its product.

4. Productivity is a measure of the amount of output produced per unit of input.

5. In general, firms will demand workers as long as the value of what those workers produce exceeds what they must be paid. Households will supply labor as long as the wage exceeds the value of leisure or the value that they derive from nonpaid work.

6. Inputs are at the same time *complementary* and *substitutable*. For example, capital raises the productivity of labor, and thus it complements labor; at the same time, capital may be substituted for labor.

7. In the short run, some factor of production is fixed. This means that all firms encounter diminishing returns in the short run. Stated somewhat differently, diminishing returns means that all firms encounter declining marginal product in the short run.

8. The *marginal revenue product (MRP)* of a variable input is the additional revenue a firm earns by employing one additional unit of the input, *ceteris paribus. MRP* is equal to the input's marginal product times the price of output.

9. Demand for an input depends on the marginal revenue product of the input. Profit-maximizing perfectly competitive firms will buy an input (e.g., hire labor) up to the point where the input's marginal revenue product equals its price. For a firm employing only one variable factor of production, the *MRP* curve *is* the firm's demand curve for that factor in the short run.

10. For a perfectly competitive firm employing one variable factor of production, labor, the condition $W = MRP_L$, is exactly the same as the condition $P = MC$. Firms weigh the value of outputs as reflected in output price against the value of inputs as reflected in marginal costs.

11. When a firm employs two variable factors of production, a change in factor price has both a *factor substitution effect* and *an output effect*.

12. A wage increase may lead a firm to substitute capital for labor and thus cause the demand for labor to decline. This is the factor substitution effect of the wage increase.

13. A wage increase increases cost, and higher cost may lead to lower output and less demand for all inputs, including labor. This is the output effect of the wage increase. The effect is the opposite for a wage decrease.

14. Every firm has an incentive to use variable inputs as long as the revenue generated by those inputs covers the costs of those inputs at the margin. Therefore, firms will employ each input up to the point that its price equals its marginal revenue product. This profit-maximizing condition holds for all factors at all levels of output.

Input Demand Curves

15. A shift in a firm's demand curve for a factor of production can be influenced by the demand for the firm's product, the amount and productivity of other inputs used, the prices of other inputs, and changes in technology.

16. The elasticity of a firm's factor demand curve depends on the size of output and substitution effects. These in turn depend on the ease of substitutability among inputs, the elasticity of demand for outputs, and the relative intensity with which that factor is used.

Resource Allocation and the Mix of Output in Competitive Markets

17. According to the *marginal productivity theory of income distribution,* because the price of a factor at equilibrium in competitive markets is equal to its marginal revenue product, the distribution of income among households depends in part on the relative productivity of factors.

REVIEW TERMS AND CONCEPTS

complementary and substitutable
  inputs   245
demand determined price   256
derived demand   245
factor substitution effect   252
marginal productivity theory
  of income distribution   266

marginal product of labor
  (MP_L)   245
marginal revenue product
  (MRP)   246
output effect of a factor price
  increase/decrease   253
productivity of an input   245

pure rent   256
technological change   262

Equations:
$$MRP_L = MP_L \times P_X$$
$$W^* = MRP_L$$

PROBLEM SET

1. The following schedule shows the technology of production at the Delicious Apple Orchard for 1994:

WORKERS	TOTAL BUSHELS OF APPLES PER DAY
0	0
1	40
2	70
3	90
4	100
5	105
6	102

If apples sell for $2 per bushel and workers can be hired in a competitive labor market for $30 per day, how many workers should be hired? What if workers unionized and the wage rose to $50? (*Hint:* Create marginal product and marginal revenue product columns for the table.) Explain your answers clearly.

2. Assume that a firm that produces widgets can produce them with one of three processes, used alone or in combination. The following table indicates the amounts of capital and labor required by each of the three processes to produce one widget.

	UNITS OF LABOR	UNITS OF CAPITAL
Process 1	4	1
Process 2	2	2
Process 3	1	3

  a. Assuming that capital costs $3 per unit and labor costs $1 per unit, which process will be employed?
  b. Plot the three points on the firm's *TVC* curve corresponding to $q = 10$, $q = 30$, and $q = 50$.

  c. At each of the three output levels, how much K and L will be demanded?
  d. Repeat parts a–c, assuming the price of capital is $3 per unit and that the price of labor has risen to $4 per unit.

3. Describe how each of the following events would affect (1) the demand for construction workers, and (2) construction wages in Portland, Oregon. Illustrate with supply and demand curves:
  a. A sharp increase in interest rates on new-home mortgages reduces the demand for new houses substantially.
  b. The economy of the area booms. Office rents rise, creating demand for new office space.
  c. A change in the tax laws in 1993 made real estate developments less profitable. As a result, three major developers cancel plans to build major shopping centers.

4. The demand for land is a derived demand. Think of a popular location near your school. What determines the demand for land in that area? What outputs are sold by businesses located there? Discuss the relationship between land prices and the prices of those products.

5. Many states provide firms with an "investment tax credit" that effectively reduces the price of capital. In theory, these credits are designed to stimulate new investment and thus create jobs. Critics have argued that if there are strong factor substitution effects, these subsidies could actually *reduce* employment in the state. Explain their arguments.

6. Suppose that the number of haircuts given by Hair, Inc. is given by the equation $q = 50L - [L^2/2]$, where L is the number of hours of labor. The MP_L is $50 - L$.
  a. Suppose that the haircut industry is perfectly competitive with a price of $10 per haircut. What is the firm's demand-for-labor schedule?
  b. How many workers will be hired at a wage of $50? A wage of $100?

The Capital Market and the Investment Decision

11

We saw in Chapter 10 that perfectly competitive firms hire factors of production (inputs) up to the point at which the marginal revenue product of each factor is equal to the price of that factor. The three main factors of production are land, labor, and capital. We also saw that factor prices are determined by the interaction of supply and demand in the factor markets (see Figure 10.10). The wage rate is determined in the labor market, the price of land is determined in the land market, and the price of capital is determined in the capital market.

In Chapter 10, we explored the labor and land markets in some detail. In this chapter we consider the demand for capital and the capital market more fully. Transactions between households and firms in the labor and land markets are direct. In the labor market, households offer their labor directly to firms in exchange for wages, and in the land market landowners rent or sell their land directly to firms in exchange for rent or an agreed-upon price. In the capital market, though, households often supply the financial resources necessary for firms to purchase capital *indirectly*. When households save and add funds to their bank accounts, for example, firms can purchase more capital by borrowing these funds from the bank to finance their capital purchases.

Earlier, in Chapter 9, we discussed the incentives of new firms to enter industries in which profit opportunities exist and the incentives that existing firms have to leave industries in which they are suffering economic losses. We also described the conditions under which existing firms have an incentive either to expand or to reduce their scales of operation. That chapter was in a preliminary way describing the process of *capital allocation*. When new firms enter an industry or an existing firm expands, someone pays to put capital (plant, equipment, and inventory) in place. Since the future is uncertain, capital investment decisions always involve risk. The essential feature of market capitalist systems is that the decision to put capital to use in a particular enterprise is made by private citizens putting their savings at risk in search of private gain. This chapter describes the set of institutions through which such transactions take place.

CAPITAL, INVESTMENT, AND DEPRECIATION

Before we proceed with our analysis of the functioning of the capital market, we need to review some basic economic principles and introduce some related concepts.

Capital

capital Those goods produced by the economic system that are used as inputs in the production of future goods and services.

One of the most important concepts in all of economics is the concept of **capital.** Recall that:

> Capital goods are those goods produced by the economic system that are used as inputs to produce other goods and services in the future. Capital goods thus yield valuable productive services over time.

physical, or tangible, capital Material things used as inputs in the production of future goods and services. The major categories of physical capital are nonresidential structures, durable equipment, residential structures, and inventories.

TANGIBLE CAPITAL   When we think of capital, we generally think of the physical capital employed by business firms. The major categories of **physical,** or **tangible, capital** are (1) nonresidential structures (office buildings, power plants, factories, shopping centers, warehouses, and docks, for example); (2) durable equipment (machines, trucks, sandwich grills, automobiles, and so on); (3) residential structures; and (4) inventories of inputs and outputs that firms have in stock.

Most firms need tangible capital, along with labor and land, to produce their products. A restaurant's capital requirements include a kitchen, ovens and grills, tables and chairs, silverware, dishes, and light fixtures. These items must be purchased up front and maintained if the restaurant is to function properly. A manufacturing firm must have a plant, specialized machinery, trucks, and inventories of parts. A winery needs casks, vats, piping, temperature-control equipment, and cooking and bottling machinery.

In addition to its shelves and display cases, the capital stock of a retail drug store is made up mostly of inventories. Drug stores do not produce the aspirin, vitamins, and toothbrushes that they sell. Those things are bought from manufacturers and put on display. The product actually produced and sold by a drug store is convenience. Like any other product, convenience is produced with labor and capital in the form of a store with lots of products, or inventory, displayed on the sales floor and kept in storerooms. The inventories of inputs and outputs that are maintained by manufacturing firms are also capital. In order to function smoothly and meet the demands of buyers, for example, the Ford Motor Company maintains inventories of both auto parts (tires, windshields, etc.) and completed cars.

An apartment building is also capital. Produced by the economic system, it yields valuable services over time, and it is used as an input to produce housing services, which are rented out.

SOCIAL CAPITAL: INFRASTRUCTURE Some physical or tangible capital is owned by the public rather than by private firms. **Social capital,** sometimes called **infrastructure,** is capital that provides services to the public. Most social capital takes the form of public works like highways, roads, bridges, mass transit systems, and sewer and water systems. Police stations, fire stations, city halls, courthouses, and police cars are all forms of social capital that are used as inputs to produce the services that government provides.

All firms use some forms of social capital in producing their outputs. Manufacturing firms transport their raw materials and products over highways and secondary roads. Even insurance companies in office towers use water pumped through publicly owned pipes and receive police and fire protection services that are produced with social capital.

Recent economic research has shown that a country's infrastructure plays a very important role in helping private firms produce their products efficiently. When public capital is not properly cared for—for example, when roads deteriorate or when airports are not modernized to accommodate increasing traffic—private firms that depend on efficient transportation networks suffer. In his economic plan presented to the Congress in early 1993, President Clinton proposed increasing government spending on infrastructure—road and bridge repair, the development of a high-speed rail network, and several other transportation projects.

> **social capital, or infrastructure** Capital that provides services to the public. Most social capital takes the form of public works (roads and bridges) and public services (police and fire protection).

INTANGIBLE CAPITAL Not all capital is physical. Some things that are intangible (nonmaterial) satisfy every part of our definition of capital. When a business firm invests in advertising to establish a brand name, it is producing a form of **intangible capital** called *goodwill*. This goodwill yields valuable services to the firm over time.

When a firm establishes a training program for employees, it is investing in the skills of its workers. One can think of such an investment as the production of an intangible form of capital called **human capital.** It is produced with labor (instructors) and capital (classrooms, computers, projectors, and books). Human capital in the form of new or augmented skills is an input—it will yield valuable productive services for the firm in the future.

When research produces valuable results, such as a new production process that reduces costs or a new formula that creates a new product, the new technology itself can be thought of as capital. Furthermore, even ideas can be patented and the rights to them can be sold.

> **intangible capital** Nonmaterial things that contribute to the output of future goods and services.

> **human capital** A form of intangible capital that includes the skills and other knowledge that workers have or acquire through education and training and which yields valuable services to a firm over time.

THE TIME DIMENSION The most important dimension of capital is that it exists through time. Labor services are used at the time they are provided. Households consume services and nondurable goods[1] almost immediately after purchase. But capital exists now and into the future. Therefore,

> The value of capital is only as great as the value of the services it will render over time.[2]

---

[1] Consumer goods are generally divided into two categories: durables and nondurables. Technically, *durable goods* are goods that are expected to last for more than one year. *Nondurable goods* are goods that are expected to last less than one year.

[2] Conceptually, consumer durable goods, such as automobiles, washing machines, and the like, are capital. They are produced, they yield services over time, and households use them as inputs to produce services such as transportation and clean laundry.

Labor is measured in hours, and land is measured in square feet or acres. But because capital comes in so many forms, it is virtually impossible to measure it directly in physical terms. The indirect measure generally used is *current market value*. The measure of a firm's **capital stock** is the current market value of its plant, equipment, inventories, and intangible assets. Using value as a measuring stick, business managers, accountants, and economists can, in a sense, add buildings, barges, and bulldozers into a measure of total capital.

Capital is measured as a stock value. That is, it is measured at a point in time. The capital stock of the XYZ Corporation on July 31 is $3,453,231. Or at the beginning of 1992, the gross nonresidential fixed capital stock (buildings and equipment) of all private industries, including farms, in the United States was $9.8 trillion, including $5.1 trillion in structures and $4.7 trillion in equipment.[3]

Although it is measured in terms of money, or value, it is very important to think of the actual capital stock itself:

> When we speak of capital, we refer not to money or to financial assets such as bonds or stocks, but rather to the physical plant, equipment, inventory, and intangible assets of the firm.

Investment and Depreciation

Recall the difference between stock and flow measures discussed in earlier chapters. *Stock measures* are valued at a particular point in time, while *flow measures* are valued over a period of time. The easiest way to think of the difference between a stock measure and a flow measure is to think about a tub of water. The volume of water in the tub is measured at a point in time and is a stock. The amount of water that flows into the tub *per hour* and the amount of water that evaporates out of the tub *per day* are flow measures. Flow measures have meaning only when the time dimension is added. Clearly, water flowing into the tub at a rate of five gallons per hour is very different than a rate of five gallons per year.

Stocks of capital are affected over time by two flows: investment and depreciation. When a firm produces or puts in place new capital—a new piece of equipment, for example—it has invested. **Investment** is a flow that increases the stock of capital. Because it has a time dimension, we speak of investment per period (by the month, quarter, or year).

Before you proceed any further, you should be careful to keep in mind that the term "investing" is not used in economics to describe the act of buying a share of stock or a bond. Although people commonly use the term this way ("I invested in some Union Carbide stock" or "he invested in Treasury bonds"), the term *investment* when used correctly refers only to the *creation of new capital*.

Table 11.1 presents data on investment in the United States economy in 1992. About half of the total was new durable equipment. Almost all the rest was investment in structures, both residential (apartment buildings, condominiums, houses, and so forth) and nonresidential (factories, shopping malls, and so forth). Inventory investment was small.

Depreciation is the decline in the economic value of an asset over time. If you have ever owned a car, you are aware that its resale value falls with age. Suppose you bought a new Pontiac in 1992 for $20,500 and you decide to

capital stock The current market value of a firm's plant, equipment, inventories, and intangible assets.

investment New capital additions to a firm's capital stock. Although capital is measured at a given point in time (a stock), investment is measured over a period of time (a flow). The flow of investment increases the stock of capital.

depreciation The decline in the economic value of an asset over time.

---

[3]U.S. Department of Commerce, *Statistical Abstract of the United States,* 1992, p. 538, table 861.

TABLE 11.1
Investment in the U.S. Economy, 1992

	BILLIONS OF CURRENT DOLLARS	AS A PERCENTAGE OF TOTAL GROSS INVESTMENT	AS A PERCENTAGE OF GDP
Nonresidential structures	168.4	21.9	2.8
Durable equipment	379.9	49.3	6.4
Inventories	4.4	0.5	0.1
Residential structures	217.7	28.3	3.7
Total gross private investment	770.4	100.0	13.0
Depreciation	653.4	−84.8	−11.0
Net investment	117.0	15.2	2.0
(gross investment minus depreciation)			

Source: U.S. Department of Commerce.

sell it two years and 25,000 miles later. Checking the newspaper and talking to several dealers, you find out that, given its condition and the mileage, you can expect to get $12,000 for it. It has depreciated $8,500 ($20,500 − $12,000). Table 11.1 shows that in 1992 depreciation in the U.S. economy was $653.4 billion.

A capital asset can depreciate because it wears out physically or because it becomes obsolete. Take, for example, a computer control system in a factory. If a new, technologically superior system is developed that does the same job for half the price, the old system may be replaced even if it still functions well. The Pontiac depreciated because of wear and tear *and* because new models were available.

THE CAPITAL MARKET

Where does capital come from? How and why is it produced? How much and what kinds of capital are produced? Who pays for it? These questions are answered in the complex set of institutional structures in which households supply their savings to firms that demand funds in order to buy capital goods. Collectively, these institutions are called the **capital market.**

Although governments and households make some capital investment decisions, most decisions to produce new capital goods—that is, to invest—are made by firms. A firm cannot invest, however, unless it has the funds to do so. Although firms can invest in many ways, it is always the case that:

capital market The market in which households supply their savings to firms that demand funds in order to buy capital goods.

> The funds that firms use to buy capital goods come, directly or indirectly, from households. When a household decides not to consume a portion of its income, it saves. Investment by firms is the *demand for capital;* saving by households is the *supply of capital.* Various financial institutions then facilitate the transfer of those savings to firms that use them for capital investment.

Let us use a simple example to see how the system works. Suppose that some firm wants to purchase a machine that costs $1000 and that some household decides at the same time that it wants to save $1000 from its income. Figure 11.1 shows one way that the household's decision to save might connect with the firm's decision to invest.

Either directly or through a financial intermediary (such as a bank), the household agrees to loan its savings to the firm. In exchange, the firm contracts to pay the household interest at some agreed-upon rate each period. If the household lends directly to the firm, the firm gives the household a *bond,* which is nothing more than a contract that promises to repay the loan at some specific time in the future. The bond also specifies the flow of interest to be paid in the meantime.

The new saving adds to the household's stock of wealth. The household's net worth has increased by the $1000, which it holds in the form of a bond.[4] The bond is an asset to the household because it represents the firm's promise to repay the $1000 at some future date with interest. The firm uses the $1000 to buy a new $1000 machine, which it adds to its stock of capital. In essence, the household has supplied the capital demanded by the firm. It's almost as if the household bought the machine and rented it to the firm for an annual fee. Presumably, this investment will generate added profits that will facilitate the payment of interest to the household.

> In general, projects are undertaken as long as the profits likely to be realized from the investment are sufficient to cover the interest payments to the household.

Sometimes the transfer of household savings through the capital market into investment is direct. Recall from Chapter 4 that an *entrepreneur* is one who organizes, manages, and assumes the risk of a firm. When an entrepreneur starts a new business by buying capital with his own savings, he is both demanding capital and supplying the resources (i.e., his savings) needed to purchase that capital; no third party is involved in the transaction. Most investment, however, is accomplished with the help of financial intermediaries (third parties such as banks, insurance companies,

---

[4]Note that it is the *act of saving* that increases the household's wealth, not the act of buying the bond. Buying the bond simply transforms one financial asset (money) into another (a bond). The household could simply have held onto the money.

FIGURE 11.1
$1000 in Saving Becomes
$1000 of Investment

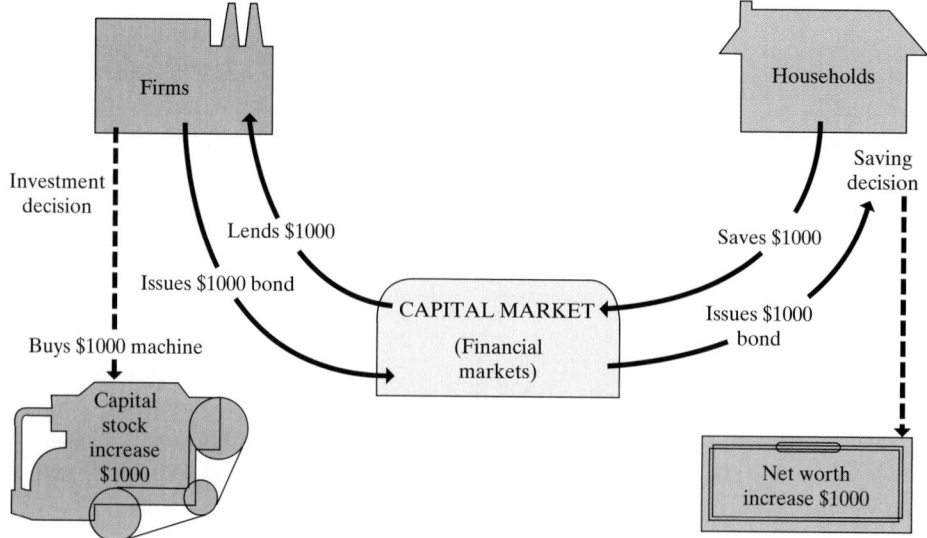

and pension funds) that stand between the supplier (saver) and the demander (investing firm). That part of the capital market in which savers and investors interact through intermediaries is often referred to as the **financial capital market**.

Capital Income: Interest and Profits

It should now be clear to you how capital markets fit into the circular flow: They facilitate the movement of household savings into the most productive investment projects. When households allow their savings to be used to purchase capital, they receive payments, and these payments (along with wages and salaries) are part of household incomes. Income that is earned on savings that have been put to use through financial capital markets is called **capital income.** Capital income is received by households in many forms, the two most important of which are *interest* and *profits.*

INTEREST   The most common form of capital income received by households is interest. In simplest terms, **interest** is the payment made for the use of money. Banks pay interest to depositors, whose deposits are loaned out to businesses or individuals who want to make investments.[5] They also *charge* interest to those who borrow money. Corporations pay interest to households that buy their bonds. The government borrows money by issuing bonds, and the buyers of those bonds receive interest payments.

Interest is almost always expressed as an annual rate. The *interest rate* is the agreed-upon annual interest payment expressed as a percentage of the loan or deposit. For example, a $1000 bond (representing a $1000 loan from a household to a firm) that carries a fixed 10% interest rate will pay the household $100 per year ($1000 × .10) in interest. A savings account that carries a 5% annual interest rate will pay $50 annually on a balance of $1000.

The interest rate is usually agreed to at the time a loan or deposit is made. Sometimes borrowers and lenders agree to adjust periodically the level of interest payments depending on market conditions. These types of loans are called *adjustable* or *floating rate loans.* (*Fixed-rate loans* are loans in which the interest rate never varies.) In recent years there have even been adjustable rates of interest on savings accounts and certificates of deposit.

The interest rate of a loan depends on a number of factors. A loan that involves more risk will generally pay a higher rate of interest than a loan with less risk. For example, many real estate developers in the Northeast and in California found themselves in serious trouble in 1991 and 1992 as the real estate market worsened. Many needed to borrow to complete projects that had been started before the downturn. Because so many developers were in financial trouble, and because banks were reeling from scores of bad real estate loans, any developer lucky enough to obtain a loan was forced to pay a very high rate of interest.

It is generally agreed that the safest borrower is the U.S. government, even though its debt is now over $4 trillion and continues to rise at a steady rate. With the "full faith and credit" of the U.S. government pledged to buyers of U.S. Treasury bonds and bills, most people believe that there is little risk that the government will *default* on (that is, not repay) its loans. For this reason, the U.S. government can borrow money at a lower interest rate than any other borrower.

financial capital market The part of the capital market in which savers and investors interact through intermediaries.

capital income Income earned on savings that have been put to use through financial capital markets.

interest The payment made for the use of money. Almost always expressed as an annual rate.

---

[5]Although we are focusing on investment by businesses, households can and do make investments also. The most important form of household investment is the construction of a new house, usually financed by borrowing in the form of a mortgage. A household may also borrow to finance the purchase of an existing house, but when it does so, no new investment is taking place.

profit The excess of revenues over cost in a given period.

PROFITS As the term is commonly used, **profit** means any excess of revenues over cost in a given period. Profits are earned by all forms of business enterprise: proprietorships, partnerships, and corporations. Profits are part of the incomes of business owners. Corporations, on the other hand, often do not pay out all of their profits to shareholders. As you saw in Chapter 3, corporate profits are divided into three categories: dividends (profits distributed to shareholders), retained earnings (profits not distributed to shareholders), and profit taxes.

Recall that when the term "profits" is used in economics, it refers to *excess* profits—that is, to profits over and above a normal return. Economic profit is defined this way because true economic cost includes the opportunity cost of capital. Suppose, for example, that I decide to open a candy store that requires an initial investment of $100,000. Clearly, if I borrow the $100,000 from a bank, I am not making a profit until I cover the interest payments on my loan.

Even if I use my own savings or raise the funds I need by selling shares, I am not making a profit until I cover the opportunity cost of using those funds to start my business. Because I always have the option of lending my funds at the current market interest rate, I earn an economic profit only when I earn a rate of return that is higher than the market interest rate. For example, if the market interest rate is 11%, the annual profits earned by my candy store would not be considered economic profits unless they were greater than $11,000 a year. The first $11,000 of my profits is actually part of the cost of capital—it is the normal return on a $100,000 investment when the interest rate is 11 percent ($100,000 × .11 = $11,000).

As another example, suppose that the Kauai Lamp Company was started in 1990, and that 100% of the $1 million needed to start up the company (to buy the plant and equipment) was raised by selling shares of stock. Now suppose that the company earns a total profit of $200,000 per year, all of which is paid out to shareholders. Since $200,000 is 20% of the company's total capital stock, we could say that the firm is enjoying a 20% rate of profit and that shareholders are earning profits of $200,000. But only a part of that $200,000 is *economic* profit. If the market interest rate is 10%, then 10% of $1 million ($100,000) is really part of the cost of capital. Not until the firm earns *over* a 10% rate of return on its investment is it earning economic profits.

FUNCTIONS OF INTEREST AND PROFIT Capital income serves several functions. First, interest and profit may function as incentives to postpone gratification. When you save, you pass up the chance to buy things that you want right now. Rather than spending and consuming something today, you decide to spend and consume something in the future, using what you hope will be increased funds. One view of interest and profit is that they are the rewards for postponing consumption.

Second, interest and profit also serve as rewards for innovation and risk taking. The entrepreneur's goal is to reap rewards in the form of profits from the new enterprise. When a new firm makes it big, the rewards can be enormous. Successful entrepreneurs have accumulated huge fortunes. Dave Thomas, founder of Wendy's, made millions. Every year *Fortune* magazine publishes the names of the richest people in America, and virtually every major fortune listed there is traceable to the founding of some business enterprise that "made it big." In recent years, big winners have included retail stores (Leslie Wexner of The Limited), high-tech companies (David Packard of Hewlett-Packard and Bill Gates of Microsoft), and candy companies (the Mars family of Mars, Inc.).

Many argue that rewards for innovation and risk taking are the essence of the United States' free enterprise system. The potential for big financial rewards is one factor that motivates innovation, and innovation is good for much of society. Ideas lead to new products and new ways of producing things. Innovation is at the core of economic growth and progress. More efficient production techniques mean that the resources saved can be used to produce new things. There is another side to this story, however: Critics of the free enterprise system claim that such large rewards are not justified and that accumulations of great wealth and power are not in society's best interests.

Financial Markets in Action

As you have seen, when a firm issues a fixed-interest-rate bond, it borrows funds and pays interest at an agreed-upon rate to the person or institution that buys the bond. Many other mechanisms, four of which are illustrated below (and see Figure 11.2), also channel household savings into investment projects. The Global Perspective box entitled "The Capital Market in Action: Rural Credit in Indonesia" offers an additional example.

Case A: Business Loans As I look around my home town, I see several ice cream stores doing very well, but I think that I can make better ice cream than they do. To go into the business, I need capital: ice cream–making equipment, tables, chairs, freezers, signs, and a store. Because I put up my house as collateral, I am not a big risk, and the bank grants me a loan at a fairly reasonable interest rate. Banks have these funds to lend only because households deposit their savings there.

Case B: Venture Capital A scientist at a leading university develops an inexpensive method of producing a very important family of virus-fighting drugs, using microorganisms created through gene splicing. This is a new process and a new business, and no one really knows whether it will be profitable or not. The business could very well fail within 12 months, but if it succeeds, the potential for profit is huge.

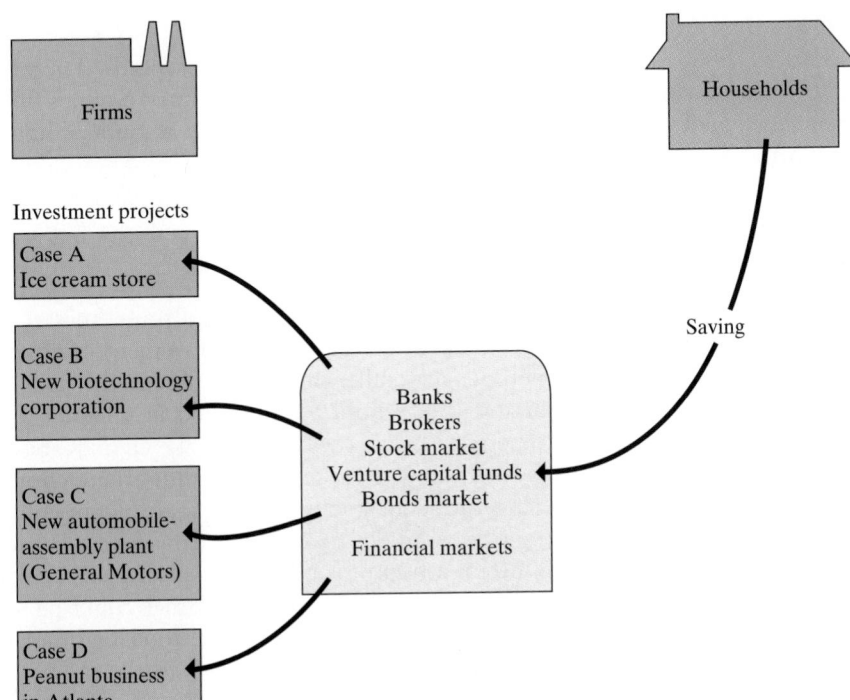

FIGURE 11.2
Financial Markets Link Household Saving and Investment by Firms

Our scientist goes to a *venture capital fund* for financing. Such funds take household savings and put them into high-risk ventures in exchange for a share of the profits if the new businesses succeed. By investing in many different projects, the funds reduce the risk of going broke. Once again, household funds make it possible for firms to undertake investments. If a venture succeeds, those owning shares in the venture capital fund receive substantial profits.

Case C: Retained Earnings General Motors Corporation decides that it wants to build a new assembly plant in Tennessee, and it discovers that it has enough funds to pay for the new facility. The new investment is thus paid for through internal funds, or *retained earnings.*

The result is exactly the same as if the firm had gone to households via some financial intermediary and borrowed the funds to pay for the new plant. General Motors is owned by its shareholders. When it earns a profit, that profit really belongs to the shareholders. If GM uses its profits to buy new capital, it does so only with the shareholders' implicit consent. When a firm takes its own profit and uses it to buy capital assets instead of paying it out to its shareholders, the total value of the firm goes up, as does the value of the shares held by stockholders. As in the other examples, GM's capital stock increases, and so does the net worth of households.

When a household owns a share of stock that *appreciates,* or increases in value, the appreciation is part of the household's income. Unless the household sells the stock and consumes the gain, that gain is part of saving. In essence, when a firm retains earnings for investment purposes, it is actually saving on behalf of its shareholders.

Case D: The Stock Market A former high-ranking government official decides to start a new peanut processing business in Atlanta, and he also decides to raise the funds needed by issuing shares of stock. Households buy the shares with income that they decide not to consume. In exchange, they are entitled to a share of the profits of the firm.

The shares of stock become part of the net worth of households. The proceeds from stock sales are used to buy plant equipment and inventory. Savings flow into investment, and the firm's capital stock goes up by the same amount as household net worth.

Capital Accumulation and Allocation

You can see from the preceding examples that various, and sometimes complex, connections between households and firms facilitate the movement of saving into productive investment. The methods may differ, but the results are the same.

Think again about Colleen and Bill, whom we discussed in Chapter 2. They found themselves alone on a deserted island. They had to make choices about how to allocate available resources, including their time. One important choice was how much energy to devote to producing goods and services for present enjoyment and how much to devote to investment that would bring future enjoyment. By spending long hours working on a house or a boat, for example, Colleen and Bill are saving and investing. First, they are using resources that could be used to produce more immediate rewards—they could gather more food or simply lie in the sun and relax. Second, they are applying those resources to the production of *capital* and capital accumulation.

THE CAPITAL MARKET IN ACTION: RURAL CREDIT IN INDONESIA

Capital markets serve the same basic functions all over the world: to transfer household savings into the hands of those who need funds for investment. Nowhere is this process more important than in the developing countries of the world, where economic growth depends critically on capital production and investment.

The case studies that follow describe the functioning of a remarkably successful capital market in rural Indonesia. Indonesia is the fifth most populous country in the world, with an estimated population of 180 million. Per capita income is about $500 per year, with many workers earning less than a dollar per day. But despite this low level of individual income, Indonesia's economy has been growing at a healthy pace. One aspect of Indonesia's success has been the development of a rural credit system that makes funds available to purchase the capital that is needed for economic expansion.

Starting a business almost always requires capital. Because most individuals do not have enough savings to finance a new business on their own, they need to turn to a credit system that will give them access to the savings of other people. This is accomplished fairly easily in the developed countries, where funds are almost always available for investment. In most developing countries, however, modern capital markets (banks, stock exchanges, and so forth) do not exist in traditional sectors of the economy and in rural areas. In those countries, it is usually the case that the only firms that have access to credit to buy capital equipment are the large, wealthy businesses.

But things may be changing. One large bank in Indonesia has recently discovered that making banking services available to relatively poor people in rural areas can be quite profitable. The Unit Desa ("Village Unit") Program, established in its present form by the Bank Rakyat Indonesia (BRI) in 1984, has collected hundreds of millions of dollars in small savings accounts at tiny branch banks throughout Indonesia. Some of this money, along with money deposited in banks in the large cities, is loaned to entrepreneurs to start or to expand small enterprises. The success of these small rural enterprises has contributed significantly to Indonesia's recent economic success.

The following descriptions of Unit Desa operations tell exactly how the capital market functions: Private savings are accumulated. Those savings are transferred to business enterprises, who use the funds to purchase capital. The profits of these enterprises are sufficient to pay back the loan, pay interest to the saver, compensate the bank for its services, and leave the business owner with something left over. The accumulation of capital leads to growth, and everybody benefits.

A Unit Desa in Java

Approximately one hour's drive south of the city of Jember in East Java lies the BRI Unit Desa Ambulu. Housed in a simple but functional office, a staff of seven has developed a highly profitable financial institution, generating net profits in 1988 of 88 million rupiah ($52,000). Total savings accounts at the branch at the end of 1988 totaled 377 million rupiah ($222,000). In an average month, the branch made 135 loans. The average loan was $315. (The minimum loan under the program is $15.) Losses from unpaid loans have been less than 1 percent of total outstanding loans.

In some parts of Indonesia, rice is still harvested by hand. Indonesia's rural villages are experiencing success with the help of a credit system that makes funds available to help farmers expand their operations.

Typical Unit Desa Loans

In January 1988, a couple borrowed 1.2 million rupiah (about $700) to buy a milling and grinding machine to be used in milling rice and corn and in grinding coffee. Before taking out the loan, the family was making a living in petty trading. After the loan, the family operated a processing service for the surrounding area and had three formal full-time employees outside the immediate family. It paid back the loan in full.

In June 1988, two partners borrowed 3 million rupiah (about $1800) to buy a steam furnace for a beancurd processing factory. At the time the loan was made, the factory employed four workers and supplied about 15 beancurd peddlers a day. With the steam processor, the output of the factory doubled and four additional workers were hired full time.

Source: Based on Richard H. Patton and Jay K. Rosengard, *Progress with Profits: The Development of Rural Banking in Indonesia* (Cambridge, MA: Harvard Institute for International Development, 1990).

Industrialized or agrarian, small or large, simple or complex, all societies exist through time and must allocate resources over time. In simple societies, investment and saving decisions are made by the same people. Colleen and Bill decide whether to forgo present pleasures (consumption) and whether to produce capital goods (a house, a boat). However,

> In modern industrial societies, investment decisions (capital production decisions) are made primarily by firms. Households decide how much to save, and in the long run saving limits or constrains the amount of investment that firms can undertake. The capital market exists in between to direct savings into profitable investment projects.

THE DEMAND FOR NEW CAPITAL AND THE INVESTMENT DECISION

We saw in Chapter 9 that firms have an incentive to expand in industries that earn economic profits (that is, profits over and above the normal rate of return) and in industries in which economies of scale lead to lower average costs at higher levels of output. We also saw that economic profits in an industry stimulate the entry of new firms into that industry. The expansion of existing firms and the creation of new firms both involve investment in new capital.

Even when there are no economic profits in an industry, however, firms must still do some investing. First, equipment wears out and must be replaced if the firm is to stay in business. Second, firms are constantly changing; a new technology may become available, sales patterns may shift, or the firm may expand or contract its product line.

With these points in mind, we now turn to a discussion of the investment decision process within the individual firm. In the end we will see (just as we did in Chapter 10) that a perfectly competitive firm invests in capital up to the point at which the marginal revenue product of capital is equal to the price of capital. (Because we based much of our discussion in Chapter 10 on the assumption of perfect competition, it makes sense to continue doing so here. Keep in mind, though, that much of what we say here also applies to firms that are not perfectly competitive. In Chapter 13, we begin relaxing the assumptions of perfect competition.)

Forming Expectations

We have already said that the most important dimension of capital is that of time. Capital produces useful services over *some period of time*. In building an office tower, a developer makes an investment that will be around for decades. In deciding where to build a branch plant, a manufacturing firm commits a large amount of resources to purchase capital that will be in place for a long time.

It is important to remember, though, that capital goods do not begin to yield benefits until they are *used*. Often the decision to build a building or purchase a piece of equipment must be made years before the actual project is completed. While the acquisition of a small business computer may take only days, the planning process for downtown development projects in big U.S. cities has been known to take decades.

THE EXPECTED BENEFITS OF INVESTMENTS Decision makers must have expectations about what is going to happen in the future. A new plant will be very valuable—that is, it will produce much profit—if the market for a firm's product grows and the price of that product remains high. The same plant will be worth little if the economy goes into a slump or consumers grow tired of the firm's product. An office tower may turn out to be an excellent investment if all the space gets rented at market rents that are as high as, or higher than, rents in other office towers, but it may be a poor investment if many new office buildings go up at the same time, flooding the office space market, pushing up the vacancy rate, and driving down rents—which is exactly what happened in Texas, New England, and California in the 1980s and 90s. It follows, then, that:

> The investment process requires that the potential investor evaluate the expected flow of future productive services that an investment project will yield.

Remember that households, business firms, and governments all undertake investments. A household must evaluate the future services that a new roof will yield. A firm must evaluate the flow of future revenues that a new plant will generate. Governments must estimate how much benefit society will derive from a new bridge or a war memorial.

An official of the General Electric Corporation once described the difficulty involved in making such predictions. GE subscribes to a number of different economic forecasting services. In 1982, those services provided the firm with ten-year predictions of new housing construction that ranged from a low of 400,000 new units per year to a high of 4 million new units per year. Because General Electric sells millions of household appliances to contractors building new houses, condominiums, and apartments, the forecast was critical. If GE decided that the high number was more accurate, it would need to spend literally billions of dollars on new plant and equipment to prepare for the extra demand. If GE decided that the low number was more accurate, it would need to begin closing several of its larger plants and disinvesting. In fact, GE took the middle road. It assumed that housing production would be between 1.5 and 2 million units—which, in fact, it turned out to be.

General Electric is not an exception. All firms must rely on forecasts to make sensible investment and production decisions, but forecasting is an inexact science because so much depends on events that cannot be foreseen.

THE EXPECTED COSTS OF INVESTMENTS   The benefits of any investment project take the form of future profits. These profits must be forecast. But costs must also be evaluated. Like households, firms have access to financial markets, both as borrowers and as lenders. If a firm borrows, it must *pay* interest over time; if it lends, it will *earn* interest. If the firm borrows to finance a project, the interest on the loan is part of the cost of the project.

Even if a project is financed with the firm's own funds, rather than by borrowing, there is an opportunity cost involved. A thousand dollars put into a capital investment project will generate an expected flow of future profit; the same $1000 put into the financial market (in essence, loaned to another firm) will yield a flow of interest payments. Clearly, the project will not be undertaken unless it is expected to yield more than the market interest rate will yield. The cost of an investment project may thus be direct or indirect because:

> The ability to lend at the market rate of interest means that there is an *opportunity cost* associated with every investment project. The evaluation process thus involves not only estimating future benefits, but also comparing them with the possible alternative uses of the funds required to undertake the project. At a minimum, those funds could earn interest in financial markets.

Comparing Costs and Expected Return

expected rate of return The annual rate of return that a firm expects to obtain through a capital investment.

Once expectations have been formed firms must quantify them—that is, they must assign some dollars-and-cents value to them. One way to quantify expectations is to calculate an **expected rate of return** on the investment project. For example, if a new computer network that costs $400,000 is likely to save $100,000 per year in data processing costs forever after, the expected rate of return on that investment is 25% per year. Each year the firm will save $100,000 as a result of the $400,000 investment. The expected rate of return will be less than 25% if the computer network wears out or becomes obsolete after a while and the cost savings cease. If, for example, the network lasts only ten years (with cost savings of $100,000 in each of the ten years), after which time it is worthless and the savings cease, the expected rate of return will be only 21.4 percent.[6] The expected rate of return will be even less if the network depreciates gradually during the ten years, resulting in cost savings of less than $100,000 in years two through ten. In sum:

> The expected rate of return on an investment project depends on the price of the investment, the expected length of time that the project provides additional cost savings or revenue, and the expected amount of revenue attributable each year to the project.

Table 11.2 presents a menu of investment choices and expected rates of return that face a hypothetical firm. Because expected rates of return are based on forecasts of future profits attributable to the investments, any change in expectations would change all the numbers in column 2.

Figure 11.3 graphs the total amount of investment in thousands of dollars that the firm would undertake at various interest rates. If the interest rate were 24%, the firm would fund only Project A, the new computer network. It can borrow at 24% and invest in a computer that is expected to yield 25 percent. At 24%, then, the firm's total investment is $400,000. (At such a high interest rate, of course, only very profitable projects would be funded if we were talking about the real world and not the hypothetical world of the table and figure.) The first vertical orange line in Figure 11.3 shows that at any interest rate above 20% and below 25%, only $400,000 worth of investment (that is, Project A) will be undertaken.

If the interest rate were 18%, the firm would fund projects A and B, and its total investment would rise to $3 million ($400,000 + $2,600,000). If the firm

---

[6]This 21.4% figure can be computed using the present-value analysis discussed in the appendix to this chapter.

TABLE 11.2

Potential Investment Projects and Expected Rates of Return for a Hypothetical Firm, Based on Forecasts of Future Profits Attributable to the Investment

PROJECT	(1) TOTAL INVESTMENT (DOLLARS)	(2) EXPECTED RATE OF RETURN (PERCENTAGE)
A. New computer network	400,000	25
B. New branch plant	2,600,000	20
C. Sales office in another state	1,500,000	15
D. New automated billing system	100,000	12
E. Ten new delivery trucks	400,000	10
F. Advertising campaign	1,000,000	7
G. Employee cafeteria	100,000	5

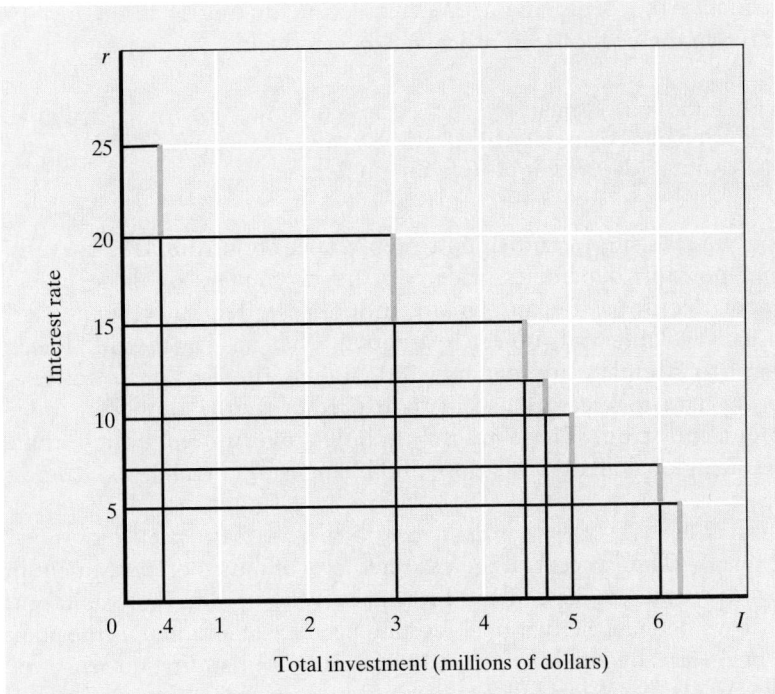

FIGURE 11.3

Total Investment as a Function of the Market Interest Rate

The demand for new capital depends on the interest rate, r. When the interest rate is low, firms are more likely to invest in new plant and equipment than when the interest rate is high. This is because the interest rate determines the direct cost (interest on a loan) or the opportunity cost (alternative investment) of each project.

could borrow at 18%, the flow of additional profits generated by the new plant and the new computer would more than cover the costs of borrowing, but none of the other projects would be justified. At an interest rate of 14%, the firm would undertake projects A, B, and C, at a total cost of $4.5 million. Only if the interest rate fell below 5% would the firm fund all seven investment projects.

The investment schedule in Table 11.2 and its graphic depiction in Figure 11.3 describe the firm's demand for new capital, expressed as a function of the market interest rate, usually represented by r. If we add the total investment undertaken by *all* firms at every interest rate, we arrive at the demand for new capital in the economy as a whole. In other words, the market demand curve for new capital is simply the sum of all the individual demand curves for new capital in the economy (see Figure 11.4). Keynes called this curve the **marginal efficiency of investment (*MEI*)**

marginal efficiency of investment (*MEI*) A curve that shows the total amount of investment that would be undertaken in an economy in a given period of time at every possible interest rate.

FIGURE 11.4

Investment Demand or Marginal Efficiency of Investment

The market investment function shows the demand for new capital in the economy as a function of the interest rate. Lower interest rates are likely to stimulate investment in the economy as a whole, while higher interest rates are likely to slow investment.

schedule. In a sense, the *MEI* schedule is a ranking of all the investment opportunities in the economy in order of expected yield.

> Only those investment projects in the economy that are expected to yield a rate of return higher than the market interest rate will be funded. At lower market interest rates, more investment projects are undertaken.

The most important thing to remember about the *MEI* curve is that its shape and position depend critically on the *expectations* of those making the investment decisions. Because many influences affect these expectations, they are usually volatile and subject to frequent change. Thus, while lower interest rates tend to stimulate investment, and higher interest rates tend to slow it, many other hard-to-measure and hard-to-predict factors also affect the level of investment spending. These might include government policy changes, election results, global affairs, inflation, and changes in currency exchange rates.

THE EXPECTED RATE OF RETURN AND THE MARGINAL REVENUE PRODUCT OF CAPITAL   The concept of the expected rate of return on investment projects is analogous to the concept of the marginal revenue product of capital (MRP_K). Recall that we defined the marginal revenue product of an input as the additional revenue a firm earns by employing one additional unit of an input, *ceteris paribus*. Also recall our earlier discussion of labor demand in a sandwich shop in Chapter 7. If an additional worker can produce 15 sandwiches in one hour (the marginal product of labor: $MP_L = 15$) and each sandwich brings in $.50 (the price of the service produced by the sandwich shop: $P_X = \$.50$), the marginal revenue product of labor is equal to $7.50 ($MRP_L = MP_L \times P_X = 15 \times \$.50 = \$7.50$).

Now think carefully about the return to an additional unit of new capital (the marginal revenue product of capital). Suppose that the rate of return on an investment in a new machine is 15 percent. This means that the investment project yields the same return as a bond yielding 15 percent. If the current interest rate is less than 15%, the investment project will be undertaken because:

> A perfectly competitive profit-maximizing firm will keep investing in new capital up to the point at which the expected rate of return is equal to the interest rate. This is analogous to saying that the firm will continue investing up to the point at which the marginal revenue product of capital is equal to the price of capital, or $MRP_K = P_K$, which is what we learned in Chapter 10.

A FINAL WORD ON CAPITAL

The concept of capital is one of the central ideas in economics. Capital is produced by the economic system itself. Capital generates services over time, and it is used as an input in the production of goods and services.

The enormous productivity of modern industrial societies is due in part to the tremendous amount of capital that they have accumulated over the years. It may surprise you to know that the average worker in the United States works with over $80,000 worth of capital. There is no question that the economic success of modern Japan resulted first and foremost from the very high rates of investment that began in that country after World War II and have continued for nearly 45 years.

The bulk of this chapter described the institutions and processes that determine the amount and types of capital produced in a market economy. Existing firms in search of increased profits, potential new entrants to the markets, and entrepreneurs with new ideas are all continuously evaluating potential investment projects. At the same time, households are saving. Each year households save some portion of their disposable incomes. This new saving becomes part of their net worth, and they want to earn a return on it. Each year a good portion of the saving finds its way into the hands of firms who use it to buy new capital goods.

Between households and firms is the financial capital market. Millions of people participate in financial markets every day. There are literally thousands of financial managers, pension funds, mutual funds, college portfolios, brokerage houses, options traders, and banks whose sole purpose is to earn the highest possible rate of return on people's saving.

Brokers, bankers, and financial managers are continuously scanning the financial horizons for profitable investments. What businesses are doing well? What businesses are doing poorly? Should we lend to an expanding firm? All the analysis done by financial managers seeking to earn a high yield for clients, by managers of firms seeking to earn high profits for their stockholders, and by entrepreneurs seeking profits from innovation serves to channel capital into its most productive uses. Within firms, the evaluation of individual investment projects involves *forecasting* costs and benefits and valuing *streams of potential income* that will be earned only in future years.

We have now completed our discussion of competitive input and output markets. We have looked at household and firm choices in output markets, labor markets, land markets, and capital markets.

We now turn to a discussion of the allocative process that we have described. How do all the parts of the economy fit together? Is the result good or bad? Can we improve on it? All this is the subject of Chapter 12.

SUMMARY

1. The central feature of market capitalist systems is that the decision to put *capital* to use in a particular enterprise is made by private citizens putting their savings at risk in search of private gain. The set of institutions through which such transactions occur is called the capital *market*.

Capital, Investment, and Depreciation

2. Capital goods are those goods produced by the economic system that are used as inputs to produce other goods and services in the future. Capital goods thus yield valuable productive services over time.

3. The major categories of *physical, or tangible, capital* are nonresidential structures, durable equipment, residential structures, and inventories. *Social capital* is capital that provides services to the public. *Intangible (nonmaterial) capital* includes *human capital* and goodwill.

4. The most important dimension of capital is that it exists through time. Therefore, its value is only as great as the value of the services it will render over time.

5. The most common measure of a firm's *capital stock* is the current market value of its plant, equipment, inventories, and intangible assets. However, in thinking about capital it is impor-

tant to think of the actual capital stock rather than its simple monetary value.

6. In economics, the term *investment* refers to the creation of new capital, not to the purchase of a share of stock or a bond. Investment is a flow that increases the stock of capital.

7. *Depreciation* is the decline in the economic value of an asset over time. A capital asset can depreciate because it wears out physically or because it becomes obsolete.

The Capital Market

8. Income that is earned on savings that have been put to use through *financial capital markets* is called *capital income*. The two most important forms of capital income are *interest* and *profits*. Interest is the fee paid by a borrower to a lender (for the use of his or her savings). Interest and profits reward households and entrepreneurs for innovation, risk taking, and postponing gratification.

9. In modern industrial societies, investment decisions (capital production decisions) are made primarily by firms. Households decide how much to save; and in the long run, saving limits the amount of investment that firms can undertake. The capital market exists in between to direct savings into profitable investment projects.

The Demand for New Capital and the Investment Decision

10. Before investing, investors must evaluate the expected flow of future productive services that an investment project will yield.

11. The availability of interest to lenders means that there is an opportunity cost associated with every investment project. This cost must be weighed against the stream of earnings that a project is expected to yield.

12. A firm will decide whether to undertake an investment project by comparing costs with expected returns. The *expected rate of return* on an investment project depends on the price of the investment, the expected length of time that the project provides additional cost savings or revenue, and the expected amount of revenue attributable each year to the project.

13. The market investment function, or the *marginal efficiency of investment* schedule, shows the demand for capital in the economy as a function of the market interest rate. Only those investment projects that are expected to yield a rate of return higher than the market interest rate will be funded. Lower interest rates should stimulate investment.

14. A perfectly competitive profit-maximizing firm will keep investing in new capital up to the point at which the expected rate of return is equal to the interest rate. This is equivalent to saying that the firm will continue investing up to the point at which the marginal revenue product of capital is equal to the price of capital, or $MRP_K = P_K$.

REVIEW TERMS AND CONCEPTS

capital   270
capital income   275
capital market   273
capital stock   272
depreciation   272

expected rate of return   282
financial capital market   275
human capital   271
intangible capital   271
interest   275

investment   272
marginal efficiency of investment (*MEI*)   283
physical, or tangible, capital   270
profit   276
social capital, or infrastructure   271

PROBLEM SET

1. The board of directors of the Quando Company in Singapore was presented with the following list of investment projects for implementation in 1994:

PROJECT	TOTAL COST SINGAPORE DOLLARS	ESTIMATED RATE OF RETURN
Factory in Kuala Lumpur	17,356,400	13%
Factory in Bangkok	15,964,200	15%
A new company aircraft	10,000,000	12%
A factory outlet store	3,500,000	18%
A new computer network	2,000,000	20%
A cafeteria for workers	1,534,000	7%

Sketch total investment as a function of the interest rate (with r on the Y-axis). Currently, the interest rate in Singapore is 8 percent. How much investment would you recommend to Quando's board?

2. Is each of the following saving, investment, or neither?
   a. Frank sells some GM stock and uses the proceeds to buy ten shares of Amex stock from Jim.
   b. Sarah's income is $20,000 this year. She spent $19,000 and put the rest into Amex stock.
   c. A Boston developer borrows $350 million from a group of banks and builds an office tower.
   d. Sarah's grandmother earns no income this year. Grandma supports herself by selling $5,000 worth of bonds.
   e. Tom's income this year was $100,000. He spent $90,000 and put the rest into Mexican government bonds. The Mexican government used the proceeds to help build a power plant.

3. "Lower interest rates are discouraging to households, and they are likely to invest less." Do you agree or disagree with this statement? Explain your answer.

4. Give at least three examples of how savings can be channeled into productive investment. Why is investment so important for an economy? What do you sacrifice when you invest today?

5. Explain what we mean when we say that "households supply capital and firms demand capital."

6. Suppose that I decide to start a small business. To raise the start-up costs, I sell 1,000 shares of stock for $100 each. For the next five years, I take in annual revenues of $50,000. My total annual costs of operating the business are $20,000. If all of my profits are paid out as dividends to shareholders, how much of my total annual profit can be considered economic profit? Assume that the current interest rate is 10 percent.

7. Describe the capital stock of your college or university. How would you go about measuring its value? Has your school made any major investments in recent years? If so, describe them. What does your school hope to gain from these investments?

APPENDIX TO CHAPTER 11
CALCULATING PRESENT VALUE

We have seen in this chapter that a firm's major goal in making investment decisions is to evaluate revenue streams that will not materialize until the future. One way for the firm to decide whether or not to undertake an investment project is to compare the expected rate of return from the investment with the current interest rate available in the financial market. This procedure was discussed in the text, although the way in which the expected rate of return is calculated was touched upon only briefly.

The purpose of this appendix is to present an alternative method of evaluating future revenue streams through present-value analysis.

PRESENT VALUE

Consider the expected flow of profits from the investment shown in Table 11A.1. If such a project cost $1200 to put in place, would the firm undertake it? At first glance, you might answer yes. After all, the total flow of profit is $1600. But this flow of profit is fully realized only after five years have passed. The same $1200 could be put into a money market account, where it would earn interest and perhaps produce a higher yield than if it were invested in the project. You can easily see that the desirability of the investment project will depend on the interest rate that is available in the market.

One way of thinking about interest is to say that it *allows us to buy and sell claims to future dollars.* Future dollars have prices in the present. That is, a contract for $1 to be delivered in one year, two years, or ten years can be purchased today. How? By simply depositing a certain amount in an interest-bearing certificate or account. Using the *present prices* of future dollars gives us a way to compare values that will be realized in the future with present costs. This method allows us to evaluate investment projects that will yield benefits into the future.

It is not difficult to figure the "price" today of $1 to be delivered in one year. You must now pay an amount (X) such that when you get X back in one year with interest you will have $1. If r is the interest rate available in the market, r times X, or rX, is the amount of interest that X will earn for you in one year. Thus, at the end of a year you will have $X + rX$, or $X(1 + r)$, and you want this to be equal to $1. Solving for X algebraically:

$$\$1 = X(1 + r), \text{ so } X = \frac{\$1}{1 + r}.$$

We say that X is the **present value (PV),** or **present discounted value,** of $1 one year from now. Actually, X is the current market price of $1 to be delivered in one year: It is the amount you have to put aside now if you want to end up with $1 a year from now.

TABLE 11A.1
Expected Profits from a $1200 Investment Project

END OF . . .	$
Year 1	100
Year 2	100
Year 3	400
Year 4	500
Year 5	500
All later years	0

Now let's go more than one year into the future and consider more than a single dollar. For example, what is the present value of a claim on $100 in two years? Using the same logic as above, let X be the present value, or current market price, of $100 payable in two years. Thus, X plus the interest it would earn compounded for two years is equal to $100.[1] After one year, you would have $X + rX$, or $X(1 + r)$. After two years, you would have this amount plus another year's interest on the whole amount:

$$X(1 + r) + r[X(1 + r)] \text{ or } X(1 + r)(1 + r), \text{ which is } X(1 + r)^2.$$

Again solving algebraically for X:

$$\$100 = X(1 + r)^2, \text{ so } X = \frac{\$100}{(1 + r)^2}.$$

If the market interest rate were 10%, or .10, then the present value of $100 in two years would be

$$X = \frac{\$100}{(1.1)^2} = \$82.65.$$

If you put $82.65 in a certificate earning 10% per year, you would earn $8.26 in interest after one year, giving you $90.91. Interest in the second year would be $9.09, leaving you with exactly $100 at the end of two years.

In general, the present value, or present discounted value, of R dollars t years from now is

$$X = \frac{\$100}{(1 + r)^2} =$$

---

[1]Thus far, all our examples have involved *simple interest*—interest that is computed on principal alone, not on principal plus interest. In the real world, however, many loans involve *compound interest*—interest that is computed on the basis of principal plus interest. If you deposit funds into an interest-compounding account at a bank and do not withdraw the interest payments as they are added to your account, you will earn interest on your previously earned interest.

Table 11A.2 calculates the present value of the income stream in Table 11A.1 at an interest rate of 10 percent. The total present value turns out to be $1126.06. This tells the firm that it can simply go to the financial market today and buy a contract that pays $100 one year from now, another that pays $100 two years from now, still another that pays $400 three years from now, and so forth, all for the low price of $1126.06. To put this another way, it could lend out or deposit $1126.06 in an account paying a 10% interest rate, withdraw $100 next year, withdraw $100 in the following year, take another $400 at the end of three years, and so forth. When it takes its last $500 at the end of the fifth year, the account will be empty—the balance in the account will be exactly zero. Thus, *at current market interest rates,* the firm has exactly duplicated the income stream that the investment project would have yielded for a total present price of $1126.06. Why then would it pay out $1200 to undertake this investment? The answer, of course, is that it would not.

We can restate the point this way:

> If the present value of the income stream associated with an investment is less than the full cost of the investment project, the investment should not be undertaken.

It is important to remember here that we are discussing the *demand for new capital.* Business firms must evaluate potential investments in order to decide whether they are worth undertaking. This involves predicting the flow of potential future profits arising from each project and comparing those future profits with the return available in the financial market at the current interest rate. The present-value method allows firms to calculate how much it would *cost today* to purchase or contract for the exact same flow of earnings in the financial market.

LOWER INTEREST RATES, HIGHER PRESENT VALUES

Now suppose that interest rates fall from 10% to 5 percent. With a lower interest rate, the firm will have to *pay more* now to purchase the same number of future dollars. Take, for example, the present value of $100 in two years. You saw that if the firm puts aside $82.65 at 10% interest, it will have exactly $100 in two years; at a 10% interest rate, the present discounted value, or current market price, of $100 in two years is $82.65. But $82.65 put aside at a 5% interest rate would generate only $4.13 in interest in the first year and $4.34 in the second year, for a total balance of $91.12 after two years. In order to get $100 in two years, the firm needs to put aside more than $82.65 now. Solving for X as we did before,

$$X = \frac{\$100}{(1+r)^2} = \frac{\$100}{(1.05)^2} = \$90.70.$$

TABLE 11A.2
Calculation of Total Present Value of a Hypothetical Investment Project (assuming r = 10 percent)

END OF ...	$(R)	DIVIDED BY $(1 + r)^t$ =	PRESENT VALUE ($)
Year 1	100	(1.1)	90.91
Year 2	100	$(1.1)^2$	82.65
Year 3	400	$(1.1)^3$	300.53
Year 4	500	$(1.1)^4$	341.51
Year 5	500	$(1.1)^5$	310.46
Total present value:			1126.06

When the interest rate falls from 10% to 5%, the present value of $100 in two years rises by $8.05 ($90.70 − $82.65).

Table 11A.3 recalculates the present value of the full stream at the lower interest rate; it shows that a decrease in the interest rate from 10% to 5% causes the total present value to rise to $1334.59. Because the investment project will yield the same stream of earnings for a present price of only $1200, it is now a better deal than the financial markets. Under these conditions, a profit-maximizing firm will make the investment. (As discussed earlier, a lower interest rate leads to more investment.)

The basic rule is:

> If the present value of an expected stream of earnings from an investment exceeds the cost of the investment necessary to undertake it, then the investment should be undertaken. But if the present value of an expected stream of earnings falls short of the cost of the investment, then the financial market can generate the same stream of income for a smaller initial investment, and the investment should not be undertaken. When the interest rate or the rate of return offered by the market exceeds the rate of return on a project, the investment is not justified at the current interest rate.

TABLE 11A.3
Calculation of Total Present Value for a Hypothetical Investment Project (assuming r = 5 percent)

END OF ...	$(R)	DIVIDED BY $(1 + r)^t$ =	PRESENT VALUE ($)
Year 1	100	(1.05)	95.24
Year 2	100	$(1.05)^2$	90.70
Year 3	400	$(1.05)^3$	345.54
Year 4	500	$(1.05)^4$	411.35
Year 5	500	$(1.05)^5$	391.76
Total present value:			1334.59

SUMMARY

1. The present value (PV) of R dollars to be paid t years in the future is the amount you need to pay today, at current interest rates, to insure that you end up with R dollars t years from now. It is the current market value of receiving R dollars in t years.

2. If the present value of the income stream associated with an investment is less than the full cost of the investment project, the investment project should not be undertaken. If the present value of an expected stream of income exceeds the cost of the investment necessary to undertake it, then the investment should be undertaken.

REVIEW TERMS AND CONCEPTS

present value (PV), or **present discounted value** The present discounted value of R dollars to be paid t years in the future is the amount you need to pay today, at current interest rates, to insure that you end up with R dollars t years from now. It is the current market value of receiving R dollars in t years.   287

Equations:

$$PV = \frac{R}{(1+r)^t}$$

PROBLEM SET

1. Your Uncle Joe has just died and left $10,000 payable to you when you turn 30 years old. You are now 20. Currently, the ten-year government bond rate is 6.5 percent. Your brother offers you $6000 cash right now to sign over your inheritance. Would you do it?

2. A special task force has determined that the present discounted value of the benefits from a bridge project comes to $23,786,000. The total construction cost of the bridge is $25,000,000. This implies that the bridge should be built. Do

you agree with this conclusion? Explain your answer. What impact could a substantial decline in interest rates have on your answer?

3. Calculate the present value of the income streams A − E, in Table 1 below, at an 8% interest rate and again at a 10% rate.
   Suppose that the investment behind the flow of income in E is a machine that cost $1235 at the beginning of year 1. Would you buy the machine if the interest rate were 8 percent? If the interest rate were 10 percent?

TABLE 1

END OF YEAR	A	B	C	D	E
1	$80	$80	$100	$100	$500
2	80	80	100	100	300
3	80	80	1100	100	400
4	80	80	0	100	300
5	1080	80	0	100	0
6	0	80	0	1100	0
7	0	1080	0	0	0

12 General Equilibrium and the Efficiency of Perfect Competition

In the last seven chapters, we have built a model of a simple perfectly competitive economy. Our discussion has revolved around the two fundamental decision-making units, *households* and *firms,* which interact in two basic market arenas, *input markets* and *output markets.* (Look again at the circular flow diagram, shown in Figure 12.1.) By limiting our discussion to perfectly competitive firms, we have been able to examine in detail how the basic decision-making units interact in the two basic market arenas.

Households make constrained choices in both input and output markets. In Chapter 5 we discussed an individual household demand curve for a single good or service. Then in Chapter 6 we went behind the demand curve and saw how income, wealth, and prices define the budget constraints within which households exercise their tastes and preferences. We soon discovered, however, that we could not look at household decisions in output markets without thinking about the decisions that are made simultaneously in input markets. Household income, for example, depends on choices made in input markets: whether to work, how much to work, what skills to acquire, and so forth. Input market choices are constrained by such factors as current wage rates, the availability of jobs, and interest rates.

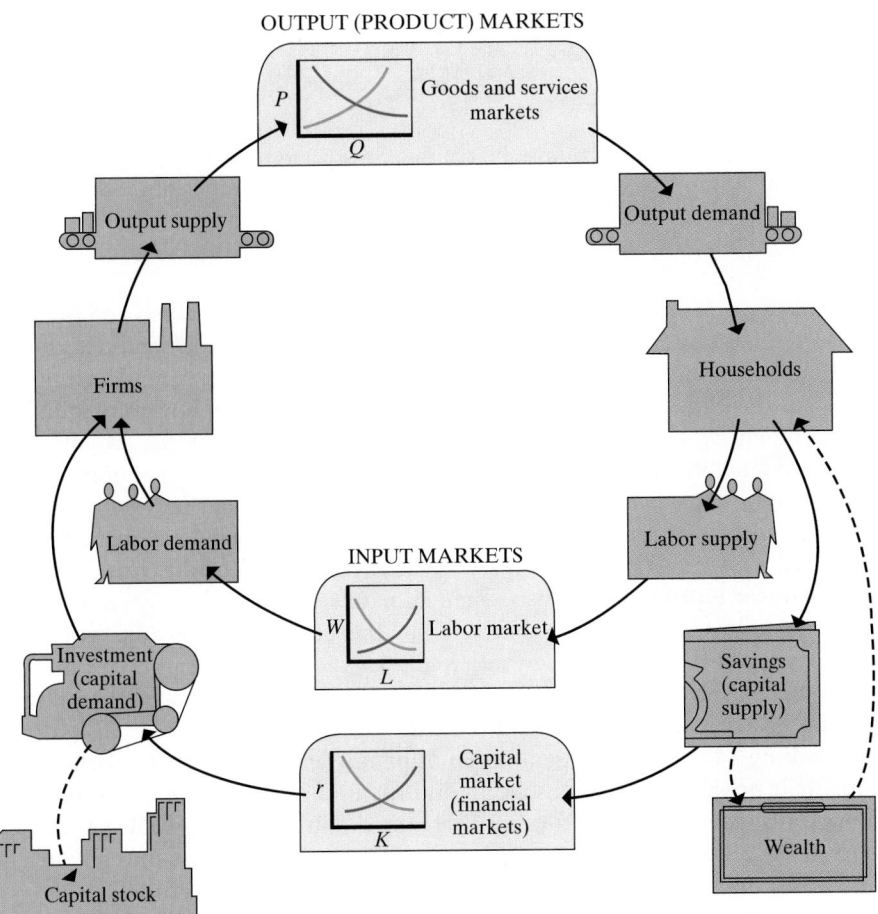

OUTPUT (PRODUCT) MARKETS

Goods and services markets

P

Q

Output supply

Output demand

Firms

Households

Labor demand

INPUT MARKETS

Labor supply

W Labor market

L

Investment (capital demand)

Savings (capital supply)

Capital market (financial markets)

r

K

Wealth

Capital stock

FIGURE 12.1

Firm and Household Decisions

Firms and households interact in both input and output markets.

Firms are the primary producing units in a market economy. Profit-maximizing firms, to which we have limited our discussion, earn their profits by selling products and services for more than it costs to produce them. With firms, as with households, output markets and input markets cannot be analyzed separately. All firms make three specific decisions simultaneously: (1) how much output to supply, (2) how to produce that output, that is, which technology to use, and (3) how much of each input to demand.

In Chapters 7–9, we explored these three decisions from the viewpoint of output markets. We saw that the portion of the marginal cost curve that lies above a firm's average variable cost curve is the supply curve of a perfectly competitive firm in the short run. Implicit in the marginal cost curve is a choice of technology and a set of input demands. In Chapters 10 and 11, we looked at the perfectly competitive firm's three basic decisions from the viewpoint of input markets.

Output and input markets are connected because firms and households make simultaneous choices in both arenas. But there are other connections among markets as well. Firms buy in both capital and labor markets, for example, and they can substitute capital for labor and vice versa. A change in the price of one factor can easily change the demand for other factors. Buying more *capital,* for instance, usually changes the marginal revenue product of *labor* and shifts the labor demand curve. Similarly, a change in the price of a single good or service usually affects household demand for other goods and services, as when a price decrease makes one good more attractive than other close substitutes. The same change also makes households better off when they find that the same amount of income will buy more. Such additional "real income" can be spent on any of the other goods and services that the household buys.

The point here is simple:

> Input and output markets cannot be considered separately or as if they operated independently. While it is important to understand the decisions of individual firms and households and the functioning of individual markets, we now need to "add it all up," to look at the operation of the system as a whole.

You have seen the concept of equilibrium applied both to markets and to individual decision-making units. In individual markets, supply and demand determine an equilibrium price. Perfectly competitive firms are in short-run equilibrium when price and marginal cost are equal ($P = MC$). In the long run, however, equilibrium in a competitive market is achieved only when economic profits are eliminated. Households are in equilibrium when they have equated the marginal utility per dollar spent on each good to the marginal utility per dollar spent on every *other* good. This process of examining the equilibrium conditions in individual markets and for individual households and firms separately is called **partial equilibrium analysis.**

A **general equilibrium** exists when all markets in an economy are in simultaneous equilibrium. An event that disturbs the equilibrium in one market may disturb the equilibrium in many other markets as well. The ultimate impact of the event depends upon the way *all* markets adjust to it. Thus, partial equilibrium analysis, which looks at adjustments in one isolated market, may be misleading.

Thinking in terms of a general equilibrium leads to some important questions. Is it possible for all households and firms and all markets to be in equilibrium simultaneously? Are the equilibrium conditions that we have discussed separately compatible with one another? Why is an event that disturbs an equilibrium in one market likely to disturb many others simultaneously?

In talking about general equilibrium, the first concept we explore in this chapter, we continue our exercise in *positive economics*—that is, we seek to understand how systems operate without making value judgments about outcomes. Later in the chapter, we turn from positive economics to *normative economics* as we begin to judge the economic system. Are its results good or bad? Can we make them better?

In judging the performance of any economic system, you will recall, it is essential first to establish specific criteria to judge by. In this chapter, we use two such criteria: *efficiency* and *equity* (fairness). First we demonstrate that the allocation of resources is **efficient**—that is, the system produces what people want and does so at least cost— if all the assumptions that we have made thus far hold. When we begin to relax some of our assumptions, however, it will become apparent that free markets may *not* be efficient. Several sources of inefficiency naturally occur within an unregulated market system. In the final part of this chapter, we introduce the potential role of government in correcting market inefficiencies and achieving fairness.

GENERAL EQUILIBRIUM ANALYSIS

Two examples will help us illustrate some of the insights that we can gain when we move from partial to general equilibrium analysis. In this section, we will consider the impact on the economy of (1) a major technological advance and (2) a shift in consumer preferences. This chapter's Issues and Applications box, "The Lumber Industry and the Price of New Housing," provides a third example. As you read, remember that we are looking for the connections between markets, particularly between input and output markets.

partial equilibrium analysis The process of examining the equilibrium conditions in individual markets and for households and firms separately.

general equilibrium The condition that exists when all markets in an economy are in simultaneous equilibrium.

efficiency The condition in which the economy is producing what people want at least possible cost.

A Technological Advance: The Electronic Calculator

Graduate students working in quantitative fields of study in the late 1960s, and even as late as the early 1970s, recall classrooms filled with noisy mechanical calculators. At that time, a calculator weighed about 40 pounds and was only able to add, subtract, multiply, and divide. These machines had no memories, and they took 20 to 25 seconds to do one multiplication problem.

Major corporations had rooms full of accountants with such calculators on their desks, and the sound when 30 or 40 of them were running was deafening. During the 1950s and 1960s, most firms had these machines, but few people had a calculator in their homes because the cost of a single machine was several hundred dollars. Some high schools had calculators for accounting classes, but most school children in the United States had never seen one.

In the 1960s, Wang Laboratories developed an electronic calculator. Bigger than a modern personal computer, it had several keyboards attached to a single main processor. It could add, subtract, multiply, and divide, but it also had a memory. Its main virtue was speed and quiet. It did calculations instantaneously without any noise. The Wang machine sold for around $1500.

The beginning of the 1970s saw rapid developments in the industry. First, calculators shrank in size. The Bomar Corporation made one of the earliest hand calculators—the Bomar Brain. These early versions could do nothing more than add, subtract, multiply, and divide, they had no memories, and they still sold for several hundred dollars. Then, in the early 1970s, a number of technological breakthroughs made it possible to mass produce very small electronic circuits (silicon chips). This, in turn, made calculators very inexpensive to produce, and it is here that we begin our general equilibrium story. Costs in the calculator industry shifted downward dramatically (see Figure 12.2b). As costs fell, profits increased. Attracted by economic profits, new firms rapidly entered the market. Instead of one or two firms producing state-of-the-art machines, dozens of firms began cranking them out by the thousands. As a result, the industry supply curve shifted out to the right, driving down prices toward the new lower costs (see Figure 12.2a).

FIGURE 12.2
Cost-Saving Technological Change in the Calculator Industry

The 1970s and 1980s brought major technological changes to the calculator industry. In 1975, 18.1 million calculators were sold at an average price of $62. As technology made it possible to produce at lower costs, cost curves shifted downward. As new firms entered the industry and existing firms expanded, output rose and market price dropped. In 1987, 33.8 million calculators were produced and sold at an average price of $30.

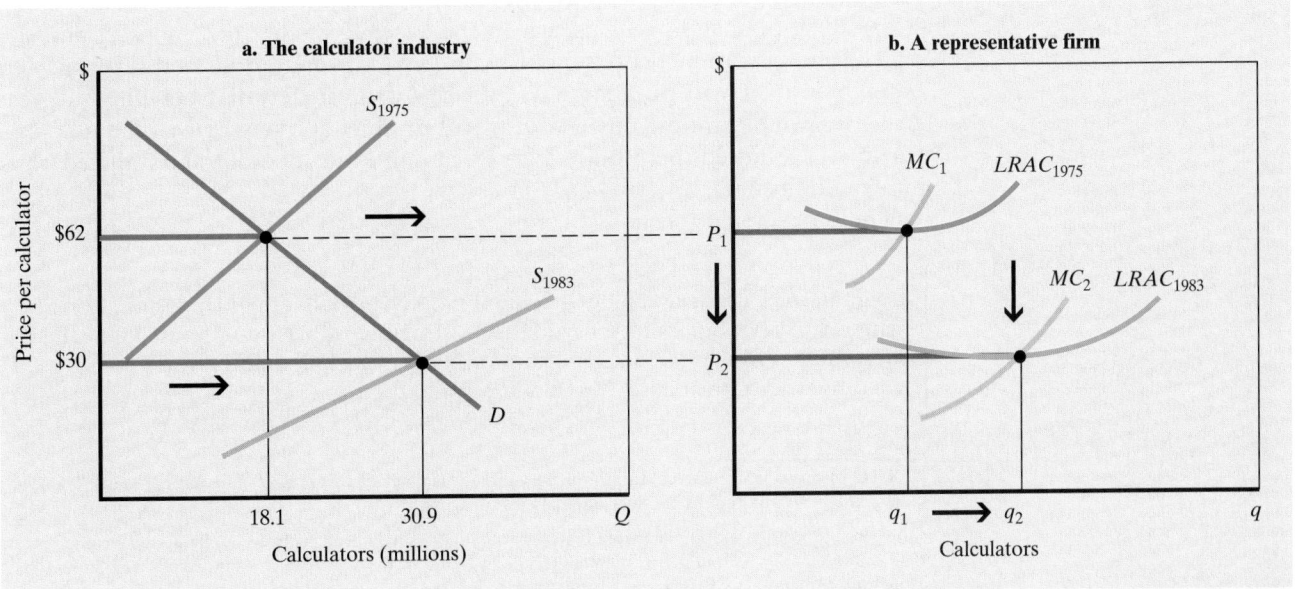

As the price of electronic calculators fell, the market for the old mechanical calculators died a quiet death. With no more demand for their product, producers found themselves suffering losses and got out of the business. As the price of electronic calculators kept falling, thousands of people who had never had a calculator began to buy them. By 1973, calculators were available at discount appliance stores for $60 to $70, and by 1975, over 18 million were produced annually and sold at an average price of $62. The average price fell to under $30 and sales hit almost 31 million by 1983. You can now buy a basic calculator for less than $5, or get one free with a magazine subscription. In 1987, 33.8 million calculators were produced.[1]

The rapid decline in the cost of producing calculators led to a rapid expansion of supply and a decline in price. (See Figure 12.2a.) The lower prices increased the quantity demanded to such an extent that most U.S. homes now have at least one calculator, and thousands of people walk around with calculators in their pockets.

This is only a partial equilibrium story, however. The events we described above, of course, had effects on many other markets; in other words, they disturbed the general equilibrium. When mechanical calculators became obsolete, many people who had over the years developed the skills required to produce and repair those complex machines found themselves unemployed. At the same time, demand for workers in the production, distribution, and sales of the new electronic calculators boomed. New skills were required, and the expansion of the industry led to an increase in demand for the kinds of labor needed. The new technology thus caused a reallocation of labor across the labor market.

Capital was also reallocated. New firms invested in the plant and equipment needed to produce electronic calculators. Old capital owned by the firms that previously made mechanical calculators became obsolete and depreciated, and it ended up on the scrapheap. The mechanical calculators themselves, once an integral part of the capital stocks of accounting firms, banks, and so forth, were scrapped as they became obsolete and were replaced by the cheaper, more efficient new models.[2]

When a new billion-dollar industry suddenly appears, it earns billions of dollars in revenues that might have been spent on other things. Even though the effects of this success on any one other industry were probably small, general equilibrium analysis tells us that in the absence of the new industry and the demand for its product, households will demand other goods and services, and other industries will produce more. In this case, society has benefited a great deal. Everyone can now buy a very useful product at a low price. The new calculators have raised the productivity of certain kinds of labor and reduced costs in many industries.

The point here is clear:

> A significant—if not sweeping—technological change in a single industry affects many markets. Households face a different structure of prices and must adjust their consumption of many products. Labor reacts to new skill requirements and is reallocated across markets. Capital is also reallocated.

---

[1] U.S. Department of Commerce, Bureau of the Census, *Statistical Abstract of the United States, 1983/1984, 1990, 1992.* Compiled from reports of associations and manufacturers.

[2] In recent years, of course, the electronic calculator has increasingly been replaced by the personal computer. In 1992, more than 50 million personal computers were in use in the United States (up from 2 million in 1981). More than 7 million new PCs are now being produced each year.

A Shift in Consumer Preferences: The Wine Industry in the 1970s

For a more formal view of the general equilibrium effects of a change in one market on other markets, consider an economy with just two sectors, X and Y. For purposes of our discussion, let us say that the wine business in the United States is industry X and everything else is industry Y. Let us also assume that the wine industry is perfectly competitive.

During the 1970s, U.S. consumer preferences in alcoholic beverages shifted significantly in favor of wine. Table 12.1 provides some data. Domestic wine production increased by 74% between 1965 and 1980. In addition, in 1980 the United States imported more than nine times as much wine as it had in 1965. Overall demand increased 86.6 percent. Part of this increase was due to increased population, part was probably due to a change in the age distribution of the population, and part was due to a simple change in preferences. Per capita consumption of wine rose 53 percent.

Figure 12.3 on the next page shows the initial equilibrium in sectors X and Y. We assume that both sectors are initially in long-run competitive equilibrium. Total output in sector X is Q_X^0, the product is selling for a price of P_X^0, and each firm in the industry produces up to where P_X^0 is equal to marginal cost—q_X^0. At that point, price is just equal to average cost, and economic profits are zero. The same condition holds initially in sector Y. The market is in zero profit equilibrium at a price of P_Y^0.

Now assume that a change in consumer preferences (or in the age distribution of the population, or in something else) shifts the demand for X out to the right from D_X^0 to D_X^1. That shift drives price up to P_X^1. If households decide to buy more X, without an increase in income they must buy *less* of something else. Since everything else is represented by Y in this example, the demand for Y must decline, and the demand curve for Y shifts to the left from D_Y^0 to D_Y^1.

With the shift in demand for X, price rises to P_X^1 and profit-maximizing firms immediately increase output to q_X^1, (the point where $P_X^1 = MC_X$). But now there are economic profits in X, profits over and above a normal rate of return. With the downward shift of demand in Y, price falls to P_Y^1. Firms in sector Y cut back to q_Y^1 (the point where $P_Y^1 = MC_Y$), and the lower price causes firms producing Y to suffer economic losses.

In the short run, adjustment is simple. Firms in both industries are constrained by their current scales of plant. Firms can neither enter nor exit their respective industries. Each firm in industry X raises output somewhat, from q_X^0 to q_X^1. Firms in industry Y cut back from q_Y^0 to q_Y^1.

TABLE 12.1
Production and Consumption of Wine in the United States, 1965–1980

YEAR	U.S. PRODUCTION (MILLIONS OF GALLONS)	IMPORTS (MILLIONS OF GALLONS)	TOTAL (MILLIONS OF GALLONS)	CONSUMPTION PER CAPITA (GALLONS)
1965	565	10	575	1.32
1970	713	22	735	1.52
1975	782	40	822	1.96
1980	983	91	1073	2.02
Percent change, 1965–1980	**+74.0**	**+81.0**	**+86.6**	**+53.0**

Source: U.S. Department of Commerce, Bureau of the Census, *Statistical Abstract of the United States, 1985*, table 1364, p. 765.

In response to the existence of economic profit in sector X, the capital market begins to take notice. In Chapter 9 we said that existing firms have an incentive to expand in, and new firms are likely to enter, an industry in which there are economic profits to be earned. In Chapter 11, we discussed the mechanics of capital allocation in more detail. Firms in an industry that is earning economic profits

FIGURE 12.3
Adjustment in an Industry with Two Sectors

Initially, demand for X shifts from D_X^0 to D_X^1. This shift pushes the price of X up to P_X^1, creating economic profits. Demand for Y shifts from D_Y^0 to D_Y^1, pushing the price of Y down to P_Y^1, and creating economic losses. Firms have an incentive to leave sector Y and an incentive to enter sector X. Exiting sector Y shifts supply in that industry to S_Y^1, raising price and eliminating losses. Entry and expansion shift supply in X to S_X^1, thus reducing price and eliminating profits.

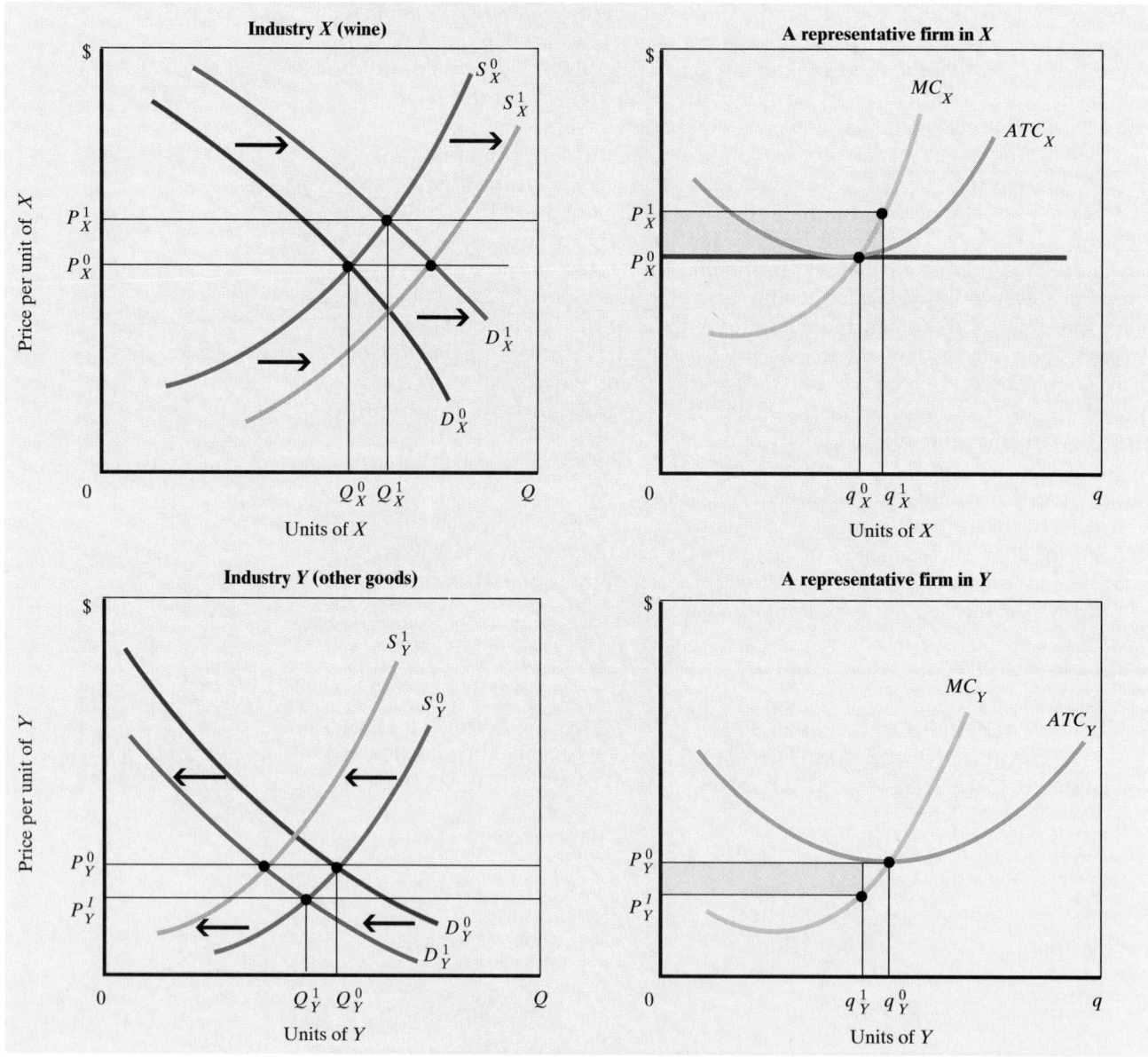

find their expectations rising and undertake investment projects that look attractive. Financial analysts also see the economic profits as a signal of future healthy growth, and entrepreneurs may become interested in the industry.

Adding all this together, we would expect to see investment begin to favor sector X. This is indeed the case: Capital begins to flow into sector X. As new firms enter and existing firms expand, the short-run supply curve in the industry shifts to the right and continues to do so until all economic profits are eliminated. In the top left diagram in Figure 12.3, the supply curve moves from S_X^0 to S_X^1, a shift that drives price back down to P_X^0.

Let us now apply our theoretical analysis to the wine industry. During the 1970s, demand for wine increased substantially. Prices began to rise, profits followed, and wine makers did very well. The high profits stimulated investment and expansion, both by existing wine companies and by new ones. Dozens of new vineyards planted vines in California, and a number of companies began mass production of wine.

Wine production is relatively "land intensive," and good wine is produced only from good land where the climate is right for grapes. Table 12.2 shows the number of vineyards and total acreage in grape production in 1974 and 1982. Between those years, over 10,000 new grape producers started up operations in the United States. In California alone, 150,000 additional acres were planted with grape vines. Thus, one of the other ways that expansion in the wine business affected the general equilibrium was that the land market was thrown off balance, and land prices in the good wine-growing regions increased.

In Figure 12.3, we saw that as sector X reaped the benefits of a shift of consumer preferences, sector Y experienced a decline in demand. With the decline, the price of Y fell to P_Y^1, creating the economic losses shown in the shaded area in the lower right diagram.

In the short run, firms in sector Y must bear those losses. Some firms may decide to shut down and take losses equal to fixed costs, but they cannot go completely out of business. In the long run, however, capital will flow out of the industry. Some firms will exit the industry and firms remaining in the industry may reduce production. Certainly financial markets will not smile on such a sector.

Since demand in sector Y has shifted to the left, reducing prices and creating losses in the industry, firms will exit the sector in the long run. As this occurs, the supply curve in Y shifts back to the left, pushing up prices and reducing losses. Capital continues to exit until all economic losses are eliminated. A new general equilibrium is not reached until equilibrium is reestablished in all markets. If costs of production remain unchanged, as they do in Figure 12.3, this equilibrium occurs at the initial product prices, but with more resources and production in X

	NUMBER OF VINEYARDS	NUMBER OF ACRES
United States		
1974	14,208	712,804
1982	24,982	874,996
Percent change	+75.8	+22.8
California		
1974	8,333	607,011
1982	10,481	756,720
Percent change	+25.8	+24.7

TABLE 12.2

Land in Grape Production in the United States and in California Alone, 1974 and 1982

Source: U.S. Department of Commerce, Bureau of the Census, *Census of Agriculture* (1974 and 1982), 1, part 51.

and less in Y. If expansion in X drives up the prices of resources used specifically in X, however, the cost curves in X shift upward and the final, post-expansion, zero-profit equilibrium occurs at a higher price. In Chapter 9 we referred to such an industry as an *increasing-cost industry*. This is exactly what happened in the case of premier California wines.[3]

Formal Proof of a General Competitive Equilibrium

Economic theorists have struggled with the question of whether a set of prices that equates supply and demand in all markets simultaneously can actually exist when there are literally thousands and thousands of markets. If such a set of prices were not possible, the result could be continuous cycles of expansion, contraction, and instability.

The nineteenth-century French economist Leon Walras struggled with the problem, but he could never provide a formal proof. Using advanced mathematical tools, economists Kenneth Arrow and Gerard Debreu and mathematicians John von Neumann and Abraham Wald have now shown the existence of at least one set of prices that *will* clear all markets in a large system simultaneously.

ALLOCATIVE EFFICIENCY AND COMPETITIVE EQUILIBRIUM

Chapters 4 through 11 built a complete model of a simple, perfectly competitive economic system. But recall that in Chapters 4 and 5 we made a number of important assumptions. We assumed that both output markets and input markets are perfectly competitive—that is, that no individual household or firm is large enough relative to the market to have any control over price. In other words, we assumed that firms and households are *price-takers*.

We also assumed that households have perfect information on product quality and on all prices available and that firms have perfect knowledge of technologies and input prices. Finally, we said that decision makers in a competitive system always consider all the costs and benefits of their decisions, that there are no "external" costs.

If all these assumptions hold, the economy will produce an efficient allocation of resources. As we relax these assumptions one by one, however, you will discover that the allocation of resources is no longer efficient and that a number of sources of inefficiency occur naturally.

Pareto Efficiency

In Chapter 1 we introduced several specific criteria used by economists to judge the performance of economic systems and to evaluate alternative economic policies. These criteria are (1) efficiency, (2) equity, (3) growth, and (4) stability. In Chapter 1 you also learned that an *efficient* economy is one that produces the things that people want and does so at least cost. The idea behind the efficiency criterion is that the economic system exists to serve the wants and needs of the people in a society; if resources can be somehow reallocated to make the people "better off," then they should be. We want to use the resources at our disposal to produce maximum well-being; the trick is defining "maximum well-being."

For many years, social philosophers wrestled with the problem of "aggregation." When we say "maximum well-being" we mean "maximum" *for society*. Societies are made up of many people, however, and the problem has always been how to maxi-

---

[3]To complete the story of the U.S. wine industry: The decade of the 1980s was one of decline. Between 1980 and the end of the decade, domestic wine production dropped to 611 million gallons, a 38% decrease from the 1980 figure. This decline caused many producers to suffer losses and contract; many others went out of business.

LINKS BETWEEN INPUT AND OUTPUT MARKETS: THE LUMBER INDUSTRY AND THE PRICE OF NEW HOUSING

Price increases in the lumber industry increase the cost of building houses and thus have an impact on the supply of new housing. The price of new homes rises as the supply of new housing falls. When demand for new housing grows, as it does when the interest rate falls, the demand for lumber increases. This in turn drives up timber prices.

You can see these connections in the following excerpt, which describes the dramatic up-swing in lumber prices in 1993:

SEATTLE, March 10 [1993]— Lumber prices have jumped 82 percent since September [1992] and are likely to continue to soar with the arrival of spring [1993], when building increases and the demand for lumber picks up.

Because the cost of lumber usually amounts to 10 to 15 percent of the cost of a new home, the shortage of lumber could eventually push up home prices.

"We haven't seen this kind of market since the late 1960's," said Robert Wulf, investor relations manager at Pope & Talbot, a 144-year-old timber company in Portland, Ore. "Panic buying started in the fourth quarter of 1992. If you're a builder and want to construct 10 houses, you want to make sure you have the lumber. Price is not as important as availability."

Behind the higher prices is a shortage of lumber, brought on in large part by the extent to which Federal forests have been closed to loggers for environmental reasons. Logging on eight million acres of timber owned by the Federal Government in the Pacific Northwest has been sharply reduced: from 1982 to 1992, sales of timber from land in Washington and Oregon owned by the United States Forest Service topped 4 billion board feet annually. Last year, they totaled a mere 385 million board feet....

In July composite framing lumber sold for $260 per thousand board feet; last Friday the cost had risen to $474.

When the lumber industry cannot cut trees as a result of legislation designed to protect the owl's habitat, the price of housing goes up.

Source: "Lumber Prices Are Soaring On Shortages and Owl Feud," *New York Times*, March 10, 1993.

mize satisfaction, or well-being, for all members of society. What has emerged is the now widely accepted concept of *allocative efficiency,* first developed by the Italian economist Vilfredo Pareto in the nineteenth century. Pareto's very precise definition of efficiency is often referred to as **Pareto efficiency** or **Pareto optimality.**

Specifically, a change is said to be efficient if it at least potentially makes some members of society better off without making other members of society worse off. An efficient, or *Pareto optimal,* system is one in which no such changes are possible. An example of a change that makes some people better off and nobody worse off is a simple voluntary exchange. I have apples; you have nuts. I like nuts; you like apples. We trade. We both gain, and no one loses.

In order for such a definition to have any real meaning, we must answer two questions: (1) What do we mean by "better off"? and (2) How do we account for changes that make some people better off and others worse off?

The answer to the first question is simple. People themselves decide what "better off" and "worse off" mean. I am the only one who knows whether I'm better off after a change. If you and I exchange one item for another because I like what you have and you like what I have, we both "reveal" that we are better off after the exchange because we agreed to it voluntarily. If everyone in the neighborhood wants a park and they all contribute to a fund to build one, they have consciously changed the allocation of resources, and they are all better off for it.

Pareto efficiency, or Pareto optimality A condition in which no change is possible that will make some members of society better off without making some other members of society worse off.

The answer to the second question is more complex. Nearly every change that one can imagine leaves some people better off and some people worse off. If some gain and some lose as the result of a change, and it can be demonstrated that the value of the gains exceeds the value of the losses, then the change is said to be *potentially efficient*. In practice, however, the distinction between a *potential* and an *actual* efficient change is often ignored, and all such changes are simply called *efficient*.

EXAMPLE: BUDGET CUTS IN MASSACHUSETTS   Several years ago, in an effort to reduce state spending, the budget of the Massachusetts Registry of Motor Vehicles was cut substantially. This meant, among other things, a sharp reduction in the number of clerks in each office. Almost immediately Massachusetts residents found themselves waiting in line for hours when they had to register their automobiles or get their driver's licenses.

Clearly, drivers and car owners began paying a price—standing in line, which uses time and energy that could otherwise be used more productively. But before we can make sensible efficiency judgments, we must be able to measure, or at least approximate, the value of both the gains and the losses produced by the budget cut. To approximate the losses to car owners and drivers, we might ask how much people would be willing to pay to avoid standing in those long lines.

One office estimated that 500 people stood in line every day for about one hour each. If each person were willing to pay just $2 to avoid standing in line, the damage incurred would be $1000 (500 × $2) per day. If the registry were open 250 days per year, the reduction in labor force at that office alone would create a cost to car owners, conservatively estimated, of $250,000 (250 × $1000) per year.

Estimates also showed that taxpayers in Massachusetts saved about $80,000 per year by having fewer clerks at that office. If the clerks were reinstated, there would be some gains and some losses. Car owners and drivers would gain, and taxpayers would lose. But since we can show that the value of the gains would substantially exceed the value of the losses, it can be argued that reinstating the clerks would be an efficient change. Note that the only *net* losers would be those taxpayers who don't own a car and don't hold driver's licenses.[4]

The Efficiency of Perfect Competition

In Chapter 2 we discussed the "economic problem" of dividing up scarce resources among alternative uses. We also discussed the three basic questions that all societies must answer, and we set out to explain how these three questions are answered in a competitive economy:

THE THREE BASIC QUESTIONS	1. How do capital, labor, and land get divided up among firms? In other words, what is the allocation of resources among producers?
	2. What determines which households get how much? In other words, what is the distribution of output among consuming households?
	3. What determines the final mix of output? In other words, what combination of things gets produced?

The following discussion of efficiency uses these three questions and their answers as the bases for an informal "proof" of the efficiency of competition. To demonstrate that the perfectly competitive system leads to an efficient, or Pareto

---

[4]But, you might ask, aren't there other gainers and losers? What about the clerks themselves? In analyses like this one, it is usually assumed that the citizens who pay lower taxes now spend their added income on other things. The producers of those other things need to expand to meet the new demand, and they hire more labor. Thus, a contraction of 100 jobs in the public sector will open up 100 jobs in the private sector. If the economy is fully employed, the transfer of labor to the private sector is assumed to create no net gains or losses to the workers themselves.

optimal, allocation of resources, we need to show that no changes are possible that will make some people better off without making others worse off. Specifically, we will show that under perfect competition (1) resources are allocated among firms efficiently, (2) final products are distributed among households efficiently, and (3) the system produces the things that people want.

EFFICIENT ALLOCATION OF RESOURCES AMONG FIRMS   The simple definition of efficiency holds that firms must produce their products using the best available—that is, lowest cost—technology. Clearly, if more output could be produced with the same amount of inputs, it would be possible to make some people better off without making others worse off.

The competitive model we have been using rests on several assumptions that assure us that resources in such a system would indeed be efficiently allocated among firms. Most important of these is the assumption that individual firms maximize profits. In order to maximize profit, a firm must minimize the cost of producing its chosen level of output. With a full knowledge of existing technologies, firms will choose the technology that produces the output it wants at least cost.

There is more to this story than meets the eye, however. Inputs must be allocated *across* firms in the best possible way. If we find that it is possible, for example, to take capital from firm A and swap it for labor from firm B and produce more product in both firms, then the original allocation was inefficient. Recall our example from Chapter 2. Farmers in Ohio and Kansas both produce wheat and corn. The climate and soil in most of Kansas is best suited to wheat production; the climate and soil in Ohio is best suited to corn production. Clearly, Kansas should produce most of the wheat and Ohio should produce most of the corn. A law that forces Kansas land into corn production and Ohio land into wheat production would result in less of both—an inefficient allocation of resources. But if markets are free and open, Kansas farmers will naturally find a higher return by planting wheat, and Ohio farmers will find a higher return in corn. The free market, then, should lead to an efficient allocation of resources among firms.

The same argument can be made more general. Misallocation of resources among firms is unlikely as long as every single firm faces the same set of prices and trade-offs in input markets. Recall from Chapter 10 that perfectly competitive firms will hire additional factors of production as long as their marginal revenue product exceeds their market price. As long as all firms have access to the *same* factor markets and the *same* factor prices, the last unit of a factor hired will produce the *same* value in each firm. Certainly firms will use different technologies and factor combinations, but at the margin, no single profit-maximizing firm can get more value out of a factor than that factor's current market price. If, for example, workers can be hired in the labor market at a wage of $6.50, *all* firms will hire workers as long as the marginal revenue product produced by the marginal worker (labor's marginal revenue product—MRP_L) remains above $6.50. *No* firms will hire labor beyond the point at which MRP_L falls below $6.50. Thus, at equilibrium, additional workers are not worth more than $6.50 to any firm, and switching labor from one firm to another will not produce output of any greater value to society. Each firm has hired the profit-maximizing amount of labor. In short:

> The assumptions that factor markets are competitive and open, that all firms pay the same prices for inputs, and that all firms maximize profits lead to the conclusion that the allocation of resources among firms is efficient.

EFFICIENT DISTRIBUTION OF OUTPUTS AMONG HOUSEHOLDS   Even if the system is producing the right things, and is doing so efficiently, these things still have to get to the right people. The Boggses shouldn't end up with the things that the Mattinglys like, and the Mattinglys shouldn't end up with the things that the Boggses like. Just as open, competitive factor markets ensure that firms don't end up with the wrong inputs, open, competitive output markets ensure that households don't end up with the wrong goods and services.

Within the constraints imposed by income and wealth, households are free to choose among all the goods and services available in output markets. A household will buy a good as long as that good generates utility, or subjective value, greater than its market price. Utility value is revealed in market behavior. You don't go out and buy something unless you are willing to pay *at least* the market price.

Figure 12.4 shows a market demand curve for a good, X. Everyone who values X at more than P^* per unit buys it and receives a "consumer surplus." Those who subjectively value it at less than P^* do not buy it. Imagine that everyone is currently consuming the bundle of goods that maximizes his or her total utility. In total, Q^* units of X will be consumed, and we end up at point A on the market demand curve. At this point, anyone who values X at more than P^* per unit buys it until the value that he places on a marginal unit of X falls to P^* (remember diminishing marginal utility). Thus, an *additional* unit of X is worth no more than P^* to *any* household, and redistributing X from one household to another will not add value to society. The reason is that the people who have bought X are the people in society who value X the most. Redistributing X would then mean giving X to people who value it less than those who had bought X. This will be true as long as everyone faces the same set of prices and is free to buy as much or as little as he or she wants.[5]

---

[5]Remember that the value you place on any one good depends on what you must give up to have that good. The trade-offs available to you depend on your budget constraint. The trade-offs that are desirable depend on your preferences. If you buy a $400 CD player for your dorm room, you may be giving up a trip home. If I buy it, I may be giving up four new tires for my car. But we've both revealed that the CD player is worth at least as much to us as all the other things that $400 can buy. As long as we are free to choose among all the things that $400 can buy, we will not end up with the wrong things; it's not possible to find a trade that will make us both better off.

FIGURE 12.4
Demand Curves Reveal Household "Willingness to Pay"

A demand curve illustrates how the market forces households to reveal their preferences. You do not get a product unless you pay for it. Those who are "willing to pay" as much as or more than the going price, P^*, buy the good; those who are not, do not.

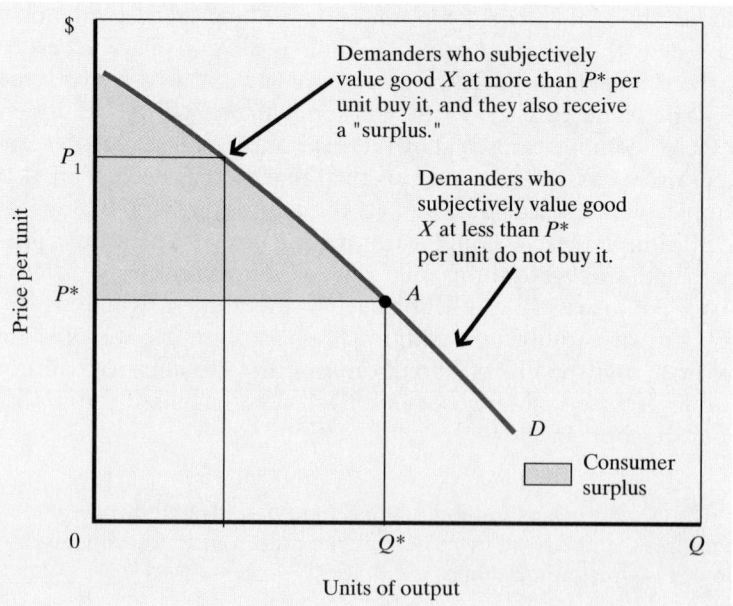

This argument is really quite intuitive:

> We all know that people have different tastes and preferences, and that they will buy very different things in very different combinations. But as long as everyone shops freely in the same markets, no redistribution of final outputs among people will make them better off. If you and I buy in the same markets and pay the same prices, and I buy what I want and you buy what you want, neither of us can possibly end up with the wrong combination of things. But free and open markets are essential to this result.

PRODUCING WHAT PEOPLE WANT: THE EFFICIENT MIX OF OUTPUT It does no good to produce things efficiently or to distribute them efficiently if the system produces the wrong things. Will competitive markets produce the things that people want?

If the system is producing the wrong mix of output, we should be able to show that producing more of one good and less of another will make people better off. In order to show that perfectly competitive markets are efficient, then, we must demonstrate that no such changes in the final mix of output are possible.

The condition that ensures that the right things are produced is $P = MC$. That is, in both the long run and the short run, a perfectly competitive firm will produce at the point where the price of its output is equal to the marginal cost of production. The logic is this: When a firm weighs price and marginal cost, it weighs the value of its product to society *at the margin* against the value of the things that could otherwise be produced with the same resources. If product Y is worth more to people than what otherwise could be produced with the same resources, then competition ensures that product Y will be produced instead of those other things. Figure 12.5 summarizes this logic.

But this is true *only if price is a good measure of the value that society places on a good and only if marginal cost is a good measure of the value of the things that might otherwise be produced with the same resources.* We have already made the argument that price *is* a good measure of the worth of a marginal unit of a good or service to society. (Review Figure 12.4.) Anyone who subjectively values a good or service at more than P^* buys that good or service; anyone who values it less than P^* does not buy it. Thus, when a *marginal* unit of product is produced, the person or household that ends up with that marginal unit is that person or household that values it just at P^*.

To see why this is so, imagine the supply of X expanding by one unit. Price will drop an infinitesimal amount to clear the market, and someone—some person or household that, before the supply expansion, was indifferent between buying

value placed on good X iety through the market, or the social value a marginal unit of X

$$P_X = MC_X$$

Market-determined value of resources needed to produce a marginal unit of X. MC is equal to the opportunity cost of those resources: lost production of other goods or the value of the resources left unemployed (leisure, vacant land, etc.)

The cost of a marginal unit of good X to society

If $P_X > MC_X$, society gains value by producing *more X*.

If $P_X < MC_X$, society gains value by producing *less X*.

FIGURE 12.5
The Key Efficiency Condition: Price Equals Marginal Cost

Society will produce the efficient mix of output if all firms equate price and marginal cost.

and not buying—will be induced to buy just that one unit. In a sense, that person is sitting right at point A on the demand curve in Figure 12.4. All of this is to say that P^* is a good measure of the actual "benefit" to society of producing an additional, or marginal, unit of product X.

To establish that marginal cost is a good measure of the societal cost, or opportunity cost, of additional production of a good, let's turn back to input markets. Resources are required to produce an added unit of output. These resources come from one of two sources: Either they were previously unused (or unemployed) or they were used, (or employed), but in the production of some other good or service.

Consider labor as an example of a factor that would otherwise have been employed producing something else. Recall that workers are paid a wage just equal to the marginal revenue product of labor ($W = MRP_L = P_X \cdot MP_L$). Thus, if a certain amount of labor is drawn out of the production of good X, society loses an amount of product X equal in value to the value of the labor withdrawn.

At equilibrium, with many firms each buying labor up to the point at which $W = MRP_L$, a unit of labor will be attracted from one firm to another only when the *product* of that unit of labor is valued more highly in the second firm. If all resources are valued in competitive markets, the marginal cost of a unit of output is just equal to the value of the goods that otherwise would have been produced with the same inputs.

Using labor as an example once again, consider what happens when resources that would otherwise have been unemployed are used in production. If each firm equates the equilibrium wage to the value of labor's marginal product, and a person chooses not to be in the labor force, that person reveals that either leisure or the value of nonpaid labor is worth more to him or her than the value that society places on his or her potential product in the market. It is therefore efficient *not* to work. Thus, if you go from being voluntarily unemployed to holding a job in which you produce goods or services for the market, you are giving up leisure that is *less* valuable to you than the wage you are paid. Those who value leisure more highly will not take a job; those who place an even lower value on leisure are already working. Remember that the "price," or opportunity cost, of each hour of leisure is the wage you could have earned by working that additional hour.

Marginal cost, then, is a good measure of what society gives up by using resources to produce more of a good or service. If the resources needed to produce something are taken away from the production of something else, MC measures the value of the *product* given up; if those resources were previously unused, MC measures the value of *leisure* that is given up.

In sum:

Because competitive firms will produce as long as the price of their product is greater than the marginal cost of production, they will produce as long as a gain for society is possible. That is, if society values good X more than it values good Y or what otherwise would be produced with the same resources needed to produce X, then more X will indeed be produced. The market guarantees that the right things are produced, and competitive markets therefore yield an efficient mix of output.[6] By this same reasoning, however, if the price of some good ends up above the marginal cost of production at equilibrium, additional production will provide benefits in excess of the real costs to society. This means that the good is being underproduced and that the outcome is inefficient.

[6]It is important to understand that firms do not act *consciously* to balance social costs and benefits. In fact, the usual assumption is that firms are self-interested, private profit-maximizers. It just works out that in perfectly competitive markets, when firms are weighing private benefits against private costs, they are actually (perhaps without knowing it) weighing the benefits and costs to society as well.

Figure 12.6 shows how a simple competitive market system leads individual households and firms to make efficient choices in input and output markets. For simplicity, the figure assumes only one factor of production, labor. Households weigh the market wage against the value of leisure and time spent in unpaid household production. But the wage is a measure of labor's potential product because firms weigh labor cost (wages) against the value of the product produced and hire up to the point at which $W = MRP_L$. Households use wages to buy market-produced goods. Thus, households implicitly weigh the value of market-produced goods against the value of leisure and household production.

When a firm's scale is balanced, it is earning maximum profit; when a household's scale is balanced, it is maximizing utility. Under these conditions, no changes can improve social welfare.

Perfect Competition versus Real Markets

So far, we have built a model of a perfectly competitive market system that produces an efficient allocation of resources, an efficient mix of output, and an efficient distribution of output. But the perfectly competitive model is built on a set of assumptions, all of which must hold for our conclusions to be fully valid. We have assumed that all firms and households are price-takers in input and output markets, that firms and households have perfect information, that all firms maximize profits, and so forth.

FIGURE 12.6
Efficiency in Perfect Competition Follows from a Weighing of Values by Both Households and Firms

For simplicity, assume that there is just one variable factor of production, labor. Households are presumed to weigh the value of market-produced goods against the value of leisure and household production. To buy products, households must earn income from wages. But, because firms weigh the cost of labor, as reflected in wages, against the value of labor's product, households are actually weighing the value of leisure and home production against the value of what they would produce ($W = MP_L \cdot P_X$) if they entered the labor force. The result is an efficient balance in both output and input markets.

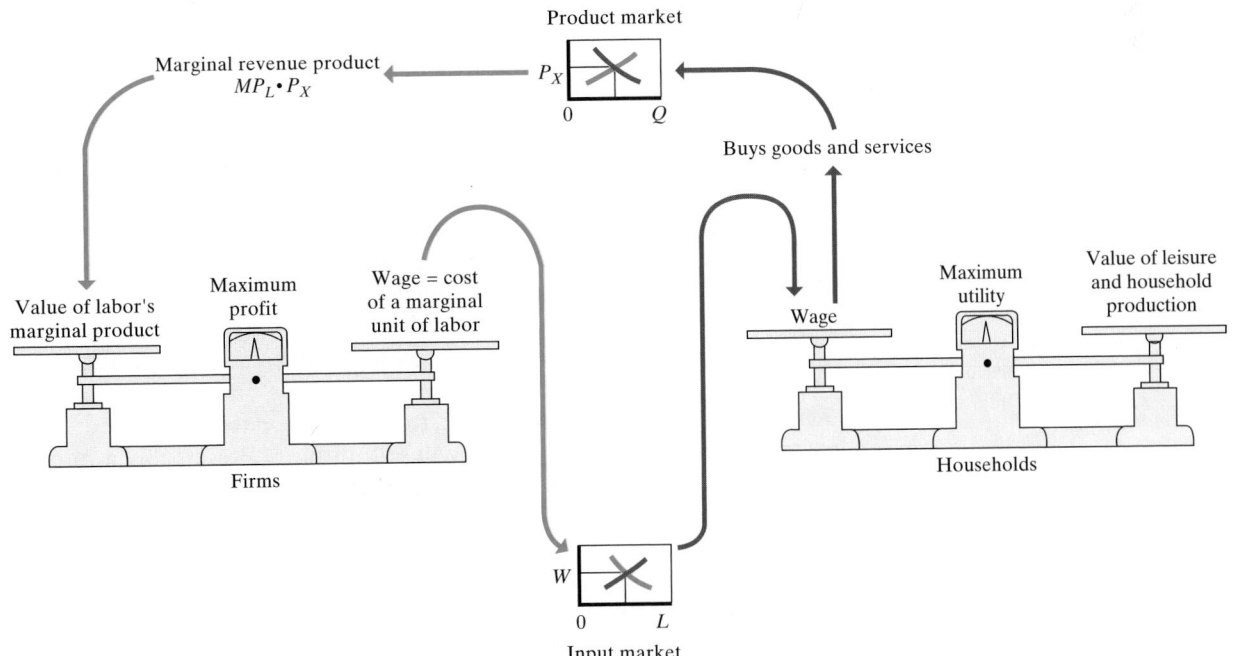

But these assumptions do not always hold in real-world markets. When this is the case, the conclusion that free, unregulated markets will produce an efficient outcome breaks down. The remainder of this chapter discusses some inefficiencies that occur naturally in markets and some of the strengths, as well as the weaknesses, of the market mechanism. We also discuss the usefulness of the competitive model for understanding the real economy.

THE SOURCES OF MARKET FAILURE

In suggesting some of the problems encountered in real markets and some of the possible solutions to these problems, the rest of this chapter previews the next part of this book, which focuses on the economics of market failure and the role of government in the economy.

market failure Occurs when resources are misallocated, or allocated inefficiently. The result is waste or lost value.

Market failure occurs when resources are misallocated, or allocated inefficiently. The result is waste or lost value. In this section, we briefly describe four important sources of market failure: (1) *imperfect market structure,* or noncompetitive behavior, (2) the existence of *public goods,* (3) the presence of *external costs and benefits,* and (4) *imperfect information.* Each condition results from the failure of one of the assumptions basic to the perfectly competitive model, and each is discussed in more detail in later chapters. Each also points to a potential role for government in the economy. The desirability and extent of actual government involvement in the economy is, as you are no doubt aware, a hotly debated subject.

Imperfect Markets

Until now we have operated on the assumption that the number of buyers and sellers in each market is large. When each buyer and each seller is only one of a great many in the market, no individual buyer or seller can independently influence price. Thus, all economic decision makers are by virtue of their relatively small size forced to take input prices and output prices as given. When this assumption does not hold—that is, when single firms have some control over price and potential competition—the result is **imperfect competition** and an inefficient allocation of resources.

imperfect competition An industry in which single firms have some control over price and competition. Imperfectly competitive industries give rise to an inefficient allocation of resources.

A Kansas wheat farmer is probably a "price-taker," but Xerox and Chrysler Corporation most certainly are not. Many firms in many industries do have some control over price. The degree of control that is possible depends on the character of competition in the industry itself.

monopoly An industry comprised of only one firm that produces a product for which there are no close substitutes and in which significant barriers exist to prevent new firms from entering the industry.

An industry that is comprised of just one firm producing a product for which there are no close substitutes is called a **monopoly.** Although a monopoly has no other firms to compete with, it is still constrained by market demand. To be successful, the firm still has to produce something that people want. Essentially, a monopoly must choose both price and quantity of output simultaneously because the amount that it will be able to sell depends on the price it sets. If the price is too high, it will sell nothing. Presumably a monopolist sets price in order to maximize profit. That price is generally significantly above average costs, and such a firm usually earns economic profits.

In competition, economic profits will attract the entry of new firms into the industry. A rational monopolist who is not restrained by the government does everything possible to block any such entry in order to preserve economic profits in the long run. As a result, society loses the benefits of more product and lower prices. A number of barriers to entry can be raised. Sometimes a monopoly is actually licensed by government, and entry into its market is prohibited by law. Taiwan has only one beer company; most areas in the United States have only one local telephone company. Ownership of a natural resource can also be the source of monopoly power. If I buy up all the coal mines in the United States and I persuade Congress to restrict coal imports, no one can enter the coal industry and compete with me.

Between monopoly and perfect competition are a number of other imperfectly competitive market structures. *Oligopolistic industries* are made up of a small number of firms, each with a degree of price-setting power. *Monopolistically competitive industries* are made up of a large number of firms that acquire price-setting power by differentiating their products or by establishing a brand name. Only General Mills can produce Wheaties, for example, and only Miles Laboratories can produce Alka-Seltzer.

> In all imperfectly competitive industries, output is lower—the product is underproduced—and price is higher than it would be under perfect competition. The equilibrium condition $P = MC$ does not hold, and the system does not produce the most efficient product mix.

In the United States, many forms of noncompetitive behavior are illegal. The Sherman Act of 1890 makes "combinations or conspiracies in restraint of trade" illegal. A firm that attempts to monopolize an industry or conspires with other firms to reduce competition risks serious penalties. The Clayton Act of 1914 strengthened the Sherman Act and made a few more practices illegal, such as buying the stock of competitive firms, interlocking boards of directors, and price discrimination. The most famous recent antitrust case ended in 1982 with the break-up of the American Telephone and Telegraph Company. The case was originally filed in 1974 by the Justice Department, which charged that AT&T had used its power to freeze out competition in the long-distance and equipment markets. This sort of behavior, the Justice Department argued, prevents society from enjoying the benefits of free competition. (All of this is discussed in much more detail in Chapters 13, 14, and 15.)

Public Goods

A second major source of inefficiency lies in the fact that private producers simply do not find it in their best interest to produce everything that members of society want. More specifically, there is a whole class of goods called **public goods,** or **social goods,** that will be underproduced or not produced at all in a completely unregulated market economy.[7]

Public goods are goods or services that bestow collective benefits on society; they are, in a sense, collectively consumed. The classic example is national defense, but there are countless others—police protection, preservation of wilderness lands, and public health, to name a few. These things are "produced" using land, labor, and capital just like any other good. Some public goods, such as national defense, benefit the whole nation. Others, such as clean air, may be limited to smaller areas—the air may be clean in a Kansas town but dirty in a Southern California city.

public goods, or social goods
Goods or services that bestow collective benefits on members of society; they are, in a sense, collectively consumed. Generally, no one can be excluded from enjoying their benefits. The classic example is national defense.

---

[7]While they are normally referred to as public *goods,* many of the things we are talking about are *services.*

Public goods are consumed by everyone, not just by those who pay for them. Once the good is produced, no one can be excluded from enjoying its benefits. Producers of **private goods,** like hamburgers, can make a profit because they don't hand over the product to you until you pay for it. (Chapters 4–11 centered on the production of private goods.)

private goods Products produced by firms for sale to individual households.

If the provision of public goods were left to private, profit-seeking producers with no power to force payment, a serious problem would arise. Suppose, for example, that I value some public good, X. If there were a functioning market for X, I would be willing to pay for it. But suppose that I am asked to contribute voluntarily to the production of X. Should I contribute? Perhaps I should on moral grounds but not on the basis of pure self-interest.

At least two problems can get in the way. First, since I cannot be excluded from using X for not paying, I get the good whether I pay or not. Why should I pay if I don't have to? Second, since public goods that provide collective benefits to large numbers of people are expensive to produce, any one person's contribution is not likely to make much difference to the amount of the good ultimately produced. Would the national defense suffer, for example, if you didn't pay your share of the bill? Probably not. Thus, nothing happens if you don't pay; the output of the good doesn't change much, and you get it whether you pay or not.

For these reasons:

> Private provision of public goods fails. A completely laissez-faire market system will not produce everything that all members of a society might want. Citizens must band together to ensure that desired public goods are produced, and this is generally accomplished through government spending financed by taxes. The purpose of government provision of public goods is to correct for a naturally occurring failure of the market to produce everything that consumers want.

Public goods are the subject of Chapter 16.

Externalities

A third major source of inefficiency in the market is the existence of external costs and benefits. An **externality** is a cost or benefit imposed or bestowed on an individual or group that is outside, or external to, the transaction—in other words, something that affects a third party. In a city, external costs are pervasive. The classic example is pollution, but there are thousands of others, such as noise, congestion, and painting your house a color that the neighbors think is ugly.

externality A cost or benefit resulting from some activity or transaction that is imposed or bestowed upon parties outside the activity or transaction.

Not all externalities are negative, however. Housing investment, for example, may yield benefits for neighbors. A farm located near a city provides residents in the area with nice views, fresher air, and a less congested environment.

Externalities are a problem only if decision makers do not take them into account. The logic of efficiency presented earlier in this chapter required that firms weigh social benefits against social costs. If a firm in a competitive environment produces a good, it is because the value of that good to society exceeds the social cost of producing it—this is the logic of $P = MC$. If social costs or benefits are overlooked or left out of the calculations, inefficient decisions result.

The market itself has no automatic mechanism that provides decision makers with an incentive to consider external effects. Through government, however, society has established over the years a number of different institutions for dealing with externalities. Tort law, for example, is a body of legal rules that deal with third-party effects. Under certain circumstances, those who impose costs are held strictly liable for them; in other circumstances, liability is assessed only if the cost results from "negligent" behavior. Tort law deals with small problems as well as larger ones. If a neighbor sprays her lawn with a powerful chemical and kills your prize shrub, you can take her to court and force her to pay for it. Huge damages were caused when a large oil tanker ran aground in the Shetland Islands off Scotland in early 1993. Most damage claims resulting from the accident will be settled in court.

The effects of externalities can be enormous. A recent example of an externality with potentially horrifying results is toxic waste dumping. For years, companies piled chemical wastes indiscriminately into dump sites near water supplies and residential areas. In some locations, those wastes seeped into the ground and contaminated the drinking water. In Love Canal, New York, an entire community was forced to abandon its homes to escape the dangers of chemical dumping. Had these potential costs been considered at the time the dumping took place, the chemicals would probably not have been disposed of in this fashion and enormous damages would have been avoided. During 1992 and 1993, several medical journals published reports linking "second-hand" smoke to lung disease and other health problems. In response to the evidence that smoking damages not only the smoker but others as well, governments have increased prohibitions against smoking in public places.

For years, economists have suggested that a carefully designed set of taxes and subsidies could help to "internalize" external effects. For example, if a paper mill that pollutes the air and waterways were taxed in proportion to the damage caused by that pollution, it would consider those costs in its decisions.

Sometimes, interaction among and between parties can lead to the proper consideration of externality without government involvement. If someone plays her radio loudly on the fourth floor of your dormitory, that person imposes an externality on the other residents of the building. The residents, however, can get together and negotiate a set of mutually acceptable rules to govern radio playing.

Calculating damages from externalities in dollar terms is a difficult, but often necessary, task. Judges in liability cases are forced to make judgments of this sort all the time. Public policies that attempt to deal with problems like acid rain will hurt one sector at the expense of another. If the costs of acid rain are as large as some suggest, for example, taxing the industrial firms that cause acid rain will make it very difficult for many of them to survive. If a power plant is forced by government mandate to install every possible measure to reduce pollution, electric bills will rise sharply. Unless absolute rights are involved, gains and losses must be weighed. There are no easy answers.

The key point here is that:

> The market does not always force consideration of all the costs and benefits of decisions. Yet for an economy to achieve an efficient allocation of resources, all costs and benefits must be weighed.

We discuss externalities in more detail in Chapter 16.

Imperfect Information

The fourth major source of inefficiency is **imperfect information** on the part of buyers and sellers:

> The conclusion that markets work efficiently rests heavily on the assumption that consumers and producers have full knowledge of product characteristics, available prices, and so forth. The absence of full information can lead to transactions that are ultimately disadvantageous.

imperfect information The absence of full knowledge regarding product characteristics, available prices, and so forth.

Some products are so complex that consumers find it difficult to judge the potential benefits and costs of purchase. Certainly demanders in the market for medical care do not fully understand what they buy. Buyers of life insurance have a very difficult time sorting out the terms of the more complex policies and determining the true "price" of the product. Consumers of almost any service that requires expertise, such as plumbing or TV repair, have a hard time evaluating what is needed, much less how well it is done. It is difficult for a used car buyer to find out the true "quality" of the cars in Big Jim's Kar Emporium.

Some forms of misinformation can be corrected with simple rules such as "truth-in-advertising" regulations. In some cases, the government provides information to citizens; job banks and consumer information services exist for this purpose. In some industries, such as medical care, there is no clear-cut solution to the problem of noninformation or misinformation. (We discuss these topics in more detail in Chapter 16.)

EVALUATING THE MARKET MECHANISM

Is the market system good or bad? Should the government be involved in the economy, or should it leave the allocation of resources to the free market? So far, our information is mixed and incomplete. To the extent that the perfectly competitive model reflects the way markets really operate, there seem to be some clear advantages to the market system. But when we relax the assumptions and expand our discussion to include noncompetitive behavior, public goods, externalities, and the possibility of imperfect information, we see at least a potential role for government.

The market system does seem to provide most participants with the incentive to weigh costs and benefits and to operate efficiently. Firms can make profits only if a demand for their products exists. If there are no externalities, or if such costs or benefits are properly internalized, firms *will* weigh social benefits and costs in their production decisions. Under these circumstances, the profit motive should provide competitive firms with an incentive to minimize cost and to produce their products using the most efficient technologies. Likewise, competitive input markets should provide households with the incentive to weigh the value of their time against the social value of what they can produce in the labor force.

But markets are far from perfect. Freely functioning markets in the real world do not always produce an efficient allocation of resources, and this provides a potential role for government in the economy. Many have called for government involvement in the economy to correct for market failure—that is, to help markets function more efficiently. As you will see, however, many feel that government involvement in the economy creates more inefficiency than it cures.

In addition, we have thus far discussed only the criterion of efficiency, and economic systems and economic policies must be judged by many other criteria, not the least of which is *equity*, or *fairness*. Indeed, some contend that the outcome of any free market is ultimately unfair, because some become rich while others remain very poor.

Part Three, which follows, explores the issue of market imperfections and government involvement in the economy in greater depth. In Chapter 13, we begin with a discussion of output and pricing decisions in monopoly markets. In Chapter 14, we move on to a discussion of output and pricing decisions in monopolistically competitive industries and oligopolistic industries. Chapters 15, 16, and 17 are all concerned with the potential role of the government in regulating industry, controlling externalities, and redistributing income.

PERFECT COMPETITION: A FINAL WORD

In this chapter we have wrapped up the perfectly competitive model described in detail in the last seven chapters. In discussing the idea of "general equilibrium," we saw how the markets described separately in earlier chapters are all interrelated and how adjustments in any one market can cause subsequent adjustments in many or all of the others. In order to understand the way an economic system functions and to think properly about public policy issues, it is essential that we consider these interconnections. Partial equilibrium analysis can lead to wrong answers.

We also turned for the first time to normative economics. We began by reviewing the concept of efficiency. Next, we took a look at the efficiency of the perfectly competitive system. If all the assumptions of perfect competition hold, the result is efficient. No changes could be made in the allocation of resources among firms, in the mix of output, or in the distribution of output among members of society that would even potentially make some better off without making some worse off.

But the assumptions of perfect competition simply do not hold in the real world. When we relax them in order to describe the world more accurately, we see some of the problems that the unconstrained market does not solve for itself.

SUMMARY

General Equilibrium Analysis

1. Both firms and households make simultaneous choices in both input and output markets. For example, input prices determine output costs and affect output supply decisions of firms; wages in the labor market affect labor supply decisions, income, and ultimately how much output households can and do purchase.

2. A *general equilibrium* exists when all markets in an economy are in simultaneous equilibrium. An event that disturbs the equilibrium in one market may disturb the equilibrium in many other markets as well. *Partial equilibrium analysis* can be misleading, because it looks only at adjustments in one isolated market.

Allocative Efficiency and Competitive Equilibrium

3. An *efficient* economy is one that produces the goods and services that people want and does so at least cost. Specifically, a change is said to be efficient if it at least potentially makes some members of society better off without making others worse off. An efficient, or *Pareto optimal*, system is one in which no such changes are possible.

4. If a change makes some people better off and some people worse off, but it can be shown that the value of the gains exceeds the value of the losses, the change is said to be potentially efficient.

5. If all the assumptions of perfect competition hold, the result is an efficient, or Pareto optimal, allocation of resources. To prove this statement, it is necessary to show that resources are allocated efficiently among firms, that final products are distributed efficiently among households, and that the system produces what people want.

6. The assumptions that factor markets are competitive and open, that all firms pay the same prices for inputs, and that all firms maximize profits lead to the conclusion that the allocation of resources among firms is efficient.

7. People have different tastes and preferences, and they buy very different things in very different combinations. But as long as everyone shops freely in the same markets, no redistribution of outputs among people will make them better off. This leads to the conclusion that final products are distributed efficiently among households.

8. Because perfectly competitive firms will produce as long as the price of their product is greater than the marginal cost of production, they will continue to produce as long as a gain for society is possible. The market thus guarantees that the right things are produced. In other words, the perfectly competitive system produces what people want.

The Sources of Market Failure

9. When the assumptions of perfect competition do *not* hold, the conclusion that free, unregulated markets will produce an efficient allocation of resources breaks down.

10. An imperfectly competitive industry is one in which single firms have some control over price and competition. Forms of *imperfect competition* include *monopoly,* monopolistic competition, and oligopoly. In all imperfectly competitive industries, output is lower and price is higher than it would be in competition. Imperfect competition is a major source of market inefficiency.

11. *Public, or social, goods* bestow collective benefits on members of society. Because the benefits of social goods are collective, people cannot in most cases be excluded from enjoying

them. Thus, private firms usually do not find it profitable to produce public goods. The need for public goods is thus another source of inefficiency.

12. An *externality* is a cost or benefit that is imposed or bestowed on an individual or group that is outside, or external to, the transaction—in other words, something that affects a third party. If such social costs or benefits are overlooked, the decisions of households or firms are likely to be wrong, or inefficient.

13. Market efficiency depends on the assumption that buyers have perfect information on product quality and price and that firms have perfect information on input quality and price. Misinformation can lead to wrong choices and inefficiency.

Evaluating the Market Mechanism

14. Sources of market failure—such as imperfect markets, social goods, externalities, and *imperfect information*—are considered by many to justify the existence of government and governmental policies that seek to redistribute costs and income on the basis of efficiency, equity, or both.

REVIEW TERMS AND CONCEPTS

efficiency   292
externality   308
general equilibrium   292
imperfect competition   306
imperfect information   309
market failure   306

monopoly   306
Pareto efficiency,
  or Pareto optimality   299
partial equilibrium analysis   292
private goods   308
public goods, or social goods   307

Equations:

Key efficiency condition in perfect
  competition: $P_X = MC_X$

PROBLEM SET

1. A medium-sized bakery has just opened in Slovakia. A loaf of bread is currently selling for 14 koruna (the Slovakian currency) over and above the cost of intermediate goods (flour, etc.). Assuming that labor is the only variable factor of production, the following table gives the production function for bread:

WORKERS	LOAVES OF BREAD
0	0
1	15
2	30
3	42
4	52
5	60
6	66
7	70

a. Suppose that the current wage rate in Slovakia is 119 koruna per hour. How many workers will the bakery employ?

b. Suppose that the economy of Slovakia begins to grow, incomes rise, and the price of a loaf of bread is pushed up to 20 koruna. Assuming no increase in the price of labor, how many workers will the bakery hire?

c. An increase in the demand for labor pushes up wages to 125 koruna per hour. What impact will this increase in cost have on employment and output in the bakery?

d. If all firms behaved like our bakery, would the allocation of resources in Slovakia be efficient? Explain your answer.

2. On February 4, 1993, the *New York Times* reported a sharp increase in timber prices in the United States: "Lumber prices have climbed steadily since early November as signs of economic recovery have sent dealers scrambling for supplies reduced by logging bans in the Northwest." One part of the reason for this increase in price is the reduced supply of timber due to environmental regulations limiting logging. Another part of the explanation has to do with an increase in demand.

a. What sectors produced in the United States are likely to use large amounts of timber products? Under what circumstances do these sectors see an increase in the demand for their products?

b. Go to the library and find data on the number of housing starts in the United States in 1991, 1992, and 1993. What pattern do you see in the numbers? Can you offer an explanation?

3. Do you agree or disagree with each of the following statements? Explain your answer.

a. "Housing is a 'public good' and should be produced by the public sector because private markets will fail to produce it efficiently."

b. "Monopoly power is inefficient, since large firms will produce too much product, dumping it on the market at artificially low prices."

c. "Medical care is an example of a potentially inefficient market because consumers do not have perfect information about the product."

4. A major source of chicken feed in the United States is anchovies, small fish that can be scooped up out of the ocean at low cost. Every seven years, the anchovies disappear to

spawn, and producers must turn to grain, which is more expensive, to feed their chickens. What is likely to happen to the cost of chicken when the anchovies disappear? What are substitutes for chicken? How are the markets for these substitutes affected? Name some complements to chicken. How are the markets for these complements affected? How might the allocation of farmland be changed as a result of the anchovies' disappearance?

5. Suppose two passengers both end up with a reservation for the last seat on a train from San Francisco to Los Angeles. Two alternatives are proposed:

a. Toss a coin.
b. Sell the ticket to the highest bidder.
   Compare the two from the standpoint of efficiency and equity.

6. Assume that there are only two sectors in an economy: housing (H) and other goods (X). Assume that housing services are produced with capital alone and no labor. Describe the adjustments that would take place if a tax were levied on profits in the housing sector. In your answer, describe the adjustment that you would expect in capital, labor, and output markets.

THE BROILER INDUSTRY–ALMOST PERFECTLY COMPETITVE

■ The chicken industry has changed significantly since Herbert Hoover declared in the 1930s that there would soon be a "chicken in every pot." In the early 1900s, numerous small farms raised chickens on the side, selling their extra eggs to townspeople. Per capita consumption of poultry was less than a pound per year at that time. By 1990, however, per capita poultry consumption had reached the level of per capita beef consumption in the United States—over 70 pounds annually.

Located primarily in the Southeast (to take advantage of lower production costs), the broiler industry is "vertically integrated." Breeder farms send chicks to grow-out farms, where the chicks spend six to eight weeks eating before being sent on to the processing plant. The majority of these transactions take place under a contract coordinated by the processing plant, which generally owns its own feed mills.

Feed represents about 70% of the costs in raising chickens. The price of chicken, which averaged close to $0.51 per pound from 1990 to 1992, is closely linked to the price of feed; bumper grain

crops are generally followed by falling prices for broilers. The price and selection of cuts at the grocery store are influenced by the level of exports, which tend to consist of dark meat that is used as a loss leader at many supermarkets.

Barriers to entry in the poultry industry seem low; one estimate of the minimum efficient scale for a processing plant indicates that a firm would need to have less than 0.5% of the market to compete on an efficient and cost-effective basis. Declines in average cost appear to taper off after a volume of 10 million birds a year is reached. Nevertheless, although the largest firm in the industry owns 30 processing plants, most of the top 10 firms operated four to seven processing plants.

The market for broilers consists of retail grocery (51%), food-service (34%), export (6%), and nonhuman consumption markets (feed and pet food). Most broilers sold to consumers are labeled as Grade A chickens by the U.S. Department of Agriculture. Although processors believe that quality varies, surveys have shown that consumers do not hold strong preferences and often fail to distinguish between brands. Although 80% of processors offer fresh chicken brand names, over half of all the chicken sold does not carry a brand name.

Although there were a number of mergers in the broiler industry during the 1980s, none of these were challenged by the Department of Justice, as the broiler industry continues to be relatively unconcentrated (see Figure 1).

Tyson Foods controlled just over 20% of the market in

1990, but only three other firms had more than 5% of the market. Nevertheless, efforts to capture market share and gain economic profits persist. Market niches such as kosher and free-range chicken are expanding. The number of value-enhanced products, which offer higher profit margins and more stable earnings, is also increasing.

QUESTIONS FOR ANALYTICAL THINKING

1. Between 1950 and 1980, there was a negative relationship between real price and per capita consumption of chicken. By the 1980s, however, increases in consumption occurred with little or no decrease in price. What explanations might account for this? The decline in the income elasticity from +1.0 to +0.38 between 1950 and 1980 and a cross-price elasticity with beef of +0.20 might be relevant to your answer.

2. The average advertising-to-sales ratio for all food and tobacco industries is 2 percent. Would you expect the advertising-to-sales ratio to be higher or lower for the processed broiler industry? Explain.

3. To what extent would you expect broiler processors to compete on price? On quality? Will this differ for the retail and food-service markets?

4. The market for broilers exhibits much more price volatility than does the market for processed (value-enhanced) chicken products; it is relatively easy for firms to expand (or contract) production. Most economists consider this volatility to be a sign of competition (and stable prices to reflect more market power). Explain why this might be true.

FIGURE 1

Broiler Industry Concentration, 1954–1990

Source: L. Deutsch, *Industry Studies*, (Englewood Cliffs, NJ, Prentice Hall, 1992) p. 100.

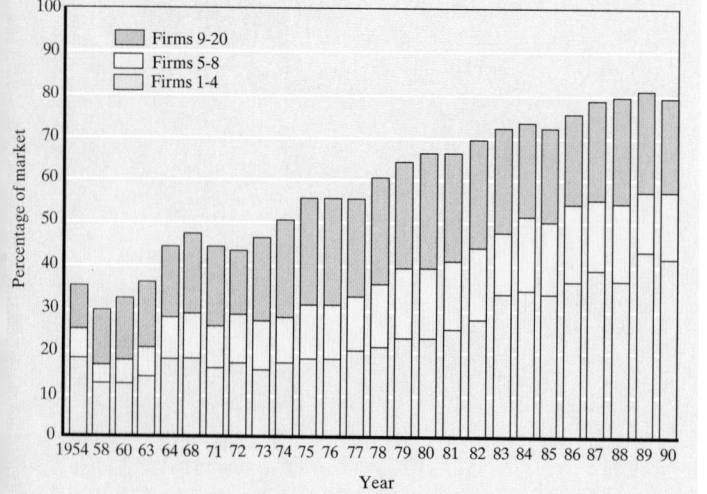

PART THREE

Market Imperfections and the Role of Government

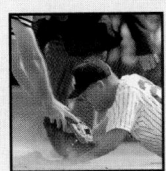

In Part Two, we discussed the components of a simple but complete perfectly competitive market system. Although the perfectly competitive model is abstract, it does provide insight into how real systems function. To build the perfectly competitive model, you will recall, we needed to make some fairly restrictive assumptions. In this part, we strip away many of these assumptions. As we do so, you will discover that there are many problems that markets do not solve. In fact, real economies frequently encounter a number of naturally occurring sources of inefficiency that government may be called upon to correct. Should the government intervene in the economy, or should it adopt a hands-off approach? As you will see, there are many opposing viewpoints but no "right answer."

For example:

■ Should government act to maintain competition? Was it in the best interests of the U.S. economy when the courts broke up American Telephone and Telegraph (AT&T) into separate competing companies in the early 1980s? Or did such a move amount to penalizing a successful company for its success? (Chapters 13–15)

■ Should some industries be regulated by government? What are the pros and cons of regulation? (Chapter 15)

■ The damage being done to our environment is a source of much concern today. How involved should the government be in controlling pollution? How can the government get industries to take the environment into account in their production and pricing decisions? (Chapter 16)

■ Is the distribution of wealth and income fair? Given the system of free enterprise in the United States, to what extent (if at all) should the government redistribute income and wealth through taxing and transfer payments? (Chapter 17)

13 Monopoly

In Chapters 6 through 12, we devoted most of our attention to building a model of a *perfectly competitive* economy. In order to do so, we needed to make some fairly restrictive assumptions. In Chapter 12 we began to see what happens when we relax some of them.

A number of very important assumptions, you will recall, underlie the logic of perfect competition. One is that a large number of firms and households interact in each individual output market. Another is that firms in a given market produce undifferentiated, or homogeneous, products. Together, these two conditions limit firms' choices. With many firms in each market, no single firm has any control over market prices. Single firms may decide how much to produce and how to produce, but the market determines output price. The assumption that new firms are free to enter industries and to compete for profits led us to conclude that opportunities for economic profit are eliminated in the long run as competition drives price to a level equal to the average cost of production.

In the next two chapters, we explore the important implications of relaxing these basic assumptions. In this chapter, we focus on the case of a single firm in an industry—a monopoly.

IMPERFECT COMPETITION AND MARKET POWER: CORE CONCEPTS

A market, or industry, in which individual firms have some control over the price of their output is **imperfectly competitive.** All firms in an imperfectly competitive market have one thing in common: They exercise **market power,** that is, the ability to raise price without losing all demand for their product. Imperfect competition and market power are major sources of inefficiency.

> Imperfect competition does not mean that *no* competition exists in the market. In fact, in some imperfectly competitive markets, competition takes place in even *more* arenas than in perfectly competitive markets. Firms can differentiate their products, improve quality, market aggressively, cut prices, and so forth.

imperfectly competitive industry An industry in which single firms have some control over the price of their output.

market power An imperfectly competitive firm's ability to raise price without losing all demand for its product.

Limiting Competition and Maintaining Market Power

For a firm to exercise control over the price of its product, it must be able to *limit competition*. If your firm produces sweatbands, and if other firms can enter freely into the sweatband industry and produce exactly the same sweatbands that you produce, the result will be the outcome that you would expect in a perfectly competitive industry: The supply of sweatbands will increase, the price of sweatbands will be driven down to their average cost, and economic profits will be eliminated.

If your firm can prevent other firms from producing exactly the same sweatbands, however, or if it can prevent other firms from entering the market, then it has a chance of preserving its economic profits. A *monopoly,* you will recall, is an industry with a single firm in which the entry of new firms is blocked. A monopoly may be able to erect barriers to entry in a number of ways.

But a firm need not be a monopoly to exercise market power. An *oligopoly* is an industry in which there is a small number of firms, each of which is large enough to have an impact on the market price of its outputs. To preserve their market power in the long run, oligopolists too must erect barriers to entry. When new firms producing the exact same product can enter the market freely, no one has market power.

Even when an industry has a large number of firms, however, individual firms may still be able to acquire market power. Establishing a brand name, gaining a reputation for producing high-quality products, or acquiring a patent have the effect of creating a separate market for the products of a single firm. Even though there are many close substitutes for Ivory brand soap, only Procter & Gamble can produce Ivory. In a sense, P&G monopolizes the market for Ivory—entry to this market is legally blocked by P&G's copyright on the brand name. Firms that differentiate their products in industries that have many producers and free entry are called *monopolistic competitors* (review Figure 3.1).

Defining Industry Boundaries

We can say that a monopoly is an industry with just one firm and that an oligopoly is an industry with just a few competitors, but where do we set the boundary of an industry? For example, although Procter & Gamble is the only firm that can produce Ivory, there are many other brands of soap. In general:

> The ease with which consumers can substitute for a product limits the extent to which a monopolist can exercise market power. The more broadly a market is defined, the more difficult it becomes to find substitutes.

Consider hamburger, for example. A firm that produces Brand X hamburger faces stiff competition from other hamburger sellers, even though it is the only producer of Brand X. The Brand X firm has no market power because near-perfect substitutes for its hamburger are available. But if a firm were the *only* producer of hamburger (or, better yet, the only producer of beef), it would have more market power, because fewer (or no) alternatives would be available. When fewer substitutes exist, a monopolist has more power to raise price because demand for its product is less elastic, as Figure 13.1 shows. A monopolist that produces all the food in an economy would exercise enormous market power because there are no substitutes at all for food as a category.

pure monopoly An industry with a single firm that produces a product for which there are no close substitutes and in which significant barriers to entry prevent other firms from entering the industry to compete for profits.

To be meaningful, therefore, our definition of a monopolistic industry must be more precise. We define **pure monopoly** as an industry with a single firm (1) that produces a product for which there are no close substitutes and (2) in which significant barriers to entry prevent other firms from entering the industry to compete for profits.

Barriers to Entry

barrier to entry Something that prevents new firms from entering and competing in imperfectly competitive industries.

Firms that already have market power can maintain that power either by preventing other firms from producing an exact duplicate of their product or by preventing firms from entering the industry. A number of **barriers to entry** can be erected.

government franchise A monopoly by virtue of government directive.

GOVERNMENT FRANCHISES Many firms are monopolies by virtue of government directive. Local telephone-operating companies, for example, are often granted exclusive licenses by states to provide "local exchange service." No other firms are permitted to offer telephone service within specific local areas. State governments also grant electric companies the sole right to supply power within given areas. The usual defense of this kind of monopoly power by **government franchise** is that it is more efficient for a single firm to produce the particular product (usually a service) than it is for many firms to produce the same product. If very large economies of scale are possible, it makes no sense to have many small firms producing the same thing at much higher costs. (These so-called natural monopolies are discussed more formally later in this chapter.)

Governments usually regulate monopolies to which they have granted exclusive licenses. Public utility commissions in each state watch over electric companies and locally operating telephone companies. Indeed, one of government's major responsibilities is to regulate the prices charged by these utilities to ensure that they don't abuse their monopoly power.

Fairness, or equity, is another frequently cited defense of government-regulated monopoly. Technological progress in the telecommunications industry has reduced the advantages that come from size, for example, but states are clearly not ready to open local exchange service to competition. The reason is that most state governments want to ensure that everyone has access to a telephone at affordable rates. In most states, private households are provided with telephone service at a price below the cost of producing it; local telephone companies earn the bulk of their

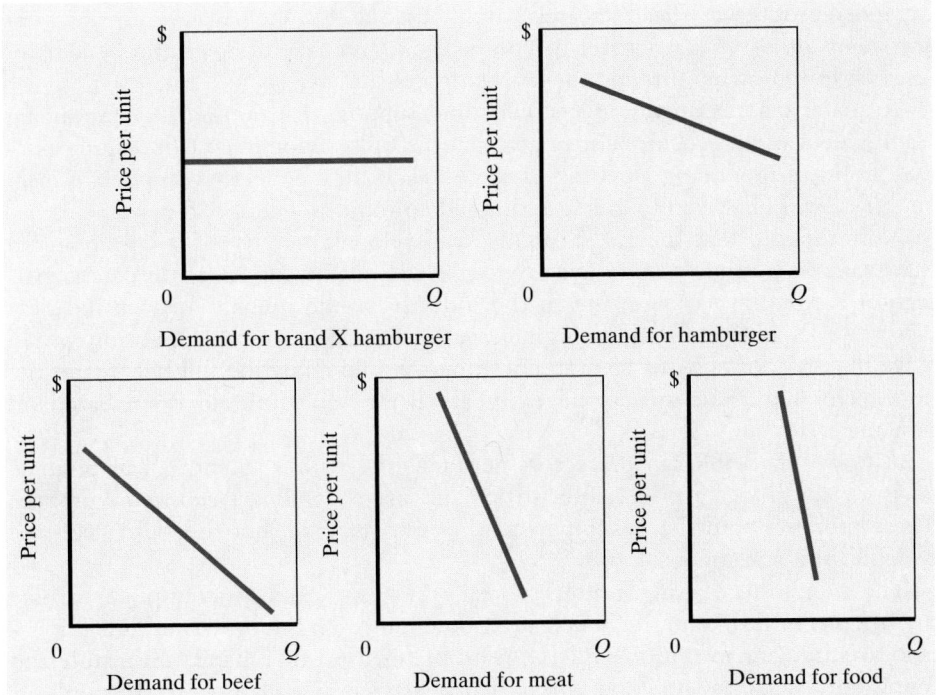

FIGURE 13.1
The Boundary of a Market
and Elasticity

We can define an industry as
broadly or as narrowly as we like.
The more broadly we define the
industry, the fewer substitutes
there are, and the less elastic
demand for that industry's product is likely to be. A monopoly is
an industry with one firm that
produces a product for which
there are *no close substitutes.*
The producer of Brand X hamburger cannot properly be called
a monopolist because this producer has no control over market
price and there are many substitutes for Brand X hamburger.

profits from business users, who are charged a price above cost. Deregulating local
service would thus mean higher telephone bills for households, a change that
would be considered "unfair" by many.

Large economies of scale and equity are not the only justifications that governments give for granting monopoly licenses, however. Sometimes government
wants to maintain control of an industry, and a monopoly is easier to control than
a competitive industry. Iowa, Maine, New Hampshire, and Ohio, for example,
permit liquor to be sold only through state-controlled and -managed liquor stores.
However, when large economies of scale do not exist in an industry, or when
equity is not a concern, the arguments in favor of government-run monopolies
are much weaker. One argument is that the state wants to prevent private parties
from encouraging, and profiting from, "sin." Another is that government monopolies are a convenient source of revenues; how can anyone criticize the state-
licensed, implicit taxation of drinking or gambling!

PATENTS   Another legal barrier that prevents entry into an industry is a **patent,**
which grants exclusive use of the patented product or process to the inventor.
Patents are issued in the United States under authority of Article I, Section 8, of
the Constitution, which gives Congress the power to "promote the progress of
science and the useful arts, by securing for limited times to authors and inventors
the exclusive right to their respective writings and discoveries." Patent protection
in the United States is currently granted for a period of 17 years.

Patents provide an incentive for invention and innovation. New products and
new processes are developed through research undertaken by individual inventors
and by firms. Research requires resources and time, which have opportunity costs.
Without the protection that a patent provides, the results of research would
become available to the general public very quickly. If research did not lead to

patent A barrier to entry that grants
exclusive use of the patented
product or process to the inventor.

expanded profits, very little research would be done. On the negative side, however, patents do serve as a barrier to competition, and they do keep the benefits of research from flowing through the market to consumers.

To understand a patent's effects on profits, suppose that the industry producing blank videocassettes is competitive and that the full economic cost (including normal profit) of producing videocassettes is $5 each. In a perfectly competitive market, price will be driven to average cost, and consumers will pay $5 per tape.

Now suppose that the BASF company develops a new type of tape material that makes it possible to produce tapes of equal quality for $3. If no patent protection existed, every company in the industry would quickly analyze the new tape material and begin producing tapes at a cost of $3. Soon competition would drive the price of tapes to $3, and consumers would enjoy the full benefits of the new technology. But this would eliminate BASF's incentive to do research on new materials.

If, however, BASF can protect its new material with a patent, it can produce tapes for $3, charge a price closer to $5, and make significant economic profits.[1] These profits reward the developers of the new material, but they also keep the benefits from consumers.

The expiration of patents after 17 years thus represents an attempt to balance the benefits of firms and the benefits of households: On the one hand, it is important to stimulate invention and innovation; on the other hand, invention and innovation do society no good unless their benefits eventually flow to the public.

Sometimes the conflict between patents as an incentive to innovation and patents as a barrier to competition is difficult to resolve. In the early 1960s, for example, General Motors developed a number of innovations that substantially improved the quality of the intercity buses that they produced. GM secured patents on these developments, of course, and proceeded to produce better buses.

Before too long, General Motors had gobbled up over 85% of the intercity bus market and found itself in trouble with the Justice Department. The courts held that GM was indeed in violation of the antitrust laws (see Chapter 15); the patents were a barrier to entry that permitted GM to monopolize the intercity bus market. As a result, the courts issued a "consent decree" forcing GM to give up its patents and to make available to the competition any new advances for several years into the future. Needless to say, not much research was done to improve the quality of intercity buses while that decree was in effect.

In recent years, public attention has been focused on the high price of health care. Indeed, one of the first problems faced by the Clinton administration in 1993 was how to deal with health care costs. As we mentioned in the Issues and Applications box in Chapter 3, one factor contributing to these costs is the very high price of many prescription drugs. Equipped with newly developed tools of bioengineering, the pharmaceutical industry has been granted thousands of patents for new drugs. When a new drug that is necessary for the treatment of a disease is developed, the patent holder can charge a very high price for it. The drug companies argue that these rewards are justified by high research and devel-

---

[1]Another alternative is *licensing*. Suppose BASF licenses the use of its material for $1 per tape produced. If other firms use the new material, costs will fall to $4 ($3 per tape plus the license fee). The price of tapes will fall to $4 and BASF will get a royalty of $1 for every tape produced using the new material. Here the new technology is used by all producers, and the inventor splits the benefits with consumers. Because forcing the non-patent-holding producers to use an inefficient technology results in waste, some analysts have proposed adding mandatory licensing to the current patent system.

opment costs; others argue that these profits are simply the result of a monopoly position protected by the patent system.

ECONOMIES OF SCALE AND OTHER COST ADVANTAGES Some products can be produced efficiently only in big, expensive production facilities. For example, the Federal Trade Commission has estimated that an oil refinery large enough to achieve maximum-scale economies in the production of gasoline would cost more than $500 million. No matter how high his or her spirits are running, a small entrepreneur is not going to jump into the refining business in search of economic profit. The need to raise an initial investment of half a billion dollars certainly limits the pool of potential entrants, a situation that is compounded by the riskiness of the business. Hence, large capital requirements are often a barrier to entry.

Sometimes large economies of scale are not production related. Breakfast cereal can be produced efficiently on a very small scale, for example; large-scale production does not reduce costs. But the breakfast cereal market is dominated by heavily advertised brand names. To compete successfully, a new firm would have to mount an advertising campaign costing millions of dollars, an enormous investment in the intangible capital called goodwill. The large front-end capital requirement in the presence of risk is certainly likely to deter would-be entrants to the cereal market.

OWNERSHIP OF A SCARCE FACTOR OF PRODUCTION You can't enter the diamond-producing business unless you own a diamond mine. There are not many diamond mines in the world, and most are already owned by a single firm, the DeBeers Company of South Africa. Once, the Aluminum Company of America (now Alcoa) owned or controlled virtually 100% of the bauxite deposits in the world and until the 1940s monopolized the production and distribution of aluminum. Obviously, if the production of a product requires a particular input, and one firm owns the entire supply of that input, that firm will control the industry. The fact of ownership alone serves as a barrier to entry.

Price: The Fourth Decision Variable

A firm has market power when it has some control over the price of its product—that is, when it can raise the price of its product without losing all demand. The exercise of market power requires that the firm be able to limit competition in some way. It does this either by erecting barriers to the entry of new firms or by preventing other firms from producing the exact same product. Regardless of the source of this market power, output price is not taken as given by the firm. Rather,

> Price is a decision variable for imperfectly competitive firms. Firms with market power must therefore decide not only (1) how much to produce, (2) how to produce it, and (3) how much to demand in each input market, but also (4) *what price to charge for their output.*

This does not mean that "market power" allows a firm to charge any price it likes, however. The market demand curve constrains the behavior even of a pure monopolist. To sell its product successfully, a firm must, of course, produce something that people want and sell it at a price they are willing to pay.

PRICE AND OUTPUT DECISIONS IN PURE MONOPOLY MARKETS

A pure monopoly market, we learned earlier, is one in which a single firm produces a product for which there are no close substitutes. For purposes of analyzing monopoly behavior, we make two basic assumptions: (1) that entry to the market is strictly blocked, and (2) that firms act to maximize profits.

Initially, we also assume that our pure monopolist buys in competitive input markets. Even though the firm is the only one producing for its product market, it is only one among many firms buying factors of production in input markets. The local telephone company, for example, must hire labor like any other firm, and to attract workers it must pay the market wage; to buy fiber-optic cable, it must pay the going price. In these input markets, therefore, the monopolistic firm is a price-taker.

On the cost side of the profit equation, then, a pure monopolist does not differ one bit from a perfect competitor. Both choose the technology that minimizes the cost of production. The cost curve of each represents the minimum cost of producing each level of output. The difference arises on the revenue, or demand, side of the equation, and this is where we begin our analysis.

Demand in Monopoly Markets

A competitive firm, you will recall, faces a fixed, market-determined price, and we assume that it can sell all that it wants to sell at that price; it is constrained only by its current capacity in the short run. The demand curve facing a competitive firm is thus a horizontal line (see Figure 13.2). Raising the price of its product means losing all demand, because perfect substitutes are available. On the other hand, the competitive firm has no incentive to charge a lower price either.

Because a competitive firm can charge only one price, regardless of the output level chosen, its *marginal revenue*—that is, the additional revenue that it earns by raising output by one unit—is simply the price of the output, or *P**. Remember that marginal revenue is important because a profit-maximizing firm will increase output as long as marginal revenue exceeds marginal cost.

The most important distinction between competition and monopoly is that:

FIGURE 13.2

The Demand Curve Facing a Perfectly Competitive Firm Is Perfectly Elastic; In a Monopoly, the Market Demand Curve is the Demand Curve Facing the Firm

Perfectly competitive firms are price-takers; they are small relative to the size of the market and thus cannot influence market price. The implication is that the demand curve facing a perfectly competitive firm is perfectly elastic. If the firm raises its price, it sells nothing, and there is no reason for the firm to lower its price if it can sell all it wants at *P**. In a monopoly, the firm is the industry. Thus the market demand curve is the demand curve facing the monopoly, and the total quantity supplied in the market is what the monopoly decides to produce.

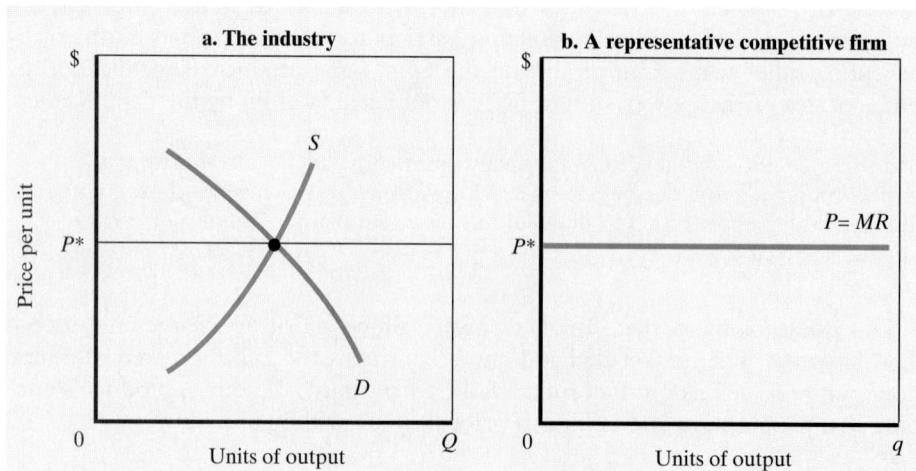

With only one firm in a monopoly market, there is no distinction between the firm and the industry—the firm *is* the industry. The market demand curve is thus the demand curve facing the firm, and the total quantity supplied in the market is what the firm decides to produce (see Figure 13.2a).

Before we proceed any further, we need to make a few more basic assumptions. First, we assume that a monopolistic firm cannot price discriminate. That is, it sells its product to all demanders at the same price. (*Price discrimination* means selling to different consumers or groups of consumers at different prices.)

We also assume that the monopoly faces a known demand curve. That is, we assume that the firm has enough information to predict how households will react to different prices. (In actuality, many firms use sophisticated statistical methods to estimate the elasticity of demand for their products. Other firms may use less formal methods, including trial and error, sometimes called "price searching." All firms with market power must have some sense of how consumers are likely to react to various prices, however.) Knowing the demand curve it faces, the firm must *simultaneously* choose both the quantity of output to supply and the price of that output. Once the firm chooses a price, the market determines how much will be sold. Stated somewhat differently, the monopoly chooses the single point on the market demand curve where it wants to be.

MARGINAL REVENUE AND MARKET DEMAND Just like a competitor, a profit-maximizing monopolist will continue to produce output as long as marginal revenue exceeds marginal cost. Because the market demand curve is the demand curve for a monopoly, however, a monopolistic firm faces a downward-sloping demand curve. Thus,

For a monopolist, an increase in output involves not just producing more and selling it, but also reducing the price of its output in order to sell it.

Consider the hypothetical demand schedule in Table 13.1. Column 3 lists the total revenue that the monopoly would take in at different levels of output. If it were to produce one unit, that unit would sell for $10, and total revenue would be $10. Two units would sell for $9 each, in which case total revenue would be $18. As column 4 shows, marginal revenue from the second unit would thus be $8 ($18

TABLE 13.1
Marginal Revenue Facing a Monopolist

(1) QUANTITY	(2) PRICE	(3) TOTAL REVENUE	(4) MARGINAL REVENUE
0	$11	$0	$—
1	10	10	10
2	9	18	8
3	8	24	6
4	7	28	4
5	6	30	2
6	5	30	0
7	4	28	-2
8	3	24	-4
9	2	18	-6
10	1	10	-18

minus $10). Notice that the marginal revenue from increasing output from one unit to two units ($8) is *less* than the price of the second unit ($9).

Now consider what happens when the firm considers setting production at four units rather than three. The fourth unit would sell for $7, but because the firm can't price discriminate, it must sell all four units for $7 each. Had the firm chosen to produce only three units, it could have sold those three units for $8 each. Thus, offsetting the revenue gain of $7 is a revenue loss of $3—that is, $1 for each of the three units that would have sold at the higher price. The marginal revenue of the fourth unit is thus $7 minus $3, or $4, which is considerably below the price of $7. (Remember, unlike a monopolistic firm, a perfectly competitive firm does not have to charge a lower price to sell more; thus $P = MR$ in competition.)

Marginal revenue can also be derived simply by looking at the change in total revenue. At three units of output, total revenue is $24; at four units of output, total revenue is $28. Marginal revenue is the difference, or $4.

Moving from six units of output to seven units of output actually reduces total revenue for the firm; at seven units of output, marginal revenue is negative. While it is true that the seventh unit will sell for a positive price ($4), the firm must sell all seven units for $4 each (for a total revenue of $28). If output had been restricted to six units, each would have sold for $5. Thus, offsetting the revenue gain of $4 is a revenue loss of $6—that is, $1 for each of the six units that the firm would have sold at the higher price. Increasing output from six to seven units actually decreases revenue by $2. Figure 13.3 graphs the marginal revenue schedule derived in Table 13.1. Notice that at every level of output except one unit, marginal revenue is *below* price. Marginal revenue turns from positive to negative after six units of output. When the demand curve is a straight line, the marginal revenue curve bisects the quantity axis between the origin and the point where the demand curve hits the quantity axis (see Figure 13.4).

Notice in the bottom panel of Figure 13.4 that:

> A monopoly's marginal revenue curve shows the change in total revenue that results as the firm moves along the segment of the demand curve that lies directly above it.

FIGURE 13.3

Marginal Revenue Curve Facing a Monopolist

At every level of output except one unit, a monopolist's marginal revenue is below price. This is so because (1) we assume that the monopolist must sell all its product at a single price (no price discrimination), and (2) to raise output and sell it, the firm must lower the price it charges. Selling the additional output will raise revenue, but this increase is offset somewhat by the lower price charged for all units sold. Therefore, the increase in revenue from increasing output by one (the marginal revenue) is less than price.

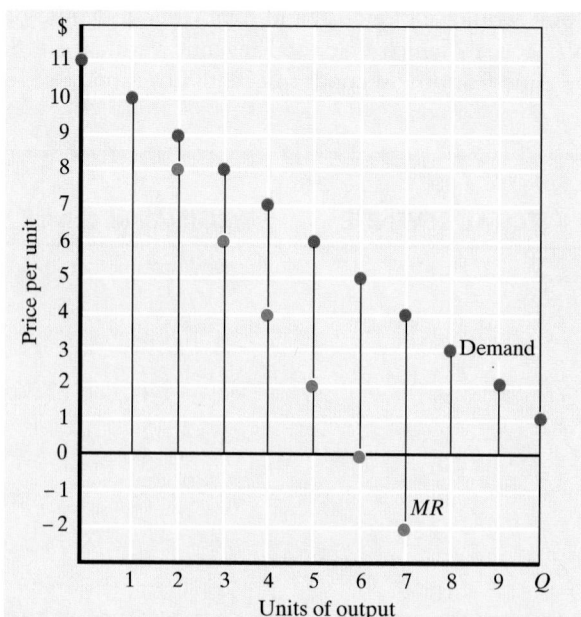

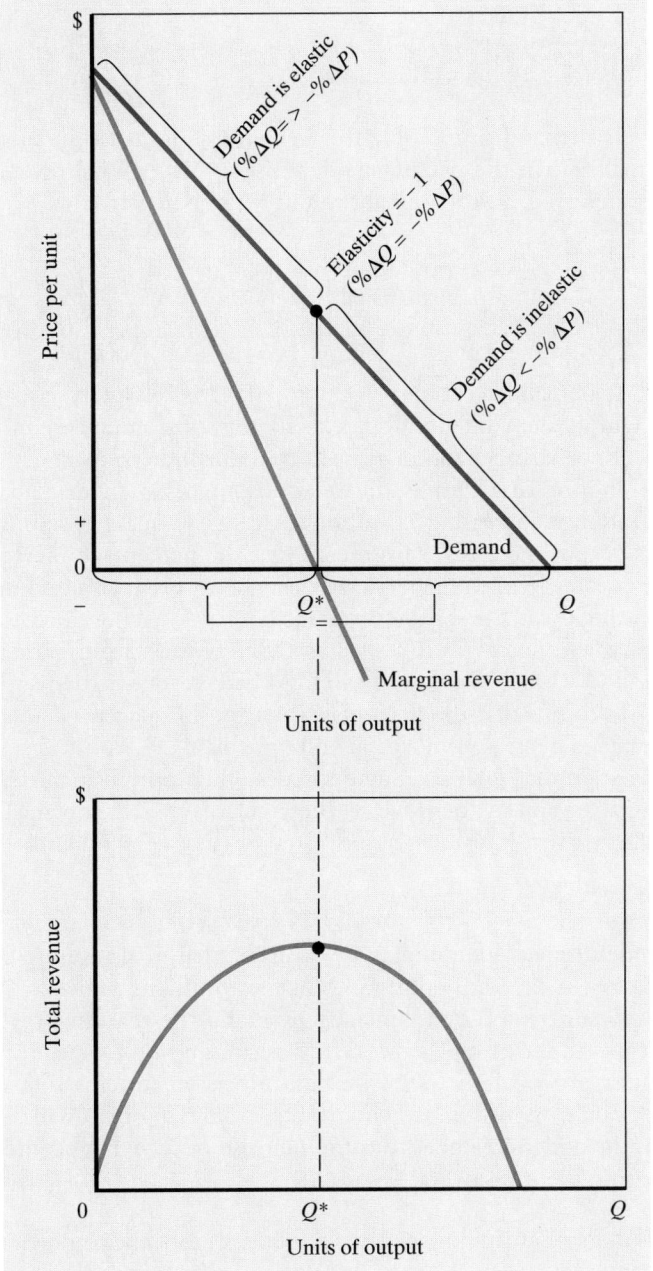

FIGURE 13.4
Marginal Revenue, Total
Revenue, and Elasticity

As you learned in Chapter 5,
elasticity changes along a
straight-line demand curve.
Marginal revenue depends on
elasticity of demand. When
demand is elastic, increasing
output increases total revenue
(*MR* is positive); when demand
is inelastic, increasing output
reduces total revenue (*MR* is
negative).

MARGINAL REVENUE AND ELASTICITY Whether an increase in output increases or
decreases total revenue in a monopolistic industry depends on the elasticity of
demand. Since total revenue is the product of price and quantity sold ($P \times Q$), the
impact of an increase in quantity sold depends on how great a price decrease
accompanies it. Recall from Chapter 5 that price elasticity of demand is the ratio
of the percentage change in quantity demanded to the percentage change in price
as the firm moves between two points along a demand curve.

If demand is *elastic,* the percentage increase in quantity demanded will be bigger
than the percentage decrease in price. Total revenue will thus increase if output is
raised, and marginal revenue will be positive:

If demand is *inelastic,* the percentage increase in quantity demanded will be smaller than the percentage decrease in price. Total revenue will thus fall if output is increased, and marginal revenue will be negative:

If demand has *unitary elasticity,* (that is, elasticity equal to −1), any increase in quantity demanded will be exactly offset by a decrease in price. Total revenue thus will not change, and marginal revenue will be zero.

Figure 13.4 graphs the relationship between marginal revenue and elasticity. Output is increasing as we move along the quantity axis. At first, demand is elastic as output increases. This means that the percentage increase in quantity demanded is greater than the percentage decrease in price at all points up to Q*. You can see in the lower part of the diagram that total revenue increases when output increases between the origin (Q = 0) and Q*. Thus, marginal revenue is positive between 0 and Q*. Once we move beyond Q*, however, the demand curve becomes inelastic. This means that the percentage increase in quantity demanded is less than the percentage decrease in price at all points past Q*. You can see in the lower part of the diagram that total revenue decreases when output increases beyond Q*. Thus, marginal revenue is negative to the right of Q*. (If you need to review elasticity and the fact that it changes along a straight-line demand curve, see Chapter 5.)

THE MONOPOLIST'S PROFIT-MAXIMIZING PRICE AND OUTPUT We have spent much time in defining and explaining marginal revenue because it is an important factor in the monopolist's choice of profit-maximizing price and output. Figure 13.5 superimposes a demand curve and the marginal revenue curve derived from it over a set of cost curves. In determining price and output, a monopolistic firm must go through the same basic decision process that a competitive firm goes through. As you know, any profit-maximizing firm will raise its production as long as the added revenue from the increase outweighs the added cost. In more specific terms, we can say that:

All firms, including monopolies, find it profitable to raise output as long as marginal revenue is greater than marginal cost. Any positive difference between marginal revenue and marginal cost can be thought of as marginal profit.

The optimal price/output combination for the monopolist in Figure 13.5 is P_m and Q_m, the quantity at which the marginal revenue curve and the marginal cost curve intersect. At any output below Q_m, marginal revenue is greater than marginal cost. At any output above Q_m, increasing output would reduce profits, because marginal cost exceeds marginal revenue. This leads us to conclude that:

The profit-maximizing level of output for a monopolist is the one at which marginal revenue equals marginal cost: *MR = MC.*

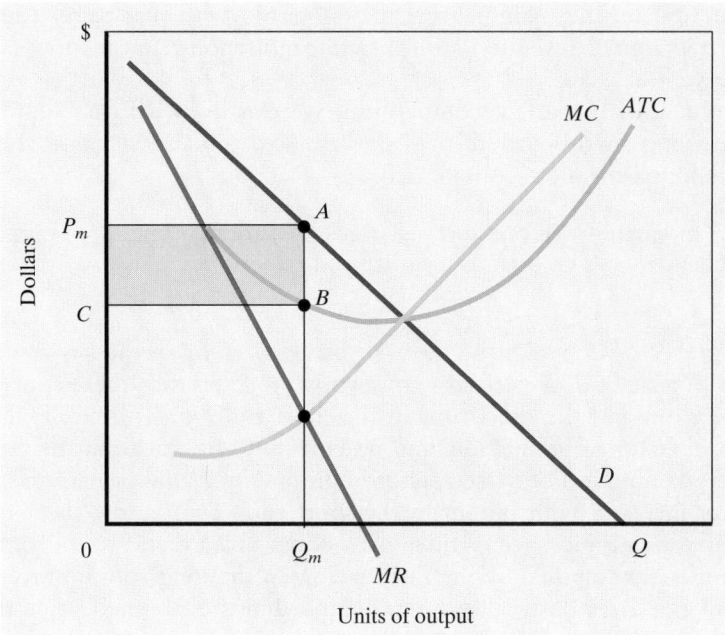

FIGURE 13.5

Price and Output Choice for a Profit-Maximizing Monopolist

A profit-maximizing monopolist will raise output as long as marginal revenue exceeds marginal cost. Maximum profit is achieved at an output of Q_m and a price of P_m. To the right of Q_m, MC is greater than marginal revenue; increasing output beyond Q_m would reduce profit.

Because marginal revenue for a monopoly lies below the demand curve, the final price chosen by the monopolist will be above marginal cost ($P_m > MC$). At Q_m, price will be fixed at P_m (point A on the demand curve), and total revenue will be $P_m \times Q_m$, or the area of rectangle $P_m A Q_m 0$. Total cost is the product of average total cost and Q_m, or the area of rectangle $CBQ_m 0$. Total profit is the difference between total revenue and total cost, or the area of $P_m ABC$.

Among competitive firms, the presence of economic profits provides an incentive for new firms to enter the industry, thus shifting supply to the right, driving down price, and eliminating profits. Remember, however, that for monopolies we assume that barriers to entry have been erected and that profits are protected.

THE ABSENCE OF A SUPPLY CURVE IN MONOPOLY In perfect competition, the supply curve of a firm in the short run is the same as the portion of the firm's marginal cost curve that lies above the average variable cost curve. As the price of the good produced by the firm changes, the perfectly competitive firm simply moves up or down its marginal cost curve in choosing how much output to produce.

As you can see, however, Figure 13.5 contains nothing that we can point to and call a supply curve. The amount of output that a monopolist produces depends on its marginal cost curve *and* on the shape of the demand curve that it faces. In other words, the amount of output that a monopolist supplies is not independent of the shape of the demand curve. Thus,

> A monopoly firm has no supply curve that is independent of the demand curve for its product.

To see why this is so, consider what a firm's supply curve means. A supply curve shows, for each price, the quantity of output the firm is willing to supply. If we ask a monopolist how much output she is willing to supply at a given price, the monopolist will say that her supply behavior depends not just on marginal cost but also on the marginal revenue associated with that price. And, to know what that marginal revenue would be, the monopolist must know what her demand curve looks like.

In sum: In perfect competition, we can draw a firm's supply curve without knowing anything more than the firm's marginal cost curve. The situation for a monopolist is more complicated:

> A monopolist sets both price and quantity, and the amount of output that it supplies depends on both its marginal cost curve and the demand curve that it faces.

MONOPOLY IN THE LONG AND SHORT RUN One of the key distinctions we made in our analysis of perfectly competitive markets was the distinction between the long run and the short run. In the short run, you will recall, all firms face some fixed factor of production, and no entry into or exit from the industry is possible. The assumption of a fixed factor of production is the primary reason that marginal cost increases with output in the short run. That is, the short-run marginal cost curve of a typical competitive firm slopes upward and to the right because of the limitations imposed by the fixed factor. In the long run, however, firms can enter and exit the industry. Long-run equilibrium is established when the entry and exit of firms drives economic profits in the industry to zero.

The distinction between the long and short runs is somewhat less important in monopoly markets. In the short run, monopolists are limited by a fixed factor of production, just as competitive firms are. The cost curves in Figure 13.5 reflect the diminishing returns to the monopoly's fixed factor of production (for example, plant size).

What will happen to the monopoly in the long run? If the monopoly is earning economic profits (profits over and above a normal return to capital), nothing will happen. In competition, profits lead to expansion and entry, but in monopoly, entry is blocked. In addition, because we assume that the monopoly is a profit-maximizing firm, it will operate at the most efficient scale of production, and it will neither expand nor contract in the long run. Thus, Figure 13.5 will not change in the long run.

It is possible for a monopoly to find itself suffering economic losses (profits below normal). A monopoly that finds itself unable to cover total costs is illustrated in Figure 13.6. The best that the firm can do is produce Q_m units of output (the point at which $MR = MC$) and charge P_m for its output (point E on the demand curve). But at Q_m total revenue (represented by rectangle P_mEQ_m0) is not sufficient to cover total costs (rectangle FDQ_m0), and the firm suffers losses equal to the shaded area (rectangle $FDEP_m$). Notice, however, that total revenue is sufficient to cover *variable* costs (rectangle GHQ_m0). Thus, operating in the short run generates a profit on operation (total revenue minus total variable costs is greater than zero) that can be used to cover some of the firm's short-run fixed costs. The basis of the monopolist's decision is thus exactly the same as that for a competitive firm:

> If a firm can reduce its losses by operating in the short run, it will do so.

Similarly, in the long run, a firm that cannot generate enough revenue to cover total costs will go out of business, whether it is competitive or monopolistic. Since the demand curve in Figure 13.6 lies completely below the average total cost curve, the monopoly will go out of business in the long run, and its product will not be produced because it is simply not worth the cost of production to buyers.

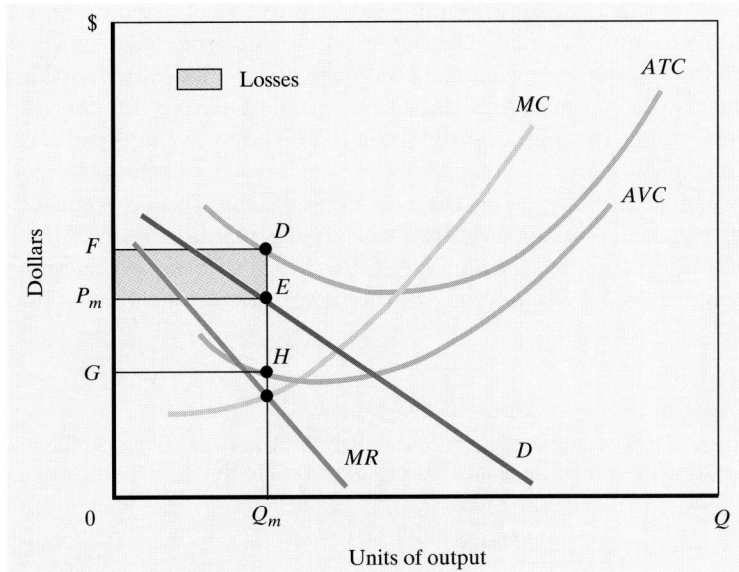

It is possible for a profit-maximizing monopolist to suffer short-run losses. At Q_m (the point at which $MR = MC$), total revenue is sufficient to cover variable cost but not to cover total cost. Thus, the firm will operate in the short run but go out of business in the long run.

Perfect Competition and Monopoly Compared

FIGURE 13.7
A Perfectly Competitive Industry in Long-Run Equilibrium

One way to understand monopoly is to compare equilibrium output and price in a perfectly competitive industry with the output and price that would be chosen if the same industry were organized as a monopoly. To make this comparison meaningful, let us exclude from consideration any technological advantage that a single large firm might enjoy.

We begin our comparison, then, with a competitive industry made up of a large number of firms operating with a production technology that exhibits constant returns to scale in the long run. (Recall that *constant returns to scale* means that average cost is the same whether the firm operates one large plant or many small plants.) Figure 13.7 shows a perfectly competitive industry at long-run equilibrium, a condition in which price is equal to long-run average costs and in which there are no economic profits.

In a perfectly competitive industry in the long run, price will be equal to long-run average cost. The market supply curve is the sum of all the short-run marginal cost curves of the firms in the industry. Here we assume that firms are using a technology that exhibits constant returns to scale: *LRAC* is flat. Big firms enjoy no cost advantage.

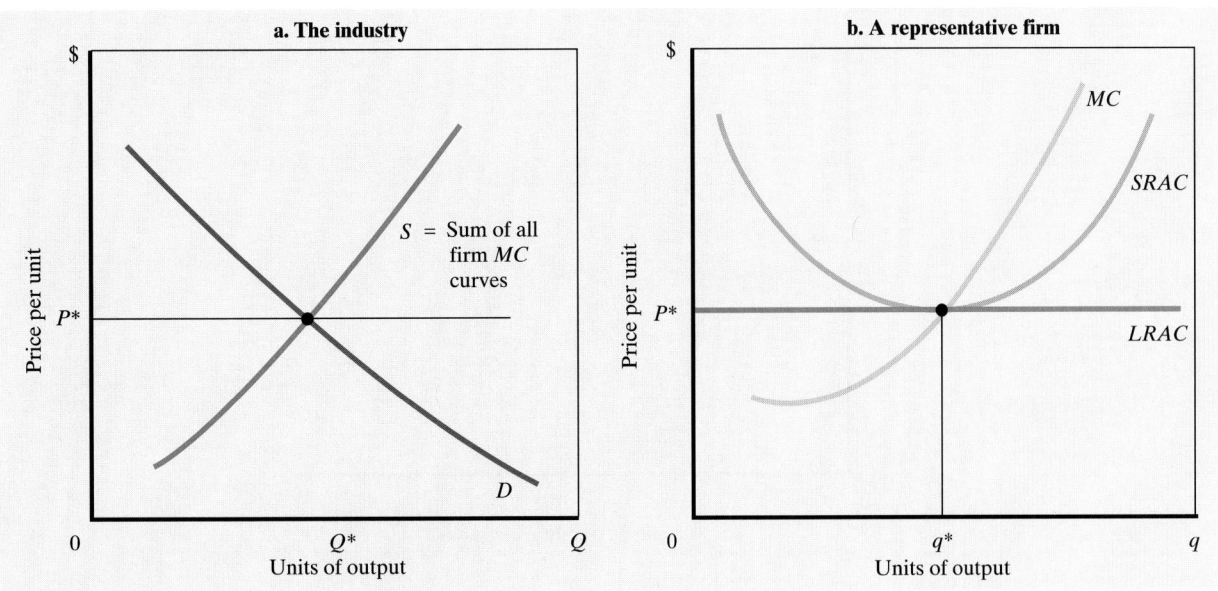

Now suppose that the industry were to fall under the control of a single private monopolist. The monopolist now owns one firm with many plants. But technology has not changed; only the locus of decision-making power has. To analyze the monopolist's decisions, we must derive the consolidated cost curves now facing the monopoly. Figure 13.8 shows average and marginal costs for a three-plant firm.

Think carefully about the cost curves facing the consolidated multiplant firm. First consider marginal costs. What is the marginal cost of the 16,000th unit of output for the new monopoly? If the firm distributes production among the three plants as shown in Figure 13.8, the marginal cost of the 16,000th unit is $10. The

FIGURE 13.8
Cost Curves for a Consolidated Multiplant Firm

The cost curves of a single, consolidated, multiplant firm are simply the sum of the cost curves of the individual plants. This is easy to see in the case where there are just three plants.

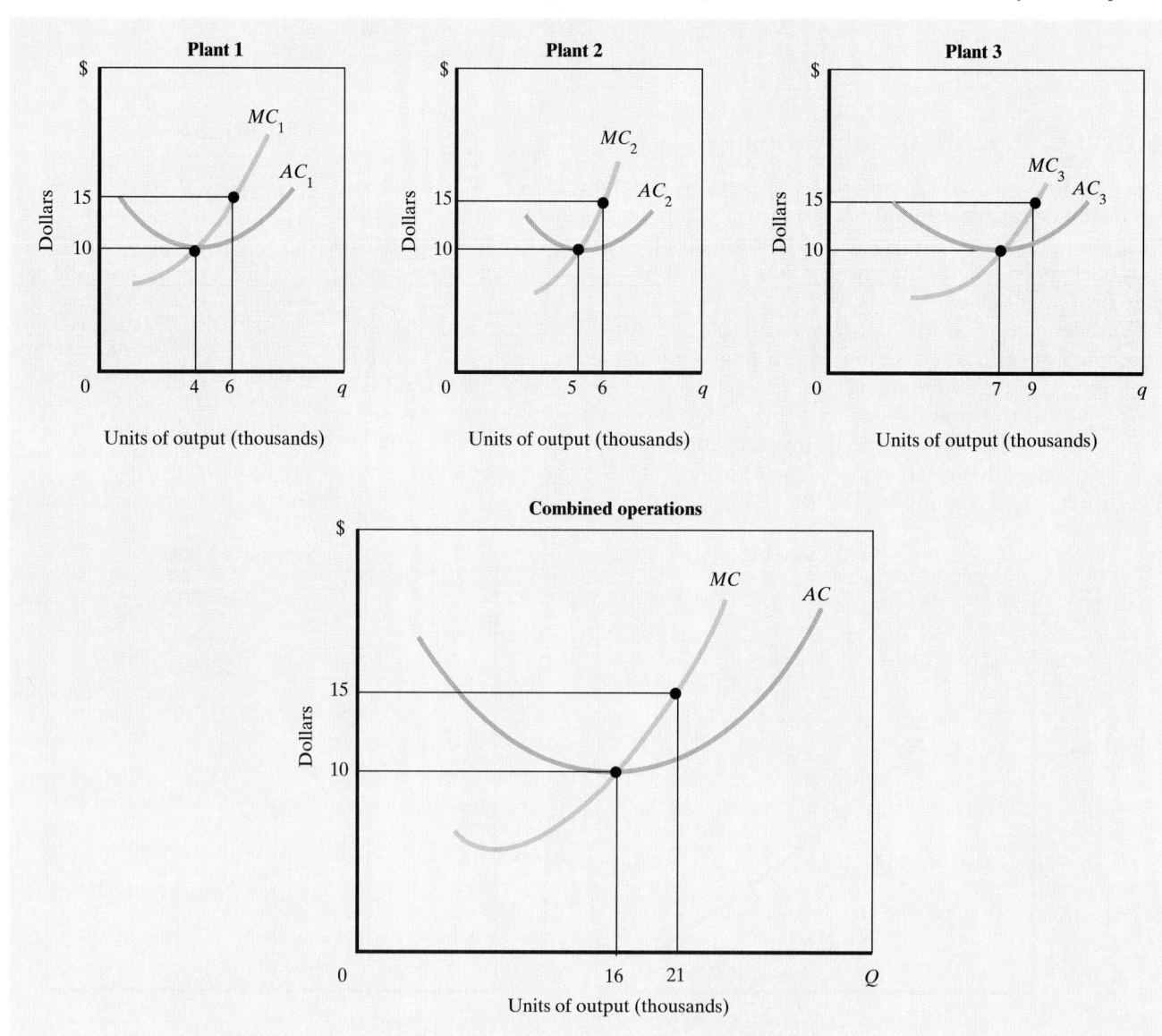

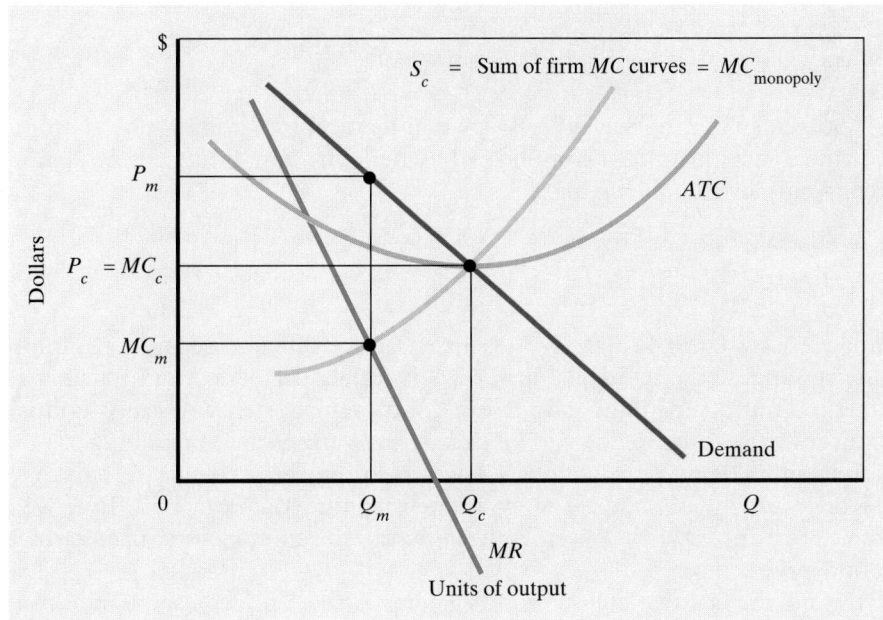

FIGURE 13.9

Comparison of Monopoly
and Perfectly Competitive
Outcomes for a Firm with
Constant Returns to Scale

In the newly organized monopoly,
the marginal cost curve is exactly
the same as the supply curve that
represented the behavior of all
the independent firms when the
industry was organized competitively. This enables us to compare
the monopoly outcome with the
competitive outcome. Quantity
produced by the monopoly will be
less than the competitive level of
output, and the monopoly price
will be higher than the price
under competition.

firm will assign Plant 1 the task of producing 4,000 units; Plant 2 a production
level of 5,000 units; and Plant 3 a production level of 7,000 units, for a grand total
of 16,000 units. At these output levels, marginal cost of production is $10 in each
of the three plants. The marginal cost of the 16,000th unit is thus $10.

Using similar reasoning, we can calculate the marginal cost of the 21,000th unit
of output. A production level of 6,000 units will be assigned to Plant 1, pushing
marginal cost up from $10 to $15; Plant 2 will also be assigned 6,000 units, pushing its marginal cost to $15; and 9,000 units will be assigned to Plant 3, where
marginal cost also rises to $15. The marginal cost of the 21,000th unit of output
produced by the monopoly is thus $15.

Based on these calculations, you should be able to see that the marginal cost
curve facing the consolidated firm (the monopoly) is equal to the sum of the marginal cost curves of the former small firms that are now small plants.[2] This means
that the marginal cost curve of the new firm is *exactly the same curve* as the supply
curve in the industry when it was competitively organized. (Recall that the industry supply curve in a perfectly competitive industry is the sum of the marginal cost
curves [above average variable cost] of all the individual firms in that industry.)

Figure 13.9 superimposes the cost curves of the consolidated monopoly industry on the diagram of the competitive industry in Figure 13.7. If the industry were
competitively organized, total industry output would have been Q_c and price
would have been P_c (which is the same as P^* in Figure 13.7). These price and
output decisions are determined by the intersection of the competitive supply
curve, S_c, and the market demand curve.

No longer faced with a price that it cannot influence, however, the monopolist
can choose any price/quantity combination along the demand curve. The output
level that maximizes profits to the monopolist is Q_m—the point at which marginal
revenue intersects marginal cost. Output will be priced at P_m. To increase output
beyond Q_m or to charge a price below P_m (which represents the amount consumers are willing to pay) would reduce profit. The final result is that:

---

[2] The same logic will show that the average cost curve of the consolidated firm is simply the sum of the average
cost curves of the individual plants.

> Relative to a competitively organized industry, a monopolist restricts output, charges higher prices, and earns economic profits.

And remember, all we did was to transfer decision-making power from the individual small firms to a consolidated owner. The new firm gains nothing at all technologically from being big.

Collusion and Monopoly Compared

collusion The act of working with other producers in an effort to limit competition and increase joint profits.

Suppose now that the industry discussed above did not become a monopoly. Instead, suppose the individual firm owners simply decide to work together in an effort to limit competition and increase joint profits, a behavior called **collusion.** In this case, the outcome would be exactly the same as the outcome of a monopoly in the industry. Firms certainly have an incentive to collude. When they act independently, they compete away whatever profits they can find. But, we saw, when price increases to P_m across the industry, the monopolistic firm earns economic profits.

Despite the fact that collusion is illegal, it has taken place in some industries. In one significant case in the 1960s, a number of executives of well-known electrical equipment manufacturers were successfully prosecuted for meeting secretly to fix prices and divide up markets. In January 1987, a judge moved to end a pricing agreement among milk producers in New York City that had existed since the 1930s. As a result, the wholesale price of milk dropped between $.30 and $.71 per gallon in one week! (See the Issues and Applications box titled "Rent-Seeking Behavior in the Milk Industry," later in this chapter, for the story behind this dramatic price decrease.)

THE SOCIAL COSTS OF MONOPOLY

So far we have seen that a monopoly produces less output and charges a higher price than a competitively organized industry, if no large economies of scale exist for the monopoly. You are probably thinking at this point that producing less and charging more to earn economic profits is not likely to be in the best interests of consumers, and you are right.

Inefficiency and Consumer Loss

In Chapter 12, we argued that price must equal marginal cost ($P = MC$) for markets to produce what people want. This argument rests on two propositions: (1) that price provides a good approximation of the social value of a unit of output, and (2) that marginal cost, in the absence of externalities (costs or benefits to external parties not weighed by firms), provides a good approximation of the social opportunity cost of the product. In pure monopoly, price ends up above marginal cost. When this happens, the firm is underproducing from society's point of view; society would be better off if the firm produced more and charged a lower price. We can therefore conclude that:

> Monopoly leads to an inefficient mix of output.

A slightly simplified version of the monopoly diagram appears in Figure 13.10, which shows how we might make a rough estimate of the size of the loss to social welfare that arises from monopoly. (For the sake of clarity here, we will ignore the short-run cost curves and assume constant returns to scale in the long run.) Under competitive conditions, firms would produce output up to Q_c, and price would ultimately settle at P_c, equal to long-run average cost. Any price above P_c will mean economic profits, which would be eliminated by the entry of new competing firms in the long run. (You should remember all this from Chapter 9.)

A monopoly firm in the same industry, however, would produce Q_m and charge a price of P_m, since $MR = MC$ at Q_m. The monopoly would make a profit equal to total revenue minus total cost, or $P_m \times Q_m$ minus $P_c \times Q_m$. Profit to the monopoly is thus equal to the area $P_m ACP_c$. (Remember $P_c = AC$ in this example.)

Now consider the gains and losses associated with increasing price from P_c to P_m and cutting output from Q_c to Q_m. You might guess that the winner will be the monopolist and the loser will be the consumer, but let us see how it works out.

At P_c, the price that would be charged under perfect competition, there are no economic profits. Consumers are paying a price of P_c, but many are willing to pay more than that. For example, a substantial number of people would pay P_m. Those people willing to pay more than P_c are receiving what we earlier called a *consumer surplus*. The demand curve shows approximately how much households are willing to pay at each level of output, and thus the area of triangle DBP_c gives us a rough measure of the "consumer surplus" being enjoyed by households when the price is P_c. Consumers willing to pay exactly P_m get a surplus equal to the length $P_m P_c$. Those who place the highest value on this good—that is, those who are willing to pay the most—get a surplus equal to DP_c.

Now the industry is reorganized as a monopoly that cuts output to Q_m and raises price to P_m. The big winner is the monopolist, who ends up earning economic profits equal to the area $P_m ACP_c$.

The big losers are the consumers. Their "surplus" now shrinks from the area of triangle DBP_c to the area of triangle DAP_m. Part of that loss (which is equal to DBP_c minus DAP_m, or the area $P_m ABP_c$) is covered by the monopolist's gain of

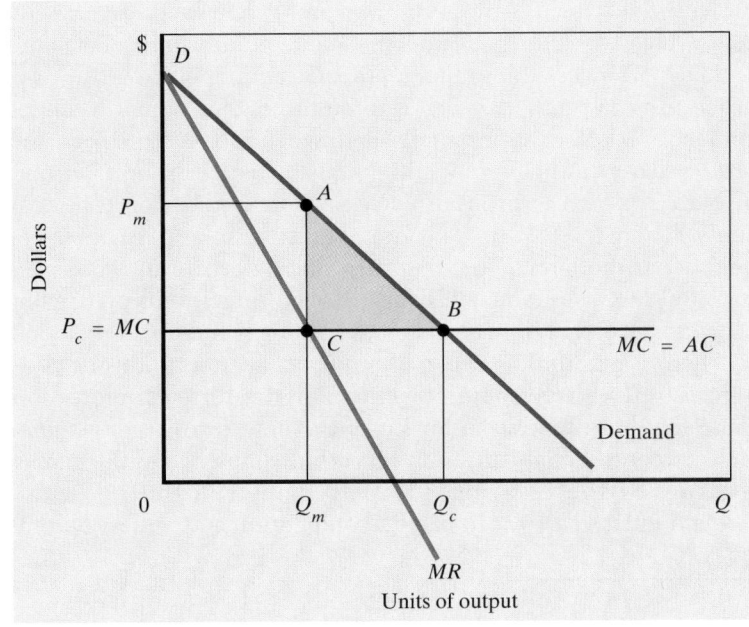

FIGURE 13.10

Welfare Loss from Monopoly

A demand curve shows the amounts that people are willing to pay at each potential level of output. Thus the demand curve can be used to approximate the benefits to the consumer of raising output above Q_m. MC reflects the marginal cost of the resources needed. The triangle ABC roughly measures the net social gain of moving from Q_m to Q_c (or the loss that results when monopoly decreases output from Q_c to Q_m).

P_mACP_c, *but not all of it.* The loss to consumers exceeds the gain to the monopoly by the area of triangle ABC (P_mABP_c minus P_mACP_c), which roughly measures the *net* loss in social welfare associated with monopoly power in this industry. If we could push price back down to the competitive level and increase output up to Q_c, however, consumers would gain more than the monopolist would lose, and the gain in social welfare would approximate the area of ABC.

In this example, the presence of a monopoly also causes an important change in the distribution of real income. In Figure 13.10, area P_mACP_c is economic profit flowing to the monopolist. If price were pushed down to P_c by competition or regulation, those excess profits would pass to consumers in the form of lower prices. Society may value this resource transfer on equity grounds in addition to efficiency grounds.

Of course, monopolies may have social costs that do not show up on these diagrams. Monopolies, which are protected from competition by barriers to entry, do not face the same pressures to cut costs and to innovate as competitive firms do. A competitive firm that does not use the most efficient technology will be driven out of business by firms that do. One of the significant arguments against tariffs and quotas to protect such industries as automobiles and steel from foreign competition is that protection removes the incentive to be efficient and competitive.

Rent-Seeking Behavior

In recent years, economists have encountered another serious worry. While triangle ABC in Figure 13.10 represents a real net loss to society, part of rectangle P_mACP_c may also end up lost. To understand why this is so, we need to think about the incentives facing potential monopolists.

The area of rectangle P_mACP_c is the difference between total revenue (P_mAQ_m0) and total cost (P_cCQ_m0). It is profit over and above a normal return to capital. If entry into the market were free and competition were open, these profits would eventually be competed to zero. Clearly, owners of businesses earning economic profits have an incentive to prevent this from happening. In fact, the diagram shows exactly how much they would be willing to pay to prevent it from happening. A rational owner of a competitive firm would be willing to pay any amount less than the entire rectangle. Any portion of profits left over after expenses is better than zero, which would be the case if free competition eliminated all profits.

There are many things that a potential monopolist can do to protect his or her profits. One obvious approach is to push the government to impose restrictions on competition. A classic example of this behavior can be seen in organizations of taxicab drivers in New York and other large cities. In order to operate a cab legally in New York City, you need a license. The number of licenses available is tightly controlled by the city. If entry into the taxi business were open, competition would hold down cab fares to the cost of operating cabs. But cab drivers have become a powerful lobbying force and have muscled the city into restricting the number of licenses issued. This restriction keeps fares high and preserves monopoly profits.

There are countless other examples. The steel industry and the automobile industry spend large sums lobbying Congress for tariff protection.[3] Some experts claim that both the establishment of the now-defunct Civil Aeronautics Board in 1937 to control competition in the airline industry and the extensive regulation of trucking by the FTC prior to deregulation in the 1970s came about partly through industry efforts to restrict competition and preserve profits.

---

[3]A tariff is a tax on imports designed to give a price advantage to domestic producers.

This kind of behavior, in which households or firms take action to preserve extranormal profits, is called **rent-seeking behavior.**[4] Recall from Chapter 10 that *rent* is the return to a factor of production in strictly limited supply. When economic profits appear in a competitive industry, they represent a return to a factor of production in limited supply in the short run. (Remember that the short run is defined as a period in which some factor of production is fixed or limited.) In the long run, resources are attracted to profit opportunities. This line of reasoning has two important implications. First, rent-seeking behavior itself consumes resources. Lobbying and building barriers to entry are not costless activities. Periodically faced with the prospect that the city of New York will issue new taxi licenses, cab owners and drivers have become so well organized that they can bring the city to a standstill with a strike or even a limited job action. Second, rent-seeking behavior presents us with a somewhat different view of government involvement in the economy. Both of these points deserve some elaboration.

In Figure 13.10, we saw the area of rectangle $P_m ACP_c$ as a transfer from consumers to monopolists that comes about as a result of the monopolization of the industry. Consumers received less consumer surplus, and monopolists received excess profits. But those profits may be consumed by the expenses of rent-seeking behavior. The resources consumed through rent-seeking behavior produce nothing of social value; all they do is help to preserve the present distribution of income. Thus, the true net social cost of monopoly is the sum of triangle *ABC and that portion of rectangle $P_m ACP_c$* that ends up paying for the rent-seeking behavior itself—lobbyists' wages, expenses of the regulatory bureaucracy, and so forth.

The frequency of rent-seeking behavior also leads us to another view of government. So far we have considered only the role that government might play in helping to achieve an efficient allocation of resources in the face of market failure—in this case, failures that arise from imperfect market structure. (In Chapter 15 we survey the measures government might take to ensure that resources are efficiently allocated when monopoly power arises.) The idea of rent-seeking behavior introduces the important notion of **government failure,** in which the government becomes the tool of the rent seeker, and the allocation of resources is made even less efficient than before.

This idea of government failure is at the center of **public choice theory,** which holds that governments are made up of people, just as business firms are. These people—politicians and bureaucrats—can be expected to act in their own self-interest, just as owners of firms can be expected to. We turn to the economics of public choice in Chapter 16.

rent-seeking behavior Actions taken by households or firms to preserve extranormal profits.

government failure Occurs when the government becomes the tool of the rent seeker and the allocation of resources is made even less efficient by the intervention of government.

public choice theory An economic theory that proceeds on the assumption that the public officials who set economic policies and regulate the players act in their own self-interest, just as firms do.

Remedies for Monopoly

It is recognized that monopoly power is not in the public interest, and numerous antimonopoly laws have been enacted. The most significant, the Sherman Act, was passed just over 100 years ago in 1890. As we will see in Chapter 15, the government has taken two basic approaches to limiting monopoly power: (1) breaking up the monopoly into a number of smaller competing firms (restructuring the indus-

---

[4]The term "rent-seeking behavior" was coined by Anne Krueger in an important article published in 1974. Much of the theory dates to earlier work by Gordon Tullock. See Anne O. Krueger, "The Political Economy of the Rent-Seeking Society," *American Economic Review* 64 (1974:291–303), and J. Buchanan, R. Tollison, and G. Tullock (eds.), *Toward a Theory of the Rent-Seeking Society* (College Station, TX: Texas A & M University Press, 1980).

try), and (2) allowing the firm to operate as a monopoly, but under strict regulations. Later in this chapter and in Chapter 15, we will see that one way the government can control monopoly is by setting the price of its output at competitive levels.

Under some circumstances, however, breaking up a monopoly would *not* be in the public interest. Some monopolies, are better left intact. It is to these "natural monopolies" that we now turn our attention.

NATURAL MONOPOLY

In comparing monopoly and competition, we assumed that the efficient scale of operation was small. When this is the case, there is no technological reason to have big firms instead of small firms. In some industries, however, there are technological economies of scale so large that it makes sense to have just one firm. Examples are rare, but public utilities—the electric company, for example, or the local telephone company—are among them. A firm that realizes such large economies of scale is called a **natural monopoly.**

natural monopoly An industry that realizes such large economies of scale in producing its product that single-firm production of that good or service is most efficient.

Although Figure 13.11 presents an exaggerated picture, it does serve to illustrate our point. One large-scale plant (Scale 2) can produce 500,000 units of output at an average unit cost of $1. If the industry were restructured into five firms, each producing on a smaller scale (Scale 1), the industry could produce the same amount, but average unit cost would be five times as high ($5). Consumers thus see a considerable gain when economies of scale are realized.

The critical point here is that:

> Economies of scale must be realized at a scale that is close to total demand in the market.

Notice in Figure 13.11 that the long-run average cost curve continues to decline almost until it hits the market demand curve. If at a price of $1 market

FIGURE 13.11
A Natural Monopoly

A natural monopoly is a firm in which the most efficient scale is very large. Here average cost declines until a single firm is producing nearly the entire amount demanded in the market. With one firm producing 500,000 units, average cost is $1 per unit. With five firms each producing 100,000 units, average cost is $5 per unit.

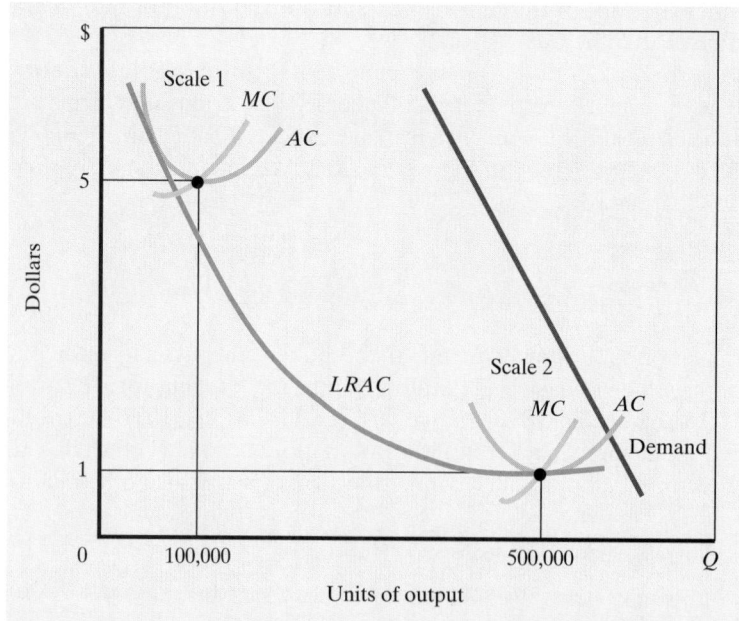

RENT-SEEKING BEHAVIOR IN THE MILK INDUSTRY

For the 50 years prior to January 1987, five dairies controlled the entire milk supply to all of New York City except for Staten Island. Entry into the city's milk market was blocked by the New York State Department of Agriculture and Markets, from which a potential entrant had to obtain a license to compete.

Not surprisingly, New Yorkers paid more for their milk than did consumers in adjacent areas. The first real evidence of this came in December 1985, when a New Jersey dairy, Farmland, was licensed to sell milk on Staten Island. Almost immediately, the price of milk there dropped more than 40 cents per gallon.

Late in 1986, New York Agriculture Commissioner Joseph Gerace denied Farmland a license to distribute milk in the rest of New York City, saying that a license for Farmland would bring "destructive competition." On December 13, 1986, the *New York Times* carried an editorial strongly critical of Governor Mario Cuomo for not firing Gerace and pointing out that Cuomo had received over $58,000 in campaign contributions from the dairy lobby. The rent-seeking behavior of the five dairies seemed to be working.

On January 3, 1987, Gerace resigned under pressure from the governor. Six days later, Farmland won in the courts what it could not win from the regulatory commission: permission to compete. On January 9, Federal District Court Judge Leonard Wexler ruled that

When barriers to entry in the New York City milk-selling business were dismantled, the price of milk dropped between 30 cents and 71 cents per gallon.

the denial of license to Farmland amounted to economic protectionism and was unconstitutional. The following day, Governor Cuomo agreed that the State would not appeal the decision and that it would pay all of Farmland's court costs and attorney fees. Thus ended the reign of a cartel that had dominated the New York City milk market for over 50 years.

On January 17, the *New York Times* carried a headline reading "Milk Prices Plunge in New York City in a Burst of Competition":

Milk prices dropped between 30 and 71 cents a gallon in New York City

supermarkets this week in the face of new competition from a New Jersey dairy. A&P, Grand Union, D'Agostino, Red Apple and Sloan's were all charging $1.99 a gallon for whole milk yesterday—a sharp drop from last week when the first shipment of milk from Farmland Dairies of Wallington, N.J. reached grocery shelves in Manhattan, Brooklyn, the Bronx and Queens. Previously, Farmland's sales had been limited to Staten Island....

Asked why Farmland's prices were lower than those of its New York competitors, its president, Marc Goldman, said, "It's not that we are so much cheaper, but that they have been overcharging."

Source: New York Times, January 17, 1987, p. 30.

demand is 5 *million* units of output, there would be no reason to have only one firm in the industry. Ten firms could each produce 500,000 units, and each could reap the full benefits of the available economies of scale.

Identifying a Natural Monopoly

Empirical studies suggest that very few true natural monopolies exist. The most often-cited example has always been the local telephone system. Would it make any sense to have two or more telephone cables running down each street? Providing local exchange service requires an enormous initial investment in switching equipment, wires, trenches, poles, and the like. Thus, fixed costs are very high, while marginal costs are very low. This means that average costs will continuously decline—one of the conditions that defines a natural monopoly.

Lately, however, this conventional wisdom has come under fire as modern technology opens up new ways of doing business in the telephone industry. For example, more and more telephone traffic is being transmitted through the air by microwave. Microwave transmitters can now be installed at relatively low cost, and no poles or connected wires are needed. Small firms are also stringing newly developed fiber-optic cable from location to location at relatively low cost. During the early 1980s, a company called The Teleport ran cable up the center of Manhattan, into the other boroughs of New York, across the Hudson River to New Jersey, and all the way to Princeton. The cable connects customers to a set of microwave antennae that communicates with over 1,000 orbiting satellites. All of this was accomplished at very low cost.

These developments have led many analysts to conclude that the monopoly power granted to local telephone exchange services can no longer be justified on the basis of large economies of scale. Nonetheless, such monopoly power is still granted. The current argument in favor of maintaining the local monopoly status is that states want to assure universal access to the telephone system at low cost. Public utility commissions, through their mandate to control basic service, can see that this happens. (For the monopolist's perspective, see the Issues and Applications box titled "The End of an Era in Telecommunications?")

Even though the argument for maintaining monopolies in local telephone service has shifted from one of efficiency to one of equity, the basic natural monopoly argument based on large efficient scale still seems valid where power companies are concerned. Electric power is still transmitted only over wires, and given this technology, huge economies of scale undeniably exist.

Regulating a Natural Monopoly

A more complete diagram of the cost structure of a natural monopoly appears in Figure 13.12. For simplicity, let us assume that the firm has very large initial fixed costs and very low constant marginal costs. Demand is fully exhausted while average cost is still in the process of declining. Like the business shown in Figure 13.11, operating this business on a small scale would make no sense because production costs would rapidly rise if firm size were reduced.

If an exclusive government license were issued to this firm, which would then be allowed to choose price and quantity freely, the firm would price at P_m, produce Q_m units of output, and earn economic profits of $P_m ABC$.[5] Such a firm, if left unregulated, would take all the benefits from the economies of scale away from consumers. All of this is simply to say that:

---

[5]You should by this point be able to figure out why economic profits are equal to rectangle $P_m ABC$. Remember: Economic profits = total revenue minus total costs. In this case, $P_m A Q_m 0 - C B Q_m 0 = P_m ABC$.

THE END OF AN ERA IN TELECOMMUNICATIONS?

In 1982, U.S. District Judge Harold H. Greene announced an agreement that broke up the world's largest telephone company, American Telephone and Telegraph (AT & T), into a number of separate companies. The purpose was to end the company's century-long virtual monopoly over the provision of telephone service in the United States. While long-distance service became openly competitive, AT & T's monopoly power did not end completely. Rather, AT & T's enforced break-up resulted in the creation of eight separate regional companies, the so-called Baby Bells, each of which was allowed to maintain monopoly power granted on a market-by-market basis by state public utility commissions.

In each local market area, one and only one company is allowed to provide local calling service. For example, if you want to get a phone line installed in your apartment in New York City, you must call New York Telephone, a subsidiary of NYNEX, one of the eight Baby Bells. The logic for allowing monopoly in local exchange service is that it is a natural monopoly (see text discussion). With very high fixed costs and low marginal costs, having many competing companies would mean higher costs. In addition, allowing competition might mean that some companies would fail and service would not be as reliable.

All local telephone monopolies are regulated by state public utility commissions (PUCs). These commissions set limits on rates, and they prevent competing companies from offering local telephone service. The PUCs thus serve as a barrier to entry. But they also restrict the ability of the Baby Bells to offer products and services other than straightforward local

The divestiture of AT&T has not stopped the company from participating in research and developing new products. In 1992, AT&T introduced the VideoPhone, which allows callers to see each other (provided both callers have a VideoPhone).

connection services and access to long-distance carriers. The commissions have argued that allowing the Baby Bells to compete in other markets would expose them to risks and drain resources from the provision of universal access to telephone service.

February 1993 saw the beginning of a new era. Ameritech, the Baby Bell servicing a number of Midwestern states, offered to end its local monopoly in exchange for the right to compete in newly emerging telecommunications markets, as the following excerpt describes.

Ameritech, the main provider of telephone service to 12 million customers in the Midwest, made a bold proposal yesterday to end its local telephone monopoly in return for freedom to offer more lucrative long-distance and cable-television services.

If approved by state and Federal regulators, the Ameritech plan would hasten the day when businesses and consumers in Ameritech's service area could choose the company that provides their local phone service,

just as they now can decide which company provides long-distance service....Ultimately at stake is the nation's $90 billion local telephone market and the $19 billion market for cable television. Cable operators are seeking to offer video and other services, including telephone service, in competition with local phone carriers....

"We're not talking mom-and-pop stores here," said William L. Weiss, chairman of Ameritech, whose 1992 revenue totaled $11.2 billion, most of it from local phone service. "We're talking Tele-Communications Inc. and Time Warner, and MCI and A.T.& T.," he said. "It would be a fair fight."...In return for giving up its local monopolies, Ameritech said it should be given the opportunity to make up for the lost revenue by competing in the long-distance and cable television markets. But the company provided few details on how it intends to enter those businesses....Under Ameritech's proposal, the Sprint Corporation, for example, could compete for these lucrative "local" toll calls—something Sprint is not currently allowed to do.

Source: Anthony Ramirez, "Ameritech Offers to End Monopoly," *New York Times*, February 23, 1993.

FIGURE 13.12

The Problem of Regulating a Natural Monopoly

An unregulated monopolist would produce only up to the point at which *marginal cost* and *marginal revenue* are equal—Q_m. If price were set at the efficient level, P_E, the firm would always suffer losses, because that price is insufficient to cover average costs. A compromise is for regulators to set price at P_A, which is just sufficient to cover costs including a normal profit rate.

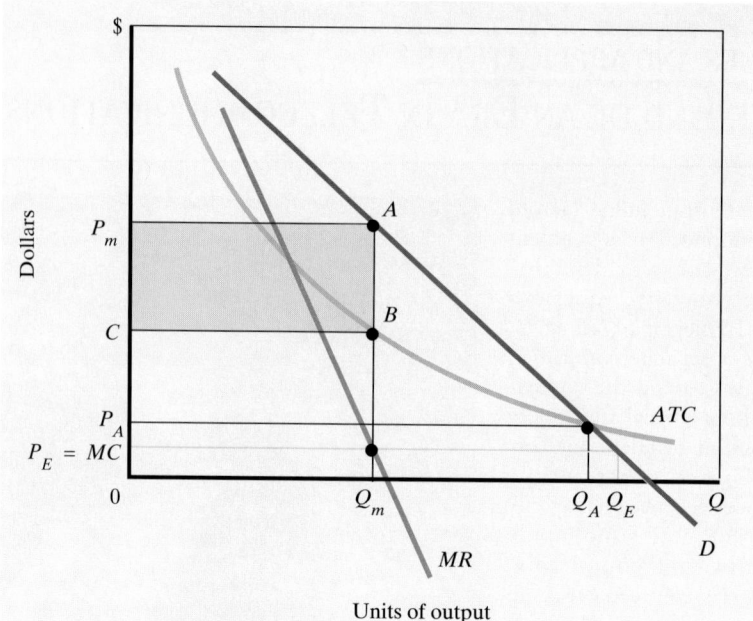

Units of output

Acknowledging a single firm as a natural monopoly and allowing it to operate under the protection of a government franchise essentially requires that the government become involved in regulating that firm.

One regulation possibility is for the government to set the price of the monopoly's output equal to marginal cost of production—that is, at $P_E = MC$. This would be the price of the output if it were produced competitively and efficiently. Notice, however, that marginal cost is *always* below average cost. Thus, if the government were to set price at $P_E = MC$, no level of output would produce enough revenue to cover total costs. If average revenue per unit (which, you will recall, equals price) is always below average cost per unit, there can be no profit. The firm would therefore suffer losses and go out of business in the long run.

Two other solutions to this regulatory dilemma are possible. The efficient solution would be to enforce a **price ceiling**—that is, a maximum price per unit above which the producer may not legally charge—at marginal cost and to subsidize the monopoly to keep it in business. Because this requires the use of tax dollars, however, it is rarely used.

By far the most common regulatory practice is to control price in a way that allows the owners of the public utility to earn a "fair rate of return." The state regulator's "fair rate of return" is very much like the economist's "normal rate of return." Because a normal return to capital is included in economic costs, a price that allows a firm to earn a normal return (which we assume is the same as the regulator's "fair return") would be a price just sufficient to cover average total costs (*ATC*). In Figure 13.12, a price ceiling set at P_A would leave the firm earning zero profits and just a normal rate of return.

While **average-cost pricing**—that is, setting price to cover average cost per unit including a fair return—will lower cost to consumers, transfer profits from monopolists, and reduce the net loss of social welfare, it does *not* produce efficient results. (Remember, economic efficiency requires production levels at which price equals marginal cost.) It is a compromise whose chief virtue is that it requires no tax revenues to subsidize utilities.

price ceiling A maximum price per unit above which the producer of a good or service may not legally charge.

average-cost pricing Setting price to cover average cost per unit including a fair return.

MARKET POWER IN INPUT MARKETS: MONOPSONY

Up to this point, we have been talking about market power in terms of output, or product, markets. Even monopolies, we assumed, were price-takers in input markets. But it is also possible for a firm to exercise control over prices in input markets. Consider, for example, a firm that is the *only buyer* in a market, the company that hires labor in a "company town." A market with only one buyer is called a **monopsony.**[6]

We have said time and time again that competitive firms are price-takers in input markets as well as output markets. The wage rate, for example, is set by the supply and demand that result when many firms demand labor and many households supply it. An individual competitive firm takes an externally determined wage rate as a given and will demand an input as long as the marginal revenue product of that input exceeds its price. The marginal revenue product of labor, for example, is the added revenue that the firm earns by hiring one additional unit of labor. The unit of labor produces some product—its marginal product—which, when sold, brings in revenues. In making input decisions, the competitive firm compares the "marginal gains" from hiring each unit of labor (that is, what the product of that unit sells for) against the "marginal cost" of that unit (that is, the wage rate). (If this sounds unfamiliar, you might want to review Chapter 10.)

When a firm hires labor competitively, it hires all the labor it needs at the current market wage. But suppose that the firm is the *only* buyer of laborers with some particular skill. This means that the firm now faces a market supply curve rather than a market-determined equilibrium wage. The wage rate thus becomes a decision variable for the firm. If the market supply curve of labor slopes upward, and the monopsony firm needs more labor, it must offer a higher wage to get that labor. The marginal cost of an additional unit of labor is no longer just equal to the wage rate. This leads us to the concept of **marginal factor cost (*MFC*),** that is, the additional cost of using one additional unit of a factor of production at the margin.

Using the supply schedule in Table 13.2, suppose that the monopsony firm wants to increase its use of labor from three units to four. The fourth unit of labor will work for a wage of $8 per hour, but because our firm cannot price discriminate, it must pay *all* workers the higher wage. When the monopsony employed three workers, it had to pay them only $6 per hour each; when the fourth unit of

monopsony A market in which there is only one buyer for a good or service.

marginal factor cost (*MFC*) The additional cost of using one more unit of a given factor of production.

---

[6]The terms "monopoly" and "monopsony" both derive from Greek root words. In both cases *mon(o)* means "sole" or "single." "Monopoly" adds a form of the Greek verb *polein,* "to sell." "Monopsony" adds a form of the Greek verb *opsonein,* "to buy food."

TABLE 13.2
Deriving Marginal Resource Cost for a Monopsonist

(1) UNITS OF LABOR SUPPLIED	(2) WAGE	(3) TOTAL FACTOR COST (TFC)	(4) MARGINAL FACTOR COST ((MFC)
0	$0	$—	$—
1	2	2	2
2	4	8	6
3	6	18	10
4	8	32	14
5	10	50	18
6	12	72	22
7	14	98	26

labor is added, those three will each earn an additional $2 per hour. The total cost of increasing labor from three to four units, therefore, is the $8 that goes to the fourth worker plus the $2 to each of the other three. The marginal factor cost is thus $14. In other words, increasing the use of labor by one unit will cost the firm $14. The marginal factor cost is higher than the wage rate at every level of labor demand except one, because the higher wage needed to attract any additional labor supply goes to all workers, not just to the marginal worker.

Figure 13.13 shows a typical marginal factor cost schedule that is above the labor supply schedule facing a monopsonist in a labor market. It is superimposed on the firm's marginal revenue product schedule. Using our now-familiar marginal logic, we can conclude that:

> A profit-maximizing firm hires labor as long as its marginal revenue product exceeds its marginal factor cost. Therefore, the profit-maximizing amount of labor for the monopsonist occurs at the point where $MRP_L = MFC$.

Note that this condition is true for all firms, not just monopsonists. In perfectly competitive labor markets, the wage equals the marginal factor cost. Thus the profit-maximizing amount of labor for a perfectly competitive firm can be written as $MRP_L = W$, which is what we learned in Chapter 10.

The monopsonist in Figure 13.13 would hire labor up to L_m (the point at which MFC and MRP_L intersect) and thus set a wage equal to W_m (point F on the supply curve). In competition, the wage would be W_c, the point at which quantity supplied and quantity demanded (marginal revenue product) are equal, and L_c units of labor would be hired. (Review Chapter 10 if this reasoning is unclear to you.) Thus, much like a monopolist who curtails production and charges a price above the level set by competition, a monopsonist cuts back on the units of labor hired and pays a wage below the level set by competition.

As you saw in Chapter 12, the condition $W = MRP_L$ ensures that households

FIGURE 13.13

A Monopsonist Will Hold Wages Below Marginal Revenue Product and Hire Less Labor Than a Perfect Competitor

For a monopsonist, the marginal cost of hiring one additional unit of labor is higher than the wage rate, because the firm must increase the wage of all workers to attract the new worker into the labor force. The monopsonist will hire only up to L_m and pay a wage W_m.

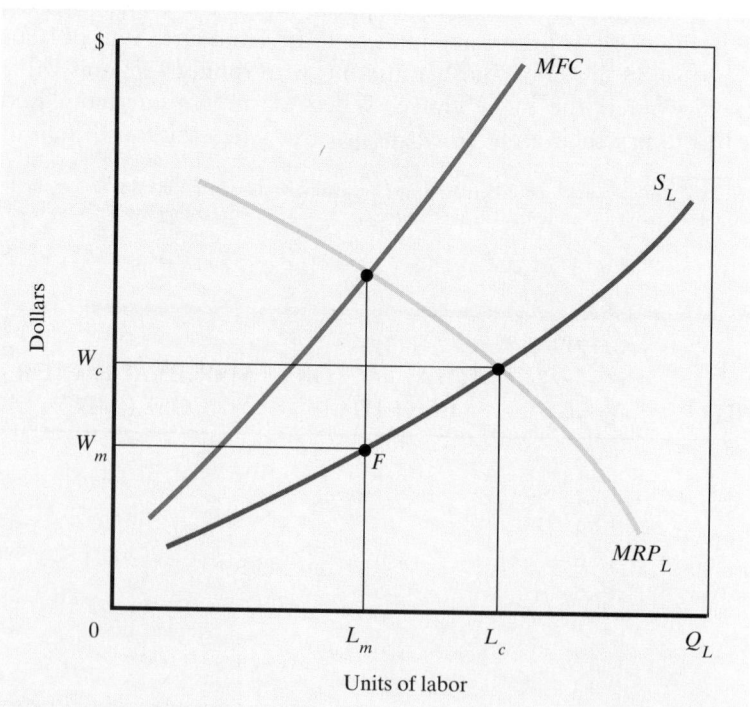

supply, and that firms hire, the efficient amount of labor. This condition implies that the market wage facing households and affecting their labor-supply behavior reflects the value of the product of labor. With monopsony, the wage rate is held considerably below MRP_L at competitive equilibrium. Because marginal revenue product is the value of labor's product, keeping the wage lower keeps people out of the work force who would otherwise be producing output that has a value to society. Thus, monopsony is inefficient.

IMPERFECT MARKETS: A REVIEW AND A LOOK AHEAD

A firm has *market power* when it exercises some control over the price of its output or the prices of the inputs that it uses. The extreme case of a firm with market power is the pure monopolist. In pure monopoly, a single firm produces a product for which there are no close substitutes in an industry in which all new competitors are barred from entry.

Our focus in this chapter on pure monopoly (which occurs only rarely) has served a number of purposes. First, the monopoly model does indeed describe a number of industries quite well. Second, the monopoly case clearly illustrates the observation that imperfect competition leads to an inefficient allocation of resources. Finally, the analysis of pure monopoly offers a number of important insights into the more commonly encountered market models of monopolistic competition and oligopoly, which we discussed briefly in this chapter and will discuss in detail in the next chapter.

SUMMARY

1. A number of important assumptions underlie the logic of pure competition. Among them are: (1) A large number of firms and households are interacting in each market; (2) firms in a given market produce undifferentiated, or homogeneous, products; and (3) new firms are free to enter industries and to compete for profits. The first two assumptions imply that firms have no control over input prices or output prices; the third implies that opportunities for economic profit are eliminated in the long run.

Imperfect Competition and Market Power: Core Concepts

2. A market in which individual firms have some control over price is imperfectly competitive; such firms exercise *market power*. The three forms of *imperfect competition* are monopoly, oligopoly, and monopolistic competition.

3. A *pure monopoly* is an industry with a single firm that produces a product for which there are no close substitutes and in which there are significant *barriers to entry*.

4. There are many barriers to entry, including government franchises and licenses, patents, economies of scale, and ownership of scarce factors of production.

5. Market power means that firms must make four decisions instead of three: (1) how much to produce, (2) how to produce it, (3) how much to demand in each input market, and (4) *what price to charge for their output*.

6. Market power does not imply that a monopolist can charge any price it wants. Monopolies are constrained by market demand. They can sell only what people will buy and only at a price that people are willing to pay.

Price and Output Decisions in Pure Monopoly Markets

7. In perfect competition, many firms supply homogeneous products. With only one firm in a monopoly market, however, there is no distinction between the firm and the industry—the firm *is* the industry. The market demand curve is thus the firm's demand curve, and the total quantity supplied in the market is what the monopoly firm decides to produce.

8. For a monopolist, an increase in output involves not just producing more and selling it but also reducing the price of its output in order to sell it. Thus marginal revenue, to a monopolist, is not equal to product price, as it is in competition. Rather, marginal revenue is lower than price because to raise

output one unit *and to be able to sell* that one unit, the firm must lower the price it charges to all buyers.

9. When demand is elastic, marginal revenue is positive—to sell more output, firms must lower price, but by a smaller percentage than the percentage increase in output. When demand is inelastic, marginal revenue is negative—to sell more output, firms must lower price by a larger percentage than the percentage increase in output. Therefore, monopolists do not produce in areas of the demand curve that are inelastic.

10. A profit-maximizing monopolist will produce up to the point at which marginal revenue is equal to marginal cost ($MR = MC$).

11. Monopolies have no identifiable supply curves. They simply choose a point on the market demand curve—that is, they choose a price and quantity to produce, which depend on both marginal cost and the shape of the demand curve.

12. In the short run, monopolists are limited by a fixed factor of production, just as competitive firms are. Monopolies that do not generate enough revenue to cover costs will go out of business in the long run.

13. Compared to a competitively organized industry, a monopolist restricts output, charges higher prices, and earns economic profits. Because MR always lies below the demand curve for a monopoly, monopolists will always charge a price higher than MC (the price that would be set by perfect competition).

The Social Costs of Monopoly

14. When firms price above marginal cost, the result is an inefficient mix of output. The decrease in consumer surplus is larger than the monopolist's profit, thus causing a net loss in social welfare.

15. Actions that firms take to preserve excess economic profits, such as lobbying for restrictions on competition, are called rent seeking. *Rent-seeking behavior* consumes resources and adds to social cost, thus reducing social welfare even further.

Natural Monopoly

16. When a firm exhibits economies of scale so large that average costs continuously decline with output, it may be efficient to have only one firm in an industry. Such an industry is called a *natural monopoly*.

17. The most common method of regulating a natural monopoly is to control the monopoly's price in a way that allows the owners of the monopoly to earn a "fair rate of return." This method, called *average-cost pricing,* will lower costs to consumers, but it does not produce efficient results.

Market Power in Input Markets: Monopsony

18. A market with only one buyer is a *monopsony*. The problem of firms that exercise market power in input markets is similar to the problems of monopoly.

19. *Marginal factor cost* is the additional cost of using one more unit of a given factor of production. A profit-maximizing firm will hire labor as long as its marginal revenue product exceeds its marginal factor cost.

REVIEW TERMS AND CONCEPTS

average-cost pricing 340
barriers to entry 318
collusion 332
government failure 335
government franchise 318

imperfect competition 317
marginal factor cost (*MFC*) 341
market power 317
monopsony 341
natural monopoly 336

patent 319
price ceiling 340
public choice theory 335
pure monopoly 318
rent-seeking behavior 335

PROBLEM SET

1. Do you agree or disagree with each of the following statements? Explain your reasoning.

a. For a monopoly, price is equal to marginal revenue because a monopoly has the power to control price.

b. A natural monopoly will produce at an efficient level of output if its price is simply set by the regulatory agency at marginal cost.

c. It is always true that if demand elasticity is equal to -1, marginal revenue is equal to zero.

d. Because a monopoly is the only firm in an industry, it can charge virtually any price for its product.

2. Explain why the marginal revenue curve facing a competitive firm differs from the marginal revenue curve facing a monopolist.

3. Assume that the potato chip industry in the Northwest in 1993 was competitively structured and in long-run competitive equilibrium; firms were earning a normal rate of return. In

1994 two smart lawyers quietly bought up *all* the firms and began operations as a monopoly called "Wonks." In order to operate efficiently, Wonks hired a management consulting firm, which estimated long-run costs and demand. These results are presented in the following figure:

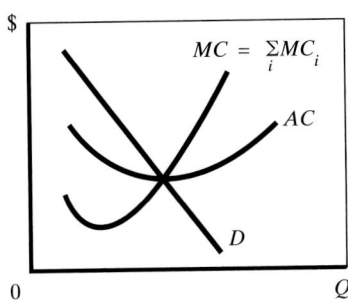

($\sum_i MC_i$ = the horizontal sum of the marginal cost = curves of the individual branches/firms)

    a. Indicate 1993 output and price on the diagram.

    b. Assuming that the monopolist is a profit-maximizer, indicate on the graph total revenue, total cost, and total profit after the consolidation.

    c. Show the perfectly competitive outcome on the graph. Compare the perfectly competitive outcome with the monopoly outcome.

    d. In 1994, an old buddy from law school files a complaint with the antitrust division of the Justice Department claiming that Wonks has monopolized the potato chip industry. Justice concurs and prepares a civil suit. Suppose you work in the White House and the President asks you to prepare a brief memo (two or three paragraphs) outlining the issues. In your response, be sure to include

    1. the economic justification for action

    2. a proposal to achieve an efficient market outcome.

4. Consider the following monopoly that produces paperback books:

$$\text{Fixed costs} = \$1000$$
$$\text{Marginal cost} = \$1 \text{ (and is constant)}.$$

    a. Draw the total cost schedule.

    b. Draw the average total cost curve and the marginal cost curve on the same graph.

    c. Assume that all households have the same demand schedule, given by the following relationship:

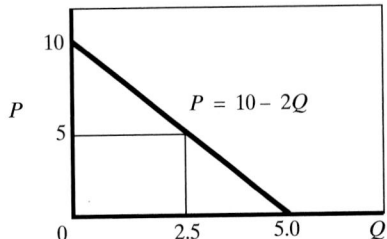

If there are 400 households in the economy, draw the market demand curve and the marginal revenue schedule facing the monopolist.

    d. What is the monopolist's profit-maximizing output? What is the monopolist's price?

    e. Calculate consumer surplus and profit for the monopolist.

    f. What is the "efficient price," assuming no externalities? What is consumer surplus at this price? How does it compare with monopoly profits and consumer surplus in e?

    g. Suppose that the government "imposed" the efficient price by setting a ceiling on price at the efficient level. What is the long-run output of the monopoly?

    h. Can you suggest an alternative approach for achieving an efficient outcome?

14 Monopolistic Competition and Oligopoly

We have now examined two "pure" market structures. At one extreme is *perfect competition,* a market structure in which many firms, each small relative to the size of the market, produce undifferentiated products and have no market power at all. Each competitive firm takes price as given and faces a perfectly elastic demand for its product. At the other extreme is *pure monopoly,* a market structure in which only one firm dominates an industry. The monopoly holds the power to set price and is protected against competition by barriers to entry. Its market power would be complete if it did not face the discipline of the market demand curve. Even a monopoly, however, must produce a product that people want and are willing to pay for.

Most industries in the United States fall somewhere between these two extremes. In this chapter, we focus on two types of industries in which firms exercise some market power but at the same time face competition. The first type, *monopolistic competition,* differs from perfect competition only in that firms can differentiate their products. Entry to a monopolistically competitive industry is free, and each industry is made up of many firms.

The second type, *oligopoly,* is an extremely broad category that covers many different kinds of firm behavior and industry structure. An oligopoly is an industry with a small number of competitors. Each firm in an oligopoly is large enough to have some control over market price, but beyond that the character of competition varies greatly from industry to industry. An oligopoly may have two firms or twenty, and those firms may produce differentiated or undifferentiated products.

Before we go on, it is useful to outline the approach that we will take to studying and analyzing monopolistic competition and oligopoly. We will start with a description of the structure of each kind of industry. How many firms are there? What portion of the industry's total sales is accounted for by the largest firms in the industry? Are there barriers to entry? If so, how do they operate? Do firms produce homogeneous or differentiated products? Are there economies of scale?

After examining structure, we analyze the behavior of firms in the industry. How are prices set? Does a dominant firm in effect set price for other, smaller firms? Do firms advertise? How much research do the firms do? How often are new product lines introduced?

Finally, we discuss the performance of each type of industry and how efficiently the firms in that industry operate. Do the industry's behavior and structure lead to inefficiency? Does the industry enhance or retard economic growth? What impact do the industry's structure and behavior have on the distribution of income?

MONOPOLISTIC COMPETITION

A **monopolistically competitive industry** has the following characteristics:

1. a large number of firms;
2. no barriers to entry;
3. product differentiation.

monopolistic competition A common form of industry (market) structure in the United States, characterized by a large number of firms, none of which can influence market price by virtue of size alone. Some degree of market power is achieved by firms producing differentiated products. New firms can enter and established firms can exit such an industry with ease.

While pure monopoly and perfect competition are rare, monopolistic competition is a very common form of organization in the United States. Take, for example, the restaurant business. The San Francisco Yellow Pages devote 26 pages to listing over 1,500 different restaurants in the area. Each of these restaurants produces a slightly different product and makes an attempt to distinguish itself in the minds of consumers. Entry to the market is certainly not blocked. One location near Union Square saw five different restaurants start up and go out of business in five years. Although many restaurants fail, small firms can nonetheless compete and survive because there are no economies of scale in the restaurant business.

The feature that distinguishes monopolistic competition from monopoly and oligopoly is that firms cannot influence market price by virtue of their size. No one restaurant is big enough to affect the market price of a prime rib dinner, for example, even though all restaurants can certainly control their *own* prices. Rather, firms gain control over price in monopolistic competition by differentiating their products. You make it in the restaurant business by producing a product that people want that others are not producing and/or by establishing a reputation for good food and good service. By producing a unique product or establishing a particular reputation, a firm becomes, in a sense, a "monopolist"—that is, no one else can produce the exact same good.

The feature that distinguishes monopolistic competition from pure monopoly is that good substitutes are available in a monopolistically competitive industry. With 1,500 restaurants in the San Francisco area, there are dozens of reasonably good Italian, Chinese, and French restaurants. San Francisco's Chinatown, for example, has about 50 small Chinese restaurants, with over a dozen packed on a single street. The menus are nearly identical, and they all charge virtually the same prices. At the other end of the spectrum are those restaurants, with very well-established names and prices far above the cost of production, that are always booked. That, of course, is the goal of every restaurateur who ever put a stockpot on the range.

Table 14.1 presents some data on eight national manufacturing industries that have the characteristics of monopolistic competition.[1] Each of these industries includes hundreds of individual firms, some of which are larger than others, but all of which are small relative to the industry. The top four firms in book publishing, for example, account for 24% of total shipments. The top 20 firms account for 62% of the market, while the market's remaining 38% is split among over 2,000 separate firms.

To review:

> Firms in a monopolistically competitive industry are small relative to the total market. New firms can enter the industry in pursuit of profit, and relatively good substitutes for the firms' products are available. Firms in monopolistically competitive industries try to achieve a degree of market power by differentiating their products—by producing something new, different, or better, or by creating a unique identity in the minds of consumers.

Before we go on to discuss the behavior of such firms, a few words about advertising and product differentiation are in order.

---

[1] The data are tabulated and reported by Standard Industrial Classification, or SIC, codes. This classification system for industries has been developed over a period of years and is administered by the Department of Commerce. The system operates in such a way that industry definitions become progressively narrower, and thus industry descriptions become more specific, with successive additions of digits. There are 20 *major groups* (SIC 20: food and kindred products), 150 *groups* (SIC 201: meat products), 450 *industries* (SIC 2011: meat-packing plants), 1,500 *product classes* (SIC 20112: bacon), and 13,000 *products* that add two more digits to make up a seven-digit code. The Census Bureau compiles its numbers from data collected in the Census of Manufacturers, done every five years. The data from the 1992 census will not be released for a few years.

TABLE 14.1

Percentage of Value of Shipments Accounted for by the Largest Firms in Selected Industries, 1987

SIC#	INDUSTRY DESIGNATION	FOUR LARGEST FIRMS	EIGHT LARGEST FIRMS	TWENTY LARGEST FIRMS	NUMBER OF FIRMS
3792	Traveler trailers and campers	34	50	66	384
2515	Mattresses and bedsprings	33	38	47	721
2521	Wood Office Furniture	26	37	50	625
2731	Book publishing	24	38	62	2182
2834	Pharmaceutical preparations	22	36	65	640
2321	Men's and boys' dress shirts	22	32	50	464
2599	Furniture and fixtures	18	24	34	1569
3564	Blowers and fans	14	23	42	445
2335	Woman's Misses,' & Juniors' Dresses	6	10	18	5398
3079	Misc. plastic products	6	9	14	7767

Source: U.S. Department of Commerce, Bureau of the Census, 1987 Census of Manufacturers, *Concentration Ratios in Manufacturing*, Subject Series MC87-S-6, Feb. 1992.

Product Differentiation, Advertising, and Social Welfare

Monopolistically competitive firms achieve whatever degree of market power they command through **product differentiation.** In order to be chosen over competitors, products must have distinct positive identities in the minds of consumers. This differentiation is often accomplished through advertising.

In 1990 firms spent over $128 billion on advertising, as Table 14.2 shows. You couldn't possibly get through life (and probably not even through a day) without hearing that "Pepsi is the choice of a new generation," or that leaving AT&T "just isn't worth it." Advertising reaches us through every medium of communication. Driving down most major highways we see billboard after billboard. Table 14.3 shows national network television advertising expenditures by major industrial category. The automobile industry leads the pack with expenditures of over $1.7 billion in television advertising in 1990. In 1993, 30 seconds of commercial advertising time during Super Bowl XXVII cost $850,000–$900,000.

The effects of product differentiation in general and advertising in particular on the allocation of resources have been hotly debated for years. Advocates claim that these forces give the market system its vitality and power; critics argue that they cause waste and inefficiency. Before we proceed to the formal models of monopolistic competition and oligopoly, the major points of this debate are worth reviewing.

THE CASE FOR PRODUCT DIFFERENTIATION AND ADVERTISING   The most important advantage of open product competition is that it provides us with the variety inherent in a steady stream of new products while ensuring that the quality of those products remains high. We have said before that one of the most important characteristics of a modern economy is the tremendous variety of tastes and preferences that it can satisfy. A walk through several neighborhoods of a big city, or even an hour in a modern department store or mall, should be enough to convince you that one thing we can say for certain about human wants is that they are infinite in their variety.

Free and open competition with differentiated products is the only way to satisfy all of us. Think of the variety of music we listen to—bluegrass, heavy metal, country, folk, rap, classical, grunge. Business firms engage in constant market research to satisfy these wants. What do consumers want? What colors? What cuts? What sizes? The only firms that succeed are the ones that answer these questions correctly and thereby satisfy an existing demand that was not previously being satisfied by the market.

In recent years, quite a few of us have taken up the sport of running. The market has responded in a very big way. Now there are numerous running magazines; hundreds of orthotic shoes designed specifically for runners with particular running styles; running suits of every imaginable color, cloth, and style; weights for the hands, ankles, and shoe laces; tiny radios to slip into your sweatbands; and so forth. Even physicians have differentiated their products: Sports medicine clinics have diets for runners, therapies for runners, and doctors specializing in shin splints or Morton's toe. There is even a running shoe with a small computer built into the heel to monitor a runner's time, distance, and calories expended.

The products that satisfy a real demand survive, but the market shows no mercy to products that no one wants. They sit on store shelves, are sold at heavy discount prices or not at all, and eventually disappear. Firms making products that don't sell go out of business, the victims of an economic Darwinism in which only the products that can thrive in a competitive environment survive.

product differentiation A strategy that firms use to achieve market power. Accomplished by producing products that have distinct positive identities in the minds of consumers.

TABLE 14.2
Total Advertising Expenditures in 1990

	DOLLARS (BILLIONS)
Newspapers	32.3
Television	28.4
Direct mail	23.4
Other	20.1
Yellow Pages	8.9
Radio	8.7
Magazines	6.8
Total	128.6

Source: McCann Erickson, Inc., Reported in U.S. Bureau of the Census, *Statistical Abstract of the United States,* 1992 table 905, p. 5590.

TABLE 14.3
Expenditures for Television Network Advertising in 1990

	DOLLARS (MILLIONS)
Automobiles	$1,781
Food and food products	1,704
Toiletries and toilet goods	944
Proprietary medicines	817
Restaurants & Drive-in's	624
Consumer Services	524
Soft drinks and confectionary	407
Laundry soap, cleansers, polishes	317
Beer and wine	293
All industries	10,132

Source: Television Bureau of Advertising, Inc. (New York). Reported in U.S. Department of Commerce, Bureau of the Census, *Statistical Abstract of the United States,* 1992, table 907, p. 560.

The standard of living rises when the technology of production improves—that is, when we learn to produce more with fewer resources. But the standard of living also rises when we have product *innovation,* when new and better products come on the market. Just think of all the things that we have and use today that didn't exist 10 or 15 years ago. Compact disc players, microwave ovens, VCRs, mountain bikes, and personal computers have all been developed in the last two decades.

Variety is also important to us psychologically. The astonishing range of products available exists not just because your tastes differ from mine. Human beings get bored easily. We grow tired of things, and diminishing marginal utility sets in. I don't go only to French restaurants; it's nice to eat Greek or Chinese food once in a while too. To satisfy many people with different preferences that change over time, the market must be free to respond with new products.

People who visit planned economies always comment on the lack of variety. Indeed, before the Berlin Wall came down in 1989 and East and West Germany were reunited in 1990, the classic story was one of driving from colorful and exciting West Berlin into dull and grey East Berlin; variety seemed to vanish. As the Wall came down, thousands of Germans from the East descended on the department stores of the West. Visitors to China since the economic reforms of the mid-1980s claim that the biggest visible sign of change is the increase in the selection of products available to the population.

Proponents of product differentiation also argue that it leads to efficiency. If my product is of higher quality than that of my competition, my product will sell more and my firm will do better. If I can produce something of high quality more cheaply—that is, more efficiently—than my competition can, I will force them to do likewise or force them out of business. Creating a brand name through advertising also helps to ensure quality. Firms that have spent millions to establish a brand name or a reputation for quality have something of value to protect.

For product differentiation to be successful, of course, consumers must know about product quality and availability. In perfect competition, where all products are alike, we assume that consumers have perfect information; without it, the market fails to produce an efficient allocation of resources. Complete information is even more important when we allow for product differentiation. How do consumers get this information? The answer is, at least in part, through advertising. The basic function of advertising, according to its proponents, is to assist consumers in making informed, rational choices.

Supporters of product differentiation and advertising also claim that these techniques promote competition. New products can compete with old, established brands only if they can get their messages through to consumers. When consumers are informed about a wide variety of potential substitutes, they can more effectively resist the power of monopolies.

To sum up:

> The advocates of free and open competition believe that differentiated products and advertising give the market system its vitality and are the basis of its power. They are the only ways to begin to satisfy the enormous range of tastes and preferences in a modern economy. Product differentiation also helps to ensure high quality and efficient production, and advertising provides consumers with the valuable information on product availability, quality, and price that they need to make efficient choices in the marketplace.

THE CASE AGAINST PRODUCT DIFFERENTIATION AND ADVERTISING Critics of product differentiation and advertising argue that these practices waste society's scarce resources. The argument is that enormous sums of money are spent to create minute, meaningless differences among products.

Drugs, both prescription and nonprescription, are a prime example. Companies spend millions and millions of dollars to "hype" brand-name drugs that contain exactly the same compounds as those available under their generic names. The antibiotics erythromycin and erythrocin have the same ingredients. Yet the latter is half as expensive as the former. Aspirin is aspirin, yet we pay twice the price for an advertised brand, because the manufacturer has convinced us that there is a tangible—or intangible—difference.

Do we really need 50 different kinds of soap, all of whose prices are inflated substantially by the cost of advertising? For a firm producing a differentiated product, advertising is part of the everyday cost of doing business; its price is built into the average cost curve and thus into the price of the product in the short run and the long run. Thus, consumers pay to finance advertising.

In a way, advertising and product differentiation turn the market system completely around. We have been talking about an economic system designed to meet the needs and satisfy the desires of members of society—that is, as a means to an end, which is the social good. Advertising is intended to change people's preferences and to create wants that otherwise would not have existed. From the advertiser's viewpoint, people exist to satisfy the needs of the economy. In other words, the *goal* of the economic system has been lost, and the *means* has become the end.[2]

Critics also argue that the information content of advertising is minimal at best and deliberately deceptive at worst. It is meant to change our minds, to persuade us, and to create brand "images." Try to determine how much real information there is in the next 10 advertisements you see on television. To the extent that no information is conveyed, critics argue, advertising creates no real value, and thus a substantial portion of the $128 billion worth of resources that we devote to advertising is wasted.

Competitive advertising can also easily turn into unproductive warfare. Suppose there are five firms in an industry and that one of these firms begins to advertise heavily. In order to survive, the others respond in kind—if one firm drops out of the race, it will certainly lose out. Advertising of this sort may not increase demand for the product or improve profitability for the industry at all. Instead, it is all too often a "zero sum game"—a game that, on balance, no one wins.

Advertising may reduce competition by creating a barrier to the entry of new firms into an industry. One famous case study taught at the Harvard Business School calculates the cost of entering the breakfast cereal market. In order to be successful, a potential entrant would have to start with millions of dollars in an extensive advertising campaign to establish a brand name recognized by consumers. Entry to the breakfast cereal game is not completely blocked, but such financial requirements make it much more difficult.

Finally, some argue that advertising by its very nature imposes a cost on society. We are continuously bombarded by bothersome jingles and obtrusive images. Driving home from work, we pass 50 billboards and listen to 15 minutes of news and 20 minutes of advertising on the radio. When we get home, we open and throw away 10 pieces of unsolicited junk mail, glance at a magazine containing 50 pages of writing and 75 pages of advertisements, and perhaps watch a television show that is interrupted every 10 minutes for a "message."

---

[2]This point was made by John Kenneth Galbraith in *The Affluent Society* (Boston: Houghton Mifflin, 1958).

In sum:

> The bottom line, critics of product differentiation and advertising argue, is waste and inefficiency. Enormous sums are spent to create minute, meaningless, and possibly nonexistent differences among products. Advertising raises the cost of products and frequently contains very little information. Often, it is merely an annoyance. Product differentiation and advertising have turned the system upside down: People exist to satisfy the needs of the economy, not vice versa. Advertising can lead to unproductive warfare and may serve as a barrier to entry, thus reducing real competition.

NO RIGHT ANSWER One of the things that you will see over and over as you study economics is that many questions have no right answers. There are strong arguments on both sides of the advertising debate, and even the empirical evidence leads to conflicting conclusions. Some studies show that advertising leads to concentration and excess profits; others, that advertising improves the functioning of the market.[3]

Price and Output Determination in Monopolistic Competition

Recall that monopolistically competitive industries are made up of a large number of firms, each small relative to the size of the total market. Thus, no one firm can affect market price by virtue of its size alone. Firms do differentiate their products, however, and by doing so, they gain some control over price.

PRODUCT DIFFERENTIATION AND DEMAND ELASTICITY Purely competitive firms face a perfectly elastic demand for their product: All firms in a perfectly competitive industry produce exactly the same product. If Firm A tried to raise price, buyers would simply go elsewhere and Firm A would sell nothing. When a firm can distinguish its product from all others in the minds of consumers, as we assume it can under monopolistic competition, it probably can raise price without losing all demand. Figure 14.1 shows how product differentiation might make demand somewhat less elastic for a hypothetical firm.

A monopoly, we said, is an industry with a single firm that produces a good for which there are no close substitutes. A monopolistically competitive firm is like a monopoly in that it is the only producer of its unique product. Only one firm can produce Cheerios, Wheat Thins, Johnson's Baby Shampoo, and Oreo cookies. But unlike the product in a monopoly market, the product of a monopolistically competitive firm has many close substitutes competing for the consumer's favor. Thus,

> While the demand curve faced by a monopolistic competitor is likely to be less elastic than the demand curve faced by a perfectly competitive firm, it is likely to be more elastic than the demand curve faced by a monopoly.

PRICE/OUTPUT DETERMINATION IN THE SHORT RUN Under conditions of monopolistic competition, a profit-maximizing firm behaves very much like a monopolist in the short run. First, marginal revenue is not equal to price, because the monopolistically competitive firm has some control over output price. Like a

---

[3]The most widely quoted study showing that advertising restricts competition is William S. Comoner and Thomas A. Wilson, *Advertising and Market Power* (Cambridge, Mass.: Harvard University Press, 1974). As one example of the opposing argument, see John M. Scheidell, *Advertising, Prices, and Consumer Reaction: A Dynamic Analysis* (Washington, D.C.: American Enterprise Institute, 1978).

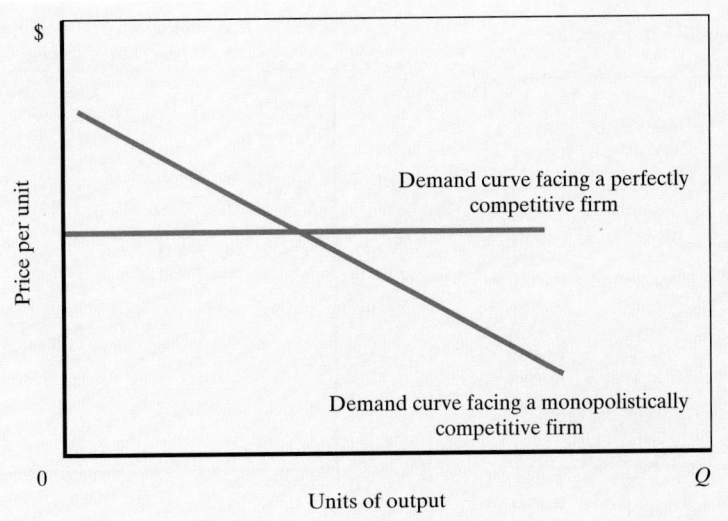

FIGURE 14.1

Product Differentiation
Reduces the Elasticity of
Demand Facing a Firm

While the demand curve faced by
a monopolistic competitor is likely to be less elastic than the
demand curve faced by a perfectly
competitive firm, it is likely to be
more elastic than the demand
curve faced by a monopolist
because close substitutes for the
products of a monopolistic competitor are available.

monopolistic firm, a monopolistically competitive firm must lower price in order
to increase output and sell it. The monopolistic competitor's marginal revenue
curve thus lies *below* its demand curve, intersecting the quantity axis midway
between the origin and the point at which the demand curve intersects it. (If necessary, review Chapter 13 to get a grip on this idea.)

The firm then chooses that combination of output and price that maximizes profit.

> In order to maximize profit, the monopolistically competitive firm will produce as
> long as the marginal revenue from increasing output and selling it exceeds the mar-
> ginal cost of producing it. This occurs at the point at which marginal revenue
> equals marginal cost: $MR = MC$.

In Figure 14.2a on the next page, the profit-maximizing output is q_0, the point
at which marginal revenue equals marginal cost. To sell q_0 units of product, the
firm must charge P_0. Total revenue is $P_0 \times q_0$, or the area of P_0Aq_00. Total cost is
equal to average total cost times q_0, or CBq_00. Total profit is equal to the difference, or the shaded area P_0ABC.

Nothing guarantees that a firm in a monopolistically competitive industry will
earn economic profits in the short run. Figure 14.2b shows what happens when a
firm with the same cost curves faces a weaker market demand. Even though the
firm does have some control over price, market demand is insufficient to make the
firm profitable.

As in pure competition, such a firm minimizes its losses by producing up to the
point where marginal revenue is equal to marginal cost. Of course, as in competition, the price that the firm charges must be sufficient to cover variable costs.
Otherwise, the firm will shut down and suffer losses equal to total fixed costs,
rather than increase losses by producing more. In other words, the firm must make
a profit on operation. In Figure 14.2b, the loss-minimizing level of output is q_1.
Total revenue is $P_1 \times q_1$, or P_1Bq_10. Total cost, or CAq_10, is greater than revenue,
and the firm suffers a loss equal to the gray shaded area, $CABP_1$.

PRICE/OUTPUT DETERMINATION IN THE LONG RUN   In analyzing monopolistic
competition, our key assumption is that entry and exit are, in the long run, free.

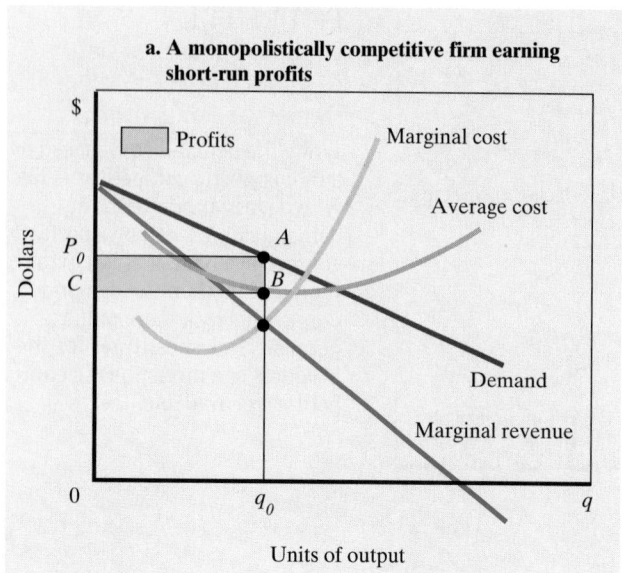

a. A monopolistically competitive firm earning short-run profits

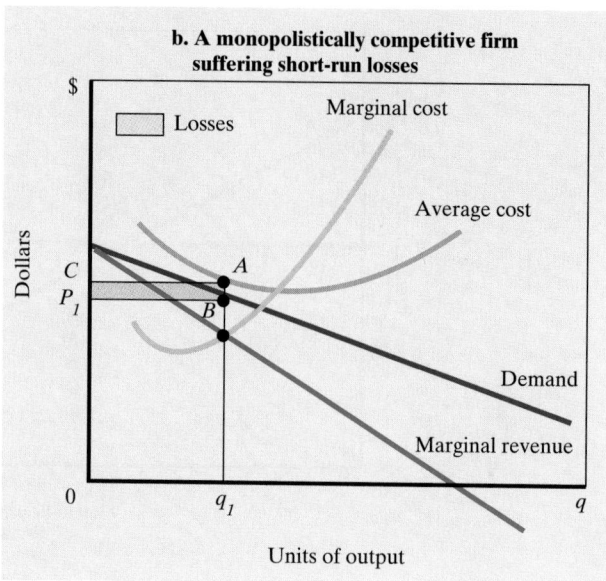

b. A monopolistically competitive firm suffering short-run losses

FIGURE 14.2
Monopolistic Competition in the Short Run

In the short run, a monopolistically competitive firm will produce up to the point at which $MR = MC$. At q_0 in panel a, the firm is earning economic profits equal to P_0ABC. In panel b, another monopolistically competitive firm with a similar cost structure is shown facing a weaker demand and suffering short-run losses at q_1 equal to $CABP_1$.

Firms can enter an industry when there are profits to be made, and firms suffering losses can fold up and go out of business. But entry into an industry of this sort is somewhat different from entry into pure competition, because products are differentiated in monopolistic competition. A firm that enters a monopolistically competitive industry is producing a close substitute for the good in question, *but not the same good.*

Let us begin with a firm earning economic profits in the short run. Those economic profits provide an incentive for new firms to enter the industry. The new firms compete by offering close substitutes, and this drives down the demand for the product of the firm that was previously earning economic profits. If several restaurants seem to be doing very well in a particular location, for example, others may start up and attract business from them.

New firms will continue to enter the market until excess profits are eliminated. As the new firms enter, the demand curve facing each old firm begins to shift to the left, pushing the marginal revenue curve along with it. (Review Chapter 13 if you are unsure why this is so.) This shift continues until profits are eliminated, which occurs when the demand curve slips down to the average total cost curve. Graphically, this is the point at which the demand curve and the average total cost curve are tangent (that is, the point at which they just touch and have the same slope). Figure 14.3 shows a monopolistically competitive industry in long-run equilibrium. At q^* and P^*, price and average total cost are equal, and there are no economic profits or losses.

Look carefully at this tangency, which in Figure 14.3 is at output level q^*. The tangency occurs at the profit-maximizing level of output. At this point, marginal cost is equal to marginal revenue. At any level of output other than q^*, ATC lies above the demand curve. This means that at any other level of output, ATC is greater than the price that the firm can charge. (Recall that the demand curve

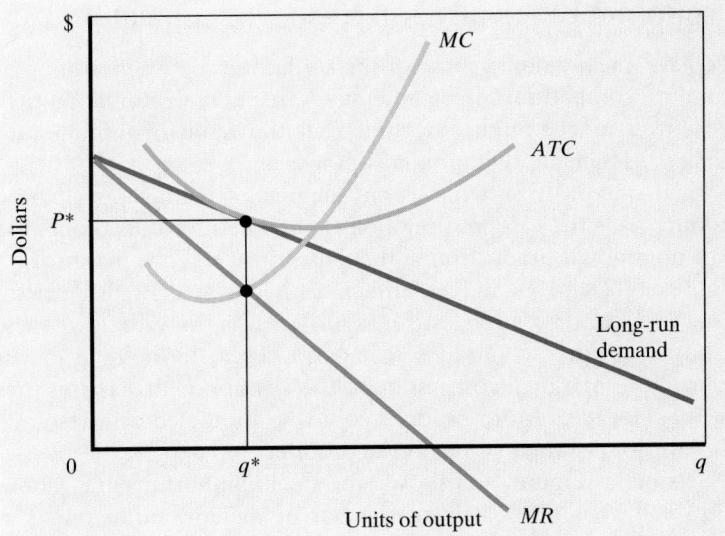

FIGURE 14.3
Monopolistically
Competitive Firm at Long-
Run Equilibrium

As new firms enter a monopolistically competitive industry
in search of profits, the demand
curves of profit-making existing
firms begin to shift to the left,
pushing marginal revenue with
them as consumers switch to
the new close substitutes. This
process continues until profits
are eliminated, which occurs
for a firm when its demand
curve is just tangent to its average cost curve.

shows the price that can be charged at every level of output.) Hence, price equals
average cost at q^* and economic profits equal zero.

This final equilibrium must occur at the point at which the demand curve is
just tangent to the average total cost curve. If the demand curve cut across the average cost curve, thus intersecting it at two points, the demand curve would be *above*
the average cost curve at some levels of output. Producing at those levels of output
would mean economic profits. Economic profits would attract entrants, thus shifting the market demand curve to the left, and thus lowering profits. If, on the
other hand, the demand curve were always *below* the average cost curve, all levels
of output would produce losses for the firm. This would cause firms to exit the
industry, thus shifting the market demand curve to the right, and thus increasing
profits (or reducing losses) for those firms still in the industry. Thus,

> The firm's demand curve must end up tangent to its average total cost curve for
> economic profits to equal zero. This is the condition for long-run equilibrium in a
> monopolistically competitive industry.

Even if a monopolistically competitive firm starts with losses, it will arrive at
the same long-run equilibrium. (Look back at Figure 14.2b, which shows a firm
suffering losses.) Suppose that too many restaurants open up in a given small area,
for example. Near Philadelphia, along a strip of highway called City Line, there
are a dozen or so "quick dinner" restaurants crowded into a very small area. Most
diners go to one or two of the popular spots, while business is slow at the others.
Given these circumstances, it seems likely that there will be a "shake-out" sometime in the near future—that is, one or more of the firms suffering losses will
decide to drop out of the industry.

When this happens, the firms remaining in the industry will get a larger share
of the total business, and their demand curves will shift to the right. Prosperous
firms will grow more prosperous, and firms that were suffering losses will find
those losses reduced by the additional demand. The demand curves of the remaining monopolistic competitors will continue to shift until losses are eliminated.
Thus, we end up with the same long-run equilibrium as we did when we started
out with a firm earning profits. At equilibrium, demand is tangent to average total
cost, and there are no economic profits or losses.

Economic Efficiency and Resource Allocation

We have already noted some of the similarities between monopolistic competition and pure competition. Because entry is free and economic profits are eliminated in the long run, we might conclude that the result of monopolistic competition is efficient. There are two problems, however.

First, once a firm achieves any degree of market power by differentiating its product (as is the case in monopolistic competition), its profit-maximizing strategy is to hold down production and charge a price above marginal cost, as you saw in Figures 14.2 and 14.3. Remember from Chapter 12 that price is the value that society places on a good, and marginal cost is the value that society places on the resources needed to produce that good. Thus, by holding production down and price above marginal cost, monopolistically competitive firms prevent the efficient use of resources. More product could be produced at a resource cost below the value that consumers place on the product.

Second, as Figure 14.3 shows, the final equilibrium in a monopolistically competitive firm is necessarily to the left of the low point on its average total cost curve. Thus, a typical firm in a monopolistically competitive industry will not realize all the economies of scale available. (In pure competition, you will recall, firms are pushed to the bottom of their long-run average cost curves, and the result is an efficient allocation of resources.)

Suppose, for example, that a number of firms enter an industry and build plants on the basis of initially profitable positions. But as more and more firms compete for those profits, individual firms find themselves with smaller and smaller market shares, and they end up eventually with "excess capacity." The firm in Figure 14.3 is not fully utilizing its existing capacity because competition drove its demand curve to the left. Thus, in monopolistic competition we end up with many firms, each producing a slightly different product at a scale that is less than optimal. Would it not be more efficient to have a smaller number of firms, each producing on a slightly larger scale?

The costs of less-than-optimal production, however, need to be balanced against the gains that can accrue from aggressive competition among products. If, as we said earlier, product differentiation leads to the introduction of new products, improvements in old products, and greater variety, then an important gain in economic welfare may counteract, and perhaps outweigh, the loss of efficiency from pricing above marginal cost or not fully realizing all economies of scale.

Most industries that comfortably fit the model of monopolistic competition are very competitive. Price competition coexists with product competition, and firms do not earn incredible profits. Nor do they violate any of the antitrust laws that we discuss in detail in the next chapter.

Monopolistically competitive firms have not been a subject of great concern among economic policy makers. Their behavior appears to be sufficiently controlled by competitive forces, and no serious attempt has been made to regulate or control them.

OLIGOPOLY

oligopoly A form of industry (market) structure characterized by a few firms, each large enough to influence market price. Products may be homogeneous or differentiated. The behavior of any one firm in an oligopoly depends to a great extent on the behavior of others.

An **oligopoly** is an industry dominated by a few firms that, by virtue of their individual sizes, are large enough to influence the market price. Oligopolies exist in many forms. In some oligopoly markets, products are differentiated—the classic example is the automobile industry. In others, products are nearly homogeneous—

in primary copper production, for example, only eight firms produce all the basic metal. Some oligopolies have a very small number of firms, each large enough to influence price—only five firms are involved in primary lead production, for example. Others have many firms, of which only a few control market price—four firms control 90% of the market for electrical lamps, but 93 firms compete in the industry.

An industry that has a relatively small number of firms that dominate the market is called a *concentrated industry*. Oligopolies are concentrated industries. Table 14.4 contains some data on nine industries that are relatively concentrated. While the largest firms account for most of the output in each of these industries, some seem to support a large number of smaller firms.

The complex interdependence that usually exists among firms in these industries makes oligopoly very difficult to analyze. The behavior of any one firm depends on the reactions it expects of all the other firms in the industry. Because individual firms make so many decisions—how much output to produce, what price to charge, how much advertising to do, whether and when to introduce new product lines, and so forth—industrial strategies can be, and usually are complex and difficult to generalize about.

Oligopoly Models

Because many different types of oligopolies exist, a number of different oligopoly models have been developed. A complete survey would exceed our purposes, but the discussion that follows provides a good sample of the alternative approaches to the behavior (or conduct) of oligopolistic firms. As you will see, all kinds of oligopoly have one thing in common:

> The behavior of any given oligopolistic firm depends on the behavior of the other firms in the industry.

THE COLLUSION MODEL   In Chapter 13, we examined what happens when a purely competitive industry falls under the control of a single profit-maximizing firm.

TABLE 14.4
Percentage of Value of Shipments Accounted for by the Largest Firms in High-Concentration Industries, 1987

SIC#	INDUSTRY DESIGNATION	FOUR LARGEST FIRMS	EIGHT LARGEST FIRMS	NUMBER OF FIRMS
3331	Primary copper	NA	100	8
2067	Chewing gum	96	100	8
2111	Cigarettes	92	99	9
2296	Tire cord and fabric	91	99	9
3641	Electric lamp bulbs	91	94	93
3711	Motor vehicles	90	95	352
3482	Small Arms Ammunition	88	96	75
2043	Cereal breakfast foods	87	99	33
3632	Household Refrigerator & Freezers	85	98	40
3996	Hard surface floor covering	82	99	14

NA = Not available.

Source: U.S. Department of Commerce, Bureau of the Census, 1987 Census of Manufacturers, *Concentration Ratios in Manufacturing*, Subject Series MC 87-S-6.

FIGURE 14.4

Market Equilibrium for a Colluding Oligopoly Is Just Like Equilibrium for a Monopoly

If all firms in a competitive industry jointly maximize their profits, the result is the same as it would be under a pure monopoly. The cartel would face market demand and produce only up to the point at which marginal revenue and marginal cost are equal. (By this point, you should be able to work out total costs, revenues, and profits for the illustrated firm.)

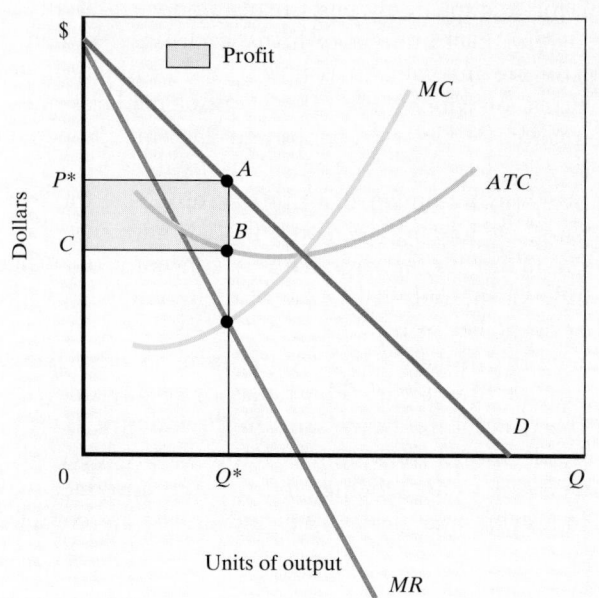

In that analysis, we assumed neither technological nor cost advantages to having one firm rather than many. We saw that when many competing firms act independently, they produce more, charge a lower price, and earn less profit than they would have if they had acted as a single unit. If these firms get together and agree to cut production and increase price—that is, if firms can agree *not* to price compete—they will have a bigger total-profit pie to carve up. When a group of profit-maximizing oligopolists colludes on price and output, the result is exactly the same as it would be if a monopolist controlled the entire industry (see Figure 14.4):

> The colluding oligopoly will face market demand and produce only up to the point at which marginal revenue and marginal cost are equal (*MR = MC*), and price will be set above marginal cost.

Review the section of Chapter 13 entitled "Collusion and Monopoly Compared" if you are unsure why this is so.

A group of firms that gets together and makes price and output decisions jointly is called a **cartel.** Perhaps the most familiar example of a cartel today is the Organization of Petroleum Exporting Countries (OPEC). As early as 1970, the OPEC cartel began to cut petroleum production. Its decisions in this matter led to a 400% increase in the price of crude oil on world markets during 1973 and 1974.

Price fixing is not controlled internationally, but it is illegal in the United States. Nonetheless, the incentive to fix prices can be irresistible, and industries are caught in the act from time to time. One famous case in the 1950s involved explicit agreements among a number of electrical equipment manufacturers. In that case, 12 people from five companies met secretly on a number of occasions and agreed to set prices and split up contracts and profits. The scheme involved rotating among the firms the winning bids on alternate contracts. Ultimately the scheme was exposed, and the participants were tried, convicted, and sent to jail.

For a cartel to work, a number of conditions must be present. First, demand for the cartel's product must be inelastic. If many substitutes are readily available, the

cartel A group of firms that gets together and makes joint price and output decisions in order to maximize joint profits.

DIAMONDS IN THE ROUGH: THE END OF A CARTEL?

For decades, DeBeers Consolidated Mines, a South African company, has been the leader of a powerful cartel that has been able to control the world's supply of diamonds. A cartel acts just like a monopoly: By restricting supply, the cartel is able to charge a higher price than would be the case if its members operated independently as competitors.

It has always been difficult for cartels to maintain their power. The following excerpt indicates that, after decades of stability, the DeBeers cartel may be coming unglued.

Less than a month ago De Beers Consolidated Mines, the secretive South African company that dominates the world diamond trade through a cartel that controls 80 percent of the world's uncut diamonds, seemed to have coasted miraculously through a recession that had rattled other luxury industries.

But in the last few weeks the industry has admitted that it is suffering its worst swoon in a decade, provoking speculation, once unthinkable, that the cartel is losing its grip.

One source of the disarray is a flood of Angolan diamonds that have begun to pour onto the normally orderly world market.

Now that Angola's civil war has ended, some 50,000 prospectors are digging for gems, mainly along the diamond-rich Cuango River. As the African drought has dried up the rivers, alluvial diamond deposits in the riverbeds and riverbanks have become more accessible to the wildcat miners, who smuggle them out to buyers in Antwerp....

For the first time since the diamond market collapsed in 1981, investors wondered openly whether the De Beers cartel could continue to dominate the gem trade....

A recent spate of prospectors digging for diamonds in the Angolan Cuango River is jeopardizing the existence of the decades-old DeBeers cartel. What is likely to happen to the price of diamonds if the DeBeers cartel breaks up?

The cartel is scrambling to hold retail prices stable by buying up the oversupply. But for now, the big industrial economies show no signs of returning to the bauble-buying euphoria of the 1980's, and there seems to be little immediate prospect of arresting the flow of gems from Angola....

De Beers has worked hard to create stability in an industry that in effect sells caprice. After all, no one really needs dia-monds. Even the gems used in industry now have synthetic alternatives. Like luxury tours and sable coats, gem diamonds have the makings of a cyclical business that should flutter with economic trends. But it does not, largely because De Beers has kept tight controls on the supply.

Source: Bill Keller, "DeBeers May Be Losing Grip on Diamond Market," *New York Times,* September 3, 1992.

cartel's price increases may become self-defeating as buyers switch to substitutes. Second, the members of the cartel must play by the rules. If a cartel is holding up prices by restricting output, there is a big incentive for members to cheat by increasing output. Breaking ranks can mean very large profits.

Both of these problems have plagued the OPEC cartel in recent years. The demand for oil has turned out to be much more elastic in the long run than it was in the short run. The high prices of the early 1980s led to sharp decreases in the demand for oil during that decade. In addition, the amount of oil produced by non-OPEC countries (including the United States) has increased significantly. Finally, at least some OPEC countries exceeded their quotas. For example, evidence exists that during the 1980s Kuwait was producing more than its OPEC quota of oil. These events caused oil prices to fall during much of the 1980s. The ups and downs of another cartel, DeBeers Consolidated Mines, are described in this chapter's Global Perspective box.

Collusion occurs when price- and quantity-fixing agreements are explicit. **Tacit collusion** occurs when firms end up fixing price without a specific agreement, or when such agreements are implicit. A small number of firms with market power may fall into the practice of setting similar prices or following the lead of one firm without ever meeting or setting down formal agreements.

tacit collusion *Collusion* occurs when price- and quantity-fixing agreements among producers are explicit. *Tacit collusion* occurs when such agreements are implicit.

THE PRICE-LEADERSHIP MODEL In another form of oligopoly, one firm dominates an industry and all the smaller firms follow the leader's pricing policy—hence the descriptive term **price leadership.** If the dominant firm knows that the smaller firms will follow its lead, it will derive its own demand curve simply by subtracting from total market demand the amount of demand that the smaller firms will satisfy.

price leadership A form of oligopoly in which one dominant firm sets prices and all the smaller firms in the industry follow its pricing policy.

The price-leadership model assumes, first, that the industry is made up of one large firm and a number of smaller, competitive firms. Second, it assumes that the dominant firm maximizes profit subject to the constraint of market demand *and* subject to the behavior of the smaller, competitive firms. Finally, the model assumes that the dominant firm allows the smaller firms to sell all they want to at the price that the leader has set. The difference between the quantity demanded in the market and the amount supplied by the smaller firms is the amount that the dominant firm will produce.

Figure 14.5 illustrates the behavior of an oligopolistic industry in which one dominant firm sets price and other smaller firms follow the dominant firm's lead. The diagram may seem complex, but it is really quite easy. Market demand in the diagram is shown by the dashed blue curve labeled *D*. The quantity that the smaller firms taken together will supply at each price is labeled "smaller firms' supply curve." The demand curve facing the dominant firm is the difference between these two curves. To derive this curve, we simply take the quantity supplied by the smaller firms at each price and subtract it (horizontally) from the quantity demanded in the market. The difference at each price lies along the line labeled *d,* which is the dominant firm's demand curve.

At price P_1, for example, the smaller firms' supply curve intersects the market demand curve. At this price, the quantity supplied by the smaller firms meets *all* of the quantity demanded in the market. Thus, at price P_1, the quantity demanded of the product of the dominant firm is zero. At the other extreme, consider what happens at price P_2. At a price this low, the quantity supplied by the smaller firms is zero. If the smaller firms don't supply any output, all of quantity demanded in the market is left for the dominant firm to supply. Thus, the dominant firm's demand curve meets the market demand curve at P_2. At all prices below P_2, the market demand curve (*D*) and the dominant firm's demand curve (*d*) are

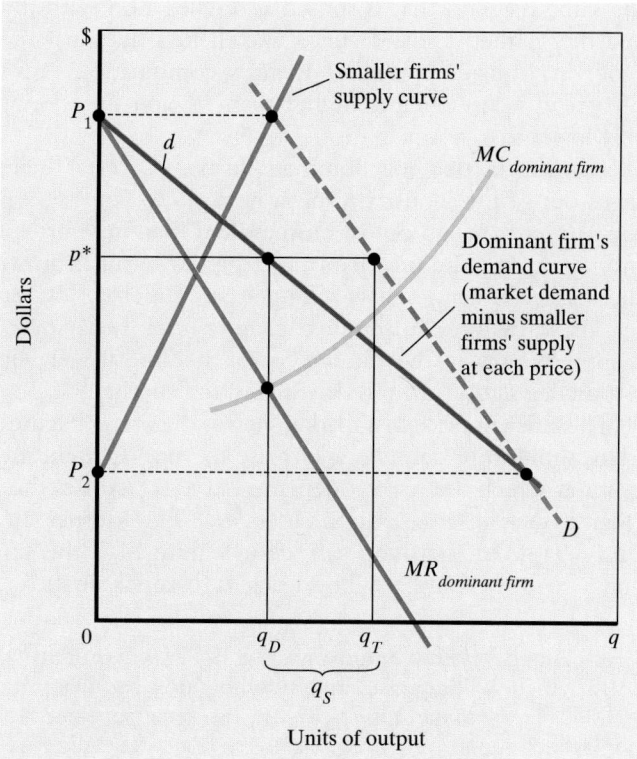

FIGURE 14.5

Price Leadership with a Single Dominant Firm

The demand curve facing the dominant firm is derived by subtracting the amount supplied by the smaller firms from market demand. When smaller firms respond to the price set by a dominant firm, the usual result is a price higher than the price that would be set by perfect competition but lower than the price that would be set by monopoly.

the same because nothing will be produced by the smaller firms when price is below P_2.

The dominant firm maximizes profit as if it were a monopoly facing demand curve d. (At this point you can ignore the market demand curve D and the smaller firms' supply curve.) In order to determine price and output, the dominant firm must first derive its marginal revenue curve from its demand curve. As with any downward-sloping demand curve, the marginal revenue curve lies below its corresponding demand curve (review Chapter 13 if this point is not clear to you). The dominant firm's marginal revenue curve is labeled $MR_{dominant\ firm}$. As you can guess, the dominant firm will maximize profits by producing as long as marginal revenue is greater than marginal cost, or up to the point at which $MR = MC$. The optimal output/price combination for the dominant firm is thus q_D and P^*.

Now look carefully at what would take place if the dominant firm were to set a price equal to P^*. At this price, the total quantity demanded in the market is q_T. The dominant firm supplies q_D units of output, leaving the smaller firms to supply the difference (q_S). Recall that at each price (including P^*) we derived the point on the dominant firm's demand curve (d) by subtracting the amount supplied by the smaller firms from the quantity demanded in the market. Thus, at P^*, we derived q_D by subtracting q_S from q_T.

The final result has the quantity demanded in the market split between the smaller firms and the dominant firm. This result is based entirely on the market power of the dominant firm. The only constraint facing a monopoly firm, you will recall, is the behavior of demanders—that is, the market demand curve. In this case, however, the presence of smaller firms acts to constrain the power of the dominant firm. If we were to assume that the smaller firms were out of the way, the dominant firm would face the market demand curve on its own. If you draw the same diagram that is shown in Figure 14.5 with just the marginal cost curve and the market demand curve, sketch in a marginal revenue curve, and find the profit-maximizing price and quantity combination, you will find that the monopoly price is considerably higher than P^* and the monopoly quantity is considerably lower than q_T.

This means that the dominant firm has a clear incentive to push the smaller firms out of the industry. One way to do so is to set a price below P_2 until all of the smaller firms go out of business and then raise price once the market has been monopolized. The practice of a large, powerful firm driving smaller firms out of the market by temporarily selling at an artificially low price is called *predatory pricing*. As we will see in the next chapter, such behavior, common during the nineteenth century in the United States, became illegal with the passage of antimonopoly legislation around the turn of the century.

The efficient price in a market such as the one in Figure 14.5 would be at $P = MC$. (This should not come as a surprise to you.) Graphically, the efficient price is the point at which the market demand curve, D, crosses the marginal cost curve, MC. (Remember, in competition, $P = MR$. This satisfies the profit-maximizing equation $MR = MC$.) As you can see in Figure 14.5, this point is at a price below P^* and a quantity above q_T. This leads us to conclude that:

> An oligopoly with a dominant price leader will produce a level of output between that which would prevail under competition and that which a monopolist would choose in the same industry. It will also set a price between the monopoly price and the competitive price. These results are generally true in oligopoly models. Some competition is usually more efficient than none at all.

THE KINKED DEMAND CURVE MODEL   Another common model of oligopolistic behavior assumes that firms believe that rivals will follow suit if they *cut* prices but not if they *raise* prices. In other words, the **kinked demand curve model** assumes that the elasticity of demand in response to an increase in price is different from the elasticity of demand in response to a price cut. The result is a "kink" in the demand for a single firm's product.

kinked demand curve model A model of oligopoly in which the demand curve facing each individual firm has a "kink" in it. The kink follows from the assumption that competitive firms will follow suit if a single firm cuts price but will not follow suit if a single firm raises price.

You can see some of these reactions by examining the demand curve in Figure 14.6. If the initial price of Firm B's product is P^*, raising its price above P^* would cause Firm B to face an elastic demand curve if its rivals did not also raise their prices. That is, in response to the price increase, demand for Firm B's product would fall off quickly. The reaction to a price *decrease* would not be as great, however, because rivals would decrease price too. Firm B would lose some of its market share by increasing price, but it would not gain a larger share by decreasing price.

Recall the very important point that a firm's marginal revenue curve reflects the changes in demand occurring along the demand curve *directly above it*. (Review the derivation of the marginal revenue curve in Chapter 13 if this is not fresh in your mind.) This being the case, MR_1 reflects the changes in P and q along demand curve segment d_1. MR_2 reflects changes in P and q along demand curve segment d_2. Since the demand curve is discontinuous at q^*, the marginal revenue curve is also discontinuous, jumping from point A all the way down to point B.

As always, profit-maximizing firms will produce as long as marginal revenue is greater than marginal cost. If, as in Figure 14.6, the marginal cost curve passes through q^* at any point between A and B, the optimal price is P^* and the optimal output is q^*. To the left of q^*, marginal revenue is greater than marginal cost; to maximize profits, then, the firm should increase output. To the right of q^*, mar-

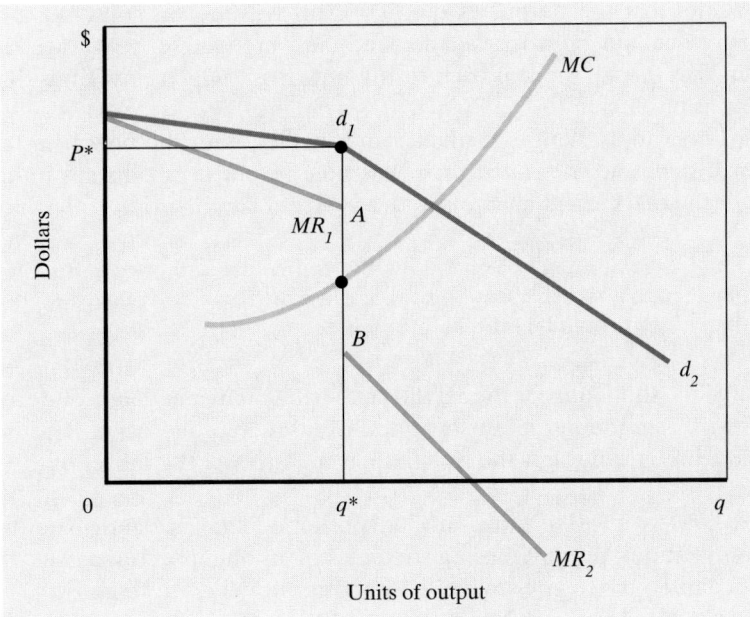

FIGURE 14.6
A Kinked Demand Curve
Oligopoly Model

The kinked demand model assumes that competing firms follow price cuts but not price increases. Thus, if Firm B increases its price, the competition will not, and quantity demanded of Firm B's product will fall off quickly. But if Firm B cuts price, other firms will also cut price and the price cut will not gain as much quantity demanded for Firm B as it would if other firms did not follow. Above d_1 demand is relatively elastic. Below d_1 demand is less elastic.

ginal cost is greater than marginal revenue; in this case the firm should not increase output, because producing above q^* will reduce profits.

Notice that this model predicts that price in oligopolistic industries is likely to be more stable than costs. In Figure 14.6, the marginal cost curve can shift up or down by a substantial amount before it becomes advantageous for the firm to change price at all. A number of attempts have been made to test whether oligopolistic prices are indeed more stable than costs. While the results do not support the hypothesis of stable prices, the evidence is far from conclusive.[4]

The kinked demand curve model has been criticized on a number of grounds. First, it fails to explain why price is at P^* to begin with. Second, the assumption that competing firms will follow price cuts but not price increases is overly simple; real-world oligopolistic pricing strategies are much more complex.

THE COURNOT MODEL   Perhaps the oldest model of oligopoly behavior was put forward by Augustin Cournot almost 150 years ago. The **Cournot model** is based on three assumptions: (1) that there are just two firms in an industry—a situation called a *duopoly;* (2) that each firm takes the output of the other as given; and (3) that both firms maximize profits.

The story begins with a new firm producing nothing and the existing firm producing everything. That is, the existing firm simply takes the market demand curve as its own, acting like a monopolist. When the new firm starts operating, it assumes that the existing firm will continue to produce the same level of output and charge the same price as before. The market demand of the new firm, then, is simply market demand less the amount that the existing firm is currently selling. In essence, the new firm assumes that its demand curve is everything on the market demand curve below the price charged by the older firm.

When the new firm starts operation, the existing firm discovers that its demand has eroded because some output is now sold by the new firm. The old firm now

Cournot model A model of a two-firm industry (duopoly) in which a series of output-adjustment decisions leads to a final level of output that is between that which would prevail if the market were organized competitively and that which would be set by a monopoly.

[4]See, for example, Julian Simon, "A Further Test of the Kinky Oligopoly Demand Curve," *American Economic Review* (December 1969), and George Stigler, "The Kinky Oligopoly Demand Curve and Rigid Prices," *Journal of Political Economy* 55 (1947).

assumes that the output of the new firm will remain constant, subtracts the new firm's demand from market demand, and produces a new, lower level of output. But that throws the ball back to the new firm, which now finds that the competition is producing *less.*

These adjustments get smaller and smaller, with the new firm raising output in small steps and the initial firm lowering output in small steps until the two firms split the market and charge the same price. Like the price leadership model:

> The Cournot model of oligopoly results in a quantity of output somewhere between that which would prevail if the market were organized competitively and that which would be set by a monopoly.

While the Cournot model illustrates the interdependence of decisions in oligopoly, its assumptions about strategic reactions are quite naive. The two firms in the model react only after the fact and never anticipate the moves of the competition.

GAME THEORY   The firms in Cournot's model do not anticipate the moves of the competition. Yet in choosing strategies in an oligopolistic market, real-world firms can and do try to guess what the opposition will do in response.

In 1944, John von Neumann and Oskar Morgenstern published a path-breaking work in which they analyzed a set of problems, or *games,* in which two or more people or organizations pursue their own interests and in which no one of them can dictate the outcome.[5]

Game theory goes something like this: In all conflict situations, and thus all games, there are decision makers (or players), rules of the game, and payoffs (or prizes). Players choose strategies without knowing with certainty what strategy the opposition will use. At the same time, though, some information that indicates how their opposition may be "leaning" may be available to the players.

Figure 14.7 illustrates what is called a "payoff matrix" for a very simple game. Each of two firms, A and B, must decide whether to mount an expensive advertising campaign. If neither firm decides to advertise, each will earn a profit of $50,000. But if one firm advertises and the other does not, the firm that does will increase its profit by 50% (to $75,000), while driving the competition into the loss column. If both firms decide to advertise, they will each earn profits of $10,000. They may generate a bit more demand by advertising, but that demand is completely wiped out by the expense of the advertising itself.

game theory Analyzes oligopolistic behavior as a complex series of strategic moves and reactive countermoves among rival firms. In game theory, firms are assumed to anticipate rival reactions.

---

[5]See J. von Neumann and O. Morgenstern, *Theory of Games and Economic Behavior* (Princeton, NJ.: Princeton University Press, 1944).

FIGURE 14.7
Payoff Matrix for Advertising Game

| | **B'S STRATEGY** | |
	DON'T ADVERTISE	ADVERTISE
DON'T ADVERTISE	A's profit = $50,000 B's profit = $50,000	A's loss = $25,000 B's profit = $75,000
ADVERTISE	A's profit = $75,000 B's loss = $25,000	A's profit = $10,000 B's profit = $10,000

A'S STRATEGY

If Firms A and B could collude (and we assume that they cannot), their optimal strategy would be to agree not to advertise. That solution maximizes the joint profits to both firms. If neither firm advertises, joint profits are $100,000. If both firms advertise, joint profits are only $20,000. If only one of the firms advertises, joint profits are $50,000.

The strategy that Firm A will actually choose depends on (1) the information available concerning B's likely strategy, and (2) A's preferences for risk. In this case, it is possible to predict behavior. Consider A's choice of strategy. Regardless of what B does, it pays A to advertise. If B does not advertise, A makes $25,000 more by advertising than by not advertising. Thus, A will advertise. If B does advertise, A must advertise to avoid a loss. The same logic holds for B. Regardless of the strategy pursued by A, it pays B to advertise. A **dominant strategy** is one that is best no matter what the opposition does. In this game, both players have a dominant strategy, and it is likely that both will advertise.

dominant strategy In game theory, a strategy that is best no matter what the opposition does.

Interestingly, the result may be different if the game is played over and over again. Clearly, the best outcome for both firms is for neither to advertise. Suppose that Firm A decided not to advertise for one period to see how Firm B would respond. If Firm B continued to advertise, A would have to resume advertising to survive. But suppose that B's strategy was to play tit for tat. That is, suppose that B decided to simply match A's strategy. In this case, both firms might—with no explicit collusion—end up not advertising after A figures out what B is doing.

There are many games in which one player does not have a dominant strategy but in which the outcome is predictable. Consider the game in Figure 14.8, in which C does not have a dominant strategy. If D plays the left strategy, C will play the top strategy. If D plays the right strategy, C will play the bottom strategy. But the question remains: What strategy will D choose to play? If C knows the options, she will see that D has a dominant strategy and is likely to play it. D does better playing the right-hand strategy regardless of what C does; he can guarantee himself a $100 win by chosing right and is guaranteed to win nothing by playing left. Since D's behavior is predictable (he will play the right-hand strategy) C will play bottom. When all players are playing their best strategy given what their competitors are doing, the result is called a **Nash equilibrium.**

Nash equilibrium In game theory, the result of all players playing their best strategy given what their competitors are doing.

Now suppose that the game in Figure 14.8 were changed. Suppose that all the payoffs are the same except that if D chooses left and C chooses bottom, C loses $10,000. While D still has a dominant strategy (playing right), C now stands to lose a great deal by choosing bottom on the off chance that D chooses left instead. When uncertainty and risk are introduced, the game changes. C is likely to play top and guarantee herself a $100 profit rather than to risk losing $10,000 to win $200, even if there is just a small chance of D's choosing left. A **maximin strategy**

maximin strategy In game theory, a strategy chosen to maximize the minimum gain that can be earned.

	D'S STRATEGY	
	LEFT	RIGHT
TOP	C wins $100 D wins $0	C wins $100 D wins $100
BOTTOM	C loses $100 D wins $0	C wins $200 D wins $100

C'S STRATEGY

FIGURE 14.8
Payoff Matrix for Left/Right-Top/Bottom Strategies

is one chosen by a player to maximize the minimum gain that it can earn. In essence, one who plays a maximin strategy assumes that the opposition will play the strategy that does the most damage.

When the game theory first appeared in the late 1940s, it seemed that it would in time be able to explain the behavior of oligopolistic firms in great detail. However, when we move from two potential strategies to three or four, and particularly when we move to more than two players, the number of potential outcomes and the properties of the strategy pairings become enormously complex. As a result, it becomes very difficult to predict the strategy, or the combination of strategies, that a firm might choose in any given circumstance.

In the end, game theory leaves us with a greater understanding of the problem of oligopoly but with an incomplete and inconclusive set of propositions about the likely behavior of oligopolistic firms. Some very interesting conclusions emerge about a fairly small number of specific game circumstances, but game theory doesn't provide much help with an industry of five firms, each simultaneously choosing product, pricing, output, and advertising strategies.

About all we are left with is the certainty of interdependence:

> The strategy that an oligopolistic firm chooses is likely to depend on that firm's perceptions of the responses of competing firms.

CONTESTABLE MARKETS Before we discuss the performance of oligopolies, we should note one relatively new theory of behavior that has limited applications but some important implications for understanding imperfectly competitive market behavior.

perfectly contestable market
A market in which entry and exit are costless.

A market is defined as **perfectly contestable** if entry to it *and* exit from it are costless. That is, a market is perfectly contestable if a firm can move into it in search of excess profits but lose nothing if it fails. To be part of a perfectly contestable market, a firm must have capital that is both mobile and easily transferable from one market to another.

Take, for example, a small airline that can move its capital stock from one market to another with little cost. Provincetown Boston Airlines (PBA) flies between Boston, Martha's Vineyard, Nantucket, and Cape Cod during the summer months. During the winter, the same planes are used in Florida, where they fly up and down that state's west coast between Naples, Fort Meyers, Tampa, and other cities. A similar situation may occur when a new industrial complex is built at a fairly remote site and a number of trucking companies offer their services. Because the trucking companies' capital stock is mobile, they can move their trucks somewhere else at no great cost if business is not profitable.

Because entry is cheap, participants in a contestable market are continuously faced with competition or the threat of competition. Even if there are only a few firms competing, the openness of the market forces all these firms to produce efficiently or be driven out of business. This threat of potential competition remains high simply because new firms face little risk in going after a new market. If things don't work out in a crowded market, they don't lose their investment. They can simply transfer their capital to a different place or different use.

> In contestable markets, even large oligopolistic firms end up behaving like perfectly competitive firms. Prices are pushed to long-run average cost by competition, and economic profits do not persist.

To recap: Oligopoly is a market structure that is consistent with a variety of behaviors.

> The only necessary condition of oligopoly is that firms are large enough to have some control over price. Oligopolies are concentrated industries. At one extreme is the cartel, in which a few firms get together and jointly maximize profits—thus, in essence, acting as a monopolist. At the other extreme, the firms within the oligopoly vigorously compete for small contestable markets by moving capital quickly in response to observed economic profits. In between the two are a number of alternative models, all of which stress the interdependence of oligopolistic firms.

Oligopoly and Economic Performance

How well do oligopolies perform? Should they be regulated or changed? Are they efficient, or do they lead to an inefficient use of resources? On balance, are they good or bad?

With the exception of the contestable-markets model, all the models of oligopoly we have examined lead us to conclude that concentration in a market leads to pricing above marginal cost and output below the efficient level. When price is above marginal cost at equilibrium, consumers are paying more for the good than it costs to produce that good in terms of products forgone in other industries. To increase output would be to create value that exceeds the social cost of the good, but profit-maximizing oligopolists have an incentive not to increase output.

Entry barriers in many oligopolistic industries also prevent new capital and other resources from responding to profit signals. Under competitive conditions or in contestable markets, excess profits would attract new firms and thus increase production. But this does not happen in most oligopolistic industries; the problem is most severe when entry barriers exist and firms explicitly or tacitly collude. The results of collusion are essentially identical to the results of a monopoly. Firms jointly maximize profits by fixing prices at a high level and splitting up the profits among themselves.

Product differentiation under oligopoly presents us with the same dilemma that we encountered in monopolistic competition. On the one hand, vigorous product competition among oligopolistic competitors produces variety and leads to innovation in response to the wide variety of consumer tastes and preferences. It can thus be argued that vigorous product competition is efficient. On the other hand, product differentiation may lead to waste and inefficiency. Product differentiation accomplished through advertising may have nothing to do with product quality, and advertising itself may have little or no information content. If it serves as an entry barrier that blocks competition, product differentiation can cause the market allocation mechanism to fail.

To sum up:

> Oligopolistic, or concentrated, industries are likely to be inefficient for several reasons. First, profit-maximizing oligopolists are likely to price above marginal cost. When price is above marginal cost, there is underproduction from society's point of view—in other words, society could get more for less, but it doesn't. Second, strategic behavior can lead to outcomes that are not in society's best interest. Specifically, strategically competitive firms can force themselves into deadlocks that waste resources. Finally, to the extent that oligopolies differentiate their products and advertise, there is the promise of new and exciting products. At the same time, however, there remains a real danger of waste and inefficiency.

Industrial Concentration and Technological Change

One of the major sources of economic growth and progress throughout history has been technological advance. Innovation, both in methods of production and in the creation of new and better products, is one of the engines of economic progress. As we have seen, much innovation starts with research and development efforts undertaken by firms in search of profit.

Several economists, most notably Joseph Schumpeter and John Kenneth Galbraith, argued in works now considered classics that industrial concentration actually increases the rate of technological advance. As Schumpeter put it in 1942:

> As soon as we . . . inquire into the individual items in which progress was most conspicuous, the trail leads not to the doors of those firms that work under conditions of comparatively free competition but precisely to the doors of the large concerns . . . and a shocking suspicion dawns upon us that big business may have had more to do with creating that standard of life than keeping it down.[6]

The Schumpeterian hypothesis caused the economics profession to pause and take stock of its theories. The conventional wisdom had always been that concentration and barriers to entry insulate firms from competition and lead to sluggish performance and slow growth.

The evidence regarding where innovation comes from is mixed. Certainly, most small businesses do not engage in research and development, and most large firms do. When R&D expenditures are considered as a percentage of sales, firms in industries with high concentration ratios spend more on research and development than firms in industries with low concentration ratios.

Oligopolistic companies such as AT&T have done a great deal of research. AT&T's Bell Laboratories has probably done more important primary research over the last several decades than any other organization in the country. It has been estimated that Bell Labs conducted 10% of *all* the basic industrial research in the United States during the 1970s. IBM, which despite its recent problems set the industry standard in personal computers, has certainly introduced as much new technology to the computer industry as any other firm.

On the other hand, the "high-tech revolution" grew out of many tiny start-up operations. Companies such as Apple Computers, LOTUS Development Corporation, INTEL, and many others barely existed only a generation ago. The new biotechnology firms that are just beginning to work miracles with genetic engineering are still tiny operations that started with research done by individual scientists in university laboratories.

As with the debate about product differentiation and advertising, significant ambiguity on this subject remains. Indeed, there may be no right answer. Technological change seems to come in fits and starts, sometimes from small firms and sometimes from large ones.

A ROLE FOR GOVERNMENT?

Certainly there is much to guard against in the behavior of large, concentrated industries. Barriers to entry, large size, and product differentiation all lead to market power and to potential inefficiency. Barriers to entry and collusive behavior stop the market from working toward an efficient allocation of resources.

---

[6]J. A. Schumpeter, *Capitalism, Socialism and Democracy* (New York: Harper, 1942), and J. K. Galbraith, *American Capitalism* (Boston: Houghton Mifflin, 1952).

For several reasons, however, economists no longer attack industry concentration with quite the same fervor that they once did. First, the theory of contestable markets shows that even firms in highly concentrated industries can be pushed to produce efficiently under certain market circumstances. Second, the benefits of product differentiation and product competition are real, at least in part. After all, a constant stream of new products and new variations of old products does come to the market almost daily. Third, the effects of concentration on the rate of research and development spending are, at worst, mixed. It is certainly true that large firms do a substantial amount of the total research in the United States. Finally, in some industries, substantial economies of scale simply preclude a completely competitive structure.

In addition to the debate over the desirability of industrial concentration, there is a never-ending debate regarding the historical role of government in regulating markets and what the proper role of government should be. One view is that high levels of concentration lead to inefficiency and that government should act in an effort to improve the allocation of resources—to help the market work more efficiently. This logic has been used to justify the laws and other regulations aimed at moderating noncompetitive behavior.

An opposing view holds that the clearest examples of effective barriers to entry are those actually created by government. This view holds that government regulation in past years has been ultimately anticompetitive and has made the allocation of resources less efficient than it would have been with no government involvement. Recall from our discussion in Chapter 13 that those who earn economic profits have an incentive to spend resources to protect themselves and their profits from competitors. This *rent-seeking* behavior may include using the power of government.

In the next chapters, we look carefully at the role of government and the potential role of government in correcting the market failure brought about by imperfectly competitive markets. We then turn to a discussion of the government's role in providing social goods and correcting externalities (Chapter 16) and an examination of the government's role in income redistribution (Chapter 17).

SUMMARY

Monopolistic Competition

1. A monopolistically competitive industry has the following structural characteristics: (1) a large number of firms, (2) no barriers to entry, and (3) *product differentiation*. Relatively good substitutes for a monopolistic competitor's products are available. Thus, monopolistic competitors try to achieve a degree of market power by differentiating their products.

2. Advocates of free and open competition believe that differentiated products and advertising give the market system its vitality and are the basis of its power. Critics argue that product differentiation and advertising are wasteful and inefficient.

3. By differentiating their products, firms hope to be able to raise price without losing all demand. The demand curve facing a monopolistic competitor is less elastic than the demand curve faced by a perfectly competitive firm but more elastic than the demand curve faced by a monopoly.

4. To maximize profit in the short run, a monopolistically competitive firm will produce as long as the marginal revenue from increasing output and selling it exceeds the marginal cost of producing it. This occurs at the point at which $MR = MC$.

5. When firms enter a monopolistically competitive industry, they introduce close substitutes for the goods being produced. This attracts demand away from the firms already in the industry. Demand faced by each firm shifts left, and profits are ultimately eliminated in the long run. This long-run equilibrium occurs at the point where the demand curve is just tangent to the average total cost curve.

6. Monopolistically competitive firms end up pricing above marginal cost. This is inefficient, as is the fact that monopolistically competitive firms will not realize all economies of scale available.

Oligopoly

7. An *oligopoly* is an industry dominated by a few firms that, by virtue of their individual sizes, are large enough to influence market price. The behavior of a single oligopolistic firm depends on the reactions it expects of all the other firms in the industry. Industrial strategies can be, and usually are, very complicated and difficult to generalize about.

8. When firms collude, either explicitly or tacitly, they jointly maximize profits by charging an agreed-upon price or by setting output limits and splitting profits. The result is exactly the same as it would be if one firm monopolized the industry: The firm will produce up to the point at which $MR = MC$, and price will be set above marginal cost.

9. The *price-leadership* model leads to a similar but not identical result as the collusion model. In this organization, the dominant firm in the industry sets a price and allows competing firms to supply all they want at that price. An oligopoly with a dominant price leader will produce a level of output between that which would prevail under competition and that which a monopolist would choose in the same industry. It will also set a price between the monopoly price and the competitive price. (These results are generally true of oligopoly models.)

10. A firm faces a kinked demand curve if competitors follow price cuts but fail to respond to price increases. The *kinked demand curve model* predicts that in oligopolistic industries price is likely to be more stable than costs.

11. The *Cournot model* is based on three assumptions: (1) that there are just two firms in an industry—a situation called duopoly; (2) that each firm takes the output of the other as a given; and (3) that both firms maximize profits. The model holds that a series of output-adjustment decisions in the duopoly leads to a final level of output between that which would prevail under perfect competition and that which would be set by a monopoly.

12. *Game theory* analyzes the behavior of firms as if their behavior were a series of strategic moves and countermoves. It helps us understand the problem of oligopoly but leaves us with an incomplete and inconclusive set of propositions about the likely behavior of individual oligopolistic firms.

13. A market is *perfectly contestable* if entry to it and exit from it are costless—that is, if a firm can move into a market in search of excess profits but lose nothing if it fails. Firms in such industries must have mobile capital. In contestable markets, even large oligopolistic firms end up behaving like perfect competitors: Prices are pushed to long-run average costs by competition, and economic profits do not persist.

14. The behavior of oligopolistic firms is likely to lead to an inefficient allocation of resources.

REVIEW TERMS AND CONCEPTS

cartel   358
Cournot model   363
dominant strategy   365
game theory   364
kinked demand curve model   362

maximin strategy   365
monopolistic competition   347
Nash equilibrium   365
oligopoly   356

perfectly contestable market   366
price leadership   360
product differentiation   349
tacit collusion   360

PROBLEM SET

1. For each of the following state whether you agree or disagree. Explain your answer carefully.

a. Successful product differentiation has the effect of increasing the elasticity of demand facing a monopolistically competitive firm.

b. Long-run equilibrium in a monopolistically competitive industry is virtually identical to long-run equilibrium in monopoly.

c. In monopolistically competitive industries, firms are able to exert market power (control prices) by virtue of their size relative to the market.

2. Suppose that a new specialty ice cream store opens in your town. Soon people are lining up outside the place every day for hours. The store sells ice cream cones, which cost $0.50 to produce, for $2.00. Describe the likely response of the market over time. Be specific. What type of industry are we dealing with?

3. Which of the following markets are likely to be perfectly contestable? Explain your answers.

a. Shipbuilding
b. Trucking
c. Housecleaning services
d. Wine production

4. The matrix in Figure 1 shows payoffs based on the strategies chosen by two firms. If they collude and hold prices at $10, each will earn profits of $5 million. If A cheats on the agreement, lowering its price, but B does not, A will get 75% of the business and earn profits of $8 million and B

FIGURE 1

	B'S STRATEGY	
	STAND BY AGREEMENT	CHEAT
STAND BY AGREEMENT	A's profit = $5 million B's profit = $5 Million	A's profit = –$2 million B's profit = $8 million
CHEAT	A's profit = $8 million B's profit = –$2 million	A's profit = $2 million B's profit = $2 million

A'S STRATEGY (label at left of rows)

will lose $2 million. Similarly, if B cheats and A does not, B will earn $8 million and A will lose $2 million. If both cut prices, they will end up with $2 million each in profits.

Which strategy minimizes the maximum potential loss for A? For B? If you were A, which strategy would you choose? Why? If A cheats, what will B do? If B cheats, what will A do? What is the most likely outcome of such a game? Explain.

5. Assume that you are in the business of building houses. You have analyzed the market carefully, and you know that at a price of $120,000 you will sell 800 houses per year. In addition, you know that at any price above $120,000 no one will buy your houses because the government provides equal quality houses to anyone who wants one at $120,000. You also know that when you lower your price by $20,000, the quantity that you can sell increases by 200 units. For example at a price of $100,000, you can sell 1,000 houses, at a price of $80,000 you can sell 1,200 houses, and so forth.

a. Sketch the demand curve facing your firm.

b. Sketch the effective marginal revenue curve facing your firm.

c. If the marginal cost of building a house is $100,000, how many will you build, and what price will you charge? What if *MC* = $85,000?

6. Examine the short-run graph in Figure 2 for a monopolistically competitive firm.

a. What is the profit-maximizing level of output?

b. What price will be charged in the short run?

c. How much is short-run total revenue? Total cost? Total profit?

d. Describe what will happen to this firm in the long run.

7. Write a position paper on industrial concentration for a new President. Is this a problem in the United States? What are some of the possible advantages and disadvantages of government actions against concentrated industries?

8. The payoff matrixes in Figure 3 show the payoffs for two games. The payoffs are given in parentheses. The figure on the left refers to the payoff to A, the figure on the right to the payoff to B.

a. Is there a dominant strategy in each game for each player?

b. If Game 1 were repeated a large number of times, and you were A and you could change your strategy, what might you do?

c. Which strategy would you play in Game 2? Why?

FIGURE 2

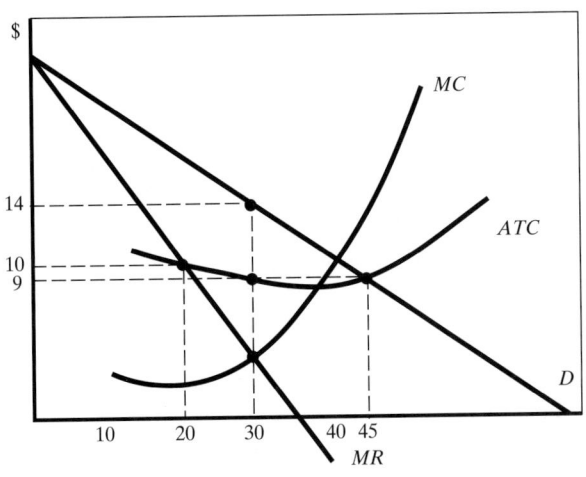

FIGURE 3

GAME 1: PRICING

		FIRM B	
		PRICE HIGH	PRICE LOW
FIRM A	PRICE HIGH	(15, 15)	(2, 25)
	PRICE LOW	(25, 2)	(5, 5)

GAME 2: CHICKEN

		BOB (B)	
		SWERVE	DON'T SWERVE
ANN (A)	SWERVE	(5, 5)	(3, 10)
	DON'T SWERVE	(10, 3)	(-10, -10)

15 Antitrust and Regulation

If all the assumptions of perfect competition hold, the allocation of resources in an economy is efficient—the system produces the goods and services that people want, and it does so at least cost. No reshuffling of resources or output can improve the welfare of some without reducing the welfare of others. This was the message of Chapter 12.

As we began to relax some of the assumptions of perfect competition, we found several naturally occurring sources of market failure. Chapters 13 and 14 examined the first of these, *imperfect markets.* Firms that are able to achieve some degree of control over the price of their products are likely to end up charging more than the socially optimal price and producing less than the socially optimal output. Thus far we have looked carefully at three different imperfect market structures that tend to be inefficient: *monopoly, monopolistic competition,* and *oligopoly.*

When unregulated markets fail to produce efficiently, governments can and do act to improve the allocation of resources. However, some government actions can lead to a *less* efficient allocation of resources. This chapter discusses in some detail the history and theory of government involvement in imperfectly competitive markets.

The Development of Antitrust Law

Historically, in market economies, governments have assumed two basic and seemingly contradictory roles with respect to imperfectly competitive industries: (1) They *promote* competition and restrict market power primarily through antitrust laws and other congressional acts, and (2) they *restrict* competition by regulating industries.

Historical Background

The period immediately following the Civil War was one of rapid growth and change in the United States. As migrants headed to the open spaces, population swelled in the West as well as in the East. Railroads were built between all major cities, and in May of 1869 a golden spike driven at Promontory Point, Utah, completed the transcontinental railroad line linking the East with California. Between 1864 and 1874, what was already a substantial rail network doubled in size. At the same time, factories sprang up to accommodate new methods of production. Between 1870 and 1913, the economy grew at a faster rate than at any other time in U.S. history.

Before the Civil War, most firms had been small and their markets local. The high cost of transportation limited access to large market areas, and production technologies were efficient only on a small scale. But the railroads opened up the nation, and firms began to compete for national markets. Many of the new technologies exhibited economies of scale; real advantages to size in some industries soon became apparent.

Communications technology also changed dramatically during the same period. In 1877 an inventor offered to sell Western Union, for $100,000, a patent on a new method of sending information over wires. Alexander Graham Bell's asking price was just too high for Western Union, and it turned down the offer. Within ten years, telephone lines operated by Bell companies crisscrossed the country, linking city after city.[1]

As all of these forces drew the United States together, the character of the economy changed. Small firms selling to local markets were replaced by large firms selling to regional and national markets. With size came power, and with power came hunger for more power. Competition was fierce and often brutal.

The successful exercise of power meant driving competition out of business and controlling markets, and for many firms these became explicit goals. Thousands of smaller firms were gobbled up by big ones. Cartels fixed prices and controlled output. Price cutting to drive competitors out of business was common. In this climate, the **trust** flourished. Under these arrangements, shareholders of independent firms agreed to give up control of their stock in exchange for trust certificates that entitled them to a share of the common profits. A group of trustees then operated the combined firm as a monopoly, controlling output and setting price.

It wasn't long before people saw that something was wrong with the system that had emerged. Small independent farmers facing large powerful railroads, monopsonistic buyers, and declining agricultural prices began to organize. Formed in 1867, the National Grange became a strong pressure group on behalf

trust An arrangement in which shareholders of independent firms agree to give up control of their stock in exchange for trust certificates that entitle them to a share of the common profits. A group of trustees then operates the combined firm as a monopoly, controlling output and setting price.

---

[1]See Gerald Brock, *The Telecommunications Industry* (Cambridge, Mass.: Harvard University Press, 1980).

The early days of antitrust enforcement, 1881. The cartoon shows Uncle Sam breaking the Gould-Vanderbilt Telegraph monopoly. Note the bags of money under the desk.

of farmers against the power of big business. At the same time, life for the laboring classes in the cities and in factory towns was grim. Child labor, long hours, meager wages, and crowded housing in slums were reminiscent of conditions in England during the Industrial Revolution, which had begun a century earlier.

"Big business" was held responsible, and its image was probably best captured in cartoons of grotesquely fat men with big cigars and diamond stickpins crushing workers and farmers underfoot. Perhaps the best known and most vilified of these "robber barons" was Jay Gould, who made a fortune manipulating railroad stocks and trying to monopolize the railroad business. In 1881 Gould controlled more miles of railroad track than any other individual or group. While recent research shows that Gould may not have been as evil as most history books portray him, there is no question that he wielded enormous power.

Landmark Antitrust Legislation

Even though public sentiment increasingly favored reform, faith in the market and in private enterprise also remained strong. In response to public pressure, Congress began to formulate antitrust legislation. In 1887, it created the **Interstate Commerce Commission (ICC)** to oversee and correct abuses in the railroad industry; in 1890, it passed the **Sherman Act,** which declared monopoly and trade restraints illegal. To control monopoly power in general, the Sherman Act turned not to regulation and public enterprise, but rather to competition and the market.

Interstate Commerce Commission (ICC) A federal regulatory group created by Congress in 1887 to oversee and correct abuses in the railroad industry.

Sherman Act Passed by Congress in 1890, the act declared every contract or conspiracy to restrain trade among states or nations illegal and declared any attempt at monopoly, successful or not, a misdemeanor. Interpretation of which specific behaviors were illegal fell to the courts.

THE SHERMAN ACT OF 1890   The real substance of the Sherman Act is contained in two short sections:

> *Section 1.* Every contract, combination in the form of trust or otherwise, or conspiracy, in restraint of trade or commerce among the several States, or with foreign nations, is hereby declared to be illegal. . . .
>
> *Section 2.* Every person who shall monopolize, or attempt to monopolize, or combine or conspire with any other person or persons, to monopolize any part of the trade or commerce among the several States, or with foreign nations, shall be deemed guilty of a misdemeanor, and, on conviction thereof, shall be punished by fine not exceeding five thousand dollars, or by imprisonment not exceeding one year, or by both said punishments, in the discretion of the court.

The biggest problem with the Sherman Act lay in its interpretation. The language of the statute seemed to declare monopolistic structure, as well as certain kinds of monopolistic conduct or behavior, to be illegal, but it was unclear what specific acts were to be considered "restraints of trade." Competition itself can act as a restraint, for example.

When a statute is unclear, it usually falls to the courts to provide clarification. Unfortunately, the courts only added to the confusion in the early years of antitrust legislation and enforcement. In 1911 two major antitrust cases were brought before the Supreme Court. The two companies involved, Standard Oil and American Tobacco, seemed to epitomize the textbook definition of monopoly, and both appeared to exhibit the structure and the conduct outlawed by the Sherman Act. Standard Oil controlled about 91% of the refining industry, and although the exact figure is still disputed, the American Tobacco Trust probably controlled between 75% and 90% of the market for all tobacco products except cigars. Both companies had used tough tactics to swallow up competition or to drive it out of business. Not surprisingly, the Supreme Court found both firms guilty of violating Sections 1 and 2 of the Sherman Act and ordered their dissolution.[2]

The court's opinion made it clear, however, that the Sherman Act did not outlaw every action that seemed to restrain trade, but only those that were "unreasonable." In enunciating this **rule of reason,** the court seemed to say that structure alone was not a criterion for unreasonableness. Thus it was possible for a near-monopoly not to violate the Sherman Act as long as it had won its market using "reasonable" tactics.

rule of reason The criterion introduced by the Supreme Court in 1911 to determine whether a particular action was illegal ("unreasonable") or legal ("reasonable") within the terms of the Sherman Act.

Subsequent court cases confirmed that a firm could be convicted of violating the Sherman Act only if it had exhibited *unreasonable conduct*. Between 1911 and 1920, cases were brought against Eastman Kodak, International Harvester, United Shoe Machinery, and United States Steel, the first three of which controlled overwhelming shares of their respective markets and the fourth of which controlled 60% of the country's capacity to produce steel. But all four cases were dismissed on the grounds that no evidence of "unreasonable conduct" on the part of these companies had been shown.

The enunciation of the rule of reason did little to clarify the language of the Sherman Act, and just what explicit acts the courts would deem "unreasonable" remained a mystery. The original supporters of the act were upset by the lack of enforcement; business simply wanted to know the rules of the game. In response, Congress went back to the drawing board in 1914 and passed the Clayton Act and the Federal Trade Commission Act.

---

[2]*U.S. v. Standard Oil Co. of New Jersey,* 221 U.S. 1 (1911); *U.S. v. American Tobacco Co.,* 221 U.S. 106 (1991).

THE CLAYTON ACT AND THE FEDERAL TRADE COMMISSION, 1914 Designed both to strengthen the Sherman Act and to clarify the "rule of reason," the **Clayton Act** of 1914 outlawed a number of very specific practices. First, it made *tying contracts* illegal. Such contracts force a customer to buy one product in order to obtain another. Second, it limited mergers that would "substantially lessen competition or tend to create a monopoly." Third, it banned *price discrimination*—that is, charging different customers different prices for reasons other than changes in cost or the matching of competitors' prices.

The **Federal Trade Commission (FTC),** created by Congress in 1914, was established to investigate "the organization, business conduct, practices, and management" of companies that engage in interstate commerce. At the same time, the act establishing the Commission added another vaguely worded prohibition to the books: "Unfair methods of competition in commerce are hereby declared unlawful." The determination of what constituted "unfair" behavior was left up to the Commission. The FTC was also given the power to issue "cease-and-desist orders" where it found behavior in violation of the law.

Nonetheless, the legislation of 1914 retained the focus on *conduct,* and thus the "rule of reason" remained central to all antitrust action in the courts.

THE ALCOA CASE, 1945 The history of antitrust law has been an ongoing struggle between the rule of reason and various actions and outcomes that the courts have declared *per se* (intrinsic) violations of antitrust law. For example, a **per se rule** against price fixing evolved over a number of years until 1926, when the Supreme Court held unequivocally that price fixing violates Section 1 of the Sherman Act whether the resulting price is reasonable or not.

Prior to 1945, most antitrust law enforcement continued to focus on *conduct.* In most cases, the rule of reason determined whether the conduct was or was not illegal. Even though United States Steel grew large enough to dominate the market for iron and steel, for example, it did not coerce its remaining rivals or conspire to fix prices, and thus it did not engage in unreasonable conduct. As the court said, "The law does not make *mere size* [italics added] an offense or the existence of unexerted power an offense." In short, the courts decreed, it was not illegal to be a benevolent monopoly.

This was the basic position of the courts until 1945, when the "rule of reason" was challenged in a different way in the landmark Alcoa case.[3] In that case, the United States charged the Aluminum Company of America (Alcoa) with violating Section 2 of the Sherman Act by monopolizing the market for newly refined aluminum. At the time, Alcoa controlled approximately 90% of the raw aluminum market.

The court did not hold that any specific behavior, or conduct, by which Alcoa achieved its monopoly position was in itself illegal. It said, in fact, that Alcoa had used "normal, prudent, but not predatory business practices. . . . These included building capacity well ahead of demand." Rather, it was the *structure* of the market itself that led Judge Learned Hand to order the dissolution of Alcoa:

> No monopolist monopolizes unconscious of what he is doing. So here "Alcoa" meant to keep, and did keep, that complete and exclusive hold upon the ingot market with which it started. That was to "monopolize" that market, however innocently it otherwise proceeded.

---

[3]*U.S. v. Aluminum Co. of America,* 148 F. 2nd 416 (1945).

Clayton Act Passed by Congress in 1914 to strengthen the Sherman Act and clarify the "rule of reason," the act outlawed specific monopolistic behaviors such as tying contracts, price discrimination, and unlimited mergers.

Federal Trade Commission (FTC) A federal regulatory group created by Congress in 1914 to investigate the structure and behavior of firms engaging in interstate commerce, to determine what constitutes unlawful "unfair" behavior, and to issue cease-and-desist orders to those found in violation of antitrust law.

per se rule A rule enunciated by the courts declaring a particular action or outcome to be a *per se* (intrinsic) violation of antitrust law, whether the result is reasonable or not.

One other case is worth a brief note here, because it extended the Sherman Act as it was interpreted in the Alcoa case to cover an oligopoly that was acting like a monopoly. In 1946 the United States brought suit against the three largest domestic cigarette producers. The court found no specific evidence of collusion, but did find that the firms had acted *as if* they were taking account of each other's behavior in setting prices. The case, in essence, extended the law to include *tacit collusion* as well as explicit conspiracy.[4]

OTHER IMPORTANT LEGISLATION   Several other pieces of legislation designed to deal with specific problem areas followed the Clayton Act. In 1921 the **Willis-Graham Act** formally exempted telephone mergers from antitrust review. The telephone industry was one of the very few industries that the government essentially declared a natural monopoly and decided to regulate rather than dissolve. Later in this chapter we discuss the telecommunications industry in some detail.

The **Wheeler-Lea Act** of 1938 extended the language of the Federal Trade Commission Act to include "deceptive" as well as "unfair" methods of competition. The act thus gave the FTC the power to deal with false and deceptive advertising and the sale of harmful products.

The **Celler-Kefauver Act** of 1950 extended the government's authority to ban mergers. The original legislation could block only *horizontal mergers* (mergers in which firms producing the same product join together). The Celler-Kefauver Act extended the government's power to block *vertical mergers* (mergers in which firms at various stages in a production process combine—movie-making companies, movie-distribution companies, and theater chains, for example) and *conglomerate mergers* (mergers in which firms producing unrelated products combine). In all cases, however, the fact that the merger would substantially lessen competition had to be established.

The Celler-Kefauver Act also closed an important loophole in the Clayton Act. Earlier legislation had prevented one firm from acquiring the stock of another company if such a purchase would lessen competition, but firms got around the legislation by buying the physical assets (plant and equipment) of a competing firm. This strategy was explicitly banned in 1950 under Celler-Kefauver.

The most recent significant piece of antitrust legislation is the **Hart-Scott-Rodino Antitrust Procedural Improvements Act** of 1980. Many large firms, such as law firms and accounting firms, are not corporations and prior to 1980 were not subject to the antitrust laws. The Hart-Scott-Rodino Act extended the antitrust laws to proprietorships and partnerships. In addition, the act requires that all proposed mergers between firms be reported to the Justice Department.

Willis-Graham Act (1921)
Declared the telephone industry a natural monopoly and exempted telephone mergers from review.

Wheeler-Lea Act (1938) Extended the language of the Federal Trade Commission Act to include "deceptive" as well as "unfair" methods of competition.

Celler-Kefauver Act (1950) Extended the government's authority to ban mergers and prevented firms from acquiring the physical stock of competitors.

Hart-Scott-Rodino Act The 1980 antitrust legislation that extended the antitrust laws to proprietorships and partnerships and requires that all proposed mergers be reported to the Department of Justice.

The Herfindahl-Hirschman Index

The Clayton Act of 1914 had given government the authority to limit mergers that might "substantially lessen competition in an industry." The Celler-Kefauver Act of 1950 enabled the Justice Department to monitor and enforce these provisions effectively.

In 1968 the Justice Department issued its first guidelines designed to reduce uncertainty about the mergers that it would find acceptable. The 1968 guidelines

---

[4]See William H. Nicholls, "The Tobacco Case of 1946," *American Economic Review* (May 1949), p. 296. Also *American Tobacco Co. et al.* v. *U.S.,* 328 U.S. 781 (1946). In the American Tobacco case, fines totaling $255,000 were levied against the tobacco companies and their executives, but no structural remedies were applied. There is little evidence that the behavior of these companies changed after the fines were paid.

were very strict. For example, if the largest four firms in an industry controlled 75% or more of a market, an acquiring firm with a 15% market share would be challenged if it wanted to acquire a firm that controlled as little as an additional 1% of the market.

In 1982 the Antitrust Division, in keeping with President Reagan's laissez-faire policy toward big business, issued a new set of far more lenient guidelines. Revised in 1984, they remain in place today. The 1982/1984 standards are based on a measure of market structure called the **Herfindahl–Hirschman Index (HHI).** The HHI is calculated by expressing the market share of each firm in the industry as a percentage, squaring these figures, and adding. For example, in an industry in which two firms each control 50% of the market, the index is

$$50^2 + 50^2 = 2500 + 2500 = 5000.$$

For an industry in which four firms each control 25% of the market, the index is

$$25^2 + 25^2 + 25^2 + 25^2 = 625 + 625 + 625 + 625 = 2500.$$

Table 15.1 shows HHI calculations for several hypothetical industries. The Justice Department's courses of action, summarized in Figure 15.1, are as follows:

> If the Herfindahl-Hirschman Index is less than 1000, the industry is considered unconcentrated, and any proposed merger will go unchallenged by the Justice Department. If the index is between 1000 and 1800, the department will challenge any merger that would increase the index by over 100 points. Herfindahl indexes above 1800 mean that the industry is considered concentrated already, and the Justice Department will challenge any merger that pushes the index up more than 50 points.

In 1982 two breweries, Pabst and Heileman, proposed a merger. At the time, the Herfindahl index in the beer industry was about 1772. Before the merger, each firm had about 7.5% of the market. Thus, after a merger, the new firm would have a combined share of 15 percent. The merger would thus raise the index by 112.5:

$$\underbrace{(15^2)}_{\text{Post-merger}} - \underbrace{(7.5^2 + 7.5^2)}_{\text{Pre-merger}} = 225 - 112.5 = 112.5$$

Because the merger increased the index by more than 100 points, it was challenged by the Justice Department.

In 1984 the same two companies reapplied to the Justice Department for permission to merge. This time Pabst agreed to sell four of its brands—which accounted for over one third of its total production—and one brewery to a

Herfindahl-Hirschman Index (HHI) A mathematical calculation that uses market share figures to determine whether or not a proposed merger will be challenged by the government.

TABLE 15.1
Calculation of a Simple Herfindahl-Hirschman Index for Four Hypothetical Industries, Each with No More than Four Firms

	PERCENTAGE SHARES OF:				HERFINDAHL-HIRSCHMAN INDEX
	FIRM 1	FIRM 2	FIRM 3	FIRM 4	
Industry A	50	50	—	—	$50^2 + 50^2 = 5000$
Industry B	80	10	10	—	$80^2 + 10^2 + 10^2 = 6600$
Industry C	25	25	25	25	$25^2 + 25^2 + 25^2 + 25^2 = 2500$
Industry D	40	20	20	20	$40^2 + 20^2 + 20^2 + 20^2 = 2800$

third party. The sale was sufficient to bring the merger within the guidelines, and the Antitrust Division dropped its objections. Ultimately, however, the merger never took place. Heileman was bought by an Australian company and in 1991 went bankrupt.

ENFORCEMENT OF ANTITRUST LAW

Now that we have briefly sketched the history of the antitrust laws, we turn to a discussion of the equally important area of antitrust enforcement.

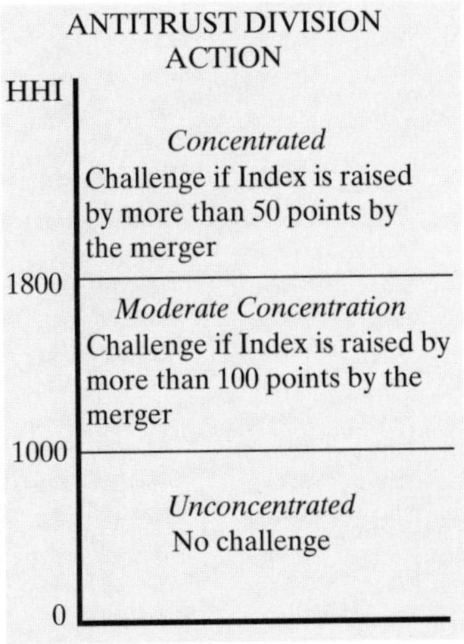

Initiating Antitrust Actions

Two different administrative bodies have the responsibility for initiating actions on behalf of the U.S. government against individuals or companies thought to be in violation of the antitrust laws. These agencies are the Antitrust Division of the Justice Department and the Federal Trade Commission.

GOVERNMENT ACTIONS: THE ANTITRUST DIVISION AND THE FTC   The 1914 legislation that established the FTC, and the Wheeler-Lea Act that followed, gave the FTC broad powers to forbid "unfair and deceptive" conduct. The FTC is comprised of five members appointed by the President and confirmed by the Senate for terms of seven years. A large staff of lawyers and economists investigates and prosecutes offenders. The FTC can issue cease-and-desist orders to offenders, but such orders carry no criminal or civil penalties for past damages or monetary fines. In essence, the FTC exists to prevent *further* unlawful action, and in practice most FTC proceedings end in formal agreements rather than in cease-and-desist orders.

The FTC has also established a set of trade regulation rules that make clear what practices it deems unfair and subject to action. One such "rule," for example, states that a service station that fails to display octane ratings clearly on gas pumps is guilty of an "unfair or deceptive act or practice." These rules simplify the process of adjudication by making the standards of conduct clear.

Along with the **Antitrust Division of the Department of Justice,** the FTC initiates actions against those who violate antitrust law. The power to impose penalties and remedies formally rests with the courts, but the Antitrust Division decides which cases to prosecute. All cases involving criminal complaints against individuals or companies originate in the Antitrust Division, but it is fairly small. Its resources are limited, and the vigor with which it pursues antitrust violators changes with the views of the President and the Attorney General.

PRIVATE ACTIONS   Antitrust cases may also be brought to the courts by private citizens. Since 1914, private persons have been empowered to bring suits as long as they can clearly demonstrate a significant injury or threat of injury. Much like the old "rule of reason," however, the law is vague about what constitutes a "significant injury or threat." The original suit against AT&T that ended in the divestiture in 1982 was brought by a private company, MCI. In 1987, major league baseball players who were free agents found that team owners seemed reluctant to bid against each other for the top players. Several actually brought private action against what they saw as a "conspiracy in restraint of trade" among

ANTITRUST DIVISION ACTION

HHI

Concentrated
Challenge if Index is raised by more than 50 points by the merger

1800

Moderate Concentration
Challenge if Index is raised by more than 100 points by the merger

1000

Unconcentrated
No challenge

0

FIGURE 15.1
Department of Justice Merger Guidelines (revised 1984)
Note: See Phillip Areeds, *Antitrust Analysis,* 3rd. ed. 1986 supplement (Boston: Little Brown, 1986), p.185.

Antitrust Division (of the Department of Justice) One of two federal agencies empowered to act against those in violation of antitrust laws. It initiates action against those who violate antitrust laws and decides which cases to prosecute and against whom to bring criminal charges.

the owners, and the courts ruled in the players' favor. A number of players were given a second chance at free agent bargaining status, and team owners were warned and reprimanded.

Sanctions and Remedies

The courts are empowered to impose a number of remedies if they find that antitrust law has been violated. Certain civil and criminal penalties can be exacted for past wrongs, and other measures can prevent future wrongs. Specifically, the courts can "(1) forbid the continuation of illegal acts, (2) force the defendant to dispose of the fruits of his or her wrong, and (3) restore competitive conditions":

> In fashioning effective relief, the courts have considerable discretion in their choice of remedy. Antitrust decrees have, for example, ordered defendants to dispose of subsidiary companies; to create a company with appropriate assets and personnel to compete effectively with defendant; to make patents, trademarks and trade secrets or know-how available to competitors at reasonable royalties or even without any royalties; to provide goods and services to all who wish to buy; to revise the terms on which defendant buys or sells; and to cancel, shorten or modify outstanding agreements with competitors, suppliers or customers.[5]

consent decrees Formal agreements on remedies between all the parties to an antitrust case that must be approved by the courts. Consent decrees can be signed before, during, or after a trial.

CONSENT DECREES Between 75% and 80% of all government-initiated civil suits are settled with the signing of a consent decree. **Consent decrees** are formal agreements between the prosecuting government and the defendants that must be approved by the courts. Such decrees can be signed before, during, or after a trial. Because antitrust cases are long and expensive to litigate, both parties benefit if settlement comes early in the process. A recent case involving allegations of price fixing by Ivy League colleges was settled before trial when eight of the nine schools involved signed a consent decree. For more details, see the Issues and Applications box titled "The Overlap Group: Price Fixing at Private Colleges."

Consent decrees have encompassed a wide variety of agreements. A company may agree to give up a patent that is serving as a barrier to effective competition, for example, or it may agree to be broken up into separate competing companies, as in the AT&T case (described in detail later in this chapter).

CRIMINAL ACTIONS In 1955 and again in 1974, the sanctions for violating the Sherman Act were changed. The original act held that violations were misdemeanors and made no distinction between individuals and corporations. Today the penalties are considerably more severe:

> Every person who shall make any contract or engage in any combination or conspiracy hereby declared to be illegal shall be deemed guilty of a *felony*, and on conviction thereof, shall be punished by a fine not exceeding *one million dollars* if a corporation, or, if any other person, *one hundred thousand dollars* or by imprisonment not exceeding three years, or by both said punishments, in the discretion of the court.[6]

The practice of the Antitrust Division has been to limit criminal proceedings to only the most outrageous violations, where intent to violate is clear. In 1961,

---

[5] Phillip Areeda, *Antitrust Analysis: Problems, Text and Cases,* 3rd ed. (Boston: Little, Brown, 1986), p. 61.
[6] 26 Stat. 209 (1890), as amended 15 U.S.C.A. 1–7 (1980). Changes to the statute are italicized in the text.

THE OVERLAP GROUP: PRICE FIXING AT PRIVATE COLLEGES

The Antitrust Division of the Justice Department began investigating the pricing practices of a number of America's most prestigious private colleges in the late 1980s. At the center of the controversy was a practice called "overlap" in which representatives from a group of institutions met each year to share information on student financial aid. The practice dated to the 1950s when the Overlap Group was formed by the Ivy League (Brown, Columbia, Cornell, Dartmouth, Harvard, Princeton, Yale, and the University of Pennsylvania) and the Massachusetts Institute of Technology (MIT).

These schools and a number of others that joined later agreed that they would not try to outbid each other in aid offers to talented students. By limiting financial aid to cases of demonstrated need and preserving resources for those who could not otherwise afford private higher education, the group hoped to allow students to choose among schools on the basis of quality or best fit, not on the basis of which school offered the best deal. Qualified students who were admitted to more than one of the Overlap schools thus got approximately the same offer of aid from each institution.

The Justice Department argued that the practices of the Overlap Group constituted anticompetitive behavior and that the Overlap schools were guilty of illegal price fixing.

The Ivy League schools decided not to incur the legal costs of fighting the case in court and voluntarily signed a "consent decree" agreeing to stop the practice. MIT did not agree to sign the decree, however. Convinced that its actions were in the best interests of society, MIT

Many colleges and universities coordinate their financial aid awards. Is this is a practice that produces a social benefit, or is it a form of price fixing that is against society's best interests? In 1992, a federal judge decided the latter.

spent over $2 million fighting the case in court. In September 1992, the court held that MIT had indeed violated the law. MIT decided to appeal the decision, even though its arguments, summarized in the following excerpt, have been clearly rejected by the court.

A Federal judge ruled yesterday that the Massachusetts Institute of Technology had violated antitrust laws by participating in a decades-long conspiracy with other elite universities to fix the amount of student financial aid packages.

Louis C. Bechtle, Chief Judge of the Federal District Court for the Eastern District of Pennsylvania, clearly and pointedly rejected M.I.T.'s argument that it was engaged in charity, not conspiracy, when it shared confidential financial information on students with other universities. . .

"M.I.T.'s attempt to disassociate the Overlap process from the commercial aspects of higher education is pure sophistry," Judge Bechtle wrote, "No reasonable person could conclude that the Ivy Overlap agreements did not suppress competition."

M.I.T. relied heavily on convincing the court that the social benefits of the agreements far outweighed any technical legal violation. It offered as proof the fact that in the last academic year, 44 percent of its undergraduates were members of minorities and 57 percent of students received more than $20 million in financial aid.

Without such agreements, M.I.T. argued, needy students would inevitably suffer as the universities would be forced to compete for the best students.

Source: Anthony DePalmar, "M.I.T. Ruled Guilty in Antitrust Case," *New York Times*, September 3, 1992.

for example, seven prominent executives of major U.S. corporations that produced electrical equipment were found guilty of flagrantly violating well-established laws. They had secretly met and agreed to fix prices. All seven received 30-day jail sentences.

TREBLE DAMAGES Any person or private company that sustains injury or financial loss because of an antitrust violation can recover damages from the guilty party over and above any fines levied. The award made by the court must be three times the actual damages (*treble damages*):

> [A]ny person injured in his business or property by reason of anything forbidden in the antitrust laws. . . .shall recover threefold the damages by him sustained, and the cost of suit, including a reasonable attorney's fee.[7]

This provision, of course, provides a powerful incentive for private parties to have recourse to the antitrust laws.

Exemptions from Antitrust Statutes

The antitrust laws specifically exempt several industries. As we noted above, the Willis–Graham Act of 1921 declared the telephone industry a natural monopoly and exempted telephone mergers from review. Over the years, Congress and the courts have added others to the list. Today this list includes, but is not limited to, lobbying organizations, labor unions, sports organizations, and regulated industries.

LOBBYING As you know, a monopoly would be willing to pay most of its monopoly profits to protect itself from competition. (Recall the discussion of rent-seeking behavior in Chapter 13.) One of the activities that monopolies could spend these profits on is lobbying for exemption from the antitrust laws. In the mid-1960s, Congress decided that representatives of any industry group can join together for purposes of lobbying Congress. Lobbying is protected under what is called the *Noerr-Pennington Doctrine,* named after the court cases in which it was first enunciated.[8]

LABOR UNIONS Although the Sherman Act was originally used to fight the power of labor unions, the Clayton Act specifically exempted collective bargaining agreements from antitrust actions.

SPORTS ORGANIZATIONS The issue of monopoly power versus competition in sports, both college and professional, is extremely complex and has been the subject of countless court cases. Players have argued, with some success, that the sports leagues enjoy monopoly power and that they have conspired against the players to hold down salaries. Similarly, entry into professional baseball, basketball, and football leagues is effectively barred. I can't simply hire a team, build a stadium, and start competing in one of the existing leagues.

---

[7]See Areeda, *Antitrust.*

[8]*Eastern Railroad Presidents Conference* v. *Noerr Motor Freight, Inc.,* 365 U.S. 127 (1961), and *United Mine Workers of America* v. *Pennington,* 381 U.S. 637 (1965).

Congress has specifically allowed the mergers of the American Football League with the National Football League as well as the merger of the National Basketball Association with the American Basketball Association despite the fact that the amount of competition was substantially decreased by the two mergers. While there is a never-ending debate about whether the sports exemption is in the public interest, it is clear that sports associations continue to enjoy considerable protection from the antitrust statutes in their dealings with players, owners, and potential competitors.

REGULATED INDUSTRIES   We discussed natural monopoly in Chapter 13, and we will discuss it again below. Here it is sufficient to say that where large economies of scale exist, it may make sense to limit competition so that firms can take advantage of the lower costs of producing on a very large scale. In such a situation, regulation may be used as an alternative to restructuring. We discuss regulation in much greater depth later in this chapter.

THE ANTITRUST ENFORCEMENT DEBATE

Should the Antitrust Division be more aggressive in prosecuting antitrust violators? Just what level of enforcement activity should we settle for? Critics of business who favor more enforcement argue that the Antitrust Division does not have the resources to enforce the law.[9] Others argue that while some level of enforcement activity is useful, the Antitrust Division is overly aggressive and should be scaled back. Administration and enforcement of the law is costly, and laws and penalties neither can nor do stop all undesirable behavior.

The break-up of AT&T in 1982 brought this debate into the public arena. Some people believe that the outcome of the AT&T case has been a disaster, that it has torn apart the greatest telephone company in the world and has made consumers worse off than before. In fact, local telephone rates have risen substantially since 1982. Others argue that the outcome of the case has been an enormous success and that we are just beginning to see the fruits of intense competition in the form of new and better products and services. They point out that the rise in local rates is due to the gradual elimination of an inefficient subsidy to local rate payers that regulators had, over the years, unwisely built into long-distance rates. They also point out that long-distance rates have fallen sharply.

The issues raised by this debate require some further discussion. In the sections that follow we review the economic logic behind the antitrust laws before turning to a discussion of recent criticism leveled at enforcement practices.

The Case for Antitrust Enforcement

In a sense, the first part of this book—particularly Chapters 13 and 14—has already made the case for antitrust laws. As you have seen, competition has many potential benefits. It drives firms to produce at least cost and provides an incentive for them to introduce new, efficient production techniques and new products. Thus, the argument goes, the government should step in when anticom-

---

[9]For fiscal years 1985–1990, the budget of the Antitrust Division was about $50 million per year. Staffing has remained between 600 and 700 full-time employees during this period. (See *Budget of the United States,* Fiscal Years 1985–1990.)

petitive behavior or monopoly power threatens to rob society of the benefits of open competition.

The antitrust laws do more than just condemn monopoly; they also restrict certain specific kinds of conduct, whether the industry is monopolistic or not. Most of the specific practices outlawed by the various antitrust laws can result in serious social costs and waste of society's scarce resources. Thus, it is easy to build an economic case for governmental enforcement of prohibitions against unfair and deceptive practices, price fixing, collusion, and price discrimination.

UNFAIR OR DECEPTIVE PRACTICES   For a market economy to work, consumers must have valid information on product availability, quality, and price. The variety and complexity of modern life forces the average consumer to consider many products that cannot be fully understood or personally evaluated. Medical care, financial services, insurance, drugs, food products, consumer electronics, and products in other areas too numerous to mention are so complicated and specialized that the consumer may well be misinformed about them, if not deliberately deceived. In such cases, it may be reasonable for the government to act on behalf of consumers to prevent "unfair and deceptive acts or practices." (We discuss this topic in more detail in Chapter 16.)

PRICE FIXING AND COLLUSION   Firms can use price fixing and collusion to protect themselves from competition. Both practices allow firms that would otherwise compete to act together as a monopoly and reap monopoly profits. Competitive markets drive product prices close to the cost of production, and in the long run competitive firms will earn only normal profits. If a monopolist were to gain control of an industry, it would clearly be in his or her interest to cut output, raise price, and do everything possible to prevent competition. If firms were permitted to set prices jointly or collude to restrict output and divide the market, they would act just like a monopoly, and consumers would lose. They would pay more for the same product than they would pay under competition, and less of the product would be produced. (In Chapter 13 you learned how the size of this net loss to society from the monopolization of an industry is calculated.)

price discrimination Occurs when a firm charges different buyers different prices for the same product. Such strategies are illegal if they drive out competition.

PRICE DISCRIMINATION   Under the Clayton Act, **price discrimination** that tends to lessen competition is illegal. For example, suppose that several companies buy rolled steel to make filing cabinets. The largest producer, by virtue of its size and bargaining power, may be able to obtain a very low price from the steel producers, a price not justified by cost savings due to large volume. The bargaining power thus gives the large producer an advantage over its smaller competitors. This can lead to monopoly power in the long run.

Not all forms of price discrimination are inefficient, however. The most common form of price discrimination in practice is *third degree price discrimination,* which involves dividing consumers into identifiable groups and charging them different prices. Third degree price discrimination goes on all around us. Airlines, druggists, movie theaters, public transportation systems, and telephone companies all charge different prices for children, senior citizens, students, military personnel, and other identifiable groups. Professional journals charge individuals and institutions (libraries) very different subscription fees. Rental car companies offer discounts to members of AAA, frequent fliers, and employees of certain businesses.

For third degree price discrimination to work, resales between groups must be prevented. Otherwise, the differences in price would be arbitraged. *Arbitrage* takes place when someone buys a good at one price and immediately sells it to someone else at a higher price. Many firms have devised methods that keep arbitrage possibilities to a minimum. This is easily accomplished for services, which must be sold directly to the person consuming them, but is more difficult for goods, which can be resold easily.

Assuming that resale cannot occur, is third degree price discrimination inefficient? There is no easy answer. Suppose, for example, that Frank and Sarah both like widgets. Suppose further that Frank is willing to pay $3 for a widget, but that he will be charged $5 for a widget. Clearly, Frank will not buy. Sarah, however, is able to buy widgets for $1 each. She is willing to pay $2 for a widget. The optimal solution, from society's point of view, is for Sarah to buy a widget for $1 and then sell it to Frank for $3. But this cannot happen if resale is prevented. Thus, because exchange is blocked, it is likely that society will end up with the wrong distribution of output. Also, when a firm charges more than one price for its product, it is clearly not selling at least some of its product at marginal cost. (Remember that one of the conditions for allocative efficiency is $P = MC$.)

Ultimately, whether or not third degree price discrimination is in society's best interests depends on the alternative market solution. If the alternative is that the firm will sell all of its product at a single, high, monopoly price, then price discrimination may be preferable. If a firm with market power finds that it can expand its output beyond the amount that it would sell at a single fixed price by selling more to certain groups at lower prices, the result will be more efficient and more socially desirable.

Perfect price discrimination occurs when a seller charges buyers the absolute maximum price that buyers are willing to pay for each unit produced. It is as if sellers know everyone's demand curve exactly and simply charge a different price for every unit sold. Perfect price discrimination cannot possibly exist because it requires so much information. However, even if it did exist, it would not be inefficient. A monopolist able to price discriminate would produce and sell all the way to the point at which the price of the last unit sold to every consumer was just equal to marginal cost. In essence, a perfectly price discriminating monopolist would produce as much as a competitive industry but would take away all consumer surplus.

HIGHLY CONCENTRATED INDUSTRIES   Arguments in favor of antitrust action against firms in highly concentrated industries on the basis of industry structure alone are more difficult to make. In theory, a monopoly can be just as efficient as a competitive industry if it does not exercise its power and if it continues to minimize costs and to innovate as if it had rivals. Those who favor antitrust action on the basis of structure alone argue, however, that such behavior is extremely unlikely.

Between 1911 and 1945, the courts and the Antitrust Division were stuck with the "rule of reason." Under this rule, months of testimony were often necessary to demonstrate "unreasonable conduct," if it could be demonstrated at all. In the Alcoa decision, Judge Hand essentially said "enough is enough." When a firm controls 90% of a clearly defined market, an illegal monopoly exists, he decided, and there is no such thing as a benevolent monopoly.

THE ANTITRUST LAWS AS A DETERRENT   Because we can only speculate about what would have happened without them, we cannot say whether the antitrust laws have "worked" or not. Some decisions have clearly produced the desired results. The Standard Oil decision, for example, gave us several regional oil companies that came to compete vigorously in the refining business. And clear evidence indicates that price-fixing complaints tend to lower prices.

But you cannot measure the success of the speed limit laws by looking only at the behavior of those who get speeding tickets; you must also look at how fast most people drive. Proponents of antitrust enforcement argue that the real gains of such a policy lie in the cases that never make it to court, because antitrust laws and rules serve as a significant deterrent. Without such laws, they argue, the temptation to fix prices, collude, and engage in deceptive advertising would be irresistible. If no prohibitions existed, can anyone doubt that firms would merge, dominate markets, and exploit monopoly power? As you saw in Chapters 13 and 14, the profit incentive for firms to do all these things is compelling.

The Case against Antitrust Enforcement

In recent years, antitrust laws have come under increasing criticism. While few complain about the laws that make certain kinds of conduct illegal, there is growing concern about remedies aimed at concentrated industries that seem to be performing fairly well. Several themes recur in this recent criticism.

REGULATIONS AS THE PENALTY FOR SUCCESS? Critics of regulation contend that the Antitrust Division and the FTC are not concerned with inefficient firms that have not done well; rather, they are interested only in the firms that, in a sense, have done *too well*. In other words, if a company produces a "better mousetrap" and comes to dominate an industry, the government nails it for being a monopoly.

We discussed one prominent example of regulation as the "penalty for success" in Chapter 13. In the early 1960s, extensive research led the General Motors Corporation to come up with a number of important improvements in the design of intracity buses. Those improvements were patented, and as a result GM came to dominate the market for intracity buses.

After a long antitrust battle, the court issued a consent decree forcing GM to give up its patents to the competition. In addition, any further design improvements that GM made through research and development would likewise have to be made available to its competitors. The result was that GM stopped developing new and better buses, and travelers ended up with worse buses than they might have had.

Many people made the same argument about the divestiture of AT&T in 1982: We had a well-managed and enormously successful private company—the best telephone company in the world. No one argued that AT&T had done anything wrong or unethical. Rather, the argument was that competition might lead to an even better result—new products, better service, and lower rates. But, the critics cried, the key word was "might." And, they added, resorting to familiar and compelling logic, "If it's not broken, don't fix it!"

THE NEED FOR BIG, STRONG COMPANIES TO FACE GLOBAL COMPETITION For most of its history, the United States did not have to worry much about global competition. Today everyone knows the names Toyota, Volvo, Sony, and many others. Giant corporations in the Far East and Europe are filling American markets with sophisticated products and masterful marketing techniques.

It is said that the old theory of competitive markets doesn't work when one country's industries face competition from foreign companies whose governments aid and abet their activities. The Japanese government, for example, does everything in its power to help its giant firms penetrate foreign markets and to grow, while the United States government forces U.S. megafirms to defend themselves in court against antitrust judgments.

It may also be that cooperation among firms (a major joint research effort, for example), if allowed, might help U.S. industries fight foreign competition. But firms in concentrated industries are unlikely to participate in joint ventures for fear of antitrust action.

NEGATIVE EFFECTS ON RESEARCH, DEVELOPMENT, AND GROWTH   The Schumpeterian hypothesis, outlined in Chapter 14, is the foundation for the argument that large firms can devote significant resources to research and development activities, while lower levels of industrial concentration lead to less R&D. But, as you have seen, the evidence regarding this hypothesis is mixed. Larger firms are indeed more likely to have research staffs than smaller firms, but the number of patents procured and the number of important developments over the years do not seem to show any systematic correlation with firm size.[10] Nonetheless, this may not be true in all industries:

> After the Alcoa case in 1945, Kaiser, Reynolds, and several other new firms entered the aluminum industry: A study examined technical progress [before and after the Alcoa case] and concluded that the reduction in seller concentration was responsible at least in part for increased progressiveness . . . . the existence of several producers has led to competitive marketing, increasing the pressures to develop new alloys and new uses for aluminum, including many consumer products such as foil. Reduced concentration seems to have provided a significant competitive stimulus to innovation.[11]

Conflicting evidence comes from the telecommunications industry. Before its break-up, for example, AT&T maintained an enormous research facility called Bell Laboratories. Founded in 1925, at its peak it had 17 research centers in nine states and employed thousands of scientists and engineers. We can safely say that no single research program was responsible for more important technological breakthroughs, including the transistor, the solar battery, and the laser. Yet research and new product development are proceeding at an amazing rate in the new companies that were broken off from AT&T in 1982 and in those that are springing up around it.

EFFICIENT CAPITAL FLOWS AND RELATIVELY CONTESTABLE MARKETS   Another argument against vigorous antitrust enforcement is that barriers to entry are not as formidable as they once were. Capital markets have become more efficient; investors are always looking for profitable ventures and are now able to mobilize the huge sums necessary to enter almost any industry if there are economic profits to be earned. The efficiency of capital markets serves to make more and more markets contestable. Critics of antitrust enforcement argue that both actual entry and the threat of new entry make market power less of a problem.

DISTRUST OF GOVERNMENT   Even if it can be shown that antitrust enforcement is a good idea in theory, many people simply do not want to put more power in the hands of government. They feel that government intervention creates more prob-

---

[10]See Richard Caves, *American Industry: Structure, Conduct, Performance*, 7th ed. (Englewood Cliffs, N.J.: Prentice Hall, 1992).

[11]See Caves, *American Industry*.

lems than it solves. Bureaucracy is slow and wasteful, the argument goes, and the people in a particular industry clearly know more about what they do than those government employees charged with regulating that industry.

The Policy Maker's Dilemma

One of the lessons that we hope you will take from this course (and from your entire college education) is that complicated questions have no simple answers. There are strong arguments for government involvement in the economy. Unchecked monopoly power, collusion, and price fixing can be enormously expensive to a society. It is also easy to show that competition provides incentives for efficient production, innovation, and a healthy economy.

It is equally clear, unfortunately, that enforcement of the antitrust laws has imposed costs on society. Successful companies have paid a price for their success. Some, such as GM, have been forced to give back markets that they won through vigorous competition. Antitrust activities may also have played a part in reducing the United States' ability to compete for international markets.

> The role of policy makers is to understand the arguments, weigh the evidence, and proceed in one direction or the other. While policy decisions must be made without knowledge of the outcome, enlightened uncertainty is better than ignorance.

REGULATION

At the beginning of this chapter we said that the government plays two basic roles that seem contradictory: (1) It *promotes* competition and restricts market power, primarily through antitrust laws and other acts of Congress, and (2) it *restricts* competition by simultaneously regulating and protecting certain industries. So far, we have looked exclusively at the way the government protects competition. Now we turn to government activities that end up protecting monopoly power.

The government regulates many areas of the economy that have nothing to do with market structure. Some of these areas (environmental protection, for example) are discussed in later chapters. In the section that follows, however, we examine only the regulation of natural monopolies.

Regulation of Natural Monopoly

In Chapter 13 we introduced you to some of the ways the market fails when market power is unrestrained. Firms that can control price and bar the entry of new firms find it advantageous to overprice and underproduce relative to what is best for society. A number of solutions to this problem are possible, at least in theory. One solution is to restructure the industry to make it more competitive. A second is to impose some sort of price regulation—a price ceiling at marginal cost, for example. Yet another is public or government ownership and operation.

The antitrust laws that we examined above are based on the proposition that competition, not regulation or public ownership, is the best way to achieve efficiency in an economy. Although the courts exercise great discretion, everything they do, from requiring firms to give up patents to breaking firms up into smaller competing units, aims at stimulating competition. Nonetheless, it has always been understood that not all markets can be, or should be, competitively structured.

Most important among these exceptions are firms or industries that can take advantage of very large economies of scale—the natural monopolies mentioned earlier in this chapter and described in Chapter 13.

Figure 15.2 reproduces a natural monopoly diagram from Chapter 13. Notice that average total cost is still declining when the demand curve intersects it. To break such a firm into smaller pieces, each producing some fraction of total demand, would mean that each of the small firms would have to produce at a much higher average cost. (All of this is implied by the existence of large economies of scale. If this is not clear to you, review Chapter 13.)

Most natural monopolies have very high fixed costs and low marginal costs. Take, for example, the local electric company. Building a power generation plant and putting up poles and wires is costly. Once they are in place, the cost of generating and distributing one additional kilowatt of electricity is low. Part of the reasoning behind the protection of such industries is that having more than one firm undertake the very large initial investment is a waste of resources.

One solution to the natural monopoly problem is to let the firm continue to exist as a monopoly but to regulate the price of its product and its rate of return. If the natural monopoly in Figure 15.2 went unregulated, it would produce Q^* units of output (the point at which $MR = MC$) and charge price P^*, far above marginal costs. But imposing a simple price ceiling at $P = MC$ would not work, because at that price marginal cost is below average cost, and the firm could not make even a normal profit. Remember that price is equal to average revenue, and if average revenue is less than average cost, total revenue will be less than total cost. This implies a loss.

Theory suggests three options for regulation: (1) Set the *efficient price* $(P = MC)$ and provide a subsidy out of general government revenues to the monopoly; (2)

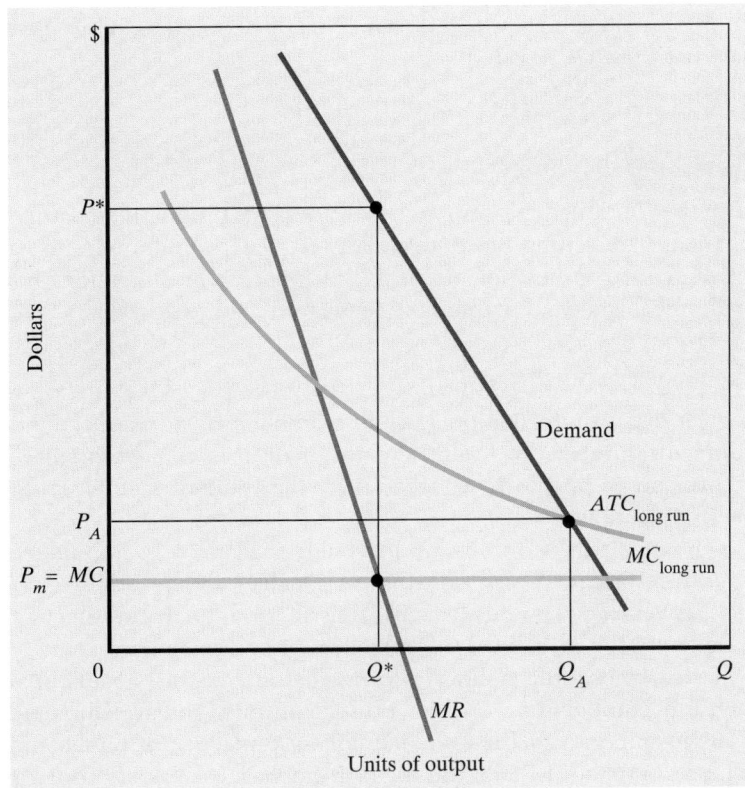

FIGURE 15.2
Regulating a Natural Monopoly

A natural monopoly exists when a firm exhibits very large economies of scale. Here long-run average costs facing the firm continue to decline with output even when a single firm is producing all the output demanded in the market. With no regulation, the firm would produce at Q^* and price at P^*. Regulating price to be equal to marginal cost results in losses. Setting price at P_A means that average cost is covered and that investors earn a normal rate of return.

set price equal to average cost (P_A), which would allow firms to charge a price that covers all costs, including a normal return on invested capital; or (3) impose a fee on each user of the monopoly's product—a basic service charge as a lump sum and a price for usage equal to marginal cost. The last two options both require that some regulatory commission set the firm's rate of return.

PUBLIC OWNERSHIP VERSUS PRIVATIZATION   A fourth solution to the natural monopoly problem is public (or government) ownership and operation of business. Many U.S. and foreign cities operate their own public utilities. The railroad systems of many countries are run by the government, often quite efficiently. France, for example, operates one of the most efficient and innovative railroads in the world.

Despite some successful examples of public ownership, however, the prevailing opinion seems to be that the government should stay out of a particular business if the private sector can do the job. In fact, one of the most popular trends of the 1980s was **privatization,** or the transfer of government businesses to the private sector. Japan sold the Japan National Railway to the public, and Britain and France have sold stock in state-owned banks, energy companies, and telecommunications firms. U.S. states and localities have privatized garbage collection, recycling services, fire fighting, prisons, and even water treatment facilities. In 1988, a special commission appointed by President Reagan recommended the privatization of air traffic control operations, public housing, prisons, and mail services.

Why the rush to privatize? The basic logic is simple. The incentive to be efficient is greater when one's own money is at risk. On the other side of the argument, those opposed to privatization argue, that natural monopoly must be regulated or nationalized because private companies do not always act in the public interest. They also point out that government does a creditable job of running its businesses: More than 70% of people receiving government services say that they are satisfied.

privatization The transfer of government business to the private sector.

The Problems of Regulation

The theory of natural monopoly sounds fairly simple: Regulatory commissions are charged with setting prices that allow regulated monopolies to earn a normal rate of return. A number of problems are inherent in regulation, however, and these will probably always perplex the regulator to some degree.

GATHERING AND ANALYZING THE NECESSARY DATA   Regulation requires analyzing a great deal of information. The first problem is calculating the base—presumably some measure of the "value" of the firm's capital investment—on which a fair return should be allowed. Debate over the value of a public utility can go on and on, for example.

The regulatory commission must also analyze costs. Should all costs be allowed in setting price? Which costs are reasonable? Public utility commissions (PUCs) have developed methods for analyzing all the information necessary, but analysis is a difficult process, subject to differences of opinion and to error.

Furthermore, the political process that attends rate regulation is time-consuming and cumbersome. Public utility commissions are impaneled to act in the "public interest." Whenever decisions are made, the public must be consulted. These consultations take the form of public hearings and open sessions. And the final decisions made by PUCs can be reviewed in the courts. Interested parties have not been shy about filing suits after an unfavorable or unpopular decision. When a private firm makes a pricing mistake, it can act quickly to change its price. When a utility commission makes a mistake, however, correcting it may take over a year.

LACK OF INCENTIVES TO BE EFFICIENT   Because the return to a regulated natural monopoly is set by a commission, the monopoly may lack the incentive to use efficient production techniques. For example, if a regulatory commission fixes the return by setting a rate expressed as a percent of the utility's assets, the dollar amount of profit depends only on the total value of those assets. Thus, firms may actually have an incentive to overinvest in capital if the allowed return exceeds the cost of capital. This tendency is called the **Averch-Johnson effect,** after the scholars who noted the proclivity of regulated firms to build more capital capacity than they need.[12]

In general, then, we can say that when regulated firms are guaranteed a standard rate of return, they have no incentive to keep costs at a minimum. When profits are not linked to some measure of performance, there is no reason for the firm to perform well and no severe penalty for weak performance.

EXCESSIVE NONPRICE COMPETITION   Regulated monopolies generally do not have a problem with nonprice competition, because they don't *have* competition. In regulated industries where several firms compete directly with each other while being required to charge the same price, however, product differentiation can become excessive.

The marketing zeal of the airlines in the early 1970s is the example most often cited of this effect. During that time, airlines offered frequent flights, designer-painted planes, a choice of five menus, free carpet slippers, and all kinds of other little frills that are hard to imagine today, in an effort to increase ticket sales. As a result of deregulation, competition now drives airlines to produce the service that people want at least cost and thus at a lower price.

> **Averch-Johnson effect** The tendency for regulated monopolies to build more capital than they need. Usually occurs when allowed rates of return are set by a regulatory agency at some percent of fixed capital stocks.

The Rise and Fall of Regulation

The Bell Telephone Company behaved like a textbook monopoly until some of its patents expired in 1894. After 1894, increasing competition in the telecommunications industry actually led Bell to argue *for* regulation. Worried about both antitrust actions and the emergence of new competition, Bell argued that it was a natural monopoly. It made little sense, it said, to have two or more sets of telephone lines down the same road. Around the same time, many other industries put forth similar arguments.

In response to these types of arguments, many states set up public utility commissions in the early years of this century. Pro-regulation sentiment reached its peak in 1907, when seven states established new regulatory bodies. Mergers between firms in the telecommunications market were finally exempted from antitrust review by the Willis-Graham Act of 1921. By that time, telephone companies were strictly regulated in all states.

---

[12]Harvey Averch and Leland Johnson, "Behavior of the Firm under Regulatory Constraint," *American Economic Review* LII (December 1962), pp. 1052–1069.

By the last part of the 1970s and the early 1980s, the feeling had grown that the government was regulating industries that were not really natural monopolies. In some cases, the arguments for regulation had eroded with technological advances in the industries; in other cases, the industries had not been natural monopolies to begin with. As a result, there has been a movement toward deregulation, and the mandates of various regulatory agencies are gradually changing.

The authority of the oldest regulatory agency granted nationwide powers, the *Interstate Commerce Commission (ICC)*, expanded for a time to include interstate trucking as well as railroads. Today, however, its control over truckers' services and rates is essentially gone, and only those railroads that exhibit "market dominance" remain under its direct control. Trucking deregulation began in 1978; by 1983, competition had pushed the real price of truckload shipments down by 25 percent.

The airlines were once tightly regulated by the *Civil Aeronautics Board (CAB)*, which controlled routes and fares for all interstate carriers. Today the CAB is out of business, and there is no lack of competition in the airline industry. In fact, when cutthroat competition during 1992 and 1993 kept airfares below costs, the airlines lost billions of dollars—prompting many to call for reregulation of the industry.

The *Federal Energy Regulatory Commission* once regulated the price of natural gas that travels through interstate pipelines. It also fixed the wholesale rates for electricity transmitted interstate. In 1978 Congress began gradually deregulating the price of natural gas which is now set competitively.

The *Federal Communications Commission* regulates interstate telephone and telegraph rates and services. Regulation of local operating companies remains the responsibility of state-run public utility commissions. Clearly an industry in transition, telecommunications is likely to see much less regulation in the future.

Technological change has made it possible—and even necessary—for long-distance telephone service to become competitive. This was signaled when a new company, MCI, filed a private action against AT&T, arguing that AT&T used its monopoly in local service areas and in the manufacture of equipment to monopolize the long-distance market. In 1982 AT&T reached a settlement in which it agreed to separate its long-distance service and equipment manufacturing business from its local operating companies. Although the FCC still regulates AT&T's long-distance rates (partly to give the new long-distance companies a chance in the face of AT&T's "100-year head start"), it is clear that the FCC sees this residual regulation of the long-distance market as transitional and that long-distance rates will ultimately be competitively set.

Even local public utility commissions have recently moved toward deregulation. In nearly every state, PUCs still regulate the price of local service and the rate of return of the local operating companies, but increasing competition from many sources has become a real challenge. Firms are setting up private networks that bypass the system altogether. "Telecommunications-enhanced real estate," or "smart buildings," are wired with private systems or microwave transmitters that bypass the local exchange network. These competitive services currently are not permitted to provide local exchange service, but they are making the life of the regulator difficult, and the local telephone companies are now asking their regulatory agencies to allow them to compete with these private companies.

Perhaps the only remaining pure natural monopolies are the electric power industry and cable television. After cable television rates were deregulated in 1987, prices for service in some areas doubled. Most consumers have no choice among competing cable companies. When the cables were first installed, several companies submitted proposals to service individual areas, but once a company was chosen, it enjoyed a "natural" monopoly.

Citing evidence that rates in areas where competing cable companies operate were two thirds the level of rates in single-company areas, Congress passed a law to reregulate the industry in 1992. In 1993, the FCC ordered rate cuts as a first step toward price regulation of the cable television industry, where more than 99% of all firms face virtually no competition.

The Case for Deregulation

Clearly, there must be a strong rationale behind the extensive deregulation that has occurred in recent years. Those who favor deregulation make two basic arguments. First, because few real natural monopolies exist, there is rarely a reason for government regulation on the basis of market structure. Second, many (if not most) instances of government regulation have succeeded in reducing competition in industries where competition might be beneficial.

It is important to understand that this chapter does not discuss *all* forms of government regulation. In later chapters, we examine other kinds of government involvement in the economy, including environmental protection, occupational health and safety, and food and drug regulation. Here we are talking simply about government regulation of firms that are allowed to operate essentially as monopolies on the grounds that economies of scale make antitrust enforcement impractical. Critics argue that even the classic natural monopoly—the electric power company—may no longer fit the definition very well. While large economies of scale may still exist in power *distribution,* power *generation* can be done on a relatively small scale at scattered sites. Small plants can efficiently produce power and feed it into the "grid." It is technologically possible, they say, for the industry to be quite competitive.

Those who contend that the government has stifled potentially beneficial competition argue that most examples of real barriers to entry are barriers *created* by governments. We have already talked about regulation in the taxicab, telephone, and airlines industries. Certainly none of these industries could be called a natural monopoly, and yet all are, or were, highly regulated.

Most of these examples are consistent with the theory of rent-seeking behavior discussed in Chapter 13. Recall that basic argument: If a firm finds that it is possible to earn economic profits and to protect those profits by preventing competition, it will expend resources to do so. These expenditures may include lobbying for regulatory protection. AT&T decided in 1905 that regulation was a better fate than all-out competition, so it actually sought regulation. Similarly, the trucking industry favored continued regulation, as did most of the airlines, when deregulation of each of those industries was first proposed.

Be careful not to confuse the criticisms of regulation with the criticisms of antitrust enforcement, however. While both call for less government, the logic behind the two arguments is quite different:

> Antitrust enforcement is undertaken to *promote* competition. In a way, it is the opposite of market regulation, which nearly always serves to *restrict* competition.

SUMMARY

The Development of Antitrust Law

1. Governments have assumed two basic roles with respect to imperfectly competitive industries: (1) They *promote* competition and restrict market power, primarily through antitrust laws and other congressional acts, and (2) they *restrict* competition by regulating industries.

2. Congress created the *Interstate Commerce Commission* in 1887 to regulate the railroads and in 1890 passed the *Sherman Act,* which declared monopoly and trade restraints illegal. In two famous cases in 1911, the Supreme Court enunciated the *rule of reason,* which implied that monopolistic structure alone was not a criterion for antitrust enforcement.

3. In 1914 Congress passed the *Clayton Act,* which was designed to strengthen the Sherman Act and to clarify exactly what specific forms of conduct were "unreasonable" restraints of trade. In the same year, the *Federal Trade Commission* was established and given broad powers to investigate and regulate unfair methods of competition. Subsequent legislation extended the government's power to limit mergers that might substantially lessen competition in an industry. Currently the Justice Department uses the *Herfindahl-Hirschman Index* to determine whether or not it will challenge a proposed merger.

Enforcement of Antitrust Law

4. Responsibility for the enforcement of the antitrust laws rests primarily with the *Antitrust Division* of the Justice Department and the Federal Trade Commission. Antitrust complaints may also be brought to the courts by private citizens.

5. The courts are empowered to impose a number of remedies if they find that antitrust law has been violated. These include civil and criminal penalties, *consent decrees* that specifically forbid future illegal acts, and treble damages.

6. The antitrust laws specifically exempt certain groups. These groups include lobbying organizations, labor unions, sports organizations, and regulated industries.

The Antitrust Enforcement Debate

7. The case for government intervention in imperfectly competitive industries is well established: Unchecked monopoly power, *price discrimination,* collusion, and price fixing can be enormously expensive to society. Proponents of antitrust enforcement point out that the real gains are in the cases that never make it to court because the antitrust rules and laws serve as a significant deterrent. Without such laws, the temptation to fix prices, collude, and engage in deceptive advertising would be irresistible.

8. The basic arguments against antitrust enforcement are that it penalizes success, that the United States needs strong companies to face foreign competition, that antitrust actions may reduce basic research and development, and that most markets are reasonably competitive.

Regulation

9. When an industry demonstrates very large economies of scale, it may be efficient to have only one large firm in that industry. Such a firm is called a natural monopoly. If a single-firm industry is protected on the grounds that it is a natural monopoly, it must be regulated to prevent exploitation of its monopoly power.

10. In past years, the government has been involved in regulating industries that are not natural monopolies. In the last decade, however, a number of these industries (including trucking, airlines, and telecommunications) have been totally or partially deregulated.

11. There are a number of problems associated with regulation. First, it is difficult to collect and analyze all the data necessary to regulate an industry. Second, firms that are guaranteed a certain rate of return lack incentives to be efficient. This may give rise to the *Averch-Johnson effect,* in which a monopoly tends to build more capital than it needs. Finally, regulation may give rise to excessive nonprice competition.

12. The proper role of government in the world of business is hard to define. Doing nothing about noncompetitive industries inevitably results in significant social losses. The antitrust laws have strengths and weaknesses, but most economists feel they deter behavior that might otherwise cost society too much. Where very large economies of scale make it logical to preserve monopoly structure in an industry, regulation is the only reasonable course of action.

REVIEW TERMS AND CONCEPTS

PROBLEM SET

1. What was the "rule of reason" enunciated by the courts in 1911? What problems did the courts encounter in implementing the rule of reason? In what ways did the Clayton Act help to clarify its meaning?

2. With the Alcoa case, the position of the courts changed dramatically. What important principle was changed by Judge Hand's opinion in the Alcoa case? List the advantages and disadvantages of the structural approach to antitrust enforcement introduced by the Alcoa decision.

3. Suppose the widget industry were made up of five firms each controlling 10% of the market, and 10 firms each controlling 5% of the market. If two firms that each control 10% of the market in this industry proposed merging, would the merger be challenged by the Justice Department under the 1982/1984 guidelines? Explain your answer. (*Hint:* Calculate the HHI.)

4. What potential problems do you see with Justice Department decisions based on the Herfindahl-Hirschman Index? For example, should the "market share" referred to in computing the HHI be national share or regional share? How useful do you think the HHI would be in the case of a merger between two multiproduct firms?

5. As head of the New Hampshire Public Utility Commission, you must make a recommendation concerning electric rates in the town of Nashua, where power is provided by a private electric company that enjoys a monopoly. Currently the price of electricity is regulated at $0.105 per kilowatt hour (kwh). Total usage is 89.3 million kwh. Assume that variable costs amount to $0.048 per kwh, fixed costs of maintaining the power plant total $1.5 million annually, and demand elasticity is zero. The commission has established that a fair return on invested capital to the owners of the electric company is 10 percent. If total invested capital in the plant was $45 million, would you recommend a rate hike or a cut? By how much?

6. Explain, using graphs, why restructuring a monopoly into a number of competing firms is likely to lead to a more efficient allocation of resources.

7. Explain why restructuring fails as a remedy in the case of a natural monopoly. Illustrate your answer with a graph. What alternatives are there to restructuring in the case of a natural monopoly? Show these on a graph. Compare consumer surplus, profits, and welfare losses under each scheme.

8. What are the arguments in favor of continued regulation of local operating companies in the telecommunications industry? What are the arguments in favor of complete deregulation of that industry?

9. One of the objectives of the AT&T divestiture was to bring lower prices to consumers through competition. Long-distance rates have indeed fallen since 1983, but the price of local service has gone up. Does this mean that restructuring and deregulation have failed? Explain.

16

Externalities, Public Goods, Imperfect Information, and Social Choice

market failure Occurs when resources are misallocated, or allocated inefficiently.

In Chapters 5 through 12, we built a complete model of a perfectly competitive economy under a set of fairly restrictive assumptions. By Chapter 12, we had demonstrated that the allocation of resources under perfect competition is efficient. At the end of that chapter, we began to relax some of the assumptions on which the competitive model is based. We introduced the idea of **market failure,** and in Chapters 13 and 14 we talked about three kinds of imperfect markets: monopoly, oligopoly, and monopolistic competition. In chapter 15 we discussed some of the ways government has responded to the inefficiencies of imperfect markets and to the development of market power.

As we continue our examination of market failure, we look first at *externalities* as a source of inefficiency. Often when we engage in transactions or make economic decisions, second or third parties suffer consequences that decision makers have no incentive to consider. For example, for many years manufacturing firms and power plants had no reason to worry about the impact of smoke from their operations on the quality of the air we breathe. Now we know that air pollution harms people, and it has become one of the most often-cited examples of an externality.

Next, we consider a second type of market failure that involves a class of products that private firms find it unprofitable to produce even if members of society want them. These products are called *public goods* or *social goods*. Public goods yield collective benefits, and in most societies, governments either produce them or arrange for their provision. The process of choosing what social goods to produce is by nature very different from the process of private choice.

A third source of market failure is *imperfect information*. In Chapters 6 through 12, we assumed that households and firms make choices in the presence of perfect information—that households know all that there is to know about product availability, quality, and price and that firms know all there is to know about factor availability, quality, and price. When information is imperfect, a misallocation of resources may result.

Finally, while the existence of public goods, externalities, and imperfect information are examples of market failure, it is not necessarily true that government involvement will always improve matters. Just as markets can fail, so too can governments. In fact, when we look carefully at the incentives facing government decision makers, we find several reasons behind government failure.

EXTERNALITIES AND ENVIRONMENTAL ECONOMICS

An **externality** exists when the actions or decisions of one person or group impose a cost or bestow a benefit on some second or third parties. Externalities are sometimes called *spillovers* or *neighborhood effects*. Inefficient decisions result when decision makers fail to consider social costs and benefits.

The presence of externalities is a significant phenomenon in modern life. Examples are everywhere: Air, water, land, sight, and sound pollution; traffic congestion; automobile accidents; abandoned housing; nuclear accidents; and cigarette smoking are only a few of them. Because so many externalities affect the environment, the study of externalities is a major concern of *environmental economics*.

The opening of Eastern Europe in 1989 and 1990 revealed that environmental externalities are not limited to free-market economies. Part of the logic of a planned economy is that when economic decisions are made socially (by the government, presumably acting on behalf of the people) rather than privately, planners can and will take all costs—private and social—into account. This has not been the case, however. When East and West Germany were reunited and the borders of Europe were opened, many were shocked by the disastrous condition of the environment in virtually all of Eastern Europe. (For more details, see the Global Perspective box titled "Environmental Problems in Eastern Europe.")

As societies become more and more urbanized, externalities become more and more important. The reason is clear: When we live closer together, our actions are more likely to affect others.

externality A cost or benefit resulting from some activity or transaction that is imposed or bestowed upon parties outside the activity or transaction. Sometimes called *spillovers* or *neighborhood effects*.

Marginal Social Cost and Marginal-Cost Pricing

Profit-maximizing perfectly competitive firms will produce output up to the point at which price is equal to marginal cost ($P = MC$). Let us take a moment here to review why this condition is essential to the proposition that competitive markets produce what people want (that is, an efficient mix of output).

When a firm weighs price and marginal cost and no externalities exist, it is in fact weighing the full benefits to society of additional production against the full costs to society of that production. Those who benefit from the production of a

ENVIRONMENTAL PROBLEMS IN EASTERN EUROPE

Pollution has become so choking in some parts of Eastern Europe that people wear protective masks while conducting daily affairs. Environmental problems have been particularly serious in Czechoslovakia, pictured here.

In theory, socialist economies are supposed to pay attention to externalities and social costs better than free-market economies, where private firms must often be prodded to consider external effects. The radical changes that have taken place in Eastern Europe over the last few years certainly challenge this once-conventional wisdom, as the following excerpt describes:

KATOWICE, Poland—In the depths of a salt mine in Poland, men, women and children lie in bed, bundled in coats and tugging at heavy blankets. In an upside-down world, they have come to this underground clinic to breathe clean and healing air....

Clean air has become a luxury here and in the industrial zones of Central Europe, where poisonous gases and toxic dust roam freely. As the secrets of the Eastern bloc's formerly Communist nations become known, this one may be the saddest. In the years when Soviet-bloc rulers claimed that they were forming "a new socialist man," they were in many instances condemning this man and his family to severe lung and heart disease, cancer, eye and skin ailments and, often, sickly children and shorter lives....

In much of Eastern Europe, comprehensive health surveys are not yet available because Communist Governments hid or ignored many of the medical statistics.

But from East Germany to Bulgaria, physicians, biologists and other health specialists are now eager to talk. And visiting experts from the United States and Western Europe have said that Central Europe's pollution is more dangerous and widespread than anything they have seen in the Western industrial nations, and that it occurs on a far greater scale than in the developing world, which does not have nearly as much industry.

Health specialists throughout the region said that diseases traceable to a poisoned environment were consuming a large portion of public health budgets and boding ill for future generations. Similar problems from pollution affect many parts of the Soviet Union as well.

A study of new mothers in the industrial region of Katowice and Cracow in southern Poland showed concentrations of lead, mercury, cadmium and other toxic metals in the placenta of every woman. The study's author, Dr. Josef Niwelinski of the University of Cracow, said more than half of the 1,000 placentas examined were deformed or damaged, "most likely by the high level of carbon monoxide and sulfur dioxide in the air."

The findings were all the more worrisome, he said, because "we studied only the most healthy mothers with normal births."...

In the former East bloc nations as well as in the Soviet Union, the quality of air, water and food has deteriorated sharply over the past two decades as heavy industries and vehicles multiplied. To Western experts, the polluting practices seem all the more ruthless because they increased at a time when their dire consequences were already widely known.

Experts said the technology to control pollution from antiquated installations was well known and in some Eastern European countries was even produced for export. Yet there are only minimal controls on much of Eastern Europe's industrial emissions, or none at all.

Source: Marlisle Simons, "Rising Iron Curtain Exposes Haunting Veil of Polluted Air," *New York Times*, April 8, 1990.

product are the people or households who end up consuming it. The price of a product (P_X) is a good measure of what an additional unit of that product is "worth," since those who value it more highly than P_X already buy it. People who value it less than P_X are not buying it. If marginal cost includes all costs—that is, all costs *to society*—of producing a marginal unit of a good, then additional pro-duction is efficient, provided that P_X is greater than *MC*. Up to the point where $P = MC$, each unit of production yields benefits in excess of cost.

Consider a firm in the business of producing laundry detergent. As long as the price per unit that consumers pay for that detergent exceeds the cost of the resources needed to produce one marginal unit of it, the firm will continue to produce. Producing up to the point where $P = MC$ is efficient, because for every unit of detergent produced, consumers derive benefits that exceed the cost of the resources needed to produce it. Producing at a point where $MC > P$ is inefficient, because marginal cost will rise above the unit price of the detergent. For every unit produced beyond the level at which $P = MC$, society uses up resources that have a value in excess of the benefits that consumers place on detergent. Figure 16.1a shows a firm and an industry in which no externalities exist.

But suppose that the production of the firm's product imposes external costs on society as well. If it does not factor those additional costs into its decisions, the firm is likely to overproduce. In Figure 16.1b, a certain measure of external costs is

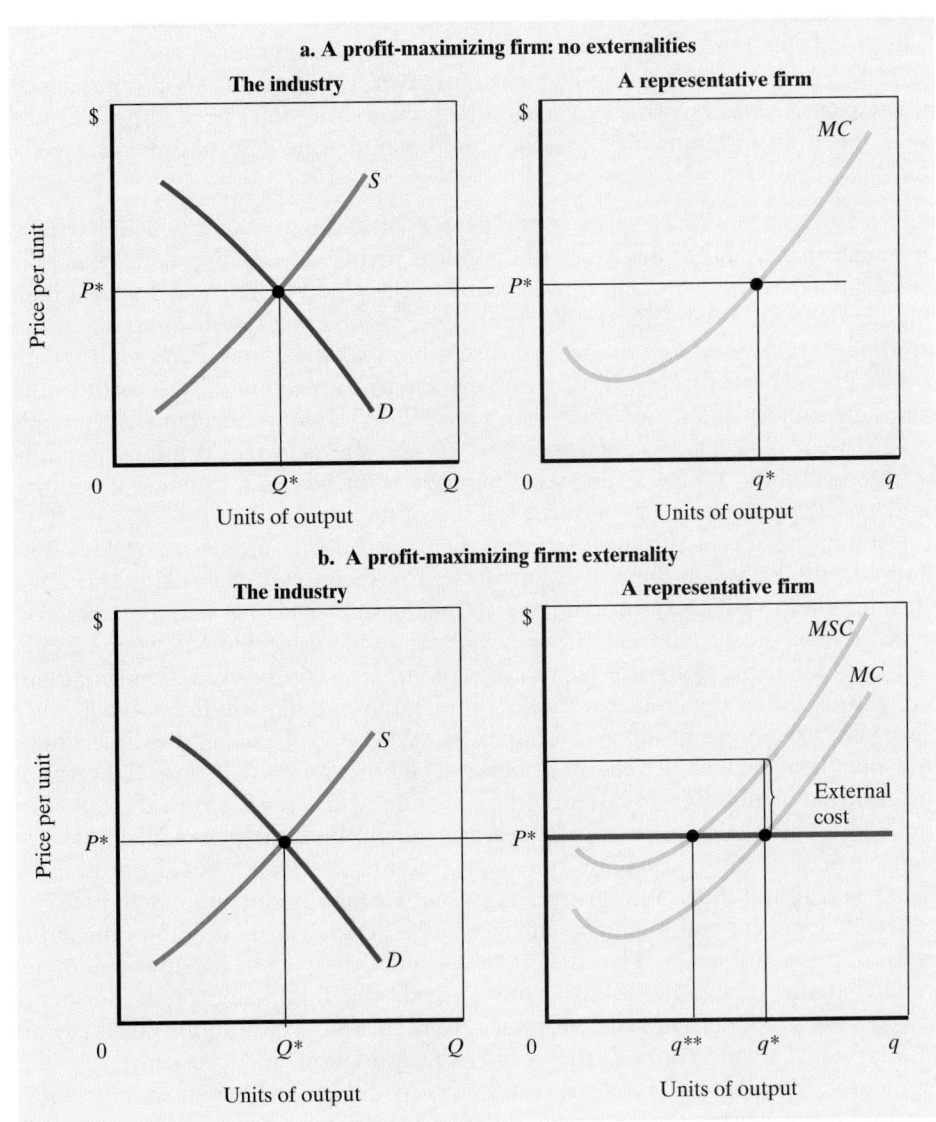

a. A profit-maximizing firm: no externalities

The industry   A representative firm

b. A profit-maximizing firm: externality

The industry   A representative firm

FIGURE 16.1

Profit-Maximizing Competitive Firms Will Produce up to the Point That Price Equals Marginal Cost ($P = MC$)

If we assume that the current price reflects what consumers are willing to pay for a product at the margin, firms that create external costs without weighing them in their decisions are like-ly to produce too much. Every unit of output produced above $q**$ in Figure 16.1b costs soci-ety more than the benefits it provides to consumers.

marginal social cost (MSC) The total cost to society of producing an additional unit of a good or service. *MSC* is equal to the sum of the marginal costs of producing the product and the correctly measured damage costs involved in the process of production.

added to the firm's marginal cost curve. We see these external costs in the diagram, but the firm is ignoring them. The curve labeled *MSC*, which stands for **marginal social cost (MSC)**, is the simple sum of the marginal costs of producing the product plus the correctly measured damage costs imposed in the process of production.

If the firm does not have to pay for these damage costs, it will produce exactly the same level of output (q^*) as before, and price (P^*) will continue to reflect only the costs that the firm actually pays to produce its product. The firms in this industry will continue to produce, and consumers will continue to consume their product, but the market price takes into account only part of the full cost of producing the good. At equilibrium (q^*), marginal social costs are considerably greater than price. (Recall that *price* is a measure of the full value to consumers of a unit of the product at the margin.)

Let us say that our detergent plant freely dumps untreated toxic waste into a river. The waste imposes a number of specific costs on people who live downstream: It kills the fish in the river, it makes the river ugly to look at and rotten to smell, and it destroys the river for recreational use. There may also be serious health hazards, depending on what chemicals the firm is dumping. Obviously, the plant's product also provides certain benefits. Its soap is valuable to consumers, who are willing and able to pay for it. The firm employs people and capital, and its revenues are sufficient to cover all costs. The issue, however, is how the *net benefits* produced by the plant compare with the damage that it does. You don't need a sophisticated economic model to know that *someone* should consider the costs of those damages.

ACID RAIN AND THE CLEAN AIR ACT The case of acid rain is an excellent example of an externality and of the issues and conflicts involved in dealing with externalities. Manufacturing firms and power plants in the Midwest burn coal with a high sulphur content. When the smoke from those plants mixes with moisture in the atmosphere, the result is a dilute acid that is blown by the prevailing winds north to Canada and east to New York and New England, where it falls to earth in the rain. The subject of a major conflict between the U.S. and Canadian governments and between industry and environmental groups, this acid rain is imposing enormous costs where it falls. Estimates of damage from fish kills, building deterioration, and deforestation range into the billions of dollars.

Decision makers at the manufacturing firms and public utilities using high-sulphur coal should weigh these costs, of course. But there is another side to this story. Burning cheap coal and not worrying about the acid rain that may be falling on someone else means jobs and cheap power for residents of the Midwest. Forcing coal-burning plants to pay for past damages from acid rain or even requiring them to begin weighing the costs that they are presently imposing will undoubtedly raise electricity prices and production costs in the Midwest. There is also little doubt that some firms will be driven out of business and that jobs will be lost. However, if the electricity and other products produced in the Midwest are worth the full costs imposed by acid rain, plants would not shut down; consumers would simply pay higher prices. If those goods are not worth the full cost, they should not be produced, at least not in current quantities or using current production methods.

The case of acid rain highlights the fact that efficiency analysis ignores the *distribution* of gains and losses. That is, to establish efficiency we need only to demonstrate that the total value of the gains exceeds the total value of the losses. If Midwestern producers and the consumers of their products were forced to pay an amount equal to the damages they cause, the gains from reduced damage in the East and in Canada would exceed costs in the Midwest. The beneficiaries of forcing Midwestern firms to consider these costs would be the households and firms in the East and in Canada. After many years of debate, Congress passed and President Bush signed the Clean Air Act of 1990. Included in the law are strict emissions standards aimed, in part, at controlling the production and distribution of acid rain. An interesting provision of the Clean Air Act is its use of "tradable pollution rights," which we discuss later in this chapter.

CHERNOBYL   One of the most significant cases of an externality that affected people in many parts of the world was the 1986 explosion and fire in a nuclear power plant at Chernobyl, a small city in the Soviet Union. Within a few hours after the fire began, radioactive particles were detected in the air in Scandinavia. Food products contaminated by the fallout had to be destroyed all over Europe. Within a week of the disaster, radioactivity was detected across the United States. The long-term health consequences of the Chernobyl explosion are still unknown.

Private Choices and External Effects

To help us understand externalities better, let us use a simple two-person example. Harry lives in a dormitory at a big public college in the Southwest, where he is a first-year student. When he graduated from high school, his family gave him an expensive stereo system. Unfortunately, when Harry's dorm was built, the university's capital budget was tight, and the walls are made of quarter-inch sheetrock over three-inch aluminum studs. You can hear people sleeping four rooms away. Harry likes bluegrass music of the particularly "twangy" kind. Because of a hearing loss after an accident on the Fourth of July some years ago, he often does not notice the volume at which he plays his music.

Jake, who lives next door to Harry, isn't much of a music lover, but when he does listen, he listens to Brahms concerti and occasionally to Mozart. Needless to say, Harry's music bothers Jake.

Let's assume for a moment that there are no further external costs or benefits to anyone other than Harry and Jake. Figure 16.2 diagrams the decision process that

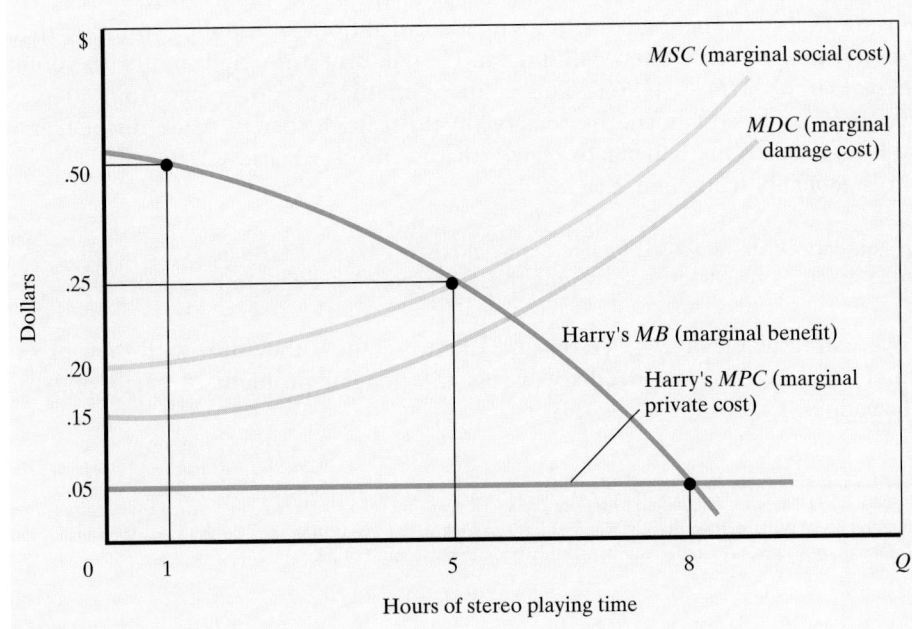

FIGURE 16.2
Externalities in a College Dormitory

The marginal benefits to Harry exceed the marginal costs he must bear to play his stereo for a period of up to eight hours. But when the stereo is playing, a cost is being imposed on Jake. When we add the costs borne by Harry to the damage costs imposed on Jake we get the full cost of the stereo to the two-person society made up of Harry and Jake. Playing the stereo more than five hours is inefficient because the benefits to Harry are less than the social cost for every hour above five. If Harry considers only his private costs, he will play the stereo for too long a time from society's point of view.

the two dorm residents face. The downward-sloping curve labeled *MB* represents the value of the marginal benefits that Harry derives from listening to his music. Of course, Harry doesn't sit down to draw this curve, any more than anyone else (other than an economics student) sits down to draw actual demand curves. Curves like this are simply abstract representations of the way people behave. But if you think carefully about it, such a curve must exist. To ask how much an hour of listening to music is worth to you is to ask how much you would be willing to pay to have it. Start at $0.01 and raise the "price" slowly in your mind. Presumably, you must stop at some point; where you stop depends on your taste for music and your income.

You can think, then, about the benefits that Harry derives from listening to bluegrass as the maximum amount of money that he would be willing to pay to listen to his music for an hour. For the first hour, let us say, the figure for *MB* is $0.50. We assume diminishing marginal utility, of course. The more hours Harry listens, the lower the additional benefits from each successive hour. As the diagram shows, the *MB* curve falls below $0.05 per hour after eight hours of listening time.

marginal private cost (MPC)
The amount that a consumer pays to consume an additional unit of a particular good.

We call the costs that Harry must pay for each additional hour of listening to music **marginal private costs,** labeled *MPC* in Figure 16.2. These include the cost of electricity and so forth. These costs are constant at $0.05 per hour.

Then there is Jake. Although Harry's music doesn't poison Jake, give him lung cancer, or even cause him to lose money, it damages him nonetheless: He gets a headache, loses sleep, and can't concentrate on his work. Jake is harmed, and it is possible (at least conceptually) to measure that harm in terms of the maximum amount that he would be willing to pay to avoid it. The damage, or cost, imposed on Jake is represented in Figure 16.2 by the curve labeled *MDC*. Formally, **marginal damage cost (MDC)** is the additional harm done by increasing the level of an externality-producing activity by one unit. Assuming that Jake would be willing to pay some amount of money to avoid the music, it is also reasonable to assume that the amount increases with each successive hour. His headache gets worse with each additional hour of being forced to listen to bluegrass.

marginal damage cost (MDC)
The additional harm done by increasing the level of an externality-producing activity by one unit. If producing product X pollutes the water in a river, MDC is the additional cost imposed by the added pollution that results from increasing output by one unit of X per period.

In the simple two-person society of Jake and Harry, it's easy to add up social benefits and costs. Consider first what would happen if Harry simply ignored Jake.[1] If Harry decides to play the stereo, Jake will be damaged. As long as Harry gains more in personal benefits from an additional hour of listening to music than he incurs in costs, the stereo will stay on. He will play it for eight hours (the point where Harry's *MB* = *MPC*). This result is inefficient; for every hour of play beyond five, the cost borne by society (in this case, a society made up of Harry and Jake) exceeds the benefits to Harry (that is, *MSC* > Harry's *MB*).

It is generally true, then, that:

> When economic decisions ignore external costs, whether those costs are borne by one person or by society as a whole, those decisions are likely to be inefficient.

We will return shortly to Harry and Jake to see how they deal with their problem. First, however, we need to discuss the general problem of correcting for externalities.

---

[1] It may actually be easier for people to ignore the social costs imposed by their actions when those costs fall on large numbers of other people that they do not have to look in the eye or that they do not know personally. For the moment, however, we simply assume that Harry takes no account of Jake.

Internalizing Externalities

A number of mechanisms are available to provide decision makers with incentives to weigh the external costs and benefits of their decisions, a process called *internalization*. In some cases, externalities are internalized through bargaining and negotiation without government involvement; in other cases, private bargains fail, and the only alternative may be government action of some kind.

Five basic approaches have been taken to solving the problem of externalities: (1) government-imposed taxes and subsidies, (2) private bargaining and negotiation, (3) legal rules and procedures, (4) the sale or auctioning of rights to impose externalities, and (5) direct government regulation. While each approach is best suited for a different set of circumstances, all five provide decision makers with an incentive to weigh the external effects of their decisions.

TAXES AND SUBSIDIES Traditionally, economists have advocated the use of marginal taxes and subsidies as a direct way of forcing firms to consider external costs or benefits. When a firm imposes an external social cost, the reasoning goes, a per unit tax should be imposed equal to the damages of each successive unit of output produced by the firm. In other words, the tax should be *exactly equal* to marginal damage costs.[2]

Figure 16.3 repeats the diagram that appears as Figure 16.1, but this time the damage costs are paid by the firm in the form of a per unit tax. The firm now faces a marginal cost curve that is the same as the marginal social cost curve. Remember that the industry supply curve is the sum of the marginal cost curves of the individual firms. This means that as a result of the tax the industry supply curve shifts back

---

[2]As we discuss later in this chapter, damage costs are difficult to measure. It is often assumed that they are proportional to the volume of pollutants discharged into the air or water. Instead of taxes, governments often impose *effluent charges*, which make the cost to polluters proportional to the amount of pollution caused. We will use the term "tax" to refer both to taxes and effluent charges.

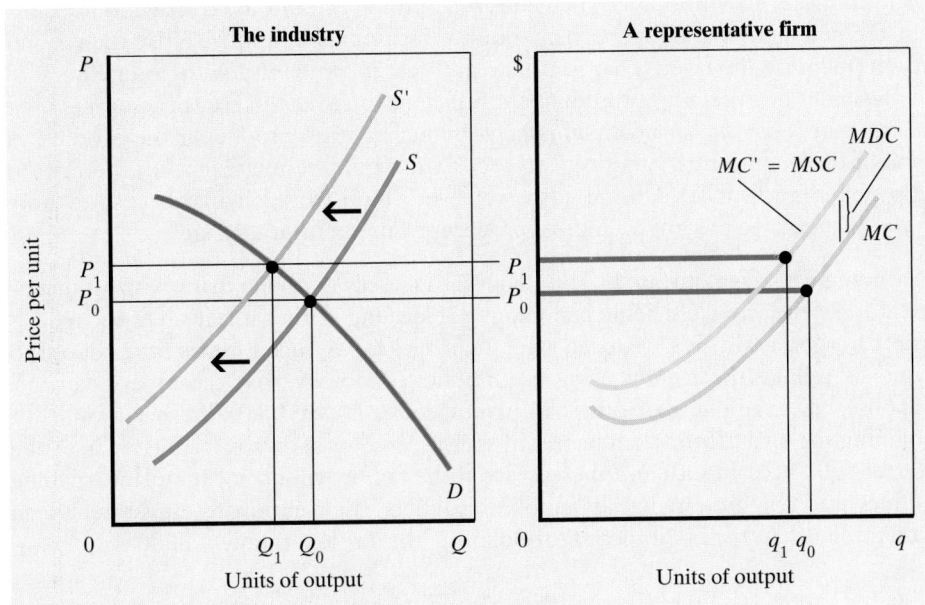

FIGURE 16.3

Tax Imposed on a Firm Equal to Marginal Damage Cost

If a per unit tax exactly equal to marginal damage costs is imposed on a firm, the firm will weigh the tax, and thus the damage costs, in its decisions. At the new equilibrium price, P_1, consumers will be paying an amount sufficient to cover full resource costs as well as the cost of damage imposed. q_1 is the efficient level of output for the firm.

to the left, driving up price from P_0 to P_1. The efficient level of output is q_1, where $P = MC'$. (Recall our general equilibrium analysis from Chapter 12.)

Because a profit-maximizing firm equates price with marginal cost, the new price to consumers now covers both the resource costs of producing the product and the damage costs. The consumer-decision process is now once again efficient at the margin, because marginal social benefit as reflected in market price is equal to the full marginal cost of the product.

Measuring Damages   The biggest problem with this approach is that damages must be estimated in financial terms. For the detergent plant polluting the nearby river to be properly taxed, the government must evaluate the damages done to residents downstream in money terms. This is a difficult, but not impossible, task. When legal remedies are pursued, judges are forced to make such estimates as they decide on compensation to be paid. Surveys of "willingness to pay," studies of property values in affected versus nonaffected areas, and sometimes the market value of recreational activities can provide basic data.

The monetary value of damages to health and loss of life is, naturally, much more difficult to estimate, and any measurement of such losses is certainly controversial. But even here, policy makers frequently make judgments that implicitly set values on life and health. Tens of thousands of deaths and millions of serious injuries result from traffic accidents in the United States every year, yet Americans are unwilling to give up driving or to reduce the speed limit to 40 miles per hour—the costs of either course of action would be too high. Indeed, in response to public demand, Congress in 1987 passed legislation to allow states to increase the speed limit to 65 miles per hour on rural parts of interstate highways. If most Americans are willing to increase the risk of death in exchange for shorter driving times, the value we place on life clearly has its limits.

It is important to note that taxing externality-producing activities may not eliminate damages. Taxes on these activities are not designed to eliminate externalities; they are simply meant to force decision makers to consider the full costs of their decisions. Even if we assume that a tax correctly measures all the damage done, the decision maker may find it advantageous to continue causing the damage. For example, the detergent manufacturer may find it most profitable simply to pay the tax and go on polluting the river. That is, it may find that it can continue to pollute because the revenues from selling its product are sufficient to cover the cost of resources used *and to compensate the damaged parties fully.* In such a case, producing the product in spite of the pollution is "worth it" to society. It would be inefficient for the firm to stop polluting. Only if damage costs were very high would it make sense to stop. Thus, you can see the importance of proper measurement of damage costs.

Reducing Damages to an Efficient Level   Taxes also provide firms with an incentive to use the most efficient technology for dealing with damage. If a tax reflects true damages, and if it is reduced when damages are reduced, firms may choose to avoid or reduce the tax by using a different technology that causes less damage. Suppose, for example, that our soap manufacturer is taxed $10,000 per month for polluting the river. If the soap plant can ship its waste to a disposal site elsewhere at a cost of $7000 per month and thereby avoid the tax, it will do so. If a plant belching sulfides into the air can install "smoke scrubbers" that eliminate emissions for an amount less than the tax imposed for polluting the air, it certainly will do so.

The Incentive to Take Care and to Avoid Harm   It is important to note that all externalities involve at least two parties and that it is not always clear which party is "causing" the damage. Take our friends Harry and Jake. Harry enjoys music; Jake enjoys quiet. If Harry plays his music, he imposes a cost on Jake. If Jake can force Harry to stop listening to music, he imposes a cost on Harry.

Often, the best solution to an externality problem may not involve stopping the externality-generating activity. Suppose, for example, that Jake and Harry's dormitory has a third resident, Pete. Pete hates silence and loves bluegrass music. The brilliant Resident Advisor on Harry's floor arranges for Pete and Jake to switch rooms. What was once an external cost has been transformed into an external benefit. Everyone is better off. Harry and Pete get to listen to music, and Jake gets the silence he craves.

Sometimes, then, the most efficient solution to an externality problem is for the damaged party to avoid the damage. But if full compensation is paid by the damager, damaged parties may have no incentive to do so. Take, for example, a laundry located next to the exhaust fans from the kitchen of a Chinese restaurant. Suppose damages run to $1000 per month because the laundry must use special air filters in its dryers so that the clothes will not smell of Szechuan spices. The laundry looks around and finds a perfectly good alternative location away from the restaurant that rents for only $500 per month above its current rent. Without any compensation from the Chinese restaurant, the laundry will move and the total damage will be the $500 per month extra rent that it must pay. But if the restaurant compensates the laundry for damages of $1000 a month, why should the laundry move? Under these conditions, a move is unlikely, even though it would be efficient.

Subsidizing External Benefits Sometimes activities or decisions generate external benefits instead of costs, as in the case of Harry and Pete. Real estate investment provides another example. When I fix up my house, I am the primary beneficiary, but those in my neighborhood also gain. Not only does my place look nicer, but the street also becomes more stable, and that is a social benefit. Investors who revitalize a downtown area—an old theater district in a big city, for example—provide benefits to many people, both in the city and in surrounding areas.

Activities that provide such external social benefits may be subsidized at the margin to give decision makers an incentive to consider them. Just as ignoring social costs can lead to inefficient decisions, so too can ignoring social benefits. Government subsidies for housing and other development, either directly through specific expenditure programs or indirectly through tax exemptions and abatements, have been justified on such grounds.

BARGAINING AND NEGOTIATION In a notable article written in 1960, Ronald Coase pointed out that the government need not be involved in every case of externality.[3] Taxes and subsidies would be irrelevant in the case of Harry and Jake, for example. Coase argued that private bargains and negotiations are likely to lead to an efficient solution in many social damage cases without any government involvement at all. This argument is referred to as the **Coase theorem.**

For Coase's solution to work, three conditions must be satisfied. First, the basic rights at issue must be clearly understood. Either Harry has the right to play his stereo or Jake has the right to silence. These rights will probably be spelled out in dorm rules. Second, there must be no impediments to bargaining. Parties must be willing and able to discuss the issues openly and without cost. Third, only a few people can be involved. Serious problems can develop when one of the parties to a bargain is a large group of people, such as all the residents of a large town.

Coase theorem Under certain conditions, when externalities are present, private parties can arrive at the efficient solution without government involvement.

[3]See Ronald Coase, "The Problem of Social Cost," *Journal of Law and Economics* (1960).

For the sake of our example, let us say that all three of these conditions hold for Harry and Jake and that no room swap with someone like Pete is possible. The dorm rules establish basic rights in this case by specifying that during certain hours of the day, Harry has the right to play his stereo as loudly as he pleases. Returning to Figure 16.2 and our earlier discussion, suppose that under the rules Harry is free to choose any number of music-playing hours between zero and eight.

Because Harry is under no legal constraint to pay any attention to Jake's wishes, you might be tempted to think that he will ignore Jake and play his stereo for eight hours. (Recall that up to eight hours, the marginal benefits to Harry exceed the marginal costs that he must pay.) Jake is, however, willing to pay Harry to play his stereo less than eight hours. For the first hour of play, the marginal damage to Jake is $0.15, so Jake would be willing to pay Harry $0.15 in the first hour to have Harry turn off his stereo. The opportunity cost to Harry of playing the first hour is thus $0.15 plus the (constant) marginal private cost of $0.05, or $0.20. Since the marginal gain to Harry in the first hour is $0.50, Harry would not accept the bribe. Likewise, for hours two through five the marginal benefit to Harry exceeds the bribe that Jake would be willing to pay plus the marginal private cost.

After five hours, however, Jake is willing to pay $0.25 per hour to have Harry turn off his stereo. This means that the opportunity cost to Harry is $0.30. But after five hours the marginal benefit to Harry of another hour of listening to his stereo falls below $0.25. Harry will thus accept the bribe not to listen to his music in the sixth hour. Similarly, a bribe of $0.25 per hour is sufficient to have Harry not play the stereo in the seventh and eighth hours, and Jake would be willing to pay such a bribe. Five hours is thus the efficient amount of playing time. More hours or fewer hours reduces net total benefits to Harry and Jake.

Coase also pointed out that bargaining will bring the contending parties to the right solution regardless of where rights are initially assigned. For example, suppose that the dorm rules state that Jake has the right to silence. This being the case, Jake can go to the dorm administrators and have them enforce the rule. Now when Harry plays the stereo and Jake asks him to turn it off, Harry must comply.

Now the tables are turned. Accepting the dorm rules (as he must), Harry knocks on Jake's door. Jake's damages from the first hour are only $0.15. This means that if he were compensated by more than $0.15, he would allow the music to be played. Now the stage is set for bargaining. Harry gets $0.45 in net benefit from the first hour of playing the stereo ($0.50 minus private cost of $0.05). Thus, he is willing to pay up to $0.45 for the privilege. If there are no impediments to bargaining, money will change hands. Harry will pay Jake some amount between $0.15 and $0.45 and, just as before, the stereo will continue to play. Jake has, in effect, sold to Harry his right to have silence. As before, bargaining between the two parties will lead to five hours of stereo playing. At exactly five hours, Jake will stop taking compensation and tell Harry to turn the stereo off. (Look again at Figure 16.2 to see that this is true.)

Note that in both cases the offer of compensation might be made in some form other than cash. Jake may offer Harry goodwill, a favor or two, or the use of his Harley Davidson for an hour.

Coase's critics are quick to point out that the conditions required for bargaining to produce the efficient result are not always present. The biggest problem with Coase's system is also a common problem. Very often one party to a bargain is a large group of people, and our reasoning may be subject to a fallacy of composition.

Suppose, for example, that a power company in Pittsburgh is polluting the air. The damaged parties are the 100,000 people who live near the plant. For the sake of argument, let's assume that the plant has the right to pollute. The Coase theorem predicts that the people who are damaged by the smoke will get together and offer a bribe (just as Jake offered a bribe to Harry). If the bribe is sufficient to induce the power plant to stop polluting or reduce the pollutants with air scrubbers, then it will accept the bribe and cut down on the pollution. If it is not, the pollution will continue, but the firm will have weighed all the costs (just as Harry did when he continued to play the stereo) and the result will be efficient.

But not everyone will contribute to the bribe fund. First, each contribution is so small relative to the whole that no single contribution makes much of a difference. Thus, making a contribution may seem unimportant or unnecessary to some. Second, everyone gets to breath the cleaner air, whether he or she contributes to the bribe or not. Many people will not participate simply because they are not compelled to, and the private bargain breaks down—the bribe that the group comes up with will be less than the full damages unless everyone participates. (These two problems—the "drop-in-the-bucket" and the "free-rider"—are discussed more fully later in this chapter.) Thus, when the number of damaged parties is large, government taxes or regulation may be the only avenue to a remedy.

LEGAL RULES AND PROCEDURES   For bargaining to result in an efficient outcome, the initial assignment of rights must be clear to both parties. When rights are established by law, more often than not some mechanism to protect those rights is also built into law. In some cases where a nuisance exists, for example, there may be injunctive remedies. In such cases, the victim can go to court and ask for an **injunction** that forbids the damage-producing behavior from continuing. When the dorm rules specifically gave Jake the right to silence, his getting the dorm administrator to speak to Harry was something like getting an injunction.

> **injunction** A court order forbidding the continuation of behavior that leads to damages.

Injunctive remedies are irrelevant when the damage has already been done. Consider accidents, for example. If your leg has already been broken as the result of an automobile accident, enjoining the driver of the other car from drinking and driving won't work—it's already too late. In these cases, rights must be protected by **liability rules**—that is, rules that require A to compensate B for damages imposed. In theory, such rules are designed to do exactly the same thing that taxing a polluter is designed to do: provide decision makers with an incentive to weigh all the consequences, actual and potential, of their decisions. Just as taxes do not stop all pollution, liability rules do not stop all accidents.

> **liability rules** Laws that require A to compensate B for damages imposed.

The threat of liability actions, however, does induce people to take more care than they might otherwise take. Product liability is a good case in point. If a person is damaged in some way because a product is defective, the producing company is in most cases held strictly liable for the damages, even if the company took reasonable care in producing the product. Thus, producers have a powerful incentive to be careful. If consumers know they will be generously compensated for any damages, however, they may not have as powerful an incentive to be careful when using the product.

SELLING OR AUCTIONING POLLUTION RIGHTS   We have already established that not all externality-generating activities should be banned. Around the world, the private automobile has become the clearest example of an externality-generating activity whose benefits (many believe) outweigh its costs.

Many externalities are imposed when we drive our cars. First, congestion is an externality. When many of us decide to drive into the city at rush hour, each of us imposes costs on the rest of us. Even though the marginal "harm" imposed by any one driver is small, the sum total is a serious cost to all who spend hours in traffic jams. Second, most of the air pollution in the United States comes from automobiles. The problem is most evident in Los Angeles, where smog loaded with harmful emissions, mostly from cars, blankets the city virtually every day. Finally, driving increases the likelihood of accidents, raising insurance costs to all.

While we do not ignore these costs from the standpoint of public policy, we certainly have not banned driving. This is also true for many other forms of pollution. In many cases we have consciously opted to allow ocean dumping, river pollution, and air pollution within limits.

There is no question that the right to impose environmental externalities is beneficial to the parties causing the damage. In a sense, the right to dump in a river or pollute the air or the ocean can be thought of as a resource. Thinking of the privilege to dump in this way suggests an alternative mechanism for controlling pollution: selling or auctioning the pollution rights to the highest bidder. The Clean Air Act of 1990 takes this approach by strictly limiting the quantity of emissions from the nation's power plants. To minimize the initial cost of compliance and to distribute the burden fairly, each plant is issued tradable pollution rights. These rights can be sold at auction to those plants whose costs of compliance are highest. (For more details, see the Issues and Applications box titled "The Clean Air Act and Pollution Auctions.")

Another example of the selling of externality rights takes place in Singapore, where the right to buy a car is auctioned off each year. Despite very high taxes and the need for special permits to drive in downtown areas, the roads in Singapore have become quite congested. The government decided to limit the number of new cars on the road because the external costs associated with them (congestion and pollution) have become very high. With these limits imposed, the decision was made to distribute car-ownership rights to those who place the highest value on them. It seems likely that taxi drivers, trucking companies, bus lines, and traveling salespeople will buy the licenses, while families who drive for convenience instead of taking public transportation will find them too expensive.

Congestion and pollution are not the only externalities that Singapore's government takes seriously. In 1993, the fine for littering was $625, for failing to flush a public toilet $94, and for eating on a subway $312. In addition, 514 people were convicted in 1992 of illegally smoking in public.

DIRECT REGULATION OF EXTERNALITIES Taxes, subsidies, legal rules, and public auction are all methods of indirect regulation designed to induce firms and households to weigh the social costs and benefits of their actions. The actual size of the external cost/benefit depends on the reaction of households and firms to the incentives provided by the taxes, subsidies, and rules.

However, for obvious reasons, many externalities are too important to be regulated indirectly. These externalities must be regulated directly. For example, dumping cancer-causing chemicals into the ground near a public water supply is simply illegal, and those who do it can be prosecuted and sent to jail.

Direct regulation of externalities takes place on both the state and federal level. The Environmental Protection Agency is a federal agency established by an act of Congress in 1970. In addition, every state has a division or department charged with regulating activities that are likely to harm the environment. Since the 1960s, Congress has passed a number of pieces of legislation that set specific standards for permissible discharges into the air and water. But direct regulation of externalities is not imposed only when damages are severe; most airports in the United States have landing patterns and hours that are regulated by local governments to minimize aggravating noise.

THE CLEAN AIR ACT AND POLLUTION AUCTIONS

The Clean Air Act of 1990 imposed strict limits on the amount of pollution that the nation's largest power plants can generate. Instead of regulating each plant separately, the act sets aggregate limits and allocates to each plant a set of pollution "rights" that can be sold to other plants at auction. The polluters who find it most costly to clean up their emissions simply buy the right to pollute from plants that can more easily reduce emissions. Allowing the market to distribute the rights, some argue, will lead to a more efficient distribution of the costs of cleanup. The following excerpt describes the United States' first-ever pollution auction:

The Clean Air Act, first approved in 1970 and amended in 1990, was designed to reduce air pollution. Pictured here is an oil refinery at Lake Charles, Louisiana.

The Environmental Protection Agency's first auction of rights to pollute the air attracted more participants than had been expected and reaped $21 million…

At stake were more than 275,000 pollution allowances, each permitting a utility to emit a ton of sulfur dioxide, the chemical that causes acid rain. Under the 1990 Clean Air Act, the E.P.A. set strict "spot" emissions limits to take effect in 1995, covering 110 of the nation's largest, dirtiest power plants. Even stricter "advance" limits, applicable to about 800 plants, will take effect by the year 2000….

The act allows utilities that can reduce emissions below the permitted levels to sell the allowances they do not need to others that are having trouble meeting the limits. In the-

ory, market forces will encourage utilities that can cut pollution the most for the least investment in scrubbers or fuel changes to lead the way. That would allow the nation to shave billions of dollars off the cost of meeting pollution-reduction goals.…

Indeed, one utility that bid in the auction, the Illinois Power Company, has already stopped construction on a $350 million scrubber and begun in private deals to stockpile permits that it will use between 1995 and 2000. "The state requires us to meet emissions standards in the least costly way," said John Dewey, a spokesman for the Decatur, Ill., utility. "Using the permits will save us at least $250 million over

the next 20 years and save Illinois coal-mining jobs as well."…

One worry, currently running strongest in New York, is that Midwestern utilities blamed for pollution in the Adirondack Mountains will be able to avoid reductions in emissions by purchasing allowances from other regions. Such fears do not take into account the size of the reductions the Midwest must make, said Joseph Goffman, a staff lawyer for the Environmental Defense Fund, a Washington-based environmental group that has been a major backer of pollution trading.

Source: Barnaby J. Feder, "Sold: $21 Million of Air Pollution," *New York Times*, March 30, 1993.

Many criminal penalties and sanctions for violating environmental regulations are like the taxes imposed on polluters. Not all violations and crimes are stopped, but violators and criminals face "costs." For the outcome to be efficient, the penalties they expect to pay should reflect the damage their actions impose on society.

PUBLIC (SOCIAL) GOODS

Another source of market failure lies in the existence of **public goods,** often called **social,** or **collective, goods.** These kinds of goods represent a market failure because they have characteristics that make it difficult for the private sector to produce them profitably:

> **public goods (social or collective goods)** Goods or services that bestow collective benefits on members of society. Such goods are both nonrival in consumption and their benefits are nonexcludable.

> In an unregulated market economy with no government to see that they are produced, public goods would at best be produced in insufficient quantity and at worst not produced at all.

Public goods are defined by two closely related characteristics: They are nonrival in consumption and/or their benefits are nonexcludable.

A good is considered **nonrival in consumption** when A's consumption of it does not interfere with B's consumption of it. This means that the benefits of the goods are collective—they accrue to everyone. National defense, for instance, benefits us all. The fact that I am protected in no way detracts from the fact that you are protected; indeed, every citizen is protected just as much as every other citizen. If the air is cleaned up, my breathing that air does not interfere with your breathing it, nor (under ordinary circumstances) is that air used up as more people breathe it. Private goods, on the other hand, are *rival in consumption*—if I eat a hamburger, you cannot eat it too.

nonrival in consumption A characteristic of public goods: One person's enjoyment of the benefits of a public good does not interfere with another's consumption of it.

Goods can sometimes generate collective benefits and still be rival in consumption. This happens when crowding occurs. A park or a pool, for example, can accommodate many people at the same time, generating collective benefits for everyone. But when too many people crowd in on a hot summer day, they begin to interfere with each other's enjoyment. Beyond a certain level of use, the park or the pool becomes rival in consumption.

Most public goods are also **nonexcludable.** This means that once the good is produced, people cannot be excluded for any reason from enjoying its benefits. Once a national defense system is established, it protects everyone. When the police department sets up a successful crime-prevention program, everyone in town is less likely to be the victim of a crime.

nonexcludable A characteristic of most public goods: Once a good is produced, no one can be excluded from enjoying its benefits.

For a private profit-making firm to produce a good and make a profit, it must be able to withhold that good from those who do not pay. McDonald's can make money selling fish sandwiches only because you don't get the fish sandwich unless you pay for it first. If payment were voluntary, McDonald's would probably not be in business for long.

Let us consider a clever entrepreneur who decides to offer better police protection to the city of Metropolis. Careful, and we will assume correct, market research reveals that the citizens of Metropolis do indeed want high-quality protection and that they are willing to pay for it. Not everyone is willing to pay the same amount; some can afford more, others can afford less, and people have different preferences and different feelings about risk. Our entrepreneur nevertheless hires a sales force and begins to sell his service. Soon, however, he encounters a problem. Because his is a private company, payment is strictly voluntary, and he can't force anyone to pay. Payment for a hamburger is voluntary too, but a hamburger can be withheld for nonpayment. The good that our new firm is selling, however, is by nature a public good.

free-rider problem A problem intrinsic to public goods: Because people can enjoy the benefits of public goods whether they pay for them or not, they are usually unwilling to pay for them.

drop-in-the bucket problem A problem intrinsic to public goods: The good or service is usually so costly that its provision generally does not depend on whether or not any single person pays.

As a potential consumer of a public good, I face a dilemma. I want more police protection, and, let's say, I'm even willing to pay $50 a month for it. But nothing is contingent upon my payment. First, if the good is produced, the crime rate falls and all residents benefit; I get that benefit whether I pay for it or not. In other words, I get a free ride, and that is why this dilemma is called the **free-rider problem.** Second, my payment is very small relative to the amount that must be collected to provide the service. Thus, the amount of police protection actually produced will not be significantly affected by the amount that I contribute, or whether I contribute at all. This is appropriately called the **drop-in-the-bucket problem.**

The outcome is clear:

> A consumer acting in his or her own self-interest has no incentive to contribute voluntarily to the production of public goods. Some will feel a moral responsibility or social pressure to contribute, and those people indeed may do so. But the economic incentive is missing, and most people do not find room in their budgets for many voluntary payments.

Income Distribution as a Public Good?

In the next chapter, we add the issues of justice and equity to the matters of economic efficiency that we are considering here. There we explain that the government may wish to change the distribution of income that results from the operation of the unregulated market on the grounds that the distribution is not fair. Before we do so, however, we need to note that some economists have argued for redistribution of income on grounds that it generates benefits that are public.

For example, let us say that many members of U.S. society want to eliminate hunger in the United States. Suppose that you are willing to give $200 per year in exchange for the knowledge that people are not going to bed hungry. Many private charities in the United States use the money they raise to feed the poor. If you want to contribute to this activity, you can certainly do so privately, through charity. So why do we need government involvement?

To answer this question, we must first consider the benefits of eliminating hunger. First, it generates collective psychological benefits; simply knowing that people are not starving helps us sleep better. Second, eliminating hunger may reduce disease, and this in turn has a number of beneficial effects. People who are fit and strong are more likely to stay in school and to get and keep jobs. This reduces welfare claims and contributes positively to the economy. If people are less likely to get sick, insurance premiums for everyone will go down. Robberies may decline because fewer people are desperate for money. This means that all of us are less likely to be victims of crime, both now and in the future, and so on.

These are goals that members of society may very well want to achieve. But just as there is no economic incentive to contribute voluntarily to national defense, so there is no economic incentive to contribute to private causes. If hunger is eliminated, you benefit whether you contributed or not—the free-rider problem again. At the same time, poverty is a huge problem, and your contribution cannot possibly have any influence on the amount of national hunger—the drop-in-the-bucket problem again. Thus, the goals of income redistribution may be more like national defense than like a fish sandwich from McDonald's.

> If we accept the idea that redistributing income generates a public good, private endeavors may fail to do what we want them to do, and government involvement may be called for.

Public Provision of Public Goods

All societies, past and present, have had to face the problem of providing public goods. When members of society get together to form a government, they do so to provide themselves with goods and services that will not be provided if they act separately. Like any other good or service, a body of laws (or system of justice) is produced with labor, capital, and other inputs. Law and the courts yield social benefits, and they must be set up and administered by some sort of collective, cooperative effort. There are hundreds of other examples of pure public goods: national defense, police and fire protection, public health, and weather forecasting, to name just a few.

Notice that we are talking about public *provision,* not public *production.* Once the government decides what service it wants to provide, it often contracts with the private sector to produce the good. Much of the material for national defense is produced by private defense contractors. Highways, government offices, data processing services, and so forth are usually produced by private firms.

One of the immediate problems of public provision, is that it frequently leads to public dissatisfaction. It is easy to be angry at government. Part, but certainly not all, of the reason for this dissatisfaction lies in the nature of the goods that government provides. Firms that produce or sell private goods post a price—we can choose to buy any quantity that we want, or we can walk away without any. It makes no sense to get mad at a shoe store, because no one can force you to shop there.

You cannot shop for collectively beneficial public goods. When it comes to national defense, for example, the government must choose one and only one kind and quantity of (collective) output to produce. Because none of us can choose how much should be spent or on what, we are all dissatisfied. Even if the government does its job with reasonable efficiency, at any given time about half of us think that we have too much national defense and about half of us think that we have too little.

Optimal Provision of Public Goods

In a famous article first published in the early 1950s, Paul Samuelson demonstrated that there exists an *optimal,* or *most efficient,* level of output for every public good.[4] The discussion of the Samuelson solution that follows leads us straight to the thorny problem of how societies, as opposed to individuals, make choices.

SAMUELSON'S THEORY   An efficient economy is one that produces what people want. Private producers, whether competitors or monopolists, are constrained by the market demand for their products. If they can't sell their products for more than it costs to produce them, they are out of business. But, because private goods permit exclusion, firms can withhold their products until households pay. This contingency of delivery upon payment forces households to reveal something about their preferences. No one is forced to buy or not to buy, but if you want a product, you must pay for it. Buying a product at a posted price reveals that it is "worth" at least that amount to you and to everyone who buys it.

Market demand for a private good is simply the sum of the quantities that each household decides to buy. The diagrams in Figure 16.4 review the derivation of a market demand curve. Assume that society consists of two people, A and B. At a price of $1, A demands 9 units of the private good and B demands 13. Thus, market demand at a price of $1 is 22 units. If price were to rise to $3, A's demand would drop to 2 units and B's would drop to 9 units; market demand at a price of $3 is thus 11 units. The point here is that:

[4]Paul A. Samuelson, "Diagrammatic Exposition of a Theory of Public Expenditure," *Review of Economics and Statistics* XXXVII (1955).

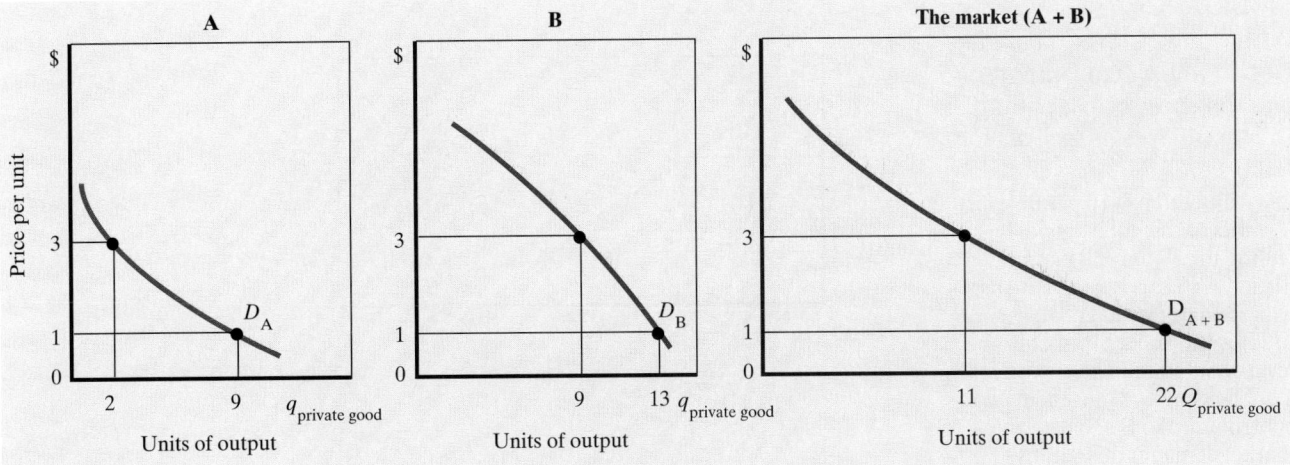

FIGURE 16.4

With Private Goods, Consumers Decide What Quantity to Buy; Market Demand
Is the Sum of Those Quantities at Each Price

At a price of $3, A buys 2 units and B buys 9 for a total of 11. At a price of $1, A buys 9 units
and B buys 13 for a total of 22. We all buy the quantity of each private good that we want.
Market demand is the horizontal sum of all individual demand curves.

> The price mechanism forces people to reveal what they want, and it forces firms to
> produce only what people are willing to pay for, but it works this way only because
> exclusion is possible.

People's preferences and demands for public goods are conceptually no different
than their preferences and demands for private goods. One may want fire protection and be willing to pay for it in the same way that one wants to listen to a CD.
To demonstrate that an efficient level of production exists, Samuelson assumes that
we know people's preferences. Figure 16.5 shows demand curves for buyers A and
B. If there were a market and the public good were available at a price of $6, A
would buy X_1 units. Or, put another way, A is willing to pay $6 per unit to obtain
X_1 units of the public good. B, on the other hand, is willing to pay only $3 per
unit to obtain X_1 units of the public good.

Remember, however, that public goods are nonrival—that benefits accrue
simultaneously to everyone. One, and only one, quantity can be produced, and
that is the amount that everyone gets. If X_1 units are produced, A gets X_1 and B
gets X_1. If X_2 units are produced, A gets X_2 and B gets X_2.

To arrive at market demand for public goods, then, we do not sum quantities.
Rather, *we add up the amounts that individual households are willing to pay for each
potential level of output.* In Figure 16.5 on the next page, A is willing to pay $6 per
unit for X_1 units and B is willing to pay $3 per unit for X_1 units. Thus, if society
consists only of A and B, society is willing to pay $9 per unit for X_1 units of public
good X. For X_2 units of output, society is willing to pay a total of $4 per unit.

In sum:

> For private goods, market demand is the horizontal sum of individual demand
> curves—we add the different *quantities* that households consume. For public goods,
> market demand is the vertical sum of individual demand curves—we add the differ-
> ent *amounts* that households are willing to pay to obtain each level of output.

FIGURE 16.5

With Public Goods, There Is Only *One* Level of Output, and Consumers Are Willing to Pay Different Amounts for Each Level

A is willing to pay $6 per unit for X_1 units of the public good. B is willing to pay only $3 per unit. Society—in this case A & B—is willing to pay a total of $9 per unit for the good. Since only one level of output can be chosen for a public good, we must add A's contribution to B's to determine market demand; this means adding demand curves vertically.

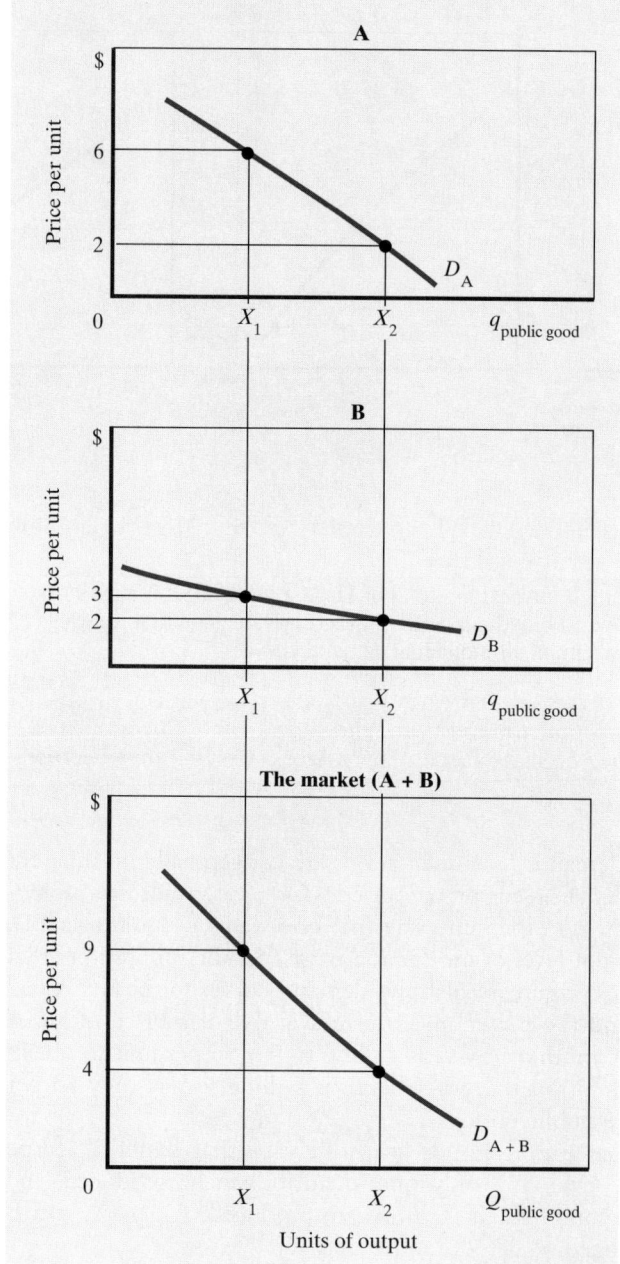

Samuelson argued that once we know how much society is willing to pay for a public good, we need only compare that amount to the cost of its production. Figure 16.6 reproduces A's and B's demand curves and the total demand curve for the public good. As long as society (in this case, A and B) is willing to pay more than the marginal cost of production, the good should be produced. If A is willing to pay $6 per unit of public good and B is willing to pay $3 per unit, society is willing to pay $9.

The efficient level of output here is X^* units. If at that level A is charged a fee of P_A per unit of X produced and B is charged a fee of P_B per unit of X, everyone should be happy. Resources are being drawn from the production of other goods and

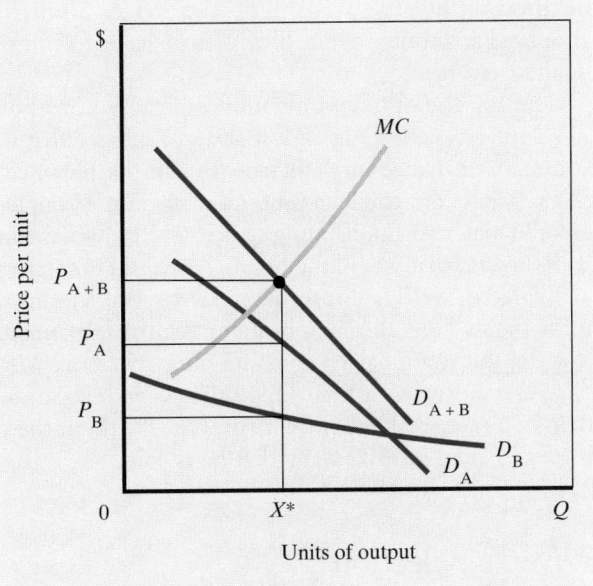

FIGURE 16.6
Optimal Production of a
Public Good

Optimal production of a public
good means producing as long as
society's total willingness to pay
per unit (D_{A+B}) is greater than
the marginal cost of producing
the good.

services only to the extent that people want the public good and are willing to pay for it. We have thus arrived at the **optimal level of provision for public goods.**

> At the optimal level, society's total willingness to pay per unit is equal to the marginal cost of producing the good.

THE PROBLEMS OF OPTIMAL PROVISION One major problem exists, however. To produce the optimal amount of each public good, the government must know something that it cannot possibly know—everyone's preferences. Because exclusion is impossible, nothing forces households to reveal their preferences. Furthermore, if we ask households directly about their willingness to pay, we run up against the same problem encountered by our "protection-services" salesman above. If my actual payment depends on my answer, I have an incentive to hide my true feelings. Knowing that I cannot be excluded from enjoying the benefits of the good and that my payment is not likely to have an appreciable influence on the level of output finally produced, what incentive do I have to tell the truth—or to contribute?

How, then, does society decide which public goods to provide? We assume that members of society want certain public goods. Private producers in the market cannot make a profit by producing these goods, and the government cannot obtain enough information to measure society's demands accurately. No two societies have dealt with this dilemma in precisely the same way. In some countries, dictators simply decide for the people. In others, representative political bodies speak for the people's preferences. In still others, people vote directly. None of these solutions works perfectly. We will return to the problem of social choice after discussing one more source of market failure.

optimal level of provision for a public good The level at which resources are drawn from the production of other goods and services only to the extent that people want the public good and are willing to pay for it. At this level, society's willingness to pay per unit is equal to the marginal cost of producing the good.

IMPERFECT INFORMATION

In Chapters 6 through 12, we assumed that households and firms possess complete information on products and inputs. To make informed choices among various goods and services available in the market, households must have full information on product quality, availability, and price. Similarly, to make sound judgments about what inputs to use, firms must have full information on input availability, quality, and price.

The absence of full information can cause households and firms to make mistakes. A voluntary exchange is almost always evidence that both parties benefit. Thus, most voluntary exchanges are efficient. But in the presence of imperfect information, not all exchanges are efficient. The most obvious example is fraud. Frank sells a bottle of colored water to Ed claiming that it will grow hair on Ed's bald head. Clearly, if Ed had known what was in the bottle, he would not have purchased it.

Firms as well as consumers can be the victims of incomplete or inaccurate information. Recall that a profit-maximizing competitive firm will hire workers as long as the marginal revenue product of labor (MRP_L) is greater than the wage rate. But how can a firm judge the *productivity* of a potential hire? Also, suppose that a worker steals from the firm. Clearly, then, the cost of employing that worker is greater than just the wage that he is paid.

Adverse Selection

adverse selection Can occur when a buyer or seller enters into an exchange with another party who has more information.

The problem of **adverse selection** can occur when a buyer or seller enters into an exchange with another party who has more information. Suppose, for example, that there are only two types of workers: lazy workers and hard workers. Each worker knows which she is, but employers cannot tell. If there is only one wage rate, lazy workers will be overpaid relative to their productivity and hard workers will be underpaid. Recall that workers weigh the value of leisure and nonmarket production against the wage in deciding whether to enter the labor force. Since hard workers will end up underpaid relative to their productivity, fewer hard workers than is optimal will be attracted into the labor force. Similarly, since lazy workers are overpaid relative to their productivity, more of them will be attracted into the labor force than is optimal. Hence, the market has selected among workers adversely.

The classic case of adverse selection is the used car market. Suppose that owners (potential sellers) of used cars have all the information about the real quality of their cars. To simplify matters, suppose further that half of all used cars are "lemons" (bad cars) and that half are "cherries" (good cars). Suppose further that consumers (potential used car buyers) are willing to pay $6000 for a cherry but only $2000 for a lemon.

If half the cars for sale were lemons and half were cherries, the market price of a car would be about $4000, and consumers would have a 50-50 chance of getting a lemon. But there is an adverse selection problem because of unequal information: Used car *sellers* know whether they have a lemon or a cherry while used car *buyers* do not. Lemon owners know that they are making out like bandits by selling at $4000, while cherry owners know that they are not getting what their car is really worth. Thus, more lemon owners are attracted into selling their cars than are cherry owners.

Over time, buyers come to understand that the probability of getting a lemon is greater than the probability of getting a cherry, and the price of used cars drops. This, of course, makes matters worse because it provides even less incentive for cherry owners to sell their cars. This process will continue until only lemons are left in the market. Once again, the unequal information leads to an adverse selection.[5]

---

[5]This discussion is based on a classic article by George Akerlof, "The Market for 'Lemons': Quality, Uncertainty, and the Market Mechanism," *Quarterly Journal of Economics* 84 (August 1970), pp. 488–500.

Adverse selection is also a problem in insurance markets. Insurance companies insure people against risks like health problems or accidents. Individuals know more about their own health than anyone else, even with required medical exams. If medical insurance rates are set at the same level for everyone, then medical insurance is a better deal for those who are unhealthy than for those who are healthy and likely never to have a claim. This means that more unhealthy people will buy insurance, which forces insurance companies to raise premiums. As with used cars, fewer healthy people and more unhealthy people will end up with insurance.

Moral Hazard

Another information problem that arises frequently in insurance markets is *moral hazard*. Often, people enter into contracts in which the result of the contract at least in part depends upon the future behavior of one of the parties. A **moral hazard** problem arises when one party to a contract passes the cost of his or her behavior on to the other party to the contract. For example, accident insurance policies are contracts that agree to pay for repairs to your car if it is damaged in an accident. Whether you have an accident or not in part depends on whether you drive cautiously. Similarly, apartment leases may specify that the landlord perform routine maintenance around the apartment. If you decide to kick the door every time you come into the house or punch the wall every time you get angry, your landlord ultimately pays the repair bill.

> **moral hazard** Arises when one party to a contract passes the cost of his or her behavior on to the other party to the contract.

Such contracts can lead to inefficient behavior. The problem is very much like the externality problem in which firms and households have no incentive to consider the full costs of their behavior. If my car is fully insured against theft, why should I lock it? If visits to the dentist are free under my dental insurance plan, why not get my teeth cleaned six times a year?

Like adverse selection, the moral hazard problem is an information problem. Contracting parties cannot always determine the future behavior of the person with whom they are contracting. If all future behavior could be predicted, contracts could be written to try to eliminate undesirable behavior. Sometimes this is possible. Life insurance companies do not pay off in the case of suicide. Fire insurance companies will not write a policy unless you have smoke detectors. If you cause unreasonable damage to an apartment, your landlord can retain your security deposit.

Nonetheless:

> It is impossible to know everything about behavior and intentions. If a contract absolves one party of the consequences of his or her actions, and people act in their own self-interest, the result is inefficient.

Market Solutions

Imperfect information violates one of the assumptions of perfect competition, but not all information problems are market failures. In fact, information is itself valuable, and there is an incentive for competitive producers to produce it. As with any other good, there is an efficient quantity of information production.

Often, information is produced by consumers and producers themselves. The information-gathering process is called *market search*. When we go shopping for a "good buy" or for the "right" sweater, we are collecting the information that we need to make an informed choice. Just as products are produced as long as the marginal benefit from additional output exceeds the marginal cost of production, consumers have an incentive to continue searching out information until the expected marginal benefit from an additional hour of search is equal to the cost of that additional hour. After I've looked in 11 different stores that sell sweaters, I know a great deal about the quality and prices available. Continuing to look takes up valuable time and effort that could be used doing other things. In shopping for a house or a car, I may spend much more time and effort searching out information than I might for a sweater since the potential benefits (or losses) are much greater.

Firms also spend time and resources searching for information. Potential employers ask for letters of reference, resumes, and interviews before offering employment. Market research helps firms respond to consumer preferences. It should come as no surprise to you that the general rule is:

> Like consumers, profit-maximizing firms will gather information as long as the marginal benefits from continued search are greater than the marginal costs of engaging in it.

Many firms produce information for consumers and businesses. *Consumer Reports* is a magazine that tests consumer products and sells the results in the form of a periodical. Credit bureaus keep track of people's credit histories and sell credit reports to firms who need them to evaluate potential credit customers. "Head-hunting" firms collect information and search out applicants for jobs. Real estate agents and independent insurance agents are paid to represent people in those markets.

The point of all this is simple: Because the market handles many information problems efficiently, we don't need to assume perfect information to arrive at an efficient allocation of resources. However, some information problems are not handled well by the market.

Government Solutions

One of the most important characteristics of information is that it is essentially a public good. If a set of test results on the safety of various products is produced, my having access to that information in no way reduces the value of that information to others. In other words, information is nonrival in consumption. When information is very costly for individuals to collect and disperse, it may be cheaper for government to produce it once for everybody.

In many cases, the government has set up special administrative agencies to ensure that accurate information reaches the public. As we noted in Chapter 15, the Federal Trade Commission was established by Congress in 1914 specifically to deal with unfair and deceptive trade practices. The FTC regulates advertising, sets standards for disclosure of contents, and so forth. The Consumer Products Safety Commission sets standards of safety for potentially unsafe products. The Food and Drug Administration regulates the content of foods and drugs that are permitted on the market. It is not legal to sell a drug that has not been demonstrated to be effective. In addition, many state governments have passed "lemon laws" that grant car buyers certain rights in case they end up with a troublesome car.

One view of government, or the public sector, holds that it exists to provide things that "society wants." A society is a collection of individuals, and each individual has a unique set of preferences. Defining "what society wants," therefore, becomes a problem of **social choice**—of somehow adding up, or aggregating, individual preferences.

It is also important to understand, however, that government is made up of individuals—politicians and government workers—whose *own* objectives in part determine what government does. To understand government, then, we must understand the incentives facing politicians and public servants, as well as the difficulties of aggregating the preferences of the members of a society.

social choice The problem of deciding what society wants. The process of adding up individual preferences to make a choice for society as a whole.

The Voting Paradox

Democratic societies use ballot procedures to determine aggregate preferences and to make the social decisions that follow from them. If all votes could be unanimous, efficient decisions would be guaranteed. Unfortunately, unanimity is virtually impossible to achieve when hundreds of millions of people, each with his or her own different preferences, are involved.

The most common social decision-making mechanism is majority rule. But this system is far from perfect. In a well-known work published in 1951, Kenneth Arrow proved what has come to be called the **impossibility theorem.**[6] Arrow has shown that it is impossible to devise a voting scheme that respects individual preferences and gives consistent, nonarbitrary results.

One example of a seemingly irrational result emerging from majority-rule voting is the voting paradox. Suppose that, faced with a decision about the future of the institution, the president of a major university opts to let her three top administrators vote on the following options: Should the university (1) increase the number of students and hire more faculty, (2) maintain the current size of the faculty and student body, or (3) cut back on faculty and reduce the student body? Figure 16.7 represents the preferences of the three administrators diagrammatically.

The vice president for finance (VP1) wants growth. He prefers A to B and B to C. The vice president for development (VP2), however, doesn't want to rock the boat. She prefers maintaining the current size of the institution, option B, to either

impossibility theorem A proposition demonstrated by Kenneth Arrow which shows that no system of aggregating individual preferences into social decisions will always yield consistent, nonarbitrary results.

---

[6] Kenneth Arrow, *Social Choice and Individual Values* (New York: Wiley, 1951).

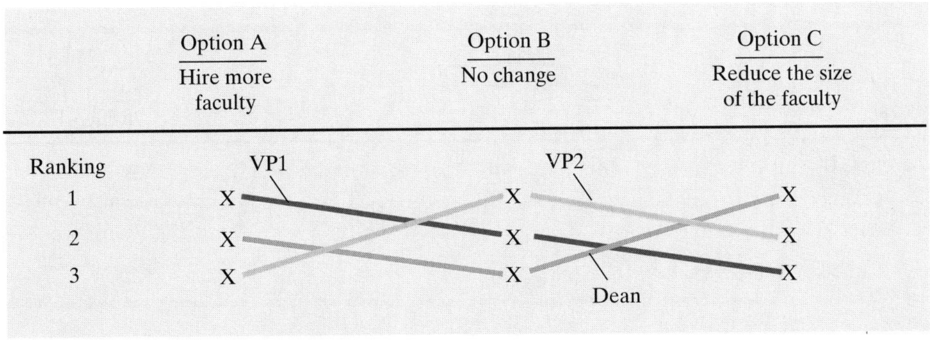

	Option A Hire more faculty		Option B No change		Option C Reduce the size of the faculty
Ranking	VP1		VP2		
1	X		X		X
2	X		X		X
3	X		X		X
			Dean		

FIGURE 16.7
Preferences of Three Top University Officials

VP1 prefers A to B and B to C. VP2 prefers B to C and C to A. The Dean prefers C to A and A to B.

of the others. If the status quo is out of the question, she would prefer option C. The dean believes in change; he wants to shake the place up, and he doesn't care whether that means increase or decrease. He prefers C to A and A to B.

Table 16.1 shows the results of the vote. When the three vote on A versus B, they vote in favor of A—that is, to increase the size of the university rather than keep it the same size. VP1 and the dean outvote VP2. Voting on B and C produces a victory for option B; two of the three would rather hold the line than decrease the size of the institution. After two votes we have the result that A (increase) is preferred to B (no change) and that B (no change) is preferred to C (decrease).

The problem arises when we then have the three vote on A against C. Both VP2 and the dean vote for C, giving it the victory; C is actually preferred to A. But if A beats B, and B beats C, how can C beat A? The results are inconsistent.

The **voting paradox** illustrates several points. Most important is the fact that when preferences for public goods differ across individuals, any system for adding up, or aggregating, those preferences can lead to inconsistencies. In addition, it illustrates just how much influence the person who sets the agenda has. If a vote had been taken on A and C first, the first two votes might never have occurred. This is why rules committees in both houses of Congress have enormous power; they establish the rules under which and the order in which legislation will be considered.

Another problem with majority-rule voting is that it leads to **logrolling.** Logrolling occurs when representatives trade votes—D helps get a majority in favor of E's program, and in exchange E helps D get a majority on her program. It is not clear whether any bill could get through any legislature without logrolling. Neither is it clear whether logrolling is, on balance, a good thing or a bad thing from the standpoint of efficiency. On the one hand, a program that benefits one region or group of people might generate enormous net social gains, but because the group of beneficiaries is fairly small, it will not command a majority of delegates. If another bill that is likely to generate large benefits to another area is also awaiting a vote, a trade of support between the two sponsors of the bills should result in the passage of two good pieces of efficient legislation. On the other hand, logrolling can also turn out unjustified, inefficient, "pork barrel" legislation.

A number of other problems also follow from voting as a mechanism for public choice. For one thing, voters do not have much of an incentive to become well informed. When you go out to buy a car or, on a smaller scale, a CD player, you are the one who suffers the full consequences of a bad choice. Similarly, you are the beneficiary of the gains from a good choice. Not so in voting. One person's vote is not likely to determine whether a bad choice or a good choice is made.

voting paradox A simple demonstration of how majority-rule voting can lead to seemingly contradictory and inconsistent results. A commonly cited illustration of the kind of inconsistency described in the impossibility theorem.

logrolling Occurs when congressional representatives trade votes, agreeing to help each other get certain pieces of legislation passed.

TABLE 16.1
Results of Voting on University's Plans: The Voting Paradox

	VOTES OF:			
VOTE	VP1	VP2	DEAN	RESULT*
A versus B	A	B	A	A wins: A > B
B versus C	B	B	C	B wins: B > C
C versus A	A	C	C	C wins: C > A

*A > B is read "A is preferred to B."

Although many of us feel that we have a civic responsibility to vote, no one really believes that his or her vote will actually determine the outcome of an election. The time and effort it takes just to get to the polls is enough to deter many people. Becoming informed involves even more costs, and it is not surprising that many people do not do it.

But beyond the fact that a single vote is not likely to be decisive is the fact that the costs and benefits of wise and unwise social choices are widely shared. If the congressman that I elect makes a bad mistake and wastes a billion dollars, I bear only a small fraction of that cost. It may be that the direct consequences of a vote are so widely shared and seem so remote that voters perceive them to be extremely small or zero. Thus, even though the sums involved are large in aggregate, individual voters find little incentive to become informed.

Two additional problems with voting are that choices are almost always limited to *bundles* of publicly provided goods, and we vote infrequently. Most of us vote for Republicans or Democrats. We vote for President only every four years. We elect senators for six-year terms. In private markets, we can look at each item separately and decide how much of each we want. We also can shop daily. In the public sector, though, we vote for a platform or a party that takes a particular position on a whole range of issues. In the public sector it is very difficult, or impossible, for voters to unbundle issues.

There is, of course, a reason why bundling occurs in the sphere of public choice. It is difficult enough to convince people to go to the polls once a year. If we voted separately on every appropriation bill, we would spend our lives at the polls. This is in fact one reason for representative democracy. We elect officials who we hope will become informed and represent our interests and preferences.

Government Inefficiency

Recent work in economics has focused not just on the government as an extension of individual preferences but also on government officials as people with their own agendas and objectives. That is, government officials are assumed to maximize their own utility, not the social good. To understand the way government functions, we need to look less at the preferences of individual members of society and more at the incentive structures that exist around public officials.

One group of officials that we seem to worry about constantly are the people who run government agencies—the Social Security Administration, the Department of Housing and Urban Development, and state registries of motor vehicles, for example. What incentive do these people have to produce a good product and to be efficient? Might such incentives be lacking?

In the private sector, where firms compete for profits, only efficient firms producing goods that consumers will buy survive. If a firm is inefficient—that is, if it is producing at a higher-than-necessary cost—the market will drive it out of business. This is not necessarily so in the public sector. If a government bureau is producing a necessary service, or one mandated by law, it does not need to worry about customers. No matter how bad the service is at the registry of motor vehicles, everyone with a car must buy its product.

The efficiency of a government agency's internal structure depends on the way incentives facing workers and agency heads are structured. If the budget allocation of an agency is based on the last period's spending alone, for example, agency heads have a clear incentive to spend more money, however inefficiently. This point is not lost on government officials, who have experimented with many ways of rewarding agency heads and employees for cost-saving suggestions.

But critics point out that such efforts to reward productivity and punish inefficiency are rarely successful. It is difficult to punish, let alone dismiss, a government employee. Elected officials are subject to recall, but it usually takes gross negligence to rouse voters into instituting such a measure. And elected officials are rarely associated with problems of bureaucratic mismanagement, which they decry on a daily basis.

Critics of "the bureaucracy" argue that no set of internal incentives can ever match the discipline of the market, and they point to studies of private versus public garbage collection, airline operations, fire protection, mail service, and so forth, all of which suggest significantly lower costs in the private sector. Indeed, one of the major themes of the Reagan and Bush administrations was "privatization." According to this argument, if the private sector can possibly provide a service, it is likely to do so more efficiently. When this is the case, the public sector should allow the private sector to take over.

One concern regarding wholesale privatization is the potential effect it may have on distribution. Late in his administration, for example, President Reagan suggested that the federal government sell its entire stock of public housing to the private sector. But would the private sector continue to provide housing to poor people? The worry is that it would not, because it may not be profitable to do so.

Like voters, public officials suffer from a lack of incentive to become fully informed and to make tough choices. Consider, for example, an elected official. If the real objective of an elected official is to get reelected, then his or her real incentive must be to provide visible goods for his or her constituency while hiding the costs or spreading them thin. Self-interest may thus easily lead to poor decisions and public irresponsibility.

Rent Seeking Revisited

Another problem with public choice is that special-interest groups can and do spend resources to influence the legislative process. As we said before, individual voters have little incentive to become well informed and to participate fully in the legislative process. But favor-seeking special-interest groups have a great deal of incentive to participate in political decision making. We saw in Chapter 13 that a monopolist should be willing to pay a substantial amount to prevent competition from eroding its economic profits. Many—if not all—industries lobby for favorable treatment, softer regulation, or antitrust exemption. This behavior, as you recall, is called *rent seeking*.

In fact, rent seeking extends far beyond those industries that lobby for government help in preserving monopoly powers. Any group that benefits from a government policy has an incentive to use its resources to lobby for that policy. Farmers lobby for farm subsidies, oil producers lobby for oil import taxes, the American Association of Retired Persons lobbies against cuts in social security, and so forth.

In the absence of well-informed and active voters, special-interest groups assume an important and perhaps a critical role. But there is another side to this story. Some have argued that favorable legislation is, in effect, for sale in the marketplace. Those willing and able to pay the most are more successful in accomplishing their goals than those with fewer resources.

GOVERNMENT FAILURE The point of the preceding sections is simple:

> Theory may well suggest that unregulated markets fail to produce an efficient allocation of resources. But this should not lead you to the conclusion that government involvement necessarily leads to efficiency. There are good reasons to believe that government attempts to produce the right goods and services in the right quantities efficiently may also fail.

GOVERNMENT AND THE MARKET

There is no question that government must be involved in both the provision of public goods and the control of externalities. While the argument is less clear-cut, a strong case can also be made for government actions to increase the flow of information. No society has ever existed in which citizens did not get together to protect themselves from the abuses of an unrestrained market and to provide for themselves certain goods and services that the market did not provide. The question is not *whether* we need government involvement. The question is *how much* and *what kind* of government involvement we should have.

Critics of government involvement correctly point out that the existence of an "optimal" level of public-goods production does not guarantee that governments will achieve it. In fact, it is easy to show that governments will generally fail to achieve the most efficient level. Nor is there any reason to believe that governments are capable of achieving the "correct" amount of control over externalities or dispersing the proper information to all those who need it. Markets do indeed fail to produce an efficient allocation of resources, but governments also fail for a number of reasons.

1. Measurement of social damages and benefits is difficult and imprecise. For example, estimates of the costs of acid rain range from practically nothing to incalculably high amounts.
2. There is no precise mechanism through which citizens' preferences for public goods can be correctly determined. All voting systems lead to inconsistent results. Samuelson's optimal solution works only if each individual in a society pays in accordance with his or her own preferences. Since this is impossible under our system, we all must be taxed to pay for the mix of public goods that the imperfect voting mechanism grants us.
3. Because government agencies are not subject to the discipline of the market, we have little reason to expect that they will be efficient producers. The amount of waste, corruption, and inefficiency in government is a hotly debated issue. Although government is not subjected to the discipline of the market, it must, however, submit to the discipline of the press, tight budgets, and the opinion of the voters.
4. Both elected and appointed officials have needs and preferences of their own, and it is naive to expect them to act selflessly for the good of society (even if they know what would be best for society). Bureaucrats in the Department of Defense, for example, have a clear incentive to increase the size of their budgets, and elected officials rely heavily on those same bureaucrats for information.

Just as critics of government involvement concede that the market fails to achieve full efficiency, defenders of government must acknowledge government's failures. Nonetheless, defenders of government involvement respond that we get closer to an efficient allocation of resources by trying to control externalities and by doing our best to produce the public goods (including information) that people want with the imperfect tools we have than we would by leaving everything to the market.

SUMMARY

Externalities and Environmental Economics

1. Often when we engage in transactions or make economic decisions, second or third parties suffer consequences that decision makers have no incentive to consider. These are called *externalities*. A classic example of an external cost is pollution.

2. When external costs are not considered in economic decisions, we may engage in activities or produce products that are not "worth it." When external benefits are not considered, we may fail to do things that are indeed "worth it." The result is an inefficient allocation of resources.

3. A number of alternative mechanisms have been used to control externalities: (1) government-imposed taxes and subsidies, (2) private bargaining and negotiations, (3) legal remedies such as *injunctions* and *liability rules,* (4) the sale or auctioning of rights to impose externalities, and (5) direct regulation.

Public (Social) Goods

4. In a free market, certain goods and services that people want will not be produced in adequate amounts. These *public goods* have characteristics that make it difficult or impossible for the private sector to produce them profitably.

5. Public goods are *nonrival in consumption;* their benefits fall collectively on members of society or on groups of members. It is generally impossible to exclude people from enjoying the benefits of public goods for not paying. An important example of a public good is national defense.

6. One of the major problems of public provision is that it leads to public dissatisfaction. We can choose any quantity of private goods that we want, or we can walk away without buying any. When it comes to public goods such as national defense, however, the government must choose one and only one kind and quantity of (collective) output to produce.

7. Theoretically, there exists an *optimal level of provision for each public good*. At this level, society's willingness to pay per unit equals the marginal cost of producing the good. To discover such a level, however, we would need to know the preferences of each individual citizen.

Imperfect Information

8. Choices made in the presence of imperfect information may not be efficient. In the face of incomplete information, consumers and firms may encounter the problem of *adverse selection*. When buyers or sellers enter into market exchanges with other parties who have more information, low-quality goods are exchanged in greater numbers than high-quality goods. *Moral hazard* arises when one party to a contract passes the cost of his or her behavior on to the other party to the contract. If a contract absolves one party of the consequences of his or her actions, and people act in their own self-interest, the result is inefficient.

9. In many cases, the market provides solutions to information problems. Profit-maximizing firms will continue to gather information as long as the marginal benefits from continued search are greater than the marginal costs of engaging in it. Consumers will follow a similar process: More time is afforded to the information search for larger decisions. In other cases, government must be called on to collect and disperse information to the public.

Social Choice

10. Because there is no way to know everyone's preferences about public goods, we are forced to rely on imperfect *social choice* mechanisms, such as majority rule.

11. The theory that suggests that free markets do not achieve an efficient allocation of resources should not lead one to conclude that government involvement necessarily leads to efficiency. Governments also fail demonstrably.

Government and the Market

12. Defenders of government involvement in the economy acknowledge its failures but believe that we get closer to an efficient allocation of resources with government than we would without it. By trying to control externalities and by doing the best we can to provide the public goods that society wants, we do better than we would if we left everything to the market.

REVIEW TERMS AND CONCEPTS

adverse selection 416
Coase theorem 405
drop-in-the-bucket problem 410
externality 397
free-rider problem 410
impossibility theorem 419
injunction 407

liability rules 407
logrolling 420
marginal damage cost (*MDC*) 402
marginal private cost (*MPC*) 402
marginal social cost (*MSC*) 400
market failure 396
moral hazard 417

nonexcludable 410
nonrival in consumption 410
optimal level of provision for
  public goods 415
public goods (social or collective goods) 409
social choice 419
voting paradox 420

PROBLEM SET

1. "If government imposes on the firms in a polluting industry penalties (taxes) that exceed the actual value of the damages done by the pollution, the result is an inefficient and unfair imposition of costs on those firms and on the consumers of their products." Discuss. Using the diagrams in Figure 16.3, show how consumers end up bearing the burden of the penalties.

2. Suppose that a city decides to sponsor a free concert series in a public park surrounded by high-rise apartment buildings. The city's economist endorses the concerts on the grounds that they will provide a number of external public benefits.

    a. Explain his logic. Would you support such a series? Could the concerts have been sponsored by the private sector?

    b. The people who reside in the buildings surrounding the park object on the grounds that an external cost is being imposed on them. How would you go about resolving the conflict? What information would you need?

3. It has been argued that the following are examples of "mixed goods." They are essentially private but partly public. For each, describe the private and public components and discuss briefly why the government should or should not be involved in their provision.

    a. Elementary and secondary education
    b. Higher education
    c. Medical care
    d. Air traffic control

4. A paper factory dumps polluting chemicals into the Snake River. Thousands of citizens live along the river, and they bring suit claiming damages. You are asked by the judge to testify at the trial as an impartial expert. The court is considering four possible solutions, and you are asked to comment on the potential efficiency and equity of each. Your testimony should be brief.

    a. Deny the merits of the case and simply affirm the polluter's right to dump. The parties will achieve the optimal solution without government.

    b. Find in favor of the plaintiff. The polluters will be held liable for damages and must fully compensate citizens for all past and future damages imposed.

    c. Order an immediate end to the dumping. No damages awarded.

    d. Refer the matter to the Environmental Protection Agency, which will impose a tax on the factory equal to the marginal damage costs. Proceeds will not be paid to the damaged parties.

5. Explain why you agree or disagree with each of the following statements:

    a. The government should be involved in providing housing for the poor because housing is a "public good."

    b. From the standpoint of economic efficiency, an unregulated market economy tends to overproduce public goods.

6. Society is made up of two individuals whose demands for public good X are given in Figure 1. Assuming that the public good can be produced at a constant marginal cost of $6, what is the optimal level of output? How much would you charge A? B?

7. Government involvement in general scientific research has been justified on the grounds that advances in knowledge are public goods—once produced, information can be shared at virtually no cost. A new production technology in an industry could be made available to all firms, reducing costs of production, thus driving down price and benefiting the public. The patent system, however, allows private producers of "new knowledge" to *exclude* others from enjoying the benefits of that knowledge. Inventors would have little incentive to produce new knowledge if there were no possibility of profiting from their inventions. If one company holds exclusive rights to an advanced production process, it produces at lower cost but can use the exclusion to acquire monopoly power and hold price up.

    a. On balance, is the patent system a good or a bad thing?

    b. Is government involvement in scientific research a good idea? Discuss.

8. "The Coase theorem implies that we never need to worry about regulating externalities because the private individuals involved will reach the efficient outcome through negotiations." Is this statement true or false? Justify your answer and use examples.

9. Explain how imperfect information problems such as adverse selection or moral hazard might affect the following markets or situations:

    a. Workers applying for disability benefits from a company
    b. The market for used computers
    c. The market for customized telephone systems for college offices and dorms
    d. The market for automobile collision insurance

FIGURE 1

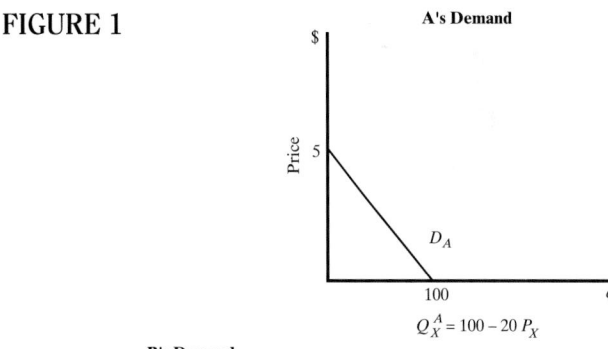

A's Demand

$Q_X^A = 100 - 20 P_X$

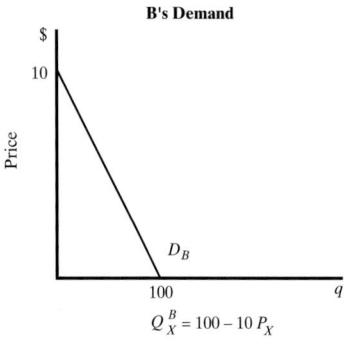

B's Demand

$Q_X^B = 100 - 10 P_X$

17 Income Distribution and Poverty

equity Fairness.

L et us now return to the question we have been considering for the last four chapters: What role should government play in the economy? Thus far, we have focused only on actions the government might be called upon to take to improve the efficiency of markets. But even if we achieved markets that are perfectly efficient, would the result be fair? We now turn to the question of **equity,** or fairness.

Somehow, the goods and services produced in every society get distributed among its citizens. Some of those citizens end up with palatial mansions in Palm Beach, weekend ski trips to Gstaad, and Maseratis; others end up without enough to eat and live in shacks. This chapter focuses on distribution. Why do some people get more than others? What are the sources of inequality? Should the government change the distribution that the market generates?

THE UTILITY POSSIBILITIES FRONTIER Ideally, in discussing distribution, we should talk not about the distribution of things but about the distribution of well-being. In the nineteenth century, philosophers used the concept of *utility* as a measure of well-being. As they saw it, people make choices among goods and services on the basis of the utility that those goods and services yield. People act so as to maximize utility. If a person prefers a night at the symphony to a rock concert, it is because that person expects to get more utility from the symphony performance. If we extend this thinking, we might argue that if household A gets more total utility than household B, A is better off than B.

Utility is not directly observable or measurable. But thinking about it as if it were can help us understand some of the ideas that underlie debates about distribution. Suppose, for example, that society consisted of only two people, "I" and "J." Next suppose that the line PP' in Figure 17.1 represents all the combinations of I's utility and J's utility that are possible, given the resources and technology available in their society. (Note that this is an extension of the production possibilities frontier discussed in Chapter 2, which plotted outputs on the X and Y axes.)

Any point inside PP', or the **utility possibilities frontier,** is inefficient, because both I and J could be better off. A is one such point. B is one of many possible points along PP' that society should prefer to A, because both members are better off at B than they are at A.

While point B is clearly preferable to point A from everyone's point of view, how does point B compare with point C? Both B and C are efficient; I cannot be made better off without making J worse off, and vice versa. Indeed, all the points along PP' are efficient, but they may not be equally desirable. If all the assumptions of competitive market theory held, the market system would lead to one of the points along PP'. The actual point reached would depend upon I's and J's initial endowments of wealth, skills, and so forth.

In practice, however, the market solution leaves some people out. The rewards of a market system are linked to productivity, and some people in every society are simply not capable of being very productive. All societies make some provision for the very poor. Most often, public expenditures on behalf of the poor are financed with taxes collected from the rest of society. Society thus makes a judgment that those who are better off should give up some of their rewards so that those at the bottom can have more than the market system would allocate to them. In a democratic state, such redistribution is presumably undertaken because a majority of the members of that society think that it is fair, or just.

utility possibilities frontier A graphical representation of a two-person world that shows all points at which A's utility can be increased only if B's utility is decreased. That is, it represents all Pareto efficient points at which A can be made better off only by making B worse off.

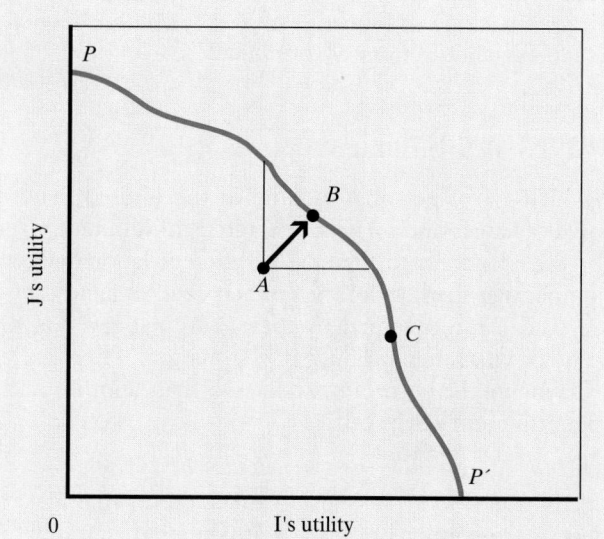

FIGURE 17.1
Utility Possibilities Frontier
If society were made up of just two people, I and J, and all of the assumptions of perfect competition held, the market system would lead to some point along PP'. Every point along PP' is Pareto optimal, or efficient; it is impossible to make I better off without making J worse off, and vice versa. But which point is best? Is B better than C?

Early economists drew analogies between social choices among alternative outcomes and consumer choices among alternative outcomes. A consumer chooses on the basis of his or her own unique utility function, or measure of his or her own well-being; a society, they said, chooses on the basis of a social welfare function that embodies the society's ethics.

Such theoretical discussions of fairness and equity focus on the distribution and redistribution of utility. But because utility is neither observable nor measurable, most discussions of social policy center on the distribution of income or the distribution of wealth as indirect measures of well-being. It is important that you remember throughout this chapter, however, that income and wealth are imperfect measures of well-being. Someone with a profound love of the outdoors may choose to work in a national park for a low wage rather than to work for a consulting firm in a big city for a high wage. The choice reveals that she is better off, even though her measured income is lower. As another example, think about five people with $1 each. Now suppose that one of those people has a magnificent voice, and that the other four give up their dollars to hear her sing. The exchange leads to inequality of measured wealth—the singer has $5 and no one else has any, but all are better off than they were before.

While income and wealth are imperfect measures of utility, they have no observable substitutes and are therefore the measures we use throughout this chapter. First, we review the factors that determine the distribution of income in a market setting. Second, we look at the data on income distribution, wealth distribution, and poverty in the United States. Third, we talk briefly about some theories of economic justice. Finally, we describe a number of current redistributional programs, including public assistance, or welfare, food stamps, Medicaid, and public housing.

THE SOURCES OF HOUSEHOLD INCOME

Why do some people and some families have more income than others? Before we turn to data on the distribution of income, let us review what we already know about the sources of inequality:

> Households derive their incomes from three basic sources: (1) from wages or salaries received in exchange for labor; (2) from property (that is, capital, land, and so forth); and (3) from government.

Wages and Salaries

About 64% of personal income in the United States in 1991 was received in the form of wages and salaries. Hundreds of different wage rates are paid to employees for their labor in thousands of different labor markets. As you saw in Chapter 9, competitive market theory predicts that all factors of production (including labor) are paid a return equal to their marginal revenue products—that is, the market value of what they produce at the margin. There are a number of reasons one type of labor might be more productive than another and why some households have higher incomes than others.

REQUIRED SKILLS, HUMAN CAPITAL, AND WORKING CONDITIONS   Clearly, some people are simply born with attributes that translate into valuable skills. Patrick Ewing, David Robinson, and Robert Parish are great basketball players, partly because they happen to be over seven feet tall. They didn't decide to go out and invest in height; they were born with the right genes. Some people have perfect pitch and beautiful voices; others are tone deaf. Some people have quick mathematical minds; others cannot add two and two.

The rewards of a skill that is in strictly limited supply depend upon the demand for that skill. Men's professional basketball is extremely popular, and the top NBA players make millions of dollars per year. There are some great women basketball players, too, but because women's professional basketball has not become popular in the United States, these women's skills go comparatively unrewarded. In tennis, however, people want to see women play, and women therefore earn prize money similar to the money earned by men. (For more on the relative earning power of men and women, see the Issues and Applications box titled "The Controversy over Comparable Worth.")

Some people with rare skills or presence can make enormous salaries in a free market economy. Luciano Pavarotti has a voice that millions of people are willing to pay to hear in person and on tapes and CDs. Garth Brooks sells a million copies of every album he makes. Before Pablo Picasso died, he could sell small sketches for vast sums of money. Were they worth it? They were worth exactly what the highest bidder was willing to pay.

Not all skills are inborn, however. Some people have invested in training and schooling to improve their knowledge and skills, and therein lies another source of inequality in wages. When we go to school, we are investing in **human capital** that we expect to yield dividends, partly in the form of higher wages, later on. Human capital is also produced through on-the-job training. People learn their jobs and acquire "firm-specific" skills as long as they are on the job. Thus, in most occupations there is a reward for experience. Pay scale often reflects numbers of years on the job, and those with more experience earn higher wages than those in similar jobs with less experience.

human capital The stock of knowledge, skills, and talents that people possess; it can be inborn or acquired through education and training.

Some jobs are more desirable than others. Entry-level positions in "glamour" industries such as publishing and television tend to be low-paying. Since talented people are willing to take entry-level jobs in these industries at salaries below what they could earn in other occupations, there must be other, nonwage rewards. It may be that the job itself is more personally rewarding, or that a low-paying apprenticeship is the only way to acquire the human capital necessary to advance. On the other hand, less desirable jobs often pay wages that include **compensating differentials.** Of two jobs requiring roughly equal levels of experience and skills that compete for the same workers, the job with the poorer working conditions usually has to pay a slightly higher wage to attract workers away from the job with the better working conditions.

compensating differentials Differences in wages that result from differences in working conditions. Risky jobs usually pay higher wages; highly desirable jobs usually pay lower wages.

Compensating differentials are also required when a job is very dangerous. Those who take great risks are usually rewarded with high wages. High-beam workers on skyscrapers and bridges command premium wages. Fire fighters in cities that have many old, run-down buildings are usually paid more than those in relatively tranquil rural or suburban areas.

MULTIPLE HOUSEHOLD INCOMES Another source of wage inequality among households lies in the fact that many households have more than one earner in the labor force. Second, and even third, incomes are becoming more the rule than the exception for U.S. families. In 1960 about 37% of women over the age of 16 were in the labor force. By 1978 the figure had increased to over 50%, and it continued to climb slowly but steadily to a level of nearly 58% by 1990.

THE CONTROVERSY OVER COMPARABLE WORTH

Although more and more women are working in traditionally male-dominated professions (such as firefighting), on average women still earn significantly less than men.

On average, women earn significantly less than men. In 1990, the median earnings of women were 56.9% of men's earnings. Since women holding full-time jobs work fewer hours than men, women's average hourly earnings are a slightly larger fraction of men's—71.6% in 1990. In addition, the degree of occupational segregation between men and women in the United States is striking. For example, in 1991, women accounted for 94.8% of registered nurses, 98.7% of kindergarten and preschool teachers, 99.0% of secretaries, and 68.0% of social workers. A study of 393 companies in California found that only 10% of established job categories had both men and women assigned to them.*

There are two views about why these differences exist. One view holds that most wage differentials can be attributed to choices women make about what jobs to take, how many hours to work, and when to enter and leave the labor force. The argument is that labor markets are efficient and that wages reflect productivity. Women earn lower wages because they have chosen to enter occupations that require little training and have low productivity, or because they avoid dangerous occupations and seek those that allow free movement into and out of the labor force.

This view also argues that the gap between women's and men's wages will close when women obtain the same amount of training as men, when they enter the same professions, and when they remain on the job without taking time off to raise families.

The second view holds that women's choices are not free and that wage differentials cannot be explained by differences in productivity. This view maintains that women are channeled into certain occupations by custom, tradition, and discrimination and that wages in those occupations are kept artificially low. It is argued that jobs requiring similar skills, contributing similar amounts to employer earnings, and having similar working conditions are likely to be paid low wages when they are traditionally filled by women.

Those who espouse this second view argue that the wage gap can be closed in a number of ways. First, employers could be persuaded or forced to accept women into jobs that were held previously only by men. Second, wages across occupations of "comparable worth" could be equalized:

*Under this approach, expert panels would evaluate the intellectual and physical demands of jobs within a particular company or controlled by a single employer (such as a state or local government). The panel would assign points to each job based on its working conditions, responsibility, and other characteristics, and would weigh each of these factors. The result would be a composite score, or index, that, it is claimed, would measure the "worth" of each job. People holding jobs of comparable worth as measured by these scores would receive equal pay.***

In 1963, Congress passed the Equal Pay Act, which prohibited unequal pay for *equal* work. The current move is to require equal pay for *comparable* work. A large number of states, including California, Iowa, Minnesota, Montana, Oregon, and Washington, have passed comparable worth laws for state employees. In the mid-1970s Australia adopted such a plan nationwide. As a result, base pay for women rose from 65% of men's to 94% between 1970 and 1980.

Critics of the comparable worth approach argue that such laws will end up hurting women. Raising wages above their equilibrium levels, it is argued, will cause employers to hire fewer women. Those who end up with jobs will earn higher wages, but some will be left out. There is mixed evidence on this score from the Australian experience. One study found that pay equalization slowed the growth of women's employment by one third and increased women's unemployment by 0.5 percentage points. Other studies found virtually no effect.

Critics also claim that the job evaluation process is hopelessly complex. They argue that the only reliable indicator of a job's worth is the wage rate that an employer must pay to fill it.

Source: Henry Aaron and Cameran Lougy, *The Comparable Worth Controversy* (Washington, D.C.: The Brookings Institution, 1986) and author's update.

*William T. Bielby and James N. Baron, "A Woman's Place Is with Other Women: Sex Segregation within Organizations," in *Sex Segregation in the Workplace: Trends, Explanations, Remedies,* ed. Barbara F. Reskin (Washington, D.C.: National Academy Press, 1984), p. 35. Other data in the first paragraph from *Statistical Abstract of the United States, 1992,* Tables 629 and 656.

**Aaron and Lougy, *The Comparable Worth Controversy,* p. 2.

Comparing two-earner and one-earner households highlights another problem of using money income as a measure of well-being. Consider, for example, a family of four with both parents working and an identical family with only one wage earner. The two-earner family will have a significantly higher money income, but the comparison ignores the value of what the non–wage-earning spouse produces. When one parent stays home, he or she normally provides services that would otherwise have to be purchased. The children are cared for, the house is maintained, food may be grown in the garden. When both parents work, there are expenses for day care, housecleaning, yard work, home repairs, and so forth.

When one parent stays home voluntarily, that family has revealed that it values the home-produced services more than the income it would otherwise earn. It is better off than it would be if both parents were working, even though it has a lower money income. Again, this means that we must exercise caution when discussing the fairness of the distribution of money income.

UNEMPLOYMENT   Before turning to property income, it is important to mention another major cause of inequality in the United States that is the subject of much discussion in macroeconomics: *unemployment.*

People earn wages only when they have jobs. In recent years, the United States has been through two severe recessions (economic downturns). In 1975, the unemployment rate hit 9%, and over 8 million people were unable to find work; in 1982, the unemployment rate was nearly 11%, and over 12 million were jobless. More recently, the recovery from the recession of 1990–1991 was slow, with more than 8.8 million unemployed in mid-1993.

Unemployment hurts primarily those who are laid off, and thus its costs are narrowly distributed. For some workers, the costs of unemployment are lowered by unemployment compensation benefits paid out of a fund accumulated with receipts from a tax on payrolls.

Income from Property

Another important source of income inequality is that some people have **property income**—that is, income from the ownership of real property and financial holdings—while many others do not. Some people own a great deal of wealth, and some have no assets at all. Overall, about 25% of personal income in the United States in 1991 came from ownership of property. In general:

property income Income from the ownership of real property and financial holdings. It takes the form of profits, interest, dividends, and rents.

> The amount of property income that a household earns depends upon (1) how much property it owns, and (2) what kinds of assets it owns. Such income generally takes the form of profits, interest, dividends, and rents.

Households come to own assets through saving and through inheritance. Many of today's large fortunes were inherited from previous generations. The Rockefellers, the Kennedys, and the Fords, to name a few, still have large holdings of property originally accumulated by previous generations. Thousands of families receive smaller inheritances each year from their parents. (Under 1993 tax laws, $600,000 can pass from one generation to another free of estate taxes.) Most families receive little through inheritance, however, and most of their wealth or property comes from saving.

Another important component of wealth today is real estate. For most people, the biggest asset they will ever own is their home, and equity accumulated in owner-occupied houses is a major source of inequality. A house earns a return just like any other asset, a return that comes in the form of "housing services"—the owner of the house lives in it rent free. In addition to these returns, houses can also *appreciate*, or increase in value. During the 1980s, the real estate market had some dramatic impacts on the distribution of income as the prices of single-family housing boomed in a number of metropolitan areas. In New England, New York, and in most of New Jersey, housing prices more than doubled between 1983 and 1987. In California, house prices increased by more than 80% between 1987 and 1989. In 1989 and 1990, house prices boomed in Seattle and Honolulu.

Those who owned houses when prices rose ended up with substantial accumulations of value in their houses. But those who did not own found themselves much worse off. Not only did their rents increase, but many families found themselves unable to make the leap from renting to home ownership because of the dramatically higher prices. In the New York metropolitan area, for example, the median sales price of existing single-family houses in 1989 was $190,000. To purchase the median house in New York required a minimum of $19,000 cash down payment (10%) and a monthly mortgage payment of over $1,600.

Some people made vast fortunes building shopping malls, office towers, and condominiums during the 1980s. Perhaps the best known is Donald Trump, who built Trump Tower in New York and several Atlantic City casinos. With his profits from real estate deals, he also bought the New York-Washington-Boston shuttle from Eastern Airlines and renamed it the Trump Shuttle.

But the late 1980s and early 1990s demonstrated that real estate values can fall as dramatically as they rise. Numerous fortunes were wiped out when the Texas economy, which is heavily dependent on oil production, became overbuilt and simultaneously ran into a worldwide oil glut and sharp drop in the value of crude oil. Even Donald Trump was on the verge of bankruptcy when the New York and New England commercial real estate markets declined. In addition, home owners all over the country, but especially those in New York, New England, and California, have seen the values of their homes fall significantly in the last few years.

Income from the Government: Transfer Payments

transfer payments Payments by government to people who do not supply goods or services in exchange.

About 11% of personal income in 1991 came from governments in the form of **transfer payments.** Transfer payments are payments made by government to people who do not supply goods or services in exchange. Some, but not all, transfer payments (such as Aid to Families with Dependent Children [AFDC] and unemployment compensation) are made to people with low incomes, precisely because they have low incomes. Transfer payments thus reduce the amount of inequality in the distribution of income.

Not all transfer income goes to the poor, however. The biggest single transfer program at the federal level is social security. Nearly everyone who is employed in the United States pays a social security tax out of his or her wages. Disabled workers, retired workers, or their survivors receive monthly benefit checks paid by the Social Security Administration out of those tax receipts. The size of the monthly payment depends on a complicated formula that takes into account the recipient's preretirement earnings and the number of years he or she worked and paid the tax.

Except for social security, however:

> Transfer programs are by and large designed to provide income to those in need. They are part of the government's attempts to offset some of the problems of inequality and poverty.

Later in this chapter we examine the basic logic of income redistribution and a number of specific programs in more detail.

THE DISTRIBUTION OF INCOME

Despite the many problems with using income as a measure of well-being, it is useful to know something about how income is actually distributed. Before we examine these data, however, we should pin down precisely what the data represent.

Economic income is defined as the amount of money that a household can spend during a given time period without increasing or decreasing its net assets. Thus, economic income includes anything that enhances your ability to spend—wages, salaries, dividends, interest received, proprietors' income, transfer payments, rents, and so forth. In addition, if you own an asset (such as a share of stock) that increases in value, that gain is part of your income, whether you sell the asset to "realize" the gain or not. Normally, we speak of "before-tax" income, with taxes considered a use of income.

economic income The amount of money a household can spend during a given time period without increasing or decreasing its net assets. Wages, salaries, dividends, interest income, transfer payments, rents, and so forth are sources of economic income.

Income Inequality in the United States

Table 17.1 presents some estimates of the distribution of several income components and of total income for family units in 1985.[1] The measure of income used to calculate these figures is very broad; it includes both taxable and nontaxable items, as well as estimates of capital gains (gains from selling shares of stock for a price above the price at which the shares were purchased).

[1] These are the most recent data available in this form. The term "family" refers both to individuals living alone—one-person families—and to households with more than one person living together, who are related by blood, marriage, or adoption.

TABLE 17.1
Distribution of Total Economic Income and Components in the United States, 1985 (percentages)

HOUSEHOLDS	TOTAL INCOME	WAGES AND SALARIES	PROPERTY INCOME	TRANSFER INCOME
Bottom fifth	4.2	6.1	1.5	27.7
Second fifth	10.0	12.9	4.7	26.1
Third fifth	15.8	19.8	9.1	18.7
Fourth fifth	22.3	26.0	15.2	13.5
Top fifth	47.7	35.2	69.5	13.9
Top 1 percent	11.9	2.7	27.4	1.2

Source: Brookings Merge File.

The data are presented by "quintiles"—that is, the total number of families is first ranked by income and then split into five groups of equal size. In 1985 the top quintile earned 47.7% of total income, while the bottom quintile earned just 4.2 percent. The top 1% (which is part of the top quintile) earned nearly three times as much as the bottom 20 percent.

Wage and salary income (that is, labor income) was more evenly distributed than total income. The top 1% earned only 2.7%, and the middle groups earned a larger share. The combined middle three quintiles, or 60% of the total, received 58.7% of wages and salaries, compared with only 48.1% of all income.

Not surprisingly, income from property is much more unevenly distributed than wages and salaries. Property income comes from owning things: Land earns rent, stocks earn dividends and appreciate in value, bonds and deposit accounts earn interest, owners of small businesses earn profits, and so forth. The top 20% of households earned nearly 70% of property income, and the top 1% earned 27.4 percent.

Transfer payments include social security benefits, unemployment compensation, and welfare payments, as well as an estimate of nonmonetary transfers from the government to households—food stamps and Medicaid and Medicare program benefits, for example. Transfers flow to low-income families, but not solely to them. Social security benefits, for example, which account for about half of all transfer payments, flow to everyone who participated in the system for the requisite number of years and who has reached the required age, regardless of income. Nonetheless, transfers represent a much more important income component at the bottom of the distribution than at the top. Although not shown in Table 17.1, transfers account for more than 80% of the income of the bottom 10% of families, but only about 3% of income among the top 10% of families.

CHANGES IN THE DISTRIBUTION OF INCOME   Table 17.2 presents the distribution of money income among U.S. families at a number of points in time. **Money income,** the measure used by the Census Bureau in its surveys and publications, is slightly less complete than the income measure used in the calculations in Table 17.1. It does not include noncash transfer benefits, for example, nor does it include capital gains.

As you can see, income distribution in the United States has remained remarkably stable over a long period of time. Between the end of World War II and 1980, there was a slight move toward equality: The share of income going to both the top 5% and the top 20% declined, while the share going to the bottom 20% increased slightly. Between 1980 and 1990, however, the trend reversed, with the top fifth gaining share and the bottom four fifths losing share.

money income The measure of income used by the Census Bureau. Because it excludes noncash transfer payments and capital gains income, it is less inclusive than "economic income."

TABLE 17.2
Distribution of Money Income of U.S. Families by Quintiles, 1947–1990 (percentages)

	1947	1960	1972	1980	1984	1990
Bottom fifth	5.0	4.8	5.4	5.2	4.7	4.6
Second fifth	11.8	12.2	11.9	11.5	11.0	10.8
Third fifth	17.0	17.8	17.5	17.5	17.0	16.6
Fourth fifth	23.1	24.0	23.9	24.3	24.4	23.8
Top fifth	43.0	41.3	41.4	41.5	42.9	44.3
Top 5 percent	17.2	15.9	15.9	15.3	16.0	17.4

Source: *Statistical Abstract of the United States,* various editions.

THE LORENZ CURVE AND THE GINI COEFFICIENT The distribution of income can be graphed in several ways. The most widely used graph is the **Lorenz Curve,** shown in Figure 17.2. Plotted along the horizontal axis is the percentage of families, and along the vertical axis is the cumulative percentage of income. The curve shown here represents the year 1990, using data from Table 17.2.

During that year, the bottom 20% of families earned only 4.6% of total money income. The bottom 40% earned 15.4 (4.6% plus 10.8%), and so forth. If income were distributed equally—that is, if the bottom 20% earned 20% of the income, the bottom 40% earned 40% of the income, and so forth—the Lorenz Curve would be a 45-degree line between zero and 100 percent. More unequal distributions produce Lorenz Curves that are farther from the 45-degree line.

The **Gini coefficient** is a commonly used measure of the degree of inequality in a distribution. It is the ratio of the shaded area in Figure 17.2 to the total triangular area below and to the right of the diagonal line *OA*.

> If income is equally distributed, there is no shaded area (because the Lorenz Curve and the 45-degree line are the same), and the Gini coefficient is zero. The Lorenz Curves for distributions with more inequality are farther down to the right, their shaded areas are larger, and their Gini coefficients are higher. The maximum Gini coefficient is one. As the Lorenz Curve shifts down to the right, the shaded arc becomes a larger portion of the total triangular area below *OA*. If one person earned all the income (with no one else receiving anything), the shaded area and the triangle would be the same, and the ratio would equal one.

DIFFERENCES BETWEEN BLACK HOUSEHOLDS, WHITE HOUSEHOLDS, AND SINGLE-PERSON HOUSEHOLDS So far we have been looking at income distribution among all families lumped together. But looking just at families without differentiating

Lorenz Curve A widely used graph of the distribution of income, with cumulative percentage of families plotted along the horizontal axis and cumulative percentage of income plotted along the vertical axis.

Gini coefficient A commonly used measure of inequality of income derived from a Lorenz Curve. It can range from zero to a maximum of one.

FIGURE 17.2
Lorenz Curve for the United States, 1990

The Lorenz Curve is the most common way of presenting income distribution graphically. The larger the shaded area, the more unequal the distribution. If distribution were equal, the Lorenz Curve would be the 45-degree line *OA*.

them in any way hides some important distinctions. First, income distribution differs significantly between black and Hispanic families and white families. Second, many people do not belong to a family—they may live alone, or they may be part of a group of unrelated people living together. In 1990 the Census Bureau estimated that 10.7 million of the total 94.3 million households in the United States had a black "householder." In the same year, about 23.6 million persons were in one-person households.

Table 17.3 presents data on the distribution of money income for households by race and for single-person households. The differences between the groupings are dramatic. Over 14% of black households, but only 4% of white households, have annual incomes below $5000. At the upper end, 26.2% of white households, but only 11.9% of black households, have incomes above $50,000.

The category of single-person households includes a diverse mixture of people, including the elderly living alone, college students, and single people in apartments. While it is hard to generalize about such a mixed bag, the income distribution of this group differs from that of families in very notable ways. Over 33% of one-person households have incomes below $10,000, and 10.9% have incomes below $5000. Only 6.1% have incomes over $50,000, compared with 24.6% of all households.

The income difference between multi-person households and single-person households is in part due to the fact that many households contain more than one earner. Of the 66.3 million families in the United States in 1990, 52.1 million had a husband and wife present and 29.5 million had at least two earners.[2]

Poverty

Most of the government's concern with income distribution and redistribution has focused on poverty. "Poverty" is a very complicated word to define, however. In simplest terms, it means the condition of people who have very low incomes. The dictionary defines the term simply as "lack of money or material possessions." But how low does your income have to be before you are classified as poor?

---

[2]*Statistical Abstract of the United States, 1992,* Table 706.

TABLE 17.3
Distribution of Money Income of Households, 1990 (percentages)

	ALL HOUSEHOLDS	BLACK HOUSEHOLDS	WHITE HOUSEHOLDS	HISPANIC HOUSEHOLDS	ONE-PERSON HOUSEHOLDS
0–5,000	5.2	14.1	4.0	7.5	10.9
5–10,000	9.7	16.7	8.8	13.7	22.5
10–15,000	9.5	11.6	9.2	12.9	15.7
15–25,000	17.7	19.1	17.7	21.1	21.9
25–35,000	15.8	13.5	16.1	16.5	13.9
35–50,000	17.5	13.1	18.0	14.8	9.0
50,000–75,000	14.9	8.1	15.8	9.1	4.2
75,000 +	9.7	3.8	10.4	4.3	1.9
Total	100.0	100.0	100.0	100.0	100.0

Source: *Statistical Abstract of the United States, 1992* Table 697.

THE PROBLEM OF DEFINITION Philosophers and social policy makers have long debated the meaning of "poverty." One school of thought argues that poverty should be measured by determining how much it costs to buy the "basic necessities of life." For many years, the Bureau of Labor Statistics published "family budget" data designed to track the cost of specific "bundles" of food, clothing, and shelter that were supposed to represent the minimum standard of living.

Critics argue that defining bundles of necessities is a hopeless task. While it might be possible to define a minimally adequate diet, what is a "minimum" housing unit? Is a car a necessity? What about medical care? In reality, low-income families end up using what income they have in an enormous variety of ways.

Some also argue that poverty is culturally defined and is therefore a relative concept, not an absolute one. Poverty in Bangladesh, for example, is very different from poverty in the United States. Even within the United States, urban poverty is very different from rural poverty. If poverty is a relative concept, the definition of it might change significantly as a society accumulates wealth and achieves higher living standards.

Although it is difficult to define precisely, the word "poverty" is one that we all understand intuitively to some degree. It conveys images of run-down, overcrowded, rat-infested housing, homeless people, untreated illness, and so forth. But it is also a word that we have been forced to define formally for purposes of keeping statistics and administering public programs.

THE OFFICIAL POVERTY LINE In the early 1960s, the U.S. government established an official poverty line. Because poor families tend to spend about one third of their incomes on food:

> The **official poverty line** has been set at a figure that is simply three times the cost of the Department of Agriculture's minimum food budget.

poverty line The officially established income level that distinguishes the poor from the non-poor. It is set at three times the cost of the Department of Agriculture's minimum food budget.

Each year the Department of Agriculture sets out a nutritionally sound minimum food bundle. For example, a week's food for a woman between 20 and 34 years old includes 4 eggs; 1 1/4 pounds of meat, fish, or poultry; 3 pounds of potatoes; 12 ounces of dark green or yellow vegetables; 3 pounds of other vegetables; and 8 ounces of fat or oil. In 1991, the department estimated that such a bundle would cost about $89.26 per week for a family of four people. Multiply that times 52 weeks for a total of $4,641 per year; triple that, and you have a poverty line for a family of four set at $13,924.

POVERTY IN THE UNITED STATES SINCE 1960 In 1962 Michael Harrington published *The Other America: Poverty in the United States,* a book that many credit with waking the American people up to the problem of poverty and stimulating the government to declare a "war on poverty" in 1964. In 1960 official figures had put the number of the poor in the United States at just under 40 million, or 22% of the total population. In his book, Harrington argued that the number had reached over 50 million.

By the late 1960s the number of those living below the official poverty line had declined to about 25 million, where it stayed for over a decade. Between 1978 and 1983, however, the number of poor jumped nearly 45%, from 24.5 million to 35.3 million, the highest number since 1964. The figure stood at 35.7 million in 1991. As a percentage of the total population, the poor accounted for between

11% and 12.6% of the population throughout the 1970s. That figure increased sharply to 15.2% between 1979 and 1983. From 1983 to 1989 the rate dropped to 12.8%, rising back to 14.2% in 1991.

While the official 1991 figures put the poverty rate at 14.2% of the population, they do not show that some groups in society experience more poverty than others. Table 17.4 shows the official poverty count for 1964 and 1991 by demographic group. One of the problems with the official count is that it considers only money income as defined by the census and is therefore somewhat inflated. Many federal programs designed to help people out of poverty include noncash benefits (sometimes called *in-kind benefits*) such as food stamps, public housing, and so forth. If added to income, these benefits would reduce the number of those officially designated as below the poverty line. The right-hand column in Table 17.4 shows how many would be classified as poor if noncash benefits were taken into account.

The poverty rate among blacks is nearly three times as high as the poverty rate among whites. Even after noncash benefits are counted, nearly one in four blacks lives in poverty. In addition, approximately the same proportion of Hispanics as blacks had incomes below the poverty line after in-kind transfers in 1991.

The group with the highest incidence of poverty in 1987 was women living in households with no husband present. In 1964, 45.9% of such women lived in poverty. By 1991 the figure was still over one third. During the 1980s there was increasing concern about the "feminization of poverty," a concern that continues today.

Poverty rates among the elderly have been reduced considerably over the last few decades, dropping from 28.5% in 1964 to 12.4% in 1991. Certainly social security, supplemental security income, and Medicare have played a role in reducing poverty among the elderly.

The only category for which poverty rates have increased since 1964 is that of children. In 1964, 20.7% of all children under 18 lived in poverty; by 1991, the figure had risen to 21.8%.

The Distribution of Wealth

Data on the distribution of wealth are not as readily available as data on the distribution of income. Periodically, however, the government conducts a detailed survey of the holdings that make up wealth. Some of the results of this survey are presented in Table 17.5. The top 10% of families ranked by income control 64.4%

TABLE 17.4
Percentage of Persons in Poverty by Demographic Group, 1964–1991

	OFFICIAL MEASURE 1964	OFFICIAL MEASURE 1991	ADJUSTED FOR IN-KIND TRANSFERS AT MARKET VALUE, 1990*
All	19.0	14.2	11.0
White	14.9	11.3	9.0
Black	49.6	32.7	24.3
Hispanic	NA	28.7	22.7
Female householder— no husband present	45.9	33.8	NA
Elderly (65 +)	28.5	12.4	NA
Children under 18	20.7	21.8	NA

Note: *Includes food, housing, and medical benefits.

Source: U.S. Bureau of the Census, 1992.

TABLE 17.5
Percent of Assets Held by
Families, 1989

	TOP 1 PERCENT	TOP 10 PERCENT
Stocks	44.6	82.7
Bonds	65.2	93.5
Business assets	67.7	93.0
Principal residence	8.4	37.7
Other real estate	43.0	82.1
Total assets*	32.8	64.4

*Note: Checking, savings, certificates of deposit, IRAs, Keogh plans, stocks, bonds, businesses, real estate, automobiles.

Source: Arthur Kennickell and R. Louise Woodburn, "Estimation of Household Net Worth Using Model-Based and Design-Based Weights: Evidence from the 1989 Survey of Consumer Finances," April 1992. Unpublished manuscript.

of all the nation's assets, and the top 1% control nearly one-third. The top 1% hold 44.6% of the stock and 65.2% of the bonds held by households.

The term "principal residence" in Table 17.5 refers to owner-occupied housing. For many families, the family home is the most important asset they own. The huge increase in the value of houses across the nation in the 1970s and 1980s, discussed earlier, exacerbated an already important source of inequality in the United States. Those who owned houses or bought into the housing market early made large gains and found housing relatively inexpensive until very recently. As house prices declined in the early 1990s, however, the gap narrowed as housing became more affordable to potential buyers, and current owners lost some of their wealth.

Clearly, the distribution of wealth is significantly more unequal than the distribution of income. Part of the reason is that wealth is passed from generation to generation and thus accumulates. Large fortunes also accumulate when small businesses become successful large businesses. Some argue that an unequal distribution of wealth is the natural and inevitable consequence of risk taking in a market economy: It provides the incentive structure necessary to motivate entrepreneurs and investors. Others believe that too much inequality can undermine democracy and lead to social conflict. Many of the arguments for and against income redistribution, discussed in the next section, apply equally well to wealth redistribution.

THE REDISTRIBUTION DEBATE

Debates about the role of government in correcting for inequity in the distribution of income revolve around two kinds of issues, philosophical and practical. *Philosophical* issues are those dealing with the "ideal." What should the distribution of income be if we could give it any shape we desired? What is "fair"? What is "just"? *Practical* issues, on the other hand, deal with what is, and what is not, possible. Suppose we wanted to eliminate poverty altogether. How much would it cost, and what would we sacrifice to do so? When we take wealth or income away from higher-income people and give it to lower-income people, do we destroy incentives? What are the effects of this kind of redistribution?

Clearly, policy makers must deal with both kinds of issues, but it seems logical to confront the philosophical issues first. If you do not know where you want to go, you cannot talk very well about how to get there or how much it costs to get there. Indeed, you may find that you do not want to go anywhere at all. Many respected economists and philosophers do, in fact, argue quite convincingly that the government should *not* redistribute income.

Arguments against Redistribution

Those who argue against government redistribution believe that the market, when left to operate on its own, is fair. This argument rests on the proposition that "one is entitled to the fruits of one's efforts."[3] Remember that if market theory is correct, rewards paid in the market are linked to productivity. In other words, labor and capital are paid in accordance with the value of what they produce.

This view also holds that property income—that is, income from land or capital—is no less justified than labor income. All factors of production have marginal products. Capital owners receive profits or interest because the capital that they own is productive. (Recall from Chapter 7 that a production function shows the relationship between inputs and output. Output can be increased by adding labor or by adding capital or land.)

The argument against redistribution also rests on the principles behind "freedom of contract" and the protection of property rights. When I enter into an agreement either to sell my labor or to commit my capital to use, I do so freely, and in return I contract to receive payment, which becomes my "property." When a government taxes me and gives my income to someone else, that action violates these two basic rights.

The more common arguments against redistribution are not philosophical. Rather, they point to more practical problems. First, it is said that taxation and transfer programs interfere with the basic incentives provided by the market. Taxing higher-income people reduces their incentive to work, save, and invest. Taxing the "winners" of the economic game also discourages risk taking. Furthermore, providing transfers to those at the bottom reduces their incentive to work as well. All of this leads to a reduction in total output that is the "cost" of redistribution.

Another practical argument against redistribution is that it does not work. Some critics point to the rise in the poverty rate during the early 1980s and again in the early 1990s as an indication that antipoverty programs simply drain money without really helping the poor out of poverty. Whether or not these programs actually help people break out of poverty, the charge of bureaucratic inefficiency in administration always exists. Social programs must be administered by people who must be paid. The Department of Health and Human Services employs over 120,000 people to run the social security system, process Medicaid claims, and so forth. Some degree of waste and inefficiency is inevitable in any sizable bureaucracy.

Arguments in Favor of Redistribution

The argument most often used in favor of redistribution is that a society as wealthy as the United States has a moral obligation to provide all its members with the basic necessities of life. The Constitution does, after all, carry a guarantee of the "right to life." In declaring "war on poverty" in 1964, President Lyndon Johnson put it this way:

> There will always be some Americans who are better off than others. But it need not follow that the "poor are always with us". . . . It is high time to redouble and to concentrate our efforts to eliminate poverty. . . . We know what must be done and this nation of abundance can surely afford to do it.[4]

---

[3]Powerful support for this notion of "entitlement" can be found in the works of the seventeenth-century English philosophers Thomas Hobbes and John Locke.

[4]*Economic Report of the President, 1964.*

Many people, often through no fault of their own, find themselves left out. Some are born with mental or physical problems that severely limit their ability to "produce." Then, of course, there are children. Even if some parents can be held accountable for their low incomes, do we want to punish innocent children for the faults of their parents and thus perpetuate the cycle of poverty? The elderly, without redistribution of income, would have to rely exclusively on savings to survive once they retire, and many conditions can lead to inadequate savings. Should the victims of bad luck be doomed to inevitable poverty? Illness is perhaps the best example. The accumulated savings of very few can withstand the drain of extraordinary hospital and doctors' bills and the exorbitant cost of nursing home care.

Proponents of redistribution refute "practical" arguments against it by pointing to empirical studies that show little negative effect on the incentives of those who benefit from transfer programs. For many of those people—children, the elderly, the mentally ill—incentives are irrelevant, they say, and providing a basic income to most of the unemployed does not discourage them from working when they have the opportunity to do so.[5] We now turn briefly to several more formal arguments.

UTILITARIAN JUSTICE The essence of the utilitarian argument in favor of redistribution is that "a dollar in the hand of a rich person is worth less than a dollar in the hand of a poor person." The rich spend their marginal dollars on luxury goods—it is very easy, for example, to spend over $100 per person for a meal in a good restaurant in New York or Los Angeles. The poor, in contrast, spend their marginal dollars on necessities—food, clothing, and medical care. If the "marginal utility" of income declines as income rises, the value of a dollar's worth of luxury goods is worth less than a dollar's worth of necessity. Thus, redistributing from the rich to the poor increases total utility. To put this notion of **utilitarian justice** in everyday language: Through income redistribution, the rich sacrifice a little and the poor gain a lot.

utilitarian justice The idea that "a dollar in the hand of a rich person buys less than a dollar in the hand of a poor person." If the marginal utility of income declines with income, transferring income from the rich to the poor will increase total utility.

Each of the various utilitarian philosophers who wrote in the late eighteenth and nineteenth centuries (including, most notably, the Englishmen Jeremy Bentham and John Stuart Mill) took a slightly different approach to the utilitarian argument. Some positions were quite formal. If, for example, the marginal utility of income declines with income and everyone has identical "utility functions,"[6] then as long as anyone has more income than anyone else, a utility gain will result from transferring income from those with more to those with less. If A has more income than B and diminishing marginal utility of income sets in, taking from A and giving to B will increase total utility, because A values those marginal dollars less than B does.

The utilitarian position is not without its problems, of course. People have very different tastes and preferences. Who is to say that you value a dollar more or less than I do? Because utility is unobservable and unmeasurable, comparisons between individuals cannot be easily made. Nonetheless, many people find the basic logic of the utilitarians persuasive. When you weigh luxuries against necessities in your own mind, you consult your own "utility function." And, as you know from your own experience, necessities are by definition worth more than luxuries.

---

[5] For a discussion of the empirical evidence on the effects of transfer programs and taxation on incentives, see Chapter 19.

[6] A "utility function" is a way of expressing the relationship between goods or income and satisfaction or utility. $U = F(X_1, X_2, X_3 \ldots X_n)$ says that utility "is a function of" the goods, X_1 through X_n, that are consumed. To say that everyone has the same utility function means that everyone places the same subjective value on those goods.

SOCIAL CONTRACT THEORY—RAWLSIAN JUSTICE The work of Harvard philosopher John Rawls has generated a great deal of recent discussion, both within the discipline of economics and between economists and philosophers.[7] In the tradition of Hobbes, Locke, and Rousseau, Rawls argues that, as members of society, we have a contract with one another. In the theoretical world that Rawls imagines, an original *social contract* is drawn up, and all parties agree to it without knowledge of who they are or who they will be in society. This condition is called the "original position," or the "state of nature." With no vested interests to protect, members of society are able to make disinterested choices.

As we approach the contract, everyone has a chance to end up very rich or homeless, male or female. On the assumption that we are all "risk averse," Rawls believes that people will attach great importance to the position of the least fortunate members of society because anyone could end up there. **Rawlsian justice,** then, is argued from the assumption of risk aversion. Rawls concludes that any contract emerging from the original position would call for an income distribution that would "maximize the well-being of the worst-off member of society."

Any society bound by such a contract would allow for inequality, but only if that inequality had the effect of improving the lot of the very poor. If inequality provided an incentive for people to work hard and innovate, for example, those inequalities should be tolerated as long as some of the benefits went to those at the bottom.

THE WORKS OF KARL MARX For many decades, the most dangerous rivalry on earth was that between the two super powers, the United States and the Soviet Union. At the heart of this rivalry was a fundamental philosophical difference of opinion about how economic systems work and how they should be managed. At the center of the debate were the writings of Karl Marx.

Marx did not write very much about socialism or communism. His major work, *Das Kapital* (published in the nineteenth century), was a three-volume analysis and critique of the capitalist system that he saw at work in the world around him. We know what Marx thought was wrong with capitalism, but he was not very clear about what would replace it. In one essay, written late in his life, he put forward the oft-quoted line "from each according to his ability, to each according to his needs,"[8] but he was not specific about the applications of this principle.

Marx's view of capital income, however, does have important implications for income distribution. In the preceding chapters, we discussed profit as a return to a productive factor: Capital, like labor, is productive and has a marginal product. By contrast, Marx attributed *all value to labor* and *none to capital*. According to Marx's **labor theory of value,** the value of any commodity depends only on the amount of labor needed to produce it. The owners of capital are able to extract profit, or "surplus value," because labor creates more value in a day than it is paid for. Like any other good, labor power is worth only what it takes to "produce" it. Translated into simple language, this means that under capitalism labor is paid a subsistence wage.

Marx saw profit as an illegitimate expropriation by capitalists of the fruits of labor's efforts. It follows, then, that Marxians see the property income component of income distribution as the primary source of inequality in the United States today. Without capital income, the distribution of income would be much more equal. (Refer again to Table 17.1.)

Rawlsian justice A theory of distributional justice that concludes that the social contract emerging from the "original position" would call for an income distribution that would maximize the well-being of the worst-off member of society.

labor theory of value Stated most simply, the theory that the value of a commodity depends only on the amount of labor required to produce it.

---

[7]See John Rawls, *A Theory of Justice* (Cambridge, Mass.: Harvard University Press, 1972).

[8]Karl Marx, "Critique of the Gotha Program" (May 1875), in *The Marx-Engels Reader,* ed. Robert Tucker (New York, W. W. Norton), p. 388.

Despite the fact that the Soviet Union no longer exists, Marxism remains a powerful force in the world. China, Vietnam, Cuba, and a number of other countries remain communist, and many believe that the Marxian critique of capitalism was correct even though one version of an alternative has failed.

INCOME DISTRIBUTION AS A PUBLIC GOOD   Those who argue that the unfettered market produces a just income distribution certainly do not believe that private charity should be forbidden. Voluntary redistribution does not involve any violation of property rights by the state.

In Chapter 16, however, you saw that there may be a problem with private charity. Suppose that people really do want to end the hunger problem, for example. As they write out their checks to charity, they encounter the classic "public-goods" problem. First, there are "free riders." If hunger and starvation are eliminated, the benefits—even the merely psychological benefits—flow to everyone, whether they contributed or not. Second, any contribution is a "drop in the bucket." One individual contribution is so small that it can have no real effect.

With private charity, as with national defense, nothing depends upon whether I pay or not—there is no contingency. Thus, private charity may fail for the same reason that the private sector is likely to fail to produce national defense and other public goods. People will find it in their interest not to contribute. Thus, we turn to government to provide things that we want that will not be provided adequately if we act separately—in this case, help for the poor and hungry.

REDISTRIBUTION PROGRAMS AND POLICIES

The role of government in changing the distribution of income from that which follows from the operation of the market is a hotly debated and very important issue. The debate involves not only what government programs are appropriate to fight poverty but the character of the tax system as well. Unfortunately, the quality of the public debate on the subject is low. Usually it consists of a series of claims and counterclaims about what social programs do to incentives rather than a serious inquiry into what our distributional goal should be.

In this section, we talk about the tools of redistributional policy in the United States. As we do so, you will have a chance to assess for yourself some of the evidence about their effects.

Financing Redistribution Programs: Taxes

Redistribution always involves two parties or groups: those who end up with less and those who end up with more. Because redistributional programs are financed by tax dollars, it is important to know who the donors and recipients are—that is, who pays the taxes and who receives the benefits of those taxes.

The mainstay of the U.S. tax system is the individual income tax, authorized in 1913 by the Sixteenth Amendment to the Constitution. The income tax is *progressive*. This means that those with higher incomes pay a higher percentage of their incomes in taxes. Even though the tax is subject to many exemptions, deductions, and so forth that allow some taxpayers to reduce their tax burdens, all studies of the income tax show that its burden as a percentage of income rises as income rises.

With the passage of the Tax Reform Act of 1986, Congress initiated a major change in income tax rates and regulations. The purpose of the reforms was to simplify the tax and make it easier for people to comply with and harder to avoid. In addition, the act significantly reduced the number of tax brackets and the overall progres-

TABLE 17.6
Effective Rates of Federal, State, and Local Taxes, 1990 (taxes as a percentage of total income)

POPULATION DECILES	PERCENTAGE OF TOTAL INCOME
Bottom tenth	22.3
Second	21.7
Third	21.8
Fourth	22.9
Fifth	23.5
Sixth	23.9
Seventh	24.1
Eighth	25.1
Ninth	25.6
Top tenth	25.7

Source: Authors' estimates, based on Brookings Merge File Data

sivity of the rates. The largest reduction was in the top rate, which was cut from 50% to 28 percent in 1986. It also substantially reduced the tax burdens of those at the very bottom by increasing the amount of income one can earn before paying any tax at all.

In 1993, President Clinton signed into law a tax bill that increased the top rate to 36% for families with taxable incomes over $140,000 and individuals with taxable incomes over $115,000. In addition, families with incomes of over $250,000 will pay a surtax of 10%, bringing the marginal rate for those families to 39.6 percent. Families with incomes below $22,100 will receive grants and credits under the plan. Overall, the new tax system is substantially more progressive.

The individual income tax is only one tax among many, however. More important to the individual is the *overall* burden of taxation, including all federal, state, and local taxes. Most studies of the effect of taxes on the distribution of income, both before and after the Tax Reform Act, have concluded that the overall burden is roughly proportional. In other words:

> Everyone pays about the same percentage of his or her income in total taxes.

Table 17.6 presents an estimate of effective tax rates paid in 1990 by families that have been ranked by income. While some progressivity is visible, it is very slight. The bottom 10% of the income earners pay 22.3% of their total incomes in tax. The top 10% pay 25.7%. Table 17.7 shows the impact of taxes on the cumulative distribution of income in 1990. After taxes have been paid, as you can see, the distribution of income is virtually unchanged. We can conclude from these data that the tax side of the equation produces very little change in the distribution of income.

Expenditure Programs

Some programs designed to redistribute income or to aid the poor provide cash income to recipients. Others provide benefits in the form of health care, subsidized housing, or food stamps. Still others provide training or help workers find jobs.

social security system The federal system of social insurance programs. It includes three separate programs that are financed through separate trust funds: the Old Age and Survivors Insurance program (OASI), the Disability Insurance program (DI), and the Health Insurance program (HI).

SOCIAL SECURITY By far the largest income redistribution program in the United States is social security. The **social security system** is really three programs that are financed through separate trust funds. The *Old Age and Survivors Insurance program (OASI),* the largest of the three, pays cash benefits to retired workers, their survivors, and their dependents. The *Disability Insurance program (DI)* pays cash benefits to disabled workers and their dependents. The third program, *Health Insurance (HI)* or *Medicare,* provides medical benefits to workers covered by OASI and DI and the railroad retirement program. Regardless of the merits or demerits of the system, social security has been credited with substantially reducing poverty among the elderly.

Most workers in the United States must participate in the social security system. For many years, federal employees and employees belonging to certain state and municipal retirement systems were not required to participate, but federal employees are now being brought into the system. Today well over 90% of all workers in the United States contribute to social security.

Participants and their employers are required to pay a *payroll tax* to the *Federal Insurance Corporation Association (FICA)* to finance the social security system. The tax in 1992 was 7.65% paid by employers and 7.65% paid by employees on wages up to 55,500. Self-employed people assume the entire FICA burden themselves.

You are entitled to social security benefits if you participate in the system for 10 years. Benefits are paid monthly to you after you retire or, if you die, to your survivors. A complicated formula based on your average salary while you were paying into the system determines your benefit level. Those who earned more receive a higher level of benefits. But there are maximum and minimum monthly benefits. By and large, low-salaried workers get more out of the system than they paid into it while they were working. High-salaried workers usually get out of the system considerably less than they put in.

The social security system is self-financing, but it is different from funded retirement systems. In a *funded system,* deposits (by the employer, the employee, or both) are made to an account in the employee's name. Those funds are invested and earn interest or dividends that accumulate until retirement, when they are withdrawn. Funded retirement plans operate very much like a savings plan that you might set up independently except that you cannot touch the contents until you retire.

In the social security system, the tax receipts from today's workers are used to pay benefits to retired and disabled workers and their dependents today. Currently, the system is collecting more than it is paying out, and the excess is accumulating in the trust funds. This is necessary to keep the system solvent, because after the year 2010 there will be a large increase in the number of retirees and a relative decline in the number of workers. These demographic changes are the result of a high birth rate between 1946 and 1964—the so-called "baby boom." In 1990, 24.8 million retired persons received social security benefits and 3.0 million received disability payments.

PUBLIC ASSISTANCE Next to social security, the biggest cash transfer program in the United States is **public assistance,** more commonly called **welfare.** Aimed specifically at the poor, welfare falls into two major categories.

Most welfare is paid in the form of *Aid to Families with Dependent Children (AFDC).* Benefit levels for AFDC are set by the states, and they vary widely. In 1990 the average monthly payment to a family was $121 per month in Alabama, $593 per month in Connecticut, and $720 per month in Alaska; the average monthly payment in the United States was $392. To participate, a family must have very low income and virtually no assets. In 1990 there were 11.4 million AFDC recipients in the United States, of whom just under 70% were children. Those adults who find jobs and enter the labor force lose benefits quickly as their incomes rise. This loss of benefits acts as a tax on beneficiaries, and some argue that it discourages welfare recipients from seeking jobs.

A second category of welfare payments is *general assistance,* which goes to the very poor regardless of family circumstances. In 1990 there were about 1.1 million general assistance recipients.

Welfare has been a source of much debate in recent years. In 1988, the welfare system was overhauled. The Issues and Applications box entitled "Welfare Reform: The Family Support Act of 1988" describes the 1988 changes in detail.

SUPPLEMENTAL SECURITY INCOME The *Supplemental Security Income program (SSI)* is a federal program that was set up under the Social Security Administration in 1974. The program is financed out of general revenues—that is, there is no trust fund, nor are there any earmarked taxes from which SSI benefits are paid out.

SSI is designed to take care of the elderly who end up very poor and have no, or very low, social security entitlement. In 1990, 4.8 million people received SSI payments, about half of whom also received some social security benefits. As with welfare, qualified recipients must have very low incomes and virtually no assets.

TABLE 17.7
Distribution of Income before and after Taxes, 1990 (percentage of income in each quintile)

	TOTAL INCOME BEFORE TAXES*	TOTAL INCOME AFTER TAXES†
Bottom Fifth	1.1	1.4
Second Fifth	7.9	8.9
Third Fifth	15.5	16.4
Fourth Fifth	24.7	25.2
Top Fifth	50.7	48.1

*Includes money income excluding transfers and including capital gains and income supplements (health insurance benefits).

†Income in * minus social security payroll taxes and federal and state individual income taxes.

Source: *Statistical Abstract of the United States, 1992,* Table 731.

public assistance, or welfare
Government transfer programs that provide cash benefits to (1) families with dependent children whose incomes and assets fall below a very low level and (2) the very poor regardless of whether or not they have children.

unemployment compensation
A state government transfer program that pays cash benefits for a certain period of time to laid-off workers who have worked for a specified period of time for a covered employer.

UNEMPLOYMENT COMPENSATION   In 1990 governments paid out over $18 billion in benefits to workers who were unemployed. The money to finance this benefit comes from taxes paid by employers into special funds. Companies that hire and fire frequently pay a higher tax rate, while companies with relatively stable employment levels pay a lower tax rate. Tax and benefit levels are determined by the states, within certain federal guidelines.

Workers who qualify for **unemployment compensation** begin to receive benefit checks soon after they are laid off. These checks continue for a period of time that is specified by the state. Most unemployment benefits continue for 20 weeks. However, in times of recession the benefit period is often extended on a state by state basis. The average unemployed worker receives only about 36% of his or her normal wages in benefits, and not all workers are covered. To qualify for benefits, an unemployed person must have worked recently for a covered employer for a specified length of time for a given amount of wages. Recipients must also demonstrate willingness and ability to seek and accept suitable employment. Although nine of ten employed persons are covered by unemployment insurance paid for by employers, only 36% of the unemployed received benefits in 1990.

Unemployment benefits are not aimed at the poor alone, although many of the unemployed are poor. Unemployment benefits are paid regardless of a person's income from other sources and regardless of assets.

Medicare and Medicaid In-kind government transfer programs that provide health and hospitalization benefits: Medicare to the aged and their survivors and to certain of the disabled, regardless of income, and Medicaid to people with low incomes.

MEDICAID AND MEDICARE   The largest in-kind transfer programs in the United States are Medicare and Medicaid. The **Medicaid** program provides health and hospitalization benefits to people with low incomes. Although the program is administered by the states, about 56% of the cost is borne by the federal government. In 1990 about 25.3 million people received benefits; in that year, total payments were $72.2 billion and rising. Sixty percent of all Medicaid recipients are technically below the poverty line, and half are AFDC recipients.

Medicare, which is run by the Social Security Administration, is a health insurance program for the aged and certain disabled persons. Most U.S. citizens over age 65 receive Medicare hospital insurance coverage regardless of their income. In addition, they may elect to enroll in a supplementary medical insurance program under Medicare by paying a premium. Medicare pays only a part of total hospital expenses. When their hospital stay is longer than 60 days, for example, patients are responsible for $130 per day.

In 1990, 29.7 million aged and 2.9 million disabled were covered by Medicare. Benefit payments in 1990 totalled $42.5 billion.

food stamps Vouchers that have a face value greater than their cost and that can be used to purchase food at grocery stores.

FOOD STAMPS   The Food Stamp program is an antipoverty program funded out of general federal tax revenues, with states bearing 50% of the program's administrative costs. **Food stamps** are vouchers that have a face value greater than their cost and that can be used to purchase food at grocery stores. The amount by which the face value of the stamps exceeds their cost depends on income and family size. Only low-income families and single persons are eligible to purchase food stamps.

It is generally acknowledged that a thriving black market in food stamps exists. Families that want or need cash can sell their food stamps to people who will buy them for less than face value but more than the original recipient paid for them. Because the program has been subject to so much abuse, the Reagan administration began reducing the program in 1981.

In 1990 there were 20.5 million participants in the Food Stamp program, down from 22 million in 1980. The total cost of the program in 1990 was $14.2 billion.

WELFARE REFORM: THE FAMILY SUPPORT ACT OF 1988

Over the years, many proposals for welfare reform have been put forth and rejected. Finally, after years of only minor reforms and adjustments to the welfare system, Congress in 1988 passed the most important welfare legislation since social security. This legislation, the Family Support Act of 1988, is designed to enhance employment prospects for the poor and thus end the vicious cycle of poverty. The following excerpt describes some of the major provisions of the act:

Welfare has few supporters and many critics, yet it has resisted repeated efforts at major reform. The fundamental dilemma is the impossibility of simultaneously maximizing the two primary policy objectives: reducing poverty and encouraging self-support. Simple logic dictates a trade-off, at least in the short run and probably in the long run. Because welfare programs are means-tested, they discourage work, since the more you work, the less assistance you receive. Moreover, any effort to increase benefits to combat poverty more effectively will only further decrease the incentives for recipients to take low-paying jobs and work.

To simplify a complex debate, in which there is more of a continuum than a dichotomy of views, liberals and conservatives stress different designs and outcomes. Liberals generally accept the premise that work is better than welfare but continue to emphasize reducing poverty over reducing dependence. They argue that welfare recipients want to work but lack the education and skills to get jobs that assure self-sufficiency and a decent standard of living, and that many of them would not be able to find adequate care for their children if they did find jobs. Thus, liberals prefer programs that serve volunteers first, offer choices, provide intensive education and training services, do not require people to take low-wage jobs or indeed any job, and assure adequate child care and health insurance to those who leave welfare to work. Liberals focus on insufficient human capital as the critical reason for continued dependence,

An important component of the Family Support Act of 1988 is increased child-care services available to women who want to return to school. Such programs are designed to help people on government assistance achieve self-sufficiency.

and they believe that countering this will have high returns.

Conservatives, on the other hand, usually emphasize reducing dependence over reducing poverty. They argue that jobs are available and believe that welfare recipients are unwilling to work, are too discouraged to try, or have unrealistic expectations about their job prospects. Thus, conservatives favor programs that set clear expectations for recipients, require participation in program activities or regular employment, provide low-cost job placement assistance rather than expensive training, and mandate "workfare" for those who remain on the rolls.

The Family Support Act of 1988 (FSA), especially its centerpiece, the Job Opportunities and Basic Skills Training (JOBS) Program, redefines federal policy on welfare employment programs and represents a compromise among these conflicting visions of welfare reform. The key elements of FSA are that parents, both fathers and mothers, should be the primary supporters of their children and that government should provide incentives and assistance to welfare recipients to find employment. For absent fathers, this translates into greater enforcement of child support collections and new obligations on welfare mothers to

cooperate with such efforts. For welfare recipients, JOBS contains features of both the conservative and liberal views: an expansion of the program participation mandate to women with younger children (as young as age 3, or age 1 at state option), a complex balance of mandatory and voluntary elements (including an emphasis on serving volunteers first and on determining services through case management and client choice), child care guarantees, and investments designed to improve the capacity of AFDC mothers to obtain jobs and, hopefully, self-sufficiency.

While JOBS gives states substantial flexibility in designing welfare employment programs, it includes incentives to move the system in new directions. In contrast to state programs of the 1980s, which typically provided job search activities followed by unpaid work experience, JOBS places much greater emphasis on education. It requires that (to the extent resources are available) education be offered to any adult on AFDC who lacks a high school diploma or does not demonstrate basic literacy.

Source: Judith Gueron, "Work and Welfare: Lessons on Employment Programs," *Journal of Economic Perspectives,* Winter 1990. Reprinted by permission of the American Economic Association.

HOUSING PROGRAMS   Over the years, the federal government and state governments have administered many different housing programs designed to improve the quality of housing for low-income people. The biggest is the Public Housing program, which is financed by the federal government but administered by local public housing authorities. Public housing tenants pay rents equal to no more than 25% of their incomes. In many cases, this means that they pay zero. The largest housing program, called "Section 8," provides housing assistance payments to tenants and slightly above-market rent guarantees to participating landlords.

In 1990 there were 32.9 million rental housing units in the United States, of which 1.4 million were in public housing projects. Another 2.5 million received a government rent subsidy. Government expenditures on housing totaled 17.5 billion in 1990.

How Effective Are Antipoverty Programs?

Recall from Table 17.4 that the number of persons officially classified as poor dropped sharply during the 1960s and early 1970s. Between 1978 and 1983, however, the number of poor increased nearly 40 percent. After falling back between 1983 and 1989, the figure hit 35.7 million in 1991, the highest total since 1964. This increase is at the center of a great debate over the effectiveness of antipoverty programs.

One view holds that economic growth is the best way to cure poverty. Poverty programs are expensive and must be paid for with tax revenues. The high rates of taxation required to support these programs, critics say, have eroded the incentive to work, save, and invest, thus slowing the rate of economic growth. In addition, the rise in poverty is cited as evidence that antipoverty programs do not work.

The opposite view is that poverty would be much more widespread without antipoverty programs. Poverty has increased not because of *increasing* programs but because the "real" level of transfer payments has actually *fallen* significantly. In other words, transfer payments have not kept up with rising prices. More than one in three women who are heads of households now live in poverty, as do more than one in five children. In addition, substantial unemployment accompanied serious recessions in the 1970s, the 1980s, and the 1990s.

Despite the anti-big-government rhetoric of the Reagan years, most of what the government did to change the distribution of income before 1981 it still does today. The volume of redistribution is less, but most major programs have remained largely intact. Many still argue that we do far too little. Poverty rates remain higher today than they were 20 years ago, and the number of homeless people continues to increase. But others continue to insist that government redistribution is taking its toll on incentives.

GOVERNMENT OR THE MARKET? A REVIEW

Part Two of this book (Chapters 6–12) introduced you to the behavior of households and firms in input and output markets. There you learned that if all the assumptions of perfect competition held in the real world, the outcome would be perfectly efficient.

But as we began to relax the assumptions of perfect competition in Part Three (Chapters 13–17), we began to see a potential role for government in the economy. Some firms acquire market power and tend to underproduce and overprice. Unregulated markets give private decision makers no incentives to weigh the social costs of externalities. Goods that provide collective benefits may not be produced in sufficient quantities without government involvement. And, as we saw in this chapter, the final distribution of well-being determined by the free market may not be considered equitable by society.

Remember, however, that government is not a cure for all economic woes. There is nothing to guarantee that public sector involvement will improve matters. In fact, many argue that government involvement may bring about even more inequity and inefficiency because bureaucrats are often driven by self-interest, not public interest.

You now have a strong foundation in microeconomic theory. Part Four of this book—Chapters 18–20—presents three topics in applied economics: public finance, labor economics, and urban economics. These chapters are meant to provide you with an overview of how the discipline addresses some of the most pressing problems of our time. They also represent a preview of what you will encounter in more advanced courses in economics.

SUMMARY

1. Even if all markets were perfectly efficient, the result might not be fair. Even in relatively free market economies, governments redistribute income and wealth, usually in the name of fairness, or *equity*.

2. Because utility is neither directly observable nor measurable, most policy discussions deal with the distributions of income and wealth as imperfect substitutes for the concept of "the distribution of well-being."

The Sources of Household Income

3. Households derive their incomes from three basic sources: (1) from wages or salaries received in exchange for labor (about 64%); (2) from property such as capital and land (about 25%); and (3) from government (about 11%).

4. Differences in wage and salary incomes across households result from differences in the characteristics of workers (skills, training, education, experience, and so on) and from differences in jobs (dangerous, exciting, glamorous, difficult, and so forth). Household income also varies with the number of household members in the labor force, and it can decline sharply if members become unemployed.

5. The amount of property income that a household earns depends on the amount and kinds of property it owns. Property income is unevenly distributed. In the United States the top 20% of income earners earn about 70% of the property income, which usually takes the form of profits, interest, dividends, and rents.

6. Transfer income from governments flows substantially, but not exclusively, to lower-income households. Except for social security, transfer payments are by and large designed to provide income to those in need.

The Distribution of Income

7. The top 20% of all income earners received 44.3% of the total income in the United States in 1990, while the bottom 20% earned just 4.6 percent. Income distribution in the United States has remained remarkably stable over a long period of time.

8. The Lorenz Curve is a commonly used graphic device for describing the distribution of income. The Gini coefficient is an index of income inequality that ranges from zero for perfect equality to one for total inequality.

9. Poverty is very difficult to define. Nonetheless, the official poverty line in the United States is fixed at three times the cost of the Department of Agriculture's minimum food budget. In 1991 the poverty line for a family of four was $13,924.

10. Between 1960 and 1970, the number of people officially classified as poor fell from 40 million to 25 million. That number did not change much between 1970 and 1978. Between 1978 and 1983, the number of poor people increased by nearly 45% to 35.3 million. In 1991 the figure was 35.7 million.

11. Data on the distribution of wealth are not as readily available as data on the distribution of income. The distribution of wealth in the United States is more unequal than the distribution of income. The wealthiest 10% of households own nearly two thirds of all household assets, while the wealthiest 1% own nearly one third of all household assets.

The Redistribution Debate

12. The basic philosophical argument against government redistribution rests on the proposition that one is entitled to the fruits of one's efforts. It also rests on the principles of freedom of contract and protection of property rights. More common arguments focus on the negative effects of redistribution on incentives to work, save, and invest.

13. The basic philosophical argument in favor of redistribution is that a society as rich as the United States has a moral obligation to provide all its members with the basic necessities of life. More formal arguments can be found in the works of the utilitarians, Rawls, Marx, and others.

Redistribution Programs and Policies

14. In the United States, redistribution is accomplished through mildly progressive taxation and through a number of government transfer programs. The largest of these are social

security, public assistance, supplemental security, unemployment compensation, Medicare and Medicaid, food stamps, and various housing subsidy programs, including public housing.

15. The increase in poverty during the early 1980s is at the center of a great debate over the effectiveness of antipoverty programs. One view holds that the best way to cure poverty is with economic growth. Poverty programs are expensive and must be paid for with tax revenues. The high rates of taxation required to support these programs have eroded the incentive to work, save, and invest, thus slowing the rate of economic growth. In addition, the rise in poverty is cited as evidence that antipoverty programs do not work. The opposite view holds that without antipoverty programs, poverty would be much worse.

REVIEW TERMS AND CONCEPTS

compensating differentials   430
economic income   433
equity   426
food stamps   446
Gini coefficient   435
human capital   430
labor theory of value   442

Lorenz Curve   435
Medicaid and Medicare   446
money income   434
poverty line   437
property income   431
public assistance, or welfare   445

Rawlsian justice   442
social security system   444
transfer payments   432
unemployment compensation   446
utilitarian justice   441
utility possibilities frontier   427

PROBLEM SET

1. In 1993, President Bill Clinton proposed, and the U.S. Congress passed, a number of measures to increase the progressivity of the U.S. individual income tax, including tax relief at the bottom of the income scale and an increase in the top bracket's rate from 31% to 39.6 percent. What are the arguments in favor of such a policy? What are some of the possible consequences of such a policy? In retrospect, were the Clinton proposals a good idea?

2. During the mid-1980s, house values and rents rose sharply in California and in the northeastern United States. Homeowners, who have higher incomes on average than renters, benefit from house-price increases and are protected from housing-cost increases. Renters experience rising rents and falling standards of living if incomes do not keep up with housing-cost increases. Using the *Statistical Abstract of the United States,* look up residential rent, home prices, and income levels for your area. What has happened in the last 10 years? Do you think the performance of the housing market in recent years has increased or decreased inequality in your area?

3. New Ph.D.'s in economics entering the job market find that academic jobs (jobs teaching at colleges and universities) pay about 30% less than nonacademic jobs such as working at a bank or a consulting firm. Those who take academic jobs are clearly worse off than those who take nonacademic jobs. Do you agree? Explain your answer.

4. Using the data in Table 1 for 1981, plot two Lorenz Curves on the same graph:
Which has the higher Gini coefficient? How do you interpret the result?

5. How is the official poverty line in the United States established? How does it change from year to year? Suggest two alternative ways of measuring poverty.

6. Should welfare benefits be higher in California and New York than they are in Mississippi? Defend your answer.

7. Poverty among the elderly has been sharply reduced in the last quarter century. How has this been accomplished?

8. Write a memo to your senator urging either an increase or a decrease in federal spending on public housing. Defend your position carefully, using both philosophical and practical arguments.

9. "Income inequality is evidence that our economic system is working well, not poorly." What arguments might this speaker use in order to support his opinion of income redistribution policies? How might he respond when racial or sexual disparities are brought to his attention?

TABLE 1

	PERCENT OF INCOME	
	BLACK	WHITE
Lowest fifth	5.4	4.1
Second fifth	11.7	9.4
Third fifth	17.5	16.0
Fourth fifth	24.2	25.7
Highest fifth	41.2	44.8

REGULATION IN THE CABLE TV INDUSTRY

Over 57 million households in the United States are customers of the $22-billion-a-year cable TV industry. In response to continuing consumer complaints of rising cable rates, Congress in 1992 followed the lead of the Federal Communications Commission (FCC) and expanded local rate regulation of cable television operators. The FCC's April 1, 1993, ruling based on the 1992 Cable Act called for a billion-dollar rollback in cable rates and sparked a 10% to 20% decrease in the price of some cable stocks.

This reversal of policy took place only six years after the 1984 Cable Act, which deregulated the industry, took effect. The 1984 act authorized the FCC to regulate only those cable companies that did not face "effective competition" (considered to be three or more over-the-air stations until 1991, when this number was raised to six). Even then, municipal authorities were able to regulate only basic service. In the wake of deregulation, cable companies combined most of their stations into one basic package and raised rates. Bills for the most popular services increased 61% from 1986 to 1991. During the same period, industry revenues almost doubled (see Figure 1).

The definition of "basic service" is now a source of controversy. When Congress first began discussing reregulating cable TV in 1989, local cable companies began to split the package of channels they offered, narrowing the number of channels included in the basic service and raising the price of the more popular "expanded" packages. This practice is called *tiering*. For example, in February of 1990, Paragon Cable in Laredo, Texas, offered 34 channels in its basic service at a monthly fee of $17.00. In June 1990, it split the package into "limited basic," ($12.00) and "Paragon preferred" ($17.00). By September of 1991, the expanded package cost $20.50, 21% more than the

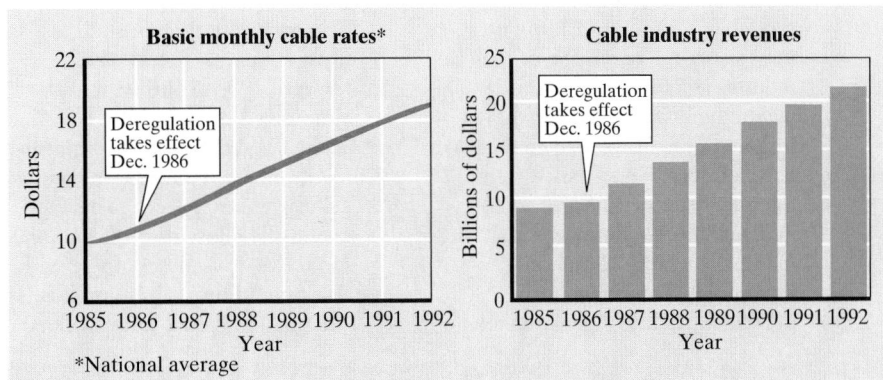

FIGURE 1

Growth in Cable Rates and Industry Revenues, 1985–1992

Source: *The Wall Street Journal*, April 2, 1993, p. B1.

same 34 channels had cost in 1990. Although the price of the new "basic" package fell to $7.95 in September 1991, subscribers were automatically signed up for the expanded service and had to pay a fee of $15.00 to switch to the limited tier. Most subscribers selected the "expanded" package.

To protect the new cable TV companies when they first began operating, television networks were prohibited from owning cable systems. Early in 1992, the FCC voted to partially rescind this ruling. In July of 1992, the FCC voted 5-0 to reduce further the protection offered to cable monopolies by allowing phone companies to offer video programming (although phone companies are barred from buying cable companies in their areas). On May 17, 1993, U.S. West Inc. announced a $2.5 billion deal with Time Warner, the second-largest cable operator in the United States, to build an advanced cable system offering interactive video and phone service.

The future of cable TV is unclear. Since 1991, the FCC has encouraged telephone companies to adopt technologies that would allow them to offer video programming and other information services to customers.

Interactive TV, which could allow MTV viewers to purchase CDs and customers at home to play along with game shows, may be the next step in the creation of the information highway. But will the FCC's recent rulings affect new or existing companies' decisions to offer new services? Some analysts predict a choice of over 500 cable channels by the end of the decade and the availability of thousands of movies upon demand, but few are willing to predict with certainty who will be offering these services.

QUESTIONS FOR ANALYTICAL THINKING

1. Most networks receive approximately 50% of their revenues from advertising. What effect would you expect a proliferation of stations to have on network profits and potential funding for new programs?

2. The president of the National Cable Television Association has said that allowing telephone companies to enter the video business is unfair, because these companies would be able to subsidize their operations with profits from the telephone business.

The president of the U.S. Telephone Association has said he fears that cable TV companies that own their own programming would deny those programs to competitors. Discuss.

3. What is the role of fixed costs in the cable TV industry? How do they justify the regulation of the industry as a monopoly? As new technologies are developed, how important might these fixed costs be? Consider that in Asia, where the infrastructure for cable is limited, satellite TV dominates the market, reaching 12 million households. Entrepreneurs have purchased satellite dishes and constructed local cable systems with as few as 1,000 subscribers in their neighborhoods. How might the industry evolve in Asia?

4. What impact would you expect cable TV regulation to have on industry plans to spend billions on new technologies, such as fiber optics?

5. In April 1993, Southwestern Bell announced plans to buy two cable TV systems in Washington, D.C., where it already operates a cellular phone system. This may eventually allow it to offer phone service that would compete with that offered by Bell Atlantic. Bell Atlantic has filed a suit in federal court to overturn a ban on phone companies supplying TV programs to their customers. These developments suggest two possible futures for the industry: (1) an increase in monopoly power, where one company controls the market for both cable TV and phone services (and could possibly supplant the video rental business and offer home shopping and banking services), or (2) increased competition, where a number of firms compete to offer information services in any geographic area. Which do you think is more likely? Explain your answer.

PART FOUR

Current Microeconomic Issues

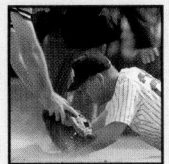

In Chapter 1, we noted that economics is a diverse field that encompasses many specialized subfields. Some are concerned with economic history; others with the economic relationships between nations; others with the formulation of government policy.

In Part Four, we provide a closer look at three areas of economic inquiry that we've found students are most interested in. These include:

■ Public finance and the economics of taxation (Chapter 18). What are some of the effects of taxes on incentives to work and invest? Who ends up bearing the burden of the various taxes in the United States?

■ The economics of labor markets and labor unions (Chapter 19). How does the labor market allocate the millions of people in an economy to the available jobs in that economy? What are the pros and cons of a minimum wage law? How widely do wages vary across regions, sexes, and ethnic groups? What role has organized labor played in the United States?

■ Urban and regional economics (Chapter 20). How do households and firms decide where to locate? How have the economic fortunes of the various regions of the United States changed over the years? What are some of the larger cities doing to rejuvenate their economies?

18 Public Finance: The Economics of Taxation

An introductory course in economics has several goals, one of which is to introduce a body of theory about how economies work. The first 17 chapters of this book contain what amounts to the core of microeconomic theory. Beginning with perfect markets in Chapters 6 through 12, we built a model of a perfectly competitive market system, with no public sector, in which households and firms made self-interested choices. The result, we saw, was efficient. The system seemed to produce what people want at least cost.

But to construct the perfectly competitive model, we made a number of restrictive assumptions. As we began to relax those assumptions in Chapters 13 through 17, we discovered some problems. We saw, for example, that imperfect market structures—monopoly, oligopoly, and so forth—can lead to underproduction and overpricing. Goods that bestow public or social benefits may not be produced by private, profit-seeking firms. External costs and benefits can lead to inefficient consumption and production decisions if these externalities are not taken into account by decision makers. Imperfect information can lead to an inefficient allocation of resources. In addition, the distribution of income and wealth may not be fair.

The previous five chapters focused on the steps that government might take to correct these market failures. In theory, governments can improve the allocation of resources in a number of ways: through production of public goods, antitrust enforcement and regulation of monopoly, and rules and regulations to control externalities, dispersal of information, and redistribution of income. In reality, however, governments are just as prone to failure as unregulated markets are.

Another purpose of an introductory course in economics is to survey the major subfields of the discipline. In Chapter 1 we briefly described a number of these subfields. This chapter is the first of several that expand on those brief descriptions. Because the discipline is so varied, we cannot possibly survey all the areas of economic inquiry. We therefore limit our discussion to three of the most widely debated economic issues of the day: public finance (Chapter 18), labor economics (Chapter 19), and urban economics (Chapter 20).

THE ECONOMICS OF TAXATION

The five chapters in Part Three analyzed the potential role of government in the economy. Taken together, those chapters discuss much of the field of *public economics.* From there, it is an easy transition to the field of *public finance,* with which we begin our survey of applied economics. No matter what functions we end up assigning to government, in order to do anything at all government must first raise revenues. The primary vehicle that the government uses to finance itself is taxation.[1]

The most important thing to remember about taxes is that ultimately they are paid by people, or by households:

> Taxes may be imposed on transactions, institutions, property, meals, and all kinds of other things, but in the final analysis they are paid by individuals or households.

Taxes: Basic Concepts

Before we begin our analysis of the U.S. tax system, we need to clarify some terms. There are many different kinds of taxes, and tax analysts use a very specific language to describe them. Every tax has two parts: a *base* and a *rate structure.* The **tax base** is the measure or value upon which the tax is levied. In the United States, taxes are levied on a variety of different bases, including income, sales, property, and corporate profits. The **tax rate structure** determines the portion of the tax base that must be paid in taxes. A tax rate of 25% on income, for example, means that I pay a tax equal to 25% of my income.

tax base The measure or value upon which a tax is levied.

tax rate structure The percentage of a tax base that must be paid in taxes—25% of income, for example.

TAXES ON STOCKS VERSUS TAXES ON FLOWS Tax bases may be either stock measures or flow measures. The local property tax is a tax on the value of residential, commercial, or industrial property. Homeowners, for instance, are taxed on the current assessed value of their homes. Current value is a stock variable—that is, it is measured or estimated at a point in time.

Other taxes are levied on flows. (Review Chapter 4 if the difference between stock and flow variables is unclear to you.) Income is a flow. Most

---

[1]Before we proceed, you may want to review the discussion of the public sector in Chapter 3. There we describe the basic sources of revenue for federal, state, and local governments, as well as the things those revenues are spent on. You will often hear the taxing and spending policies of federal or state governments referred to as "fiscal policies." The word "fiscal" comes from "fisc," another word for a government treasury.

people are paid on a weekly, biweekly, or monthly basis, and they have taxes deducted from every paycheck. Retail sales take place continuously, and a retail sales tax takes a portion of that flow.

PROPORTIONAL, PROGRESSIVE, AND REGRESSIVE TAXES All taxes are ultimately paid out of income. A tax whose burden is a constant proportion of income for all households is called a **proportional tax.** A comprehensive tax of 20% on all forms of income, with no deductions or exclusions, is an example of a proportional tax.

proportional tax A tax whose burden is the same proportion of income for all households.

A tax that exacts a higher proportion of income from higher-income households than it does from lower-income households is a **progressive tax.** Because its rate structure increases with income, the U.S. individual income tax is a progressive tax. Under current law, for example, a family with a taxable income of $30,000 would pay a tax of roughly 15%, while a family with an income of $60,000 would fall into the 28% bracket.

progressive tax A tax whose burden, expressed as a percentage of income, increases as income increases.

A tax that exacts a lower proportion of income from higher-income families than it does from lower-income families is a **regressive tax.** The retail sales tax is a good example of a regressive tax. Suppose the retail sales tax in your state is 5 percent. You might assume that it is a proportional tax because everyone pays 5 percent. But all people do not spend the same fraction of their income on taxable goods and services. In fact, higher-income households save a larger fraction of their incomes. Thus, even though they spend more money on more expensive things and may pay more taxes in *dollars* than lower-income families do, they end up paying a smaller *proportion* of their incomes in sales tax.

regressive tax A tax whose burden, expressed as a percentage of income, falls as income increases.

Table 18.1 shows this principle at work in three families. The lowest-income family saves 20% of its $10,000 income, leaving $8000 for consumption. With a 5% sales tax, the household pays $400, or 4% of total income, in tax. The $50,000 family saves 50% of its income, or $25,000, leaving $25,000 for consumption. With the 5% sales tax, the household pays $1250, only 2.5% of its total income, in tax.

Figure 18.1 graphs an estimate of the actual burden of individual income taxes—federal, state, and local—and of state and local sales taxes in 1990. As you can see, income taxes are progressive and sales taxes are regressive. *Excise taxes* (taxes on specific commodities) are also regressive.

MARGINAL VERSUS AVERAGE TAX RATES When discussing a specific tax or taxes in general, it is often useful to distinguish between average tax rates and marginal tax rates. Your *average tax rate* is the total amount of tax you pay divided by your total income. For example, if you earned a total income of $15,000 and paid income taxes of $1500, your average income tax rate would be 10% ($1500 divided by $15,000). If you paid $3000 in taxes, your rate would be 20% ($3000 divided by $15,000).

TABLE 18.1
The Burden of a Hypothetical 5% Sales Tax Imposed on Three Households with Different Incomes

HOUSE-HOLD	INCOME	SAVING RATE, %	SAVING	CONSUMPTION	5% TAX ON CONSUMPTION	TAX AS A % OF INCOME
A	$ 10,000	20	$ 2,000	$ 8,000	$ 400	4.0
B	20,000	40	8,000	12,000	600	3.0
C	50,000	50	25,000	25,000	1250	2.5

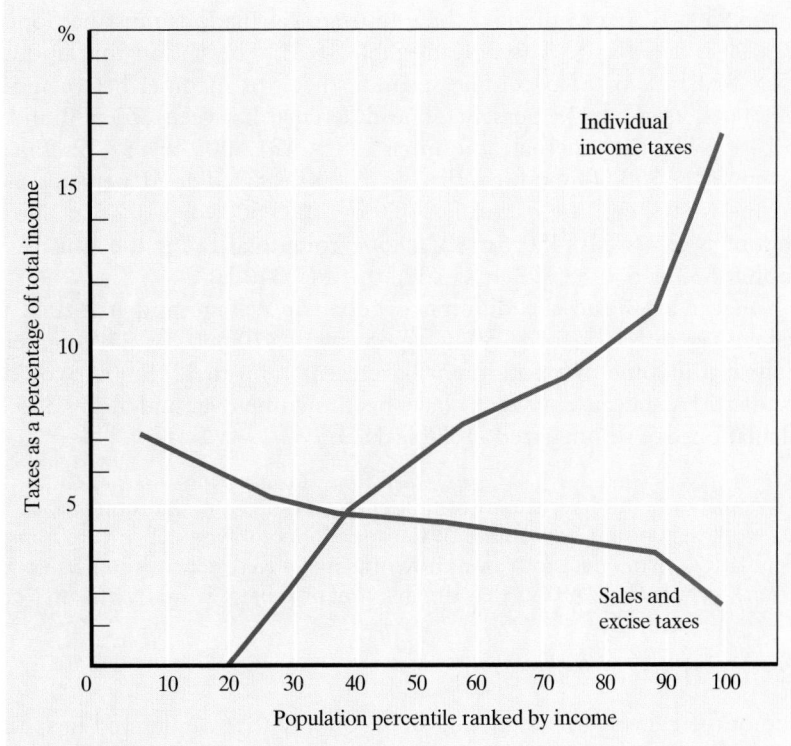

FIGURE 18.1

Income, Sales, and Excise Taxes as a Percentage of Total Income in 1990

The individual income tax is progressive; sales and excise taxes are regressive.

Sources: Joseph Pechman, "The Future of the Income Tax," *American Economic Review,* March 1990, Table 8, and authors' estimates.

Your *marginal tax rate* is the tax rate that you pay on any additional income that you earn. If you take a part-time job and pay an additional $280 in tax on the extra $1000 you've earned, your marginal tax rate is 28% ($280 divided by $1000).

Marginal and average tax rates are usually different. The U.S. individual income tax provides an excellent example of how and why marginal tax rates can differ. Each year, you must file a tax return with the Internal Revenue Service on or before April 15. On that form you first figure out the total tax that you are responsible for paying. Next, you determine how much was withheld from your income and sent to the IRS by your employer. If too much was withheld, you get a refund. If not enough was withheld, you have to write a check to the government for the difference.

In figuring out the total amount of tax that you are responsible for paying, you first add up all your income. You are then allowed to subtract certain items from it. Among the things that virtually all taxpayers can subtract are the *personal exemption* and the *standard deduction.*[2] After everything is subtracted, you are left with *taxable income.* Taxable income is then subject to a set of marginal rates that rise with income. Table 18.2 presents the marginal individual income tax rates for 1993.

Suppose that you are a single taxpayer who earned $70,000 in 1993. To calculate your tax, you first subtract the personal exemption ($2350) and the standard deduction ($3700) from your gross income. This leaves you with a taxable income

TABLE 18.2

Individual Income Tax Rates, 1993

MARRIED COUPLES FILING JOINTLY	
TAXABLE INCOME	TAX RATE
$0—$36,900	15%
$36,900—$89,150	28%
$89,150—$140,000	31%
$140,000—$250,000	36%
Over $250,000	39.6%

SINGLE TAXPAYERS	
TAXABLE INCOME	TAX RATE
$0—$22,100	15%
$22,100—$53,500	28%
$53,500—$115,000	31%
$115,000—$250,000	36%
Over $250,000	39.6%

Source: Internal Revenue Service.

---

[2]Deductions and exemptions have no definition other than that they are amounts that you are allowed to subtract from income before figuring your tax. In 1993, a single taxpayer could subtract a *personal exemption* of $2,350. A married couple could subtract twice that amount plus $2,350 for every dependent child in the family. If your parents claim you as a dependent, you cannot claim an exemption for yourself when you file as an individual. Taxpayers in 1993 were also permitted to subtract either a *standard deduction* of $3,700 or itemized deductions if they exceeded $3,700. Expenditures that can be itemized and deducted include extraordinary medical expenses, state and local income and property taxes, mortgage interest paid, and charitable contributions. The standard deduction is larger for those who are over 65 and/or blind.

of $63,950. To figure the tax, three separate calculations must be done.[3] The first $22,100 is taxed at 15% (see again Table 18.2). The tax on this amount is simply .15 × $22,100, or $3,315. The second "slice" of income, between $22,100 and $53,500 is taxed at 28 percent. The difference between $53,500 and $22,100 is $31,400. The tax on that amount is .28 × $31,400, or $8,792. Finally, taxable income over $53,500 and less than $115,000 is taxed at 31 percent. Since taxable income is $63,950, the excess is $63,950 − $53,500, or $10,450. The tax on that amount is .31 × $10,450, or $3239.50. Your total tax is the sum of these three amounts: $3,315 + $8,792 + $3,239.50 = $15,346.50.

You can now see the difference between average and marginal rates. Your average tax rate is $15,346.50 as a percent of $70,000, or 21.9 percent. But any additional income that you might have earned, up to $115,000, would have been taxed at 31%, because it would have been income over and above $53,500. These calculations are summarized in Table 18.3.

> Marginal tax rates have the most influence on behavior. Decisions about how much to work depend on how much of the added income you get to take home. Similarly, a firm's decision about how much to invest depends in part on the additional, or marginal, profits that the investment project would yield after tax.

Tax Equity

One of the criteria for evaluating the economy that we defined in Chapter 1 (and returned to in Chapter 17) was fairness, or *equity*. Everyone agrees that tax burdens should be distributed fairly, that all of us should pay our "fair share" of taxes, but there is endless debate about what constitutes a fair tax system.

One theory of fairness is called the **benefits-received principle.** Dating back to the eighteenth-century economist Adam Smith and earlier writers, the benefits-received principle holds that taxpayers should contribute to government according to the benefits that they derive from public expenditures. This principle ties the tax side of the fiscal equation to the expenditure side. For example, the owners and users of cars pay gasoline and automotive excise taxes, which are paid into the Federal Highway Trust Fund that is used to build and maintain the federal

benefits-received principle A theory of fairness which holds that taxpayers should contribute to government (in the form of taxes) in proportion to the benefits that they receive from public expenditures.

---

[3]Taxpayers do not have to do these calculations. Rather, filers simply look up the tax due for their particular income level in the tax table that accompanies their tax form package.

TABLE 18.3
Tax Calculations for a Single Taxpayer Who Earned $70,000 in 1993

Total income	$70,000
– Personal exemption	2,350
– Standard deduction	3,700
=Taxable income	$63,950
Tax calculation	
$0 – $22,100 taxed at 15% → ($22,100) × .15 =	$3,315.00
$53,500 – $22,150 taxed at 28% →	
($53,500 – $22,100) × .28 = $31,400 × .28 =	$8,792.00
> $53,500 taxed at 31% →	
($63,950 – $53,500) × .31 = $10,450 × .31 =	$3,239.50
Total tax = $15,346.50	$15,346.50
Average tax rate = $15,346.50/70,000 =	21.9%
Marginal tax rate =	31%

highway system. The beneficiaries of public highways are thus taxed in rough proportion to their use of those highways.

The difficulty with applying the benefits principle is that the bulk of public expenditures are for public goods—national defense, for example. The benefits of public goods fall collectively on all members of society, and there is no way to determine what value individual taxpayers receive from them.

A different principle, and one that has dominated the formulation of tax policy in the United States for decades, is the **ability-to-pay principle**. This principle holds that taxpayers should bear tax burdens in line with their ability to pay. Here the tax side of the fiscal equation is viewed separately from the expenditure side. Under this system, the problem of attributing the benefits of public expenditures to specific taxpayers or groups of taxpayers is avoided.

ability-to-pay principle A theory of taxation which holds that citizens should bear tax burdens in line with their ability to pay taxes.

HORIZONTAL AND VERTICAL EQUITY   If we accept the idea that ability to pay should be the basis for the distribution of tax burdens, two principles follow. First, the principle of *horizontal equity* holds that those with equal ability to pay should bear equal tax burdens. Second, the principle of *vertical equity* holds that those with greater ability to pay should pay more.

Although these notions seem appealing, we must have answers to two interdependent questions before they can be meaningful. First, how is ability to pay measured? What is the "best" tax base? Second, if A has a greater ability to pay than B, *how much* more should A contribute?

What Is the "Best" Tax Base?

The three leading candidates for best tax base are *income, consumption,* and *wealth.* Before we debate the merits of each as a basis for taxation, however, let us review the meanings of these terms.

Income—or, to be precise, *economic income*—is anything that enhances one's ability to command resources. The most used technical definition of economic income is the value of what one consumes plus any change in the value of what one owns:

$$\text{Economic Income} = \text{Consumption} + \text{Change in Net Worth}$$

This broad definition includes many items that are not counted by the Internal Revenue Service and some items that the Census Bureau does not include in its definition of "money income." Economic income includes all money receipts, whether from employment, profits, or transfers from the government. It also includes the value of benefits not paid or received in money form, such as medical benefits, employer retirement contributions, paid country club memberships, and so forth. Increases or decreases in the value of stocks or bonds, whether or not they are "realized" through sale, are part of economic income. For income tax purposes, capital gains count as income only when they are realized, but for purposes of defining economic income, all increases in asset values count, whether they are realized or not.

A few other items that we do not usually think of as income are included in a comprehensive definition of income. If I own my house outright and live in it rent free, income flows from my house just as interest flows from a bond or profit from a share of stock. By owning the house, I enjoy valuable housing benefits that I would otherwise have to pay rent for. I am my own landlord and I am, in essence, earning my own rent. Other components of economic income include any gifts and bequests received and food grown at home.

The point here is that:

> In economic terms, income is income, regardless of source and regardless of use.

Consumption is the total value of things that a household consumes in a given period. It is equal to income minus saving, or:

> Consumption = Income − Saving (Change in Net Worth)

Wealth, or *net worth,* is simply the value of all the things that one owns after one's liabilities are subtracted. If you were to sell off today everything of value that you own—stocks, bonds, houses, cars, and so forth—at their current market prices and pay off all your debts—loans, mortgages, and so forth—you would end up with your net worth. In other words:

> Net Worth = Assets − Liabilities

For years, conventional wisdom among economists held that income was the best measure of ability to pay taxes. Many who feel that consumption is a better measure have recently challenged that assumption. The following arguments are not just arguments about fairness and ability to pay; they are also arguments about the best base for taxation.

CONSUMPTION AS THE BEST TAX BASE   The view favoring consumption as the best tax base dates back at least to the seventeenth-century English philosopher Thomas Hobbes, who argued that people should pay taxes in accordance with "what they actually take out of the common pot, not what they leave in." The standard of living, the argument goes, depends not on income but on how much income is spent. If we want to redistribute well-being, therefore, the tax base should be consumption, because consumption is the best measure of well-being.

A second argument with a distinguished history dates back to work done by Irving Fisher in the early part of this century. Fisher and many others have argued that a tax on income discourages saving by taxing savings twice. A story told originally by Fisher illustrates this theory quite nicely.[4]

Suppose that Alex builds a house for Frank. For this service, Alex is paid $10,000 and given an orchard containing 100 apple trees. Alex spends the $10,000 today, but he saves the orchard, and presumably he will consume or sell the fruit it bears every year in the future. Suppose that at year's end the state levies a 10% tax on Alex's total income, which includes the $10,000 and the orchard. First, the government takes 10% of the $10,000, which is 10% of Alex's consumption. Second, it takes 10% of the orchard—10 trees—which is 10% of Alex's saving. If this is all the government did, there would be no double taxation of saving. If, however, the income tax is also levied in the following year, Alex will be taxed on the income generated by the 90 trees that he still owns. If the income tax is levied in the year after that, Alex will again be taxed on the income generated by his orchard, and so on. The income tax is thus taxing Alex's saving more than once. It taxes the initial saving *plus* all the future income generated from the saving. To avoid the double taxation of saving, either the original saving of 100 trees should not be taxed or the income generated from the after-tax number of trees (90) should not be taxed.

---

[4]Irving Fisher and Herbert Fisher, *Constructive Income Taxation: A Proposal for Reform* (New York: Harper, 1942), Ch. 8, p. 56.

The same logic can be applied to cash saving. Suppose that the income tax rate is 25% and that you earn $20,000. Out of the $20,000 you consume $16,000 and save $4000. At the end of the year, you owe the government 25% of your total income, or $5000. You can think of this as a tax of 25% on consumption ($4000) and 25% on savings ($1000). Why, then, do we say that the income tax is a double tax on saving? To understand the argument you have to think about the $4000 that is saved.

If you save $4000, you will no doubt put it to some use. Safe possibilities include putting it in an interest-bearing account or buying a bond with it. If you do either of these, you will earn interest that you can consume in future years. In fact, when we save and earn interest we are spreading some of our present earnings over future years of consumption. Just as the orchard yields future fruit, so the bond yields future interest, which is considered income in the year it is earned, and is taxed as such. The only way that you can earn that future interest income is if you leave your money tied up in the bond or the account. You can consume the $4000 today *or* you can have the future flow of interest; you can't have both. Yet both are taxed.

Suppose that the interest rate is 10 percent. If you save $4000 and put that money into a long-term bond that pays 10% annual interest, you have converted your $4000 into an additional income flow of $400 per year. That flow will be taxed at 25%, or $100 per year. Thus, your saving is taxed both when you earn it *and* as you consume it in the future. Many people think this is unfair.

It is also inefficient. As you will see in more detail later, a tax that distorts economic choices creates *excess burdens*. By double taxing saving, an income tax distorts the choice between consumption and saving, which is really the choice between present consumption and future consumption. Double taxing also tends to reduce the saving rate and the rate of investment—and ultimately the rate of economic growth.

INCOME AS THE BEST TAX BASE   Your ability to pay is your ability to command resources, and your income is the best measure of your capacity to command resources today. According to proponents of income as a tax base, you should be taxed not on what you actually draw out of the common pot, but rather on the basis of your *ability,* to draw from that pot. In other words, your decision to save or consume is no different from your decision to buy apples, to go out for dinner, or to give money to your mother. It is your *income* that enables you to do all these things, and it is income that should be taxed, regardless of its sources and regardless of how you use it. Saving is just another use of income.

If income is the best measure of ability to pay, the double taxation argument doesn't hold water. An income tax taxes savings twice only if consumption is the measure used to gauge a person's ability to pay. It does not do so if income is the measure used. Acquisition of the orchard enhances your ability to pay today; a bountiful crop of fruit enhances your ability to pay when it is produced. Interest income is no different than any other form of income; it too enhances your ability to pay. Taxing both is thus fair.

WEALTH AS THE BEST TAX BASE   Still others argue that the real power to command resources comes not from any single year's income but from accumulated wealth. Aggregate net worth in the United States is many times larger than aggregate income.

If two people have identical annual incomes of $10,000, but one also has an accumulated net worth of $1 million, is it reasonable to argue that these two people have the same ability to pay, or that they should pay equal taxes? Most people would answer no. Those who favor income taxation, however, argue that net wealth comes from after-tax income that has been saved. An income tax taxes consumption and saving correctly, they say. To subsequently take part of what has been saved would be an unfair second hit—*real* double taxation.

NO SIMPLE ANSWER As you can see, the "best-base" debate has a number of sides. Before the 1970s, most tax economists favored a comprehensive income base. Today, many economists favor a comprehensive personal consumption tax. Part of the reason for the increasing popularity of consumption taxes is a growing concern with the low saving rate in the United States. Since 1978 there has been concern with productivity growth, and many point to the inadequacy of saving as the culprit. As we saw in earlier chapters, household saving provides resources for firms to invest in capital that raises the productivity of labor.

Many of these issues were debated in 1993 as part of President Clinton's proposals to bring the national deficit under control and reform the health care system. The final bill included a substantial increase in progressivity to be achieved by raising the top marginal tax rate from 31% to 39.6% (36% plus a surcharge of 10% for the very wealthiest taxpayers) and a tax on gasoline. In addition, some in the administration favored the imposition of a national value-added tax (VAT), which is essentially a national sales tax. Most European countries rely heavily on value-added taxes. The average VAT rate among members of the European community is 17 percent.

TAX INCIDENCE: WHO PAYS?

When a government levies a tax, it writes a law assigning responsibility for payment to specific people or specific organizations. To understand a tax, however, we must look beyond those named in the law as the initial taxpayers.

First, remember the cardinal principle of tax analysis: The burden of a tax is ultimately borne by individuals or households; institutions have no real taxpaying capacity. Second, the burden of a tax is not always borne by those initially responsible for paying it. Directly or indirectly, tax burdens are often *shifted* to others. When we speak of the **incidence of a tax,** we are referring to the ultimate distribution of its burden.

The simultaneous reactions of many households and/or firms to the presence of a tax may cause relative prices to change, and price changes affect the well-being of households. Households may feel the impact of a tax on the sources side or on the uses side of the income equation. (We use the term "income equation" because the amount of income from all *sources* must be exactly equal to the amount of income allocated to all *uses*—including saving—in a given period.) On the **sources side,** a household is hurt if the net wages or profits that it receives fall; on the **uses side,** a household is hurt if the prices of the things that it buys rise. If your wages remain the same but the price of every item that you buy doubles, you are in the same position you would have been in if your wages had been cut by 50% and prices hadn't changed. In short:

> The imposition of a tax or a change in a tax can change behavior. Changes in behavior can affect supply and demand in markets and cause prices to change. When prices in input or output markets change, some households are made better off and some are made worse off. These final changes determine the ultimate burden of the tax.

Tax shifting takes place when households can alter their behavior and do something to avoid paying a tax. This is especially easily accomplished when only certain items are singled out for taxation. For example, suppose a heavy tax were levied on bananas. Initially the tax would make the price of bananas much higher, but there are many potential substitutes for bananas. Consumers can avoid the tax

tax incidence The ultimate distribution of tax's burden.

sources side/uses side The impact of a tax may be felt on one or the other or on both sides of the income equation. A tax may cause net income to fall (damage on the sources side), or it may cause prices of goods and services to rise so that income buys less (damage on the uses side).

tax shifting Occurs when households can alter their behavior and do something to avoid paying a tax.

by not buying bananas, and that is exactly what many of them will do. But, as demand drops, the market price of bananas falls and banana growers lose money. Thus, the tax shifts from consumers to the growers, at least in the short run.

A tax such as the retail sales tax, which is levied at the same rate on *all* consumer goods, is harder to avoid. The only thing that consumers can do to avoid such a tax is to consume less of everything. If consumers do so, saving will increase, but otherwise there are few opportunities for tax avoidance and therefore for tax shifting. The general principle here is that:

> Broad-based taxes are less likely to be shifted and more likely to "stick" where they are levied than "partial taxes" are.

The Incidence of Payroll Taxes

In 1992 nearly 40% of federal revenues came from social insurance taxes, also called "payroll taxes." The revenues from the various payroll taxes go to support social security, unemployment compensation, and other health and disability benefits for workers. (These are discussed in Chapter 17.) Some of these taxes are levied on employers as a percentage of payroll, and some are levied on workers as a percentage of wages or salaries earned.

To analyze the payroll tax, let us take a tax of $\$T$ per unit of labor levied on employers and briefly sketch the reactions that are likely to follow. When the tax is first levied, firms find that the price of labor is higher. Before the tax was levied, they paid $\$W$ per hour; now they must pay $\$W + \$T$. Firms may react in two ways. First, they may substitute capital for the now-more-expensive labor. Second, higher costs and lower profits may lead to a cut in production. Both reactions mean a lower demand for labor. Lower demand for labor, in turn, reduces wages, and part of the tax is thus passed on, or *shifted to,* the workers, who end up earning less. The extent to which the tax is shifted to workers depends on how workers react to the lower wages.

We can develop a more formal analysis of this situation with a picture of the market before the tax is levied. Figure 18.2 shows equilibrium in a hypothetical labor market with no payroll tax. Before we proceed, however, we should review the factors that determine the shapes of the supply and demand curves.

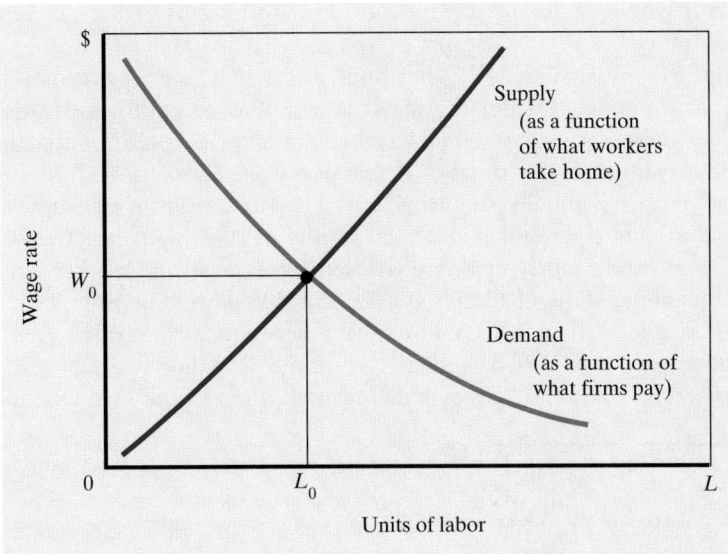

FIGURE 18.2

Equilibrium in a Competitive Labor Market— No Taxes

With no taxes on wages, the wage that firms pay is the same as the wage that workers take home. At a wage of W_0, the quantity of labor supplied and the quantity of labor demanded are equal.

Recall that the demand for labor in competitive markets depends on its productivity. As you saw in Chapter 10, a competitive, profit-maximizing firm will hire labor up to the point at which the market wage is equal to labor's marginal revenue product. The shape of the demand curve for labor shows how responsive *firms* are to changes in wages. Several factors determine a firm's reactions to changes in wage rates: how easy it is to substitute capital for labor, whether labor costs are large or small relative to total costs, and how elastic the demand for the firm's product is.[5]

The shape of the labor supply curve shows how responsive *workers* are to changes in wages. As you saw in Chapter 6, lower wages may affect workers' behavior in two ways. First, lower wages mean that workers will earn less income for the same amount of effort. They will therefore be able to buy fewer goods and services. They will also buy less leisure by working more. This is the *income effect* of a decrease in wages.

Second, a lower wage means that leisure is less expensive relative to other goods—an additional hour of leisure means an hour of lost wages, and wages are now lower. Workers "substitute" leisure for other goods by working less and buying less of other goods with the lower income. This is the *substitution effect* of a decrease in wages. An upward-sloping labor supply curve means that, on balance, the substitution effect is stronger than the income effect, and that lower wages lead to less work effort. If the opposite were true, the labor supply curve would bend back.[6]

In either case, the labor supply curve represents the reaction of workers to changes in the wage rate. Their behavior depends on the *after-tax* wage that they actually take home per hour of work. Labor demand is, of course, a function of the full amount that firms must pay per unit of labor, an amount that may include a tax if it is levied directly on payroll, as it is in our example. Such a tax, when present, drives a "wedge" between the price of labor that firms face and take-home wages.

IMPOSING A PAYROLL TAX: WHO PAYS?   In Figure 18.2, there were no taxes, and the wage that firms paid was the same as the wage that workers took home. At a wage of W_0, quantity of labor supplied and quantity of labor demanded were equal, and the labor market was in equilibrium.[7]

But now suppose that employers must pay a tax of $\$T$ per unit of labor. Figure 18.3 shows a new supply curve that is parallel to the old supply curve but above it by a distance, T. The new curve, S', shows labor supply as a function of what firms pay. Regardless of how the ultimate burden of the tax is shared, there is a difference between what firms pay and what workers take home.

If the initial wage is W_0 per hour, firms will face a price of $W_0 + T$ per unit of labor immediately after the tax is levied. Workers still receive only W_0, however. The higher wage rate—that is, the higher price of labor that firms now face—reduces the quantity of labor demanded from L_0 to L_d, and the firms lay off workers. Workers initially still receive W_0, so that amount of labor supplied does not change, and the result is an excess supply of labor equal to $(L_0 - L_d)$.

The excess supply applies downward pressure to the market wage, and wages fall, thus shifting some of the tax burden onto workers. The issue, of course, is: How far will wages fall? Figure 18.3 shows that a new equilibrium is achieved at W_1, with firms paying $W_1 + T$. When workers take home W_1, they will *supply* L_1 units of labor; if firms must pay $W_1 + T$, they will *demand* L_1 units of labor, and the market clears.

---

[5]If demand for output is highly inelastic, increases in costs from a rise in wages generally flow through to consumers in the form of higher prices.

[6]Evidence regarding the relative size of the income and substitution effects is presented in Chapter 19.

[7]Although the supply curve has a positive slope here, that slope implies nothing about the actual shape of the labor supply curve in the United States. Empirical estimates of supply elasticities are treated more fully in Chapter 19.

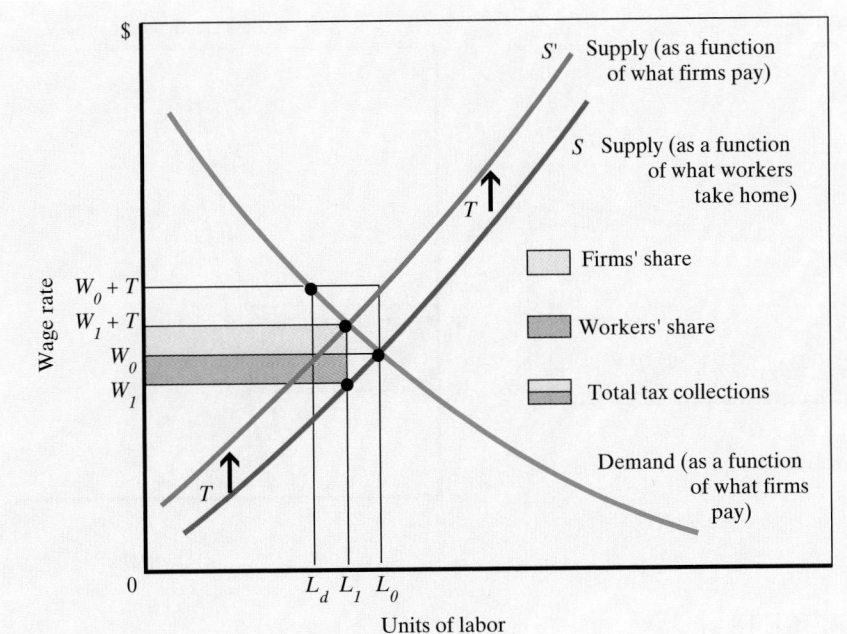

FIGURE 18.3

Incidence of a Per Unit Payroll Tax in a Competitive Labor Market

With a tax on firms of $T per unit of labor hired, the market will adjust, shifting the tax partially to workers. When the tax is levied, firms must at first pay $W_0 + T$. This reduces labor demand to L_d. The result is excess supply, which pushes wages down to W_1 and passes some of the burden of the tax on to workers.

In this case, then, the burden of the payroll tax is shared by employers and employees. Initially, firms paid W_0; after the tax, they pay $W_1 + T$. Initially, workers received W_0; after the tax, they end up with W_1. Total tax collections by the government are equal to $T \times L_1$; geometrically, they are equal to the entire shaded area in Figure 18.3. The workers' share of the tax burden is the lower portion, $(W_0 - W_1) \times L_1$; the firms' share is the upper portion, $[(W_1 + T) - W_0] \times L_1$.

Notice that the relative sizes of the firms' share and the workers' share of the total tax burden depend on the shapes of the demand and supply curves. For example, Figure 18.4 shows how the relative burden of a tax depends on the elasticity of labor supply. The same demand curve is depicted in both part a and part b of the figure. In addition, the initial equilibrium wage (W_0) is the same in the two diagrams. Finally, an identical tax of $T per unit of labor is levied on firms in both diagrams.

In both diagrams, the final equilibrium is labeled W_1 and $W_1 + T$. In Figure 18.4a on the next page, the labor supply curve is very elastic (that is, the quantity of labor supplied is very responsive to wages). In this diagram, the equilibrium wage paid to workers does not fall very much (from W_0 to W_1), while the total wage paid by firms rises sharply, to $W_1 + T$. Thus,

Firms bear the bulk of the tax burden when labor supply is very elastic.

In Figure 18.4b, however, the supply curve is very inelastic. Here, the quantity of labor supplied is less responsive to wage changes. In this diagram, the equilibrium wage falls significantly from W_0 to W_1, while the total wage paid by firms rises only modestly, to $W_1 + T$. Thus,

Workers bear the bulk of the tax burden when labor supply is less elastic.

Empirical studies of labor supply behavior in the United States suggest that for most of the work force, the elasticity of labor supply is close to zero. This leads to the conclusion that:

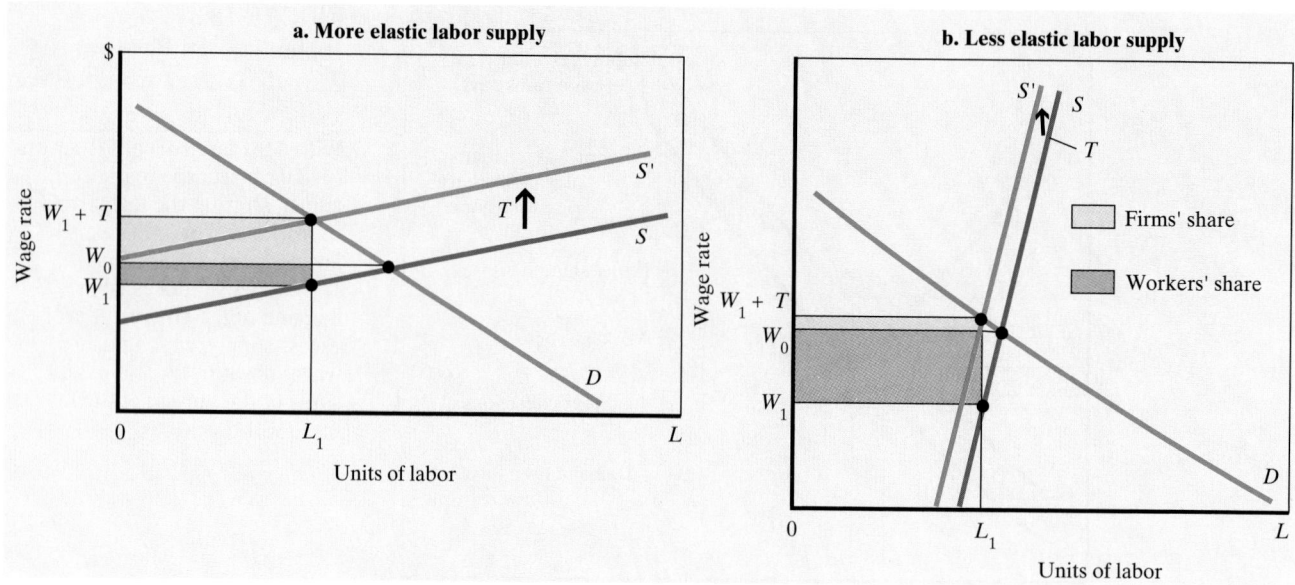

FIGURE 18.4

Payroll Tax with (a) More Elastic and (b) Less Elastic Labor Supply

The ultimate burden of a payroll tax depends on the elasticities of labor supply and labor demand. If labor supply is relatively elastic, as in part a, the tax burden falls largely on employers. If labor supply is relatively inelastic, as in part b, the burden falls largely on workers.

> Most of the payroll tax in the United States is probably borne by workers.

The result would be exactly the same if the tax were initially levied on workers rather than on firms. Suppose we go back to the equilibrium in Figure 18.3, with wages at W_0. But now assume the tax of $\$T$ per hour is levied on workers rather than firms. The burden will end up being shared by firms and workers in the *exact same proportions*. Initially, take-home wages will fall to $W_0 - T$. Workers will supply less labor, creating excess demand and pushing market wages up. That shifts part of the burden back to employers. The "story" is different, but the result is the same.

Table 18.4 presents an estimate of the incidence of payroll taxes (social security taxes) in the United States in 1992. This estimate assumes that both the employers' share and employees' share of the payroll taxes are ultimately *borne by employees.*

The payroll tax is regressive for two reasons. First, in 1992 most of the tax (6.2% of total income levied on both employers and employees) did not apply to wages and salaries above $55,500. The remainder of the total 7.65% tax—1.45% earmarked for Medicare—applied to all income only up to $130,200. Income over $130,200 was not subject to any payroll taxation. Second, wages and salaries fall as a percentage of total income as we move up the income scale. Those with higher incomes earn a larger portion of their incomes from profits, dividends, rents, and so forth, and these kinds of income are not subject to the payroll tax.

Some economists dispute the conclusion that the payroll tax is borne entirely by wage earners. Even if labor supply is inelastic, some wages are set in the process of collective bargaining between unions and large firms. If the payroll tax results in a higher gross wage in the bargaining process, firms may find themselves faced with higher costs. Higher costs, in turn, either reduce profits to owners or are passed on to consumers in the form of higher product prices.

POPULATION RANKED BY INCOME	TAX AS A % OF TOTAL INCOME
Bottom 10%	8.6
Second	8.7
Third	9.2
Fourth	9.2
Fifth	8.6
Sixth	8.4
Seventh	8.2
Eighth	7.2
Ninth	6.6
Top 10%	3.4
Top 5%	2.5
Top 1%	1.3

Source: Authors' estimates based on IRS data.

TABLE 18.4

Estimated Incidence of Payroll Taxes in the United States in 1992

But as you will see in Chapter 19, a smaller and smaller portion of the labor force is unionized; about 16% of those employed currently belong to unions. In spite of arguments to the contrary, then, to the extent that markets are competitive, the burden of the payroll tax does fall heavily on employees.

The Incidence of Corporate Profits Taxes

Another tax that requires careful analysis is the corporate profits tax that is levied by the federal government, as well as by most states. The *corporate profits tax,* or *corporation income tax,* is a tax on the profits of firms that are organized as corporations. The owners of partnerships and proprietorships do not pay this tax; rather, they report the income from their firms directly on their individual income tax returns.

Thus, we can think of the corporate tax as a tax on capital income, or profits, in one sector of the economy. For the sake of simplicity we will assume that there are only two sectors of the economy, corporate and noncorporate, and only two factors of production, labor and capital. Owners of capital receive profits, and workers are paid a wage.

Like the payroll tax, the corporate tax may affect households on the sources or the uses side of the income equation. The tax may affect profits earned by owners of capital, wages earned by workers, or prices of corporate and noncorporate products. Once again, the key question is how large these changes are likely to be.

The corporate profits tax, when first imposed, initially reduces net, or after-tax, profits in the corporate sector. Assuming that the economy was in long-run equilibrium before the tax was levied, firms in both the corporate and noncorporate sectors were earning a *normal rate of return;* there was no reason to expect higher profits in one sector than in the other. All of a sudden, firms in the corporate sector become significantly less profitable as a result of the tax. (In 1993, for example, the tax rate applicable to most corporations was 34 percent.)

In response to these lower profits, capital investment begins to favor the nontaxed sector because after-tax profits are higher there. Firms in the taxed sector contract in size or, in some cases, go out of business, while firms in the nontaxed sector expand and new firms enter its various industries. As this happens, the flow of capital from the taxed to the nontaxed sector reduces the profit rate in the nontaxed sector; more competition springs up, and product prices are driven down. Some of the tax burden now shifts to capital income earners in the noncorporate sector, who end up earning lower profits.

As capital flows out of the corporate sector in response to lower after-tax profits, the profit rate in that sector rises somewhat because fewer firms means less supply, which means higher prices, and so forth. Presumably, capital will continue to favor the nontaxed sector until the after-tax profit rates in the two sectors are equal. Thus, even though the tax is imposed on just one sector, it eventually depresses profits in all sectors equally.

Under these circumstances, the products of corporations will probably become more expensive and products of proprietorships and partnerships will probably become less expensive. But because almost everyone buys both corporate and noncorporate products, these "excise effects" (that is, effects on the prices of products) are likely to have a minimal impact on the distribution of the tax burden; in essence, they cancel each other out.

Finally, what effect does the imposition of a corporate income tax have on labor? If the contracting sector were more labor intensive than the expanding sector—that is, if it used more labor relative to capital—wages might fall even though employment in the economy as a whole remained full. If the expanding sector were the more labor intensive, however, wages might actually be driven up. Furthermore, because the corporate profits tax essentially taxes the use of capital, firms might be pushed to substitute more labor-intensive methods of production. This would increase the demand for labor and reduce the demand for capital, thus raising wage rates relative to returns from capital.

THE BURDEN OF THE CORPORATE TAX The ultimate burden of the corporate tax appears to depend on several factors: the relative capital/labor intensity of the two sectors, the ease with which capital and labor can be substituted in the two sectors, and elasticities of demand for the products of each sector. In 1962 Arnold Harberger of the University of Chicago analyzed this problem rigorously and concluded that:

> Owners of corporations, proprietorships, and partnerships all bear the burden of the corporate tax in rough proportion to profits, even though it is directly levied only on corporations.

He also found that wage effects of the corporate tax were small and that excise effects, as we noted above, probably cancel each other out.[8]

Although most economists accept Harberger's view of the corporate tax, there are arguments against it. For example, a profits tax on a monopoly firm earning above-normal profits is *not* shifted to other sectors unless the tax drives profits below the competitive level.

You might be tempted to conclude that because monopolists can control market price, they will simply pass on the profits tax in higher prices to consumers of monopoly products. But theory predicts just the opposite: that the tax burden will remain with the monopolist.

Remember that monopolists are constrained by market demand. That is, they choose the combination of price and output that is consistent with market demand and that maximizes profit. If a proportion of that profit is taxed, the choice of price and quantity will not change. Why not? Quite simply, if you behave so as to maximize profit, and then I come and take half of your profit, you maximize your half by maximizing the whole, which is exactly what you would do in the absence of the tax. Thus, your price and output do not change, the tax

---
[8]Arnold Harberger, "The Incidence of the Corporate Income Tax," *Journal of Political Economy,* Vol. LXX (June 1962).

is not shifted, and you end up paying the tax. In the long run, capital will not leave the taxed monopoly sector, as it did in the competitive case. Even with the tax, the monopolist is earning higher profits than are possible elsewhere.

The great debate about whom the corporate tax hurts illustrates the advantage of broad-based direct taxes over narrow-based indirect taxes. Because it is levied on an institution, the corporate tax is indirect, and therefore it is always shifted. Furthermore, it taxes only one factor (capital) in only one part of the economy (the corporate sector). The income tax, on the other hand, taxes all forms of income in all sectors of the economy, and it is virtually impossible to shift. It is difficult to argue that a tax is a good tax if we can't be sure who ultimately ends up paying it.

Table 18.5 presents an estimate of the actual incidence of the U.S. corporation income tax in 1992. These figures have been calculated on the basis of compromise assumptions—that is, half of the burden is assumed to fall fully on owners of corporations (as in the monopoly model) and half of the burden is assumed to be shared equally by all those who earn capital income (as in the competitive model). None of the burden is assumed to fall on consumers or wage earners. Under such assumptions, the burden of the corporate income tax is clearly progressive, because profits and capital income make up a much bigger part of the incomes of high-income households.

The Overall Incidence of Taxes in the United States: Empirical Evidence

A complete treatment of tax incidence, one that includes an analysis of each individual tax, would take more space than we have here. Many researchers have done complete analyses under varying assumptions about incidence, and in most cases their results are similar:

> State and local taxes (with sales taxes playing a big role) seem as a group to be mildly regressive. Federal taxes, dominated by the individual income tax but increasingly affected by the regressive payroll tax, are mildly progressive. The overall system is mildly progressive.

Data on international income tax rates and incidence can be found in Chapter 3.

TABLE 18.5
Estimated Burden of the U.S. Corporation Income Tax in 1992

POPULATION RANKED BY INCOME	CORPORATE TAX BURDEN AS A % OF TOTAL INCOME
Bottom 10%	0.6
Second	0.7
Third	0.7
Fourth	0.8
Fifth	0.8
Sixth	0.9
Seventh	1.0
Eighth	1.0
Ninth	1.4
Top 10%	3.8
Top 5%	4.6
Top 1%	5.7

Source: Authors' estimate.

EXCESS BURDENS AND THE PRINCIPLE OF NEUTRALITY

You have seen that when households and firms make decisions in the presence of a tax that differ from those they would make in its absence, the burden of the tax can be shifted from those for whom it was originally intended. Now we can take the same logic one step further:

> When taxes distort economic decisions, they impose burdens on society that in aggregate exceed the revenue collected by the government.

excess burden The amount by which the burden of a tax exceeds the total revenue collected. Also called "dead weight losses."

The amount by which the burden of a tax exceeds the revenue collected by the government is called the **excess burden** of the tax. The *total burden* of a tax is the sum of the revenue collected from the tax and the excess burden created by the tax. Because excess burdens are a form of waste, or lost value, tax policy should be written with an eye toward minimizing them. (Excess burdens are also sometimes called "dead weight losses.")

The size of the excess burden imposed by a tax depends on the extent to which economic decisions are distorted. Thus, the general principle that emerges from the analysis of excess burdens is the **principle of neutrality.** That is,

principle of neutrality All else equal, taxes that are neutral with respect to economic decisions (that is, taxes that do not distort economic decisions) are generally preferable to taxes that distort economic decisions. Taxes that are not neutral impose excess burdens.

> *Ceteris paribus* or all else equal,[9] a tax that is neutral with respect to economic decisions is preferred to one that distorts economic decisions.

In practice, all taxes change behavior and distort economic choices. A product-specific excise tax raises the price of the taxed item, and people can avoid the tax by buying substitutes. An income tax distorts the choice between present and future consumption and between work and leisure. The corporate tax influences investment and production decisions—investment is diverted away from the corporate sector, and firms may be induced to substitute labor for capital.

How Do Excess Burdens Arise?

The idea that a tax can impose an extra cost, or excess burden, by distorting choices can be illustrated by a simple numerical example. Consider a competitive industry that produces an output, *X,* using the technology shown in Figure 18.5. Using technology A, firms can produce one unit of output with seven units of capital *(K)* and three units of labor *(L).* Using technology B, the production of one unit of output requires four units of capital and seven units of labor. A is thus the more capital-intensive technology.

If we assume that labor and capital each cost $2 per unit, it costs $20 to produce each unit of output with technology A and $22 with technology B. Thus, firms will choose technology A. Because we assume competition, output price will be driven to cost of production, and the price of output will in the long run be driven to $20 per unit.

Now let us narrow our focus to the distortion of technology choice that is brought about by the imposition of a tax. We assume that demand for the good in

---

[9]The phrase *ceteris paribus* (all else equal) is important. In judging the merits of a tax or a change in tax policy, the degree of neutrality is only one criterion among many, and it often comes into conflict with others. For example, tax A may impose a larger excess burden than tax B, but tax B may be deemed more equitable by members of society.

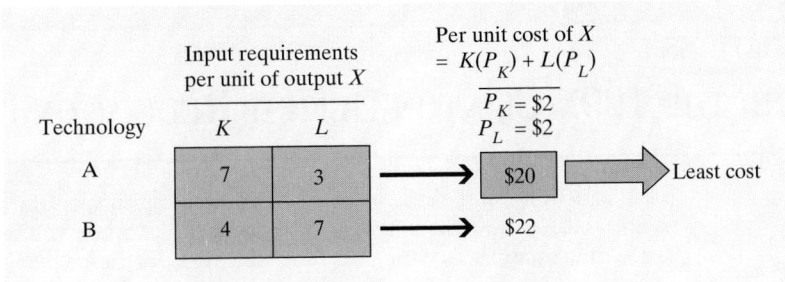

If the industry is competitive,
long-run equilibrium price will
be $20 per unit of X. If 1,000
units of X are sold, consumers
will pay a total of $20,000 for X.

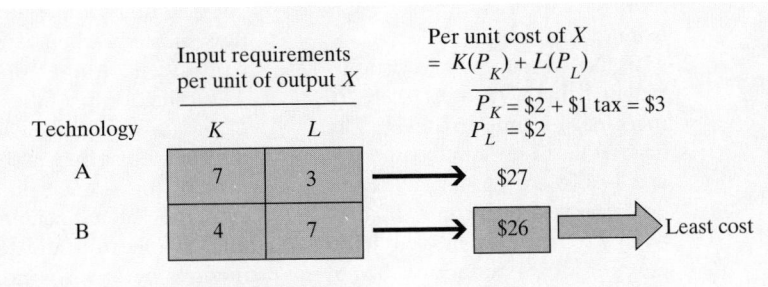

FIGURE 18.6
Imposition of a Tax on
Capital Distorts the Choice
of Technology

If the industry is competitive,
price will be $26 per unit of X
when a tax of $1 per unit of capi-
tal is imposed. If technology B is
used, and if we assume that total
sales remain at 1,000 units, total
tax collections will be 1,000 × 4
× $1 = $4000. But consumers
will pay a total of $26,000 for the
good—$6000 more than before
the tax. Thus, there is an excess
burden of $2000.

question is perfectly inelastic at 1,000 units of output. That is, regardless of price,
households will buy 1,000 units of product. A price of $20 per unit means con-
sumers pay a total of $20,000 for 1,000 units of X.

Now suppose that the government comes along and levies a tax of 50% on
capital. This has the effect of raising the price of capital, P_K, to $3. Figure 18.6
shows what would happen to unit cost of production after the tax is imposed.
With capital now more expensive, the firm switches to the more labor-intensive technology B. With the tax in place, X can be produced at a unit cost of
$27 per unit using technology A but for $26 per unit using technology B.

If we assume that demand is inelastic, buyers continue to buy 1,000 units of
X regardless of its price. (We shall ignore any distortions of consumer choices
that might result from the imposition of the tax.) Recall that the tax is 50%, or
$1 per unit of capital used. Because it takes four units of capital to produce
each unit of output, firms now using technology B will pay a total tax to the
government of $4 per unit of output produced. With 1,000 units of output
produced and sold, total tax collections amount to $4000.

But if you look carefully, you will see that the burden of the tax exceeds
$4000. After the tax, consumers will be paying $26 per unit for the good.
Twenty-six dollars is now the unit cost of producing the good using the best
available technology in the presence of the capital tax. Thus, consumers will
pay $26,000 for 1,000 units of the good. This represents an increase of $6000
over the previous total of $20,000. The revenue raised from the tax is $4000,
but its total burden is $6000. Thus, there is an *excess burden* of $2000.

How did this excess burden arise? Look back at Figure 18.5. You can see
that technology B is less efficient than technology A (unit costs of production
are $2 higher per unit using technology B). But the tax on capital has caused
firms to switch to this less efficient, labor-intensive mode of production. The
result is a waste of $2 per unit of output. The total burden of the tax is equal to
the revenue collected plus the loss due to the wasteful choice of technology,
and the excess burden is $2 per unit times 1,000 units, or $2000.

TAX REFORM AND THE 1993 CLINTON DEFICIT REDUCTION BILL

The Tax Reform Act of 1986

The Tax Reform Act of 1986 was, to quote the *Wall Street Journal* (August 18, 1986), "virtually unprecedented in the 73-year history of the nation's income tax."

The 1986 act had three major goals: (1) to simplify the tax system so that people can understand it better, (2) to reduce the marginal rates to increase the incentive to work, save, and invest, and (3) to make more income subject to the tax in order to compensate for the revenue loss from the lower rates and reduce the distortion of economic decisions. The approach was to try to broaden the base by cutting the number of things that people can subtract. With fewer things to subtract, the law is simpler, and revenue goals can be achieved with lower rates.

Here are a few of the major changes.

1. A significant increase was made in the standard deduction and the personal exemption. These reduce taxes significantly at the very bottom of the income distribution. For example, in 1986 the personal exemption was only $1050 and the standard deduction was $2300 for a single person. Thus the tax rates began to bite in at just over $3000 of income for a single person. The personal exemption and standard deduction were raised in total to $5000, and because of some other less important provisions, the income at which an individual would begin to pay taxes is a bit higher than that. Estimates are that these provisions removed 4.8 million poor people from the tax roles.

2. Marginal tax rates were drastically reduced. In 1978 there were 26 marginal income brackets. The first $1000 of taxable income was taxed at 14 percent for all taxpayers, regardless of income. Income over $200,000 was taxed at 70 percent. Rate reduction began with the 1978 tax act, which cut the number of brackets to 16. The Economic Recovery Tax Act of 1981 kept the 16 brackets but cut the rates. The top rate, for example, was reduced to 50 percent. The 1986 act reduced the 16 brackets to two, and the rates to 15 percent on the first $17,850 for single persons ($29,750 for married couples) and 28 percent on income over that amount. (Actually, there is also a hidden bracket of 33 percent for incomes over $89,560 for single persons and over $149,250 for married couples.)

3. A number of provisions broadened the tax base. The ability to deduct losses from tax shelters was greatly reduced. Income from realized capital gains (for example, your profits when you sell a share of stock for more than you paid for it) is now taxed at a rate of 28%; before the act, 60 percent of any profit was simply excluded. All unemployment benefits are now subject to the tax. Sales taxes paid are no longer deductible. The category of "other itemized deductions" has been limited to the extent that they exceed 2 percent of income. Deductions for consumer interest paid was phased out. Scholarship and fellowship income previously excluded is now taxable. The two-earner deduction was eliminated.

Overall, these provisions led to a decrease in revenue from the income tax. Because the overall bill was meant to be revenue neutral, these lost revenues had to be made up somewhere. The place they found was the corporate income tax.

Two major provisions account for most of the increase in corporate tax receipts. The first was the repeal of the investment tax credit (ITC). Prior to 1987, corporations (and proprietorships and partnerships as well) were permitted to take up to 10 percent of the total amount of every investment that they made and subtract it from their tax liability. The ITC no longer exists.

The same principle holds for taxes that distort consumption decisions. Suppose that I prefer to consume bundle X to bundle Y when there is no tax but choose bundle Y when there is a tax in place. Not only do I pay the tax, I also end up with a bundle of goods that is worth less than the bundle I would have chosen if the tax had not been levied. Again, we have the burden of an extra cost.

In general:

> The larger the distortion that a tax causes in behavior, the larger the excess burden of the tax. Taxes levied on broad bases tend to distort choices less and impose smaller excess burdens than taxes on more sharply defined bases.

The second major provision of the 1986 law that led to increased corporate taxes was the substantial lengthening of the period over which capital assets can be depreciated. Longer depreciation periods mean that the expenses taken for capital depreciation in any given period are lower, and thus profits on the books are higher. Also, corporations, like individuals, now have to pay taxes on capital gains as if they were ordinary income.

The 1993 Clinton Bill

In February 1993, President Clinton proposed a comprehensive program of spending cuts and tax increases to cut the federal deficit by $500 billion over a four-year period. The program was passed by Congress in August with a number of changes. The highlights of the final bill included the following provisions:

Despite the fact that the United States has one of the lowest overall tax rates in the developed world, many U.S. citizens believe that they pay too much in taxes.

1. The top tax rate, which was 31% in 1992, increased to 36% for couples with a taxable income over $140,000 and for individuals with a taxable income over $115,000. Families with taxable incomes over $250,000 would pay a surcharge of 10%, bringing the effective top tax rate to 39.6% (36% + 3.6%).

2. The top rate for corporate income was raised from 34% to 35% for corporations with net income of over $10 million.

3. The Medicare tax, which in 1992 was 1.45% paid by employers and employees on wage and salary income up to $135,000 was extended to all wage and salary income.

4. Realized capital gains will continue to be taxed at a maximum of 28 percent.

5. Gasoline for most uses will be subject to an increased tax of 4.3¢ per gallon. Aviation fuel is exempt for two years.

6. Families with incomes below $25,300 received a tax cut through an increase in the "earned income credit."

7. Beginning in 1994, Social Security recipients with incomes of over $34,000 for singles and $44,000 for married couples will be taxed on 85% of their social security benefits instead of 50 percent.

8. A special capital gains break is now available for investments in small businesses held for more than five years.

This follows from our discussion earlier in this chapter: The more partial the tax, the easier it is to avoid. An important part of the logic behind the tax reforms of 1986 was that broader bases and lower rates reduce the distorting effects of the tax system and minimize excess burdens.[10] (For a full discussion of the 1986 Act and recent proposals, see the Issues and Applications box titled "Tax Reform and the 1993 Clinton Deficit Reduction Bill.")

[10]Charles McClure, "Rationale Underlying the Treasury Proposals," *Economic Consequences of Tax Simplification,* Federal Reserve Bank of Boston (1986).

Measuring Excess Burdens

It is possible to measure the size of excess burdens if we know something about how people respond to price changes. Look at the demand curve in Figure 18.7. The product in question originally sold for a price, P_0, equal to marginal cost that, for the sake of simplicity, we assume is constant. As you recall, when input prices are determined in competitive markets, marginal cost reflects the real value of the resources used in producing the product. Wages, for example, reflect the marginal revenue product of labor; the cost of capital reflects the marginal revenue product of capital. That means that if $25 worth of resources flow out of the sector represented in Figure 18.7, they will end up being used in other sectors to produce final products worth exactly $25 to consumers.

P_0 is a very good approximation of the value to society of one marginal unit of product X. Anyone who values X more highly has already bought it at P_0; anyone who values it at less than P_0 per unit simply will not buy it. But now suppose that the government comes along and imposes an excise tax at rate t on product X. The price of the product to consumers rises in the long run to $P_0(1 + t) = P_1$. The higher price drives demanders to seek substitutes, and quantity demanded falls from X_0 to X_1.

In order to measure the total burden of the tax we need to recall the notion of consumer surplus from Chapter 6. At any price, some people pay less for a product than it is worth to them. All we reveal when we buy a product is that it is worth *at least* the price being charged. For example, if only one unit of product X were auctioned, someone would pay a price close to D in Figure 18.7. By paying only P_0, that person received a "surplus" equal to $(D - P_0)$. The next demander is willing to pay a bit less, but that person still receives a significant "surplus" that is only slightly less than $(D - P_0)$. Moving down the demand curve a little further, the person sitting on the demand curve at point A receives a surplus equal to $(P_1 - P_0)$ when the price is P_0. If we were to continue down the demand curve to point C, we would discover that the total consumer surplus from the production of good X for sale at P_0 is equal to the area of the large triangle DCP_0. (If this is unclear, review the discussion of consumer surplus in Chapter 6.)

Now consider what happens as the excise tax raises the price of X from P_0 to P_1. First, the government collects revenue. The amount of revenue collected is

FIGURE 18.7

The Excess Burden of a Distorting Excise Tax

A tax that alters economic decisions imposes a burden that exceeds the amount of taxes collected. An excise tax that raises the price of a good above marginal cost drives some consumers to buy less desirable substitutes, reducing consumer surplus.

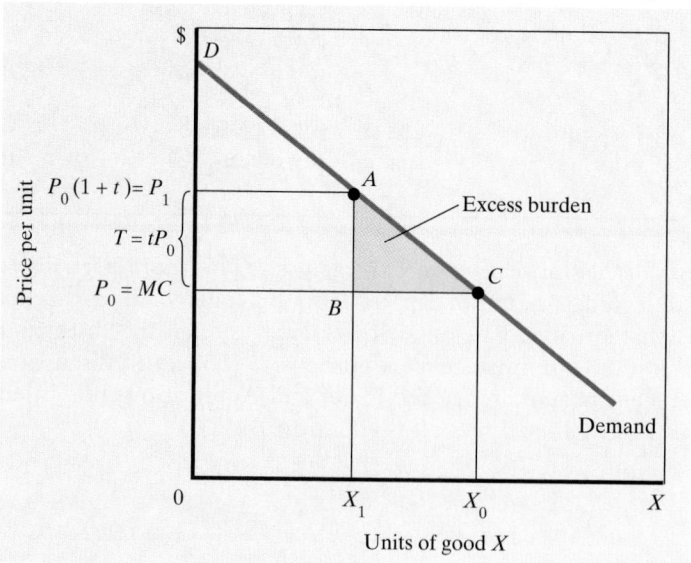

equal to the tax per unit of X (T) times the number of units of X purchased (X_1). If you look carefully at Figure 18.7, you can see that $T \times X_1$ is equal to the area of rectangle P_1ABP_0. Second, since consumers must now pay a price of P_1, the consumer surplus generated in the market is reduced from the area of triangle DCP_0 to the area of the smaller triangle DAP_1.

Now think for a moment about the consumers lined up along the demand curve between points D and C. Those who value the good most (by virtue of preferences and ability to pay) are lined up between D and A. Those people continue to buy the good at P_1, but they receive a smaller consumer surplus as some of it (total taxes, or P_1ABP_0) is taxed away. Those consumers who are lined up between A and C value the good less. In fact, they are unwilling to pay the price P_1. These people stop buying X and switch to some other goods and services and thus avoid paying any tax. But despite the fact that they pay no tax, they still bear a cost and thus some of the burden of the tax. Before the tax, consumers between A and C received a surplus because X was available at a price of P_0. By switching to another, less valuable, bundle of goods and services, they lose that surplus. The amount that they lose is equal to the area of triangle ACB. The excess burden is thus equal to the original (pre-tax) consumer surplus *minus* the after-tax surplus *minus* the total taxes collected by the government.

In sum, the original value of consumer surplus (triangle DCP_0) has been broken up into three parts: the area of triangle DAP_1 that is still consumer surplus; the area of rectangle P_1ABP_0 that is tax revenue collected by the government; and the area of triangle ACB that is lost. Thus, the area ACB is an approximate measure of the excess burden of the tax. The total burden of the tax is the sum of the revenue collected and the excess burden: the area of P_1ACP_0.

EXCESS BURDENS AND THE DEGREE OF DISTORTION   The size of the excess burden that results from a decision-distorting tax depends on the degree to which decisions change in response to that tax. In the case of an excise tax, consumer behavior is reflected in elasticity of demand:

> The more elastic the demand curve, the greater is the distortion caused by any given tax rate.

Figure 18.8 on the next page shows how the size of the consumer response determines the size of the excess burden. At price P_0, the quantity demanded by consumers is X_0. Now suppose that the government imposes a tax of $\$T$ per unit of X, just as it did in Figure 18.7. The two demand curves (D_1 and D_2) illustrate two possible responses by consumers. The change in quantity demanded along D_1 (from X_0 to X_1) is greater than the change in quantity demanded along D_2 (from X_0 to X_2). In other words, the response of consumers illustrated by D_1 is more elastic than the response of consumers along D_2.

The excess burdens that would result from the tax under the two alternative assumptions about demand elasticity are approximately equal to the areas of the shaded triangles in Figure 18.8. As you can see, where demand is more responsive (more elastic), the excess burden is larger.

If demand were perfectly inelastic, no distortion would occur, and there would be no excess burden. The tax would simply transfer part of the surplus being earned by consumers to the government. That is why some economists favor uniform land taxes over other taxes. Because land is in perfectly inelastic supply, a uniform tax on all land uses distorts economic decisions less than taxes levied on other factors of production that are in variable supply.

FIGURE 18.8

The Size of the Excess Burden of a Distorting Excise Tax Depends on the Elasticity of Demand

The size of the excess burden from a distorting tax depends on the degree to which decisions or behaviors change in response to it. For an excise tax, relevant consumer behavior is reflected in the elasticity of demand. An estimate of demand elasticity permits us to measure roughly the size of the excess burden.

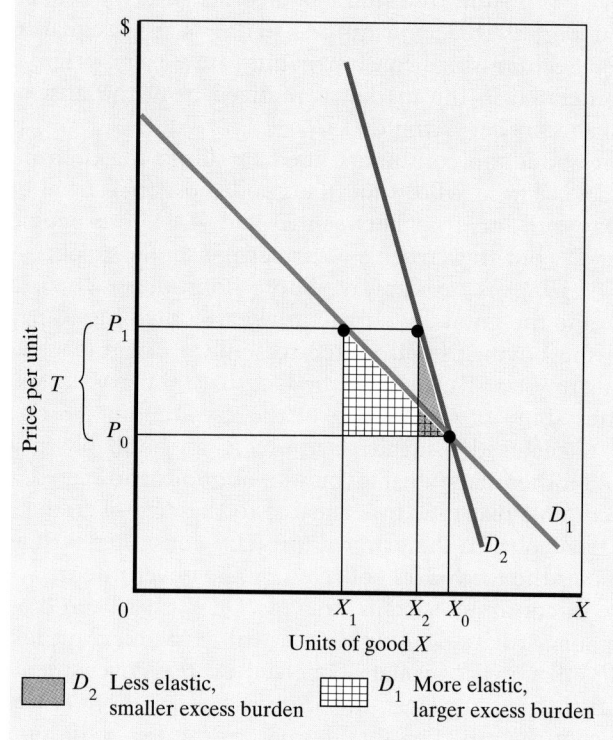

D_2 Less elastic, smaller excess burden

D_1 More elastic, larger excess burden

THE PRINCIPLE OF SECOND BEST Now that we have established the connection between taxes that distort decisions and excess burdens, we can add more complexity to our earlier discussions. Although it may seem that distorting taxes always create excess burdens, this is not necessarily the case. In fact, a distorting tax is sometimes actually desirable when other distortions already exist in the economy. This is called the **principle of second best.**

principle of second best The fact that a tax distorts an economic decision does not always imply that such a tax imposes an excess burden. If previously existing distortions exist, such a tax may actually improve efficiency.

> At least two kinds of circumstances favor nonneutral (that is, distorting) taxes: the presence of externalities and the presence of other distorting taxes.

We have already examined externalities at some length in Chapter 16. If some activity by a firm or household imposes costs on society that are not considered by decision makers, then firms and households are likely to make bad, economically inefficient choices. Pollution is the classic example of an externality, but there are thousands of others. An efficient allocation of resources can be restored if a tax is imposed on the externality-generating activity that is exactly equal to the value of the damages caused by it. Such a tax forces the decision maker to consider the full economic cost of the decision.

Because taxing for externalities changes decisions that would otherwise be made, it does in a sense "distort" economic decisions. But its purpose is to force decision makers to consider real costs that they would otherwise ignore. In the case of pollution, for example, the distortion caused by a tax is desirable. Instead of causing an excess burden, it results in a gain of efficiency. (Review Chapter 16 if this is not clear in your mind.)

A distorting tax can also improve economic welfare when there are other taxes present that already distort decisions. Suppose, for example, that there were only three goods, *X, Y,* and *Z.* Suppose further that there was a 5% excise tax on both

Y and Z. The taxes on Y and Z distort consumer decisions away from those goods and toward X. Imposing a similar tax on X reduces the distortion of the existing system of taxes. When consumers face equal taxes on all goods, they cannot avoid the tax by changing what they buy. Thus, the distortion caused by imposing a tax on X corrects for a pre-existing distortion—the taxes on Y and Z.

Let's return to the example described earlier in Figures 18.5 and 18.6. Imposing the tax of 50% on the use of capital generated revenues of $4000 but imposed a burden of $6000 on consumers. A distortion now exists. But consider what would happen if the government now imposed an additional tax of 50%, or $1 per unit, on labor. Such a tax would push our firm back toward the more efficient technology A. In fact, the labor tax will generate a total revenue of $6000, but the burden it imposes on consumers would be only $4000. (It is a good idea for you to work these figures out yourself.)

OPTIMAL TAXATION   The idea that taxes work together to affect behavior has led tax theorists to search for optimal taxation systems. Knowing how people will respond to taxes would allow us to design a system that would minimize the overall excess burden. For example, if we know the elasticity of demand for all traded goods, we can devise an optimal system of excise taxes that are heaviest on those goods with relatively inelastic demands and lightest on those goods with relatively elastic demands.

Of course, it is impossible to collect all the information required to implement the optimal tax systems that have been suggested. This point brings us full circle, and we end up where we started, with the *principle of neutrality*: All else equal, taxes that are neutral with respect to economic decisions are generally preferable to taxes that distort economic decisions. Taxes that are not neutral impose excess burdens.

SUMMARY

The Economics of Taxation

1. Public finance is one of the major subfields of applied economics. A major interest within this subfield is the economics of taxation.

2. Taxes are ultimately paid by people. Taxes may be imposed on transactions, institutions, property, and all kinds of other things, but in the final analysis, taxes are paid by individuals or households.

3. The *base* of a tax is the measure, or value, upon which the tax is levied. The *rate structure* of a tax determines the portion of the base that must be paid in tax.

4. A tax whose burden is a constant proportion of income for all households is a *proportional tax*. A tax that exacts a higher proportion of income from higher-income households is a *progressive tax*. A tax that exacts a lower proportion of income from higher-income households is a *regressive tax*. In the United States, income taxes are progressive, and sales and excise taxes are regressive.

5. Your average tax rate is the total amount of tax you paid divided by your total income. Your marginal tax rate is the tax rate that you pay on any additional income that you've earned. Marginal tax rates have the most influence on behavior.

6. There is much disagreement over what constitutes a fair tax system. One theory contends that people should bear tax burdens in proportion to the benefits that they receive from government expenditures. This is the *benefits-received principle*. Another contends that people should bear tax burdens in line with their ability to pay. This *ability-to-pay principle* has dominated U.S. tax policy.

7. The three leading candidates for best tax base are income, consumption, and wealth.

Tax Incidence: Who Pays?

8. As a result of behavioral changes and market adjustments, tax burdens are often not borne by those initially responsible for paying them. When we speak of the *incidence of a tax,* we are referring to the ultimate distribution of its burden.

9. Taxes change behavior, and changes in behavior can affect supply and demand in markets, causing prices to change. When prices change in input markets or in output markets, some people may be made better off and some may be made worse off. These final changes determine the ultimate burden of a tax.

10. *Tax shifting* occurs when households can alter their behavior and do something to avoid paying a tax. In general, broad-based taxes are less likely to be shifted and more likely to stick where they are levied than partial taxes are.

11. When labor supply is very elastic, firms bear the bulk of a tax imposed on labor. When labor supply is less elastic, workers bear the bulk of the tax burden. Because the elasticity of labor supply in the United States is close to zero, most economists conclude that most of the payroll tax in the United States is probably borne by workers.

12. The payroll tax is regressive for two reasons. First, in 1992 most of the tax (6.2% of total income levied on both employers and employees) did not apply to wages and salaries above $55,500. The remainder of the total 7.65%—1.45% earmarked for Medicare—applied to all income only up to $130,200. Income over $130,200 was not subject to any payroll taxation. Second, wages and salaries fall as a percentage of total income as we move up the income scale. Those with higher incomes earn a larger portion of their incomes from profits, dividends, rent, and so forth, and these kinds of income are not subject to the payroll tax.

13. The ultimate burden of the corporate tax appears to depend on several factors. One generally accepted study shows that the owners of corporations, proprietorships, and partnerships all bear the burden of the tax in rough proportion to profits, even though it is directly levied only on corporations;

that wage effects are small; and that excise effects are roughly neutral. However, there is still much debate about whom the corporate tax "hurts." The burden of the corporate tax is likely to be progressive, because profits and capital income make up a much bigger part of the incomes of high-income households.

14. Taken together under a reasonable set of assumptions about tax shifting, state and local taxes seem as a group to be mildly regressive. Federal taxes, dominated by the individual income tax but increasingly affected by the regressive payroll tax, are mildly progressive. The overall system is mildly progressive.

Excess Burdens and the Principle of Neutrality

15. When taxes distort economic decisions, they impose burdens that in aggregate exceed the revenue collected by the government. The amount by which the burden of a tax exceeds the revenue collected by the government is called the *excess burden*. The size of excess burdens depends on the degree to which economic decisions are changed by the tax. The *principle of neutrality* holds that the most efficient taxes are broad-based taxes that do not distort economic decisions.

16. The *principle of second best* holds that a tax that distorts economic decisions does not necessarily impose an excess burden. If previously existing distortions or externalities exist, such a tax may actually improve efficiency.

REVIEW TERMS AND CONCEPTS

ability-to-pay principle   459
benefits-received
    principle   458
excess burden   470
principle of neutrality   470

principle of
    second best   476
progressive tax   456
proportional tax   456
regressive tax   456

sources side/uses side   462
tax base   455
tax incidence   462
tax rate structure   455
tax shifting   462

PROBLEM SET

1. A citizens' group in the Pacific Northwest has the following statement in its charter:

"Our goal is to ensure that large, powerful corporations pay their fair share of taxes in this country."

To implement this goal, the group has recommended and lobbied for an increase in the corporation income tax and a reduction in the individual income tax. Would you support such a petition? Explain your logic.

2. President Clinton's original deficit reduction plan called for an increase in the top rate of the individual income tax and the broad-based energy tax. Suppose that before passage, Senator Phil Gramm of Texas, a Ph.D. economist, had asked for your opinion. Present economic arguments either for or against these two provisions using the concepts of efficiency and equity. Did the proposals pass the Congress? What changes were part of the final bill?

3. "Taxes imposed on necessities that have low demand elasticities impose large excess burdens because consumers can't avoid buying them." Do you agree or disagree? Explain.

4. For each of the following, do you agree or disagree? Why?
    a. "Economic theory predicts unequivocally that a payroll tax reduction will increase the supply of labor."
    b. "Corporation income taxes levied on a monopolist are likely to be regressive, because the monopoly can simply pass on their burden to consumers."
    c. "All nonneutral taxes are undesirable."

5. In calculating total faculty compensation, the administration of Doughnut University includes payroll taxes (social security taxes) paid as a *benefit* to faculty. After all, those tax payments are earning future entitlements for the faculty under social security. However, the American Association of

University Professors has argued that, far from being a benefit, the employer's contribution is simply a tax, and that its burden actually falls on the faculty, even though it is paid by the university. Discuss both sides of this debate.

6. Developing countries rarely have sophisticated income tax schemes like that in the United States. The primary means of raising revenues in many developing countries is through commodity taxes. What problems do you see with taxing particular goods in these countries? (*Hint:* Think about elasticities of demand.)

7. Some members of the Clinton economic team favor a value-added tax (VAT), a form of national sales tax, to fund a new national health care system. Would you favor such a tax? Discuss.

8. Suppose a special tax were introduced that used the value of one's automobile as the tax base. Each person would pay taxes equal to 10% of the value of his or her car. Would the tax be proportional, regressive, or progressive? What assumptions do you make in answering this question? What distortions do you think would appear in the economy if such a tax were introduced?

19 The Economics of Labor Markets and Labor Unions

In 1993, 118.6 million people in the United States' civilian labor force of 127.4 million held jobs. Somehow 118.6 million people sorted themselves into thousands of different occupations and jobs, performing an enormous variety of tasks in exchange for wages that range from a few dollars an hour to millions of dollars a year. Some have little or no formal education; others have invested many years and thousands of dollars in education and training. Some work only part time; others hold more than one job. Some large employers hire hundreds of people each year into well-defined jobs with specific job descriptions. Small firms may hire only one or two people every few years for very loosely defined jobs. And, of course, many people work for themselves.

The second of several chapters designed to survey some of the subfields of applied economics, this chapter addresses a number of important questions. How do people and jobs get matched? How are wage rates determined? Under what circumstances do people get trained? When do firms hire? What happens when people lose their jobs? These questions, by and large, are answered in what we refer to collectively as "the labor market," but in fact there are many labor markets. There is a market for professional basketball players, a market for lawyers, a market for carpenters, and a market for unskilled workers. Each market operates under a different set of rules and through a different set of institutions, but the basic forces that drive all of them are the same.

The importance of the labor market to the economy should not be underestimated. Indeed, perhaps the most dramatic of all the changes currently underway in the republics of the former Soviet Union and Eastern Europe is the introduction of a labor market. Under the central planning systems that dominated Eastern Europe before 1989, national planning agencies determined the economies' staffing needs. Training programs were then designed to meet those needs, and people were channeled through them into jobs. The introduction of a labor market into these systems means that the responsibility for finding a job is left to workers and the responsibility for finding workers is left to firms. Firms can exercise choice in hiring and firing. Presumably, employment and advancement in the Eastern European economies will begin to depend more on productivity.

Several earlier chapters have touched on the economics of labor markets. In Chapter 6 we looked at some of the decisions that lie behind the labor supply curve; in Chapter 10 we discussed the factors that determine the demand for labor; in Chapter 17 we listed several reasons for the inequality of wages. After a quick review, this chapter discusses the workings of labor markets in a more systematic fashion.

In the final part of the chapter, we take up the topic of labor unions. Labor unions have existed for about 200 years now, and their effects are the subject of considerable controversy. Do they succeed in raising wages? Do they create unemployment? What is their impact on productivity? Almost everyone has a strong opinion about unions. Some say they are responsible for all of our economic woes; others believe that they are the only hope for economic justice.

COMPETITIVE LABOR MARKETS: A REVIEW

A brief review of a few key concepts is in order before we begin to examine the theory of labor markets. (You may also wish to review Chapter 10 at this point.)

MARGINAL REVENUE PRODUCT AND THE DEMAND FOR LABOR Remember that firms make several decisions simultaneously: They decide how much to produce, they choose among alternative techniques of production, and they decide how much of each input to demand. If they have market power, they also decide what price to charge. In making these decisions, they use information from product markets, from input markets, and from their knowledge of technology.

The concept of *marginal revenue product (MRP)* is central to an understanding of the demand for labor. The **marginal revenue product of labor (MRP$_L$)** is the additional revenue that a firm would take in by hiring one additional unit of labor, *ceteris paribus*. Because labor is presumed to be productive, hiring more yields more product. The product produced by one marginal unit of labor is called the *marginal physical product of labor* or simply *marginal product of labor*. To be turned into revenue, that product must be sold. Product prices are determined in output markets, and purely competitive firms take them as given. Thus, for perfectly competitive firms the added revenue from hiring one more unit of labor is the marginal product of labor *(MP$_L$)* times the price of output: $MP_L \times P_X.$[1]

marginal revenue product of labor *(MRP$_L$)* The additional revenue that a firm will take in by hiring an additional unit of labor, *ceteris paribus*. For perfectly competitive firms, marginal revenue product of labor is equal to the marginal physical product of labor times the price of output.

---

[1]For firms in imperfect markets where output price is set by the firm, marginal revenue product is equal to marginal physical product times marginal revenue—$MRP_L = MP_L \times MR$. MRP_L is still the revenue gained by hiring an added unit of labor.

Figure 19.1 graphs a firm's decision to hire in a competitive labor market. The market-determined wage rate is W^*. The firm can hire all the labor it wants at that wage. Thus, we can think of W^* as the marginal cost of a unit of labor. Firms will hire as long as the marginal gains in revenue from hiring additional units of labor (MRP_L) exceed W^*. When labor is the only variable input, the MRP curve is the firm's demand curve for labor. When more than one factor of production can vary, the demand curve is more complicated but essentially the same. (These points are explained fully in Chapter 10.)

The point is that:

> Demand for labor depends on what labor can produce and how much its product sells for in output markets. The *physical* product of labor is technologically determined. Given the state of the technology, machinery, and other equipment available, and the level of effort required to produce something, there is a limit to what one unit of labor can produce. But the *revenue* product of labor depends on the market value of its product; if no one wants to buy a product, that product has no market value.

THE SUPPLY OF LABOR   Households supply labor. In any given labor market, the supply of labor depends on some factors that households control and some that they do not.

First, each household member must decide whether to work. The alternatives to working for a wage are either working for no pay or enjoying one's leisure. In this regard, households face a trade-off. Working yields a wage as well as some nonpecuniary rewards and/or costs—you may like your working environment and derive satisfaction from being creative or productive, or you may hate your job because it is dull or dangerous. The opportunity cost of working is either the value of what can be produced using the same time *or* the value of leisure. If you are not in the labor force working for a wage, you can paint your house, raise children, or sleep in the sun. All these alternatives have a value that must be weighed in a decision to take a job.

Beyond this basic decision to work or not to work, a more complicated set of choices and constraints comes into play. Not everyone can supply his or her labor in every market. A 110-pound man would probably not offer his services to the National Football League as a football player. A carpenter with no medical training would be breaking the law if she sold herself as a surgeon. Each market requires its own set of skills that workers are either born with or that they must acquire.

FIGURE 19.1

Demand for Labor in Competitive Markets Depends on Labor's Productivity

Competitive firms will hire labor as long as marginal revenue product of labor ($MRP_L = MP_L \times P_X$) exceeds the market wage, W^*. When labor is the only variable factor of production, the marginal revenue product curve is the demand curve for labor.

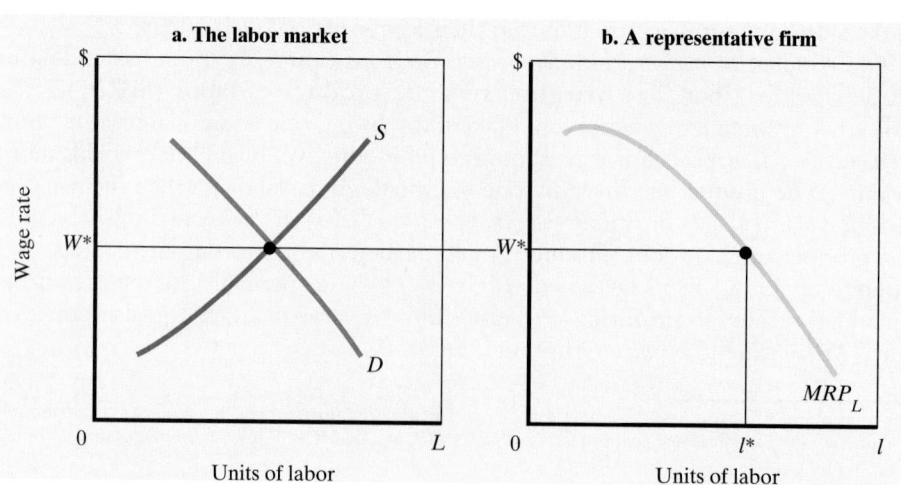

HUMAN CAPITAL   The stock of knowledge, skills, and talents that human beings possess by nature or through education and training is called **human capital.** When people who have special skills or knowledge earn higher wages, a part of their wage can be thought of as a return on human capital.

human capital The stock of knowledge, skills, and talents that people possess; it can be inborn or acquired through education and training.

Both households and firms invest in human capital. The principal form of human capital investment financed primarily by *households* is education. When parents send their children to school, they are investing in human capital that they hope will pay dividends later on. The principal form of human capital investment financed primarily by *firms* is **on-the-job training.** Presumably, training workers raises their productivity and yields dividends to the firms that provide such training.

on-the-job training The principal form of human capital investment financed primarily by firms.

Governments also invest in human capital. Federal and state governments have sponsored and subsidized numerous training programs over the years. Local governments are responsible for public elementary and secondary education, state governments have built excellent state university systems, and the federal government provides billions of dollars in student financial aid. Some argue that public health expenditures are also essentially human capital investment. A healthy labor force is a prerequisite for a productive labor force. (This argument was used by those favoring comprehensive health can reform during the Clinton administration.)

THE EQUILIBRIUM WAGE   Wage rates in competitive markets are determined by supply and demand:

> If quantity of labor demanded exceeds quantity of labor supplied, wages should rise until the quantity demanded and the quantity supplied are equal. The resulting higher wages should then reduce the quantity of labor demanded and increase the quantity of labor supplied.

Figure 19.2a shows excess demand for labor; as you can see, the initial wage of W_0 rises until the market clears at W^*.

When an excess supply of labor exists, we would expect to see market wages fall. At W_0 in Figure 19.2b quantity supplied exceeds quantity demanded; this sit-

FIGURE 19.2
Excess Demand and Supply in Labor Markets
When excess demand exists, wages will usually rise. When excess supply exists, wages will usually fall.

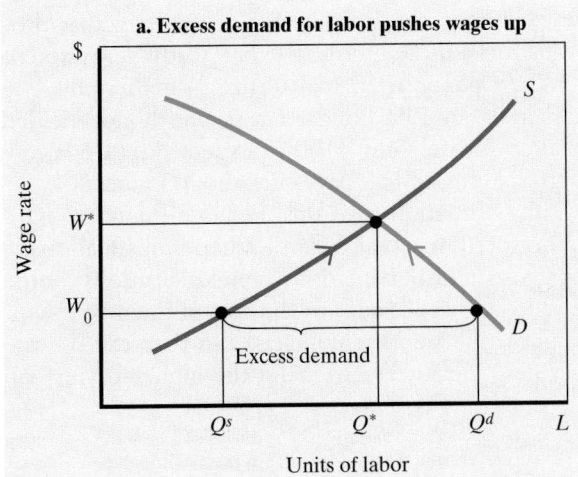

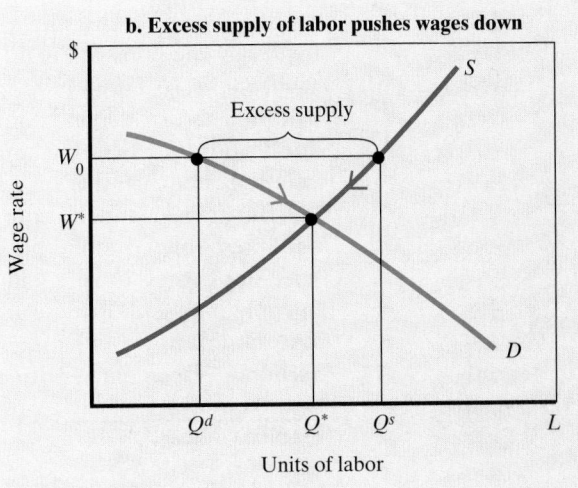

uation creates a downward pressure on wages. If wages fall, quantity demanded will increase and quantity supplied will fall until equilibrium is restored at W^*.

Disequilibria sometimes persist, however. Minimum wage laws may prevent wages from falling in response to a surplus. Union contracts may hold wages above the equilibrium level. Even in competitive markets, some prices are slow to adjust in response to surpluses.

THE LABOR MARKET IN ACTION

So far we have discussed the labor market only in the abstract. A better way to grasp the basic economic logic of labor markets is to work through a number of concrete examples of the theory as it applies in everyday decisions.

INVESTING IN HUMAN CAPITAL: SHOULD I GO TO SCHOOL? Cathy graduated from Liberty State College with an associate degree two years ago. Currently she works as a technical assistant in a small firm that trains people to work with personal computers. She likes the job, but she feels trapped; there isn't any room for her to move up in the company without more training. She makes $7.50 per hour.

A technical school located near Cathy's home is offering a one-year program leading to a certificate of proficiency in two computer languages. With this training, which would move her up a notch in the labor market, she is all but assured of a job paying $9.50 per hour. But tuition at the school is $5000, and students must attend full time. If going to school full time for a year means that Cathy must give up her job, she will incur an opportunity cost of $12,000 in take-home pay ($15,000 less taxes of $3000) in addition to the $5000 tuition. If the books and materials that she needs for the program cost $1000, the full cost of a year's training is $18,000. Cathy must decide if the investment is worth making.

Cathy is considering an investment in human capital. The training will increase her productivity and thus her wages in the future. Table 19.1 shows some simple calculations. If we assume that Cathy works 40 hours per week and 50 weeks per year, her gross wages will increase by $4000 each year. To determine the *net* return, we must remember to subtract taxes. At her income level, the *marginal tax rate* (that is, the rate applicable to marginal dollars of income) is about 25 percent.[2] This figure includes social security (7.65%), federal income taxes (15%), and a city income tax (2.5%). (There are no state income taxes in her state.) After taxes, then, Cathy's income will be $3000 a year higher if she gets the training.

If we assume that these flows will continue into the future—that is, that they will stay the same in "real," or inflation-adjusted, dollars—then Cathy's investment will yield 16.7% ($3000 ÷ $18,000) per year in real terms. Whether this is a "good" return depends on the market. In 1993 long-term savings bonds yielded only about 5% before taking inflation into account. Cathy's expected return is certainly better than that on a savings account, which pays only about 3 percent.

But there is much more to Cathy's situation than this. For one thing, we have counted only costs and benefits measured in actual dollars. When individuals make decisions, they usually add other costs and benefits into their calculations. Some people hate school and can't stand to study; this adds to the cost of the investment. At school, however, students might make valuable contacts, and they can use the school's placement service to get new job interviews. And the higher-paying job

---

[2]Notice that Cathy's *average tax rate* is only 20 percent. She is currently paying a total of $3000 in taxes on an income of $15,000. What matters when we calculate her gains from the new job at the margin is her *marginal tax rate,* which is 25 percent. (Review Chapter 18 if you are unsure why this is so.)

Annual return to investment

Wage rate with no training	= $7.50 per hour	
Wage rate with training	= $9.50 per hour	

Assuming 40 hours per week, 50 weeks per year

Annual pay with training	($9.50 × 40 × 50) =	$19,000
Annual pay with no training	($7.50 × 40 × 50) =	15,000
Gross increase	($2.00 × 40 × 50) =	+$4,000
Marginal tax rate = 25%		
Tax on increase	(.25 × $4,000)	$1,000
Net annual increase in pay		**$3,000**

Cost of training

Tuition	$5,000
Books and materials	1,000
Forgone wages, one year (after taxes)	12,000
Total cost	**$18,000**

Annual return on investment $\dfrac{\$3,000}{\$18,000} = 16.7\%$

might offer intangible psychological rewards and nicer people to work with. All of these benefits would add to the yield of the investment.

Often these "utility" gains and losses dominate the pecuniary costs and benefits. Someone might decide to pursue a Ph.D. in classics even if the probability of landing a good faculty position in the field was very low. The yield on such an investment would lie entirely in psychological rewards.

For another thing, taxes and financial aid affect the yields of different courses of action and have an impact on decisions. For example, a $5000 tuition scholarship would reduce the cost of Cathy's investment considerably—to $13,000. This raises the yield on the investment to 23% ($3000 ÷ $13,000) and might well tip the balance in favor of school.

A cut in taxes would have the conflicting effects of increasing the cost of the training while increasing the net benefits. Cathy would sacrifice more take-home pay (higher forgone earnings) to attend school, but she would get to keep more of the $4000 annual wage increase in the foreseeable future. The net effect will probably be to increase the return on an investment made now. (See if you can perform the calculations to show that reducing both average and marginal tax rates to 15% would increase the yield to 18.1 percent.)

WHAT DOES MCDONALD'S PAY? At two locations about 40 minutes apart, McDonald's hires workers at very different wage rates. At one franchise, a small sign on the counter reads "Help wanted, full or part time." If you ask about a job, you will find that only one part-time opening is available, and that the wage rate offered is the minimum wage, $4.25 per hour. At the other location, a large sign says "Full-time or part-time positions available, day or night shifts, excellent benefits and $7.50 per hour." There are six positions available at this location.

Why would one restaurant pay wages nearly twice as high as an identical restaurant with identical jobs in the same metropolitan area? Quite simply, because the franchise owner finds that she has no applicants—and thus no workers—at lower wages. Even at the higher wage rates, she has a very difficult time keeping her positions filled.

Clearly, the two restaurants are buying labor in different labor markets. If people could get from one point to another at no cost, such wage differences would disappear. But there are costs. Neither of these restaurants is accessible by public transportation. Thus, to take a job at one of them, you must live nearby or have a car. Fast food restaurants like McDonald's draw much of their labor from the supply of high school students who want to work part time. Most of them don't have cars. The high-wage franchise is on a major highway at some distance from local high schools and residential areas; the low-wage franchise is in the center of town.

There are probably other factors that affect the available labor supplies at the two locations as well. Suppose, for example, that the average income of the four towns surrounding the high-wage franchise is 50% higher than the average income of the four towns surrounding the low-wage franchise. To the extent that the labor supply is made up of students, parents' income may well have an effect. Higher-income families may spend some of their money buying leisure for their children, while many lower-income families expect older children to contribute to the family income.

This example illustrates three important points:

First, labor supply depends on a number of factors, including wage rates, nonlabor income, and wealth. Second, individual firms have very little control over the market wage; firms are forced to pay the wage that is determined by the market. Finally, because people cannot get from one place to another free of charge, and because most people do not reside at their work places—as capital does—there is an important spatial dimension to labor markets.

Different supply and demand conditions can and do prevail at different geographical locations. This is true across regions as well as within cities. Labor markets in different regions of the country—Northeast, South, and so forth—are very different.

THE IMPORTANCE OF INDIVIDUAL PREFERENCES   David was a highly paid young lawyer with a major Chicago law firm. Three years ago he made partner, and his share of the firm's earnings last year was over $150,000. This year he resigned, sold his North Side condominium, and moved to Jackson, Wyoming, where he bought a small restaurant and a cabin near the edge of the Grand Teton National Park. The best he can hope to earn from the restaurant is about $20,000 per year, and even that is an optimistic forecast.

Were David's decisions irrational? If we add up the dollars and calculate the monetary gains and losses, as we did for Cathy, we can see that David is giving up a great deal. But economic theory in no way suggests that such decisions are irrational. David made his decision to accept a lower income in exchange for a number of things from which he derives utility. The hectic life of a big city may have been a significant cost to him. The beauty of Wyoming and the climate may be invaluable benefits. He may like to ski, or he might simply have wanted to buy more leisure time.

The critical point is that:

Preferences play a very important role in the decisions we make about labor supply and in the decisions we make about what to consume.

As you saw at the beginning of this chapter, there are 118.6 million jobholders in the United States. Every one of them has a unique set of talents and preferences. Every one of them has made a different set of decisions about investing in human capital. Some go to college and some do not. Some stay in high school and some do not. Those differences help to explain the way people end up being sorted across jobs.

A WORD OF CAUTION Do not assume that the importance of individual preferences and choices makes generalization about labor market behavior impossible. An enormous amount of empirical work has documented that labor behaves in predictable ways in response to incentives. The manager of the McDonald's franchise in the high-wage area got the desired response by raising wages, not by lowering them. People with high nonwage incomes do supply less labor than people with low nonwage incomes.

The fact that labor responds to incentives is important for public policy. In fact, one of the central themes behind the economic policies pursued during the 1980s was that workers would respond to tax cuts (and therefore higher after-tax wages) by supplying more labor and working harder.

Let us now turn to a more detailed discussion of several important public policy issues that involve the labor market.

LABOR MARKETS AND PUBLIC POLICY

The government influences the operation of the labor market in a variety of ways. This section examines a number of important current public policy issues that affect the labor market. Specifically, we examine the effects of minimum wage legislation, tax policy, welfare programs, and unemployment insurance.

The Minimum Wage Controversy

One strategy for reducing poverty that has been used for almost 100 years in many countries is the **minimum wage.** A minimum wage is the lowest wage that firms are permitted to pay workers. The first minimum wage law was adopted in New Zealand in 1894. The United States adopted a national minimum wage with the passage of the Fair Labor Standards Act of 1938, although many individual states had laws on the books much earlier. Since April 1, 1991, the federal minimum wage has been $4.25 per hour, although firms are permitted to hire teenagers at $3.61 per hour during their first three months of employment.

In recent years, the minimum wage has come under increasing attack. Opponents argue that minimum wage legislation interferes with the smooth functioning of the labor market and creates unemployment. Proponents argue that it has been successful in raising the wages of the poorest workers and alleviating poverty without creating much unemployment.

These arguments can best be understood with a simple supply and demand diagram. Figure 19.3 on the next page shows hypothetical demand and supply curves for unskilled labor. The equilibrium wage rate is $3.40; at that wage, the quantity of unskilled labor supplied and the quantity of unskilled labor demanded are equal. Now suppose that a law is passed setting a minimum wage of $4.25. At that wage rate, the quantity of labor supplied increases from the equilibrium level, L^*, to L_S. At the same time, the higher wage reduces the quantity of labor demanded by firms from L^*, to L_D. As a result, firms lay off $L^* - L_D$ workers.

It is true that those workers who remain on payrolls receive higher wages. With the minimum wage in effect, unskilled workers receive $4.25 per hour instead of $3.40. But is it worth it? Some gain while others (including those who had been employed at the equilibrium wage) suffer unemployment.

A very high unemployment rate among teenage workers is cited as evidence that the unemployment problem caused by the minimum wage is significant. In 1993, while the overall unemployment rate stood at 7%, the unemployment rate for teenagers (16 to 19 years) stood at 19.5 percent. For black teenagers,

minimum wage The lowest wage that firms are permitted to pay workers.

FIGURE 19.3

Effect of Minimum Wage Legislation

If the equilibrium wage in the market for unskilled labor is below the legislated minimum wage, the result is likely to be unemployment. The higher wage will attract new entrants to the labor force (quantity supplied will increase from L^* to L_S), but firms will hire fewer workers (quantity demanded will drop from L^* to L_D).

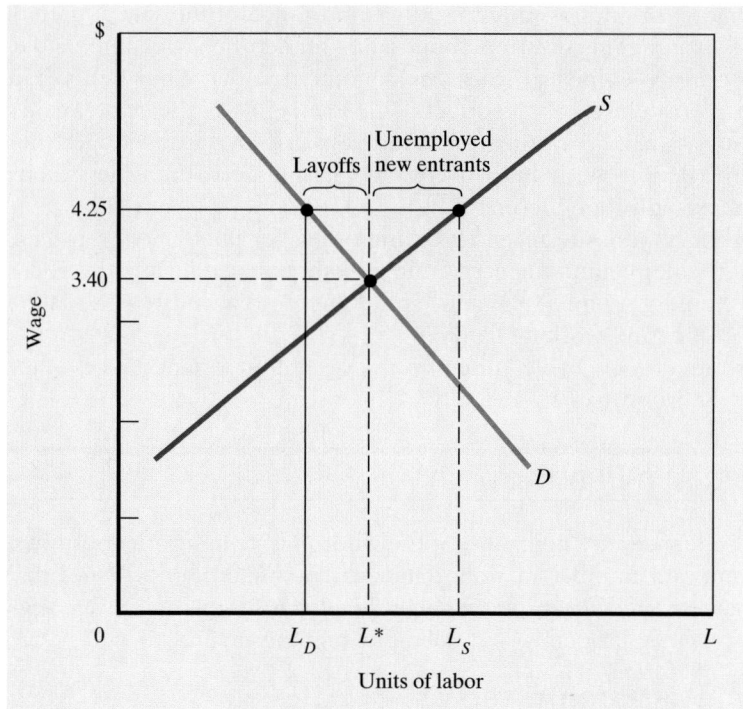

the rate stood at over 40 percent. Proponents of the minimum wage argue that such data are irrelevant, that the demand for unskilled labor is relatively inelastic with respect to the wage rate, and that only a small part of the unemployment problem is due to the minimum wage.

Between 1981 and 1990, proponents and opponents of the minimum wage were locked in a political battle. Although the minimum wage remained on the books, it was not changed between 1981 and 1990 despite the fact that prices rose nearly 40% during that period. In 1981 the minimum wage was $3.35 per hour. Adjusting for the increased cost of living, $3.35 in 1990 was enough to buy the same quantity of goods and services that $2.41 bought in 1981. Some of this erosion in purchasing power was restored when the minimum wage was raised to $4.25 in 1991, but the purchasing power of today's minimum wage is still more than 25% below the purchasing power of the 1981 minimum wage.

When the Congress and the President reached an agreement to raise the minimum wage in the fall of 1989, a compromise was worked out. The legislation added a subminimum wage for teenagers. As of April 1991, teenagers can be hired for three months at a wage of $3.61. In 1993, the debate reemerged, with many in Congress calling for a $5.00 minimum wage. (See the Issues and Applications box titled "The Debate Continues: The Minimum Wage in 1993" for more details.)

Taxes and Labor Supply

One of the basic beliefs of the Reagan administration (which took office in 1981) was that high rates of taxation were at the root of the economic problems faced by the United States during the 1970s. High tax rates had reduced the incentive to work, save, and invest, it was said. If tax rates were to go down (thus increasing take-home pay), it was argued, more people would go to work, people already working would work harder, and more investment and capital formation would take place. All of this would expand the *supply* of goods and services.

THE DEBATE CONTINUES: THE MINIMUM WAGE IN 1993

In February 1993, Peter Passell described the latest round of debates on the minimum wage, summarizing what we know and don't know from recent research. The following excerpt tells the story:

According to the textbooks, the minimum wage cuts both ways. A higher minimum does indeed mean higher incomes for low-wage workers who are employed. But over the decades, myriad studies have confirmed that employers respond to wage regulation by cutting their payrolls; most put the damages at roughly a 1 percent loss in jobs for a 10 percent increase in the minimum.

This apparent dilemma was sharpened by Ed Gramlich of the University of Michigan. Many minimum-wage workers, he discovered, were the dependent children of the middle class. Thus, much of the gain from a higher minimum would go into surfboards and stereos—not into rent and baby formula. It is far better, then, mainstream economists concluded, to increase the living standards of the working poor with tax breaks or to improve their earning power with training.

But this near-consensus has broken down. For one thing, today's opponents of the minimum wage do not have much to offer the food stamp generation. There is little public support in the deficit-ridden 1990's for an expensive attack on poverty. . . .

For another, there have been a handful of intriguing studies—two by David Card of Princeton University and one by Lawrence Katz of Harvard and Alan Kreuger of Princeton—suggesting that the 27 percent increase in the Federal minimum wage in

Fast-food restaurants like Burger King often pay their employees the minimum wage. Many of these companies have instituted procedures to offset the effects of the high employee turnover that results as workers leave to take better-paying jobs.

1990–91 had virtually no effect on jobs. And these studies will probably weigh heavily on Administration thinking: Mr. Katz is now the chief economist for the Labor Department.

If the Card-Katz-Kreuger analysis were as widely accepted outside the Clinton Administration as in, everyone could relax. At very worst, patrons of Taco Bell would end up paying an extra dime for their chicken fajitas so that the nice college kids behind the counter could spend spring break in Fort Lauderdale.

No such luck. The Employment Policies Institute, a Washington organization financed

by big retailers who oppose the minimum wage, is publicizing a critique by David Neumark of the University of Pennsylvania and William Wascher of the Federal Reserve Board. Their findings support the once-universal academic view that the minimum has modest but noticeable effects on employment.

So, too, does a freshly minted study of California labor by Lowell Taylor and Taeil Kim of Carnegie Mellon University that used more detailed—and arguably more accurate—data than the New View analyses.

Source: Peter Passell, "Does Raising the Minimum Wage Still Mean Fewer Jobs?" *New York Times*, February 18, 1993.

These principles were subsequently embodied in the Economic Recovery Tax Act passed by Congress in 1981. This act cut individual income tax rates across the board and substantially reduced the burden of taxes on corporations. The same argument underlay the continuing tax reform debates that climaxed in the substantial changes to the tax code enacted in 1986. The President's reform proposals in May of 1985 enunciated the logic of this thinking explicitly: "By taxing workers' earnings at excessively high rates. . . [the current system]. . . discourages work. . . . and prevents workers from reaching their full potential."[3]

---

[3]"The President's Tax Proposals to the Congress for Fairness, Growth, and Simplicity" (May 1985).

The tax cuts proposed for individuals and families were designed to increase the supply of labor. But economic theory shows that tax cuts could increase *or decrease* labor supply. Nobody disagrees with the fact that reducing taxes on income increases the "net wage." The debatable issue is, instead: What is the likely impact of higher net wages on the supply of labor?

INCOME AND SUBSTITUTION EFFECTS OF TAXES ON LABOR SUPPLY   As you recall from Chapter 6, higher wages have both a **substitution effect** and an **income effect.** Higher net wages increase the price of leisure. Increasing the price, or opportunity cost, of leisure leads to additional work effort as people find an incentive to substitute other goods, bought with income from working, for leisure. This is the *substitution effect* of higher wages. But higher net wages also make people better off. By working the same number of hours, workers can earn more income. That added income can be spent on any combination of goods, including leisure. Because I have a higher income, I may decide to consume more leisure; the result is that I actually work less. This is the *income effect* of higher wages.

> The income and substitution effects of higher wages work in opposite directions. If the income effect is larger than the substitution effect, higher net wages will actually reduce the supply of labor.

WAGES AND ELASTICITY OF LABOR SUPPLY   Many studies have attempted to measure the effect of changes in net wages on labor supply. One major survey looked at 28 studies of the behavior of adult males and 22 studies of the behavior of adult females.

Twenty of the 28 studies of men's labor-force behavior found that the overall elasticity of labor supply with respect to wages is negative but small. A negative wage elasticity means that an increase in wages actually reduces labor supply. Thus, the supply of labor curve for adult males seems to bend back (see Figure 6.11b). The negative income effect is therefore larger than the positive substitution effect. All but two of the studies reported positive substitution effects and negative income effects.

Table 19.2 summarizes the results of the general survey. The overall average of wage elasticities for men is −.06. In other words, a net wage increase of 10% would reduce the supply of male labor by 0.6 percent. Thus, the tax cuts of the 1980s probably had a tiny negative effect on the supply of adult male labor.

The evidence shows the opposite effect for women, however. Of the 22 studies, all but two found a positive overall wage elasticity. This suggests that for women, the substitution effect of a wage increase is greater than the income effect. The average of all 22 studies is +.94. In other words, an increase in net wages of 10% would increase the supply of adult female labor by a full 9.4 percent. All but one study of women found a negative income effect, while all the studies that reported substitution elasticities found them to be positive.

substitution effect of higher wages Consuming an additional hour of leisure means sacrificing the wages that would be earned by working. Thus, when the wage rate rises leisure becomes a more expensive commodity, and households may "buy" less of it. This means working more.

income effect of higher wages When wages rise, people are better off. If leisure is a normal good, they may decide to consume more of it and to work less.

TABLE 19.2
Survey of Labor Supply Elasticity Studies

	TOTAL WAGE ELASTICITY	INCOME ELASTICITY	SUBSTITUTION ELASTICITY
Men (28 studies)	−.06	−.16	+.12
Women (22 studies)	+.94	−.17	+.80
Overall median	+.10	−.15	+.25

Source: Ingemar Hanson and Charles Stuart, "Tax Revenue and the Marginal Cost of Public Funds," *Journal of Public Economics* (August 1985).

The tax reforms of 1986 were designed to have a maximum effect on the labor supply by cutting marginal rates but expanding the tax base at the same time. (Recall from Chapter 18 that the income tax base is the amount of income that is subject to taxation.) Such a change in the tax system makes leisure more expensive relative to other goods, but it does not provide households with more income to buy leisure. There is thus a substitution effect but no income effect to counteract it.

Welfare and Labor Supply

There has always been some worry that, by providing a "guaranteed" minimum standard of living, welfare programs available to those at the bottom of the income distribution give potential workers a disincentive to enter the labor force and go to work. Are such worries justified?

When we examined the incentive effects of taxes (Chapter 18), we discovered that income and substitution effects work in opposite directions. Imposing a tax reduces income; if people think of leisure as a good, they will choose to buy less of it and will instead tend to work more. But it is also true that imposing a tax or increasing marginal tax rates reduces the opportunity cost, or price, of leisure. With leisure less expensive at the margin, people will tend to buy more of it and work less. Because the two effects counteract each other, theory cannot tell us whether taxes will increase or decrease the supply of labor.

Unlike taxes, however,

Income maintenance programs produce income and substitution effects that work in the same direction. Theory predicts that both effects will reduce work effort and labor supply. Nearly all income maintenance programs are targeted to households with low incomes. Because households with higher incomes are ineligible, households that increase their incomes by working will lose some or all of their income maintenance benefits. The system, then, imposes an *implicit tax* on income from labor earned by those who are eligible for welfare.

Because of the number of income-tested programs, such as food stamps and public housing, this implicit tax on earnings can be quite high. If you earn $3000 and lose $2000 worth of benefits, your implicit tax rate would be 66 percent. For some people, the loss of benefits has been estimated at over 100% of marginal income earned.

When we think of loss of benefits as an implicit tax, we come to the conclusion that income and substitution effects do not offset each other when an income maintenance program is involved. Labor supply is likely to be lower in the presence of the program. Income maintenance programs obviously provide income, some of which is "spent" on leisure. Withdrawing benefits as income rises also reduces the opportunity cost of leisure. Suppose, for example, that for every dollar of income I earn, I lose $0.50 in benefits. If the hourly wage available is $4.00, then consuming an extra hour of leisure would cost me only $2.00 ($4.00 × 0.50); I give up $4.00 in income but retain $2.00 in benefits. Thus, the substitution effect also leads to a decrease in labor supply.

Policy makers must try to determine how much of a reduction in labor supply actually results from the programs that exist today. A major review of modern studies estimates that overall labor supply is 4.8% lower than it would be if all transfer programs were eliminated.[4] Another paper by two Harvard professors who currently serve as senior officials in the Clinton administration concludes:

---

[4]Sheldon Danziger, Robert Haveman, and Robert Plotnick, "How Income Transfer Programs Affect Work, Savings and the Income Distribution: A Critical Review," *Journal of Economic Literature* (September 1981).

There are undoubtedly some reductions in labor supply by female family heads induced by the current program. But, studies suggest that AFDC [Aid to Families with Dependent Children] has had a modest effect in reducing work. Welfare mothers do not seem to be very sensitive to work incentives. Most recently, changes have been made in the AFDC program which essentially eliminate all work incentives. After four months, benefits are reduced at least one dollar for each dollar the woman earns over $30. Yet there apparently has been little change in the work of single mothers.[5]

This is an important conclusion. Budget cuts in the early 1980s did indeed increase the rate at which benefits are withdrawn from welfare recipients. As a result, effective implicit tax rates are very high, in many cases over 100 percent. If millions of people continue to work in spite of such a large disincentive (and they do), there must be significant nonpecuniary rewards associated with holding a job.

Matching Jobs and Workers: Job Search

One important fact about the labor market is that the flow of workers into and out of the labor force is continuous. Some enter school, some graduate, others are promoted. As the population ages, some retire. Some people quit jobs, some are fired, and some take leaves or drop out of the labor force temporarily. At the same time, some firms expand and must hire new workers, changes in technology generate needs for new skills and make others obsolete, and some firms fall on hard times and must lay people off.

This constant flux results in a continuous process of sorting available workers among available jobs. New entrants into the labor force expend time and effort searching for the best possible jobs; firms send out recruiters to schools or raid competing firms, often bringing in candidates from long distances. But no matter how well these systems work:

> The distribution of skills and abilities among the available work force never corresponds exactly to the skills and abilities currently in demand.

Some people find it puzzling that the newspaper is full of available job listings while the headlines of the same paper lament very high unemployment rates. In the spring of 1993, when almost 9 million people were unemployed, the classified ads carried pages and pages of available jobs. The problem is that the skills and abilities of available job seekers often do not match the needs of firms. And, of course, unemployment also has a regional dimension. Not only do the skills demanded not always match the skills supplied, the location of jobs (labor demand) does not always correspond to the location of job seekers. In 1993, 9.4% of the labor force in California was out of work, while in North Carolina the unemployment rate was just 5.3 percent.

A person who is entering the labor force for the first time or who is considering a job change must carefully sift through the set of jobs that might be available given his or her skills, experience, ability, and location. People, even those without highly specialized skills, might have hundreds of possibilities open to them. The problem is finding out about them. Job searching is a process of gathering data. By making phone calls, applying, being rejected, or perhaps even turning down job offers, job hunters find out about what is available and what they can expect. The **job search** is thus an extended process of information gathering.

job search The process of gathering information about job availability and job characteristics.

[5]David Ellwood and Lawrence Summers, "Poverty in America: Is Welfare the Answer or the Problem?" National Bureau of Economic Research, working paper 1171 (October 1985).

To be counted as unemployed by the Bureau of Labor Statistics, one must actively be looking for a job. If a person stops looking, he or she is no longer considered a part of the labor force and thus is no longer technically "unemployed." This is why full-time homemakers and students are not counted as unemployed. Because workers without jobs who are seeking work are unemployed, the efficiency of the search process can have a significant impact on the amount of measured unemployment.

Thinking about the job search as an information-gathering process is revealing. We all want the best available job, the one that matches our abilities and aspirations and pays the highest possible wage. For many people, there are readily available jobs that are not desirable; every college graduate could get a job working the counter at Burger Baby's, but most have higher expectations.

In theory:

> Job hunting by an individual should continue as long as the expected gains from continuing the search exceed the costs of doing so.

The opportunity costs of search are those things that are lost by continuing the search, the most important of which are *forgone earnings* and *time*. Other costs include transportation, dressing for interviews, paper, postage, and telephone bills. The potential benefits from continued search depend on the job seeker's expectations. As the person gathers more and more information, expectations should become more and more accurate.

Both the government and the marketplace have responded to the problem of providing information to job hunters. In recent years, employment agencies have become more and more common. Many employers are making use of "headhunters," specialized firms that quietly and confidentially gather information from people interested in senior positions, people who are currently employed and do not want it known that they are looking to change jobs. This keeps costs low, both to the potential applicant and to society. Acutely aware of the unemployment problem, the government also sponsors a number of programs to help match jobs and workers. Most state unemployment agencies have job banks, and in many states unemployment recipients are required to check in and take job referrals.

The government can have other impacts on the search process. Consider, for example, the unemployment insurance program. Being laid off or spending an extended period of time unemployed—that is, actively looking for a job—can be a devastating experience. During periods of unemployment, suicide rates increase, the crime rate increases, and other indicators of "pain" appear in the economy. To alleviate some of this pain, the United States has an unemployment compensation system that pays benefits to workers who lose their jobs. Although rules are set state by state, most states pay benefits for 20 weeks. In 1992 and 1993, Congress authorized extended benefits in a number of states that had experienced severe economic problems.

Unemployment benefits reduce the cost of job search, and some researchers have argued that this results in inefficiency. Until recently, unemployment benefits were not taxable, and for some people benefits make up as much as 80% of lost after-tax wages. With the costs of looking for a job reduced in this fashion, people have an incentive to prolong the process. Prolonged job search drains tax revenues, artificially increases the unemployment rate, and keeps productive workers off the job—another example of a trade-off between efficiency and equity.

We have already said that the labor market is not one market—it is made up of many separate, but often closely related, markets. Nonetheless, a general sorting process is always going on. As a result, different occupational groups end up earning different wages, and the distribution of income reflects these differences. As you recall from Chapter 17, wages differ across jobs for two basic reasons: differences in jobs and differences in workers.

Some jobs are more desirable than others. Some jobs, like those in coal mining or heavy construction, involve higher levels of risk than others. *Ceteris paribus*, jobs that are more desirable and less risky tend to pay less than jobs that are less desirable and more risky. These wage differences are called **compensating differentials.**

In competitive markets, equilibrium wages are equal to the productivity of the marginal worker. And the product of a highly skilled machine operator is clearly worth more than that of an unskilled laborer. An unskilled laborer working on a routine set of tasks adds little to the final value of a product compared to the value added by a skilled machinist working with complex capital equipment. Workers who supply their labor in markets that demand unusual or highly developed skills can expect to earn higher wages, *ceteris paribus.*

But wages are determined by the forces of supply *and* demand. At most major American universities, you must have a Ph.D. to be appointed to the humanities faculty. The training and skills required are quite high. But because there are few positions relative to the number of qualified applicants, wages for humanities professors have remained low. In contrast, many elementary and high school systems have had difficulty filling open positions, particularly in math and science. As a result, teachers' salaries have increased significantly in recent years.

Earnings and Occupational Segregation

Tables 19.3 and 19.4 present some data on trends in the U.S. labor market and on actual wage rate and income differentials. During the last three decades, the labor force has changed significantly. For example, in 1960 only 36.5% of all white women were in the labor force. This figure is now approaching 60 percent. Nearly 50% of black women were in the labor force as early as 1960. Male labor-force participation has dropped for both races, with a very sharp drop for black men during the early 1970s.

Table 19.4 gives a very rough breakdown of occupations in the United States. An examination of the number of workers shows evidence of **occupational segregation** by sex. About 45% of all employed women work in the categories of administrative support (including clerical support) and service workers, while only 16% of all men work at jobs in these categories. The executive, administrative, and management category includes about 50% more men than women. Women also earn substantially lower wages than men in virtually every category, and the overall median earnings of women are only 57% of the median earnings of men.

Labor Market Discrimination, Crowding, and Inefficiency

The above data make it clear that women and men are not randomly distributed across occupations. It also shows that women, on average, earn significantly less than men. One explanation for these observations is gender discrimination in the labor market.

compensating differentials
Differences in wages that result from differences in working conditions. Risky jobs usually pay higher wages, and highly desirable jobs usually pay lower wages.

occupational segregation The concentration of men and women in certain occupations. Women are concentrated in administrative support positions, men in executive, administrative, and management positions.

TABLE 19.3
Labor-Force Participation Rates for Those 16 Years of Age and Over, 1960–1993

	MEN	WOMEN
	BLACK	
1960	83.0	48.2
1970	76.5	49.5
1975	71.0	48.9
1980	70.6	53.2
1986	71.2	56.9
1990	68.9	58.2
1993	72.3	59.1
	WHITE	
1960	83.4	36.5
1970	80.0	42.6
1975	78.7	45.9
1980	78.2	51.2
1986	76.9	55.0
1990	76.4	57.0
1993	77.6	58.1

Source: Bureau of Labor Statistics, April, 1993.

TABLE 19.4
Earnings Differences by Sex and Occupation, 1990

OCCUPATION	WOMEN		MEN		RATIO OF WOMEN TO MEN	
	NUMBER*	MEDIAN EARNINGS	NUMBER*	MEDIAN EARNINGS	NUMBER	MEDIAN EARNINGS
Total	61,732	12,250	72,348	21,522	.85	.57
Executive, administrative, management	6,577	22,551	9,244	37,010	.71	.61
Professional specialty	8,814	23,113	8,035	36,942	1.09	.63
Sales	8,393	7,307	7,871	22,955	1.06	.32
Administrative support, including secretarial	16,728	14,292	4,141	20,287	4.04	.70
Machine operators, assemblers, and operators	3,773	10,983	5,389	19,389	.70	.57
Service workers	11,722	5,746	7,801	10,514	1.66	.55

* In thousands.

Source: U.S. Bureau of the Census, *Statistical Abstract of the United States, 1992,* Table 656, p. 414.

Labor market discrimination occurs when one group of workers receives inferior treatment from employers because of some characteristic irrelevant to job performance. Inferior treatment may involve being systematically barred from certain occupations, receiving lower wages, or inability to win promotion or obtain training.

Suppose that women (the same argument can be made for African-Americans and other minorities) were systematically barred from a number of occupations. To simplify our example, let's call the occupations reserved for men (or whites) sector X, and the rest of the economy sector Y. Since women (or African-Americans) are excluded from X, the supply of labor in sector X is reduced, and wages are higher than they would otherwise be. On the other hand, women (African-Americans) must *crowd* into the occupations reserved for them. Such crowding increases the supply of labor in sector Y and pushes wages down. Thus, occupational segregation resulting from discrimination is sufficient to cause a wage differential if the number of restricted jobs is significant.

But there is more to the story than wage differentials. Occupational discrimination also results in a net loss of welfare in the economy. To understand this argument, you need to recall that the demand for labor depends on the productivity of that labor. When extra workers are crowded into sector Y, wages fall. Because wages are lower, more workers will be hired. (Recall that workers will be hired as long as the value of their product at the margin exceeds the going wage.) With more workers working at a lower wage, the marginal product of workers in Y will end up lower than it otherwise would be.

The opposite situation occurs in sector X. With fewer workers supplying their labor in the reserved sector, wages remain high. The marginal product of workers in X, then, remains high. Now consider what would happen if we transferred one worker at a time from sector Y to sector X. If we assume that the discrimination was unrelated to job qualifications, workers will be moving from a sector in which their productivity was low at the margin to a sector where it is high. Thus, the value of the product gained in sector X is greater than the value of the product lost in sector Y. There is thus a net gain in value. *Ending discrimination, then, should increase national income.* The logic behind this argument is simple:

labor market discrimination
Occurs when one group of workers receives inferior treatment from employers because of some characteristic irrelevant to job performance.

> If workers vary in their talents in ways unrelated to gender or race, rules or behaviors that force one group into specific occupations are clearly inefficient.

Critics of discrimination theory argue that competition should put an end to discrimination rather quickly. If women (or African-Americans, or any other group that is discriminated against) were more productive than the current wage would suggest, some firms would hire them into the restricted occupations, thus driving those who persist in their discrimination out of business.

Those who defend the discrimination and crowding theory rejoin that the pure-competition scenario is naive and unrealistic. They argue that the link between productivity and wages is difficult to establish, and that those in positions of power (often white men) have both the incentive and the ability to maintain discriminatory practices over long periods of time.

A lively and emotional debate among labor economists that has ended up in the courts in recent years is the controversy over *comparable worth*. The basic argument is that women are systematically paid less than men for work of equal, or at least comparable, value. This controversy is discussed in Chapter 17.

LABOR UNIONS

Thus far we have focused on the behavior of firms and workers in competitive labor markets. This is by no means the whole story, however. For many years, a substantial number of workers have been and still are employed under contracts negotiated between their employers and their labor unions. In 1991 just over 16 million workers—about 16% of all wage and salary workers in the United States—belonged to unions. The bargaining that takes place between parties acting on behalf of firms and of workers does not necessarily produce the same outcome as the operation of an unregulated, competitive labor market.

Nearly all eligible workers in a number of major industries, including automobiles, mining, and steel, belong to unions. But workers in many other industries (perhaps the most significant of which are the high-tech industries) have not been unionized. While unions are still a major force in the economy and in U.S. society, they do not enjoy the influence and power that they once did. Union membership has fallen dramatically as a percentage of all those employed. In absolute numbers, union membership is about the same as it was in 1954, but the number of jobs has nearly doubled. In 1954 nearly 35% of workers were in unions. Since 1960, the figure has declined in every year but two, and it now stands at its lowest level since 1937.

We begin our discussion of labor unions with a brief history of the labor movement in the United States. We then turn to economic theory and an analysis of the potential effects of an organized labor force on the economy. Finally, we present some issues and controversies concerning what is known about the actual effects of unions.

The Labor Movement in the United States: A Brief History

Some scholars have associated unions with the medieval craft guilds, but there are important differences between the two. The guild members were master craftsmen who owned capital and often employed workers. Unions as we know them today first appeared in Great Britain and the United States in the late eighteenth and early nineteenth centuries as associations of workers with similar skills.

At that time, individual workers had no control over the conditions of their working lives; political and economic power was concentrated in the hands of wealthy business owners. Workers found, however, that there was strength in uniting. From their earliest years, union objectives have been higher wages and improved working conditions.

Employers resisted, of course. They used the law, coercion, and brute force in an effort to stop union organizing and activity. Union members were fired, workers were forced to sign **yellow-dog contracts** in which they promised not to join a union, and companies hired strikebreakers, thugs, and even gunmen to intimidate organizers. Without laws on their side, the unions had no hope of success. Because changes in existing law and passage of new law follow only from political power, that power became an important union goal, and politics remains at the heart of the labor movement today.

yellow-dog contracts Contracts in which workers agree not to join unions.

One of the earliest successful labor organizations in the United States was the **Knights of Labor,** founded in 1869. The Knights, which included both skilled and unskilled workers, attempted to organize all workers into one great union. After it successfully struck the Wabash railroad owned by "robber baron" Jay Gould in 1885, its popularity and power grew dramatically. In 1886 the Knights had 700,000 members.

Knights of Labor One of the earliest successful labor organizations in the United States, it recruited both skilled and unskilled laborers. Founded in 1869, the power of the Knights declined after the Chicago Haymarket bombing in 1886.

The decline of the Knights of Labor came quickly. Although allegations of its association with the 1886 Haymarket bombing in Chicago that killed seven policemen were false, the strike against Gould was gradually broken, and the Knights' radical positions on social issues cost them public support. In the end, a lack of unanimity, as well as the rapid inflow of unskilled immigrants, weakened the union's economic power, and the organization gradually disintegrated.

THE AMERICAN FEDERATION OF LABOR Founded in 1881, the **American Federation of Labor (AFL)** was meant to be a practical, nonideological movement. While its goal was to improve the lot of skilled workers, it fully accepted the existing social *and economic* system.[6]

American Federation of Labor (AFL) Founded in 1881, the AFL was successfully led by Samuel Gompers from 1886 until 1924. A practical, nonideological union, the AFL existed as a "confederation" of individual craft unions representing skilled workers, each with an independent organization and an exclusive jurisdiction. Now merged with the CIO, the AFL maintains a preeminent position among unions today.

The AFL was led for many years by Samuel Gompers, a cigar maker who was elected its president in 1886 and who served in that capacity until his death in 1924. Made up of independent organizations, each was given exclusive jurisdiction over its particular craft or area. Between 1900 and the beginning of World War I, its membership grew from about half a million to about two million, and by 1920 it had doubled to nearly four million.

During the 1920s, however, the labor movement stagnated. A major antiunion offensive by employers, widespread antilabor sentiments, conservative U.S. presidents, and hostile courts all contributed to a significant drop in union membership. Gompers died in 1924, and the AFL was left without strong leadership.

THE DEPRESSION AND THE NEW DEAL The Great Depression began in 1929, and with it came a new start for unions. In 1932 Congress passed the *Norris-LaGuardia Act,* which stopped the use of court-ordered injunctions to prevent strikes. Franklin Roosevelt was elected president in 1932, and pro-labor legislation was a major part of his "New Deal" (the Roosevelt prescription for economic recovery).

---

[6]Many critics of the capitalist system find the fact that this principle has characterized the American labor movement from the beginning an anathema. The Marxist critique of capitalism argues that workers are inevitably exploited to the point that they rise up and overthrow the capitalist system, replacing it with a socialist or communist state. To Marxists, the labor union is the instrument of revolt. In Western Europe, union ideology has always been much closer to that envisioned by Marx than in the United States. For example, the United States has never seen a more committed anticommunist than George Meany, who served as president of the AFL-CIO for many years.

collective bargaining The process by which union leaders bargain with management as the representatives of all union employees.

National Labor Relations Board (NLRB) A watchdog board established by the Wagner Act in 1935 whose duties include ensuring that all workers are guaranteed the right to join unions and that firm managers participate fairly in collective bargaining if so requested by a majority of their employees.

Congress of Industrial Organizations (CIO) Founded by John L. Lewis, president of the United Mine Workers, after the AFL rejected his plan to organize the steel, rubber, automobile, and chemical industries in 1935, the CIO was the first union to organize semiskilled laborers in the mass production industries. After 20 years of independence, it merged with the AFL in 1955.

The most important piece of New Deal labor legislation came in 1935. The *Wagner Act,* also called the *National Labor Relations Act,* guaranteed workers the right to join unions. It also required management to engage in **collective bargaining** if a majority of its employees so desired. To enforce the law, the act set up the **National Labor Relations Board (NLRB).** In 1938 the Fair Labor Standards Act established the "minimum wage" at $0.25 an hour. By 1991, the minimum wage had risen to $4.25 an hour.

THE CONGRESS OF INDUSTRIAL ORGANIZATIONS   The AFL was an association of craft unions representing skilled workers. Prior to the 1930s, however, no real attempt had been made to organize the growing numbers of semiskilled workers in mass production industries, such as steel and automobiles.

John L. Lewis, president of the United Mine Workers, and a number of other unions within the AFL independently tried to organize the steel, automobile, rubber, and chemical industries. In 1935, when the AFL decided not to endorse his plan, Lewis founded the Committee for Industrial Organization, which later became the **Congress of Industrial Organizations (CIO).** The AFL subsequently expelled the unions involved in the rebellion. The new competition between the AFL and the CIO led to organization drives that pushed total union membership up rapidly in the late 1930s and early 1940s. By the end of World War II in 1945, union membership had risen to nearly 15 million, over 35% of all workers.

Not surprisingly, the rapid rise in union power triggered some reaction. The *Smith-Connally Act* of 1943 and the *Taft-Hartley Act* of 1947 introduced new government controls over unions. Any strike that was deemed to "imperil the national health or safety" could be suspended by the courts through an injunction for an 80-day "cooling off period." President Reagan used such an injunction to stop a railroad strike in 1986. The Taft-Hartley Act also gave states the right to pass "right-to-work" laws. Such laws, currently enforced in 20 states, make illegal union shop agreements requiring workers to join unions. Right-to-work laws have seriously hampered union organizing in the states that have them.

THE MERGER OF THE AFL AND THE CIO   The AFL and CIO coexisted independently for 20 years until they merged in 1955 under the leadership of two men who would dominate the movement for many years, Walter Reuther and George Meany. In 1968 Reuther's United Automobile Workers left the AFL-CIO and joined the International Brotherhood of Teamsters, the truck drivers' union that the AFL-CIO had earlier expelled for corrupt practices.

RECENT HISTORY AND CONTINUED DECLINE   The 1980s were not kind to the labor movement. First, in 1981 President Reagan "broke" a national strike of air traffic controllers. Public employees do not have the same right to strike as workers in other industries, and when Reagan fired 11,400 controllers, the controllers' union went bankrupt. The traveling public had been greatly inconvenienced by the strike, and the union did not receive a great deal of public sympathy.

Second, the labor movement moved decisively in 1984 to throw all its political muscle behind the Democratic presidential candidate, Walter Mondale. Partly because of intense early union organizing, Mondale received the nomination but was later overwhelmingly defeated by Ronald Reagan. Many people felt that Mondale was simply too closely associated with unions at a time when they were falling from favor with the voting public. Mondale's overwhelming defeat certainly contributed to the difficulties faced by union organizers.

Third, international competition for U.S. markets as well as for markets around the world has increased tremendously in recent years. The U.S. steel and automobile industries, for example, have found themselves losing markets rapidly to Japanese and European producers. Justifiable fear of foreign competition has weighed in powerfully on the side of firms when contracts come up for negotiation. In the last few years, major unions, including the United Automobile Workers, have signed contracts calling for major *reductions* in wages to make various industries more competitive.

Finally, deregulation and increased domestic competition have reduced the power of unions in several key industries. For example, the airline industry was deregulated in 1978. Since then a number of new firms have entered the industry, offering low fares by employing only nonunion employees at much lower salaries. Airline pilots at nonunion airlines earn half to two thirds of the salaries of their union counterparts. Increased competition also threatens the power of unions in trucking and telecommunications.

Economic Effects of Labor Unions

One way to analyze union power is to think of a union as a monopolistic seller of labor in a market. If there were many buyers, the union's situation would be very similar to that of a pure monopolist selling in output markets: The union would restrict the supply of labor and charge a wage rate above the competitive equilibrium wage rate. But wages may not be the only concern of unions. Other objectives might include keeping all of their members employed or improving working conditions.

UNIONS AS MONOPOLIES Let us assume for a moment that a union is the only seller of labor in some market. Let us also suppose that, as an initial condition, union membership is less than the number of workers that would be employed if the market were competitively organized and that the union's objective is to maximize its members' wages and keep them all employed. In Figure 19.4, if L_u is the number of union members, the union would set a wage W_u above the competitive

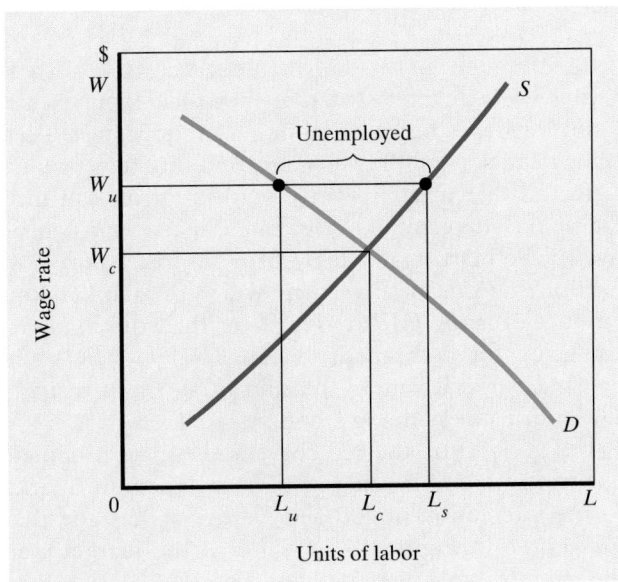

FIGURE 19.4
A Competitive Labor Market and a Monopoly Union

If the union imposes a wage of W_u, demand for labor will be limited to L_u. But there will be a labor supply of L_s. Thus, many will not be able to find jobs. But if union membership is L_u, all the unemployed would be nonunion workers.

wage rate W_c. At W_u, the quantity of labor supplied is L_s, but firms will demand only L_u units of labor. There would thus be an excess supply of workers, or unemployment, in this market equal to the difference between L_s and L_u, but the unemployed would all be nonunion workers.

For wage W_u to hold, the union would have to restrict membership, because increasing the number of union members would also mean decreasing the wages that union members receive. (This is implied by the downward-sloping demand curve, of course.) Restriction of union membership is a common practice. Some unions simply refuse to admit new members; others have long apprenticeship programs that must be completed before a worker is admitted. Unions have also been accused of using racial and gender barriers to restrict membership.

You can see the trade-off in Figure 19.4. If wages were set lower than W_u, more workers would be employed. If union membership were greater than L_u, the leadership would have to make a tough decision. They could get more members into jobs, but only by accepting a lower wage for everyone or by somehow increasing demand for the services of their members.

Over the years, unions have shown great concern for keeping members in jobs. The preferred route has been to increase demand for workers rather than to take pay cuts. Unions have used many techniques for shifting the demand curve to the right. Union contracts now include provisions for job security, especially for those with seniority. Some contracts have clauses that preserve jobs even when it is inefficient to do so. The most often-cited example of this widely used and widely criticized policy, called **featherbedding,** involves the coal shovelers that trains had to carry for years after they were all powered by diesel engines rather than by coal.

featherbedding The common union practice of preserving jobs even when it is inefficient to do so.

Unions have actively sought protective trade measures such as tariffs (taxes on imports) and quotas to prevent foreign producers from cutting into the demand for domestic, union-made goods. Parking your new Toyota in the parking lot of a General Motors plant in Detroit would certainly not make you popular with your fellow union members. Some unions have even gone so far as to advertise union-produced products. The International Ladies Garment Workers for many years has run an ad accompanied by a popular jingle that tells you to "look for the union label."

UNION POWER VERSUS MONOPSONY POWER   In Chapter 13, we examined *monopsony*, a market structure in which there is just one buyer. To maximize profits, a single buyer of labor—a monopsonist—that could control part of the labor market would lower wages and hire fewer workers.

Recall that in competitive markets, firms can hire all the labor they need at the market-determined wage rate. Since every firm in competition is small relative to the market, no single firm has any control over the wage rate. A profit-maximizing competitive firm will hire labor as long as the marginal revenue product of labor (MRP_L) is greater than the market wage rate; the equilibrium condition for a competitive firm is $W = MRP_L$. In competition, the market demand curve is simply the sum of all the marginal revenue product curves of all the firms demanding labor.

In Figure 19.5, the red curve is the market demand curve for labor (the sum of the firms' MRP_L curves). The equilibrium market wage rate is determined by the interaction of competitive demanders and the supply of labor (the lower blue curve in Figure 19.5). Thus, if the market were organized competitively, the equilibrium wage rate would be W_c.

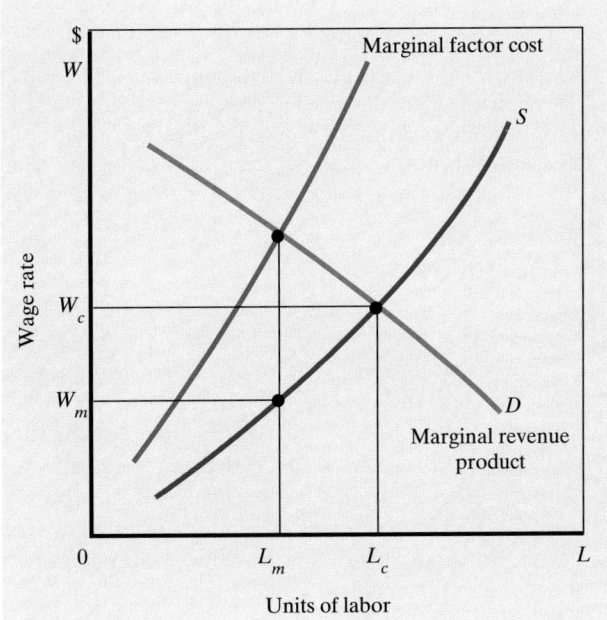

FIGURE 19.5

A Profit-Maximizing Monopsonist

A profit-maximizing monopsonist would pay a wage, W_m, below the competitive level, W_c.

But now suppose that instead of many firms demanding labor, there is only one firm demanding labor (a *monopsonist*). This changes our analysis significantly. Under competition, firms can hire all the labor they want at the market wage. But now the large firm faces the *market* labor supply curve. This means that the more labor the firm decides to hire, the higher is the wage that the firm must pay. At lower wages, less labor is supplied.

The upper blue curve in Figure 19.5 is called the *marginal factor cost* curve for labor (MFC_L). See Chapter 13 for a review of this concept. It represents the added cost of hiring an additional unit of labor. The supply of labor curve *(S)* shows the wage that must be paid to attract each level of labor supply. Marginal factor cost at every level of output is *higher* than the wage because to attract added workers at the margin, the wage paid to *all* workers must be raised. For example, suppose that at a wage of $5, six units of labor are supplied, and that at a wage of $6, seven units of labor are supplied. Hiring six units of labor costs $30 (6 units × $5), while hiring seven units of labor costs $42 (7 units × $6). The marginal factor cost of the seventh unit of labor is thus $12 ($42 − $30), which is higher than the $6 wage rate.

A profit-maximizing firm that is the only buyer of labor in a market (i.e., our monopsonist) will hire labor as long as the marginal revenue product of labor (MRP_L) exceeds the marginal factor cost (MFC_L). Thus, in Figure 19.5, the optimal quantity of labor is L_m (the point at which $MRP_L = MFC_L$), and the wage paid to workers is W_m (the lowest wage required to attract L_m units of labor). In essence, monopsony power leads to lower wages and fewer jobs than would be the case under competitive conditions.

When a monopsonist faces a monopolistic *seller* of labor such as a union, the story is different. The union, of course, tries to impose a wage rate above the going wage, W_c. The monopsonist wants to pay a wage below W_c. The final result depends on the relative bargaining strengths of the union and the firm. In a sense, the union in this model exists to resist and exercise *countervailing power* on the buying side of the labor market. Indeed, many of the most highly unionized markets are in concentrated monopsonist like industries such as steel and automobiles.

To summarize:

> Union power in a competitive labor market is likely to be inefficient. Pushing up wages reduces labor demand and can actually cause unemployment and restrictions on union membership. In markets where the buying side is highly concentrated, however, unions may actually drive wages closer to their efficient levels.

EMPIRICAL EVIDENCE: DO UNIONS RAISE WAGES? The answer to this question, not surprisingly, is yes:

> An overwhelming number of studies using very different sets of data and techniques have found that unions have succeeded in raising wages.

An early and well-known study by H. Gregg Lewis surveyed the existing literature in 1963 and found that unions succeeded in increasing wages by 10% to 15 percent.[7]

Modern cross-sectional studies using more sophisticated statistical techniques to control for characteristics of union and nonunion workers found that unions have succeeded in increasing wages by 20% to 30 percent.[8]

DO UNIONS DECREASE OR INCREASE PRODUCTIVITY? The picture of unions that has emerged from our discussion so far is not very positive. The monopoly model leads us to the same unflattering conclusions. First, unions raise wages above the competitive level, which leads to unemployment and the underuse of labor. Second, union work rules and featherbedding reduce productivity. Third, unions create inequities by forcing wage differentials between similar workers. And finally, unions may discriminate to limit membership and hold down labor supply.

Another view has recently been put forth by two Harvard economists, Richard Freeman and James Medoff, who argue that unions in fact have a *positive* effect on the allocation of resources. According to Freeman and Medoff, unions actually raise productivity. Union members, they say, have lower quit rates, remain more loyal to the firm, maintain a higher morale, and are more likely to cooperate on the job. By communicating with management, they help to put efficient policies into effect. They collect information on workers' preferences that leads to more efficient design of benefits packages and better personnel administration.[9]

Freeman and Medoff present a very convincing argument supported with a great deal of data. Their conclusions have been debated, however, and they are still far from becoming "conventional wisdom."

---

[7]H. Gregg Lewis, *Unionism and Relative Wages* (Chicago: University of Chicago Press, 1963).

[8]See Richard Freeman and James Medoff, *What Do Unions Do?* (New York: Basic Books, 1984), Ch. 2, "The Union Wage Effect."

[9]Freeman and Medoff, *Unions.*

SUMMARY

Competitive Labor Markets: A Review

1. Demand for labor in competitive markets depends on labor's productivity. Firms will hire labor as long as the marginal revenue product exceeds the market wage. The *marginal revenue product of labor* depends on the market value of its product; if no one wants to buy a product, that product has no market value.

2. Households supply labor. The supply of labor depends on some factors that households control and some that they do not. The alternatives to working for a wage are working for no pay or enjoying one's leisure. Labor supply decisions depend to a large extent on preferences for work and leisure.

3. The stock of knowledge, skills, and talents that human beings possess by nature or through education and training is called *human capital*. The principal form of human capital investment financed primarily by households is education. The principal form of human capital investment financed primarily by firms is *on-the-job training*. Governments invest heavily in human capital.

4. Wages in competitive markets are determined by supply and demand. When a surplus exists in a labor market, we can usually expect to see wages fall, but sometimes disequilibria persist.

The Labor Market in Action

5. Labor supply depends on a number of factors, including wage rates, tax rates, nonlabor income, and wealth. Individual firms have very little control over the market wage; firms are forced to pay the wage that is determined by the market. Because people cannot get from one point to another free of charge and because most people do not reside at their work places—as capital does—there is an important spatial dimension to labor markets.

6. Personal preferences play a very important role in the decisions that households make about labor supply and in the decisions they make about what to consume.

Labor Markets and Public Policy

7. The *minimum wage* is the lowest wage that firms are permitted to pay workers by law. Opponents argue that minimum wage legislation interferes with the smooth functioning of the labor market and creates unemployment. Proponents argue that the minimum wage has been successful in raising the wages of the poorest workers and alleviating poverty without creating much unemployment. The current minimum wage is $4.25 per hour.

8. Depending on the relative size of the *income and substitution effect*, tax cuts could increase or decrease labor supply.

9. Empirical evidence suggests that men's labor supply does not respond very much to changes in wage rates. In fact, higher net wages actually seem to reduce slightly men's labor supply. Women seem to be more responsive to changes in wage rates, and, in contrast to men, tend to work more when net wages rise.

10. Unlike taxes, income maintenance programs produce income and substitution effects that work in the same direction. Both effects will reduce work effort and labor supply. Because households on welfare lose some or all of their benefits by working, the system imposes an implicit tax on any income that those households earn.

11. The distribution of skills and abilities among the available work force never corresponds exactly to the skills and abilities currently in demand.

12. *Job searching* is a process of gathering data. In theory, job hunting should continue as long as the expected gains from continuing to search exceed the costs of doing so.

13. Unemployment benefits reduce the cost of the job search. Some have argued that this results in inefficiency. Until recently, unemployment benefits were not taxable, and for some people they make up as much as 80% of lost wages. With the costs of looking for a job reduced in this fashion, people have an incentive to prolong the process. Prolonged job search drains tax revenues, artificially increases the unemployment rate, and keeps productive workers off the job.

Wage and Income Differentials in the United States

14. *Ceteris paribus*, jobs that are more desirable and less risky tend to pay less than jobs that are less desirable and more risky. These wage differences are called *compensating differentials*.

15. Recent data regarding the U.S. labor force show evidence of *occupational segregation* by sex. Women are concentrated in administrative support positions; men are concentrated in executive, administrative, and management positions.

16. *Labor market discrimination* occurs when one group of workers receives inferior treatment from employers because of some characteristic irrelevant to job performance. Inferior treatment may involve being systematically barred from certain occupations, receiving lower wages, or being unable to win promotion or obtain training. If workers vary in their talents in ways unrelated to gender or race, rules or behaviors that force one group into specific occupations are inefficient.

Labor Unions

17. While unions are still a major force in the economy and in U.S. society, they do not enjoy the power or the influence that they once did. As a percentage of those employed, union membership now stands at its lowest level since 1937. The decline of unionism has been attributed to politics, antiunion sentiment in both the business community and the general public, and increased foreign competition.

18. Union power in a competitive labor market is likely to be inefficient. Pushing up wages reduces labor demand and can cause unemployment and restrictions on union membership. In markets where the buying side is highly concentrated, however, unions may actually drive wages closer to their efficient levels.

19. An overwhelming number of studies have found that unions have succeeded in raising wages. Modern cross-sectional studies find that unions have raised wages by 20% to 30 percent.

20. One school of thought holds that unions lead to unemployment, the underuse of labor, lower productivity, and artificial wage differentials. Another school argues that unions raise productivity because union members have lower turnover, maintain higher morale, and are more likely to cooperate on the job.

REVIEW TERMS AND CONCEPTS

American Federation
   of Labor (AFL) 497
collective bargaining 498
compensating differentials 494
Congress of Industrial
   Organizations (CIO) 498
featherbedding 500

human capital 483
income effect of higher wages 490
job search 492
Knights of Labor 497
labor market discrimination 495
marginal revenue product
   of labor (MRP_L) 481

minimum wage 487
National Labor Relations Board
   (NLRB) 498
occupational segregation 494
on-the-job training 483
substitution effect of higher wages 490
yellow-dog contracts 497

PROBLEM SET

1. Jane is considering returning to school to get an MBA. She currently makes $30,000 and pays $9000 in taxes (30%). Tuition at the school of her choice is $15,000 per year, and the program requires two years to complete. She must attend full time and would receive no financial aid.

  a. What is the total cost of acquiring an MBA?

  b. What other information might you need to get a better picture of the full cost of acquiring an MBA? (*Hint:* What about summers?)

  c. If the degree would raise Jane's expected after-tax wage by $5000 per year in real terms for a long time, what is the rate of return on investment in an MBA for Jane? What if the increase were $15,000?

  d. To make a final decision, what other factors might Jane want to consider?

2. Draw a diagram to illustrate each of the following situations:

  a. A labor supply curve for a group of households for whom the income effect of a wage increase is stronger than the substitution effect.

  b. The effect of a general increase in the productivity of labor (an overall rise in the marginal product of labor).

  c. The effect of a union contract that succeeds in raising wage rates above the competitive equilibrium.

  d. The effect of a minimum wage above equilibrium in a competitive labor market.

  e. The effect of a minimum wage at competitive equilibrium on a monopsony buyer in the labor market.

3. Some people have suggested that the Department of Labor should establish a computerized national and regional job bank to provide people with listings of available jobs. Is this a good idea, or is it an unwarranted intrusion of the government into the private sector? Explain your answer.

4. Explain how the functioning of income-tested programs such as welfare acts as a tax on the poor that can have an effect on their work effort.

5. Explain how the 1993 extension of unemployment insurance benefits could actually lead to unemployment. If evidence were found to support this claim, should we repeal the extension or abandon the unemployment compensation system altogether? Explain your answer.

6. If you had to drop out of school and fully support yourself and your parents, how would you begin the task of searching for a job? Whom would you talk to first? Second? How would you go about finding and getting the best possible job?

7. In many developing countries, the government sector pays a much higher wage for workers than the private sector does. This practice has been widely criticized on the grounds that it creates unemployment as people queue for government jobs in the cities rather than staying in the countryside working for market-determined wages. Using supply and demand curves, show how this situation could lead to higher wages and less employment in the private sector job market.

8. The American Brotherhood of Widget Makers has 15,000 members. Today all are employed at a wage rate of $15 per hour. The union is considering a push to raise wages by $1.50 per hour. A union economist has pointed out that evidence for the industry suggests a labor demand elasticity of −1. What is the potential cost of a new wage contract that accepts the 10% hike? What further contract provisions might you suggest to reduce or eliminate these potential losses?

9. What factors are important in determining a person's wages? Connect these factors to explanations of why some groups (e.g., women, African-Americans, teenagers) earn less than others.

The Location of Economic Activity: Urban and Regional Economics

20

Since Chapter 4, we have been discussing the economic decisions made by individual firms and households: how much to produce, what to produce, which technology to use, how much of each input to demand, what to consume, and how much to save. But we have not yet touched on one equally important decision—*where to locate.* Every household must live somewhere, and every firm must locate its facilities. In fact, our world has been shaped by the collective location decisions of millions of households and firms. The collection of factories, office buildings, roads, houses, apartment buildings, stores, museums, and schools that we know as a city exists only because people once decided that those things needed to be close together.

Location decisions are similar to other decisions made by firms and households. For households, location decisions depend on preferences, incomes, and relative prices. A graduate of Florida State University who decides to look for a job in Atlanta may like the Atlanta area, but her decision is also likely to be influenced by factors such as job opportunities, wage rates, and the cost of living. For firms, decisions depend on potential revenues, costs, and profits. Digital Equipment Corporation opened a production facility in Ireland because it seemed profitable to do so. Honda opened a large plant in Ohio for the same reason.

Our exploration of the economics of locational choices begins with a discussion of the microeconomics of locational choice. Location is determined in the market for land. In theory, land use is determined by a market that allocates space to its most productive use. But land markets are highly regulated. In many areas, land use is carefully planned and must conform to strict zoning rules and regulations.

We conclude our study of microeconomics by discussing some of the social consequences of past locational choices: the high concentrations of poor people and minorities in cities and high-income families in separate suburban jurisdictions; the struggles of central cities to maintain schools and essential public services on declining revenue bases; and the problems some regions have with the flight of jobs, high unemployment, and poverty.

THE LOCATION OF BUSINESS FIRMS

No topic is of greater concern for state governors than employment, and employment in a state or a region depends upon location decisions made by business firms. Just as presidents rise and fall with the national economy, governors rise and fall with the economies of their states. Most states have development departments charged with the responsibility of attracting new firms and encouraging established firms to stay and expand. Within the last dozen years, many states have established tax reform commissions. A top item on the agenda of practically every one of them has been a study of the impact of state taxes on industrial location decisions.

The single most important thing to understand about business location decisions is that they are complicated. The easiest way to see just how complicated they are is to look at the profit function of a single firm. *Profits,* you will recall, are the difference between total revenue and total cost of production:

$$\text{Profit} = TR - TC = P \times q - (P_1 X_1 + P_2 X_2 + \cdots P_n X_n).$$

Total revenue is the price of output times the quantity of output sold. *Total cost* is the total cost of all the inputs required. In the equation above, we have n inputs, which we presume include various kinds of labor, capital, land, transport costs, and so forth. P_1 is the price of the first input, X_1 is the quantity of the first input used, and so forth.

Before we introduced the question of location to our analysis of profit-maximizing firms, we assumed that each firm knew the price of output, the price of each input required, and the technologies of production available. That information was used to pick one profit-maximizing level of output. The addition of the location question brings with it a significant complication. The fact is that:

Every single variable in a profit function may change from location to location.

In other words, when a firm shops around for a location, it must think about the price it can charge, the amount it might sell, the costs of transportation, wage rates, rent levels, the taxes it must pay, and so forth *at every possible location.* Once these factors are calculated, the firm will presumably pick the location where its profit will be highest.

Location and Profits

For a perfectly competitive firm selling a homogeneous product to a national market, demand is perfectly elastic regardless of location. That is, price is determined by the market and firms can sell all that they can produce. For all other firms, however, revenues depend, to some extent, on location.

LOCATIONAL VARIATION IN REVENUES As you have seen, revenues depend on demand, but, more specifically, they depend on price (P) and how much the firm can sell (q). A gas station located on a deserted country road would not sell much gasoline. A store that sells deep-sea fishing equipment exclusively would probably not last long in Nebraska. A retail outlet that sells goods or services directly to people must be accessible to its customers. Many firms comfortably located along major state and U.S. highways found themselves in deep trouble when the interstate highway system diverted traffic away from them.

The price that a firm can charge for its product also may vary with location. Take, for example, the corner convenience store. Everyone knows that small neighborhood grocery and drug stores charge higher prices than the big supermarkets and chain drug stores. They can do so and not go out of business because they are conveniently located. Because there is a cost associated with getting in the car and driving the two or three miles to the supermarket, the convenience of the corner store may be worth the extra cost to me.

But location can also work to keep prices down. Most college towns, for example, have several stores that sell tapes and CDs to students. In such places, this business is quite competitive—items are heavily discounted, and any store that charges higher prices for popular CDs will lose most of its business. But if you want to buy a CD in a relatively isolated suburban community with only one small music store, you will probably pay a substantially higher price. For the same reason, the lowest gasoline prices are found along roads that are well traveled by local residents and that have several gas stations. When competitors are not very accessible, prices tend to be higher. You encounter the highest gas prices of all in remote areas, in the centers of large cities, and at rest stops along interstate highways.

LOCATIONAL VARIATION IN COSTS Some costs vary from location to location and some do not. For many firms, the cost of transporting inputs to the point of production and outputs to the point of sale make up a large component of final cost. Clearly, transport costs depend upon what needs to be transported where.

Automobiles are a prime example. Components must be produced, then assembled, and the final product must be shipped to dealers all over the world. Many of an automobile's component parts are produced from steel and aluminum. Moving iron ore, bauxite, and coal to the sites of aluminum and steel production, transporting the raw materials to production facilities, moving finished parts to assembly plants, and shipping assembled automobiles to dealers is an enormously complex set of tasks. The costs of all these tasks clearly depend on the sites of ore sources, production facilities, assembly plants, and dealers.

Wage rates also vary significantly across the country. The highest average wages are in the Pacific Northwest and in the north central industrial states of Michigan, Ohio, Indiana, and Iowa. The lowest-priced labor is found in the deep South and in northern New England. Average wage rates in October 1992 ranged from $9.09 in Arkansas and $9.58 in North Carolina to $12.82 in Indiana and $14.98 in Michigan. Average wages in Michigan were 65% higher than those in Arkansas.

Firms that employ people to work in offices face wide variations in the cost of office space, both within and across metropolitan areas. The rental price of floor space in office buildings is normally quoted in terms of dollars per square foot per year. These prices are usually tied in to the state of the economy. Between 1984 and 1987, for example, the economies of New England and New York experienced a boom. Employment grew, and office vacancy rates fell. As demand exceeded supply, rents increased; by 1987 rents ranged from $25 to $75 per square foot in New York City and Boston office buildings. At the same time, dramatic overbuilding combined with a declining economy in Texas and other southwestern cities drove rents to below $10 per square foot. (In a few cases, leases were signed for space in high-quality buildings at rents of $5 per square foot!) Clearly, such differences can affect business decisions. Firms found that locating a branch office or an operations center in the Southwest was much cheaper than locating the same facility in the Northeast. Cheap real estate (low rents) and wage rates gave southwestern firms an incentive to expand, while high rents and high wage costs provided disincentives to expansion for New England firms in the 1980s.

Office rents have proven very volatile. National overbuilding in the 1980s caused rents to fall sharply in the early 1990s. The biggest rent decreases have been in the Northeast—which suddenly finds itself competitive again—and in California.

The cost of capital to a firm depends to a great extent on the cost of financing. Neither the cost of borrowing nor the cost of raising funds through bond or stock offerings varies significantly across cities and regions, because the banking industry is highly integrated. If interest rates in Phoenix increase, Phoenix banks can obtain funds from outside the region, or firms themselves may turn directly to credit markets outside the area. Money can thus move quickly from low-demand regions to high-demand regions. The stock market and the bond market are national markets. A household in Columbus, Ohio, may save and deposit some of its income in a local brokerage account, with the proceeds going to finance a new wing on a fiberglass plant near San Diego.

Location and Public Policy

As we noted above, public officials have sought for decades to influence firms' locational choices. Both tax and expenditure policies have been continued to encourage businesses. Several years ago, New York State included in its Corporate Franchise Tax a number of provisions designed to promote the expansion of firms within the state. The "jobs-incentive-credit" program, for example, reduced a firm's taxes if it expanded its employment in the state by a minimum of 1% during the year. More recently, the federal government has designated a number of "enterprise zones" in which locating firms receive special tax treatment.

Some states and cities negotiate property tax rates with new firms, offering juicy abatements and other perquisites. Others build access roads or new freeway interchanges that benefit new firms. During the 1960s, when urban renewal was seen as the salvation of run-down inner cities, city governments paid for most of the land and site-improvement costs before developments even began.

For years, economists have debated whether state tax and expenditure policies have a significant effect on business location decisions. The evidence is mixed. Those who find no effect argue that state and local taxes represent a very small portion of total costs for most firms, and that tax rates vary less across states than most people think. When decision makers are asked in surveys about the factors that played a key role in their location decisions, taxes and other special incentives do not score high. Most, but not all, statistical studies find that state and local taxes and expenditure policies are insignificant in the location decision. The factors that do seem to play a major role include the availability of a trained labor force, wage rates, and transport costs. But the view that state taxes and expenditures have little or no effect on location decisions is not universally held by economists. Some studies have found statistical evidence that site choice *is* sensitive to tax rates. Others point to specific examples of firms that claim to have been influenced by tax incentives.

Whether or not location-specific incentives work, it is not at all clear from the standpoint of national policy that intense competition among state governments for employment is a good thing. Because firms are naturally drawn to the locations that best suit their own circumstances, the nation as a whole benefits when a firm is able to move from one state to another and reduce real costs. If state policies succeed in changing those decisions, the result may be inefficient. And if many states compete by throwing money at firms to attract them, one state's gain may become another state's loss. Suppose, for example, that an automobile company decides to build a new plant in state X for cost reasons. The company then tells states W, X, Y, and Z that they are all in the running. The resulting competition ultimately forces state X into offering a substantial subsidy that wastes state tax dollars and has no effect on the firm's decision.

But there is another side to this story. The fact that firms may react either positively or negatively to differences in tax rates and state spending policies forces state officials to be more responsible. Interstate tax competition, some economists argue, forces public officials to look long and hard at potentially wasteful tax and expenditure policies.

Land Costs and Density of Development

One of the most important factors that shows a significant variation within a city or a metropolitan area is land costs. If you think about a city or metropolitan area as a series of concentric rings around the city center, land area increases significantly as you move out from the center. Space near the center is also the most accessible. It is not surprising, then, that:

> In nearly all cities, land value decreases with its distance from the city center.

Figure 20.1 shows a land price gradient for a typical U.S. city. The highest prices are those in the center of the city ("downtown"). The highest land prices in the world are in downtown Tokyo, where land parcels were sold for over $5000 per square foot in 1992! In 1993, Japan's land values declined somewhat while those in China increased. See the Global Perspective box titled "Property Fever in Beijing" for more details.

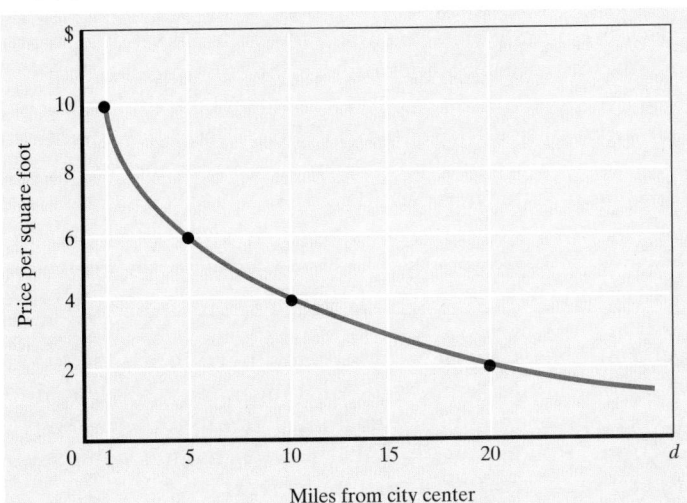

FIGURE 20.1
Typical Land Price Gradient in a U.S. City, 1993

Land prices are high in the center of U.S. cities and decline as one moves out toward the periphery.

As you recall from the discussion of factor prices and technological choice in Chapter 7, most firms can produce their output in a number of alternative ways, using a number of different combinations of inputs. They may be able to substitute capital for labor, labor for capital, capital for land, and so forth. The substitutability of capital for land is of particular importance to the discussion of industrial location.

A firm that spreads out in a sprawling one-story plant complex, for example, is using a lot of land relative to capital. A firm that builds a skyscraper uses a lot of capital relative to land. Near the center of a city, where land is very expensive, we would expect firms to substitute capital for land; and, indeed, we see tall buildings near the center of cities and sprawling one-story plants near the periphery.

The possibility of substituting capital for land has implications for the kinds of firms that locate downtown and the kinds that locate out in the suburban ring. Firms whose employees work in offices find it relatively easy to operate efficiently in tall buildings. These include firms in such industries as business services, finance, insurance, and real estate. Manufacturing firms, which must move materials through many stages of production, find it impractical, and in many cases impossible, to produce in a multistory plant. (Imagine assembling a car in a 20-story building!) Because manufacturing firms find it very difficult to substitute capital for land, manufacturing plants tend to locate farther and farther away from the city center on less expensive land. At the same time, corporate headquarters, law firms, accounting firms, insurance companies, and the like are more likely to locate in the center city on more expensive land.

This is not to say that there are no office-based firms on the periphery and no manufacturing firms in the central city. Many firms that occupy office buildings are in business to serve people and to serve other firms. Insurance companies, banks, brokerage houses, and the like find it important to locate in or near suburban residential areas, and major manufacturing firms located in the suburbs require the services of lawyers, accountants, consultants, and so on. As a consequence, many office buildings have sprung up in suburban rings around major cities. At the same time, many manufacturing plants are still located in or near central cities.

THE COMPLEXITY OF BUSINESS LOCATION DECISIONS   We have already said that the economics of location decisions are extremely complicated. Choosing the optimal level of output when input and output prices are known with certainty is hard enough. When you then allow all prices to vary from location to location, the decision becomes much more complex. Because of this complexity, it is difficult to generalize about, or to predict, industrial location patterns. It is even more difficult to design public policies that significantly change patterns of economic development to benefit a particular state or region. Such policies are expensive and they often fail.

THE LOCATION OF HOUSEHOLDS

Everyone needs a place to live. Furthermore, at least one person in almost every household is employed. This means that residential locations depend to a large extent on workplace locations. Because of the costs associated with getting from home to work and back, the natural tendency is for households to cluster around areas of high employment.

PROPERTY FEVER IN BEIJING

The Chinese city of Beijing is much more famous for its state-owned slums than it is for luxury housing. Now, thanks to new laws that allow the "use of land" (but not the land itself) to be sold, property fever has come to Beijing. The following excerpt describes the situation in detail.

Although China is officially Communist, the nation's leaders have allowed certain private industries to develop. Now that "land use" rights can be sold in China, the market for luxury housing has boomed. Pictured here is Beijing's Ritan Park with luxury high-rise apartment buildings in the background.

The deputy mayor of Beijing, Zhang Baifa, says he has received applications from every district in the capital to build luxury villas, and he is going to turn down all of them. The market in luxury housing, says Mr Zhang, has got "out of control". . . .

The people who run the capital have actually been slow in taking advantage of the concession. Shanghai and the provinces of Guangdong, Hainan and Fujian have all experienced property booms. Bai Mei, an eager young real-estate dealer in one of China's booming special economic zones, says she bought her first villa for $80,000 and made a profit of more than 100% when she sold it after 18 months. "I started doing this two years ago," she says, "and now that people have seen how much money I've made, everyone is doing it."

Flats which sold for $120,000 last August are now selling for more than $160,000. Miss Bai believes there is plenty of scope for prices to rise further. "Most buyers don't want to live in the properties they buy. They just want to sell again for a profit." Of the 230 properties sold at prices ranging from $200,000 to $700,000 on a

new estate near Beijing's airport, only 50 buyers have moved in, suggesting that many others plan to resell at a profit . . . .

The boom in luxury housing depends on foreign money. Although Chinese are now encouraged to buy their own housing, even those with capital can afford only tiny flats. On the day of Mr Zhang's ban on new villas, the official news agency reported that 30 Taiwanese would come to Beijing in March to do deals involving

everything from villas and office buildings to holiday villages.

At least office buildings will have Mr Zhang's approval. In Guangzhou, too, it was reported this month, there is to be less luxury housing and more business buildings. The astute Miss Bai says she is moving into office development.

Source: "Nice Property, Nice Price," *The Economist,* February 20, 1993.

Monocentric City Models

The earliest models constructed to analyze residential location were based on the assumption that all employment was located at the center of the city and that households bid against each other for the locations most accessible to the central city. Most models also assumed that land and capital were substitutable in the production of housing.

These models argued that those who end up living close to the center city bear lower transportation costs because their commute is shorter. This desirability of location is reflected in bids for land. But as people move away from the center, their transportation costs increase. Location therefore becomes less desirable and bids for housing fall. An equilibrium can exist only where the land prices just off-set the lower transport costs closer to the center. If, at current land prices, a household on the periphery could increase its welfare by moving closer to the center, it would bid the closer land away from its current occupant.

With higher land prices at the center, theory predicts that we will find substitution of capital for land. And, indeed, high-rise apartment buildings do appear most frequently in downtown areas, while garden apartments and single-family homes are usually found farther out. Despite the simplicity of the assumptions, these **monocentric,** or "single-center," **models** that assume central employment are a good way to gain an understanding of residential location.

But job location is not the only factor that affects residential location decisions. Housing is an enormously complicated "product." It has many different dimensions, and people have different preferences, which also shift over time. Some families have a taste for space; others feel lost in it. Some love urban living; others are afraid of crime. Some want to be near water; others prefer mountains. Many people never leave their home towns; others can't wait to get away. Some people have high incomes and others are poor. This heterogeneity of tastes and incomes is reflected in the diversity of the housing stock in the United States—from huge, single-family country estates to million-dollar downtown condominiums, from small urban apartments to rural shacks.

Discrimination in the Housing Market

Bidding for accessible locations tells only a small part of the residential location story. Census data reveal that African-Americans and white Americans still live, by and large, in separate neighborhoods, both in urban and rural parts of the country. The South has many rural blacks, and there is virtually complete segregation in its small towns. In the North, African-Americans tend to live in the cities. While more mixed neighborhoods exist today than existed 20 years ago, they are few and far between.

Many theories to explain why blacks and whites tend to live apart from each other have been offered. African-Americans earn lower average incomes than whites. Income differences, however, explain only a small fraction of actual segregation. The hypothesis that blacks live separately by choice and do not want to live in predominantly white neighborhoods is not supported by evidence. Ample evidence does support a third hypothesis, however—that African-Americans are denied equal access to the housing market through discrimination.

Racial discrimination in the housing market has been documented in many forms. Until recent years, many property deeds carried provisions that restricted an owner's ability to sell to blacks. These **racial covenants** were actually enforceable until the 1950s, when the courts found them to be unconstitutional. Even with such agreements declared illegal, however, owners and real estate agents in all-white neighborhoods often do everything possible to prevent selling or renting to blacks or to those who belong to ethnic groups that form the underclass of a given region.

During the 1950s and 1960s, many African-Americans moved from the rural South to the urban North. When they arrived, they found their access to the housing market limited. Certain neighborhoods were designated for black occupancy, and few were able to buy or rent elsewhere. As demand for housing increased in the designated black areas, prices rose. Dozens of studies during the 1960s and early 1970s documented the existence of **ghetto premiums.** African-Americans were paying more to live in the ghetto than whites of comparable means were paying to live in virtually identical housing in white neighborhoods.

monocentric models Models of residential location that assume central employment. As people move farther from the center, their costs of commuting increase. Equilibrium in the housing market exists only where land prices just offset the lower transport costs closer to the center.

racial covenants Provisions spelled out in property deeds that prohibit sale of that property to members of specific racial or ethnic groups.

ghetto premium Evidence suggests that during the 1960s and 1970s, housing in sections of U.S. cities inhabited predominantly by African-Americans was more expensive than comparable housing in white neighborhoods. The price difference came to be called a ghetto premium.

Although ghetto premiums seemed to disappear during the 1970s, they probably did so more because blacks stopped moving to the city in great waves than because discrimination had ended. A number of studies have shown that racial and ethnic discrimination in housing continues to be widespread today, despite decades of efforts to stop it. One study using matched pairs of "auditors," one black and one white, revealed that blacks seeking apartments are invited to inspect 36.3% fewer units than their white counterparts.[1]

The African-American population in the United States is an urban population. In 1993, more than 80% lived in metropolitan areas, and the vast majority of those lived in central cities. Table 20.1 presents data on eight U.S. cities from the 1990 census. In all of the cities except Los Angeles, the African-American population in the central city exceeded 25 percent. The African-American population located outside the central city in the suburbs was much smaller. Typical in 1990 was Chicago, where African-Americans represented just under 40% of the city's population but less than 9% of the suburban population.

Table 20.1 also presents similar data for the Hispanic population in eight U.S. cities. In all the cities except St. Louis and Atlanta, both of which have very few Hispanic residents, Hispanics are more heavily represented in central cities. The differences are not as sharp as they are for African-Americans, however.

The Filtering Process and Housing for the Poor

Most poor people today live in old housing once occupied by higher-income people, housing that has declined in quality and value over the years. Virtually all unsubsidized new housing in the United States is built for those at the upper- and middle-income levels. As rich people buy the new homes, their old homes become available to those in lower-income brackets.

As housing "filters" down the income-distribution ladder, it depreciates. The cheapest housing, the housing available to poor people, is often housing that is the oldest or that has depreciated the fastest from lack of upkeep. Housing subsidies and tax advantages offered to middle- and upper-income households and to new construction are often justified on the grounds that such programs speed up the **filtering** process. If the filtering chain works faster than the rate at which the older housing stock deteriorates, everyone will end up in better housing.

filtering The process whereby the newest and best housing goes to the wealthy, whose former housing passes down to those of middle income, whose former housing passes down to those of low income. Thus housing "filters" down the income-distribution ladder.

[1]See John Yinger, "Measuring Racial Discrimination with Fair Housing Audits: Caught in the Act," *American Economic Review* (December 1986).

TABLE 20.1
Distribution of African-American and Hispanic Populations in Cities and Metropolitan Areas, 1990

	% AFRICAN-AMERICAN		% HISPANIC	
	CENTRAL CITY	METRO AREA OUTSIDE CENTRAL CITY	CENTRAL CITY	METRO AREA OUTSIDE CENTRAL CITY
ATLANTA	67.1	19.4	1.9	2.0
BOSTON	25.6	2.5	10.8	3.6
CHICAGO	39.1	8.6	19.6	6.6
DALLAS	29.5	9.0	20.9	10.8
LOS ANGELES	14.0	6.8	39.9	30.7
NEW YORK CITY	28.7	11.1	24.4	9.3
PHILADELPHIA	39.9	10.9	5.6	3.1
ST. LOUIS	47.5	11.4	1.3	1.1

Source: U.S. Bureau of the Census, 1990.

AFFORDABLE HOUSING AND RENT CONTROL

Several U.S. cities have confronted the problem of affordable housing by passing *rent control laws,* which impose a price ceiling on the monthly rent that landlords can charge. Although these laws have been almost universally criticized by economists, they remain in force in many cities, including New York.

The basic argument against rent control is illustrated in Figure 1. The quantity of housing services is measured along the x-axis; monthly rent per unit is measured along the y-axis. Without rent control, the market is in equilibrium at a rent of R^*. At that price, Q^* units of housing services are supplied and the same number of units (Q^*) of housing services are demanded.

The imposition of a ceiling on rents (shown by $\overline{R}$ in Figure 1) causes excess demand as the quantity of housing services demanded increases (from Q^* to Q_D) and the quantity supplied decreases (from Q^* to Q_S). The lower rents, critics argue, reduce landlords' incentives to maintain their property and to invest in new units. And even if new units are not subject to rent control (as is the case in New York City), detractors claim, the mere existence of rent control deters would-be developers from building new units for fear of being subject to control later. Thus, far from increasing the supply of affordable housing, rent control actually *reduces* the stock of affordable housing. Furthermore, because the occupancy of rent-controlled units is not limited to the poor, rent control laws may end up providing a subsidy to upper-income households.

But there is another side to this story. Those who favor rent control argue that it simply brings about a transfer from landlords to tenants, and that such laws do not change the behavior of landlords very much. Because state and federal budgets for direct housing subsidies are limited, many see rent control as the only alternative to increased homelessness.

The following excerpt highlights some recent research into the economic effects of rent control:

With rents slipping and vacancies on the rise, a loose coalition of landlords and university housing experts is preparing a challenge to New York's 43-year-old system of rent regulations, which is facing renewal this spring. . . .

Studies and papers challenging the underlying justification for rent control have been prepared over the last few years, arguing that the rules, which control everything from rent increases to the frequency of paint jobs, benefit well-to-do renters most, let housing deteriorate, and cost the city taxes. . . .

Every three years, when the rent rules come up for renewal, landlords fight to have them repealed. But this time, they are hoping that their academic backers and the current housing slump will give new force to their argument.

To strengthen their case, landlords have gone armed with studies. Among them are the following:

- *A study by the Joint Center for Housing Studies at Harvard University found that the rent rules may benefit rich New Yorkers more than poor ones. In poor neighborhoods, some landlords are already charging less than they are legally entitled to, while in Manhattan's wealthiest neighborhoods, rent regulations save affluent tenants hundreds of dollars a month over what they would pay for similar apartments at market rates, the study found.*
- *A study by the chairman of the Hunter College Planning and Urban Studies Department comparing New York rental housing with that of other*

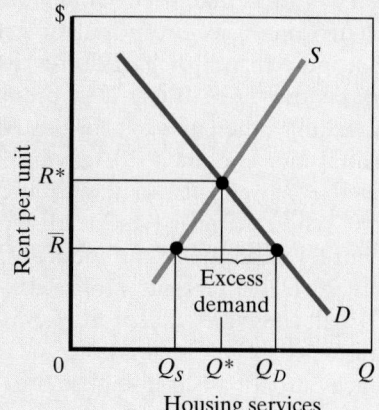

FIGURE 1
Rent Control Increases the Quantity of Housing Demanded While Reducing the Quantity Supplied

cities found that the rent rules reduced incentives to maintain housing so much that New York buildings had, on average, more broken boilers, outmoded wiring, cracked walls and other problems than other cities' buildings did.

- *A study by the accounting firm of Peat, Marwick concluded that the city would collect $370 million more a year in real estate taxes by dropping protections for tenants earning over $40,000 a year, since the taxable value of the buildings these renters live in would rise with higher rents.*

Rent controls are an emotional issue with a huge constituency, and for many politicians, the issue is simply taboo. Nearly three million people—about 40 percent of New York City's population and a huge voting block—live in the city's roughly one million rent-regulated apartments.

Source: Iver C. Peterson, "Wielding New Studies, Landlords Ask Albany to Undo Rent Laws," *New York Times,* February 16, 1991.

The central parts of cities are usually the oldest parts. Because the oldest housing falls to the poorest people, low-income housing has in many places become concentrated in the inner city.

For many years, rent control has been used in major U.S. cities as a way of providing affordable housing. Rent control remains a controversial issue; the Issues and Applications box titled "Affordable Housing and Rent Control" discusses the debate in more detail.

THE LAND MARKET, RENT, AND LOCATION

Before you can fully understand the location of economic activity, you need to understand the land market. Land is the ticket to location. In the absence of restrictions, you would expect to see locations going to the user who is willing to pay the most. A small commercial space in Harvard Square might end up occupied by a restaurant, a clothing store, a copy center, or some other kind of firm. Under ordinary circumstances, the firm that ends up in a space should be the one that is willing to pay the most for it.

Rent as a Function of Location

The amount that a firm is willing to pay for a location depends on how profitable the firm can be at that particular location. A restaurant at a popular, accessible downtown location will sell more meals than a comparable restaurant in a dangerous neighborhood. It will probably be able to charge higher prices, also. The owners of the restaurant would probably earn large profits at the popular location, but they would also have to pay a much higher rent if they did not own the land. Remember, there is no such thing as a free lunch. The land—that is, location—is the critical factor in the restaurant's success, and the owner of the land will not just give it away or rent it cheaply.

Suppose I own a lot near a new interchange that is being built on an interstate highway. The land had previously been farmed, but now I want to sell or rent it. What is it worth? It is worth exactly what some person or some firm is willing to pay for it. The best use of the land will probably turn out to be a gas station, a fast food restaurant, or a motel. What such an establishment is willing to pay depends on how much business it expects to get at that location. Cheap land doesn't do a retail or a service firm any good if it can't get customers to come there.

To see how the land market operates, let us consider a small vacant lot near a popular square in a major metropolitan area. Suppose that the lot has two potential uses: a suite of offices or four small apartments. Table 20.2 gives revenue and cost

TABLE 20.2

Hypothetical Revenue, Cost, and Profit Calculations for Competing Uses of a Building Lot

	OFFICES	FOUR STUDIO APARTMENTS
CAPITAL INVESTMENT REQUIRED	$100,000	$150,000
Expected annual revenues	50,000	28,000
Expected annual costs (excluding rent and capital cost)	– 30,000	– 8,000
Accounting profit (before rent and capital cost)	$20,000	$20,000
Normal return to capital (10% yield)*	– 10,000	– 15,000
Potential bid rent	$10,000	$5,000

* Note: This figure could also be thought of as the annual cost of borrowing at 10% to finance the capital investment required.

estimates for these two projects. First, each of the two projects will require a capital investment: A structure must be built. Constructing the office suite will cost a flat $100,000, while building a set of four small apartments will cost $150,000. Notice that these are *capital expenditures.* When a firm (the developer) invests $100,000 in a new piece of capital, it acquires an asset, but it does not incur a cost—at least not as an accountant or an economist would define a cost.[2] We assume that the building maintains its value as long as it is maintained. As long as the building maintains its value, the buyer has really not incurred a cost—he can always sell. The same is true for the apartments. In both cases, the cost of maintaining the structure's value is included in the expected annual costs.

If the offices generate a stream of $50,000 per year in revenues against costs of $30,000, cash profit before rent and capital costs will equal $20,000. The initial capital expenditure required for the offices is $100,000, and, let us assume, the normal rate of return is 10%—that is, to get an investor (developer) interested in making the $100,000 investment, she must get a return of at least 10%, or $10,000 per year, on her investment. (This is the cost of the use of the capital, or *capital cost.*) If our developer were to borrow the money from a bank at a cost of 10% or to use her own money at an opportunity cost of 10%, then that $10,000 per year of the $20,000 profit from the building would go back to the developer as a normal return on investment.

With capital cost subtracted from cash profits, the office building yields a flow of $10,000 per year. Thus, the office project developer could theoretically be pushed to pay up to $10,000 per year in rent to the landowner. At a rent of $10,000 per year, the developer would earn only a normal profit but no economic profits. At any rent higher than $10,000, she would not earn sufficient revenues to cover basic costs, including capital costs.

What about the apartment complex? The apartments would rent for $583 per month each, yielding a total of $28,000 per year in rental income. Maintenance and other costs are only $8000. The cash income before land rent and capital costs is thus $20,000, the same as for the offices. But the capital costs are higher. The initial capital expenditure required is $150,000; normal profits must be 10% of this amount, or $15,000 a year. This means that the potential apartment developer could not pay a rent of more than $5000. Thus, the apartment developer would lose interest and drop out of the bidding if rent at the location went over $5000.

The office building project would win the location because it would generate a greater net flow of profit from the location, and its developer would be willing to bid the most. The best use of the location, from the landowner's point of view, is to provide office space. This is also true from society's point of view, because using the land as office space would create more value. Any rational landlord would want to charge a rent closer to $10,000 per year. Thus, you can see that:

> Rents are determined by the amount that potential users of a location are willing to pay for that location. That amount, in turn, depends on the profits that are likely to be generated from locating at the site in question.

This insight also helps us to explain a seeming paradox. There are many locations at which profits seem to be high but at which the firms that occupy

---

[2]Throughout the discussion that follows, we assume that the landowner and the person who owns the business (and the capital stock of the business) are separate people. Many businesses own the land on which they are located, but this does not change the story.

them go out of business. Why should this be so? If the high profits are the result of a prime location, the rent on that location is also likely to be very high. The landowner is not likely to sell the benefits of what he or she owns at a cheap price. But what makes sense for the location owner may squeeze the occupying firm's profits. Thus,

> Even at prime locations, new investors (or firms) cannot expect to make much over a normal rate of profit because they need to buy the ticket to the location—they must rent the land.

Restraints on a Free Land Market: Zoning and Planning

So far we have been discussing the market for land as if it were a free, unregulated market. But land markets are rarely free. Generally they are regulated by locally appointed bodies that are responsible for what is sometimes called **land use planning.** Towns, understandably, will not let a steel mill locate next to a residential neighborhood. Building a house or locating a business next to, or near, other homes and businesses obviously has a number of external effects. These effects may be costs, or they may be benefits; either way, they can be insignificant or they can be huge. A new business could cause traffic congestion or generate sight, air, or noise pollution, particularly if it moves into an area that is already highly congested. A run-down abandoned mansion in a residential area could, on the other hand, be converted into a beautifully landscaped and well-maintained conference center.

Nearly all cities and towns are zoned. **Zoning** is the designation of certain areas for commercial activities, industrial activities, residences, and so on. Within the residential zone category, many cities and towns have specific subzones for multifamily housing and for single-family housing. Some towns have been accused of using zoning powers to restrict development to exclude all but the very wealthy. A town that sets a rule that only single-family houses can be built and that each must be built on a minimum of five acres of land, for example, is probably leaning in this direction. Local governments also issue building permits, and some towns have limited the number of building permits that may be issued in order to slow population growth. Such procedures have been challenged successfully in the courts.

Zoning can significantly affect the value of a location by changing its use. Suppose, for example, that the town board zoned the location we have been describing (see Table 20.2) for residential use only. The owner of the land would then be able to rent it only to the developer that wanted to build the apartments. Instead of earning a rent of $10,000 per year as an office location, the property could earn only $5000 per year at most, and the offices would be forced to look for a second-best place to locate.

Is it more efficient not to regulate the land market and to let locations go to the highest bidder? In the absence of regulations, the office building, which is willing to pay the most for the location, would get the location. The goal of the market is to channel resources to their best use, and the office building, in one sense, is the best use. There may, however, be negative externalities associated with building the offices. The use of the land in question for offices might lead to congestion, loss of privacy, an increase in crime, and so forth. If these external costs exceed $5000 per year, the apartments, not the offices, would be a more efficient use of the space.

land use planning A regulatory system, generally overseen by local zoning boards, that stipulates what kinds of industries, businesses, and housing may locate in an area, and under what conditions.

zoning The designation of certain areas for industry, commerce, and housing. Often these categories are broken down into subcategories that specify the number of families allowed within a single residential building, how much land a residence must have around it, and so on.

REGIONAL GROWTH AND CHANGE

As we noted earlier in this chapter, one of the primary concerns of the states and their governors is jobs. A major goal of most state-level policy makers is to attract industry and increase employment in the state. But states are part of regions, and regions are part of the country. No governor of an individual state could in any way influence, much less stop, the recessions of 1982 or 1991. National recessions do not respect geographical boundaries; although some states fared better than others, all states suffered during those downturns.

REGIONAL CHANGES   During the last 25 years, the various regions of the United States have experienced major economic changes. The most dramatic changes have been in the Southwest and in New England. The economies of the southwestern states, particularly Texas, have traditionally been heavily dependent on oil and gas production. When oil prices are high, production increases, and the oil-producing states prosper. This was the case in the late 1970s, when oil prices were very high. The prosperity of the period led to a building boom that provided jobs for thousands of construction workers in the Southwest.

But the economy of the Southwest was not immune to changes in the world. The 1980s saw a steady decline in world oil prices as world production increased and demand declined. The price of crude oil dropped from a high of $40 per barrel in 1980 to $10 per barrel in 1988. The impact on Texas and on the rest of the Southwest was devastating. Employment and earnings dropped sharply. Oil and gas exploration ground to a halt because the costs of producing oil exceeded potential revenues. The decrease in incomes, profits, and employment in the region meant a sharp drop in the demand for office space and housing just as millions of square feet of new office space and thousands of new houses were coming on the market. The result was a glutted market, and rents and home values dropped sharply. Falling real estate values and a declining economy led to hundreds of bank failures, and the area sank deeper and deeper into a regional recession.

At the same time that the Southwest was declining, the Northeast was booming. In 1975 New England had the highest unemployment of any region in the country. But as traditional industries (such as textiles, leather, and furniture) went out of business or moved out of the region (often to locations in the South or in Asia), a group of new industries began to prosper. A number of firms producing high-technology products experienced enormous growth. In Massachusetts, the Digital Equipment Corporation and Wang Laboratories, both very small companies in the early 1970s, employed a total of over 100,000 people by the mid-1980s. As employment and incomes grew, real estate prices exploded, new housing was built at a record pace, and office buildings went up everywhere. By 1987 states in the region had the lowest unemployment rates in the country.

The fates of the Southwest and the Northeast reversed again in the 1990s. By late 1990, New England looked a lot like the Texas of five years earlier. The regional boom ran out of gas as high home prices, a labor shortage, and rising wages caused business to curtail their operations or look elsewhere for expansion. At the same time, the building boom glutted the housing and office markets, and the result was very similar to what had happened earlier in the Southwest. Construction workers hired during the boom lost their jobs, and banks whose lending fueled the boom ran into serious problems as loans went bad. By 1991 the region once again had the highest unemployment rate in the country.

Never has a region gone from boom to bust faster than California in the 1990s. In 1988 and 1989, California was in the midst of a boom similar to that experienced in the Northeast two years earlier. In mid-1988, home prices were rising at rates approaching 50% per year. The unemployment rate in the state was 5.1%, one of the lowest in the United States. But by 1989, the situation began to change, and California slid into a deep recession. In March 1993, California's unemployment rate hit 9.4%, the highest in the United States. The reasons for the California bust were similar to the reasons for the bust in the Northeast a few years earlier: the high cost of doing business and high living costs, overbuilding during the boom, and troubles in high-technology manufacturing and defense-related industries (New England and California have high concentrations of both).

All this was happening while the economies of the Southwest were making a comeback. The dark days of the mid-1980s left the Southwest with cheap real estate and low wages, which worked together to spur a major economic recovery. By the end of 1991, the economy of the Southwest was back on a healthy growth path.

By and large, these changes were the result of natural economic events that occurred at different times in different regions of the country. Most had nothing to do with government economic policies. The rise of high-technology industries, fluctuation in energy prices, the increase in home prices, and the like were the result of perfectly normal market adjustment processes that were not caused by government, and governments probably could not have stopped them from happening.

THE ECONOMICS OF URBAN DECLINE AND RECOVERY

Many large U.S. cities endured a host of troubles during the 1960s and 1970s. Firms began moving to the suburbs, creating unemployment in the central cities. Buildings were abandoned. Crime rates rose. City governments found themselves with a declining tax base at the same time that the demand for public services was increasing. Many cities faced serious fiscal crises; many lost their bond ratings and came close to defaulting on their debts.

The Sources of Urban Decline

Urban decline results directly from lack of investment. In one sense, we can see a city as a huge agglomeration of capital: factories, houses, office buildings, warehouses, government buildings, roads, water and sewer systems, bridges, and so forth. Some of this is private capital, and some of it is public capital. But all capital depreciates, and unless it is maintained, repaired, and periodically replaced, it deteriorates very quickly.

Abandoned housing is simply housing that has not been maintained. Roofs need to be replaced every ten years or so, walls must be painted, and plumbing systems and heating systems need to be repaired and replaced. When owners stop investing, deterioration accelerates, and soon the building is ready for the scrap dealer and the rats.

Run-down buildings often have a positive value. It is sometimes advantageous to walk away from a property, not when its value is zero but when its value has fallen lower than the obligations of its owners. Building owners, for example, must pay property taxes in addition to maintenance costs, and they usually hold heavy mortgages. If I owe $100,000 to a bank on a mortgage for an apartment building but have allowed the building to deteriorate to a point where it is worth only $40,000, I am better off defaulting on the mortgage and letting the bank take the building. If I have not paid my property taxes for 10 years, and the bill for back taxes plus penalties exceeds $40,000, I am better off if I let the building go than I would be if I paid the overdue taxes.

urban decline The deterioration of the private and social capital stock of a city that results from the lack of investment by both private and public sectors.

Social capital decays when governments do not continuously invest in maintaining it. In many cities, water systems, sewer systems, roads and bridges, and transit systems are in a very bad state of repair. The task of maintaining public capital is staggering. The New York subway system, which carries 1.1 billion passengers per year, consists of 231 miles of track, 461 stations, and 6,700 cars. The New York water system contains 6,150 miles of main water lines, 95% of which is made of old cast iron pipe of various ages, strengths, and sizes. Anyone who has driven in New York knows what the streets are like. One 1979 estimate put the costs of needed replacement and repair to New York's streets, water systems, and subways at nearly $12 billion.[3] That figure is undoubtedly much higher now.

Urban economists point to a number of factors that explain the lack of investment in social capital during the last quarter century. Since the end of World War II, firms have been gradually moving out of the central cities and into the suburban ring. Improvement in both transportation and communications technology has made the suburbs a more attractive location. Of course, people wanted to be close to their jobs, so they began to move out of the cities toward the new suburban business centers. As a result, suburban housing investment boomed, while inner-city housing began to decay. Then, during the 1950s and 1960s, poor rural African-Americans moved to northern cities in record numbers. Discrimination limited their housing choices, and they became concentrated in central cities. Because very little low-income family housing, subsidized or unsubsidized, is located in the suburbs of America, the urban poor have had little choice but to live in central cities.

All of this had a devastating effect on city budgets. First, the tax base declined because business firms were moving to the suburbs. Inner-city housing filtered down the depreciation ladder, property values decreased, and some properties fell off the tax rolls altogether. Second, the expenditures required to run city government increased. Old, poorly maintained buildings are more likely to catch fire, increasing the need for fire protection. Because crime rates are higher in poor areas than in high-income areas, more police and courts are needed. In addition, poor and homeless people need more social services.

With the squeeze on city budgets, it is not surprising that the social capital stock in many cities is inadequately maintained. Roads, water systems, and government buildings are all in various states of disrepair.

THE PROPERTY TAX PROBLEM   Property tax policies, together with local responsibility for public services, education, and a substantial portion of the social welfare system, have led to increasing segregation by income and have exacerbated the problem of urban decay.

Local government has always been responsible for elementary and secondary education and for the provision of most local public services, such as police and fire protection. Nationally, about three quarters of all local tax receipts come from the *property tax,* which is a proportional tax on the assessed value of all property. This can have important implications for the economic development of localities.

Consider two towns, A and B. A is the older town with a depreciating housing stock occupied by lower-income people. Because a significant proportion of A's population is poor, social welfare expenditures and the need for social services will be high in A. These needed services put added pressure on the tax system. If property *values* are lower in A, the tax *rates* required to support the higher level of service may be extraordinary.

---

[3]David Grossman, *The Future of New York City's Capital Plant* (Washington, D.C.: The Urban Institute, 1979).

The arithmetic is simple. Suppose the average house in A is valued at $30,000 and the average house in B is valued at $120,000. Suppose also that citizens of both towns have an average of one school-age child per household. A property tax rate of 2% in town A would yield enough to finance $600 per student per year, while the same rate in town B would yield $2400 per student per year. In many U.S. cities, suburban school districts boast much lower tax rates *and* higher expenditures for education.[4]

Together, the higher tax rate and lower quality of education and public services in cities put added pressure on those who can afford it to move to the suburbs. The increased income segregation that results then further exacerbates the problem of decline. In the extreme, if all the poor lived together and all the rich lived together, no redistribution of income could take place through local governments, and public services would be produced only in proportion to income.

Urban Renewal and Recent Public Policy

The first major federal program designed to deal with the problem of urban decay was the **urban renewal** program enacted in 1949. By the mid-1960s, billions of dollars had been spent in hundreds of cities to clear slums and bring investment back into the city. The federal government provided the money, and local governments evicted the people, cleared the land, and sold it to private developers—usually at a price that amounted to about 30% of the cost of clearing.

urban renewal Government programs designed to confront and correct the problems of urban decay.

By the mid-1960s, it had become clear that the urban renewal program was not the answer to the nation's urban woes. It was true that many projects increased the local tax base, but serious costs went uncounted. Wherever they were undertaken, renewal projects reduced the supply of low- and moderate-income housing and drove up house prices and rents. Many poor and middle-income families were uprooted and displaced, and a great deal of useful capital was destroyed. Renewal projects often cleared stable lower-middle-income neighborhoods because developers did not want to build in the worst parts of town. Some urban "blight" was cleared, but it simply moved to other locations.

During the 1970s, the urban renewal program was all but abandoned. It had treated the symptoms and not the disease, and it had had severe side effects. To replace it, policy makers began to search for other programs to slow or reverse urban decline without destroying valuable capital or displacing people.

One way to help the situation, it was argued, would be to relieve some of the pressure on local governments by shifting responsibility for financing some local public services to higher levels of government or simply by sharing federal and state revenues with localities. Between 1960 and 1980 the percentage of local expenditures financed with local sources of revenue declined steadily from just under 70% to 55.9 percent. Since 1980, however, this trend has been reversed as progressive, significant cuts in federal aid to states and localities have been made. In 1980, 9.1% of local spending was financed by the federal government and 35% was financed by states. In 1990, the federal government's share had dropped to 3.6% and the state's share had dropped to 33.6 percent.

In addition to reducing tax burdens and improving public services, literally hundreds of different urban development programs emerged from the dust of the urban renewal program: urban development grants, neighborhood housing services, low-interest loans to small business, and so forth. But although all of these

---

[4]The system of financing education using local property tax revenues has been challenged in the courts on numerous occasions. The best-known cases were *Serrano v. Priest* in the California Supreme Court in 1971 and the *San Antonio Independent School District v. Rodriguez,* which went to the U.S. Supreme Court in 1972. In 1987 the same issue was raised in New Jersey when Camden, a relatively poor, declining city, brought suit against the state, pointing to nearby Cherry Hill, where property tax rates were lower and school expenditures higher.

programs have had some impact, the fundamental economic forces that bring about decay in our central cities have not changed. There are many poor people in the United States, and they have become increasingly concentrated in the cities. People with low incomes cannot pay high rents, and they generate a disproportionate demand for local public services.

During the mid-1980s, a number of cities that were in serious trouble in the 1970s experienced a resurgence of investment. Warehouses, fishing piers, factories, and other eighteenth- and nineteenth-century structures have been rehabilitated and converted into popular downtown shopping areas, sometimes with spectacular results. The Cannery in San Francisco, Seattle's Waterfront, Boston's Faneuil Hall Market Place, and many other restorations have been tremendously successful. Many cities have experienced a boom in the construction of hotels and office buildings.

Whether or not these trends signal the revitalization of the city remains to be seen. Although many of the jobs in the new high-rise office buildings are white-collar jobs in finance, insurance, real estate, and service firms, the people who hold those jobs are often not residents of the city but of the suburbs. In addition, many new young professionals are moving back into the city, and the urban housing market is feeling pressure from added demand.

BEYOND THIS CHAPTER

This chapter has introduced you to another decision that must be made by every firm and every household: where to locate. It has also introduced you to another field of applied microeconomics: *urban economics,* or the economics of the city. The location decisions of millions of economic agents have given us the physical environment in which we live. Cities first arose because of economic forces and have become what they are today because of economic forces.

The urban decline of recent years is the result of disinvestment, both public and private. The increasing concentration of poor people in central cities has led to private disinvestment in central-city housing. Improved transport technology and high land prices have caused the decentralization of jobs. Eroding tax bases and increased demand for services have put enormous pressure on local government finances. The result has been a low level of maintenance of city roads, water systems, public transit systems, and so forth.

If cities as we have known them are to make a comeback, both the public and private sectors will have to invest in them, and it is unclear whether this will happen. If cities are to change in some important ways—if they are to become largely nonresidential, for example—the same analysis holds, of course. For these reasons, the further study of urban economics may be one of the most exciting enterprises you can undertake.

SUMMARY

The Location of Business Firms

1. The world has been shaped by the location decisions of millions of households and firms. For households, location decisions depend on preferences, incomes, and relative prices. For firms, location decisions depend on potential revenues, costs, and profits.

2. Firm location decisions are complex because costs and revenues are likely to be different at every potential location.

3. Public officials have sought for decades to influence the locational choices that firms make. There is mixed evidence on the effectiveness of such efforts.

4. Because of the costs associated with traveling between home and work, the natural tendency is for households to cluster around areas of high employment. If employment is concentrated at the center of a city, land values and population density should decline with distance from the center.

The Location of Households

5. Black and white Americans still live, by and large, in separate neighborhoods, in part because discrimination has denied African-Americans equal access to the housing market.

6. Most poor people today live in old housing once occupied by higher-income people, housing that has declined in quality and value over the years. Virtually all unsubsidized new housing in the United States is built for those at the upper- and middle-income levels. As rich people buy the new homes, their old homes become available to those in lower-income brackets.

The Land Market, Rent, and Location

7. The location of economic activity is determined by the functioning of land markets. The activity that ends up occupying a given space is the one that is willing to pay the most for it. The amount that a firm is willing to pay for a location depends on how profitable it is likely to be at that location.

8. Land use is generally regulated by locally appointed bodies that are responsible for what is sometimes called *land use planning*. Some towns have been accused of using zoning powers to restrict development to exclude all but the very wealthy. *Zoning* can also affect the value of a location by changing its allowed uses.

Regional Growth and Change

9. During the last 25 years, the various regions of the United States have experienced major economic changes. Currently, the Southwest is experiencing an upturn and the Northeast is experiencing a downturn. Population and employment have been shifting to the South and West for many decades.

The Economics of Urban Decline and Recovery

10. Many large cities in the United States experienced decline and decay during the 1960s and 1970s. *Urban decline* results directly from lack of investment, both public and private. Housing stocks have deteriorated, businesses have moved to the suburbs, and social capital—roads, bridges, and transit systems—have fallen into disrepair.

11. Property tax policies, together with local responsibility for public services, education, and a substantial portion of the social welfare system, have led to increasing segregation by income and have exacerbated the problem of urban decay.

12. Early *urban renewal* efforts were not successful, but more recent public policies to stimulate investment in cities have been more effective. However, the fundamental forces that lead to decay in many central cities have not changed.

REVIEW TERMS AND CONCEPTS

filtering 513
ghetto premiums 512
land use planning 517

monocentric model 512
racial covenants 512
urban decline 519

urban renewal 521
zoning 517

PROBLEM SET

1. Recently retired from academic life, Emily is considering opening a gas station. Her research suggests the following:

	LOCATION A	LOCATION B
Expected annual sales	1 million gallons	2 million gallons
Price of lot	$250,000	$1,000,000

Gasoline sells for $1.10 per gallon at all locations (there is only one grade of gasoline).

Gasoline can be purchased from wholesalers for $1 per gallon. It would cost $300,000 to build a gasoline station, regardless of location.

Annual costs of running a station are $50,000, regardless of how much gasoline is sold—this includes maintenance and full upkeep on the building.

The interest rate is 10 percent.

Emily is considering locations A and B. Each is a one-acre lot. Would you advise Emily to go into business? If so, where should she locate?

2. The largest single federal housing subsidy is the provision of the individual income tax that allows homeowners to deduct property taxes and mortgage interest payments from their income for tax purposes. Describe in detail how a subsidy that accrues almost exclusively to middle- and upper-income families might raise the quality of housing occupied by lower-income families. (*Hint:* Recall the filtering process.) What specific assumptions would one have to make in order to predict such a result?

3. H. Ross Perot, in his unsuccessful run for the presidency, proposed a 50-cent-per-gallon gasoline tax. If gasoline prices remained high for a long time, in what ways might you expect a stiff gasoline tax to affect the spatial arrangement of households and firms?

4. Land prices and housing prices in China were booming during 1993. What lessons might real estate buyers and investors in China learn from the experiences of the United States (Texas, the Northeast, and California) and from Japan?

5. Some cities in the United States have experienced renewed development in their central business districts.

High-rise office buildings were built at a record pace in the early 1980s in some older U.S. cities that had earlier experienced decline. That growth has been denounced by some community leaders on the grounds that the benefits do not accrue to city residents, but rather to suburban residents. Make a list of all the benefits and costs you can think of that might result from a modern office tower in an older city. What groups benefit? What groups lose out? Be sure to include some discussion of the housing market.

6. How does the provision of public goods affect people's decisions about where to live? What effects do taxes have? Welfare benefits? (All of these vary from state to state and even from city to city.)

7. In the 1960s, a good deal of evidence revealed that the urban housing market was in fact a "dual" market divided along racial lines. That is, there were completely separate supply and demand forces at work in black and white "submarkets." Blacks could buy housing only in certain areas, and the supply of housing in these areas was relatively fixed. The empirical evidence also indicated that the price of housing in the black submarket was higher than in the white submarket—that is, that houses in the black areas were selling for more than identical houses in white areas. Urban economists attributed this differential to "demand pressure" because demand trends showed that blacks had been moving from the rural South to the urban North in large numbers.

A recent economic study of discrimination in the rural South found the same sort of "dual" housing market. Rural black populations have been declining, both relatively and absolutely, and the researchers had anticipated finding a price differential favoring blacks. In other words, they expected to find blacks paying a lower price for housing. Instead, despite the decline in black population, the price of housing in black neighborhoods was in fact higher than the price of identical housing in white neighborhoods.

Give at least two possible explanations for this seeming paradox. Use simple supply and demand graphs in your explanation.

8. What externalities, both positive and negative, are most frequently encountered by city dwellers? By suburb dwellers?

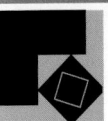

REBUILDING AMERICA'S CITIES WITH ENTERPRISE ZONES

■ The Los Angeles riots of 1992 sparked a national debate over what role the federal government should play in tackling the problems facing America's cities. Although there are many views regarding the causes of poverty and unemployment in the inner cities, the use of *enterprise zones* as a tool to help solve these problems has received wide support.

The term "enterprise zone" was first used in 1978 to describe a project to redevelop part of London, England. Shortly afterward, the concept crossed the Atlantic, and by 1993, 38 states had created enterprise zones of their own. Although some have been created in rural areas, enterprise zones are usually designed to promote urban renewal, particularly in inner cities that were left behind as cities moved from manufacturing to services. Typical incentives offered to attract businesses to the zones include reductions in local property tax and utility rates, tax credits for each employee, and exemption from sales taxes on items sold in the zone or those items used in the construction of the business. Critics argue that access to credit may be more important than future tax breaks and that the jobs created in an enterprise zone are often filled by individuals who live outside the zone. Nonetheless, enterprise zones have created jobs (see Table 1).

Although members of Congress and the Reagan and Bush administrations had discussed the idea of federal enterprise zones for a decade, no bill passed Congress until 1992. Republicans envisioned the zones as a means of empowering the poor by encouraging firms to locate or expand in the targeted areas, thus creating stable jobs and wealth. Democrats viewed the zones as one part of a larger plan that would include increased spending on education, job training, and community health centers, among other social programs. Nonetheless, President Bush vetoed the bill, which would have created 50 zones.

In May 1993, President Clinton proposed a $4.1 billion Economic

TABLE 1
Jobs Created by Enterprise Zones, 1981-1991

	YEAR ENACTED	NUMBER OF EZ AREAS	JOBS* CREATED	INVESTMENT* ($ BILLIONS)
Illinois	1982	82	54,422	$4.0
New York	1983	10	34,705	$2.9
Ohio	1982	193	34,000	$12.0
Louisiana	1981	750	25,361	$2.2
Kentucky	1982	10	18,154	$1.7

* Cumulative from the year the zone was enacted to June 1991.
Source: Housing and Urban Development, Office of Economic Development, Division of Community Development, State Enterprise Zone Update, Washington D.C., 1991.

Empowerment Act that would select 110 zones (71 urban, 33 rural, and 6 on Indian reservations) to qualify for business tax incentives (primarily wage credits) and federal money. Because federal taxes are a larger part of operating expenses than either local or state taxes, federal involvement could have a potentially larger impact than earlier state and city initiatives. Whatever the outcome, renewed attention to urban policy at the federal level has been welcomed by those who fear that the deterioration of the cities will lead to reduced U.S. competitiveness in the long run.

QUESTIONS FOR ANALYTICAL THINKING

1. An IKEA (furniture) store located in a New Jersey enterprise zone took out ads in New York newspapers calling attention to the 3% sales tax that customers of the store will pay. (The usual New Jersey state tax is 6 percent.) Does this mean that growth is a "zero-sum" game? Are tax and regulatory relief in enterprise zones more likely to create jobs that would otherwise not exist or to influence only the location of those jobs? If the former, why not implement this type of relief on a national level?

2. Many cities are already having trouble balancing their budgets, and some suffer from falling revenues. Why, then, would they offer tax relief to businesses locating in the city? Consider both the expenditure and revenue/tax expenditure points of view.

3. What sort of requirements might a city choose to enact on wage credits if it wants to have the greatest impact on unemployment in the inner city? Also consider the type of firm (employment) the city should attempt to attract and the type of tax credits (capital gains, wage, sales, and so forth) or regulatory relief that it might seek to offer in each case.

4. The Trenton, New Jersey, enterprise zone encouraged some inner-city development through tax incentives and credits (although it failed to lower the city's unemployment rate). Nevertheless, the zone is still slightly more expensive than suburban areas as a business location. Why might this be? What other policies might localities follow to attract firms through lower costs?

MACROECONOMICS

PART FIVE

Concepts and Problems in Macroeconomics

As we noted in Part One, microeconomics concentrates on individual units—the household, the firm, the industry. It sees and examines the "trees." Macroeconomics looks at the whole, the aggregate— total household income, total employment, total output. It sees and analyzes the "forest."

This part is designed to acquaint you with the macroeconomy as a whole. In it, you'll encounter some of the concepts that are most important to macroeconomists. You'll learn about the relationship of the U.S. economy to the economies of the rest of the world. You'll learn how economists measure gross domestic product (GDP), which is an important indicator of a country's economic health. You'll also learn some economic history and see how the United States has been affected by the major macroeconomic events of the last two decades.

In addition, you'll explore topics like the following:

■ The Great Depression and the birth of macroeconomics as a discipline (Chapter 21).

■ Foreign investment in the United States and U.S. investment abroad (Chapter 22).

■ What the Consumer Price Index is and how it is calculated (Chapter 23).

21 Introduction to Macroeconomics

microeconomics The branch of economics that deals with the functioning of individual industries and the behavior of individual decision-making units—business firms and households.

macroeconomics The branch of economics that deals with the economy as a whole. Macroeconomics focuses on the determinants of total national income, deals with aggregates such as aggregate consumption and investment, and looks at the overall level of prices rather than individual prices.

We now begin our study of macroeconomics. We touched on the differences between microeconomics and macroeconomics in Chapter 1. **Microeconomics** is the branch of economics that examines the functioning of individual industries and the behavior of *individual decision-making units,* typically business firms and households. With a few simple assumptions about how these units behave (firms maximize profits, households maximize satisfaction, or utility), we can derive useful conclusions about how markets work, how resources are allocated, and so forth.

Macroeconomics takes a different perspective. Instead of focusing on the factors that influence the production of particular products and the behavior of individual industries, macroeconomics focuses on the determinants of *total national output.* Macroeconomics studies not household income but *national* income, not individual prices but the *overall* price level. It does not analyze the demand for labor in the automobile industry but rather total employment in the economy.

Both microeconomics and macroeconomics are concerned with the decisions of households and firms. Microeconomics deals with *individual decisions,* while macroeconomics deals with the *sum of these individual decisions.* The word "aggregate" is used in macroeconomics to refer to sums. When we speak of

aggregate behavior, we mean the behavior of all households and firms taken together. We also speak of aggregate consumption and aggregate investment, which refer to total consumption and total investment in the economy.

Since microeconomists and macroeconomists look at the economy from different perspectives, you may expect that they will reach somewhat different conclusions about the way the economy behaves. This is true to some extent. Microeconomists generally conclude that markets work well. They see prices as flexible, adjusting to maintain equality between quantity supplied and quantity demanded. Macroeconomists, however, observe that important prices in the economy—for example, the wage rate (or price of labor)—often seem "sticky." **Sticky prices** are prices that do not always adjust rapidly to maintain equality between quantity supplied and quantity demanded. Microeconomists do not expect to see the quantity of apples supplied exceeding the quantity of apples demanded, because the price of apples is not sticky. But macroeconomists—who analyze aggregate behavior—examine periods of high national unemployment, where the quantity of labor supplied appears to exceed the quantity of labor demanded. At such times, it appears that wage rates do not adjust fast enough to equate the quantity of labor supplied and the quantity of labor demanded.

Until fairly recently, macroeconomists tended to be relatively uninterested in reconciling their analyses with the postulates and conclusions of microeconomic theory. The new trend among macroeconomists, however, is to try to make macroeconomic analysis consistent with microeconomic postulates—that is, with the idea that firms and households make their decisions along the lines suggested by microeconomic theory. If prices do not appear to adjust to equate the quantity supplied and the quantity demanded, for example, macroeconomists now look for solid microeconomic reasons why this is the case.

The task of reconciling macroeconomics and microeconomics is an extremely difficult one. Much less agreement about the way things work is apparent in macroeconomics than in microeconomics. In recent years, however, this chaos has partly (but only partly) subsided, largely as a result of the increasing use of microeconomic principles to help explain macroeconomic events. One of the aims of this book is to explain the **microeconomic foundations of macroeconomics.**

aggregate behavior The behavior of all households and firms taken together.

sticky prices Prices that do not always adjust rapidly to maintain equality between quantity supplied and quantity demanded.

microeconomic foundations of macroeconomics The underlying microeconomic principles behind macroeconomic analysis.

THE ROOTS OF MACROECONOMICS

The Great Depression

Economic events of the 1930s, the decade of the **Great Depression,** spurred a great deal of thinking about macroeconomic issues. The 1920s had been generally prosperous years for the U.S. economy. Virtually everyone who wanted a job could get one, incomes rose substantially, and prices were stable. Beginning in late 1929, however, things took a sudden turn for the worse. In 1929, 1.5 million people were unemployed. By 1933, that number had increased to 13 million out of a labor force of 51 million. In 1929, the United States produced $103 billion worth of new goods and services; by 1933, production had fallen to $55 billion, a drop of nearly 50 percent. In October of 1929, when stock prices collapsed on Wall Street, billions of dollars of personal wealth were lost. Unemployment remained above 14% of the labor force until 1940.

The 1930s saw enormous suffering across the United States and around the world as the depression spread to Europe and beyond. In the United States, the number of suicides increased nearly 30%, and millions of families were pushed into poverty.

Great Depression The period of severe economic contraction and high unemployment that began in 1929 and continued throughout the 1930s.

CLASSICAL MODELS   Before the Great Depression, economists generally applied microeconomic models, sometimes referred to as "classical models," to economy-wide problems. (In fact, the word "macroeconomics" was not even invented until after World War II.) For example, classical supply and demand analysis assumed that an excess supply of labor would drive down wages to a new equilibrium level; as a result, unemployment would not persist.

In other words, classical economists believed that recessions (downturns in the economy) were self-correcting. As output falls and the demand for labor shifts to the left, the argument went, the wage rate will decline, thereby raising the quantity demanded for labor by firms who would want to hire more workers at the new lower wage rate. (Graph this movement along the demand curve yourself.)

In fact, however, during the Great Depression unemployment levels remained very high for nearly ten years. In large measure, the failure of simple classical models[1] to explain the prolonged existence of high unemployment provided the impetus for the development of macroeconomics. Thus, it is not surprising that the application of what we now call macroeconomics was born in the 1930s.

THE KEYNESIAN REVOLUTION   One of the most important works in the history of economics, *The General Theory of Employment, Interest and Money,* by John Maynard Keynes, was published in 1936. Building on what was already understood about markets and their behavior, Keynes set out to construct a theory that would explain the confusing economic events of his time.

Much of macroeconomics has deep roots in Keynes's work. According to Keynes, it is not prices and wages that determine the level of employment, as classical models had suggested, but rather the level of aggregate demand for goods and services. Keynes also believed that governments could intervene in the economy and affect the level of output and employment. The government's role during periods when private demand is low, Keynes argued, is to stimulate aggregate demand and, by so doing, to lift the economy out of recession. (For more on Keynes see the Issues and Applications box entitled "The Great Depression and John Maynard Keynes.")

Recent Macroeconomic History

After World War II, and especially in the 1950s, Keynes's views began to gain increasing influence over both professional economists and government policy makers. Governments came to believe that they could intervene in their economies to attain specific employment and output goals, and they began to use their powers to tax and spend, as well as their ability to affect interest rates and the money supply, for the explicit purpose of controlling the ups and downs of the business cycle. This view of government policy became firmly established in the United States with the passage of the Employment Act of 1946. This act established the President's Council of Economic Advisors, a group of economists who advise the President on macroeconomic and other economic issues. It also committed the federal government to intervening in the economy to prevent large declines in output and employment.

FINE TUNING IN THE 1960S   The notion that the government could, and should, act to stabilize the macroeconomy reached the height of its popularity in the 1960s. During these years, Walter Heller, the chairman of the Council of Economic Advisors under both President Kennedy and President Johnson, coined the phrase **fine tuning** to refer to government's role in regulating inflation and unemployment.

fine tuning The phrase coined by Walter Heller to refer to the government's role in regulating inflation and unemployment.

---

[1]Classical models are also sometimes known as "market clearing" models because they emphasize that prices and wages adjust to insure that markets always clear—that is, that the quantity supplied is equal to the quantity demanded.

THE GREAT DEPRESSION AND JOHN MAYNARD KEYNES

Much of the framework of modern macroeconomics comes from the works of John Maynard Keynes, whose *General Theory of Employment, Interest and Money* was published in 1936. The following excerpt by Robert L. Heilbroner provides some insights into Keynes's life and work.

By 1933 the nation was virtually prostrate .... On street corners, in homes, in Hoovervilles, 14 million unemployed sat, haunting the land ....

It was the unemployment that was hardest to bear. The jobless millions were like an embolism in the nation's vital circulation; and while their indisputable existence argued more forcibly than any text that something was wrong with the system, the economists wrung their hands and racked their brains ... but could offer neither diagnosis nor remedy. Unemployment—this kind of unemployment—was simply not listed among the possible ills of the system: it was absurd, impossible, unreasonable, and paradoxical. But it was there.

It would seem logical that the man who would seek to solve this impossible paradox of not enough production existing side by side with men fruitlessly seeking work would be a Left-winger, an economist with strong sympathies for the proletariat, an angry man. Nothing could be further from the fact. The man who tackled it was almost a dilettante with nothing like a chip on his shoulder. The simple truth was that his talents inclined in every direction. He had, for example, written a most recondite book on mathematical probability, a book that Bertrand Russell had declared "impossible to praise too highly"; then he had gone on to match his skill in abstruse logic with a flair for making money—he accumulated a fortune of £500,000 by way of the most treacherous of all roads to riches: dealing in international currencies and commodities. More impressive yet, he had written his mathematics treatise on the side, as it were, while engaged in

Source: Robert L. Heilbroner, *The Worldly Philosophers* (New York: Simon & Schuster, 1961). Reprinted by permission.

As people lost their homes or were evicted from their apartments during the Great Depression, communities of makeshift shacks sprang up across the United States. The "Hooverville" pictured here was photographed in Seattle in July, 1934.

Government service, and he piled up his private wealth by applying himself for only half an hour a day while still abed.

But this is only a sample of his many-sidedness. He was an economist, of course— a Cambridge don with all the dignity and erudition that go with such an appointment .... He managed to be simultaneously the darling of the Bloomsbury set, the cluster of Britain's most avant-garde intellectual brilliants, and also the chairman of a life insurance company, a niche in life rarely noted for its intellectual abandon. He was a pillar of stability in delicate matters of international diplomacy, but his official correctness did not prevent him from acquiring a knowledge of other European politicians that included their ... neuroses and financial prejudices .... He ran a theater, and he came to be a Director of the Bank of England. He knew Roosevelt and Churchill and also Bernard Shaw and Pablo Picasso ....

His name was John Maynard Keynes, an old British name (pronounced to rhyme with "rains") that could be traced back to one William de Cahagnes and 1066. Keynes was a traditionalist; he liked to think that greatness ran in families, and it is true that his own father was John Neville Keynes, an illustrious enough economist in his own right. But it took more than the ordinary gifts of heritage to account for the son; it was as if the talents that would have sufficed half a dozen men were by happy accident crowded into one person.

By a coincidence he was born in 1883, in the very year that Karl Marx passed away. But the two economists who thus touched each other in time, although each was to exert the profoundest influence on the philosophy of the capitalist system, could hardly have differed from one another more. Marx was bitter, at bay, heavy and disappointed; as we know, he was the draftsman of Capitalism Doomed. Keynes loved life and sailed through it buoyant, at ease, and consummately successful to become the architect of Capitalism Viable.

During the 1960s, many economists believed that the government could use the tools available to it to manipulate unemployment and inflation levels fairly precisely.

Since 1970, the U.S. economy has been through a series of dramatic fluctuations in employment, output, and inflation. In 1974–1975 and again in 1980–1982, the United States experienced severe recessions. While not as catastrophic as the Great Depression of the 1930s, these recessions left millions without jobs and resulted in billions of dollars of lost output and income. In 1974–1975 and again in 1979–1981, the United States experienced very high rates of inflation. The U.S. economy also experienced a moderate recession in 1990–1991 and very slow growth for about two years after the recession. (We discuss these events in more detail in later chapters.)

Moreover, the 1970s witnessed the birth of a new phenomenon called **stagflation** (stagnation + inflation). Stagflation occurs when the overall price level rises rapidly (inflation) during periods of recession or high and persistent unemployment (stagnation). Until the 1970s, rapidly rising prices had been observed only in periods when the economy was prospering and unemployment was low (or at least declining). The problem of stagflation proved to be a vexing one, both for macroeconomic theorists and for policy makers concerned with the health of the economy.

It was clear by 1975 that the macroeconomy was considerably more difficult to control than either Heller's words or textbook theory had led economists to believe. The events of the 1970s and 1980s had an important influence on macroeconomic theory. Much of the faith in the simple Keynesian model and the "conventional wisdom" of the 1960s has been lost. New ways of understanding the behavior of the macroeconomy have been proposed, but as yet there is no consensus as to which explanation is best. It is precisely this flux in macroeconomics, the sense that the discipline is wide open and that many of the most important issues have yet to be resolved, that makes it so exciting to study.

stagflation Occurs when the overall price level rises rapidly (inflation) during periods of recession or high and persistent unemployment (stagnation).

MACROECONOMIC CONCERNS

Having established the aggregate focus of macroeconomics, we can now turn to some of the major questions and problems with which the discipline is concerned. Many of these questions do not have agreed-upon answers, and all the questions will require more exploration before we can hope to answer them. Our object here is to give you a sense of what the coming chapters are about.

There is no standard list of the crucial topics in macroeconomics, but we can easily identify four major concerns of the discipline (not necessarily in order of importance):

- First, macroeconomics is concerned with the *aggregate price level*. Increases in the overall price level (inflation) are, of course, of great concern to policy makers and citizens at large, as well as to economists.
- Second, macroeconomics is concerned with *aggregate output* (the quantity of goods and services being produced in the economy), particularly when the economy does not seem to be producing as much as it is capable of producing.
- The third concern, which is closely related to the second, is *total employment*. An economy may not be producing as much as it is capable of producing because it is not employing all the people who want jobs (unemployment).
- Fourth and finally, the *rest of the world* and its *relationship to the domestic economy* must be considered. The U.S. economy has a profound impact on the economies of the rest of the world, and developments in other countries have important effects on the United States as well.

Each of these issues is of great concern to the government, which would like to have low inflation, high output and employment, and a prosperous world economy. In fact, several of these goals were embodied in the Employment Act of 1946. How effective the government can be in achieving these goals is a matter of considerable debate, but the goals themselves are clear. (The effectiveness of government policies is the subject of later chapters.)

One troublesome fact should be kept in mind throughout all our discussions:

> Almost all macroeconomic events are interrelated, and making progress on one front often means making conditions worse on another front.

For example, some economists believe that the only way to cure inflation is to put the economy into a recession (thereby increasing unemployment and lowering output). Not all the good things we want may be compatible with each other, and thus macroeconomics is rife with trade-offs. One of the main aims of the following chapters is to explore and explain the nature of these trade-offs. But now let us return to the key concerns of macroeconomics for a more detailed examination.

Inflation

Inflation is an increase in the overall price level. The reduction of inflation has long been a goal of government policy. Especially problematic are **hyperinflations,** or periods of very rapid increases in the overall price level.

inflation An increase in the overall price level.

hyperinflation A period of very rapid increases in the overall price level.

Most Americans are unaware of what life is like under very high inflation. In some countries, however, people are accustomed to prices rising by the day, by the hour, or even by the minute. During the hyperinflation in Bolivia in 1984 and 1985, for example, the price of one egg rose from 3,000 pesos to 10,000 pesos in one week. In 1985, three bottles of aspirin sold for the same price as a luxury car had sold for in 1982. At the same time, the problem of handling money became quite burdensome. Banks stopped counting deposits—a $500 deposit was equivalent to about 32 million pesos, and it just did not make sense to count a huge mail sack full of bills. Bolivia's currency, printed in West Germany and England, was the country's third biggest import in 1984, surpassed only by wheat and mining equipment.

The almost unbelievable rise in prices in Bolivia is really only a small part of the story, however. When inflation approaches the stratospheric rates of 2000% per year, the economy, and indeed the whole organization, of a country begin to break down. Workers may go on strike to demand wage increases commensurate with the high inflation rate, firms find it almost impossible to secure credit, and the economy grinds to a halt. Fortunately, dramatic hyperinflations usually end very abruptly. In the course of only a few months, Bolivia went from having the highest inflation rate in the world to having one of the lowest inflation rates in the Western Hemisphere.

Luckily, hyperinflations are quite rare. Nonetheless, economists have devoted much effort to identifying the costs and consequences of even moderate inflation. Who gains from inflation, and who loses? What costs does inflation impose on society, and how severe are they? What causes inflation, and what is the best way of stopping it? We will focus on some of these questions in Chapters 23 and 29. It will be obvious throughout the following chapters that inflation is a major issue in macroeconomics.

Aggregate Output and the Business Cycle

business cycle The cycle of short-term ups and downs in the economy.

aggregate output The total quantity of goods and services produced in an economy in a given period.

recession A period during which aggregate output declines. Conventionally, a period in which aggregate output declines for two consecutive quarters.

depression A prolonged and deep recession.

Rather than moving along on a perfectly even keel at all times, economies tend to experience ups and downs in their performance. The technical name for these ups and downs is the **business cycle.** The main measure of how an economy is doing is **aggregate output,** the total quantity of goods and services produced in the economy in a given period. Clearly, when less is produced (in other words, when aggregate output decreases), there are fewer goods and services to go around, and the standard of living declines. When firms cut back on production, they also lay off workers, thus increasing the rate of unemployment.

Recessions are periods of time during which aggregate output declines. It has become conventional to classify an economic downturn as a "recession" when aggregate output declines for two consecutive quarters. A prolonged and deep recession is called a **depression,** although economists do not agree on when a recession becomes a depression. Since the beginning of the twentieth century, the U.S. economy has experienced one depression (during the 1930s), three severe recessions (1946, 1974–1975, and 1980–1982), and a number of less severe, shorter recessions (1954, 1958, 1970, and 1990–1991).

Devising explanations for and predicting the business cycle is one of the main concerns of macroeconomics. The key questions are: Why does the economy fluctuate so much, and why at times does it not seem to respond to the simple forces of supply and demand?

Unemployment

unemployment rate The percentage of the labor force that is unemployed.

You cannot listen to the news or read a newspaper without noticing that data on the unemployment rate are released each month. The **unemployment rate**—that is, the percentage of the labor force that is unemployed—is a key indicator of the health of the economy. Because the unemployment rate is usually closely related to the economy's aggregate output, announcements of each month's new figure are followed with great interest by economists, politicians, and policy makers.

Although macroeconomists are interested in learning why the unemployment rate has risen or fallen in a given period, they also try to answer a more basic question: Why is there any unemployment at all? Of course, we do not expect to see zero unemployment. At any given time, some firms may go bankrupt due to competition from rival firms, bad management, or just bad luck. Employees of such firms typically are not able to find new jobs as soon as they have lost their old ones, and while they are looking for work, they will be counted as unemployed. Also, workers entering the labor market for the first time may require a few weeks, or even months, to find a job.

If we base our analysis on supply and demand, as we have in all our discussions so far, we would expect conditions to change in response to the existence of unemployed workers. Specifically, when there is unemployment beyond some minimum amount, there is an excess supply of workers—at the going wage rates, there are people who want to work who cannot find work. In microeconomic theory, the response to excess supply is a decrease in the price of the commodity in question and therefore an increase in the quantity demanded, a reduction in the quantity supplied, and the restoration of equilibrium. With the quantity supplied equal to the quantity demanded, the market clears.

The existence of unemployment seems to imply that the aggregate labor market is not in equilibrium—that something prevents the quantity supplied and the quantity demanded from equating. But why do labor markets not clear when so many other markets do? Or is it that labor markets are clearing and the unemployment data are reflecting something different? The implications of the unemployment data are a major puzzle in macroeconomics and a major focus of Chapters 23 and 30.

Global Issues

Finally, economic conditions in the rest of the world have important effects on the U.S. economy. If the value of the dollar falls relative to the Japanese yen, are unemployment or inflation levels in the United States affected? What happens to the United States if Germany expands its money supply? How does an increase in oil prices affect the global economy?

Clearly, a complete analysis of the economy must take into account the effects of the events in the United States on the rest of the world and the effects of the events in the rest of the world on the United States. These issues are addressed throughout the chapters that follow; Chapter 37 provides a more detailed look at macroeconomics in an open economy.

THE ROLE OF GOVERNMENT IN THE MACROECONOMY

A major part of our discussion of macroeconomics concerns the potential role of government in influencing the economy. Here we mention briefly four kinds of policy that the government has used to influence the macroeconomy:

GOVERNMENT POLICIES FOR INFLUENCING THE MACROECONOMY:	1. fiscal policy 2. monetary policy 3. incomes policies 4. supply-side policies

FISCAL POLICY One of the major ways in which the federal government affects the economy is through its tax and expenditure decisions, or **fiscal policy.** The federal government collects taxes from households and firms and spends these funds on various items ranging from missiles to parks to social security payments to interstate highways. Both the magnitude and composition of these taxes and expenditures have a major effect on the economy.

fiscal policy Government policies regarding taxes and expenditures.

One of Keynes's main ideas in the 1930s was that fiscal policy could and should be used to stabilize the level of output and employment in the economy. More specifically, Keynes believed that the government should cut taxes and/or raise spending—so-called *expansionary fiscal policies*—to get the economy out of a slump. Conversely, he held that the government should raise taxes and/or cut spending—so called *contractionary fiscal policies*—to bring the economy out of an inflation.

MONETARY POLICY Taxes and spending are not the only variables that the government controls, however. Through the Federal Reserve, the nation's central bank,[2] the government can determine the quantity of money in the economy. The effects and proper role of **monetary policy** are among the most hotly debated subjects in macroeconomics. Most economists agree that the quantity of money

monetary policy The tools used by the Federal Reserve to control the money supply.

---

[2]The Federal Reserve is a quasi-independent agency, and it does not always do what the President or Congress wants it to do. Nevertheless, because it is part of the government rather than part of the private sector, we consider it in this section.

supplied affects the overall price level, interest rates and exchange rates, the unemployment rate, and the level of output. The main controversies arise regarding how monetary policy manifests itself and exactly how large its effects are.

INCOMES POLICIES   Although monetary and fiscal policies are the two major tools that the government uses to control the U.S. economy, other instruments are also available. **Incomes policies** are direct attempts by government to control prices and wages. They generally take the form of regulations specifying the maximum amount by which prices or wages are permitted to rise. Sometimes, voluntary guidelines are used instead of rigid controls—the government may simply plead with firms and labor unions to show restraint in their price- and wage-setting behavior. The efficacy of wage and price controls is a point of some controversy, although such controls are generally viewed with disfavor in the United States because they are believed to prevent the price system from functioning as an efficient allocator of resources.

incomes policies Direct attempts by the government to control prices and wages.

supply-side policies Government policies that focus on aggregate supply and increasing production rather than stimulating aggregate demand.

SUPPLY-SIDE POLICIES   More recently, some economists have advocated **supply-side policies** for managing the economy. Advocates of supply-side economics reject the Keynesian notion that the government should act to stimulate aggregate demand; they focus instead on aggregate supply and on increasing production. In practice, the main instrument of supply-side policy has been the tax system. (In this sense, supply-side policy is just a special case of fiscal policy.) Personal taxes were reduced in 1981 and again in 1986. The goal was to increase the labor supply by increasing the incentive to work and to increase the supply of capital by increasing the incentive to save. (We discuss the relationship between saving and capital investment in Chapter 24.) In addition, the 1981 tax cuts sharply reduced business taxes and provided extra tax incentives to stimulate investment. Proponents of these policies argued that stimulating the supply of labor and capital and increasing investment was the best way to increase the supply of goods and services.

The effects of these dramatic personal and business tax cuts are hotly debated among economists and politicians. One legacy of the massive tax cuts has been a federal budget deficit that is larger than it otherwise would have been. A *budget deficit* arises when the government spends more than it receives in current tax revenues. In such a case, the government covers its expenses by borrowing from the public, to whom it issues bonds payable in the future. Some supply-side advocates claimed that the tax cuts would not increase the deficit. The argument was that with lower taxes, people would work harder and save more. As a result, the economy would expand and the total amount of tax collected would rise, despite the cut in individual rates.[3] Unfortunately, this did not prove to be the case; the deficit rose substantially after the tax cuts.

The magnitude of recent government deficits has renewed interest in their effects. How, exactly, did these deficits arise? Are all deficits the same? What are their consequences, and do they pose a problem for the economy? What, if any, is the relationship between budget deficits, the exchange rate, and interest rates?

Large deficits also imply large increases in the government debt, and the size of the debt is of considerable concern to policy makers. What are the consequences of a large government debt? Should the government try to reduce it, and if so, how? We return to the pressing issue of the government debt in later chapters.

---

[3]For example, suppose the tax rate were initially 50% and the tax base were $100. Tax revenues would be $50 or .5 × $100. By cutting the rate to 25%, one would ordinarily expect revenues to decline to $25 (.25 × $100). If, however, the tax base rose to $200 (because lower tax rates provide incentive for everyone to work harder, thereby generating more income to be taxed), tax revenues would stay the same.

THE COMPONENTS OF THE MACROECONOMY

Macroeconomics focuses on four groups in the economy: *households* and *firms* (the private sector), the *government* (the public sector), and the *rest of the world* (the international sector). (We provided data on each of these sectors in Chapter 3.) These four groups interact in a variety of ways, many of which involve either the receipt or payment of income.

The Circular Flow Diagram

A useful way of seeing the economic interactions among the four groups in the economy is to examine a **circular flow** diagram, which shows the income received and payments made by each sector. A simple circular flow diagram is pictured in Figure 21.1.

Let's walk through the circular flow step by step. Households work for firms and the government, and they receive wages for their work. Hence our diagram shows a flow of wages *into* the household sector as payment for those services. Households also receive interest on corporate and government bonds and dividends from firms. Many households receive other payments from the government, such as social security benefits, veterans' benefits, and welfare payments. Economists call these kinds of payments from the government (for which the recipients do not supply goods, services, or labor) **transfer payments.** Together, these receipts make up the total income received by the households.

Households spend by buying goods and services from firms and by paying taxes to the government. These items make up the total amount paid out by the households. The difference between the total receipts and the total payments of the

circular flow A diagram showing the income received and payments made by each sector of the economy.

transfer payments Cash payments made by the government to people who do not supply goods, services, or labor in exchange for these payments. They include social security benefits, veterans' benefits, and welfare payments.

FIGURE 21.1
The Circular Flow of Payments

Households receive income from firms and the government, purchase goods and services from firms, and pay taxes to the government. They also purchase foreign-made goods and services (imports). Firms receive payments from households and the government for goods and services; they pay wages, dividends, interest, and rents to households, and taxes to the government. The government receives taxes from both firms and households, pays both firms and households for goods and services—including wages to government workers—and pays interest and transfers to households. Finally, people in other countries purchase goods and services produced domestically (exports).

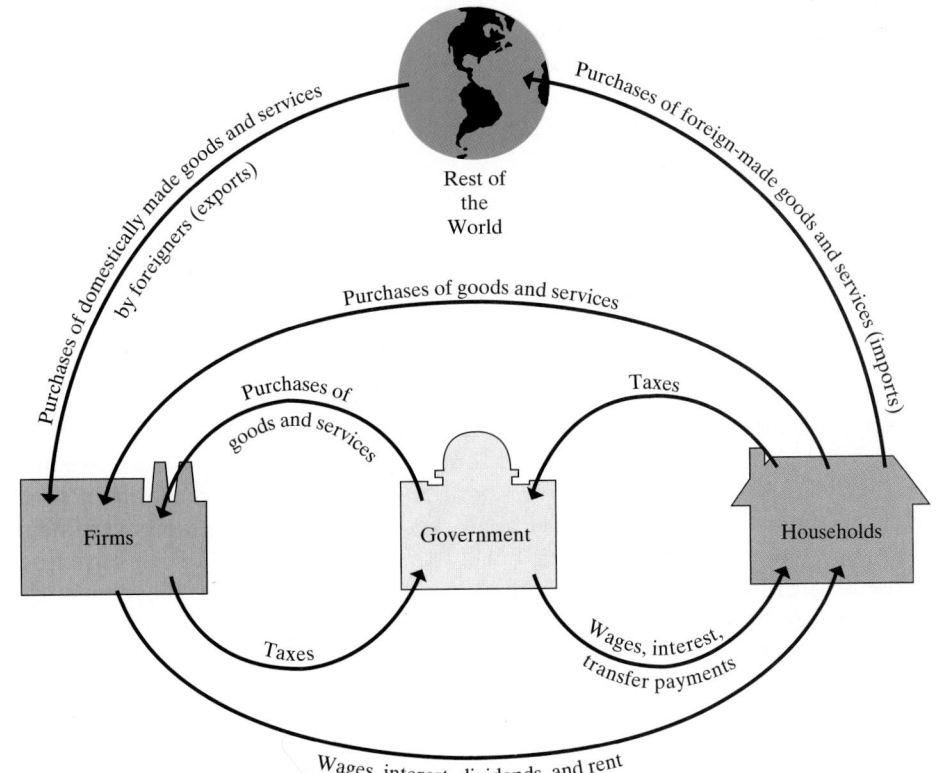

households is the amount that the households save or dissave.[4] If households receive more than they spend, they *save* during the period. If they receive less than they spend, they *dissave*. A household can dissave by using up some of its previous savings or by borrowing. In the circular flow diagram, household spending is shown as a flow *out* of the household sector.

Firms sell goods and services to households and the government. These sales earn revenue, which shows up in the circular flow diagram as a flow of funds *into* the firm sector. Firms pay wages, interest, and dividends to households, and they pay taxes to the government. These payments are shown as flowing *out* of the firm sector.

The government collects taxes, which provide revenue from households and firms. The government also makes payments. It buys goods and services from firms, pays wages and interest to households, and makes transfer payments to households. If the government's revenue is less than its payments, the government is dissaving.

Finally, households spend some of their income on *imports*—goods and services produced in the rest of the world. Similarly, people in foreign countries purchase *exports*—goods and services produced by domestic firms.

One of the major lessons of the circular flow diagram is that everyone's expenditure is someone else's receipt. If you buy a personal computer from IBM you make a payment to IBM and IBM receives income. If IBM pays taxes to the government, it has made a payment and the government has received revenue. In short:

> Everyone's expenditures go somewhere. It is impossible to sell something without there being a buyer, and it is impossible to make a payment without there being a recipient. Every transaction must have two sides.

The Three Market Arenas

Another way of looking at the ways households, firms, the government, and the rest of the world relate to each other is to consider the markets in which they interact. The three broadly defined market arenas in which households, firms, the government, and the rest of the world interact, as depicted in Figure 21.2, are:

> THE THREE MARKET ARENAS:
> 1. goods-and-services market
> 2. labor market
> 3. money (financial) market

GOODS-AND-SERVICES MARKET   Households and the government purchase goods and services from firms in the *goods-and-services market*. In this market, firms also purchase goods and services from each other. For example, Levi Strauss buys denim from other firms to make its blue jeans. In addition, firms buy capital goods from other firms. If General Motors needs new robots on its assembly lines, it will probably buy them from another firm rather than make them itself. Firms *supply* to the goods-and-services market, and households, the government, and firms *demand* from this market. Finally, the rest of the world both buys from and sells to the goods-and-services market. As we mentioned in Chapter 3, the United States now imports hundreds of billions of dollars worth of automobiles, VCRs, oil, and other goods. At the same time, the United States exports hundreds of billions of dollars worth of computers, airplanes, and agricultural goods.

---

[4]Saving by households is sometimes termed a "leakage" from the circular flow because it withdraws income, or current purchasing power, from the system.

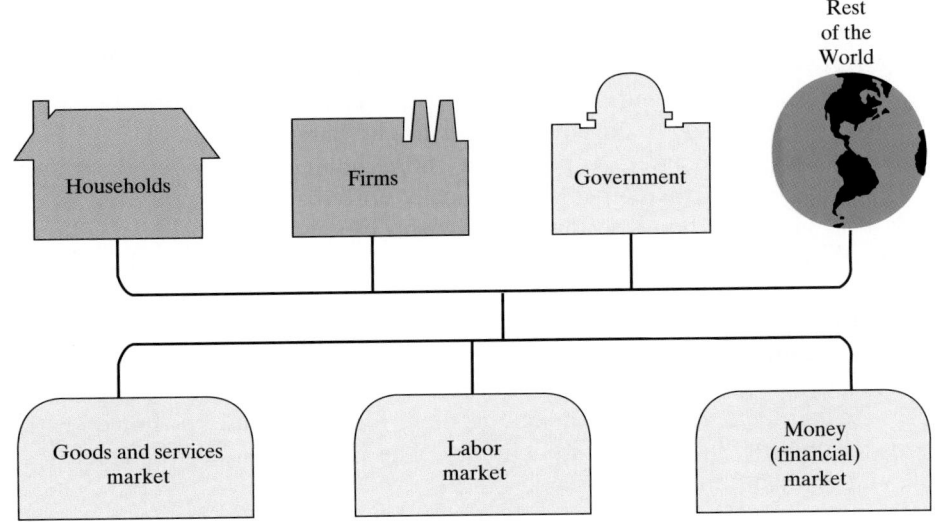

LABOR MARKET Interaction in the *labor market* takes place when firms and the government purchase labor from households. Households *supply* labor, and firms and the government *demand* labor in this market. In the U.S. economy, firms are the largest demanders of labor, although the government is also a substantial employer. The total supply of labor in the economy depends on the sum of decisions made by households. Individuals must decide whether to enter the labor force (whether to look for a job at all) and how many hours to work.

Labor is also supplied to and demanded from the rest of the world. In recent years, the labor market has become an international market. For example, vegetable and fruit farmers in California would find it very difficult to bring their product to market if it were not for the labor of migrant farm workers from Mexico. For years, Turkey has provided Germany with "guest workers" who are willing to take low-paying jobs that more prosperous German workers avoid. Even the United States exports some labor. When Iraq invaded Kuwait in 1990, thousands of U.S. citizens working in Kuwait (for foreign as well as U.S. firms) were trapped and held hostage for a few months.

MONEY MARKET In the *money market*—sometimes called the *financial market*—households purchase stocks and bonds from firms. Households *supply* funds to this market in the expectation of earning extra income in the form of dividends on stocks and interest on bonds. Households also *demand* (borrow) funds from this market to finance various purchases. Firms borrow to build new facilities in the hope of earning more in the future. The government borrows by issuing bonds. The rest of the world both borrows from and lends to the money market; every morning you can now hear reports on the radio about the Japanese and British stock markets. Much of the borrowing and lending of households, firms, the government, and the international sector is coordinated by financial institutions—commercial banks, savings and loan associations, insurance companies, and the like. These institutions take deposits from one group and lend them to others.

When a firm, a household, or the government borrows to finance a purchase, it has an obligation to pay that loan back, usually at some specified time in the future. Most loans also involve payment of interest as a fee for the use of

promissory notes Promises to pay that are signed by a borrower and given to a lender.

Treasury bonds, notes, and bills Promissory notes issued by the federal government when it borrows money.

corporate bonds Promissory notes issued by corporations when they borrow money.

shares of stock Financial instruments that give to the holder a share in the ownership of a firm and therefore the right to share in the profits of the firm.

capital gain An increase in the value of an asset over the price initially paid for it.

dividends The portion of a corporation's profits that the firm pays out each period to its shareholders.

the borrowed funds. When a loan is made, the borrower nearly always signs a "promise to repay," or **promissory note,** and gives it to the lender. When the federal government borrows, it issues "promises" called **Treasury bonds, notes,** or **bills** in exchange for money. Corporations issue **corporate bonds** at fixed interest rates. A corporate bond might state, for example, "General Electric Corporation agrees to pay $5000 to the holder of this bond on January 1, 1995, and interest thereon at 8.3% annually until that time."

Instead of issuing bonds to raise funds, firms can also issue shares of stock. A **share of stock** is a financial instrument that gives to the holder a share in the ownership of the firm and therefore the right to share in the profits of the firm. If the firm does well, the value of the stock increases, and the stockholder receives a **capital gain**[5] on the initial purchase. In addition, the stock may pay **dividends**—that is, the firm may choose to return some of its profits directly to its stockholders, rather than retaining them for its own use. If, however, the firm does poorly, so does the stockholder. The capital value of the stock may fall, and dividends may not be paid.

It is important to realize that stocks and bonds are simply contracts, or agreements, between parties. I agree to loan you a certain amount, and you agree to repay me this amount plus something extra at some future date. Or I agree to buy part ownership in your firm, and you agree to give me a share of the firm's future profits.

One of the critical variables in the money market is the *rate of interest.* Although we sometimes talk as if there were only one interest rate, there is never just one rate of interest at any given time. Rather, the rate of interest on a given loan reflects the length of the loan and the perceived risk to the lender. A business that is just getting started, for example, will have to pay a higher rate than will IBM. A 30-year mortgage has a different interest rate than a 90-day loan. Nevertheless, interest rates tend to move up and down together, and their movement reflects general conditions in the financial market. (We discuss the complexities of interest rates in later chapters.)

THE METHODOLOGY OF MACROECONOMICS

Macroeconomists build models based on theories, and they test their models using data. In this sense, the methodology of macroeconomics is similar to the methodology of microeconomics. As we noted earlier, however, microeconomists study the behavior of *individual* households and firms, while macroeconomists study the *aggregate behavior* of all households and all firms in the economy.

Connections to Microeconomics

How do macroeconomists try to explain aggregate behavior? One approach assumes that the same factors that affect individual behavior also affect aggregate behavior. For example, we know from microeconomics that an individual's wage rate should affect that person's consumption habits and the amount of labor he or she is willing to supply. If we were to apply this microeconomic hypothesis to the aggregate data, we would say that the average wage rate in the economy should affect total consumption and total labor supply (which, in fact, seems to be true).

---

[5]A *capital gain* occurs whenever the value of an asset increases. If you bought a stock for $1000 and it is now worth $1500, you have earned a capital gain of $500. A capital gain is "realized" when you sell the asset. Until you sell, the capital gain is *accrued* but not *realized.*

The reason for looking to microeconomics for help in explaining macroeconomic events is quite simple:

> Macroeconomic behavior is the sum of all the microeconomic decisions made by individual households and firms. If the movements of macroeconomic aggregates, such as total output or total employment, reflect decisions being made by individual firms and households, we cannot possibly understand the former without some knowledge of the factors that influence the latter.

Consider the problem of unemployment. The unemployment rate is the number of people unemployed as a fraction of the labor force. To be classified as "in the labor force," a person must either have a job or be seeking one actively. To understand aggregate unemployment, then, we need to understand individual household behavior in the labor market. Why do people choose to enter the labor force? Under what circumstances will they drop out? Why does unemployment exist even when the economy seems to be doing very well? A knowledge of microeconomic behavior is the logical starting point for macroeconomic analysis.

Aggregate Demand and Aggregate Supply

A major theme as we work our way through the next few chapters is the behavior of *aggregate demand* and *aggregate supply*. **Aggregate demand** is the total demand for goods and services in an economy. **Aggregate supply** is the total supply of goods and services in an economy.

Figure 21.3 shows *aggregate demand* and *aggregate supply curves.* Measured on the horizontal axis is the total amount of all goods and services demanded *or* supplied in a given period of time. Measured on the vertical axis is the *overall price level,* not the price of a particular good or service. (This is a very important point—be sure to keep it in mind.)

As you will discover, aggregate demand and supply curves are much more complicated than the simple demand and supply curves that we described in Chapters 4 and 5. The simple logic of supply, demand, and equilibrium in individual markets does not explain what is depicted in Figure 21.3. Indeed, it will take us the entire next chapter just to describe what is meant by "aggregate out-

aggregate demand The total demand for goods and services in an economy.

aggregate supply The total supply of goods and services in an economy.

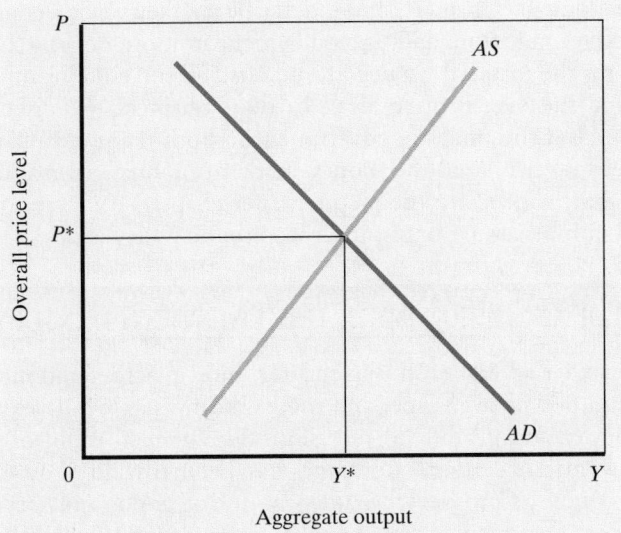

FIGURE 21.3
The Aggregate Demand and Aggregate Supply Curves

A major theme in macroeconomics is the behavior of aggregate demand and aggregate supply. The aggregate quantity demanded and the aggregate quantity supplied are both a function of the overall price level. The logic behind these curves, however, is much more complex than the logic underlying the simple supply and demand curves described in Chapters 4 and 5.

put" and the "overall price level." Furthermore, although we will look to the behavior of households and firms in individual markets for clues about how to analyze aggregate behavior, there are important differences when we move from the individual to the aggregate level.

Consider, for example, *demand,* one of the most important concepts in economics. When the price of a *specific good* increases, the most important determinant of consumer response is the availability of other goods that can be substituted for the good whose price has increased. Part of the reason that an increase in the price of airline tickets causes a decline in the quantity of airline tickets demanded is that a higher price relative to other goods means that the opportunity cost of buying a ticket is higher. The sacrifice required in terms of other goods and services has increased. But when the *overall price level* changes, there may be no changes at all in relative prices. When analyzing the behavior of aggregate demand, the availability of substitutes is irrelevant.

Microeconomics teaches us that, *ceteris paribus,* the quantity demanded of a good falls when its price rises and rises when its price falls. (This is the microeconomic law of demand.) In other words, individual demand curves and market demand curves slope downward to the right. The reason that the *aggregate* demand curve in Figure 21.3 slopes downward to the right is much more complex, however. As we will see later, the downward slope of the aggregate demand curve is related to what goes on in the money (financial) market.

The aggregate supply curve is also very different from the supply curve of an individual firm or market. A firm's supply curve is derived under the assumption that all its input prices are fixed. In other words, the firm's input prices are assumed to remain unchanged as the price of the firm's output changes. When we derived Clarence Brown's soybean supply schedule in Chapter 4, for example, we took his input prices as fixed. A change in an input price leads to a shift in Brown's supply curve, not a movement along it. If we are examining changes in the overall price level, however, *all* prices are changing (including at least some input prices), so the aggregate supply curve cannot be based on the assumption of fixed input prices. We will see later that the aggregate supply curve is a source of much controversy in macroeconomics.

Because of the complexity of the aggregate demand and aggregate supply curves shown in Figure 21.3, we will need to build our analysis piece by piece. In Chapter 22, we discuss the methods of measuring economic activity and aggregate output. In Chapter 23, we describe the key macroeconomic problems of business cycles, inflation, and unemployment in more detail. Chapters 24 through 29 present the material we need to understand the equilibrium levels of aggregate output and the overall price level. In these chapters, we discuss the behavior of households, firms, and the government in both the goods market (the market for goods and services) and the money market (the financial market). Chapter 30 brings the labor market into the picture. Later chapters elaborate on this material and discuss a number of important macroeconomic policy issues.

THE U.S. ECONOMY IN THE TWENTIETH CENTURY: TRENDS AND CYCLES

As we said earlier in this chapter, most macroeconomic variables go through ups and downs over time, and the economy as a whole experiences periods of prosperity and periods of recession. The general trend of the U.S. economy in the twentieth century, however, has been toward prosperity. One measure of an economy's prosperity is the amount of goods and services that it produces during a year, or its gross domestic product (GDP). (GDP is the subject of the next chapter.) An economy is said to grow from one year to another if GDP is larger in the second year than in the first. Between 1900 and 1992, the U.S. economy grew at an average rate of 3% per year. In other words, during those years the economy was on average 3% richer each year than it had been the year before.

It is important to remember that we are discussing the average growth rate here. The economy did not actually grow by 3% every year. In some years, growth was less than 3%, and in some years growth was actually negative (that is, GDP fell). In other years, the growth rate was greater than 3 percent. It is thus important to distinguish between *long-term,* or *secular, trends* in economic performance and *short-term,* or *cyclical, variations.*

Consider, for instance, the world's climate. Measurements have revealed that the earth's average temperature has been slowly but steadily rising for the past 18,000 years (a long-term secular trend). This does not mean, however, that every day, week, month, and year since 16,000 B.C. has been slightly warmer than the one before. There are seasonal fluctuations in climate as well as day-to-day variations, and there are even centuries-long cooling and warming periods within this 18,000-year span.

Expansion and Contraction: The Business Cycle

Macroeconomics is concerned both with long-run trends—Why has the U.S. economy done so well over the past 100 years while Great Britain's has done rather poorly?—and with short-run fluctuations in economic performance—Why did the world experience a severe recession in the early 1980s? Most of this part of the text focuses on short-run fluctuations, because they are somewhat better understood. As we mentioned earlier in this chapter, these short-term ups and downs in the economy are known as the *business cycle.* A typical business cycle is illustrated in Figure 21.4.

Because the U.S. economy on average grows over time, the business cycle in Figure 21.4 shows an overall positive trend—the *peak* (that is, the highest point) of a new business cycle is higher than the peak of the previous cycle. The period from a *trough,* or bottom of the cycle, to a peak is called an **expansion** or a **boom.** During an expansion, output and employment are growing. The period from a peak to a trough is called a **contraction, recession,** or **slump.** During a recession, output and employment are falling.

In judging whether an economy is expanding or contracting, it is important to note the difference between the level of economic activity and its rate of change. If, for example, the economy has just left a trough (point *A* in Figure 21.4), it will be grow-

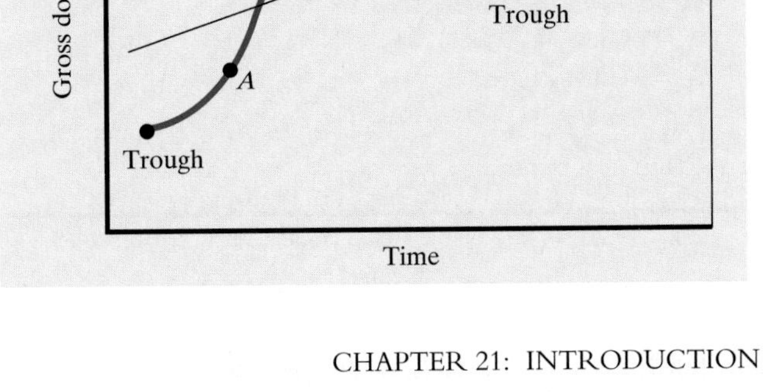

expansion, or boom The period in the business cycle from a trough up to a peak, during which output and employment rise.

contraction, recession, or slump The period in the business cycle from a peak down to a trough, during which output and employment fall.

FIGURE 21.4
A Typical Business Cycle

In this business cycle, the economy is expanding as it moves through point *A* from the trough to the peak. When the economy moves from a peak down to a trough, through point *B,* the economy is in recession.

ing (rate of change is positive), but its level of output will still be low. Conversely, if the economy has just started to decline from a peak (point *B* in Figure 21.4), it will be contracting (rate of change is negative), but its level of output will still be high.

The business cycle in Figure 21.4 is symmetric, which means that the length of an expansion is the same as the length of a contraction. All business cycles are not symmetric, however. It is possible, for example, for the expansion phase to be longer than the contraction phase. When contraction comes, it may be fast and sharp, while expansion may be slow and gradual. Moreover, the economy is not nearly as regular as the business cycle in Figure 21.4 indicates. While there are ups and downs in the economy, they tend to be fairly erratic.

What do actual business cycles in the United States look like? You can see the answer to this question in Figure 21.5, where the percentage deviation of U.S. GDP around its trend is plotted for the 1900–1992 period. Although many business cycles have occurred in the last nine decades, the cycles have not been very regular. Each business cycle is unique, and it is extremely important to keep this in mind. The economy is not so simple that it has regular cycles.

The periods of the Great Depression and World War II are clearly the low and high points of Figure 21.5, although other large contractions and expansions have taken place. In particular, the expansion in the 1960s is noteworthy, as are the recessions at the beginning of the 1980s and 1990s. Some of the cycles have been long in duration, and some have been very short. Note also that GDP actually increased between 1933 and 1937, even though at its peak in 1937 GDP was still quite low. The economy did not really come out of the Depression until the defense build up prior to the start of World War II.

FIGURE 21.5
Percentage Deviation of Real GDP around Its Trend, 1900–1992

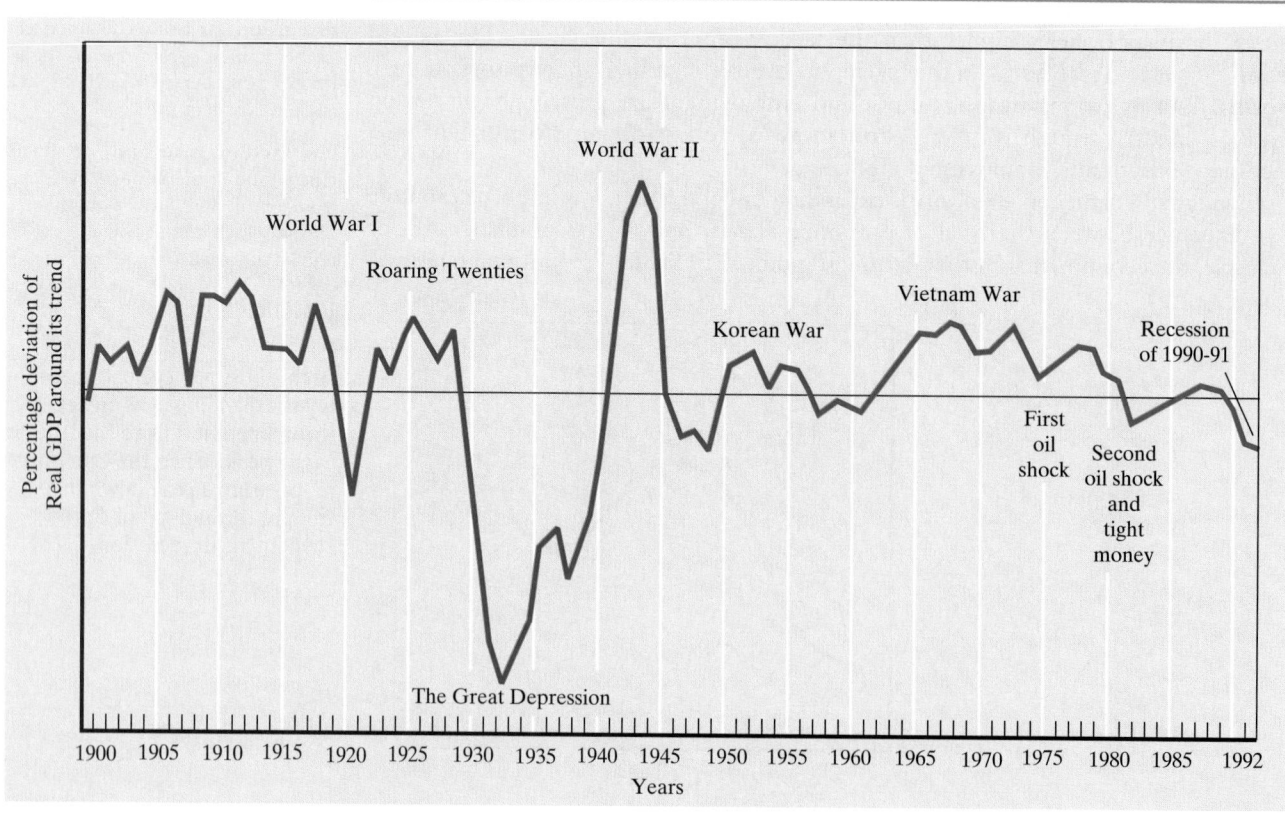

The U.S. Economy Since 1970

Since 1970, the U.S. economy has seen three recessions and large fluctuations in the rate of inflation. By analyzing how the various parts of the economy behaved during these hectic times, we can learn a lot about macroeconomic behavior. The following chapters thus concentrate on these years.

Figures 21.6, 21.7 and 21.8 show the behavior of three key variables during the period since 1970: *GDP,* the *unemployment rate,* and the *rate of inflation.* These graphs are based on *quarterly data* (that is, data compiled for each quarter of the year) rather than on annual data. The first quarter of a year consists of January, February, and March; the second quarter consists of April, May, and June; and so on. The Roman numerals I, II, III, and IV denote the four quarters. (For example, "1972 III" refers to the third quarter, or summer, of 1972.)

Figure 21.6 plots GDP for the period 1970 I–1992 IV. In the following chapters we will look at three recessionary periods within this period: 1974 I–1975 IV, 1980 II–1983 I, and 1990 III–1991 I. These periods make useful reference points when we examine how other variables behave during the three periods.[6]

One of the main concerns of macroeconomics is unemployment, as we said earlier. Unemployment generally rises during recessions and falls during expansions. This can be seen clearly in Figure 21.7, which plots the unemployment rate for the period 1970 I –1992 IV. Note that unemployment rose

---

[6]As Figure 21.6 shows, GDP rose in the middle of 1981 before falling again in the last quarter of 1981. Given this fact, one possibility would be to treat the 1980 II–1983 I period as if it included two separate recessionary periods: 1980 II–1981 I and 1981 IV–1983 I. Because the expansion in 1981 was so short-lived, however, we have chosen not to separate the period into two parts.

FIGURE 21.6
Real GDP, 1970 I–1992 IV

Real GDP in the United States since 1970 has risen overall, but there have been three recessionary periods: 1974 I–1975 IV, 1980 II–1983 I, and 1990 III–1991 I.

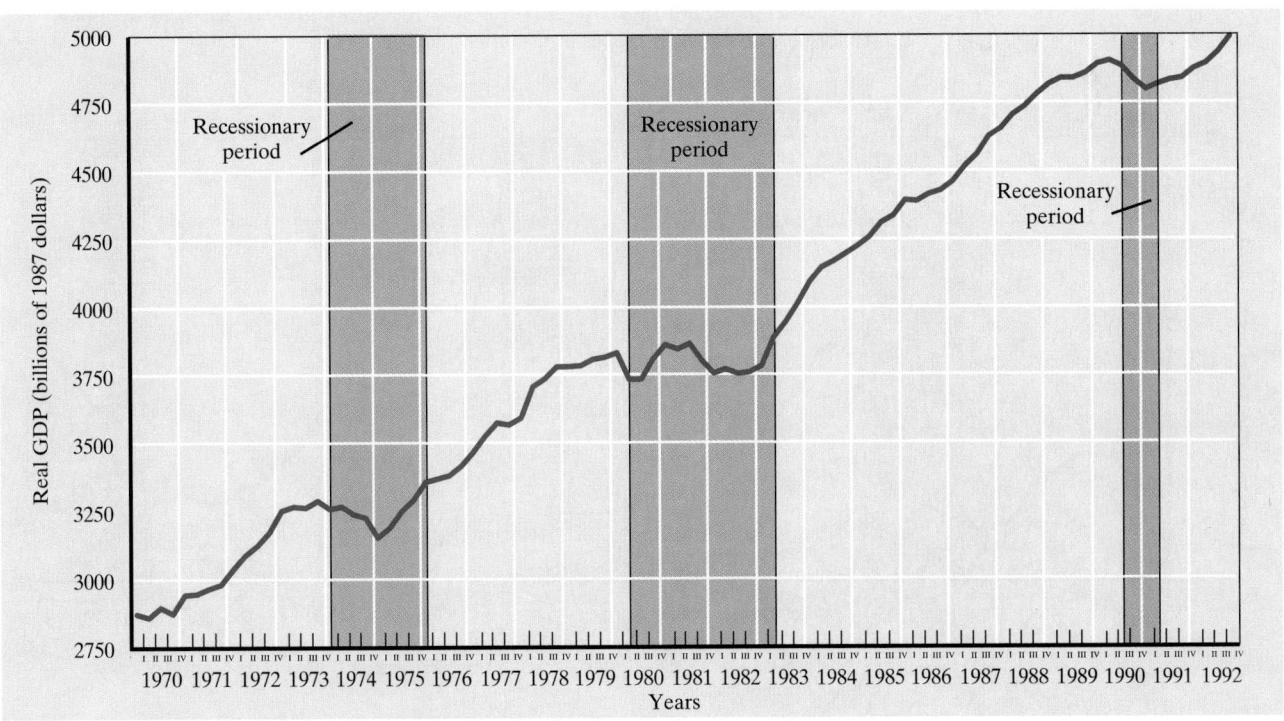

in all three recessions. In the 1974–1975 recession, the unemployment rate reached a maximum of 8.8% in the second quarter of 1975. During the 1980–1982 recession, it reached a maximum of 10.7% in the fourth quarter of 1982. The unemployment rate continued to rise after the 1990–1991 recession and reached a peak of 7.5% in 1992 III.

Macroeconomics is also concerned with the inflation rate. A measure of the overall price level is the GDP *deflator,* an economy-wide price index. (The construction of the GDP deflator is discussed in the next chapter. It is an index of prices of all domestically produced goods in the economy.) The percentage change in the GDP deflator provides one measure of the overall rate of inflation. Figure 21.8 plots the percentage change in the GDP deflator for the 1970 I–1992 IV I period.[7] For reference purposes, we have picked two periods within this time as showing particularly high inflation: 1973 IV–1975 IV and 1979 I–1981 IV. In the first period, the inflation rate peaked at 10.9% in the first quarter of 1975. In the second period, it peaked at 10.6% in the first quarter of 1981. Since 1983, the rate of inflation has been quite low by the standards of the 1970s. In the fourth quarter of 1992 it was only 2.5 percent.

One of the main concerns of macroeconomics is to explain the behavior of and the connection between variables such as GDP, the unemployment rate, and the GDP deflator. When you can understand the movements shown in Figures 21.6, 21.7, and 21.8, you will have come a long way in understanding how the economy works.

---

[7]The percentage change in Figure 21.8 is the percentage change over four quarters. For example, the value for 1970 I is the percentage change from 1969 I, the value for 1970 II is the percentage change from 1969 II, and so on.

FIGURE 21.7
Unemployment Rate, 1970 I–1992 IV

The U.S. unemployment rate since 1970 shows wide variations. The three recessionary reference periods show increases in the unemployment rate.

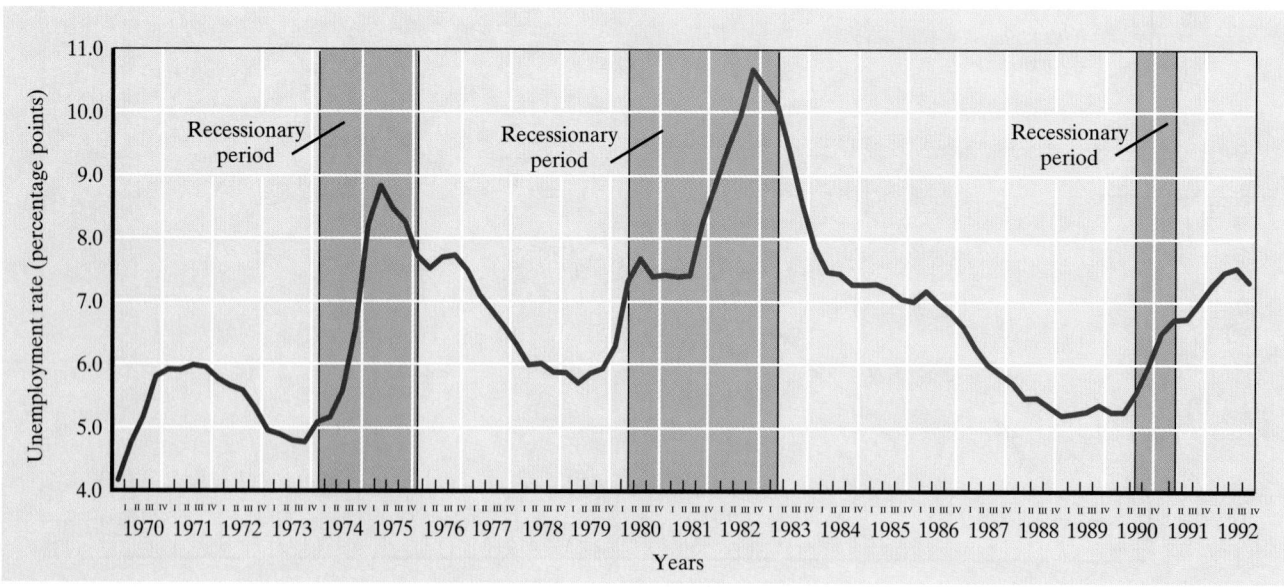

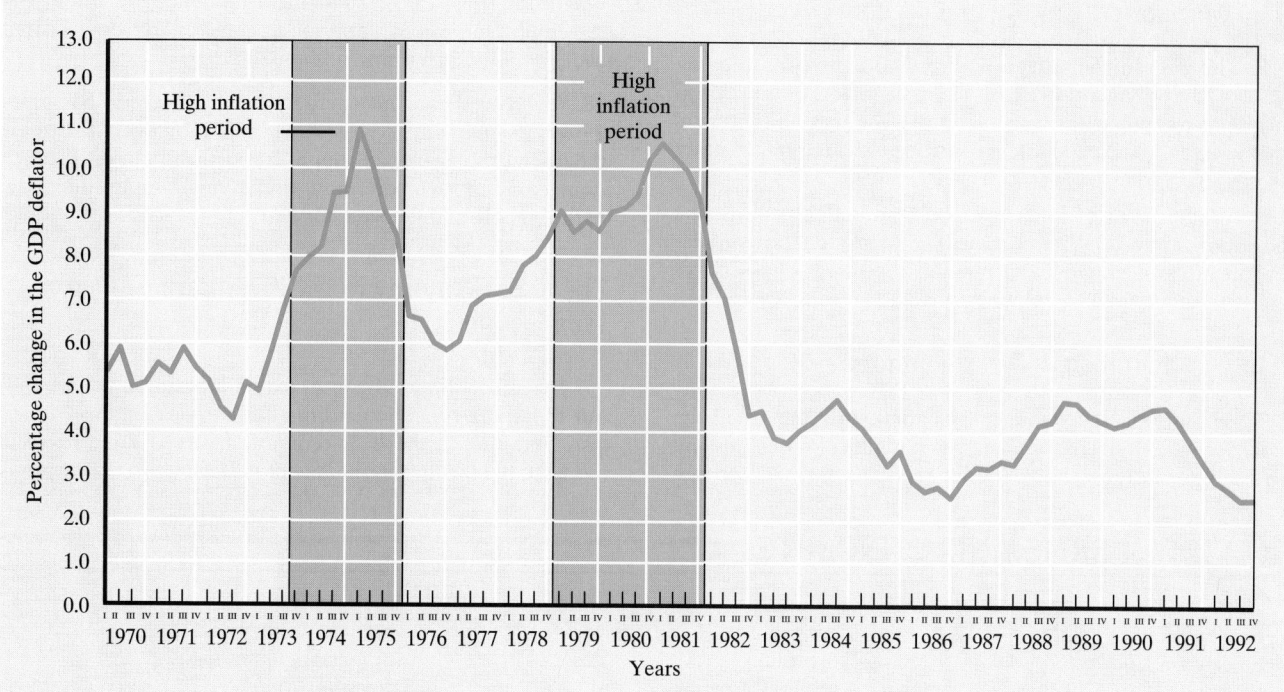

FIGURE 21.8

Percentage Change in the GDP Deflator (four-quarter average), 1970 I–1992 IV

The percentage change in the GDP deflator measures the overall rate of inflation. Since 1970, inflation has been high in two periods: 1973 IV–1975 IV and 1979 I–1981 IV. Inflation since 1983 has been moderate.

SUMMARY

1. *Microeconomics* is the branch of economics that examines the functioning of individual industries and the behavior of individual decision-making units. *Macroeconomics* is concerned with the sum, or aggregate, of these individual decisions—the consumption of *all* households in the economy, the amount of labor supplied and demanded by *all* individuals and firms, the total amount of *all* goods and services produced.

The Roots of Macroeconomics

2. Macroeconomics was born out of the effort to explain the *Great Depression* of the 1930s. Since that time, the discipline has evolved, concerning itself with new issues as the problems facing the economy have changed. Through the late 1960s, it was believed that the government could "fine tune" the economy to keep it running on an even keel at all times. The poor economic performance of the 1970s, however, showed that *fine tuning* does not always work.

Macroeconomic Concerns

3. The four topics of primary concern to macroeconomists are increases in the overall price level, or *inflation;* the level of aggregate output in the economy; the level of aggregate employment and the rate of unemployment; and the country's economic relationships with the rest of the world.

The Role of Government in the Macroeconomy

4. Among the tools that governments have available to them for influencing the macroeconomy are *fiscal policy* (decisions on taxes and government spending); *monetary policy* (control of the money supply); *incomes policies* (direct controls over wages and prices); and *supply-side policies* (policies that focus on aggregate supply and increasing production).

The Components of the Macroeconomy

5. The *circular flow* diagram shows the flow of income received and payments made by the three sectors of the economy—private, public, and international. The diagram illustrates that everybody's expenditure is someone else's receipt. In other words, every transaction must have two sides.

6. Another way of looking at how households, firms, the government, and the international sector relate is to consider the markets in which they interact: the goods-and-services market, labor market, and money market.

The Methodology of Macroeconomics

7. Because macroeconomic behavior is the sum of all the microeconomic decisions made by individual households and firms, we cannot possibly understand the former without

some knowledge of the factors that influence the latter. The movements of macroeconomic aggregates reflect decisions made by individual firms and households.

8. A major theme in macroeconomics is the behavior of *aggregate supply* and *aggregate demand*. However, the logic underlying the aggregate supply and demand curves is much more complex than the logic underlying simple individual market supply and demand curves.

The U.S. Economy in the Twentieth Century: Trends and Cycles

9. Macroeconomics is concerned with both long-run trends and the short-run fluctuations that are part of the *business cycle*. Since 1970, the U.S. economy has seen three *recessions* and large fluctuations in the rate of *inflation*.

REVIEW TERMS AND CONCEPTS

aggregate behavior   531
aggregate demand   543
aggregate output   536
aggregate supply   543
business cycle   536
capital gain   542
circular flow   539
contraction, recession, or slump   546
corporate bonds   542
depression   536
dividends   542

expansion, or boom   546
fine tuning   532
fiscal policy   537
Great Depression   531
hyperinflation   535
incomes policy   538
inflation   535
macroeconomics   530
microeconomic foundations of
   macroeconomics   531
microeconomics   530

monetary policy   537
promissory notes   542
recession   536
shares of stock   542
stagflation   534
sticky prices   531
supply-side policy   538
transfer payments   539
Treasury bonds, notes, bills   542
unemployment rate   536

PROBLEM SET

1. The economy was the number one issue during the 1992 presidential campaign. Most people believed that the economy was in recession. However, a careful look at the data shows that GDP stopped falling and began growing in the spring of 1991. In other words, the recession ended a full year and a half before the election. What was it about the economy that led the public to perceive things as so bad? In what ways do members of society actually benefit during a "recovery" from recession? (*Hint:* Think about the labor market.)

2. In 1993, the various regions of the United States were behaving very differently from one another. California, for example, was in recession with rising unemployment. The Texas economy had suffered a dramatic decline in employment during the mid-1980s and was recovering, as was New England. Describe the economy of your state. What is the current unemployment rate? Has it been rising or falling over the last few months? What explanations have been offered in the press? How does the performance of your state compare to the performance of the U.S. economy over the last few months?

3. Explain briefly how macroeconomics is different from micro-

economics. How can macroeconomists use microeconomic theory to guide them in their work, and why might they wish to do so?

4. In 1993, a company paid its blue-collar employees $7.50 per hour but its white-collar employees only $5 per hour. It gave all employees a $1 raise in 1994, so that blue-collar employees were making $8.50 and white-collar employees $6 per hour. Yet the average wage paid to all employees in the company actually declined between 1993 and 1994. How is this possible? How does this question have anything to do with macroeconomics?

5. List, and briefly define, the four major concerns of macroeconomics. How would you rank these four in order of their importance to you personally? Why? Why might others assess the relative importance differently?

6. Figure 21.5 shows that many of the expansionary periods during the twentieth century have occurred during wars. Why do you think this is true?

7. In the 1940s, one could buy a can of soda for 5¢, eat dinner at a restaurant for less than a dollar, and purchase a house for $10,000. From this statement, it follows that consumers today are worse off than consumers in the 1940s. Comment.

Measuring National Output and National Income

22

GROSS DOMESTIC PRODUCT
    Final Goods and Services
    Exclusion of Used Goods and Paper Transactions
    Exclusion of Output Produced Abroad by
        Domestically Owned Factors of Production

CALCULATING GDP
    The Expenditure Approach
    The Income Approach

FROM GDP TO PERSONAL INCOME

NOMINAL VERSUS REAL GDP
    Distinguishing between Production and Price
        Increases
    The GDP Deflator

LIMITATIONS OF THE GDP CONCEPT
    GDP and Social Welfare
    The Underground Economy
    Per Capita GDP/GNP

LOOKING AHEAD

M acroeconomics relies heavily on data, much of it collected by the government. In order to study the economy, we need data on total output, total income, total consumption, and the like. One of the main sources of these data are the **national income and product accounts,** which describe the various components of national income in the economy.

The national income and product accounts do more than just convey data about the performance of the economy, however. They also provide an important conceptual framework that macroeconomists use to think about how the various pieces of the economy fit together. When an economist thinks about the macroeconomy, the categories and vocabulary he or she uses come from the national income and product accounts.

The national income and product accounts can be compared to the mechanical or wiring diagrams for an automobile engine. The diagrams by themselves do not explain how an engine works, but they do identify and name the key parts of an engine and show how they are connected. Trying to understand the macroeconomy without having an understanding of national income accounting is like trying to fix an engine without a mechanical diagram and with no names for the engine parts.

national income and product accounts Data collected and published by the government describing the various components of national income and output in the economy.

GROSS DOMESTIC PRODUCT

gross domestic product (GDP) The total market value of all final goods and services produced within a given period by factors of production located within a country.

The key concept in the national income and product accounts is **gross domestic product,** or **GDP.** GDP is the total market value of a country's output. More specifically, it is the market value of all final goods and services produced within a given period of time by factors of production located within a country. U.S. GDP for 1992—in other words, the value of all the output produced by factors of production in the United States in 1992—was $5950.7 billion.

Final Goods and Services

final goods and services Newly produced goods that are not resold to someone else.

intermediate goods Goods that are produced by one firm for use in further processing by another firm.

The phrase "goods and services produced" in the definition of GDP refers to **final goods and services**—newly produced goods that are not resold to someone else. Many goods are **intermediate goods;** that is, they are produced by one firm for use in further processing by another firm. Tires sold to automobile manufacturers, for example, are intermediate goods. The value of intermediate goods that are resold is not counted in the definition of GDP. Newly produced goods that are *not* resold are counted as a part of GDP.

Why aren't intermediate goods counted in GDP? Suppose that in producing a car GM pays $100 to Goodyear for tires. GM uses these tires (among other components) to assemble a car, which it then sells for $12,000. The value of the car (including its tires) is $12,000, not $12,000 + $100. In other words, the final price of the car already reflects the value of all its components. To count in GDP both the value of the tires sold to the automobile manufacturers and the value of the automobiles sold to the consumers would result in *double counting.*

> GDP is simply the sum of all goods and services produced for final use in a given period of time.

value added The difference between the value of goods as they leave a stage of production and the cost of the goods as they entered that stage.

Double counting can also be avoided by counting only the *value added* to a product by each firm in its production process. The **value added** during some stage of production is the difference between the value of goods as they leave that stage of production and the cost of the goods as they entered that stage. Value added is illustrated in Table 22.1. The four stages of the production of a gallon of gasoline are (1) oil drilling, (2) refining, (3) shipping, and (4) retail sale. In the first stage of production, value added is simply the value of sales. In the second stage, the refiner purchases the oil from the driller, refines it into gasoline, and sells it to the shipper. The refiner pays the driller $0.50 per gallon and charges the shipper $0.65. The value added by the refiner is thus $0.15 per gallon. The shipper then sells the gasoline to retailers for $0.80. The value added in the third stage of production is thus $0.15. Finally, the retailer sells the gasoline to consumers for $1.00. The value added at the fourth stage is $0.20, and the total value added in the pro-

TABLE 22.1
Value Added in the Production of a Gallon of Gasoline (Hypothetical Numbers)

STAGE OF PRODUCTION	VALUE OF SALES	VALUE ADDED
(1) Oil drilling	$0.50	$0.50
(2) Refining	0.65	0.15
(3) Shipping	0.80	0.15
(4) Retail sale	1.00	0.20
Total value added		$1.00

duction process is $1.00, the same as the value of sales at the retail level. Adding the total values of sales at each stage of production ($0.50 + $0.65 + $0.80 + $1.00 = $2.95) would significantly overestimate the value of the gallon of gasoline.

The point of this example is simple:

> In calculating GDP, we can either sum up the value added at each stage of production or we can take the value of final sales. We do not want to use the value of total sales in an economy to measure how much output that economy has produced.

Exclusion of Used Goods and Paper Transactions

GDP is concerned only with new, or current, production. Old output is not counted in current GDP because it was already counted back at the time it was produced. It would be double counting to count sales of used goods in current GDP. For example, if someone sells her used car to you, the transaction is not counted in GDP, because no new production has taken place. Similarly, a house is counted in GDP only at the time it is built, not each time it is resold. In short,

> GDP ignores all transactions in which money or goods change hands but in which no new goods and services are produced.

Sales of stocks and bonds are also not counted in GDP. These sales are merely exchanges of paper assets and do not correspond to current production. But what if I sell the stock or bond for more than I originally paid for it? Profits from the stock or bond market have nothing to do with current production, and thus they are not counted in GDP either. If, on the other hand, I pay a fee to a broker for selling a stock of mine to someone else, this fee is counted in GDP, because the broker is performing a service for me. This service is part of current production. You should thus be careful to distinguish between exchanges of stocks and bonds for money (or for other stocks and bonds), which do not involve current production, and fees for performing such exchanges, which do.

Exclusion of Output Produced Abroad by Domestically Owned Factors of Production

> GDP is the value of output produced by factors of production *located within a country.*

The three basic factors of production are land, labor, and capital. The labor of U.S. citizens counts as a domestically owned factor of production for the United States. The output produced by U.S. citizens abroad (for example, U.S. citizens working for a foreign company) is *not* counted in U.S. GDP because the output is not produced within the United States. Likewise, profits earned abroad by U.S. companies are not counted in U.S. GDP. However, the output produced by foreigners working in the United States is counted in U.S. GDP because the output is produced within the United States. Also, profits earned in the United States by foreign-owned companies are counted in U.S. GDP.

It is sometimes useful to have a measure of the output produced by factors of production owned by a country's citizens regardless of where the output is produced. This measure is called **gross national product,** or **GNP.** For most countries, including the United States, the difference between GDP and GNP

gross national product (GNP)
The total market value of all final goods and services produced within a given period by factors of production owned by a country's citizens, regardless of where the output is produced.

is small.[1] In 1992 GNP for the United States was $5961.9 billion, which is close to the $5950.7 billion value for U.S. GDP.

The distinction between GDP and GNP can be tricky. Consider, for example, the Honda plant in Marysville, Ohio. The plant is owned by the Honda Corporation, a Japanese firm, although most of the workers employed at the plant are U.S. workers. Although all of the output of the plant is included in U.S. GDP, only part of it is included in U.S. GNP. The wages paid to U.S. workers are part of U.S. GNP, while the profits from the plant are not. The profits from the plant are counted in Japanese GNP because this is output produced by Japanese-owned factors of production (Japanese capital in this case). The profits, however, are not counted in Japanese GDP because they were not earned in Japan.

The centrality of GDP as a working concept can hardly be overestimated. Just as an individual firm needs to evaluate the success or failure of its operations each year, so the economy as a whole needs to assess itself. GDP, as a measure of the total production of an economy, provides us with a country's economic report card.

Calculating GDP

expenditure approach, income approach Two methods of computing GDP. The *expenditure approach* measures the amount spent on all final goods during a given period. The *income approach* measures the income—wages, rents, interest, and profits—received by all factors of production in producing final goods.

GDP can be computed in two ways. One way is to add up the amount spent on all final goods during a given period. This is the **expenditure approach** to calculating GDP. The other way is to add up the income—wages, rents, interest, and profits—received by all factors of production in producing final goods. This is the **income approach** to calculating GDP. These two methods of computation lead to the same value for GDP for the reason we discussed in the previous chapter: *Every payment (expenditure) by a buyer is at the same time a receipt (income) for the seller.* We can measure either income received or expenditures made, and we will end up with the same total output.

Suppose, for example, that the economy is made up of just one firm and that the firm's total output this year sells for $1 million. Because the total amount *spent* on output this year is $1 million, this year's GDP is $1 million. Remember: The expenditure approach calculates GDP on the basis of total expenditures for final goods and services in the economy.

But *every one* of the million dollars of GDP is either paid to someone or remains with the owners of the firm as profit. Using the income approach, we add up the wages paid to employees of the firm, the interest paid to those who lent money to the firm, and the rents paid to those who leased land, buildings, or equipment to the firm. What is left over is profit, which is, of course, income to the owners of the firm. Thus, if we add up the *incomes* of all the factors of production, including profits to the owners, we get a GDP of $1 million.

The expenditure and income approaches to GDP are discussed in more detail in the sections that follow.

---

[1]In some countries, however, there is a large difference between GDP and GNP. For instance, the tiny country of Lesotho (surrounded entirely by South Africa) has an extremely poor and rudimentary domestic economy. Most residents of Lesotho earn their living by working in the mines and industries of neighboring South Africa. These payments from abroad are not counted in GDP, although they are part of GNP. According to most recent International Financial Statistics published by the International Monetary Fund, Lesotho's GNP exceeded its GDP by 72% in 1988.

The Expenditure Approach

Recall from Chapter 21 that there are four main groups in the economy: *households, firms,* the *government,* and the *rest of the world.* There are also four main categories of expenditure:

Expenditure Categories:	• Consumption (*C*)—household spending on consumer goods. • Investment (*I*)—spending by firms and households on new capital: plant, equipment, inventory, and new residential structures. • Government purchases of goods and services (*G*). • Net exports (*EX* − *IM*)—net spending by the rest of the world, or exports minus imports.

The expenditure approach calculates GDP by adding together these four components of spending. Stated in equation form:

$$\text{GDP} = C + I + G + (EX - IM).$$

U.S. GDP was $5950.7 billion in 1992. The four components of the expenditure approach are shown in Table 22.2, along with their various categories.

CONSUMPTION (*C*)   A large part of GDP consists of **personal consumption expenditures (C)**. Table 22.2 shows that in 1992 the amount of personal consumption expenditures accounted for 68.8% of GDP. These are expenditures by consumers on goods and services.

There are three main categories of consumer expenditures: durable goods, nondurable goods, and services. **Durable goods,** such as automobiles, furniture, and household appliances, are goods that last a relatively long time. **Nondurable goods,** such as food, clothing, gasoline, and cigarettes, are used up fairly quickly. Payments for **services**—those things that we buy that do not involve the production of physical items—include expenditures for doctors, lawyers, and educational institutions. As Table 22.2 shows, in 1992 durable goods expenditures accounted for 8.1% of GDP, nondurables for 21.7%, and services for 39.1 percent.

personal consumption expenditures (C) A major component of GDP: expenditures by consumers on goods and services.

durable goods Goods that last a relatively long time, such as cars and household appliances.

nondurable goods Goods that are used up fairly quickly, such as food and clothing.

services The things we buy that do not involve the production of physical things, such as legal and medical services and education.

TABLE 22.2
Components of GDP, 1992: The Expenditure Approach

	BILLIONS OF DOLLARS	PERCENTAGE OF GDP
Total Gross Domestic Product	5950.7	100.0
Personal Consumption Expenditures (C)	4095.8	68.8
Durable goods	480.4	8.1
Nondurable goods	1290.7	21.7
Services	2324.7	39.1
Gross Private Domestic Investment (I)	770.4	12.9
Nonresidential	548.2	9.2
Residential	217.7	3.7
Change in business inventories	4.4	0.0
Government Purchases of Goods and Services (G)	1114.9	18.7
Federal	449.1	7.5
State and local	665.8	11.2
Net Exports (EX – IM)	−30.4	−0.5
Exports (EX)	636.3	10.7
Imports (IM)	666.7	11.2

Note: Numbers do not add exactly because of rounding.

Source: U.S. Department of Commerce, Bureau of Economic Analysis, *Survey of Current Business,* March 1993.

INVESTMENT *(I)* The term "investment," as we use it in economics, refers to the purchase of new housing, plants, equipment, and inventory. The economic use of the term is in contrast to its everyday use, where "investment" often refers to purchases of common stocks, bonds, or mutual funds ("He 'invested' in some 8% corporate bonds.") Two subjects that have generated much interest lately, foreign investment in the United States and U.S. investment abroad, are discussed in this chapter's Global Perspective box.

Total investment by the private sector is called **gross private investment (I)** It accounted for 12.9% of GDP in 1992. Of this 12.9%, 9.2% was *nonresidential investment* and 3.7% was *residential investment.* Business inventories were virtually unchanged in 1992. Expenditures by firms for machines, tools, plants, and so forth make up **nonresidential investment.**[2] Because these items are goods that firms buy and do not resell to anyone else, they are part of "final sales" in the economy and are therefore counted in GDP. Expenditures for new houses and apartment buildings constitute **residential investment.** The third component of gross private investment, the **change in business inventories,** is the amount by which firms' inventories change during a period. Business inventories can be looked at as the goods that firms produce now but intend to sell later.

Change in Business Inventories It is sometimes confusing to students that inventories should be counted as capital and that changes in inventory should be counted as investment. But conceptually it makes some sense. The inventory that a firm owns has a value, and it serves a purpose, or provides a service, to the firm. The fact that it has value is obvious. Just think of the inventory of a new car dealer or of a clothing store, or stocks of newly produced but as yet unsold computers awaiting shipment. All these things certainly have value.

But what *service* does inventory provide? Firms keep stocks of inventory for a number of reasons. One obvious reason is to meet unforeseen demand. Firms are never sure how much they will sell from period to period. Sales go up and down. To maintain the goodwill of their customers, therefore, firms need to be able to respond to unforeseen increases in sales. The only way to do that is with inventory.

Other firms provide direct services to customers with inventory. In fact, that is the main function of a retail store. A grocery store provides a service—convenience. The store itself doesn't produce any food at all. It simply assembles a wide variety of items and puts them on display so that consumers with widely varying tastes can come and shop in one place for what they want. The same is true for a clothing or hardware store. In order to provide their services, such stores need light fixtures, counters, cash registers, buildings, and lots of inventory.

Thus, capital stocks are made up of plant, equipment, and inventory; inventory accumulations are part of the change in capital stocks, or investment.

It is important to remember that GDP is not the market value of total final *sales* during a period, but rather the market value of total *production.* The relationship between total production and total sales is this: The amount of total final sales of domestic goods equals total production (GDP) minus the change in business inventories, or:

> Final Sales = GDP – Change in Business Inventories.

---

gross private investment (I)
Total investment—that is, the purchase of new housing, plants, equipment, and inventory—by the private (or nongovernment) sector.

nonresidential investment
Expenditures by firms for machines, tools, plants, and so on.

residential investment
Expenditures by households and firms on new houses and apartment buildings.

change in business inventories
The amount by which firms' inventories change during a period. Inventories are the goods that firms produce now but intend to sell later.

---

[2]The distinction between what is considered investment and what is considered consumption is sometimes fairly arbitrary. A firm's purchase of a car or a truck is counted as investment, but a household's purchase of a car or a truck is counted as consumption of durable goods. In general, expenditures by firms for items that last longer than a year are counted as investment expenditures. Expenditures for items that last less than a year are seen as purchases of intermediate goods.

In 1992, production exceeded sales by $4.4 billion. Thus, inventories at the end of 1992 were $4.4 billion *more* than they were at the beginning of 1992.

Gross Investment versus Net Investment During the process of production, capital (especially machinery and equipment) produced in previous periods gradually wears out. Thus, GDP does not give us a true picture of the real ("net") production of an economy. GDP includes newly produced capital goods but does not take account of capital goods that are "consumed" in the production process.

Capital assets *depreciate* when they decline in value. The amount by which an asset's value falls each period is called its **depreciation.**[3] For example, a personal computer purchased by a business today may be expected to have a useful life of four years before becoming worn out or obsolete. Over that period of time, the PC steadily depreciates.

Recall that *I* stands for *gross* private investment. What, then, is the relationship between *I* and depreciation? **Gross investment** is the total value of all newly produced capital goods (plant, equipment, housing, and inventory) produced in a given period. It takes no account of the fact that some capital wears out and must be replaced. **Net investment** is equal to gross investment minus depreciation (capital consumption allowances). Net investment is a measure of how much the stock of capital *changes* during a period. If net investment is positive, the capital stock has increased; if net investment is negative, the capital stock has decreased. If *K* is the total value of a firm's (or the country's) capital stock, then:

$$K_{\text{end of period}} = K_{\text{beginning of period}} + \text{Net Investment}$$

GOVERNMENT PURCHASES OF GOODS AND SERVICES (G) **Government purchases of goods and services (G)** include expenditures by federal, state, and local governments for final goods (bombs, pencils, school buildings) and labor (military salaries, congressional salaries, school teachers' salaries). Government transfer payments (social security benefits, veterans' disability stipends, etc.) are not included in government purchases of goods and services because these transfers are not purchases of anything currently produced. The payments are not made in exchange for any goods or services. Because interest payments on the government debt are also counted as transfers, they are also excluded from GDP on the grounds that they are not payments for current services.

As Table 22.2 shows, government purchases accounted for $1114.9 billion, or 18.7% of U.S. GDP in 1992. Federal government spending in 1992 accounted for 7.5% of GDP, and state and local government spending accounted for 11.2 percent.

NET EXPORTS (EX − IM) The value of **net exports (EX − IM)** is the difference between *exports* (sales to foreigners of U.S.-produced goods and services) and *imports* (U.S. purchases of goods and services from abroad). This figure can be positive or negative. In 1992, the United States exported less than it imported; the level of net exports was thus negative (–$30.4 billion). Before 1983, the United States had generally been a net exporter. That is, exports exceeded imports, so the net export figure was positive.

depreciation The amount by which an asset's value falls in a given period.

gross investment The total value of all newly produced capital goods (plant, equipment, housing, and inventory) produced in a given period.

net investment Gross investment minus depreciation.

government purchases of goods and services (G) Expenditures by federal, state, and local governments for final goods and labor.

net exports (EX − IM) The difference between exports (sales to foreigners of U.S.-produced goods and services) and imports (U.S. purchases of goods and services from abroad). The figure can be positive or negative.

---

[3]This is the formal definition of economic depreciation. Because depreciation is difficult to measure precisely, accounting rules allow firms to use shortcut methods to approximate the amount of depreciation that they incur each period. To complicate matters even more, the U.S. tax laws allow firms to deduct depreciation for tax purposes under a different set of rules.

The reason for including net exports in the definition of GDP is fairly simple. First, consumption, investment, and government spending (C, I, and G) include expenditures on goods produced both domestically and by foreigners. Therefore, $C + I + G$ overstates domestic production because it contains expenditures on foreign-produced goods—i.e., imports. Thus, imports (IM) have to be subtracted out of GDP to obtain the correct figure. However, $C + I + G$ understates domestic production because some of what a nation produces is sold abroad and is therefore not included in C, I, or G. Thus, exports (EX) have to be added in. For example, if a U.S. firm produces computers and sells them in Germany, the computers are clearly part of U.S. production and should thus be counted as part of U.S. GDP.

The Income Approach

We have seen already that GDP can be obtained by adding up the final spending (on goods and services produced by factors of production located within the country) of households, firms, the government, and the rest of the world. As we have mentioned, however, there is another way of computing GDP. Table 22.3 presents the income approach to calculating GDP, which looks at GDP in terms of who receives it as income rather than in terms of who purchases it.

The income approach to GDP breaks down GDP into four components: national income, depreciation, indirect taxes minus subsidies, and net factor payments to the rest of the world:

$$\text{GDP} = \text{National Income} + \text{Depreciation} + (\text{Indirect Taxes} - \text{Subsidies}) + \text{Net Factor Payments to the Rest of the World.}$$

We examine each of these components in the sections that follow. As you proceed, keep in mind the cardinal rule that total expenditures always equal total income.

NATIONAL INCOME   National income is the total income earned by factors of production owned by a country's citizens. Table 22.3 shows that national income is the sum of five items: (1) compensation of employees, (2) proprietors' income, (3) corporate profits, (4) net interest, and (5) rental income. **Compensation of employees**, which is the largest of the five items by far, includes wages and salaries paid to households by firms and by the government, as well as various supplements to wages and salaries such as contributions that employers make to social insurance and private pension funds. **Proprietors' income** is the income of unincorporated businesses, and **corporate profits** are the income of corporate businesses. **Net interest** is the interest paid by business. (Interest paid by households and by the government is not counted in GDP because it is not assumed to flow from the production of goods and services.) Finally, **rental income**, a very minor item, is the income received by property owners in the form of rent.

DEPRECIATION   Recall from our discussion of net versus gross investment that when capital assets wear out or become obsolete, they decline in value. The measure of that decrease in value is called *depreciation*. This depreciation is a part of GDP in the income approach.

compensation of employees Includes wages, salaries, and various supplements—employer contributions to social insurance and pension funds, for example—paid to households by firms and the government.

proprietors' income The income of unincorporated businesses.

corporate profits The income of corporate businesses.

net interest The interest paid by business.

rental income The income received by property owners in the form of rent.

	BILLIONS OF DOLLARS	PERCENTAGE OF GDP
Total Gross Domestic Product	5950.7	100.0
National Income	4744.1	79.7
Compensation of employees	3525.2	59.2
Proprietors' income	404.5	6.8
Corporate profits	394.5	6.6
Net interest	415.2	7.0
Rental income	4.7	0.1
Depreciation	653.4	11.0
Indirect Taxes Minus Subsidies	564.4	9.5
Net Factor Payments to the Rest of the World	–11.2	–0.2

Source: See Table 22.2.

TABLE 22.3
Components of GDP, 1992: The Income Approach

It may seem odd that we must *add* depreciation to national income when we calculate GDP by the income approach, as Table 22.3 shows. But remember that we want a measure of *all* income, including income that results from the replacement of existing plant and equipment. Because national income does not include depreciation, to get to total income (gross domestic product) we need to add depreciation.

More specifically, firms subtract costs from revenues to calculate profits. One component of cost is depreciation. When a firm's capital becomes obsolete, it clearly incurs a cost, and that cost (depreciation) must be subtracted from revenues when computing profits. But depreciation does not involve the actual expenditure of any of the receipts of a firm. Thus, to equal GDP as calculated on the expenditure side, we must add depreciation back on the income side.

In 1992, depreciation accounted for $653.4 billion, or 11% of U.S. GDP.

INDIRECT TAXES MINUS SUBSIDIES The next income component in Table 22.3 is indirect taxes minus subsidies. In calculating final sales on the expenditures side, **indirect taxes**—sales taxes, customs duties, and license fees, for example—are included. These taxes must thus be accounted for on the income side.

indirect taxes Taxes like sales taxes, customs duties, and license fees.

A simple example will help to clarify this point. Suppose that the sales tax is 7% and that a firm sells 100,000 jellybeans for $100 plus tax. The total sales price is thus $107, and this is the value of output recorded in the expenditure approach to calculating GDP. Of this $107, $7 goes to pay the tax to the government, some goes to pay wages to the workers in the jellybean factory, and some goes to pay interest. The rest is profits plus depreciation of the firm.

In order to have the income and expenditure sides match, the sales tax must be recorded on the income side. If it were not included as part of income, then the basic rule that everyone's expenditure is someone else's income would be violated. After all, indirect taxes are an expenditure of the households or firms who buy things, but they are not income of firms that sell the products. (One way of thinking about indirect taxes is to consider them as income of the government.) We must thus add indirect taxes on the income side to make things balance.

Subsidies are payments made by the government for which it receives no goods or services in return. These subsidies are subtracted from national income to get GDP. (Remember that in the definition of GDP above is indirect taxes *minus* subsidies). For example, farmers receive substantial subsidies from the government. Subsidy payments to farmers are income to farm pro-

subsidies Payments made by the government for which it receives no goods or services in return.

FOREIGN INVESTMENT IN THE UNITED STATES AND U.S. INVESTMENT ABROAD

In recent years, a great deal of concern has been expressed over the fact that many U.S. assets have been sold to foreign investors. For example, Japanese investors have bought hotels, banks, movie companies, and office towers and have invested in factories, colleges, and retail stores in the United States. In 1990, a Japanese firm bought Rockefeller Center in New York City.

Should the United States be worried about profits earned on these investments leaving the country? Exactly how much of the United States' capital stock is owned by foreign investors? And how much of the capital stock of the rest of the world does the United States own?

As Table 1 shows, total foreign direct investment in the United States did indeed increase dramatically during the 1980s, jumping from $54.5 billion in 1979 to over $400 billion in 1991. Japan's holdings of U.S. capital assets increased from $3.5 billion at the end of 1979 to $86.7 billion at the end of 1991. That's $25 in 1991 for every dollar in 1979.

Interestingly, the largest foreign owner of U.S. assets is Great Britain. The British owned 26% of all foreign-owned assets in the United States in 1991. The Japanese were second at 21.3%, with the Dutch third at 15.7 percent.

Table 2 presents data on U.S. ownership of capital assets abroad. Currently, about three fourths of U.S. foreign holdings are in developed countries. About half of these are in Europe. The remaining one quarter of U.S. foreign holdings are located in developing countries, mostly in Latin America. Investment by U.S. multinational firms in developing countries has been very controversial, with some arguing that these companies exert political pressure on host governments. The most famous case of this type involved the alleged participation of IT&T in a military coup in Chile in the early 1970s.

At the beginning of the 1980s, the United States owned nearly 3.5 times as much capital in foreign countries as foreigners owned in the United States. By 1991, however, foreign direct investment in the United States was almost as large as U.S. direct investment abroad. Interestingly, in spite of the dramatic increases during the 1980s, foreign holdings of U.S. capital assets represented only 2.4% of total U.S. fixed capital in 1991.

TABLE 1 Foreign Direct Investment in the United States (Total Holdings at Year's End, 1979 and 1991)

	1979		1991	
	BILLIONS OF DOLLARS	PERCENT OF TOTAL	BILLIONS OF DOLLARS	PERCENT OF TOTAL
Country				
Canada	7.2	13.2	30.0	7.4
Europe	37.4	68.6	258.1	63.3
U. K.	9.8	18.0	106.1	26.0
Netherlands	NA	NA	63.8	15.7
Japan	3.5	6.4	86.7	21.3
Other	6.4	11.7	32.8	8.0
Total	**54.5**	**100.0**	**407.6**	**100.0**
Percent of total U.S. fixed capital	0.6	–	2.4	–

Note: NA = not applicable.
Source: Survey of Current Business, August 1981 and August 1992, and *Statistical Abstract of the United States,* 1992.

TABLE 2 U.S. Direct Investment in Foreign Countries (Total Holdings at Year's End, 1979 and 1991)

	1979		1991	
	BILLIONS OF DOLLARS	PERCENT OF TOTAL	BILLIONS OF DOLLARS	PERCENT OF TOTAL
Country				
Developed countries	138.6	74.2	335.4	74.5
Europe	82.6	44.2	224.6	49.9
Canada	40.2	21.5	68.5	15.2
Developing countries	44.5	23.8	111.6	24.8
Latin America	35.1	18.8	77.3	17.2
Other	3.6	1.9	3.2	0.7
Total	186.8	100.0	450.2	100.0

Source: Survey of Current Business, August 1981 and August 1992.

prietors and are thus part of national income, but they do not come from the sale of agricultural products and thus are not part of GDP. To balance the expenditure side with the income side, then, these subsidies must be subtracted on the income side.

NET FACTOR PAYMENTS TO THE REST OF THE WORLD   The last component in Table 22.3 is **net factor payments to the rest of the world**, which equals the payments of factor income (that is, income to the factors of production) to the rest of the world *minus* the receipts of factor income from the rest of the world. This item is added for the following reason. National income is defined as the income of factors of production *owned* by the country. GDP, however, is output produced by factors of production located *within* the country. Therefore, in calculating GDP via the income approach, we must add payments of factor income to the rest of the world (the income of foreign factors of production located within the country whose GDP we are calculating) and subtract receipts of factor income from the rest of the world (the citizens' income of the country whose GDP we are calculating that is earned abroad). In other words, national income includes some income that should not be counted in GDP—namely, the income a country's citizens earn abroad—and this income must be subtracted. In addition, national income does not include some income that is counted in GDP—namely, the foreigners' income in the country whose GDP we are calculating—and this income must be added. Table 22.3 shows that the value of net factor payments to the rest of the world was negative in 1992 (–$11.2 billion). This means that U.S. receipts of factor income from the rest of the world exceeded U.S. payments of factor income to the rest of the world in 1992.

As you can see in Table 22.3, U.S. GDP as calculated by the income approach was $5950.7 billion in 1992—the same amount that we calculated by using the expenditure approach.

> **net factor payments to the rest of the world** Payments of factor income to the rest of the world minus the receipt of factor income from the rest of the world.

From GDP to Personal Income

Although GDP is the most important item in national income accounting, some other concepts are also useful to know. Some of these are presented in Table 22.4. The first part of Table 22.4 shows how GNP is calculated from GDP. Remember that a country's GDP is total production by factors of production located within that country, while its GNP is total production by factors of production owned by that country. If we take U.S. GDP, add to it factor income earned by U.S. citizens from the rest of the world (receipts of factor income from the rest of the world), and subtract from it factor income earned in the United States by foreigners (payments of factor income to the rest of the world), we get GNP.

From GNP, we can calculate *net national product (NNP)*. First, recall that the expenditure approach to GDP includes gross investment as one of the components of GDP (and of GNP). Gross domestic product does not, therefore, account for the fact that some of the nation's capital stock is used up in the process of producing the nation's product. **Net national product** (NNP) is gross national product minus depreciation. In a sense, it is total product minus (or "net of") what is required to maintain the value of the capital stock. Because GDP does not take into account any depreciation of the capital stock that may have occurred, NNP is sometimes a better measure of how the economy is doing than is GDP.

To calculate national income, we subtract indirect taxes minus subsidies from NNP (i.e., we subtract indirect business taxes and add subsidies). We subtract indirect taxes because they are included in NNP but do not represent payments to fac-

> **net national product (NNP)** Gross national product minus depreciation; a nation's total product minus what is required to maintain the value of its capital stock.

	DOLLARS (BILLIONS)
GDP	5950.7
Plus: Receipts of factor income from the rest of the world	+128.8
Less: Payments of factor income to the rest of the world	−117.6
Equals: **GNP**	5961.9
Less: Depreciation	−653.4
Equals: **Net national product (NNP)**	5308.5
Less: Indirect taxes minus subsidies	−564.4
Equals: **National income**	4744.1
Less: Retained corporate earnings	
(Corporate profits minus dividend and corporate profit taxes)	−253.7
Less: Social insurance payments	−553.5
Plus: Personal interest income received from the government and consumers	+255.0
Plus: Transfer payments	+866.1
Equals: **Personal income**	5058.1
Less: Personal taxes	−627.3
Equals: **Disposable personal income**	4430.8

Note: Numbers do not add exactly because of rounding.
Source: See Table 2.2.

tors of production and are thus not part of national income. We add subsidies because they are payments to factors of production but are not included in NNP.

personal income The total income of households. Equals (national income) minus (retained corporate profits) minus (social insurance payments) plus (interest income received by households) plus (transfer payments to households). The income received by households after paying social insurance taxes but before paying personal income taxes.

Personal income is the total income of households. To calculate personal income from national income, two items are subtracted: (1) corporate profits minus dividends, and (2) social insurance payments. Both of these items need some explanation. First, some corporate profits are paid to households in the form of dividends, and dividends are clearly part of personal income. The profits that remain after dividends are paid—corporate profits minus dividends—are not paid to households as income. Therefore, corporate profits minus dividends must be subtracted from national income when computing personal income. Second, social insurance payments are payments made to the government, some by firms and some by employees. Because these payments are not received by households, they too must be subtracted from national income when computing personal income.

In addition, two items must be added to national income to calculate personal income: (1) personal interest income received from the government and consumers, and (2) transfer payments. As we have pointed out, interest payments made by the government and consumers (households) are not counted in GDP and thus are not reflected in national income figures.[4] But these payments are income received by households, so they must be added to national income when computing personal income.[5] Similarly, transfer payments are not counted in GDP because they do not represent the production of any goods or services. But social security checks and

---

[4]The reason that interest payments on government bonds are not included in national income, while interest payments on bonds of private firms are, is that government debt is typically the result of past wars, recessions, and overspending. In contrast, it is presumed that firms sell bonds to finance investment that does add to current production. Similarly, interest payments by households are not included in national income because they are not considered to add to current production.

[5]Note that households can both pay and receive interest. As a group, households receive more interest than they pay.

	DOLLARS (BILLIONS)
Disposable personal income	$4430.8
Less:	
Personal consumption expenditures	−4095.8
Interest paid by consumers to business	−112.1
Personal transfer payments to foreigners	−10.3
Equals: **Personal saving**	212.6
Personal saving as a percentage of disposable personal income:	4.8%

Source: See Table 22.2.

TABLE 22.5
Disposable Personal Income and Personal Saving, 1992

other cash benefits are obviously income received by households, and they must therefore also be added to national income when computing personal income.

Personal income is the income received by households before paying personal income taxes but after paying social insurance contributions. The amount of income that households have to spend or save is called **disposable personal income,** or **after-tax income.** It is equal to personal income minus personal taxes. (These calculations are summarized in Table 22.4.)

Because disposable personal income is the amount of income that households can spend or save, it is an important income concept. As Table 22.5 shows, there are three categories of spending: (1) personal consumption expenditures, (2) interest paid by consumers to business, and (3) personal transfer payments to foreigners. The amount of disposable personal income that is left after total personal spending is **personal saving.** For example, if your monthly disposable income is $500 and you spend $450 of it, you have $50 left over at the end of the month. Your personal saving is thus $50 for the month. Your personal saving level can be negative: If you earn $500 and spend $600 during the month, you have *dissaved* $100. In order to spend $100 more than you earn, of course, you will either have to borrow the $100 from someone, take the $100 from your savings account, or sell an asset that you own.

The **personal saving rate** is the percentage of disposable personal income that is saved, and it is an important indicator of household behavior. A low saving rate means that households are spending a large amount of their income. A high saving rate means that households are cautious in their spending behavior. As Table 22.5 shows, the U.S. personal saving rate in 1992 was 4.8 percent. Saving rates tend to rise during recessionary periods, when consumers become anxious about their future, and fall during boom times, as pent-up spending demand gets released.

This completes our discussion of the various components of gross domestic product, gross national product, net national product, national income, and personal income. We now turn to another key concept, the distinction between nominal and real GDP. In the process, we will also discuss the aggregate price level and how it is measured.

disposable, or after-tax, personal income Personal income minus personal income taxes. The amount that households have to spend or save.

personal saving The amount of disposable income that is left after total personal spending in a given period.

personal saving rate The percentage of personal disposable income that is saved. If the personal saving rate is low, households are spending a large amount relative to their incomes; if it is high, households are spending cautiously.

NOMINAL VERSUS REAL GDP

So far, we have looked at GDP measured in **current dollars,** or the current prices that one pays for things. When a variable is measured in current dollars, it is said to be described in *nominal terms.* **Nominal GDP** is thus GDP measured in current dollars—that is, with all components of GDP valued at their current prices.

current dollars The current prices that one pays for goods and services.

nominal GDP Gross domestic product measured in current dollars.

In many applications of macroeconomics, nominal GDP is not a very desirable measure of production. Why is this so? Assume that there is only one good—say, pizza—produced in the economy. Suppose that in both years 1 and 2, 100 units (slices) of pizza were produced. Production thus remained the same for year 1 and year 2. But suppose that the price of pizza increased from $1.00 per slice in year 1 to $1.10 per slice in year 2. Nominal GDP in year 1 is thus $100 (100 units × $1.00 per unit), and nominal GDP in year 2 is $110 (100 units × $1.10 per unit). Nominal GDP has thus increased by $10, even though no more slices of pizza were produced. If we use nominal GDP to measure growth, we can be misled into thinking that production has grown when all that has really happened is a rise in the price level, or inflation.

real GDP Gross domestic product measured in the prices of a fixed, or base, year.

A better measure of production is real GDP. **Real GDP** is GDP measured in the prices of a fixed, or *base,* year. With year 1 as the base year for our pizza economy, real GDP in year 1 is $100 (100 units × $1.00 per unit) and real GDP in year 2 is also $100 (100 units × $1.00 per unit). Using the base year price as the basis of our calculations in year 2, we see that the increase in real GDP from year 1 to year 2 is zero; there has been no change in production.

Distinguishing between Production and Price Increases

Let us now consider a more complicated example, one in which there is both a production increase and a price increase, to see how the concept of real GDP can help us distinguish between the two. Assume that pizza production in year 1 is 100 slices and 105 slices in year 2. Production has thus increased by five slices. Suppose that the price of the good increased from $1.00 in year 1 to $1.10 in year 2. Nominal GDP in year 1 is $100 (100 units × $1.00 per unit) and $115.50 in year 2 (105 units × $1.10 per unit). Nominal GDP has thus increased by $15.50 ($115.50 − $100.00). Real GDP in year 1 is $100 (100 units × $1.00 per unit), and $105 in year 2 (105 units × $1.00 per unit). Real GDP has thus increased by $5, an amount that correctly measures the actual increase in production. Production has increased by $5 when valued at year 1's price (five extra units × $1.00 per unit).

So far we have assumed that the economy produces only one good. The calculation of real GDP is somewhat more complicated when we consider an economy that produces more than one good, however. Table 22.6 shows what is involved in the calculation of real GDP when there are two goods. Each year we record the real (the physical volume of) production of each good and its price that year. When we multiply the amount of each good produced in a year by the price of the good in that year, we get the dollar value of the production of each good in the current year's prices. Nominal GDP is simply the sum of the dollar values. In Table 22.6, nominal GDP is $175.00 in year 1, $178.50 in year 2, and $201.00 in year 3.

TABLE 22.6
Calculation of Real GDP

	PRODUCTION			PRICE PER UNIT			VALUE OF NOMINAL GDP (PRODUCTION × PRICE PER UNIT)			VALUE OF REAL GDP (YEAR 1'S PRICES)		
	YEAR 1	YEAR 2	YEAR 3	YEAR 1	YEAR 2	YEAR 3	YEAR 1	YEAR 2	YEAR 3	YEAR 1	YEAR 2	YEAR 3
Good A	100	105	110	$1.00	$1.10	$1.10	$100.00	$115.50	$121.00	$100.00	$105.00	$110.00
Good B	50	45	50	$1.50	$1.40	$1.60	75.00	63.00	80.00	75.00	67.50	75.00
Total							$175.00	$178.50	$201.00	$175.00	$172.50	$185.00

If we take year 1 as the base year, real GDP in year 1 is the same as nominal GDP. In year 2, the amount of each good produced is multiplied by year 1's price of the good. Real GDP for year 2 is the sum of these values, where the values are calculated in year 1's prices: $1.00 as the price of good A and $1.50 as the price of good B. The total value of good A produced in year 2 is thus $105.00 (105 × $1.00) and the total value of good B produced in year 2 is $67.50 (45 × $1.50). Real GDP for the two-good economy in Table 22.6 thus fell from $175.00 in year 1 to $172.50 in year 2. The production of good A increased and the production of good B decreased. Although production of one good increased and production of the other good decreased, the value of real GDP shows that there was an overall drop in production from year 1 to year 2.

Real GDP for year 3 is the sum of the amount of each good produced in year 3 multiplied by the year 1 price of each good. As Table 22.6 shows, real GDP increased from $172.50 in year 2 to $185.00 in year 3. The production of each good increased by five units (from year 2). In year 1's prices, this is a total increase of $5.00 for good A and a total increase of $7.50 for good B. The sum of these two increases is the total increase in real GDP for year 3: $12.50.

The government uses thousands of categories of goods in the actual calculation of real GDP. The nominal amount spent in each category is divided by the price index (discussed in the next chapter) for that category, giving the amount spent in each category in the base year's prices. Real GDP is the sum of all these amounts. (Nominal GDP is simply the sum of the nominal amounts.)

The GDP Deflator

Using real and nominal GDP, we can calculate an overall measure of prices called the GDP deflator. The **GDP deflator** is the ratio of nominal GDP to real GDP multiplied by 100:

GDP deflator An overall measure of prices in the economy. Equal to the ratio of nominal GDP to real GDP multiplied by 100.

$$\text{GDP Deflator} = \frac{\text{Nominal GDP}}{\text{Real GDP}} \times 100.$$

For the data in Table 22.6, the GDP deflator in year 1 is simply 100, because year 1 is the base year. In year 2 the GDP deflator is 103.5 [(178.50 ÷ 172.50) × 100], and in year 3 it is 108.6 [(201.00 ÷ 185.00) × 100].

The percentage change in the GDP deflator is a measure of the overall rate of inflation in the economy. In the example above, the rate of inflation was 3.5% in year 2 and 4.9% in year 3. (To calculate the rate of inflation when the deflator rises from 100.0 to 103.5 we take [(103.5 − 100.0)/100] and multiply by 100. Similarly, [(108.6 − 103.5)/103.5] × 100 = 4.9%.) Note that an increase in the GDP deflator does not necessarily mean that *all* prices in the economy have risen. In Table 22.6, for example, the price of good B fell in year 2. The GDP deflator rose in year 2 because the increase in the price of good A more than offset the decrease in the price of good B.

As a final point, note that:

Nominal GDP generally grows faster than real GDP. Nominal GDP rises both from an increase in output and from an increase in the price level, while real GDP grows only from an increase in output. Nominal GDP usually rises faster than real GDP because the price level tends to increase over time.

The GDP deflator is only one of a number of measures of the overall price level. An alternative measure is the *consumer price index (CPI)*, which includes the prices for a "typical" basket of consumer goods. The CPI focuses on a narrower category of goods than does the GDP deflator. While the GDP deflator is the price index of *all* the goods produced in the country, both consumption goods and investment goods, the CPI represents the prices of only *consumption* goods. We discuss alternative measures of the price level and inflation in detail in the next chapter.

LIMITATIONS OF THE GDP CONCEPT

We generally think of increases in GDP as good. Indeed, increasing GDP (or preventing its decrease) is usually considered one of the chief goals of the government's macroeconomic policy. Because some serious problems arise when we try to use GDP as a measure of happiness or well-being, however, we now point out some of the limitations of the GDP concept as a measure of welfare.

GDP and Social Welfare

A decrease in crime clearly increases social welfare, but crime levels are not measured in GDP. If crime levels went down, society as a whole would be better off, but a decrease in crime is not an increase in output, and thus it is not reflected in GDP. Neither is an increase in leisure time. Yet, to the extent that households desire extra leisure time (rather than having it forced on them by a lack of jobs in the economy), an increase in leisure is also an increase in social welfare. Furthermore, some increases in social welfare are associated with a *decrease* in GDP. An increase in leisure during a time of full employment, for example, leads to a decrease in GDP because less time is spent on producing output.

In addition, most nonmarket and domestic activities, such as housework and child care, are not counted in GDP even though they amount to real production. However, if I decide to send my children to day care or hire someone to clean my house or to drive my car for me, GDP increases. The salaries of day-care staff, cleaning people, and chauffeurs are counted in GDP, but the time I spend doing the same things is not counted. In other words, a mere change of institutional arrangements, even though no more output is being produced, can show up as a change in GDP.

Furthermore, GDP seldom reflects losses or social ills. GDP accounting rules do not adjust for production that pollutes the environment. The more production there is, the larger is GDP, regardless of how much pollution results in the process.

GDP also has nothing to say about the distribution of output among individuals in a society. It does not distinguish, for example, between the case in which most output goes to a few people and the case in which output is evenly divided among all people. One cannot use GDP to measure the effects of redistributive policies (which take income from some people and give income to others). Such policies have no direct impact on GDP. GDP is also neutral about the kinds of goods that an economy produces. Symphony performances, handguns, cigarettes, professional football games, Bibles, soda pop, milk, economics textbooks, and comic books all get counted, regardless of the different weights that society might attach to these items.

TABLE 22.7
Per Capita GNP for Selected Countries, 1990

COUNTRY	U.S. DOLLARS
Switzerland	32,680
Finland	26,040
Japan	25,430
Sweden	23,660
Norway	23,120
West Germany*	22,320
Denmark	22,080
United States	21,790
Canada	20,470
France	19,490
Austria	19,060
Australia	17,000
United Kingdom	16,100
Spain	11,020
Israel	10,920
Greece	5,990
Portugal	4,900
Mexico	2,490
Botswana	2,040
Chile	1,940
Turkey	1,630
Jamaica	1,500
Jordan	1,240
Philippines	730
Bolivia	630
Egypt	600
Indonesia	570
Haiti	370
Mali	270
Mozambique	80

* Before unification

Source: World Bank, *World Development Report,* 1992.

In spite of these limitations, GDP is still a highly useful measure of economic activity and well-being. If you doubt this assertion, answer this simple question: Would you rather live in the United States of 200 years ago, when rivers were less polluted and crime rates were probably lower, or in the United States of today? Most people would say that they prefer the present. Even with all the "negatives," GDP per person and the average standard of living are dramatically higher today than they were 200 years ago.

The Underground Economy

Many transactions in the economy are simply missed in the calculation of GDP, even though in principle they should be counted. Most illegal transactions are missed unless they are "laundered" back into legitimate business. Income that is earned but not reported as income for tax purposes is usually missed, although some adjustments are made in the GDP calculations to take misreported income into account. The part of the economy that should be counted in GDP but is not is sometimes called the **underground economy.**

> **underground economy** The part of the economy in which transactions take place and in which income is generated that is unreported and therefore not counted in GDP.

Tax evasion is usually thought to be the major incentive for people to participate in the underground economy. A number of studies[6] have attempted to estimate the size of the U.S. underground economy, with estimates ranging from 5% to 30% of GDP. While these figures may seem quite dramatic, the estimated size of the U.S. underground economy is comparable to the size of the underground economy in most European countries and is probably much smaller than the size of the underground economy in the Eastern European countries. Estimates of Italy's underground economy range from 10% to 35% of Italian GDP. At the lower end of the scale, estimates for Switzerland range from 3% to 5 percent.

Why should we care about the underground economy? To the extent that GDP reflects only a part of economic activity rather than being a complete measure of what the economy produces, it is obviously misleading. Unemployment rates, for example, may be lower than officially measured if people work in the underground economy without reporting this fact to the government. Also, if the size of the underground economy varies between countries—as it certainly does—we can be misled when we compare GDP between countries. For example, Italy's GDP would be much higher if we considered its underground sector as part of the economy, while Switzerland's GDP would change very little.

Per Capita GDP/GNP

GDP and GNP are sometimes measured in per capita terms. **Per capita GDP or GNP** is simply a country's GDP or GNP divided by its population. It is a better measure of well-being for the average person than is total GDP or GNP. Table 22.7 lists the per capita GNP of various countries for 1990. Switzerland is the country with the highest per capita GNP, followed next by Finland, Japan, and Sweden. Many European countries, plus Canada and the United States, had per capita GNP values over $20,000 in 1990.

> **per capita GDP or GNP** A country's GDP or GNP divided by its population.

---

[6]See, for example, Carol Carlson, "The Underground Economy," *Survey of Current Business* (May 1984), pp. 21–37; and Edgar Feige, "How Big Is the Irregular Economy," *Challenge* (Nov./Dec. 1979).

LOOKING AHEAD

This chapter has introduced you to many of the key variables that macroeconomists are interested in, including GDP and its various components. There is, however, much more to be learned regarding the main data that macroeconomists use. In the next chapter we discuss the data on employment, unemployment, and the labor force, and in Chapters 26 and 27 we discuss the data on money and interest rates. Finally, in Chapter 37 we discuss in more detail the data on the relationship between the United States and the rest of the world.

SUMMARY

1. One of the main sources of data on the key variables in the macroeconomy are the national income and product accounts. These accounts provide an important conceptual framework that macroeconomists use to think about how the various pieces of the economy fit together.

Gross Domestic Product

2. *Gross domestic product* (GDP) is the key concept in national income accounting. GDP is the total market value of all *final goods and services* produced within a given period by factors of production located within the country. GDP excludes *intermediate goods*, because to include goods both when they are purchased as inputs and when they are sold as final products would be double counting and thus an overstatement of the value of production.

3. GDP excludes all transactions in which money or goods change hands but in which no new goods and services are produced. GDP includes the income of foreigners working in the United States and the profits that foreign companies earn in the United States. GDP excludes the income of U.S. citizens working abroad and profits earned by U.S. companies in foreign countries.

4. *Gross national product* (GNP) is the market value of all final goods and services produced during a given period by factors of production owned by a country's citizens.

Calculating GDP

5. The *expenditure approach* to computing GDP adds up the amount spent on all final goods and services during a given period. The four main categories of expenditures are *personal consumption expenditures (C), gross private domestic investment (I), government purchases of goods and services (G)*, and *net exports (EX − IM)*. The sum of these four equals GDP.

6. The three main components of personal consumption expenditures *(C)* are *durable goods, nondurable goods*, and *services.*

7. *Gross private domestic investment (I)* is the total investment made by the private sector in a given period of time. There are three kinds of investment: *nonresidential investment, residential investment*, and *changes in business inventories.* Gross investment does not take *depreciation*—the decrease in the value of assets—into account. *Net investment* is equal to gross investment minus depreciation.

8. Government purchases of goods and services *(G)* include expenditures by state, federal, and local governments for final goods and labor. The value of *net exports (EX − IM)* equals the differences between exports (sales to foreigners of U.S.-produced goods and services) and imports (U.S. purchases of goods and services from abroad).

9. Because every payment (expenditure) by a buyer is at the same time a receipt (income) for the seller, GDP can also be computed in terms of who receives it as income. This is the *income approach* to calculating gross domestic product. The GDP equation using the income approach is GDP = National Income + Depreciation + (Indirect Taxes − Subsidies) + Net Factor Payments to the Rest of the World.

From GDP to Personal Income

10. GNP minus depreciation is known as *net national product* (NNP). *National income* is the total amount earned by the factors of production in the economy; it is equal to NNP less indirect taxes minus subsidies. *Personal income* is the total income of households. *Disposable income* is what households have to spend or save after paying their taxes. The *personal saving rate* is the percentage of disposable income that is saved rather than spent.

Nominal versus Real GDP

11. GDP that is measured in current dollars (the current prices that one pays for goods) is called *nominal GDP.* If we use nominal GDP to measure growth, we can be misled into thinking that production has grown when all that has really happened is a rise in the price level, or inflation. A better measure of production is *real GDP*, which is GDP measured in the prices of a fixed, or base, year.

TABLE 23.1
Real GDP and
Unemployment Rates,
1929–1933 and 1980–1982

THE EARLY PART OF THE GREAT DEPRESSION, 1929–1933

	REAL GDP (BILLIONS OF 1987 DOLLARS)	PERCENTAGE CHANGE IN REAL GDP	UNEMPLOYMENT RATE	NUMBER OF UNEMPLOYED (MILLIONS)
1929	846.9		3.2	1.5
1930	767.2	-9.4	8.9	4.3
1931	701.6	-8.6	16.3	8.0
1932	607.4	-13.4	24.1	12.1
1933	594.9	-2.1	25.2	12.8

Note: Percentage fall in real GDP between 1929 and 1933 was 29.8 percent.

THE RECESSION OF 1980–1982

	REAL GDP (BILLIONS OF 1987 DOLLARS)	PERCENTAGE CHANGE IN REAL GDP	UNEMPLOYMENT RATE	NUMBER OF UNEMPLOYED (MILLIONS)	CAPACITY UTILIZATION (PERCENTAGE)
1979	3796.8		5.8	6.1	85.2
1980	3776.3	-0.5	7.0	7.6	80.9
1981	3843.1	1.8	7.5	8.3	79.9
1982	3760.3	-2.2	9.5	10.7	72.1

Note: Percentage fall in real GDP between 1979 and 1982 was 1.0 percent.
Sources: Historical Statistics of the United States and U.S. Department of Commerce, Bureau of Economic Analysis.

comparison. However, Table 23.1 does show that capacity utilization fell from 85.2% in 1979 to 72.1% in 1982. Clearly, although the recession in the early 1980s was severe, it did not come close to the severity of the Great Depression.

Defining and Measuring Unemployment

The most frequently discussed symptom of a recession is unemployment. In September of 1982, the United States' unemployment rate was over 10% for the first time since the 1930s. But although unemployment is widely discussed, most people are unaware of what unemployment statistics mean or how they are derived.

The unemployment statistics released to the press on the first Friday of each month are based on a survey of households conducted by the Bureau of Labor Statistics (BLS), a branch of the Department of Labor. Each month the BLS draws a sample of 65,000 households and completes interviews with all but about 2,500 of them. Each interviewed household answers questions regarding the work activity of household members 16 years of age or older during the calendar week that contains the twelfth of the month. (The survey is conducted in the week that follows the week that contains the twelfth of the month.)

If a household member 16 years of age or older worked one hour or more as a paid employee, either for someone else or in his or her own business or farm, that person is classified as **employed.** A household member is also considered employed if he or she worked 15 hours or more without pay in a family enterprise. Finally, a

employed Any person 16 years old or older (1) who works for pay, either for someone else or in his or her own business for one or more hours per week, (2) who works without pay for 15 or more hours per week in a family enterprise, or (3) who has a job but has been temporarily absent, with or without pay.

household member is counted as employed if he or she held a job from which he or she was temporarily absent due to illness, bad weather, vacation, labor-management disputes, or personal reasons, whether that person was paid or not.

Those who are not employed fall into one of two categories: (1) *unemployed* or (2) *not in the labor force.* To be considered **unemployed,** a person must be available for work and have made specific efforts to find work during the previous four weeks. Persons who are not looking for work, either because they do not want a job or because they have given up looking, are classified as **not in the labor force.** People not in the labor force include full-time students, retirees, individuals in institutions, and those staying home to take care of children or elderly parents.

The total **labor force** in the economy is the number of people employed plus the number of unemployed:

unemployed A person 16 years old or older who is not working, is available for work, and has made specific efforts to find work during the previous four weeks.

not in the labor force The subset of unemployed people who are not looking for work, either because they do not want a job or because they have given up looking.

labor force The number of people employed plus the number of unemployed.

$$\text{Labor Force} = \text{Employed} + \text{Unemployed.}$$

The total population 16 years of age or older is equal to the number of people in the labor force plus the number not in the labor force:

$$\text{Population} = \text{Labor Force} + \text{Not in Labor Force.}$$

unemployment rate The ratio of the number of people unemployed to the total number of people in the labor force.

With these numbers, several ratios can be calculated. The **unemployment rate** is the ratio of the number of people unemployed to the total number of people in the labor force:

$$\text{Unemployment Rate} = \frac{\text{Unemployed}}{\text{Employed} + \text{Unemployed}}.$$

In January 1993, the labor force contained 128.6 million people, 119.6 million of whom were employed and 9 million of whom were looking for work. The unemployment rate was thus 7 percent:

$$\frac{9.0}{119.6 + 9.0} = 7.0\%$$

labor-force participation rate The ratio of the labor force to the total population 16 years old or older.

The ratio of the labor force to the population 16 years old or over is called the **labor-force participation rate:**

$$\text{Labor-force Participation Rate} = \frac{\text{Labor Force}}{\text{Population}}.$$

Table 23.2 shows the relationship among these numbers for selected years since 1953. As you can see, 1982 has been added to show the effects of the recession. Although the unemployment rate has gone up and down, the labor-force participation rate has grown steadily since 1953. Most of this increase is due to the growth in the participation rate of women between the ages of 25 and 54.

Looking at column 3 in Table 23.2, you can see how many new workers the U.S. economy has managed to absorb in recent years. The number of employed workers increased by nearly 38 million between 1953 and 1982 and by 18 million between 1982 and 1992.

TABLE 23.2
Employed, Unemployed, and the Labor Force, 1953–1992

	(1) POPULATION 16 YEARS OLD OR OVER (MILLIONS)	(2) LABOR FORCE (MILLIONS)	(3) EMPLOYED (MILLIONS)	(4) UNEMPLOYED (MILLIONS)	(5) LABOR-FORCE PARTICIPATION RATE	(6) UNEMPLOYMENT RATE
1953	109.3	65.2	63.4	1.8	59.7	2.8
1960	119.1	71.5	67.6	3.9	60.0	5.5
1970	139.2	84.9	80.8	4.1	61.0	4.8
1980	169.3	108.5	100.9	7.6	64.1	7.0
1982	173.9	111.9	101.2	10.7	64.3	9.6
1992	193.1	128.5	119.2	9.4	66.5	7.3

Source: U.S. Department of Labor, Bureau of Labor Statistics.

Components of the Unemployment Rate

Because the unemployment rate is a single number, it can convey only a limited amount of information. To understand the level of unemployment better, we must look at unemployment rates across groups of people, regions, and industries.

UNEMPLOYMENT RATES FOR DIFFERENT DEMOGRAPHIC GROUPS   Marked differences in rates of unemployment exist across demographic groups. Table 23.3 shows the unemployment rate for November 1982—the worst month of the recession in 1982—and for January 1993, broken down by race, sex, and age. In November of 1982, when the overall unemployment rate hit 10.8%, the rate for whites stood at 9.2%, while the rate for blacks stood at more than twice that level—19.5 percent.

During the recession in 1982, men fared worse than women. In November 1982, 9.5% of all white men, but only 8.9% of all white women, were unem-

		NOVEMBER 1982	JANUARY 1993
Total		10.8	7.0
White		9.2	6.2
Men	20 years and over	9.5	5.8
	16–19 years	24.1	18.1
Women	20 years and over	8.9	5.5
	16–19 years	19.5	14.9
Black		19.5	14.2
Men	20 years and over	21.0	13.0
	16–19 years	54.9	39.0
Women	20 years and over	17.9	12.5
	16–19 years	46.9	38.5

TABLE 23.3
Unemployment Rates by Demographic Group (Race, Sex, and Age), 1982 and 1993

Source: U.S. Department of Labor, Bureau of Labor Statistics.

ployed. For blacks: 21% of black men and 17.9% of black women were unemployed. Teenagers between 16 and 19 years of age fared worst. Black males between 16 and 19 experienced an unemployment rate of 54.9% in 1982. The figure was nearly as high (46.9%) for black females in the same age bracket.

While the rates were much lower for all groups in January 1993, the pattern was similar. The highest unemployment rates were for black teenagers—39% for black males and 38.5% for black females. Among both blacks and whites, the January 1993 unemployment rate for women was slightly lower than the rate for men.

The main point of Table 23.3 is that an unemployment rate of 7% does not mean that every group in society has a 7% unemployment rate. In fact,

> There are large differences in unemployment rates across demographic groups.

UNEMPLOYMENT RATES IN STATES AND REGIONS   Unemployment rates vary by geographical location. For a variety of reasons, not all states and regions have the same level of unemployment. For one thing, states and regions have different combinations of industries, which do not all grow and decline at the same time and at the same rate. For another, the labor force is not completely mobile—that is, workers often cannot or do not want to pack up and move to take advantage of job opportunities in other parts of the country.

The last 20 years have seen remarkable changes in the relative prosperity of regions. None have been quite as dramatic as the changing fortunes of the Northeast and the oil-rich Southwest. During the early 1970s, the Northeast (and New England in particular) was hit by a serious decline in its industrial base. Textile mills, leather goods plants, and furniture factories closed up in the face of foreign competition or moved south to states with lower wages. During the recession of 1975, Massachusetts and Michigan had very high unemployment rates (11.2% and 12.5% respectively). Riding the crest of rising oil prices, Texas had one of the lowest unemployment rates at that time (5.6%) (see Table 23.4).

During the recession of 1982, Texas continued to do well, and the fortunes of Massachusetts took a sharp turn for the better. In fact, the unemployment rate in Massachusetts went from nearly three points above the national average during the 1975 recession to nearly two points below the national average during the 1982 recession.

By 1987, things had changed dramatically. Although not shown in Table 23.4, Massachusetts had one of the lowest unemployment rates in the country in

TABLE 23.4
Regional Differences in Unemployment Rates during Recessions, 1975, 1982, and 1991

	1975	1982	1991
U.S. average	8.5	9.7	6.7
California	9.9	9.9	7.5
Florida	10.7	8.2	7.3
Illinois	7.1	11.3	7.1
Massachusetts	11.2	7.9	9.0
Michigan	12.5	15.5	9.2
New Jersey	10.2	9.0	6.6
New York	9.5	8.6	7.2
North Carolina	8.6	9.0	5.8
Ohio	9.1	12.5	6.4
Texas	5.6	6.9	6.6

Source: Statistical Abstract of the United States, various editions.

1987—an amazing 2.8%—and Texas—at 8.5%—had one of the highest. In Massachusetts, high-technology firms such as Wang Laboratories and Digital Equipment, two firms that employed a total of over 100,000 people, had grown dramatically. In contrast, the fall in crude oil prices from over $30 per barrel to under $15 per barrel in the early 1980s forced the oil-based economy of Texas into a deep and prolonged recession. Then, in 1991, Massachusetts experienced yet another reversal of fortune, with an unemployment rate of 9 percent.

The economy of Michigan is heavily tied to the fortunes of the automobile industry. During the recession of 1982, Michigan had the highest unemployment rate in the country at 15.5%. Not only did the automobile industry suffer from the decline in the U.S. economy, it also faced stiff foreign competition, primarily from Japan. Michigan also suffered in 1991, with an unemployment rate of 9.2 percent.

The important point here is that:

> The unemployment rate does not tell the whole story. A low national rate of unemployment does not mean that the entire nation is growing and producing at the same rate.

UNEMPLOYMENT RATES IN DIFFERENT INDUSTRIES   Unemployment rates also differ from industry to industry. Table 23.5 shows that in 1992 workers in the construction industry experienced unemployment rates over twice the national average. The three lowest unemployment rates were for finance and service industries (6.5%), transportation and public utilities (5.9%), and government (2.9%).

DISCOURAGED-WORKER EFFECTS   Remember that people who decide to stop looking for work are classified as having dropped out of the labor force rather than as being unemployed. During recessions people often become so discouraged about ever finding a job that they stop looking. This actually lowers the unemployment rate, because those no longer looking for work are no longer counted as being unemployed.

A simple example can demonstrate how this **discouraged-worker effect** lowers the unemployment rate. Suppose that there are 10 million unemployed out of a labor force of 100 million. This would mean an unemployment rate of 10/100 = .10, or 10 percent. If 1 million of these 10 million unemployed people simply stop looking for work and drop out of the labor force, there would be 9 million

discouraged-worker effect The decline in the measured unemployment rate that results when people who want to work but cannot find jobs grow discouraged and stop looking, thus dropping out of the ranks of the unemployed and the labor force.

TABLE 23.5
Unemployment in Different Industries, 1992

	OCTOBER 1992
Mining	8.6
Construction	16.0
Manufacturing	8.3
Durable goods	9.2
Nondurable goods	7.2
Transportation and public utilities	5.9
Wholesale and retail trade	8.1
Finance and service industries	6.5
Agriculture	12.4
Government	2.9
National average	7.4

Source: Bureau of Labor Statistics, *Monthly Labor Review* (December 1992).

TABLE 23.6
Average Duration of
Unemployment, 1979–1992

	WEEKS
1979	10.8
1980	11.9
1981	13.7
1982	15.6
1983	20.0
1984	18.2
1985	15.6
1986	14.8
1987	13.7
1988	13.5
1989	11.9
1990	12.1
1991	13.8
1992*	19.4

Note: As of October 1992.
Source: Statistical Abstract of the United States, 1987 and Bureau of Labor Statistics, *Monthly Labor Review* (December 1992).

unemployed out of a labor force of 99 million. The unemployment rate would then drop to 9/99 = .091, or 9.1 percent.

The Bureau of Labor Statistics survey provides some evidence on the size of the discouraged-worker effect. Respondents who indicate that they have stopped searching for work are asked why they have done so. If the respondent cites inability to find employment as the sole reason for not searching, that person might reasonably be classified as a discouraged worker.

The number of discouraged workers seems to hover around 1% of the labor force in normal times. During the 1980–1982 recession, the number of discouraged workers increased steadily to a peak of 1.5 percent. By the end of the first quarter of 1991, the recession of 1990–1991 had produced 997,000 discouraged workers.[3] Some economists argue that adding the number of discouraged workers to the number who are now classified as unemployed gives a better picture of the unemployment situation.

THE DURATION OF UNEMPLOYMENT   The unemployment rate measures unemployment at a given point in time. It tells us nothing about how long the average unemployed worker is out of work.

Table 23.6 shows that during recessionary periods, not only are there more workers unemployed, but the average duration of unemployment rises. In fact, between 1979 and 1983, the average duration of unemployment rose from 10.8 weeks to 20 weeks. The slow growth following the 1990–1991 recession resulted in an increase in duration of unemployment to 19.4 weeks by October 1992.

The Costs of Unemployment

In the Employment Act of 1946, the Congress of the United States declared that it was the

> continuing policy and responsibility of the federal government to use all practicable means. . . to promote maximum employment, production, and purchasing power.

In 1978, Congress passed the Full Employment and Balanced Growth Act, commonly referred to as the *Humphrey-Hawkins Act,* which formally established a specific unemployment target of 4 percent.

Why should full employment be a policy objective of the federal government? What costs does unemployment impose on society?

SOME UNEMPLOYMENT IS INEVITABLE   Before we discuss the costs of unemployment, it must be noted that some unemployment is simply part of the natural workings of the labor market. Remember that in order to be classified as unemployed, a person must be looking for a job. Every year, thousands of people enter the labor force for the first time. Some have dropped out of high school, some are high school or college graduates, and still others are finishing graduate programs. At the same time, new firms are starting up and others are expanding and creating new jobs, while other firms are contracting or going out of business. In April 1991, for example, the Defense Department announced the closing of 31 major military installations. As a result of these closings, tens of thousands of civilian workers were forced to find other work, and businesses near those bases contracted. In short, the economy is dynamic: People grow and acquire skills and the structure of the job market is continuously changing.

---

[3] *New York Times,* April 6, 1991, p. 1.

At any given moment, then, there is a set of job seekers and a set of jobs that must be matched with one another. It is important that the right people end up in the right jobs. The right job for a person will depend on that person's particular skills, his or her preferences regarding work environment (large firm or small, formal or informal), where he or she lives, and his or her willingness to commute. At the same time, firms want workers that can meet the requirements of the job and grow with the company.

In order to make a good match, workers must acquire information on job availability, wage rates, location, and work environment. Firms must acquire information on worker availability and skills. This information-gathering process is time consuming and resource consuming. The search process may involve travel, interviewing, preparation of a résumé, telephone calls, and hours spent going through the newspaper. But to the extent that these efforts lead to a better match of workers and jobs, they are well spent. Specifically, as long as the gains to firms and workers exceed the costs of search, the result is efficient.

FRICTIONAL AND STRUCTURAL UNEMPLOYMENT When the BLS does its survey about work activity during the week containing the twelfth of each month, it interviews many people who are involved in the normal search for work. Some of these people are involved either in entering the labor force or in switching jobs. This unemployment is both natural and beneficial for the economy.

The portion of unemployment that is due to the normal working of the labor market is called **frictional unemployment.** The frictional unemployment rate can never be zero. It may, however, change over time. As jobs become more and more differentiated and the number of required skills increases, matching skills and jobs becomes more complex, and the frictional unemployment rate may rise.

The concept of frictional unemployment is somewhat abstract because it is hard to know just what the phrase "the normal working of the labor market" means. The industrial structure of the U.S. economy is continually changing. Manufacturing, for instance, has yielded part of its share of total employment to services and to finance, insurance, and real estate. Within the manufacturing sector, the steel and textiles industries have contracted sharply, while high-technology sectors, such as electronic components, have expanded.

Although the unemployment that arises from such structural shifts could be classified as frictional, it is usually called **structural unemployment.** The term *frictional unemployment* is used to denote short-run job/skill matching problems, problems that last a few weeks. *Structural unemployment* denotes longer-run adjustment problems—those that tend to last for years.

Although structural unemployment is to be expected in a dynamic economy, it is no less painful to the workers who experience it. In some ways, those who lose their jobs because their skills are obsolete are the ones who experience the greatest pain. The fact that structural unemployment is natural and inevitable does not mean that it costs society nothing.

Economists sometimes use the phrase **natural rate of unemployment** to refer to unemployment that occurs as a normal part of the functioning of the economy. This concept is also somewhat vague, because "naturally" is not a precise word. It is probably best to think of the natural rate as the sum of the frictional rate and the structural rate. Estimates of the natural rate range from 4% to 7%, but most labor market analysts assume that it lies somewhere in the 5% to 6% range.

> **frictional unemployment** The portion of unemployment that is due to the normal working of the labor market; used to denote short-run job/skill matching problems.

> **structural unemployment** The portion of unemployment that is due to changes in the structure of the economy that result in a significant loss of jobs in certain industries.

> **natural rate of unemployment** The unemployment that occurs as a normal part of the functioning of the economy. Sometimes taken as the sum of frictional unemployment and structural unemployment.

CYCLICAL UNEMPLOYMENT AND LOST OUTPUT Although some unemployment is indeed "natural," there are times when the unemployment rate seems to be above the natural rate. In 1979, the unemployment rate stood at 5.8%, but it did not fall below 6% again until 1987, a full eight years later. In the meantime, the United States experienced a major recession, during which the unemployment rate rose substantially. The increase in unemployment that occurs during recessions and depressions is called **cyclical unemployment.**

cyclical unemployment The increase in unemployment that occurs during recessions and depressions.

In one sense, an increase in unemployment during a recession is simply a manifestation of a more fundamental problem. The basic problem is that firms are producing less. Remember that a recession entails a decline in real GDP, or real output. When firms cut back and produce less, they employ fewer workers and less capital. Thus, the first and most direct cost of a recession is the loss of real goods and services that otherwise would have been produced.

Never was the loss of output more dramatic than during the Great Depression. In Table 23.1 you saw that real output fell about 30% between 1929 and 1933. It is, of course, the real output of the economy that matters most—the food we eat, the medical care we get, the cars we drive, the movies we watch, the new houses that are built, the pots we cook in, and the education that we receive. When output falls by 30%, life changes dramatically for a lot of people.

During the recession of 1980–1982, the decline in real GDP was significant but not nearly as dramatic. Consider Table 23.1 again. Had real GDP grown at 3% each year from 1979 on—a good, but not outstanding, growth rate—real GDP would have been $3910.7 billion in 1980, $4028 in 1981, and $4148.9 in 1982. Comparing these values to the actual values presented in Table 23.1, the differences in output are $134.4 billion in 1980, $184.9 billion in 1981, and $388.6 billion in 1982. The $388.6 billion in 1982 is obviously a large number. It corresponds to $1672 per man, woman, and child in the United States. These figures show the substantial amount of output that would have been produced had the economy grown at the rate of 3% per year rather than actually contracting between 1979 and 1982.

SOCIAL CONSEQUENCES The costs of recessions and depressions are neither evenly distributed across the population nor easily quantifiable. The real costs of unemployment, whether in 1933, 1982, or 1993, are borne by the unemployed themselves.

The social consequences of the depression of the 1930s are perhaps the hardest to comprehend. Most people who are alive today did not live through the Great Depression and can only read about it in books or hear stories told by parents and grandparents. Few emerged from this period unscathed. At the bottom were the poor and the fully unemployed, about 25% of the labor force. But even those who kept their jobs found themselves working part time. Many people lost all or part of their savings as the stock market crashed and thousands of banks failed.

Congressional committees heard story after story. From Cincinnati, where the labor force totaled about 200,000, 48,000 were wholly unemployed, 40,000 more were on short time, and relief payments to the needy averaged $7 to $8 per week:

> Relief is given to a family one week and then they are pushed off for a week in the hope that somehow or other the breadwinner may find some kind of work. . . . We are paying no rent at all. That, of course, is a very difficult problem because we are continually having evictions, and social workers. . . are hard put to find places for people whose furniture has been put out on the street.[4]

---

[4]U.S. Senate Hearings before a subcommittee of the Committee of Manufacturers, 72nd Congress, first session (1931), p. 239. Cited in Lester Chandler, *America's Greatest Depression, 1929–1941* (Harper and Row, 1970), p. 43.

From Birmingham, Alabama, in 1932:

> . . . we have about 108,000 wage and salary workers in my district. Of that number, it is my belief that not exceeding 8000 have their normal incomes. At least 25,000 men are altogether without work. Some of them have not had a stroke of work for more than 12 months. Perhaps 60,000 or 70,000 are working from one to five days a week, and practically all have had serious cuts in wages and many of them do not average over $1.50 per day.[5]

From a transient labor camp in California in 1932:

> Many of them were laborers, but there were also businessmen and tradesmen. There were many professional men and many high-school and college graduates. . . . We have graduates of some of the largest colleges in the United States. . . . We have a doctor and a dentist. . . . We have men who had been bankers and brokers. . . . many gave a false name as a matter of pride.[6]

One historian summarized the Depression this way:

> Mass unemployment is both a statistic and an empty feeling in the stomach. To fully comprehend it, you have to both see the figures and feel the emptiness.[7]

Economic hardship accompanied the more recent recessions as well. Between 1979 and 1983, the number of people officially classified as living in poverty in the United States rose from 26.1 million (11.7% of the population) to 35.5 million (15.3%). In addition to economic hardship, prolonged unemployment may also bring with it a number of social and personal ills: anxiety, depression, a deterioration of physical and psychological health, drug abuse (including alcoholism), and suicide.

LOWER INVESTMENT AND LONG-TERM GROWTH   In addition to lost output today and serious, immediate social consequences, recessions may lead to lost output in the future. When the economy experiences a recession, the level of investment tends to fall. (We cover the determinants of investment spending in later chapters.) Common sense should tell you, however, that declining real output tends to lower the rate of investment and capital production.

The production of capital—that is, *investment*—is one of the keys to future economic growth and progress. Thus, eliminating or reducing contractions in output could increase the level of investment and ultimately the rate of growth.

The Benefits of Recessions

Do recessions have any benefits? Yes: Recessions are likely to slow down the rate of inflation. We saw in Figure 21.8 that there have been two serious inflationary periods since 1970: 1974–1975 and 1979–1981. Each of these periods was followed by a recession during which the rate of inflation decreased. As Table 23.7 shows, the inflation rate fell from a 1974 rate of 11.1% to a rate of 5.8% in 1976. In 1983, the inflation rate also fell, to 3.0%, from a 1980 rate of 13.5 percent.

In short, it appears that recessions do help to counteract inflation, but much more analysis is needed before we can understand just why this is so. (We will do this analysis in Chapter 29.) The main point here is simply that:

Recessions may help to reduce inflation.

---

[5]Senate Hearings, in Lester Chandler, *Depression*, p. 43.

[6]Senate Hearings, in Lester Chandler, *Depression*, p. 47.

[7]Cabell Phillips, *From the Crash to the Blitz, 1929–1939* (New York: Macmillan, 1969), p. xii.

TABLE 23.7
Inflation Rates, 1974–1976
and 1980–1983

		INFLATION RATE
Recession begins →	1974	11.1
	1975	9.2
	1976	5.8
Recession begins →	1980	13.5
	1981	10.3
	1982	6.1
	1983	3.0

Source: See Table 23.9.

In addition, some argue that recessions may increase efficiency by driving the least efficient firms in the economy out of business and forcing surviving firms to trim waste and manage their resources better. Finally, as we will discuss in detail in Chapter 37, a recession leads to a decrease in the demand for imports, which improves a nation's balance of payments (that is, its record of trade with other countries).

INFLATION

Ups in the business cycle often, but not always, seem to encourage inflation. Table 23.8 shows the rate of inflation during the three most recent periods of expansion. The inflation rate rose from 3.3% to 11.1% from 1972 to 1974. The general trend in inflation was also upward from 1976 to 1980. The sustained growth that began in 1983, however, did not seem to bring rapid inflation with it. (Wars, too, are frequently accompanied by inflation. As the Issues and Applications box titled "Wars and Inflation" explains, however, this was not the case following the Persian Gulf War in 1991.)

Why is inflation a problem? If you understand that wages and salaries, as well as other forms of income, increase along with prices during periods of inflation, you will understand that this question is more subtle than you might think at first. If my income doubles and the prices of the things I buy double, am I any worse off? I can buy exactly the same things that I bought yesterday, so to the extent that my well-being depends on what I am able to buy, the answer is no.

However, incomes and prices do not all increase at the same rate during inflations. For some people, income increases faster than prices; for others, prices increase faster. Consequently, some people actually benefit from inflations, while others are hurt.

The remainder of this chapter focuses on the problem of inflation: its measurement, its costs, and the gains and losses experienced during inflationary periods.

TABLE 23.8
Inflation during the Last
Three Expansions

	INFLATION RATE
1972	3.3
1973	6.1
1974	11.1
1976	5.8
1977	6.5
1978	7.6
1979	11.3
1980	13.5
1984	4.1
1985	3.6
1986	1.9
1987	3.6
1988	4.1
1989	4.8

Source: See Table 23.9.

Defining and Measuring Inflation

What is inflation? Clearly, not all price increases constitute an inflation. Prices of individual goods and services are determined in a number of ways. In competitive markets, the interaction of many buyers and many sellers— the operation of supply and demand—determines prices. In imperfectly

ISSUES AND APPLICATIONS
WARS AND INFLATION

Historically, periods of high inflation in the United States have occurred during and after wars. Yet, as the following excerpt points out, this did not seem to be the case during or after the brief Persian Gulf War in 1991:

From the Revolution to Vietnam, virtually every American war has sparked a round of inflation. But the Persian Gulf War looks as if it will be an exception. A barrage of signals—including cheaper oil and raw materials, softer prices at factories, swelling cattle herds and shrinking bonuses for sales workers—suggests that inflation may retreat.

If inflation stays low, the economy would benefit. The United States would fall closer in line with such rich and powerful nations as Germany and Japan, whose inflation rates have averaged half of the United States rate, or less, in the last decade. And long-term interest rates could edge down as investors' fears of future inflation eases. . . .

Among the reasons the Persian Gulf War seems not to have been inflationary are that it lasted only 42 days, quickly contained the

TABLE 1
Wars and Prices
Price increases during the period of inflation caused by war.

WAR	% PRICES ROSE	WAR	% PRICES ROSE
Revolutionary War 1775–1783	201	**Spanish-American War** 1898	8
War of 1812 1812–1815	39	**World War I** 1917–1918	126
Mexican War 1846–1848	8	**World War II** 1941–1945	108
Civil War (Union) 1861–1865	117	**Korean War** 1950–1953	2
Civil War (Confederacy) 1861–1865	9,210	**Vietnam War** 1964–1973	69

Source: Claudia D. Goldin, Harvard University.

threat to oil supplies, was financed in part by American allies and was fought with arms taken from inventory. Ordinarily, military spending overheats the economy as production surges to supply the war effort, leaving fewer goods available for civilian consumption. As a result prices rise.

Source: Sylvia Nasar, "An Exception to the Rule of War: Inflation Threat is Receding," *New York Times,* March 10, 1991.

competitive markets, prices are determined by producers' decisions. (This is the core of microeconomic theory.)

In any economy, prices are continuously changing as markets adjust to changing conditions. Lack of rain may dry up corn and wheat fields, thus reducing supply and pushing up the price of agricultural products. At the same time, high levels of production by oil producers may be driving down the price of oil and petroleum products. Simultaneously, the United Auto Workers may be negotiating a contract with the Ford Motor Company that raises (or lowers) wage rates.

When the price of one good rises, that price increase may or may not be part of a larger inflation. As we explained earlier, an **inflation** is an increase in the overall price level. It happens when many prices increase simultaneously. We measure inflation by looking at a large number of goods and services and calculating the average increase in their prices during some period of time. A **deflation** is a decrease in the overall price level. It occurs when many prices decrease simultaneously.

inflation An increase in the overall price level.

deflation A decrease in the overall price level.

It is often useful to distinguish between a *one-time* increase in the overall price level and an increase in the overall price level that continues over a period of time. For example, the overall price level could rise 10% in a single month and stop rising, or it could increase steadily over some years. Economists often use the term *inflation* to refer only to increases in the price level that continue over some significant period of time. We will refer to such periods as periods of **sustained inflation.**

In the previous chapter we distinguished between "real" and "nominal" GDP. Recall that *nominal GDP* is the value of the goods and services produced in an economy in a given year. If we want to measure *real GDP*, we must adjust for any changes in prices that occur from year to year. For example, if all prices double, but total output remains the same, nominal GDP will double. If we want to measure the real increase in output and calculate real GDP, we need to eliminate the effects of the price increase on GDP. As we saw in the last chapter, these adjustments can be made by using a single set of prices to value GDP in different years.

sustained inflation An increase in the overall price level that continues over a significant period of time.

PRICE INDEXES   One way to measure changes in the overall price level is to calculate a **price index,** which shows how the average price of a bundle of goods changes over time. Government agencies compute a number of different price indexes each month. Before we discuss any individual index, however, we need to describe how price indexes are constructed.

To construct a price index, we must first identify the specific set of prices that we are concerned with. Suppose that only three goods, X, Y, and Z, are produced in an economy. Figure 23.1 constructs an index based on changes in the prices of

price index A measurement showing how the average price of a bundle of goods changes over time.

FIGURE 23.1
Constructing a Price Index

	Units consumed	Price period 1	Price period 2	Percentage change in price
Good X	2	$1.00	$1.50	50
Good Y	1	$3.00	$4.00	33
Good Z	3	$2.00	$4.00	100

Bundle = 2 units of X + 1 unit of Y + 3 units of Z

Bundle price, period 1 = $(2 \times \$1) + (1 \times \$3) + (3 \times \$2) = \$11$

Bundle price, period 2 = $(2 \times \$1.50) + (1 \times \$4) + (3 \times \$4) = \$19$

Price index (period 1 = base period)

$$\text{Period 1 index} = \frac{\text{bundle price 1}}{\text{bundle price 1}} \times 100 = \frac{\$11}{\$11} \times 100 = 100$$

$$\text{Period 2 index} = \frac{\text{bundle price 2}}{\text{bundle price 1}} \times 100 = \frac{\$19}{\$11} \times 100 = 172.7$$

Inflation = percent change in price index from period 1 to period 2:

$$\text{Percent change} = \frac{\text{period 2 index} - \text{period 1 index}}{\text{period 1 index}} \times 100$$

$$= \frac{172.7 - 100}{100} \times 100 = 72.7\%$$

The price level has risen 72.7 percent.

these goods. Between period 1 and period 2, the price of X went up 50%, the price of Y went up 33.3%, and the price of Z went up 100 percent. The question is: How much did the *general* level of prices increase?

One way to calculate the increase in the general level of prices is to take the simple average of all price increases. The simple average of 50, 33.3, and 100 is $(50 + 33.3 + 100)/3 = 61.1$. But this method assumes that all price changes are of equal importance. If we are interested in constructing an index that measures the increase in the cost of living, we would not want to assign equal weight to rent and pepper. Most of us spend a tiny fraction of our income on pepper, and even if the price of pepper were to quadruple, the change would have little impact on the cost of living. But many people spend a sizable portion of their income on rent, so a doubling of rents would have a major impact on the cost of living.

To take into account the relative importance of various items in the construction of a price index, we need to look at the quantity of each item consumed or produced. Let us assume that we are interested in the cost of living in an economy where the average household consumes two units of X, one unit of Y, three units of Z, and nothing else. In Figure 23.1, we calculate the price of that "bundle" of goods in each of the two periods. In period 1, the average bundle of consumer goods cost $11. In period 2, the same bundle cost $19.

To construct a price index using the bundle approach, we must first choose a base year. Once a base year is chosen and an index is constructed, the index can be used to compare any given year with any other year. To construct the index in Figure 23.1, we will choose period 1 as the base year. The index for each period is defined as the bundle price in that year divided by the bundle price in the base year multiplied by 100. Thus, the index for the base year is always equal to 100—the bundle price (base year) divided by the bundle price (base year) equals one, and one times 100 equals 100. To determine the index for period 2, we use the same formula: (bundle price/base year bundle price) $\times$ 100 = 19/11 $\times$ 100 = 172.7. A quick glance at Figure 23.1 shows us that the price level has increased by $[(172.7 - 100)/100] \times 100$, or 72.7 percent.

As we noted earlier, the particular index chosen—or the particular bundle used to construct the index—depends on what the index is to be used for. Let us now describe briefly three commonly used indexes that are used to measure inflation.

Consumer Price Index (CPI) The index most often used to measure inflation is the **Consumer Price Index,** commonly referred to in the press as the **CPI.** The CPI was first constructed during World War I as a basis for adjusting shipbuilders' wages, which were controlled by the government during the war.

Currently, the CPI is computed by the Bureau of Labor Statistics every month, using a bundle that is meant to represent the "market basket" purchased monthly by the typical urban consumer. The quantities of each good in the bundle are based on extensive surveys of consumers.

Table 23.9 shows values of the CPI since 1950. The percentage changes in the table on the left are calculated from the index on the right. For example, from 1970 to 1971, the CPI increased from 38.8 to 40.5. To calculate the percentage change, we simply take $[(40.5 - 38.8)/38.8] \times 100$, which is $[1.7/38.8] \times 100 = .044 \times 100 = 4.4\%$.

One problem with any fixed-bundle index as a measure of cost of living is that it does not account for substitutions that consumers might make in response to price changes. If the price of bananas were to triple, most people would simply stop buying them and switch to apples or some other substitute. Thus, if good substitutes are available, a specific price increase may have only a minimal effect on the cost of living.

consumer price index (CPI) A price index computed each month by the Bureau of Labor Statistics using a bundle that is meant to represent the "market basket" purchased monthly by the typical urban consumer.

TABLE 23.9

U.S. Consumer Price Indexes and Inflation Rates, 1950–1992

PERCENTAGE CHANGES IN THE CONSUMER PRICE INDEX				ANNUAL INDEXES			
1950	1.3	1972	3.2	1950	24.1	1972	41.8
1951	7.9	1973	6.2	1951	26.0	1973	44.4
1952	1.9	1974	11.0	1952	26.5	1974	49.3
1953	0.8	1975	9.1	1953	26.7	1975	53.8
1954	0.7	1976	5.8	1954	26.9	1976	56.9
1955	-0.4	1977	6.5	1955	26.8	1977	60.6
1956	1.5	1978	7.6	1956	27.2	1978	65.2
1957	3.3	1979	11.3	1957	28.1	1979	72.6
1958	2.8	1980	13.5	1958	28.9	1980	82.4
1959	0.7	1981	10.3	1959	29.1	1981	90.9
1960	1.7	1982	6.2	1960	29.6	1982	96.5
1961	1.0	1983	3.2	1961	29.9	1983	99.6
1962	1.0	1984	4.3	1962	30.2	1984	103.9
1963	1.3	1985	3.6	1963	30.6	1985	107.6
1964	1.3	1986	1.9	1964	31.0	1986	109.6
1965	1.6	1987	3.6	1965	31.5	1987	113.6
1966	2.9	1988	4.1	1966	32.4	1988	118.3
1967	3.1	1989	4.8	1967	33.4	1989	124.0
1968	4.2	1990	5.4	1968	34.8	1990	130.7
1969	5.5	1991	4.2	1969	36.7	1991	136.2
1970	5.7	1992	3.0	1970	38.8	1992	140.3
1971	4.4			1971	40.5		

Source: Economic Report of the President, 1993, and updates.

A *fixed-weight*, or *fixed-bundle*, *index* like the CPI keeps quantities constant in measuring price changes. When the price of gasoline jumped dramatically during the oil crises in 1974 and 1979, for example, consumers drove less and car pooled more—they used less gasoline—but the CPI bundle, which included some fixed amount of gasoline, did not change. Because of the failure of the CPI to account for the substitution away from high-priced goods on the part of consumers,

> The CPI somewhat overstates changes in the cost of living.

producer price indexes measures of prices that producers receive for products at all stages in the production process.

Producer Price Indexes   Producer price indexes—once called *wholesale price indexes*—measure prices that producers receive for products at all stages in the production process, not just final goods and services. The indexes are calculated separately for various stages in the production process. The three main categories are *finished goods, intermediate materials,* and *crude materials,* although there are subcategories within each of these categories.

One advantage of some of the producer price indexes is that they detect price increases early in the production process. And, because their movements sometimes seem to foreshadow future changes in consumer prices, they might be considered leading indicators of future inflation rates.

CORE INFLATION IN 1992: THE LOWEST IN TWENTY YEARS

The core inflation rate in the United States rose by only 3.3% in 1992, the lowest increase in twenty years, as the following excerpt from the January 16, 1993, *New York Times* points out:

[T]he so-called core inflation rate, which excludes food and energy, eased to 3.3 percent. This was the slimmest rise since 1972, when the economy was subject to price controls imposed by the Nixon Administration.

Since food and energy prices often gyrate wildly, as they did in 1986 when the price of a barrel of oil collapsed into single digits, economists tend to consider the core rate a better gauge of underlying inflation trends.

The year finished with the best overall performance since July. In December, the Consumer Price Index rose only one-tenth of one percent, an increase that was heavily influenced by holiday discounting of women's and girls' clothing.

While the results reported today came as no particular surprise, they represent powerful evidence that inflation is strongly in check despite an economic rebound that has been under way since early 1991 and has gained significant momentum since last summer.

. . . For 1992 as a whole, inflation eased for every major category but transportation, where higher costs of gasoline pushed prices ahead 3 percent after falling

The Kmart chain of discount stores began to flourish during the inflationary period in the early 1980s and is experiencing continued success in the low-inflation 1990s. The core inflation rate rose only 3.3% in 1992.

1.5 percent in 1991. Food, housing, apparel, entertainment, "other" goods and services and even medical care all rose at a noticeably slower pace.

In medical care, weighted to account for 6.7 percent of the consumer's market basket, prices advanced 6.6 percent, the lowest since 1987. For 1991, medical inflation was 7.9 percent, down from 9.6 percent in 1990.

At 3.3 percent, the 1992 core rate compared with 4.4 percent in 1991 and 5.2 percent in 1990. It was also the lowest rate since the 3 percent recorded in 1972.

Source: Robert D. Hershey, Jr., "'92 Consumer Prices Rose 2.9%, The Lowest Inflation in Six Years," *New York Times,* January 16, 1993.

GDP Deflator The **GDP deflator,** which we introduced in the previous chapter, is a price index for GDP. Thus, it is the broadest based price index available. It is also calculated in a slightly different way from the consumer and producer price indexes. To review: First, the value of all newly produced final goods is calculated using today's prices. The result is nominal GDP. Then the same set of goods is valued at the prices that prevailed in the base year; the result is real GDP. The GDP deflator is the ratio of nominal GDP to real GDP. Since the composition of GDP changes each period, the GDP deflator is not based on a fixed bundle of goods.

The main advantage of the GDP deflator is its breadth. Although it is not often discussed in the popular press, many economists consider it the best overall indicator of inflationary pressures in the economy. Another gauge of inflationary trends, the core inflation rate, is discussed in the Issues and Applications box titled "Inflation in 1992: The Lowest in Twenty Years."

GDP deflator An overall measure of prices in the economy. Equal to the ratio of nominal GDP to real GDP multiplied by 100.

The Costs of Inflation

If you asked most people why inflation is "bad," they would tell you that it lowers the overall standard of living by making goods and services more expensive. That is, it cuts into people's purchasing power. People are fond of recalling the days when a bottle of Coca-Cola cost a dime and a hamburger cost a quarter. Just think what we could buy today if prices had not changed!

What people usually do not think about is what their incomes were in the "good old days." The fact that the cost of a Coke has increased from 10¢ to 50¢ does not mean anything in real terms if people who once earned $5000 now earn $25,000. Why? The reason is simple:

> People's income comes from wages and salaries, profits, interest and rent, and income from these sources increases during inflations as well. The wage rate is the price of labor, rent is the price of land, and so forth. During inflations, most prices—including input prices—tend to rise together, and input prices determine both the incomes of workers and the incomes of owners of capital and land.

INFLATION CHANGES THE DISTRIBUTION OF INCOME   Whether you gain or lose during a period of inflation depends on whether your income rises faster or slower than the prices of the things you buy. The group most often mentioned when the impact of inflation is discussed is the group of people living on fixed incomes. Clearly, if your income is fixed and prices rise, your ability to purchase goods and services falls proportionately. But who are the fixed-income earners?

Most people think of the elderly. Indeed, many retired workers living on private pensions receive monthly checks that will never increase. Many pension plans, however, pay benefits that are *indexed* to inflation. That is, the benefits these plans provide automatically increase when the general price level rises. If prices rise 10%, for example, benefits also rise 10 percent. The biggest source of income for the elderly is social security. In 1990, 25 million retired workers received about $14 billion per month—an average of $560 per recipient—in social security benefits. These benefits are fully indexed; when prices rise (that is, when the CPI rises) by 5%, social security benefits also increase by 5 percent.

The poor have not fared so well. Welfare benefits, which are not indexed, have not kept pace with the price level over the last two decades. Indeed, benefits to families with dependent children under the AFDC program declined 33% in real terms between 1970 and 1988. In five states—Idaho, Illinois, Kentucky, New Jersey, and Texas—the average benefits fell by more than 50% in real terms.[8]

Effects on Debtors and Creditors   It is also commonly believed that debtors benefit at the expense of creditors during an inflation. Certainly, if I loan you $100 to be paid back in a year, and prices increase 10% in the meantime, I get back 10% less in real terms than what I loaned you.

But suppose that we had both anticipated that prices would rise 10 percent. Of course, I would have taken this into consideration in the deal that I made with you. That is, I would charge you an interest rate high enough to cover the decrease in value due to the anticipated inflation. If, for example, we agree on a 15% interest rate, then you must pay me $115 at the end of a year. The difference between the interest rate on a loan and the inflation rate is referred to as the **real interest rate.** In our deal, I will earn a real interest rate of 5 percent. By charging a 15% interest rate, I have taken into account the anticipated 10% infla-

real interest rate The difference between the interest rate on a loan and the inflation rate.

---

[8]Alicia H. Munnell, "The Current Status of Our Social Welfare System," Federal Reserve Bank of Boston, monograph (1987).

tion rate. In this sense, I am not hurt by the inflation—I keep pace with inflation and earn a profit on my money, too—despite the fact that I am a creditor.

On the other hand, an unanticipated inflation—that is, an inflation that takes people by surprise—can hurt creditors. If the actual inflation rate during the period of my loan to you turns out to be 20%, then I as a creditor will be hurt. I charged you 15% interest, expecting to get a 5% real rate of return, when I needed to charge you 25% to get the same 5% real rate of return. Because inflation turned out to be higher than expected, I got a negative real return of 5 percent. Thus, we can say that:

> Inflation that is higher than expected benefits debtors and inflation that is lower than expected benefits creditors.

ADMINISTRATIVE COSTS AND INEFFICIENCIES There are, of course, costs, or losses, associated even with anticipated inflation. One obvious cost is the administrative cost associated with simply keeping up. During the rapid inflation in Israel in the early 1980s, a telephone hotline was set up to give the hourly price index! Store owners have to recalculate and re-post prices frequently, and this takes time that could be used more efficiently.

More frequent banking transactions may be required of people as well. For example, interest rates tend to rise with anticipated inflation. When interest rates are high, the opportunity costs of holding cash outside of banks is high. People therefore hold less cash and need to stop at the bank more often. (We discuss this in more detail in the next part of this book.) In addition, if people are not fully informed, or if they do not understand what is happening to prices in general, they may make mistakes in their business dealings. These mistakes can lead to a misallocation of resources.

INCREASED RISK AND SLOWER ECONOMIC GROWTH When unanticipated inflation occurs regularly, the degree of risk associated with investments in the economy increases. Increases in uncertainty may make investors reluctant to invest in capital and to make long-term commitments. To the extent that the level of investment falls, the prospects for long-term economic growth are lessened.

Inflation: Public Enemy Number One?

Economists have debated the seriousness of the costs of inflation for decades. Some, like Alan Blinder, claim that "inflation, like every teenager, is grossly misunderstood, and this gross misunderstanding blows the political importance of inflation out of all proportion to its economic importance."[9] Others, like Phillip Cagan and Robert Lipsey, argue that "it was once thought that the economy would in time make all the necessary adjustments [to inflation], but many of them are proving to be very difficult. . . . for financial institutions and markets, the effects of inflation have been extremely unsettling."[10]

No matter what the real economic cost of inflation, it seems clear that people don't like it. It makes us uneasy and unhappy. In 1974, President Ford verbalized some of this discomfort when he said that "our inflation, our public enemy number one, will unless whipped destroy our country, our homes, our liberties, our property, and finally our national pride, as surely as any well-

---

[9]Alan Blinder, *Hard Heads, Soft Hearts: Tough-Minded Economics for a Just Society* (Reading, Mass.: Addison-Wesley, 1987).

[10]Phillip Cagan and Robert Lipsey, "The Financial Effects of Inflation," National Bureau of Economic Research (Cambridge, Mass.: General Series #103, 1978), pp. 67–68.

armed wartime enemy."[11] In this belief, our elected leaders have vigorously pursued policies designed to stop inflation. This brings us around to where we started. If, as we suggested earlier, the recessions of 1975 and 1982 were the price we had to pay to stop inflation, stopping inflation is indeed costly.

LOOKING AHEAD

This ends our introduction to the basic concepts and problems of macroeconomics. The first chapter of this part introduced the field, the second discussed the measurement of national product and national income, and this chapter discussed two of the macroeconomy's major problems—unemployment and inflation—in detail.

Thus far, however, we have said nothing about what *determines* the level of national output, the number of employed and unemployed workers, and the rate of inflation in an economy. The following chapters provide you with the background in macroeconomic theory you need to understand *how* the macroeconomy functions. With this knowledge, you will also be able to understand how the government can influence the economy through its taxing, spending, and monetary policies.

[11]U.S. President, *Weekly Compilation of Presidential Documents,* vol. 10, no. 41, p. 1247. Cited in Blinder, *Hard Heads.*

SUMMARY

Recessions, Depressions, and Unemployment

1. A *recession* is a period in which real GDP declines for at least two consecutive quarters. When less output is produced, employment declines, the unemployment rate rises, and a smaller percentage of capital stock is used. When real output falls, real income declines.

2. A *depression* is a prolonged and deep recession, although there is disagreement over how severe and how prolonged a recession must be in order to be called a depression.

3. Based on a survey of households conducted by the Bureau of Labor Statistics each month, the *unemployment rate* is the ratio of the number of unemployed people to the number of people in the labor force. To be considered unemployed and in the labor force, a person must be looking for work.

4. Marked differences in rates of unemployment exist across demographic groups, regions, and industries. Blacks, for example, experience much higher unemployment rates than whites.

5. When a person decides to stop looking for work, that person is considered to have dropped out of the labor force and is no longer classified as unemployed. People who stop looking because they are discouraged about ever finding a job are sometimes called *discouraged workers.*

6. Some unemployment is inevitable. Because new workers are continually entering the labor force, because industries and firms are continuously expanding and contracting, and because people switch jobs, there is a constant process of job search as workers and firms try to match the best people to the available jobs. This unemployment is both natural and beneficial for the economy.

7. The unemployment that occurs because of short-run job/skill matching problems is called *frictional unemployment.* The unemployment that occurs because of longer-run structural changes in the economy is called *structural unemployment.* The *natural rate of unemployment* is the sum of the frictional rate and the structural rate. The increase in unemployment that occurs during recessions and depressions is called *cyclical unemployment.*

8. The major costs associated with recessions and unemployment are decreased real output, the damage done to the people who are unemployed, and lost output in the future. Benefits of recessions are that they may help to reduce inflation, increase efficiency, and improve a nation's balance of payments.

Inflation

9. An *inflation* is an increase in the overall price level. It happens when many prices increase simultaneously. Inflation is measured by calculating the average increase in the prices of a large number of goods during some period of time. A *deflation* is a decrease in the overall price level. A *sustained inflation* is an increase in the overall price level that continues over a significant period of time.

10. A number of different indexes are used to measure the overall price level. Among them are the *Consumer Price Index (CPI), producer price indexes,* and the *GDP deflator.* Many economists consider the GDP deflator the best measure of the overall price level.

11. Whether a person gains or loses during a period of inflation depends on whether his or her income rises faster or slower than the prices of the things he or she buys. The elderly are more insulated from inflation than most people think, because social security benefits and many pensions are indexed to inflation. Welfare benefits, which are not indexed to inflation, have not kept pace with inflation since 1970.

12. Inflation that is higher than expected benefits debtors, and inflation that is lower than expected benefits creditors.

REVIEW TERMS AND CONCEPTS

consumer price index (CPI) 585
cyclical unemployment 580
deflation 584
depression 572
discouraged-worker
   effect 577
employed 573
frictional unemployment 579
GDP deflator 587
inflation 583
labor force 574

labor-force participation rate 574
natural rate of unemployment 579
not in the labor force 574
price index 584
producer price indexes 586
real interest rate 588
recession 572
structural unemployment 579
sustained inflation 584
unemployed 574
unemployment rate 574

Equations:
labor force = employed + unemployed
population = labor force + not in force
  unemployment rate =

$$\frac{\text{unemployed}}{\text{employed} + \text{unemployed}}$$

labor-force participation rate =

$$\frac{\text{labor force}}{\text{population}}$$

PROBLEM SET

DATE	REAL GDP (BILLIONS OF 1987 DOLLARS)	%CHANGE REAL GDP	EMPLOYMENT (MILLIONS)	UNEMPLOYMENT (MILLIONS)	UNEMPLOYMENT RATE
1969–1	2867.3	6.16	81.20	2.72	0.0338
1969–2	2872.5	0.73	81.68	2.77	0.0342
1969–3	2888.0	2.18	82.24	2.93	0.0359
1969–4	2880.8	−0.99	82.62	2.94	0.0358
1970–1	2872.9	−1.09	82.69	3.44	0.0416
1970–2	2860.3	−1.74	82.42	3.95	0.0475
1970–3	2896.6	5.17	82.31	4.32	0.0517
1970–4	2873.8	−3.11	82.25	4.88	0.0580
1971–1	2943.0	9.99	82.23	4.98	0.0591
1971–2	2947.4	0.60	82.37	4.99	0.0591
1971–3	2966.0	2.55	82.85	5.10	0.0598

1. The table above shows that between early 1969 and late 1971, real GDP in the United States grew by about $100 billion and employment grew by 1.65 million, but that the unemployment rate nearly doubled, going from 3.38% to 5.98 percent. How can this be?

2. Using the data in Table 23.2, calculate the changes in the unemployment rate and the labor-force participation rate that would occur if one million unemployed persons dropped out of the labor force in 1992.

3. "When an inefficient firm or a firm producing a product that people no longer want goes out of business, people are unemployed, but that's part of the normal process of economic growth and development; the unemployment is part of the natural rate and need not concern policy makers." Discuss this statement and its relevance to the economy today.

4. What is the unemployment rate in your state today? What was it in 1970, 1975, and 1982? How has your state done relative to the national average? Do you know, or can you determine, why?

5. Suppose that all wages, salaries, welfare benefits, and other sources of income were indexed to inflation. Would inflation still be considered a problem? Why or why not?

6. Using 1992 as the base year, construct price indexes for 1992, 1993, and 1994 using the data in the following table:

	QUANTITY CONSUMED	PRICE, 1992	PRICE, 1993	PRICE, 1994
Good X	100	$1.00	$1.50	$1.75
Good Y	150	1.50	2.00	2.00
Good Z	25	3.00	3.25	3.00

Calculate the percentage change in the price index between 1992 and 1993 and between 1993 and 1994. Was there inflation between 1993 and 1994?

7. Consider the following statements:
  a. "More people are employed in Tappania now than at any time in the past 50 years."
  b. "The unemployment rate in Tappania is higher now than it has been in 50 years."
Can both of these statements be true at the same time? Explain.

THE UNDERGROUND ECONOMY

In Vladivostok, Russia, auto parts are frequently sold in underground markets.

■ When most people hear about the underground economy, they think of organized crime, street gangs, or drug smugglers. In fact, there is a great deal more economic activity that occurs legally, but "off-the-books," than criminal activity of the type that captures media attention. The term "underground" simply means that the income derived from "off-the-books" activity is not reported to either the Internal Revenue Service or the Labor Department.

How many of you have ever been paid by a friend or relative for odd jobs like mowing a lawn or painting a house? If you failed to report this income to the IRS, then you and they have participated in the underground economy. The fact that this income is never reported means not only lost tax revenue for the government but also unmeasured economic activity because income and expenditures in the underground economy are not included in GDP.

The "underground economy" has many different names. Sometimes referred to as the "invisible" or "shadow" economy, it shares many characteristics with the black market for goods and services often found in foreign countries. We don't generally think of a black market existing in the United States, but in many nations the black market serves an important role in keeping governments afloat when state-run enterprises fail to meet demand. Cambodia and Vietnam, for example, have put up with a dose of black-market capitalism to help boost commerce and trade.

In the United States, the underground economy provides an important cushion during periods of recession. People who lose their "surface" jobs can often find part-time work in a variety of "subterranean" jobs that provide them with income until economic conditions improve. Furthermore, the underground economy benefits consumers by providing a wider range of goods and services at lower prices.

The reasons for the existence of an underground economy in the United States can be traced to a number of factors. Most of these relate to attempts to evade taxes or circumvent government restrictions. Regulations governing zoning ordinances (home offices), licensing and registration requirements (doctors and plumbers), working conditions (health and safety regulations, minimum wage laws), and eligibility requirements (employment of minors or nonunion workers) all contribute to the existence of a healthy underground economy in the United States. Sole proprietorships appear to be the biggest players in the underground economy. Establishments like the neighborhood grocery store, the local diner, and self-employed professionals account for about $205 billion in unreported income each year.

How healthy is the U.S. underground economy? The IRS estimates that the underground economy produces annual income of more than $500 billion, or roughly 10% of total GDP. Some economists believe the size to be closer to 15 percent. Add another $200 billion or so for criminal activity and you've got an underground economy that's doing better than the combined economies of Canada, Australia, and Sweden.

Probably the most important problem facing policy makers is the "tax gap" created by the underground economy. In 1992, this gap was about $127 billion—enough to reduce the federal budget deficit by about one third. In addition, income earned through the underground economy may enable some individuals to circumvent eligibility requirements for income-support programs. This leads to questions of fairness and equity and may put at risk the nation's ability to fund social programs.

QUESTIONS FOR ANALYTICAL THINKING

1. How healthy is the underground economy in your area? Is there an underground economy on campus? What impacts, both positive and negative, does it have on the local economy?

2. What changes in the laws would you recommend to a member of Congress to help recover some of the lost revenue that has been attributed to the underground economy?

3. Illegal aliens are an important factor in the underground economy. What are the benefits and costs of hiring illegal aliens? Should illegal aliens pay income and social security taxes? Should they collect social security?

4. In what ways has increased trade with other nations fueled the growth of the underground economy in the United States?

5. Should illegal activities be included in computing GDP?

PART SIX

Macroeconomic Principles and Policy

Macroeconomic variables— the number of jobs in the economy, import and export volumes, the rate of inflation, and the like—are determined by the decisions of millions of people interacting in the macroeconomy. To understand the macroeconomy as a whole, we must begin with the individual pieces. As mentioned in Chapter 21, there are three macroeconomic markets: the goods market, the money market, and the labor market. In this part, we consider the goods market and the money market. An important focus in the next four chapters will be on the role of government in the macroeconomy. In what ways, if at all, can the taxing and spending powers of the government (fiscal policy) and the central bank's control over the money supply (monetary policy) affect the course of economic events? Other questions we consider include:

■ What determines the level of national income and output? What determines the total spending of households on consumer goods? What determines the total investment undertaken by firms? (Chapter 24)

■ In recent years, the federal deficit and the national debt have received a great deal of attention. What is the federal deficit? What impact does the deficit have on the functioning of the economy? How large is the national debt? What are the consequences of a huge national debt? (Chapter 25)

■ We use and talk about money every day, but most people do not really understand the role of money in an economy. Where does money come from? How can private banks "create" money? (Chapter 26)

■ Interest rates can affect your ability to buy a house or afford a new car. They can also affect a firm's decision to invest in new equipment. But what determines the level of the interest rate? What is the Federal Reserve System, and what role does it play in determining the supply of money and the interest rate? (Chapters 26 and 27)

24

Aggregate Expenditure and Equilibrium Output

AGGREGATE OUTPUT AND AGGREGATE INCOME (Y)
Income, Consumption, and Saving (*Y, C,* and *S*)
Planned Investment *(I)*
Planned Aggregate Expenditure *(AE)*

EQUILIBRIUM AGGREGATE OUTPUT (INCOME)
The Saving/Investment Approach to
Equilibrium

Adjustment to Equilibrium
The Multiplier

LOOKING AHEAD: THE GOVERNMENT AND
INTERNATIONAL SECTORS

APPENDIX: DERIVING THE MULTIPLIER
ALGEBRAICALLY

We now begin our discussion of macroeconomic theory. We know how to calculate national income, but what factors *determine* national income? We know how to define and measure inflation and unemployment, but what circumstances *cause* inflation and unemployment? And what, if anything, can government do to reduce unemployment, inflation, and other macroeconomic maladies?

Analyzing the various components of the macroeconomy is a complex undertaking. The level of national income and the overall price level—two of the chief concerns of macroeconomists—are influenced by events in three broadly defined "markets": *goods-and-services markets, financial (money) markets,* and *labor markets.* We will explore each of these markets, as well as the links between these markets and the corresponding markets in the rest of the world, in more detail in the chapters that follow.

MACROECONOMIC MARKETS Figure 24.1 presents the plan of the next seven chapters of this book, which form the core of macroeconomic theory. In Chapters 24 and 25, we describe the market for goods and services, often called simply the *goods market.* In Chapter 24, we explain several basic concepts and show how the

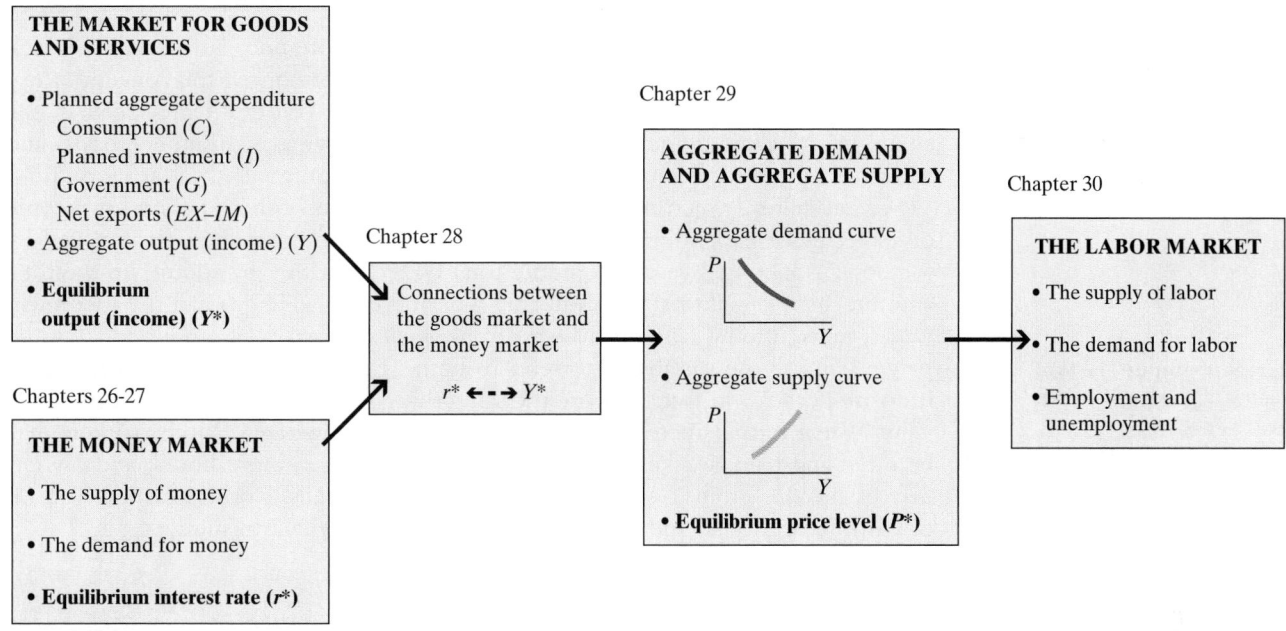

FIGURE 24.1
Understanding Markets in the Macroeconomy

equilibrium level of national income is determined in a very simple economy with no government and no imports or exports. In Chapter 25, we provide a more complete picture of the economy by adding government purchases, taxes, and net exports to the analysis.

In Chapters 26 and 27, we focus on the *money market*. Chapter 26 introduces the money market and the banking system and discusses the way the central bank of the United States (the Federal Reserve) controls the supply of money. Chapter 27 analyzes the demand for money and the way interest rates are determined. Chapter 28 then examines the relationship between the goods market and the money market. Chapter 29 explores the aggregate demand and supply curves first mentioned in Chapter 21. Chapter 29 also analyzes how the overall price level is determined as well as the relationship between national income and the price level. Finally, Chapter 30 discusses the supply of and demand for labor and the functioning of the *labor market* in the macroeconomy. This material is essential to an understanding of employment and unemployment.[1]

Before we begin our discussion of aggregate output and aggregate income, however, we need to stress that production, consumption, and the other activities that we will be discussing in this and the following chapters are ongoing activities. Nonetheless, it is helpful to think about these activities as if they took place in a series of *production periods.* During each period, some output is produced, income is generated, and spending takes place. At the end of each period we can examine the results. Was everything that was produced in the economy sold? What percentage of income was spent? What percentage was saved? Is output (income) likely to rise or fall in the next period? The answers to these questions help us to keep track of the economy's performance.

---

[1]Throughout Chapters 24–30, we provide examples and policy applications relevant to our discussion in each chapter. In Chapter 31, we use everything we know about the three broadly defined markets to analyze such macroeconomic topics as stabilization policy and the federal budget deficit.

AGGREGATE OUTPUT AND AGGREGATE INCOME (Y)

Each period, firms produce some aggregate quantity of goods and services, which we refer to as *aggregate output* (Y). In Chapter 22, we introduced the concept of real gross domestic product as a measure of the quantity of output produced in the economy, Y. Output includes the production of services, consumer goods, and investment goods. It is important to think of these as components of "real" output.

We have already seen that GDP (Y) can be calculated either in terms of income or in terms of expenditures. Because every dollar of expenditure is received by someone as income, we can compute total GDP (Y) either by adding up the total amount spent on all final goods during a period *or* by adding up all the income—wages, rents, interest, and profits—received by all the factors of production.

We will use the variable Y to refer to both **aggregate output** and **aggregate income** because, in fact, they are the same thing seen from two different points of view. When output increases, additional income is generated. More workers may be hired and paid; workers may put in, and be paid for, more hours; and owners may earn more profits. When output is cut, income falls, workers may be laid off or work fewer hours (and be paid less), and profits may fall. In sum:

> In any given period, there is an exact equality between aggregate output (production) and aggregate income. You should be reminded of this fact whenever you encounter the combined term **aggregate output (income)**.

Aggregate output can also be looked on as the aggregate quantity supplied, because it is the amount that firms are supplying (producing) during the period. In the discussions that follow, we use the phrase "aggregate output (income)," rather than "aggregate quantity supplied," but keep in mind that the two are equivalent. Also remember that "aggregate output" means "real GDP."

Income, Consumption, and Saving (Y, C, and S)

Each period (weeks, months, years, etc.), households receive some aggregate amount of income (Y). In a simple world with no government, no taxes, and no imports, a household can do two, and only two, things with its income: It can buy domestically produced goods and services—that is, it can *consume*—or it can save. The part of its income that a household does not consume in a given period is called **saving** (see Figure 24.2). Thus, total household saving in the economy (represented by the letter S) is by definition equal to income minus consumption (represented by the letter C):

$$\text{Saving} \equiv \text{Income} - \text{Consumption}$$
$$S \equiv Y - C$$

The triple equal sign simply means that this equation is an **identity,** or something that must be true at all times. You will encounter several important identities in this chapter; be sure to commit them to memory.

It is very important to remember that saving does *not* refer to the total savin*gs* that have been accumulated over time. Saving (without the final *s*) refers to the portion of a *single period's* income that is not spent in that period. Saving (S) is the amount that is added to (or subtracted from) *accumulated savings* in any given period. *Saving* is a flow variable; *savings* is a stock variable. (Review Chapter 4 if you are unsure of the difference between stock and flow variables.)

aggregate output The total quantity of goods and services produced (or supplied) in an economy in a given period.

aggregate income The total income received by all factors of production in a given period.

aggregate output (income) (Y) A combined term used to remind you of the exact equality between aggregate output and aggregate income.

saving (S) The part of its income that a household does not consume in a given period. To be distinguished from *savings,* which is the current stock of accumulated saving.

identity Something that must be true at all times.

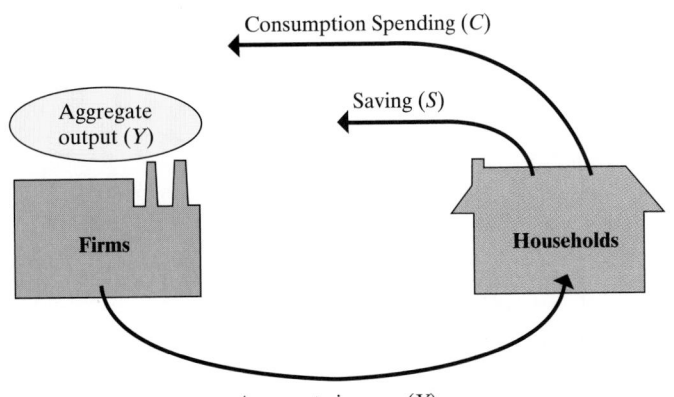

Consumption Spending (*C*)

Saving (*S*)

Aggregate output (*Y*)

Firms

Households

Aggregate income (*Y*)

FIGURE 24.2

Saving ≡ Aggregate
Income – Consumption

All income is either spent on consumption or saved in an economy in which there is no government. Thus, $S \equiv Y - C$.

EXPLAINING SPENDING BEHAVIOR   At this point, we have said absolutely nothing about behavior. We have not described the consumption and saving behavior of households, nor have we speculated about how much aggregate output firms will decide to produce in a given period. Rather, we have only a framework and a set of definitions to work with.

But macroeconomics, you will recall, is the study of behavior. To understand the functioning of the macroeconomy, we must understand the behavior of households and firms. In our simple economy in which there is no government, there are two types of spending behavior: spending by households, or *consumption,* and spending by firms, or *investment.*

Household Consumption and Saving   How do households decide how much to consume? In any given period, the amount of aggregate consumption in the economy depends on a number of factors, including:

SOME	1. Household income
DETERMINANTS OF	2. Household wealth
AGGREGATE	3. Interest rates
CONSUMPTION:	4. Households' expectations about the future.

That these factors work together to determine the spending and saving behavior of households, both individually and in the aggregate, should not be surprising. Households with higher income and higher wealth are likely to spend more than households with less income and less wealth. Lower interest rates reduce the cost of borrowing, so lower interest rates are likely to stimulate spending. (The reverse is true for higher interest rates, which increase the cost of borrowing and are likely to decrease spending.) Finally, positive expectations about the future are likely to increase current spending, while uncertainty about the future is likely to decrease current spending. In 1990, for example, households began consuming less partly because of their uncertainty about the outcome of the Persian Gulf conflict.

While all these factors are important, we will concentrate for now on the relationship between income and consumption.[2] In *The General Theory,* Keynes argued that the amount of consumption undertaken by a household is directly related to its income:

The higher someone's income is, the higher his or her consumption is likely to be. Thus, people with more income tend to consume more than people with less income.

---

[2]The assumption that consumption is dependent solely on income is, of course, overly simplistic. Nonetheless, many important insights about how the economy works can be obtained through this simplification. In Chapter 32, we relax this assumption and consider the behavior of households and firms in the macroeconomy in more detail.

FIGURE 24.3

A consumption function for an
individual household shows the
level of consumption at each
level of household income.

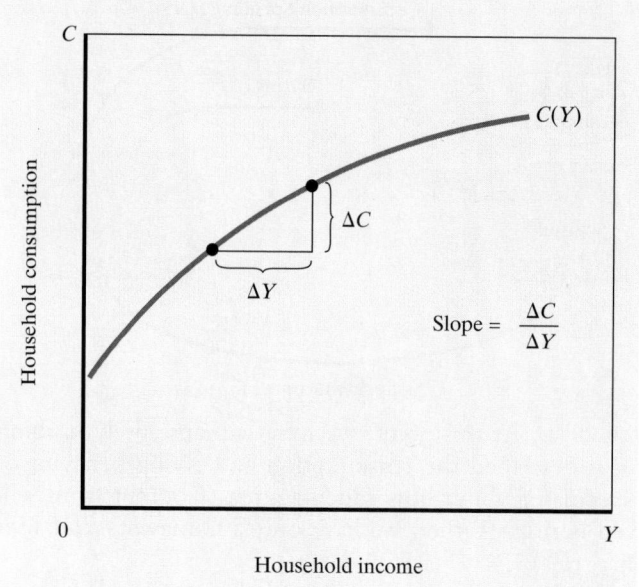

consumption function The
relationship between consumption
and income.

The relationship between consumption and income is called a **consumption function.** Figure 24.3 shows a hypothetical consumption function for an individual household. The curve is labeled $C(Y)$, which is read "C as a function of Y." There are several things you should notice about the curve. First, it has a positive slope. In other words, $\Delta C/\Delta Y$ is positive:[3] As Y increases, so does C. Second, the curve intersects the C axis above zero. This means that even at an income of zero, consumption is positive. Even if a household found itself with a zero income, it still must consume to survive. It would borrow or live off its savings, but its consumption could not be zero.

Keep in mind that Figure 24.3 shows the relationship between consumption and income for an individual household. But also remember that macroeconomics is concerned with aggregate consumption. Specifically, macroeconomists want to know how *aggregate* consumption (the total consumption of all households) is likely to respond to changes in *aggregate* income. If all individual households increase their consumption as income increases, and we assume that they do, it is reasonable to assume that a positive relationship exists between aggregate consumption (C) and aggregate income (Y).

For the sake of simplicity, let us assume that points of aggregate consumption, when plotted against aggregate income, lie along a straight line, as in Figure 24.4. Because the aggregate consumption function is a straight line, we can write the following equation to describe it:

$$C = a + bY.$$

Y, as you know, represents aggregate output (income). C stands for aggregate consumption. The letter a is the point at which the consumption function intersects the C axis; it is a constant. The letter b is the slope of the line. Note that the slope of the line in this case is $\Delta C/\Delta Y$ (since consumption [C] is measured on the vertical axis, and income [Y] is measured on the horizontal axis). Every time that income (Y) increases (say by ΔY), consumption (C) increases by b times that amount, or b times ΔY. Thus, $\Delta C = b \times \Delta Y$ and $\Delta C/\Delta Y = b$.

---

[3]The Greek letter Δ (delta) means "change in." For example, ΔY (read "delta Y") means the "change in income." If income (Y) in 1993 is \$100 and income in 1994 is \$110, then ΔY for this period is \$110 — \$100 = \$10. For a review of the concept of slope, see the Appendix to Chapter 1.

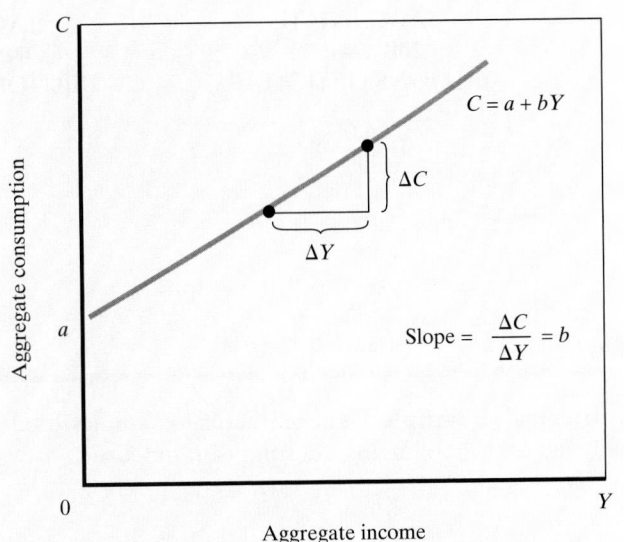

FIGURE 24.4
An Aggregate
Consumption Function

The consumption function shows
the level of consumption at every
level of income. The upward
slope indicates that higher levels
of income lead to higher levels of
consumption spending.

Suppose, for example, that the slope of the line in Figure 24.4 were .75 (that is, $b = .75$). In this case, an increase in income (ΔY) of $100 would increase consumption (ΔC) by $b\Delta Y = .75 \times \$100$, or $75.

The **marginal propensity to consume (MPC)** is the fraction of a change in income that is consumed. In the consumption function above, b is the MPC. An MPC of .75 simply means that consumption changes by three quarters (.75) of the change in income. The slope of the consumption function is thus the MPC:

marginal propensity to consume (MPS) That fraction of a change in income that is consumed, or spent.

$$\text{Marginal Propensity to Consume} \equiv \text{Slope of Consumption Function} \equiv \frac{\Delta C}{\Delta Y}.$$

There are only two places income can go: consumption or saving. Thus, if $0.75 of a $1.00 increase in income goes to consumption, the remaining $0.25 must go to saving. Likewise, if income decreases by $1.00, consumption will decrease by $0.75 and saving will decrease by $0.25. The **marginal propensity to save (MPS)** is the fraction of a change in income that is saved: $\Delta S/\Delta Y$. Because everything not consumed is saved, the MPC and the MPS must add up to one:

marginal propensity to save (MPS) That fraction of a change in income that is saved.

$$MPC + MPS \equiv 1.$$

Because the MPC and the MPS are such important concepts, it may help to review their definitions one more time:

The marginal propensity to consume (MPC) is the fraction of an increase in income that is consumed (or the fraction of a decrease in income that comes out of consumption). The marginal propensity to save (MPS) is the fraction of an increase in income that is saved (or the fraction of a decrease in income that comes out of saving).

Since C is aggregate consumption and Y is aggregate income, it follows that the MPC is *society's* marginal propensity to consume out of national income and that the MPS is *society's* marginal propensity to save out of national income.

TABLE 24.1

Consumption Schedule
Derived from the Equation
$C = 100 + .75Y$

AGGREGATE INCOME, Y (BILLIONS OF DOLLARS)	AGGREGATE CONSUMPTION, C (BILLIONS OF DOLLARS)
0	100
80	160
100	175
200	250
400	400
600	550
800	700
1000	850

Numerical Example The numerical examples used in the rest of this chapter are based on the following consumption function:

$$C = 100 + .75Y.$$

This equation is simply an extension of the generic $C = a + bY$ consumption function we have been discussing. At a national income of zero, consumption is $100 billion ($a$). As income rises, so does consumption. We will assume that for every $100 billion increase in income (ΔY), consumption rises by $75 billion ($\Delta C$). This means that the slope of the consumption function (b) is equal to $\Delta C/\Delta Y$, or $75 billion/$100 billion = .75. The marginal propensity to consume (MPC) out of national income is therefore .75; the marginal propensity to save (MPS) is .25.

Some numbers derived from this consumption function appear in Table 24.1 and are graphed in Figure 24.5.

We already know that $Y \equiv C + S$. That is, income equals consumption plus saving. Therefore, once we know how much consumption will result from a given level of income, we also know how much saving there will be. Recall that saving is everything that is not consumed:

$$S \equiv Y - C.$$

From the numbers in Table 24.1, we can easily derive the saving schedule in Table 24.2. At an income of $200 billion, consumption is $250 billion; saving is thus a negative $50 billion ($S \equiv Y - C = $200 billion $-$ $250 billion $= -$50 billion). At an aggregate income of $400 billion, consumption is exactly $400 billion, and saving is zero. At $800 billion in income, saving is a positive $100 billion.

TABLE 24.2

Deriving a Saving
Schedule from a
Consumption Schedule

Y AGGREGATE INCOME (BILLIONS OF DOLLARS)	−	C AGGREGATE CONSUMPTION (BILLIONS OF DOLLARS)	≡	S AGGREGATE SAVING (BILLIONS OF DOLLARS)
0		100		−100
80		160		−80
100		175		−75
200		250		−50
400		400		0
600		550		50
800		700		100
1000		850		150

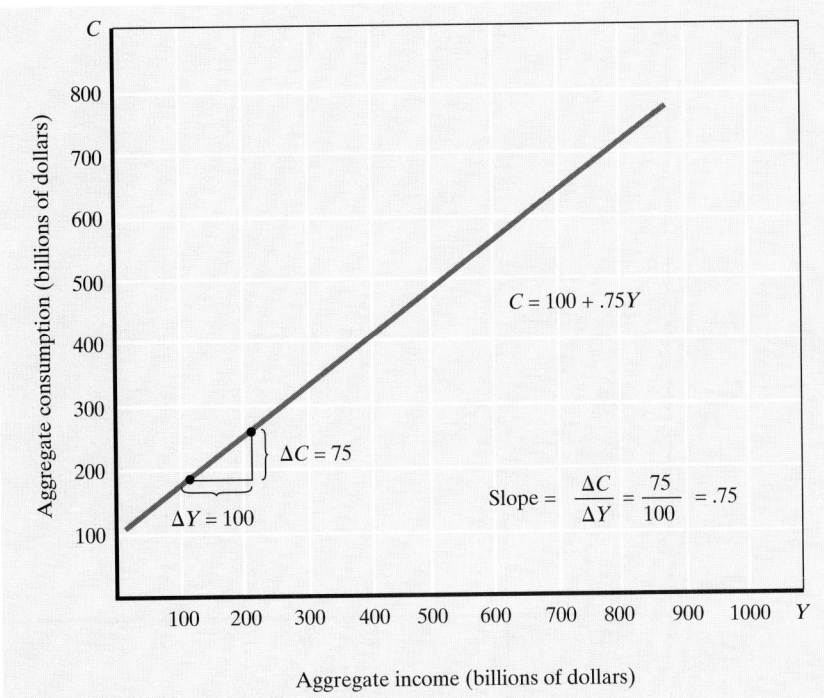

FIGURE 24.5

An Aggregate Consumption Function Derived from the Equation $C = 100 + .75Y$

In this simple consumption function, consumption is $100 billion at an income of zero. As income rises, so does consumption. For every $100 billion increase in income, consumption rises by $75 billion. The slope of the line is .75.

These numbers are graphed as a saving function in Figure 24.6 on the next page. The 45° line, which appears as a dashed line in the top part of Figure 24.6, provides us with a convenient way of comparing C and Y. (Remember that all the points along a 45° line are points at which the value on the horizontal axis equals the value on the vertical axis. Thus, the 45° line in Figure 24.6 represents all the points at which aggregate income equals aggregate consumption.) Where the consumption function is *above* the 45° line, consumption exceeds income, and saving is negative. Where the consumption function *crosses* the 45° line, consumption is equal to income, and saving is zero. Where the consumption function is *below* the 45° line, consumption is less than income, and saving is positive. Note that the slope of the saving function is $\Delta S/\Delta Y$, which is the marginal propensity to save (*MPS*).

> The consumption function and the saving function are mirror images of one another. No information appears in one that does not also appear in the other. These functions tell us how households in the aggregate will divide income between consumption spending and saving at every possible income level. In other words, they embody aggregate household behavior.

Planned Investment (I)

Consumption, as we've seen, is the spending by households on goods and services. But what kind of spending do firms engage in? The answer is *investment*.

WHAT IS INVESTMENT? Let us begin with a brief review of terms and concepts. In everyday language, we use "investment" to refer to what we do with our savings: "I invested in a mutual fund and some IBM stock." In the language of economics, however, "investment" always refers to the creation of capital stock. To an economist, an investment is something that is used to create value in the future.

It is very important that you not confuse the two uses of the term. When a firm builds a new plant or adds new machinery to its current stock, it is investing. When

FIGURE 24.6

Deriving a Saving Function from a Consumption Function

Since $S \equiv Y - C$, it is easy to derive a saving function from a consumption function. A 45° line drawn from the origin can be used as a convenient tool to compare consumption and income graphically. At $Y = 200$, consumption is 250. The 45° line shows us that consumption is larger than income by 50. Thus $S \equiv Y - C = -50$. At $Y = 800$, consumption is less than income by 100. Thus, $S = 100$ when $Y = 800$.

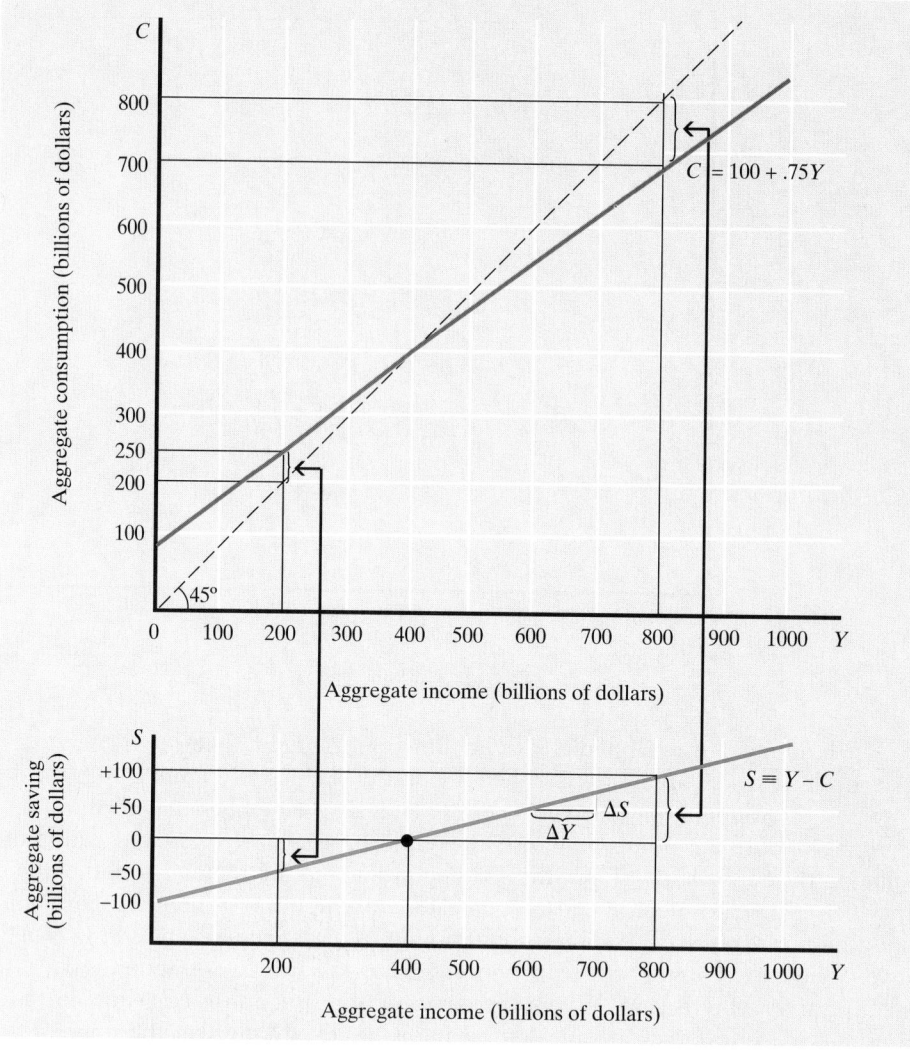

investment Purchases by firms of new buildings and equipment and additions to inventories, all of which add to firms' capital stock.

a restaurant owner buys tables, chairs, cooking equipment, and silverware, he or she is investing. When a college builds a new sports center, it is investing. From now on, we use the term **investment** only in this sense, to refer to purchases by firms of new buildings and equipment and inventories, all of which add to firms' capital stocks.

Recall that inventories are part of the capital stock. When firms add to their inventories, they are investing—they are buying something that creates value in the future. Most of the capital stock of a clothing store, for example, consists of its inventories of unsold clothes in its warehouses and on its racks and display shelves. The service provided by a grocery or department store is the convenience of having a large variety of commodities in inventory that are available for purchase at a single location.

Manufacturing firms generally have two kinds of inventories: *inputs,* or raw materials, and *final products.* General Motors, for example, has stocks of tires, rolled steel, engine blocks, valve covers, and thousands of other things in inventory, all waiting to be used in producing new cars. In addition, GM has an inventory of finished automobiles awaiting shipment.

Investment is a flow variable; that is, it represents additions to capital stock in a specific period. A firm's decision on how much to invest each period is determined by many factors. For now, we will focus simply on the effects that given investment levels have on the rest of the economy.

ACTUAL VERSUS PLANNED INVESTMENT One of the most important insights of macroeconomics is deceptively simple: A firm may not always end up investing the exact amount that it planned to. The reason for this is that a firm does not have complete control over its investment decision; some parts of that decision are made by other actors in the economy. (This is not true of consumption, however. Because we assume that households have complete control over their consumption, planned consumption is always equal to actual consumption.)

Generally, firms can choose how much new plant and equipment they wish to purchase in any given period. If GM wants to buy a new robot to stamp fenders or McDonald's decides to buy an extra french-fry machine, it can usually do so without difficulty. There is, however, another component of investment over which firms have less control—inventory investment.

Suppose GM expects to sell one million cars this quarter and has inventories at a level that it considers proper. If the company produces and sells one million cars, it will keep its inventories just where they are now (at the desired level). Now suppose that GM produces one million cars but that a sudden shift of consumer interest enables it to sell only 900,000 cars. By definition, GM's inventories of cars must go up by 100,000 cars. The firm's **change in inventory** is equal to production minus sales. The key point here is simply:

> One component of investment—inventory change—is partly determined by how much households decide to buy, which is not under the complete control of firms. If households do not buy as much as firms expect them to, inventories will be higher than expected, and firms will have made an inventory investment that they did not plan to make.

Because involuntary inventory adjustments are neither desired nor planned, we need to distinguish between actual and **desired,** or **planned, investment.** We will use the symbol I to refer to desired or planned investment only. In other words, I will refer to planned purchases of plant and equipment and planned inventory changes. **Actual investment,** on the other hand, is the *actual* amount of investment that takes place. If, for example, actual inventory investment turns out to be higher than firms planned, then actual investment is greater than I, planned investment.

desired, or planned, investment Those additions to capital stock and inventory that are planned by firms.

actual investment The actual amount of investment that takes place; it includes items such as unplanned changes in inventories.

For the purposes of this chapter, we will take the amount of investment that firms plan to make each period (I) as fixed at some given level. We assume that this level does not vary with income. For purposes of the example that follows, we will assume that $I = \$25$ billion, regardless of income. As Figure 24.7 shows, this means that the planned investment function is simply a horizontal line.

Planned Aggregate Expenditure (*AE*)

Until now, we have assumed that there are only two kinds of spending in the economy: *consumption,* or spending by households, and *investment,* or spending by firms. We've used the letter C to represent consumption and assumed that actual and planned consumption are always the same. The letter I refers to planned investment. Actual investment will differ from I if there are unplanned inventory changes.

Total **planned aggregate expenditure (AE)** in the economy is simply equal to consumption (C) plus planned investment (I):

planned aggregate expenditure (AE) The total amount the economy plans to spend in a given period. Equal to consumption plus planned investment: $AE \equiv C + I$.

$$\text{Planned Aggregate Expenditure} \equiv \text{Consumption} + \text{Planned Investment}$$
$$AE \equiv C + I.$$

FIGURE 24.7

The Planned
Investment Function

For the time being, we will
assume that planned investment
is fixed. It does not change when
income changes, so its graph is
just a horizontal line.

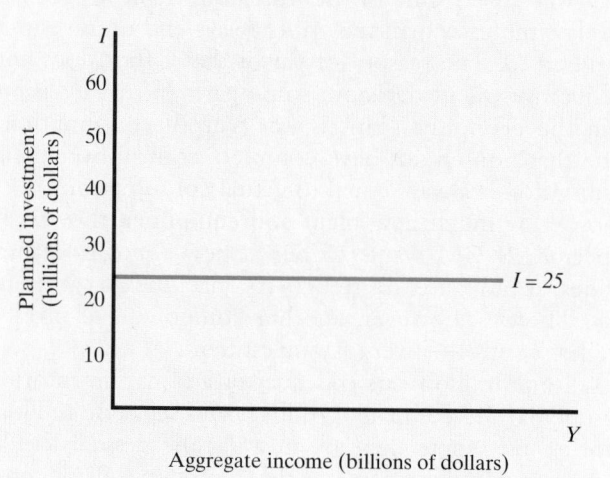

AE is the total amount that the economy plans to spend in a given period.
We will now use the concept of planned aggregate expenditure to discuss the
equilibrium level of output in the economy.

EQUILIBRIUM AGGREGATE OUTPUT (INCOME)

Thus far, we have described only the behavior of firms and households. We
must now discuss the nature of equilibrium in the macroeconomy and explain
how the economy achieves such an equilibrium.

A number of definitions of "equilibrium" are used in economics. However,
they all refer to the idea that at equilibrium, there is no tendency for change. In
microeconomics, equilibrium is said to exist in a particular market (for example, the market for bananas) at the price for which the quantity demanded is
equal to the quantity supplied. At this point, both suppliers and demanders are
satisfied. The equilibrium price of a good is the price at which suppliers want
to furnish the amount that demanders want to buy.

In macroeconomics, however, we define **equilibrium** in the goods market as
that point at which planned aggregate expenditure is equal to aggregate output:

equilibrium Occurs when there is
no tendency for change. In the
macroeconomic goods market,
equilibrium occurs when planned
aggregate expenditure is equal to
aggregate output.

$$\text{aggregate output} \equiv Y;$$
$$\text{planned aggregate expenditure} \equiv AE \equiv C + I;$$
$$\text{equilibrium: } Y = AE, \text{ or } Y = C + I.$$

This definition of equilibrium can hold if, and only if, planned investment and
actual investment are equal. (Remember that we are assuming there is no
unplanned consumption.)

To understand why this is true, consider the cases where Y does not equal AE.
First, suppose that aggregate output is greater than planned aggregate expenditure:

$$Y > C + I.$$
$$\text{aggregate output} > \text{planned aggregate expenditure}$$

When output is greater than planned spending, there is unplanned inventory
investment. Firms planned to sell more of their goods than they did, and the difference shows up as an unplanned increase in inventories.

Next, suppose that planned aggregate expenditure is greater than aggregate output:

$$C + I > Y.$$
planned aggregate expenditure $>$ aggregate output

When planned spending exceeds output, firms have sold more than they planned to. Thus, inventory investment is smaller than planned. Again, planned and actual investment are not equal. Only when output is exactly matched by planned spending will there be no unplanned inventory investment.

To summarize, we can say that:

Equilibrium in the goods market is achieved only when aggregate output (Y) and planned aggregate expenditure $(C + I)$ are equal, or when actual and planned investment are equal.

Table 24.3 derives a planned aggregate expenditure schedule and shows the point of equilibrium for our numerical example. (Remember, all our calculations are based on the equation $C = 100 + .75Y$.) To determine planned aggregate expenditure, we add consumption spending (C) to planned investment spending (I) at every level of income. Glancing down columns 1 and 4, we discover one, and only one, level at which aggregate output and planned aggregate expenditure are equal: the point where $Y = 500$.

Figure 24.8 on the next page illustrates the same equilibrium graphically. Figure 24.8a adds planned investment, constant at $25 billion, to consumption at every level of income. Since planned investment is a constant, the planned aggregate expenditure function is simply the consumption function displaced vertically by that constant amount. Figure 24.8b plots the planned aggregate expenditure function with the 45° line. The 45° line, which represents all points on the graph where the variables on the horizontal and vertical axes are equal, allows us to compare measurements along the two axes. The planned aggregate expenditure function crosses the 45° line at a single point, where $Y = \$500$ billion.

Now let us look at some other levels of aggregate output (income). First, consider $Y_1 = \$800$ billion. Is Y_1 an equilibrium output? Clearly not. At $Y = \$800$ billion, planned aggregate expenditure is $725 billion. (See Table 24.3.)

TABLE 24.3
Deriving the Planned Aggregate Expenditure Schedule and Finding Equilibrium (all figures in billions of dollars)
The figures in column 2 are based on the equation $C = 100 + .75Y$.

(1) AGGREGATE OUTPUT (INCOME) (Y)	(2) AGGREGATE CONSUMPTION (C)	(3) PLANNED INVESTMENT (I)	(4) PLANNED AGGREGATE EXPENDITURE (AE) C + I	(5) UNPLANNED INVENTORY CHANGE Y – (C + I)	(6) EQUILIBRIUM? (Y = AE?)
100	175	25	200	−100	No (1 < 4)
200	250	25	275	−75	No (1 < 4)
400	400	25	425	−25	No (1 < 4)
500	475	25	500	0	Yes (1 = 4)
600	550	25	575	+25	No (1 > 4)
800	700	25	725	+75	No (1 > 4)
1000	850	25	875	+125	No (1 > 4)

FIGURE 24.8
Equilibrium Aggregate Output

Equilibrium occurs when planned aggregate expenditure and aggregate output are equal. Planned aggregate expenditure is the sum of consumption spending and planned investment spending.

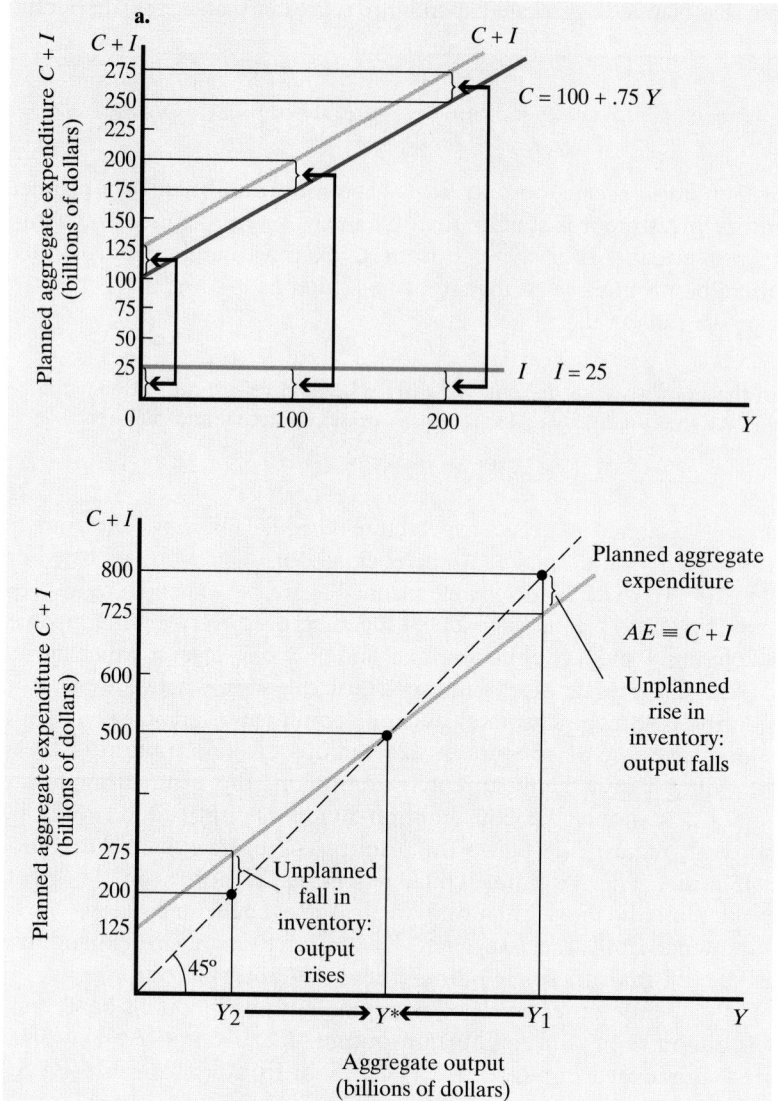

This amount is less than aggregate output, which is $800 billion. Because output is greater than planned spending, the difference ends up in inventory as unplanned inventory investment. In this case, unplanned inventory investment is $75 billion.

Next, consider $Y_2 = \$200$ billion. Is Y_2 an equilibrium output? Again, clearly not. At $Y = \$200$ billion, planned aggregate expenditure is $275 billion. Thus, planned spending (AE) is greater than output (Y), and there is unplanned inventory disinvestment of $75 billion.

At Y_1 and Y_2, planned investment and actual investment are unequal. There is unplanned investment, and the system is out of balance. Only at Y^*, where planned aggregate expenditure and aggregate output are equal, will planned investment equal actual investment.

Finally, let us find the equilibrium level of output (income) algebraically. Recall that we know the following:

(1) $Y = C + I$ (equilibrium),
(2) $C = 100 + .75Y$ (consumption function),
(3) $I = 25$ (planned investment).

Substituting (2) and (3) into (1) we get

$$Y = \underbrace{100 + .75Y}_{C} + \underbrace{25}_{I}.$$

There is only one value of Y for which this statement is true, and we can find it by rearranging terms:

$$Y - .75Y = 100 + 25$$
$$Y - .75Y = 125$$
$$.25Y = 125$$
$$Y = \frac{125}{.25} = 500.$$

The equilibrium level of output is thus 500, as we have already seen in Table 24.3 and Figure 24.8.

The Saving/Investment Approach to Equilibrium

We have already noted that aggregate income must either be saved or spent. By definition, then, $Y \equiv C + S$, which, you remember, is an identity. The equilibrium condition is $Y = C + I$, but this is not an identity because it does not hold when we are out of equilibrium.[4] Substituting $C + S$ for Y, the equilibrium condition can thus be written:

> Saving/Investment Approach to Equilibrium: $C + S = C + I$.
> Since we can subtract C from both sides of this equation, we are left with $S = I$.
> Thus, only when planned investment equals saving will there be equilibrium.

This saving/investment approach to equilibrium stands to reason intuitively if we recall two things: (1) Output and income are equal, and (2) saving is income that is not spent. Saving, then, is like a leakage out of the system—that is, it is not spent. Only if that leakage is counterbalanced by some other component of planned spending can the resulting planned aggregate expenditure equal aggregate output. This other component is planned investment (I).

This counterbalancing effect can be seen clearly in Figure 24.9. Aggregate income flows into the households, and consumption and saving flow out. The

---

[4]It would be an identity if I included unplanned inventory accumulations—in other words, if I were actual investment rather than planned investment.

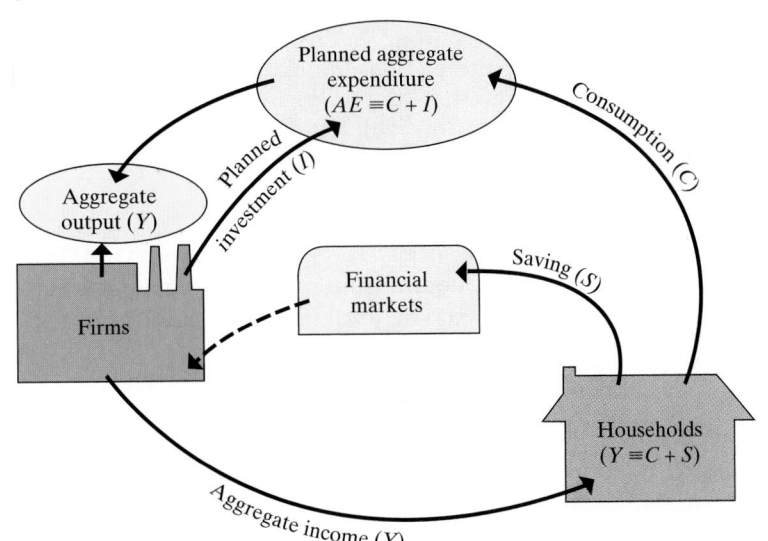

FIGURE 24.9
Planned Aggregate Expenditure and Aggregate Output (Income)

Saving (S) is a leakage out of household income. If planned investment (I) is exactly equal to S, then planned aggregate expenditure (AE) is exactly equal to aggregate output (Y), and there is equilibrium.

diagram shows saving flowing from households into the financial (money) market, which can be used by firms to finance investment projects. If the planned investment of firms equals the saving of households, then planned aggregate expenditure ($AE \equiv C + I$) equals aggregate output (income) (Y), and there is equilibrium. In this case, the leakage out of the system—saving—is matched by an equal injection of planned investment spending into the system. For this reason, the saving/investment approach to equilibrium is also called the *leakages/injections approach* to equilibrium.

Figure 24.10 reproduces the saving schedule derived in Figure 24.6 and the horizontal investment function from Figure 24.7. Notice that $S = I$ at one, and only one, level of aggregate output, $Y = 500$. At $Y = 500$, $C = 475$ and $I = 25$. In other words, $Y = C + I$, and therefore equilibrium exists.

Adjustment to Equilibrium

We have now defined equilibrium and learned how to find it, but we have said nothing about how firms might react to *disequilibrium*. Now let us consider the actions that firms might take when planned aggregate expenditure exceeds aggregate output (income).

We already know that the only way firms can sell more than they produce is by selling some inventory. This means that when planned aggregate expenditure exceeds aggregate output, unplanned inventory reductions have occurred. It seems reasonable to assume that firms will respond to unplanned inventory reductions by increasing output. If firms increase output, then income must also increase (since output and income are simply two ways of measuring the same thing). As General Motors builds more cars, for example, it hires more workers (or pays its existing work force for working more hours), buys more steel, uses more electricity, and so on. These purchases by GM represent income for the producers of labor, steel, electricity, and so on. Therefore, if GM (and all other firms) try to keep their inventories intact by increasing production, they will generate more income in the economy as a whole. This in turn will lead to more consumption. Remember, when income rises, consumption also rises.

> The adjustment process will continue as long as output (income) is below planned aggregate expenditure. Thus, if firms react to unplanned inventory reductions by increasing output, an economy with planned spending greater than output will adjust to equilibrium, with Y higher than before. Similarly, if planned spending is less than output, there will be unplanned increases in inventories. In this case, firms will respond by reducing output. As output falls, income falls, consumption falls, and so forth, until equilibrium is restored, with Y lower than before.

As Figure 24.8 shows, at any level of output above Y^* such as Y_1, output will fall until it reaches equilibrium at Y^*, and at any level of output below Y^*, such as Y_2, output will rise until it reaches equilibrium at Y^*.

The Multiplier

Now that we know how the equilibrium value of income is determined, we need to ask: How does the equilibrium level of output change when planned investment changes? In other words, if there is a sudden change in planned investment, how will output respond, if it responds at all? As we will see, the

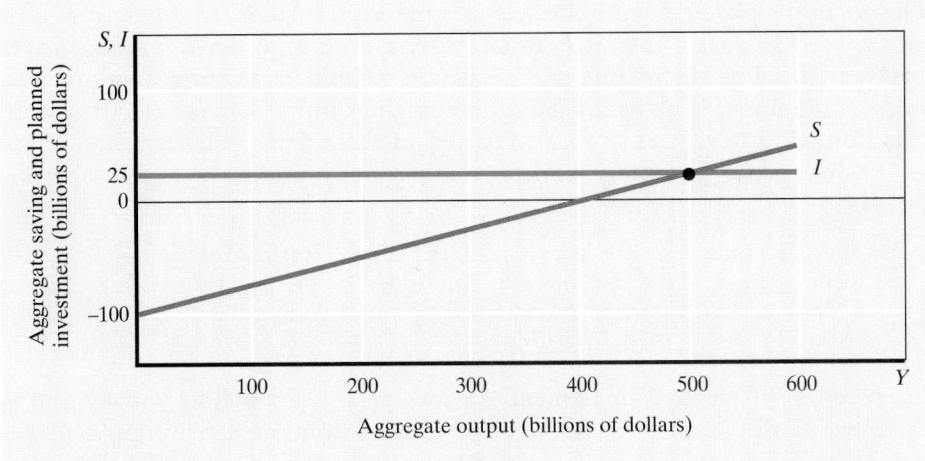

FIGURE 24.10
The $S = I$ Approach to Equilibrium

Aggregate output will be equal to planned aggregate expenditure only when saving equals planned investment ($S = I$). Saving and planned investment are equal at $Y = 500$.

change in output is *greater* than the initial change in planned investment. Output changes by a multiple of the change in planned investment. Not surprisingly, this multiple is called the **multiplier.** The basic idea behind the multiplier is that the initial change in planned investment stimulates multiple spending increases.

More formally, the multiplier is defined as the ratio of the change in the equilibrium level of output to a change in some autonomous variable. A variable is **autonomous** when it is taken as a given. For the purposes of this chapter, we consider planned investment to be autonomous. This simplifies our analysis and provides a strong foundation for our later discussions.

With planned investment taken as a given, we can now ask the question of how much the equilibrium level of output changes when planned investment changes. Remember that we are not trying here to explain *why* planned investment changes; we are simply asking the question of how much the equilibrium level of output changes when (for whatever reason) planned investment changes. Beginning in Chapter 28, we will no longer take planned investment as a given and will explain how planned investment is determined. (This should give you something to look forward to!)

Let's now move from theory to practice. Consider, as an example, a sustained increase in planned investment of $25 billion—that is, suppose that I increases from $25 billion to $50 billion and stays at $50 billion. If equilibrium existed at $I = $25 billion, an increase in planned investment of $25 billion will cause a disequilibrium, with planned aggregate expenditure greater than aggregate output by $25 billion. Firms immediately see unplanned reductions in their inventories, and, as a result, they begin to increase output.

For the sake of illustration, let us say that the increase in planned investment comes from an anticipated increase in travel that leads airlines to purchase more airplanes, car rental companies to increase purchases of automobiles, and bus companies to purchase more buses. (These are, of course, capital goods.) The firms experiencing unplanned inventory declines will therefore be automobile manufacturers, bus producers, and aircraft producers—General Motors, Ford, McDonnell Douglas, Boeing, and so forth. These firms will gear up and increase output.

Now suppose that these firms raise output by the full $25 billion increase in planned investment. Does this restore equilibrium? No, because when output goes up, people earn more income and a part of that income will be spent.

multiplier The ratio of the change in the equilibrium level of output to a change in some autonomous variable. For purposes of this chapter, the autonomous variable is planned investment.

autonomous variable A variable that is taken as a given.

This increases planned aggregate expenditure even further. In other words, an increase in *I* also leads indirectly to an increase in *C*. In order to produce more airplanes, Boeing has to hire more workers or ask its existing employees to work more hours. It also must buy more engines from General Electric, more tires from Goodyear, and so forth. Owners of these firms will earn more profits, produce more, hire more workers, and pay out more in wages and salaries.

> This added income does not just vanish into thin air. It is paid to households that spend some of it and save the rest. The added production thus leads to added income, which leads to added consumption spending.

Therefore, if planned investment (*I*) goes up by $25 billion initially and is sustained at this higher level, an increase of output of $25 billion will *not* restore equilibrium, because it generates even more consumption spending (*C*). People buy more consumer goods. There are unplanned reductions of inventories of basic consumption items—washing machines, food, clothing, and so forth—and this prompts other firms to increase output. Thus, the cycle starts all over again.[5]

Clearly, then, output and income can rise by significantly more than the initial increase in planned investment. The question is: By how much? In other words, *How large is the multiplier?* This question is answered graphically in Figure 24.11. Assume that the economy is in equilibrium at point *A*, where equilibrium output is 500. The increase in *I* of 25 shifts the $AE \equiv C + I$ curve up by 25, because *I* is higher by 25 at every level of income. The new equilibrium occurs at point *B*, where the equilibrium level of output is 600. Like point *A*, point *B* is on the 45° line and is thus an equilibrium value. Output (*Y*) has thus increased by 100 (600 − 500), or four times the initial increase in planned investment of 25, between point *A* and point *B*. The multiplier in this example is therefore four. At point *B*, aggregate spending is also higher by 100. If 25 of this additional 100 is investment (*I*), as we know it is, the remaining amount—75—is added consumption (*C*). From point *A* to point *B* then, $\Delta Y = 100$, $\Delta I = 25$, and $\Delta C = 75$.

The size of the multiplier depends on the slope of the planned aggregate expenditure line. The steeper the slope of this line, the greater the change in output for a given change in investment. When planned investment is fixed, as it is in our example, the slope of the $AE \equiv C + I$ line is just the marginal propensity to consume ($\Delta C/\Delta Y$). The greater the *MPC*, the greater the multiplier. This should not be surprising. A large *MPC* means that consumption increases a lot when income increases. The more consumption changes, the more output has to change to achieve equilibrium.

---

[5]Figure 24.9 can help you understand the multiplier effect more clearly. Note in the figure how an increase in planned investment makes its way through the circular flow. Initially, aggregate output is at equilibrium with $Y = C + I$. That is, every period, aggregate output is produced by firms, and every period, planned aggregate expenditure is just sufficient to take all those goods and services off the market.

Now note what happens when planned investment spending increases and is sustained at a higher level. Firms experience unplanned declines in inventories and they increase output of investment goods. But the added output means more income; thus we see added income flowing to households. This, in turn, means more spending. Households spend some portion of their added income (equal to the added income times the *MPC*) on consumer goods.

The higher consumption spending means that even if firms responded fully to the increase in investment spending in the first round, the economy is still out of equilibrium. Follow the added spending back over to firms in Figure 24.9 and you can see that with higher consumption, planned aggregate expenditure will be greater. Firms again see an unplanned decline in inventories and they respond by increasing the output of consumer goods. This sets off yet another round of income and expenditure increases.

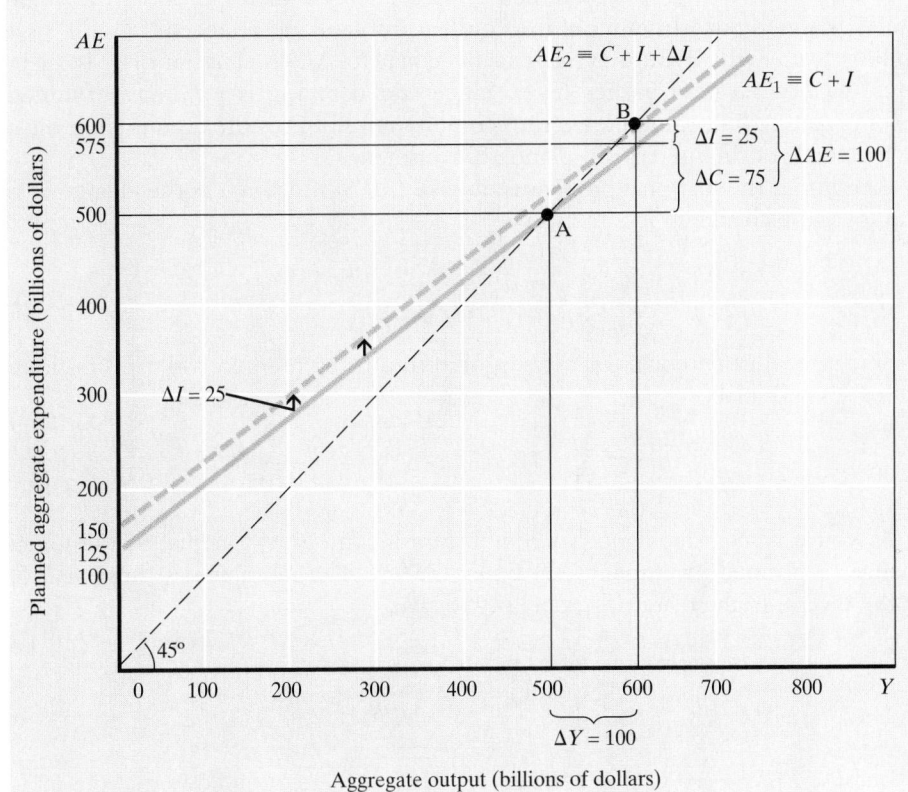

At point A, the economy is in equilibrium at $Y = 500$. When I increases by 25, planned aggregate expenditure is initially greater than aggregate output. As output rises in response, additional consumption is generated, pushing equilibrium output up by a multiple of the initial increase in I. The new equilibrium is found at point B, where $Y = 600$. Equilibrium output has thus increased by 100 ($600 - 500$), or *four times* the amount of the increase in planned investment.

THE MULTIPLIER EQUATION Is there a way to determine the size of the multiplier without using graphic analysis? The answer is yes.

Consider the following. Assume, as we did above, that the market is in equilibrium at an income level of $Y^* = 500$. Now suppose that planned investment (I), and thus planned aggregate expenditure (AE), increases and remains higher by some amount ΔI—say, \$25 billion. Planned aggregate expenditure is thus greater than output, there is an unplanned inventory reduction, and firms respond by increasing output (income) (Y). This leads to a second round of increases, and so on.

What will restore equilibrium? Look back at Figure 24.10 and recall that planned aggregate expenditure ($AE \equiv C + I$) is not equal to aggregate output (Y) unless $S = I$; the leakage of saving must exactly match the injection of planned investment spending for the economy to be in equilibrium. Recall also that we assumed that planned investment jumps to a new higher level and stays there; it is a *sustained* increase of \$25 billion in planned investment spending. As income rises, consumption rises and so does saving. Our $S = I$ approach to equilibrium thus leads us to conclude that:

> Equilibrium will be restored only when saving has increased by exactly the amount of the initial increase in I.

Otherwise, I will continue to be greater than S, and $C + I$ will continue to be greater than Y. (The $S = I$ approach to equilibrium leads to an interesting paradox in the macroeconomy. For more details, see the Issues and Applications box titled "The Paradox of Thrift.")

It is possible to figure how much Y must increase in response to the additional planned investment before equilibrium will be restored. Y will rise, pulling S up with it until ΔS is exactly equal to ΔI—that is, until S is again equal to I at its new higher level. Since added saving is a *fraction* of added income (the MPS), the increase in income required to restore equilibrium must be a *multiple* of the increase in planned investment.

Recall that the marginal propensity to save (MPS) is defined as the change in S (ΔS) over the change in income (ΔY):

$$MPS \equiv \frac{\Delta S}{\Delta Y}.$$

Since ΔS must be equal to ΔI for equilibrium to be restored, we can substitute ΔI for ΔS and solve:

$$MPS = \frac{\Delta I}{\Delta Y}. \text{ Therefore, } \Delta Y = \Delta I \times \frac{1}{MPS}.$$

As you can see, the change in equilibrium income (ΔY) is equal to the initial change in planned investment (ΔI) times $1/MPS$. The multiplier is thus $1/MPS$, or the inverse of the marginal propensity to save:

$$\text{Multiplier} \equiv \frac{1}{MPS}.$$

Because $MPS + MPC \equiv 1$, $MPS \equiv 1 - MPC$. It therefore follows that the multiplier is also equal to:

$$\text{Multiplier} \equiv \frac{1}{1 - MPC}.$$

In our example, the MPC is .75 ($\Delta C/\Delta Y = 75/100 = .75$), so the MPS must equal $1 - .75$, or .25. Thus, the multiplier is 1 divided by .25, or four. The change in the equilibrium level of Y is thus $4 \times \$25$ billion, or $\$100$ billion.[6] It is also important to note that the same analysis holds when planned investment falls. If planned investment falls by a certain amount and is sustained at this lower level, output will fall by a multiple of the reduction in I. As the initial shock is felt and firms cut output, they lay people off. The result: Income, and subsequently consumption, falls. This is exactly what happened in Germany and Japan in 1993, as this chapter's Global Perspective box, "The Multiplier Around the World in 1993" discusses.

THE SIZE OF THE MULTIPLIER IN THE REAL WORLD In considering the size of the multiplier, it is important to realize that the multiplier we derived in this chapter is based on a *very* simplified picture of the economy. First, we have assumed that planned investment is fixed and does not respond to changes in the economy. Second, we have thus far ignored the role of government, financial markets, and the rest of the world in the macroeconomy. For these reasons, it would be a mistake to move on from this chapter thinking that national income can be increased by $\$100$ billion simply by increasing planned investment spending by $\$25$ billion.

---

[6]The multiplier can also be derived algebraically, as the appendix to this chapter demonstrates.

The multiplier story is not complicated: When the real output of an economy grows, real income also grows. Firms expand production, hire workers, and pay out wages and dividends. In turn, households devote one part of their higher incomes to saving and the rest to consumption spending. Higher consumption expenditure leads to higher aggregate expenditure. As expenditure expands, inventories of firms fall and real output rises.

Unfortunately, the multiplier also works on the way down. When real output falls, workers are laid off, incomes fall, and both consumption spending and saving fall. When income and consumption spending decrease, aggregate expenditure drops off, inventories rise, and real output falls even further.

In 1993, some of the world's economies were expanding and others were contracting. The most dramatic expansion was taking place in China, where a real boom seemed to be in progress and a multiplier was at work. The following excerpt tells part of the story:

"China has 60 million to 300 million consumers, people who can spend real money for goods, and that's a wholly new phenomenon in China."... said Jerome A. Cohen, a lawyer.... As the Chinese grow more affluent and trade restrictions are eased, they are increasingly becoming an important market for foreign sellers. In the south, Chinese consumers are buying Lux soap, Heinz baby food and Pabst beer.... Demand for steel caused by the Chinese construction boom has helped increase world steel prices by 10 to 15 percent in the last six months.

Much of the world, however, was in recession. The new Eastern European republics and the former Soviet Union experienced sharply falling GDP. Times were particularly tough in Germany:

As Japan's economy has entered a period of downturn, China's economy has experienced strong growth. Kerry's Department Store in Beijing, pictured here, sells (among other things) Japanese fashions and fragances to the newly-affluent Chinese.

Crippled by the disappearance of markets in the former Soviet bloc and an inability to compete in the West, the old-fashioned, bloated and often environmentally poisonous industries of [the former East Germany] have suffered a collapse far more devastating than what was foreseen by German leaders in 1990.

"Nobody imagined anything on this scale," said Richard Gardner, an executive at Deutsche Bank in Berlin. "The more we looked at the eastern part of the country, the more decrepit we realized it really was."

Of the 9.75 million people employed in eastern Germany in 1989, Deutsche Bank estimates that 5.35 million still have jobs in the eastern regions. In three years, 4.4 million jobs have been lost.

The unemployment rate, including people in the temporary work programs, has soared to more than 30 percent, and reaches 45 percent if early retirees and those obliged to work in the west are included. Industrial output has slumped by 70 percent...

Weighed down by the higher-than-expected costs of unification, Germany has plunged into its first recession since 1982. The

Government predicted last month that the economy would shrink five-tenths of 1 percent this year; Deutsche Bank said this month the decline could be as much as 2 percent.

Even Japan, whose economy had been growing steadily for years, experienced a slowdown. Particularly hard hit was the Japanese steel industry:

The NKK Corporation, a Japanese steelmaker, announced deep job cuts today, and industry analysts said they expected similar moves from the country's other steel producers, which have been hard hit by the recession here.

NKK said it would eliminate 3,200 jobs—18 percent of its work force—by the end of 1995.... NKK's president, Yoshinari Miyoshi, said the company was expecting a prolonged period of low growth.

Sources: Sheryl WuDunn, "Booming China," *New York Times,* Feb. 15, 1993; "Deep Cutbacks in Japan," *New York Times,* March 11, 1993; Roger Cohen, "In Three Years, 4.4 Million Eastern German Jobs Have Been Lost," *New York Times,* March 8, 1993.

As we relax these assumptions in the following chapters, you will see that most of what we add to make our analysis more realistic has the effect of *reducing* the size of the multiplier. For example:

1. The appendix to Chapter 25 shows that when tax payments depend on income (as they do in the "real world"), the size of the multiplier is reduced. As the economy expands, tax payments increase and act as a drag on the economy. The multiplier effect is thus smaller.

2. As you will see in Chapter 28, planned investment (*I*) is not fixed; rather, it depends on the interest rate in the economy. This too has the effect of reducing the size of the multiplier.

3. Thus far we have not discussed how the overall price level is determined in the economy. When we do so in Chapter 29, we will see that part of an expansion of the economy is likely to take the form of an increase in the price level rather than an increase in output. When this happens, the size of the multiplier is reduced.

4. We introduce the role of imports and exports in Chapter 25 and treat them fully in Chapter 37. In these chapters, you will see that the multiplier effect on domestic production will be reduced if some domestic spending leaks into foreign markets.

These juicy tidbits give you something to look forward to as you proceed through the rest of this book. For now, however, it is enough to point out that:

> In many applications, the actual size of the multiplier is about 1.4.

This is a far cry from the value of 4.0 that we used in this chapter.

THE MULTIPLIER IN ACTION: RECOVERING FROM THE GREAT DEPRESSION The Great Depression began in 1930 and lasted nearly a decade. Real output in 1938 was lower than real output in 1929, and the unemployment rate never fell below 14% of the labor force between 1930 and 1940. How is it possible that the economy got "stuck" at such a low level of income and a high level of unemployment? The essentially Keynesian model that we have analyzed in this chapter can help us to answer this question.

If firms do not wish to undertake much investment (*I* is low) or if consumers decide to increase their saving and cut back on consumption, then planned spending will be low. Firms do not want to produce more because, with many workers unemployed, households do not have the income to buy the extra output that firms might produce. And households, who would purchase more if they had more income, cannot find jobs that would enable them to earn additional income. The economy is thus caught in a vicious cycle.

How might such a cycle be broken? One possibility is for planned aggregate expenditure to increase, thereby increasing aggregate output via the multiplier effect. This increase in *AE* may occur naturally, or it may be caused by a change in government policy.

In the late 1930s, for example, the economy experienced a surge of both residential and nonresidential investment. Between 1935 and 1940, total investment spending (in real terms) increased 64% and residential investment more than doubled. There can be no doubt that this increased investment had a multiplier effect. In just five years, employment in the construction industry increased by more than 400,000, employment in manufacturing industries jumped by more than one million, and total employment grew by more than five million. As more workers were employed, more income was generated, and some of this added income was

THE PARADOX OF THRIFT

An interesting paradox can arise when households attempt to increase their saving. What happens if households become concerned about the future and want to save more today to be prepared for hard times tomorrow? If households increase their planned saving, the saving schedule in the figure below shifts upward, from S to S'. The plan to save more is, of course, a plan to consume less, and the resulting drop in spending leads to a drop in income. Income drops by a multiple of the initial shift in the saving schedule. Before the increase in saving, equilibrium exists at point A, where $S = I$ and $Y = \$500$ billion. Increased saving shifts the equilibrium to point B, the point at which $S' = I$. New equilibrium output is thus $\$300$ billion—a $\$200$ billion decrease (ΔY) from the initial equilibrium.

Thus, by consuming less, households have actually *caused* the hard times about which they were apprehensive. What is worse, the new equilibrium finds saving at the same level as it was before consumption dropped ($\$25$ billion). In their attempt to save more, households have caused a contraction in output, and thus in income. They end up consuming less, but they have not saved any more.

It should be clear why saving at the new equilibrium is equal to saving at the old equilibrium. Equilibrium requires that saving equal planned investment, and since planned investment is unchanged, saving must remain unchanged for equilibrium to exist. This paradox shows that the interactions among sectors in the economy can be of crucial importance.

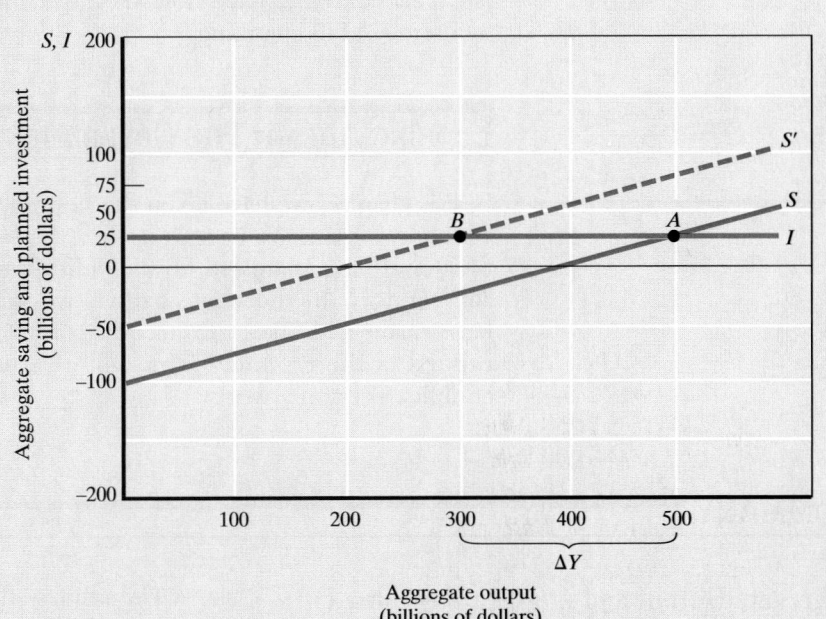

FIGURE 1
The Paradox of Thrift

An increase in planned saving from S to S' causes equilibrium output to decrease from $\$500$ to $\$300$ billion. The decreased consumption that accompanies increased saving leads to a contraction of the economy and thus to a reduction of income. But at the new equilibrium, saving is the same as it was at the initial equilibrium. Thus, increased efforts to save have caused a drop in income but no overall change in saving.

The **paradox of thrift** is "paradoxical" because it contradicts the widely held belief that "a penny saved is a penny earned." This may be true for an individual, but when society as a whole saves more, the result is a drop in income but no increased saving.

Does the paradox of thrift always hold? Recall our assumption that planned investment is fixed. Let us drop this assumption for a moment. If the extra saving that households want to do to ward off hard times is channeled into additional investment through financial markets, there is a shift up in the I schedule. The paradox could then be averted. If investment increases, a new equilibrium can be achieved at a higher level of saving and income. This result, however, depends critically on the existence of a channel through which additional household saving finances additional investment.

spent on consumption goods. Inventories declined and firms began to expand output. Between 1935 and 1940, real output (income) increased by more than one third and the unemployment rate dropped from 20.3% to 14.6 percent.

But 14.6% is still a very high rate of unemployment; the depression was not yet over. Between 1940 and 1943, however, the depression ended, with the unemployment rate dropping to 1.9% in 1943. This recovery was triggered by the mobilization for World War II and the significant increase in government purchases of goods and services, which rose from $14 billion in 1940 to $88.6 billion in 1943. In the next chapter, we will explore this *government spending multiplier,* and you'll see how the government can help stimulate the economy by increasing its spending.

LOOKING AHEAD: THE GOVERNMENT AND INTERNATIONAL SECTORS

In this chapter, we have taken the first important step in understanding how the economy works. We have described the behavior of two sectors (household and firm) and have discussed how equilibrium is achieved in the market for goods and services. In the next chapter, we will relax some of the assumptions we have made and take into account the roles of government spending and net exports in the economy. This will give us a more realistic picture of how our complex economy works.

SUMMARY

Aggregate Output and Aggregate Income (Y)

1. Each period, firms produce an aggregate quantity of goods and services called *aggregate output* (Y). Because every dollar of expenditure is received by someone as income, aggregate output and aggregate income are the same thing.

2. The total amount of aggregate consumption that takes place in any given period of time depends on factors such as household income, household wealth, the interest rate, and households' expectations about the future.

3. In an economy in which there are no imports or exports and no government, households can do only two things with their income: They can either spend on consumption or they can save. The letter C is used to refer to aggregate consumption by households. The letter S is used to refer to aggregate saving by households. By definition, saving equals income minus consumption: $S \equiv Y - C$.

4. The higher someone's income is, the higher his or her consumption is likely to be. This also holds true for the economy as a whole: There is a positive relationship between aggregate consumption (C) and aggregate income (Y).

5. The *marginal propensity to consume (MPC)* is the fraction of a change in income that is consumed, or spent. The *marginal propensity to save (MPS)* is the fraction of a change in income that is saved. Because all income must be either saved or spent, $MPS + MPC \equiv 1$.

6. The primary form of spending that firms engage in is investment. Strictly speaking, *investment* refers to the purchase by firms of new buildings and equipment and additions to inventories, all of which add to firms' capital stock.

7. *Actual investment* can differ from planned investment because changes in firms' inventories are part of actual investment and inventory changes are not under the complete control of firms. Inventory changes are partly determined by how much households decide to buy. The letter I is used to refer to planned investment only.

8. In an economy with no government, no imports, and no exports, *planned aggregate expenditures* (AE) equal consumption plus planned investment: $AE \equiv C + I$. *Equilibrium* in the goods market is achieved when planned aggregate expenditure equals aggregate output: $C + I = Y$. This holds if, and only if, planned investment and actual investment are equal.

Equilibrium Aggregate Output (Income)

9. Because aggregate income must be saved or spent, the equilibrium condition $Y = C + I$ can be rewritten as $C + S = C + I$, or $S = I$. Thus, only when planned investment equals saving will there be equilibrium. This approach to equilibrium is called the *saving/investment approach* to equilibrium or the *leakages/injections approach* to equilibrium.

10. When aggregate expenditure exceeds aggregate output *(income),* there is an unplanned fall in inventories. Firms will therefore increase output. This increased output leads to

increased income and even more consumption. This process will continue as long as output (income) is below planned aggregate expenditure. If firms react to unplanned inventory reductions by increasing output, an economy with planned spending greater than output will adjust to equilibrium, with Y higher than before.

11. Equilibrium output changes by a multiple of the change in planned investment. The multiplier is equal to $1/MPS$.

12. When households increase their planned saving, income decreases and saving does not change. Saving does not increase because in equilibrium saving must equal planned investment and planned investment is fixed. If planned investment also increased, this paradox of thrift could be averted and a new equilibrium could be achieved at a higher level of saving and income. This result, however, depends critically on the existence of a channel through which additional household saving finances additional investment.

REVIEW TERMS AND CONCEPTS

actual investment   603
aggregate income   596
aggregate output   596
aggregate output (income) (Y)   596
autonomous variable   609
change in inventory   603
consumption function   598
desired, or planned,
   investment (I)   603
equilibrium   604
identity   596
investment   601

marginal propensity to consume
   (MPC)   599
marginal propensity to save
   (MPS)   599
multiplier   609
paradox of thrift   615
planned aggregate expenditure
   (AE)   604
saving (S)   596

Equations:
$S \equiv Y - C$
$MPC \equiv$
   slope of consumption function $\equiv \dfrac{\Delta C}{\Delta Y}$

$MPC + MPS \equiv 1$
$AE \equiv C + I$
equilibrium condition: $Y = AE$ or
   $Y = C + I$
saving/investment approach to
   equilibrium: $S = I$

$$\text{Multiplier} \equiv \dfrac{1}{MPS} \equiv \dfrac{1}{1 - MPC}.$$

PROBLEM SET

1.   The following is the consumption schedule for the Republic of Nurd in 1994:

Y	50	60	70	80	90	100	110	120	130	140	150
C	52	62	71.5	80.5	89	97	104	110	115	119	122.5

a. Construct a graph of the consumption function.
b. Compute the marginal propensity to consume over each income range. What is the geometrical meaning of the *MPC*? Explain why.
c. Compute and graph the saving schedule (saving as a function of income, Y) for Nurd. Also compute the marginal propensity to save over each income range.
d. Suppose that planned investment spending (I) is constant at $10. What is the equilibrium level of Nurd's domestic product (Y)? Graph the equilibrium level of income/output (Y) in two ways.
e. Suppose that planned investment (I) on Nurd increases to $16 and remains at that level. Assuming a constant *MPC* of 0.5, what will Nurd's new equilibrium level of income/output (Y) be? Compute and show this equilibrium point graphically.

2. Explain how planned investment can differ from actual investment.

3. You are given the following data regarding Freedonia, a legendary country:

(1)   Consumption function: $C = 200 + 0.8Y$
(2)   Investment function: $I = 100$
(3) $AE \equiv C + I$
(4) $AE = Y$

a. What is the marginal propensity to consume in Freedonia? The marginal propensity to save?
b. Graph equations (3) and (4) and solve for equilibrium income.
c. Suppose equation (2) were changed to
          (2') $I = 110$.

What is the new equilibrium level of income? By how much does the $10 increase in planned investment change equilibrium income? What is the value of the multiplier?
d. Calculate the saving function for Freedonia. Plot this saving function on a graph with equation (2). Explain why the equilibrium income in this graph must be the same as in part b.

4. If I decide to save an extra dollar, my saving goes up by that amount. But if everyone decides to save an extra dollar, income falls and saving does not rise. Explain.

5. How can my choosing to buy a $10 pizza, by decreasing my saving this period, cause total income to rise by more than $10?

6. In Chapter 21, you learned that expenditures and income should always be equal. In this chapter, you've learned that AE and aggregate output (income) can be different. Is there an inconsistency here?

APPENDIX TO CHAPTER 24
DERIVING THE MULTIPLIER ALGEBRAICALLY

In addition to deriving the multiplier using the simple substitution we used in the chapter, we can also derive the formula for the multiplier by using simple algebra.

Recall that our consumption function is

$$C = a + bY,$$

where b is the marginal propensity to consume. In equilibrium,

$$Y = C + I.$$

All we have to do now is solve these two equations for Y in terms of I. Substituting the first equation into the second, we get

$$Y = \underbrace{a + bY}_{C} + I.$$

This equation can be rearranged to yield

$$Y - bY = a + I$$
$$Y(1 - b) = a + I.$$

We can then solve for Y in terms of I by dividing through by $(1 - b)$:

$$Y = \left(\frac{1}{1-b}\right)(a+I).$$

Now look carefully at this expression and think about increasing I by some amount, ΔI, with a held constant. If I increases by ΔI, income will increase by

$$\Delta Y = \Delta I \times \frac{1}{1-b}.$$

Since $b \equiv MPC$, the expression becomes

$$\Delta Y = \Delta I \times \frac{1}{1-MPC}.$$

The multiplier is thus

$$\frac{1}{1-MPC}.$$

Finally, since $MPS + MPC \equiv 1$, MPS is equal to $1 - MPC$, making the alternative expression for the multiplier $1/MPS$, just as we saw in the chapter.

The Government and Fiscal Policy

25

Few areas in either macroeconomics or microeconomics arouse as much controversy as the question of the proper role of government in the economy. In microeconomics, the active presence of government in regulating competition, providing roads and education, and redistributing income is much applauded by those who believe that a free market simply does not work well if left to its own devices. Opponents of government intervention argue that it is the government, rather than the market, that performs badly. These critics point to bureaucracy and inefficiency that they argue could be eliminated or reduced if the government played a smaller role in the economy.

In macroeconomics, the debate over what the government can and should do has a similar flavor, although the issues are somewhat different. At one end of the spectrum are the Keynesians and their intellectual descendants, who believe that the macroeconomy is likely to fluctuate too much if left on its own and that the government should play an important role in smoothing out fluctuations in the business cycle. These ideas can be traced back to Keynes's analysis in *The General Theory*, which suggests that governments can use their taxing and spending powers to increase aggregate expenditure (and thereby stimulate aggregate output) in times of recessions or depressions. At the other end of the spectrum are those who claim that government spending is at best incapable of stabilizing the economy and at worst destabilizing and harmful.

Perhaps the one thing most people can agree on is that, like it or not, governments are important actors in the economies of virtually all countries. On these grounds alone, then, it is worth our while to analyze the way in which the government influences the functioning of the macroeconomy.

While the government has a wide variety of powers, including regulating firms' entry into and exit from an industry, setting standards for the quality of products, setting minimum wage levels, and regulating the disclosure of information, in macroeconomics we study a government with general, but more limited, powers. Specifically, government can affect the macroeconomy through two specific policy channels: *fiscal policy* and *monetary policy*. **Fiscal policy,** the focus of this chapter, refers to the government's spending and taxing behavior—in other words, its budget policy.[1] Fiscal policy is generally divided into three categories: (1) policies regarding government purchases of goods and labor, (2) policies regarding taxes, and (3) policies regarding transfer payments (such as unemployment compensation, social security benefits, welfare payments, and veterans' benefits) to households. **Monetary policy,** the focus of the next two chapters, refers to the behavior of the nation's central bank, the Federal Reserve, regarding the nation's money supply.

fiscal policy The spending and taxing policies used by the government to influence the economy.

monetary policy The behavior of the Federal Reserve regarding the nation's money supply.

GOVERNMENT PARTICIPATION IN THE ECONOMY

Given the scope and power of local, state, and federal governments in the U.S. economy, it should be stressed that there are some matters over which these governments exert great control and some matters that are beyond their control. There is an important distinction between variables that a government controls directly and variables that are a consequence of government decisions *combined with the state of the economy.*

Tax rates, for example, are controlled by the government. By law, Congress has the authority to levy taxes: It decides who and what should be taxed and at what rate. Tax *revenue,* on the other hand, is not subject to complete control by the government. Revenue from the personal income tax system depends both on personal tax rates (which Congress sets) *and* on the income of the household sector (which depends on many factors that are not under direct government control, such as how much households decide to work). Revenue from the corporate profits tax depends both on corporate profits tax rates and on the size of corporate profits. The government controls corporate tax rates but not the size of corporate profits.

Government spending also depends both on government decisions and on the state of the economy. For example, one of the most important transfer programs in the United States is the unemployment insurance program, which pays benefits to people who are unemployed. When the economy goes into a recession, the number of unemployed workers increases and so does the level of government unemployment insurance payments.

Government Purchases (G), Net Taxes (T), and Disposable Income (Y_d)

In the previous chapter, we explored the equilibrium level of national output for a simple economy with no government and no imports and exports. The purpose of that chapter was to provide you with a general idea of how the macroeconomy operates.

---

[1] The word "fiscal" comes from the root *fisc,* which refers to the "treasury" of a government.

Clearly, though, it is much more realistic to consider an economy in which government is an active participant. After all, there are no countries in the world without a government. We therefore begin our discussion of fiscal policy by adding the government sector into the simple economy described in the previous chapter.

To keep things simple, we will combine two major government activities—the collection of taxes and the payment of transfer payments—into a category we will call **net taxes (T)**. Specifically, net taxes are equal to the tax payments made by firms and households to the government minus transfer payments made to households by the government. The other variable we will consider is government purchases of goods and services (G).

Our earlier discussions of household consumption did not take taxes into account. We simply assumed that all the income generated in the economy was either spent or saved by households. However, when we take into account the role of government in the economy, as Figure 25.1 does, we see that as income (Y) flows toward households, the government takes income from households in the form of net taxes (T). The income that ultimately gets to households is called **disposable, or after–tax, income (Y_d)**:

$$Y_d \equiv Y - T.$$

Y_d excludes taxes paid by households and includes transfer payments made to households by the government. Note that for now we are assuming that T does not depend on Y, i.e., net taxes do not depend on income. This assumption is relaxed in Appendix B to this chapter. Taxes that do not depend on income are sometimes called *lump-sum taxes*.

As Figure 25.1 also shows, the disposable income (Y_d) of households must end up either as consumption (C) or saving (S). Thus, it follows that

$$Y_d \equiv C + S.$$

net taxes (T) Taxes paid by firms and households to the government minus transfer payments made to households by the government.

disposable, or after–tax, income (Y_d) Total income minus net taxes: $Y - T$.

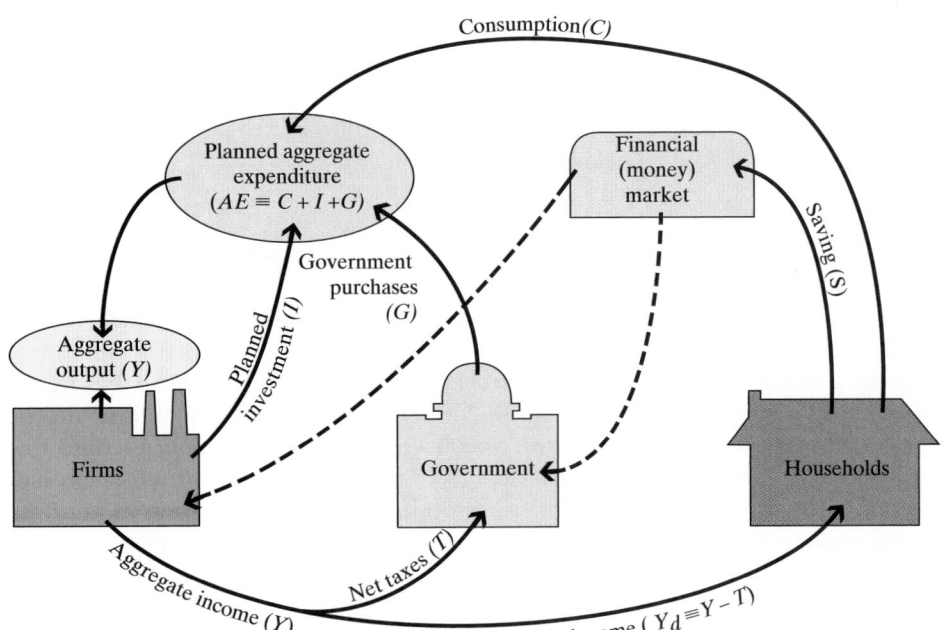

FIGURE 25.1
Adding Net Taxes (T) and Government Purchases (G) to the Circular Flow of Income

Remember that the triple equal sign means that this equation is an *identity*, or something that is always true.

Because disposable income is simply aggregate income (Y) minus net taxes (T), we can write another identity:

$$Y - T \equiv C + S.$$

Adding T to both sides, we get:

$$Y \equiv C + S + T.$$

This identity simply says that aggregate income gets cut into three pieces. Government takes a slice (net taxes, T), and then households divide the rest between consumption and saving (C and S).

Because governments spend money on goods and services, we also need to expand our definition of planned aggregate expenditure. Planned aggregate expenditure (AE) is thus equal to the sum of consumption spending by households (C), planned investment by business firms (I), *and* government purchases of goods and services (G):

$$AE \equiv C + I + G.$$

budget deficit The difference between what a government spends and what it collects in taxes in a given period: $G - T$.

A government's **budget deficit** is the difference between what it spends (G) and what it collects in taxes (T) in a given period:

$$\text{Budget Deficit} \equiv G - T.$$

If G exceeds T, the government must borrow from the public to finance the deficit. It does so by selling Treasury bonds and bills (more on this later). In this case, a part of household saving (S) goes to the government. Observe from the dotted line in Figure 25.1 that some S goes to firms to finance investment projects and some goes to the government to finance its deficit.[2]

ADDING TAXES TO THE CONSUMPTION FUNCTION In the last chapter, we examined the consumption behavior of households and noted that aggregate consumption (C) depends on aggregate income (Y): In general, the higher aggregate income is, the higher is aggregate consumption. For the sake of illustration, we used a specific linear consumption function:

$$C = a + bY,$$

where a is the amount of consumption that would take place if national income were zero and b is the marginal propensity to consume.

We need to modify this consumption function slightly now that we have added government to the economy. With taxes now a part of the picture, it makes sense to assume that disposable income (Y_d), rather than before-tax income (Y), determines consumption behavior. If you earn a million dollars, but have to pay $950,000 in taxes, you have no more disposable income than someone who earns only $50,000 but pays no taxes. In terms of what you have available for spending on current consumption, then, what matters is your disposable income, not your before-tax income.

---

[2]Although it is almost unheard of these days, governments do sometimes run budget surpluses. A *surplus* occurs when net taxes are greater than government purchases of goods and services. A surplus is simply a negative deficit.

It is very easy to modify our aggregate consumption function to incorporate disposable income rather than before-tax income. Instead of $C = a + bY$, we can simply write

$$C = a + bY_d$$

or

$$C = a + b(Y - T).$$

Our new consumption function now has consumption depending on disposable income rather than on before-tax income.

INVESTMENT   What about investment? The government can have an important effect on investment behavior through its tax treatment of depreciation and its other tax policies. Investment may also vary with economic conditions and interest rates, as we will see a little later. For our present purposes, however, we shall continue to assume that planned investment (I) is fixed.

Equilibrium Output: $Y = C + I + G$

We know from the previous chapter that equilibrium occurs where $Y = AE$, that is, where aggregate output equals planned aggregate expenditure. Remember that planned aggregate expenditure in an economy with a government is $C + I + G$. We can thus write the equilibrium condition as:

> Equilibrium Condition: $Y = C + I + G$.

The equilibrium analysis we presented in the previous chapter holds here also. If output (Y) exceeds planned aggregate expenditure ($C + I + G$), there will be an unplanned increase in inventories. In other words, actual investment will exceed planned investment. Conversely, if $C + I + G$ exceeds Y, there will be an unplanned decrease in inventories.

Let us work through a numerical example to illustrate the government's effect on the macroeconomy and the equilibrium condition. First, our specific consumption function, which was $C = 100 + .75Y$ before we introduced the government sector, now becomes

$$C = 100 + .75Y_d$$

or

$$C = 100 + .75(Y - T).$$

Second, we assume that the government is currently purchasing $100 billion of goods and services and collecting net taxes (T) of $100 billion.[3] In other words, the government is running a balanced budget, financing all of its spending with taxes. Third, we assume that planned investment (I) is $100 billion.

Table 25.1 calculates planned aggregate expenditure at several levels of disposable income. For example, at $Y = 500$, disposable income is $Y - T$, or 400. Therefore, $C = 100 + .75(400) = 400$. Assuming that I is fixed at $100 billion, and

---

[3]As we pointed out earlier, the government does not have complete control over tax revenues and transfer payments. We ignore this problem here, however, and set tax revenues minus transfers at a fixed amount. Things will become more realistic later in this chapter and in Appendix B.

TABLE 25.1
Finding Aggregate Expenditures and Equilibrium with *C, I,* and *G* (all figures in billions of dollars)

(1) OUTPUT (INCOME) Y	(2) NET TAXES T	(3) DISPOSABLE INCOME $Y_d \equiv Y - T$	(4) CONSUMPTION SPENDING $(C = 100 + .75\,Y_d)$	(5) SAVING S $(Y_d - C)$	(6) PLANNED INVESTMENT SPENDING I	(7) PLANNED GOVERNMENT PURCHASES G	(8) AGGREGATE EXPENDITURE $C + I + G$	(9) UNPLANNED INVENTORY CHANGE $Y - (C + I + G)$	(10) ADJUST-MENT TO DISEQUILI-BRIUM
300	100	200	250	-50	100	100	450	-150	Output↑
500	100	400	400	0	100	100	600	-100	Output↑
700	100	600	550	50	100	100	750	-50	Output↑
900	100	800	700	100	100	100	900	0	Equilibrium
1100	100	1000	850	150	100	100	1050	+50	Output↓
1300	100	1200	1000	200	100	100	1200	+100	Output↓
1500	100	1400	1150	250	100	100	1350	+150	Output↓

assuming that G is fixed at \$100 billion, planned aggregate expenditure is 600 ($C + I + G = 400 + 100 + 100$). Since output ($Y$) is only 500, planned spending is *greater* than output by 100. As a result, there is an unplanned inventory decrease of 100, giving firms an incentive to raise output. Thus, output of \$500 billion is below equilibrium.

If $Y = 1300$, however, then $Y_d = 1200$, $C = 1000$, and planned aggregate expenditure is 1200. Here, planned spending is *less* than output, there will be an unplanned inventory increase of 100, and firms will have an incentive to cut back output. Thus, output of \$1300 billion is above equilibrium. Only at $Y = 900$ are output and planned aggregate expenditure equal, and only at $Y = 900$ does equilibrium exist.

In Figure 25.2, we derive the same equilibrium level of output graphically. First, the consumption function must be drawn, taking into account the net taxes of 100. The old function was $C = 100 + .75Y$. The new function is $C = 100 + .75(Y - T)$ or $C = 100 + .75\,(Y - 100)$. This can be rewritten as $C = 100 + .75Y - 75$, or $C = 25 + .75Y$. The marginal propensity to consume has not changed—we assume that it remains .75. Thus, for example, consumption at an income of zero is \$25 billion ($C = 25 + .75Y = 25 + .75(0) = 25$). Note that the consumption function in Figure 25.2 plots the points in columns 1 and 4 of Table 25.1.

Planned aggregate expenditure, you will recall, is arrived at by adding planned investment to consumption. But now we have government purchases of 100 as well. Thus, because I and G are constant at 100 each at all levels of income, we add $I + G = 200$ to consumption at every level of income. The result is the new AE curve. This curve is just a plot of the points in columns 1 and 8 of Table 25.1. The 45° line helps us find the equilibrium level of real output, which, as we already know, is 900. If you examine any level of output above or below 900, you will find disequilibrium. Look, for example, at $Y = 500$ on the graph. At this level, planned aggregate expenditure is 600, but output is only 500. Inventories will fall below what was planned, and firms will have an incentive to increase output.

THE LEAKAGES/INJECTIONS APPROACH TO EQUILIBRIUM As we did in the last chapter, we can also examine equilibrium using the leakages/injections approach. Look again at the circular flow of income in Figure 25.1. The government takes out net taxes (T) from the flow of income—a leakage—and households save (S) some of their income—also a leakage from the flow of income. The planned

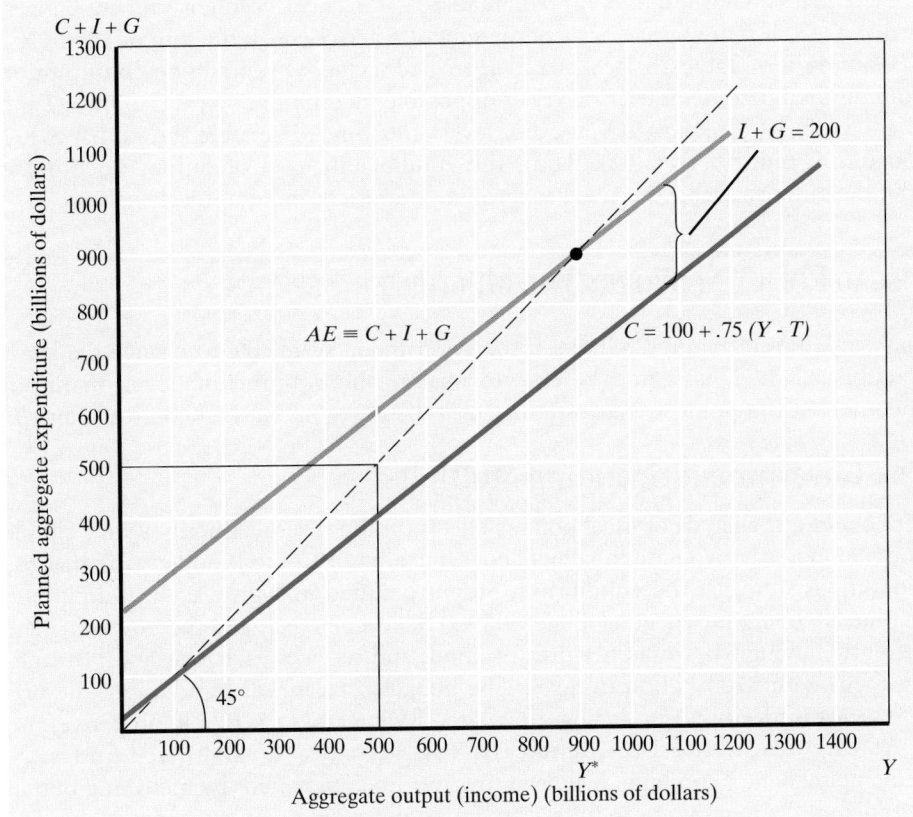

FIGURE 25.2
Finding Equilibrium
Output/Income Graphically

Since G and I are both fixed at $100 billion, the aggregate expenditure function is the new consumption function ($C = 25 + .75\,Y$) displaced upward by $I + G = 200$. Equilibrium occurs at $Y = AE = \$900$ billion.

spending injections are government purchases (G) and planned investment (I). If leakages ($S + T$) equal planned injections ($I + G$), there is equilibrium:

Leakages/Injections Approach to Equilibrium: $S + T = I + G$.

This equilibrium condition is easy to derive. We know that in equilibrium, aggregate output (income) (Y) equals planned aggregate expenditure (AE). By definition, AE equals $C + I + G$, and by definition Y equals $C + S + T$. Therefore, at equilibrium

$$C + S + T = C + I + G.$$

Subtracting C from both sides leaves

$$S + T = I + G.$$

Finally, it is revealing to rearrange terms. If we subtract T from both sides of the equation, we get the following expression:

$$S = I + (G - T).$$

Since we have defined the government deficit as $G - T$, this way of writing the equilibrium condition says that:

Equilibrium is achieved when saving is exactly equal to the sum of planned investment plus the government deficit.

Note that equilibrium does *not* require that $G = T$ (a balanced government budget) or that $S = I$. It is only necessary that the sum of S and T equals the sum of I and G.

Column 5 of Table 25.1 calculates aggregate saving by subtracting consumption from disposal income at every level of disposable income ($S \equiv Y_d - C$). Since I and G are fixed, $I + G$ equals 200 at every level of income. The table shows that $S + T$ equals 200 only at $Y = 900$. Thus, the equilibrium level of output (income) is 900, the same answer we arrived at through numerical and graphical analysis.

FISCAL POLICY AT WORK: THE MULTIPLIER EFFECTS

You can see from Figure 25.2 that if the government were able to change the levels of either G or T, it would be able to change the equilibrium level of output (income). At this point, we are assuming that the government does control G and T.

The Government Spending Multiplier

Let's begin our analysis of fiscal policy's effects on the macroeconomy with a simple story. Suppose that you are the chief economic advisor to the President and that the economy is sitting at the equilibrium output pictured in Figure 25.2. Output and income are being produced at a rate of $900 billion per year, and the government is currently buying $100 billion worth of goods and services each year and is financing them with $100 billion in taxes. The budget is balanced. In addition, the private sector is investing (producing capital goods) at a rate of $100 billion per year.

At this point, the President calls you into the Oval Office and says, "Unemployment is too high. We need to lower unemployment by increasing output and income." After some careful research, you determine that an acceptable unemployment rate could be achieved only if aggregate output increases to $1100 billion.

The question you now need to answer is: How can the government use taxing and spending policy—fiscal policy—to increase the equilibrium level of national output? Suppose that the President has let it be known that taxes must remain at present levels—the Congress just passed a major tax reform package—so adjusting T is out of the question for several years. That leaves you with G. Your only option, then, is to increase government spending while holding taxes constant.

To increase spending without raising taxes (which provides the government with revenue to spend), the government must borrow. When G is bigger than T, the government runs a *deficit,* and the difference between G and T must be borrowed. For the moment we will ignore the possible effect of the deficit and focus only on the effect of a higher G with T constant.

Meanwhile, the President is awaiting your answer. How much of an increase in spending would be required to generate a $200 billion increase in the equilibrium level of output, pushing it from $900 billion up to $1100 billion and reducing unemployment to "the President's acceptable level"?

You might be tempted to say that since we need to increase income by 200 (1100 − 900), we should increase government spending by the same amount.[4] But consider what would happen if we do. The increased government spending will throw the economy out of equilibrium. Since G is a component of aggregate spending, planned aggregate expenditure will increase by 200. Planned spending will be greater than output, inventories will be lower than planned, and firms will have an incentive to increase output. Suppose output rises by the desired 200. You might be tempted to think, "Well, we increased spending by 200 and output by 200, so equilibrium is restored."

---

[4]For the rest of this discussion, we will assume but not state that figures are in billions of dollars.

TABLE 25.2
Finding Equilibrium with *C, I,* and *G* After a $50 Billion Government Spending Increase
(all figures in billions of dollars)

(1) OUTPUT (INCOME) Y	(2) NET TAXES T	(3) DISPOSABLE INCOME $Y_d \equiv Y - T$	(4) CONSUMPTION SPENDING $(C = 100 + .75\,Y_d)$	(5) SAVING S $(Y_d - C)$	(6) PLANNED INVESTMENT SPENDING I	(7) GOVERNMENT PURCHASES G	(8) PLANNED AGGREGATE EXPENDITURE $C + I + G$	(9) UNPLANNED INVENTORY CHANGE $Y - (C + I + G)$	(10) ADJUST-MENT TO DISEQUI-LIBRIUM
300	100	200	250	-50	100	150	500	-200	Output↑
500	100	400	400	0	100	150	650	-150	Output↑
700	100	600	550	50	100	150	800	-100	Output↑
900	100	800	700	100	100	150	950	-50	Output↑
1100	100	1000	850	150	100	150	1100	0	Equilibrium
1300	100	1200	1000	200	100	150	1250	+50	Output↓
1500	100	1400	1150	250	100	150	1400	+100	Output↓

As we know, however, there is more to the story than this. The moment that output rises, the economy is generating more income—after all, this was the desired effect: the creation of more employment. Some of the newly employed workers become consumers and some of their income gets spent. With higher consumption spending, planned spending will be greater than output, inventories will be lower than planned, and firms will raise output, and thus income, again. This time firms are responding to the new consumption spending. Already, total income is over 1100.

This story should sound familiar. It is the multiplier in action. Although this time it is government spending (*G*) that is changed rather than planned investment (*I*), the effect is the same as the multiplier effect we described in the previous chapter. An increase in government spending has exactly the same impact on the equilibrium level of output and income as an increase in planned investment. A dollar of extra spending from either *G* or *I* is identical with respect to its impact on equilibrium output. Thus, the equation for the government spending multiplier is the same as the equation for multiplier for a change in planned investment.[5]

$$\text{Government spending multiplier} \equiv \frac{1}{MPS}.$$

The fact that the government spending multiplier equals $1/MPS$ means that an increase (decrease) in *G* will cause equilibrium output (*Y*) to increase (decrease) by the change in *G* times the government spending multiplier: $\Delta Y = \Delta G(1/MPS)$.

Formally, the **government spending multiplier** is defined as the ratio of the change in the equilibrium level of output to a change in government spending. This is the same definition we used in the previous chapter, but now the autonomous variable is government spending rather than planned investment.

Remember that we were thinking of increasing government spending (*G*) by 200. We can use the multiplier analysis to see what the new equilibrium level of *Y* would be for an increase in *G* of 200. Because the multiplier in our example is 4 (since *b*—the *MPC*—is .75, the *MPS* must be 1 − .75, or .25), *Y* will increase by 800 (4 × 200). Since the initial level of *Y* was 900, the new equilibrium level of *Y* is 1700 when *G* is increased by 200.

government spending multiplier The ratio of the change in the equilibrium level of output to a change in government spending.

[5]We derive the government spending multiplier algebraically in Appendix A to this chapter.

The level of 1700 is much larger than the level of 1100 that we calculated as necessary to lower unemployment to the desired level. Let us back up, then. If we want Y to increase by 200 and if the multiplier is four, we need G to increase by only $200/4 = 50$. In other words, if G changes by 50, the equilibrium level of Y will change by 200, and the new value of Y will be 1100 (900 + 200), as desired.

Looking at Table 25.2, we can check our answer to be sure that it is an equilibrium. Look first at the old equilibrium of 900. When government purchases (G) were equal to 100, aggregate output (income) was equal to planned aggregate expenditure ($AE \equiv C + I + G$) at $Y^* = 900$. But now G has increased to 150. Thus, at $Y = 900$, $(C + I + G)$ is greater than Y, there's an unplanned fall in inventories and output will rise. The question is: By how much? The multiplier told us that income would rise by four times the change in G, which was 50. Thus, Y should rise by 4×50, or 200, to 1100 before equilibrium is restored. Let's check. If $Y = 1100$, then consumption is $C = 100 + .75 \, Y_d = 100 + .75(1000) = 850$. Since I equals 100 and G now equals 100 (the original level of G) + 50 (the additional G brought about by the fiscal policy change) = 150, then $C + I + G = 850 + 100 + 150 = 1100$. Thus, $Y = AE$, and the economy is in equilibrium.

The graphic solution to the President's problem is presented in Figure 25.3. An increase in G of 50 shifts the planned aggregate expenditure function up by 50. As you can see, the new equilibrium income occurs where the new AE line (AE_2) crosses the 45° line, which is at $Y_2 = 1100$.

The Tax Multiplier

Remember that fiscal policy involves policies regarding government spending *and* policies regarding taxation. What effect does a change in tax policy have on the economy? To shed some light on this question, imagine the following situation. You are still chief economic advisor to the President, but now the President instructs you to devise a plan to reduce unemployment to an acceptable level *without* increasing the level of government spending. In your plan, instead of increasing government spending (G), you decide to cut taxes and maintain the current level of spending. A tax cut increases disposable income, which is likely to lead to added consumption spending. (Remember our general rule that increased income leads to increased consumption.) Would the impact of a decrease in taxes on aggregate output (income) be the same as it would be for an increase in G?

Clearly, a decrease in taxes would increase income. The government spends no less than it did before the tax cut, and households find they have a larger after-tax, or disposable, income than they had before. This leads to an increase in consumption. Thus, planned aggregate expenditure will increase, which will lead to inventories being lower than planned, which will lead to a rise in output. When output rises, more workers will be employed and more income will be generated, causing a second-round increase in consumption, and so on. Thus, income will increase by a multiple of the decrease in taxes.

But there is a wrinkle:

The multiplier for a change in taxes is *not the same* as the multiplier for a change in government spending.

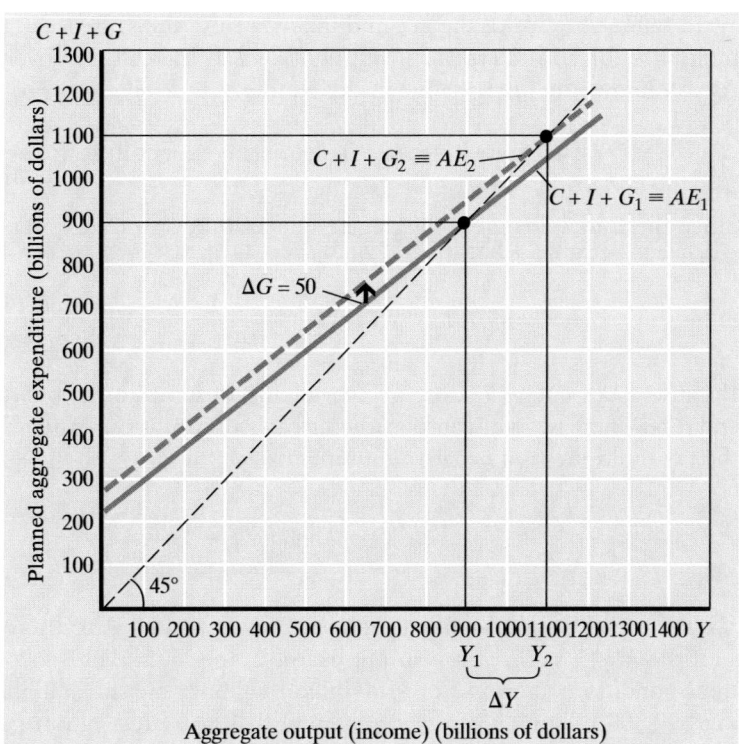

FIGURE 25.3
The Government Spending
Multiplier

Increasing government spending by $50 billion shifts the *AE*
function up by 50. As *Y* rises in
response, additional consumption is generated. Overall, the
equilibrium level of *Y* increases
by 200, to 1100.

Why does the **tax multiplier**—that is, the ratio of change in the equilibrium level of output to a change in taxes—differ from the spending multiplier? To answer this question, it is helpful to compare the ways in which a tax cut and a spending increase work their way through the economy.

Look back at Figure 25.1. When the government increases its spending, there is an immediate and direct impact on the economy's *total* spending. Because *G* is a component of planned aggregate expenditure, an increase in *G* leads to a dollar-for-dollar increase in planned aggregate expenditure. When taxes are cut, however, there is no direct impact on spending. Taxes enter the picture only because they have an effect on the disposable income of households, and households' disposable income influences their consumption (which is part of total spending). As Figure 25.1 shows, the tax cut flows through households before affecting aggregate expenditure.

Let's assume that the government decides to cut taxes by $1. By how much would spending increase? We already know the answer to this question. The marginal propensity to consume tells us how much consumption spending changes when disposable income changes. In the example we have been using throughout this chapter, the marginal propensity to consume out of disposable income is .75. This means that if households' after-tax incomes rise by $1, they will increase their consumption not by the full $1, but by only $0.75.[6]

To summarize: When government spending increases by $1, planned aggregate expenditure increases initially by the full amount of the rise in *G*, or $1. When taxes are cut, however, the initial increase in planned aggregate expenditure is only the *MPC* times the change in taxes. Because the initial increase in planned aggregate expenditure is smaller for a tax cut than it is for a government spending increase, the final effect on the equilibrium level of income will be smaller.

tax multiplier The ratio of change in the equilibrium level of output to a change in taxes.

---

[6]What happens to the other $.25? Remember that whatever households do not consume is, by definition, saved. The missing $.25 thus gets allocated to saving.

To figure the size of the tax multiplier, we use the same logic used to derive the multiplier for an increase in investment and an increase in government purchases. As you know, the final change in the equilibrium level of output (income) (Y) is:

$$\Delta Y = (\text{initial increase in aggregate expenditure}) \times \left(\frac{1}{MPS}\right).$$

Since the initial change in aggregate expenditure caused by a tax change of ΔT is ($-\Delta T \times MPC$), we can solve for the tax multiplier by simple substitution:

$$\Delta Y = \left(-\Delta T \times MPC\right) \times \left(\frac{1}{MPS}\right) = -\Delta T \times \left(\frac{MPC}{MPS}\right).$$

Because a tax cut will cause an *increase* in consumption expenditures and output and a tax increase will cause a *reduction* in consumption expenditures and output, the tax multiplier is a negative multiplier:

$$\text{Tax multiplier} \equiv -\left(\frac{MPC}{MPS}\right).$$

We derive the tax multiplier algebraically in Appendix A to this chapter.

If the *MPC* is .75, as it is in our example, the multiplier is $-.75/.25 = -3$. Under these conditions, a tax cut of $100 billion will increase the equilibrium level of output by $300 billion. This is very different than the effect of our government spending multiplier of 4. Under these same conditions, a $100 billion increase in G will increase the equilibrium level of output by $400 billion ($100 billion $\times$ 4).

The Balanced-Budget Multiplier

We have now discussed (1) changing government spending with no change in taxes, and (2) changing taxes with no change in government spending. But what happens if government spending and taxes are increased by the same amount? That is, what if the government decides to pay for its extra spending by increasing taxes by the same amount? Such a move would not change the government's budget deficit, since the increase in expenditures would be exactly matched by an increase in tax income.

You might think in this case that equal increases in government spending and taxes have no effect on equilibrium income. After all, the extra government spending is just equal to the extra amount of tax revenues collected by the government. But careful thought should convince you that this is not so. Take, for example, a government spending increase of $40 billion. We know from the analysis above that an increase in G of $40 billion, with taxes ($T$) held constant, should increase the equilibrium level of income by $40 billion $\times$ the government spending multiplier. The multiplier is $1/MPS$ or $1/.25 = 4$. Thus, the equilibrium level of income should rise by $160 billion ($40 billion $\times$ 4).

Now let us suppose that instead of keeping tax revenues constant, we finance the $40 billion increase in government spending with an equal increase in taxes, so as to maintain a balanced budget. What happens to aggregate spending as a result of both the rise in G and the rise in T? There are two initial effects. First, government spending rises by $40 billion. This effect is direct, immediate, and positive. But now the government also collects $40 billion more in taxes. The tax increase has a *negative* impact on overall spending in the economy, but it does not fully offset the increase in government spending.

The final impact of a tax increase on aggregate expenditure depends on how households respond to it. The only thing we know about household behavior so far is that households spend 75% of their added income and save 25 percent. We know that when disposable income falls, both consumption and saving are reduced. A tax *increase* of $40 billion reduces disposable income by $40 billion, and that means consumption falls by $40 billion × *MPC*. Since *MPC* = .75, consumption falls by $30 billion ($40 billion × .75).

The net result in the beginning is thus that government spending rises by $40 billion and consumption spending falls by $30 billion. This means that aggregate expenditure increases by $10 billion right after the simultaneous balanced-budget increases in *G* and *T*.

So we know that a balanced-budget increase in *G* and *T* will raise output. But the question is: By how much? How large is this **balanced-budget multiplier**? The answer may surprise you:

$$\text{Balanced-budget Multiplier} \equiv 1.$$

Let us combine what we know about the tax multiplier and the government spending multiplier to explain why this is so. To find the final effect of a simultaneous increase in government spending and increase in net taxes, we need to add the multiplier effects of the two. The government spending multiplier is $1/MPS$. The tax multiplier is $-MPC/MPS$. The sum of the two is $(1/MPS) + (-MPC/MPS) \equiv (1 - MPC)/MPS$. Because $MPC + MPS \equiv 1$, then $1 - MPC \equiv MPS$. This means that $(1 - MPC)/MPS \equiv MPS/MPS \equiv 1$.[7]

Now let us work through our numerical example. Using the government spending multiplier, we discovered that a $40 billion increase in *G* would *raise* output at equilibrium by $160 billion ($40 billion × the government spending multiplier of 4). Using the tax multiplier, we know that a $40 billion tax hike will *reduce* the equilibrium level of output by $120 billion ($40 billion × the tax multiplier of − 3). The net effect is thus $160 billion minus $120 billion, or $40 billion. It should be clear, then, that the effect on equilibrium *Y* is equal to the balanced increase in *G* and *T*. In other words, the net increase in the equilibrium level of *Y* resulting from the change in *G* and the change in *T* is exactly the size of the initial change in *G* or *T* itself.

If the President wanted to raise *Y* by $200 billion without increasing the deficit, a simultaneous increase in *G* and *T* of $200 billion would do the trick. To see that this is so, look at the numbers in Table 25.3. Back in Table 25.1, we discovered an

balanced-budget multiplier The ratio of change in the equilibrium level of output to a change in government spending where the change in government spending is balanced by a change in taxes so as not to create any deficit. The balanced-budget multiplier is equal to one: The change in *Y* resulting from the change in *G* and the equal change in *T* is exactly the same size as the initial change in *G* or *T* itself.

[7]We also derive the balanced-budget multiplier in Appendix A to this chapter.

TABLE 25.3
Finding Equilibrium with Government After a $200-Billion Balanced-Budget Increase in *G* and *T* (all figures in billions of dollars)

(1) OUTPUT (INCOME) Y	(2) NET TAXES T	(3) DISPOSABLE INCOME $Y_d \equiv Y - T$	(4) CONSUMPTION SPENDING C $(C = 100 + .75\, Y_d)$	(5) PLANNED INVESTMENT SPENDING I	(6) GOVERNMENT PURCHASES G	(7) PLANNED AGGREGATE EXPENDITURE $C + I + G$	(8) UNPLANNED INVENTORY CHANGE $Y - (C + I + G)$	(9) ADJUST-MENT TO DISEQUI-LIBRIUM
500	300	200	250	100	300	650	-150	Output↑
700	300	400	400	100	300	800	-100	Output↑
900	300	600	550	100	300	950	-50	Output↑
1100	300	800	700	100	300	1100	0	Equilibrium
1300	300	1000	850	100	300	1250	+50	Output↓
1500	300	1200	1000	100	300	1400	+100	Output↓

TABLE 25.4
Summary of Fiscal Policy
Multipliers

	POLICY STIMULUS	MULTIPLIER	FINAL IMPACT ON EQUILIBRIUM Y
Government-spending multiplier	Increase or decrease in the level of government purchases: ΔG	$\dfrac{1}{MPS}$	$\Delta G \cdot \dfrac{1}{MPS}$
Tax multiplier	Increase or decrease in the level of net taxes: ΔT	$\dfrac{-MPC}{MPS}$	$\Delta T \cdot \dfrac{-MPC}{MPS}$
Balanced-budget multiplier	Simultaneous balanced-budget increase or decrease in the level of government purchases and net taxes: $\Delta G = \Delta T$	1	ΔG or ΔT

equilibrium level of output of $900. With both G and T up by $200, the new equilibrium is $1100—higher by $200 billion. At no other level of Y do we find $(C + I + G) = Y.$ In sum:

> An increase in government spending has a direct initial effect on planned aggregate expenditure; a tax increase does not. The initial effect of the tax increase is that households cut consumption by the *MPC* times the change in taxes. This change in consumption is less than the change in taxes, because the *MPC* is less than one. The positive stimulus from the government spending increase is thus greater than the negative stimulus from the tax increase. The net effect is that the balanced-budget multiplier is one.

Table 25.4 summarizes everything that we have said about fiscal policy multipliers. If any of these effects are still unclear to you, go back and review the relevant discussions in this chapter.

A WARNING Although we have now added the role of government to our discussion, the story we have told about the multiplier is still incomplete and oversimplified. As noted at the end of the previous chapter, adding more realism to our story has the effect of reducing the size of the multiplier.

One example of this is the case in which taxes depend on income, which is the case in the "real world." For the sake of simplicity, we have been treating net taxes (*T*) as a lump-sum, fixed amount. Appendix B to this chapter shows that the size of the multiplier is reduced when we make the more realistic assumption that taxes depend on income. We continue to add more realism to our analysis in the next section and in the chapters that follow. (See also the Issues and Applications box titled "Fiscal Policy During the Recessions of 1974–1975, 1980–1982, and 1990–1991" for a discussion of the government's use of fiscal policy during the last three recessions.)

ADDING THE INTERNATIONAL SECTOR

In Chapter 21, we noted that the U.S. economy does not operate in a vacuum. Rather, it influences and is influenced by the rest of the world. Up until this point, though, we have not taken into account the role of imports and exports in the macroeconomy.

FISCAL POLICY DURING THE RECESSIONS OF 1974–1975, 1980–1982, AND 1990–1991

As we've seen throughout this chapter, the government can stimulate a sluggish economy by increasing government expenditures (G) and cutting taxes (T). Such policies have the effect of increasing aggregate expenditure (demand) and increasing equilibrium output (income). For this reason, you might expect the government to increase G and/or cut T whenever the economy is in a recession.

In fact, the government has taken very different actions to deal with the three recessions that the U.S. economy has experienced since 1970. The last time that the President and Congress consciously used fiscal policy to fight a recession was in 1975, during the administration of President Gerald Ford. The following passage from the *Economic Report of the President, 1976* suggests that the policy succeeded in accomplishing its goals:

During the first part of 1975 the economy moved rapidly through the final stages of the most severe recession of the postwar period. Real gross national product (GNP) fell at an annual rate of 9.2 percent in the first quarter and then began to increase ....

Economic policy shifted early in the year to counter the decline in output. The President proposed a $16-billion tax reduction in the State of the Union message in January and the Congress enacted a $21-billion net reduction in March. Because of these tax cuts, and associated one-time social security payments, real disposable personal income rose sharply in the second quarter ....

GNP rose sharply in the second half of the year; and by the end of the year the initial phase of a recovery was clearly evident ....

As the economy enters a recession, national output decreases and households have less income. Lower household spending was one of the reasons the House of Grossman—an upscale furniture and interior decorating chain—went out of business in 1991. With lower income, people began shopping in less expensive stores, where they paid less for furniture.

The idea of using fiscal policy to stimulate aggregate expenditure and increase output during a recession was explicitly rejected by President Reagan in the 1980s. Instead, the Reagan administration favored policies designed to stimulate the supply side (rather than the demand side) of the market. These **supply-side policies** (which we discuss in more detail in Chapter 34) focused on cutting taxes (a fiscal policy tool) to increase incentives to work, save, and invest. Reagan believed that the added labor supply and investment brought about by the lower taxes would lead to an expansion of the supply of goods and services, which, in turn, would reduce inflation and unemployment.

President Reagan's policy worked, at least partially for reasons he did not intend. There is no question that the major supply-side tax cuts enacted in 1981 with President Reagan's blessing had the effect of stimulating aggregate demand (spending). This outcome makes perfect sense if you remember the theory we've developed so far: Lower taxes mean higher disposable income, and higher disposable income means more consumption and ultimately greater output.

This trend against using fiscal policy to stimulate the economy continued into the 1990s. Just as the recession of 1990–1991 was beginning, Congress and President Bush passed the Omnibus Budget Reconciliation Act, which *cut* federal expenditures and *increased* taxes in an effort to reduce the federal deficit. Clearly, this policy did not serve to stimulate the economy, which remained sluggish until the end of 1992.

Opening the economy to foreign trade adds a fourth component to planned aggregate expenditure—exports of goods and services, which we denote *EX*. Exports are foreign purchases of goods and services produced in the United States. Opening the economy to the rest of the world also means that U.S. consumers and businesses have greater choice because they can decide to buy foreign-produced goods and services (imports, or *IM*) in addition to domestically produced goods and services.

We can therefore think of imports (*IM*) as a leakage from the circular flow and exports (*EX*) as an injection into the circular flow. (Review Figure 21.1.) With imports and exports accounted for, the equilibrium condition for the economy becomes:

$$\text{Open-economy equilibrium position: } Y = C + I + G + (EX - IM).$$

net exports An economy's total exports (*EX*) minus its total imports (*IM*).

The expression (*EX* − *IM*) is referred to as **net exports.**

Increases or decreases in net exports can throw the economy out of equilibrium and cause national income to change. For example, a large decrease in exports, *ceteris paribus,* would mean a drop in spending on domestically produced goods and services. The result would be an unplanned rise in inventories and a fall in output. Furthermore, if some domestic spending leaks into foreign markets (imports), the multiplier effect on domestic production will be reduced.

We discuss the international sector and its effects on the macroeconomy in much more detail in Chapter 37. For now, though, we continue to use the equation $Y = C + I + G$ as the basis of our analysis. Doing so allows us to keep our discussions clear and concise. Keep in mind, though, that the international sector is an important player in the macroeconomy.

THE FEDERAL BUDGET

Because fiscal policy is the manipulation of items in the federal budget, we need to consider those aspects of the budget that are most relevant to our study of macroeconomics. The **federal budget** is an enormously complicated document, running to thousands of pages each year. It lists in great detail all the things the government plans to spend money on and all the sources of government revenues for the coming year. It is the product of a complex interplay of social, political, and economic forces.

federal budget The budget of the federal government.

In fact, "the budget" is really three different budgets. First, it is a *political document* that dispenses favors to certain groups or regions (the elderly benefit from social security, farmers from agricultural price supports, students from federal loan programs, and so on) and places burdens (taxes) on others. Second, it is a *reflection of certain goals* the government wants to achieve. For example, in addition to assisting farmers, agricultural price supports are meant to preserve the "family farm." Tax breaks for corporations engaging in research and development of new products are meant to encourage such research. Finally, the budget may be an *embodiment of some beliefs about how (if at all) the government should manage the macroeconomy.* The macroeconomic aspects of the budget are thus only a part of a more complicated story, a story that may at times be of more concern to political scientists than to economists.

An Overview of the Budget

A highly condensed version of the federal budget is shown in Table 25.5 (Some of this reviews material from Chapter 3, but here we highlight the budget com-

	AMOUNT	PERCENTAGE OF TOTAL
Receipts		
Personal taxes	474.1	40.8
Corporate taxes	115.3	9.9
Indirect business taxes	81.5	7.0
Contributions for social insurance	489.7	42.2
Total	**1160.6**	**100.0**
Expenditures		
Purchases of goods and services: defense	315.8	21.7
nondefense	133.4	9.1
Transfer payments	623.3	42.7
Grants-in-aid to state and local governments	173.0	11.9
Net interest payments	186.7	12.8
Net subsidies of government enterprises	26.2	1.8
Total	**1458.4**	**100.0**
Surplus (+) or deficit (-) (Receipts − Expenditures)	-297.8	

Source: U.S. Department of Commerce, Bureau of Economic Analysis.

ponents of particular importance to macroeconomics.) In 1992, the government had total receipts of $1160.6 billion, largely from personal income taxes ($474.1 billion) and contributions for social insurance ($489.7 billion).[8] Receipts from corporate taxes accounted for $115.3 billion, or only 9.9% of total receipts. Not everyone is aware of the fact that corporate taxes as a percentage of government receipts are quite small relative to personal taxes and social security taxes.

The federal government also made $1458.4 billion in expenditures in 1992. Of this amount, $623.3 billion represented transfer payments (social security, military retirement benefits, and unemployment compensation).[9] Defense spending ($315.8 billion) was the next largest component of government expenditures, followed by interest on the federal debt ($186.7 billion).

The Federal Budget Deficit and the Federal Debt

Table 25.5 makes it clear that the federal government spent substantially more than it took in during 1992. The result was a deficit of $297.8 billion in 1992.

The 1992 deficit, though high, was nothing new. In fact, the federal deficit has been quite high since the early 1980s. You can see this in Figure 25.4 on the next page, where the federal deficit as a percentage of GDP is plotted for the 1970 I–1992 IV period. As the figure clearly shows, the deficit has been positive throughout the entire period. In no quarter within this 92-quarter period were revenues greater than expenditures. The deficit has varied from a low of 0.2% of GDP in 1970 I to highs of 6.5% in 1975 II and 5.7% in 1982 IV. The deficit as a percentage of GDP fell in the late 1980s, but it rose sharply in 1991 and 1992.

---

[8]Contributions for social insurance are employer and employee social security taxes.

[9]Remember that there is an important difference between transfer payments and government spending. Much of the government budget goes for things that an economist would classify as transfers (payments that are grants or gifts) rather than purchases of goods and services. It is only the latter that are included in our variable G. Transfers are counted as part of net taxes.

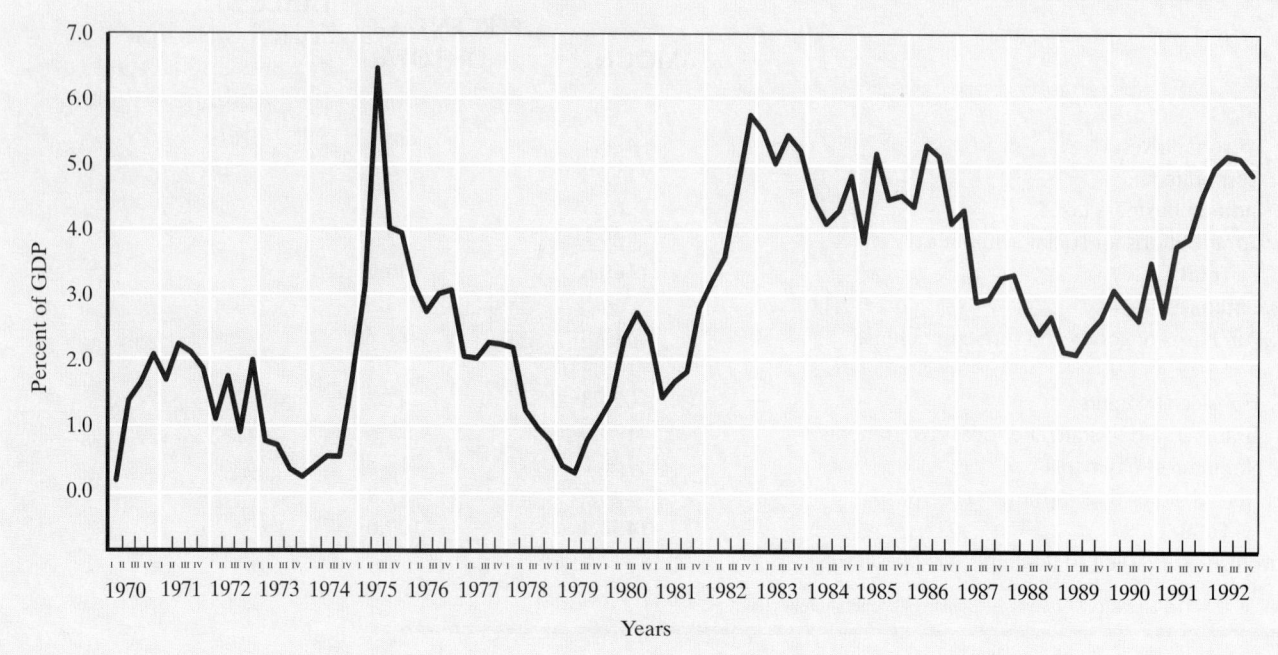

FIGURE 25.4

The Federal Government Deficit as a Percentage of GDP, 1970 I-1992 IV

While the federal deficit was positive over the entire 1970–92 period, the deficits in the 1980s were particularly large by historical standards.

How did such large deficits come about? There are several reasons. First, government purchases as a percentage of GDP have generally risen since 1980. This increase primarily reflects the defense build-up of the Reagan years. Second, interest payments as a percentage of GDP have risen substantially since 1980. Third, personal income tax rates have fallen since 1981 as a result of the Economic Recovery Tax Act of 1981. With defense spending and interest payments rising rapidly and personal tax rates falling, it is not surprising that the deficit rose substantially during the 1980s. The government has simply been spending a lot more than it has been collecting in taxes.

When the government runs a deficit, it must borrow to finance it. To borrow, the federal government sells government securities to the public. It issues pieces of paper promising to pay a certain amount, with interest, in the future. In return, it receives funds from the buyers of the paper and uses these funds to pay its bills. This borrowing increases the **federal debt,** the total amount owed by the government to the public. The federal debt is the total of all accumulated deficits minus surpluses over time.

Given the large deficits that the federal government has run up since the early 1980s, it should not be surprising that the federal debt has risen sharply from the early 1980s on. You can see this in Figure 25.5, where the federal debt as a percentage of GDP is plotted for the 1970 I-1992 IV period. The debt has risen rapidly since 1982—from 19.6% of GDP in 1982 I to 44.9% in 1992 IV.

In 1986, the U.S. Congress became alarmed enough about the deficit and the federal debt to pass a bill popularly known as the *Gramm-Rudman-Hollings bill* (after its three Congressional sponsors). This bill was designed to lower the

federal debt The total amount owed by the federal government to the public.

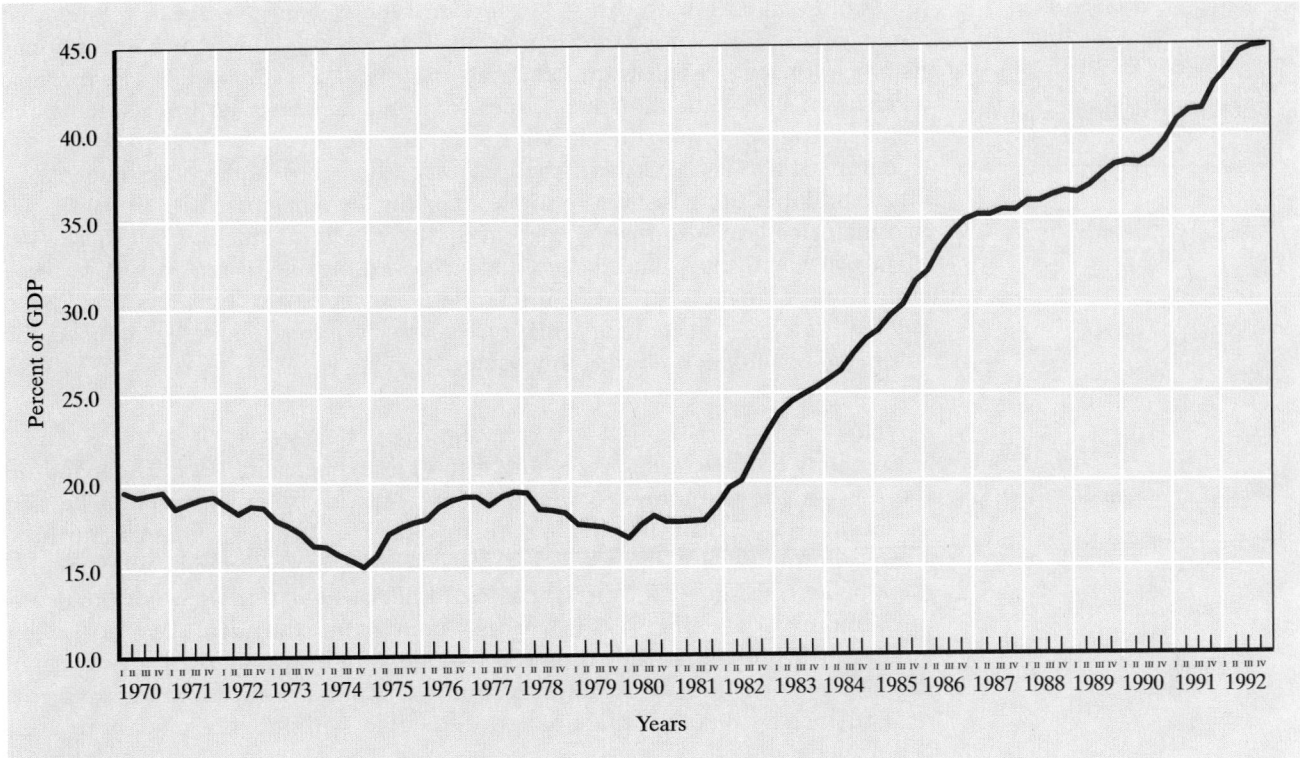

FIGURE 25.5

The Federal Government Debt as a Percentage of GDP, 1970 I-1992 IV

The federal government debt increased dramatically in the 1980s as a result of the large deficits.

deficit by a certain amount each year until a zero deficit is achieved. In effect, the bill made the deficit a direct target variable, with fiscal policy tools automatically adjusting if necessary to achieve the given target value for the year. This bill, which never accomplished its goal, has a number of interesting macroeconomic issues associated with it and is discussed in detail in Chapter 31.

The Economy's Influence on the Deficit

As we said earlier, some parts of the government's budget depend on the state of the economy, over which the government has no direct control. Take, for example, the revenue side of the budget. The government passes laws that set tax rates and tax brackets. These are clearly variables that the government does control. Tax revenue, on the other hand, depends on taxable income, and income depends on the state of the economy, which the government does *not* control. The government can set a personal income tax rate of 20%, but the revenue that the tax brings in will depend on the average income earned by households. Clearly, the government will collect much more revenue when average income is $40,000 than it will when average income is $20,000.

FISCAL DRAG   If the economy is doing well, income will be high and so will tax revenue. Tax revenue increases with increases in income for two reasons. First, there is simply more income to be taxed when people are earning more. Second, as people earn more income, they move into higher tax brackets and the average tax rate that they pay increases. This type of increase in tax rates is sometimes called **fiscal drag,** because the increase in average tax rates that results when people move into higher brackets acts as a "drag" on the economy. As the economy expands and income increases, the automatic tax increase mechanism built into the system goes to work. Tax rates go up, reducing the after-tax wage, and this slows down the expansion.

Before 1982, people found themselves pushed into higher tax brackets by inflation alone. Suppose, for example, that my income rose 10% in 1981, but that the price level also rose by 10% in that year. My income did not increase at all in real terms, but since the tax brackets were not legislated in real terms, I ended up paying more taxes. Since 1982, however, tax brackets have been *indexed*—that is, adjusted for inflation—and this has substantially reduced the automatic fiscal drag built into the system.

GOVERNMENT EXPENDITURES THAT DEPEND ON THE STATE OF THE ECONOMY
Some items on the expenditure side of the government budget also depend on the state of the economy. As the economy expands, unemployment falls, and the result is a decrease in unemployment benefits. Welfare payments and food stamp allotments also decrease somewhat. Some of the people who receive these benefits during bad times are able to find jobs when the state of the economy improves, and they begin earning enough income that they no longer qualify. Transfer payments thus tend to go down automatically during an expansion. (The reverse is true in a slump. During a slump, transfer payments tend to increase because there are more people without jobs and more poor people generally.)

Another reason that government spending is not completely controllable is that inflation often picks up when the economy is expanding. This can lead the government to spend more than it had planned to spend. Suppose the government has ordered 20 planes at $2 million per plane and that inflation causes the actual price per plane to be higher than expected. If the government decides to go ahead and buy the planes anyway, it will be forced to increase its spending.

Finally, any change in the interest rate changes government interest payments as well. An increase in interest rates means that the government spends more in interest payments. When interest rates are high and the government debt is relatively large, interest payments can be an important component of the total budget, as we have already seen.

AUTOMATIC STABILIZERS   We have just seen that as the economy expands, the government's tax receipts increase. Also, transfer payments fall as the economy expands which leads to a decrease in government expenditures. The revenue and expenditure items that change in response to changes in economic activity are known as **automatic stabilizers.** As the economy expands or contracts, "automatic" changes in government revenues and expenditures take place, and these tend to reduce the change in, or stabilize, GDP.

The fact that some revenues *automatically* tend to rise and some expenditures *automatically* tend to fall in an expansion means that the government surplus is larger, or the deficit is smaller, in an expansion than it otherwise would be. Suppose we wanted to assess whether a government is practicing a policy designed to increase desired spending and income. If we looked only at the size of the government budget deficit, we might be fooled into thinking that the government is trying to stimulate the economy when, in fact, the real source of the deficit is a slump in the economy that caused revenues to fall and transfer payments to increase.

This may seem like an obscure point, but it is tremendously important. During the 1980–1982 recession, there was considerable public outcry about the ballooning federal deficit. Some of this concern was well founded, because by cutting tax rates the government did increase the deficit. In large part, however, the deficit grew simply because the economy was in a severe recession during those years. In fact, the tendency for the deficit to rise automatically (without any change in tax laws or spending programs) during recessions provides an important stabilizer for the economy. Such changes in the budget work to increase spending when spending would otherwise be low. This, in turn, helps to keep output on a more even keel than would otherwise be the case.

FULL-EMPLOYMENT BUDGET Because the condition of the economy affects the budget deficit so strongly, we cannot accurately judge either the intent or the success of fiscal policies just by looking at the deficit. Instead of looking simply at the size of the deficit, economists have developed an alternative way to measure how effective fiscal policy actually is. By examining what the budget would be like if the economy were producing at the full-employment level of output—the so-called **full-employment budget**—we can establish a benchmark for evaluating fiscal policy.

The distinction between the actual and full-employment deficits is an important one. Suppose that the economy is in a slump and that the deficit is $250 billion. Also suppose that if there were full employment, the deficit would fall to $75 billion. The $75 billion deficit that would remain even with full employment would be due to the structure of tax and spending programs rather than to the state of the economy. This deficit—the deficit that remains at full employment—is sometimes called the **structural deficit.** The structural deficit is the deficit of the full-employment budget. The $175 billion ($250 billion − $75 billion) part of the deficit that is caused by the fact the economy is in a slump is known as the **cyclical deficit.** The existence of the cyclical deficit depends on where the economy is in the business cycle, and it ceases to exist when full employment is reached. By definition, the cyclical deficit of the full-employment budget is zero.

DEBT AND DEFICITS IN THE REST OF THE WORLD

The United States is not the only country in the world that has a problem with budget deficits. Table 25.6 shows the deficit in 1990 as a percent of GDP for six countries. Italy's government borrowed more than 10% of its total national output in 1990. Japan, on the other hand, has been running a surplus ($G < T$) for several years.

Figure 25.6 shows the total debt for the same six countries as a percentage of GDP in 1990. Japan's debt is small while Italy's debt is nearly equal to its yearly GDP.

TABLE 25.6
Surpluses (+) and Deficits (-) of Selected Countries, Expressed as a Percentage of Nominal GDP, 1990

Japan (FY1990)	3.6
Germany	-1.9
France	-1.7
Italy	-10.6
United Kingdom	-1.0
Canada	-3.8

Source: J. P. Morgan, 1993.

full-employment budget What the federal budget would be if the economy were producing at a full-employment level of output.

structural deficit The deficit that remains at full employment.

cyclical deficit The deficit that occurs because of a downturn in the business cycle.

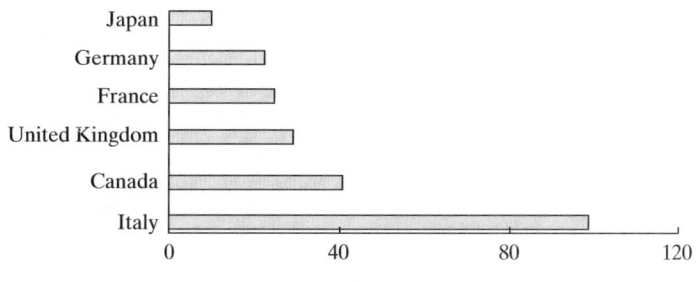

FIGURE 25.6
Total Debt for Selected Countries, Expressed as a Percentage of Nominal GDP, 1990

Japan's debt is small relative to its GDP, while Italy's is quite large.

THE MONEY MARKET AND MONETARY POLICY: A PREVIEW

We have now seen how households, firms, and the government interact in the goods market, how equilibrium output (income) is determined, and how the government uses fiscal policy to influence the economy. (We've also provided a brief introduction to the international sector's influence on aggregate expenditure and equilibrium output.) Our next task, which we undertake in the following two chapters, is to analyze the money market and monetary policy—the government's other major tool for influencing the economy.

SUMMARY

1. The government can affect the macroeconomy through two specific policy channels: fiscal policy and monetary policy. *Fiscal policy* refers to the government's taxing and spending behavior. *Monetary policy* refers to the tools the government uses to control the nation's money supply.

Government Participation in the Economy

2. The government does not have complete control over tax revenues and certain expenditures, which are partially dictated by the state of the economy.

3. As a participant in the economy, the government makes purchases of goods and services (G), taxes, and makes transfer payments to households. *Net taxes* (T) is equal to the tax payments made by firms and households to the government minus transfer payments made to households by the government.

4. *Disposable*, or after-tax, *income* (Y_d) is equal to the amount of income received by households after taxes: $Y_d \equiv Y - T$. After-tax income determines households' consumption behavior.

5. The *budget deficit* is equal to the difference between what the government spends and what it collects in taxes: $G - T$. When G exceeds T, the government must borrow from the public to finance its deficit.

6. In an economy in which a government is a participant, planned aggregate expenditures equal consumption spending by households (C) plus planned investment spending by firms (I) plus government spending on goods and services (G): $AE \equiv C + I + G$. Because the condition $Y = AE$ is necessary for the economy to be in equilibrium, it follows that $Y = C + I + G$ is the macroeconomic equilibrium condition. The economy is also in equilibrium when leakages out of the system equal injections into the system: This occurs when savings and net taxes (the leakages) equal planned investment and government purchases (the injections): $S + T = I + G$.

Fiscal Policy at Work: The Multiplier Effects

7. Fiscal policy has a multiplier effect on the economy. A change in government spending gives rise to a multiplier equal to $1/MPS$. A change in taxation brings about a multiplier equal to $-MPC/MPS$. A simultaneous equal increase or decrease in government spending and taxes has a multiplier effect of one.

Adding the International Sector

8. Opening the economy to foreign trade adds two additional components to the equilibrium condition: exports (EX) and imports (IM). Exports are an injection into the circular flow; imports are a leakage from the circular flow. Thus the equilibrium condition for the economy becomes $Y = C + I + G + (EX - IM)$ when the international sector is taken into account. The expression $(EX - IM)$ is referred to as *net exports*.

The Federal Budget

9. The federal deficit has been quite large in recent years. Reasons for the deficit include the defense build-up of the Reagan years, the high amount of interest paid on already-existing debt, and cuts in personal tax rates. With defense spending and interest payments rising rapidly and personal income tax rates falling, the government has simply been spending more than it has been collecting in taxes. In 1986, Congress passed the Gramm-Rudman-Hollings bill, which was designed to lower the federal deficit to zero. The bill has not succeeded in its goal, however.

10. *Fiscal drag* is the negative effect on the economy that occurs when average tax rates increase because taxpayers have moved into higher income brackets during an expansion. These higher taxes reduce disposable income and slow down the expansion. Since 1982, tax brackets have been indexed to inflation, and this has reduced the fiscal drag built into the tax system.

11. *Automatic stabilizers* are revenue and expenditure items in the federal budget that automatically change with the state of the economy and thus tend to stabilize GDP. For example, during expansions the government automatically takes in more revenue, because people are making more money that is taxed. Higher income and tax brackets also mean fewer transfer payments.

12. The *full-employment budget* is an economist's construction of what the federal budget would be if the economy were producing at a full-employment level of output. The *structural deficit* is the federal deficit that remains even at full employment. *Cyclical deficits* occur when there is a downturn in the business cycle.

REVIEW TERMS AND CONCEPTS

automatic stabilizers 638
balanced-budget multiplier 631
budget deficit 622
cyclical deficit 639
disposable, or after-tax, income (Y_d) 621
federal budget 634
federal debt 636
fiscal drag 638
fiscal policy 620
full-employment budget 639
government purchases of goods and services (G) 621

government spending multiplier 627
monetary policy 620
net exports ($EX - IM$) 634
net taxes (T) 621
structural deficit 639
supply-side policies 633
tax multiplier 629

Equations:
Disposable income (Y_d) $\equiv Y - T$
$AE \equiv C + I + G$
Government budget deficit $\equiv G - T$

Equilibrium in an economy with government: $Y = C + I + G$
Leakages/injections approach to equilibrium in an economy with government: $S + T = I + G$

Government spending multiplier $\equiv \dfrac{1}{MPS}$

Tax multiplier $\equiv -\left(\dfrac{MPC}{MPS}\right)$

Balanced-budget multiplier $\equiv 1$

PROBLEM SET

1. Crack economists in the economy of Yuk estimate the following:

Real output/income	1000 billion Yuks
Government purchases	200 billion Yuks
Total net taxes	200 billion Yuks
Investment spending (planned)	100 billion Yuks

Assume that Yukkers consume 75% of their disposable incomes and that they save 25 percent.

a. You are asked by the business editor of the *Weird Harold* to predict the events of the next few months. Using the data above, can you make a forecast? (Assume that investment is constant.)

b. If no changes were made, at what level of GDP (Y) would the economy of Yuk settle?

c. Some local conservatives blame Yuk's problems on the size of the government sector. They suggest cutting government purchases by 25 billion Yuks. What effect would such cuts have on the economy? (Be specific.)

2. "A $1 increase in government spending will raise equilibrium income by more than a $1 tax cut, yet both have the same impact on the budget deficit. So if we care about the budget deficit, the best way to stimulate the economy is through increases in spending, not cuts in taxes." Comment.

3. Assume that in 1994, the following situation prevails in the Republic of Nurd:

$Y = \$200 \quad C = \$160 \quad S = \$40 \quad I \text{ (planned)} = \$30$

Assume that households consume 80% of their income, that they save 20% of their income, that MPC = .8, and MPS = .2. That is, $C = .8Y$ and $S = .2Y$.

    a. Is the economy of Nurd in equilibrium? What is Nurd's equilibrium level of income? What is likely to happen in the coming months if the government takes no action?

    b. If $200 is the "full employment" level of Y, what fiscal policy might the government follow if its goal is full employment?

    c. If the full employment level of Y is $250, what fiscal policy might the government follow?

d. Suppose that $Y = \$200$, $C = \$160$, $S = \$40$, and $I = \$40$. Is Nurd's economy in equilibrium?

e. Starting with the situation in d., suppose that the government starts spending $30 each year with no taxation and continues to spend $30 every period. If I remains constant, what will happen to the equilibrium level of Nurd's domestic product (Y)? What will the new levels of C and S be?

f. Starting with the situation in d., suppose that the government starts taxing the population $30 each year without spending anything and continues to tax at that rate every period. If I remains constant, what will happen to the equilibrium level of Nurd's domestic product (Y)? What will be the new levels of C and S? How does your answer to f. differ from your answer to e.? Why?

4. Suppose that all tax collections are fixed (rather than dependent on income), and that all spending and transfer programs are also fixed (in the sense that they do not depend on the state of the economy, as, for example, unemployment benefits now do). If this were the case, would there be any automatic stabilizers in the government budget? Would there be any distinction between the full-employment deficit and the actual budget deficit? Explain.

5. What is the relationship between the government budget deficit and the government debt? Suppose that the United States managed to balance its budget in fiscal year 1994. Would there be any effect on the size of the debt?

6. Answer the following questions:

    a. $MPS = .4$. What is the government spending multiplier?

    b. $MPC = .9$. What is the government spending multiplier?

    c. $MPS = .5$. What is the government spending multiplier?

    d. $MPC = .75$. What is the tax multiplier?

    e. $MPS = .1$. What is the tax multiplier?

    f. If the government spending multiplier is 6, what is the tax multiplier?

    g. If the tax multiplier is -2, what is the government spending multiplier?

    h. If government purchases and taxes are both increased by $100 billion simultaneously, what will the effect be on equilibrium output (income)?

Deriving the Fiscal Policy Multipliers

The Government Spending and Tax Multipliers

In the chapter, we noted that the government spending multiplier is equal to $1/MPS$. (This is the same as the investment multiplier.) We can also show that the government spending multiplier is the same as the investment multiplier by using our hypothetical consumption function:

$$C = a + b (Y - T),$$

where b is the marginal propensity to consume. As you know, the equilibrium condition is

$$Y = C + I + G.$$

Substituting for C, we get

$$Y = a + b(Y - T) + I + G$$
$$Y = a + bY - bT + I + G.$$

This equation can be rearranged to yield

$$Y - bY = a + I + G - bT$$
$$Y(1 - b) = a + I + G - bT.$$

We can then solve for Y by dividing through by $(1 - b)$:

$$Y = \frac{1}{(1 - b)}\left(a + I + G - bT\right)$$

We see from this last equation that if G increases by one with the other determinants of Y (a, I, and T) remaining constant, Y increases by $1/(1 - b)$. Thus, the multiplier is, as before, simply $1/(1 - b)$, where b is the marginal propensity to consume. And, of course, $1 - b$ equals the marginal propensity to save, so the government spending multiplier is $1/MPS$.

We can also derive the tax multiplier. The last equation above says that when T increases by \$1, holding a, I, and G constant, income decreases by $b/(1 - b)$ dollars. The tax multiplier is thus $-b/(1 - b)$, or $-MPC/(1 - MPC) = -MPC/MPS$. (Remember that we add the negative sign to the tax multiplier because the tax multiplier is a *negative* multiplier.)

The Balanced-Budget Multiplier

It is quite easy to show formally that the balanced-budget multiplier is equal to one. As you know, when taxes and government spending are simultaneously increased by the same amount, there are two effects on planned aggregate expenditure: one positive and one negative. The initial impact of a balanced-budget increase in government spending and taxes on aggregate expenditure would be the *increase* in government purchases (ΔG) *minus* the *decrease* in consumption (ΔC) caused by the tax increase. The decrease in consumption brought about by the tax increase is equal to $\Delta C = \Delta T(MPC)$.

Increase in spending :	ΔG
−Decrease in spending :	$\Delta C = \Delta T\left(MPC\right)$
= Net increase in spending	$\Delta G - \Delta T\left(MPC\right)$

In a balanced-budget increase, $\Delta G = \Delta T$, so we can substitute:

Net initial increase in spending:
$$\Delta G - \Delta G(MPC) = \Delta G(1\text{-}MPC)$$

Since $MPS = (1 - MPC)$, the initial increase in spending is

$$\Delta G(MPS).$$

We can now apply the expenditure multiplier $\left(\dfrac{1}{MPS}\right)$ to this net initial increase in spending:

$$\Delta Y = \Delta G \left(MPS\right) \left(\frac{1}{MPS}\right) = \Delta G.$$

Thus, the final total increase in the equilibrium level of Y is just equal to the initial balanced increase in G and T. In other words, the balanced-budget multiplier is 1.

APPENDIX B TO CHAPTER 25

THE CASE IN WHICH TAX REVENUES DEPEND ON INCOME

In this chapter, we used the simplifying assumption that the government collects taxes in a lump sum. This made our discussion of the multiplier effects somewhat easier to follow. But now suppose that the government collects taxes not solely as a lump sum that is paid regardless of income, but also partly in the form of a proportional levy against income. As we noted earlier, this is clearly a more realistic assumption. Typically, tax collections are either based on income (as with the personal income tax) or they closely follow the ups and downs in the economy (as with sales taxes). Thus, instead of setting taxes equal to some fixed amount, let us say that tax revenues depend on income. If we call the amount of net taxes collected T, we can write: $T = T_0 + tY$.

This equation contains two parts. First, we note that net taxes (T) will be equal to an amount T_0 if income (Y) is zero. Second, the tax rate (t) indicates how much net taxes change as income changes. Suppose that T_0 is equal to –200 and t is 1/3. The resulting tax function is $T = -200 + 1/3Y$, which is graphed in Figure 25A.1. Note that when income is zero, the government collects "negative net taxes," which simply means that it makes transfer payments of 200. As income rises, tax collections increase because every extra dollar of income generates $.33 in extra revenues for the government.

How do we incorporate this new tax function into our discussion? It is actually quite simple. All we need to do is replace the old value of T (in the example in the chapter, T was set equal to 100) with the new value, –200 + 1/3Y. Look first at the consumption equation. Consumption (C) still depends on disposable income, as it did before. Also, disposable income is still $Y - T$, or income minus taxes. Instead of disposable income equaling $Y - 100$, however, the new equation for disposable income is

$$Y_d \equiv Y - T$$

$$Y_d \equiv Y - (-200 + 1/3Y)$$

$$Y_d \equiv Y + 200 - 1/3Y.$$

Since consumption still depends on after-tax income, exactly as it did before, we have

$$C = 100 + .75Y_d$$

$$C = 100 + .75 (Y + 200 - 1/3Y).$$

Nothing else needs to be changed. We solve for equilibrium income exactly as before, by setting planned aggregate expenditure equal to aggregate output. Recall that planned aggregate expenditure is $C + I + G$, and aggre-

FIGURE 25A.1
The Tax Function

This graph shows net taxes (taxes minus transfer payments) as a function of aggregate income.

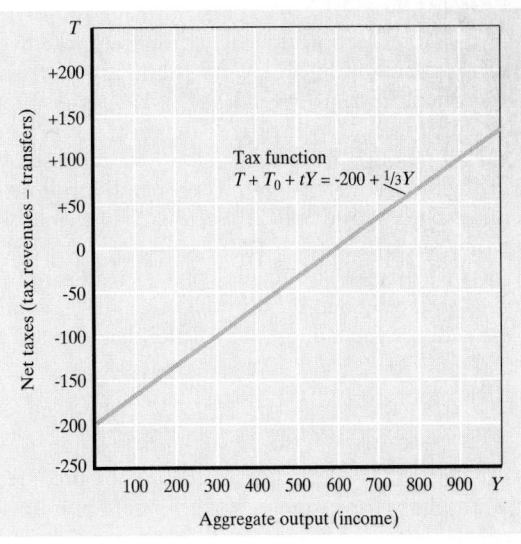

gate output is Y. If we assume, as before, that $I = 100$ and $G = 100$, the equilibrium is

$$Y = C + I + G$$

$$Y = 100 + .75 (Y + 200 - 1/3Y) + 100 + 100.$$

This equation may look difficult to solve, but it is not. It simplifies to

$$Y = 100 + .75Y + 150 - .25Y + 100 + 100$$

$$Y = 450 + .5Y$$

$$.5Y = 450.$$

This means that $Y = 450/.5 = 900$. The new equilibrium level of income is thus 900.

It is useful to consider the graphic analysis of this equation as shown in Figure 25A.2. The most important thing you should note from Figure 25A.2 is that when we make taxes a function of income (instead of merely a lump-sum amount), the AE function becomes *flatter* than it was before. Why is this so? When tax collections do not depend on income, an increase in income of $1 means that disposable income also increases by a dollar. Because taxes are a constant amount, adding more income does not raise the amount of taxes paid. Disposable income therefore changes dollar-for-dollar with any change in income.

When taxes depend on income, however, a $1 increase in income does not increase disposable income by a full dollar, because some of the additional dollar must go to pay extra taxes. In fact, under the modified tax function of Figure 25A.2, an extra dollar of income will increase disposable income by only $.67, because $.33 of the extra dollar goes to the government in the form of taxes.

No matter how taxes are calculated, the marginal propensity to consume out of disposable (or after-tax) income is the same—each extra dollar of disposable income will increase consumption spending by $.75. But a $1 change in before-tax income does not have the same effect on disposable income in each case. Suppose we were to increase income by $1. With the lump-sum tax function, disposable income would rise by $1, and consumption would increase by $MPC \times Y_d$, or $.75. When taxes depend on income, disposable income would rise by only $.67 from the $1 increase in income, and consumption would rise by only the MPC times the change in disposable income, or $.75 \times .67 = $.50$.

Clearly, if a $1 increase in income raises expenditure by $.75 in one case, and by only $.50 in the other, the second aggregate expenditure function must be flatter than the first.

THE GOVERNMENT-SPENDING AND TAX MULTIPLIERS ALGEBRAICALLY

All of this means that if taxes are a function of income, the three multipliers (investment, government spending, and tax) are less than they would be if taxes were a lump-sum amount. Using the same linear consumption function we used in the last two chapters, we can derive the multiplier:

$$C = a + b (Y - T)$$
$$C = a + b (Y - T_0 - tY)$$
$$C = a + bY - bT_0 - btY.$$

We know that $Y = C + I + G$. Through substitution we get:

$$Y = \underbrace{a + bY - bT_0 - btY}_{C} + I + G.$$

Solving for Y:

$$Y = \left(\frac{1}{1 - b + bt}\right)\left(a + I + G - bT_0\right)$$

FIGURE 25A.2
Different Tax Systems

When taxes are strictly lump-sum ($T = 100$) and do not depend on income, the aggregate expenditure function is steeper than when taxes depend on income.

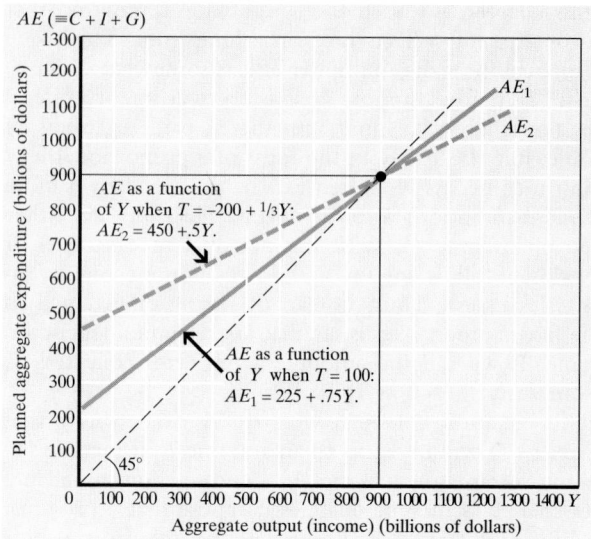

This means that a $1 increase in G or I (holding a and T_0 constant) will increase the equilibrium level of Y by:

$$\frac{1}{\left(1 - b + bt\right)}$$

Thus, if b = MPC = .75 and t = .20, the spending multiplier is 2.5. (Compare this to 4, which would be the value of the spending multiplier if taxes were a lump sum—that is, if $t = 0$.)

Holding a, I, and G constant, a fixed or lump-sum tax cut (a cut in T_0) will increase the equilibrium level of income by:

$$\frac{b}{\left(1 - b + bt\right)}$$

Thus, if b = MPC = .75 and t = .20, the tax multiplier is -1.875. (Compare this to − 3, which would be the value of the tax multiplier if taxes were a lump sum.)

SUMMARY

1. When taxes depend on income, a $1 increase in income does not increase disposable income by a full dollar, because some of the additional dollar must go to pay extra taxes. This means that if taxes are a function of income, the three multipliers (investment, government spending, and tax) are less than they would be if taxes were a lump-sum amount.

PROBLEM SET

1. You are given the following model for the economy of a country:

   (1) Consumption function: $C = 85 + 0.5Y_d$
   (2) Investment function: $I = 85$
   (3) Government spending: $G = 60$
   (4) Net taxes: $T = -40 + 0.25Y$
   (5) Disposable income: $Y_d \equiv Y - T$
   (6) Equilibrium: $Y = C + I + G$.

Solve for equilibrium income. (*Hint:* Be very careful in doing the calculations. They are not difficult, but it is easy to make careless mistakes that produce dramatically wrong results.) How much does the government collect in net taxes when the economy is in equilibrium? What is the government's budget deficit or surplus?

26

The Supply of Money and the Federal Reserve System

In the last two chapters, we explored how consumers, firms, and the government interact in the goods market. We now turn to a discussion of the *money market*. This chapter and the chapter that follows show how money markets work in the macroeconomy. We begin with an overview of what money is and what role it plays in the U.S. economy. We then discuss the forces that determine the supply of money and show how money is created by banks. Finally, we discuss the workings of the nation's central bank, the Federal Reserve, and the tools it has at its disposal to control the money supply.

It is interesting to note that microeconomics has little to say about money. Microeconomic theories and models are concerned primarily with *real* quantities (apples, oranges, hours of labor) and *relative* prices (the price of apples relative to the price of oranges, the price of labor relative to the prices of other goods). Most of the key ideas in microeconomics simply do not require that one know anything about money. As we shall see, this is clearly not the case in macroeconomics.

AN OVERVIEW OF MONEY

You often hear people say things like "He makes a lot of money" (in other words, "He has a high income") or "She's worth a lot of money" (meaning, "She is very wealthy"). It is true that your employer uses money to pay you your income, and your wealth may be accumulated in the form of money. But *money is not income, and money is not wealth*. We will soon get to a formal definition of money, but it is important that you start out with the right basic idea:

> Money is anything that is generally accepted as a medium of exchange.

As a way of understanding that money and income are not the same thing, think of a $20 bill. That single bill may pass through a thousand hands in a year, and it may never be used to pay anyone a salary. Suppose, for example, that I get a crisp, new $20 bill from an automatic teller machine, and I spend it on dinner. The restaurant puts that $20 bill in a bank in the next day's deposit. The bank gives it to a woman cashing a check the following day; she spends it at a baseball game that night. The bill has been through many hands and it has yet to be part of anyone's income.

What Is Money?

Most people take the ability to obtain and use money for granted. When the whole monetary system works well, as it generally does in the United States, the basic mechanics of the system are virtually invisible. People simply take it for granted that they can walk into any store, restaurant, boutique, or gas station and buy whatever they want, as long as they have enough little green pieces of paper in their pockets.

Indeed, the idea that you can buy things with money is so natural and obvious that it seems almost absurd to mention it. But stop and ask yourself the following questions: "How is it that a shop owner is willing to part with a steak and a loaf of bread that I can eat in exchange for some pieces of paper that are intrinsically worthless?" And why, on the other hand, are there times and places where it takes a shopping cart full of money to purchase a dozen eggs? The answers to these questions lie in what money is: a means of payment, a store of value, and a unit of account.

A MEANS OF PAYMENT, OR MEDIUM OF EXCHANGE Money is vital to the working of a market economy. You can see why if you imagine what life would be like without it. The alternative to a monetary economy is **barter,** a process by which people exchange goods and services for other goods and services directly instead of exchanging via the medium of money.

barter The direct exchange of goods and services for other goods and services.

How does a barter system work? Suppose you wake up in the morning and decide you want bacon, eggs, and orange juice for breakfast. Instead of going to the store and buying these things with money, you would have to find someone who has these items and is willing to trade them. You would also have to have something the bacon seller, the orange juice purveyor, and the egg vendor want. Having lots of pencils to trade will do you no good if the bacon, orange juice, and egg sellers do not want pencils.

double coincidence of wants The condition necessary for successful barter: Both parties to an exchange must want what the other has.

A barter system requires a **double coincidence of wants** for trade to take place. That is, in order to effect a trade, I not only have to find someone who has what I want, but that person must also want what I have. Where the range of goods traded is small, as it is in relatively unsophisticated economies, it is not difficult to find someone to trade with, and barter is often used. In a complex society with many goods, however, barter exchanges involve an intolerable amount of effort. Imagine trying to find people who offer for sale all the things you buy in a typical trip to the grocery store, and who are willing to accept goods that you have to offer in exchange for their goods.

medium of exchange, or means of payment What sellers generally accept and buyers generally use to pay for goods and services.

Some agreed-upon **medium of exchange** (or, as it is sometimes called, **means of payment**) neatly eliminates the double-coincidence-of-wants problem. Under a monetary system, money is exchanged for goods or services when people buy things; goods or services are exchanged for money when people sell things. No one ever has to trade goods for other goods directly. The importance of money as a lubricant in the functioning of a market economy can hardly be overstated.

store of value An asset that can be used to transport purchasing power from one period of time to another.

A STORE OF VALUE   Economists have identified other roles for money aside from its primary function as a medium of exchange. Money also serves as a **store of value**—that is, as an asset that can be used to transport purchasing power from one period of time to another. If you raise chickens and at the end of the month sell them for more than the amount you want to consume immediately, you may decide to keep some of your earnings in the form of money that you will hold until the time you want to spend it.

There are many other stores of value besides money. You could have decided to hold your "surplus" earnings by buying such things as antique paintings, baseball cards, or diamonds, which you could sell later when you want to spend your earnings. Money has several important advantages over these other stores of value, however. First, it comes in convenient denominations and is easily portable. You don't have to worry about making change for a Renoir to buy a gallon of gasoline. Second, because money is also a means of payment, it is easily exchanged for goods at all times. (A Renoir, of course, is not easily exchanged for other goods.) These two factors comprise the **liquidity property of money.** Money is easily spent, flowing out of your hands like liquid. Renoirs and ancient Aztec statues are neither convenient nor portable and are not readily accepted as a means of payment.

liquidity property of money The property of money that makes it a good medium of exchange as well as a store of value: It is portable and readily accepted and thus easily exchanged for goods.

The main disadvantage of using money as a store of value is that the value of money actually falls when the prices of goods and services rise. If, for example, the price of potato chips rises from $1 per bag to $2 per bag, the value of a dollar bill, in terms of potato chips, falls from one bag to half a bag. When this happens, it may be better to use potato chips (or perhaps antiques or real estate) as a store of value.

unit of account A standard unit that provides a consistent way of quoting prices.

A UNIT OF ACCOUNT   Finally, money also serves as a **unit of account**—that is, as a consistent way of quoting prices. All prices are quoted in monetary units. A textbook is quoted as costing $35, not 140 bananas or 4 videotapes, and a banana is quoted as costing 25¢, not 1.4 apples or 16 pages of a textbook.

Obviously, a standard unit of account is extremely useful when quoting prices. This function of money may have escaped your notice—after all, what else would people quote prices in except money? Life is not always so simple, however, especially in times when the prices of goods rise very rapidly. (See the Global Perspective box entitled "Long-Term Contracts and Inflation in Israel" for more details.)

GLOBAL PERSPECTIVE
LONG-TERM CONTRACTS AND INFLATION IN ISRAEL

In Israel, many apartment leases quote rents in dollars, not in Israeli shekels. When it comes time to pay the rent, however, the landlord does not insist on payment in dollars. Dollars are simply used as a unit of account for posting the rent on apartments, not as a means of payment. Why should this be so? Why would landlords in one country want to quote rents in another country's currency, and why would tenants agree to this practice?

The answer has to do with inflation. When prices rise very rapidly, all long-term contracts have to be written so that they are automatically adjusted to the inflation rate. This process is called *indexing*. If inflation were running at 400% per year, an apartment that rented for 1,000 shekels at the beginning of the year would have to rent for 5,000 shekels at the end of the year in order to compensate for the rise in prices over this time. Also, when inflation is not only high but variable (with prices rising by 10% one month, 20% another, 5% the next, and so on), indexing can be very cumbersome. Each month the tenant and landlord must agree on how much prices rose and decide

A residential apartment complex in Maale Adomin, Israel. Because of high inflation rates, tenants of the apartment buildings may have their leases quoted in U.S. dollars rather than Israeli shekels.

how much the rent should increase.

Suppose instead that rents are quoted in a relatively stable foreign currency, such as the U.S. dollar, whose value is almost automatically linked to domestic inflation. (That is, if Israeli prices rise by 10%, 20%, or 5% in a month, the Israeli shekel tends to fall in value by 10%, 20%, or 5% against the U.S. dollar.) By multiplying the shekels-per-dollar exchange rate by the apartment rent quoted in dollars, the landlord and tenant have a fair and convenient way of indexing the shekel price of the apartment to changes in the price level. When inflation is high, quoting prices for long-term contracts in another currency can be a convenient way of avoiding the difficulties inherent in haggling over adjustments to inflation.

Commodity and Fiat Monies

Introductory economics textbooks are full of stories about the various items that have been used as money by various cultures–candy bars, cigarettes (in World War II prisoner-of-war camps), huge wheels of carved stone (on the island of Yap in the South Pacific), cowrie shells (in West Africa), beads (among North American Indians), cattle (in southern Africa), small green scraps of paper (in contemporary North America)–the list goes on and on. These various kinds of money are generally divided into two groups, *commodity monies* and *fiat money*.

Commodity monies are those items used as money that also have an intrinsic value in some other use. For example, prisoners of war made purchases with cigarettes, quoted prices in terms of cigarettes, and held their wealth in the form of accumulated cigarettes. Of course, cigarettes could also be smoked–they had an

commodity monies Items used as money that also have intrinsic value in some other use.

alternative use apart from serving as money. Gold represents another form of commodity money. For hundreds of years gold could be used directly to buy things, but it also had other uses, ranging from jewelry to dental fillings.

By contrast, money in the United States today is mostly fiat money. **Fiat money,** sometimes called **token money,** is money that is intrinsically worthless. The actual value of a one-, ten-, or fifty-dollar bill is basically zero; what other uses are there for a small piece of paper with some green ink on it?

Why would anyone agree to use worthless scraps of paper as money instead of something that has at least some value, such as gold, cigarettes, or cattle? If you think the answer is "Because the paper money is backed by gold or silver," you are wrong. True, there was a time when dollar bills were convertible directly into gold. The government backed each dollar bill in circulation by holding a certain amount of gold in its vaults. If the price of gold were $35 per ounce, for example, the government agreed to sell one ounce of gold for 35 dollar bills. It is no longer the case, however, that dollar bills are backed by any commodity–gold, silver, or anything else. They are exchangeable only for dimes, nickels, pennies, other dollars, and so on.

In essence, paper money is accepted by the public as a means of payment and a store of value simply because the government has taken steps to ensure that its money is accepted. The government declares its paper money to be **legal tender.** That is, the government declares that its money must be accepted in settlement of debts. It does this by fiat (hence the term *fiat money*). It passes laws defining certain pieces of paper printed in certain inks on certain plates to be legal tender, and that is that. Printed on every Federal Reserve note in the United States is the phrase, "This note is legal tender for all debts, public and private." Often, the government can get a start on gaining acceptance for its paper money by requiring that it be used to pay taxes. (Note that you cannot use chickens, baseball cards, or Renoir paintings to pay your taxes, only checks or currency.)

Aside from declaring its currency legal tender, the government usually does one other thing to ensure that paper money will be accepted: It promises the public that it will not print paper money so fast that it loses its value. The practice of expanding the supply of currency so rapidly that it loses much of its value has been a problem throughout history and is known as **currency debasement.** Debasement of the currency has been a special problem of governments that lack the strength to take the politically unpopular step of raising taxes. Printing money to be used on government expenditures of goods and services can serve as a substitute for tax increases, and weak governments have often relied on the printing press to finance their expenditures. A recent example of this is Brazil, where the inflation rate hit a record of 1,759% in 1990. We will discuss the links between money and inflation at great length in later chapters.

Measuring the Supply of Money in the United States

We now turn to a more detailed look at the various kinds of money in the United States. Recall that money possesses the following properties: It is usable to buy things (a means of payment); it is usable as a means of holding wealth (a store of value); and it is used to quote prices (a unit of account). Unfortunately, however, these characteristics apply to a broad range of assets in the U.S. economy. As we will see, it is not at all clear where we should draw the line and say, "Up to this is money, beyond this is something else."

To solve the problem of multiple monies, economists have given different names to different measures of money. The two most common measures of money are transactions money, or *M*1, and broad money, or *M*2.

fiat, or token, money Items designated as money that are intrinsically worthless.

legal tender Money that a government has required to be accepted in settlement of debts.

currency debasement The decrease in the value of money that occurs when its supply is increased rapidly.

M1: TRANSACTIONS MONEY   What should be counted as money? Clearly, coins and dollar bills, as well as higher denominations of currency, must be counted as money—they fit all the requirements. But what about checking accounts? Checks too can be used to buy things and can serve as a store of value. In fact, bankers call checking accounts *demand deposits,* because depositors have the right to go to the bank and cash in (demand) their entire checking account balances at any time. Thus, your checking account balance is virtually equivalent to bills in your wallet, and it should be included as part of the amount of money you hold.

If we take the value of all currency (including coins) held outside of bank vaults and add to it the value of all demand deposits, travelers checks, and other checkable deposits, we have defined **M1,** or **transactions money.** As its name suggests, this is the money that can be directly used for transactions—to buy things:

> $M1 \equiv$ Currency Held Outside Banks + Demand Deposits + Travelers Checks + Other Checkable Deposits.

M1, or transactions money
Money that can be directly used for transactions.

A *checkable deposit* is any deposit account with a bank or other financial institution on which a check can be written. Checkable deposits include demand deposits (discussed above); *negotiable order of withdrawal (NOW) accounts,* which are like checking accounts that pay interest; and *automatic-transfer savings (ATS) accounts,* which automatically transfer funds from savings to checking (or vice versa) when the balance on one of those accounts reaches a predetermined level.

M1 on March 1, 1993, was $1,036.1 billion. Notice that M1 is a stock measure. That is, it is measured at a point in time. It is the total amount of coins and currency outside of banks and the total dollar amount in checking accounts *on a specific day.* Until now, we have considered supply as a flow—a variable with a time dimension: the quantity of wheat supplied *per year,* the quantity of automobiles supplied to the market *per year,* and so forth. Remember, however, that M1 is a stock variable.

M2: BROAD MONEY   Although M1 is the most widely used measure of the money supply, there are others with which you should be familiar. Should savings accounts be considered money, for example? Many of these accounts cannot be used for transactions directly, but it is easy to convert them into cash or to transfer funds from a savings account into a checking account. And what about money market accounts operated by your bank and money market mutual funds operated by your stockbroker? These can be used to write checks and make purchases, although such purchases are generally limited to sums over a certain amount.

If we add these **near monies,** close substitutes for transactions money, to M1, we arrive at **M2,** sometimes called **broad money** because it includes various not-quite-money monies such as savings accounts, money market accounts, and other near monies.

near monies Close substitutes for transactions money, such as savings accounts and money market accounts.

> $M2 \equiv$ M1 + Savings Accounts + Money Market Accounts + Other Near Monies.

M2, or broad money
M1 plus savings accounts, money market accounts, and other near monies.

On March 1, 1993, M2 was $3443.2 billion, considerably larger than the total M1 of $1,036.1 billion. The main advantage of looking at M2 instead of M1 is that M2 is sometimes more stable. For instance, when banks introduced new forms of interest-bearing checking accounts in the early 1980s, M1 shot up dramatically as people switched their funds from savings accounts to checking accounts. M2 remained fairly constant during this period, however, because the fall in savings account deposits and the rise in checking account balances were both part of M2 and thus canceled each other out.

BEYOND M2 As we noted earlier, a wide variety of financial instruments bear some resemblance to money, and some economists have advocated including almost all of them as part of the money supply. In recent years, for example, credit cards have come to be used extensively in exchange. Everyone who has a credit card has a credit limit—you can charge only a certain amount on your card before you have to pay it off. Usually we pay our credit card bills with a check. One of the very broad definitions of money includes the amount of available credit on credit cards (your charge limit minus what you have charged but not paid) as part of the money supply.

There are no hard and fast rules for deciding what is money and what is not money. This poses problems for economists and for those in charge of economic policy. However, *for our purposes here, "money" will always refer to transactions money, or M1.* For the sake of simplicity, we will say that $M1$ is the sum of two *general* categories: currency in circulation and deposits. Keep in mind, however, that $M1$ has *four* specific components: currency held outside banks, demand deposits, travelers checks, and other checkable deposits.

The Private Banking System

Most of the money in the United States today is "bank money" of one sort or another. $M1$ is made up largely of checking account balances rather than currency, and currency makes up an even smaller part of $M2$ and other broader definitions of money. Thus, any understanding of money requires some knowledge of the structure of the private banking system.

Banks and other financial intermediaries borrow from individuals or firms with excess funds and lend to those who need funds. For example, commercial banks receive funds in various forms, including deposits in checking and savings accounts. They take these funds and loan them out in the form of car loans, mortgages, commercial loans, and so forth. Banks and banklike institutions are called **financial intermediaries** because they "mediate," or act as a link between people who have funds to lend and those who need to borrow.

The main types of financial intermediaries are commercial banks, followed by savings and loan associations, life insurance companies, and pension funds. Since about 1970, the legal distinctions between the different types of financial intermediaries have narrowed considerably. It used to be the case, for example, that checking accounts could be held only in commercial banks and that commercial banks could not pay interest on checking accounts. Savings and loan associations were prohibited from offering certain kinds of deposits and were restricted primarily to making loans for mortgages.

The Depository Institutions Deregulation and Monetary Control Act, enacted by Congress in 1980, eliminated many of the previous restrictions on the behavior of financial institutions. Many types of institutions now offer checking accounts, and interest is paid on many types of checking accounts. Savings and loan associations now make loans for many things besides home mortgages. The Sears Financial Network is one of a number of financial service firms offering, under one roof, a wide variety of services that used to be offered by separate providers such as banks, brokerage houses, insurance companies, and financial planners.

The U.S. and international banking system experienced major difficulties in the 1980s. This topic is explored in more detail in the Issues and Applications box titled "The Credit Crunch of 1992–1993."

financial intermediaries Banks and other institutions that act as a link between those who have money to lend and those who want to borrow money.

THE CREDIT CRUNCH OF 1992–1993

The U.S. banking system went on a wild roller coaster ride in the 1980s. In the early part of the decade, a number of the world's largest banks found themselves with hundreds of billions of dollars of bad loans made to developing countries, particularly in Latin America. These loans, in combination with deregulation, fierce competition, and deep regional recessions (particularly in the Southwest) led to what many have called the "savings and loan" crisis. Hundreds of S&L's went bankrupt. And because most S&L deposits were insured by the federal government through the Federal Savings and Loan Insurance Corporation (FSLIC), the cost to the U.S. Treasury was staggering. Some estimates put the figure at over $300 billion.

Similar problems are facing the commercial banking industry in the 1990s, and some analysts argue that the resulting "credit crunch" has contributed to the very slow rate of economic growth in recent years.

To understand this argument, remember that the function of the capital (money) market, of which the banking system is a major component, is to channel household saving into productive capital investment—that is, new equipment and inventory. In the late 1980s, many bank deposits were loaned to real estate developers who built office towers, shopping centers, and condominiums. In many regions of the country, particularly New England and California, overbuilding resulted in declining rents and building values. As a result, the builders found themselves unable to repay their loans.

All loans involve some element of risk. During the 1980s real estate loans were not perceived as risky, though. A loan to a builder or developer is nearly always "secured" with the project being developed; that is,

Freedom National Bank in New York City closed its doors in December, 1990. After suffering from bad investments and hard times in the late 1980s and early 1990s, the banking industry is beginning to rebound.

if the borrower *defaults* (that is, fails to repay the loan), the bank can foreclose and sell the building to pay off the remaining amount of the loan. Because building values in the United States had been rising for a long time, bankers did not see much risk in making real estate loans.

But in a market economy, supply and demand can sometimes be out of balance. Thus, a nationwide excess supply of office space and retail space that hit the market in the early 1990s drove down rents and pushed many building owners into default. At the same time, an excess supply of housing on the East Coast and in California drove down house and condominium prices. The banking system, particularly in New England, was hit by heavy losses as a result. Many banks, including the multibillion dollar Bank of New England, failed in 1990 and 1991. During 1992, virtually all banks in the Northeast had lost money on bad loans.

During 1992 and 1993, banks worked hard to regain what had been lost, and they were largely successful. The environment of the early 1990s made it possible for banks to earn

profits without taking on added risk. The interest rate that banks had to pay on deposits in 1993 was very low—in most cases, around 2 percent. At the same time, the interest rate that the government paid on long-term government bonds and bills remained quite high. In February 1993, the interest rate paid on 30-year government bonds dropped to 7% for the first time. Many banks took advantage of these large "spreads" by simply investing deposits in risk-free government bonds rather than making loans to businesses. Some analysts claim that this behavior, while good for the banks, had a negative effect on the economy by creating a "credit crunch" that prevented many businesses from borrowing to build new plant and investing in new equipment—and, in the process, creating new jobs.

Some bankers, however, claim that the low volume of loans in 1992 and 1993 was not the result of any reluctance to lend on the part of banks but rather a lack of demand for credit on the part of business. Their argument is that the slowly growing economy is the *cause* of the low level of loans, not the result of it.

HOW BANKS CREATE MONEY

So far we have described the general way that money works and the way the supply of money is measured in the United States. But how much money is there available at a given time? Who supplies it, and how does it get supplied? The time has now come to analyze these questions in detail. In particular, we want to explore a process that many find mysterious: the way that banks *create money*.

A Historical Perspective: Goldsmiths

A useful way of understanding how banks create money is to consider the origins of the modern banking system. In the fifteenth and sixteenth centuries, citizens of many lands used gold as money, particularly for large transactions. Because gold is both inconvenient to carry around and susceptible to theft, people began to place their gold with goldsmiths for safekeeping. Upon receiving the gold, a goldsmith would issue a receipt to the depositor, charging him a small fee for looking after his gold. After a time, these receipts themselves, rather than the gold that they represented, began to be traded for goods. The receipts thus became a form of paper money, making it unnecessary to go to the goldsmith to withdraw gold each time a transaction took place.

At this point, all the receipts issued by goldsmiths were backed 100% by gold. If a goldsmith had 100 ounces of gold in his safe, he would issue receipts for only 100 ounces of gold, and no more. Goldsmiths thus functioned as mere warehouses where people stored gold for safekeeping. The goldsmiths found, however, that people did not come often to withdraw gold. Why should they, when paper receipts that could easily be converted to gold were "as good as gold"? (In fact, receipts were better than gold–more portable, safer from theft, and so on.) As a result, goldsmiths had a large stock of gold continuously on hand.

Since they had what amounted to "extra" gold sitting around, goldsmiths gradually realized that they could lend out some of this gold to would-be borrowers without any fear of running out of gold. Why would they do this? Quite simply, because it was to their advantage to do so–instead of just keeping their gold idly in their vaults, they earned interest on the loans they made. Something subtle, but quite dramatic, happened at this point. The goldsmiths changed from mere depositories for gold into banklike institutions that had the power to create money. This transformation occurred as soon as goldsmiths began making loans. Without adding any more real gold to the system, the goldsmiths increased the amount of money in circulation by creating additional claims to gold (that is, receipts, which entitled the bearer to receive a certain number of ounces of gold on demand).[1] There were thus more claims than there were ounces of gold.

A more detailed example may help to clarify this point. Suppose you go to a goldsmith who is functioning only as a depository, or warehouse, and ask for a loan to buy a plot of land that costs 20 ounces of gold. Also suppose that the goldsmith has 100 ounces of gold on deposit in his safe and receipts for exactly 100 ounces of gold out to the various people who deposited the gold. If the goldsmith decides he is tired of being a mere goldsmith and wants to become a real bank, he will loan you some gold. You don't want the gold itself, of course; rather, you want a slip of paper that represents 20 ounces of gold. The goldsmith in essence "creates" money for you by simply giving you a receipt for 20 ounces of gold (even though his entire supply

---

[1]Remember, these receipts circulated as money, and people used them to make transactions without feeling the need to cash them in–that is, to exchange them for gold itself.

of gold already belongs to various other people).[2] When he does so, there will be receipts for 120 ounces of gold in circulation instead of the 100 ounces worth of receipts before your loan, and the supply of money will have increased.

People often think that the creation of money is mysterious, perhaps even magical. In fact, far from being mystical, the creation of money is, as we shall see, simply an accounting procedure, among the most mundane of human endeavors. You may also harbor a suspicion that the whole process is fundamentally unsound, or somehow dubious. After all, the banking system began when someone issued claims for gold that already belonged to someone else. Here you may be on slightly firmer ground.

Goldsmiths-turned-bankers did face certain problems. Once they started making loans, their receipts outstanding (claims on gold) were greater than the amount of gold they had in their vaults at any given moment. If the owners of the 120 ounces worth of gold receipts in the example above all presented their receipts and demanded their gold at the same time, the goldsmith would find himself in trouble. With only 100 ounces of gold on hand, there would be no way to pay off everyone at once.

In normal times, people would be quite happy to hold receipts instead of real gold, and this problem would never arise. If, however, people began to worry about the financial safety of the goldsmith, they might begin to have doubts about whether their receipts really were as good as gold. Knowing that there were more receipts outstanding than there were ounces of gold in the goldsmith's vault, people might start to demand gold for receipts.

This situation leads to a paradox. It makes perfect sense to hold paper receipts (instead of gold) if you know you can always get gold for your paper. In normal times, goldsmiths could feel perfectly safe in loaning out more gold than they actually had in their possession. But once you (and everyone else) start to doubt the safety of the goldsmith, then you (and everyone else) would be foolish not to demand your gold back from the vault.

A **run** on a goldsmith (or in our day, a **run on a bank**) occurs when many people present their claims at the same time. These runs tend to feed on themselves. If I see you going to the goldsmith to withdraw your gold, I may become nervous and decide to withdraw my gold as well. In fact, it is the *fear* of a run that usually causes the run to take place. Runs on a bank can be triggered by a variety of causes: rumors that an institution may have made loans to dubious borrowers who cannot repay them, wars, failures of other institutions that have borrowed money from the bank, and so on. As you will see, today's bankers differ from goldsmiths, in that today's banks are subject to a "required reserve ratio." Goldsmiths had no legal reserve requirements, although the amount that they loaned out was subject to the restriction imposed on them by their fear of running out of gold.

run on a bank Occurs when many of those who have claims on a bank (deposits) present them at the same time.

The Modern Banking System

To understand how the modern banking system works, you need to have a passing familiarity with some basic principles of accounting. Once you are comfortable with the way banks keep their books, the whole process of money creation will seem quite logical.

A BRIEF REVIEW OF ACCOUNTING   Central to accounting practices is the statement that "the books always balance." In practice, this means that if we take a snapshot of a firm–any firm, including a bank–at a particular moment in time, then by definition:

$$\text{Assets} - \text{Liabilities} \equiv \text{Capital (or Net Worth), or}$$
$$\text{Assets} \equiv \text{Liabilities} + \text{Capital.}$$

---

[2]In return for lending you the receipt for 20 ounces of gold, the goldsmith expects to get an IOU promising to repay the amount (in gold itself or with a receipt from another goldsmith) with interest after a certain period of time.

Federal Reserve System (the Fed) The central bank of the United States.

Assets are things that a firm owns that are worth something. For a bank, these assets include the bank building, its furniture, its holdings of government securities, cash in its vaults, bonds, stocks, and so forth. Most important among a bank's assets, for our purposes at least, are its *loans.* When a bank makes a loan, the borrower gives the bank an *IOU,* a promise to repay a certain sum of money on or by a certain date. This promise is an asset of the bank because it is worth something. The bank could (and sometimes does) sell the IOU to another bank for cash.

Other bank assets include cash on hand (sometimes called *vault cash*) and deposits with the United States' central bank–the **Federal Reserve Bank (the Fed).** As we will see later in this chapter, federal banking regulations require that banks keep a certain portion of their deposits on hand as vault cash or on deposit with the Fed.

A firm's *liabilities* are simply its debts–what it owes. Stated another way, a bank's liabilities are the promises to pay, or IOUs, that it has issued. A bank's most important liabilities are its deposits. *Deposits* are debts owed to the depositors, because when you deposit money in your account, you are in essence making a loan to the bank.

The basic rule of accounting says that if we add up a firm's assets and subtract from this the total amount it owes to all those who have lent it funds, the difference is the firm's net worth. *Net worth* represents the value of the firm to its stockholders or owners. How much would you pay for a firm that owns $200,000 of diamonds and had borrowed $150,000 from a bank to pay for them? Clearly, the firm is worth $50,000–the difference between what it owns and what it owes. If the price of diamonds were to fall, bringing their value down to only $150,000, the firm would be worth nothing at all.

We can keep track of a bank's financial position using a simplified balance sheet called a T account. By convention, the bank's assets are listed on the left-hand side of the T account, its liabilities and net worth on the right-hand side. By definition, the balance sheet always balances, so that the sum of the item(s) on the left side of the T account is exactly equal to the sum of the item(s) on the right side of the T account.

reserves The deposits that a bank has at the Federal Reserve bank plus its cash on hand.

The T account of a hypothetical bank is shown in Figure 26.1. The bank has $110 million in *assets,* of which $20 million are **reserves**–the deposits that the bank has made at the Fed and its cash on hand (coins and currency). Reserves are an asset to the bank because the bank can go to the Fed and get cash for them, just the way you can go to the bank and get cash for the amount in your savings account. Our bank's other asset is its loans, worth $90 million.

Why do banks hold reserves/deposits at the Fed? There are many reasons, but perhaps the most important is the legal requirement that they hold a certain percentage of their deposit liabilities as reserves. The percentage of its deposits that a bank must keep as reserves at the Fed is known as the **required reserve ratio.** If the reserve ratio is 20%, then a bank with deposits of $100 million must deposit $20 million with the Fed.

required reserve ratio The percentage of its total deposits that a bank must keep as reserves at the Federal Reserve.

FIGURE 26.1

T Account for a Typical Bank (millions of dollars)

The balance sheet of a bank must always balance, so that the sum of assets (reserves and loans) equals the sum of liabilities (deposits and net worth).

	Assets	Liabilities	
Reserves	20	100	Deposits
Loans	90	10	Net worth
Total	110	110	Total

On the liabilities side of the T account, the bank has taken deposits of $100 million, so it owes this amount to its depositors. This means that the bank has a net worth of $10 million to its owners ($110 million in assets − $100 million in liabilities = $10 million net worth). The net worth of the bank is what "balances" the balance sheet.

A rule worth remembering is as follows:

> When some item on a bank's balance sheet changes, there must be at least one other change somewhere else to maintain balance.

For example, if a bank's reserves increase by $1, then one of the following must also be true: (1) its other assets (say, loans) decrease by $1; (2) its liabilities (deposits) increase by $1; or (3) its net worth increases by $1. Of course, various fractional combinations of these are also possible.

THE CREATION OF MONEY Like the goldsmiths, today's bankers seek to earn income by lending money out at a higher interest rate than they pay depositors for use of their money.

In modern times, the chances of a run on a bank are fairly small; and, even if there is a run, the central bank protects the private banks in various ways. Therefore,

> Banks usually make loans up to the point where they can no longer do so because of the reserve requirement restriction.

A bank's required amount of reserves is equal to the required reserve ratio times the total deposits in the bank. If, for example, a bank has deposits of $100 and the required ratio is 20%, the required amount of reserves is $20. The difference between a bank's actual reserves and its required reserves is its **excess reserves:**

$$\text{Excess Reserves} \equiv \text{Actual Reserves} - \text{Required Reserves.}$$

If banks make loans up to the point where they can no longer do so because of the reserve requirement restriction, this means that banks make loans up to the point where their excess reserves are zero.

To see why this is so, note that when a bank has excess reserves, it has credit available, and it can make loans. Actually, a bank can make loans *only* if it has excess reserves. When a bank makes a loan, it simply creates a demand deposit for the borrower. This creation of a demand deposit causes the bank's excess reserves to fall because the extra deposits created by the loan use up some of the excess reserves the bank has on hand.

Assume for simplicity that there is only one private bank in the country, that the required reserve ratio is 20%, and that the bank starts off with nothing, as shown in Panel 1 of Figure 26.2. Now suppose that dollar bills are in circulation and that someone deposits 100 of them in the bank. The bank deposits the $100 with the central bank, so it now has $100 in reserves, as shown in Panel 2. The bank now has assets (reserves) of $100 and liabilities (deposits) of $100. If the required reserve ratio is 20%, the bank now has excess reserves of $80.

FIGURE 26.2
Balance Sheets of a Bank in a Single-Bank Economy

Panel 1

Assets	Liabilities
Reserves 0	0 Deposits

Panel 2

Assets	Liabilities
Reserves 100	100 Deposits

Panel 3

Assets	Liabilities
Reserves 100 Loans 400	500 Deposits

excess reserves The difference between a bank's actual reserves and its required reserves.

How much can the bank lend and still meet the reserve requirement? For the moment, let's suppose that anyone who gets a loan keeps the entire proceeds in the bank or pays them to someone else who does. Nothing is withdrawn as cash. In this case, the bank can lend $400 and still meet the reserve requirement, as you can see in Panel 3 of Figure 26.2. With $80 of excess reserves, the bank can have up to $400 of additional deposits. The $100 in deposits plus $400 in loans (which are made as deposits) equal $500 in deposits. With $500 in deposits and a required reserve ratio of 20%, the bank must have reserves of $100 (20% of $500)—and it does. The bank can lend no more than $400 because if it were to do so, its reserve requirement would exceed $100. When a bank has no excess reserves and thus can make no more loans, it is said to be *loaned up*.

Remember, the money supply (M1) equals cash in circulation plus deposits. Before the initial deposit, the money supply was $100 ($100 cash and no deposits). After the deposit and the loans, the money supply is $500 (no cash outside of bank vaults and $500 in deposits). It is clear, then, that when cash is converted into deposits, the supply of money can change.

The bank whose T accounts are presented in Figure 26.2 is allowed to make loans of $400 based on the assumption that loans that are made *stay in the bank* in the form of deposits. Now suppose that I borrow from the bank to buy a personal computer, and I write a check to the computer store. If the store also deposits its money in the bank, my check merely results in a reduction in my account balance and an increase to the store's account balance within the bank. No cash has left the bank. As long as the system is closed in this way—remember that we have so far assumed that there is only one bank—the bank knows that it will never be called upon to release any of its $100 in reserves. It can thus expand its loans up to the point where its total deposits are $500.

In practice, of course, there are many banks in the country, a situation that is depicted in Figure 26.3. As long as the banking system as a whole is closed, it is still possible for an initial deposit of $100 to result in an expansion of the money supply to $500, but more steps are involved when there is more than one bank.

An example will help to clarify this point. Assume that Mary makes an initial deposit of $100 in Bank 1, and that the bank deposits the entire $100 with the Fed. (See Panel 1 of Figure 26.3.) Also assume that all loans that a bank makes are withdrawn from the bank as the individual borrowers write checks to pay for merchandise. After Mary's deposit, Bank 1 can make a loan of up to $80 to its customer Bill, because it needs to keep only $20 of its $100 deposit as reserves. (We are assuming a 20% required reserve ratio.)

The balance sheet of Bank 1 at the moment of the loan to Bill appears in Panel 2 of Fig 26.3. The bank now has loans of $80. It has credited Bill's account with the $80, so its total deposits are $180 ($80 in loans plus $100 in reserves). Bill then writes a check for $80 for a set of shock absorbers for his car. Bill wrote his check to Sam's Car Shop, and Sam deposits Bill's check in his bank, Bank 2. When the check clears, Bank 1 transfers $80 in reserves to Bank 2. Bank 1's balance sheet now looks like that in Panel 3 of Fig 26.3. Its assets include reserves of $20 and loans of $80; its liabilities are $100 in deposits. Both sides of the T-account balance: The bank's reserves are 20% of its deposits, as required by law, and it is fully loaned up.

Now look at Bank 2. Since Bank 1 has transferred $80 in reserves to Bank 2, it now has $80 in deposits and $80 in reserves. (See Panel 1, Bank 2). Since its reserve requirement is also 20%, it has excess reserves of $64 on which it can make loans.

Panel 1			Panel 2			Panel 3	

Panel 1

	Assets	Liabilities
Bank 1	Reserves 100	100 Deposits
Bank 2	Reserves 80	80 Deposits
Bank 3	Reserves 64	64 Deposits

Panel 2

	Assets	Liabilities
Bank 1	Reserves 100 Loans 80	180 Deposits
Bank 2	Reserves 80 Loans 64	144 Deposits
Bank 3	Reserves 64 Loans 51.20	115.20 Deposits

Panel 3

	Assets	Liabilities
Bank 1	Reserves 20 Loans 80	100 Deposits
Bank 2	Reserves 16 Loans 64	80 Deposits
Bank 3	Reserves 12.80 Loans 51.20	64 Deposits

Summary:	Deposits
Bank 1	100
Bank 2	80
Bank 3	64
Bank 4	51.20
⋮	
Total	500.00

FIGURE 26.3
The Creation of Money: Balance Sheets of Three Banks

Now assume that Bank 2 loans the $64 to Kate to pay for a college text-book and that Kate writes a check for $64 payable to the Manhattan College Book Store. The final position of Bank 2, after it honors Kate's $64 check by transferring $64 in reserves to the bookstore's bank, is reserves of $16, loans of $64, and deposits of $80 (Panel 3).

The Manhattan College Book Store deposits Kate's check in its bank account with Bank 3. Bank 3 now has excess reserves, because it has added $64 to its reserves. With a reserve ratio of 20%, Bank 3 can loan out $51.20 (80% of $64, leaving 20% in required reserves to back the $64 deposit).

As the process is repeated over and over, the total amount of deposits created is $500, the sum of the deposits in each of the banks. Because the banking system can be looked upon as one big bank, the outcome here for many banks is the same as the outcome in Figure 26.2 for one bank.[3]

THE MONEY MULTIPLIER   In practice, the banking system is not completely closed–some leakage out of the system does take place. Still, the important point here is that:

An increase in bank reserves leads to a greater than one-for-one increase in the money supply. Economists call the relationship between the final change in deposits and the change in reserves that caused this change the **money multiplier.** Stated somewhat differently, the money multiplier is the multiple by which deposits can increase for every dollar increase in reserves.

money multiplier The multiple by which deposits can increase for every dollar increase in reserves; equal to one divided by the required reserve ratio.

[3]If banks create money when they make loans, does repaying a loan "destroy" money? The answer is yes.

Do not confuse the money multiplier with the spending multipliers we discussed in the last two chapters. They are not the same thing.

In the example we just examined, reserves increased by $100 when the $100 in cash was deposited in a bank, and the amount of deposits increased by $500 ($100 from the initial deposit, $400 from the loans made by the various banks). The money multiplier in this case is thus $500/$100 = 5. Mathematically, the money multiplier can be defined as:

$$\text{Money Multiplier} \equiv \frac{1}{\text{Required Reserve Ratio}}.$$

In the United States, the required reserve ratio varies, depending on the size of the bank and the type of deposit. For large banks and for checking deposits, the ratio is currently 10%, which makes the potential money multiplier $1/.10 = 10.0$. This means that an increase in reserves of $1 could cause an increase in deposits of $10.00 if there were no leakage out of the system.

THE FED AND THE MONEY SUPPLY We have now seen how the private banking system creates money by making loans. However, private banks are not free to create money at will. Their ability to create money is controlled by the volume of reserves in the system, which is in turn controlled by the Federal Reserve. The Federal Reserve, therefore, has the ultimate control over the money supply. We examine the structure and function of the Federal Reserve in the sections that follow.

THE FEDERAL RESERVE SYSTEM

Founded in 1913 by an act of Congress (to which major reforms were added in the 1930s), the Federal Reserve is the central bank of the United States. The Fed is a complicated institution with many responsibilities, including the regulation and supervision of over 10,000 commercial banks. The organization of the Federal Reserve System is presented in Figure 26.4.

The *Board of Governors* is the most important group within the Federal Reserve System. The board consists of seven members, each appointed for 14 years by the President of the United States. The *chair* of the Federal Reserve, who is appointed by the President and whose term runs for four years, usually dominates the entire Federal Reserve System and is sometimes said to be the second most powerful person in the United States. The Fed is an independent agency in that it does not take orders from the President or from Congress.

The United States is divided into 12 Federal Reserve districts, each of which has its own Federal Reserve bank. These districts are indicated on the map in Figure 26.4. The district banks are like branch offices of the Federal Reserve in that they carry out the rules, regulations, and functions of the central system in their districts and report to the Board of Governors on local economic conditions.

U.S. monetary policy, that is, the behavior of the Federal Reserve regarding the money supply, is formally set by the **Federal Open Market Committee (FOMC).** The FOMC consists of the seven members of the Federal Reserve System's Board of Governors, the president of the New York Federal Reserve Bank, and, on a rotating basis, four of the presidents of the 11 other district banks. The FOMC sets goals regarding the money supply and interest rates, and it directs the **Open Market Desk** in the New York Federal Reserve Bank to buy and/or sell government securities. (We discuss the specifics of open market operations at length later in this chapter.)

Federal Open Market Committee (FOMC) A group composed of the seven members of the Fed's Board of Governors, the president of the New York Federal Reserve Bank, and four of the other 11 district bank presidents on a rotating basis; it sets goals regarding the money supply and interest rates and directs the operation of the Open Market Desk in New York.

Open Market Desk The office in the New York Federal Reserve Bank from which government securities are bought and sold by the Fed.

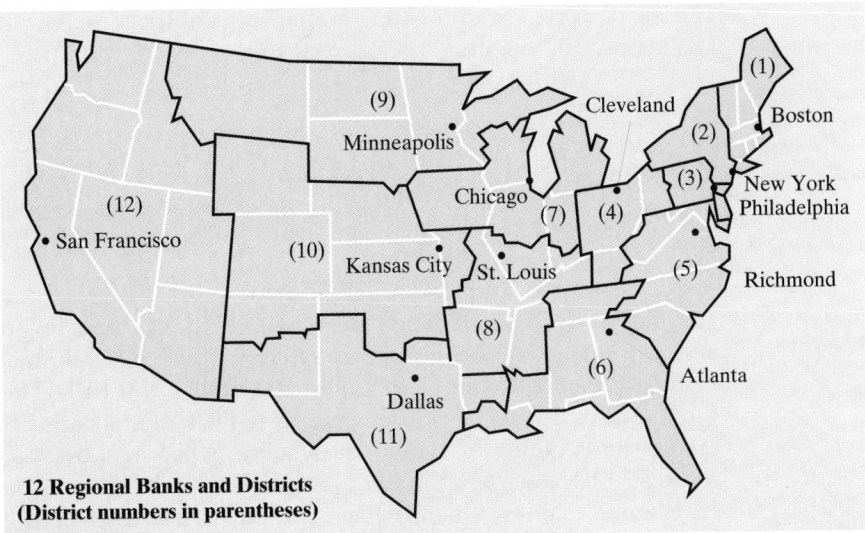

12 Regional Banks and Districts
(District numbers in parentheses)

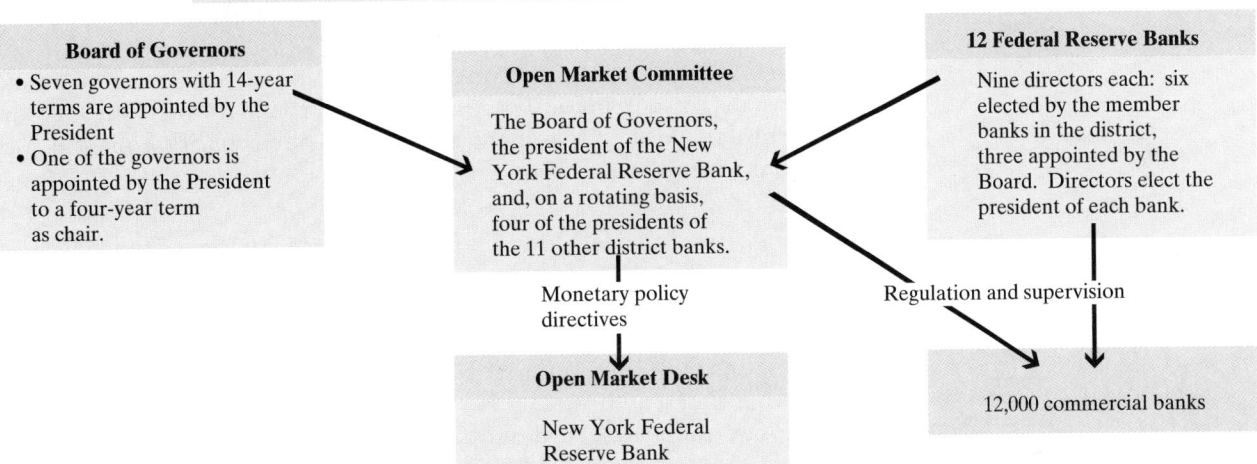

Board of Governors
- Seven governors with 14-year terms are appointed by the President
- One of the governors is appointed by the President to a four-year term as chair.

Open Market Committee

The Board of Governors, the president of the New York Federal Reserve Bank, and, on a rotating basis, four of the presidents of the 11 other district banks.

Monetary policy directives

12 Federal Reserve Banks

Nine directors each: six elected by the member banks in the district, three appointed by the Board. Directors elect the president of each bank.

Regulation and supervision

Open Market Desk

New York Federal Reserve Bank

12,000 commercial banks

Functions of the Fed

FIGURE 26.4
The Structure of the Federal Reserve System

As noted above, the Fed is the central bank of the United States. Central banks are sometimes known as "bankers' banks" because only banks (and occasionally foreign governments) can have accounts in them. As a private citizen, you cannot go to the nearest branch of the Fed and open a checking account or apply to borrow money.

Although from a macroeconomic point of view the Fed's crucial role is to control the money supply, the Fed also performs several important functions for banks. These functions include clearing interbank payments, regulating the banking system, and assisting banks that are in a difficult financial position. The Fed is also responsible for managing exchange rates and the nation's foreign exchange reserves.[4] In addition, it is often involved in intercountry negotiations on international economic issues. In the early 1980s, for example, then Chair Paul Volcker played a major role in negotiations with foreign governments on issues relating to the serious debt problems of developing countries. More recently, Chair Alan Greenspan has been involved in discussions with European

---

[4] *Foreign exchange reserves* are holdings of the currencies of other countries (for example, French francs) by the U.S. government. We discuss exchange rates and foreign exchange markets at length in Chapter 37.

central bankers regarding the monetary problems of reuniting East and West Germany and "opening up" Eastern Europe.

CLEARING INTERBANK PAYMENTS   Suppose you write a $100 check, drawn on your bank, the First Bank of Fresno (FBF), to pay for some tulip bulbs from Crockett Importers of Miami, Florida. Since Crockett Importers does not bank at FBF, but rather at Banco de Miami, how does your money get from your bank to the bank in Florida?

The answer is simple: The Fed does it. Both FBF and Banco de Miami have accounts at the Federal Reserve. When Crockett Importers receives your check and deposits it at the Banco de Miami, the bank submits the check to the Federal Reserve, asking it to collect the funds from FBF. The Fed then presents the check to FBF and is instructed to debit FBF's account for the $100 and to credit the account of Banco de Miami. Since accounts at the Fed count as reserves, FBF loses $100 in reserves and Banco de Miami gains $100 in reserves. In essence, the two banks have traded ownerships of their deposits at the Federal Reserve. Note that the *total* volume of reserves has not changed, however, and neither has the money supply.

This function of clearing interbank payments allows banks to shift money around virtually instantaneously. All they need to do is wire the Fed and request a transfer, and the funds move at the speed of electricity from one computer account to another.

OTHER DUTIES OF THE FED   Besides facilitating the transfer of funds between banks, the Fed performs several other important duties. It is responsible for many of the regulations governing banking practices and standards. For example, the Federal Reserve has the authority to control mergers between banks, and it is responsible for examining banks to ensure that they are financially sound and that they conform to a host of government accounting regulations. And, as we saw earlier, the Fed also sets reserve requirements for all financial institutions.

lender of last resort One of the functions of the Fed: It provides funds to troubled banks that cannot find any other sources of funds.

One of the most important responsibilities of the Fed is to act as the **lender of last resort** for the banking system. As our discussion of goldsmiths suggested, banks are subject to the possibility of runs on their deposits. In the United States, most deposits of less than $100,000 are insured by the Federal Deposit Insurance Corporation (FDIC). The existence of deposit insurance makes panics less likely. Because depositors know they can always get their hands on their money, even if the bank fails, they are less likely to withdraw their deposits. Not all deposits are insured, however, and the possibility of bank panics remains real. Thus, the Federal Reserve stands ready to provide funds to a troubled bank that cannot find any other sources of funds.

The Fed is the ideal lender of last resort for two reasons. First, providing funds to a bank that is in dire straits is risky and not likely to be very profitable, and it is hard to find private banks or other private institutions that are willing to perform this function. The Fed, by contrast, is a nonprofit institution whose function is to serve the overall welfare of the public. Thus, the Fed would certainly be interested in preventing catastrophic banking panics such as those that occurred in the late 1920s and the 1930s.

Second, the Fed has an essentially unlimited supply of funds with which to bail out banks that are facing the possibility of runs. The reason, as we shall see, is that the Fed can simply create reserves at will. A promise by the Fed that it

ASSETS		LIABILITIES	
Gold	$11,060	$300,010	Federal Reserve notes (outstanding)
Loans to banks	80		Deposits:
U.S. government		29,339	Bank reserves (from depository institutions)
securities	282,877	4,413	U.S. Treasury
All other assets	52,317	12,572	All other liabilities and net worth
Total	346,334	346,334	Total

Source: *Federal Reserve Bulletin* (January 1993).

TABLE 26.1

Assets and Liabilities of the Federal Reserve System, October 31, 1992 (millions of dollars)

will support a bank is thus a very convincing one. Unlike any other lender, the Fed can never run out of money. Therefore, the explicit or implicit support of the Fed should be enough to assure depositors that they are in no danger of losing their funds.

The Fed's Balance Sheet

Although it is a special bank, the Federal Reserve is in some ways very similar to an ordinary commercial bank. Like an ordinary bank, the Fed has a balance sheet that records its asset and liability position at any moment in time. The balance sheet for the Federal Reserve is presented in Table 26.1.

As the asset side of the balance sheet shows, the Fed owns about $11 billion of gold. *Do not think that this gold has anything to do with the supply of money.* Most of the gold was acquired during the 1930s, when it was purchased from the U.S. Treasury Department. Since 1934, the dollar has not been backed by (that is, it is not convertible into) gold. You cannot take a dollar bill to the Fed and ask to receive gold for it; all you can get for your old dollar bill is a new dollar bill.[5] Although it is unrelated to the money supply, the Fed's gold nevertheless counts as an asset on its balance sheet, because it is something of value that the Fed owns.

The balance sheet also mentions an asset called "loans to banks." These loans are an asset of the Federal Reserve in just the same way that a private commercial bank's loans are among its assets. The Fed sometimes makes loans to commercial banks that are short of reserves.[6] The $80 million in Table 26.1 represents these kinds of loans.

The largest of the Fed's assets by far consist of government securities: about $283 billion worth in 1992. Government securities are obligations of the federal government, such as Treasury bills and government bonds, which the Fed has purchased over the years. The way in which these bonds are acquired has important implications for the Fed's control of the money supply. (We return to this topic after our survey of the Fed's balance sheet.)

The bulk of the Fed's liabilities are Federal Reserve notes. The dollar bill you carry in your pocket when you go to the store to buy a quart of milk is clearly an asset from your point of view—it is something you own that has value. But

---

[5]The fact that the Fed is not obliged to provide gold for currency means that it can never go bankrupt. When the currency was backed by gold, it would have been possible for the Fed to run out of gold if too many of its depositors came to it at the same time and asked to exchange their deposits for gold. But if depositors come to the Fed and wish to withdraw their deposits today, all they can get are dollar bills, which the Fed can print as quickly as it needs to. In addition, it should be noted that the dollar was convertible into gold internationally until August 15, 1971.

[6]Recall that commercial banks are required to keep a set percentage of their deposit liabilities on deposit at the Fed. If a bank suddenly finds itself short of reserves, one of its alternatives is to borrow the reserves it needs from the Fed.

since every financial asset is by definition a liability of some other agent in the economy, whose liability is that dollar bill? Quite simply: That dollar bill, and bills of all other denominations in the economy, are a liability—an IOU—of the Federal Reserve. They are, of course, rather strange IOUs, because all they can be redeemed for are other IOUs of exactly the same type. They are, nonetheless, classified as liabilities of the Fed.

The Fed's balance sheet also shows that, like an ordinary commercial bank, the Fed has accepted deposits. These deposits are recorded as liabilities. The bulk of the Fed's deposits come from commercial banks. Remember that commercial banks are required to keep a certain share of their own deposits as deposits at the Fed. Since a bank's deposits at the Fed—its reserves—are an asset from the bank's point of view, those same reserves must be a liability from the Fed's point of view.

Table 26.1 also shows that the Fed has accepted a small volume of deposits from the U.S. Treasury. In effect, the Fed acts as the bank for the U.S. government. When the government needs to pay for something it has bought—a new aircraft carrier, for example—it may write out a check to the supplier of the ship drawn on its "checking account" at the Federal Reserve. Similarly, when the government receives revenues from tax collections, fines, or sales of government assets, it may deposit these funds in its account at the Fed.

HOW THE FED CONTROLS THE MONEY SUPPLY

The key to understanding how the Fed controls the supply of money in the U.S. economy is an appreciation of the role of reserves. (Reserves on the Fed's balance sheet are the deposits of depository institutions.) As we have said, the required reserve ratio establishes a link between the reserves of the commercial banks and the deposits (money) that commercial banks are allowed to create.

The reserve requirement, in essence, determines how much a given bank has available to lend. If, for example, the required reserve ratio is 20%, then each $1 of reserves can support $5 in deposits. A bank that has reserves of $100,000 cannot have more than $500,000 in deposits. If it did, it would fail to meet the required reserve ratio.

If you recall that the *money supply* is equal to the sum of deposits inside banks and the currency in circulation outside of banks, you can see that reserves provide the leverage that the Fed needs to control the money supply:

> If the Fed wants to increase the supply of money, it creates more reserves, thereby freeing banks to create additional deposits by making more loans. If it wants to decrease the money supply, it reduces reserves.

The key question then becomes, of course: How does the Fed control the supply of reserves? There are three major tools available to the Fed for changing the money supply. These are (1) changing the required reserve ratio, (2) changing the discount rate, and (3) open market operations. We shall explore each of these in turn.

The Required Reserve Ratio

The simplest way for the Fed to alter the supply of money is to change the required reserve ratio. An analysis of how this process works is presented in Table 26.2. Let us assume that the initial required reserve ratio is 20 percent.

TABLE 26.2

A Decrease in the Required Reserve Ratio from 20% to 12.5% Increases the Supply of Money

Panel 1: Required Reserve Ratio = 20%

FEDERAL RESERVE				COMMERCIAL BANKS			
ASSETS		LIABILITIES		ASSETS		LIABILITIES	
Government securities	$200	$100	Reserves	Reserves	$100	$500	Deposits
		$100	Currency	Loans	$400		

Note: Money supply (*M*1) = Currency + Deposits = $600.

Panel 2: Required Reserve Ratio = 12.5%

FEDERAL RESERVE				COMMERCIAL BANKS			
ASSETS		LIABILITIES		ASSETS		LIABILITIES	
Government securities	$200	$100	Reserves	Reserves	$100	$800	Deposits (+$300)
		$100	Currency	Loans (+$300)	$700		

Note: Money supply (*M*1) = Currency + Deposits = $900.

In Panel 1, a simplified version of the Fed's balance sheet (in billions of dollars) shows that reserves are $100 billion and currency outstanding is another $100 billion. The total value of the Fed's assets is $200 billion, which we assume to be all in the form of government securities. Assuming that there are no excess reserves—that banks stay fully loaned up—the $100 billion in reserves supports $500 billion in deposits at the commercial banks. (Remember that the money multiplier equals 1/required reserve ratio—in this case 1/.20 = 5. Thus, $100 billion in reserves can support $500 billion [$100 billion × 5] in deposits when the required reserve ratio is 20 percent.) The supply of money (*M*1, or transactions money) is therefore equal to $600 billion: $100 billion in currency and $500 billion in (checking account) deposits at the commercial banks.

Now suppose that the Fed wants to increase the supply of money to $900 billion. If it lowers the required reserve ratio from 20% to 12.5% (as shown in Panel 2 of Table 26.2), then the same $100 billion of reserves could support $800 billion in deposits instead of only $500 billion. In this case, the money multiplier is 1/.125, or 8. At a required reserve ratio of 12.5% then, $100 billion in reserves can support $800 billion in deposits. The total money supply would then be $800 billion in deposits plus the $100 billion in currency, for a total of $900 billion.[7]

Put another way, with the new lower reserve ratio, banks have excess reserves of $37.5 billion. They now need only $62.5 billion of reserves to back their $500 billion of deposits, so the remaining $37.5 billion of the existing $100 billion in reserves are "extra." With that $37.5 billion of excess reserves, banks can lend out more money. If we assume that the system loans money and creates deposits to the *maximum* extent possible, the $37.5 billion of reserves will support an additional $300 billion of deposits ($37.5 billion × the money multiplier of 8 = $300 billion). The change in the required reserve ratio has thus

---

[7]To find the maximum volume of deposits (*D*) that can be supported by an amount of reserves (*R*), simply divide *R* by the required reserve ratio. If the required reserve ratio is *g*, since $R = gD$, then $D = \dfrac{R}{g}$.

injected an additional $300 billion into the banking system, at which point the banks will be fully loaned up and unable to increase their deposits further.

In sum:

> Decreases in the required reserve ratio allow banks to have more deposits with the existing volume of reserves. As banks create more deposits by making loans, the supply of money (currency + deposits) increases. The reverse is also true: If the Fed wants to restrict the supply of money, it can raise the required reserve ratio, in which case banks will find that they have insufficient reserves and must therefore reduce their deposits by "calling in" some of their loans.[8] The result is a decrease in the money supply.

For a variety of reasons, the Fed has tended not to use changes in the reserve requirement as a means of controlling the money supply. In part, this reluctance stems from the era when only some banks were members of the Federal Reserve System and thus subject to reserve requirements. The Fed reasoned that if it raised the reserve requirement in order to contract the money supply, banks might choose to stop being members. (Since reserves pay no interest, the higher the reserve requirement, the more the penalty imposed on those banks holding reserves.) This argument, however, no longer applies. Since the passage of the Depository Institutions Deregulation and Monetary Control Act in 1980, all depository institutions are subject to Federal Reserve requirements.

It is also true that changing the reserve requirement ratio is a fairly crude tool. Because of lags in banks' reporting to the Fed on their reserve and deposit positions, a change in the requirement today does not affect banks for about two weeks. (On the other hand, the fact that changing the reserve requirement expands or reduces credit in every bank in the country makes it a very powerful tool when the Fed does use it.) A much better tool for controlling week-to-week changes in the money supply, as we shall see shortly, is open market operations.

The Discount Rate

Banks are allowed to borrow from the Fed. The interest rate that they pay the Fed for this privilege is called the **discount rate.** When banks increase their borrowing, the money supply increases.

To simplify our analysis, let us assume that there is only one bank in the country and that the required reserve ratio is 20 percent. The initial position of the bank and the Fed appear in Panel 1 of Table 26.3, where the money supply (currency + deposits) is $480. In Panel 2, the bank has borrowed $20 from the Fed. By using this $20 as a reserve, the bank can increase its loans by $100, from $320 to $420. (Remember that a required reserve ratio of 20% gives a money multiplier of 5. Thus, an additional $20 in reserves allows the bank to create an additional 20×5, or $100, in deposits.) Thus,

> Bank borrowing from the Fed leads to an increase in the money supply.

Of course, banks that borrow from the Fed must eventually repay their borrowings. When they do, the money supply goes back down by exactly the amount by which it initially increased.

---

[8] In fact, banks never really have to "call in" loans before they are due in order to reduce the money supply. First, the Fed is almost always expanding the money supply slowly because the real economy grows steadily and, as we shall see, growth brings with it the need for more circulating money. So when we speak of "contractionary monetary policy," we mean that the Fed is slowing down the rate of money growth, not reducing the money supply. Second, even if the Fed were actually to cut reserves (rather than merely curb their expansion), banks would no doubt be able to comply by reducing the volume of new loans that they make while old ones are coming due.

TABLE 26.3

The Effect on the Money
Supply of Commercial Bank
Borrowing from the Fed

Panel 1: No Commercial Bank Borrowing from the Fed

FEDERAL RESERVE				COMMERCIAL BANKS			
ASSETS		LIABILITIES		ASSETS		LIABILITIES	
Securities	$160	$80	Reserves	Reserves	$80	$400	Deposits
		$80	Currency	Loans	$320		

Note: Money supply (*M*1) = Currency + Deposits = $480.

Panel 2: Commercial Bank Borrowing $20 from the Fed

FEDERAL RESERVE				COMMERCIAL BANKS			
ASSETS		LIABILITIES		ASSETS		LIABILITIES	
Securities	$160	$100	Reserves	Reserves	$100	$500	Deposits
			(+$20)	(+$20)			(+$100)
Loans	$20	$80	Currency	Loans	$420	$20	Amount owed
				(+$100)			to Fed (+$20)

Note: Money supply (*M*1) = Currency + Deposits = $580.

The Fed can exercise some influence over bank borrowing through the discount rate:

> The higher the discount rate, the higher the cost of borrowing, and the less borrowing banks will want to do.

If the Fed wants to curtail the growth of the money supply, for example, it raises the discount rate, discourages banks from borrowing from it, and thus restricts the growth of reserves (and ultimately deposits).

In practice, the Fed does not use the discount rate very often to control the money supply. It does change the discount rate from time to time to keep it in line with other interest rates, but most often the discount rate follows the other rates rather than leads them.

Changing the discount rate in order to control the supply of money has several problems associated with it. First, although raising the discount rate does discourage borrowing by banks (and therefore reduces their ability to expand the money supply), it is never clear in advance exactly how much of an effect any given change in the discount rate will have. If banks are very short of reserves, they may decide to borrow from the Fed even though the discount rate is quite high. In short:

> The discount rate cannot be used to control the money supply with great precision, because its effects on banks' demand for reserves are uncertain.

Second, changes in the discount rate can be largely offset by movements in other interest rates. For example, if the discount rate is set at 10% and the rate paid by Treasury bills is 9%, banks will obviously not find it profitable to borrow from the Fed to purchase Treasury bills. Since they would be paying more in borrowing costs than they would be making in interest revenue, they would lose by borrowing from the Fed. If the Treasury bill rate were to rise to 11%, however, then banks could profitably borrow from the Fed to purchase Treasury bills. Thus, a discount rate that is high enough to discourage borrowing in some circumstances may not be high enough in others.

You may be wondering whether the discount rate can ever be below the rate banks charge their customers for loans or below the rate offered on Treasury bills. If this were the case, wouldn't banks borrow enormous quantities from the Fed at the lower rate and lend at the higher rate? In practice, the discount rate is at times lower than the rate that banks charge for their loans, and yet this kind of behavior is not common. This is because the Fed places other constraints on the borrowing behavior of banks. The Fed practices what is sometimes called **moral suasion** to discourage heavy borrowing. Because member banks know that the Fed would look askance at heavy borrowing, they do not borrow heavily, and the amount that they do borrow responds only slightly to changes in the discount rate.

moral suasion The pressure exerted by the Fed on member banks to discourage them from borrowing heavily from the Fed.

Open Market Operations

By far the most significant of the Fed's tools for controlling the supply of money is **open market operations.** Congress has authorized the Federal Reserve to buy and sell U.S. government securities in the open market. When the Fed purchases a security, it pays for it by writing a check which, when cleared, *expands* the quantity of reserves in the system and thus the money supply. When the Fed sells a bond, private citizens or institutions pay for it with a check which, when cleared, *reduces* the quantity of reserves in the system.

Before we look at how open market transactions and reserve controls work, however, we need to review several key ideas.

open market operations The purchase and sale by the Fed of government securities in the open market; a tool used to expand or contract the amount of reserves in the system and thus the money supply.

TWO BRANCHES OF GOVERNMENT DEAL IN GOVERNMENT SECURITIES   The fact that the Fed is able to buy and sell government securities–bills and bonds–is a source of much confusion to students. In fact, *two* branches of government deal in financial markets for very different reasons, and it is critical that you keep the two separate in your mind.

First, keep in mind that the Treasury Department is responsible for collecting taxes and paying the bills of the federal government. Salary checks paid to government workers, payments to General Dynamics for a new Navy ship, social security checks to retirees, and so forth are all written on accounts maintained by the Treasury. Tax receipts collected by the Internal Revenue Service, a Treasury branch, are deposited to these accounts.

If total government spending exceeds tax receipts, the law requires the Treasury to borrow the difference. Recall that the government deficit is $(G - T)$, or government purchases minus net taxes. $(G - T)$ is the amount the Treasury must borrow each year to finance the deficit. This means that:

The Treasury *cannot* print money to finance the deficit.

The Treasury borrows by issuing bills, bonds, and notes that pay interest. These government securities, or IOUs, are sold to the general public. Often foreign countries, as well as U.S. citizens, buy them. The total amount of outstanding government securities held by the public (that is, by U.S. citizens and foreigners) is the **national debt.** At the end of 1992, the national debt stood at about $3 trillion.

The Fed is not the Treasury. Rather, it is a quasi-independent agency authorized by Congress to buy and sell *outstanding* (that is, pre-existing) U.S. government securities on the open market. The bonds and bills initially sold by the Treasury to finance the deficit are continuously resold and traded among ordinary

national debt The total amount of outstanding government securities held by the public.

citizens, firms, banks, pension funds, and so forth. The Fed's participation in that trading affects the quantity of reserves in the system, as we will see below.

Because the Fed owns some government securities, some of what the government owes, it owes to itself. Recall that the Federal Reserve System's largest single asset is government securities. These securities are nothing more than bills and bonds initially issued by the Treasury to finance the deficit. They were acquired by the Fed over time through direct open market purchases that the Fed made in order to expand the money supply as the economy expanded.

THE MECHANICS OF OPEN MARKET OPERATIONS   How do open market operations affect the money supply? Look again at Table 26.1. As you can see, most of the Fed's assets consist of the government securities we have just been talking about.

Suppose, now, that the Fed wants to decrease the supply of money. If it can reduce the volume of bank reserves on the liabilities side of its balance sheet, it will force banks in turn to reduce their own deposits (in order to meet the required reserve ratio). Since these deposits are part of the supply of money, the supply of money will contract.

We must now ask ourselves what will happen if the Fed sells some of its holdings of government securities to the general public. Clearly, the Fed's holdings of government securities must decrease, since some of the securities it used to own will now be owned by someone else. How do the purchasers of securities pay for what they have bought? Quite simply, by writing checks that are drawn on their banks and payable to the Fed.

Let's look a bit more carefully at how this process works, with the help of Table 26.4 on the next page. In Panel 1, the Fed initially has $100 billion of government securities. Its liabilities consist of $20 billion of deposits (which, you recall, are the reserves of commercial banks) and $80 billion of currency. With the required reserve ratio at 20%, the $20 billion of reserves can support $100 billion of deposits in the commercial banks. The commercial banking system is thus fully loaned up. Panel 1 also shows the financial position of a private citizen, Jane Q. Public. Jane has assets of $5 billion (a rather large checking account deposit in the bank) and no debts, so her net worth is $5 billion.

Now imagine that the Fed sells $5 billion in government securities to Jane. Jane pays for the securities by writing a check to the Fed, drawn on her bank. The Fed then reduces the reserve account of her bank by $5 billion. The balance sheets of all the participants after this transaction are shown in Panel 2. Note that the supply of money (currency plus deposits) has fallen from $180 billion to $175 billion.

This is not the end of the story, however. As a result of the Fed's sale of securities, the amount of reserves has fallen from $20 billion to $15 billion, while deposits have fallen from $100 billion to $95 billion. With a required reserve ratio of 20%, banks must have .20 × $95 billion, or $19 billion in reserves. Banks are thus under their required reserve ratio by $4 billion ($19 billion [the amount they should have] minus $15 billion [the amount they do have]). In order to comply with the federal regulations, therefore, banks must decrease their loans and their deposits.[9]

The final equilibrium position is shown in Panel 3, where commercial banks have reduced their loans by $20 billion. Notice that the change in deposits from Panel 1 to Panel 3 is $25 billion, which is five times the size of the change in reserves that the Fed brought about through its $5 billion open market sale of securities. This corresponds exactly to our earlier analysis of the money multiplier. The change in money (− $25 billion) is equal to the money multiplier (five) times the change in reserves (− $5 billion).

---

[9]Once again, banks never really have to call in loans. Loans and deposits would probably be reduced by slowing the rate of new lending as old loans come due and are paid off.

TABLE 26.4
Open Market Operations
The boxed numbers in Panels 2 and 3 show the differences between those panels and Panel 1. All numbers are quoted in billions.

Panel 1

FEDERAL RESERVE			COMMERCIAL BANKS			JANE Q. PUBLIC		
ASSETS	LIABILITIES		ASSETS	LIABILITIES		ASSETS	LIABILITIES	
Securities $100	$20 Reserves $80 Currency		Reserves $20 Loans $80	$100 Deposits		Deposits $5	$0 Debts $5 Net Worth	

Note: Money supply (*M*1) = Currency + Deposits = $180.

Panel 2

FEDERAL RESERVE			COMMERCIAL BANKS			JANE Q. PUBLIC		
ASSETS	LIABILITIES		ASSETS	LIABILITIES		ASSETS	LIABILITIES	
Securities $95 (-$5)	$15 Reserves (-$5)		Reserves $15 (-$5)	$95 Deposits (-$5)		Deposits $0 (-$5)	$0 Debts	
	$80 Currency		Loans $80			Securities $5 (+$5)	$5 Net Worth	

Note: Money supply (*M*1) = Currency + Deposits = $175.

Panel 3

FEDERAL RESERVE			COMMERCIAL BANKS			JANE Q. PUBLIC		
ASSETS	LIABILITIES		ASSETS	LIABILITIES		ASSETS	LIABILITIES	
Securities $95 (-$5)	$15 Reserves (-$5)		Reserves $15 (-$5)	$75 Deposits (-$25)		Deposits $0 (-$5)	$0 Debts	
	$80 Currency		Loans $60 (-$20)			Securities $5 (+$5)	$5 Net Worth	

Note: Money supply (*M*1) = Currency + Deposits = $155.

Now consider what happens when the Fed *purchases* a government security. Suppose that I hold $100 in Treasury bills, which the Fed buys from me. The Fed writes me a check for $100, and I turn in my Treasury bills. I then take the $100 check and deposit it in my local bank. This increases the reserves of my bank by $100 and begins a new episode in the money expansion story. With a reserve requirement of 20%, my bank can now lend out $80. If that $80 is spent and ends up back in a bank, that bank can lend $64, and so forth. (Review Figure 26.3.) The Fed can thus expand the money supply by buying government securities from people who own them, just the way it reduces the money supply by selling these securities.

Each business day, the Open Market Desk in the New York Federal Reserve Bank buys or sells millions of dollars worth of securities, usually to large security dealers who act as intermediaries between the Fed and the private markets. We can sum up the effect of these open market operations this way:

- An open market *purchase* of securities by the Fed results in an *increase* in reserves and an *increase* in the supply of money by an amount equal to the money multiplier times the change in reserves.

- An open market *sale* of securities by the Fed results in a *decrease* in reserves and a *decrease* in the supply of money by an amount equal to the money multiplier times the change in reserves.

Open market operations are the Fed's preferred means of controlling the money supply for several reasons. First, open market operations can be used with some precision. If the Fed needs to change the money supply by just a small amount, it can buy or sell a small volume of government securities. If it wants a larger change in the money supply, it can simply buy or sell a larger amount. Second, open market operations are extremely flexible. If the Fed decides to reverse course, it can easily switch from buying securities to selling them. Finally, open market operations have a fairly predictable effect on the supply of money. Since banks are obliged to meet their reserve requirements, an open market sale of $100 in government securities will reduce reserves by $100, which will reduce the supply of money by $100 times the money multiplier.

But where does the Fed get the money to buy government securities when it wants to expand the money supply? The Fed simply creates it. In effect, it tells the bank from which it has bought a $100 security that its reserve account (deposit) at the Fed now contains $100 more than it did previously. This is where the power of the Fed, or any central bank, lies. The Fed has the ability to create money at will. In the United States, the Fed exercises this power when it creates money to buy government securities.

The Supply Curve for Money

The main point of our discussion thus far is that the Fed can control the money supply by controlling the amount of reserves in the economy. If the Fed wants the quantity of money to be $900 billion on a given date, it can aim for this target by changing the discount rate, by changing the required reserve ratio, or by engaging in open market operations. In this sense, the supply of money is completely determined by the Fed, and we can draw the money supply curve in Figure 26.5 as a vertical line.

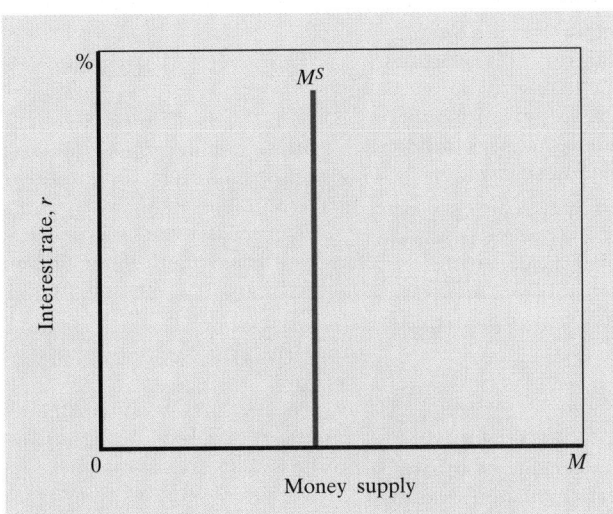

FIGURE 26.5
The Supply of Money

If the Fed's money supply behavior is not influenced by the interest rate, the money supply curve is a vertical line.

A vertical money supply curve says that the Fed sets the money supply independent of the interest rate. In other words, a vertical money supply curve means that the interest rate does not affect the Fed's decision on how much money to supply. We will see in Chapter 31 that the Fed's money supply behavior is in fact influenced by the state of the economy, and perhaps by the interest rate. In practice, then, the money supply curve is not likely to be vertical. It would, however, complicate matters too much at this stage of our analysis to consider Fed behavior in more detail, so we will assume for now that the money supply curve is vertical. This assumption is relaxed in Chapter 31.[10]

LOOKING AHEAD

This chapter has discussed only the supply side of the money market. We have seen what money is, how banks create money by making loans, and how the Fed controls the money supply. In the next chapter we turn to the demand side of the money market. There we examine the demand for money and how the supply of and demand for money determine the equilibrium interest rate.

---

[10]There is another reason that the money supply curve may not be vertical. If bank borrowing from the Fed responds positively to the difference between the market interest rate and the discount rate, then as the market interest rate rises (with the discount rate fixed), banks will borrow more. We have seen that an increase in bank borrowing leads to an increase in the money supply. Therefore, the supply of money responds positively to the market interest rate, so the money supply schedule should have a positive slope. In practice this effect is fairly small, and for the sake of simplicity we will ignore it. The Fed could, of course, offset this effect completely if it raised the discount rate in line with the market interest rate.

SUMMARY

An Overview of Money

1. Money has three distinguishing characteristics. It is (1) a means of payment, or medium of exchange, (2) a store of value, and (3) a unit of account. The alternative to using money is a *barter* system, in which goods are exchanged directly for other goods. Barter is costly and inefficient in an economy with many different kinds of goods.

2. *Commodity monies* are those items used as money that also have an intrinsic value in some other use (for example, gold and cigarettes). *Fiat monies* are intrinsically worthless apart from their use as money. In order to ensure the acceptance of fiat monies, governments use their power to declare money *legal tender* and promise the public that they will not debase the currency by expanding its supply rapidly.

3. There are various definitions of money. Currency plus demand deposits plus travelers checks plus other checkable deposits comprise *M*1, or *transactions money*–money that can be used directly to buy things. The addition of savings accounts and money market accounts (*near monies*) to *M*1 gives *M*2, or *broad money*.

How Banks Create Money

4. The *required reserve ratio* is the percentage of a bank's deposits that must be kept as *reserves* at the nation's central bank, the Federal Reserve.

5. Banks create money by making loans. When a bank makes a loan to a customer, it simply creates a deposit in that customer's account. This deposit becomes part of the money supply. Banks can create money only when they have *excess reserves*–that is, reserves in excess of the amount set by the required reserve ratio.

6. The *money multiplier* is the multiple by which the total supply of money can increase for every dollar increase in reserves. The money multiplier is equal to 1/the required reserve ratio.

The Federal Reserve System

7. The Fed's most important function is controlling the nation's money supply. However, the Fed also performs several other important functions: It clears interbank payments, is responsible for many of the regulations governing banking practices and standards, and acts as a *lender of last resort* for troubled banks that cannot find any other sources of funds. The Fed also acts as the bank for the U.S. government.

How the Fed Controls the Money Supply

8. The key to understanding how the Fed controls the money supply is an appreciation of the role of reserves. If the Fed wants to increase the supply of money, it creates more reserves, thereby freeing banks to create additional deposits. If it wants to decrease the money supply, it reduces reserves.

9. The Fed has three tools at its disposal to control the money supply. It can (1) change the required reserve ratio, (2) change the *discount rate* (the interest rate that member banks pay when they borrow from the Fed), or (3) engage in *open market operations* (that is, the buying and selling of already-existing government securities). To increase the money supply, the Fed can create additional reserves by decreasing the required reserve ratio, by lowering the discount rate, or by buying government securities. To decrease the money supply, the Fed can reduce reserves by increasing the required reserve ratio, by raising the discount rate, or by selling government securities.

10. If the Fed's money supply behavior is not influenced by the interest rate, the supply curve for money is a vertical line.

Review Terms and Concepts

barter 647
commodity monies 649
currency debasement 650
discount rate 666
double coincidence of wants 648
excess reserves 657
Federal Open Market Committee (FOMC) 660
Federal Reserve System (the Fed) 656
fiat, or token, money 650

financial intermediaries 652
legal tender 650
lender of last resort 662
liquidity property of money 648
M1, or transactions money 651
M2, or broad money 651
medium of exchange, or means of payment 648
money multiplier 659
moral suasion 668

national debt 668
near monies 651
Open Market Desk 660
open market operations 668
required reserve ratio 656
reserves 656
run on a bank 655
store of value 648
unit of account 648

Equations:

M1 ≡ Currency held outside banks + Demand deposits + Travelers checks + Other checkable deposits
M2 ≡ M1 + Savings accounts + Money market accounts + Other near monies
Assets ≡ Liabilities + Capital (or Net Worth)
Excess reserves ≡ Actual reserves − Required reserves

$$\text{Money multiplier} \equiv \frac{1}{\text{Required Reserve Ratio}}$$

Problem Set

1. As King of Medivalia, you are constantly strapped for funds to pay your army. Your chief economic wizard suggests the following plan: "When you collect your tax payments from your subjects, insist on being paid in gold coins. Take these gold coins, melt them down, and then remint them with an extra 10% of brass thrown in. You will then have 10% more money than you started with." What do you think of the plan? Will it work?

2. Why is *M2* sometimes a more stable measure of money than *M1*? Explain in your own words, using the definitions of *M1* and *M2*.

3. Do you agree or disagree with each of the following statements? Explain your answers.

a. "When the Treasury of the United States issues bonds and sells them to the public to finance the deficit, the money supply remains unchanged because every dollar of money taken in by the Treasury goes right back into circulation through government spending. This is not true when the Federal Reserve System sells bonds to the public."

b. "The money multiplier depends on the marginal propensity to save."

c. "In 1991 the Federal Reserve moved to lower the reserve requirement for banks. This move was designed to reduce the supply of money in circulation."

4. When the Fed adds new reserves to the system, some of these new reserves find their way out of the country into foreign banks or foreign investment funds. In addition, some portion of new reserves ends up in people's pockets and mattresses rather than in bank vaults. These "leakages" reduce the money multiplier and sometimes make it very difficult for the Fed to control the money supply precisely.

a. Explain why this is true.

b. Suppose that the reserve requirement is 12%, but that 25% of all U.S. cash assets end up in foreign accounts. If the Fed buys $1000 worth of securities on the open market, how much will the money supply expand? What is the impact of a 25% leakage on the size of the money multiplier?

5. You are given the following simplified T account for a bank:

ASSETS		LIABILITIES	
Reserves	$500	$3500	Deposits
Loans	3000		

The required reserve ratio is 10 percent.
a. How much is the bank required to hold as reserves, given its deposits of $3500?
b. How much are its excess reserves?
c. By how much can the bank increase its loans?
d. Suppose a depositor comes to the bank and withdraws $200 in cash. Show the bank's new balance sheet, assuming that the bank obtains the cash by drawing down its reserves. Does the bank now hold excess reserves? Is it meeting the required reserve ratio? If not, what can it do?

6. What are the major functions of the Federal Reserve? Do you think any of these functions could be performed by private banks, or is the central bank the only agent capable of filling these roles? Explain.

7. The Banco Central de Erehwon (the central bank of an imaginary country) has assets of 1,000 quetzales (the local unit of currency), which consist of government securities that it holds. It has liabilities of 800 quetzales of currency and 200 quetzales of deposits by banks in the central bank.
a. Draw a T account showing the central bank's financial position.
b. If the required reserve ratio is 10%, what is the money supply ($M1$ = currency plus deposits) in Erehwon? What assumptions did you have to make about banks' holdings of excess reserves to arrive at this answer?
c. Suppose the Banco Central wants to expand the supply of money by 200 quetzales by changing the required reserve ratio. What should the new required reserve ratio be?
d. If, instead of changing the required reserve ratio, the Banco Central decides to use open market operations to increase the money supply, how many quetzales worth of government securities should it buy or sell? Explain, with reference to the money multiplier.
e. Suppose that the discount rate charged by the Banco Central is 12 percent. If the BC still wants to increase the supply of money by 200 quetzales, by how much should it change the discount rate? Why isn't it possible to give an exact answer here?

The Demand for Money, the Equilibrium Interest Rate, and Monetary Policy

27

THE DEMAND FOR MONEY
The Transaction Motive for Holding Money
Money Management and the Optimal Balance
The Speculation Motive for Holding Money
The Total Demand for Money
Transactions Volume and the Price Level
The Determinants of Money Demand (Review)

THE EQUILIBRIUM INTEREST RATE
Supply and Demand in the Money Market

The Fed: Changing the Money Supply to Affect the Interest Rate
Increases in *Y* and Shifts in the Money Demand Curve

LOOKING AHEAD: FED BEHAVIOR AND MONETARY POLICY

APPENDIX A: THE VARIOUS INTEREST RATES IN THE U.S. ECONOMY

APPENDIX B: THE DEMAND FOR MONEY: A NUMERICAL EXAMPLE

H aving discussed the *supply* of money in the last chapter, we now turn to a discussion of the *demand* for money. One of the main goals of this chapter and the previous chapter is to provide a theory of how the interest rate is determined in the macroeconomy. Once we have seen how the interest rate is determined, we can turn to the question of how the Fed affects the interest rate through **monetary policy.**

Because the interest rate plays such an important role in the economy, it is important that you understand exactly what it is. **Interest** is the fee that a borrower pays to a lender for the use of his or her funds. Firms and the government borrow funds by issuing bonds, and they pay interest to the firms and households (the lenders) that purchase those bonds. Households and firms that have borrowed from a bank must pay interest on those loans to the bank.

The **interest rate** is the annual interest payment on a loan expressed as a percentage of the loan. For example, a $1000 bond (representing a $1000 loan from a household to a firm) that pays $100 in interest per year has an interest rate of 10 percent. Note that the interest rate is expressed as an *annual* rate. It is the amount of interest received *per year* divided by the amount of the loan.

While there are many different interest rates, for the purposes of our analysis we

monetary policy The behavior of the Federal Reserve regarding the money supply.

interest The fee that a borrower pays to a lender for the use of his or her funds.

interest rate The annual interest payment on a loan expressed as a percentage of the loan. Equal to the amount of interest received per year divided by the amount of the loan.

will assume that there is only one interest rate in the economy. This simplifies our analysis but still provides us with a valuable tool for understanding how the various parts of the macroeconomy relate to each other. (Appendix A to this chapter provides a more detailed discussion of the various types of interest rates.)

THE DEMAND FOR MONEY

The question of what factors and forces determine the demand for money is one of the central issues in macroeconomics. As we shall see, the interest rate and the level of national income (Y) are important in determining how much money households and firms wish to hold.

Before we proceed, however, we must stress one point that students often find troublesome. When we speak of the demand for money, we are not asking "How much cash do you wish you could have?" or "How much income would you like to earn?" or "How much wealth would you like?" (The answer to these questions is presumably "as much as possible.") Rather, we are concerned with the question of how much of your financial assets you want to hold *in the form of money,* which does not earn interest, versus how much you want to hold in interest-bearing securities, such as bonds. We take as given the *total* amount of financial assets; our concern here is with how these assets are divided between money and interest-bearing securities.

The Transaction Motive for Holding Money

The choice of how much money to hold involves a trade-off between the liquidity of money and the interest income offered by other kinds of assets. The main reason for holding money instead of interest-bearing assets is that money is useful for buying things. Economists call this rather obvious motive the **transaction motive** for holding money. This rationale for holding money is at the heart of the discussion that follows.[1]

transaction motive The main reason that people hold money—to buy things.

ASSUMPTIONS   In order to keep our analysis of the demand for money clear, we need to make a few simplifying assumptions. First, we assume that there are only two kinds of assets available to households: bonds and money. By "bonds" we mean interest-bearing securities of all kinds. By "money" we mean currency in circulation and deposits, neither of which is assumed to pay interest.[2]

Second, we assume that income for the typical household is "bunched up." It arrives once a month, at the beginning of the month. Spending, by contrast, is spread out over time; we assume that spending occurs at a completely uniform rate throughout the month—that is, that the same amount is spent each day.

---

[1]The model that we discuss here is known in the economics profession as the Baumol/Tobin model, after the two economists who independently derived it, William Baumol of Princeton University and James Tobin of Yale University.

[2]Remember that the category "deposits" includes checking accounts. Many checking accounts do pay interest. This turns out not to matter for the purposes of our discussion, however. Suppose that bonds pay 10% interest and checking accounts pay 5 percent. (Checking accounts must pay less than bonds. Otherwise, everyone would hold all their wealth in checking accounts and none in bonds, because checking accounts are more convenient.) When it comes to choosing whether to hold bonds or money, it is the difference in the interest rates on the two that matters. People are concerned about how much extra interest they will get from holding bonds rather than money. Therefore, in the example above, we could just as well say that bonds pay 5% and money pays 0%, which makes our discussion simpler.

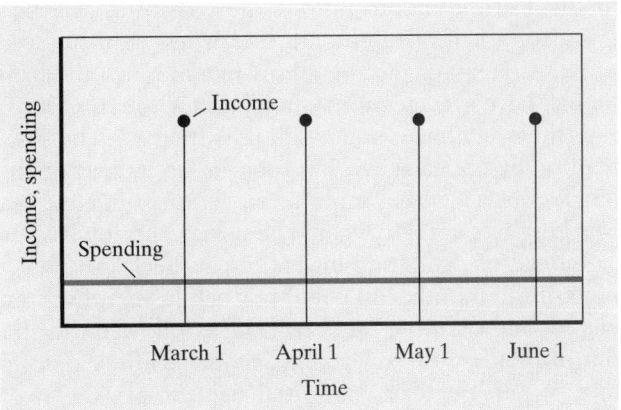

FIGURE 27.1
The Nonsynchronization of Income and Spending

Income arrives only once a month, but spending takes place continuously.

(See Figure 27.1.) The mismatch between the timing of money inflow and the timing of money outflow is sometimes called the **nonsynchronization of income and spending.**

Finally, we assume that spending for the month is exactly equal to income. Because we are focusing on the transactions demand for money and not on its use as a store of value, this assumption is perfectly reasonable.

nonsynchronization of income and spending The mismatch between the timing of money inflow to the household and the timing of money outflow for household expenses.

Money Management and the Optimal Balance

Given the assumptions above, how would a rational person (household) go about deciding how much of her or his monthly income to hold as money and how much to hold as interest-bearing bonds? Suppose our hypothetical person, Jim, decides to deposit his entire paycheck in his checking account. Let us say that Jim earns $1200 per month. The pattern of Jim's bank account balance is illustrated in Figure 27.2. At the beginning of the month, Jim's balance is $1200. As the month rolls by, Jim draws down his balance, writing checks or withdrawing cash to pay for the things he buys. At the end of the month, Jim's bank account balance is down to zero. Just in time, he receives his next month's paycheck, deposits it, and the process begins all over again.

One useful statistic that we will need to calculate is the *average balance* in Jim's account. Jim spends his money at a constant $40 per day ($40 per day times 30 days per month = $1200). Thus, his average balance is just his starting balance ($1200) plus his ending balance (0) divided by 2, or $(1200 + 0)/2 = 600. For the

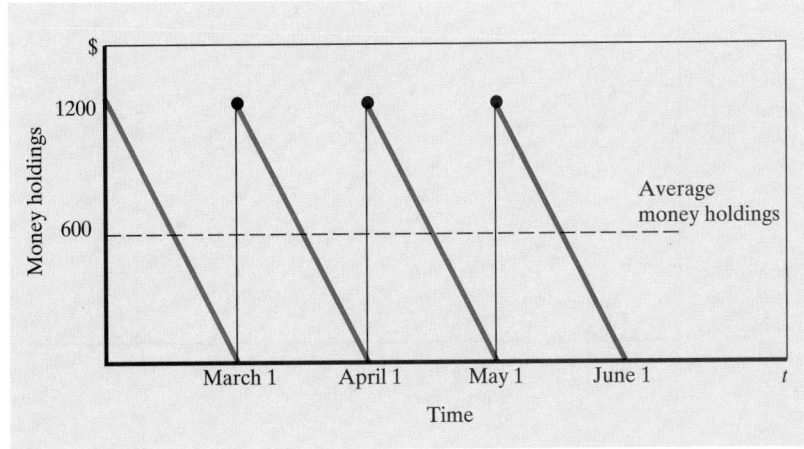

FIGURE 27.2
Jim's Monthly Checking Account Balances: Strategy 1

Jim could decide to deposit his entire paycheck ($1200) into his checking account at the start of the month and run his balance down to zero by the end of the month. In this case, his average balance would be $600.

first half of the month Jim has more than his average of $600 on deposit, and for the second half of the month he has less than his average. Thus, if he follows the simple strategy of putting all his income into the bank at the start of the month, he will have average money holdings for the month of $600.

Is there anything wrong with Jim's strategy? The answer is clearly yes. If he follows the plan described above, Jim is giving up interest on his funds, interest that he could be earning if he held some of his funds in interest-bearing bonds instead of in his checking account. How could he manage his funds to give himself more interest?

Instead of depositing his entire paycheck in his checking account at the beginning of the month, Jim could put half his paycheck into his checking account and buy a bond with the other half. If he followed this strategy, though, he would run out of money in his checking account halfway through the month. At a spending rate of $40 per day, his initial deposit of $600 would last him only 15 days. Obviously, then, Jim would have to sell his bond halfway through the month and deposit the $600 from the sale of the bond in his checking account in order to pay his bills during the second half of the month.

Jim's money holdings (checking account balances) if he follows this strategy are shown in Figure 27.3. As you can see, when he follows the "buy-a-$600-bond" strategy, Jim reduces the average amount of money in his checking account. In fact, comparing the dashed green lines (old strategy) with the solid green lines (new strategy), his average bank balance is exactly half of what it was with the first strategy.[3]

The "buy-a-$600-bond" strategy seems sensible. After all, the whole object of this strategy was to keep some of his funds in bonds, where they could earn interest, instead of as "idle" money. But why stop there? Another possibility would be for Jim to put only $400 into his checking account on the first of the month and buy two $400 bonds with the rest. The $400 in his account will last him only 10 days if he spends $40 per day, so after 10 days he must sell one of the bonds and deposit the $400 from the sale of the bond in his checking account. This will last him through the 20th of the month, at which point he

[3]Jim's average balance for the first half of the month is (starting balance + ending balance)/2, or (600 + 0)/2 = $300. His average for the second half of the month is also $300. His average for the month as a whole is thus $300.

FIGURE 27.3

Jim's Monthly Checking Account Balances: Strategy 2

Jim could also choose to put one half of his paycheck into his checking account and buy a bond with the other half of his income. At mid-month, Jim would sell the bond and deposit the $600 into his checking account to pay the second half of the month's bills. Following this strategy, Jim's average money holdings would be $300.

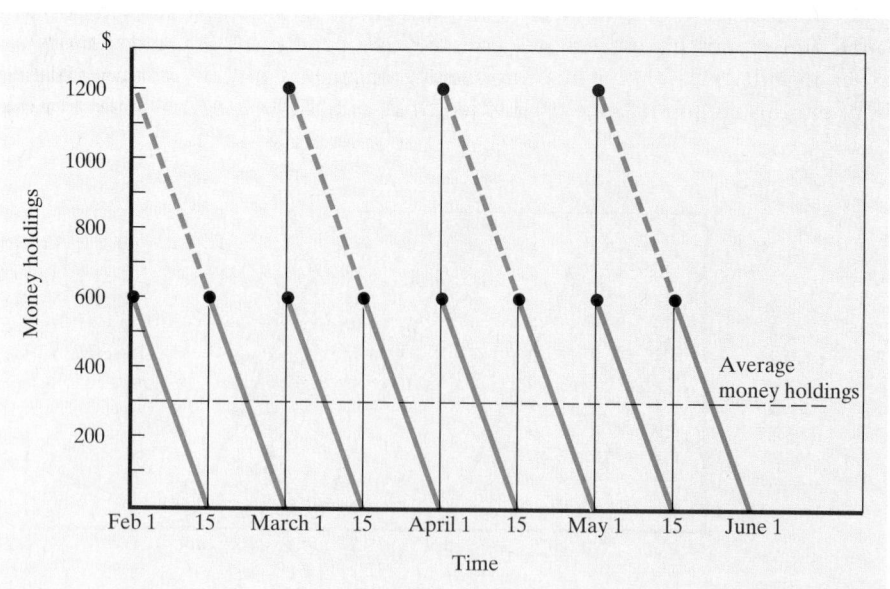

must sell the second bond and deposit the other $400. This strategy lowers Jim's average money holding (checking account balance) even further. Here Jim has reduced his money holdings to an average of only $200 per month, with correspondingly higher average holdings of interest-earning bonds.

You can imagine Jim going even further. Why not hold all wealth in the form of bonds (where it earns interest) and make transfers from bonds to money every time a purchase has to be made? If selling bonds, transferring funds to checking accounts, and making trips to the bank were without cost, Jim would never hold money for more than an instant. Each time he needed to pay cash for something or to write a check, he would go to the bank or call the bank, transfer the exact amount of the transaction to his checking account, and either withdraw the cash or write the check to complete the transaction. If he did this constantly, he would squeeze the most interest possible out of his funds because he would never hold assets that did not earn interest.

In practice, however, money management of this kind is costly. There are brokerage fees and other costs when one buys or sells bonds, and time must be spent waiting in line at the bank. However, it is also costly to hold assets in non-interest-bearing form, because they lose potential interest revenue.

We thus have a standard trade-off problem of the type that is so pervasive in economics. Switching more often from bonds to money raises the interest revenue Jim earns (since the more times he switches, the less, on average, he has to hold in his checking account and the more he can keep in bonds), but doing this increases his money management costs. Less switching means more interest revenue lost (because average money holdings are higher) but lower money management costs (fewer purchases and sales of bonds, less time spent waiting in bank lines, fewer trips to the bank, and so on).

THE OPTIMAL BALANCE   It is not hard to demonstrate that there is some level of average money balances that earns Jim the most profit, taking into account both the interest earned on bonds and the costs paid for switching from bonds to money. This *optimal balance* is the one Jim will choose to hold if he behaves optimally regarding his money holdings.

The really important question we wish to answer, however, is: How does the interest rate affect the number of switches that Jim makes and thus the average money balance he chooses to hold? It is easy to see why an increase in the interest rate lowers the optimal money balance. If the interest rate were only 2%, for example, it would not be worthwhile to give up much liquidity by holding bonds instead of cash or checking balances. But if the interest rate were 30%, the opportunity cost of holding money instead of bonds would be quite high, and we would expect people to keep most of their funds in bonds and thus to spend considerable time in managing their money balances. This leads us to conclude the following:

> When interest rates are high, people want to take advantage of the high return on bonds, so they choose to hold very little money.

Appendix B to this chapter provides an extended numerical example of this important principle.

Another way of looking at this situation is to note that the interest rate represents the opportunity cost of holding money (and therefore not holding bonds, which pay interest). The higher the interest rate, the higher the opportunity cost of holding money, and the less money people will want to hold. In other words, when interest rates rise, the amount of money people wish to hold goes down.

FIGURE 27.4

The Demand Curve for Money Balances

The quantity of money demanded (the amount of money households and firms wish to hold) is a function of the interest rate. Because the interest rate is the opportunity cost of holding money balances, increases in the interest rate will reduce the quantity that firms and households want to hold, and decreases in the interest rate will increase the quantity that they want to hold.

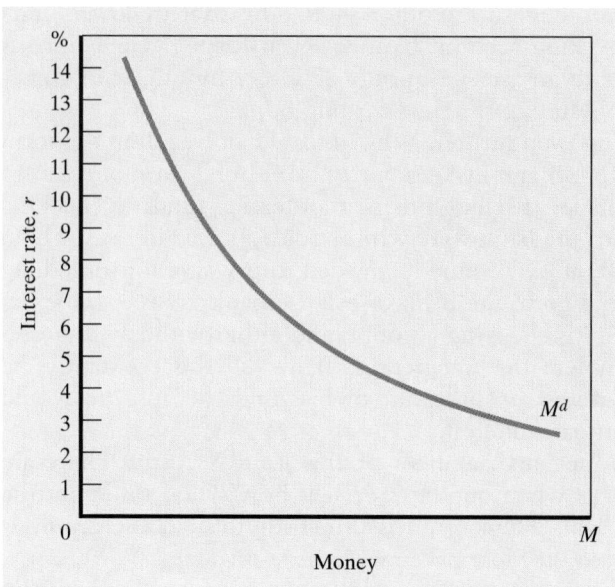

A demand curve for money, with the interest rate representing its "price," would look like the graph depicted in Figure 27.4. At higher interest rates, bonds are more attractive than money, so people hold less money because they must make a larger sacrifice in interest for each dollar of money they hold. At lower interest rates, the interest earned on bonds is lower, so people choose to hold more money. The curve in Figure 27.4 thus slopes downward, just like an ordinary demand curve for, say, oranges or shoes. There is, in other words, an inverse relationship between the interest rate and the quantity of money demanded.

The Speculation Motive For Holding Money

A number of alternative theories have been offered to explain why the quantity of money that households desire to hold may rise when interest rates fall, and fall when interest rates rise. One of these theories involves household expectations and the relationship of interest rates to bond values.

To understand this theory, it is important to understand that the market value of most interest-bearing bonds is inversely related to the interest rate. Suppose, for example, that I bought an 8% bond a year ago for $1000. Now suppose that the interest rate rises to 10 percent. If I offered to sell my bond for $1000, no one would buy it because anyone can buy a new bond and earn 10% rather than 8 percent. But at some lower price, my bond becomes attractive to buyers. This is true because a lower price increases the actual yield to the buyer of my bond. Suppose I were to sell you my bond for $500. Since the bond is paying 8% annually on the original $1000 (that is, $80 per year), it is actually paying you an annual amount that comes to 16% of your investment in the bond ($500 × .16 = $80). If you bought that same bond from me for about $800, it would effectively pay you 10% interest.

The key point here is simple:

When interest rates fall, bond values rise; when interest rates rise, bond values fall.

Now consider my desire to hold money balances rather than bonds. If interest rates are higher than normal, I may expect them to come down in the future. If and when interest rates fall, the bonds that I bought when interest rates were high will increase in value. Thus, when interest rates are high, the opportunity cost of holding cash balances is high *and* there is a **speculation motive** for holding bonds in lieu of cash. I am "speculating" that interest rates will fall in the future.

Similarly, when interest rates are lower than normal, I may expect them to rise in the future. Rising interest rates will bring about a decline in the value of bonds. Thus, when interest rates are low, it is a good time to be holding money and not bonds. When interest rates are low, not only is the opportunity cost of holding cash balances low, but there is also a speculative motive for holding a larger amount of money. Why should I put money into bonds now when I expect interest rates to rise in the future?

speculation motive One reason for holding bonds instead of money: Because the market value of interest-bearing bonds is inversely related to the interest rate, investors may wish to hold bonds when interest rates are high with the hope of selling them when interest rates fall.

The Total Demand For Money

So far we have talked only about household demand for checking account balances. But the total quantity of money demanded in the economy is the sum of the demand for checking account balances *and cash* by both households *and firms*.

The trade-off for firms is the same as it was for Jim. Like households, firms must manage their money. They have payrolls to meet and purchases to make; they receive cash and checks from sales; and many firms that deal with the public must make change—they need cash in the register. Thus, just like Jim, firms need money to engage in ordinary transactions.

But firms as well as households can hold their assets in interest-earning form. As was true for Jim, holding cash and maintaining checking account balances has an opportunity cost for firms. Firms manage their assets just as households do, keeping some in cash, some in their checking accounts, and some in bonds. A higher interest rate raises the opportunity cost of money for firms as well as for households and thus reduces the demand for money. A lower interest rate reduces the opportunity cost of holding money and increases the demand for it.

The same trade-off holds for cash. We all walk around with some money in our pockets, but not thousands of dollars, for routine transactions. We carry, on average, about what we think we will need. Why not more? Because there are costs—risks of being robbed and forgone interest.

In sum:

> At any given moment, there is a demand for money—for cash and checking account balances. Although households and firms need to hold balances for everyday transactions, their demand has a limit. For both households and firms, the quantity of money demanded at any moment depends on the opportunity cost of holding money, a cost determined by the interest rate.

Transactions Volume and the Price Level

The money demand curve in Figure 27.4 is drawn as a function of the interest rate. There are other factors besides the interest rate, however, that influence total desired money holdings. One of the most important of these is the dollar value of transactions made during a given period of time.

Suppose that Jim's income were to double. Instead of making $1200 in purchases each month, he now makes $2400 in purchases. Clearly, he needs to hold more money. Why? The answer is simple: If you want to buy more things, you need more money to buy things with.

What is true for Jim in this case is true for the economy as a whole. The total demand for money in the economy depends on the total dollar volume of transactions made. The total dollar volume of transactions in the economy, in turn, depends on two things: the total *number* of transactions and the average transaction *amount*. While there are no data on the actual number of transactions in the economy, a reasonable indicator is likely to be aggregate output (income) (Y). A rise in aggregate output—real GDP—means that there is more economic activity. Firms are producing and selling more output, more people are on payrolls, and household incomes are higher. In short, there are more transactions, and firms and households together will hold more money when they are engaging in more transactions. Thus, an increase in aggregate output (income) will increase the demand for money.

Figure 27.5 shows a shift of the money demand curve resulting from an increase in Y:

> For a given interest rate, a higher level of output means an increase in the *number* of transactions and thus more demand for money. The money demand curve shifts to the right when Y rises. Similarly, a decrease in Y means a decrease in the number of transactions and a lower demand for money. The money demand curve shifts to the left when Y falls.

The amount of money needed by firms and households to facilitate their day-to-day transactions also depends on the average dollar *amount* of each transaction. In turn, the average amount of each transaction depends on prices, or rather, on the *price level*. If all prices, including the price of labor (the wage rate) were to double, firms and households would need more money balances to carry out their day-to-day transactions—each transaction would require twice as much money. If the price of your lunch increases from $3.50 to $7.00, you will no doubt begin carrying more cash. If your end-of-the-month bills are twice as high as they used to be, you will keep more money in your checking account. Thus,

> Increases in the price level shift the money demand curve to the right, and decreases in the price level shift the money demand curve to the left. Even though the number of transactions may not have changed, the quantity of money needed to engage in them has.

FIGURE 27.5

An Increase in Aggregate Output (Income) (Y) Will Shift the Money Demand Curve to the Right

An increase in Y means that there is more economic activity. Firms are producing and selling more, and households are earning more income and buying more. There are thus more transactions, for which money is needed. As a result, both firms and households are likely to increase their holdings of money balances at a given interest rate.

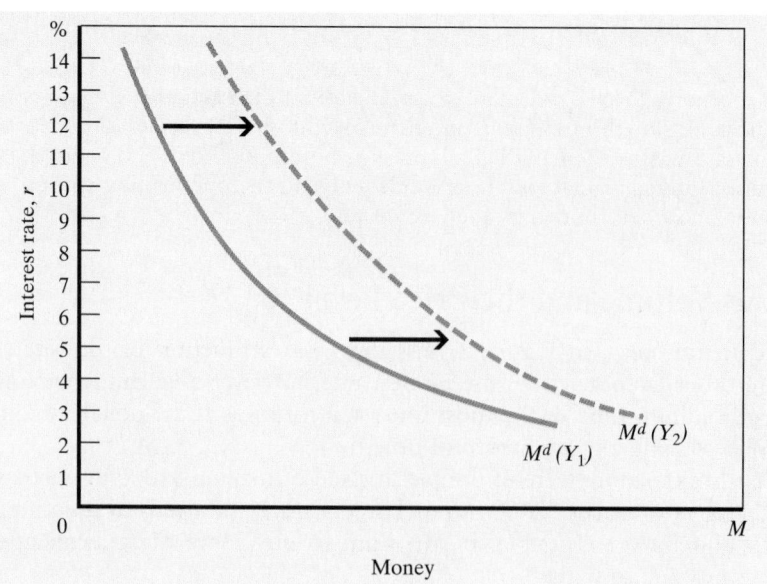

FIGURE 27.6
Determinants of Money
Demand

1. The interest rate: r (negative effect)
2. The dollar volume of transactions (positive effect)
   a. Aggregate output (income): Y (positive effect)
   b. The price level: P (positive effect)

The Determinants of Money Demand (Review)

Figure 27.6 summarizes everything we have said about the demand for money. First, because the interest rate (r) is the opportunity cost of holding money balances for both firms and households, increases in the interest rate are likely to decrease the demand for money. Similarly, decreases in the interest rate will increase the demand for money. Thus, the demand for money is a negative function of the interest rate.

The demand for money also depends on the dollar volume of transactions in a given period. The dollar volume of transactions depends on both aggregate output (income), Y, and the price level, P. The relationship of money demand to Y and the relationship of money demand to P are both positive. Increases in Y or in P will shift the money demand curve to the right, and vice versa.

THE EQUILIBRIUM INTEREST RATE

We are now in a position to consider one of the key questions in macroeconomics: How is the interest rate determined in the economy?

Financial markets—what we are calling the money market—work very well in the United States. Almost all financial markets clear—that is, almost all reach an equilibrium where quantity demanded equals quantity supplied. In the money market,

> The point at which the quantity of money demanded equals the quantity of money supplied determines the equilibrium interest rate in the economy.

As simple as this sounds, the point requires some elaboration.

Supply and Demand in the Money Market

We saw in the previous chapter that the Fed controls the money supply through its manipulation of the amount of reserves in the economy. Because we are assuming that the Fed's money supply behavior does not depend on the interest rate, the money supply curve is simply a vertical line. (Review Figure 26.5.) In other words, we are assuming that the Fed uses its three tools (the required reserve ratio, the discount rate, and open market operations) to achieve its fixed target for the money supply.

Figure 27.7 on the next page superimposes the vertical money supply curve on the downward-sloping money demand curve. Only at interest rate r^* is the quantity of money in circulation (the money supply) equal to the quantity of money demanded. To understand why r^* is an equilibrium, we need to ask what adjustments would take place if the interest rate were not r^*.

To understand the adjustment mechanism, we need to keep in mind that borrowing and lending is a continuous process. The Treasury sells U.S. government securities (bonds) more or less continuously to finance the deficit. When it does so, it is borrowing, and it must pay interest to attract bond buyers. Buyers of government bonds are, in essence, lending money to the government, just as buyers of corporate bonds are lending money to corporations that wish to finance investment projects.

FIGURE 27.7
Adjustments in the Money Market

Equilibrium exists in the money market when the supply of money is equal to the demand for money: $M^d = M^s$. At r_1, the quantity of money supplied exceeds the quantity of money demanded, and the interest rate will fall. At r_2, the quantity demanded exceeds the quantity supplied, and the interest rate will rise. Only at r^* is equilibrium achieved.

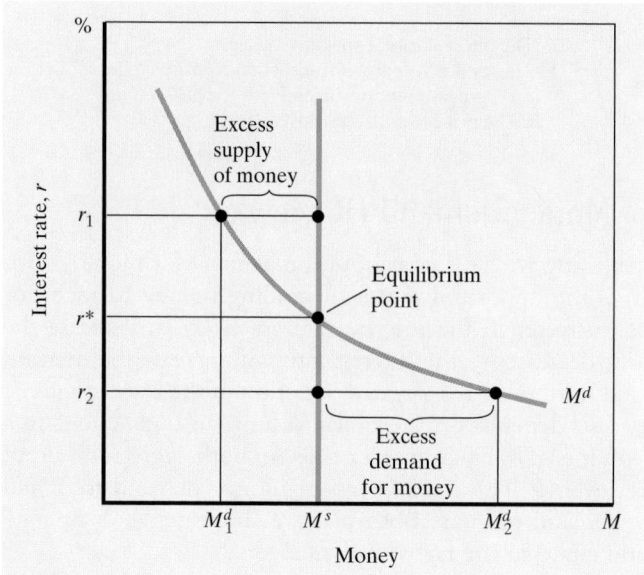

Consider first r_1 in Figure 27.7. At r_1, the quantity of money demanded is M_1^d, and the quantity of money supplied exceeds the quantity of money demanded. This means that there is more money in circulation than households and firms want to hold. At r_1, then, firms and households will attempt to reduce their money holdings by buying bonds. When there is money in circulation looking for a way to earn interest—that is, when demand for bonds is high—those looking to borrow money by selling bonds will find that they can do so at a lower interest rate. Thus,

> If the interest rate is initially high enough to create an excess supply of money, the interest rate will immediately fall, thus discouraging people from moving out of money and into bonds.

Now consider r_2. At interest rate r_2, the quantity of money demanded (M_2^d) exceeds the supply of money currently in circulation. In such a circumstance, households and firms do not have enough money on hand to facilitate ordinary transactions. As a result, they will try to adjust their holdings by shifting assets out of bonds and into their checking accounts. At the same time, the continuous flow of new bonds being issued must also be absorbed. The Treasury and corporations can sell bonds in an environment where people are adjusting their asset holdings to shift *out* of bonds only by offering a higher interest rate to the people who buy them. Thus,

> If the interest rate is initially low enough to create an excess demand for money, the interest rate will immediately rise, thus discouraging people from moving out of bonds and into money.

The Fed: Changing the Money Supply to Affect the Interest Rate

With an understanding of equilibrium in the money market under our belts, we can now see how the Federal Reserve can affect the interest rate. Suppose, for example, that the current interest rate is 14% and that the Fed wants to

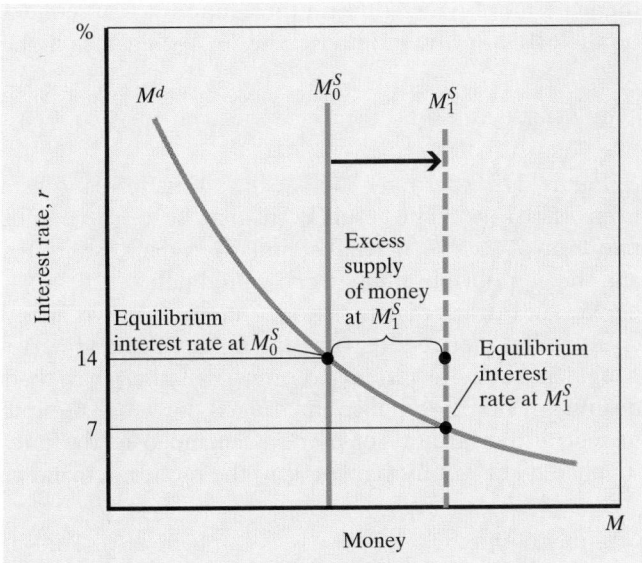

FIGURE 27.8
The Effect of an Increase in
the Supply of Money on the
Interest Rate

An increase in the supply of
money from M_0^s to M_1^s lowers the
rate of interest from 14% to 7
percent.

reduce the interest rate. To do so, it would expand the money supply. Figure 27.8 shows how such an expansion would work. To expand M^s, the Fed can reduce the reserve requirement, cut the discount rate, or buy U.S. government securities on the open market. All of these practices expand the quantity of reserves in the system. Banks can thus make more loans, and the money supply expands. (Review Chapter 26 if you are unsure why this is so.) In Figure 27.8, the initial money supply curve, M_0^s, shifts to the right, to M_1^s.

At the initial interest rate of 14%, there is now an excess supply of money. This immediately puts downward pressure on the interest rate as households and firms try to buy bonds with their money in order to earn that high interest rate. As this happens, the interest rate falls, and it will continue to fall until it reaches the new equilibrium interest rate of 7 percent. At this point, $M_1^s = M^d$, and the market is in equilibrium. (For another example of the actions taken by a central bank to decrease the interest rate, see the Global Perspective box titled "The German Central Bank (the Bundesbank) and German Interest Rates in 1992.")

If the Fed wanted to drive the interest rate *up,* it would contract the money supply. It could do so by increasing the reserve requirement, by raising the discount rate, or by selling U.S. government securities in the open market. Whichever tool the Fed chooses, the result would be lower reserves and a lower supply of money. M_0^s in Figure 27.8 would shift to the left, and the equilibrium interest rate would rise. (As an exercise, draw a graph of this situation.)

Increases in Y and Shifts in the Money Demand Curve

Changes in the supply of money are not the only factors that influence the interest rate. Shifts in money demand can do the same thing.

Recall that the demand for money depends on both the interest rate and the volume of transactions. As a rough measure of the volume of transactions, we use Y, the level of aggregate output (income). Remember that the relationship between money demand and Y is positive. That is, increases in Y mean a higher level of real economic activity. More is being produced, income is higher, and there are more transactions in the economy. Consequently, the demand for money on the part of firms and households in aggregate is higher. Thus,

An increase in Y shifts the money demand curve to the right.

Figure 27.9 illustrates such a shift. Y increases, causing money demand to shift from M_0^d to M_1^d. The result is an increase in the equilibrium level of the interest rate from 7% to 14 percent. Similarly, a decrease in Y would shift M^d to the left, and the equilibrium interest rate would fall.

We saw earlier that the money demand curve also shifts when the price level changes. If the price level rises, the money demand curve shifts to the right, because people need more money to engage in their day-to-day transactions. With the quantity of money supplied unchanged, however, the interest rate must rise in order to reduce the quantity of money demanded to the unchanged quantity of money supplied. (This is a movement *along* the money demand curve.) Thus, it follows that:

An increase in the price level is like an increase in Y in that both events increase the demand for money. The result is an increase in the equilibrium interest rate.

If the price level *falls*, the money demand curve shifts to the left, because people need less money for their transactions. But with the quantity of money supplied unchanged, the interest rate must fall in order to increase the quantity of money demanded to the unchanged quantity of money supplied. Therefore,

A decrease in the price level leads to a decrease in the equilibrium interest rate.

We explore this relationship in more detail in Chapter 29.

LOOKING AHEAD: FED BEHAVIOR AND MONETARY POLICY

We now know that the Fed can change the interest rate by changing the quantity of money supplied. If the Fed increases the quantity of money, the interest rate falls; if it decreases the quantity of money, the interest rate rises.

FIGURE 27.9

The Effect of an Increase in Income on the Interest Rate

An increase in aggregate output (income) shifts the money demand curve from M_0^d to M_1^d, which raises the equilibrium interest rate from 7% to 14 percent.

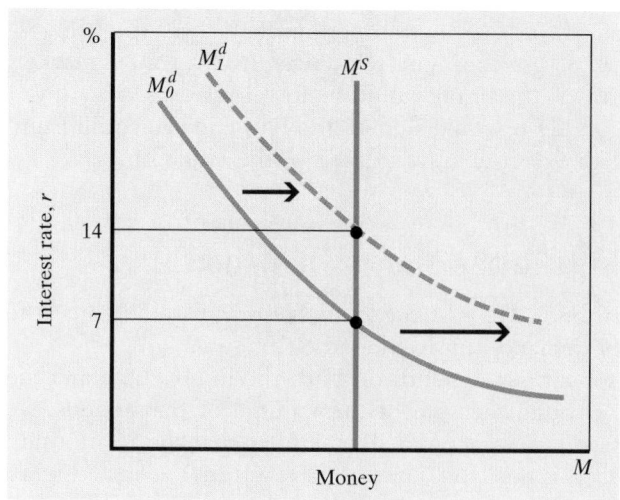

THE GERMAN CENTRAL BANK (THE BUNDESBANK) AND GERMAN INTEREST RATES IN 1992

In September 1992, the German Central bank, the Bundesbank, announced that it would take steps to increase the money supply and lower interest rates in Germany. The move was good news for the United States and the rest of Europe. For more than a year, Germany had been holding interest rates high and money supply growth low in an effort to control inflation. But with inflation seemingly in check, and international pressure mounting, the Bundesbank gave in, as the following excerpt describes:

After days of turmoil on European money markets, Germany promised tonight to lower its high interest rates . . .

"The opportunities created by the will of the Bundesbank to lower its lending rates are of considerable significance," Finance Minister Michel Sapin of France *said after the German announcement. The German promise, he said, "demonstrated the true solidarity of Germany towards its European partners and opened the way to an easing of interest rates in Europe, which is necessary to support growth and employment . . ."*

Not everyone was delighted. Peter Pietsch, an economist at Commerz-bank, said: "The Bundesbank has let itself be blackmailed. This is sensational that for the first time, they have let their independence

be compromised. This clearly has come from political pressure."

Why are low German interest rates good for the United States and for the rest of Europe? First, as you will see in more detail in the next chapter, lower interest rates act to stimulate aggregate expenditure and to increase economic growth. The United States and some European countries export a great deal of their output to Germany. Thus, a growing German economy means a growing demand for U.S. and European goods.

Second, low German interest rates are good for the United States because high interest rates attract world saving. Many U.S. citizens, both directly and through mutual funds, have been earning high interest rates on their saving by buying German securities. This made it very difficult for the U.S. Federal Reserve System and the central banks of other European countries to lower their interest rates to stimulate their own economies. Why? Because the high German interest rates made it hard to find buyers for U.S. government bonds at low interest rates in the United States.

The German central bank recently announced plans to lower interest rates. The result has been a spate of new building spurred by increased investment.

Source: Alan Cowell, "Germany Promises Interest-Rate Cut to Revive Growth," *New York Times,* September 14, 1992.

Thus far, however, we have said nothing about *why* the Fed might want to change the interest rate or what happens to the economy when the interest rate changes. We have hinted at the reason, though. A low interest rate stimulates spending, particularly investment. Similarly, a high interest rate reduces spending. This means that by changing the interest rate the Fed can also change aggregate output (income). In the next chapter, we will combine our discussions of the goods and money markets and discuss the ways that the interest rate affects the equilibrium level of aggregate output (income) (Y) in the goods market.

The Fed's use of its power to influence events in the goods market, as well as in the

tight monetary policy Fed policies designed to contract the money supply in an effort to restrain the economy.

easy monetary policy Fed policies designed to expand the money supply in an effort to stimulate the economy.

money market, is the centerpiece of the government's monetary policy. When the Fed moves to contract the money supply in an effort to restrain the economy, economists refer to the Fed's policy as a **tight monetary policy.** Conversely, when the Fed moves to stimulate the economy by expanding the money supply, economists refer to the Fed's policy as an **easy monetary policy.** The Fed moved aggressively to expand the money supply and lower interest rates in 1975, in 1982, and early in 1991. These easy money policies contributed to economic recovery from the recessions of those years. On the other side, tight money policies caused aggregate spending to decline in 1974 and 1981, thereby contributing to the recessions of those years. During the summer of 1981, tight money helped to push some key interest rates above 20 percent!

We will discuss the way in which the economy affects the Fed's behavior in Chapter 31. In that chapter, we'll also discuss some of the Fed's recent policies in more detail and examine the effects of these policies on the economy.

SUMMARY

The Demand For Money

1. *Interest* is the fee that a borrower pays to a lender for the use of his or her funds. The *interest rate* is the annual interest payment on a loan expressed as a percentage of the loan; it is equal to the amount of interest per year divided by the amount of the loan. Although there are many different interest rates in the United States, we assume that there is only one interest rate in the economy. This simplifies our analysis but still provides us with a valuable tool for understanding how the various parts of the macroeconomy relate to each other.

2. The demand for money depends negatively on the interest rate. The higher the interest rate, the higher the opportunity cost (more interest forgone) from holding money, and the less money people will want to hold. Thus, an increase in the interest rate reduces the demand for money, and the money demand curve slopes downward.

3. Increases in the volume of transactions in the economy increase money demand. The total dollar volume of transactions depends on both the *total number of transactions* and the *average transaction amount.*

4. A reasonable measure of the number of transactions in the economy is aggregate output (income) (Y). When Y rises, there is more economic activity, more is being produced and sold, and more people are on payrolls—in short, there are more transactions in the economy. Thus, an increase in Y causes the money demand curve to shift to the right. This follows because households and firms need more money when they are engaging in more transactions. A decrease in Y causes the money demand curve to shift left.

5. Changes in the price level affect the average dollar amount of each transaction. *Increases* in the price level will increase the demand for money because households and firms will need more money for their expenditures. *Decreases* in the price level will decrease the demand for money.

The Equilibrium Interest Rate

6. The point at which the quantity of money supplied equals the quantity of money demanded determines the equilibrium interest rate in the economy. An excess supply of money will cause households and firms to hold more of their assets in bonds and will drive the interest rate down. An excess demand for money will cause households and firms to shift their asset holdings out of bonds and will drive the interest rate up.

7. The Fed can affect the equilibrium interest rate by changing the supply of money using one of its three tools—the required reserve ratio, the discount rate, or open market operations.

8. An increase in the price level is like an increase in Y in that both events cause an increase in money demand. The result is an increase in the equilibrium interest rate. A decrease in the price level leads to reduced money demand and a decrease in the equilibrium interest rate.

9. *Tight monetary policy* refers to Fed policies designed to contract the money supply in an effort to restrain the economy. *Easy monetary policy* refers to Fed policies designed to expand the money supply in an effort to stimulate the economy. The Fed chooses between these two types of policies for different reasons at different times.

REVIEW TERMS AND CONCEPTS

PROBLEM SET

1. During a recession, interest rates may fall even if the Federal Reserve takes no action to expand the money supply. Why is this true? Use a graph to explain your answer.

2. Illustrate the following situations using supply and demand curves for money:
   a. The Fed buys bonds in the open market during a recession.
   b. During a period of rapid inflation, the Federal Reserve increases the reserve requirement.
   c. The Fed acts to hold interest rates constant during a period of high inflation.
   d. During a period of no growth in GDP and zero inflation, the Federal Reserve lowers the discount rate.
   e. During a period of rapid real growth of GDP, the Fed acts to increase the reserve requirement.

3. In February of 1993, Alan Greenspan, Chair of the Federal Reserve Board of Governors, was very supportive of President Clinton's proposed deficit reduction plan. The Clinton plan, as presented to the Congress in March, called for substantial cuts in government purchases (G) and increases in taxes (T). Greenspan declared himself ready to act to keep this contractionary fiscal policy from dragging the economy back into recession. What specific steps might he take? What would you expect to see happening to interest rates assuming that Congress had passed the Clinton plan? Explain your answer.

4. The demand for money in a country is given by the equation

$$M^d = 10,000 - 10,000r + Y,$$

where M^d is money demand in dollars, r is the interest rate (a 10% interest rate means $r = 0.1$), and Y is national income. Assume that Y is initially equal to 5000.

   a. Graph the amount of money demanded (on the horizontal axis) against the interest rate (on the vertical axis).

   b. Suppose the money supply (M^s) is set by the Central Bank at $10,000. On the same graph you drew for part a, add the money-supply curve. What is the equilibrium rate of interest? Explain how you arrived at your answer.

   c. Suppose that income rises from $Y = 5000$ to $Y = 7500$. What happens to the money-demand curve you drew in part a? Draw the new curve, if there is one. What happens to the equilibrium interest rate if the Central Bank doesn't change the supply of money?

   d. If the Central Bank wants to keep the equilibrium interest rate at the same value as it was in part b, by how much should it increase or decrease the supply of money given the new level of national income?

   e. Suppose that the Central Bank wants the equilibrium interest rate to stay the same as in part b, but also wants the supply of money not to change. What should it do?

APPENDIX A TO CHAPTER 27
THE VARIOUS INTEREST RATES IN THE U.S. ECONOMY

At the beginning of this chapter, we noted that there are many different interest rates in the economy. Although these different interest rates tend to move up or down with one another, it is useful to have some knowledge of their differences. In this appendix, we will first discuss the relationship between interest rates on securities with different *maturities,* or terms. We then discuss briefly some of the main interest rates in the U.S. economy.

THE TERM STRUCTURE OF INTEREST RATES

The *term structure of interest rates* is the relationship between the interest rates offered on securities of different maturities. The key question here is: How are these different rates related? Does a two-year security (that is, an IOU that promises to repay principal, plus interest, after two years) pay a lower annual rate than a one-year security (an IOU to be repaid, with interest, after one year)? What happens to the rate of interest offered on one-year securities if the rate of interest on two-year securities increases?

For the sake of example, assume that you want to invest some money for two years and that at the end of the two years you want it back. Assume also that you want to buy government securities. For the purposes of this analysis, we will restrict your choices to two: (1) You can buy a two-year security today and simply hold onto it for two years, at which time you cash it in (we will assume that the interest rate on the two-year security is 9% per year), or (2) You can buy a one-year security today. At the end of one year, you must cash this security in; and you can then buy another one-year security. At the end of the second year, you will cash in the second security. We will assume that the interest rate on the first one-year security is 8 percent.

Which of these choices would you prefer? Currently, you don't have enough data to answer this question. To consider choice 2 sensibly, you need to know the interest rate on the one-year security that you intend to buy in the second year. This rate, however, will not be known until the second year. All you know now is the rate on the two-year security and the rate on the current one-year security. In order to decide what to do, you must form an *expectation* of the rate on the one-year security a year from now. If you expect the one-year rate (8%) to remain the same in the second year, you should obviously buy the two-year security. You would earn 9% per year on the two-year security but only 8% per year on the two one-year securities. If, on the other hand, you expect the one-year rate to rise to 12% a year from now, you should make the second choice. You would earn 8% in the first year, and you expect to earn 12% in the second year. The expected rate of return over the two years is thus about 10%, which is better than the 9% you can get on the two-year security. If you expected the one-year rate a year from now to be 10%, it would not matter very much which of the two choices you made. The rate of return over the two-year period would be roughly 9% for both choices.

We must now alter the focus of our discussion to get to the topic we are really interested in—how the two-year rate is determined. Let us assume that the one-year rate has been set by the Fed and that it is 8 percent. Let us also assume that people expect the one-year rate a year from now to be 10 percent. What, then, is the two-year rate? According to a theory called the *expectations theory of the term structure of interest rates,* the two-year rate is equal to the average of the current one-year rate and the one-year rate expected a year from now. In this example, the two-year rate would be 9% (the average of 8% and 10 percent).

If the two-year rate were lower than the average of the two one-year rates, people would not be indifferent as to which security they held. They would want to hold only the short-term, one-year securities. Thus, in order to find a buyer for a two-year security, the seller would be forced to increase the interest rate being offered on the two-year security until it is equal to the average of the current one-year rate and the expected one-year rate for next year. The interest rate on the two-year security will continue to rise until people are once again indifferent between one two-year security and two one-year securities.[1]

Let us now return to Fed behavior. We know that the Fed can control the short-term interest rate through open market operations. But does it also control long-term interest rates? The answer is "somewhat." Since the two-year rate is an average of the current one-year rate and the expected one-year rate a year from now, the Fed influences the two-year rate to the extent that it influences the current one-year rate. The same holds for three-year rates and beyond. In other words, the current short-term rate is a means by which the Fed can influence longer-term rates.

In addition, Fed behavior may directly affect people's expectations of the future short-term rates, which will then affect long-term rates. If the chair of the Federal

Reserve testifies before Congress that he or she is thinking about raising short-term interest rates, people's expectations of higher future short-term interest rates are likely to increase. These expectations will then be reflected in current long-term interest rates.

TYPES OF INTEREST RATES

The following are some of the most widely followed interest rates in the United States.

Three-month Treasury Bill Rate

Government securities that mature in less than a year are called *Treasury bills,* or sometimes *T bills.* The interest rate on three-month Treasury bills is probably the most widely followed short-term interest rate.

Government Bond Rate

Government securities with terms of one year or more are called *government bonds*. There are 1-year bonds, 2-year bonds, and so on up to 30-year bonds. Bonds of different terms have different interest rates. The relationship among the interest rates on the various maturities is the term structure of interest rates that we discussed in the first part of this appendix.

Federal Funds Rate

Banks borrow not only from the Fed but also from each other. If one bank has excess reserves, it can lend some of those reserves to other banks through the federal funds market. The interest rate in this market is called the *federal funds rate*—the rate banks are charged to borrow reserves from other banks.

The federal funds market is really a desk in New York City. From all over the country, banks with excess reserves to lend and banks in need of reserves call the desk and negotiate a rate of interest. Account balances with the Fed are changed for the period of the loan without any physical movement of money.

This borrowing and lending which takes place near the close of each working day, is generally for one day ("overnight"), so the federal funds rate is a one-day rate. It is the rate that the Fed controls most closely through its open market operations.

Commercial Paper Rate

Firms have several alternatives for raising funds. They can sell stocks, issue bonds, or borrow from a bank. Large firms can also borrow directly from the public by issuing "commercial paper," which are essentially short-term corporate IOUs that offer a designated rate of interest. The interest rate offered on commercial paper depends on the financial condition of the firm and the maturity date of the IOU.

[1]For longer terms, additional future rates must be averaged in. For a three-year security, for example, the expected one-year rate a year from now and the expected one-year rate two years from now are added to the current one-year rate and averaged.

Prime Rate

Banks charge different interest rates to different customers. You would expect to pay a higher interest rate for a car loan than General Motors would pay for a $1 million loan to finance investment. Also, you would pay more interest for an unsecured loan, a "personal" loan, than for one that was secured by some asset, such as a house or car, to be used as collateral.

The *prime rate* is a "benchmark" that banks often use in quoting interest rates to their customers. A very low-risk corporation might be able to borrow at (or even below) the prime rate. A less well-known firm might be quoted a rate of "prime plus three fourths," which means that if the prime rate is say, 10%, the firm would have to pay interest of 10.75 percent. Since the prime rate depends on the cost of funds to the bank, it moves up and down with changes in the economy.

AAA Corporate Bond Rate

Corporations finance much of their investment by selling bonds to the public. Corporate bonds are classified by various bond dealers according to their degree of risk. Bonds issued by General Motors are in less risk of default than bonds issued by a new biotech research firm.

Bonds are graded in much the same way students are. The highest grade is AAA, the next highest AA, and so on. The interest rate on bonds rated AAA is the *triple A corporate bond rate,* the rate that the least risky firms pay on the bonds that they issue.

PROBLEM SET

1. The following table gives three key U.S. interest rates in 1980 and again in April 1993:

	1980	1993
Three-month U.S. government bills	11.39%	2.92%
Long-term U.S. government bonds	10.81%	6.85%
Prime rate	15.26%	6.00%

Can you give an explanation for the extreme differences that you see? Specifically, comment on the following: (1) the fact that rates in 1980 were much higher than they were in 1993, and (2) the long-term rate was higher than the short-term rate in 1993 but below it in 1980.

APPENDIX B TO CHAPTER 27
THE DEMAND FOR MONEY: A NUMERICAL EXAMPLE

This appendix presents a numerical example showing how optimal money management behavior can be derived.

We have seen that the interest rate represents the opportunity cost of holding funds in non-interest-bearing checking accounts (as opposed to bonds, which yield interest). We have also seen that there are costs involved in switching from bonds to money. Given these costs, our objective is to determine the optimum amount of money for an individual to hold. The optimal average level of money holdings is the amount that maximizes the profits from money management. Interest is earned on average bond holdings, but the cost per switch multiplied by the number of switches must be subtracted from interest revenue to obtain the net profit from money management.

Suppose the interest rate is .05 (5%), it costs $2 each time a bond is sold, and the proceeds from the sale are deposited in one's checking account. Suppose also that the individual's income is $1200 and that this income is spent evenly throughout the period. This situation is depicted in the top half of Table 27A.1. The optimum value for average money holdings is the value that achieves the largest possible profit in column 6 of the table. When the interest rate is 5%, the optimum average money holdings are $150 (which means the individual makes three switches from bonds to money).

In the bottom half of Table 27A.1, the same calculations are performed for an interest rate of 3% rather than 5 percent. In this case, the optimum average money holding is $200 (which means the person/household makes two switches from bonds to money rather than three). The lower interest rate has thus led to an increase in the optimum average money holdings. Under the assumption that people behave optimally, the demand for money is thus a negative function of the interest rate: The lower the rate, the more money on average is held, and the higher the rate, the less money on average is held.

TABLE 27A.1
Optimum Money Holdings

1 NUMBER OF SWITCHES[1]	2 AVERAGE MONEY HOLDINGS[2]	3 AVERAGE BOND HOLDINGS[3]	4 INTEREST EARNED[4]	5 COST OF SWITCHING[5]	6 NET PROFIT[6]
Assumptions: Interest rate $r = 0.05$. Cost of switching from bonds into money equals $2 per transaction.					
		$r = 5$ percent			
0	$600.00	$0.00	$0.00	$0.00	$0.00
1	300.00	300.00	15.00	2.00	13.00
2	200.00	400.00	20.00	4.00	16.00
3	150.00*	450.00	22.50	6.00	16.50
4	120.00	480.00	24.00	8.00	16.00
Assumptions: Interest rate $r = 0.03$. Cost of switching from bonds into money equals $2 per transaction.					
		$r = 3$ percent			
0	$600.00	$0.00	$0.00	$0.00	$0.00
1	300.00	300.00	9.00	2.00	7.00
2	200.00*	400.00	12.00	4.00	8.00
3	150.00	450.00	13.50	6.00	7.50
4	120.00	480.00	14.40	8.00	6.40

*Optimum money holdings. [1]That is, the number of times you sell a bond.   [2]Calculated as 600/(col. 1 + 1).   [3]Calculated as 600 – col. 2.
[4]Calculated as $r \times$ col. 3, where r is the interest rate.   [5]Calculated as $t \times$ col. 1, where t is the cost per switch ($2).   [6]Calculated as col. 4 – col. 5.

PROBLEM SET

1. Sherman Peabody earns a monthly salary of $1500. He spends the entire amount each month, at the rate of $50 per day. (Assume that there are 30 days in a month.) The interest rate paid on bonds is 10% per month. It costs $4 every time Peabody sells a bond.

   a. Describe briefly how Mr. Peabody should go about deciding how much money to hold.

   b. Calculate Peabody's optimal money holdings. (*Hint:* It may help to formulate a table such as the one in this appendix. You can round to the nearest $.50, and you need to consider only average money holdings of more than $100.)

   c. Suppose the interest rate rises to 15 percent. Find Peabody's optimal money holdings at this new interest rate. What would happen if the interest rate increases to 20 percent?

   d. Graph your answers to b. and c. with the interest rate on the vertical axis and the amount of money demanded on the horizontal axis. Explain why your graph slopes downward.

COMMODITY MONEY ON THE ISLAND OF YAP

In the Pacific Ocean between Guam and the Philippines you'll find the island of Yap and its population of about 10,000 people. Although Yap is a U.S. trust territory, and U.S. dollars will buy you gasoline and groceries there, historically the currency of choice has been large wheels of limestone.

Almost 2,000 years ago a Yapese warrior named Anagumang brought huge pieces of the stone to Yap from a nearby island and fashioned them into large circles. Most of the stones are between two and five feet in diameter, but some measure as much as 12 feet across.

Because of their obvious drawbacks in terms of portability, the stones are generally used only for major purchases, like land or a new home. In addition, they don't move around much because they are worthless if broken. Rather, ownership of the stones is exchanged in much the same fashion as gold bars found in the vaults of the New York Federal Reserve Bank—ownership of the bars is traded internationally, but the gold itself usually stays put. On Yap, people trade shares in the stones.

Stones do have some advantages as a form of money. The money supply is fixed—only about 6,600 stones are left on Yap. They are heavy, and it is hard to hide a stolen stone. This, plus the fact that the stones are valued according to the time of their arrival on the island and how difficult it was to get them there, makes them virtually immune from black-market trading.

But there are some drawbacks. The stones do not earn any interest and the major financial institutions affiliated with the island will not accept them for investment purposes. Retail stores also do not accept them as a means of payment, so you can't buy clothes with stone money.

To overcome some of these shortcomings, the people of Yap use other commodities as a means of payment. For example, beer is commonly used as a means of payment in exchange for light duty construction work. *Gaw*—which are necklaces of stone beads strung around a whale's tooth—and currency made from large sea shells called *yar* can also be spent.

Yap is not unique in its use of commodity money. Most schoolchildren know that New York City was purchased from Native Americans for a few beads and trinkets. *Wampum* was a form of Native American currency that consisted of beads made from sea shells. Tobacco was a form of currency in the colonial days of the United States, and cigarettes were a common form of money in POW camps during World War II.

Tribes in Africa have traded in commodities for centuries and still do so. These commodities can be alive (cattle) or inanimate (cloth strips, cowrie shells). Often, African currencies have taken the form of metals like iron or copper or silver, which were never minted into coins but served all the functions of money. Indeed, there persists a debate among economic historians as to the purpose of money and whether or not today's modern currencies are necessarily the result of an evolutionary process of economic exchange that begins with bartering and ends with fiat money.

More recently, the disintegration of the Soviet Union has created a need for new currency among the emerging republics. In the Ukraine, for example, rising prices caused an increase in demand for rubles. Because Russia does not supply enough rubles to keep up with demand, the Ukrainian government was forced to use old food-rationing tickets that it had on hand as currency. Salaries in the Ukraine were paid in equal proportions of rubles and ration coupons. In January 1992, these coupons were trading on the black market at a rate of 16 per U.S. dollar.

Some of Yap's stone money wheels are so large that they are never moved.

QUESTIONS FOR ANALYTICAL THINKING

1. Which of the properties of money do the stones of Yap satisfy? Which properties of money does beer satisfy? How about ration coupons in the Ukraine?

2. Is fiat money a necessary result of the evolutionary process of a developing economy, or is it simply a matter of convenience?

3. What difficulties may a developing nation face when it decides to produce its own currency?

4. Some bartering exists in the United States today. Rural physicians sometimes get paid in chickens and a dentist may exchange braces for a new roof. Have you, or someone you know, ever bartered for goods or services?

PART SEVEN

Macroeconomic Analysis and Issues

Throughout our study of macroeconomics, we've been talking about the various components of the economy. In the previous part, we discussed the goods market and the money market. In this part, we will discuss the interactions between the goods market and the money market. We will also examine the factors that determine the overall price level in the economy and analyze the third macroeconomic market, the labor market. By the time you've reached the end of this part, you will have analyzed and understood:

■ The effects of the government's fiscal and monetary policy in the three recessions of the last two decades: 1973–1974, 1980–1982, and 1990–1991 (Chapter 28).

■ The various causes of inflation and the role of import price increases, expectations, and money in creating inflations (Chapter 29).

■ The debate over whether unemployment really exists, and, if it does, some of the factors that may cause it (Chapter 30).

■ The relationship between inflation and unemployment (Chapter 30).

■ The debate over deficit-reduction policies and the effects these policies are likely to have on the economy (Chapter 31).

■ The actions that the nation's central bank—the Fed—is likely to take in response to the state of the economy (Chapter 31).

■ The problem of time lags and how they affect government policy (Chapter 31).

28

Money, the Interest Rate, and National Income: Analysis and Policy

goods market The market in
which goods and services are
exchanged and in which the
equilibrium level of aggregate
output is determined.

money market The market in
which financial instruments are
exchanged and in which the
equilibrium level of the interest rate
is determined.

In Chapters 24 and 25, we discussed the market for goods and services—the **goods market**—without ever mentioning money, the money market, or the interest rate. We described in some detail how the equilibrium level of aggregate output (income) (Y) is determined in the goods market. At given levels of planned investment spending (I), government spending (G), and net taxes (T), we were able to determine the equilibrium level of output in the economy.

In Chapters 26 and 27, we discussed the financial market, or **money market,** with only passing references to the goods market. In those chapters, we explained how the equilibrium level of the interest rate is determined in the money market.

The goods market and the money market do not operate independently, however. Events in the money market have important effects on the goods market, and events in the goods market have important effects on the money market. Only by analyzing the two markets together can we determine the values of aggregate output (income) (Y) and the interest rate (r) that are consistent with the existence of equilibrium in *both* markets.

Looking at both markets simultaneously also reveals how fiscal policy affects the money market and how monetary policy affects the goods market. This is our task in this chapter. By establishing how the two markets affect each other, we will be able to show how open market purchases of government securities (which expand the money supply) affect the equilibrium level of national output and income. Similarly, we will be able to show how fiscal policy measures (such as tax cuts) affect interest rates and investment spending.

THE LINKS BETWEEN THE GOODS MARKET AND THE MONEY MARKET

There are two key *links,* or connections, between the goods market and the money market.

LINK 1: INCOME AND THE DEMAND FOR MONEY   The first link between the goods market and the money market exists because the demand for money depends on income. As aggregate output (income) (Y) increases, the number of transactions requiring the use of money increases. (This point should be fresh in your mind from the previous chapter.) Thus, an increase in output, with the interest rate held constant, leads to an increase in the quantity of money demanded. This leads us to conclude that:

> Income, which is determined in the goods market, has an important influence on the demand for money in the money market.

LINK 2: PLANNED INVESTMENT SPENDING AND THE INTEREST RATE   The second link between the goods market and the money market exists because planned investment spending (I) depends on the interest rate (r). In Chapters 24 and 25 we assumed that planned investment spending is fixed at a certain level, but we did so only to simplify our initial discussion. In practice, investment is not fixed; rather, it depends on a number of key economic variables. One of these variables is the interest rate. The higher the interest rate, the lower the level of planned investment spending. Therefore,

> The interest rate, which is determined in the money market, has important effects on planned investment in the goods market.

We examine these links in more detail in the sections that follow.

Investment, the Interest Rate, and the Goods Market

It should come as no surprise to you that the relationship between the level of planned investment and the interest rate is a negative one. Stated simply,

> When the interest rate falls, planned investment rises.
> When the interest rate rises, planned investment falls.

It is easy to see why this is so.* Recall that *investment* refers to the purchase of new capital—new machines and plants. Firms undertake investment projects because they expect those projects to yield profits in the future. Thus, whether a firm decides to invest in a project depends upon whether the expected profits from the project justify its costs. One of the important costs of an investment project is the interest cost.

---

*The discussion that follows is simply a review of Chapter 11, "The Capital Market and the Investment Decision."

Consider, for example, a firm that is opening a new plant, or the investment required to open a new ice cream store. When a manufacturing firm builds a new plant, the contractor must be paid at the time the plant is built. When an entrepreneur decides to open a new ice cream parlor, she needs freezers, tables, chairs, light fixtures, and signs. These too must be paid for when they are installed.

The money needed to carry out such projects is generally borrowed and paid back over an extended period of time. Thus, the real cost of an investment project depends in part on the interest rate—that is, the cost of borrowing. When the interest rate rises, it becomes more expensive to borrow, and fewer projects are likely to be undertaken. Therefore, increasing the interest rate, *ceteris paribus*, is likely to reduce the level of planned investment spending. Similarly, when the interest rate falls, it becomes less costly to borrow, and more investment projects are likely to be undertaken. Therefore, reducing the interest rate, *ceteris paribus*, is likely to increase the level of planned investment spending.

The relationship between the interest rate and planned investment is illustrated by the downward-sloping demand curve in Figure 28.1. The higher the interest rate, the lower the level of planned investment. At interest rate r_0, planned investment is I_0. When the interest rate rises from r_0 to r_1, planned investment falls from I_0 to I_1.[†] As the interest rate falls, however, more projects become profitable, so more investment is undertaken.

We can now use the fact that planned investment depends on the interest rate to consider how this relationship affects planned aggregate expenditure (AE). Recall that planned aggregate expenditure is the sum of consumption, planned investment, and government purchases.[1] That is,

$$AE \equiv C + I + G.$$

We now know that there are actually many possible levels of I, each corresponding to a different interest rate (as illustrated in Figure 28.1). When the inter-

---

[1] As we saw in Chapter 25, planned aggregate expenditure also includes net exports ($EX - IM$). The impact of adding exports and imports to our analysis is complex and will be discussed in Chapter 37. For now, we ignore net exports.

[†] Figure 28.1 is in fact the same as the *marginal efficiency of investment (MEI) schedule* in Figure 11.4 in Chapter 11. The MEI schedule is derived by ranking investment projects by their expected yields and choosing all projects whose yield is greater than the interest rate.

FIGURE 28.1
Planned Investment Schedule

Planned investment spending is a negative function of the interest rate.

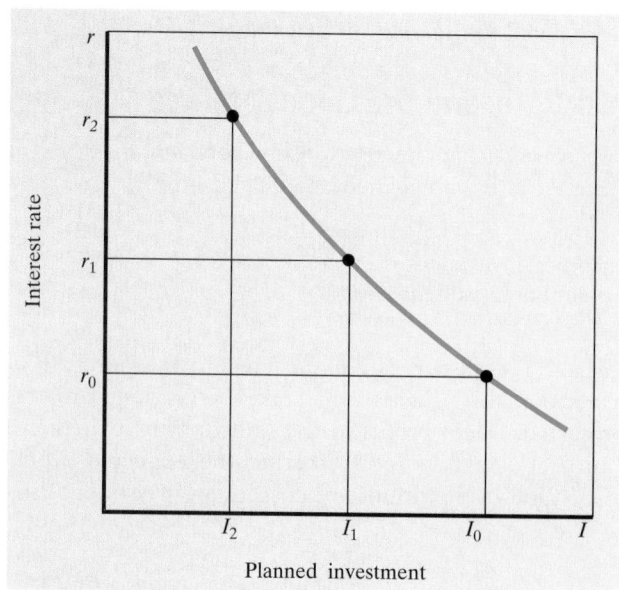

Planned investment

est rate changes, planned investment changes. Therefore, a change in the interest rate (r) will lead to a change in total planned spending ($C + I + G$) as well.[2]

Figure 28.2 shows what happens to planned aggregate expenditure when the interest rate rises from r_0 to r_1. At the higher interest rate, planned investment is lower; planned aggregate expenditure thus shifts *downward*. As you should recall from Chapters 24 and 25, a fall in any component of aggregate spending has an even larger (or "multiplier") effect on equilibrium income (Y). Thus, when the interest rate rises, planned investment (and thus planned aggregate expenditure) falls, and equilibrium output (income) falls by even more than the fall in planned investment. As you can see in Figure 28.2, the fall in equilibrium income from Y_0 to Y_1 is larger than the fall in planned investment from I_0 to I_1.

We can now summarize the effects of a change in the interest rate on the equilibrium level of output:

| The effects of a change in the interest rate: | ■ A high interest rate (r) discourages planned investment (I).
■ Planned investment is a part of planned aggregate expenditure (AE).
■ Thus, when the interest rate rises, planned aggregate expenditure (AE) at every level of income falls.
■ Finally, a decrease in planned aggregate expenditure lowers equilibrium output (income) (Y) by a multiple of the initial decrease in planned investment.
Using a convenient shorthand: |

$$r{\uparrow} \rightarrow I{\downarrow} \rightarrow AE{\downarrow} \rightarrow Y{\downarrow}.$$
$$r{\downarrow} \rightarrow I{\uparrow} \rightarrow AE{\uparrow} \rightarrow Y{\uparrow}.$$

Thus, as you can see, the equilibrium level of output (Y) is not determined solely by events in the goods market, as we assumed in our earlier simplified discussions. The reason is that the money market affects the level of the interest rate, which then affects planned investment in the goods market. There is a different equilibrium level of Y for every possible level of the interest rate (r). The final level of equilibrium Y depends on what the interest rate turns out to be, which depends on events in the money market.

---

[2]When we look at the behavior of households in the macroeconomy in detail in Chapter 32, you will see that consumption spending (C) is also stimulated by lower interest rates and discouraged by higher interest rates.

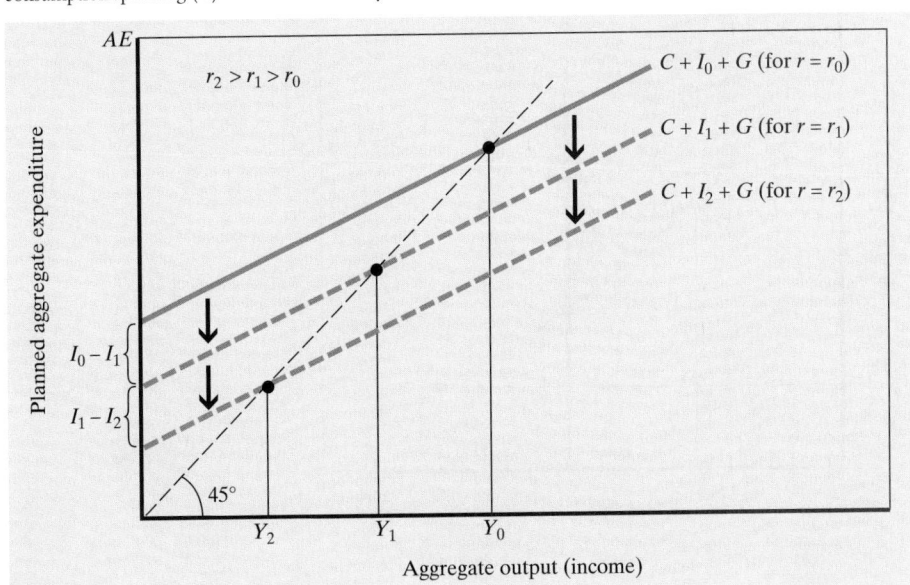

FIGURE 28.2
The Effect of an Interest Rate Increase on Planned Aggregate Expenditure

An increase in the interest rate from r_0 to r_1 lowers planned aggregate expenditure and thus reduces equilibrium income from Y_0 to Y_1. A further increase in the interest rate to r_2 reduces equilibrium income to Y_2.

Money Demand, Aggregate Output (Income), and the Money Market

We have just seen how the interest rate—which is determined in the money market—influences the level of planned investment spending and thus the goods market. Now let us look at the other half of the story: the ways in which the goods market affects the money market.

In the last chapter, we explored the demand for money by households and firms and explained why the demand for money depends negatively on the interest rate. An increase in the interest rate raises the opportunity cost of holding non-interest-bearing money (as compared to interest-bearing bonds), thus encouraging people to keep more of their funds in bonds and less of their funds in checking account balances. The downward-sloping money demand curve (M^d) is shown in Figure 28.3.

We also saw in the previous chapter that the demand for money depends on the level of income in the economy. More income means that there are more transactions, and an increased volume of transactions implies a greater demand for money. With more people earning higher incomes and buying more goods and services, more money will be demanded to meet the increased volume of transactions. An increase in income therefore shifts the money demand curve to the right. (Review Figure 27.5 if necessary.)

If, as we are assuming, the Fed's choice of the amount of money to supply does not depend on the interest rate, then the money supply curve is simply a vertical line. The equilibrium interest rate is the point at which the quantity of money demanded equals the quantity of money supplied. This equilibrium is shown at interest rate r^* in Figure 28.3. If the amount of money demanded by households and firms is less than the amount in circulation as determined by the Fed, as it is at level r_0 in Figure 28.3, the interest rate will fall. If the amount of money demanded is greater than the total money supply, as it is at r_1 in Figure 28.3, the interest rate will rise.

Now consider what will happen to the interest rate when there is an increase in aggregate output (income) (Y). As you know, this increase in Y will cause the

FIGURE 28.3

Equilibrium in the Money Market

If the interest rate were r_0, the quantity of money in circulation would exceed the amount that households and firms want to hold. The excess money balances would cause the interest rate to drop as people try to shift their funds into interest-bearing bonds. At r_1 the opposite is true. Excess demand for money balances would push interest rates up. Only at r^* would the actual quantity of money in circulation be equal to what the economy wants to hold in money balances.

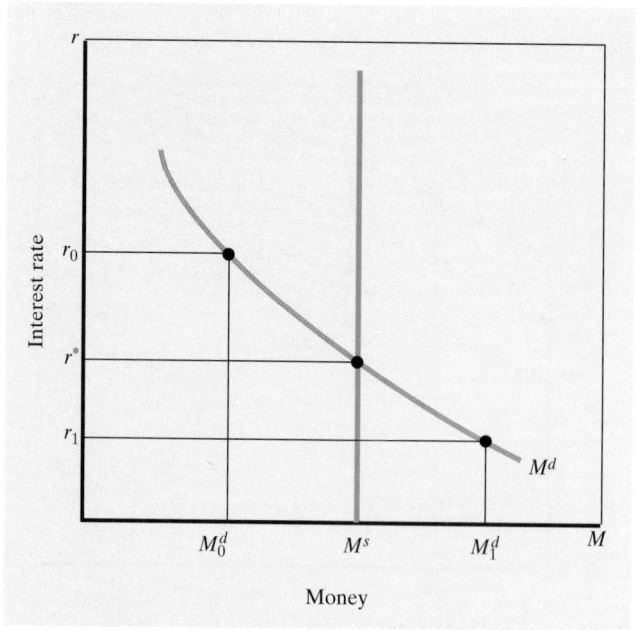

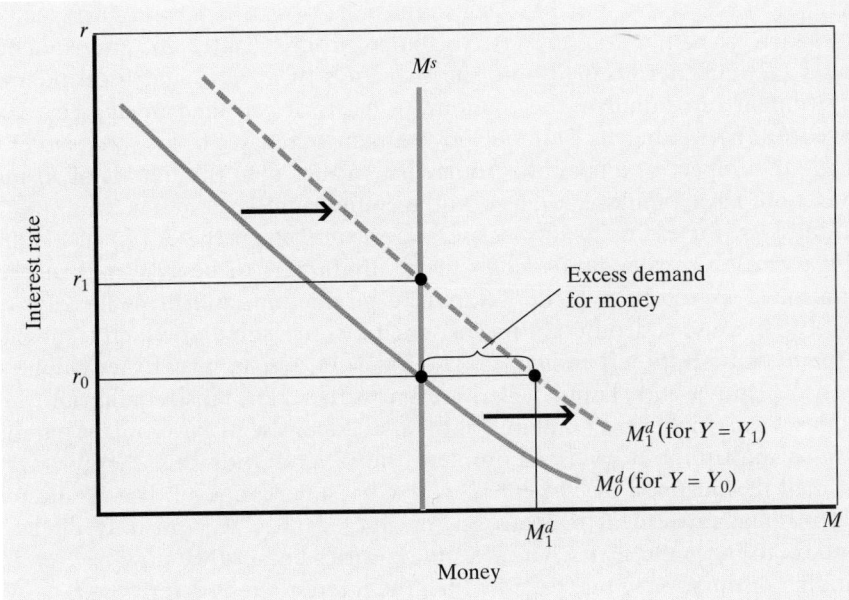

An increase in income from Y_0 to Y_1 shifts the M^d curve to the right. With a fixed supply of money, there is now an excess demand for money ($M^d > M^s$) at the initial interest rate r_0. This causes the interest rate to rise. At r_1 the money market is again in equilibrium with $M^s = M^d$, but at a higher interest rate than before the increase in income.

money demand curve to shift to the right. This situation is illustrated in Figure 28.4, where an increase in income from Y_0 to Y_1 has shifted the money demand curve from M_0^d to M_1^d. At the old interest rate r_0, there is now excess demand for money, and the interest rate rises from r_0 to r_1. It should be clear, then, that:

> The equilibrium level of the interest rate is not determined exclusively in the money market. Changes in aggregate output (income) (Y), which take place in the goods market, shift the money demand curve and cause changes in the interest rate. With a given quantity of money supplied, higher levels of Y will lead to higher equilibrium levels of r. Lower levels of Y will lead to lower equilibrium levels of r. To use our convenient shorthand:
>
> $$Y \uparrow \rightarrow M^d \uparrow \rightarrow r \uparrow.$$
> $$Y \downarrow \rightarrow M^d \downarrow \rightarrow r \downarrow.$$

COMBINING THE GOODS MARKET AND THE MONEY MARKET

Now that we are fully aware of the links between the goods market and the money market, we can examine the two markets simultaneously. To see how the two markets interact, it will be convenient to consider the effects of changes in fiscal and monetary policy on the economy. Specifically, we want to examine what happens to the equilibrium levels of aggregate output (income) (Y) and the interest rate (r) when certain key variables—notably government spending (G), net taxes (T), and the money supply (M^s)—increase or decrease.

Expansionary Policy Effects

Any government policy that is aimed at stimulating aggregate output (income) (Y) is said to be *expansionary*. An **expansionary fiscal policy** is an increase in government spending (G) or a reduction in net taxes (T) aimed at increasing aggregate output (income) (Y). An **expansionary monetary policy** is an increase in the money supply aimed at increasing aggregate output (income) (Y).

expansionary fiscal policy An increase in government spending or a reduction in net taxes aimed at increasing aggregate output (income) (Y).

expansionary monetary policy An increase in the money supply aimed at increasing aggregate output (income) (Y).

EXPANSIONARY FISCAL POLICY: AN INCREASE IN GOVERNMENT PURCHASES (G) OR DECREASE IN NET TAXES (T)   As you know from Chapter 25, government purchases (G) and net taxes (T) are the two tools of government fiscal policy. The government can stimulate the economy—that is, it can increase aggregate output (income) (Y)—either by *increasing* government purchases or by *reducing* net taxes. While the impact of a tax cut is somewhat smaller than the impact of an increase in G, both have a multiplier effect on the equilibrium level of Y.

Consider, for example, an increase in government purchases (G) of $10 billion. This increase in expenditure causes firms' inventories to be smaller than planned. Unplanned inventory reductions stimulate production, and firms increase output (Y). But because added output means added income, some of which is subsequently spent, consumption spending (C) also increases. Again, inventories will be smaller than planned and output will rise even further. The final equilibrium level of output is thus higher by a multiple of the initial increase in government purchases.

This multiplier story is incomplete, however. Until this chapter, we have assumed that planned investment (I) is fixed at a certain level. But we now know that planned investment depends on the interest rate. We can now discuss what happens to the multiplier when investment varies because we now have an understanding of the money market, in which the interest rate is determined.

Let's return to our multiplier story at the point that firms first begin to raise output in response to an increase in government purchases. As aggregate output (income) (Y) increases, an impact is felt in the money market. Specifically, the increase in income (Y) increases the demand for money (M^d). (For the moment, we assume that the Fed holds the quantity of money supplied [M^s] constant.) The resulting disequilibrium, with the quantity of money demanded greater than the quantity of money supplied, causes the interest rate to rise. An increase in G thus increases both Y and r.

The increase in r has a side effect, however. Remember that a higher interest rate causes planned investment spending (I) to decline. Because planned investment spending is a component of planned aggregate expenditure ($C + I + G$), the decrease in I works against the increase in G. An increase in government spending (G) increases planned aggregate expenditure and increases aggregate output, but a decrease in planned investment reduces planned aggregate expenditure and *decreases* aggregate output.

crowding-out effect The tendency for increases in government spending to cause reductions in private investment spending.

This tendency for increases in government spending to cause reductions in private investment spending is called the **crowding-out effect.** Without any expansion in the money supply to accommodate the rise in income and increased money demand, planned investment spending is partially crowded out by the higher interest rate. The extra spending created by the rise in government purchases is somewhat offset by the fall in planned investment spending. Income still rises, but the multiplier effect of the rise in G is lessened because of the higher interest rate's negative effect on planned investment.

This crowding-out effect is illustrated graphically in Figure 28.5. An increase in government purchases from G_0 to G_1 shifts the planned aggregate expenditure curve ($C + I_0 + G_0$) upward. The increase in (Y) from Y_0 to Y_1 causes the demand for money to rise, which results in a disequilibrium in the money market. The excess demand for money raises the interest rate (r) from r_0 to r_1, causing I to decrease from I_0 to I_1 (see Figure 28.1). The fall in I pulls the planned aggregate expenditure curve back down, which lowers the equilibrium level of income to Y^*. (Remember that equilibrium is achieved when $Y = AE$.)

Note that the size of the crowding-out effect, and thus the ultimate size of the government spending multiplier, depends on several things. The first of these is the assumption that the Fed did not change the quantity of money supplied. If we

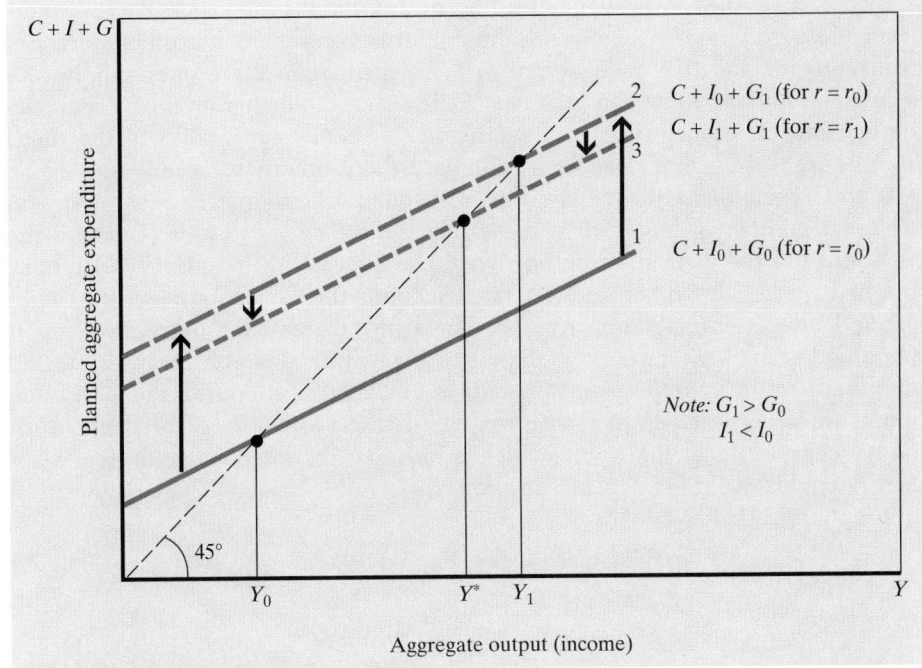

FIGURE 28.5
The Crowding-out Effect

An increase in G from G_0 to G_1 shifts the planned aggregate expenditure schedule from 1 to 2. The crowding-out effect of the decrease in planned investment (brought about by the increased interest rate) then shifts the planned aggregate expenditure schedule from 2 to 3.

Figure content labels:

2 $C + I_0 + G_1$ (for $r = r_0$)

$C + I_1 + G_1$ (for $r = r_1$)

3

1 $C + I_0 + G_0$ (for $r = r_0$)

Note: $G_1 > G_0$
$I_1 < I_0$

$45°$

Y_0 Y^* Y_1 Y

Aggregate output (income)

were to relax this assumption and assume instead that the Fed expanded the quantity of money to accommodate the increase in G, the multiplier would be larger. In this case, the higher demand for money would be satisfied with a higher quantity of money supplied, and the interest rate would not rise. Without a higher interest rate, there would be no crowding out.

Second, the crowding-out effect depends on the **sensitivity** or **insensitivity of planned investment** spending to changes in the interest rate. Crowding out occurs because a higher interest rate reduces planned investment spending. Investment depends on factors other than the interest rate, however, and investment may at times be quite insensitive to changes in the interest rate. If planned investment does not fall when the interest rate rises, there is no crowding-out effect.

To summarize the effects of an expansionary fiscal policy, we can write:

Effects of an expansionary fiscal policy:	$G\!\uparrow\,\rightarrow Y\!\uparrow\,\rightarrow M^d\!\uparrow\,\rightarrow r\!\uparrow\,\rightarrow I\!\downarrow$
	$\longrightarrow Y$ increases less than if r did not increase.

interest sensitivity or insensitivity of planned investment The responsiveness of planned investment spending to changes in the interest rate. *Interest sensitivity* means that planned investment spending changes a great deal in response to changes in the interest rate; *interest insensitivity* means little or no change in planned investment as a result of changes in the interest rate.

Exactly the same reasoning holds for changes in net taxes. The ultimate effect of a tax cut on the equilibrium level of output depends on how the money market reacts. The expansion of Y that a tax cut brings about will lead to an increase in the interest rate and thus a decrease in planned investment spending. The ultimate increase in Y will therefore be less than it would be if the interest rate did not rise.

EXPANSIONARY MONETARY POLICY: AN INCREASE IN THE MONEY SUPPLY Now let us consider what will happen when the Fed decides to increase the supply of money through open market operations. At first, open market operations inject new reserves into the system and expand the quantity of money supplied (that is, the money supply curve shifts to the right). Because the quantity of money supplied is now greater than the amount households want to hold, the equilibrium rate of interest falls. Planned investment spending (which is a component of planned aggregate expenditure) increases when the interest rate falls.

Increased planned investment spending means that planned aggregate expenditure is now greater than aggregate output. Firms experience unplanned decreases in inventories, and they raise output (Y). An increase in the money supply thus decreases the interest rate and increases Y. However, the higher level of Y increases the demand for money (that is, the demand for money curve shifts to the right) and this keeps the interest rate from falling as far as it otherwise would.

If you review the sequence of events that follows the monetary expansion, you can see a number of links between the injection of reserves by the Fed into the economy and the increase in output. First, the increase in the quantity of money supplied pushes down the interest rate. Second, the lower interest rate causes planned investment spending to rise. Third, the increased planned investment spending means higher planned aggregate expenditure, which means increased output as firms react to unplanned decreases in inventories. Fourth, the increase in output (income) leads to an increase in the demand for money (the demand for money curve shifts to the right), which means that the interest rate decreases less than it would have if the demand for money had not increased. These connections can be summarized as:

Effects of an expansionary monetary policy:	$M^s\uparrow \rightarrow r\downarrow \rightarrow I\uparrow \rightarrow Y\uparrow \rightarrow M^d\uparrow$ $\hookrightarrow r$ decreases less than if M^d did not increase.

The power of monetary policy to affect the goods market depends on how much of a reaction occurs at each link in this chain. Perhaps the most critical link is the link between r and I. Monetary policy can be effective *only* if I reacts to changes in r. If firms sharply increase the number of investment projects undertaken when the interest rate falls, expansionary monetary policy works well at stimulating the economy. If, however, firms are reluctant to invest even at a low interest rate, expansionary monetary policy will have limited success. In other words, the effectiveness of monetary policy depends on the shape of the investment function. If it is nearly vertical, indicating very little responsiveness of investment to the interest rate, the middle link in this chain is weak, rendering monetary policy ineffective.

EXPANSIONARY POLICY IN ACTION: THE RECESSIONS OF 1974–1975 AND 1980–1982
The United States has experienced three recessions since 1970. In two of these recessions, 1974–1975 and 1980–1982, the government engaged in tax cuts that had the effect of stimulating consumer spending (C). Because C is a component of planned aggregate expenditure, these tax cuts had the effect of increasing aggregate output (income) (Y).

Consider the recession of 1974–1975. The Tax Reduction Act of 1975 resulted in a 1974 tax rebate of $8 billion that was paid to consumers in the second quarter of 1975. This rebate and other tax reductions led to increased consumer spending, which contributed to the economic recovery that began soon after the new tax laws went into effect.

But what about the crowding-out effect? Did the 1975 expansionary fiscal policy drive up interest rates and crowd out private spending? The answer in this case is no. At the same time that Congress was cutting taxes to stimulate spending, the Fed was trying to stimulate the economy by expanding the money supply. Thus, even though the increased output during the expansion caused the *demand* for money to rise, the Fed was simultaneously expanding the *supply* of money, and interest rates did not change very much. This situation is illustrated in Figure 28.6.

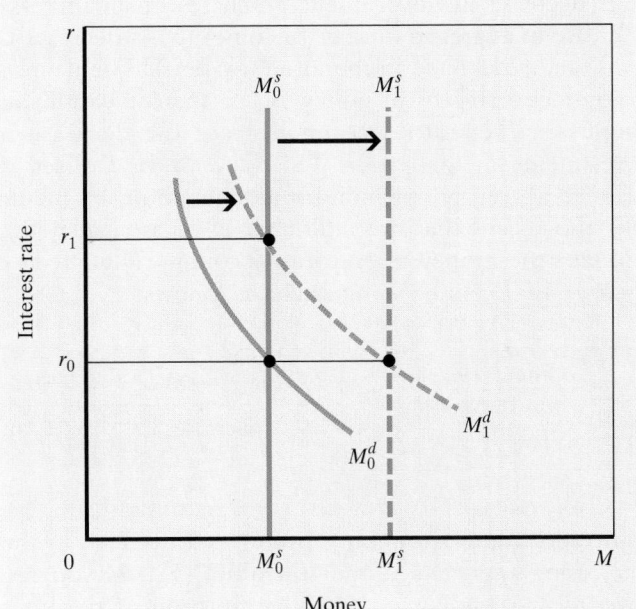

FIGURE 28.6
Fed Accommodation of an
Expansionary Fiscal Policy

An expansionary fiscal policy, like the 1975 tax cut, will increase aggregate output (income) and shift the money demand curve to the right, from M_0^d to M_1^d. If the money supply were unchanged, the interest rate would rise from r_0 to r_1 and planned investment would be negatively affected. But if the Fed were to "accommodate" the fiscal expansion by increasing the money supply from M_0^s to M_1^s, the interest rate would not rise.

A similar sequence of events took place during the recession of 1980–1982. On the recommendation of President Reagan, Congress passed a huge tax cut during the summer of 1981. Like the 1975 tax cut, the 1981 tax cut led to an increase in consumer spending, which helped lift the economy out of the recession.

Recovery from the 1980–1982 recession was also helped along by the Fed, which began to increase the supply of money sharply in the spring of 1982. So, even though output and income were expanding by late 1982, thereby increasing the demand for money, interest rates actually *declined* because the supply of money was expanding at the same time. There was thus no crowding-out effect.

Contractionary Policy Effects

Any government policy that is aimed at reducing aggregate output (income) (Y) is said to be *contractionary*. Where expansionary policy is used to boost the economy, contractionary policy is used to slow the economy.

Considering that one of the four major economic goals is economic growth (see Chapter 1), why would the government adopt policies designed to reduce aggregate spending? As we will see in more detail in the next two chapters, one of the ways to fight inflation is to reduce aggregate spending. Thus, when the inflation rate is high, the government may feel compelled to use its powers to contract the economy. Before we discuss the contractionary policies that the government has undertaken in recent years, however, we need to discuss how contractionary fiscal and monetary policy work.

CONTRACTIONARY FISCAL POLICY: A DECREASE IN GOVERNMENT SPENDING (G) OR AN INCREASE IN NET TAXES (T)   A **contractionary fiscal policy** is a decrease in government spending (G) or an increase in net taxes (T) aimed at decreasing aggregate output (income) (Y). The effects of this policy are the opposite of the effects of an expansionary fiscal policy.

contractionary fiscal policy A decrease in government spending or an increase in net taxes aimed at decreasing aggregate output (income) (Y).

A decrease in government purchases or an increase in net taxes leads to a decrease in aggregate output (income) (Y), a decrease in the demand for money (M^d), and a decrease in the interest rate (r). The decrease in Y that accompanies a contractionary fiscal policy is less than it would be if we did not take the money market into account because the decrease in r also causes planned investment (I) to *increase*. This increase in I offsets some of the decrease in planned aggregate expenditure brought about by the decrease in G. (Of course, this also means that the multiplier effect is smaller than it would be if we did not take the money market into account.) The effects of a decrease in G, or an increase in T, can be summarized as follows:

Effects of a contractionary fiscal policy:	$G\downarrow$ or $T\uparrow \rightarrow Y\downarrow \rightarrow M^d\downarrow \rightarrow r\downarrow \rightarrow I\uparrow$ $\hookrightarrow Y$ decreases less than if r did not decrease.

CONTRACTIONARY MONETARY POLICY: A DECREASE IN THE MONEY SUPPLY A **contractionary monetary policy** is a decrease in the money supply aimed at decreasing aggregate output (income) (Y). As you recall, the level of planned investment spending is a negative function of the interest rate: The higher the interest rate, the less planned investment there will be. The less planned investment there is, the lower planned aggregate expenditure will be, and the lower the equilibrium level of output (income) (Y) will be. The lower equilibrium income results in a decrease in the demand for money, which means that the increase in the interest rate will be less than it would be if we did not take the goods market into account. The effects of a decrease in the money supply can be summarized as:

Effects of a contractionary monetary policy:	$M^s\downarrow \rightarrow r\uparrow \rightarrow I\downarrow \rightarrow Y\downarrow \rightarrow M^d\downarrow$ $\hookrightarrow r$ increases less than if M^d did not decrease.

contractionary monetary policy A decrease in the money supply aimed at decreasing aggregate output (income) (Y).

CONTRACTIONARY POLICY IN ACTION: 1973–1974 AND 1979–1980 The Fed has pursued strong contractionary policies twice in the last two decades: first in 1973–1974 and again in 1979–1980. In both cases, the tight monetary policies led to very high interest rates. In 1974, short-term rates exceeded 12%, and in 1981, some short-term rates exceeded 20 percent! These high interest rates had a negative effect on planned aggregate expenditure and contributed to the recessions that followed. The Fed's purpose in following a tight monetary policy was to slow the inflation rate. We will see in the next chapter why a contractionary policy may bring the inflation rate down.

The Macroeconomic Policy Mix

Thus far, we've been treating fiscal and monetary policy separately. However, it should be clear that fiscal and monetary policy can be used simultaneously. For example, both government purchases (G) and the money supply (M^s) can be increased at the same time. We have seen that an increase in G by itself raises both Y and r, while an increase in M^s by itself raises Y but lowers r. Therefore, if the government wanted to increase Y without changing r, it could do so by increasing both G and M^s by the appropriate amounts.

The term **policy mix** refers to the combination of monetary and fiscal policies in use at a given time. A policy mix that consists of a decrease in government

policy mix The combination of monetary and fiscal policies in use at a given time.

FISCAL POLICY, MONETARY POLICY, THE PRESIDENT, AND THE FED: 1993

The following excerpt, which appeared in the *New York Times* just prior to President Clinton's inauguration in 1993, shows the tension that was already developing between the Fed—which is responsible for the nation's monetary policy—and the President and Congress, who are jointly responsible for the nation's fiscal policy:

Presidents have often pressured the Federal Reserve to keep interest rates down, but . . . Bill Clinton seems to have gone them one better: his lieutenants are jawboning the Fed even before he takes office.

And the Fed is jawboning right back.

Mr. Clinton and the governors of the Fed are on a collision course, because the central bank wants economic growth to continue its slow takeoff, hoping to keep inflation heading downward even though inflationary pressures are at their lowest level in more than two decades. But Mr. Clinton's advisers have a quite different goal: far faster economic growth to fulfill his campaign pledge of slashing the nation's 7.3 percent unemployment rate.

Federal Reserve governors, in interviews last week, cautioned that if Mr. Clinton hit the growth accelerator too hard he just might repeat the mistakes of the one President he seems least eager to emulate: Jimmy Carter, who the governors say overstimulated the economy and ignited double-digit inflation. . . .

Many governors do not squirm at the

President Bill Clinton and Fed Chairman Alan Greenspan met in January, 1993 to discuss the president's plans for stimulating the economy. To the surprise of many, Mr. Greenspan has been supportive of many of President Clinton's proposals.

Clinton economic team's plans for a modest, short-term increase in deficit spending, probably around $20 billion. A stimulus program of this magnitude, Federal Reserve officials say, is unlikely to overaccelerate growth or fuel inflation, especially if it is tied to a multiyear plan to reduce the budget deficit in the long term.

Inside the Fed there is a huge worry, however, that Congress might transform a modest Clinton plan into a $40 billion to $50 billion package. . . . [A] stimulus plan of that size, Fed officials fear, could overstimulate the economy. That would be counterproductive, they say, because it would fuel fears of inflation and push up long-term interest rates. That could cut the

legs out from under faster growth by hurting business investment and homebuilding.

Soon after his election, President Clinton proposed a deficit-reduction package that substantially increased taxes (T) and reduced government purchases (G). The proposal was strongly supported by Fed Chair Alan Greenspan, who agreed to cooperate by keeping rates low as long as Congress went along with the plan.

Source: Steven Greenhouse, "Clinton Goes Head to Head with the Fed," *New York Times,* January 18, 1993.

spending and an increase in the money supply would favor investment spending over government spending. This is because both the increased money supply and the fall in government purchases would cause the interest rate to fall, which would lead to an increase in planned investment. The opposite is true for a mix that consists of an expansionary fiscal policy and a contractionary monetary policy. This mix favors government spending over investment spending. Such a policy will have the effect of increasing government spending and reducing the money supply. Tight money and expanded government spending would drive the interest rate up and planned investment down, as the Issues and Applications box titled "Fiscal Policy, Monetary Policy, the President, and the Fed: 1993" discusses in detail.

FIGURE 28.7
The Effects of the
Macroeconomic Policy Mix

		Fiscal	
		Expansionary ($\uparrow G$ or $\downarrow T$)	Contractionary ($\downarrow G$ or $\uparrow T$)
Monetary	Expansionary ($\uparrow M^s$)	$Y\uparrow, r?, I?, C\uparrow$	$Y?, r\downarrow, I\uparrow, C?$
	Contractionary ($\downarrow M^s$)	$Y?, r\uparrow, I\downarrow, C?$	$Y\downarrow, r?, I?, C\downarrow$

KEY:
$\uparrow$: variable increases.
$\downarrow$: variable decreases.
? : forces push the variable in different directions. Without additional information, we cannot specify which way the variable moves.

There is no hard-and-fast rule about what constitutes the "best" policy mix or the "best" composition of output. On this, as on many other issues, economists (and others) disagree. In part, one's preference for a certain composition of output—say, one weighted heavily toward private spending with relatively little government spending—depends on how one stands on such issues as the proper role of government in the economy.

Figure 28.7 summarizes the effects of various combinations of policies on several important macroeconomic variables. If you can explain the reasoning underlying each of the effects shown in the figure, you can be satisfied that you have a good understanding of the links between the goods market and the money market.

OTHER DETERMINANTS OF PLANNED INVESTMENT

We have assumed in this chapter that planned investment depends only on the interest rate. In reality, however, planned investment depends on other factors as well. We will discuss these factors in more detail in Chapter 32, but provide a brief description of them here.

EXPECTATIONS Firms' expectations about their future sales play an important role in their investment decisions. When a firm invests, it adds to its capital stock, and capital is used in the production process. If a firm expects that its sales will increase in the future, it may begin to build up its capital stock (that is, to invest) now so that it will be able to produce more in the future to meet the increased level of sales. The optimism or pessimism of entrepreneurs about the future course of the economy can thus have an important effect on current planned investment.

CAPITAL UTILIZATION RATES The degree of utilization of a firm's capital stock is also likely to affect planned investment. If the demand for a firm's output has been decreasing and the firm has been lowering output in response to this decline, the firm may have a low rate of capital utilization. It can be costly to get rid of capital quickly once it is in place, and firms sometimes respond to a fall in output by keeping the capital in place but utilizing it less (for example, by running machines fewer hours per day or at slower speeds). For obvious reasons, firms tend to invest less in new capital when their capital utilization rates are low than when they are high.

RELATIVE LABOR AND CAPITAL COSTS   The cost of capital (of which the interest rate is the main component) *relative* to the cost of labor can affect planned investment. If labor is expensive relative to capital (high wage rates), firms tend to substitute away from labor toward capital. They aim to hold more capital relative to labor when wage rates are high than when they are low.

To summarize:

The determinants of planned investment:	■ The interest rate ■ Expectations of future sales ■ Capital utilization rates ■ Relative capital and labor costs.

LOOKING AHEAD: THE PRICE LEVEL

Our discussion of aggregate output (income) and the interest rate in the goods market and the money market is now complete. By now you should have a good understanding of how the two markets work together. Thus far, however, we have not yet discussed the price level in any detail.

One cannot begin to understand the economic events of the last two decades without an understanding of the aggregate price level. The two periods of rapid increases in the price level, 1974–1975 and 1979–1981, had dramatic effects on the economy. What causes the price level to change? Are there policies that might prevent large changes in the price level or stop them once they have started? Before we can answer such questions, we must understand the factors that affect the overall price level. This is the task of the next chapter. Up to this point we have taken the price level as fixed, and it is now time to relax this assumption.

SUMMARY

1. The *goods market* and the *money market* do not operate independently. Events in the money market have important effects on the goods market, and events in the goods market have important effects on the money market.

The Links Between the Goods Market and the Money Market

2. There are two important links between the goods market and the money market. First, the level of real output (income) (Y), which is determined in the goods market, determines the volume of transactions each period and thus affects the demand for money in the money market. Second, the interest rate (r), which is determined in the money market, affects the level of planned investment spending in the goods market.

3. There is a negative relationship between planned investment and the interest rate because the interest rate determines the cost of investment projects. When the interest rate rises, planned investment will decrease; when the interest rate falls, planned investment will increase.

4. For every value of the interest rate, there is a different level of planned investment spending and a different equilibrium level of output. The final level of equilibrium output depends on what the interest rate turns out to be, which depends on events in the money market.

5. For a given quantity of money supplied the interest rate depends on the demand for money. Money demand depends on the level of output (income). With a given money supply, then, increases and decreases in Y will affect money demand, which will affect the equilibrium interest rate.

Combining the Goods Market and the Money Market

6. An *expansionary fiscal policy* is an increase in government spending (G) or a reduction in net taxes (T) aimed at increasing aggregate output (income) (Y). An expansionary fiscal policy based on increases in government spending tends to lead to a *crowding-out effect:* Because increased government expenditures mean more transactions in the economy and thus an increased demand for money, the interest rate will rise. The decrease in planned investment spending that accompanies the higher interest rate will then partially offset (crowd out) the increase in aggregate expenditures brought about by the increase in G.

7. The size of the crowding-out effect, and thus the size of the government-spending multiplier, depends on two things: the assumption that the Fed does not change the quantity of money supplied and the *sensitivity* or *insensitivity of planned investment* to changes in the interest rate.

8. An *expansionary monetary policy* is an increase in the money supply aimed at increasing aggregate output (income) (Y). An increase in the money supply leads to a lower interest rate, increased planned investment, increased planned aggregate expenditure, and ultimately a higher equilibrium level of aggregate output (income) (Y). Expansionary policies have been used to lift the economy out of recessions.

9. A *contractionary fiscal policy* is a decrease in government spending or an increase in net taxes aimed at decreasing aggregate output (income (Y). A decrease in government spending or an increase in net taxes leads to a decrease in aggregate output (income) (Y), a decrease in the demand for money, and a decrease in the interest rate. However, the decrease in Y is somewhat offset by the additional planned investment that is undertaken as a result of the lower interest rate.

10. A *contractionary monetary policy* is a decrease in the money supply aimed at decreasing aggregate output (income) (Y). The higher interest rate brought about by the reduced money supply causes a decrease in planned investment spending and a lower level of equilibrium output. However, the lower equilibrium level of output brings about a decrease in the demand for money, which means that the increase in the interest rate will be less than it would be if we did not take the goods market into account. Contractionary policies have been used to fight inflation.

11. The *policy mix* is the combination of monetary and fiscal policies in use at a given time. There is no hard-and-fast rule about what constitutes the best policy mix or the best composition of output. In part, one's preference for a certain composition of output depends on one's stance regarding such issues as the proper role of government in the economy.

Other Determinants of Planned Investment

12. In addition to the interest rate, the level of planned investment in the economy also depends on expectations, capital utilization rates, and relative capital and labor costs.

REVIEW TERMS AND CONCEPTS

contractionary fiscal policy   705
contractionary monetary policy   706
crowding-out effect   702
expansionary fiscal policy   701

expansionary monetary policy   701
goods market   696
interest sensitivity or insensitivity of
    planned investment   703

money market   696
policy mix   706

Equations:
$AE \equiv C + I + G$

PROBLEM SET

1. What are the limitations of analyzing the goods market and the money market independently of each other? What happens to the size of the government spending multiplier when events in the money market are taken into account?

2. Some economists argue that the "animal spirits" of investors are so important in determining the level of investment in the economy that interest rates don't matter at all. Suppose that this were true—that investment in no way depends on interest rates.
    a. How would the first figure in this chapter be different?
    b. What would happen to the level of planned aggregate expenditures if the interest rate were to change?
    c. What would be different about the relative effectiveness of monetary and fiscal policy?

3. Occasionally, the Federal Reserve Open Market Committee sets a policy designed to "track" the interest rate. This means that the OMC is pursuing policies designed to keep the interest rate constant. If, in fact, the Fed were acting to counter any increases or decreases in the interest rate to keep it constant, what specific actions would you expect to see the Fed take if the following were to occur? (In answering, indicate the effects of each set of events on Y, C, S, I, M^s, M^d, and r.)
    a. There is an unexpected increase in investor confidence, leading to a sharp increase in orders for new plant and equipment.

    b. A major New York bank fails, causing a number of neurotic people (not trusting even the FDIC) to withdraw a substantial amount of cash from other banks and put it in their cookie jars.

4. Paranoia, the largest country in Central Antarctica, receives word of an imminent penguin attack. The news causes expectations about the future to be shaken. As a consequence, there is a sharp decline in investment spending plans; the investment schedule shifts left.
    a. Explain in detail the effects of such an event on the economy of Paranoia, assuming no response on the part of the Central Bank or the Treasury (M^s, T, and G all remain constant). Be sure to discuss the adjustments in the goods market and the money market.
    b. To counter the fall in investment, the King of Paranoia calls for a proposal to increase government spending. To finance the program, the Chancellor of the Exchequer has proposed three alternative options:
      1. Finance the expenditures with an equal increase in taxes.
      2. Keep tax revenues constant and borrow the money from the public by issuing new government bonds.
      3. Keep taxes constant and finance the expenditures by printing new money.

Consider the three financing options and rank them from most expansionary to least expansionary. Explain your ranking.

5. Why might investment not respond positively to low interest rates during a recession? Why might investment not respond negatively to high interest rates during a boom?

6. In the early 1980s, the Federal Reserve was tightening the money supply in order to fight inflation at the same time that President Reagan was increasing defense spending and reducing taxes. What would you expect the effects of this policy mix to be?

APPENDIX TO CHAPTER 28
THE *IS-LM* DIAGRAM

There is a useful way of depicting graphically the determination of aggregate output (income) and the interest rate in the goods and money markets. Two curves are involved in this diagram, the *IS* curve and the *LM* curve. In this appendix, we will derive these two curves and use them to see how changes in government purchases (*G*) and the money supply (*M*s) affect the equilibrium values of aggregate output (income) and the interest rate. The effects we describe here are the same as the effects we described in the main text; the only difference is that here we illustrate the effects graphically rather than verbally.

THE *IS* CURVE

We know that in the goods market, there is an equilibrium level of aggregate output (income) (*Y*) for each value of the interest rate (*r*). For a given value of *r*, we can determine the equilibrium value of *Y*. We also know from Figure 28.5 that the equilibrium value of *Y* falls when *r* rises and rises when *r* falls. There is thus a *negative* relationship between the equilibrium values of *Y* and *r*. The reason for this negative relationship is the negative relationship between planned investment and the interest rate. When the interest rate rises, planned investment (*I*) falls, and this decrease in *I* leads to a decrease in the equilibrium value of *Y*. The negative relationship between the equilibrium value of *Y* and *r* is shown in Figure 28A.1. This curve is called the **IS curve.**[1] Each point on the *IS* curve represents the equilibrium point in the goods market for the given interest rate.

We also know from our earlier analysis of the goods market that when government purchases (*G*) increase with a constant interest rate, the equilibrium value of *Y* increases. This means that the *IS* curve shifts to the right when *G* increases. With the same value of *r* and a higher value of *G*, the equilibrium value of *Y* is larger. Conversely, when *G* decreases, the *IS* curve shifts to the left.

FIGURE 28A.1
The *IS* Curve

Each point on the *IS* curve corresponds to the equilibrium point in the goods market for the given interest rate. When government purchases (*G*) increase, the *IS* curve shifts to the right, from IS_0 to IS_1.

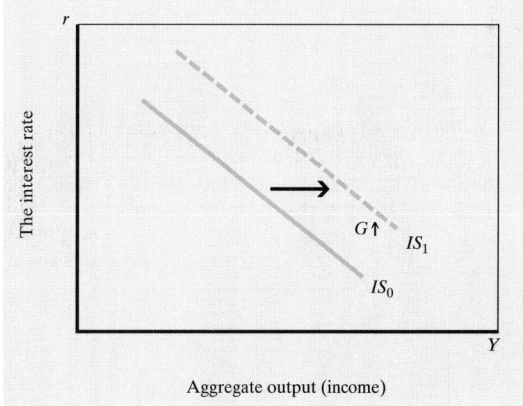

Aggregate output (income)

THE *LM* CURVE

In the money market, as we know, there is an equilibrium value of the interest rate (*r*) for every value of aggregate output (income) (*Y*). The equilibrium value of *r* is determined at the point at which the quantity of money demanded equals the quantity of money supplied. For a given value of *Y*, then, we can determine the equilibrium value of *r* in the money market. We also know from Figure 28.4 that the equilibrium value of *r* rises when *Y* rises and falls when *Y* falls. There is thus a *positive* relationship between the equilibrium values of *r* and *Y*. The reason for this positive relationship is the positive relationship between the demand for money and *Y*. When *Y* increases, the demand for money increases because more money is demanded for the increased volume of transactions in the economy. An increase in the demand for money, in turn, increases the equilibrium value of *r*. There is thus a positive relationship between the equilibrium values of *r* and *Y*.

---
[1]The letter *I* stands for investment, and the letter *S* stands for saving. *IS* refers to the fact that in equilibrium in the goods market, planned investment equals saving.

FIGURE 28A.2
The *LM* Curve

Each point on the *LM* curve corresponds to the equilibrium point in the money market for the given value of aggregate output (income). When the money supply (*M*^{s}) increases, the *LM* curve shifts to the right, from LM_0 to LM_1.

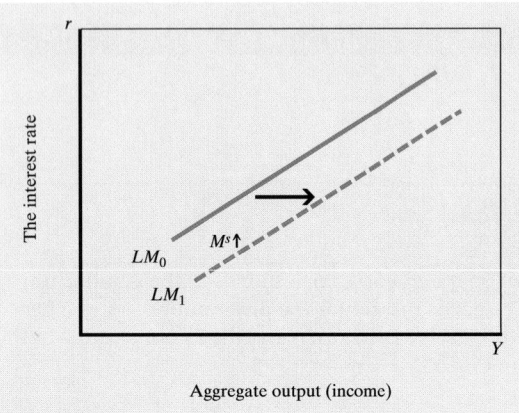

FIGURE 28A.3
The *IS-LM* Diagram

The point at which the *IS* and *LM* curves intersect corresponds to the point at which both the goods market and the money market are in equilibrium. The equilibrium values of aggregate output and the interest rate are Y_0 and r_0.

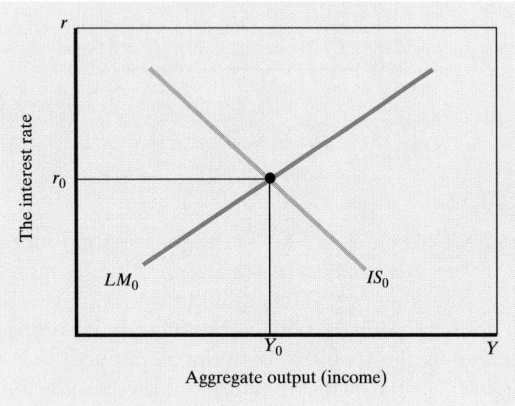

The positive relationship between the equilibrium values of *r* and *Y* is shown in Figure 28A.2. This curve is called the **LM curve**.[2] Each point on the *LM* curve represents equilibrium in the money market for the given value of aggregate output (income).

We also know from our analysis of the money market that when the money supply (*M*^{s}) increases with a constant level of *Y*, the equilibrium value of *r* decreases. As

[2]The letter *L* stands for liquidity, a characteristic of money, and the letter *M* stands for money.

FIGURE 28A.4
An Increase in Government Purchases (*G*)

When *G* increases, the *IS* curve shifts to the right. This increases the equilibrium value of both *Y* and *r*.

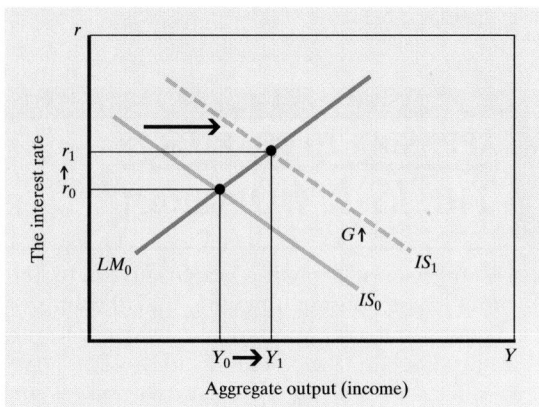

Figure 28A.2 shows, this means that the *LM* curve shifts to the right when *M*^{s} increases. With the same value of *Y* and a higher value of *M*^{s}, the equilibrium value of *r* is lower. Conversely, when *M*^{s} decreases, the *LM* curve shifts to the left.

THE *IS-LM* DIAGRAM

Figure 28A.3 shows the *IS* and *LM* curves together on one graph. The point at which the two curves intersect is the point at which equilibrium exists in *both* the goods market and the money market. There is equilibrium in the goods market because the point is on the *IS* curve, and there is equilibrium in the money market because the point is on the *LM* curve.

We now have only two tasks left. The first is to see how the equilibrium values of *Y* and *r* are affected by changes in *G*—that is, by fiscal policy. This is easy to do. We have just seen that an increase in *G* shifts the *IS* curve to the right. Thus, an increase in *G* leads to higher equilibrium values of *Y* and *r*. This situation is illustrated in Figure 28A.4. Conversely, a decrease in *G* leads to lower equilibrium values of *Y* and *r* because the lower level of *G* causes the *IS* curve to shift to the left. (The effects are similar for changes in net taxes, *T*.)

Our second task is to see how the equilibrium values of *Y* and *r* are affected by changes in *M*^{s}—that is, by monetary policy. This is also easy to do. We have just seen that an increase in *M*^{s} shifts the *LM* curve to the right. Thus, an increase in *M*^{s} leads to a higher equilibrium value of *Y* and a lower equilibrium value of *r*. This is illustrated in Figure 28A.5. Conversely, a decrease in *M*^{s} leads to a lower equilibrium value of *Y* and a higher equilibrium value of *r* because a decreased money supply causes the *LM* curve to shift to the left.

The *IS-LM* diagram is a useful way of seeing the effects of changes in monetary and fiscal policies on equilibrium aggregate output (income) and the interest rate through shifts in the two curves. You should always keep in mind, however, the economic theory that lies *behind* the two curves. Do not just memorize what curve shifts when, but always be able to go back and explain *why* the curves shift as they do. This means always going back to the behavior of households and firms in the goods and money markets.

On a final note, it is easy to use the *IS-LM* diagram to see how there can be a monetary and fiscal policy mix that leads to, say, an increase in aggregate output (income) but no increase in the interest rate. If both G and M^s increase, both curves shift to the right, and the shifts can be controlled in such a way as to bring about no change in the equilibrium value of the interest rate.

FIGURE 28A.5
An Increase in the Money Supply (M^s)

When M^s increases, the *LM* curve shifts to the right. This increases the equilibrium value of Y and decreases the equilibrium value of r.

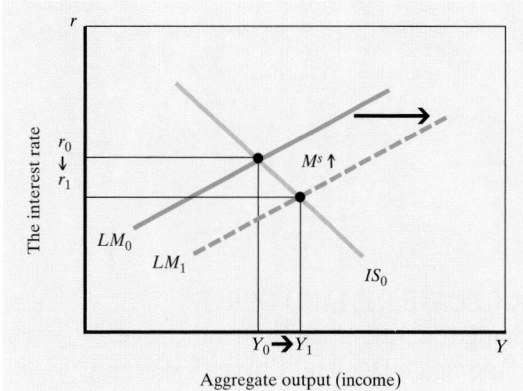

Aggregate output (income)

SUMMARY

1. An *IS curve* illustrates the negative relationship between the equilibrium values of aggregate output (income) *(Y)* and the interest rate in the goods market. An *LM curve* illustrates the positive relationship between the equilibrium values of aggregate output (income) *(Y)* and the interest rate in the money market. The point at which the IS and LM curves intersect is the point at which equilibrium exists in both the goods market and the money market.

REVIEW TERMS AND CONCEPTS

IS curve A curve illustrating the negative relationship between the equilibrium values of aggregate output (income) *(Y)* and the interest rate in the goods market.   711

LM curve A curve illustrating the positive relationship between the equilibrium values of aggregate output (income) *(Y)* and the interest rate in the money market.   712

PROBLEM SET

1. Illustrate each of the following situations with *IS/LM* curves:
   a. An increase in G with the money supply held constant by the Fed.
   b. An increase in G with Fed accommodation designed to hold interest rates constant.

   c. The president cuts G and increases T while the chair of the Fed expands M^s.
   d. The president increases G and holds T constant while the chair of the Fed holds M^s constant during a period of inflation.

29 Aggregate Demand, Aggregate Supply, and Inflation

This chapter considers one of the most important issues in macroeconomics: the determination of the overall price level. Recall that inflation—an increase in the overall price level—is one of the key concerns of macroeconomists and government policy makers. An understanding of the factors that affect the price level is essential to an understanding of macroeconomics.

In Chapter 23, we discussed how inflation is measured and the costs of inflation but made no mention of the *causes* of inflation. For simplicity, the analysis we did in Chapters 24 through 28 took the price level as fixed. This allowed us to discuss the links between the goods market and the money market without the added complication of a changing price level. Having considered how the two markets work, we are now ready to take up the case of flexible prices.

We begin this chapter by discussing the *aggregate demand curve* and the *aggregate supply curve,* which were introduced briefly in Chapter 21. We then put the two curves together and discuss how the equilibrium price level is determined in the economy. This analysis allows us to see both how the price level affects the economy and how the economy affects the price level. Finally, we consider monetary and fiscal policy effects and the causes of inflation.

THE AGGREGATE DEMAND CURVE

The best place to begin our exploration of the price level is the money market. (If you have forgotten some of the details of how the overall price level is calculated or what it means, you may wish to review Chapters 22 and 23.) As we saw in Chapter 27, people's demand for money depends on income (Y), the interest rate (r), and the price level (P).

It is not hard to understand why the price level affects the demand for money. Suppose you plan to purchase one pound of chocolate, one bag of potato chips, and a Hostess Twinkie. If these items cost $2.00, $1.00, and $.50 respectively, you would need $3.50 in cash or in your checking account in order to make your purchases. Now suppose that the price of these goods doubles. In order to make the same purchases, you now need $7.00.

In general, the amount of money required to facilitate a given number of transactions depends directly and proportionally on the average price of those transactions. A doubling of the price level will double the demand for money. As prices and wages rise, households will want to keep more in their wallets and in their checking accounts, firms will need more in their cash drawers, and so forth. If prices and wages are rising at 6% per year, for example, we can expect the demand for money to increase at about 6% per year, *ceteris paribus*.

To summarize what we know about money demand so far:

> Money demand is a function of three variables: the interest rate (r), the level of real income (Y), and the price level (P). (Remember that Y is real output, or income. It measures the actual volume of output, without regard to changes in the price level.) Money demand will increase if the real level of output (income) increases, the price level increases, or the interest rate declines.

Deriving the Aggregate Demand Curve

To derive the aggregate demand curve, we need to examine what happens to aggregate output (income) (Y) when the price level (P) changes. Does it increase, decrease, or remain constant when the price level increases? Our earlier discussions of the goods market and the money market provide us with the tools to answer this question.

The aggregate demand curve is derived under the assumption that the fiscal policy variables—government purchases (G) and net taxes (T)—and the monetary policy variable (M^s)—remain unchanged. In other words, it is assumed that the government does not take any action to affect the economy in response to changes in the price level. (Later in this chapter, we will see how the aggregate demand curve shifts in response to changes in G, T, and M^s.)

As you know, an increase in the price level increases the demand for money and shifts the money demand curve to the right. This situation is illustrated graphically in Figure 29.1a. At the initial interest rate of r_0, an increase in the price level leads to an excess demand for money. Because of the higher price level, households and firms need to hold larger money balances than they did before. However, the quantity of money supplied remains the same. (Remember, we are assuming that the Fed takes no action to change the money supply.) The money market is now out of equilibrium. Equilibrium is reestablished at a higher interest rate, r_1.

As indicated in Figure 29.1b, with the interest rate now higher, fewer investment projects are desirable, and planned investment spending (I) falls from I_0 to I_1. Lower I means that planned aggregate expenditure (AE) is lower. This effect is

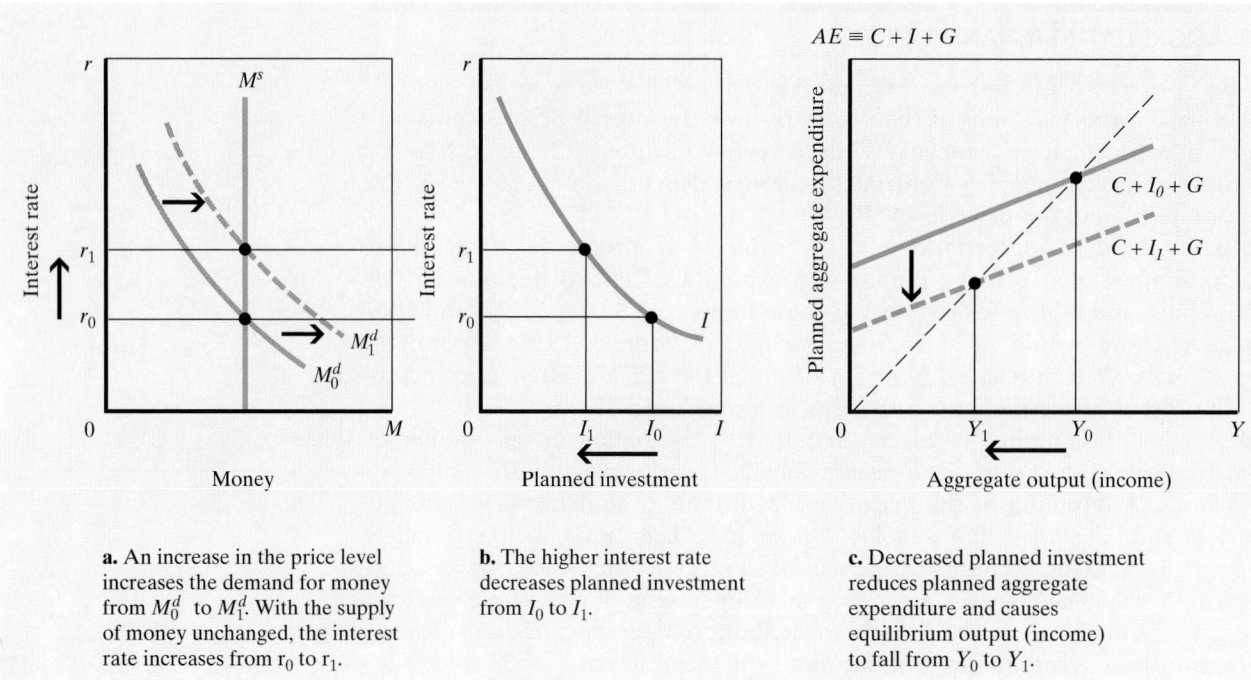

a. An increase in the price level increases the demand for money from M_0^d to M_1^d. With the supply of money unchanged, the interest rate increases from r_0 to r_1.

b. The higher interest rate decreases planned investment from I_0 to I_1.

c. Decreased planned investment reduces planned aggregate expenditure and causes equilibrium output (income) to fall from Y_0 to Y_1.

FIGURE 29.1
The Impact of an Increase in the Price Level on the Economy—Assuming No Changes in *G, T,* and M^s

shown in Figure 29.1c as a downward shift of the *AE* curve. Lower *AE* in turn means that inventories are greater than planned, firms cut back on output, and *Y* falls from Y_0 to Y_1. Thus, we can conclude that:

> An increase in the price level causes the level of aggregate output (income) to fall.

The situation is reversed when the price level declines. A lower price level causes money demand to fall, which leads to a lower interest rate. A lower interest rate stimulates planned investment spending and thus increases planned aggregate expenditure, which leads to an increase in *Y*. Thus, it is clear that:

> A decrease in the price level causes the level of aggregate output (income) to rise.

The curve that shows this negative relationship between aggregate output (income) and the price level is called the **aggregate demand (*AD*) curve.** The *AD* curve is plotted in Figure 29.2.

It is important to recognize that each point on the aggregate demand curve represents equilibrium in both the goods market *and* the money market. We have derived the *AD* curve by using the analysis we did in Chapter 28, in which the goods market and the money market were linked together. Therefore,

> Each pair of values of *P* and *Y* on the aggregate demand curve corresponds to a point at which both the goods market and the money market are in equilibrium.

aggregate demand (*AD*) curve
A curve that shows the negative relationship between aggregate output (income) and the price level. Each point on the AD curve is a point at which both the goods market and the money market are in equilibrium.

The Aggregate Demand Curve: A Warning

It is very important that you realize what the aggregate demand curve represents. As we pointed out in Chapter 21, the aggregate demand curve is much more complex than a simple individual or market demand curve. The *AD* curve is *not* a market demand curve, and it is *not* the sum of all market demand curves in the economy.

To understand why this is so, recall the logic behind a simple downward-sloping household demand curve. A demand curve shows the quantity of output demanded (by an individual household or in a single market) at every possible price *ceteris paribus*, or all else equal. Thus, in drawing a simple demand curve, we are assuming that *other prices* and *income* are fixed. From these assumptions, it follows that one of the reasons that the quantity demanded of a particular good falls when its price rises is that other prices do *not* rise. The good in question therefore becomes more expensive relative to other goods, which leads households to substitute other goods for the good whose price increased. In addition, if income does not rise when the price of a good does, real income falls. This may also lead to a lower quantity demanded of the good whose price has risen.

Things are different, however, when the *overall price level* rises. When the overall price level rises, many prices—including many wage rates (and thus many people's income)—rise together. For this reason, we cannot use the *ceteris paribus* assumption to draw the *AD* curve. Thus, the logic that explains why a simple demand curve slopes downward fails to explain why the *AD* curve also has a negative slope.

> Aggregate demand falls when the price level increases because the higher price level causes the demand for money (M^d) to rise. With the money supply constant, the interest rate will rise to reestablish equilibrium in the money market. *It is the higher interest rate that causes aggregate output to fall.*

To state this warning somewhat differently, you do not need to understand anything about the money market to understand a simple individual or market demand curve. However, to understand what the *aggregate* demand curve represents, you must understand the interaction between the goods market and the money market. Thus, the *AD* curve in Figure 29.2 embodies everything we have learned about the goods market and the money market up to now.

To reiterate:

> The *AD* curve is *not* the sum of all the market demand curves in the economy. It is *not* a market demand curve.

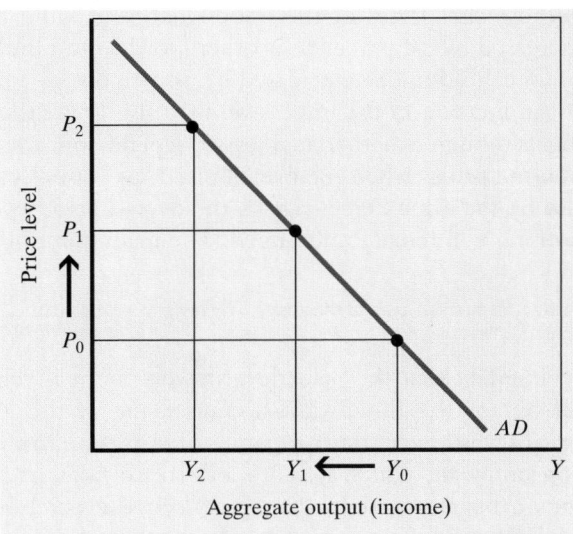

FIGURE 29.2

The Aggregate Demand (*AD*) Curve

At all points along the *AD* curve, both the goods market and the money market are in equilibrium.

Other Reasons for a Downward-Sloping Aggregate Demand Curve

In addition to the effects of money supply and money demand on the interest rate, two other factors lie behind the downward slope of the *AD* curve. These are the consumption link and the real wealth effect.

THE CONSUMPTION LINK   We noted in Chapter 24 (and will discuss in detail in Chapter 32) that, in reality, both consumption (*C*) and planned investment (*I*) depend on the interest rate. Other things being equal, consumption expenditures tend to rise when the interest rate falls and to fall when the interest rate rises—just as planned investment does. This provides another link between the goods market and the money market. If something happens to change the interest rate in the money market, both consumption and planned investment are affected in the goods market.

This *consumption link* provides another reason for the *AD* curve's downward slope. An increase in the price level increases the demand for money, which leads to an increase in the interest rate, which leads to a decrease in consumption (as well as planned investment), which leads to a decrease in aggregate output (income). The initial decrease in consumption (brought about by the increase in the interest rate) contributes to the overall decrease in output. Thus:

> Planned investment does not bear all the burden of providing the link from a higher interest rate to a lower level of aggregate output. Decreased consumption brought about by a higher interest rate also contributes to this effect.

THE REAL WEALTH EFFECT   We also noted in Chapter 24 (and will discuss in detail in Chapter 32) that consumption depends on wealth. Other things being equal, the more wealth households have, the more they consume. Wealth includes holdings of money, stocks, bonds, and housing, among other things. If household wealth decreases, the result will be less consumption both now and in the future.

The price level has an effect on some kinds of wealth. Suppose, for example, that you are holding $1000 in a checking account or in a money market fund and that the price level rises by 10 percent. Your holding is now worth 10% less because the prices of the goods that you could buy with your $1000 have all increased by 10 percent. In other words, the purchasing power (or "real value") of your holding has decreased by 10 percent.

An increase in the price level may also lower the real value of stocks and housing, although whether it does so depends on what happens to stock prices and housing prices when the overall price level rises. If stock prices and housing prices rise by the same percentage as the overall price level, the real value of stocks and housing will remain unchanged. The main point here, however, is that:

> An increase in the price level lowers the real value of *some* types of wealth.

real wealth, or real balance, effect The change in consumption brought about by a change in real wealth that results from a change in the price level.

The fact that the price level lowers the real value of wealth provides another reason for the downward-sloping shape of the *AD* curve. An increase in the price level lowers the real value of wealth. This, in turn, leads to a decrease in consumption, which leads to a decrease in aggregate output (income). There is thus a negative relationship between the price level and output through this **real wealth effect or real balance effect.**

Aggregate Expenditure and Aggregate Demand

Throughout our discussion of macroeconomics so far, we have referred to the total planned spending by households (C), firms (I), and the government (G) as planned aggregate expenditure. At equilibrium, planned aggregate expenditure ($AE \equiv C + I + G$) and aggregate output (Y) are equal:[1]

$$\text{Equilibrium condition: } C + I + G = Y.$$

Very often, economists use the term "aggregate demand" to refer to $C + I + G$, and the term "aggregate supply" to refer to actual output, Y. To avoid confusion, we have chosen to reserve the term *aggregate demand* to refer to the relationship between planned aggregate expenditure and the price level.

Nonetheless,

> At every point along the aggregate demand curve, the aggregate quantity demanded is exactly equal to planned aggregate expenditure, $C + I + G$.

You can see this in Figures 29.1 and 29.2. When the price level rises, it is planned aggregate expenditure that decreases, thus moving us down the aggregate demand curve.

But the term "aggregate demand," as we use it here, represents more than just planned aggregate expenditure. Each point on the AD curve represents the *particular* level of planned aggregate expenditure that is consistent with equilibrium in the goods market and money market. Notice that the variable on the horizontal axis of the aggregate demand curve in Figure 29.2 is Y. At every point along the AD curve, $Y = C + I + G$.

Shifts of the Aggregate Demand Curve

The aggregate demand curve in Figure 29.2 is based on the assumption that the government policy variables G, T, and M^s are fixed. If any of these variables change, the aggregate demand curve will shift.

Consider, for example, an increase in the quantity of money supplied. If the quantity of money is expanded at any given price level, the interest rate will fall, causing planned investment spending (and thus planned aggregate expenditure) to rise. The result is an increase in output at the given price level. Thus, as Figure 29.3 shows:

[1]If we include the rest of the world, the equilibrium condition is $C + I + G + (EX - IM) = Y$.

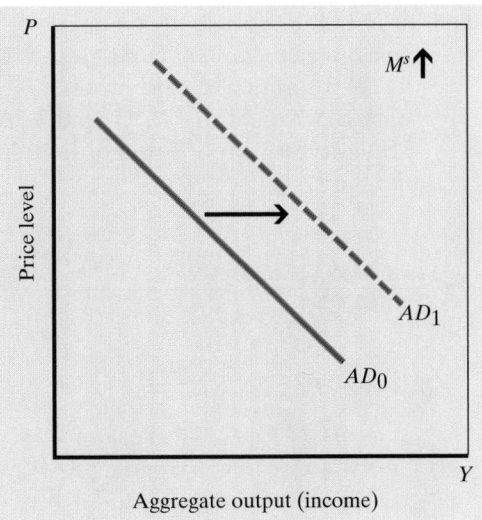

FIGURE 29.3

The Effect of an Increase in Money Supply on the *AD* Curve

An increase in the money supply (M^s) causes the aggregate demand curve to shift to the right, from AD_0 to AD_1. This shift occurs because the increase in M^s lowers the interest rate, which increases planned investment (and thus planned aggregate expenditure). The final result is an increase in output at each possible price level.

FIGURE 29.4

The Effect of an Increase in Government Purchases or a Decrease in Net Taxes on the *AD* Curve

An increase in government purchases (*G*) or a decrease in net taxes (*T*) causes the aggregate demand curve to shift to the right, from AD_0 to AD_1. The increase in *G* increases planned aggregate expenditure, which leads to an increase in output at each possible price level. A decrease in *T* causes consumption to rise. The higher consumption then increases planned aggregate expenditure, which leads to an increase in output at each possible price level.

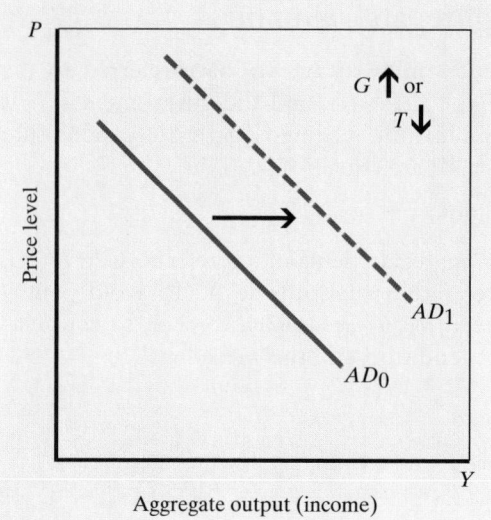

> An increase in the quantity of money supplied at a given price level shifts the aggregate demand curve to the right.

An increase in government purchases or a decrease in net taxes also increases aggregate output (income) at each possible price level, even though some of the increase will be crowded out if the money supply is held constant. (If you are unsure of what the crowding-out effect is, review the last chapter.) An increase in government purchases directly increases planned aggregate expenditure, which leads to an increase in output. A decrease in net taxes results in a rise in consumption, which increases planned aggregate expenditure, which also leads to an increase in output. Thus, as Figure 29.4 shows:

> An increase in government purchases or a decrease in net taxes shifts the aggregate demand curve to the right.

The same kind of reasoning applies to decreases in the quantity of money supplied, decreases in government purchases, and increases in net taxes. All of these cause the aggregate demand curve to shift to the *left*.

Figure 29.5 summarizes the ways in which the aggregate demand curve shifts in response to changes in M^s, *G,* and *T.* A good way to test your understanding of the *AD* curve is to go through the figure piece by piece and explain each of its components.

FIGURE 29.5

Shifts in the Aggregate Demand Curve: A Summary

Expansionary monetary policy

$M^s \uparrow \rightarrow AD$ curve shifts to the right.

Expansionary fiscal policy

$G \uparrow \rightarrow AD$ curve shifts to the right.

$T \downarrow \rightarrow AD$ curve shifts to the right.

Contractionary monetary policy

$M^s \downarrow \rightarrow AD$ curve shifts to the left.

Contractionary fiscal policy

$G \downarrow \rightarrow AD$ curve shifts to the left.

$T \uparrow \rightarrow AD$ curve shifts to the left.

THE AGGREGATE SUPPLY CURVE

The Aggregate Supply Curve: A Warning

The **aggregate supply (*AS*) curve** shows the relationship between the aggregate quantity of output supplied by all the firms in an economy and the overall price level. To understand the aggregate supply curve, we need to understand something about the behavior of the individual firms that make up the economy.

It may seem logical to think that we can derive the aggregate supply curve by simply adding together the supply curves of all the individual firms in the economy. However, the logic behind the relationship between the overall price level in the economy and the level of aggregate output (income)—that is, the *AS* curve—is very different from the logic behind an individual firm's supply curve. The aggregate supply curve is *not* a market supply curve, and it is *not* the simple sum of all the individual supply curves in the economy. (Recall that a similar warning holds for the aggregate demand curve.)

To understand why this is so, recall the logic behind a simple supply curve, which we first introduced in Chapter 4. A supply curve shows the quantity of output that an individual firm would supply at each possible price *ceteris paribus,* or all else equal. When we draw a firm's supply curve, we assume that input prices, including wage rates, are constant. Thus, an individual firm's supply curve shows what would happen to the firm's output if the price of its output changes with *no* corresponding increase in costs. Such an assumption for an individual firm is reasonable because an individual firm is small relative to the economy as a whole. (It is unlikely that one firm raising the price of its output will lead to significant increases in input prices in the economy.) If the price of a profit-maximizing firm's output rises with *no* increase in the costs of any inputs, the firm is likely to increase output.

But what would happen if there were an increase in the overall price level? It is unrealistic to believe that costs are constant for individual firms if the overall price level is increasing, for two reasons. First, the outputs of some firms are the inputs of other firms. Therefore, if output prices rise, there will be an increase in at least some input prices. Second, it is unrealistic to assume that wage rates (an important input cost) do not rise at all when the overall price level rises. Because all input prices (including wage rates) are not constant as the overall price level changes, individual firms' supply curves *shift* as the overall price level changes, so we cannot sum them to get an aggregate supply curve.

Another reason that the aggregate supply curve cannot be the sum of the supply curves of all the individual firms in the economy is that many firms (some would argue most firms) do not simply respond to prices determined in the market. Rather, they actually *set prices.* Only in perfectly competitive markets do firms simply react to prices determined by market forces. Firms in other kinds of industries (imperfectly competitive industries, to be exact) make both output *and* price decisions based on their perceptions of demand and costs. Price-setting firms do not have individual supply curves because these firms are choosing both output and price at the same time. To derive an individual supply curve, we need to imagine calling out a price to a firm and having the firm tell us how much output it will supply at that price. We cannot do this if firms are also setting prices.* Thus, if supply curves do not exist for imperfectly competitive firms, we certainly cannot add them together to get an aggregate supply curve!

What, then, can we say about the relationship between aggregate output and the overall price level? Because input prices change when the overall price level changes and because many firms in the economy set prices as well as output, it is clear that an "aggregate supply curve" in the traditional sense of the word "supply" does not exist. What does exist is what one might call a "price/output response" curve—that is, a curve that traces out the price decisions and output decisions of all the markets and firms in the economy under a given set of circumstances.

What might such a curve look like?

Aggregate Supply in the Short Run

Many would argue that the aggregate supply curve (or, better, the "price/output response" curve) has a positive slope, at least in the short run. (We will discuss the short-run/long-run distinction in more detail later in this chapter.) In addition, many would argue that at very low levels of aggregate output (for example, when the economy is in a recession), the aggregate supply curve is fairly flat, and at high levels of output (for example, when the economy is experiencing a boom), it is vertical or nearly vertical. Such a curve is shown in Figure 29.6.

To understand the logic behind the shape of the *AS* curve in Figure 29.6, consider the output and price response of markets and firms to a steady increase in aggregate demand brought about by an increasingly expansionary fiscal or monetary policy. The reaction of firms to such an expansion is likely to depend on two important factors: (1) how close the economy is to capacity at the time of the expansion, and (2) how rapidly input prices (such as wage rates) respond to increases in the overall price level.

---

*A much more complete discussion of the output and pricing behavior of imperfectly competitive firms (monopolists, oligopolists, and monopolistic competitors) is found in Chapters 13 and 14. See in particular Chapter 13 for a more detailed discussion of why supply curves do not exist for imperfectly competitive firms.

FIGURE 29.6

The Short-Run Aggregate Supply Curve

In the short run, the aggregate supply curve (the price/output response curve) has a positive slope. At low levels of aggregate output, the curve is fairly flat. As the economy approaches capacity, the curve becomes nearly vertical. At capacity, the curve is vertical.

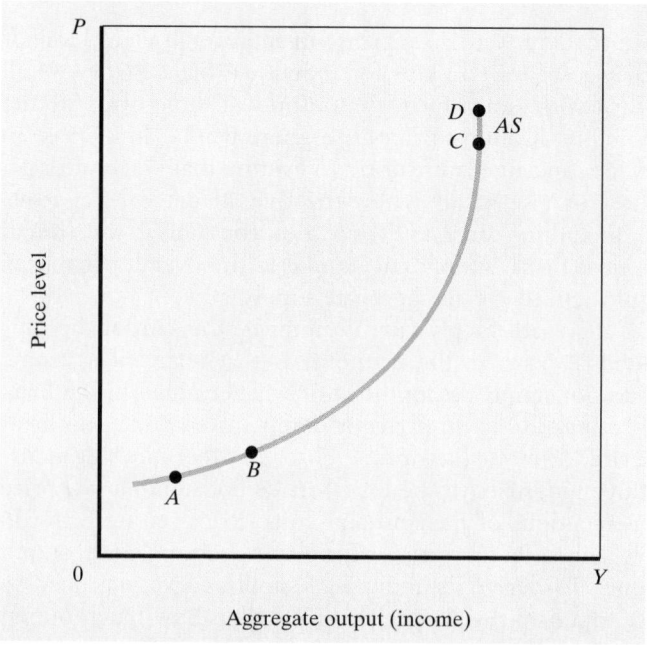

CAPACITY CONSTRAINTS   In microeconomics, the term "short run" is used to describe the period of time in which firms' decisions are constrained by some *fixed factor of production*. For example, a farmer is constrained in the short run by the number of acres of land on his or her farm—the amount of land owned is the fixed factor of production. Short-run production decisions of manufacturing firms are constrained by the size of their physical production facilities. In the longer run, these types of constraints for individual firms can be overcome by investing in greater capacity—for example, by purchasing more acreage or by building a new factory.

The idea of a fixed capacity in the short run also plays a role in macroeconomics. Macroeconomists tend to focus on the question of whether or not *individual firms* are producing at or close to full capacity. A firm is producing at full capacity if it is fully utilizing the capital and labor that it has on hand. As we will discuss in more detail in Chapter 32, firms may at times have *excess capital* and *excess labor* on hand—that is, capital and labor that are not needed to produce the current level of output. If, for example, there are costs of getting rid of capital once it is in place, a firm may choose to hold onto some of this capital, even if the economy is in a downturn and the firm has decreased its output. In this case, the firm will not be fully utilizing its capital stock. Firms may be especially likely to behave this way if they expect that the downturn will be short and that they will need the capital in the future to produce a higher level of output. Firms may have similar reasons for holding excess labor. It may be costly, both in worker morale and administrative costs, to lay off a large number of workers.

The Federal Reserve reports on the nation's "capacity utilization rate" monthly. In December of 1990, for example, during the recession of 1990–1991, the capacity utilization rate for manufacturing firms was 79.3 percent. This suggests that about 20% of the nation's factory capacity was idle.

Macroeconomists also focus on the question of whether or not the *economy as a whole* is operating at full capacity. If there is cyclical unemployment (that is, unemployment above the frictional and structural amounts), the economy is not fully utilizing its labor force. There are people who want to work at the current wage rates who cannot find jobs. Therefore,

> Even if firms are not holding excess labor and capital, the economy may be operating below its capacity if there is cyclical unemployment.

Output Levels and Price/Output Responses   At low levels of output in the economy, there is likely to be excess capacity both in individual firms and in the economy as a whole. Firms are likely to be producing at levels of output below their existing capacity constraints—that is, they are likely to be holding excess capital and labor. It is also likely that there will be cyclical unemployment in the economy as a whole in periods of low output. When this is the case, it is likely that firms will respond to an increase in demand by increasing output much more than they increase prices. Firms are below capacity, so the extra cost of producing more output is likely to be small. In addition, firms can get more labor (from the ranks of the unemployed) without much, if any, increase in wage rates. Thus,

> An increase in aggregate demand when the economy is operating at low levels of output is likely to result in an increase in output with little or no increase in the overall price level. That is, the aggregate supply (price/output response) curve is likely to be fairly flat at low levels of aggregate output.

Refer again to Figure 29.6. Aggregate output is considerably higher at point *B* than at point *A,* but the price level at point *B* is only slightly higher than it is at point *A*.

If aggregate output continues to expand, however, things will change. As firms and the economy as a whole begin to move closer and closer to capacity, the response of firms to an increase in demand is likely to change from one of primarily increasing output to one of primarily increasing prices. Why? As firms continue to increase their output, they will begin to bump into their short-run capacity constraints. In addition, unemployment will be falling as firms hire more workers to produce the increased output, so the economy as a whole will be approaching its capacity. As aggregate output rises, the prices of labor and capital (that is, input costs) will begin to rise more rapidly, thus leading firms to increase their output prices.

At some level of output, it is virtually impossible for firms to expand any further. At this level, all sectors are fully utilizing their existing factories and equipment. Plants are running double shifts, and many workers are on overtime. In addition, there is little or no cyclical unemployment in the economy. At this point, firms will respond to any further increases in demand only by raising prices. In other words:

> When the economy is producing at its maximum level of output—that is, at capacity—the aggregate supply curve becomes vertical.

Look again at Figure 29.6. Between points *C* and *D,* the *AS* curve is vertical. Moving from point *C* to point *D* results in no increase in aggregate output but a large increase in the price level.

THE RESPONSE OF INPUT PRICES TO CHANGES IN THE OVERALL PRICE LEVEL Whether or not the economy is producing a level of output close to capacity, there must be some time lag between changes in input prices and changes in output prices for the aggregate supply (price/output response) curve to slope upward. If input prices changed at exactly the same rate as output prices, the *AS* curve would be vertical.

It is easy to see why this is so. It is generally assumed that firms make decisions with the objective of maximizing profits. If all output and input prices increase 10%, no firm would find it advantageous to change its level of output. Why? Because the output level that maximized profits before the 10% increase will be the same as the level that maximizes profits after the 10% increase.[2] Thus, if input prices adjusted immediately to output prices, the aggregate supply (price/output response) curve would be vertical.

Wage rates may increase at exactly the same rate as the overall price level if the price-level increase is *fully anticipated.* For example, if inflation were expected to be 5% this year, this expected increase might be built into wage and salary contracts. Most employees, however, do not receive automatic pay raises as the overall price level increases, and sometimes increases in the price level are unanticipated. In fact, input prices—particularly wage rates—tend to lag behind increases in output prices for a variety of reasons. (We discuss these in the next chapter.) At least in the short run, wage rates tend to be slow to adjust

---

[2]All prices going up by the same percentage is analogous to changing the monetary unit of account from, say, green dollars to red dollars, where 1.1 red dollars equals one green dollar. A change in the monetary unit of account has no effect on the profit-maximizing decisions of firms. If the nominal value of all output and input prices increases by 10%, then nothing *real* happens. When all nominal values go up by 10%, firms' decisions regarding *real* output will not change.

to overall macroeconomic changes. It is precisely this point that has led to an important distinction between the *AS* curve in the long run and the *AS* curve in the short run.[3] We will return to this distinction shortly, but for now we will assume that the *AS* curve is shaped like the one in Figure 29.6.

Shifts of the Short-Run Aggregate Supply Curve

Just as the aggregate demand curve can shift, so too can the aggregate supply (price/output response) curve. Recall the individual firm behavior that we have just considered in describing the shape of the short-run *AS* curve. Firms with the power to set prices choose the price/output combinations that maximize their profits. Firms in perfectly competitive industries choose the quantities of output to supply at given price levels. The *AS* curve traces out these price/output responses to economic conditions.

Anything that affects these individual firm decisions can shift the *AS* curve. Some of these factors include cost shocks, economic growth, stagnation, public policy, and natural disasters.

COST SHOCKS Firms' decisions are heavily influenced by *costs*. Some costs change at the same time that the overall price level changes, some costs lag behind changes in the price level, and some may not change at all. Changes in costs that occur at the same time that the price level changes are built into the shape of the short-run *AS* curve. For example, when the price level rises, wage rates might rise by half as much in the short run. (This could happen if half of all wage contracts in the economy had cost-of-living increase clauses and half did not.) The shape of the short-run *AS* curve would reflect this response.

But sometimes cost changes occur that are *not* the result of changes in the overall price level. Perhaps the best recent example is the cost of energy. During the fall of 1990, world crude oil prices doubled from about $20 to $40 a barrel. Once it became clear that the Persian Gulf War would not lead to the destruction of the Saudi Arabian oil fields, the price of crude oil on world markets fell back to below $20 per barrel. On the other hand, in 1973–1974 and again in 1979, the price of oil increased substantially and remained at a higher level. Oil is an important input in many firms and industries, and when the price of firms' inputs rises, firms respond by raising prices and lowering output. (We will have more to say about the effects of import prices on costs in the next chapter.) At the aggregate level, this means that an increase in the price of oil (or a similar cost increase) *shifts* the *AS* curve to the left, as shown in Figure 29.7a. A leftward shift of the *AS* curve means a higher price level for a given level of output. Conversely, a decrease in costs shifts the *AS* curve to the right, as shown in Figure 29.7b. A rightward shift of the *AS* curve means a lower price level for a given level of output. Shifts in the *AS* curve brought about by a change in costs are referred to as **cost shocks** or **supply shocks**.

cost shock, or supply shock A change in costs that shifts the aggregate supply (AS) curve.

ECONOMIC GROWTH Economic growth shifts the *AS* curve to the right. Recall that the vertical part of the short-run *AS* curve represents the economy's maximum (capacity) output. This maximum output is determined by the existing resources of

---

[3]Some textbooks derive the short-run aggregate supply curve by assuming that *all* input prices are fixed. "Fixed input prices" means that input prices do not change as the overall price level changes. This assumption is obviously not realistic because the outputs of some firms (such as intermediate goods and capital goods) are the inputs of other firms. It is also unrealistic to assume that wage rates do not respond at all to changes in the overall price level. It is more realistic to assume that wage rates do not *fully* respond in the short run than it is to assume no response at all.

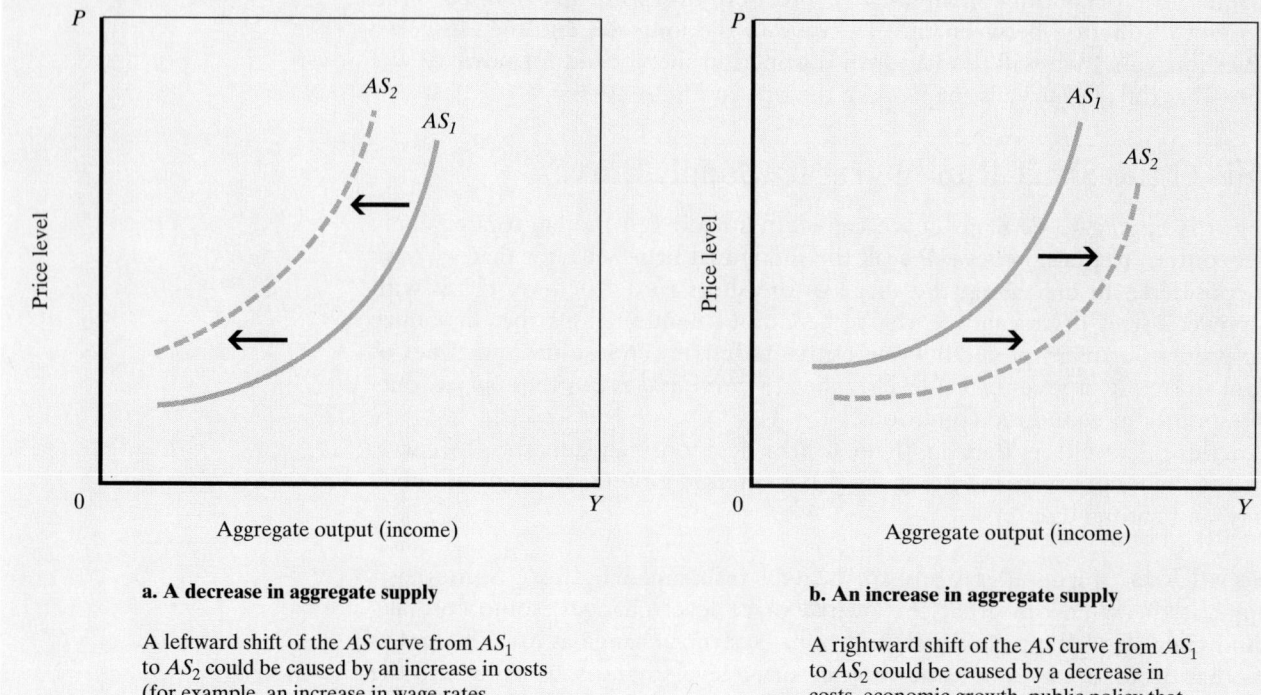

a. A decrease in aggregate supply

A leftward shift of the AS curve from AS_1 to AS_2 could be caused by an increase in costs (for example, an increase in wage rates or energy prices), natural disasters, economic stagnation, and the like.

b. An increase in aggregate supply

A rightward shift of the AS curve from AS_1 to AS_2 could be caused by a decrease in costs, economic growth, public policy that stimulates supply, and the like.

FIGURE 29.7
Shifts of the Aggregate Supply Curve

the economy and the current state of technology. If the supply of labor increases or the stock of capital grows, the AS curve will shift to the right. The labor force grows naturally with the population, but it can also increase for other reasons. Since the 1960s, for example, the percentage of women in the labor force has grown sharply, partly as a result of changing social attitudes toward women who work. This increase in the supply of women workers has shifted the AS curve to the right.

Immigration can also shift the AS curve. During the 1970s, Germany, faced with a serious labor shortage, opened its borders to large numbers of "guest workers," largely from Turkey. The United States has recently experienced significant immigration, legal and illegal, from Mexico, other Central and South American countries, and Asia. Increases in the stock of capital over time and technological advances can also shift the AS curve to the right. We will discuss economic growth in more detail in Chapter 35.

STAGNATION AND LACK OF INVESTMENT   The opposite of economic growth is stagnation and decline. Over time, capital deteriorates and eventually wears out completely if it is not properly maintained. If an economy fails to invest in both public capital (sometimes called *infrastructure*) and private capital (plant and equipment) at a sufficient rate, the stock of capital will decline. If the stock of capital declines, the AS curve will shift to the left.

PUBLIC POLICY   Public policy can also be used to shift the AS curve. In the 1980s, for example, the Reagan administration put into effect a form of public policy based on supply-side economics. The idea behind these supply-side policies was to deregulate the economy and reduce taxes to increase the incentives to work, engage in entrepreneurial activity, and invest. The main purpose of these policies was to shift the AS curve to the right. (We discuss supply-side economics in Chapter 34.)

FIGURE 29.8
Factors That Shift the
Aggregate Supply Curve

Shifts to the Right (Increases in Aggregate Supply)	Shifts to the Left (Decreases in Aggregate Supply)

■ *Lower costs*
  lower oil prices
  lower wage rates
	■ *Higher costs*
	  higher oil prices
	  higher wage rates

■ *Economic growth*
  more capital
  more labor
  technological change
	■ *Stagnation*
	  capital deterioration

■ *Public policy*
  supply-side policies
  tax cuts
  deregulation
	■ *Public policy*
	  waste and inefficiency
	  over-regulation

■ *Good weather*	■ *Bad weather, natural disasters, destruction from wars*

WEATHER, WARS, AND NATURAL DISASTERS   Changes in weather can also shift the *AS* curve. A severe drought, for example, will reduce the supply of agricultural goods, while the perfect mix of sun and rain will produce a bountiful harvest. If an economy is damaged by war or natural disaster, the *AS* curve will shift to the left. Whenever part of the resource base of an economy is reduced or destroyed, the *AS* curve shifts to the left.

Figure 29.8 summarizes some of the factors that might cause the *AS* curve to shift.

THE EQUILIBRIUM PRICE LEVEL

The **equilibrium price level** in the economy occurs at the point at which the *AD* curve and the *AS* curve intersect. This equilibrium is shown in Figure 29.9, where the equilibrium price level is P_0 and the equilibrium level of aggregate output (income) is Y_0.

Although Figure 29.9 looks simple, it is a powerful device for analyzing a number of important macroeconomic questions. Consider first what is true at the intersection of the *AS* and *AD* curves. Each point on the *AD* curve corresponds

equilibrium price level The point at which the aggregate demand and aggregate supply curves intersect.

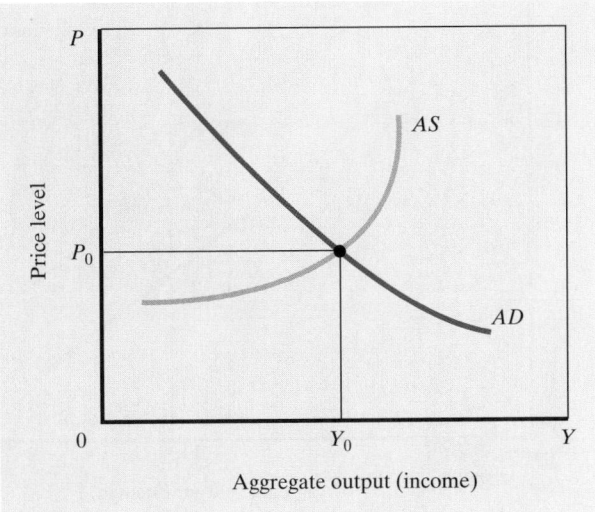

FIGURE 29.9
The Equilibrium Price Level
At each point along the *AD* curve, both the money market and the goods market are in equilibrium. Each point on the *AS* curve represents the price/output decisions of all the firms in the economy. P_0 and Y_0 correspond to equilibrium in the goods market and the money market and to a set of price/output decisions on the part of all the firms in the economy.

to equilibrium in both the goods market and the money market. Each point on the *AS* curve represents the price/output responses of all the firms in the economy. Thus, we can conclude that:

> The intersection of the *AS* and *AD* curves corresponds to equilibrium in the goods and money markets *and* to a set of price/output decisions on the part of all the firms in the economy.

We will use this *AS/AD* framework to analyze the effects of monetary and fiscal policy on the economy and to analyze the various causes of inflation. Before turning to these topics, however, we need to return to the *AS* curve and discuss its shape in the long run.

THE LONG-RUN AGGREGATE SUPPLY CURVE

As we noted earlier, for the *AS* curve not to be vertical, some costs must lag behind increases in the overall price level. If all prices (that is, both input and output prices) change at the same rate, the level of aggregate output does not change. We have assumed that in the short run at least some cost changes lag behind price level changes. But what happens in the long run?

Many economists believe that costs lag behind price-level changes in the short run but ultimately move with the overall price level. For example, wage rates tend to move very closely with the price level *over time*. If the price level increases at a steady rate, inflation may come to be fully anticipated and built into most labor contracts.

If costs and the price level move in tandem in the long run, the *AS* curve is vertical. To see why this is so, look carefully at Figure 29.10. Initially, the economy is in equilibrium at a price level of P_0 and aggregate output of Y_0 (the point at

FIGURE 29.10

The Long-Run Aggregate Supply Curve

When the *AD* curve shifts from AD_0 to AD_1, the equilibrium price level initially rises from P_0 to P_1 and output rises from Y_0 to Y_1. Costs respond in the longer run, shifting the *AS* curve from AS_0 to AS_1. If costs ultimately increase by the same percentage as the price level, the quantity supplied will end up back at Y_0. Y_0 is sometimes called "potential GDP."

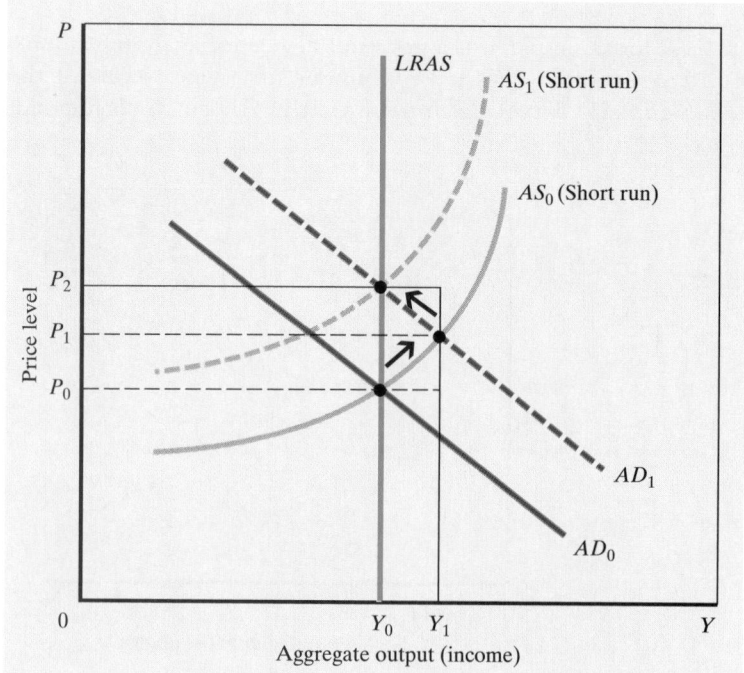

which AD_0 and AS_0 intersect). Now imagine a shift of the AD curve from AD_0 to AD_1. In response to this shift, both the price level and aggregate output rise in the short run, to P_1 and Y_1 respectively. But recall that the movement along the upward-sloping AS curve as Y increases from Y_0 to Y_1 assumes that some costs lag behind the increase in the overall price level.

Now suppose that costs *fully* adjust to prices in the long run. For example, suppose that labor unions renegotiate wage contracts to catch up with the increase in prices. These kinds of cost increases, which come in later periods, cause the AS curve to shift to the left, from AS_0 to AS_1. If, in the final analysis, costs and prices have risen by exactly the same percent, aggregate output will be back at Y_0 (the point at which AD_1 and AS_1 intersect). Thus,

> If wage rates and other costs fully adjust to changes in prices in the long run, then the long-run AS curve is vertical.

Potential GDP

Recall that even the short-run AS curve becomes vertical at some particular level of output. The vertical portion of the short-run AS curve exists because there are physical limits to the amount that an economy can produce in any given time period. At the physical limit, all plants are operating around the clock, many workers are on overtime, and there is no cyclical unemployment.

Note that the vertical portions of the short-run AS curves in Figure 29.10 are to the right of Y_0. If the vertical portions of the short-run AS curves represent "capacity," then what is the nature of Y_0, the level of output corresponding to the long-run AS curve?

Y_0 represents the level of aggregate output that can be *sustained* in the long run without inflation. It is sometimes called **potential output** or **potential GDP.** Output can be pushed above Y_0 under a variety of circumstances, but when it is, there is upward pressure on costs. As the economy approaches short-run capacity, wage rates tend to rise as firms try to attract more people into the labor force and to induce more workers to work overtime. Rising costs shift the short-run AS curve to the left (in Figure 29.10, from AS_0 to AS_1) and drive output back to Y_0.

The underlying idea here is simple. It is possible to try to squeeze too much from an existing resource base. Labor can be overemployed. In recent years, some states experienced unemployment rates below 3 percent. When the unemployment rate is this low, there is an upward pressure on wages that ultimately constrains growth.

potential output, or potential GDP The level of aggregate output that can be sustained in the long run without inflation.

MONETARY AND FISCAL POLICY EFFECTS

We are now ready to use the AS/AD framework to consider the effects of monetary and fiscal policy. We will first consider the short-run effects.

Recall that the two fiscal policy variables are government purchases (G) and net taxes (T). The monetary policy variable is the quantity of money supplied (M^s). An *expansionary* policy aims at stimulating the economy through an increase in G or M^s or a decrease in T. A *contractionary* policy aims at slowing the economy down through a decrease in G or M^s or an increase in T. We saw earlier in this chapter that an expansionary policy shifts the AD curve to the right and that a contractionary policy shifts the AD curve to the left. But how do these policies affect the equilibrium values of the price level (P) and the level of aggregate output (income)?

When considering the effects of a policy change, we must be careful to note where along the (short-run) AS curve the economy is at the time of the change. If the economy is initially on the flat portion of the AS curve, as shown by point A in Figure 29.11, then an expansionary policy, which shifts the AD curve to the right, results in a small price increase relative to the output increase: The increase in equilibrium Y (from Y_0 to Y_1) is much greater than the increase in equilibrium P (from P_0 to P_1). This is the case in which an expansionary policy works well. There is an increase in output with little increase in the price level.

If, on the other hand, the economy is initially on the steep portion of the AS curve, as shown by point B in Figure 29.12, then an expansionary policy results in a small increase in equilibrium output (from Y_0 to Y_1) and a large increase in the equilibrium price level (from P_0 to P_1). In this case, an expansionary policy does not work well. It results in a much higher price level with little increase in output. The multiplier is therefore close to zero: Output is initially close to capacity, and attempts to increase it further lead mostly to a higher price level.

Figures 29.11 and 29.12 show clearly that it is important to know where the economy is *before* a policy change is put into effect. The economy is producing on the nearly flat part of the AS curve if most firms are producing well below capacity. When this is the case, firms will respond to an increase in demand by increasing output much more than they increase prices. The opposite is true if the economy is producing on the steep part of the AS curve. In this case, firms are close to capacity, and they will respond to an increase in demand by increasing prices much more than they increase output.

To see what happens when the economy is on the steep part of the AS curve, consider the effects of an increase in G with no change in the money supply. Why, since G is increased, will there be virtually no increase in Y? In other words, why will the expansionary fiscal policy fail to stimulate the economy? To answer this question, we need to go back to the analysis we did in Chapter 28 and consider what is behind the AD curve.

The first thing that happens when G increases is an unanticipated decline in firms' inventories. However, because firms are very close to capacity output when the economy is on the steep part of the AS curve, they cannot increase their output very much. The result, as Figure 29.12 shows, is a substantial

FIGURE 29.11

A Shift of the Aggregate Demand Curve When the Economy Is on the Nearly Flat Part of the AS Curve

Aggregate demand can shift to the right for a number of reasons, including an increase in the money supply, a tax cut, or an increase in government spending. If the shift occurs when the economy is on the nearly flat portion of the AS curve, the result will be an increase in output with little increase in the price level.

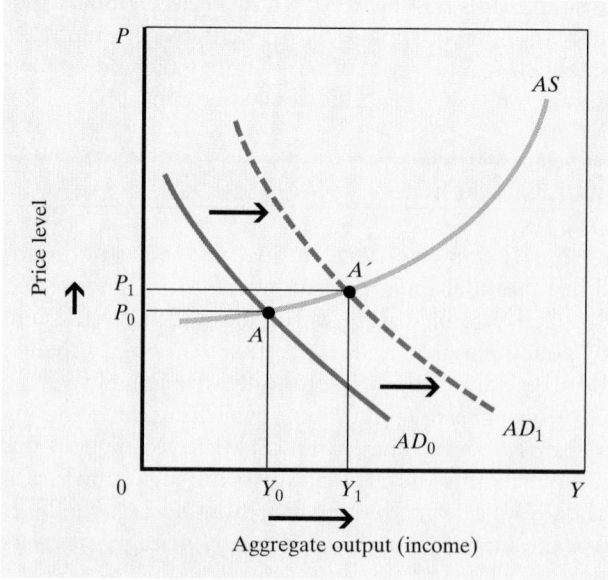

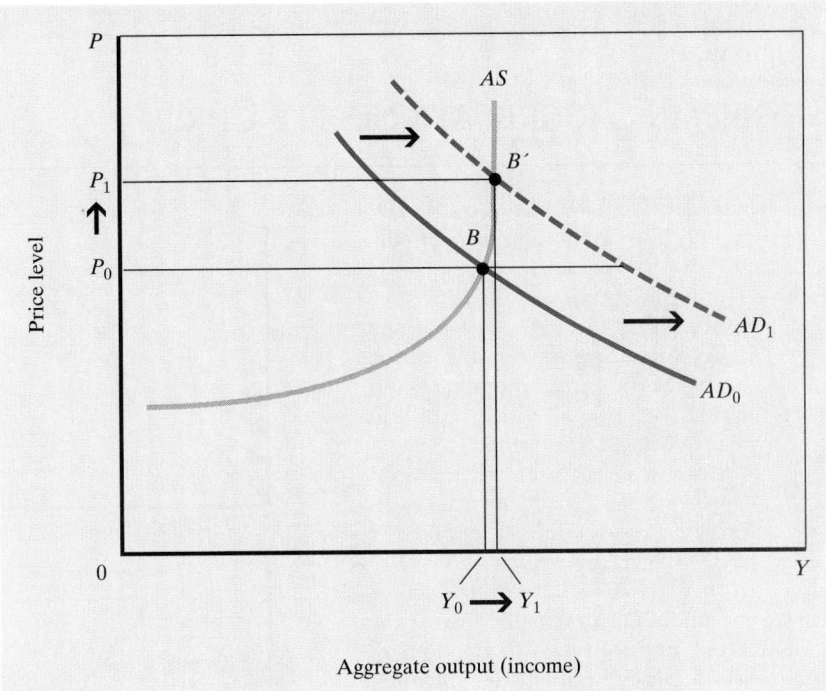

FIGURE 29.12

A Shift of the Aggregate Demand Curve When the Economy Is Operating at or Near Maximum Capacity

If a shift of aggregate demand occurs while the economy is operating near full capacity, the result will be an increase in the price level with little increase in output.

increase in the price level. The increase in the price level increases the demand for money, which (with a fixed money supply) leads to an increase in the interest rate and thus a decrease in planned investment. *There is nearly complete crowding out of investment.* If firms are producing at capacity, prices and interest rates will continue to rise until the increase in G is completely matched by a decrease in planned investment and there is complete crowding out.

Long-Run Aggregate Supply and Policy Effects

We have so far been considering monetary and fiscal policy effects in the short run. Regarding the long run, it is important to note that:

> If the AS curve is vertical in the long run, neither monetary policy nor fiscal policy has any effect on aggregate output in the long run.

Look back at Figure 29.10. Monetary and fiscal policy shift the AD curve. If the long-run AS curve is vertical, output always comes back to Y_0. In this case, policy affects *only* the price level in the long run, and the multiplier effect of a change in government spending on aggregate output in the long run is zero. Under the same circumstances, the tax multiplier is also zero.

The conclusion that policy has no effect on aggregate output in the long run is perhaps startling. Do most economists agree that the aggregate supply curve is vertical in the long run?

Most economists do agree that input prices tend to lag behind output prices in the short run, thus giving the AS curve some positive slope. Most also agree that the AS curve is likely to be steeper in the long run. The pressing question is: How long is the long run? The longer the lag time, the greater the potential impact of monetary and fiscal policy on aggregate output. If the long run is only three to six months, policy has little chance to affect output, but if the long run is three or four years, policy can have significant effects. It should not be surprising that a

THE SIMPLE "KEYNESIAN" AGGREGATE SUPPLY CURVE

As noted in the text, there is a great deal of disagreement regarding the shape of the AS curve. One view of the aggregate supply curve, often called the simple "Keynesian" view, holds that at any given moment, the economy has a clearly defined capacity, or maximum, output. This maximum output, denoted by the term Y_F, is defined by the existing labor force, the current capital stock, and the existing state of technology. If planned aggregate expenditure increases when the economy is producing *below* this maximum capacity, this view holds, inventories will be lower than planned and firms will increase output, but the price level will not change. Firms are operating with underutilized plants (excess capacity) and there is unemployment. Thus, expansion does not exert any upward pressure on prices. However, if planned aggregate expenditure increases when the economy is producing near or at its maximum (Y_F), inventories will be lower than planned, but firms cannot increase their output. The result will be an increase in the price level, or inflation.

This view is illustrated in Figure 1. In the top half of the diagram, aggregate output (income) (Y) and planned aggregate expenditure (AE) are initially in equilibrium at AE_1, Y_1, and price level P_1. Now suppose that a tax cut or an increase in government spending increases planned aggregate expenditure. If such an increase shifts the AE curve from AE_1 to AE_2 and the corresponding

aggregate demand curve from AD_1 to AD_2, the equilibrium level of output will rise from Y_1 to Y_F. (Remember that an expansionary policy shifts the AD curve to the right.) Since we were initially producing below capacity output (Y_1 is lower than Y_F), the price level will be unaffected, remaining at P_1.

But now consider what would happen if AE were to increase even further. For example, suppose that planned aggregate expenditure were to shift from AE_2 to AE_3, with a corresponding shift of AD_2 to AD_3. If the economy were producing below capacity output, the equilibrium level of output would rise to Y_3. But the output of the economy cannot exceed the maximum output of Y_F. Thus, as inventories fall below what was planned, firms encounter a fully employed labor market and fully utilized plants. Therefore, they cannot increase their output. The result is that aggregate supply becomes perfectly inelastic at Y_F, and the price level is driven up to P_3.

The difference between planned aggregate expenditure and aggregate output at full capacity is sometimes referred to as an **inflationary gap.** You can see the inflationary gap in the top half of Figure 1. At Y_F (capacity output), planned aggregate expenditure (shown by AE_3) is greater than Y_F. Thus, the price level rises to P_3 until the aggregate quantity supplied and the aggregate quantity demanded are equal.

Despite the fact that the kinked aggregate supply curve provides some

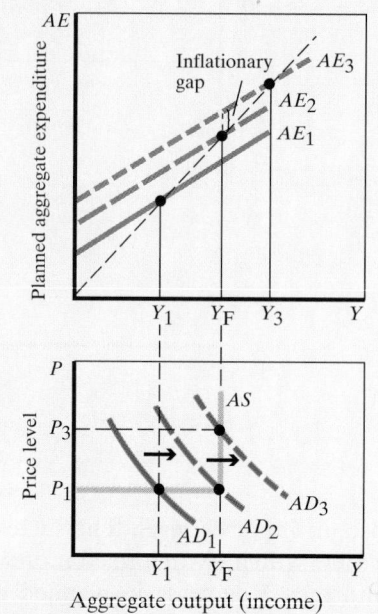

FIGURE 1

With planned aggregate expenditure of AE_1 and aggregate demand of AD_1, equilibrium output is Y_1. A shift of planned aggregate expenditure to AE_2, corresponding to a shift of the AD curve to AD_2, causes output to rise but the price level to remain at P_1. If planned aggregate expenditure and aggregate demand exceed Y_F, however, there is an inflationary gap and the price level rises to P_3.

insights, most economists find it unrealistic. It does not seem likely that the whole economy suddenly runs into a capacity "wall" at a specific level of output. As output expands, some firms and industries will hit capacity before others.

good deal of research in macroeconomics focuses on the length of time lags between input and output prices. In a sense, the length of the long run is one of the most important open questions in macroeconomics.

The "new classical" economics, which we discuss at length in Chapter 34, assumes that prices and wages are fully flexible and adjust very quickly to changing conditions. New classical economists believe, for example, that wage rate changes do not lag behind price changes. The new classical view is thus consistent with the existence of a vertical AS curve, even in the short run. At the other end of the spectrum is what is sometimes called the simple "Keynesian" view of aggregate supply. Those who hold this view believe that there is a kink in the AS curve at capacity output, as we discuss in the Issues and Applications box titled "The Simple 'Keynesian' Aggregate Supply Curve."

CAUSES OF INFLATION

We now turn to the question of inflation and use the AS/AD framework to consider the various causes of inflation.

INFLATION VERSUS SUSTAINED INFLATION: A REMINDER Before we discuss the specific causes of inflation, it is important to recall the distinction we made in Chapter 23. **Inflation,** as you know, is an increase in the overall price level. Thus, anything that shifts the AD curve to the right or the AS curve to the left causes inflation. But it is often useful to distinguish between a *one-time increase* in the price level (that is, a one-time inflation) and an inflation that is sustained. A **sustained inflation** occurs when the overall price level continues to rise over some fairly long period of time. When we speak of an inflation rate of 7%, for example, we generally mean that the price level has been rising at a rate of 7% per year over a number of years.

It is generally accepted that there are many possible causes of a one-time increase in the price level. (We discuss the main causes below.) But for the price level to continue to increase period after period, most economists believe that it must be "accommodated" by an expanded money supply. This leads to the assertion that a sustained inflation, whatever the initial cause of the increase in the price level, is essentially a monetary phenomenon.

Demand-Pull Inflation

Inflation that is initiated by an increase in aggregate demand is called **demand-pull inflation.** You can see how demand-pull inflation works by looking back at Figures 29.11 and 29.12. In both figures, the inflation begins with a shift of the aggregate demand schedule from AD_0 to AD_1, which causes the price level to increase from P_0 to P_1. (Output also increases, from Y_0 to Y_1.) If the economy is operating on the steep portion of the AS curve at the time of the increase in aggregate demand, as it is in Figure 29.12, most of the effect will be an increase in the price level rather than an increase in output. If the economy is operating on the flat portion of the AS curve, as it is in Figure 29.11, most of the effect will be an increase in output rather than an increase in the price level.

Remember that in the long run the initial increase in the price level will cause the AS curve to shift to the left as input prices (costs) respond to the increase in output prices. If the long-run AS curve is vertical, as depicted in Figure 29.10, the increase in costs will shift the short-run AS curve (AS_0) to the left to AS_1, pushing the price level even higher, to P_2. Thus, if the long-run AS curve is vertical, a shift in aggregate demand from AD_0 to AD_1 will result, in the long run, in *no* increase in output and a price-level increase from P_0 to P_2.

inflation An increase in the overall price level.

sustained inflation Occurs when the overall price level continues to rise over some fairly long period of time.

demand-pull inflation Inflation that is initiated by an increase in aggregate demand.

Cost-Push, or Supply-Side, Inflation

cost-push, or supply-side, inflation Inflation caused by an increase in costs.

Inflation can also be caused by an increase in costs. Such inflation is referred to as **cost-push,** or **supply-side, inflation.** As we noted above, several times in the last two decades oil prices on world markets increased sharply. Because oil is used in virtually every line of business, costs increased.

An increase in costs (a cost shock) shifts the AS curve to the left, as Figure 29.13 shows. If we assume that the government does not react to this shift in AS by changing fiscal or monetary policy, the AD curve will not shift. The supply shift will cause the equilibrium price level to rise (from P_0 to P_1) and the level of aggregate output to decline (from Y_0 to Y_1). Recall from Chapter 21 that **stagflation** occurs when output is falling at the same time that prices are rising—in other words, when the economy is experiencing both a contraction and inflation simultaneously. Figure 29.13 thus shows that one possible cause of stagflation is an increase in costs.

stagflation Occurs when output is falling at the same time that prices are rising.

To return to monetary and fiscal policy for a moment, note from Figure 29.13 that the government could counteract the increase in costs (the cost shock) by engaging in an expansionary policy (an increase in G or M^s or a decrease in T). This would shift the AD curve to the right, and the new AD curve would intersect the new AS curve at a higher level of output. The problem with this policy, however, is that the price level would be even higher than before. The intersection of the new AS and AD curves would take place at a price even higher than P_1 in Figure 29.13.

In sum:

> Cost shocks are bad news for policy makers. The only way they can counter the output loss brought about by a cost shock is by having the price level increase even more than it would without the policy action.

This situation is illustrated in Figure 29.14.

FIGURE 29.13

Cost-Push, or Supply-Side, Inflation

An increase in costs shifts the AS curve to the left. Assuming the government does not react to this shift so that the AD curve does not shift, the price level rises and output falls.

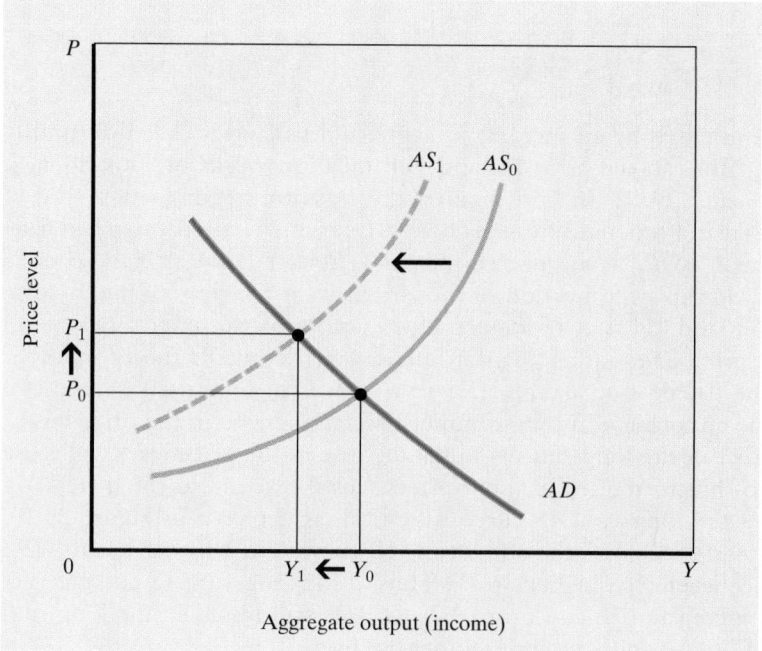

Expectations and Inflation

When firms are making their price/output decisions, their *expectations* of future prices may affect their current decisions. If a firm expects that its competitors will raise their prices, it may raise its own price in anticipation of this.

Take, for example, a firm that manufactures toasters. The toaster maker must decide what price to charge retail stores for its toaster. If it overestimates price and charges much more than other toaster manufacturers are charging, it will lose many customers. Conversely, if it underestimates price and charges much less than other toaster makers are charging, it will gain customers but at a considerable loss in revenue per sale. The firm's *optimum price*—that is, the price that maximizes the firm's profits—is presumably not too far from the average of its competitors' prices. If it does not know its competitors' projected prices before it sets its own price, as is often the case, it must base its price on what it expects its competitors' prices to be.

Suppose that inflation has been running at a rate of about 10% per year. Our firm probably expects that its competitors will raise their prices about 10% this year, so it is likely to raise the price of its own toaster by about 10 percent. This is how expectations can get "built into the system." If every firm expects every other firm to raise prices by 10%, every firm will raise prices by about 10 percent. Thus, every firm ends up with the price increase it expected.

The story is the same for the pricing of an economics textbook. Every publisher finds the optimal price for its textbook close to the price that other publishers are charging for their economics textbooks. A publisher thus bases its price on what its competitors are doing now and what it expects them to do in the future. At the same time, the publisher's competitors base *their* prices on what their rivals are doing now and what they expect them to do in the future.

The fact that expectations can affect the price level is vexing. Expectations can lead to an inertia that makes it difficult to stop an inflationary spiral. If prices have been rising, and if people's expectations are *adaptive*—that is, if they form their

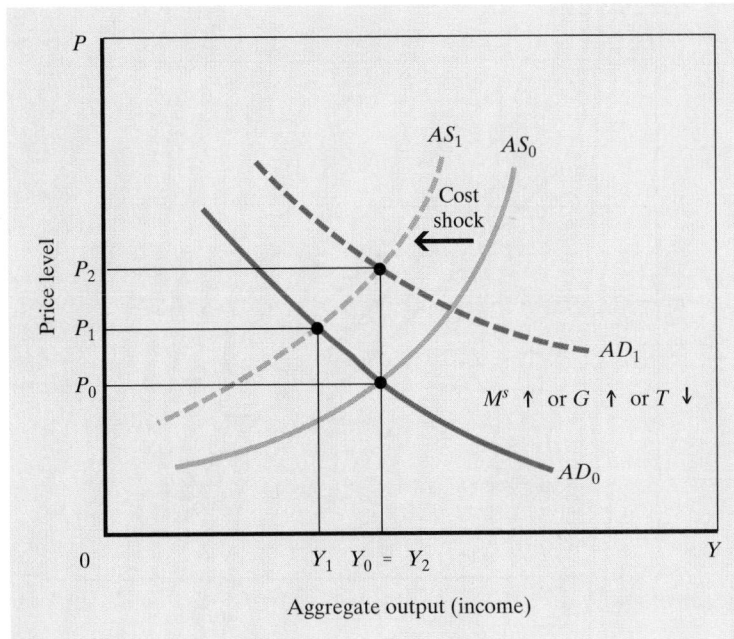

FIGURE 29.14
Cost Shocks Are Bad News for Policy Makers

A cost shock with no change in monetary or fiscal policy would shift the aggregate supply curve from AS_0 to AS_1, lower output from Y_0 to Y_1, and raise the price level from P_0 to P_1. Monetary or fiscal policy could be changed enough to have the AD curve shift from AD_0 to AD_1. This would prevent output from falling, but it would raise the price level further, to P_2.

expectations on the basis of past pricing behavior—then firms may continue raising prices even if demand is slowing or contracting.

In terms of the AS/AD diagram, an increase in inflationary expectations that causes firms to increase their prices shifts the AS curve to the left. Remember that the AS curve represents the price/output responses of firms. If firms increase their prices because of a change in inflationary expectations, the result is a leftward shift of the AS curve.

Money and Inflation

It is easy to see that an increase in the money supply can lead to an increase in the aggregate price level. As Figure 29.14 shows, an increase in the money supply (M^s) shifts the AD curve to the right and results in a higher price level. This is simply a demand-pull inflation.

But the supply of money may also play a role in creating a sustained inflation. Consider an initial increase in government spending (G) with the money supply (M^s) unchanged. Because the money supply is unchanged, this is an increase in G that is not "accommodated" by the Fed. The increase in G shifts the AD curve to the right and results in a higher price level. This is shown in Figure 29.15 as a shift from AD_0 to AD_1. (In Figure 29.15, the economy is assumed to be operating on the vertical portion of the AS curve.)

Remember what happens when the price level increases. The higher price level causes the demand for money to increase. With an unchanged money supply and an increase in the quantity of money demanded, the interest rate will rise, and the result will be a decrease in planned investment (I) spending. The new equilibrium corresponds to higher G, lower I, a higher interest rate, and a higher price level.

Now let's take our example one step further. Suppose that the Fed is sympathetic to the expansionary fiscal policy (the increase in G we just discussed) and decides to expand the supply of money to keep the interest rate constant. Thus, as

FIGURE 29.15

Sustained Inflation from an Initial Increase in G and Fed Accommodation

An increase in G with the money supply constant shifts the AD curve from AD_0 to AD_1. Although not shown in the figure, this leads to an increase in the interest rate and crowding out of planned investment. If the Fed tries to keep the interest rate unchanged by increasing the money supply, the AD curve will shift farther and farther to the right. The result is a sustained inflation, perhaps a hyperinflation.

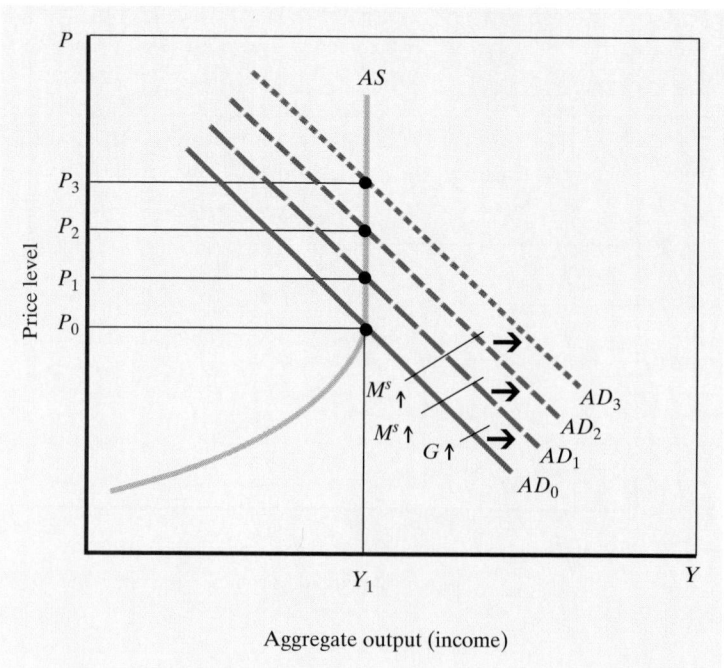

the higher price level pushes up the demand for money, the Fed expands the supply of money with the goal of keeping the interest rate unchanged and thus eliminating the crowding-out effect of a higher interest rate.

When the supply of money is expanded, the AD curve shifts to the right again, from AD_1 to AD_2. This shift of the AD curve, brought about by the increased money supply, pushes prices up even further. Higher prices in turn increase the demand for money further, which requires a further increase in the money supply, and so on.

What would happen if the Fed tried to keep the interest rate constant when the economy is operating on the steep part of the AS curve? The situation could lead to a **hyperinflation,** a period of very rapid increases in the price level. If no more output can be coaxed out of the economy and if planned investment is not allowed to fall (because the interest rate is kept unchanged), then it is not possible to increase G. As the Fed keeps pumping more and more money into the economy to keep the interest rate unchanged, the price level will keep rising.

hyperinflation A period of very rapid increases in the price level.

Sustained Inflation as a Purely Monetary Phenomenon

As we mentioned earlier, virtually all economists agree that an increase in the price level can be caused by anything that causes the AD curve to shift to the right or the AS curve to shift to the left. These include expansionary fiscal policy actions, monetary expansion, cost shocks, changes in expectations, and so forth. It is also generally agreed, however, that for a *sustained* inflation to occur, the Federal Reserve must accommodate it. In this sense, a sustained inflation can be thought of as a purely monetary phenomenon.

This argument, first put forth by monetarists (see Chapter 34), has gained wide acceptance. It is easy to show, as we just did, how expanding the money supply can continuously shift the AD curve. However, it is not as easy to come up with other reasons for continued shifts of the AD curve. One possibility is for the government to increase spending continuously without increasing taxes. But this process cannot continue forever. To finance spending without taxes, the government must borrow. Without any expansion of the money supply, the interest rate will rise dramatically, making the cost of borrowing very high. But more importantly, the public must be willing to buy the government bonds that are being issued to finance the spending increases. At some point, the public may be unwilling to buy any more bonds even though the interest rate is very high.[4] At this point, the government is no longer able to increase non-tax-financed spending without the Fed's cooperation. If this is true, then a sustained inflation cannot exist without the Fed's cooperation.

LOOKING AHEAD

Let us review where we have been and where we are going. In Chapters 24 and 25, we discussed the concept of an equilibrium level of aggregate output and income, the idea of the multiplier, and the basics of fiscal policy. Our discussion in those two chapters centered on the workings of the goods market alone.

---

[4]This means that the public's demand for money no longer depends on the interest rate. Even though the interest rate is very high, the public cannot be induced to have its real money balances fall any further. In other words, there is a limit regarding how much the public can be induced to have its real money balances fall.

In Chapters 26 and 27, we analyzed the money market by discussing the supply of money, the demand for money, the equilibrium interest rate, and the basics of monetary policy. Chapter 28 brought our analysis of the goods market together with our analysis of the money market.

In this chapter, we used everything learned up to this point to discuss the aggregate supply and aggregate demand curves, first mentioned in Chapter 21. Using aggregate supply and aggregate demand curves, we can determine the equilibrium price level in the economy and understand some of the causes of inflation.

There is still one piece missing to our story, however. We have said little about employment, unemployment, and the functioning of the labor market in the macroeconomy. The next chapter will link everything we have done so far to this third major market arena—the labor market—and to the problem of unemployment.

SUMMARY

The Aggregate Demand Curve

1. Money demand is a function of three variables: (1) the interest rate (r); (2) the level of real income (Y); and (3) the price level (P). Money demand will increase if the level of output (income) increases, the price level increases, or the interest rate declines.

2. At a higher price level, households and firms need to hold larger money balances than they did before. If the money supply remains the same, this increased demand for money will cause the interest rate to increase and planned investment spending to fall. As a result, planned aggregate expenditure will be lower, inventories will be greater than planned, firms will cut back on output, and Y will fall. Thus, an increase in the price level causes the level of aggregate output (income) to fall. Conversely, a decrease in the price level causes the level of aggregate output (income) to rise.

3. *The aggregate demand (AD) curve* illustrates the negative relationship between aggregate output (income) and the price level. Each point on the AD curve is a point at which both the goods market and the money market are in equilibrium. The AD curve is *not* the sum of all the market demand curves in the economy.

4. At every point along the aggregate demand curve, the aggregate quantity demanded in the economy is exactly equal to planned aggregate expenditure.

5. An increase in the quantity of money supplied, an increase in government purchases, or a decrease in net taxes at a given price level shifts the aggregate demand curve to the right. A decrease in the quantity of money supplied, a decrease in government purchases, or an increase in net taxes shifts the aggregate demand curve to the left.

The Aggregate Supply Curve

6. The *aggregate supply (AS) curve* shows the relationship between the aggregate quantity of output supplied by all the firms in an economy and the overall price level. The AS curve is *not* a market supply curve, and it is *not* the simple sum of all the individual supply curves in the economy. For this reason, it is helpful to think of the AS curve as a "price/output response" curve—that is, a curve that traces out the price decisions and output decisions of all the markets and firms in the economy under a given set of circumstances.

7. The shape of the AS curve is a source of much controversy in macroeconomics. Many economists believe that at very low levels of aggregate output the AS curve is fairly flat, and at high levels of aggregate output the AS curve is vertical or nearly vertical. Thus, the AS curve slopes upward and becomes vertical when the economy reaches its capacity, or maximum, output.

8. Anything that affects individual firms' decisions can shift the AS curve. Some of these factors include cost shocks, economic growth, stagnation, public policy, and natural disasters.

The Equilibrium Price Level

9. The *equilibrium price level* in the economy occurs at the point at which the AS and AD curves intersect. The intersection of the AS and AD curves corresponds to equilibrium in the goods and money markets *and* to a set of price/output decisions on the part of all the firms in the economy.

The Long-Run Aggregate Supply Curve

10. For the AS curve to slope upward, some input prices must lag behind increases in the overall price level. If wage rates and other costs fully adjust to changes in prices in the long run, then the long-run AS curve is vertical.

11. The level of aggregate output that can be sustained in the long run without inflation is called *potential output* or *potential GDP*.

Monetary and Fiscal Policy Effects

12. If the economy is initially producing on the flat portion of the AS curve, an expansionary policy—which shifts the AD curve to the right—will result in a small increase in the equilibri-

um price level relative to the increase in equilibrium output. If the economy is initially producing on the steep portion of the *AS* curve, an expansionary policy results in a small increase in equilibrium output and a large increase in the equilibrium price level.

13. If the *AS* curve is vertical in the long run, neither monetary nor fiscal policy has any effect on aggregate output in the long run. For this reason, the exact length of the long run is one of the most pressing questions in macroeconomics.

Causes of Inflation

14. *Inflation* is an increase in the overall price level. A *sustained inflation* occurs when the overall price level continues to rise over some fairly long period of time. Most economists believe that sustained inflations can occur only if the Fed continuously increases the money supply.

15. *Demand-pull inflation* is inflation initiated by an increase in aggregate demand. *Cost-push, or supply-side, inflation* is inflation initiated by an increase in costs. An increase in costs may also lead to *stagflation*—the situation in which the economy is experiencing both a contraction and inflation simultaneously.

16. Inflation can become "built into the system" as a result of expectations. If prices have been rising and people form their expectations on the basis of past pricing behavior, firms may continue raising prices even if demand is slowing or contracting.

17. When the price level increases, so too does the demand for money. If the economy is operating on the steep part of the *AS* curve and the Fed tries to keep the interest rate constant by increasing the supply of money, the result could be a *hyperinflation*—a period of very rapid increases in the price level.

REVIEW TERMS AND CONCEPTS

aggregate demand (*AD*) curve   716
aggregate supply (*AS*) curve   721
cost-push, or supply-side,
    inflation   734
cost shock, or supply shock   725

demand-pull inflation   733
equilibrium price level   727
hyperinflation   737
inflation   733
inflationary gap   732

potential output, or potential GDP   729
real wealth, or real balance,
    effect   718
stagflation   734
sustained inflation   733

PROBLEM SET

1. "The aggregate demand curve slopes downward, because when the price level is lower, people can afford to buy more, and aggregate demand rises. When prices rise, people can afford to buy less, and aggregate demand falls." Is this a good explanation of the shape of the *AD* curve? Why or why not?

2. Using aggregate supply and demand curves to illustrate your points, discuss the impacts of the following events on the price level and on equilibrium GDP (*Y*) in the *short run:*
    a. A tax cut holding government purchases constant with the economy operating at near full capacity.
    b. An increase in the money supply during a period of high unemployment and excess industrial capacity.
    c. An increase in the price of oil caused by a war in the Middle East, assuming that the Fed attempts to keep interest rates constant by accommodating inflation.
    d. The Clinton plan from early 1993: an increase in taxes and a cut in government spending, supported by a cooperative Fed acting to keep output from falling.

3. Using aggregate supply and demand curves to illustrate, describe the effects of the following events on the price level and on equilibrium GDP in the *long run* assuming that input prices fully adjust to output prices after some lag:
    a. An increase in the money supply above potential GDP.
    b. A decrease in government spending and in the money supply with GDP above potential GDP.
    c. Starting with the economy at potential GDP, a war in the Middle East pushes up energy prices. The Fed expands the money supply to accommodate the inflation.

4. Two separate capacity constraints are discussed in this chapter: (1) the actual physical capacity of existing plants and equipment, shown as the vertical portion of the short-run *AS* curve, and (2) potential GDP, leading to a vertical *LRAS* curve. Explain the difference between the two. Which is greater, full-capacity GDP or potential GDP? Why?

5. In country A, all wage contracts are indexed to inflation. That is, each month wages are adjusted to reflect increases in the cost of living as reflected in changes in the price level. In country B, there are no cost-of-living adjustments to wages, but the work force is completely unionized. Unions negotiate three-year contracts. In which country is an expansionary monetary policy likely to have a larger effect on aggregate output? Explain your answer using aggregate supply and aggregate demand curves.

6. In an effort to fight inflation in 1974 and 1975, the U.S. government acted with contractionary monetary policy. Using aggregate supply and aggregate demand curves, illustrate the effects that the government expected this policy to have on aggregate output and on the price level.

The contractionary monetary policy had the effect of reducing aggregate output; the United States experienced a recession in 1975. But although output was reduced, prices continued to increase throughout the recession. Give two alternative explanations for why prices might continue to rise even though output is falling.

30 The Labor Market, Unemployment, and Inflation

In Chapter 21, we stressed that there are three broadly defined markets in which households, firms, the government, and the rest of the world interact: (1) the *goods market,* which we discussed in Chapters 24 and 25, (2) the *money market,* which we discussed in Chapters 26 and 27, and (3) the *labor market.* In Chapter 23 we described some of the features of the U.S. labor market and explained how the unemployment rate is measured. Then, in Chapter 29, we considered the labor market briefly in our discussion of the aggregate supply curve. Because labor is an input, the workings of the labor market affect the shape of the *AS* curve. If wages and other input costs lag behind price increases, the *AS* curve will be upward-sloping; if wages and other input costs are completely flexible and rise every time prices rise by the same percentage, the *AS* curve will be vertical.

In this chapter we take a closer look at the labor market's role in the macroeconomy. First, we consider the classical view, which holds that wages always adjust to clear the labor market. We then consider why the labor market may not always clear and why unemployment may sometimes exist. Finally, we discuss the relationship between inflation and unemployment.

THE LABOR MARKET: BASIC CONCEPTS   Before beginning, it is useful to review briefly what the unemployment rate measures. Recall that the **unemployment rate** is the number of people unemployed as a percentage of the labor force. To be unemployed, a person must be out of a job and actively looking for work. When a person stops looking for work, he or she is considered *out of the labor force* and is no longer counted as unemployed. (See the Issues and Applications box later in this chapter titled "The Supply of Labor During the Recession of 1990–1991" for a discussion of the effects of discouraged workers on the unemployment rate.)

It is important to remember that even if the economy is running at or near full capacity, the unemployment rate will never be zero. The economy is dynamic. Students graduate from schools and training programs; some businesses make profits and grow, while others suffer losses and go out of business; people move in and out of the labor force and change careers. It takes time for people to find the right job and for employers to match the right worker with the jobs they have to fill. This **frictional** and **structural unemployment** is inevitable and in many ways desirable. (Review Chapter 23 if these terms are hazy to you.)

In this chapter, we are concerned with **cyclical unemployment,** the increase in unemployment that occurs during recessions and depressions. When the economy contracts, the number of people unemployed and the unemployment rate rise. The United States has experienced several periods of high unemployment. During the Great Depression, the unemployment rate remained over 17% for nearly a decade. In December of 1982, more than 12 million people were unemployed, putting the unemployment rate at 10.8 percent.

In one sense, the reason that employment falls when the economy experiences a downturn is obvious. When firms cut back on production, they need fewer workers, so people get laid off. Thus,

> Employment tends to fall when aggregate output falls and rise when aggregate output rises.

But a decline in the demand for labor does not necessarily mean that unemployment will rise. If markets work as we described in Chapters 4 and 5, a decline in the demand for labor will initially create an excess supply of labor. As a result, the wage rate will fall until the quantity of labor supplied again equals the quantity of labor demanded, thus restoring equilibrium in the labor market. At the new lower wage rate, everyone who wants a job will have one.

If the quantity of labor demanded and the quantity of labor supplied are brought into equilibrium by rising and falling wage rates, there should be no persistent unemployment above the frictional and structural amount. Indeed, this was the view held by the classical economists who preceded Keynes, and it is still the view of a number of economists today.

THE CLASSICAL VIEW OF THE LABOR MARKET

The classical view of the labor market is illustrated in Figure 30.1 on the next page. Classical economists assumed that the wage rate adjusts to equate the quantity of labor demanded with the quantity of labor supplied, thereby implying that unemployment does not exist. To see how this adjustment takes place, assume that there is a decrease in the demand for labor that shifts the demand curve in Figure 30.1 from D_0 to D_1. This decreased demand will cause the wage rate to fall from W_0 to W^* and the amount of labor demanded to fall from L_0 to L^*. The decrease in the quantity of labor supplied is a movement along the labor supply curve.

unemployment rate The ratio of the number of people unemployed to the total number of people in the labor force.

frictional unemployment The portion of unemployment that is due to the normal working of the labor market; used to denote short-run job/skill matching problems.

structural unemployment The portion of unemployment that is due to changes in the structure of the economy that result in a significant loss of jobs in certain industries.

cyclical unemployment The increase in unemployment that occurs during recessions and depressions.

FIGURE 30.1
The Classical Labor Market

Classical economists believe that the labor market always clears. If the demand for labor shifts from D_0 to D_1, the equilibrium wage will fall from W_0 to W^*. Everyone who wants a job at W^* will have one.

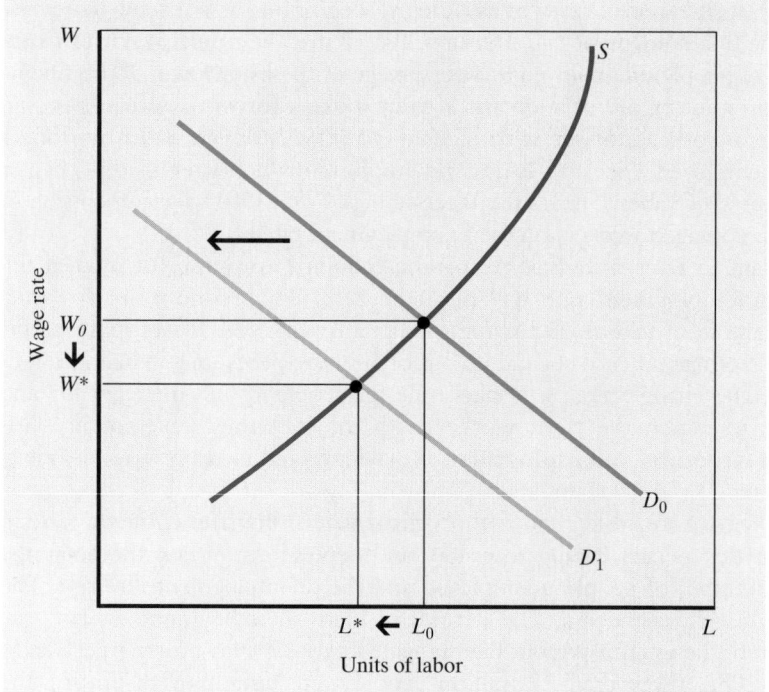

labor supply curve A graph that illustrates the amount of labor that households want to supply at the particular wage rate.

Each point on the **labor supply curve** in Figure 30.1 represents the amount of labor that households want to supply at the particular wage rate. Each household's decision regarding how much labor to supply is part of the overall consumer choice problem of a household.* Each household member looks at the market wage rate, the prices of outputs, and the value of leisure time (including the value of staying at home and working in the yard or raising children) and chooses the amount of labor to supply (if any). If a household member is not in the labor force, it is because he or she has decided that the value of his or her time is more valuable in nonmarket activities.

It is easy to see why this is so. If you choose to stay out of the labor force, it is because you (a member of society) place a higher value on the use of your time than society is currently placing on the product that you would produce if you were employed. Consider, for example, households in less-developed countries. In many of these countries, the alternative to working for a wage is subsistence farming. If the wage rate in the labor market is very low, many will choose to farm for themselves. In this case, the value of what these people produce in farming must be greater than the value that society currently places on what they would produce if they worked for a wage. If this were not true, wages would rise and more people would join the labor force.

labor demand curve A graph that illustrates the amount of labor that firms want to employ at the particular wage rate.

Each point on the **labor demand curve** in Figure 30.1 represents the amount of labor that firms want to employ at the particular wage rate. Each firm's decision about how much labor to demand is part of its overall profit-maximizing decision.† A firm makes a profit by selling output to households. It will hire workers if the value of its output is sufficient to justify the wage that is being paid. Thus, the amount of labor that a firm hires depends on the value of the output that workers produce.

---

*The household choice problem is discussed in detail in Chapter 6.

†The demand for inputs by firms, including the demand for labor, is discussed in Chapter 10.

The classical economists saw the workings of the labor market—that is, the behavior of labor supply and labor demand—as optimal from the standpoint of both individual households and firms and from the standpoint of society. If households want more output than is currently being produced, output demand will increase, output prices will rise, the demand for labor will increase, the wage rate will rise, and more workers will be drawn into the labor force. (That is, some of those who preferred not to be a part of the labor force at the lower wage rate will be lured into the labor force at the higher wage rate.) At equilibrium, prices and wages reflect a trade-off between the value that households place on outputs and the value of time spent in leisure and nonmarket work. At equilibrium, the people who are not working are those who have *chosen* not to work at that market wage. Thus, the classical economists believed, the market will achieve the optimal result if left to its own devices, and there is nothing that the government can do to make things better.

The Classical Labor Market and the *AS* Curve

We can now relate the classical view of the labor market to the theory of the vertical *AS* curve that we encountered in Chapter 29. The classical idea that wages adjust to clear the labor market is consistent with the view that wages respond quickly to price changes. For example, if something causes the overall price level to increase and if the wage rate clears the labor market quickly, the wage rate is likely to rise at roughly the same time as the price level rises, thus implying a vertical (or nearly vertical) *AS* curve. Remember that if the *AS* curve is vertical, monetary and fiscal policy cannot affect the level of output and employment in the economy. It therefore follows that those who believe that the wage rate adjusts quickly to clear the labor market are likely to believe that the *AS* curve is vertical (or almost vertical) and that monetary and fiscal policy have little or no effect on output and employment.

Reconciling the Unemployment Rate to the Classical View

If, as the classical economists assumed, the labor market works well, how can we account for the fact that the unemployment rate at times seems high? There seem to be times when millions of people who want jobs at prevailing wage rates cannot find them. How can we reconcile this situation with the classical assumption about the labor market?

Some economists answer this question by arguing that the unemployment rate is not a good measure of whether the labor market is working well. We know that the economy is dynamic and that at any given time some industries are expanding and some are contracting. In New England, for example, the construction industry has been contracting. Consider a carpenter who is laid off because of the industry's contraction. This person had probably developed specific skills related to the construction industry—skills that are not necessarily useful for jobs in other industries. If he were earning $30,000 per year as a carpenter, it may be that he could earn only $20,000 per year in another industry. He may eventually work his way back up to a salary of $30,000 in the new industry as he develops new skills, but this will take time. Will the carpenter take a job at $20,000? There are at least two reasons he may not. First, he may believe that the slump in the construction industry is temporary and that he will soon get his job back. Second, he may believe that he can earn more than $20,000 in another industry and will continue to look for a better job.

If our carpenter decides to continue looking for a job paying more than $20,000 per year, he will be considered unemployed because he is actively looking for work. This does not necessarily mean, however, that the labor market is not working properly. The carpenter has *chosen* not to work for a wage of $20,000 per year, but if his value to any firm outside the construction industry is no more than $20,000 per year, we would not expect him to find a job paying more than $20,000. The unemployment rate as measured by the government is thus not necessarily an accurate indicator of whether the labor market is working properly.

If the degree to which industries are changing in the economy fluctuates over time, there will be more people like our carpenter at some times than at others. This will, of course, cause the measured unemployment rate to fluctuate. Thus, some economists argue, the measured unemployment rate may sometimes *seem* high even though the labor market is working well. The quantity of labor supplied at the current wage is equal to the quantity demanded at the current wage. The fact that there are people willing to work at a wage higher than the current wage does not mean that the labor market is not working. Whenever there is an upward-sloping supply curve in a market (as is usually the case in the labor market), the quantity supplied at a price higher than the equilibrium price is always greater than the quantity supplied at the equilibrium price.

Economists who view unemployment in this way do not see it as a major problem. Yet the images of the bread lines in the 1930s are still with us, and many find it difficult to believe that everything was optimal when over 12 million people were looking for work at the end of 1982. Not surprisingly, there are other views of unemployment, and to these we now turn.

EXPLAINING THE EXISTENCE OF UNEMPLOYMENT

If unemployment is a major macroeconomic problem—and many economists believe that it is—then it is worthwhile to explore some of the reasons that have been suggested for its existence. Among these are sticky wages, efficiency wage theory, imperfect information, and minimum wage laws.

Sticky Wages

sticky wages The downward rigidity of wages as an explanation for the existence of unemployment.

One explanation for unemployment (above and beyond normal frictional and structural unemployment) is that wages are "**sticky**" on the downward side. That is, the equilibrium wage gets stuck at a particular level and does not fall when the demand for labor falls. This situation is illustrated in Figure 30.2, where the equilibrium wage gets stuck at W_0 and does not fall to W^*. The result is unemployment of the amount $L_0 - L_1$, where L_0 is the quantity of labor that households want to supply at wage rate W_0 and L_1 is the amount of labor that firms want to hire at wage rate W_0. $L_0 - L_1$ is thus the number of workers who would like to work at wage rate W_0 but cannot find jobs.

Unfortunately, the sticky wage explanation of unemployment begs the question. We need to know *why* wages are sticky, if they are, and why wages do not fall to clear the labor market during periods of high unemployment. Many answers to this question have been proposed, but as yet no one answer has been agreed upon. This is one of the reasons that macroeconomics has been in a state of flux for so long. The existence of unemployment continues to be a puzzle. Although we will discuss the major theories that have been proposed to explain why wages may not clear the labor market, we can offer no conclusions. The question is still very much open.

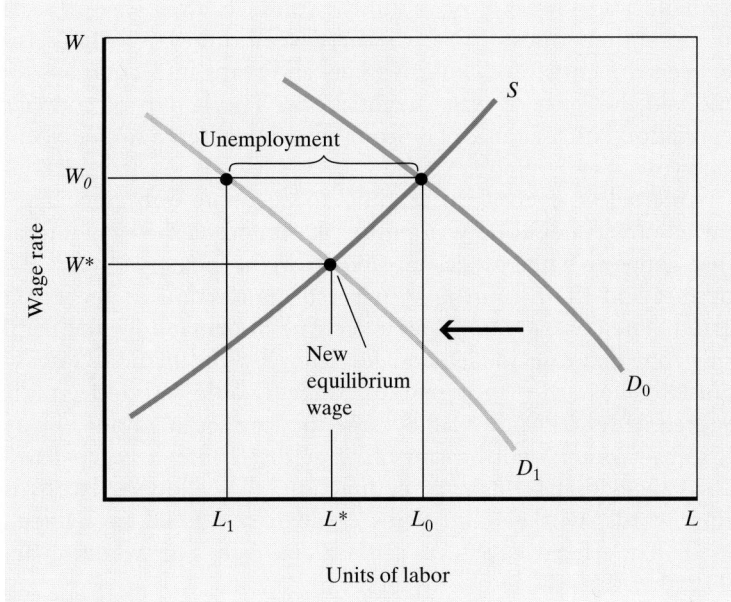

FIGURE 30.2
Sticky Wages
If wages "stick" at W_0 rather than fall to the new equilibrium wage of W^* following a shift of demand from D_0 to D_1, the result will be unemployment equal to $L_0 - L_1$.

SOCIAL, OR IMPLICIT, CONTRACTS One explanation for downwardly sticky wages is that firms enter into **social, or implicit, contracts** with workers not to cut wages. It seems that extreme events—a deep recession, deregulation, or threat of bankruptcy—are necessary for firms to cut wages. Wage cuts did occur during the Great Depression, in the airline industry following deregulation of the industry in the 1980s, and recently when some U.S. manufacturing firms found themselves in danger of bankruptcy from stiff foreign competition. These are exceptions to the general rule, however. For reasons that may be more sociological than economic, cutting wages seems close to being a taboo.

A related argument, the **relative-wage explanation of unemployment,** holds that workers are concerned about their wages *relative* to the wages of other workers in other firms and industries and may be unwilling to accept wage cuts unless they know that other workers are receiving similar cuts. Because it is difficult to reassure any one group of workers that all other workers are in the same situation, workers may resist any cut in their wages. There may thus be an implicit understanding between firms and workers that firms will not do anything that would make their workers worse off relative to workers in other firms.

EXPLICIT CONTRACTS Many workers—in particular, unionized workers—sign one- to three-year employment contracts with firms. These contracts stipulate the workers' wages for each year of the contract. Wages set in this way do not fluctuate with economic conditions, either upward or downward. Thus, if the economy slows down and firms demand fewer workers, the wage will not fall. Rather, some workers will be laid off.

Although the existence of **explicit contracts** can explain why some wages are sticky, a deeper question must also be considered. Workers and firms surely know at the time a contract is signed that unforeseen events may cause the wages set by the contract to be too high or too low. Why, then, do firms and workers bind themselves in this way? One explanation is that negotiating wages is a costly process. Negotiations between unions and firms can take a considerable amount of time—time that could be spent producing output—and it would be very costly to

social, or implicit, contracts
Unspoken agreements between workers and firms that firms will not cut wages.

relative-wage explanation of unemployment An explanation for sticky wages (and therefore unemployment): If workers are concerned about their wages relative to other workers in other firms and industries, they may be unwilling to accept a wage cut unless they know that all other workers are receiving similar cuts.

explicit contracts Employment contracts that stipulate workers' wages, usually for a period of one to three years.

negotiate wages weekly or monthly. Contracts are a way of bearing these costs at no more than one-, two-, or three-year intervals. There is thus a trade-off between the costs of locking workers and firms into contracts for long periods of time and the costs of wage negotiations. The length of contracts that minimizes negotiation costs seems to be (from what we observe in practice) between one and three years.

Nonetheless, even if it is optimal to negotiate only once a year or every other year, contracts could be written to take unforeseen events into account. Consider what happens when wages are fixed for the next two years by an employment contract and there is an unanticipated contraction in the economy during that period. The contraction causes a decrease in demand for the firm's product, which leads to a decrease in demand for labor by the firm. If wages were allowed to adjust to clear the labor market, wages would fall and equilibrium would be restored. If wages cannot fall because they are set in advance by a contract, however, some workers will be laid off. But that contract could have been written to allow wages to fall during a contraction, thus allowing layoffs to be avoided. In other words, workers and firms could have agreed to a fixed *employment* level rather than a fixed *wage* level in their contract. This would guarantee the level of jobs rather than the level of wages.

Contracts that guarantee jobs rather than wages are exceedingly rare, however. Why? One theory postulates that there are two basic types of workers: senior workers and junior workers. *Senior workers* are those workers who have been with a firm for a long time and have seniority. *Junior workers* are relatively new workers. When layoffs take place, it is usually the junior workers who are laid off. If senior workers have most of the power in the union (or other bargaining unit), they may be quite content to write a contract that calls for layoffs rather than wage cuts during hard times. Clearly, if you do not need to worry about being laid off, it is better to have wages stay where they are than to have them fall.

Another theory about why workers sign contracts that in effect call for layoffs instead of wage cuts during hard times centers on the *monitoring of information*. Suppose, for example, that there is a shift of demand away from a firm's product because of a decrease in aggregate expenditure. If the firm could reduce wages immediately, it might be able to lower the price of its product and restore some or all of the lost demand. If the strategy worked, no layoffs would be necessary. But this plan requires wage concessions from workers. To accept pay cuts, workers must believe that the firm will really cut prices, and they may not believe this. Monitoring prices is often difficult because many firms produce different versions of the same product and sometimes different products. Workers may simply not agree to an arrangement in which their wages are cut (which they can definitely see) and in which prices may or may not be cut.

In the case of layoffs, the information available to workers is much clearer. It is obvious to workers when output is cut, and most workers understand that layoffs are necessary when output falls. At any rate, in practice it certainly seems that workers more readily accept layoffs than wage cuts.

On a final note, it should be mentioned that some contracts adjust for unforeseen events by **cost-of-living adjustments (COLAs)** written into the contract. COLAs tie wages to changes in the cost of living: The greater the rate of inflation, the more wages are raised. COLAs thus protect workers from unexpected inflation. Not all contracts contain COLAs, however. Many contracts provide workers with little or no protection from unanticipated inflation, and many COLAs end up adjusting wages by a smaller percentage than the percentage increase in prices.

cost-of-living adjustments (COLAs) Contract provisions that tie wages to changes in the cost of living. The greater the inflation rate, the more wages are raised.

Efficiency Wage Theory

Another explanation for unemployment centers on the **efficiency wage theory,** which holds that the productivity of workers increases with the wage rate. If this is indeed true, firms may have an incentive to pay wages *above* the wage at which the quantity of labor supplied is equal to the quantity of labor demanded.

An individual firm has an incentive to hire workers as long as the value of what they produce is equal to or greater than the wage rate. With no efficiency effects, the market illustrated in Figure 30.1 would produce an equilibrium wage of W^*. But suppose that the firm could increase the productivity of all its workers by raising the wage rate above W^*. The firm's demand for labor would be no lower, but the higher wage rate would cause the quantity of labor supplied to increase. The quantity of labor supplied would thus exceed the quantity of labor demanded at the new higher wage—the *efficiency wage*—and the result is unemployment.

A number of empirical studies of labor markets have identified several potential benefits that firms receive from paying workers more than the market-clearing wage. Among them are lower turnover, improved morale, and reduced "shirking" of work.[1] But even though the efficiency wage theory predicts the existence of some unemployment, it is unlikely that the behavior it is describing accounts for much of the observed large cyclical fluctuations in unemployment over time.

efficiency wage theory An explanation for unemployment that holds that the productivity of workers increases with the wage rate. If this is so, firms may have an incentive to pay wages above the market clearing rate.

Imperfect Information

Thus far we have been assuming that firms know exactly what wage rates they need to set to clear the labor market. They may not choose to set their wages at this level, but at least they know what the market-clearing wage is. In practice, however, firms may not have enough information at their disposal to know what the market-clearing wage is. In this case, firms are said to have *imperfect information*. If firms have imperfect or incomplete information, they may simply set wages wrong—wages that do not clear the labor market.

If a firm sets its wages too high, more workers will want to work for that firm than the firm wants to employ, and some potential workers will be turned away. The result is, of course, unemployment. One objection to this explanation is that it explains the existence of unemployment only in the very short run. As soon as a firm sees that it has made a mistake, why wouldn't it immediately correct its mistake and adjust its wage to the correct, market-clearing level? In other words, why would unemployment *persist?*

If the economy were simple, it should take no more than a few months for firms to correct their mistakes. But in fact the economy is very complex. Although firms may be aware of their past mistakes and may try to correct them, new events are happening all the time. Because constant change—including constantly changing equilibrium wage level—is characteristic of the economy, firms may find it hard to adjust wages to the market-clearing level. The labor market is not like the stock market or the market for wheat, where prices are determined in organized exchanges every day. Rather, thousands of firms are setting wages and millions of workers are responding to these wages. It may take considerable time for the market-clearing wages to be determined after they have been disturbed from an equilibrium position.

---

[1]For a good summary, see George Akerlof and Janet Yellen, *Efficiency Wage Models of the Labor Market* (Cambridge University Press, 1986).

Minimum Wage Laws

minimum wage laws Laws that set a floor for wage rates—that is, a minimum hourly rate for any kind of labor.

The existence of **minimum wage laws** explains at least a small fraction of unemployment. These laws set a floor for wage rates—that is, a minimum hourly rate for any kind of labor. In 1994, the federal minimum wage was $4.25 per hour. If the market-clearing wage for some groups of workers is below this amount, this group will be unemployed. Refer again to Figure 30.2. If the minimum wage is W_0 and the market-clearing wage is W^*, then the number of unemployed will be $L_0 - L_1$.

Teenagers, who have relatively little job experience, are most likely to be hurt by minimum wage laws. If some teenagers can produce only $4.00 worth of output per hour, no firm would be willing to hire them at a wage of $4.25. To do so would be to incur a loss of $0.25 per hour. In an unregulated market, these teenagers would be able to find work at the market-clearing wage of $4.00 per hour. If the minimum wage laws prevent the wage from falling below $4.25, however, these workers will not be able to find jobs, and they will be unemployed.

In response to this argument against the minimum wage, Congress established a subminimum wage for teenagers. The subminimum wage was set at 85% of the minimum wage and is payable to teenagers in entry-level training programs for up to six months. As of April 1, 1991, the subminimum wage was $3.61 per hour.

Minimum wage laws setting rates of $4.25 and $3.61 per hour are clearly not important to steel workers earning $17.00 per hour or for doctors, lawyers, and most economists. It is possible, however, that the existence of minimum wage laws (even with the subminimum wage provisions in place) is one of the factors contributing to high unemployment rates among teenagers.

An Open Question

As we've seen, there are many explanations for why the labor market may not clear. The theories we have just set forth are not necessarily mutually exclusive, and there may be elements of truth in all of them. The aggregate labor market is very complicated, and there are no simple answers to the question of unemployment. In fact, much current work in macroeconomics is concerned directly or indirectly with this question, and it is an exciting area of study. Which argument or arguments will win out in the end is an open question.

THE RELATIONSHIP BETWEEN THE UNEMPLOYMENT RATE AND INFLATION

As you know, two of the most important variables in macroeconomics are the unemployment rate and the inflation rate. The relationship between these two variables is thus of considerable interest, and it has been the subject of much debate. We now have enough knowledge of the macroeconomy to explore this relationship.

We must begin by considering the relationship between aggregate output (income) (Y) and the unemployment rate (U). An increase in Y means that firms are producing more output. In order to produce more output, more labor is needed in the production process. Therefore, an increase in Y leads to an increase in employment. An increase in employment means more people working (fewer people unemployed) and thus a lower unemployment rate. An increase in Y thus corresponds to a *decrease* in U. Thus U and Y are *negatively* related:[2]

> When Y rises, the unemployment rate falls, and when Y falls, the unemployment rate rises.

---

[2]We will see in Chapter 33 that this relationship is not a simple one, but all we need to know for now is that the two variables are negatively related.

THE SUPPLY OF LABOR DURING THE RECESSION OF 1990–91

During recessions, the demand for labor declines. The immediate effect is that people lose their jobs and begin to look for work. In simplest terms, the quantity of labor demanded is less than the quantity of labor supplied.

When there is an excess supply of labor, the equilibrium wage tends to fall. As we discuss in the text, however, wages do not seem to be as downwardly flexible as classical models suggest. Nonetheless, empirical evidence has shown that when an excess supply of labor persists for a long time, wages ultimately begin to drop and the quantity of labor supplied declines.

Between 1989 and 1991, the economy of the northeastern United States was in decline, with falling output and high unemployment. The unemployment rate in Massachusetts hit 9.7% in March of 1991. It was then a major surprise to most economists when the unemployment rate in Massachusetts dropped to 8.3% in April.

Does this decline in the unemployment rate mean that the economy of the Northeast is starting to recover and that output is increasing? Not necessarily. Recall that the unemployment rate is the number of unemployed as a fraction of the labor force. To be in the labor force, you must be working or actively seeking work. When workers stop searching and drop out of the labor force, they are no longer classified as unemployed. (Review the discussion of the discouraged-worker effect in Chapter 23, if necessary.) Should we view the following article from the *Boston Globe* as good news or bad news?

The Massachusetts unemployment rate fell unexpectedly in April to 8.3 percent from 9.7 percent in March, the first decline in seven months and a tentative sign that the state's economic free fall is over.

State officials were encouraged by yesterday's report from the US Labor Department, but they warned that it was too early to start celebrating the end of the recession ....

While the number of people with jobs rose, the total work force has been shrinking. For example, the government survey that determines the jobless rate found that 44,000 fewer people in the Bay State classified themselves as unemployed in April than had the month before. Of those, only 14,000 had actually found jobs. The remaining 30,000 dropped out of the labor pool and were not factored into the unemployment rate [emphasis added].

As jobs have become harder to find, the unemployed have turned to innovative ways of looking for employment. In some areas of the United States, cable television networks have begun to offer video want-ad channels.

Some of the 14,000, said Cynthia Latta, an economist with DRI/McGraw-Hill in Lexington, may be listing themselves as self-employed and may be bringing in sharply reduced incomes. "I bet most of these people, if offered a job, would jump at it," she said.

[A government official] said it was not clear what happened to those who withdrew from the labor pool. "Some could be retired; some could be young mothers. Some may not be bothering to look," he said.

Source: Lawrence Edelman, "Jobless Rate in Mass. Declines," *Boston Globe*, May 4, 1991.

Next consider an upward-sloping aggregate supply (*AS*) curve, as shown in Figure 30.3 on the next page. This curve represents the relationship between *Y* and the overall price level (*P*). The relationship is a positive one: When *Y* increases, *P* increases, and when *Y* decreases, *P* decreases.

As you will recall from the last chapter, the shape of the *AS* curve is determined by the behavior of firms and how they react to an increase in demand. If aggregate demand shifts to the right and the economy is operating on the nearly flat part of the *AS* curve—far from capacity—output will increase but the price level will not change much. However, if the economy is operating on the steep part of the *AS* curve—close to capacity—an increase in demand will drive up the price level, but output will be constrained by capacity and will not increase much.

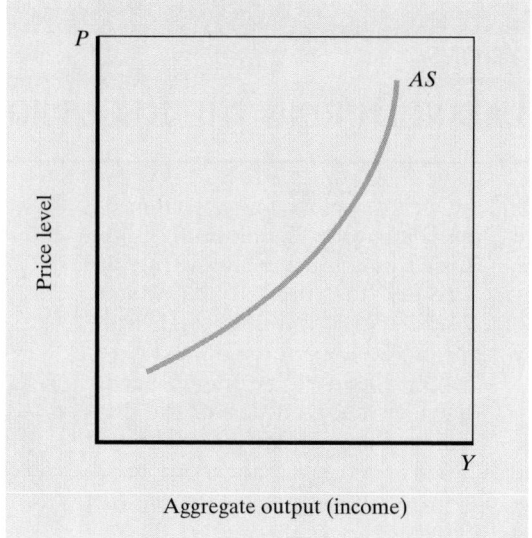

FIGURE 30.3

The Aggregate Supply Curve

The *AS* curve shows a positive relationship between the price level (*P*) and aggregate output (income) (*Y*).

Now think carefully about what will happen following an event that leads to an increase in aggregate demand. First, firms experience an unanticipated decline in inventories. They respond by increasing output (*Y*) and hiring workers. Thus, the unemployment rate falls. If the economy is not close to capacity, there will be little increase in the price level. But if aggregate demand continues to grow, the ability of the economy to increase output will eventually reach its limit. As aggregate demand shifts further and further to the right along the *AS* curve, the price level increases more and more, and output begins to reach its limit. At the point at which the *AS* curve becomes vertical, output cannot rise any further. If output cannot grow, the unemployment rate cannot be pushed any lower. Thus, we can see that:

> There is a negative relationship between the unemployment rate and the price level. As the unemployment rate declines in response to the economy moving closer and closer to capacity output, the overall price level rises more and more, as shown in Figure 30.4.

FIGURE 30.4

The Relationship between the Price Level and the Unemployment Rate

There is a negative relationship between the price level (*P*) and the unemployment rate (*U*). As the unemployment rate declines in response to the economy's moving closer and closer to capacity output, the price level rises more and more.

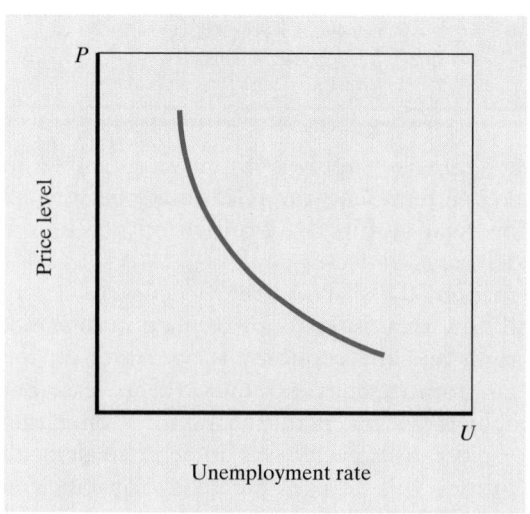

The curve depicted in Figure 30.4 has not been a major focus of attention in macroeconomics. Rather, the curve that has been extensively studied is shown in Figure 30.5, which plots the inflation rate on the vertical axis and the unemployment rate on the horizontal axis. The **inflation rate** is the percentage change in the price level, not the price level itself.

The implications of Figures 30.4 and 30.5 are different. Figure 30.4 says that the *price level* remains the same if the unemployment rate remains unchanged. Figure 30.5, on the other hand, says that the *inflation rate* remains the same if the unemployment rate remains unchanged. The curve in Figure 30.5 is called the **Phillips Curve,** after A. W. Phillips, who first examined it using data for the United Kingdom. In simplest terms, the Phillips Curve is a graph showing the relationship between the inflation rate and the unemployment rate.

The rest of this chapter focuses on the Phillips Curve depicted in Figure 30.5 because it is the macroeconomic relationship that has been studied the most. You should keep in mind, however, that it is not easy to go from the *AS* curve to the Phillips Curve. We have moved from graphs in which the price level is on the vertical axis (Figures 30.3 and 30.4) to a graph in which the *percentage change* in the price level is on the vertical axis (Figure 30.5). Put another way, the theory behind the Phillips Curve is somewhat different from the theory behind the *AS* curve. Fortunately, however, most of the insights gained from the *AS/AD* analysis regarding the behavior of the price level also apply to the behavior of the inflation rate.

inflation rate The percentage change in the price level.

Phillips Curve A graph showing the relationship between the inflation rate and the unemployment rate.

The Phillips Curve: A Historical Perspective

In the 1950s and 1960s, there was a remarkably smooth relationship between the unemployment rate and the rate of inflation, as Figure 30.6 shows for the 1960s. As you can see, the data points fit fairly closely around a downward-sloping curve; in general, the higher the unemployment rate, the lower the rate of inflation. The Phillips Curve in Figure 30.6 thus shows a trade-off between inflation and unemployment. To lower the inflation rate, we must accept a higher unemployment rate, and to lower the unemployment rate, we must accept a higher rate of inflation.

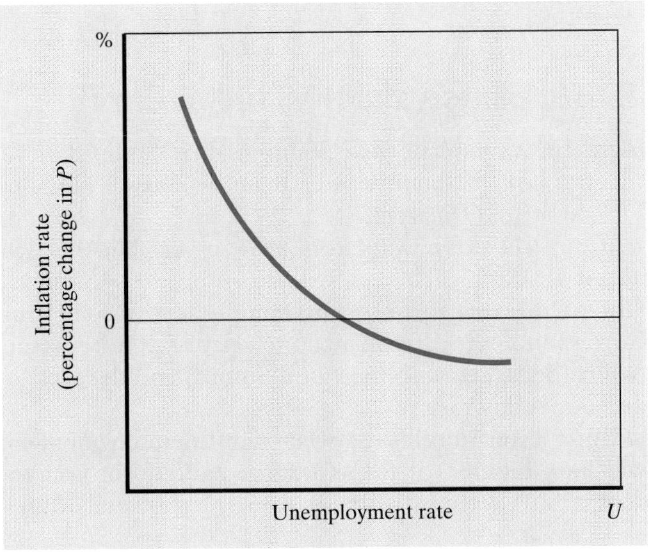

FIGURE 30.5
The Phillips Curve

The Phillips Curve shows the relationship between the inflation rate and the unemployment rate.

FIGURE 30.6

Unemployment and
Inflation, 1960–1969
(Source: *Economic Report of the President, 1988*.)

During the 1960s there seemed
to be an obvious trade-off
between inflation and unemployment. Policy debates during the period revolved around
this apparent trade-off.

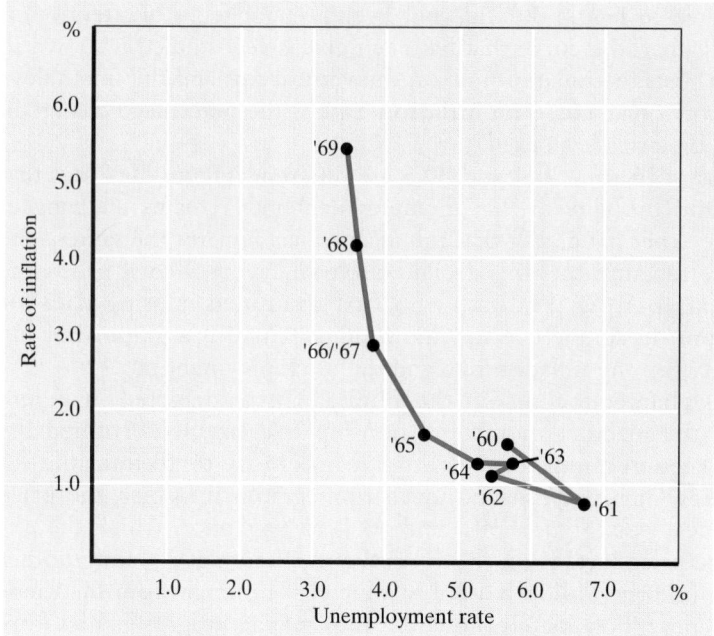

Textbooks written in the 1960s and early 1970s relied on the Phillips Curve as the main explanation of inflation. Things seemed fairly simple—inflation appeared to respond in a fairly predictable way to changes in the unemployment rate. For this reason, policy discussions in the 1960s revolved around the Phillips Curve. The role of the policy maker, it was thought, was to choose a point on the curve. Conservatives usually argued for choosing a point with a low rate of inflation and were willing to accept a higher unemployment rate in exchange for this. Liberals usually argued for accepting more inflation to keep unemployment at a low level.

Life did not turn out to be quite so simple, however. The Phillips Curve broke down in the 1970s and 1980s. This is easily seen in Figure 30.7, which graphs the unemployment rate and inflation rate for the period from 1970 to 1992. The points in Figure 30.7 show no particular relationship between inflation and unemployment.

AS/AD Analysis and the Phillips Curve

How can we explain the stability of the Phillips Curve in the 1950s and 1960s and the lack of stability after that? To answer this question, we need to turn back to *AS/AD* analysis.

If the *AD* curve shifts from year to year but the *AS* curve does not, the values of *P* and *Y* each year will lie along the *AS* curve (see Figure 30.8a). The plot of the relationship between *P* and *Y* will thus look upward-sloping. Correspondingly, the plot of the relationship between the unemployment rate (which decreases with increased output) and the rate of inflation will be a curve that slopes downward.

But the relationship between the unemployment rate and the inflation rate will look different if the *AS* curve shifts from year to year but the *AD* curve does not. A leftward shift of the *AS* curve will cause an *increase* in the price

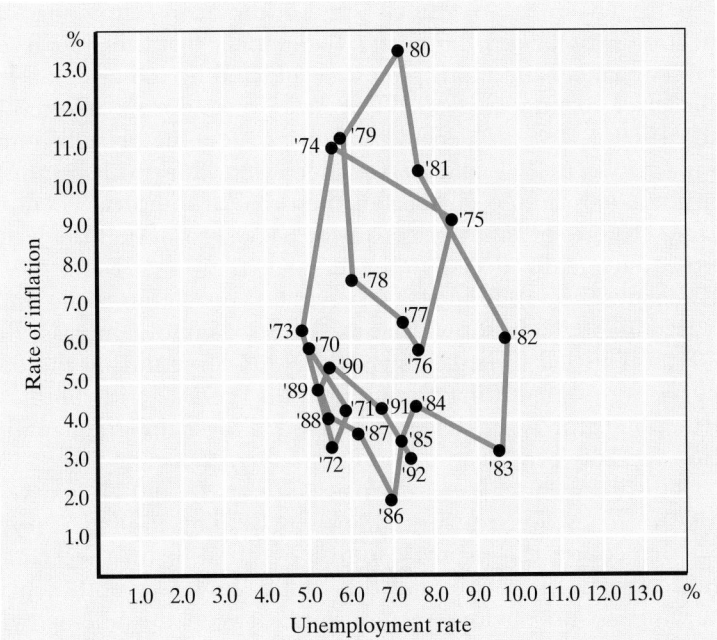

FIGURE 30.7

Unemployment and
Inflation, 1970–1992
(Source: *Economic Report of the President, 1993.*)

During the 1970s and 1980s, it
became clear that the relationship between unemployment and inflation was anything but simple.

level (*P*) and a *decrease* in aggregate output (*Y*) (see Figure 30.8b). Thus, when
the *AS* curve shifts to the left, the economy experiences both inflation *and* an
increase in the unemployment rate (because decreased output means increased
unemployment). In other words, if the *AS* curve is shifting from year to year,
we would expect to see a positive relationship between the unemployment rate
and the inflation rate.

   If both the *AS* and the *AD* curves are shifting simultaneously, however, there
is no systematic relationship between *P* and *Y* (see Figure 30.8c) and thus no
systematic relationship between the unemployment rate and the inflation rate.

FIGURE 30.8

Changes in the Price Level
and Aggregate Output
Depend on Both Shifts in
Aggregate Demand and
Shifts in Aggregate Supply

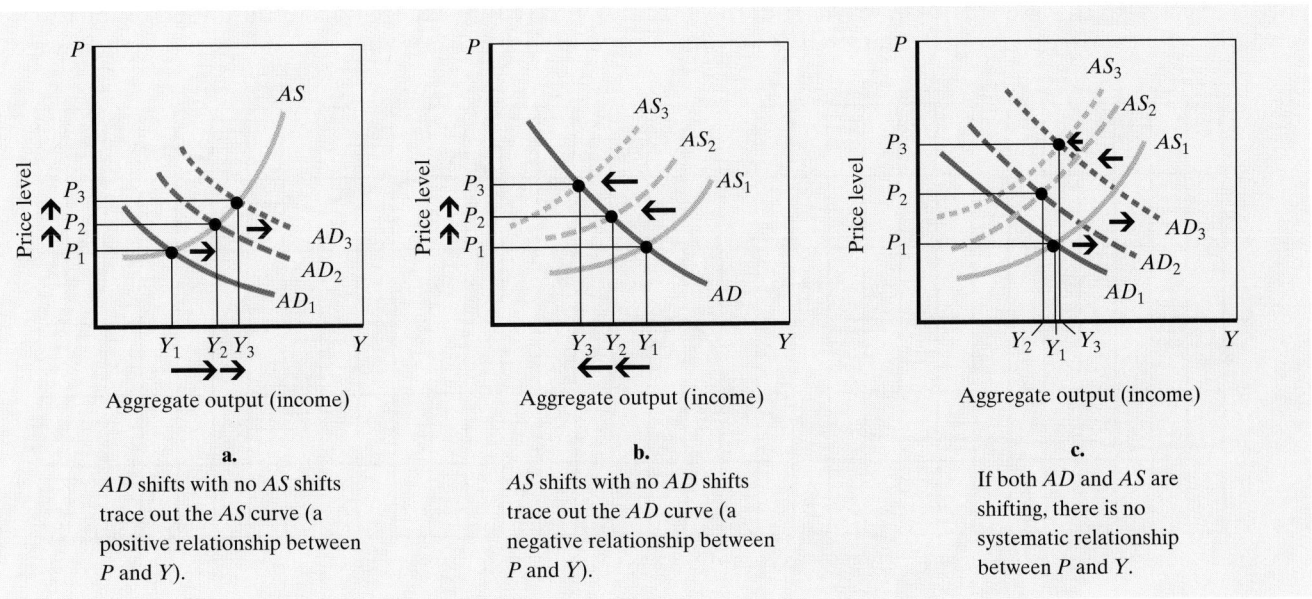

a.
AD shifts with no *AS* shifts
trace out the *AS* curve (a
positive relationship between
P and *Y*).

b.
AS shifts with no *AD* shifts
trace out the *AD* curve (a
negative relationship between
P and *Y*).

c.
If both *AD* and *AS* are
shifting, there is no
systematic relationship
between *P* and *Y*.

THE ROLE OF IMPORT PRICES One of the main factors that causes the *AS* curve to shift is the price of imports. (Remember that the *AS* curve shifts when input prices change, and input prices are affected by the price of imports, particularly the price of imported oil.) The price of imports is plotted in Figure 30.9 for the 1960 I–1992 IV period. As you can see, the price of imports changed very little between 1960 and 1970. There were thus no large shifts in the *AS* curve in the 1960s due to changes in the price of imports. There were also no other large changes in input prices in the 1960s, so overall the *AS* curve shifted very little during the decade. The main variation in the 1960s was in aggregate demand, so the shifting *AD* curve traced out points along the *AS* curve.

Figure 30.9 also shows that the price of imports increased dramatically in the 1970s. This led to large shifts in the *AS* curve during the decade. But the *AD* curve was also shifting throughout the 1970s. With both curves shifting, the data points for *P* and *Y* were scattered all over the graph, and the observed relationship between *P* and *Y* was not at all systematic.

This story about import prices and the *AS* and *AD* curves in the 1960s and 1970s carries over to the Phillips Curve. The Phillips Curve was stable in the 1960s because the primary source of variation in the economy was demand, not costs. In the 1970s (and the 1980s), however, both demand *and* costs were varying, so no obvious relationship between the unemployment rate and the inflation rate was apparent.

To some extent, what is remarkable about the Phillips Curve is not that it was not smooth after the 1960s but that it ever was smooth.

Expectations and the Phillips Curve

Another reason that the Phillips Curve is not stable concerns expectations. We saw in the last chapter that if a firm expects other firms to raise their prices, the firm may raise the price of its own product. If all firms are behaving in this way, then prices will rise because they are expected to rise. In this sense, expectations are self-fulfilling. Similarly, if inflation is expected to be high in the future, negotiated wages are likely to be higher than if inflation is expected to be low. Wage inflation is thus affected by expectations of future price inflation. Because wages are input costs, prices rise as firms respond to the higher wage

FIGURE 30.9
The Price of Imports, 1960 I–1992 IV

The price of imports changed very little in the 1960s and early 1970s. It increased substantially in 1974 and again in 1979–1980. Since 1981, the price of imports has changed very little.

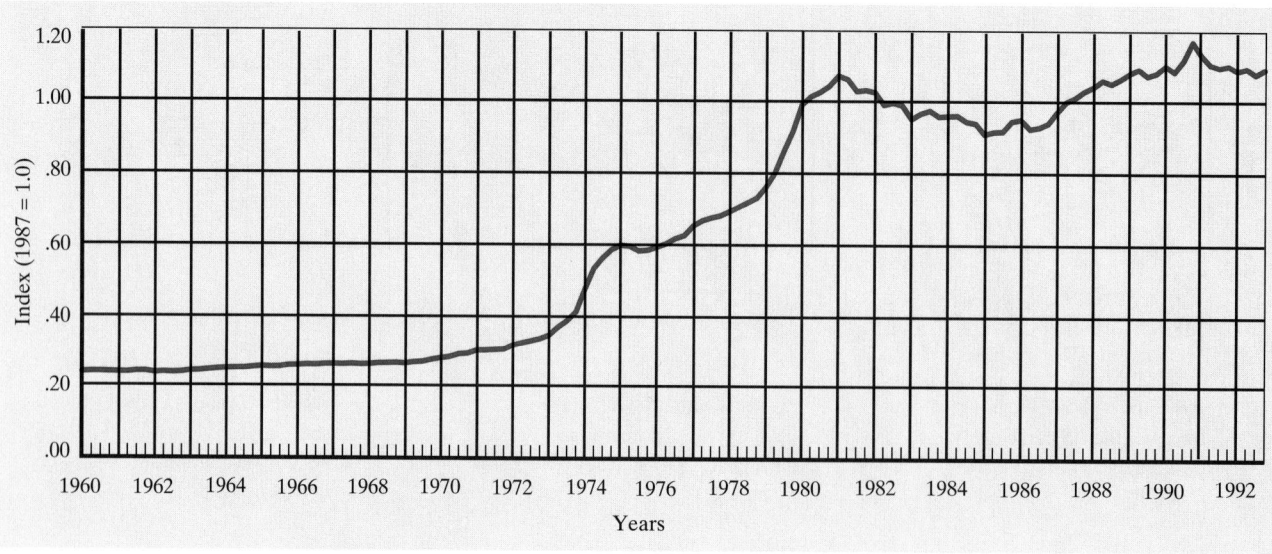

costs. Thus, price expectations that affect wage contracts eventually affect prices themselves.

If the rate of inflation depends on expectations, then the Phillips Curve will shift as expectations change. If, for example, inflationary expectations increase, the result will be an increase in the rate of inflation even though the unemployment rate may not have changed. In this case, the Phillips Curve will shift to the right. Conversely, if inflationary expectations decrease, the Phillips curve will shift to the left—there will be less inflation at any given level of the unemployment rate.

It so happened that inflationary expectations were quite stable in the 1950s and 1960s. The inflation rate was moderate during most of this period, and people expected it to remain moderate. With inflationary expectations not changing very much, there were no major shifts of the Phillips Curve, which helps explain its stability during the period.

Near the end of the 1960s, however, inflationary expectations began to increase, primarily in response to the actual increase in inflation that was occurring because of the tight economy caused by the Vietnam War. Inflationary expectations increased even further in the 1970s as a result of large oil price increases. These changing expectations led to shifts of the Phillips Curve, which is another reason the curve was not stable during the 1970s.

Is There a Trade-Off between Inflation and Unemployment?

Does the fact that the Phillips Curve broke down during the 1970s and 1980s mean that there is no trade-off between inflation and unemployment? Not at all. It simply means that other things affect inflation aside from unemployment. Just as the relationship between price and quantity demanded along a standard demand curve shifts when income or other factors change, so too does the relationship between unemployment and inflation change when other factors change.

In 1975, for example, inflation and unemployment were both high. As we explained earlier, this stagflation was caused partly by an increase in oil costs that shifted the aggregate supply curve to the left and partly by expectations of continued inflation that kept prices rising despite high levels of unemployment. In response to this situation, the Fed pursued a contractionary monetary policy, which shifted the *AD* curve to the left and led to even higher unemployment. This resulted in a lower inflation rate. By 1977, the rate of inflation had dropped from over 11% to about 6 percent. In sum:

> There *is* a trade-off between inflation and unemployment, but other factors besides unemployment affect inflation. Policy involves much more than simply choosing a point along a nice, smooth curve.

Back in Chapter 23, we mentioned that recessions may be the price that the economy pays to eliminate inflation. We can now understand this statement better. When unemployment rises, *other things being equal,* inflation falls. We explore the trade-off between inflation and unemployment in other nations—and caution against generalizing too much—in the Global Perspective box titled "Inflation and Unemployment Around the World, 1990–91."

The Long-Run *AS* Curve, Potential GDP, and the Natural Rate of Unemployment

Recall from the previous chapter that many economists believe that the *AS* curve is vertical in the long run. In the short run, we know that some input prices (which are costs to firms) lag behind increases in the overall price level. If the price level rises without a full adjustment of costs, firms' profits will be higher and output will increase. In the long run, however, input prices may catch up to output price increases. If input prices rise in subsequent periods, thus driving up costs, the short-run aggregate supply curve will shift, and aggregate output will fall.

This situation is illustrated in Figure 30.10. Assume that aggregate demand shifts from AD_0 to AD_1. If input prices lag behind changes in the overall price

FIGURE 30.10

The Long-Run Phillips Curve: The Natural Rate of Unemployment

If the *AS* curve is vertical in the long run, so is the Phillips Curve. In the long run, the Phillips Curve corresponds to the natural rate of unemployment—that is, the unemployment rate that is consistent with the notion of a fixed long-run output at potential GDP.

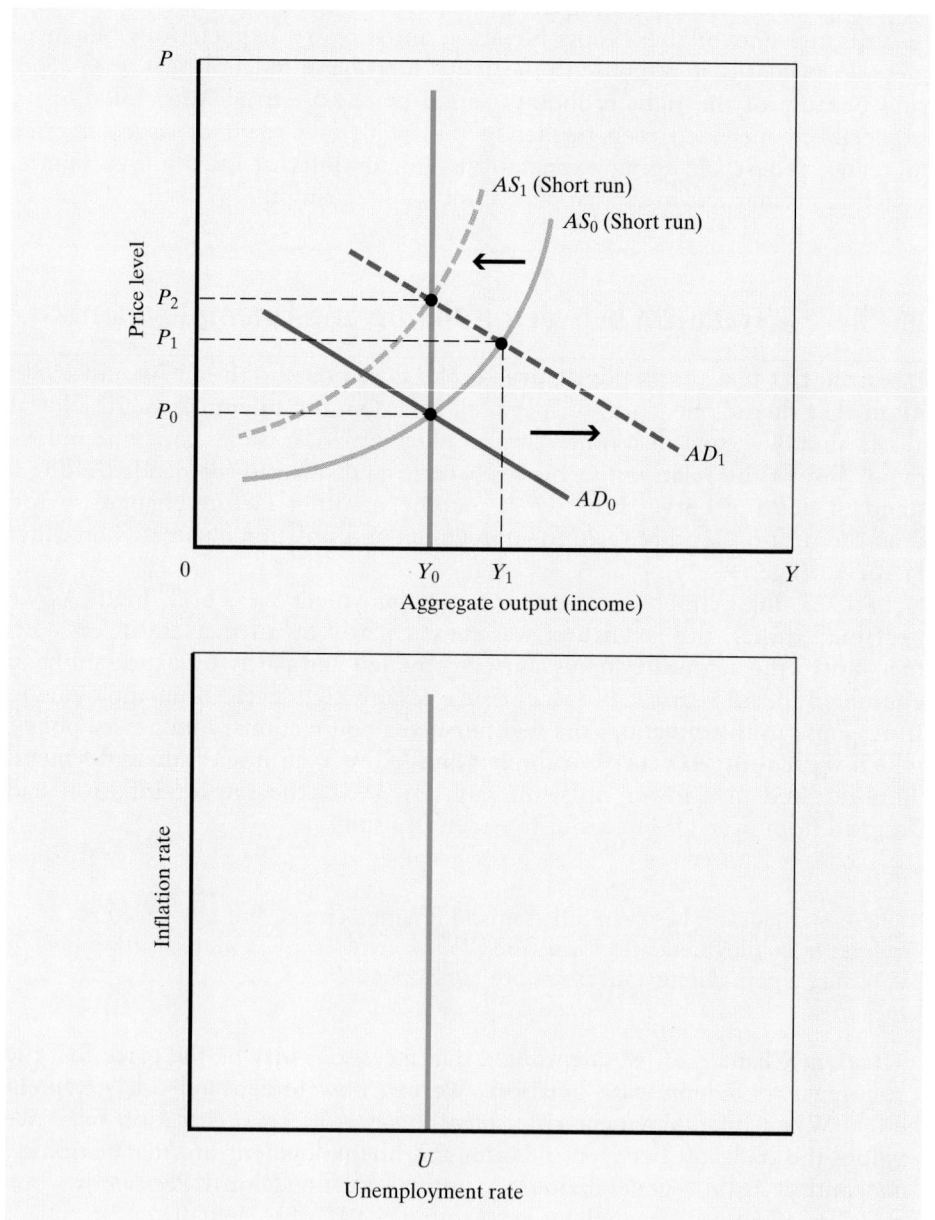

level, aggregate output will rise from Y_0 to Y_1. (This is a movement along the short-run AS curve AS_0.) But in the longer run, input prices may catch up. For example, next year's labor contracts may make up for the fact that wage increases did not keep up with the cost of living this year. If input prices catch up in the longer run, the AS curve will shift from AS_0 to AS_1 and drive aggregate output back to Y_0. If input prices ultimately rise by exactly the same percentage as output prices, firms will produce the same level of output as they did before the increase in aggregate demand.

In the last chapter, we referred to Y_0 as *potential GDP*. Aggregate output can be pushed above Y_0 in the short run. When aggregate output exceeds Y_0, however, there is upward pressure on input prices and costs. The unemployment rate is already quite low, firms are beginning to encounter the limits of their plant capacities, and so forth. At levels of aggregate output above Y_0, costs will rise, the AS curve will shift to the left, and the price level will rise. Thus potential GDP is the level of aggregate output that can be sustained in the long run without inflation.

This story is directly related to the Phillips Curve. Those who believe that the AS curve is vertical in the long run at potential GDP also believe that the Phillips Curve is vertical in the long run at some **natural rate of unemployment.** The *natural rate of unemployment* is the rate of unemployment that is consistent with the notion of a fixed long-run output at potential GDP. The logic behind the vertical Phillips Curve is that whenever the unemployment rate is pushed below the natural rate, wages begin to rise, thus pushing up costs. This leads to a *lower* level of output, which pushes the unemployment rate back up to the natural rate.

Why is the natural rate of unemployment higher than zero? We have said several times that in the normal functioning of a healthy economy, some firms are contracting while others are expanding. Some people switch jobs; others graduate from high school or college and begin looking for jobs. This means that even in good times, there are people out looking for work. These normal frictional and structural unemployment rates make up the natural rate. The measured unemployment rate can be pushed below the natural rate, but only in the short run and not without inflation.

If the natural rate is fixed in the long run, what role can policy play in reducing unemployment? If some event like a cost shock drives the level of unemployment above the natural rate, policy can be used to accelerate its return to the sustainable natural rate. The key point here, however, is that:

> There is a limit to how low the unemployment rate can be pushed without setting off a round of inflation.

We will return to the notion of the natural rate of unemployment when we discuss new classical economics in Chapter 34.

LOOKING AHEAD

This chapter concludes our basic analysis of how the macroeconomy works. In the last seven chapters, we have examined how households and firms behave in the three market arenas—the goods market, the money market, and the labor market. We have seen how aggregate output (income), the interest rate, and the price level are determined in the economy, and we have examined the relationship between two of the most important macroeconomic variables, the inflation rate and unemployment rate. In the next chapter, we use everything we have learned up to this point to examine a number of important policy issues.

natural rate of unemployment is consistent with the notion of a fixed long-run output at potential GDP. Generally considered the sum of the frictional and structural unemployment rates.

GLOBAL PERSPECTIVE
INFLATION AND UNEMPLOYMENT AROUND THE WORLD, 1990–1991

Job resource centers throughout France provide listings of jobs for which the unemployed can apply. The French unemployment rate was one of the highest in the world in 1990.

Table 1 presents unemployment and inflation figures for a number of industrial economies in 1990. The countries are ranked by unemployment rate from highest to lowest.

As you might guess, France–the country with the highest 1990 unemployment rate (9.2%), had the lowest inflation rate (3.1 percent). Sweden–the country with the lowest unemployment rate (1.5%) had the highest inflation rate (9.3 percent). Beyond these numbers, however, there is no real pattern. Japan had the second-lowest unemployment rate (2.1%), yet prices in Japan remained remarkably stable in 1990, rising only 3.3% that year (the second-lowest inflation rate among the countries listed). Italy had a year of both relatively high inflation (6.4%)

and relatively high unemployment (7.0 percent).

These numbers make it clear that economic generalizations across countries can be hazardous. This is true for two reasons. First, the economic events experienced by one country in a given time period may be very different than the economic events experienced by another country during the same period. (For example, one country may encounter a supply shock that shifts its aggregate supply curve at the same time that another is experiencing demand-pull inflation.) Second, the trade-off between inflation and unemployment, to the extent that one exists, is determined by the institutions within the country. For example, Japan has had a

tradition of "lifetime" employment for male workers in the country's largest industries. Although 1992 and 1993 saw the rules beginning to change, Japanese firms are still more reluctant than their U.S. counterparts to lay off workers during economic hard times. This means that Japanese workers do much less "job searching" and that Japan probably has a lower natural rate of unemployment than the United States. The opposite is true in the Netherlands, which has a very liberal unemployment insurance program that pays virtually 100% of lost wages to the unemployed for an extended period of time. Such a system is likely to lead to a higher natural rate because it makes the cost of being unemployed quite low. Indeed, despite 3% real growth in the Netherlands in 1990, the unemployment rate held at 8%.

TABLE 1

UNEMPLOYMENT AND INFLATION RATES IN SELECTED COUNTRIES, 1990–91

	1990 UNEMPLOYMENT RATE	1990–1991 INFLATION RATE
France	9.2	3.1
Canada	8.1	5.6
Netherlands	8.0	3.9
Italy	7.0	6.4
Australia	6.9	7.2
United Kingdom	6.9	5.9
United States	5.5	4.2
Germany	5.2	3.5
Japan	2.1	3.3
Sweden	1.5	9.3

Source: *Statistical Abstract of the United States, 1992,* Tables 1384, 1386.

SUMMARY

1. Because the economy is dynamic, *frictional* and *structural unemployment* are inevitable and in some ways desirable. Nonetheless, there are times of *cyclical unemployment* that concern macroeconomic policy makers.

2. In general, employment tends to fall when aggregate output falls and rise when aggregate output rises.

The Classical View of the Labor Market

3. Classical economists believe that the interaction of supply and demand in the labor market brings about equilibrium and that unemployment (beyond the frictional and structural amounts) does not exist.

4. The classical view of the labor market is consistent with the theory of a vertical aggregate supply curve.

Explaining the Existence of Unemployment

5. Some economists argue that the unemployment rate is not an accurate indicator of whether the labor market is working properly. Unemployed people who are considered part of the labor force may be offered jobs but may be unwilling to take those jobs at the offered salaries. Thus, some of the unemployed may have chosen not to work, but this does not mean that the labor market has malfunctioned.

6. Those who do not subscribe to the classical view of the labor market have suggested several reasons why unemployment exists. Downwardly *sticky wages* may be brought about by *implicit* or *explicit contracts* not to cut wages. If the equilibrium wage rate falls but wages are prevented from falling also, the result will be unemployment.

7. *Efficiency wage theory* holds that the productivity of workers increases with the wage rate. If this is true, firms may have an incentive to pay wages above the wage at which the quantity of labor supplied is equal to the quantity of labor demanded. At all wages above the equilibrium, there will be an excess supply of labor and therefore unemployment.

8. If firms are operating with incomplete or imperfect information, they may not know what the market-clearing wage is. As a result, they may set their wages incorrectly and bring about unemployment. Because the economy is so complex, it may take considerable time for firms to correct these mistakes.

9. *Minimum wage laws,* which set a floor for wage rates, are one of the factors contributing to unemployment among teenagers. If the market-clearing wage for some groups of workers is below the minimum wage, some members of this group will be unemployed.

10. There is a negative relationship between the unemployment rate (U) and aggregate output (income) (Y): When Y rises, U falls; when Y falls, U rises.

The Relationship Between the Unemployment Rate and Inflation

11. The relationship between the unemployment rate and the price level is negative: As the unemployment rate declines and the economy moves closer to capacity, the price level rises.

12. The *Phillips Curve* is a graph illustrating the relationship between the *inflation rate* and the *unemployment rate*. During the 1950s and 1960s, this relationship was fairly stable, and there seemed to be a predictable trade-off between inflation and unemployment. As a result of import price increases (which led to shifts in aggregate supply) and shifts in aggregate demand brought about partially by inflationary expectations, however, the relationship between the inflation rate and the unemployment rate since 1970 has been erratic. There *is* a trade-off between inflation and unemployment, but other things besides unemployment affect inflation.

13. Those who believe that the *AS* curve is vertical in the long run also believe that the Phillips Curve is vertical in the long run at the *natural rate of unemployment*. The natural rate is generally taken to be the sum of the frictional and structural rates. If the Phillips Curve is vertical in the long run, then there is a limit to how low government policy can push the unemployment rate without setting off inflation.

REVIEW TERMS AND CONCEPTS

PROBLEM SET

1. Suppose the government passes a law making it illegal to fire any employee. Would such a law ensure that the unemployment rate would be zero? Explain. Can you think of reasons why such a law might actually raise the unemployment rate?

2. Japan has traditionally had a substantially lower unemployment rate than the United States, at least since the 1960s. Japanese workers rarely move from one city to another and rarely switch employers, staying with one firm for their entire career. How, if at all, do these factors help to explain the difference in unemployment rates between the two countries?

3. The following policies have at times been advocated for coping with the problem of unemployment. Briefly explain how each policy might work, and explain which type or types of unemployment (frictional, structural, or cyclical) the policy is designed to alter.
   a. Developing a computer list of job openings and a service that matches employees with job vacancies (sometimes called an "economic dating service").
   b. Lowering the minimum wage for teenagers.
   c. Retraining programs for workers who need to learn new skills in order to find employment.
   d. Public employment for people without jobs.
   e. Improving information about available jobs and current wage rates.
   f. The President going on nationwide TV and attempting to convince firms and workers that the inflation rate next year will be low.

4. In 1994, the country of Ruba was suffering a period of high unemployment. The newly elected President Clang appointed as his chief economist Laurel Tiedye. Ms. Tiedye and her staff estimated the following supply and demand curves for labor from data obtained from the secretary of labor, Robert Small:

$$Q_D = 100 - 5W$$
$$Q_S = 10W - 20,$$

where Q is the quantity of labor supplied/demanded in millions of workers and W is the wage rate in slugs, the currency of Ruba.
   a. Currently, the law in Ruba states that no worker shall be paid less than nine slugs per hour. Estimate the size of the labor supply, the number of unemployed, and the unemployment rate in Ruba.
   b. President Clang, over the objection of Secretary Small, has recommended to the Congress that the law be changed to allow the wage rate to be determined in the market. If such a law were passed, and the market adjusted quickly, what would happen to total employment, the size of the labor force, and the unemployment rate? Show the results graphically.
   c. Do you think that the Rubanese labor market would adjust quickly to such a change in the law? Why or why not?

5. Your boss offers you a wage increase of 10 percent. Is it possible that you are worse off, even with the wage increase, than you were before?

6. How will the following affect labor-force participation rates? Labor supply? Unemployment?
   a. Because the retired elderly are comprising a larger and larger fraction of the U.S. population, Congress and the President decide to raise the social security tax on individuals in order to continue paying benefits to the elderly.
   b. A national child care program is enacted, requiring employers to provide free child care services.
   c. The U. S. government reduces restrictions on immigration into the United States.
   d. The welfare system is eliminated.
   e. The government subsidizes the purchase of new capital by firms (an investment tax credit).

7. Draw a graph to illustrate the following:
   a. A Phillips Curve based on the assumption of a vertical long-run aggregate supply curve.
   b. The effect of accelerating inflationary expectations on a recently stable Phillips Curve.
   c. Unemployment caused by a recently enacted minimum wage law.

8. Suppose economists have predicted an upcoming recession. Also suppose that, as a result, firms plan to reduce workers' wages, but also expect the price level to fall (thus keeping the real wage constant). Would you expect to observe an increase in unemployment? Why or why not?

9. Suppose that the inflation-unemployment relationship depicted by the Phillips Curve was, in fact, stable. Do you think that the U.S. trade-off and the Japanese trade-off would be identical? If not, what kinds of factors might make the trade-offs dissimilar?

10. What conditions would need to exist in the economy of the 1990s for the stable Phillips Curve to reappear? How likely is this to happen?

The Budget Deficit, Stabilization Policy, and Other Macroeconomic Issues

31

As we've noted throughout this book, macroeconomics is filled with important policy questions. Newspapers carry articles dealing with macroeconomic problems daily, and macroeconomic issues play an important role in many political campaigns. Using what we've learned about how the macroeconomy works, we can now examine some current issues and problems in greater depth.

In this chapter, we take up four policy issues that have received a great deal of attention in recent years: (1) fiscal policy, the government budget deficit (which we discussed briefly in Chapter 25), and the Gramm-Rudman-Hollings legislation regarding the deficit; (2) monetary policy and the ways the Fed reacts to the state of the economy; (3) the lags that exist in the economy's response to monetary and fiscal policy changes; and (4) the way voters respond to the state of the economy and how a political business cycle might come about.

THE FEDERAL DEFICIT AND THE FEDERAL DEBT

We noted in Chapter 25 that the size of the federal deficit since the early 1980s has been a subject of great concern. Recall that the **federal deficit** is

federal deficit The difference between what the government spends and what it receives in tax revenue $(G - T)$.

federal debt The total of all accumulated federal deficits minus surpluses over time, or the total amount of U.S. government obligations (bills, notes, and bonds) outstanding.

the difference between what the government spends and what it receives in tax revenue ($G - T$). In 1992, the federal deficit was $297.8 billion. Recall also that the **federal debt** is the total of all accumulated deficits minus surpluses over time. Because the U.S. Treasury must borrow by issuing securities when the government spends more than it collects in tax revenues, the federal debt is also the total amount of U.S. government obligations (bills, notes, and bonds) outstanding.

Some of the securities that the government issues end up being held by the federal government itself at the Federal Reserve or in trust funds. For this reason, the term **public debt** often refers only to the *privately held* debt of the U.S. government. At the end of 1992, total outstanding U.S. government obligations amounted to $4,002.7 billion, of which $3,309.7 billion was held in private accounts and abroad.

public debt The privately held (non-government-owned) debt of the U.S. government.

The Size of the Federal Debt

One way to measure the size of the federal debt is to compare it to the size of national output (income) (Y). Figure 31.1 shows the total privately held public debt as a percentage of GDP between the years 1940 and 1992. (A similar figure is found in Chapter 25, Figure 25.5, where the percentage is shown for each quarter between 1970 I and 1992 IV.) A large debt was incurred to fight World War II, pushing the debt-to-GDP ratio from 44.8% in 1940 to 113.8% in 1946. After 1946, the ratio dropped each year for nearly 30 years to a low of 24.5% in 1974. Between 1974 and 1981, there was little change. But between 1981 and 1992, the debt increased dramatically. The large deficits of the 1980s began with the significant tax cuts and military spending increases in the early years of the Reagan administration. As Congress and the President fought over the budget throughout the 1980s, the debt grew to over $2 trillion by the end of the 1980s. As just noted, by the end of 1992, the debt was $3,309.7 billion, or 51.1% of GDP.

Table 31.1 shows the federal deficit in billions of dollars and as a percentage of GDP for 1970 to 1992. The sharp increases after 1980 are obvious. The deficit hit 4.7% of GDP in 1986, fell somewhat for the next four years, and then rose sharply to reach 5.0% of GDP in 1992.

FIGURE 31.1

Ratio of Privately Held U.S. Government Debt to GDP, 1940–1992

(Source: *Economic Report of the President, 1993*, Table B-76.)

The large deficits of the 1980s began with the tax cuts and military spending increases in the early years of the Reagan administration. By the end of 1992, the debt stood at 51.1% of U.S. GDP.

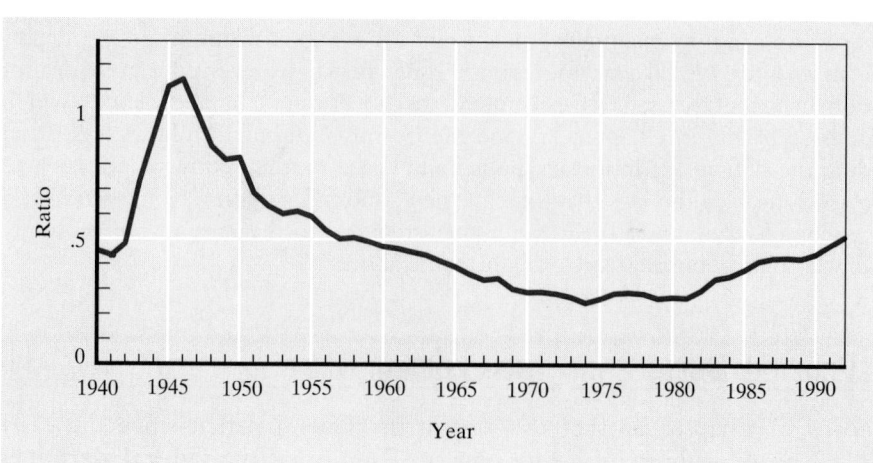

The Burden of the Debt

It is easy to determine where the burden of a household's debt falls. When a family borrows to buy a house or a car or to finance college for one or more of its members, it takes out loans that must be paid off over time. Interest must be paid on these loans while they are being held. The more a household must spend on principal and interest payments, the less it has to spend elsewhere.

In some respects, the federal government is like a household. In order to borrow, it must pay interest. The more debt it incurs, the higher its interest payments will be. Columns 5 and 6 of Table 31.1 show the annual interest cost of financing the federal debt as a percentage of GDP and as a percentage of total federal expenditures. Interest payments represented less than 10% of total federal expenditures and less than 2% of GDP until 1982. By the end of the 1980s, the figures had jumped to about 14% of total federal expenditures and to over 3% of GDP. Interest payments now rank third behind national defense and social security payments as a percentage of the total federal budget, and they far exceed total federal expenditures on education, employment training, social services, and housing assistance.

In another sense, however, the federal government is different from a household. While households are obligated to pay off their debts at a specific point in time, the federal government has an infinite life. That is, there is no particular moment when the federal debt becomes due and must be paid off. Specific bills, notes, and bonds come due periodically, but the government simply pays these off with the proceeds of another bill, note, or bond sale.

It is interesting to note that most of the federal debt is owned by U.S. citizens. Since 88% of the federal debt is owned by U.S. citizens, most interest payments are simply a transfer from one group (taxpayers) to another (bondholders). (See the Issues and Applications box titled "Who Owns the Public Debt?".)

TABLE 31.1
Deficit and Interest
Payments, 1970–1992

YEAR	CONSOLIDATED FEDERAL DEFICIT (BILLIONS OF $)	DEFICIT AS A % OF GDP	NET INTEREST PAYMENTS (BILLIONS OF $)	INTEREST AS A % OF GDP	INTEREST AS A % OF FEDERAL EXPENDITURES
1970	13.3	1.3	14.1	1.4	6.9
1972	17.3	1.4	14.4	1.2	5.8
1974	11.5	0.8	20.7	1.4	6.8
1976	52.8	3.0	26.8	1.5	6.8
1978	28.1	1.3	34.6	1.6	7.4
1980	60.0	2.2	52.7	1.9	8.6
1982	135.6	4.3	84.4	2.7	11.0
1984	166.8	4.4	113.1	3.0	12.7
1986	201.1	4.7	131.0	3.1	12.7
1987	151.8	3.3	136.5	3.0	12.8
1988	136.6	2.8	146.0	3.0	13.2
1989	122.3	2.3	164.7	3.1	13.9
1990	166.2	3.0	176.6	3.2	13.9
1991	210.4	3.7	186.9	3.3	14.0
1992	297.8	5.0	186.7	3.1	12.8

Source: U.S. Department of Commerce (NIPA data)

WHO OWNS THE PUBLIC DEBT?

At the end of 1990, the total obligations of the United States Treasury amounted to $3.2 trillion. This figure is the total of all the Treasury bills, notes, and bonds that are currently outstanding. Who owns these bills, notes, and bonds—the public debt?

Table 1 presents an estimate of the ownership of the public debt in 1990. Perhaps the most surprising thing about this table is that almost one third of the total debt is owned by various branches of the federal government itself. The Federal Reserve System owns $234.4 billion, or 7.3% of the total.

Why so much? The Fed is responsible for controlling the U.S. money supply. As the economy grows, the money supply must be expanded to accommodate that growth. In 1980, the broadly defined money supply (*M2*) stood at $1.63 trillion; in 1990, it was $3.32 trillion.

The Fed expands the money supply primarily through open market operations—that is, by buying U.S. government securities in the open market. The Fed pays for these securities by writing a check or by expanding a bank's reserve account at the Fed. In either case, reserves are injected into the system. These additional reserves allow banks to lend more money, which ultimately expands the money supply. In essence, the Fed is creating money when it buys securities.

As a result, the Fed has come to own more than $234 billion worth of Treasury securities. The Fed uses the interest it receives on these obligations to finance its operations. It turns the excess interest back to the Treasury each year.

The rest of the Treasury securities that are held by the federal government—$795.9 billion worth—are held by various trust funds. Of this

TABLE 1
Estimated Ownership of Public Debt, 1990

	BILLIONS OF $	% OF TOTAL
PUBLIC ACCOUNTS (Debt owned by the Federal Government)		
Federal Reserve System	234.4	7.3
Other (including social security trust funds)	795.9	24.8
Total public	1030.3	32.1
PRIVATE ACCOUNTS (Debt not owned by the Federal Government)		
Commercial banks	185.5	5.8
Individuals	235.1	7.3
Insurance companies	136.9	4.3
Money market funds	33.1	1.0
Corporations	97.7	3.1
State and local governments	339.1	10.6
Foreigners	399.0	12.4
Other*	749.6	23.4
Total Private	2176.0	67.9
TOTAL	$3206.3	100%

*Note: Includes savings and loans, credit unions, pension funds, etc.
Source: *Economic Report of the President, 1991*, Tables B-77, B-86, adj. for 1990 fourth qtr. changes.

$795.9 billion is currently held in trust funds administered by the Social Security Administration. To date, nearly $300 billion has accumulated in the social security trust funds.

What happens to these funds? They are used to buy Treasury securities! This makes deficit accounting a very tricky business. Table 31.1 shows that the consolidated deficit was $166.2 billion in 1990. If we remove the social security surplus for 1990, the deficit is $230.2 billion.

Other federal trust funds that own U.S. Treasury obligations include federal employees' retirement funds, highway trust funds, the military retirement fund, and the airport and airway trust fund.

"Private accounts" in Table 1 refers to nonfederal government accounts. Some of these are administered by state and local governments. Most of the $339.1 billion owned by

states and localities is in pension funds administered by those governments for their employees. For example, many states have a teachers' retirement fund, and many of the dollars in those funds are invested in Treasury securities. These funds are not really owned by the government, because each dollar in them represents an obligation of the state or local government to a retiree.

Private ownership of Treasury obligations is widespread. Individuals directly own $235.1 billion, or 7.3% of the total. Banks, insurance companies, and money market mutual funds together account for a total of $355.5 billion, or just over 11% of the total.

In recent years, there has been some concern that the United States is relying on foreign countries (particularly Japan) to finance its deficits. As of 1990, foreigners held a total of $399 billion, or 12.4% of the total.

THE DEFICIT AND THE FUTURE STANDARD OF LIVING   It is sometimes argued that one of the burdens of large government deficits (which lead to a large government debt) is the crowding out of investment. Recall from Chapter 28 that when government spending (G) increases or the level of net taxes (T) decreases (both of which increase the deficit, $G - T$) with the money supply unchanged, the interest rate rises and crowds out (decreases) planned investment spending. The cost of decreased investment spending is then a smaller capital stock.

As you know, one of the key decisions all economies make is how much to consume today and how much to consume in the future. Put another way, resources must be allocated between consumption goods and capital goods. Capital goods (investment in plant and equipment) increase future productivity and lead to economic growth. Our friends Bill and Colleen faced this decision on their desert island. They had to decide how to allocate their time between building a boat (capital investment) and gathering food (consumption). If the government through its tax and expenditure policies is crowding out investment (by spending more than it receives in tax revenues), future economic growth is being hurt. This is why many argue that the real burden of the government deficits will fall on U.S. children, whose standards of living will be lower in the future than they would have been if the government had not spent so much relative to its income in the past.

WHAT DOES THE DEFICIT MEASURE?   Much of the concern over the federal debt centers around the fact that it represents a claim on the government in the future. Recent economic analysis of the federal budget suggests that the annual budget deficit may be a misleading indicator of the impact of the overall government budget, however. This may be true because the borrowing undertaken in a given year is only one aspect of the total "obligations" that the government incurs in that year.

As an extreme example, suppose that the government decides to reduce the level of social security benefits for retirees starting in 1998. Such a policy would have no impact on the actual budgets between now and 1998, but the total public obligations of the government are now lower. Similarly, changes in loan guarantee programs (such as government guarantees of the mortgages of some veterans) or in deposit insurance laws can have significant impacts on the future obligations of the federal government. If the government were a corporation, accountants would insist that all future obligations be recognized on the books, just as if a bond had been issued.

FIGURE 31.2

Deficit Reduction Targets Under Gramm-Rudman-Hollings

The GRH legislation, passed in 1986, set out to lower the federal deficit by $36 billion per year. If the plan had worked, a zero deficit would have been achieved by 1991.

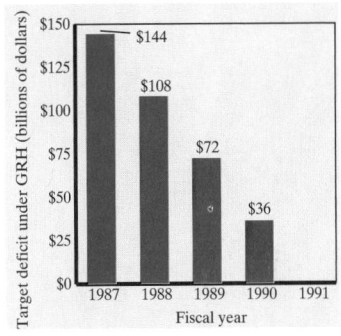

DEFICIT REDUCTION AND MACROPOLICY: GRAMM-RUDMAN-HOLLINGS

As Table 31.1 shows, in 1986 the deficit of the federal government reached an unprecedented $201.1 billion, or 4.7% of GDP. Concern over the deficit was widespread, and elected officials felt that something should be done about what was perceived as a major problem confronting the U.S. economy. As a result of this concern, the U.S. Congress passed, and President Reagan signed, a bill known popularly as the **Gramm-Rudman-Hollings Bill,** after its three congressional sponsors. Hereafter, we will refer to this bill as the GRH legislation, or just GRH.

In essence, GRH set a target for reducing the federal deficit by a set amount each year. As Figure 31.2 shows, the deficit was to decline by $36 billion per year between 1987 and 1991, with a deficit of zero slated for fiscal year 1991. What was particularly interesting about the GRH legislation was that the targets were not merely guidelines. If Congress, through its decisions about taxes and spending programs, produced a budget with a deficit larger than the targeted amount, GRH

Gramm-Rudman-Hollings Bill
Passed by the U.S. Congress and signed by President Reagan in 1986, this law set out to reduce the federal deficit by $36 billion per year, with a deficit of zero slated for 1991. The law has not succeeded in its goal, and the deficit remains very high.

called for automatic spending cuts. The cuts were divided proportionately among most federal spending programs, so that a program that comprised 5% of total spending was to endure a cut equal to 5% of the total spending cut.[1]

In 1986, the U.S. Supreme Court declared part of the GRH bill unconstitutional. In effect, the court said that the "automatic" spending cuts had to be approved by Congress before taking place. The law was changed in 1986 to meet the Supreme Court ruling and again in 1987, when new targets were established. The new targets had the deficit reaching zero in 1993 rather than 1991. The targets were changed again in 1991, when the year to achieve a zero deficit was changed from 1993 to 1996.

You can see from the actual deficit values in Table 31.1 that these targets never came close to being achieved. As time wore on even the revised targets became completely unrealistic, and by 1988 it was clear that Congress was not going to take the original GRH legislation seriously.

The Effects of Government Spending Cuts on the Deficit

Although GRH is interesting from both a historical and a political perspective, it also provides an excellent framework for talking about government deficits and the consequences of trying to reduce the deficit.

Suppose that the terms of the GRH bill, or some other deficit-reduction bill, dictate that the deficit be cut by $20 billion. By how much must government spending be cut to achieve this goal? You might be tempted to think that the spending cuts should simply add up to the amount by which the deficit is to be cut—in this case, $20 billion. (This is in fact what GRH dictated: If the deficit needed to be cut by a certain amount, automatic spending cuts were to be equal to this amount.) This course of action seems reasonable from an individual household's point of view. If you decrease your personal spending by $100 over the course of a year, your personal deficit will fall by the full $100 of your spending cut.

But the government is not an individual household. A cut in government spending shifts the AD curve to the left and results in a decrease in aggregate output (income) (Y) and thus a contraction in the economy. When the economy contracts, both the taxable income of households and the profits of firms fall. This means that revenue from the personal income tax and the corporate profits tax will fall.

How does this affect the size of the deficit? To estimate the response of the deficit to changes in government spending, we need to go through two steps. First, we must decide how much a $1 change in government spending will change GDP. In other words, we need to know the size of the government spending multiplier. (Recall that the government spending multiplier measures the increase [or decrease] in GDP [Y] brought about by a $1 increase [or decrease] in government spending.) Based on empirical evidence, a reasonable value for the government spending multiplier seems to be around 1.4 after one year, and this is the value that we will use here. This means that a $1 billion decrease in government spending lowers GDP by about $1.4 billion after one year.

Next, we must see what happens to the deficit when GDP changes. We have just noted that when GDP falls (that is, when the economy contracts), taxable income and corporate profits fall and thus tax revenues fall. In addition, some categories of government expenditures tend to rise when the economy contracts. For example, unemployment insurance benefits (a transfer payment) rise as the econo-

---

[1]Certain programs, notably Social Security, were exempt from cuts or were treated somewhat differently. Interest payments on the federal debt were also immune from cuts.

my contracts because more people become unemployed and thus eligible for unemployment benefits. Both the decrease in tax revenues and the rise in government expenditures cause the deficit to increase. Thus,

> The deficit tends to rise when GDP falls. Conversely, the deficit tends to fall when GDP rises.

For the sake of illustration, let us assume that the **deficit response index (DRI)** is −.22. That is, for every $1 billion decrease in GDP, the deficit rises by $0.22 billion. This number seems close to what is true in practice.

deficit response index (DRI) The amount by which the deficit changes with a one dollar change in GDP.

We can now use the multiplier and the *DRI* to answer the question that began this section. Suppose that government spending is reduced by $20 billion, the exact amount of the necessary deficit reduction. This will lower GDP by 1.4 × $20 billion, or $28 billion, if the value of the multiplier is 1.4. A $28 billion fall in GDP will increase the deficit by .22 × $28 billion, or $6.2 billion, if the value of the *DRI* is −.22. Because we initially cut government spending (and therefore lowered the deficit from this source) by $20 billion, the net effect of the spending cut is to lower the deficit by $20 billion − $6.2 billion = $13.8 billion.

A $20 billion government spending cut thus does not lower the deficit by the required $20 billion. To lower the deficit by the full $20 billion, we need to cut government spending by about $30 billion. Using 1.4 as the value of the government spending multiplier and −.22 as the value of the *DRI*, we see that a spending cut of $30 billion lowers GDP by 1.4 × $30 billion, or $42 billion. This raises the deficit by .22 × $42 billion, or $9.2 billion. The net effect on the deficit is thus −$30 billion (from the government spending cut) + $9.2 billion, which is −$20.8 billion (an amount slightly larger than the necessary $20 billion reduction). This means that the spending cut must be nearly 50% larger than the deficit reduction we wish to achieve! Clearly, then, Congress would have had trouble achieving the deficit targets even if it had allowed GRH's automatic spending cuts to take place.

GRH: BAD MACROECONOMICS Is Congress really so poorly informed about macroeconomics that it would pass legislation that could not possibly work? In other words, are there any conditions under which it would be reasonable to assume that a spending cut needs to be only as large as the desired reduction in the deficit? If the government spending multiplier is zero, government spending cuts will not contract the economy, and there will be no effect from this source on the deficit. In this case, the only effect on the deficit will be the initial cut in government spending.

But are there times when it is reasonable to assume that the government spending multiplier is zero? Before the GRH bill was passed, some argued that there were. If households and firms are worried about the large government deficits and hold back on consumption and investment because of these worries, the argument went, the passage of GRH might make them more optimistic and induce them to consume and invest more. This increased consumption and investment, the argument continued, would offset the effects of the decreased government spending, and the net result would be a multiplier effect of zero.

Another argument in favor of the GRH bill centered on the Fed and monetary policy. We know from Chapter 29 that an increase in the money supply shifts the *AD* curve to the right. Because a cut in government spending shifts the *AD* curve to the left, the Fed could respond to the spending cut by increasing the money supply enough to shift the *AD* curve back (to the right) to its original position, thus preventing any change in aggregate output (income). Some argued that the

Fed would be likely to behave in this way after the passage of the GRH bill because it would see that Congress finally "got its house in order."

We know from Chapter 28 that an increase in the money supply leads to a decrease in the equilibrium interest rate. Therefore, if the Fed were to offset the effects of a decrease in government spending by increasing the money supply, the interest rate would fall, thus stimulating planned investment and offsetting the effects of the decrease in G. Again, this would be a multiplier of zero. However, studies done at the time of the original GRH bill showed that the decrease in the interest rate that would be necessary to have the multiplier be zero (that is, for a government spending cut to have no effect on aggregate output [income]) is quite large. The Fed would have had to engage in extreme behavior with respect to interest rate changes for the multiplier to be zero.

To summarize:

> A zero multiplier can come about through renewed optimism on the part of households and firms or through very aggressive behavior on the part of the Fed. But because neither of these situations is very plausible, the multiplier is likely to be greater than zero. Thus, it is likely that in order to lower the deficit by a certain amount, the cut in government spending must be larger than that amount.

Economic Stability and Deficit Reduction

If the GRH legislation had been implemented, it would have had a significant impact on the way the economy responds to a variety of stimuli. By analyzing what the effects of GRH would have been, we can see some of the ways that other deficit-reduction policies would affect the economy.

In a world with no GRH or similar bill, the Congress and the President make decisions each year about how much to spend and how much to tax. The federal government deficit is a result of these decisions and the state of the economy. With GRH, on the other hand, the size of the deficit is set in advance. Taxes and government spending must be adjusted to produce the required deficit. In this situation, the deficit is no longer a consequence of the tax and spending decisions; rather, taxes and spending become a consequence of the deficit decision.

What difference does it make whether Congress chooses a target deficit and adjusts government spending and taxes to achieve this target or decides how much to spend and tax and lets the deficit adjust itself? The difference may be substantial. Consider a leftward shift of the AD curve caused by some negative demand shock. A **negative demand shock** is something that causes a shift in consumption or investment schedules or that leads to a decrease in U.S. exports.

We know that a leftward shift of the AD curve lowers aggregate output (income), which causes the government deficit to increase. In a world without GRH, the increase in the deficit during contractions provides an **automatic stabilizer** for the economy. (Review Chapter 25 if this term is hazy to you.) The contraction-induced decrease in tax revenues and increase in transfer payments tends to boost consumer incomes and stimulate consumer spending at a time when spending would otherwise be weak. Thus, the decrease in aggregate output (income) caused by the negative demand shock is lessened somewhat by the growth of the deficit (see Figure 31.3a).

In a world with GRH, the deficit is not allowed to rise. The GRH rules require some combination of tax increases and government spending cuts to offset what would have otherwise been an increase in the deficit. We know that increases in taxes or cuts in spending are contractionary in themselves. The contraction in the econo-

negative demand shock
Something that causes a shift in consumption or investment schedules or that leads to a decrease in U.S. exports.

automatic stabilizers Revenue and expenditure items in the federal budget that automatically change with the economy in such a way as to stabilize GDP.

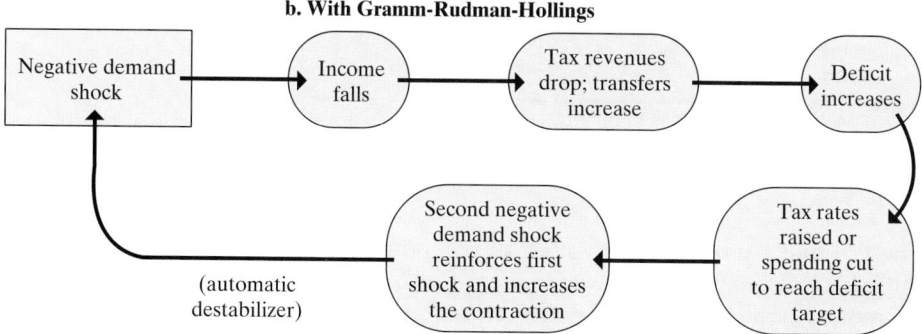

a. Without Gramm-Rudman-Hollings

Positive boost to demand reduces the shock

(automatic stabilizers)

Negative demand shock → Income falls → Tax revenues drop; transfers increase → Deficit increases

b. With Gramm-Rudman-Hollings

Negative demand shock → Income falls → Tax revenues drop; transfers increase → Deficit increases

(automatic destabilizer)

Second negative demand shock reinforces first shock and increases the contraction ← Tax rates raised or spending cut to reach deficit target

FIGURE 31.3

Gramm-Rudman-Hollings as an Automatic Destabilizer

Bills like GRH change the way the economy responds to negative demand shocks because they do not allow the deficit to increase. The result is a smaller deficit, but a larger decline in income than would have otherwise occurred.

my will therefore be larger than it would have been without the GRH rules in place, because the initial effect of the negative demand shock is worsened by the rise in taxes or the cut in government spending necessitated by the GRH rules. As Figure 31.3b shows, the GRH legislation acts as an **automatic destabilizer.** It requires taxes to be raised and government spending to be cut during a contraction, which reinforces, rather than counteracts, the shock that started the contraction.

automatic destabilizers Revenue and expenditure items in the federal budget that automatically change with the economy in such a way as to destabilize GDP.

SUMMARY   The preceding discussion should make it clear that the GRH legislation was an exercise in bad macroeconomics. It assumed a zero multiplier, which is not realistic in most cases, and it cut spending or raised taxes at the wrong times. This is not to say, of course, that Congress should ignore the deficit. (Recall that a higher government debt means that we must bear higher interest costs. In addition, higher deficits may lead to slower growth in the future.) It just means that the way the GRH legislation locked the economy into spending cuts is not a good way to manage the economy.

The size of the federal deficit was an important issue in the 1992 presidential campaign, with Bill Clinton campaigning on a promise to cut the deficit in half in four years. In addition, H. Ross Perot entered the race during the campaign with a platform of dramatic tax increases and expenditure cuts designed to cut even more deeply into the deficit. Whether President Clinton will ultimately succeed in his goal is unclear. A start in this direction, however, was the passage of the deficit reduction bill in August 1993, which was designed to reduce the deficit by a total of about $500 billion over a five-year period. Previous attempts to lower the deficit suggest that this goal will not be easy to achieve.

THE FED'S RESPONSE TO THE STATE OF THE ECONOMY

We know from Chapter 26 that the Fed can control the money supply through open market operations, and we know from Chapters 28 and 29 that changes in the money supply can affect aggregate output (income) (Y), the interest rate, and the price level.

FIGURE 31.4

The Fed's Response to Low Output/Low Inflation

During periods of low output/low inflation, the economy is on the relatively flat portion of the *AS* curve. In this case, the Fed is likely to expand the money supply. This will shift the *AD* curve to the right, from AD_0 to AD_1, and lead to an increase in output with very little increase in the price level.

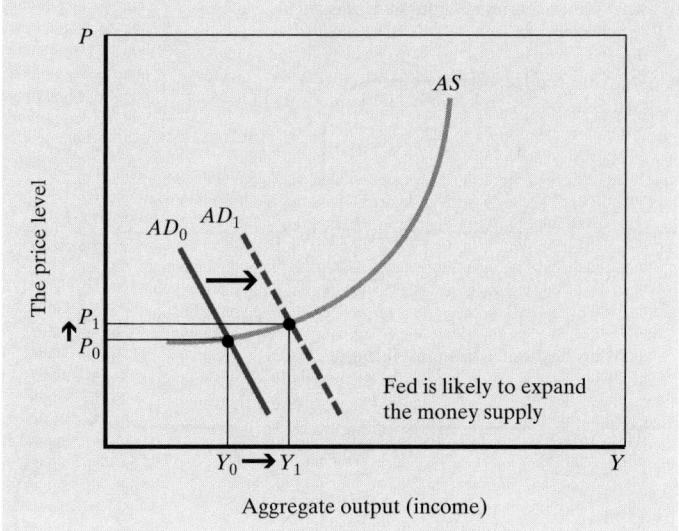

Aggregate output (income)

The Fed thus has the power to affect the economy through open market operations. But what factors affect its decisions? Why does the Fed sometimes choose to increase the money supply and sometimes choose to decrease the money supply?

Two of the Fed's main goals are high levels of output and employment and a low rate of inflation. From the Fed's point of view, the best situation is a fully employed economy with a low inflation rate. The worst situation is *stagflation*—a period of high unemployment and high inflation.

If the economy is in a low output/low inflation situation, it will be producing on the relatively flat portion of the *AS* curve (see Figure 31.4). In this case, the Fed can increase output by increasing the money supply with very little effect on the price level. The increase in the money supply will shift the *AD* curve to the right, which will lead to an increase in output with very little change in the price level. Thus,

> The Fed is likely to increase the money supply during times of low output and low inflation.

The opposite is true in times of high output and high inflation. In this situation, the economy is producing on the relatively steep portion of the *AS* curve (see Figure 31.5), and the Fed can decrease the money supply with very little effect on output. The decrease in the money supply will shift the *AD* curve to the left, which will lead to a fall in the price level and little effect on output.[2] Thus,

> The Fed is likely to decrease the money supply during times of high output and high inflation.

Stagflation is a more difficult problem to solve. If the Fed expands the money supply, output will rise, but so will the inflation rate (which is already too high). If the Fed contracts the money supply, the inflation rate will fall, but so will output (which is already too low). (You should be able to draw *AS/AD* diagrams to see

---

[2]In practice, the price level rarely falls. What the Fed actually achieves in this case is a decrease in the *rate of inflation* (that is, in the percentage change in the price level), not a decrease in the price level itself. The discussion here is sliding over the distinction between the price level and the rate of inflation. Recall our discussion of this distinction in Chapter 30.

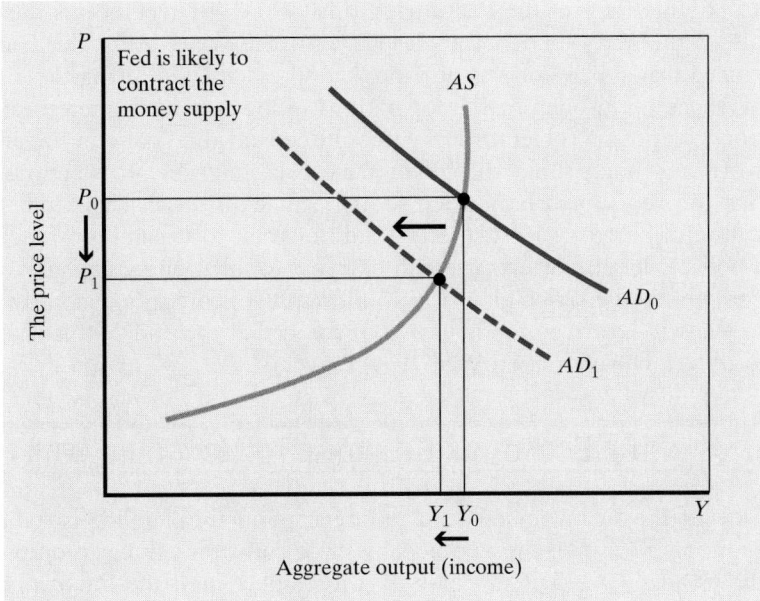

FIGURE 31.5
The Fed's Response to High Output/High Inflation
During periods of high output/high inflation, the economy is on the relatively steep portion of the AS curve. In this case, the Fed is likely to contract the money supply. This will shift the AD curve to the left, from AD_0 to AD_1, and lead to a decrease in the price level with very little decrease in output.

why this is true.) The Fed is thus faced with a trade-off. In this case, the Fed's decisions depend on how it weighs output relative to inflation. If it dislikes high inflation more than low output, it will contract the money supply; if it dislikes low output more than high inflation, it will expand the money supply. In practice, the Fed probably dislikes high inflation more than low output, but this in part depends on the beliefs of the chair of the Fed.

The Fed is sometimes said to "lean against the wind." This means that as the economy expands, the Fed uses open market operations to raise interest rates gradually to try to prevent the economy from expanding too quickly. Conversely, as the economy contracts, the Fed lowers interest rates gradually to lessen (and eventually stop) the contraction. This type of stabilization is not easily achieved, however, as we will see later in this chapter.

THE BEHAVIOR OF THE FED DURING THE 1990–1991 RECESSION Sometime in the second half of 1990, it seemed likely that the U.S. economy was in a recession. Since inflation seemed to be under control at the time, experts expected the Fed to begin following an expansionary monetary policy to lessen the contraction of the economy.

The Fed followed this policy exactly. On December 19, 1990, it lowered the discount rate from 7.0% to 6.5%, and on February 1, 1991, it lowered the discount rate further, to 6.0 percent. (Review the discussion of the discount rate in Chapter 26 if necessary.) The Fed's move on February 1 was quite interesting, as it responded almost immediately to the Labor Department's announcement that day that the unemployment rate had risen to 6.2% in January. Usually the Fed does not respond quite so rapidly, but in this case it seemed clear that the Fed was becoming alarmed that the U.S. economy was sinking fast. On April 30, 1991, the Fed lowered the discount rate again, to 5.5 percent.

During this same period, the Fed was also engaging in open market operations to lower market interest rates. The three-month Treasury bill rate fell from 7.7% in July 1990 to 6.8% in December 1990, then to 5.7% in April 1991. All of these policies were designed, of course, to stimulate private spending and bring the economy out of the recession.

The behavior of the Fed during the 1990–1991 recession is thus a clear example of the Fed's tendency to lean against the wind. After the Fed became convinced that a recession was at hand, it responded by lowering the discount rate and by engaging in open market operations to lower market interest rates. Since inflation was not a problem, the Fed could expand the economy in this way without worrying much about the inflationary consequences of its actions. Some argued that the Fed should have acted sooner, but with the Persian Gulf situation uncertain until February 1991, the Fed did not want to expand too much in the face of a possibly lengthy war that could have led to inflationary pressures. Once the outcome of the Persian Gulf War was known, the Fed responded fairly rapidly.

We will return to the behavior of the Fed at the end of this chapter, where we discuss its behavior after April 1991.

LAGS IN THE ECONOMY'S RESPONSE TO MONETARY AND FISCAL POLICY

One of the main objectives of monetary and fiscal policy is stabilization of the economy. Consider the two possible time paths for aggregate output (income) (Y) shown in Figure 31.6. In path B (the dashed line), the fluctuations in GDP are smaller than those in path A (the solid line). One aim of **stabilization policy** is to smooth out fluctuations in output, to try to move the economy along a path like B instead of A. Stabilization policy is also concerned with the stability of prices. Here the goal is not to prevent the overall price level from rising at all but rather to achieve an inflation rate that is as low as possible given the government's other goals—high and stable levels of output and employment.

Stabilization goals are not necessarily easy to achieve. The existence of various kinds of **time lags,** or delays in the response of the economy to stabilization policies, can make the economy difficult to control. Economists generally recognize three kinds of time lags: *recognition lags, implementation lags,* and *response lags.* We will consider each of these in turn, but it is useful to begin with an analogy.

"THE FOOL IN THE SHOWER" Milton Friedman, a leading critic of stabilization policy, once likened the government's attempts to stabilize the economy to a "fool in the shower." The shower starts out too cold, because the pipes have not yet warmed up. So the fool turns up the hot water. Nothing happens right away, so

stabilization policy A term used to describe both monetary and fiscal policy, the goals of which are to smooth out fluctuations in output and employment and to keep prices as stable as possible.

time lags Delays in the economy's response to stabilization policies.

FIGURE 31.6
Two Time Paths for GDP
Path A is less stable—that is, it shows more variation over time—than path B. Other things being equal, society prefers path B to path A.

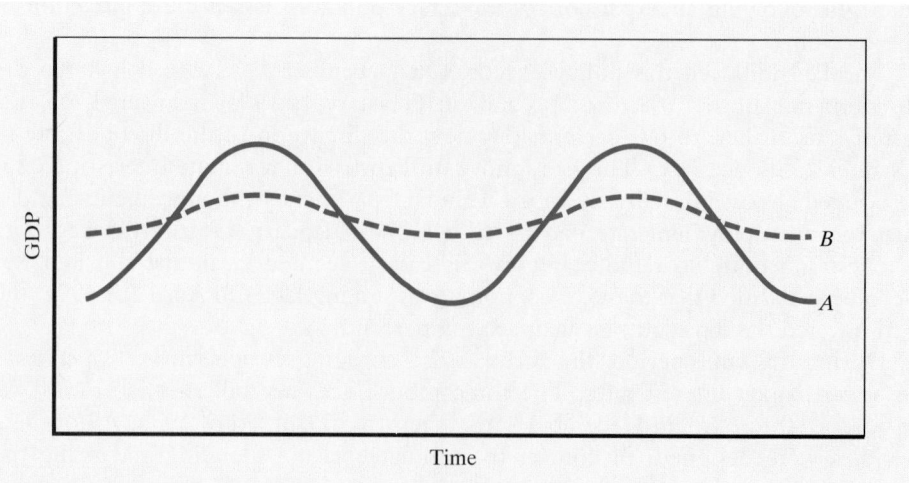

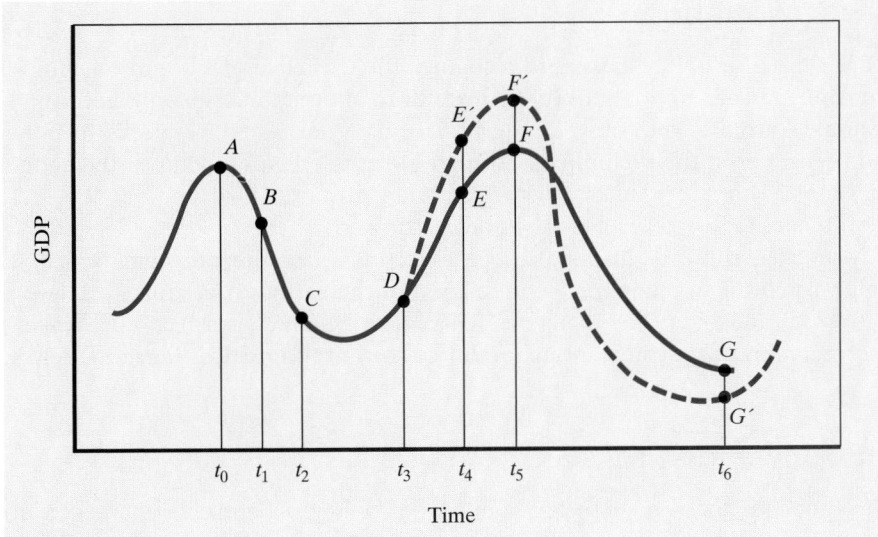

FIGURE 31.7
"The Fool in the Shower"—
How Government Policy Can
Make Matters Worse

Attempts to stabilize the economy can prove to be destabilizing because of time lags. An expansionary policy that should have begun to take effect at point A does not actually begin to have an impact until point D, when the economy is already on an upswing. Hence the policy pushes the economy to points F' and G' (rather than points F and G). Income varies more widely than it would have if no policy had been implemented.

he turns up the hot water a bit further. The hot water then comes on and scalds him. He immediately turns up the cold water. Again, nothing happens right away, so he turns up the cold still further. When the cold water finally starts to come up, he has succeeded in making the shower too cold. And so it goes.

In Friedman's view, the government is constantly behaving like the fool in the shower, stimulating or contracting the economy at the wrong time. An example of how this might happen is shown in Figure 31.7. Suppose the economy reaches a peak and begins to slide into recession at point A (at time t_0). Policy makers do not observe the decline in GDP until it has sunk to point B (at time t_1). By the time they have begun to stimulate the economy (point C, time t_2), the recession is well advanced and the economy has almost bottomed out. When the policies finally begin to take effect (point D, time t_3), the economy is already on its road to recovery. The policies thus push the economy to point F'—a much greater fluctuation than point F, which is where the economy would have been without the stabilization policy. Sometime after point D, policy makers may begin to realize that the economy is expanding too quickly. But by the time they have implemented contractionary policies and the policies have made their effects felt, the economy is starting to weaken. The contractionary policies therefore end up pushing GDP to point G' instead of point G.

In short: Because of the various time lags, the expansionary policies that should have been instituted at time t_0 do not begin to have an effect until time t_3, when they are no longer needed. The dashed lines in Figure 31.7 show how the economy behaves as a result of the "stabilization" policies; the solid lines show the time path of GDP if the economy had been allowed to run its course and no stabilization policies had been attempted. In this case, stabilization policy clearly succeeds in making income more erratic rather than less erratic—the policy results in a peak income of F' as opposed to F and a trough income of G' instead of G.

Critics of stabilization policy argue that the situation described in Figure 31.7 is typical of the interaction between the government and the rest of the economy. This is not necessarily true, however. We need to know more about the exact nature of the various kinds of lags before deciding whether stabilization policy is good or bad. We will now consider these lags.

Recognition Lags

It takes time for policy makers to recognize the existence of a boom or slump. For one thing, many important data—those from the national income accounts, for example—are available only quarterly. It usually takes several weeks to compile and prepare even the preliminary estimates for these figures. Thus, if the economy goes into a slump on January 1, the recession may not show up until the data for the first quarter are available at the end of April.

Moreover, the early national income accounts data are only preliminary estimates, based on an incomplete compilation of the various data sources. These estimates can, and often do, change as better data become available. This makes the interpretation of the initial estimates difficult, and **recognition lags** are the result.

recognition lag The time it takes for policy makers to recognize the existence of a boom or slump.

Implementation Lags

The problems that lags pose for stabilization policy do not end once economists and policy makers recognize that the economy is in a slump or a boom. Even if everyone knows that the economy needs to be stimulated or reined in, it takes time to put the desired policy into effect, especially for actions that involve fiscal policy. **Implementation lags** are the result.

Each year Congress decides on the federal government's budget for the coming year. The tax laws and spending programs embodied in this budget are not subject to change once they are in place. If it becomes clear that the economy is entering a recession and is in need of a fiscal stimulus during the middle of the year, there is relatively little that can be done. Until Congress authorizes more spending or a cut in taxes, changes in fiscal policy are not possible.[3]

implementation lag The time that it takes to put the desired policy into effect once economists and policy makers recognize that the economy is in a slump or a boom.

Implementation lags vary in length. In May of 1975, for example, it was clear that the U.S. economy was in the midst of a deep recession and needed immediate stimulation. Although many economists had called for government action earlier, general agreement that action was necessary did not come about until late spring. Once the consensus emerged, President Ford asked Congress for an immediate tax cut retroactive to 1974. (See the Issues and Applications box on this topic in Chapter 25.) Congress responded, and rebate checks were mailed to millions of people within weeks. As those dollars were spent, the economy began to recover.

Monetary policy is less subject to the kinds of restrictions that slow down changes in fiscal policy. As we saw in Chapter 26, the Fed's chief tool to control the supply of money or the interest rate is open market operations—the buying and selling of government securities. Transactions in these securities take place in a highly developed market, and if the Fed wishes, it can buy or sell a large volume of securities in a very short period of time. Therefore,

> The implementation lag for monetary policy is generally much shorter than it is for fiscal policy.

Whenever the Fed wishes to increase the supply of money, it simply goes into the open market and purchases government securities. This instantly increases the stock of money (that is, bank reserves held at the Fed), and an expansion of the money supply begins.

---

[3]Don't forget, however, about the existence of automatic stabilizers. Many programs contain built-in counter-cyclical features that expand spending or cut tax collections automatically (without the need for congressional or executive action) during a recession.

Response Lags

Even after a macroeconomic problem has been recognized and the appropriate policies to correct it have been implemented, another set of lags remains. These are **response lags**—the lags that occur because of the operation of the economy itself. Even after the government has formulated a policy and put it into place, the economy takes time to adjust to the new conditions.

Although monetary policy can be adjusted and implemented more quickly than fiscal policy, it may actually take longer to make its effect felt on the economy. What is most important is the total lag between the time a problem first occurs and the time the corrective policies are felt. Even if monetary policy has a smaller implementation lag than does fiscal policy, it may nevertheless have a longer lag in total, once response lags are also considered.

RESPONSE LAGS FOR FISCAL POLICY One way to think about the response lag in fiscal policy is through the concept of the government spending multiplier. Remember that this multiplier measures the change in GDP caused by a given change in government spending or net taxes. It takes time for the multiplier to reach its full value. There is thus a lag between the time a fiscal policy action is first initiated and the time when the full change in GDP is realized.

The reason for the response lag in fiscal policy—the delay in the multiplier process—is quite simple. During the first few months after an increase in government spending or a tax cut, there simply is not enough time for the firms or individuals who benefit directly from the extra government spending or the tax cut to increase their own spending. A simple example will help to make this clear.

Suppose that you are the owner of Transylvania Trucking, a small fleet of trucks. The government decides to increase its spending, and one of the things it spends more on is trucking services, including some extra purchases from your company. In the first months after you receive this extra business from the government, however, you are unlikely to increase your own purchases. Most of the things you buy—trucks, office furniture, stationery—are already contained in your inventories. It will generally take you some time before your own purchases are increased to reflect the extra income that you have received, and the multiplier effect of government spending will not be felt until this occurs. In short:

> Neither individuals nor firms revise their spending plans instantaneously. Until they can make those revisions, extra government spending does not stimulate extra private spending.

Changes in government purchases have the virtue of being a component of aggregate expenditure. When G rises, aggregate expenditure increases directly; when G falls, aggregate expenditure decreases directly. When personal taxes are changed, however, an additional step intervenes, and this gives rise to another lag. Suppose, for example, that a tax cut has lowered personal income taxes across the board. Each household must now decide what portion of its tax cut to spend and what portion to save. This decision is the extra step. Before the tax cut gets translated into extra spending, households must take the step of increasing their spending, and it usually takes some time for this to be done.

With a business tax cut, there is a further complication. Firms must decide what to do with their added after-tax profits. If they pay out their added profits to households as dividends, the result is the same as that of a personal tax cut.

response lag The time that it takes for the economy to adjust to the new conditions after a new policy is implemented; the lag that occurs because of the operation of the economy itself.

Households must decide whether to spend or to save the extra funds. Firms may also retain their added profits and use them for investment, but investment is a component of aggregate expenditure that requires planning and time.

In practice, it takes about a year for a change in taxes or in government spending to have its full effect on the economy. This means that if we increase spending to counteract a recession today, the full effects will not be felt for 12 months. By that time, the state of the economy might be very different from what it is now.

RESPONSE LAGS FOR MONETARY POLICY   As you know, monetary policy works by changing interest rates, which then change planned investment. Interest rates can also affect consumption spending, as we discuss in more detail in the next chapter. For now, though, it is enough to know that lower interest rates usually stimulate consumption spending and higher interest rates decrease consumption spending.

The response of consumption and investment to interest rate changes takes time. Even if interest rates were to drop by five percentage points overnight, firms would not immediately increase their investment purchases. Firms generally make their investment plans several years in advance. If General Motors wants to respond to a decrease in interest rates by investing more, for example, it will take some time—perhaps up to a year—for the firm to come up with plans for a new factory or assembly line. While such plans are being drawn up, GM may spend very little on new investments. Thus, the effect of the decrease in interest rates may not make itself felt for quite some time.

It is likely that the response lags for monetary policy will be even longer than those for fiscal policy. When government spending changes, there is a direct change in the sales of firms, which sell more as a result of the increased government purchases. When interest rates change, however, the sales of firms do not change until households change their consumption spending and/or firms change their investment spending. As we have just said, it takes time for households and firms to respond to interest rate changes. In this sense, interest rate changes are like tax rate changes. The resulting change in firm sales must wait for households and firms to change their purchases of goods.

SUMMARY   From this analysis it should be clear that stabilization is not easily achieved. It takes time for policy makers to recognize the existence of a problem, more time for them to implement a solution, and yet more time for firms and households to respond to the stabilization policies taken. Monetary policy can be adjusted more quickly and easily than taxes or government spending, and this makes it a useful instrument in stabilizing the economy. But because the economy's response to monetary changes is probably slower than its response to changes in fiscal policy, tax and spending changes can also play a useful role in macroeconomic management.

THE POLITICAL BUSINESS CYCLE

Most work in macroeconomics treats the behavior of the government in a rather stylized fashion. Although we assume that firms and households are motivated by self-interest, we usually do not think of the government in this way. Instead, in most macroeconomic analysis, the government is seen as purely benevolent—its goal is to further the overall welfare of society. Both fiscal and monetary policies are thought of as tools used to stabilize the economy for the good of everyone.

It may be useful, however, to consider a different approach to the behavior of government. We know that Congress and the President of the United States, along with the Board of Governors of the Federal Reserve (especially its chair), are responsible for setting the government's macroeconomic policies. We also know that with the exception of the Fed chair, who is appointed by the President, macroeconomic policy makers are answerable to the electorate. If these policy makers take actions that displease the voting public, they may be turned out of office, later if not sooner. Assuming that elected officials wish to remain in office, they have an incentive to manipulate the economy in such a way as to maximize their chances for being reelected.[4]

For purposes of our discussion, it will help to consider an extreme case. Let us say for the purposes of argument that elected officials are concerned solely with getting themselves and their parties reelected. How, then, would we expect elected officials to behave regarding their management of the economy? In order to answer this question, we first need to know how the state of the economy influences voters' behavior.

VOTING BEHAVIOR The empirical evidence suggests, not surprisingly, that voters dislike both inflation and recessions. If they feel that the party in power in the White House has done a poor job of managing the economy, they tend to vote against that party in the next election. If they feel that that party has done well, they tend to vote to keep that party in power.

Consider a voter on election day deciding how to vote. You might think that a typical voter would look back over the entire period that the party has been in power to judge how well the party has managed the economy. In particular, you might think that voters look at the party's record on inflation and output. Prior to the 1992 election, however, empirical studies suggested that voters look back only about a year or two. Furthermore, the evidence suggested that it is not the *level* of output, but rather the *change* in output, that voters care most about. If output has risen in the past year, for example, voters take this as a good sign, even though the level of output may still be fairly low. The evidence suggested that voters tend to vote for the party in power (1) if the inflation rate has been low in the two-year period before the election, and (2) if output has been rising in the year of the election. They vote for the other party if the opposite is true. We will see below that voters may no longer behave in this way, but assume for now that they do.

BEHAVIOR OF POLITICIANS If voters do behave in the way just described, how should the party in power manage the economy if its only goal is to get reelected? Obviously it will want inflation to be as low as possible in the two-year period before the election and output to be rising as quickly as possible in the election year. The party in power thus has an incentive to have a recession early in its term in office. By engineering a recession early on, it can pump up the economy during the later part of its term so that by the time election day rolls around, the economy will be booming. Remember from Chapter 29 that the economy is operating on the relatively flat (horizontal) part of the *AS* curve during a recession. A shift in aggregate demand, therefore, tends to have more of an impact on real output and less of an effect on the price level when the economy is in a recession.

---

[4]Do not interpret political theories of the business cycle to mean that the government is wicked or that elected officials are corrupt or cynical. We are merely interested in looking at the incentives that influence real-world political behavior, just as in earlier chapters we looked at the incentives that influence real-world behavior of households and firms.

FIGURE 31.8
The Political Business Cycle

By using macroeconomic policies, office holders can attempt to manipulate the economy to improve their chances for reelection. Under certain assumptions about voting behavior, the optimal strategy is to contract the economy soon after being elected, then stimulate the economy during the second half of the four-year term, thus producing a recovery in income and a fall in unemployment (while maintaining a low rate of inflation) just before the next election.

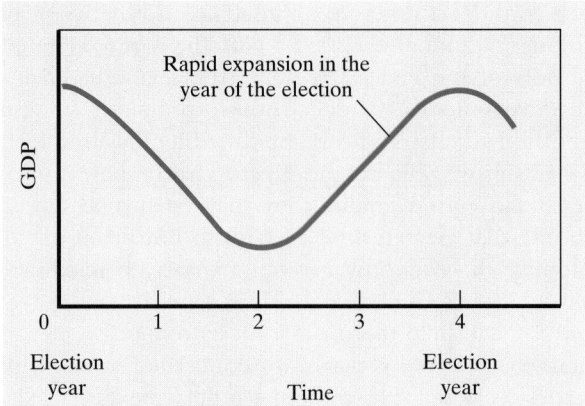

political business cycle A business cycle generated by policy makers for the purpose of maximizing their chances of being reelected.

A simplified version of this situation is shown in Figure 31.8. An election is held in year zero and again in year four. Early in its term, the party in power cuts back on aggregate expenditure through cuts in spending or tax increases. This generates a recession. By year three, the government is ready to start stimulating the economy, perhaps through a tax cut or a spending increase, or by pressuring the Federal Reserve to increase the money supply. Because the economy is in a recession and thus on the flat part of the *AS* curve, the increase in expenditure raises output and employment but has relatively little effect on the price level. The economy thus looks good to voters at the time of the election (low inflation and a rising level of output), so they tend to reelect the party in power.

Once the election is over, the party in power needs to slow down the economy to prepare for the next stimulus in about two years. And so it goes. You can see that if this policy were practiced, there would be a regular four-year cycle brought about by the policy makers. Hence the term **political business cycle,** a business cycle generated by policy makers for the purpose of maximizing their chances of being reelected.

Because the board of the Federal Reserve is not directly elected by the public, it is probably less likely to set monetary policy with political purposes in mind. Indeed, part of the reason for making the Fed independent was to insulate monetary policy from politics. Nonetheless, the members of the board and the chair of the Fed are appointed by the President, subject to the approval of Congress. The chair also serves a relatively short four-year term and is likely to be in tune with the political leanings of the President. Thus, it is not unreasonable to expect some easing of monetary policy early in an election year. Arthur Burns was accused of such a policy prior to President Nixon's reelection campaign in 1972, and Alan Greenspan, appointed by President Reagan in 1987, was grilled by senators at his confirmation hearings about the likelihood that he would stimulate the economy and risk inflation to aid the Republicans in 1988.

The Defeat of President Bush in 1992

Many, if not most, people felt that President Bush lost the 1992 election because of the state of the economy. Is this view consistent with the assumption we made about voting behavior above? To answer this question we need to examine how the economy fared during the four years of the Bush administration. Data pertaining to this period are presented in Table 31.2. As you can see, the GDP growth rate in the first six quarters of the Bush administration averaged 1.7%, a modest growth rate that was followed by a recession in the next three quarters. This recession was followed by five more quarters of only modest growth with an average rate of only 1.6 percent. Thus, by the middle of 1992—about four months before the election—the American people had had no really good news about real output for three and a half years.

As Table 31.2 also shows, the unemployment rate rose from 5.3% in mid-1990 (before the recession) to 7.5% by mid-1992. The federal deficit rose substantially as well between mid-1990 and mid-1992. The only good news was the inflation rate, which was already fairly low and falling even further. This good news seemed to be completely overwhelmed by the bad news, however, and by mid-1992, many Americans were very fearful and pessimistic about the economy.

Although the growth rate picked up to 3.4% in the third quarter of 1992, this seemed to be too little and too late in voters' minds, and President Bush received only 47% of the vote. What made the 1992 election different from previous elections is that voters seemed to look back further than just a year or two before the election. For example, the growth rate in 1992 was about 3 percent. If voters had looked only at this and at the low inflation rate, history suggests that President Bush would have won the election. The fact that he didn't win may have been due to voters' being heavily influenced by the country's poor economic performance in the first three years of the Bush administration.

If voters are looking back more than two years, then the optimal strategy of the party in power is *not* to generate a cycle like the one in Figure 31.8, even if its only interest is maximizing its chances for reelection. Instead, it needs to be concerned about the performance of the economy over the entire period.

Where was the Fed all this time and why didn't it help out President Bush? When we last left the Fed in this chapter, it had by April 30, 1991, lowered the discount rate to 5.5% and moved the T-bill rate to about the same percentage. As Table 31.2 shows, the Fed continued to force the T-bill rate lower, with the rate reaching 3.1% in the third quarter of 1992. Also, in September 1991 the Fed lowered the dis-

TABLE 31.2
Data for Selected Variables for the Period of the Bush Administration, 1989–1992

QUARTER	GDP GROWTH RATE (%)	UNEMPLOYMENT RATE (%)	INFLATION RATE (%)	T-BILL RATE	BOND RATE	FEDERAL GOVERNMENT DEFICIT	DEFICIT/GDP
1989 I	3.2	5.2	5.2	8.5	9.7	110.1	0.021
II	1.8	5.2	4.4	8.4	9.5	109.6	0.021
III	0.0	5.3	3.8	7.8	9.0	128.1	0.024
IV	1.5	5.4	3.5	7.6	8.9	141.4	0.026
1990 I	2.8	5.3	4.8	7.8	9.2	167.8	0.031
II	1.0	5.3	4.8	7.8	9.4	156.7	0.028
III	−1.6	5.6	4.5	7.5	9.4	145.5	0.026
IV	−3.9	6.0	4.1	7.0	9.3	194.7	0.035
1991 I	−3.0	6.5	4.9	6.1	8.9	150.0	0.027
II	1.6	6.7	3.5	5.6	8.9	212.2	0.038
III	1.2	6.7	2.7	5.4	8.8	220.9	0.039
IV	0.6	7.0	2.3	4.6	8.4	258.7	0.045
1992 I	2.9	7.3	3.2	3.9	8.3	289.2	0.050
II	1.6	7.5	2.7	3.7	8.3	302.9	0.051
III	3.4	7.5	1.8	3.1	8.0	304.4	0.051
IV	4.7	7.3	2.3	3.1	8.0	294.6	0.048

Source: U.S. Department of Commerce.

count rate to 5%, in November 1991 to 4.5%, in December 1991 to 3.5%, and in July 1992 to 3.0 percent. Clearly, the Fed was trying to stimulate the economy, but the stimulus was not very effective. (We will discuss in the next chapter why monetary policy may be much less effective now than it was in the past.)

Another possible reason for the ineffectiveness of monetary policy during this period is that the bond rate did not fall nearly as fast as the bill rate. Thus long-term borrowing costs remained fairly high. In addition, with the inflation rate falling at about the same rate as the nominal bond rate, the real bond rate was little changed, and so real long-term borrowing costs were little changed. The modest fall in the bond rate was a source of concern for the Fed at the time. The fact that long-term rates remained high meant that the bond market expected short-term rates to rise substantially in the future. The Fed wanted to see those expectations change, but it could not convince the bond market that it would keep short-term interest rates low in the future. Among other things, the bond market appeared worried about inflation picking up in the future and the Fed responding by raising short-term rates.

SUMMARY

The Federal Deficit and the Federal Debt

1. The *federal deficit* is the difference between what the government spends and what it receives in tax revenues ($G - T$). In 1992, the federal deficit was $296.2 billion. To finance the deficit, the U.S. Treasury issues government securities (bills, notes, and bonds).

2. The *federal debt* is the total of all accumulated deficits minus surpluses over time. The current federal debt is over $4 trillion. The term *public debt* refers to the privately held (non-government-held) debt of the U.S. government. Because most of the federal debt (88%) is owned by U.S. citizens, most interest payments on the federal debt are simply a transfer from one group (taxpayers) to another (bondholders).

3. When government spending increases or the level of net taxes decreases (both of which increase the deficit, $G - T$) with the money supply unchanged, the interest rate rises and crowds out planned investment spending. Less investment means less capital stock, which means decreased future productivity and lower economic growth. Thus large deficits may cause future standards of living to be lower than they would have been if the government had not incurred such large deficits.

Deficit Reduction and Macropolicy: Gramm-Rudman-Hollings

4. In fiscal year 1986, Congress passed and President Reagan signed the *Gramm-Rudman-Hollings Bill,* which set out to reduce the federal deficit by $36 billion per year, with a zero deficit slated for fiscal year 1991. If Congress passed a budget with a deficit larger than the targeted amount, the law called for automatic spending cuts. A Supreme Court ruling later overturned this provision, and the actual figures for each year have not even come close to the targets. Although Congress keeps revising the dates for a zero deficit, it seems clear that GRH is not being taken seriously any longer.

5. The deficit tends to rise when GDP falls, and to fall when GDP rises. The *deficit response index (DRI)* is the amount by which the deficit changes with a one dollar change in GDP.

6. For spending cuts of a certain amount to reduce the deficit by the same amount, the government spending multiplier must be zero. Before GRH was passed, some argued that a government spending multiplier of zero can be achieved through renewed optimism on the part of households or through very aggressive behavior by the Fed to decrease the interest rate. Empirical evidence has shown that neither of these situations is very plausible. Therefore, in order to lower the deficit by a certain amount, government spending cuts must be larger than that amount.

7. Laws that call for automatic spending cuts to eliminate or reduce the deficit, such as GRH, may have the effect of destabilizing the economy because they prevent automatic stabilizers from working.

The Fed's Response to the State of the Economy

8. Because the Fed can control the money supply through open market operations, it has the ability to affect aggregate output (income) (Y), the interest rate, and the price level. The Fed is likely to increase the money supply during times of low output and low inflation, and to decrease the money supply during periods of high output and high inflation. The Fed's behavior during stagflation (periods of high unemployment and high inflation) depends on how the Fed weighs output relative to inflation.

9. As the economy expands, the Fed tends to use open market operations to raise interest rates gradually to try to prevent the economy from expanding too quickly. Conversely, the Fed lowers interest rates gradually to lessen (and eventually stop) a contraction. This tendency is called "leaning against the wind."

Lags the Economy's Response to Monetary and Fiscal Policy

10. *Stabilization policy* is an inclusive term used to describe both fiscal and monetary policy, the goals of which are to smooth out fluctuations in output and employment and to keep prices as stable as possible. Stabilization goals are not necessarily easy to achieve because of the existence of certain *time lags,* or delays in the response of the economy to macropolicies.

11. A *recognition lag* is the time it takes for policy makers to recognize the existence of a boom or slump. An *implementation lag* is the time it takes to put the desired policy into effect once economists and policy makers recognize that the economy is in a boom or a slump. A *response lag* is the time that it takes for the economy to adjust to the new conditions after a new policy is implemented—in other words, a lag that occurs because of the operation of the economy itself. In general, monetary policy can be implemented more rapidly than fiscal policy, but fiscal policy generally has a shorter response lag than monetary policy.

The Political Business Cycle

12. Prior to the 1992 presidential election, empirical evidence suggested that voters tended to vote for the party in power (1) if the inflation rate had been low in the two-year period before the election, and (2) if output had been rising in the year of the election. During the 1992 election, however, voters seemed to look back further than just a year or two before the election, and as a result, President Bush was not reelected. This suggests then that the optimal strategy of the party in power is not to generate a recession early in their term of office and a boom in the last two years of their term—a *political business cycle*—but to be concerned about the performance of the economy over the entire period.

REVIEW TERMS AND CONCEPTS

automatic destabilizer 769
automatic stabilizer 768
deficit response index (*DRI*) 767
federal debt 762
federal deficit 761

Gramm-Rudman-
  Hollings Bill 765
implementation lag 774
negative demand shock 768
political business cycle 778

public debt 762
recognition lag 774
response lag 775
stabilization policy 772
time lag 772

PROBLEM SET

1. During his 1993 State of the Union message, President Clinton promised a budget with new taxes and a number of specific expenditure reductions. During the year, the Congress debated the budget and finally passed a budget bill. Using the *Readers Guide to Periodical Literature* to assist you in your search, find an article or two about the 1993 budget bill. How much deficit reduction has actually been achieved? Write a short report on the new taxes and spending cuts enacted.

2. You are given the following information about the economy in 1994 (all amounts are in billions of dollars):
(1) Consumption function:	$C = 100 + 0.8 \times Y_d$
(2) Taxes:	$T = -150 + 0.25 \times Y$
(3) Investment function:	$I = 60$
(4) Disposable income:	$Y_d = Y - T$
(5) Government spending:	$G = 80$
(6) Equilibrium:	$Y = C + I + G$

   (*Hint:* Deficit is $D = G - T = G - [-150 + 0.25 \times Y]$)
   a. Find equilibrium income. Show that the government budget deficit (the difference between government spending and tax revenues) is $5 billion. Explain why the multiplier is equal to 2.5 in this example.
   b. Congress passes the Foghorn-Leghorn amendment, which requires that the deficit be zero this year. If the budget adopted by Congress has a deficit that is larger than zero, the deficit target must be met by cutting spending. Suppose spending is cut by $5 billion (to $75 billion). What is the new value for equilibrium GDP? What is the new deficit? Explain carefully why the deficit is not zero.
   c. What is the deficit response index and how is it defined? Explain why the *DRI* must equal 0.25 in this example. Using this information, by how much must we cut spending to achieve a deficit of zero?
   d. Suppose that the Foghorn-Leghorn amendment was not in effect and that planned investment falls to $I = 55$. What is the new value of GDP? What is the new government budget deficit? What happens to GDP if the F-L amendment is in effect and spending is cut to reach the deficit target? (*Hint:* Spending must be cut by $21.666 billion to balance the budget.)

3. During the 1993 State of the Union message, Federal Reserve Chair Alan Greenspan (a Republican who is known to place a high value on keeping inflation low) sat with Hillary Rodham Clinton and Tipper Gore in the gallery of the Congress and clearly seemed to support the President's deficit-reduction plan. Many were surprised but very pleased with this show of support. If the government were going to increase taxes and cut spending at a time when the economy was weak and when many were unemployed, what role could the Fed play to ensure the plan's success? Be specific.

4. Some states are required to balance their budgets. Is this measure stabilizing or destabilizing? Suppose all states were committed to a balanced-budget philosophy and the economy moved into a recession. What effects would this philosophy have on the size of the federal deficit?

5. Describe the Fed's tendency to "lean against the wind." Do the Fed's policies tend to stabilize or destabilize the economy?

6. Explain why stabilization policy may be difficult to carry out. How is it possible that stabilization policies can actually be destabilizing?

7. It takes about one year for the multiplier to reach its full value. How can you explain this phenomenon? Does this fact have any implications for fiscal policy?

8. "Voters care less about whether there's a chicken in every pot, and more about whether the size and price of the chicken is increasing." How does this statement relate to theories of the political business cycle?

CASE STUDY
AN ECONOMY IN CRISIS: THE BRAZILIAN EXPERIENCE

■ Currently, Brazil is in deep economic trouble. This hasn't always been the case, however. Between 1940 and 1980, Brazil grew to become the world's tenth-largest economy. Fueled primarily by strong export demand during that period, Brazilian real GDP grew at an average rate of 7% each year. But this growth came at tremendous cost, and a series of economic and political disasters since 1980 have put the country on the brink of collapse.

Since the early 1980s Brazil has suffered runaway price inflation. Prices rose nearly 3000% in 1990 alone. Today, consumer prices are rising at a rate of more than 20% per month (see Figure 1). This hyperinflation presents serious economic and social problems to the nation as the poor find themselves getting poorer while the rich get richer. The top 10% of the population controls about half of the nation's wealth, while the bottom tenth owns less than 1%—and the gap continues to widen.

Part of Brazil's problem lies in the fact that much of the formal economy is indexed to the rising cost of living, thus creating "inertial inflation." Two thirds of Brazilians have monthly incomes that are roughly equal to 100 U.S. dollars. Minimum wages vary across industries, but almost all are indexed to the inflation rate, which the government reports monthly. Now consider the Brazilian who collects $100 at the beginning of the month. With inflation running at about 25% per month, that worker would receive $125 next month. But prices are rising continuously throughout the month. Thus most Brazilians spend nearly all of their earnings immediately upon receipt of their paychecks, creating temporary shortages of food and fuel. By the end of the month, they have little left to spend—and what they have

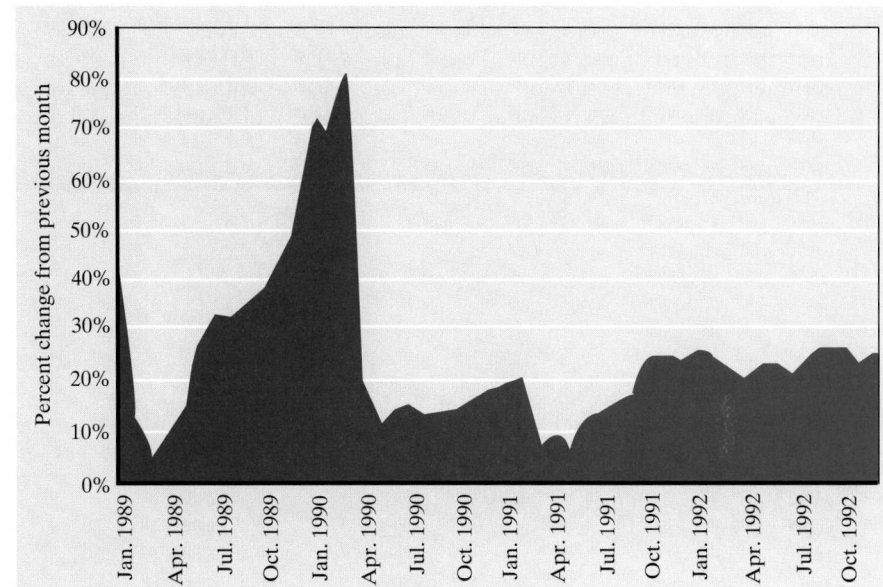

FIGURE 1
Consumer Price Inflation in Brazil, 1989–1992
Source: *International Financial Statistics*

doesn't buy very much. Indexation provides a temporary "fix" but also institutionalizes the inflationary pressures into the economy. Both sellers and buyers find themselves on an inflationary treadmill as they constantly try to keep up with rising prices.

Services are also indexed. Want to make a phone call? The pay phones in Brazil require tokens that you must buy at the local newsstand and whose prices rise with inflation. If you take a taxi in Brazil, you don't pay what the meter reads; rather, the cabby uses a table to translate the reading into current prices. (Apparently, it is easier for the government to print tables each month than it is to recalibrate the meters.) Taxicab rides are cheaper at the end of the month, prior to the table updates, than they are at the beginning of the month.

Also contributing to Brazil's hyperinflation problem is the fact that

much of the population works in the underground economy, which is estimated at nearly one third of official GDP. There is no indexation of prices or earnings in the underground economy. Hyperinflation thus acts almost as a "tax" on the poor people of Brazil.

To get things under control, the Brazilian government has frozen some prices, like that of public transit. But each time it raises the prices to catch up with rising costs, riots break out. Several different programs in the last six years designed to rein in the rising costs of living have failed, and a series of political scandals and failed legislative attempts to revise the constitution have left the government with little credibility.

Given the tightrope the Brazilian government must walk between economic stability and civil unrest, a path of slow but steady reforms seems the only way out. High interest rates and little or no growth in the money supply are the government's only real weapons for the time being. Some economists have argued for privatization of many state-owned enterprises, similar to the path adopted by Argentina. This would not only remove some of the domestic debt held by the public but also enable the government to replace current subsidy expenditures with tax revenues.

QUESTIONS FOR ANALYTICAL THINKING

1. How might a reduction in Brazil's government budget deficit help curb inflation? Illustrate your answer using aggregate supply and aggregate demand curves.

2. What would happen if the government of Brazil stopped indexing wages and the price of services and removed all price controls? Would this solve the problem of hyperinflation?

3. What impact might high inflation have on investment in Brazil?

4. Why would privatization of some of Brazil's state-owned industries help curb hyperinflation in the country?

PART EIGHT

Household and Firm Behavior in the Macroeconomy: A Closer Look

In recent years, many macroeconomists have placed increasing emphasis on the microfoundations of macroeconomics. While the connections between microeconomics and macroeconomics have been emphasized throughout this book, we have created this optional part for those who wish to learn even more about the microfoundations of macroeconomics. Its highlights include:

■ A closer look at household and firm behavior in the macroeconomy. Chapter 32 discusses theories of consumer behavior, interest rate and government effects on consumption, the role of "animal spirits" in determining investment behavior, and excess-labor and excess-capital effects on investment. The chapter also provides data on household and firm behavior in the U.S. economy since 1970.

■ Further analysis of the effects of monetary and fiscal policy on the economy in Chapter 33.

■ A discussion of the role of the stock market in the economy, plus boxed features that explain how to read stock and bond pages, also in Chapter 33.

32 Household and Firm Behavior in the Macroeconomy

In Chapters 24 through 30, we considered the interactions of households, firms, the government, and the rest of the world in the goods, money, and labor markets. The macroeconomy is complicated, and there is a lot to learn about these interactions. To keep our discussions as uncomplicated as possible, we have so far assumed fairly simple behavior on the part of households and firms—the two basic decision-making units in the economy. For example, we assumed that household consumption (C) depends only on income and that planned investment by firms (I) depends only on the interest rate. Furthermore, we did not consider the fact that households make consumption and labor supply decisions simultaneously and that firms make investment and employment decisions simultaneously.

Now that we have an understanding of the basic interactions in the economy, we are in a position to relax these restrictive assumptions. In the first part of this chapter, we present a more realistic picture of the influences on households' consumption and labor supply decisions. In the second part, we present a more detailed and realistic picture of the influences on firms' investment and employment decisions. In the next chapter, we use what we've learned in this chapter to analyze some more macroeconomic issues.

HOUSEHOLDS: CONSUMPTION AND LABOR SUPPLY DECISIONS

Before discussing the theories of household behavior, it is useful to review what we have learned up to this point.

The Keynesian Theory of Consumption: A Review

The assumption that household consumption (C) depends on income, which we have used as the basis of our analysis so far, is one that Keynes stressed in his *General Theory of Employment, Interest, and Money*. While Keynes believed that many factors, including interest rates and wealth, are likely to influence the level of consumption spending, he focused on current income:

> The amount of aggregate consumption depends mainly on the amount of aggregate income. The fundamental psychological law, upon which we are entitled to depend with great confidence both … from our knowledge of human nature and from the detailed facts of experience, is that men [and women, too] are disposed, as a rule and on average, to increase their consumption as their incomes increase, but not by as much as the increase in their income.[1]

Keynes is making two points here. First, he suggests that consumption is a positive function of income–that is, the more income one has, the more consuming one is likely to do. Except for a few rich misers who save scraps of soap and bits of string despite million-dollar incomes, this proposition seems to make sense. Rich people typically consume more than poor people do.

Second, Keynes suggests, high-income households consume a smaller proportion of their income than low-income households. (If rich households consume relatively less of their incomes, then by definition they save a higher proportion of their incomes than poor households do.) The proportion of income that households spend on consumption is measured by the **average propensity to consume (APC)**.[2] The *APC* is defined as consumption divided by income:

average propensity to consume (APC) The proportion of income households spend on consumption. Determined by dividing consumption (C) by income (Y).

$$APC \equiv \frac{C}{Y}$$

If, for example, a household earns $30,000 per year and spends $25,000 (and thus saves the remaining $5000), it has an *APC* of $25,000/$30,000, or 0.833. Keynes argues that someone who earns, say, $30,000 is likely to spend a larger portion of his or her income than is someone who earns $100,000.

Although the idea that consumption depends on income is a useful starting point, it is far from a complete description of the consumption decision. We need to consider other theories of consumption.

The Life-Cycle Theory of Consumption

The **life-cycle theory of consumption** is an important extension of Keynes's theory. The fundamental idea of the life-cycle theory is that people make lifetime consumption plans. Realizing that they are likely to earn more in their prime

life-cycle theory of consumption A theory of household consumption: Households make lifetime consumption decisions based on their expectations of lifetime income.

---

[1]John Maynard Keynes, *The General Theory of Employment, Interest, and Money* (1936), First Harbinger Ed. (New York: Harcourt Brace Jovanovich, 1964), p. 96.

[2]While the *APC* measures the proportion of total income households spend on consumption, the marginal propensity to consume (*MPC*), which we introduced in Chapter 24, measures the proportion of a *change* in income that households spend on consumption. One could interpret Keynes's theory as implying that the marginal propensity to consume falls as income rises. If the *MPC* falls as income rises, it follows that the average propensity to consume (*APC*) falls also.

working years than they earn earlier or later, they make consumption decisions based on their expectations of lifetime income. People tend to consume less than they earn during their main working years—that is, they *save* during these years—and they tend to consume more than they earn during their early and later years—that is, they *dissave,* or use up savings, during these years. Students in medical school, for example, generally have very low current incomes, but few live in the poverty that those incomes might predict. Instead, they borrow now and plan to pay back later when their incomes improve.

The lifetime income and consumption pattern of a representative individual is shown in Figure 32.1. As you can see, this person has a low income during the first part of her life, high income in the middle, and low income again in retirement. (Her income in retirement is not zero because she has income from sources other than her own labor–social security payments, interest and dividends, and the like.)

The consumption path as drawn in Figure 32.1 is constant over the person's life. This is an extreme assumption, but it illustrates an important point, namely that the path of consumption over a lifetime is likely to be much more stable than the path of income. We consume an amount greater than our incomes during our early working careers. We do this by borrowing against future income, by taking out a car loan, a mortgage to buy a house, or a loan to pay for college. This debt is repaid when our incomes have risen and we can afford to use some of our income to pay off past borrowing without substantially lowering our consumption. The reverse is true for our retirement years. Here, too, our incomes are low. But because we consume less than we earn during our prime working years, we can save up a "nest egg" that allows us to maintain an acceptable standard of living during retirement.

Fluctuations in wealth are also an important component of the life-cycle story. Many young households go into debt by borrowing in anticipation of higher income in the future. Some households actually have *negative wealth*—that is, the value of their assets is less than the debts they owe. A household in its prime working years saves to pay off debts and to build up assets for its later years, when income typically goes down. Such households, whose assets are greater than the debts they owe, are said to have *positive wealth*. With its wage earners retired, a household consumes its accumulated wealth. Generally speaking, wealth starts out negative, turns positive, and then approaches zero near the end of life. Wealth, therefore, is intimately linked to the cumulative saving and dissaving behavior of households.

FIGURE 32.1

Life-Cycle Theory of Consumption

In their early working years, people consume more than they earn. This is also true in the retirement years. In between, people save (consume less than they earn) to pay off debts from borrowing and to accumulate savings for retirement.

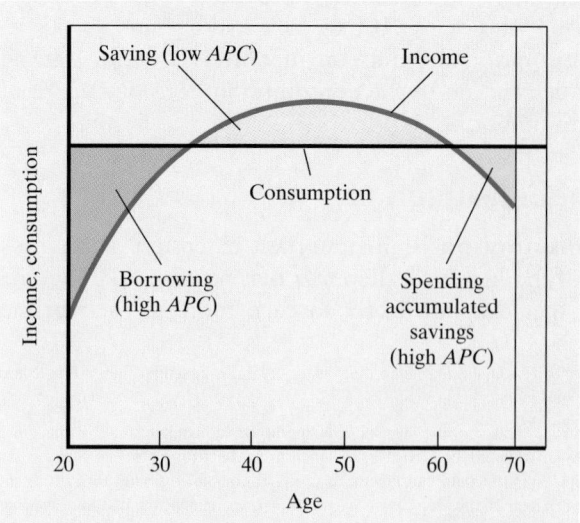

The key difference between the Keynesian theory of consumption and the life-cycle theory is that the life-cycle theory suggests that consumption and saving decisions are likely to be based not just on current income but on expectations of future income as well. The consumption behavior of households immediately following World War II clearly supports the life-cycle story. Just after the war ended, income fell as wage earners moved out of war-related work. Consumption spending did not fall commensurately, however, as Keynesian theory would predict. People expected to find jobs in other sectors eventually, and they did not adjust their consumption spending to the temporarily lower incomes they were earning in the meantime.

The phrase **permanent income** is sometimes used to refer to the average level of one's expected future income stream. If you expect that your income will be high in the future (even though it may not be high now), your permanent income is said to be high. With this concept, we can sum up the life-cycle theory by saying that current consumption decisions are likely to be based on permanent income rather than on current income.[3]

But although this insight enriches our understanding of the consumption behavior of households, the analysis is still missing a number of important pieces. To complete the picture, we need to bring in the other main decision of households—the labor supply decision.

permanent income The average level of one's expected future income stream.

The Labor Supply Decision

Households decide not only how much to consume but also how much to work. These decisions are not made separately. Rather,

> Households make consumption and labor supply decisions simultaneously. Consumption cannot be considered separately from labor supply, because it is precisely by selling one's labor that one earns the income that makes consumption possible.

This may seem obvious to you, but it is an important point that is sometimes forgotten.

Clearly, then, it does not make sense to have one theory that explains consumption and another that explains labor supply. Consumption requires income (either current income or the promise of future income that can be borrowed against), and in order to earn income, one must supply labor. Unless you are lucky enough to have a large inheritance or to win a lottery, you are going to have to work to buy the things you need and want. If you want more, you are going to have to work more.

The theories of consumption that we have discussed so far assume that consumption depends on current or permanent income. The view that consumption and labor supply are determined jointly complicates matters somewhat. If households make decisions about consumption and labor supply together, then it is not (strictly speaking) correct to say that income determines consumption. Rather, income is the byproduct of the labor supply/consumption decisions.

The theory of consumer choice in microeconomics treats consumption and labor supply decisions together. This is an important area where we can gain macroeconomic insights from microeconomic theory. The following is a brief discussion of what microeconomics tells us about the factors that affect consumption and labor supply decisions.

---

[3]The pioneering work on this topic was done by Milton Friedman, *A Theory of the Consumption Function* (Princeton, N.J.: Princeton University Press, 1957). In the mid-1960s, Franco Modigliani did closely related work that included the formulation of the life-cycle theory.

WAGES   The wage rate that a household is paid and the prices of the goods that it buys affect the household's consumption and labor supply decisions. If you work, you are paid a wage. Your wage income is the number of hours that you work times your hourly wage rate. Wage income enables you to buy market-produced goods and services. If you do not work, you may consume leisure or you may do tasks that do not pay a wage. People may choose not to do paid work for a variety of reasons—because they are bringing up children, keeping house, going to school, etc. Thus,

> There is a trade-off between the goods and services that wage income will buy and leisure or other nonmarket activities. The wage rate is the key variable that determines how a household responds to this trade-off.

Consider what would happen if the wage rate were to increase. First, an increase in the wage rate means that the opportunity cost of leisure (or of nonmarket production) is higher. The opportunity cost of leisure is the bundle of market-produced goods and services that you give up by not working—in other words, your wage rate. If the wage rate rises, the true price of each additional hour of leisure you consume is higher. That is, when the wage rate increases, you must sacrifice a larger bundle of market-produced goods and services for each hour of leisure you consume. Since leisure is now more costly, you are likely to "consume" less of it, which means you will work more after the wage rate increase. This effect is called the **substitution effect of a wage rate increase,** and it should lead to an increase in the quantity of labor supplied and a decrease in leisure (or nonmarket production).

If the wage rate declines, the substitution effect takes the opposite turn. A lower wage rate means the opportunity cost of leisure (or of nonmarket production) is lower. In this case, a decision to spend more hours at home in the garden or with the kids means less of a sacrifice in terms of market-produced goods and services. Thus, the substitution effect suggests that a lower wage rate should lead to a decrease in the quantity of labor supplied.

But the substitution effect is only part of the story. A higher wage rate also means that a person can earn a higher amount of income for a given number of hours worked. This higher income may be spent on more goods, or it may be spent on leisure. If we assume that leisure is a normal good (that is, a good for which demand increases when income increases and for which demand decreases when income decreases), we would expect to see a higher wage rate lead to more leisure and thus less labor supplied. This effect is called the **income effect of a wage rate increase.** Conversely, the income effect of a wage rate decrease is less leisure and therefore more labor supplied.

When we combine the income and substitution effects, we are left with an ambiguous result. A higher wage rate means that the opportunity cost of not working is higher. This leads to more work—that is, a larger quantity of labor supplied. But a higher wage rate also means that people can earn more wage income by working the same amount, and they spend some of this added income on leisure. The evidence suggests that the substitution effect seems to dominate for most people, which means that the aggregate labor supply responds positively to an increase in the wage rate.[4]

---

[4]Keep in mind, however, that this need not be the case. There may be times when the income effect dominates the substitution effect, in which case the aggregate labor supply falls when the wage rate rises.

Let us now return to the consumption decision. If the wage rate rises, *both* the income and substitution effects work in the same direction to increase consumption. There is a positive income effect, which leads to more consumption, and there is a substitution effect away from leisure toward work (and therefore higher income and increased consumption of goods and services). Thus,

> Consumption increases when the wage rate increases.

PRICES Prices also play a major role in the consumption/labor supply decision. As we have been discussing the possible effects of an increase in the wage rate, we have been implicitly assuming that the prices of goods and services do not rise at the same time. If the wage rate and all other prices rise simultaneously, the story is different. To keep the two cases clear, we need to distinguish between the *nominal wage rate* and the *real wage rate.*

The **nominal wage rate** is the wage rate in current dollars. The **real wage rate** is the nominal wage rate adjusted for changes in the price level over time. The real wage rate measures the amount that wages can buy in terms of goods and services. Workers do not care about their nominal wage per se; they care about the purchasing power of this wage, that is, the real wage.

nominal wage rate The wage rate in current dollars.

real wage rate The nominal wage rate adjusted for changes in the price level over time.

For example, suppose that skilled workers in Indianapolis were paid a wage rate of $15 per hour in 1993. Now suppose that their wage rate rose to $18 in 1994, a 20% increase. If the prices of goods and services were exactly the same in 1994 as they were in 1993, the real wage rate would have increased by 20 percent. That is, an hour of work in 1994 ($18) buys 20% more than an hour of work in 1993 ($15).

But what if the prices of all goods and services also increased by 20% between 1993 and 1994? In this case, the purchasing power of an hour's wages has not changed. That is, the real wage rate has not increased at all. Eighteen dollars in 1994 buys the same quantity of goods and services that $15 bought in 1993. Thus, the real wage rate in 1994 is still $15.

To measure the real wage rate, we simply adjust the nominal wage rate with a price index. As we saw in Chapter 23, there are several such indexes that we might use, including the Consumer Price Index and the GDP Deflator.[5]

We can now apply what we have learned from the life-cycle theory to our wage/price story. Recall that life-cycle theory holds that people look ahead in making their decisions. Translated to real wage rates, this idea says that:

> Households look at expected future real wage rates as well as the current real wage rate in making their current consumption and labor supply decisions.

Consider again the medical student who expects that his or her real wage rate will be higher in the future. This expectation obviously has an effect on current decisions about things like how much to buy and whether or not to take a part-time job.

---

[5]To calculate the real wage rate, we simply divide the nominal wage rate by the price index. For example, suppose that the wage rate rose from $5.00 per hour in 1984 to $9.00 per hour in 1994 and that the price level rose 50% during the same period. Using 1984 as the base year, the price index would be 1.00 in 1984 and 1.50 in 1994. The real wage rate is W/P, where W is the nominal, or money, wage rate and P is the price level (or the current value of the price index). The real and nominal wage rates in 1984 were $5.00 ($5.00/1.00), and the real wage rate in 1990 was $6.00 ($9.00/1.50). Stated another way, in 1984 dollars, the wage rate in 1994 was $6.00 per hour.

WEALTH AND NONLABOR INCOME Life-cycle theory holds that wealth fluctuates over the life cycle. Households accumulate wealth during their working years to pay off debts accumulated when they were young and to support themselves in retirement. This role of wealth is clear, but the existence of wealth also poses another question. Consider two households that are at the same stage in their life cycle and have pretty much the same expectations about future wage rates, prices, and so forth. They expect to live the same length of time, and both plan to leave the same amount to their children. They differ only in their wealth. Because of a past inheritance, Household 1 has more wealth than Household 2. Which household is likely to have a higher consumption path for the rest of its life? The answer should be obvious: Household 1 would, because it has more wealth to spread out over the rest of its life. In other words:

> Holding everything else constant (including the stage in the life cycle), the more wealth a household has, the more it will consume, both now and in the future.

Now consider a household that has a sudden unexpected increase in wealth, perhaps an inheritance from a distant relative. How will the household's consumption pattern be affected? It should be obvious that the household will increase its consumption, both now and in the future, as it spends the inheritance over the course of the rest of its life.

An increase in wealth can also be looked upon as an increase in nonlabor income. **Nonlabor,** or **nonwage, income** is income that is received from sources other than working—inheritances, interest, dividends, and transfer payments such as welfare payments and social security payments. As with wealth:

> An unexpected increase in nonlabor income will have a positive effect on a household's consumption.

But what about the effect of an increase in wealth or nonlabor income on labor supply? Nonlabor income effects are pure income effects. Unlike increases in wage rates, which have both income and substitution effects, increases in nonlabor income have *only* income effects. We already know that an increase in income results in an increase in the consumption of normal goods, including leisure. Therefore, an unexpected increase in wealth or nonlabor income results in both an increase in consumption and an increase in leisure. With leisure increasing, labor supply must fall, so we see that:

> An unexpected increase in wealth or nonlabor income leads to a *decrease* in labor supply.

This point should be fairly obvious. If I suddenly win a million dollars in the state lottery, I will probably work less in the future than I otherwise would have.

One major source of fluctuations in the wealth of the household sector is the stock market. Stock prices change considerably over time. Many households hold much of their wealth in stocks, and as stock prices rise or fall, so does household wealth. This is one of the ways in which the stock market affects the economy. By increasing or decreasing household wealth, the stock market influences how much households decide to spend and how much they decide to work. (We shall have more to say about this point in the next chapter.)

nonlabor, or nonwage, income Any income that is received from sources other than working—inheritances, interest, dividends, transfer payments, and so on.

Interest Rate Effects on Consumption

We have seen earlier that the interest rate affects planned investment (I). The interest rate can also affect consumption. In fact, a change in the interest rate has both income and substitution effects on consumption. Consider first the substitution effect. A change in the interest rate affects households' choices between present and future consumption. Every dollar I earn today can either be spent—that is, used for present consumption—or saved, allowing me to buy things in the future. Suppose I put a dollar of my income in the bank now at an interest rate of 5% per year. A year from now, my dollar will have earned $0.05 in interest, and I can then spend the $1.05 on whatever I choose. If, instead of a 5% interest rate, my bank offers a 10% rate, my dollar will grow to $1.10 at the end of a year.

The rate of interest thus represents one type of opportunity cost. Each dollar I spend today means either $1.05 or $1.10 less of future consumption, depending on the interest rate. If the interest rate rises from 5% to 10%, the opportunity cost of present consumption rises. Instead of sacrificing $1.05 of future consumption each time I spend (fail to save) a dollar today, I must now sacrifice $1.10 worth of future consumption. Hence, an increase in the interest rate should encourage me to spend less (save more) than before. Put another way, when the interest rate rises, households substitute away from current consumption toward future consumption due to the increase in the relative price of current consumption. Through this *substitution effect*, an increase in the interest rate has a negative effect on current consumption.

Now consider the *income effect*, which works in the opposite direction from the substitution effect for households that have positive wealth. Consider a household that has positive wealth and is earning interest on that wealth. When the interest rate rises, the household earns more in interest income than it did before; this is an increase in its nonlabor income. As we saw above, a rise in nonlabor income has a positive effect on consumption. This is the income effect at work. The interest rate rises, interest (nonlabor) income rises, and consumption increases due to the increase in nonlabor income.

An increase in the interest rate thus has a negative effect on consumption through the substitution effect and a positive effect on consumption through the income effect. Which effect dominates for a given household varies from situation to situation. The only time the total effect is unambiguous is when a household is a debtor, in which case an increase in the interest rate leads to a corresponding increase in the interest payments that the household must make. This situation is similar to a decrease in nonlabor income, which has a negative effect on consumption. In this case, the income effect is in the same direction as the substitution effect.

The income and substitution effects are not just theoretical niceties that have nothing important to say about the real world. In fact, they may help to explain why monetary policy was less effective in stimulating the U.S. economy after the 1990–1991 recession than it was after previous recessions.

Why is this so? Households as a group have positive wealth, and they own a considerable fraction of the federal debt. Although some of the increase in the government debt has been financed by foreigners, most of this increase has been financed by domestic households. Because the government debt is so much larger now than it was ten years ago, the effect of a change in the interest rate on government interest payments is also much larger now than it used to be.

All this means that the larger a decrease in government interest payments today (as a result of a given decrease in the interest rate), the larger the decrease in the interest income of households. This in turn means that the income effect on households is larger now than it used to be. In fact, some experiments have suggested that the income effect is now almost as large as the substitution effect. Monetary policy may thus be less effective today than in the past, which would help to explain why the easing of monetary policy in 1991 and 1992 was not very effective in stimulating the economy.

Interestingly, the news media have been busy reporting the income effect at work. As interest rates fell in 1991 and 1992, there were numerous newspaper articles and television programs interviewing retirees who were hurt by the decrease in their interest income. Interest income for many retirees is a fairly large fraction of their total income. These individuals undoubtedly consume less when their interest income falls, which at least partly offsets the stimulative effect that the Fed tries to achieve when it lowers the interest rate.

Government Effects on Consumption and Labor Supply: Taxes and Transfers

The government influences household behavior mainly through tax rates and transfer payments.

When the government raises tax rates, after-tax real wages decrease. This, in turn, lowers consumption. Conversely, when the government lowers tax rates, after-tax real wages increase. The result is an increase in consumption.

A change in tax rates also affects labor supply. If, as we are generally assuming, the substitution effect dominates, then an increase in tax rates, which lowers after-tax wages, will lower labor supply. Conversely, a decrease in tax rates will increase labor supply.

Recall that *transfer payments* are payments such as social security benefits, veterans benefits, and welfare benefits. An increase in transfer payments is an increase in nonlabor income, and we have seen that nonlabor income has a positive effect on consumption and a negative effect on labor supply. Increases in transfer payments thus increase consumption and decrease labor supply, while decreases in transfer payments decrease consumption and increase labor supply. Figure 32.2 summarizes these results.

Precisely how labor supply responds to transfer payments is a question that greatly concerns government policy makers, whose objective is a welfare system that helps people truly in need while maintaining an incentive to work for those who are able to do so. Because welfare payments are a form of nonlabor income, we expect some accompanying decrease in work, but the key question for government policy is how large this effect is. A number of income maintenance experiments have attempted to estimate the size of this response, and, in general, the response seems fairly small.

Using this information, we can again come back to the life-cycle theory and the idea that people look ahead to make lifetime consumption decisions. If people look ahead, then changes in tax rates that are expected to be permanent have a greater effect on current consumption and labor supply than those that are expected to be temporary. If tax rates are lowered this year, but people expect them to go back up next year, the effect of the tax cut on current consumption is likely to be small.

FIGURE 32.2

The Effects of Government on Household Consumption and Labor Supply

	Tax rates		Transfer payments	
	Increase	Decrease	Increase	Decrease
Effect on consumption	Negative	Positive	Positive	Negative
Effect on labor supply	Negative*	Positive*	Negative	Positive

*If the substitution effect dominates.

A Possible Employment Constraint on Households

Our discussion of the labor supply decision has so far proceeded as if households were free to choose how much to work each period. If, for example, a member of a household decides to work five additional hours a week at the current wage rate, we have implicitly assumed that the person *can* work five hours more—that work is available. If someone who has not been working decides to work at the current wage rate, we have assumed that the person *can find a job*. Implicitly, then, we have been assuming that the economy is in a situation of full employment.

As we've said all along, however, there are times when the economy does not seem to be at full employment. Indeed, it was the Great Depression, when unemployment rates reached 25% of the labor force, that led to the birth of macroeconomics in the 1930s. Since the mid-1970s, the United States has experienced three recessions, with millions of unemployed workers unable to find work.

All households face a budget constraint, regardless of the state of the economy. This budget constraint is determined by income, wealth, and prices, and separates those bundles of goods that are available to a household from those that are not. When there is less-than-full employment, some households feel an additional constraint on their behavior. Some people may want to work 40 hours per week at the current wage rates but can find only part-time work. Others may not find any work at all.

How does a household respond when it is constrained from working as much as it would like? Most importantly, it consumes less than it otherwise would. This should be fairly obvious. If your current wage rate is $10 per hour and you normally work 40 hours a week, your normal income from wages is $400 per week. If your average tax rate is 20%, your after-tax wage income is $320 per week. You are likely to spend much of this income during the week. If you are prevented from working, this income will not be available to you, and you will have less to spend.

You will spend something, of course. You may receive some form of nonlabor income, and you may have assets, such as savings deposits or stocks and bonds, that can be withdrawn or sold. You may also be able to borrow during your period of unemployment. But even though you will spend something during the week, it is almost certain that you will spend less than you would have if you had your usual income of $320 in after-tax wages. Thus,

> Households consume less if they are constrained from working.

A household constrained from working as much as it would like to at the current wage rate faces a different decision from the one facing a household that can work as much as it wants to. The work decision of the former household is, in effect, forced on it. The household works as much as it can—a certain number of hours per week or perhaps none at all—but this amount is less than the household would choose to work at the current wage rate if it could find more work. The amount that a household would like to work at the current wage rate if it could find the work is called its **unconstrained supply of labor.** The amount that the household actually works in a given period at current wage rates is called its **constrained supply of labor.**

A household's constrained supply of labor is not a variable over which it has any control. The amount of labor the household supplies is imposed on it from the outside by the workings of the economy. On the other hand, the household's consumption *is* under its control. We have just seen that the less a household works—that is, the smaller the household's constrained supply of labor–the lower its consumption is. Constraints on the supply of labor are thus an important determinant of consumption when there is less-than-full employment.

unconstrained supply of labor
The amount a household would like to work within a given period at the current wage rate if it could find the work.

constrained supply of labor The amount a household actually works in a given period at the current wage rate.

KEYNESIAN THEORY REVISITED   Recall the simple Keynesian theory that current income determines current consumption. We now know that the consumption decision is made jointly with the labor supply decision and that the two depend on the real wage rate. Thus, it is incorrect to argue that consumption depends only on income, at least when there is full employment. But if there is unemployment, Keynes's simple story is closer to being correct because income is not determined by households. When there is unemployment, the level of income (at least workers' income) depends exclusively on the employment decisions made by firms. There are unemployed workers who are willing to work at the current wage rate, and their income is in effect determined by the hiring decisions of firms. This income in turn affects current consumption, which is consistent with Keynes's theory. This is one of the reasons that Keynesian theory is generally considered to pertain to periods of less-than-full employment. It was, of course, precisely during such a period that the theory was developed.

A Summary of Household Behavior

This completes our discussion of household behavior in the macroeconomy. Clearly, household consumption depends on more than current income. Households determine consumption and labor supply simultaneously, and they look ahead in making their decisions. To summarize:

The following factors affect household consumption and labor supply decisions:
- current and expected future real wage rates
- the initial value of wealth
- current and expected future nonlabor income
- interest rates
- current and expected future tax rates and transfer payments.

If households are constrained in their labor supply decisions, income is directly determined by firms' hiring decisions. In this case, we can say (in the traditional, Keynesian way) that "income" affects consumption.

The Household Sector Since 1970

To gain a better understanding of household behavior, it is useful to examine how some of the aggregate household variables have changed over time. We will confine our discussion here to the period 1970 I–1992 IV. (Remember that the Roman numerals refer to quarters. 1970 I means the first quarter of 1970.) Within this time span, there have been three recessionary periods, 1974 I–1975 IV, 1980 II–1983 I, and 1990 III–1991 I. How did the household variables behave during each of these three periods?

CONSUMPTION   Data on the total consumption of the household sector are available from the national income and product accounts. As we saw in Table 22.2, personal consumption expenditures accounted for about 69% of GDP in 1992. The three basic categories of consumption expenditures are services, nondurable goods, and durable goods.

Figure 32.3 presents the data for consumption of services and nondurable goods combined and for durable goods. The data are in constant (1987) dollars, which means that they reflect changes in the volume of units consumed, not changes in prices. You can see from the figure that expenditures on services and nondurable goods are "smoother" over time than expenditures on durable goods. For example, the decrease in expenditures on services and nondurable goods was much smaller during the three recessionary periods than the decrease in expenditures on durable goods.

Why do expenditures on durables fluctuate more than expenditures on services and nondurables? The reason is simple. When times are bad, people can postpone the purchase of durable goods, and they do. It follows, then, that expenditures on these goods change the most. When times are tough, you do not *have* to have a new car or a new washer-dryer; you can make do with your old Chevy or Maytag until things get better. On the other hand, when your income falls, it is less easy to postpone the service costs of day care or health care. Nondurables fall into an intermediate category, with some items—new clothes, for example—easier to postpone than others (food, for example).

HOUSING INVESTMENT   Another important expenditure of the household sector is housing investment, plotted in Figure 32.4 on the next page. This variable fluctuates greatly, for at least two reasons. First, housing investment is the most easily postponable of all household expenditures. Second, housing investment is sensitive to the general level of interest rates, and interest rates fluctuate considerably over time. When interest rates are low, housing investment is generally high, and vice versa.

FIGURE 32.3
Consumption Expenditures, 1970 I–1992 IV

Over time, expenditures for services and nondurable goods are "smoother" than expenditures for durable goods.

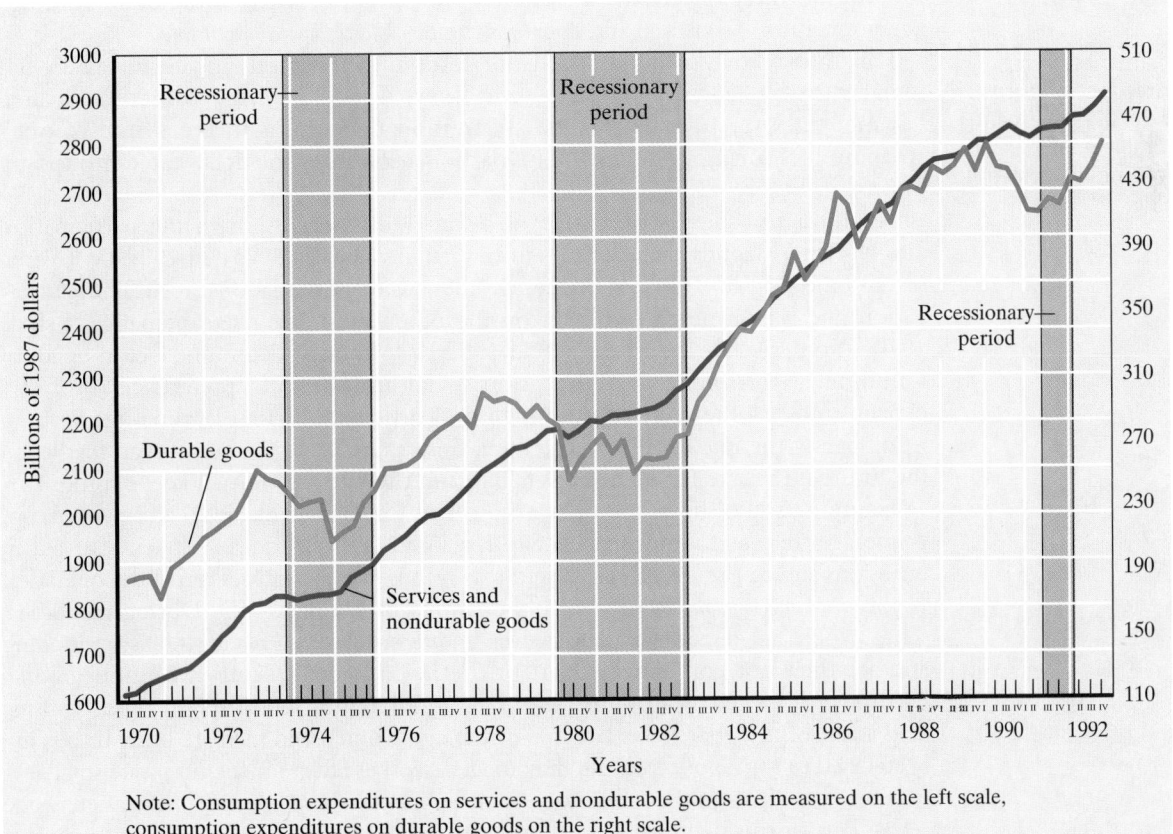

Note: Consumption expenditures on services and nondurable goods are measured on the left scale, consumption expenditures on durable goods on the right scale.

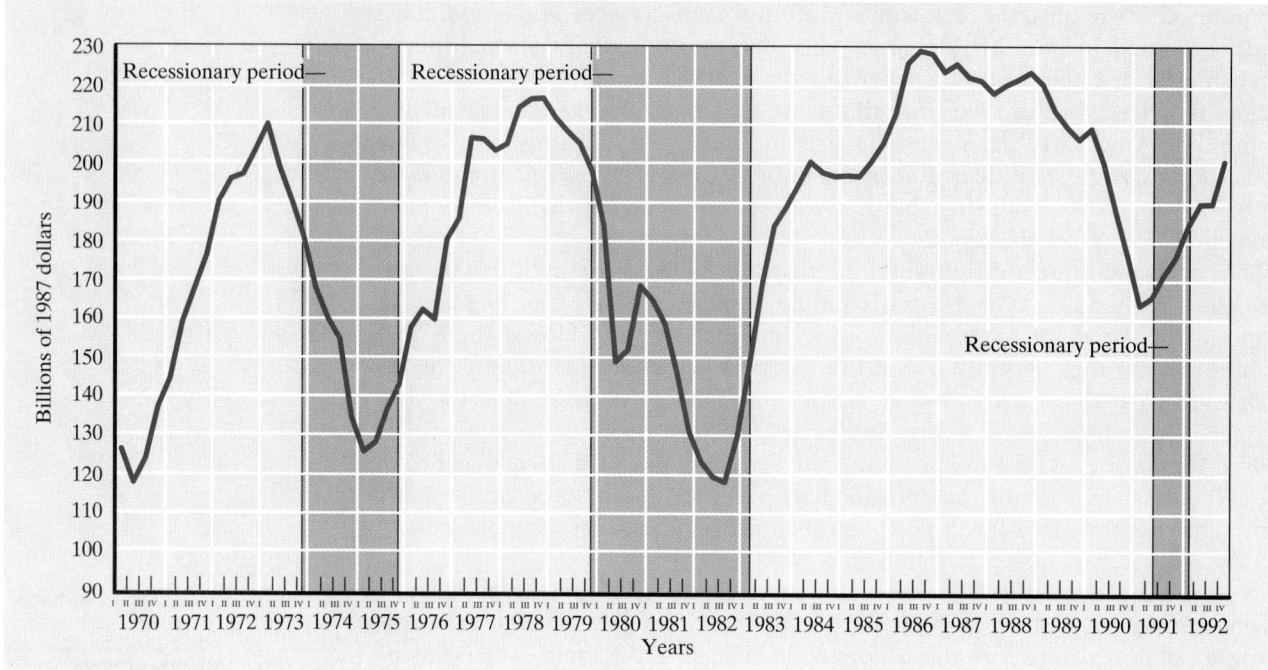

FIGURE 32.4

Housing Investment of the Household Sector, 1970 I–1992 IV

Housing investment fell sharply during the three recessionary periods since 1970. Like expenditures for durable goods, expenditures for housing investment are postponable.

LABOR SUPPLY As we noted in Chapters 23 and 30, a person is considered a part of the labor force when he or she is either working or has been actively looking for work in the past few weeks. The ratio of the labor force to the total working-age population—those 16 and over—is the *labor-force participation rate.*

It is informative to divide the labor force into three categories: males 25–54, females 25–54, and all others 16 and over. Ages 25–54 are sometimes called "prime" ages, presumably on the assumption that one is in the prime of one's working life during these ages. The participation rates for these three groups are plotted in Figure 32.5.

As the figure shows, most men of prime age work, although the participation rate has fallen slightly since 1970—from .961 in 1970 I to .931 in 1992 IV. (A rate of .931 means that 93.1% of prime-age men were in the labor force.) The participation rate for prime-age women, on the other hand, has risen dramatically since 1970—from .501 in 1970 I to .748 in 1992 IV. Although economic factors account for some of this increase, a change in social attitudes and preferences probably explains most of the increase. Although the participation rate of prime-age women is still below the rate for prime-age men, this difference will narrow even further in the future if the rate for men keeps falling and the rate for women keeps rising.

Figure 32.5 also shows the participation rate for all individuals 16 and over except prime-age men and women. This rate has some cyclical features—it tends to fall in recessions and to rise or fall less during expansions. These features reveal the operation of the *discouraged-worker effect,* which we discussed in Chapter 23. During recessions, some people get discouraged about ever finding a job. As a result, they stop looking and are then not considered a part of the labor force. During expansion, people become encouraged again. Once they begin looking for jobs, they are again considered a part of the labor force. Because prime-age women and men are likely to be fairly attached to the labor force, the discouraged-worker effect for them is quite small.

The participation rate for non–prime-age men and women has fallen since 1970. Part of this decrease reflects an increase in early retirement. When someone retires, he or she is no longer considered a part of the labor force.

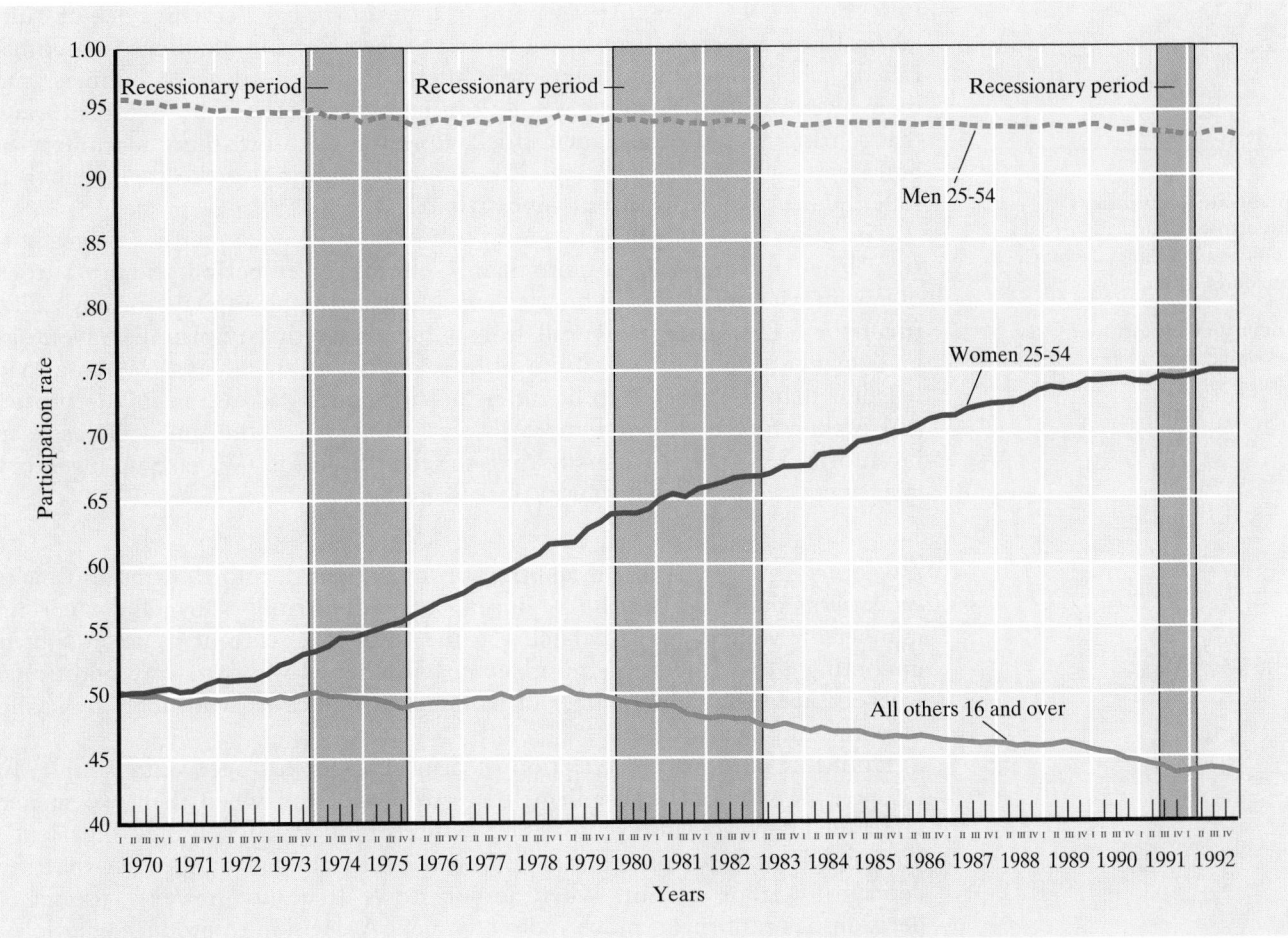

FIGURE 32.5

Labor-Force Participation
Rates for Men 25–54, Women
25–54, and All Others 16 and
Over, 1970 I–1992 IV

FIRMS: INVESTMENT AND EMPLOYMENT DECISIONS

Having taken a closer look at the behavior of households in the macroeconomy, we now turn to a closer look at the behavior of firms—the second major decision-making unit in the economy. In discussing firm behavior earlier, we simply assumed that planned investment depends only on the interest rate. However, there are several other determinants of planned investment. We now turn to a discussion of these factors. We will also discuss the factors that affect firms' employment decisions. Once again, microeconomic theory can help us gain some insights into the working of the macroeconomy.

In a market economy, firms determine which goods and services are available to consumers today and which will be available in the future, how many workers are needed for what kinds of jobs, and how much investment will be undertaken. Stated in macroeconomic terms, the decisions of firms, taken together, determine output, labor demand, and investment.

In this section, we concentrate on the input choices made by firms. By **inputs,** we mean the goods and services that firms purchase and turn into output. Two important inputs that firms use are capital and labor (others include energy, raw materials, and semifinished goods). Each period, firms must decide how much capital and labor they wish to use in producing output. Let us first look at the decision about how much capital to use.

Since 1970, the labor-force participation rate for prime-age men has been decreasing slightly. The rate for prime-age women has been increasing dramatically. The rate for all others 16 and over has been declining since 1979 and shows a tendency to fall during recessions (the discouraged-worker effect).

inputs The goods and services that firms purchase and turn into output.

INVESTMENT DECISIONS   At any point in time a firm has a certain stock of capital on hand. By *stock of capital* we mean the factories and buildings (sometimes called "plant") that firms own, the equipment they need to do business, and their inventories of partly or wholly finished goods. There are two basic ways that a firm can add to its capital stock. One way is to buy more machinery or build new factories or buildings. This kind of addition to the capital stock is called **plant-and-equipment investment.**

The other way for a firm to add to its capital stock is to increase its inventories. When a firm produces more than it sells in a given period, the firm's stock of inventories increases.[6] This type of addition to the capital stock is called **inventory investment.** Recall from Chapter 24 that unplanned inventory investment is quite different from planned inventory investment. When a firm sells less than it expected to, it suffers an unplanned increase in its inventories and is thus forced to invest more than it planned to. Unplanned increases in inventories result from factors beyond the firm's control. (We take up inventory investment in more detail later in this chapter.)

EMPLOYMENT DECISIONS   In addition to investment decisions, firms also make *employment* decisions. At the beginning of each period, a firm has a certain number of workers on its payroll. On the basis of its current situation and its upcoming plans, the firm must decide whether it wants to hire additional workers, keep the same number of workers, or reduce its work force by laying off some employees.

Until this point, our description of firm behavior has been quite simple. In Chapter 24 we argued that firms increase production when they experience unplanned decreases in inventory and reduce production when they experience unplanned increases in inventory. We have also alluded to the fact that the demand for labor increases when output grows. In reality, however, the set of decisions facing firms is much more complex. A decision to produce additional output is likely to involve additional demand for both labor *and* capital.

The demand for labor is of obvious importance in macroeconomics. If the demand for labor increases at a time of less-than-full employment, the unemployment rate will fall. If the demand for labor increases when there is full employment, wage rates will rise. The demand for capital (which, as you know, is partly determined by the interest rate) is important as well. Recall that planned investment spending is a component of planned aggregate expenditure. When planned investment spending (*I,* the demand for new capital) increases, the result is additional output (income). We discussed the investment multiplier effect in Chapter 24. Another important aspect of capital is that it increases the productivity of labor and leads to growth.

DECISION MAKING AND PROFIT MAXIMIZATION   To understand the complex behavior of firms in input markets, it is important to recall our assumption that firms make decisions to maximize their profits. One of the most important profit-maximizing decisions that a firm must make is how to produce its output. In most cases, a firm must choose among alternative methods of production, or *technologies.* Different technologies generally require different combinations of capital and labor.

---

[6]Remember from Chapter 22 that the change in inventories is exactly equal to the difference between production and sales. If a firm sells 20 units more than it produces in the course of a month, its inventories fall by 20 units; if it produces 20 units more than it sells, its inventories rise by 20 units.

Take, for example, a factory that manufactures shirts. Shirts can be made entirely by hand, with workers cutting the pieces of fabric and sewing them together. But those same shirts can also be made on huge complex machines that cut and sew and produce shirts with very little human supervision. Between these two extremes are dozens of alternative technologies. For example, shirts can be partly hand sewn, with the stitching done on electric sewing machines.

All of this is to say that firms' decisions regarding the amount of capital and labor that they will use in production are closely related. If firms maximize profits, they will choose the technology that minimizes the cost of production. That is, it is logical to assume that firms will choose the technology that is most efficient.

Clearly, the most efficient technology depends on the relative prices of capital and labor. A shirt factory in the Philippines that decides to increase its production faces a large supply of relatively inexpensive labor. Wage rates in the Philippines are quite low. Capital equipment, on the other hand, must be imported and is very expensive. A shirt factory in the Philippines is thus likely to choose a **labor-intensive technology**—that is, one that uses a large amount of labor relative to capital. When labor-intensive technologies are used, expansion is likely to increase the demand for labor substantially while increasing the demand for capital only modestly.

Conversely, a shirt factory in Germany that decides to expand production is likely to buy a large amount of capital equipment and to hire relatively few new workers. In other words, it will probably choose a **capital-intensive technology**—that is, a technique that uses a large amount of capital relative to labor. German wage rates are quite high, higher in many occupations than in the United States. Capital, however, is in plentiful supply.

In sum:

> Firms' decisions about labor demand and investment are likely to depend on the relative costs of labor and capital. The relative impact of an expansion of output on employment and on investment demand depends on the wage rate and the cost of capital.

labor-intensive technology A technique of production that uses a large amount of labor relative to capital.

capital-intensive technology A technique of production that uses a large amount of capital relative to labor.

Expectations and Animal Spirits

In addition to the cost of capital and the cost of labor, firms' expectations about the future also play an important role in investment and employment decisions. This should not come as a surprise to you, given the importance we have attached to expectations in this book.

Time is a key factor in investment decisions. Capital has a life that typically extends over many years. A developer who decides to build an office tower is making an investment that will be around (barring earthquakes, floods, or tornadoes) for several decades. In deciding where to build a plant, a manufacturing firm is committing a large amount of resources to purchase capital that will presumably yield services over a long period of time. Furthermore, the decision to build a building or to purchase a piece of large equipment must often be made years before the actual project is completed. While the acquisition of a small business computer may take only a few days, the planning process for downtown developments in large U.S. cities has been known to take decades.

For these reasons, investment decisions necessarily involve looking into the future and forming expectations about it. In forming their expectations, firms consider numerous factors. At a minimum, they usually gather information about the demand for their specific line of products, about what their competitors are planning to do, and about the overall health of the macroeconomy. A firm is not likely to increase its production capacity if it does not expect to sell more of its product in the future. Hilton will not put up a new hotel if it does not expect to fill the rooms at a profitable rate. Ford will not build a new plant if it expects the economy to enter a prolonged recession.

Forecasting the future is, of course, fraught with dangers. Many important events simply cannot be foreseen. Investments, therefore, are always made with imperfect knowledge. Keynes pointed this out in 1936:

> The outstanding fact is the extreme precariousness of the basis of knowledge on which our estimates of prospective yield have to be made. Our knowledge of the factors which will govern the yield of an investment some years hence is usually very slight and often negligible. If we speak frankly, we have to admit that our basis of knowledge for estimating the yield ten years hence of a railway, a copper mine, a textile factory, the goodwill of a patent medicine, an Atlantic liner, a building in the City of London amounts to little and sometimes nothing.

animal spirits of entrepreneurs
A phrase coined by Keynes to describe the feelings of investors.

Keynes concludes from this that much depends on psychology and on what he calls the **animal spirits of entrepreneurs:**

> Our decisions … can only be taken as a result of animal spirits. In estimating the prospects of investment, we must have regard, therefore, to nerves and hysteria and even the digestions and reactions to the weather of those upon whose spontaneous activity it largely depends.[7]

Because expectations about the future are, as Keynes points out, subject to great uncertainty, they may be changed quite often. This, in turn, helps to make investment a volatile component of GDP.

THE ACCELERATOR EFFECT   It is clear that expectations at least in part determine the level of planned investment spending. At any given interest rate, the level of investment is likely to be higher if businesses are optimistic and confident. If businesses are pessimistic and gloomy, the level of planned investment will be lower. But what determines expectations?

One possibility that seems to be borne out empirically is that expectations are optimistic when aggregate output (Y) is rising and pessimistic when aggregate output is falling. In other words:

> At any given level of the interest rate, expectations are likely to be more optimistic and planned investment is likely to be higher when output is growing rapidly than when it is growing slowly or falling.

It is not difficult to see why this is so. If firms expect future output to grow, they must plan now to add productive capacity. One indicator of future prospects is the current growth rate.

accelerator effect The tendency for investment to increase when aggregate output increases and decrease when aggregate output decreases, thus accelerating the growth or decline of output.

If this is indeed the case in reality, and the evidence indicates that it is, the ultimate result will be an **accelerator effect.** If aggregate output (income) (Y) is rising, investment will increase even though the level of Y may be low. Higher investment spending leads to an added increase in output, further "accelerating" the growth of aggregate output. Conversely, if Y is falling, expectations are dampened, and investment spending will be cut even though the level of Y may be high, thus accelerating the decline.

---

[7]John Maynard Keynes, *The General Theory of Employment, Interest, and Money* (1936), First Harbinger Ed. (New York: Harcourt Brace Jovanovich, 1964), pp. 149, 152.

Excess Labor and Excess Capital Effects

We need to make one further point about the investment and employment decisions of firms: Firms may sometimes choose to hold **excess labor** and/or **excess capital**. A firm holds excess labor (or capital) if it could reduce the amount of labor it employs (or capital it holds) and still produce the same amount of output.

Why would a firm ever want to employ more workers or have more capital on hand than it needs? After all, both labor and capital are costly—a firm has to pay wages to its workers, and it forgoes interest on its funds if they are tied up in machinery or buildings. Why would a firm want to incur costs that do not yield it anything in the way of revenue?

A simple example may help to shed some light on this question. Suppose that a firm suffers a sudden and fairly large decrease in sales, but that it expects the lower sales level to last only a few months, after which it believes that sales will pick up again. In this case, the firm is likely to lower production in response to the sales change in order to avoid too large an increase in its stock of inventories. This decrease in production means that the firm could get rid of some workers and some machines, because it now needs less labor and less capital to produce the now-lower level of output.

But things are not this simple. Decreasing its work force and capital stock quickly can be quite costly for a firm. Abrupt cuts in the work force hurt worker morale and may increase personnel administration costs, and abrupt reductions in capital stock may be disadvantageous because of the difficulty of selling used machines. These types of costs are sometimes called **adjustment costs** because they are the costs of adjusting to the new level of output. There are also adjustment costs to increasing output. For example, it is usually costly to recruit and train new workers.

Adjustment costs may be large enough that a firm chooses not to decrease its work force and capital stock when production falls. In other words, the firm may at times choose to have more labor and capital on hand than it needs to produce its current amount of output, simply because it would be more costly to get rid of them than to keep them. In practice, excess labor takes the form of workers not working at their normal level of activity (more coffee breaks and more idle time, for instance). Some of this excess labor may receive new training so that productivity will be higher when production picks up again. This is exactly what happened to the staff at the Honda plant in Marysville, Ohio in 1993. (See the Global Perspective box titled "Putting Excess Labor into the Classroom: Honda in 1993" for more details.) Excess capital takes the form of idle or partially idle machines.

The existence of excess labor and capital at any given moment is likely to affect future employment and investment decisions. Suppose that a firm already has excess labor and capital due to a fall in its sales and production. When production picks up again, the firm will not need to hire as many new workers or acquire as much new capital as it otherwise would have. In general:

> The more excess capital a firm already has, the less likely it is to invest in new capital in the future; the more excess labor it has, the less likely it is to hire new workers in the future. In fact, if it finds itself holding excess capital, the firm may try to decrease its capital stock in the future, even if demand is actually increasing. The same is true for excess labor.

excess labor, excess capital Labor and capital that are not needed to produce the firm's current level of output.

adjustment costs The costs that a firm incurs when it changes its production level—for example, the administration costs of laying off employees or the training costs of hiring new workers.

PUTTING EXCESS LABOR INTO THE CLASSROOM: HONDA IN 1993

Rather than lay off workers when the demand for its cars decreased, managers of the Honda plant in Marysville, Ohio have sent assembly-line workers back to the class-room for additional training.

Not all firms announce layoffs when demand for their products decreases. The following excerpt from the *New York Times* is a perfect example of a firm willing to hold "excess labor" during a period of slack demand:

MARYSVILLE, Ohio—For the 5,400 workers who assemble the popular Honda Accord at a factory here, the unthinkable finally happened. Tougher competition from the Big Three and tepid demand for cars has forced the Honda Motor Company to trim production significantly for the first time in the plant's 10-year history. . . .

But instead of laying off hundreds of workers until business improves, or spreading the pain by imposing a holiday on everyone, as American car makers often do in similar situations, Honda is using the extra time to intensify training.

"We've never guaranteed there won't be layoffs," Roger Lambert, a Honda spokesman, said. Nevertheless, "when we decided we would have to reduce output, we didn't see this as a way to cut 200 workers, we saw it as 5 percent more time for training."

In Big Three plants, workers who are laid off receive what amounts to a paid vacation under their union contracts. Honda decided to use this time to teach its workers new skills, reasoning that it would be an investment in future productivity.

Honda says its commitment to training is a strategy for enlarging the capability of its work force so that its rebound will be magnified when tough times improve. For Honda and other Japanese auto makers operating factories in the United States, constant training has been a key tactic in their battle against American auto makers. . . .

Last fall, Honda announced it would build 110,000 Accords in the first quarter of 1993, down almost 11 percent from the 123,483 built in the first quarter last year. The rate translates to about 200 fewer cars a day. Rather than stopping production, Honda slowed assembly slightly–which allowed it to move people from the assembly line to the classroom.

Source: Doron P. Levin, "Back to School for Honda Workers," *New York Times,* March, 1993.

Inventory Investment

We now turn to a brief discussion of the inventory-investment decision. This decision is quite different from the plant-and-equipment investment decision.

THE BASIC ROLE OF INVENTORIES   Recall that there is an important distinction between a firm's sales and its output. If a firm can hold goods in inventory, which is usually the case unless the good is perishable or unless the firm produces services, then within a given period it can sell a quantity of goods that differs from the quantity of goods it produces during that period. When a firm sells more than it produces, its stock of inventories decreases; when it sells less than it produces, its stock of inventories increases. The following relationship thus holds:

Stock of Inventories (End of Period) =   Stock of Inventories (Beginning of Period)
+ Production – Sales.

If, for example, a firm starts a period with 100 umbrellas in inventory, produces 15 umbrellas during the period, and sells 10 umbrellas in this same interval of time, it will have at the end of the period 105 umbrellas (100 + 15 − 10) left in inventory. A change in the stock of inventories is actually investment because inventories are counted as part of a firm's capital stock. In our example, inventory investment during the period is a positive number, five umbrellas (105 − 100). When the number of goods produced is less than the number of goods sold, inventory investment is negative.

THE OPTIMAL INVENTORY POLICY We can now consider firms' inventory decisions. Firms are, of course, concerned with what they are going to sell and produce in the future, as well as what they are selling and producing currently. At each point in time, a firm has some idea of how much it is going to sell in the current period and in future periods. Given these expectations and its knowledge of how much of its good it already has in stock, a firm must decide how much to produce in the current period.

Inventories are costly to a firm because they take up space and they tie up funds that could otherwise be earning interest. On the other hand, if a firm's stock of inventories gets too low, the firm may have difficulty meeting the demand for its product, especially if demand increases unexpectedly. As a result, the firm may lose sales. The point between too low a stock of inventory and too high a stock of inventory is called the **desired,** or **optimal, level of inventories.** This is the level at which the extra cost (in lost sales) from decreasing inventories by a small amount is just equal to the extra gain (in interest revenue and decreased storage costs).

A firm that had no costs other than inventory costs would always aim to produce in a period exactly the volume of goods necessary to make its stock of inventories at the end of the period equal to the desired stock. If the stock of inventory fell lower than desired, the firm would produce more than it expected to sell to bring the stock up. If the stock of inventory grew above the desired level, the firm would produce less than it expected to sell in order to reduce the stock.

There are other costs to running a firm besides inventory costs, however. In particular, large and abrupt changes in production can be extremely costly because it is often disruptive to change a production process geared to a certain rate of output. If production is to be increased, there may be adjustment costs involved in hiring more labor and in increasing the capital stock. If production is to be decreased, there may be adjustment costs in laying off workers and decreasing the capital stock.

Because holding inventories and changing production levels are both costly, firms face a trade-off between these two courses of action. Because of adjustment costs, a firm is likely to smooth its production path relative to its sales path. This means that a firm is likely to have its production fluctuate less than its sales, with changes in inventories being used to absorb the difference each period. However, because of inventory holding costs, fluctuations in production are not eliminated completely. Production is still likely to fluctuate somewhat, just not as much as sales fluctuate.

Two other points need to be made here. First, if a firm's stock of inventories is unusually or unexpectedly high, the firm is likely to produce less in the future than it otherwise would have, in order to decrease its high stock of inventories. In other words, although the stock of inventories fluctuates over time because production is smoothed relative to sales, at any point in time

desired, or optimal, level of inventories The level of inventory at which the extra cost (in lost sales) from lowering inventories by a small amount is just equal to the extra gain (in interest revenue and decreased storage costs).

inventories may be unexpectedly high or low because sales have been unexpectedly low or high. An unexpectedly high stock will have a negative effect on production in the future, and an unexpectedly low stock will have a positive effect on production in the future. To recap:

> An unexpected increase in inventories has a negative effect on future production, and an unexpected decrease in inventories has a positive effect on future production.

Second, firms do not know their future sales exactly. In practice, firms have only expectations of future sales, and these expectations may not turn out to be exactly right.

This fact has important consequences. If sales turn out to be less than expected, inventories will be higher than expected, and there will be less production in the future. Furthermore, *future* sales expectations are likely to have an important effect on *current* production. If a firm expects its sales to be high in the future, it will adjust its planned production path accordingly. Even though a firm smoothes production relative to sales, over a long period of time it must produce as much as it sells; if it did not, it would have an indefinitely falling stock of inventories. In sum:

> The level of a firm's planned production path depends on the level of its expected future sales path. If a firm's expectations of the level of its future sales path decrease, the firm is likely to decrease the level of its planned production path, including its actual production in the current period. Thus, current production depends on expected future sales.

Because production is likely to depend on expectations of the future, "animal spirits" may once again play an important role. If firms become more optimistic about the future, they are likely to produce more now. Thus, Keynes's view that animal spirits affect investment is also likely to pertain to output.

A Summary of Firm Behavior

To summarize our discussion of firm behavior:

> The following factors affect firms' investment and employment decisions:
>
> - the wage rate and the cost of capital. (An important component of the cost of capital is the interest rate.)
> - firms' expectations of future output.
> - the amount of excess labor and excess capital on hand.
>
> The most important points to remember about the relationship between production, sales, and inventory investment are:
>
> - inventory investment (that is, the change in the stock of inventories) equals production minus sales.
> - an unexpected increase in the stock of inventories has a negative effect on future production.
> - current production depends on expected future sales.

The Firm Sector Since 1970

To close our discussion of firm behavior in the macroeconomy, we now turn to an examination of some aggregate investment and employment variables for the period 1970 I–1992 IV.

PLANT AND EQUIPMENT INVESTMENT   Plant and equipment investment by the firm sector is plotted in Figure 32.6. As you can see, investment fared poorly in the first three recessionary periods after 1970. This observation is consistent with the observation that investment depends in part on output. An examination of the plot of real GDP in Figure 21.7 and the plot of investment in Figure 32.6 shows clearly that investment generally does poorly when GDP does poorly and that investment generally does well when GDP does well.

Figure 32.6 also shows that investment fluctuates greatly. This is not surprising. The "animal spirits" of entrepreneurs are likely to be volatile, and if animal spirits affect investment, it follows that investment too will be volatile.

Despite the volatility of plant and equipment investment, however, it is still true that housing investment fluctuates more than plant and equipment investment (as you can see by comparing Figures 32.4 and 32.6). Plant and equipment investment is not the most volatile component of GDP.

EMPLOYMENT   Employment in the firm sector is plotted in Figure 32.7, which shows that employment fell in all three recessionary periods. This is consistent with the theory that employment depends in part on output. Otherwise, employment has grown over time in response to the growing economy. Employment in the firm sector rose from 71.8 million in 1970 I to 105.2 million in 1992 IV.

INVENTORY INVESTMENT   Recall that *inventory investment* is the difference between the level of output and the level of sales. Recall also that some inventory investment is usually unplanned. This occurs when the actual level of sales is different from the expected level of sales.

FIGURE 32.6

Plant and Equipment Investment of the Firm Sector, 1970 I–1992 IV

Overall, plant and equipment investment declined in the three recessionary periods since 1970.

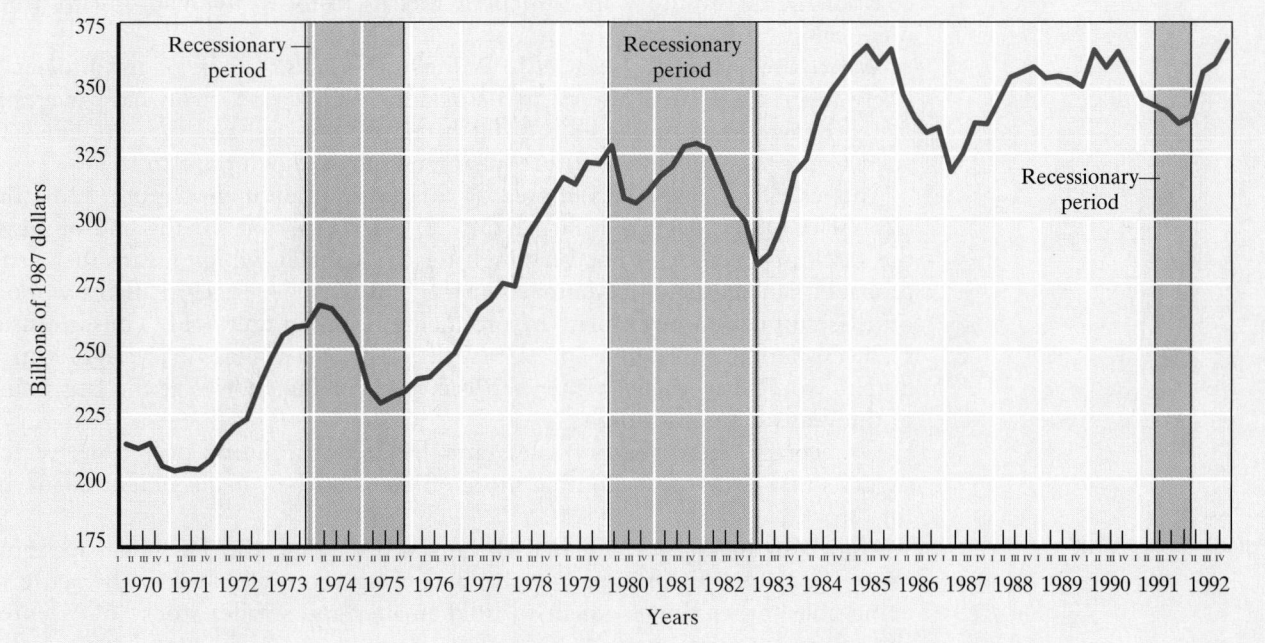

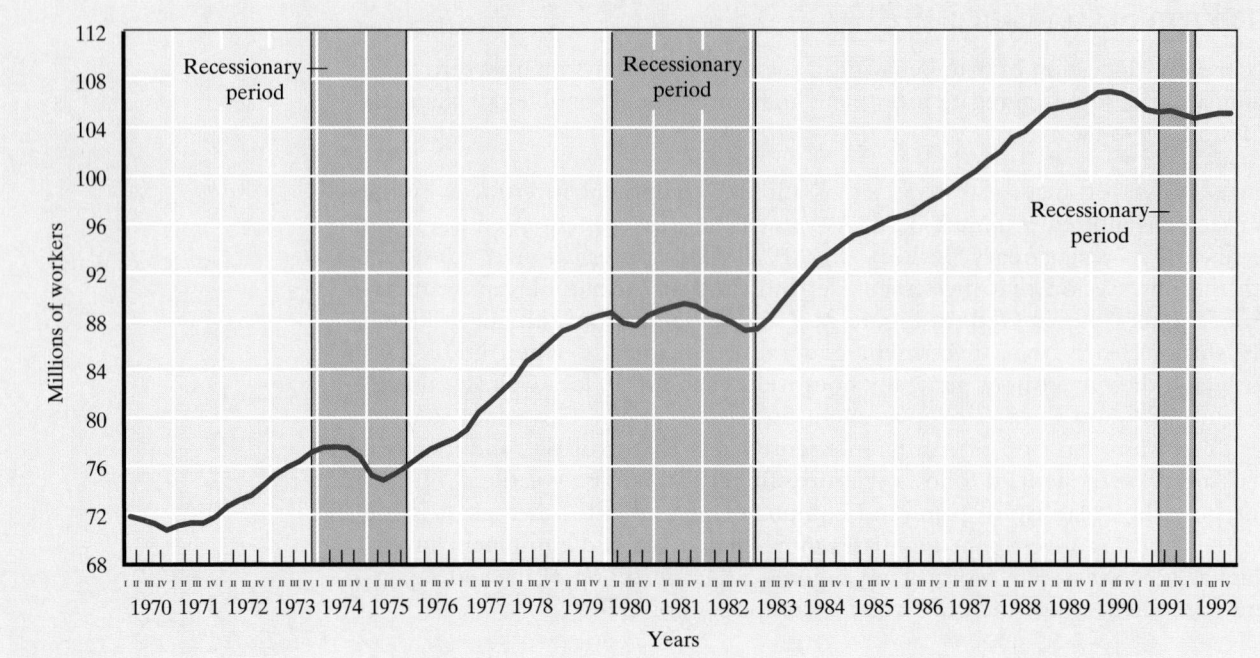

FIGURE 32.7
Employment in the Firm Sector, 1970 I–1992 IV

Growth in employment was generally negative in the three recessions the U.S. economy has experienced since 1970.

Inventory investment of the firm sector is plotted in Figure 32.8. Also plotted in this figure is the ratio of the stock of inventories to the level of sales—the *inventory/sales ratio*. The figure shows that inventory investment is very volatile—more volatile, in fact, than housing investment and plant and equipment investment. Some of this volatility is undoubtedly due to the unplanned component of inventory investment, which is likely to fluctuate greatly from one period to the next.

When the inventory/sales ratio is high, the actual stock of inventories is likely to be larger than the desired stock. In such a case, firms have overestimated demand and produced too much relative to sales, and they are likely to want to produce less in the future in order to draw down their stock.

You can find several examples of this phenomenon in Figure 32.8, the clearest of which occurred during the 1974–1975 period. At the end of 1974, the stock of inventories was very high relative to sales, which means that firms probably had undesired inventories at the end of 1974. In 1975, firms worked off these undesired inventories by producing less than they sold. Thus inventory investment was negative in 1975. The year 1975 is clearly a year in which output would have been higher had the stock of inventories at the beginning of the year not been so high.

On average the inventory/sales ratio has been declining over time, which suggests that firms are becoming more efficient in their management of inventory stocks.

Note also in Figure 32.8 that the inventory/sales ratio has been declining since 1982. U.S. firms appear to be becoming more efficient in the sense of being able (other things equal) to hold smaller and smaller stocks of inventories relative to sales.

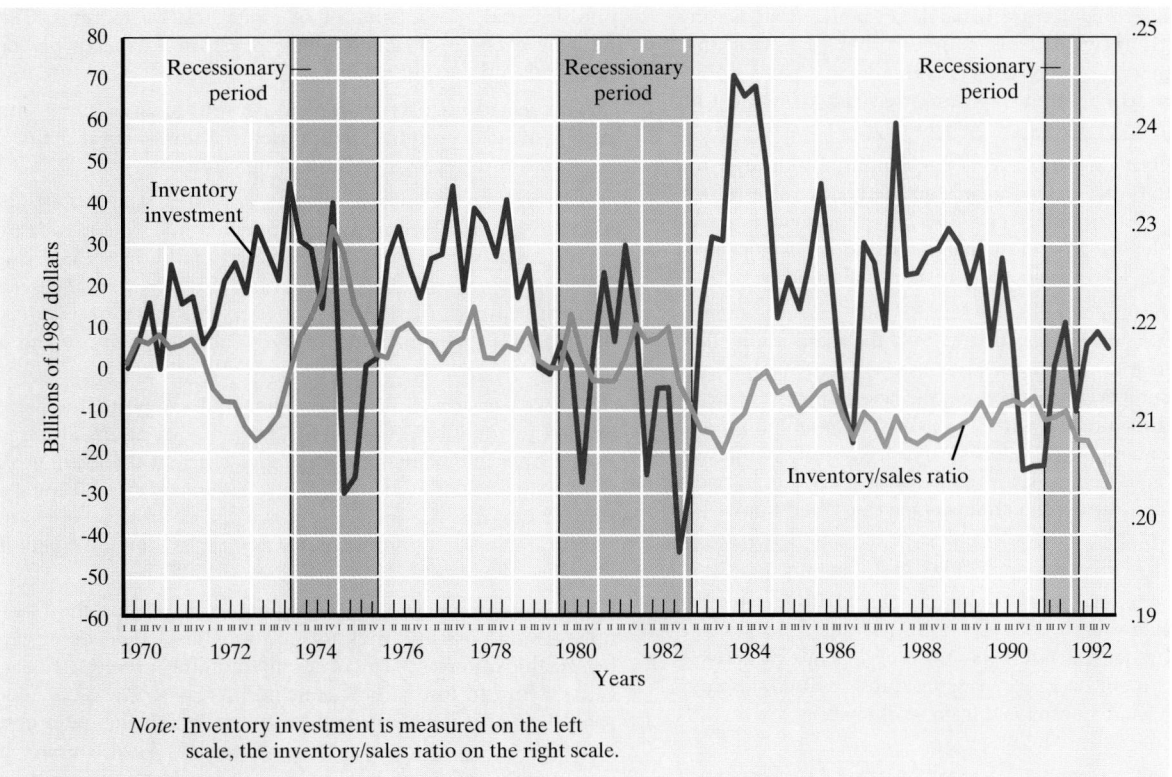

FIGURE 32.8

Inventory Investment of the Firm Sector and the Inventory/Sales Ratio, 1970 I–1992 IV

The inventory/sales ratio is the ratio of the firm sector's stock of inventories to the level of sales. Inventory investment is very volatile.

SUMMARY

Households: Consumption and Labor Supply Decisions

1. The Keynesian theory of consumption holds that household consumption (C) is positively related to income: The more income one has, the more consumption one is likely to do. Keynes also believed that high-income households consume a smaller proportion of their income than do low-income households. The proportion of income that households spend on consumption is measured by the *average propensity to consume* (*APC*), which is equal to consumption divided by income (*C/Y*).

2. The *life-cycle theory of consumption* holds that households make lifetime consumption decisions based on their expectations of lifetime income. Generally, households consume an amount less than their incomes during their prime working years and an amount greater than their incomes during their early working years and after they have retired.

3. Households make consumption and labor supply decisions simultaneously. Consumption cannot be considered separately from labor supply, because it is precisely by selling

one's labor that one earns the income that makes consumption possible.

4. There is a trade-off between the goods and services that wage income will buy and leisure or other nonmarket activities. The wage rate is the key variable that determines how a household responds to this trade-off.

5. Changes in the wage rate have both an income effect and a substitution effect. The evidence suggests that the substitution effect seems to dominate for most people, which means that the aggregate labor supply responds positively to an increase in the wage rate.

6. Consumption increases when the wage rate increases.

7. The *nominal wage rate* is the wage rate in current dollars. The *real wage rate* is the nominal wage rate adjusted for changes in the price level over time. Households look at expected future real wage rates as well as the current real wage rate in making their consumption and labor supply decisions.

8. Holding all else constant (including the stage in the life cycle), the more wealth a household has, the more it will consume, both now and in the future.

9. An unexpected increase in *nonlabor income* (that is, any income that is received from sources other than working, such as inheritances, interest, and dividends) will have a positive effect on a household's consumption and will lead to a decrease in labor supply.

10. The interest rate also affects consumption, although the direction of the total effect depends on the relative sizes of the income and substitution effects. There is some evidence that the income effect is larger now than it used to be, thus making monetary policy less effective now than it used to be.

11. The government influences household behavior mainly through tax rates and transfer payments. If the substitution effect dominates, an increase in tax rates lowers after-tax income, decreases consumption, and decreases the labor supply; a decrease in tax rates raises after-tax income, increases consumption, and increases labor supply. Increases in transfer payments increase consumption and decrease labor supply, while decreases in transfer payments decrease consumption and increase labor supply.

12. During times of less-than-full employment, households' labor supply may be constrained. That is, households may wish to work a certain number of hours at current wage rates but may not be allowed to do so by firms. In this situation, the level of income (at least workers' income) depends exclusively on the employment decisions made by firms. Households consume less if they are constrained from working.

Firms: Investment and Employment Decisions

13. Firms purchase *inputs* and turn them into outputs. Each period, firms must decide how much capital and labor (two major inputs) they wish to use in producing output. Firms can invest in plants and equipment or in inventory.

14. Because output can be produced using many different technologies, firms must make capital and labor decisions simultaneously. A *labor-intensive technique* is one that uses a large amount of labor relative to capital. A *capital-intensive technique* is

one that uses a large amount of capital relative to labor. The ultimate decision of which technology to use depends on the wage rate and the cost of capital.

15. Expectations play an important role in investment and employment decisions. Keynes used the term *animal spirits of entrepreneurs* to refer to feelings of investors.

16. At any given level of the interest rate, expectations are likely to be more optimistic and planned investment is likely to be higher when output is growing rapidly than when it is growing slowly or falling. The ultimate result is an *accelerator effect* that can cause the economy to expand more rapidly during an expansion and contract more quickly during a recession.

17. *Excess labor and capital* are labor and capital that are not needed to produce a firm's current level of output. Holding excess labor and capital may be more efficient than laying off workers or selling used equipment. The more excess capital a firm already has, the less likely it is to invest in new capital in the future, and the more excess labor it has, the less likely it is to hire new workers in the future.

18. Holding inventories is costly to a firm because they take up space and because they tie up funds that could otherwise be earning interest. However, not holding inventories can cause a firm to lose sales if demand increases. The *desired, or optimal, level of inventories* is the level at which the extra cost (in lost sales) from lowering inventories by a small amount is just equal to the extra gain (in interest revenue and decreased storage costs).

19. An unexpected increase in inventories has a negative effect on future production, and an unexpected decrease in inventories has a positive effect on future production.

20. The level of a firm's planned production path depends on the level of its expected future sales path. If a firm's expectations of its future sales path decrease, the firm is likely to decrease the level of its planned production path, including its actual production in the current period.

REVIEW TERMS AND CONCEPTS

Equations: $APC \equiv \dfrac{C}{Y}$

PROBLEM SET

1. In 1993, President Clinton proposed and Congress enacted an increase in taxes. One of the increases was in the income tax rate for higher-income wage earners. Republicans claimed that reducing the rewards for working (the net after-tax wage rate), would lead to less work effort and a lower labor supply. Supporters of the tax increase replied that this criticism was baseless because it "ignored the income effect of the tax increase (net wage reduction)." Explain what these supporters meant.

2. During the late 1980s the price of houses increased dramatically in both the Northeast and California. During the early 1990s home prices dropped sharply in both of these regions. During the late 1980s the economies of both the Northeast and California boomed, and during the 1990s both went into deep recessions.
What impact would you expect increases and decreases in home value to have on the consumption behavior of home owners? Explain. In what ways might events in the housing market have influenced the rest of the economy through their effects on consumption spending? Be specific.

3. Graph the following two consumption functions:

$$(1) \ C = 300 + 0.5 \ Y$$

$$(2) \ C = 0.5Y.$$

a. For each function, calculate and graph the average propensity to consume (APC) when income is $100, $400, and $800.
b. In both examples, what happens to the APC as income rises?
c. In both examples, what is the relationship between the APC and the marginal propensity to consume?
d. Under consumption function (1), a family with an income of $50,000 consumes a smaller proportion of its income than a family with an income of $20,000; yet if we take a dollar of income away from the rich family and give it to the poor family, total consumption by the two families does not change. Explain how this could be so.

4. Adam Smith is 45 years old. He has assets (wealth) of $20,000 and has no debts or liabilities. He knows he will work for 20 more years and that he will live five years after that, and during those five years he will earn nothing. His salary each year for the rest of his working career is $14,000. (There are no taxes.) He wants to distribute his consumption over the rest of his life in such a way that he consumes the same amount each year. Of course, he cannot consume in total more than his current wealth plus the sum of his income for the next 20 years. Assume that the rate of interest is zero and that Smith decides not to leave any inheritance to his children.

a. How much will Adam consume this year? Next year? How did you arrive at your answer?
b. Plot on a graph Adam's income, consumption, and wealth from the time he is 45 until the time he is 70 years old.
What is the relationship between the annual increase in Adam's wealth and his annual saving (income − consumption)? In what year does Adam's wealth start to decline? Why? How much wealth does he have when he dies?
c. Suppose that Adam receives a tax rebate of $100 per year, so that his income is $14,100 per year for the rest of his working career. By how much does his consumption increase this year? Next year?
d. Now suppose that Adam receives a one-year-only tax refund of $100. That is, his income this year is $14,100, but in all succeeding years, his income is back to $14,000. What happens to his consumption this year? In succeeding years?

5. Explain why a household's consumption and labor supply decisions are interdependent. What impact does this interdependence have on the way in which consumption and income are related?

6. Compile a list of factors that are important in determining how much labor you will supply during the summer. How might your list differ from that of a 40-year-old breadwinner?

7. Why do expectations play such an important role in investment demand? How, if at all, does this explain why investment is so volatile?

8. Explain why the size of its existing stock of inventories is negatively related to the amount of output a firm wishes to produce in a period.

9. How can a firm maintain a smooth production schedule even when sales are fluctuating? What are the benefits of a smooth production schedule? What are the costs?

33

Further Topics in Macroeconomic Analysis

The last chapter presented a more complete and realistic picture of the behavior of households and firms in the macroeconomy. Using what we learned there, we can now analyze the effects of fiscal and monetary policy on the macroeconomy in more detail. We can also consider some interesting new topics, including the impact of the stock market on the economy and the relationship between aggregate output and the unemployment rate. We begin our discussion with a brief review of basic monetary and fiscal policy.

MONETARY AND FISCAL POLICY REVISITED

fiscal policy The spending and taxing policies used by the government to influence the economy.

A major focus of our discussion of macroeconomics has been on the role of government. As you know, the government can influence the behavior of the economy through **fiscal policy**—that is, through its taxing and spending decisions. About 30% of U.S. GDP goes to the government in the form of taxes. In recent years, the government has been spending a good deal more than it has been collecting in taxes. The result has been high annual budget deficits and a large national debt.

The government can also influence the economy by using **monetary policy** to change the interest rate. In the United States, the Federal Reserve controls the money supply. By expanding and contracting the quantity of money in circulation, the Fed indirectly controls the interest rate and thus influences the behavior of households and firms.

Let us now consider monetary and fiscal policy in more detail.

monetary policy The behavior of the Federal Reserve regarding the money supply.

Temporary versus Permanent Changes in Taxes and Spending

Thus far, our analysis of fiscal policy has been quite simple. If the government cuts taxes, we said, households consume more. The cut in taxes shifts the aggregate expenditure (*AE*) curve up and the aggregate demand (*AD*) curve to the right. The result is a higher level of equilibrium national output, at least in the short run, and a higher price level.

With the expanded discussion of household and firm behavior in the previous chapter, we are in a position to understand better the full impacts of fiscal policy. Consider, for example, the effect of a tax cut on household behavior. We now know that household consumption and saving behavior is influenced not by current income alone, but also by households' expectations about future income. Thus,

> If a tax cut is expected to be temporary rather than permanent, it will have less of an effect on household behavior because it will have less of an impact on households' permanent income.

Examples of temporary tax changes include the lump-sum tax rebate on 1974 income granted by the Ford administration in 1975 and the temporary income tax "surcharge" enacted in the late 1960s by the Nixon administration to help pay for the Vietnam War. On the other hand, the tax cuts in 1981 and 1986 (which we have discussed several times in this book) were intended by Congress to be permanent.

The fact that household decisions depend on expectations also means that changes in government policies that have little or no impact on this year's budget, but that do have impacts in the future, can affect behavior. Perhaps the most important example of this is social security policy. As we discussed briefly in Chapter 3, virtually everyone employed in the United States belongs to the social security system. Employers and employees are required to pay a fairly stiff tax out of each week's pay. When a worker retires, he or she receives a check from the Social Security Administration every month for as long as he or she lives.

Some economists believe that the saving rate in the United States is low partly because of the social security system. If workers expect to receive social security benefits, they may decrease their personal saving for retirement and consume more today. In this sense, the social security system may act as a substitute for private saving.

The effects of tax changes on firm behavior also depend on whether these changes are perceived to be permanent or temporary. Even more than consumption decisions, investment decisions are based on expectations of the future. Clearly, the future returns on an investment project depend, at least in part, on the tax laws that will be in effect in the future. Nothing is more frustrating to private business than a government that is constantly changing the rules. In 1986, Roger Smith, then chairman of the board of General Motors, decided to speak out in favor of the Tax Reform Act of 1986 in spite of the fact that the act increased corporation income taxes by about $120 billion and in spite of opposition from many other chief executive officers. He did so because members of Congress promised that if the act were passed, they would strongly resist changing the tax laws again for a long time.

Policies That Affect Real Wages versus Policies That Affect Nonlabor Income

The analysis we did in the last chapter also makes it clear that policies that affect real after-tax wages are likely to have a different effect on labor supply and consumption than policies that affect income alone. Remember that households make both labor supply decisions *and* consumption decisions simultaneously.

In 1991, in testing the waters for a possible run for the presidency in 1992, Senator John D. Rockefeller suggested a $1000 "refundable income tax credit." Through this credit, everyone's taxes would be cut by $1000, regardless of their income. If a taxpayer paid less than $1000 in taxes, he or she would receive a check for the difference.

Now imagine the effect of a tax cut of the same magnitude enacted in the form of reduced tax *rates* rather than as a lump-sum credit. When tax rates are cut, the after-tax wage rate rises (because workers take home a bigger part of each hour's wages). Thus, the rewards of an added hour of work are higher when tax rates are cut. The rewards of an added hour of work do *not* change if the tax cut is simply $1000, regardless of how much one works.

Assuming that both the $1000 across-the-board tax cut and the rate reduction increase disposable income by the same amount initially, one might think that both would have the same impact on consumption spending and ultimately on output. But this is not the case. Why? Because the two proposals can have very different effects on the supply of labor. Both proposals make households better off, and this *income effect* leads workers to consume more leisure (that is, to work less). But the reduced tax rate also produces a *substitution effect* away from leisure, while the lump-sum reduction does not. The lower tax rate means that the opportunity cost (or the "price") of leisure is higher, which may cause people to work more. The lump-sum tax reduction, however, does *not* affect the trade-off between work and leisure. (Review the last chapter if you are unsure of how the income and substitution effects work.)

This is precisely the point made by policy makers during the Reagan administration. Between 1981 (when President Reagan first took office) and 1986, Congress sharply reduced personal income tax rates twice. In 1981, the highest income tax rate was reduced from 70% to 50 percent. Then, in 1986, it was reduced from 50% to 33 percent. The expressed purpose of these cuts was to "increase the incentive to work." This was part of the logic of what came to be called *supply-side economics*. (We touched briefly on supply-side economics earlier and will return to the topic in the next chapter.)

Transfer Payments and Other Nonlabor Income

transfer payments Cash payments made by the government directly to households.

nonlabor income Any income that is received from sources other than working.

The refundable credit we discussed above is a **transfer payment.** Other transfer payments include social security payments, welfare benefits, and unemployment compensation. (Review Chapter 3 if necessary.) Transfer payments, in turn, are part of a larger category of income called **nonlabor income**—income received from non-wage-earning activities. Interest income received by households is one type of nonlabor income.

The effect of a change in nonlabor income on households is a pure income effect. There is no substitution effect because a change in nonlabor income does not change the trade-off between work and leisure. (A change in nonlabor income does not affect the wage rate.) Therefore:

> Any increase in nonlabor income unambiguously leads to an increase in consumption and a decrease in labor supply. Conversely, any decrease in nonlabor income unambiguously leads to a decrease in consumption and an increase in labor supply.

Dividend payments by firms to households are part of nonlabor income. When the economy expands, firms' profits increase, and some of these profits go to households in the form of **dividends.** This increase in nonlabor income then leads households to consume more and work less. Firm profits are thus another channel through which policy changes can affect the economy. Any policy change that initially stimulates the economy and increases firms' profits will lead to an increase in the nonlabor income of households, which will further affect the economy through the (increased) consumption and (decreased) labor supply responses of households.

dividends The portion of a corporation's profits the firm pays out each period to shareholders.

The Importance of Interest Rates

We know that monetary policy works primarily through changes in the interest rate. Until the last chapter, we focused on the effects of changes in the interest rate on planned investment spending (I) by firms. We assumed that lower interest rates stimulate I and that higher interest rates reduce I. In the last chapter, however, we saw that consumption is also likely to depend on the interest rate. If the substitution effect is greater than the income effect, then a decrease in the interest rate has a positive effect on consumption. If the income effect is greater than the substitution effect, a decrease in interest rates has a negative effect on consumption. Because the interest rate affects both investment and consumption, there are two channels through which monetary policy can influence behavior in the goods market.

In the last chapter, we discussed the fact that the income effect of a change in the interest rate on consumption may be larger today than it was in the past. For this reason monetary policy may now be less effective than before. The income effect may be larger today due to the recent huge increase in the government debt, much of which is owned by households. A decrease in the interest rate leads to a large decrease in the interest income of households; this has a negative effect on consumption. Current evidence suggests that this effect offsets much of the positive substitution effect on consumption and the positive effect on investment from a decrease in the interest rate.

Policy Effects in High-Output versus Low-Output Periods

When we discussed the short-run aggregate supply curve in Chapter 29, we argued that the AS curve is likely to be fairly flat at low levels of output and fairly steep at high levels of output. This means that policies designed to stimulate or contract the economy are likely to have a larger impact on output when output is low rather than high.

We are now in a position to understand exactly why this is so. At low levels of output, firms may be holding excess capital and excess labor. That is, firms may have idle plant capacity and workers who are not working at their potential even though they are on the payroll. If firms believe that a downturn in sales and output is temporary and that increased output will be needed in the future, they may choose to close a plant temporarily or to reassign workers rather than to sell off the plant and fire the workers. If firms behave this way, then an expansionary policy can lead to more output without the need for more workers or more plant capacity; existing plants and current workers can simply be put back to work.

Recall that when output is low, there is likely to be unemployment. During periods of unemployment, households are constrained from working as much as they would like to at current wage rates. Thus, when firms expand during such periods, labor is available from the ranks of the unemployed, and higher wages are not needed to attract them. For this reason, output can be expanded with little or no increase in wage rates, input costs, or the overall price level.

At high levels of output, however, firms are holding very little excess capital and labor, and the unemployment rate is low. In this case, an expansionary policy can work only if the labor supply expands. The policy will create an excess demand for labor, which will push up wages (labor/input costs). Higher wages are required to induce the needed number of workers away from leisure and into the work force. This means upward pressure on wages and on the aggregate price level.

The size of the multiplier depends on whether excess labor and capital exist and whether workers are willing to take jobs at the current wage rate. If output can expand with little or no increase in costs, the multiplier is likely to be large. If, however, added output leads to higher wages and other costs, firms are not likely to expand output as much. Thus:

> During periods of high output and low unemployment, the multiplier is likely to be smaller.

The Role of Inventories

Finally, the effectiveness of monetary and fiscal policy also depends on the size of inventory stocks. During periods of low output, inventory stocks are likely to be high (because sales have presumably been weak), so part of any increase in sales brought about by an expansionary policy can come out of inventories. In periods of high output, on the other hand, inventory stocks are likely to be low, so sales increases are likely to be matched fairly closely by output increases. Thus:

> Output is likely to respond more to sales increases in high-output periods than in low-output periods, provided that firms have enough capital and labor to support the output increase.

If firms do not have sufficient capital and labor to support an output increase, their inventory stocks will fall further as sales increase, even though they would like to build their stocks back up. In this case, the economy is in effect on the steep part of the AS curve, and there is likely to be a large price response to any increase in aggregate demand.

THE EFFECTS OF THE STOCK MARKET ON THE ECONOMY

In the last chapter, we pointed out that one of the factors that affects consumption is wealth. If a household has a sudden increase in wealth, its current and future consumption levels will increase. One of the main components of household wealth is the value of stocks held by households. When stock prices rise, household wealth increases, and when stock prices fall, household wealth decreases. Stock prices thus affect the economy by affecting household wealth, which affects household consumption. (This chapter's Issues and Applications boxes explain in detail how to follow both the stock market and the bond market by reading the financial pages of the daily newspaper.)

As you should recall from Chapter 3, one of the key aspects of the modern corporation is its limited liability feature. Stockholders are entitled to a share of the firm's profits, but if the firm incurs losses, stockholders' liability is limited to the amount of their initial contribution. This is not true with partnerships or other forms of business organization.

To see how events in the stock market affect the economy, it is informative to consider a particular episode in the history of the stock market, namely the stock market crash of October 1987. The value of stocks in the United States fell by about a trillion dollars between August 1987 and the end of October 1987. In one day—October 19, 1987—the value of stocks fell nearly $700 billion. This corresponded to a large drop in household wealth.

In practice, it seems to be the case that a $1.00 decrease in wealth leads roughly to a $0.05 decrease in consumption spending per year. In other words, consumption seems to be lower in each future year by about 5% of the decrease in wealth. Using this estimate, we can see that the $1 trillion decrease in wealth in 1987 implies a $50 billion lower level of consumption in 1988. The level of GDP was around $4 trillion in 1987, so a $50 billion decrease in consumption is around 1.25% of GDP. A multiplier effect would also be at work in this case: A decrease in consumption spending leads to a decrease in aggregate output (income), which leads to a further decrease in spending, and so on. The total decrease in GDP would thus be somewhat larger than the initial decrease in consumption of $50 billion. If the multiplier is 1.4, the total decrease in GDP would be about 1.4 × $50 billion = $70 billion, or about 1.75% of GDP.

While 1.75% of GDP is a large amount, it is not large enough to imply that a recession would necessarily result from the crash. The life-cycle theory we discussed in the previous chapter is useful for understanding why this is so. If households are making lifetime decisions and want to have as smooth a consumption path as possible over their lifetimes, they will respond to a decrease in wealth by cutting consumption a little each year. They certainly will *not* decrease their consumption in the current year by the full amount of the decrease in wealth. As we noted above, it has been estimated that households adjust their consumption by about 5% of the decrease in wealth each year.

Why, then, were people predicting that the economy would go into a severe recession, if not a depression, after the crash? The reasons all pertain to expectations. If households and firms expected that the economy would contract sharply after the crash, they probably would have cut back on consumption and investment. (This would be Keynes's "animal spirits" at work.) These expectations would have become self-fulfilling in the sense that the economy would have gone into a recession because of the cuts in consumption and investment brought about by lowered expectations.

In fact, the economy did not go into a recession in 1988. It seems that expectations were not changed drastically following the crash. The Fed helped out by easing monetary policy right after the crash to counteract any large negative reaction. The three-month Treasury bill rate fell from 6.4% to 5.8% between October and November of 1987. In addition, the value of stocks gradually increased over time to their earlier levels. Because the initial decrease in wealth turned out to be temporary, the negative wealth effect was not nearly as large as it otherwise would have been. In the end, consumption was affected only slightly by the crash.

PRODUCTIVITY AND THE BUSINESS CYCLE

Productivity, sometimes called **labor productivity,** is defined as output per worker hour. If output is Y and the number of hours worked in the economy is H, then productivity is Y/H. Simply stated, productivity measures how much output an average worker produces in one hour.

productivity, or labor productivity Output per worker hour; the amount of output produced by an average worker in one hour.

READING A BOND TABLE

What Is a Bond?

When a business wishes to make a large purchase—to build a new factory, for example, or to buy an expensive piece of machinery—it often finds that it cannot pay for the purchase all at once, entirely out of its normal revenues. The obvious solution is for the firm to borrow the money, make the purchase, and then repay the lender of the funds over a longer period of time. This process is called "financing" an investment, and the "pieces of paper" that are involved in these transactions are called **financial instruments.** *Bonds* are one type of financial instrument that firms issue in exchange for cash. If you buy a bond, you are making a loan to the firm that sold it to you.

Bonds have several important properties. First, they are issued with a face value, typically in denominations of $1000, that represent the amount you (the buyer) agree to lend the bond issuer. They also come with a *maturity date* on which the firm promises to pay back the funds you lent it. (However, you can sell the bond to someone else before the maturity date if you want.) Finally, there is a fixed payment (usually made annu-

FIGURE 1

Bondholder's Outlays and Receipts from a $10,000, 10%, 15-Year Bond

Your initial expenditure is –$10,000. At the beginning of each year, you receive $1000 (10% of the bond's face value) from the firm that issued the bond. When the bond matures, you get your $10,000 back plus the last year's interest. If we were to graph the *firm's* schedule of outlays and receipts, it would be exactly the opposite of the one shown here.

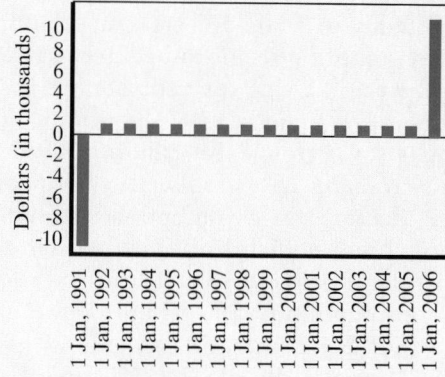

ally) of a specified amount, paid by the bond issuer to the bondholder. This payment, known as the *coupon,* is calculated using the prevailing interest rate at the time the bond is issued. Even if interest rates change over the life of the bond, which they almost always do, the amount you receive as interest on your bond remains fixed. (That is why bonds are sometimes referred to as "fixed-income securities." The bondholder receives a set amount, known in advance, no matter what happens to interest rates, stock prices, and so on.)

For example, if you bought a $10,000, 10%, 15-year bond from Company XYZ on January 1, 1991, this is what would happen.

You would give XYZ, or perhaps your broker, a check for $10,000. Every January for the next 14 years, XYZ would send you a check for $1000 (10% of the $10,000 face value). On January 1, 2006, XYZ would send you a check for the face value of the bond—$10,000—plus the interest for that year—$1000—and that would square all accounts. A graph of the transaction from the point of view of you, the bond buyer, is shown in Figure 1.

Does the fact that the annual interest payment (coupon) on a bond does not change with fluctuations in the interest rate mean that bonds are completely insulated from interest rate movements?

Productivity fluctuates over the business cycle, tending to rise during expansions and fall during contractions. In the previous chapter, we discussed why firms may at times choose to hold excess labor. This facet of firm behavior explains why productivity fluctuates in the same direction that output does.

A simple example will help to explain how the existence of excess labor can explain cyclical movements in productivity. Consider what happens at The Feed Bag restaurant over the course of the business cycle. We will assume that The Feed Bag produces and sells only one item, hamburgers, which makes it easy to keep track of its total output—simply the number of hamburgers sold.

When times are good, The Feed Bag maintains a staff of 12 people and serves an average of 960 burgers each day. Labor productivity is therefore 10

Absolutely not! Instead of the coupon responding to a change in the interest rate, it is the *price of the bond* that changes. To see why this is so, suppose you had a choice of putting $10,000 into the bond described above or into a bank account that pays 10% per year interest. In either case, you would earn $1000 per year in interest payments, so you should be indifferent between the two choices.

But now suppose that the interest rate on the bank account goes up to 20% instead of 10 percent. The bond still promises to pay $1000 per year. If you want to earn $1000 in interest, you need to put only $5000 into the bank account (since .20 × $5000 = $1000). You would obviously prefer to put $5000 into the bank rather than tie up $10,000 in the bond. The only way anyone would willingly buy the bond is if it cost no more than other investments that yield the same stream of income in the future. The bond would thus be worth much less than $10,000 if the interest rate were 20 percent. It follows, then, that when interest rates rise, bond prices fall, and bondholders suffer a *capital loss*—that is, a reduction in the value of the securities they own.

How to Read a Bond Table

Figure 2 shows a small section of the *New York Times's* corporate bond price quotations for February 3, 1993. What do all these signs and symbols mean?

The first column, under the heading "Bonds," gives the name of the corporation that issued the bond and certain information about the terms under which the bond was originally issued. Let's take the second bond listed for ConEd (the Consolidated Edison Company) as an example. The "$7\frac{3}{4}$" means that the bond pays a coupon of $7\frac{3}{4}$, or $7.75, per $100 of face value of the bond and matures in 2003. The column entitled "Current Yield" shows the annual rate of return on the bond if the bond were purchased at the current price. If the current price were $100, then the annual rate of return would be 7.75 percent. Since the bond yields only 7.5%, however, the current price of the bond must be higher than its face value of $100. (A decrease in the interest rate raises the value of a bond, as we saw above.) The third column, "Sales in $1000," tells how many thousands of dollars in bonds were traded during the day in question. Here we see that $15,000 (at face value) of the ConEd bond was

Bonds	Current Yield	Sales in $1000	Last	Chge.	
ClevEl 8 3/8 12	8.5	50	98 1/8	+	1/8
Coastl 11 1/4 96	11.0	4	102	−	1/4
Coastl 11 3/4 06	10.3	45	113 3/4	−	1/8
Coastl 11 1/8 98	10.3	46	107 5/8	+	5/8
Coeur 7s02	cv	65	98 3/4	−	5/8
viColG 9s94f	...	5	104 7/8		...
viColuG 7 1/2 970 f	...	50	99 1/2	−	3/8
viColuG 7 1/2 98f	...	5	98 1/2	−	1 1/2
viColuG 9s93f	...	27	106 5/8		
viColuG 10 1/2 12f	...	4	109 7/8	−	1 1/8
CmwE 7 5/8 03F	7.6	10	99 7/8	−	1/8
CmwE 8 3/4 05	8.5	10	103 1/2	+	3/8
CmwE 8 1/8 07J	8.0	15	101 1/4	+	3/8
CmwE 9 1/8 08	8.7	8	104 5/8	+	3/8
ConrPer 6 3/4 01	cv	137	99 1/2	−	1/2
Consec 12 3/4 97	12.0	20	106 1/4		...
ConEd 7.9s01	7.7	36	102 1/2	−	1 1/8
ConEd 7 3/4 03	7.5	15	102 3/4	+	1/4
CnNG 9s95	8.8	2	102		...
CnPw 5 7/8 96	6.0	4	98 3/8		...
CnPw 8 3/8 00	8.4	30	102 1/2		...
CnPw 8 5/8 03	8.4	15	102 1/2	+	3/4
viCtlInf 9s06f	cv	8	8		...
CoopCo 10 5/8 05	cv	69	74 1/2	-	1 1/2
CrayRs 6 1/8 11	cv	148	81	+	1/2
Crestr 7 3/4 97	7.7	35	101	+	1
CumE zr05	...	5	40 1/2		...

FIGURE 2
New York Stock Exchange Bonds

Source: New York Times, February 4, 1993.

traded on February 3, 1993.

"Last" is the last (closing) price of the bond. The ConEd bond's closing price was $102\frac{3}{4}$, which means that a bond with a face value of $100 was worth $102.75 at the end of the trading day. The last column, "Change," tells us by how much the closing bond price differs from the closing price on the previous day. In this case, the price of the ConEd bond rose by one fourth of a point—that is, by $0.25.

burgers per person/hour [960 burgers/(12 people × 8 hours each)]. If the economy goes into a slump, however, the demand for burgers tends to fall off. Instead of selling 960 burgers per day, the restaurant sells only 720—a drop in sales of 25 percent. But what happens to the work force at The Feed Bag when the slump hits?

If the restaurant is typical of most firms in the economy, it will lay off some workers or cut back on the length of the work shift. These cuts are almost always smaller, however, than they need to be. In other words, if output falls by 25%, the number of work hours should also fall by 25% if the same level of productivity is to be maintained. However, the number of work hours will probably fall by less than this amount—say by only 12.5% (or by 12 hours,

ISSUES AND APPLICATIONS

READING THE STOCK PAGE

What Is a Stock?

In addition to issuing bonds, firms can finance investments by borrowing money directly from a bank or other lending institution. A third alternative is for firms to issue additional shares of stock. When a corporation issues new shares of stock, it does not add to its debt. Instead, it brings in additional "owners" of the firm, owners who agree to supply it with funds. The contributions of such owners are treated differently from loans made by outsiders, which are considered liabilities.

What is a share of stock, exactly? If you buy one share of Company QRS, and the firm has 1 million total shares outstanding, you have purchased a one-millionth ownership of the firm. You have a right—along with the owners of the other 999,999 shares—to select the management of the firm and to share in its profits.* (This is not true of bondholders and other creditors of the firm, who have no say in its management.) Unlike bonds or direct borrowing, however, your stock does not promise a fixed annual payment. Rather, the returns you receive on your investment depend on how well Company QRS performs. If its profits are high, the firm may elect to pay dividends to its shareholders, although it is not required to do so. If the firm does well, you may also find that the price of QRS stock has gone up, in which case you could realize a capital gain by selling your stock for more than you originally paid for it.

*As you should recall from Chapter 3, one of the key aspects of the modern corporation is its limited liability feature. Stockholders are entitled to a share of the firm's profits, but if the firm incurs losses, stockholders' liability is limited to the amount of their initial contribution. This is not true with partnerships or other forms of business organization.

How to Read the Stock Page

Once you buy a stock, you are free to sell it to someone else at any time. Developments in the stock market, where such transactions take place, are constantly followed in the news.

Figure 1 reproduces part of the stock quotations from the *New York Times* for February 3, 1993. Let us take the stock of Atlantic Richfield (AtlRich) and see what information the stock pages provide.

365-Day				Yld		Sales				
High	Low	Stock	Div	%	P/E	100s	High	Low	Last	Chg
17	12 5/8	AsiaPc s	.09e	.07	q	112	13 1/8	12 7/8	13 1/8	...
2	3/4	AsiaPc rt		...	11	152	7/8	3/4	3/4	1/8
13 1/2	6 1/2	AsetInv	.40	5.7	10	107	7	6 7/8	7	+ 1/8
30 7/8	18 1/8	AsdNG	.12	0.4	32	68	29 3/8	28 1/4	29 3/8	+1 3/8
6 7/8	4 1/2^	AtalSos		...	11	50	7	6 7/8	7	+ 1/8
16 1/2	12 1/4	Athine	1.00	6.5	15	135	15 5/8	14 7/8	15 3/8	+ 1/2
39	30 1/4	AtlGas	2.08	5.3	17	127	39	38 3/4	39	+ 1/4
26 1/2	24 5/8	AtlGas pf	.92	3.5	12	28	26 1/2	26 3/8	26 1/2	...
25/8	19 15/16	AltEng s	1.52	6.5	14	326	23 1/4	22 7/8	23 1/4	+ 3/8
121 3/4	98 1/8	AtlRich	5.50	4.7	16	1971	118	117 1/2	118	+ 1/2
290 3/4	235 5/8	AtlRc pfC	2.80	1.0	...	1	281 1/2	281 1/2	281 1/2	...
7	3 1/2	Atlas		...	...	13	4 5/8	4 1/2	4 1/2	...
23 7/8	19	ATMOS	1.28	5.4	16	40	23 3/4	23 1/4	23 1/2	+ 3/8
13 7/8	8 5/8	Attwood	.70e	7.2	14	509	9 3/4	9 1/2	9 3/4	− 1/8
11 1/4	4 3/4	AudVd		...	22	485	11 1/4	11	11 1/8	...
13 1/4	8 1/2	Augat		...	35	1217	12 7/8	12 3/8	12 1/2	− 3/8
10 5/8	6 5/8	Austr		...	q	570	7 1/8	6 7/8	7	...
24 3/4	12 1/8^	AuthFit		...	...	266	26 1/8	24 1/8	26 1/8	+2 5/8
5 1/2	2 7/8	AutSec	.23e	5.6	...	1143	4 1/8	4	4 1/8	...
55 5/8	38 3/4	AutoDt s	.46	0.8	28	7192	54 3/4	52 7/8	54 3/8	+1 1/2
40 5/8	25 1/8	Autozn s		...	38	3646	36 1/4	34 3/8	35 3/4	+1 3/8
28	21	AVMCO s	.40	1.7	28	30	23 1/4	23 1/4	23 1/4	...
29 1/8	23 5/8	AveryD	.88	3.3	21	2997	27	26 5/8	27	+ 1/4
37	23 1/2	Avent	.60	1.8	20	1946	33 3/4	33 1/4	33 1/4	− 1/8
60 1/4	44 1/8	Avon	1.60a	2.7	26	3647	59 3/4	59	59 3/8	+ 1/2
27 7/8	13	Aydin		...	9	173	16 1/8	15 3/4	16	+ 1/4

FIGURE 1
New York Stock Exchange Issues

Source: New York Times, February 4, 1993.

The first two columns, under the general heading "365-Day," give the stock's highest and lowest prices over the past year. The price of a share of Atlantic Richfield stock reached a high of $121\frac{3}{4}$ and a low of $98\frac{1}{8}$ during this period. (Stock prices are quoted in dollars per share, so "$121\frac{3}{4}$" means that the stock sold for $121.75 per share at its high point during the past 365 days.) The column labeled "Div" gives the dividend paid (in dollars) per share over the past year. If you had owned a share of Atlantic Richfield stock, you would have received a payment of $5.50 during the year. What sort of return is this? The next column, "Yld %" (yield percent), takes the dividend as a percentage of the day's closing price. (The day's closing price in this case is 118, which is given in the column titled "Last.") If you had purchased a share of stock for $118.00 and received a dividend of $5.50 for the year, your interest would be returning, or "yielding," 4.7% per year.

The column labeled "P/E" (price-earnings ratio) calculates the ratio of the price of a share of stock to the company's *total earnings per share* (which includes not only dividends paid to shareholders but also retained earnings). The PE ratio is a widely used measure of how highly a stock is valued. Atlantic Richfield's PE ratio is 16. The column labeled "Sales 100s" tells how many hundreds of shares changed hands during the day's trading. On February 3, 1993, 197,100 shares of Atlantic Richfield's stock were traded. The last four columns of the table give the stock's highest, lowest, and closing price during the day's trading, as well as the change in the closing price from the closing price of the previous day.

since .125 × 96 = 12).[1] The restaurant therefore uses only 84 hours of labor (instead of 96), perhaps by employing 10 workers for eight hours each and one additional worker for four hours, or 12 workers for seven hours each, or some other combination. Why should The Feed Bag hold excess labor?

As we discussed in the last chapter, it is costly to fire and hire workers. Furthermore, if a firm is unsure whether a decrease in sales is temporary or permanent, it may decide to keep "extra" workers on hand for the not-so-distant future when they will again be needed.

The implications of excess labor with regard to labor productivity should be clear. In good times, The Feed Bag used 96 hours of labor per day to produce 960 hamburgers, for a labor productivity ratio of 10 burgers per hour worked. In a slump, the restaurant sells only 720 burgers and uses 84 worker hours each day. Output per worker hour during the slump is therefore 720/84 = 8.57 burgers per worker hour—lower than the previous figure of 10 burgers per hour.

Figure 33.1 shows the pattern of employment and output for a hypothetical economy over time. The figure shows that employment does not fluctuate as much as output over the business cycle. It is precisely this pattern that leads to higher productivity during periods of high output and lower productivity during periods of low output. During expansions in the economy, output rises by a larger percentage than employment, and the ratio of output to workers rises. During downswings, output falls faster than employment and the ratio of output to workers falls.

The existence of excess labor when the economy is in a slump means that productivity as measured by the ratio Y/H tends to fall at such times. Does this mean that labor is in some sense "less productive" during recessions than it was previously? Not really: It means only that firms choose to employ more labor than they need. For this reason, some workers are in effect idle some of the time, even though they are considered employed. They are not less productive in the sense of having less potential to produce output; they are merely not working part of the time that they are *counted* as working.

---

[1]In terms of the notation we developed above, Y, or output, falls by more than H, or labor hours. It follows, then, that the ratio Y/H, or labor productivity, must fall when the numerator falls by more than the denominator.

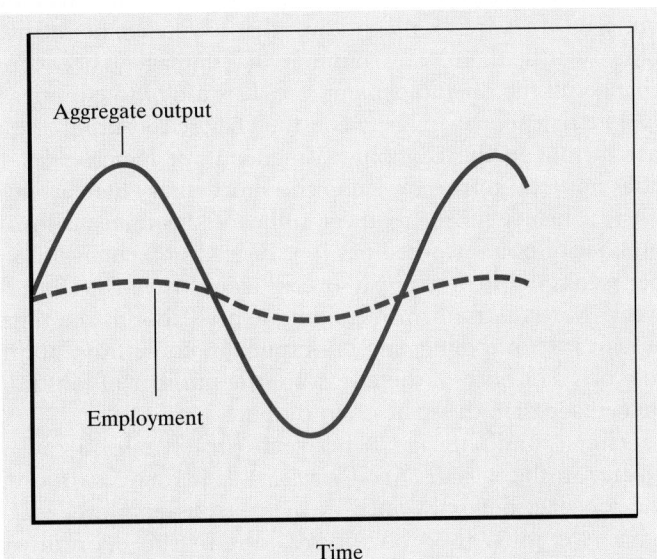

Aggregate output

Employment

Time

FIGURE 33.1
Output and Employment over the Business Cycle

In general, employment does not fluctuate as much as output over the business cycle. As a result, measured productivity (the output-to-labor ratio) tends to rise during expansionary periods and decline during contractionary periods.

PRODUCTIVITY IN THE LONG RUN Theories of long-run economic behavior, which attempt to explain how and why economies grow over time, focus a great deal of attention on productivity. *Output per worker,* or its closely related measure, *GDP per capita,* is the key index of an economy's performance over the long run. For example, in comparing how the economies of the United States and Japan have performed over the past 90 years, we would probably begin by noting that while the United States had a substantially higher income per person in 1900, the two countries' incomes per person are now comparable. As we shall see in Chapter 35, the growth of output per worker depends on technological progress and on the growth of the capital stock, both of which have been more rapid in Japan than in the United States.

For now, the crucial point is this:

> Productivity figures can be misleading when used to diagnose the health of the economy over the short run, because business cycles can distort the meaning of productivity measurements. Output per worker falls in recessions simply because firms hold excess labor during slumps. Output per worker rises in expansions because firms put the excess labor back to work. Neither of these conditions has anything to do with the long-run potential of the economy to produce output.

THE RELATIONSHIP BETWEEN OUTPUT AND UNEMPLOYMENT

When we discussed the connections between the *AS/AD* diagram and the Phillips Curve in Chapter 30, we mentioned that output (Y) and the unemployment rate (U) are inversely related. When output rises, the unemployment rate falls, and when output falls, the unemployment rate rises.

At one time, it was believed that the relationship between the two variables was fairly stable. **Okun's Law** (named after Arthur Okun, who first studied the relationship) stated that the unemployment rate decreased about one percentage point for every 3% increase in GDP. As with the Phillips Curve, however, Okun's Law has not turned out to be a "law" at all. The economy is far too complex for there to be such a simple and stable relationship between two macroeconomic variables.

Although the relationship between output and the unemployment rate is not the simple relationship Okun believed it to be, it is true that a 1% increase in output tends to correspond to a less than 1% decrease in the unemployment rate. In other words, there are a number of "slippages" between changes in output and changes in the unemployment rate. It is useful to consider what these slippages are.

The first slippage is between the change in output and the change in the number of jobs in the economy. When output increases by 1%, the number of jobs does not tend to rise by 1% in the short run. There are two reasons why this is so. First, a firm is likely to meet some of the increase in output by increasing the number of hours worked per job. Instead of having the labor force work 40 hours per week, the firm may pay overtime and have the labor force work 42 hours per week. Second, if a firm is holding excess labor at the time of the output increase, at least part of the increase in output can come from putting the excess labor back to work. For both of these reasons, the number of jobs is likely to rise by a smaller percentage than the increase in output.

The second slippage is between the change in the number of *jobs* and the change in the *number of people employed.* If I have two jobs, I am counted twice in the job data but only once in the persons-employed data. Because some people have two jobs, there are more jobs in the economy than there are people employed. When the number of jobs increases, some of the new jobs are filled by people who already have one job (rather than by people who are unemployed). This means that the increase in the number of people employed is less than the increase in the number of jobs. This is a slippage between output and the unemployment rate because the unemployment rate is calculated from data on the number of people employed, not the number of jobs.

The third slippage concerns the response of the labor force to an increase in output. Let E denote the number of people employed, let L denote the number of people in the labor force, and let U denote the unemployment rate. In these terms, the unemployment rate is equal to

$$U = 1 - E/L.$$

In other words, the unemployment rate is one minus the employment rate, E/L.

When we discussed how the unemployment rate is measured in Chapter 23, we introduced the notion of the **discouraged-worker effect.** A discouraged worker is one who would like a job but who has stopped looking for one because the prospects seem so bleak. When output increases, job prospects begin to look better, and some people who had stopped looking for work begin looking again. When they do so, they are once again counted as part of the labor force. Thus, the labor force increases when output increases because discouraged workers are moving back into the labor force. This is another reason that the unemployment rate does not fall as much as one might expect when output increases: As the economy expands, more people enter the labor force, and this means that the measured unemployment rate does not fall as much as it would have if discouraged workers had not reentered the labor force.

These three slippages show that the link from changes in output to changes in the unemployment rate is fairly complicated. All three slippages combine to make the change in the unemployment rate less than the percentage change in output in the short run. They also show that the relationship between changes in output and changes in the unemployment rate is not likely to be stable. The size of the first slippage, for example, depends on how much excess labor is being held at the time of the output increase, and the size of the third slippage depends on what else is affecting the labor force (like changes in real wage rates) at the time of the output increase. In general:

> The relationship between output and unemployment depends on the state of the economy at the time of the output change.

Table 33.1 on the next page shows the percentage change in aggregate output (real GDP) and the change in the unemployment rate for each year between 1975 and 1992. You can see that increases in the level of real output tend to be associated with decreases in the unemployment rate, and vice versa. But you can also see that the pattern is anything but uniform.

THE SIZE OF THE MULTIPLIER

We mentioned in Chapter 24 that much of the analysis we would do after deriving the simple multiplier would have the effect of decreasing the size of the multiplier. Now that we have a better understanding of how the macroeconomy works, we can review why the multiplier is smaller than the analysis in Chapter 24 might indicate.

discouraged-worker effect The decline in the measured unemployment rate that results when people who want to work but cannot find work grow discouraged and stop looking for jobs, thus dropping out of the ranks of the unemployed and the labor force.

YEAR	% CHANGE IN REAL GDP	CHANGE IN UNEMPLOYMENT RATE	YEAR	% CHANGE IN REAL GDP	CHANGE IN UNEMPLOYMENT RATE
1975	−0.8	+2.9	1984	6.2	−2.1
1976	4.9	−0.8	1985	3.2	−0.3
1977	4.5	−0.6	1986	2.9	−0.2
1978	4.8	−1.0	1987	3.1	−0.8
1979	2.5	−0.3	1988	3.9	−0.7
1980	−0.5	+1.3	1989	2.5	−0.2
1981	1.8	+0.5	1990	0.8	+0.2
1982	−2.2	+2.1	1991	−1.2	+1.2
1983	3.9	−0.1	1992	2.1	+0.7

* over the previous year.

Source: *Economic Report of the President,* February 1993, Tables B-2 and B-37. Updates for 1992.

TABLE 33.1
The Relationship between
Output and Unemployment

■ First, there are *automatic stabilizers.* We saw in the appendix to Chapter 25 that if taxes are not a fixed amount but rather depend on income (which is surely the case in practice), the size of the multiplier is decreased. When the economy expands and income increases, the amount of taxes collected increases. This acts to offset some of the expansion (thus a smaller multiplier). Conversely, when the economy contracts and income decreases, the amount of taxes collected decreases. This helps to lessen the contraction. Some transfer payments also respond to the state of the economy and act as automatic stabilizers, thus lowering the value of the multiplier. Unemployment benefits are the best example of transfer payments that increase during contractions and decrease during expansions.

■ Second, there is the interest rate. We saw in Chapter 28 that if government spending increases and the money supply remains unchanged, the interest rate increases, which decreases planned investment and thus aggregate output (income). This *crowding out* of planned investment decreases the value of the multiplier. And, as we saw in Chapter 32, increases in the interest rate also have a negative effect on consumption. Consumption is thus also crowded out in the same way that planned investment is, and this lowers the value of the multiplier even further.

■ Third, there is the response of the *price level.* We saw in Chapter 29 that some of the effect of an expansionary policy is to increase the price level. The multiplier is smaller than it otherwise would be because of this price response. The multiplier is particularly small when the economy is on the steep part of the *AS* curve, where most of the effect of an expansionary policy is to increase prices.

■ Fourth, there is the existence of *excess capital* and *excess labor.* If firms are holding excess labor and capital, then part of any output increase can come from putting the excess labor and capital back to work rather than from increasing employment and investment. This lowers the value of the multiplier because (1) investment increases less than it would have if there were no excess capital, and (2) the employment constraint on households is relaxed less than it would be if there were no excess labor, so that household income changes less than otherwise. There is thus less of a change in consumption.

■ Fifth, there is the existence of *inventories.* Part of any initial increase in sales can come from drawing down inventories rather than increasing output. To the extent that firms draw down their inventories in the short run, the value of the multiplier is lower because output does not respond as quickly to demand changes.

■ Sixth, there is the *life-cycle story* and *expectations.* People look ahead, and they respond less to temporary changes than to permanent changes. The multiplier effects for policy changes that are perceived to be temporary are smaller than those for policy changes that are perceived to be permanent.

- Finally, the fact that the United States imports a good deal of what it consumes makes the multiplier smaller than it would be if the U.S. economy were closed. Consider the effects of an increase in government purchases. Initially, most government spending is spending on domestically produced goods and services. But the multiplier effect results from consumption spending by those who earn more income as a result of the additional government spending. Consumers in the United States buy automobiles from Germany and Japan, electronics from Korea, and textiles from the Philippines. When spending "leaks" into imports, the size of the multiplier is reduced. (We will discuss this topic fully in Chapter 37.)

THE SIZE OF THE MULTIPLIER IN PRACTICE   In practice, the multiplier probably has a value of around 1.4. Its size also depends on how long ago the spending increase began. For example, in the first quarter of an increase in government spending, the multiplier is only about 1.1. If government spending rises by $1 billion, then GDP increases by only about $1.1 billion during the first quarter. In the second quarter, the multiplier rises to about 1.3. The multiplier then rises to its peak of about 1.4 in the third or fourth quarter.

One of the main points to remember here is that if the government is contemplating a monetary or fiscal policy change, the response of the economy to the change is not likely to be large and quick. It takes time for the full effects to be felt, and in the final analysis the effects are much smaller than the simple multiplier we discussed in Chapter 24 would lead one to believe.

A good way to review much of the material since Chapter 24 is to make sure that you clearly understand how the value of the multiplier is affected by each of the additions to the simple model in Chapter 24. We have come a long way since then, and this review may help you to put all the pieces together.

SUMMARY

Monetary and Fiscal Policy Revisited

1. The government influences the economy through *fiscal policy* (its taxing and spending behavior) and through *monetary policy* (the Fed's direct control over the money supply and indirect control over the interest rate).

2. Changes in taxes and spending that are expected to be permanent have a larger effect on household and firm behavior than changes that are expected to be temporary.

3. Policies that change tax rates have both an income *and* a substitution effect because they change the trade-off between work and leisure. Thus, reducing tax rates may lead to a *decrease* in the quantity of labor supplied through the income effect dominating or to an *increase* in the quantity of labor supplied through the substitution effect dominating.

4. Income received from non-wage-earning activities is called *nonlabor income*. The effect of a change in nonlabor income on households is a pure income effect. Any increase in nonlabor income therefore unambiguously leads to an increase in consumption and a decrease in labor supply. Conversely, any decrease in nonlabor income unambiguously leads to a decrease in consumption and an increase in labor supply.

5. The interest rate affects consumption as well as investment, and so there are two channels through which monetary policy can affect the economy.

6. Policies designed to stimulate or contract the economy are likely to have a larger impact when output is low rather than high. During periods of high output and low unemployment, the multiplier is likely to be smaller.

7. Output is likely to respond more to sales increases in high-output periods than in low-output periods, provided that firms have enough capital and labor to support the output increase. If firms do not have excess capacity to support an output increase, their inventory stocks will fall further as sales increase. In this case, the economy is on the steep part of the *AS* curve.

The Effects of the Stock Market on the Economy

8. When stock prices rise, household wealth increases. When stock prices fall, household wealth decreases. Stock prices thus affect the economy by affecting household wealth, which affects household consumption.

Productivity and the Business Cycle

9. *Productivity,* or *labor productivity,* is defined as output per worker. It is the amount of output produced by an average worker in one hour. Productivity fluctuates over the business cycle, tending to rise during expansions and fall during contractions. The fact that workers are less productive during

contractions does not mean that workers have less potential to produce output; it simply means that excess labor exists and that workers are not working at their capacity.

The Relationship Between Output and Unemployment

10. There is a negative relationship between output and unemployment: When output (Y) rises, the unemployment rate (U) falls, and when output falls, the unemployment rate rises. *Okun's Law* stated that the unemployment rate decreases about one percentage point for every 3% increase in GDP. However, Okun's Law is not a "law" at all—the economy is far too complex for there to be such a stable relationship between two macroeconomic variables. In general, the relationship between output and unemployment depends on the state of the economy at the time of the output change.

The Size of the Multiplier

11. There are several reasons why the actual value of the multiplier is smaller than the size that would be predicted by a simple model of a closed economy: (1) Automatic stabilizers help to offset contractions or limit expansions. (2) When government spending increases, the increased interest rate crowds out planned investment and consumption spending. (3) Expansionary policies increase the price level. (4) Firms sometimes hold excess capital and excess labor. (5) Firms may meet increased demand by drawing down inventories rather than increasing output. (6) Households and firms change their behavior less when they expect changes to be temporary rather than permanent. (7) A significant portion of spending is spent on foreign-produced goods.

12. In practice, the size of the multiplier at its peak is about 1.4.

REVIEW TERMS AND CONCEPTS

dividends 815	fiscal policy 812	Okun's Law 822
discouraged-worker effect 823	monetary policy 813	productivity, or labor productivity 817
financial instruments 818	nonlabor income 814	transfer payments 814

PROBLEM SET

1. The recession of 1990–1991 officially ended when real GDP began to rise in the second quarter of 1991. GDP continued to rise in each of the next six quarters, yet by early 1993 employment had hardly grown at all. What do these facts imply about U.S. productivity? Is what happened consistent with what you would expect to happen during a slow expansion? In what ways is the U.S. economy better off as a result of the recession and slow expansion? Who is worse off? Is this a trade-off that you as a policy analyst would be willing to accept? Why or why not?

2. The chair of the Council of Economic Advisors has recommended several options for dealing with the current recession. The President has asked you, as a member of the domestic policy staff, to evaluate the options. For each of the following options, describe the likely effects on consumer spending, labor supply, planned aggregate investment, the overall price level, aggregate output, and the unemployment rate.
   a. A temporary tax cut of 10% in place for two years or until the recession ends, with a continued tight monetary policy
   b. A permanent tax cut of 5% with a continued tight monetary policy
   c. An expansionary monetary policy with no change in fiscal policy
   d. An increase in transfer payments (unemployment benefits) with no tax cut and a continued tight monetary policy

3. Between January and July of 1993, the Dow Jones Industrial Average rose by 300 points, from 2,700 to 3,000. Assume that the household sector held $2 trillion worth of stocks in January of 1993 and that these stocks increased in value at about the same rate as the Dow increased. How much of an effect would you expect such an increase to have on annual consumer spending? How would such an increase affect the supply of labor? The unemployment rate?

4. Okun's Law suggests that a fairly simple negative relationship exists between the rate of unemployment and the level of aggregate output—that an increase in aggregate output should lead to a decrease in the unemployment rate. Between 1980 and 1981, aggregate output in the United States rose by 1.9%, but the unemployment rate *increased* from 7% to 7.5 percent. Give several possible explanations for this phenomenon.

5. Do you agree or disagree with the following statements? Explain your answers.
   a. The primary reason that productivity tends to increase during periods of increased output is that higher wages attract better workers into the labor force.
   b. The fact that the United States exports nearly a tenth of its total output and imports a good deal of what it consumes implies that the multiplier is significantly larger than what it otherwise would be.
   c. If an economy is operating at a level of output along its short-run *AS* curve above the level of potential GDP, the multiplier is likely to be large and output is likely to increase.

CASE STUDY
DOES SOCIAL SECURITY DISCOURAGE SAVING?

■ Social security. It's your guaranteed retirement fund when you turn 65, right? Maybe not. Many people believe that the Social Security system is in serious trouble and that there will be nothing left in the system by the time today's college graduates are ready for retirement. How can this be, given the fact that together employers and employees pay a 12.4% payroll tax on earnings specifically earmarked for social security?

The Social Security Act of 1935 established social security as a *pay-as-you-go* system. This means that payroll taxes paid by workers today are paid out in the form of benefits to the elderly. As of 1993, the system had over $330 billion in reserves. But what you pay in today is *not* held in your name to be paid back with interest when you retire.

In reality, the social security system can't go bankrupt simply because it is an income-transfer program. As long as Congress is willing to tax sufficiently to pay for the benefits, they will always be paid. So what's all the fuss about?

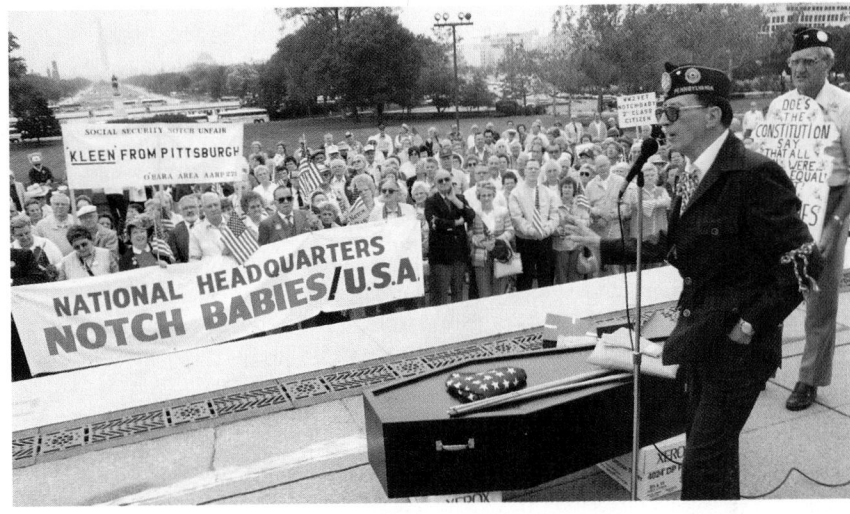

The senior citizen lobby in the United States is quite vocal in its disapproval of any program that reduces Social Security benefits. Here, a group of senior citizens gathers to protest the unfairness of the "social security notch," which penalizes recipients born in 1917.

The problem lies in the demographic makeup of the United States. Currently there are about 48 million people who were born prior to 1945. However, the "baby-boom" generation (people born between 1946 and 1964) is made up of over 77 million

Americans. Right now the baby boomers are experiencing their greatest income growth. Thus annual surpluses in the social security system are projected to continue until sometime around the year 2020. Total reserves at that time are expected to be nearly $2 trillion in constant 1992 dollars! But this is exactly the time that the system will begin to experience the most strain.

Why? The baby boomers will begin retiring sometime around 2010. The number of people on the benefit rolls in the following two decades will increase by about 50% while the number of workers paying into the system will probably remain about the same. By the year 2036, the social security system will be unable to meet benefits and the entire $2 trillion surplus, in addition to what is being paid into the system, will have been spent.

This problem is compounded by the fact that much of today's social security surplus is being used to fund current government spending. A large portion of the social security trust fund is held in the form of U.S. Treasury bonds, IOUs from the Treasury Department.

FIGURE 1
Projected Social Security Surpluses and Deficits, 1995-2070
Source: *Federal Old-Age and Survivors Insurance and Disability Insurance Trust Funds, The 1992 Annual Report of the Board of Trustees.*

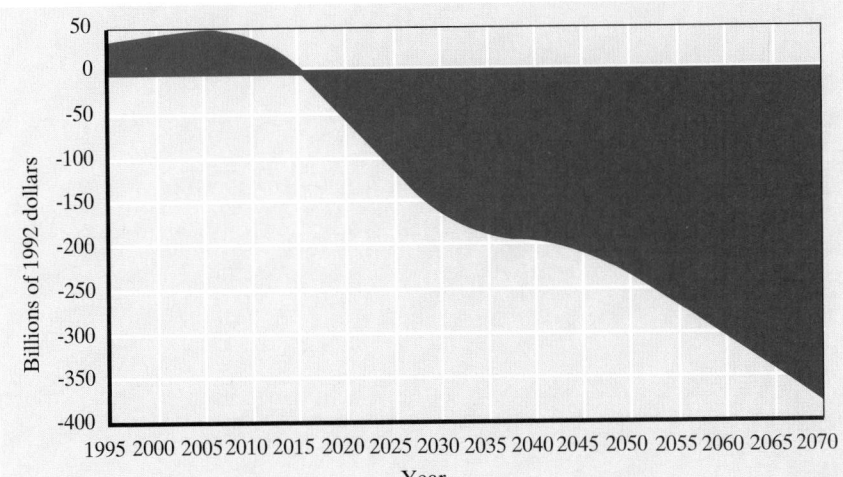

In fact, the Social Security Administration is rapidly becoming the largest owner of U.S. debt.

Some economists believe that the social security system is at least partly responsible for the low savings rate in the United States. As social security payments rose from about $30 billion in 1970 to nearly $250 billion in 1990, the personal savings rate declined from over 8% to about 4% of disposable income. It would appear that the system has reduced the incentive for individuals to save for their retirement because they could count on social security to be there when they need it. Indeed, people who retired as recently as 1985 could expect to receive over 160% of what they and their employers paid into the system. But many of today's baby boomers can expect to receive only about 85% of what they paid in on retirement. Clearly, the incentives for retirement saving are changing.

Some of the proposals put forth for fixing the system include raising the retirement age, perhaps to as high as 70; increasing social security taxes; increasing the personal income tax on benefits received by the wealthiest retirees; and privatizing the system into an insurance program that is *fully funded* and managed by a group of private investors.

It would take an increase of 3.5 percentage points in social security taxes today, and kept in place for the next 75 years, to ensure revenues sufficient to make scheduled benefit payments as the twenty-first century begins. If we wait until the year 2030, payroll taxes will need to be much higher just to meet scheduled social security payments, and additional revenue would be required to replace the deficit financing available today through the surplus in the social security trust fund.

QUESTIONS FOR ANALYTICAL THINKING

1. Would privatizing social security help or hinder the prospects for long-term economic growth in the United States?

2. What supply- and demand-side impacts would an increase in social security taxes have on employment and output?

3. Some countries have financial incentives designed to *increase* the birth rate. Would this be a viable solution to the social security problem in the United States?

4. Is using the social security trust fund to finance government spending a good or a bad idea? Should the current surplus in the trust fund be included in calculations of the federal deficit (thereby reducing it)?

5. Use the life-cycle theory of consumption to explain the impact of social security or consumption over a worker's lifetime. Do the implications of the theory differ for baby boomers?

PART NINE

Debates in Macroeconomics and Economic Growth

As we've noted throughout this book, macroeconomics is an exciting area of study because of the many open questions in the discipline. We have touched on some of these questions in earlier chapters. In Chapter 34, we take a closer look at some of the modern schools of macroeconomic thought and the differences that characterize them. We also discuss some of the problems involved in testing the assertions made by each of the various schools.

Finally, to close our study of macroeconomics, we examine the process of economic growth. While economic growth is often considered desirable, many critics point to the problems that arise as a result of growth. In Chapter 35, we present both sides of this debate–with the warning, as usual, that there is "no right answer."

34

Debates in Macroeconomics: Monetarism, New Classical Theory, and Supply-Side Economics

Throughout this book, we have noted that there are many disagreements and open questions in macroeconomics. For example, economists disagree on whether the aggregate supply curve is vertical, either in the short run or the long run. (Some even doubt that the aggregate supply curve is a useful macroeconomic concept!) There are also different views on whether cyclical employment exists and, if it does, what causes it. Economists disagree as well about whether monetary and fiscal policies are effective at stabilizing the economy, and they espouse different views on the primary determinants of consumption and investment spending.

We discussed some of these disagreements in previous chapters, but only briefly. In this chapter, we discuss in more detail a number of alternative views of how the macroeconomy works.

KEYNESIAN ECONOMICS

John Maynard Keynes's *General Theory of Employment, Interest and Money*, first published in 1936, remains one of the most important works in the history of economics. While a great deal of the material in the previous ten chapters of this book is drawn from modern research that postdates Keynes, much of it is built around a framework first constructed by Keynes.

But what exactly is *Keynesian economics?* In one sense, Keynesian economics is the foundation of all of macroeconomics. Keynes was the first to stress aggregate demand and the links between the money market and the goods market. In addition, it was Keynes who stressed the possible problem of sticky wages. In fact, virtually all the debates that we discuss in this chapter can be understood in terms of the aggregate output/aggregate expenditure framework suggested by Keynes.

In recent years, the term "Keynesian" has been used more narrowly. Keynes believed in an activist federal government. That is, he believed that the government had an important role to play in fighting inflation and unemployment, and he argued that monetary and fiscal policy should be used to manage the macroeconomy. Thus, the term "Keynesian" is sometimes used to refer to economists who advocate active government intervention in the macroeconomy.

During the 1970s and 1980s, it became clear that managing the macroeconomy was much more easily accomplished on paper than in practice. The inflation problems of the 1970s and early 1980s and the seriousness of the recessions of 1974–1975 and 1980–1982 led many economists to challenge the idea of active government intervention in the economy. Some of these challenges were simple attacks on the bureaucracy's ability to act in a timely manner; others were theoretical assaults that claimed to show that monetary and fiscal policy could have *no effect whatsoever* on the economy, even if it were efficiently managed.

In particular, in recent years two major schools of thought that are decidedly *against* government intervention have developed: monetarism and new classical economics. It is to these schools of thought that we now turn.

MONETARISM

Much has been written about the debate between monetarist and Keynesian economics. This debate is complicated by the fact that these terms mean different things to different people. If one takes the main monetarist message to be that "money matters," then almost all economists would agree. In the *AS/AD* story, for example, an increase in the money supply shifts the *AD* curve to the right, which leads to an increase in both aggregate output (Y) and the price level (P). Monetary policy thus has an effect on output and the price level. **Monetarism,** however, is usually considered to go beyond the notion that money matters.

The Velocity of Money

To understand monetarist reasoning, you must understand a new term, the **velocity of money.** You can think of velocity as the number of times a dollar bill changes hands, on average, during the course of a year.

Suppose, for example, that on January 1 you buy a new ball point pen with a $5 bill. The owner of the stationery store does not spend your $5 right away. She may hold onto it until, say, May 1, at which point she uses it to buy a dozen doughnuts. The doughnut store owner, in turn, does not spend the $5 he receives until July 1, when he uses it (along with other cash) to buy 100 gallons of oil. The oil distributor uses the bill to buy an engagement ring for his fiancée on September 1, but the $5 bill is not used again in the remaining three months of the year. Because this $5 bill has changed hands four times during the year, its velocity of circulation is four. Stated another way, a velocity of four means that the $5 bill stays with each owner for an average of three months, or one quarter of a year.

velocity of money The number of times a dollar bill changes hands, on average, during the course of a year; the ratio of nominal GDP to the stock of money.

In practice, we usually use GDP, rather than the total value of all transactions in the economy, to measure velocity,[1] simply because GDP data are more readily available. The income velocity of money (V) is the ratio of nominal GDP to the stock of money (M):

$$V \equiv \frac{GDP}{M}.$$

If $6 trillion worth of final goods and services are produced in a year and if the money stock is $1 trillion, then the velocity of money is $6 trillion ÷ $1 trillion, or 6.0.

We can expand this definition slightly by noting that nominal income (GDP) is equal to real output (income) (Y) times the overall price level (P):

$$GDP \equiv P \bullet Y.$$

Through simple substitution, we can write

$$V \equiv \frac{P \bullet Y}{M},$$

or

$$M \bullet V \equiv P \bullet Y.$$

At this point, it is worth pausing to ask if our definition has provided us with any insights into the workings of the economy. The answer is no. Because we defined V as the ratio of GDP to the money supply, the statement $M \bullet V \equiv P \bullet Y$ is an identity—that is, it is true by definition. It contains no more useful information than the statement "a bachelor is an unmarried man." Suppose that M doubles. Does this mean that nominal income ($P \bullet Y$) will also double? Not necessarily. The final value of $P \bullet Y$ depends on what happens to V. If V falls when M increases, the product $M \bullet V$ could stay the same, in which case a doubling of the money supply would have no effect whatsoever on nominal income.

To give our definition of velocity some economic content, we must look at a simple version of monetarism known as the **quantity theory of money.**

quantity theory of money
The theory based on the identity $M \bullet V \equiv P \bullet Y$ and the assumption that the velocity of money (V) is constant (or virtually constant).

The Quantity Theory of Money

The identity $M \bullet V \equiv P \bullet Y$ can be given economic content by a simple assumption that has a long history in economics, namely that the velocity of money is constant (or virtually constant). If velocity is fairly stable over time, then the equation $M \bullet V \equiv P \bullet Y$ provides an easy and accurate way to explain nominal GDP. Given M, which can be considered a policy variable set by the Federal Reserve, $P \bullet Y$ equals $M \bullet \overline{V}$, where $\overline{V}$ is the constant value of V. In this case, the effects of monetary policy are very clear. Changes in M cause equal percentage changes in nominal GDP. For example, if the money supply doubles, nominal GDP also doubles. If the constant velocity assumption holds, it is also true that nominal GDP ($P \bullet Y$) cannot change *unless the money supply changes.*

---

[1] Recall that GDP does not include transactions in intermediate goods (such as the flour sold to a baker to be made into bread) or in existing assets (such as the sale of a used car). If these transactions are made using money, however, they do influence the number of times money changes hands during the course of a year. GDP is thus an imperfect measure of transactions to use in calculating the velocity of money.

The key question is, of course, whether the velocity of money is really constant. Early economists believed that the velocity of money was determined largely by institutional considerations, such as how often people are paid and how the banking system clears transactions between banks. Because these factors change gradually, early economists believed that velocity was essentially constant.

However, our analysis in Chapter 27 suggests that the demand for money depends on the interest rate as well as on institutional factors. This, in turn, implies that the velocity of money may also be a function of the interest rate and that it is therefore *not* likely to be constant. The analysis we have worked through suggests that *velocity should change with changes in the interest rate.*

An example will help to make this point clear. Suppose the Fed decides to increase the supply of money by 10 percent. If we believe that velocity is constant, then we can safely predict that the 10% increase in M will lead to a 10% increase in nominal income $(P \cdot Y)$. If money demand depends on the interest rate, however, the story is quite different. When the Fed expands the supply of money, and thus creates an excess supply, the way in which equilibrium is restored in the money market is for the interest rate to fall, thereby encouraging households and firms to hold larger money balances. When the interest rate falls and the quantity of money demanded rises, the velocity of money decreases because there is now more money held per dollar of income. Hence an increase in the money supply (M) tends to lower velocity (V), so that $M \cdot V$ does not increase by as large a percentage as M itself does. This, in turn, means that nominal GDP does *not* rise by the same percentage as the money supply, contrary to the suggestion of simple quantity-theory monetarism.

To summarize what we have said so far:

> If the demand for money depends on the interest rate, velocity is not constant. In this case, the quantity theory of money does not hold. If, on the other hand, the demand for money does not depend on the interest rate, velocity may very well be constant. In this case, the quantity theory of money does hold.

TESTING THE QUANTITY THEORY OF MONEY One way to test the validity of the quantity theory of money is to look at the demand for money using recent data on the U.S. economy. The key question is: Does money demand depend on the interest rate? Most empirical work finds that the answer is yes. When demand-for-money equations are estimated (or "fit to the data"), the interest rate usually turns out to be an important explanatory variable. This implies, then, that the quantity-theory-of-money version of monetarism is probably not correct, because velocity is not constant but rather is a function of the interest rate.

Another way of testing the quantity theory is simply to plot velocity over time and see how it behaves. Figure 34.1 on the next page plots the velocity of money for the 1960 I–1992 IV period. The data in the figure clearly show that velocity is far from constant. There is a long-term trend—on average, velocity has been rising during these years—but fluctuations around this trend have also occurred, and some of them have been quite large. Velocity rose from 6.8 in 1980 III to 7.2 in 1981 III; fell to 6.7 in 1983 I; rose to 7.0 in 1984 III; and fell to 6.1 in 1986 IV. Changes of a few tenths of a point may seem small, but they are actually quite large. For example, the money supply in 1986 IV was $709 billion. If velocity changes by 0.3 with a money supply of this amount, and if the money supply is unchanged, we have a change in nominal GDP $(P \cdot Y)$ of $213 billion $(0.3 \times \$709 \text{ billion})$, which is about 5% of GDP.

FIGURE 34.1

The Velocity of Money, 1960 I–1992 IV

Velocity has not been constant over the period from 1960 to 1992. There is a long-term trend—velocity has been rising. There are also fluctuations, some of them quite large, around this trend.

The debate over monetarist theories is more subtle than our discussion so far indicates, however. First, there are many definitions of the money supply. M1 is the money supply variable used for the graph in Figure 34.1, but there may be some other measure of the money supply that would lead to a smoother plot. For example, many people shifted their funds from checking account deposits to money market accounts when the latter became available in the late 1970s. Because GDP did not change as a result of this shift while M1 decreased, velocity—the ratio of GDP to M1—must have gone up. But suppose instead that we measured the supply of money by M2 (which includes both checking accounts and money market accounts). In this case, the decrease in checking deposits would be exactly offset by the rise in money market account deposits, and M2 would remain unchanged. With no change in GDP and no change in M2, the velocity of money would not change either. Thus, whether velocity is constant or not may depend partly on how we choose to measure the money supply.

Second, there may be a time lag between a change in the money supply and its effects on nominal GDP. Suppose that we experience a 10% increase in the money supply today, but that it takes one year for nominal GDP to increase by 10 percent. If we measured the ratio of today's money supply to today's GDP, it would seem that velocity had fallen by 10 percent. But if we measured today's money supply against GDP one year from now, when the increase in the supply of money had its full effect on income, then velocity would prove to have been constant after all.

The debate over the usefulness of monetarist theory is thus primarily an empirical one. That is, it is a debate that can be resolved by looking at facts about the real world and seeing whether they are in accord with the predictions of theory. Is there a measure of the money supply and a choice of the lagged response of GDP to the money supply such that V is in effect constant? If so, then the monetarist theory is a useful approach to understanding how the macroeconomy works. If not, then some other theory is likely to be more appropriate. (We discuss the testing of alternative theories at the end of this chapter.)

Inflation as a Purely Monetary Phenomenon

One of the main insights of monetarism is that sustained inflation (that is, inflation that continues over many periods) is a purely monetary phenomenon. Almost all economists agree with this view. We pointed out in Chapter 29 in the context of the *AS/AD* framework that inflation cannot continue indefinitely unless the Fed "accommodates" it by increasing the money supply. It is useful to review this argument here.

Consider the case of a continuously increasing level of government spending (*G*) without any corresponding increase in taxes. The increases in *G* keep shifting the *AD* curve to the right, which leads to an increasing price level (*P*). (You may find it useful to draw a graph here.) With a fixed money supply, the increases in *P* lead to a higher and higher interest rate, but there is a limit to how far this process can go. Because taxes are unchanged, the government must finance the increases in *G* by issuing bonds, and there is a limit to how many bonds the public is willing to hold regardless of how high the interest rate goes. At the point at which the public cannot be induced to hold any more bonds, the government will be unable to borrow any more to finance its expenditures. Only if the Fed is willing to increase the money supply (that is, buy some of the government bonds) can the government spending (with its inflationary consequences) continue. In sum:

> Inflation cannot continue indefinitely without increases in the money supply.

We can also see the monetary explanation of sustained inflation by examining the $M \cdot V \equiv P \cdot Y$ equation. Suppose that V is constant and that Y (real output) has been pushed to its capacity level (and thus is in effect constant). In this situation, P must increase when M increases. Also, since V and Y are constant, the *only way* that P can increase is if M increases. Inflation (an increase in P) is a purely monetary phenomenon. End of story.

In our *AS/AD* analysis, however, V is not constant (because the demand for money depends on the interest rate). Does this have any effect on the story we are telling? Let us rewrite the above equation as $V \equiv (P \cdot Y)/M$, and continue to assume that Y has been pushed to its capacity level (and thus is constant). Now consider what happens when we increase G with M constant in the *AS/AD* story. We know that the increase in G increases P, so it follows that V must also increase. As we noted above, this process must stop at some point, which means that at some point V cannot be driven any higher. At this point, V is constant (equal to its upper limit), and the monetarist story holds thereafter: For the price level to continue increasing, the money supply must also be increasing.

The Keynesian/Monetarist Debate

The leading spokesman for monetarism over the last few decades has been Professor Milton Friedman, formerly of the University of Chicago and currently at the Hoover Institute in California. Most monetarists, including Friedman, blame most of the instability in the economy on the federal government, arguing that the inflation that the United States encountered over the years could have been avoided if only the Fed had not expanded the money supply so rapidly.

Interestingly, most monetarists do not advocate an activist monetary stabilization policy. That is, they do not advocate expanding the money supply during bad times and slowing the growth of the money supply during good times. By and large, monetarists tend to be very skeptical of the government's ability to "manage" the macroeconomy. The argument against such management that is most often voiced is the one expressed in Chapter 31: That time lags make it likely that conscious attempts to stimulate and contract the economy make the economy more, not less, unstable.

Friedman has for many years advocated a policy of steady and slow money growth. Specifically, he argues that the money supply should grow at a rate equal to the average growth of real output (income) (Y). That is, the Fed should pursue a constant policy that accommodates real growth but not inflation.

It is clear, then, that Keynesianism and monetarism are at odds with each other. As we said earlier, many Keynesians advocate the application of coordinated monetary and fiscal policy tools to reduce instability in the economy— that is, to fight inflation and unemployment. It is important to point out, though, that not all Keynesians advocate an activist federal government. Some Keynesian economists reject the strict monetarist position that only money matters in favor of the view that both monetary and fiscal policies make a difference and *at the same time* believe that the best possible policy for government to pursue is basically noninterventionist.

Most Keynesians do agree after the experience of the 1970s that monetary and fiscal tools are not finely calibrated. The notion that monetary and fiscal expansions and contractions can "fine tune" the economy is gone forever. Still, many feel that the experiences of the 1970s also show that stabilization policies can help prevent even bigger economic disasters. Had we not cut taxes and expanded the money supply in 1975 and in 1982, they argue, the recessions of those years might have been significantly worse. The same people would argue that had we not resisted the inflations of 1974–1975 and 1979–1981 with tight monetary policies, they would probably have become much worse.

Twenty years ago, the debate between Keynesians and monetarists was the central controversy in macroeconomics. That controversy, while still alive today, is out of fashion. For the past decade, the focus of current thinking in macroeconomics has been on the new classical macroeconomics.

NEW CLASSICAL MACROECONOMICS

The key challenge to Keynesian and related theories has come from a school that is sometimes referred to as the **new classical macroeconomics.**[2] Like the terms "monetarism" and "Keynesianism," this term is somewhat vague. No two new classical macroeconomists think exactly alike, and no single model completely represents this school. The following discussion, however, conveys the general flavor of the new classical views.

The Development of New Classical Macroeconomics

New classical macroeconomics has developed from two different, though related, sources. These sources are the theoretical and the empirical critiques of existing, or traditional, macroeconomics.

---

[2]The term "new classical" is used because many of the assumptions and conclusions of this group of economists resemble those of the classical economists—that is, those who wrote before Keynes.

On the theoretical level, there has been growing dissatisfaction with the way traditional models treat expectations. Keynes himself recognized that expectations (in the form of "animal spirits") play an important role in economic behavior. The problem is that traditional models have generally assumed that expectations are formed in rather naive ways. A common assumption, for example, is that people form their expectations of future inflation by assuming a continuation of present inflation. If they turn out to be wrong, they adjust their expectations by some fraction of the difference between their original forecast and the actual inflation rate. Suppose that I expect 10% inflation next year. When next year rolls around, the inflation rate turns out to be only 5%, so I have made an error of five percentage points. I might then predict an inflation rate for the following year of 7.5%, halfway between my earlier expectation (10%) and actual inflation last year (5%).

The problem with this traditional treatment of expectation formation is that it is not consistent with the assumptions of microeconomics. Specifically, it implies that people systematically overlook information that would allow them to make better forecasts, even though there are costs to being wrong. If, as microeconomic theory assumes, people are out to maximize their satisfaction and firms are out to maximize their profits, they should form their expectations in a smarter way. Instead of just blindly or naively assuming that the future will be like the past, they should actively seek to forecast the future. Any other behavior is not in keeping with the microeconomic view of the forward-looking, rational people who compose households and firms.

The second major source of the development of new classical macroeconomics lay in empirical observation of the stagflation in the U.S. economy during the 1970s. Remember that stagflation is the simultaneous existence of high unemployment and rising prices. The Phillips Curve theory of the 1960s predicted that demand pressure pushes up prices, so that when demand is weak—in times of high unemployment, for example—prices should be stable (or perhaps even falling). The new classical theories were an attempt to explain the apparent breakdown in the 1970s of the simple inflation-unemployment trade-off predicted by the Phillips Curve. Just as the Great Depression of the 1930s motivated the development of Keynesian economics, so the stagflation of the 1970s helped motivate the formulation of new classical economics.

Rational Expectations

In previous chapters, we stressed the importance of households' and firms' expectations about the future. A firm's decision to build a new plant depends on its expectations of future sales. The amount of saving a household chooses to undertake today depends on its expectations about future interest rates, wages, and prices. The list of situations in which expectations come into play could be greatly expanded.

How are expectations formed? Do people simply assume that things will continue as they are at present? (This would be equivalent to predicting rain tomorrow because it is raining today.) What information do people use to make their guesses about the future? Questions like these have become central to current macroeconomic thinking and research. One theory, the **rational-expectations hypothesis,** offers a powerful way of thinking about expectations.

Suppose we want to forecast inflation. What does it mean to say that my expectations of inflation are "rational"? The rational-expectations hypothesis assumes that people know the "true model" that generates inflation—that is, they know how inflation is determined in the economy—and that they use this model to

rational-expectations hypothesis The hypothesis that people know the "true model" of the economy and that they use this model to form their expectations of the future.

forecast future inflation rates. If there were no random, unpredictable events in the economy, and if people knew the true model generating inflation, then their forecasts of future inflation rates would be perfect. Because it is true, the model would not permit mistakes, and thus the people using it would not make mistakes either.

In practice, however, many events that affect the inflation rate are not predictable—they are, in fact, random. By "true" model, then, we mean a model that is *on average* correct in forecasting inflation. Sometimes the random events have a positive effect on inflation, which means that the model underestimates the inflation rate, and sometimes they have a negative effect, which means that the model overestimates the inflation rate. On average, however, the model is correct. Therefore, rational expectations are correct on average, even though their predictions are not exactly right all the time.

A noneconomic example may help at this point. Suppose that you have to make a forecast about how many times a fair coin will come up heads out of 100 tosses. The true model in this case is that the coin has a 50-50 chance of coming up heads on any one toss. Because the outcome of the 100 tosses is random, you cannot be sure of guessing correctly. If you know the true model, namely that the coin is fair, your rational expectation of the outcome of 100 tosses is 50 heads. You are not likely to be exactly right—the actual number of heads is likely to be slightly higher or slightly lower than 50—but *on average* you will be correct.

Sometimes people are said to have rational expectations if they use "all available information" in forming their expectations. This definition is somewhat vague, because it is not always clear what the phrase "all available information" means. The definition is precise, however, if by "all available information" we mean that people know and use the true model. One cannot have more or better information than the true model.

If information can be obtained at no cost, then someone is not behaving rationally if he or she fails to use all available information. Because there are almost always costs to making a wrong forecast, it is not rational to overlook information that could help improve the accuracy of one's estimate as long as the costs of acquiring that information do not outweigh the benefits of improving the accuracy of one's forecasts.

RATIONAL EXPECTATIONS AND MARKET CLEARING If firms have rational expectations and if they set prices and wages on this basis, then, on average, prices and wages will be set at levels that ensure equilibrium in the goods and labor markets. When a firm has rational expectations, it knows the demand curve for its output and the supply curve of labor that it faces, except when random shocks disrupt those curves. Therefore, on average the firm will set the market-clearing prices and wages. The firm knows the true model, and it will not set wages different from those it expects will attract the number of workers it wants. If all firms behave this way, then wages will be set in such a way that the total amount of labor supplied will, on average, be equal to the total amount of labor that firms demand. In other words, on average there will be no unemployment.

In Chapter 30, we argued that there might be disequilibrium in the labor market (either in the form of unemployment or in excess demand for workers) because firms may make mistakes in their wage-setting behavior because of expectation errors. If, on average, firms do not make errors, then, on average, there is equilibrium. In other words, when expectations are rational, disequilibrium exists only temporarily as a result of random, unpredictable shocks. This is obviously an important conclusion. If true, it means that disequilibrium in any market is only a temporary phenomenon, because firms, on average, set market-clearing wages and prices.

The assumption that expectations are rational radically changes the way one views the economy. We go from a world in which unemployment can exist for substantial periods of time and the multiplier can operate to a world in which (on average) all markets clear and there is full employment. In this new world there is no need for government stabilization policies. Unemployment is not a problem that governments need to worry about; if it exists at all, it is simply because of unpredictable shocks which, on average, amount to zero. There is no more reason for the government to try to change the outcome in the labor market than there is for it to change the outcome in the banana market. On average, prices and wages are being set at market-clearing levels.

The Lucas Supply Function

The **Lucas supply function,** named after its originator, Robert E. Lucas of the University of Chicago, is an important part of a number of new classical macroeconomic theories. It yields, as we shall see, a surprising policy conclusion. The function is deceptively simple. It says that real output (Y) depends on the difference between the actual price level (P) and the expected price level (P^e):

$$Y = f(P - P^e)$$

The actual price level minus the expected price level $(P - P^e)$ is the **price surprise.** Before considering the policy implications of this function, we should look at the theory behind it.

Lucas begins by assuming that people and firms are specialists in production but generalists in consumption. Take, for example, someone you know. If she is a manual laborer, the chances are she sells only one thing—labor. If she is a lawyer, she sells only legal services. And so on. On the other hand, people buy a large bundle of goods—ranging from gasoline to ice cream and pretzels—on a regular basis. The same is true for firms. Most companies tend to concentrate on producing a relatively small range of products, but they typically buy a much larger range of inputs—raw materials, labor, energy, capital. According to Lucas, this divergence between people's buying and selling experience creates an asymmetry. People know much more about the prices of the things they sell than they do about the prices of the things they buy.[3]

At the beginning of each period, a firm has some expectation of the average price level for that period. If the actual price level turns out to be different from what the firm expected, there is a price surprise. Say that the average price level is higher than expected. Because the firm learns about the actual price level slowly, some time goes by before it realizes that all prices have gone up. The firm does learn rather quickly, however, that the price of *its output* has gone up. The firm thus perceives—incorrectly, as it turns out—that its price has risen relative to other prices, and this leads it to produce more output.

A similar argument holds for workers. When there is a positive price surprise, workers at first believe that their "price"—that is, their wage rate—has increased relative to other prices. In other words, workers believe that their real wage rate has risen. We know from theory that an increase in the real wage is likely to

Lucas supply function The supply function, originated by Robert Lucas, that embodies the idea that output (Y) depends on the difference between the actual price level and the expected price level.

price surprise The actual price level minus the expected price level.

---

[3]It is not entirely obvious why this should be true, and, indeed, some critics of the new classical school have argued that this assumption is unrealistic. Some have also criticized the Lucas supply function as being too simple, arguing that other things besides price surprises affect aggregate output.

encourage workers to work more hours.[4] The real wage has not actually risen, but it takes workers a while to figure this out. In the meantime, they will supply more hours of work than they otherwise would have. This means that the economy will produce more output when prices are unexpectedly higher than when prices are at their expected level.

This, in essence, is the rationale for the Lucas supply function. As long as people's expectations are on target, the amount of output they produce is not related to the price level. Unexpected increases in the price level can fool workers and firms into thinking that relative prices have changed, however, and this causes them to alter the amount of labor or goods they choose to supply.

POLICY IMPLICATIONS OF THE LUCAS SUPPLY FUNCTION The Lucas supply function in combination with the assumption that expectations are rational implies that anticipated policy changes have no effect on real output. Consider, for example, a change in monetary policy. In general, such a change will have some effect on the average price level. If the policy change is announced to the public, then people know what the effect on the price level will be, because they have rational expectations (and thus know the way that changes in monetary policy affect the price level). This means that the change in monetary policy affects both the actual price level and the expected price level in the same way. The new price level minus the new expected price level is thus zero—there is no price surprise. In such a case, there will be no change in real output, because the Lucas supply function states that real output can change from its fixed level only if there is a price surprise.

The general conclusion is thus that *any* announced policy change—in fiscal policy or any other policy—has no effect on real output, because the policy change affects both actual and expected price levels in the same way. In other words, if people have rational expectations, known policy changes can produce no price surprises and thus no increases in real output. The only way that any change in government policy can affect real output is if it is kept in the dark so that it is not generally known. Government policy can affect real output only if it surprises people; otherwise, it cannot. Obviously, rational-expectations theory combined with the Lucas supply function proposes a very small role for government policy in the economy.

Evaluating Rational-Expectations Theory

What are we to make of all this? It should be clear by now that the key question regarding the new classical macroeconomics is how realistic the assumption of rational expectations is. If it does approximate the way that expectations are actually formed, then it calls into question any theory that relies at least in part on expectation errors for the existence of disequilibrium. The arguments in favor of the rational-expectations assumption sound persuasive from the perspective of microeconomic theory. If expectations are not rational, there are likely to be unexploited profit opportunities around, and most economists believe that such opportunities are rare and short-lived.

The argument *against* the rational-expectations assumption is that it requires households and firms to know too much. According to this argument, it is unrealistic to think that these basic decision-making units know as much as they need to know in order to form rational expectations. People must know the true model

---

[4]This is true if we assume that the substitution effect dominates the income effect (see Chapter 32).

(or at least a good approximation of the true model) to form rational expectations, and this is a lot to expect. Even if firms and households are smart enough in principle to learn the true model, it may be costly to take the time and gather the relevant information to do so. The gain from learning the true model (or a good approximation of it) may not be worth the cost. In this sense, there may not be unexploited profit opportunities around. Gathering information and learning economic models may simply be too costly to bother with, given the expected gain from improving one's forecasts.

Although the assumption that expectations are rational seems consistent with the satisfaction-maximizing and profit-maximizing postulates of microeconomics, the rational-expectations assumption is more extreme and demanding because it requires more information on the part of households and firms. Consider a firm engaged in maximizing profits. In some way or other, it forms expectations of the relevant future variables, and given these expectations, it figures out the best thing to do from the point of view of maximizing profits. Given a set of expectations, the problem of maximizing profits may not be too hard. What may be hard, however, is forming accurate expectations in the first place. This requires firms to know much more about the overall economy than they are likely to, so the assumption that their expectations are rational is not necessarily realistic. Firms, like the rest of us—so the argument goes—grope around in a world that is difficult to understand, trying to do their best but not always understanding enough to avoid mistakes.

In the final analysis, the issue is an empirical one. Does the assumption of rational expectations stand up well against empirical tests? This is a difficult question to answer, and much work is currently proceeding along these lines. There are no conclusive results as yet, but it is one of the questions that makes macroeconomics an exciting area of research.

SUPPLY-SIDE ECONOMICS

If you think back to our discussion of equilibrium in the goods market, beginning with the simple multiplier in Chapter 24 and continuing through Chapter 29, you will recall that we have focused primarily on *demand*. Supply increases and decreases in response to changes in aggregate expenditure (which, as you recall, is closely linked to aggregate demand). Fiscal policy works by influencing aggregate expenditure through tax policy and government spending. Monetary policy works by influencing investment and consumption spending through increases and decreases in the interest rate. In essence, the theories we have been discussing are "demand oriented."

As we have said a number of times, the 1970s were difficult times for the U.S. economy. The United States found itself in 1974–1975 with stagflation—high unemployment and inflation. The late 1970s saw inflation return to the high levels of 1974–1975. It seemed as if policy makers were incapable of controlling the business cycle.

As a result of these seeming failures, orthodox economics came under fire. One assault was from a group of economists who expounded what came to be called **supply-side economics.** The essential argument of the supply-siders was quite simple. Basically, they said, all the attention to demand in orthodox macro theory distracted our attention from the real problem with the U.S. economy. The real problem, according to the supply-siders, was that high rates of taxation and heavy regulation had reduced the incentive to work, to save, and to invest. What was needed was not a demand stimulus but rather better incentives to stimulate *supply*.

If we cut taxes so that people take home more of their paychecks, the argument continued, they will work harder and save more. If businesses get to keep more of their profits and can get away from government regulations, they will invest more. This added labor supply and investment, or capital supply, will lead to an expansion of the supply of goods and services, which, in turn, will reduce inflation and unemployment at the same time. The ultimate solution to the economy's woes, the supply-siders concluded, was to be found on the *supply side* of the economy.

At their most extreme, supply-siders argued that the incentive effects of supply-side policies were likely to be so great that a major cut in tax rates would actually *increase* tax revenues. That is, even though tax *rates* would be lower, more people would be working and earning income and firms would earn more profits, so that the increases in the tax *bases* (profits, sales, and income) would outweigh the decreases in rates, resulting in increased government revenues.

This chapter's Issues and Applications box titled "Supply-Side Economics and Public Policy" presents a clear statement of supply-side reasoning in supply-siders' words.

THE LAFFER CURVE   Figure 34.2 presents one of the key diagrams of supply-side economics. The tax rate is measured on the vertical axis, and tax revenue is measured on the horizontal axis. The assumption behind this curve is that there is some tax rate beyond which the supply response is large enough to lead to a decrease in tax revenue for further increases in the tax rate. There is obviously some tax rate between zero and 100% at which tax revenue is at a maximum. At a tax rate of zero, work effort is high, but there is no tax revenue. At a tax rate of 100, the labor supply is presumably zero, since no one is allowed to keep any of his or her income. Somewhere in between zero and 100 is the maximum-revenue rate.

The major debate in the 1980s was whether tax rates in the United States put the country on the upper or lower part of the curve in Figure 34.2. The supply-side school claimed that the United States was at a point like *A* and that taxes should be cut. Others argued that the United States was at a point like *B* and that tax cuts would lead to lower tax revenue.

The diagram in Figure 34.2 is called the **Laffer Curve,** after Arthur Laffer, who, legend has it, first drew it on the back of a napkin at a cocktail party. The Laffer Curve had some influence on the passage of the Economic Recovery Tax Act of 1981, the tax package put forward by the Reagan administration that brought with it substantial cuts in both personal and business taxes. The individual

Laffer Curve The graph, named after Arthur Laffer, with the tax rate measured on the vertical axis and tax revenue measured on the horizontal axis. The Laffer Curve shows that there is some tax rate beyond which the supply response is large enough to lead to a decrease in tax revenue for further increases in the tax rate.

FIGURE 34.2
The Laffer Curve

The Laffer Curve shows that the amount of revenue that the government collects is a function of the tax rate. It also shows that when tax rates are very high, an increase in the tax rate could cause tax revenues to fall. Similarly, under the same circumstances, a cut in the tax rate could generate enough additional economic activity to cause revenues to rise.

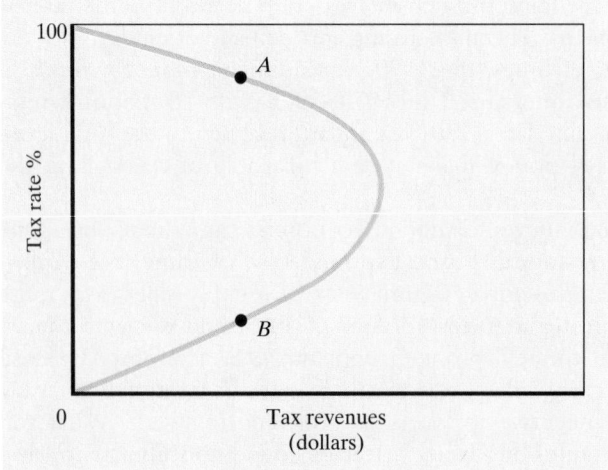

SUPPLY-SIDE ECONOMICS AND PUBLIC POLICY

Even before the election of 1980, traditional macroeconomics that emphasized the management of aggregate demand was being hotly debated in the political arena. The following excerpt from the *Joint Economic Report* of the 96th Congress, published early in the spring of 1980, is a clear statement of the supply-side logic of many in Congress:

> The 1980 Joint Economic Committee Report is not a vague compromise of mushy logic. It is a clarion call to get this country moving again. And it offers a new, clear set of policies to generate real, sustainable economic growth without inflation. It is forthright, revolutionary, and important.
>
> These are tense times. The United States and the free world are threatened militarily and economically. Americans struggle with each other for a bigger slice of a shrinking pie. It should not be this way....
>
> Faster growth, higher real incomes, and plentiful jobs are exactly what the minorities, the unemployed, and the underprivileged of this country have been seeking for years. It is no accident that the greatest gains in income, jobs, and dignity for such workers have come during periods of rapid expansion.
>
> Therefore, growth is critical; and saving, investment, and productivity are critical to growth. They must be encouraged, as the Minority [members of the Joint Economic Committee] has been saying for years. The hour is very late. It is high time the Nation got started.
>
> We have not gotten started because the Administration has clung to an outdated economic doctrine, forged in other economic circumstances decades ago. The political leadership that has dominated our Nation for more than a generation has not adopted modern solutions to address America's current economic problem....
>
> This report provides the needed

Early advocates of supply-side economics saw supply-side policies as a potential cure for many of the nation's economic problems.

approach that repudiates the myth perpetuated by the Administration that to fight inflation we must increase unemployment. That is manipulative demand management economics of the old-fashioned variety, and it is outdated by today's circumstances.

Our Nation should have three major goals: Price stability, real growth, and full employment.

We cannot hit these diverse economic targets if all our policy options are aimed at slowing the economy to wring out inflation. The proper policy "mix," as outlined in this report, is:

(1) To fight inflation by a gradual (but sustained) reduction in the growth of the money supply and a gradual reduction of the ratio of Federal direct and regulatory spending to GNP.

(2) To fight general unemployment by increasing real economic growth through tax reductions designed, not to pump money into the economy, but to restructure the tax code to increase the after-tax reward to additional saving, investment, production, and employment.

[emphasis in original] The tax structure must direct more of our annual economic effort into modernization for competitiveness and growth rather than immediate consumption....

These policies ... are consistent and mutually reinforcing. The tax cuts to stimulate saving, investment, and competitiveness will put more goods on the shelves and lower prices, thus reinforcing the anti-inflation monetary policy. The anti-inflation monetary policy will reduce the biases against saving and investment (now in the tax code) which occur as inflation destroys the depreciation allowances and savings returns and pushes people into higher tax brackets. The lowering of inflation will thus reinforce the tax changes in generating more production, real growth, and profits to operate government programs at lower tax rates. Both policies will raise labor productivity, increase the demand for labor, and reinforce the incentives to hire and train the unemployed.

Source: 1980 Joint Economic Report, 96th Congress, March 1980.

income tax was to be cut 25% over three years. Corporate taxes were cut sharply in a way designed to stimulate capital investment. The new law allowed firms to depreciate their capital at a very rapid rate for tax purposes, and the bigger deductions led to taxes that were significantly lower than before.

EVALUATING SUPPLY-SIDE ECONOMICS   Supply-side economics has been criticized on a number of counts. Critics point out that it is unlikely that a tax cut would increase the supply of labor substantially.

Supporters of supply-side economics claim that Reagan's tax policies were quite successful in stimulating the economy. They point to the fact that almost immediately after the tax cuts of 1981 were put into place, the economy expanded and the recession of 1980–1982 came to an end. In addition, inflation rates fell sharply from the high rates of 1980 and 1981. And, except for one year, federal receipts continued to rise throughout the 1980s despite the cut in tax rates.

Critics of supply-side policies do not dispute these facts but offer an alternative explanation of how the economy recovered. The Reagan tax cuts were enacted just as the U.S. economy was in the middle of its deepest recession since the Great Depression. The unemployment rate stood at 10.8% in the fourth quarter of 1982. It was the recession, critics argue, that was responsible for the reduction in inflation— not the supply-side policies. In addition, in theory, a tax cut could even lead to a *reduction* in labor supply. Recall our discussion of income and substitution effects in Chapter 4. While it is true that a higher after-tax wage rate provides a higher reward for each hour of work and thus more incentive to work, a tax cut also means that households receive a higher income for a given number of hours of work. Because they can earn the same amount of money working fewer hours, households might actually choose to work *less*. In other words, they might spend some of their added income on leisure. Research done during the 1980s suggests that tax cuts do seem to increase the supply of labor somewhat but that the increases are very modest.

But what about the recovery from the recession? Why did real output begin to grow rapidly in late 1982, precisely when the supply-side tax cuts were taking effect? Two reasons have been suggested. First, the supply-side tax cuts had large *demand*-side effects that stimulated the economy. Second, the Federal Reserve dramatically expanded the money supply and drove interest rates down at the same time that the tax cuts were being put into effect. The money supply expanded about 20% between 1981 and 1983, and interest rates dropped dramatically. In 1981, the average three-month U.S. Treasury bill paid 14% interest. In 1983, the figure had dropped to 8.6 percent.

Certainly, traditional theory suggests that a huge tax cut will lead to an increase in disposable income and, in turn, an increase in consumption spending (a component of aggregate expenditure). In addition, although an increase in planned investment (brought about by a lower interest rate) leads to added productive capacity and added supply in the long run, it also increases expenditures on capital goods (new plant and equipment investment) in the short run.

Whether the recovery from the 1981–1982 recession was the result of supply-side expansion or supply-side policies that had demand-side effects, one thing is clear: The extreme promises of the supply-siders did not materialize. President Reagan argued that because of the effect depicted in the Laffer Curve, the government could maintain expenditures (and even increase defense expenditures sharply), cut tax rates, *and* balance the budget. This was clearly not the case. Government revenues fell sharply from levels that would have been realized without the tax cuts. And, since 1982, the federal government has been running huge deficits, with more than $4 trillion added to the national debt in twelve years. Bill Clinton now faces a total debt of nearly $5 trillion.

TESTING ALTERNATIVE MACROECONOMIC MODELS

At this point, you may be wondering why there is so much disagreement in macroeconomics. Why cannot macroeconomists simply test their models against one another and see which one performs best?

One problem is that macroeconomic models differ in ways that are hard to standardize for. If, for example, one model takes the price level to be given, or not explained within the model, and another one does not, the model with the given price level may do better in, say, predicting output—not because it is a better model but simply because the errors in predicting prices have not been allowed to affect the predictions of output. The model that takes prices as given has a head start, so to speak.

Another problem arises in the testing of the rational-expectations assumption. Remember that if people have rational expectations, they are using the true model to form their expectations. Therefore, to test this assumption one needs the true model. One is never sure, of course, that whatever model is taken to be the true model is in fact the true one. Any test of the rational-expectations hypothesis is therefore a *joint* test (1) that expectations are formed rationally, and (2) that the model that is being used is the true one. If the test rejects the hypothesis, it may be that the model is wrong rather than that expectations are not rational.

Another problem that macroeconomists have is that the amount of data available is fairly small. Most empirical work uses data beginning in about 1950, which in 1994 was about 44 years' (176 quarters) worth of data. While this may seem like a lot of data, it is not. Macroeconomic data are fairly "smooth," which means that a typical variable does not vary all that much from quarter to quarter or year to year. For example, the number of business cycles within this 44-year period is quite small, about seven. Testing various macroeconomic hypotheses on the basis of seven business cycle observations is not easy, and any conclusions drawn from such an exercise must be interpreted with considerable caution.

To give an example of the problem of a small number of observations, consider trying to test the hypothesis that import prices affect domestic prices. Import prices changed very little in the 1950s and 1960s. Because of this, it would have been very difficult at the end of the 1960s to estimate the effect of import prices on domestic prices. The variation in import prices was simply not great enough to show any effects. One cannot demonstrate that changes in import prices explain changes in domestic prices if import prices do not change! The situation was quite different by the end of the 1970s, however, because by then import prices had varied considerably. By the end of the 1970s, there were fairly good estimates of the import price effect, but not before then. This kind of problem is encountered again and again in empirical macroeconomics. In many cases there are simply not enough observations for much to be said, and thus there is considerable room for disagreement.

We pointed out in Chapter 1 that it is difficult in economics to perform controlled experiments. Economists are for the most part at the mercy of the historical data. If we were able to perform experiments, we could probably learn more about the economy in a shorter period of time. Since this is not the case, we must wait. In time, the current range of disagreements in macroeconomics should be considerably narrowed.

SUMMARY

Keynesian Economics

1. In a broad sense, Keynesian economics is the foundation of all macroeconomics. In a narrower sense, the term "Keynesian" is used to refer to economists who advocate active government intervention in the economy.

Monetarism

2. The monetarist analysis of the economy places a great deal of emphasis on the *velocity of money,* which is defined as the number of times a dollar bill changes hands, on average, during the course of a year. The velocity of money is the ratio of nominal GDP to the stock of money, or $V \equiv GDP/M \equiv P \cdot Y/M$. Alternately, $M \cdot V \equiv P \cdot Y$.

3. The *quantity theory of money* assumes that velocity is constant (or virtually constant). This implies that changes in the supply of money will lead to equal percentage changes in nominal GDP.

4. The velocity of money may be a function of the interest rate as well as institutional factors, and it is therefore not likely to be a constant. For example, when interest rates fall and the quantity of money demanded increases, the velocity of money decreases. Hence an increase in the money supply (M) tends to lower velocity (V), so $M \cdot V$ does not increase by as large a percentage as M itself does and nominal GDP does not rise by the same percentage as the money supply.

5. Most economists believe that inflation is a purely monetary phenomenon. Inflation cannot continue indefinitely unless the Fed "accommodates" it by expanding the money supply.

6. Most monetarists blame most of the instability in the economy on the federal government.

7. Most monetarists are skeptical of the government's ability to manage the macroeconomy. They argue that the money supply should grow at a rate equal to the average growth of real output (income) (Y). That is, the Fed should expand the money supply to accommodate real growth but not inflation.

New Classical Macroeconomics

8. The *new classical macroeconomics* has developed from two different but related sources: the *theoretical* and the *empirical* cri-

tiques of traditional macroeconomics. On the theoretical level, there has been growing dissatisfaction with the way traditional models treat expectations. On the empirical level, the stagflation in the U.S. economy during the 1970s caused many people to look for alternative theories to explain the breakdown of the Phillips Curve.

9. The *rational-expectations hypothesis* assumes that people know the "true" model that generates economic variables. For example, rational expectations assumes that people know how inflation is determined in the economy and use this model to forecast future inflation rates.

10. The *Lucas supply function* assumes that real output (Y) depends on the actual price level minus the expected price level, or the *price surprise*. This function in combination with the assumption that expectations are rational implies that anticipated policy changes have no effect on real output.

Supply-Side Economics

11. *Supply-side economics* focuses on incentives to stimulate supply. Supply-side economists believe that if we lower taxes, workers will work harder and save more and firms will invest more and produce more. At their most extreme, supply-siders argue that incentive effects are likely to be so great that a major cut in taxes will actually increase tax revenues.

12. The *Laffer Curve* shows the relationship between tax rates and tax revenues collected. Supply-side economists use it to argue that it is possible to generate higher revenues by cutting tax rates, but evidence does not appear to support this proposition. The lower tax rates put into place by the Reagan administration decreased tax revenues significantly and contributed to the massive increase in the federal debt during the 1980s.

Testing Alternative Macroeconomic Models

13. Economists disagree about which macroeconomic model is best for several reasons: (1) macroeconomic models differ in ways that are hard to standardize for; (2) when testing the rational-expectations assumption, one is never sure that whatever model is taken to be the true model is in fact the true one; (3) the amount of data available is fairly small.

REVIEW TERMS AND CONCEPTS

Laffer Curve   842
Lucas supply function   839
monetarism   831
new classical macroeconomics   836
price surprise   839

quantity theory of money   832
rational-expectations
   hypothesis   837
supply-side economics   841
velocity of money (V)   831

Equations:

$V \equiv GDP/M$
$M \cdot V \equiv P \cdot Y$

PROBLEM SET

1. When Bill Clinton took office in January 1993, he faced two major economic problems: a large federal budget deficit and high unemployment resulting from a very slow recovery from the recession of 1990–1991. In his first State of the Union message, the President called for spending cuts and substantial tax increases to reduce the deficit. Most of these proposed spending cuts were in the defense budget. The following day, Alan Greenspan, chair of the Federal Reserve Board of Governors, signaled his support for the President's plan. Many elements of the President's original plan were later incorporated into the deficit reduction bill passed in August, 1993.

   a. Some say that without the Fed's support, the Clinton plan would be a disaster. Explain this argument.

   b. Supply-side economists and monetarists are very worried about the plan and the support that it has received from the Fed. Why are these two groups worried? What specific problems might a monetarist worry about? A supply-side economist?

   c. Suppose that you were hired by the Federal Reserve Bank of St. Louis to report on the events of 1994 and 1995. What specific evidence would you look for to see if the Clinton plan was effective or whether the critics were right to be skeptical?

2. A cornerstone of new classical economics is the notion that expectations are "rational." What do you think will happen to the prices of single-family homes in your community over the next several years? On what do you base your expectations? Is your thinking consistent with the notion of rational expectations? Explain.

3. You are a monetarist, and you are given the following information. The money supply is $1000. The velocity of money is five. What is nominal income? What is real income? What happens to nominal income if the money supply is doubled? To real income?

4. "In an economy with reasonably flexible prices and wages, full employment is almost always maintained." Explain why this statement is true.

5. During the 1980 presidential campaign, Ronald Reagan promised to cut taxes, increase expenditures on national defense, and balance the budget. During the New Hampshire primary of 1980, George Bush called this "voodoo economics." The two men were arguing about the relative merits of supply-side economics. Explain their disagreement.

6. Assume that in a hypothetical economy there is a simple proportional tax on wages imposed at a rate t. Suppose further that there are plenty of jobs around so that if people enter the labor force they can find work. We define total government receipts from the tax as

$$T = t \cdot W \cdot L$$

where t = the tax rate, W = the gross wage rate, and L = the total supply of labor.
The net wage rate is

$$W_N = (1 - t)W.$$

The elasticity of labor supply is defined as

$$\frac{\%\Delta L}{\%\Delta W_N}.$$

Suppose that t were cut from .25 to .20. In order for such a cut to *increase* total government receipts from the tax, how elastic must the supply of labor be? (Assume a constant gross wage and full employment.) What does your answer imply about the supply-side assertion that a cut in taxes can increase tax revenues?

35 Economic Growth

economic growth An increase in the output of an economy. Defined by some economists as an increase of real GDP per capita.

modern economic growth The period of rapid and sustained increase in real output per capita that began in the Western World with the Industrial Revolution.

As you may recall from Chapter 1, **economic growth** occurs when an economy experiences an increase in total output. However, the increase in real output that began in the Western World with the Industrial Revolution and continues today has been so sustained and so rapid that economists have given the period a special name: **modern economic growth.** These three simple words describe the complex phenomenon that is the subject of this chapter.

Modern economic growth is the subject of much debate. It is through economic growth that living standards improve. But growth also brings change. New things are produced, while others become obsolete. Some believe that growth is the fundamental objective of a society, because it lifts people out of poverty and enhances the quality of their lives. Others argue that economic growth erodes traditional values and leads to exploitation, environmental destruction, and corruption.

The first part of this chapter describes the economic growth process in some detail and identifies some sources of economic growth. Following a review of the U.S. economy's growth record since the nineteenth century, we turn to an examination of the role of public policy in the growth process. The chapter concludes with a review of the debate over the benefits and costs of growth.

The Growth Process: From Agriculture to Industry

The easiest way to understand the process of growth and to identify its causes is to think about a simple economy. Recall from Chapter 2 our friends Colleen and Bill who were washed up on a desert island. At first they had only a few simple tools and whatever human capital they brought with them to the island. They gathered nuts and berries and built a small cabin. Their "GDP" consisted of basic food and shelter.

Over time, things improved. The first year, they cleared some land and began to cultivate a few vegetables that they found growing on the island. They made some tools and dug a small reservoir to store rainwater. As their agricultural efforts became more efficient, they shifted their resources (that is, their time) into building a larger, more comfortable home.

Colleen and Bill were accumulating capital in two forms. First, they built *physical capital,* material things used in the production of goods and services—a better house, tools, and a water system. Second, they acquired more *human capital*—knowledge, skills, and talents. Through trial and error, they learned about the island, its soil and its climate, what worked and what didn't. Both kinds of capital made them more efficient and increased their productivity. Because it took less time to produce the food that they needed to survive, they could devote more energy to producing other things or to leisure.

At any given time, Colleen and Bill faced limits on what they could produce. These limits were imposed by the existing state of their technical knowledge and the resources at their disposal. Over time, they expanded their possibilities, developed new technologies, accumulated capital, and made their labor more productive. In Chapter 2, you will recall, we defined a society's *production possibilities frontier (ppf)*, which shows all possible combinations of output that can be produced given present technology and available resources. Economic growth expands those limits and shifts society's production possibilities frontier out to the right, as Figure 35.1 shows.

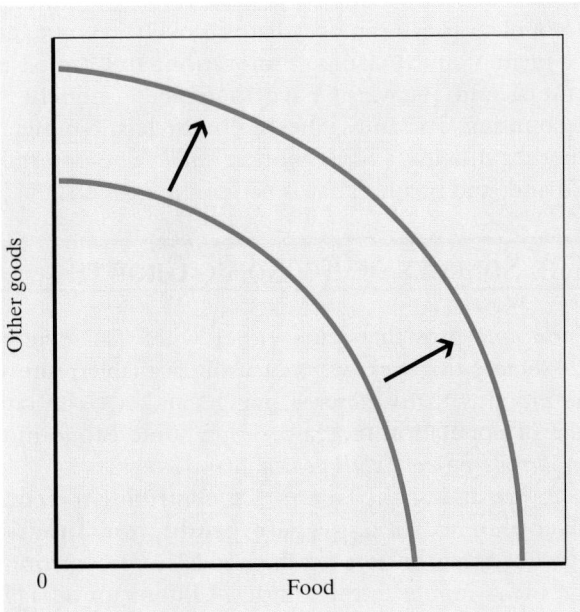

FIGURE 35.1
Economic Growth Shifts Society's Production Possibility Frontier Up and to the Right

The production possibility frontier shows all the combinations of output that can be produced if all of society's scarce resources are fully and efficiently employed. Economic growth expands society's production possibilities, shifting the ppf up and to the right.

FROM AGRICULTURE TO INDUSTRY: THE INDUSTRIAL REVOLUTION Before the Industrial Revolution in Great Britain, every society in the world was agrarian. Towns and cities existed here and there, but almost everyone lived in rural areas. People spent most of their time producing food and other basic subsistence goods. Then, beginning in England around 1750, technical change and capital accumulation increased productivity dramatically in two very important industries: agriculture and textiles. New and more efficient methods of farming were developed. New inventions and new machinery in spinning, weaving, and steel production meant that more could be produced with fewer resources. Just as new technology, capital equipment, and the resulting higher productivity made it possible for Colleen and Bill to spend time working on other projects and new "products," the British turned from agricultural production to industrial production. In both cases, growth meant new products, more output, and wider choice.

There was one major difference, however. Colleen and Bill were fully in charge of their own lives. But peasants and workers in eighteenth-century England ended up with a very different set of choices. It was no longer possible to make a living as a peasant farmer. The cities offered the only real alternative, and a rural agrarian society was very quickly transformed into an urban industrial society.

GROWTH IN AN INDUSTRIAL SOCIETY The process of economic growth in an industrial society such as the United States is more complex but follows the same steps we have just described for growth in an agrarian society.

Consider the development of the electronic calculator. Prior to 1970, calculators that could add, subtract, multiply, and divide weighed fifty pounds, performed calculations very slowly, and were very expensive (a good calculator cost hundreds of dollars). Today, electronic calculators retail for as low as $3 or come free with a magazine subscription. Some are even small enough to fit into a wristwatch.

Everyone with a checkbook knows the value of owning a small calculator. The increase in the efficiency and speed with which basic mathematical functions are performed by inexpensive calculators saves us all time and effort that can be spent doing other things. Tasks that once took days now take minutes, and one accountant today can do what it took 10 accountants to do 20 years ago.

Technological change, innovation, and capital production (calculators, computers, and software) have increased productivity. If a diner spends less on accounting, its sandwiches will cost less. Sandwich buyers thus may go to see another movie or have another soda. The entertainment and soft drink sectors expand, and so on. That is economic growth.

THE SOURCES OF ECONOMIC GROWTH

Economic growth occurs either when (1) society acquires more resources, or (2) society discovers ways of using available resources more efficiently. For economic growth to increase living standards, the rate of growth must exceed the rate of population increase. Thus, some economists define economic growth as *an increase in real GDP per capita.*

As we discuss the factors that contribute to economic growth, it will be helpful to think of an **aggregate production function.** An individual firm's production function is a mathematical representation of the relationship between the firm's inputs and its output. Output for an aggregate production function is domestic output, or gross domestic product. Stated simply, gross domestic prod-

aggregate production function
The mathematical representation of the technological relationship between inputs and national output, or gross domestic product.

uct (output) (Y), depends upon the amount of labor (L) and the amount of capital (K) available in the economy (assuming that the amount of land is fixed).[1]

If you think of GDP as a function of both labor and capital, you can see that:

> An increase in GDP can come about in three ways: (1) through an increase in labor, (2) through an increase in physical or human capital, or (3) through an increase in the amount of product produced by each unit of capital or labor.

An Increase in Labor Supply

It stands to reason that an increasing labor supply can generate more output. Consider, for example, what would happen if another person joined Colleen and Bill on the island. She would join in the work and produce, and so GDP would rise. Or suppose that a person who had not been a part of the labor force were to begin to work and use his time and energy to produce pottery. Real output would rise in this case also.

Whether output *per capita* rises when the labor supply increases is another matter. If the capital stock remains fixed while labor increases, it is likely that the new labor will be less productive than the old labor. This phenomenon is called *diminishing returns,* and it worried Thomas Malthus, David Ricardo, and other early economists.

Malthus and Ricardo, who lived in England during the nineteenth century, were concerned that the fixed supply of land would ultimately lead to diminishing returns. With land in strictly limited supply, population increases would mean encountering the constraints of the ppf very quickly. To increase agricultural output, people would be forced to farm less productive land or to farm land more intensively. In either case, the returns to successive increases in population would diminish. Both Malthus and Ricardo predicted a gloomy future as population outstripped the land's capacity to produce. What both economists left out of their calculations, however, was technological change and capital accumulation. New and better farming techniques have raised agricultural productivity so dramatically that less than 3% of the U.S. population now provides enough food for the country's entire population and much of the rest of the world as well.

Diminishing returns can also occur if a nation's stock of capital grows more slowly than its work force. Capital enhances the productivity of workers. A person with a shovel digs a bigger hole than a person without one, and a person with a steam shovel outdoes them both. If a society's stock of plant and equipment does not grow, marginal workers will not be as productive, because they do not have machines to work with.

Table 35.1 illustrates how growth in the labor force, without a corresponding

---

[1]All the numbers in the tables to follow were derived from the simple production function: $Y = 3 \cdot K^{1/3}L^{2/3}$.

TABLE 35.1
Economic Growth from an Increase in Labor—More Output but Diminishing Returns and Lower Labor Productivity

PERIOD	QUANTITY OF LABOR L (UNITS)	QUANTITY OF CAPITAL K (UNITS)	TOTAL OUTPUT Y (UNITS)	MEASURED LABOR PRODUCTIVITY Y/L
1	100	100	300	3.0
2	110	100	320	2.9
3	120	100	339	2.8
4	130	100	357	2.7

increase in the stock of capital or technological change, might lead to growth of output but declining productivity and a lower standard of living. As labor increases, output rises from 300 units in Period 1 to 320 in Period 2, to 339 in Period 3, and so forth, but output per worker (Y/L) per period falls. Output per worker, Y/L, is a measure of labor's productivity.

The fear that new workers entering the labor force will displace existing workers and generate unemployment has been with us for a long time. New workers can come from many places. They might be immigrants, young people looking for their first jobs, or older people entering the labor force for the first time. Between 1947 and 1992, the number of women in the labor force more than tripled, jumping from 16.7 million to 56.7 million. Table 35.2 shows that in the United States since World War II, the civilian noninstitutional population (that is, those not in jails or mental institutions) over 16 years of age grew by 88.2%, while the labor force more than doubled. The U.S. economy, however, has shown a remarkable ability to expand right along with the labor force. The number of persons employed jumped by over 60 million—more than 100%—during the same period.

> As long as the economy and the capital stock are expanding rapidly enough, new entrants into the labor force do not displace other workers.

Increases in Physical Capital

An increase in the stock of capital can also increase output, even if it is not accompanied by an increase in the labor force. Physical capital both enhances the productivity of labor and provides valuable services directly.

It is easy to see how capital provides services directly. Consider, for example, what happened on Bill and Colleen's island. In the first few years, they built a house, putting many hours of work into it that could have gone into producing other things for immediate consumption. With the house for shelter, Colleen and Bill live in relative comfort and can thus spend time on other things. In the same way, capital equipment produced in one year can add to the value of a product over many years. For example, we still derive use and value from bridges and tunnels built decades ago.

TABLE 35.2

Employment, Labor Force, and Population Growth, 1947–1992

	CIVILIAN NONINSTITUTIONAL POPULATION OVER 16 YEARS OLD (MILLIONS)	CIVILIAN LABOR FORCE		EMPLOYMENT (MILLIONS)
		NUMBER (MILLIONS)	PERCENTAGE OF POPULATION	
1947	101.8	59.4	58.3	57.0
1960	117.3	69.6	59.3	65.8
1970	137.1	82.8	60.4	78.7
1980	167.7	106.9	63.7	99.3
1990	188.0	124.8	66.4	117.9
1992	191.6	127.0	66.3	117.6
Percentage change, 1947—1992	+88.2%	+113.8%		+106.3%
Annual Rate	+1.4%	+1.7%		+1.6%

Source: Department of Labor, Bureau of Labor Statistics, *Monthly Labor Review,* February 1993.

TABLE 35.3
Economic Growth from an
Increase in Capital—More
Output, Diminishing
Returns to Added Capital,
Higher Measured Labor
Productivity

PERIOD	QUANTITY OF LABOR	QUANTITY OF CAPITAL	TOTAL OUTPUT	MEASURED LABOR PRODUCTIVITY
	L (UNITS)	K (UNITS)	Y (UNITS)	Y/L
1	100	100	300	3.0
2	100	110	310	3.1
3	100	120	319	3.2
4	100	130	327	3.3

It is also easy to see how capital used in production enhances the productivity of labor. Computers enable us to do almost instantly tasks that once were impossible or might have taken several years to complete. An airplane with a relatively small crew can transport hundreds of people thousands of miles in a few hours. A bridge over a river at a critical location may save thousands of labor hours that would be spent transporting materials and people the long way around. It is precisely this yield in the form of future valuable services that provides both private and public investors with the incentive to devote resources to capital production.

Table 35.3 shows how an increase in capital without a corresponding increase in labor might increase output. Several things about these numbers are notable. First, additional capital increases measured productivity; output per worker (Y/L) increases from 3.0 to 3.1, to 3.2, and finally to 3.3 as the quantity of capital (K) increases. Second, there are diminishing returns to capital. Increasing capital by 10 units first increases output by 10 units—from 300 in Period 1 to 310 in Period 2. But the second increase of 10 units yields only 9 units of output, and the third increase yields only eight.

Table 35.4 shows the value of gross nonresidential capital stocks in the United States since 1960. The increase in capital stock is the difference between gross investment and depreciation. (Remember that some capital becomes obsolete and some capital wears out every year.) Over the last 31 years, the capital stock has increased at a rate of 3.5% per year. The stock of equipment has increased faster than the stock of structures.

By comparing Tables 35.2 and 35.4, you can see that capital has been increasing faster than labor since 1960. In all economies experiencing modern economic growth, capital expands at a more rapid rate than labor. That is, the ratio of capital to labor (K/L) increases, and this too is a source of increasing productivity. Another important source of increased productivity is public capital, the subject of the Issues and Applications box titled "Infrastructure and Economic Growth."

	GROSS STOCK	EQUIPMENT	STRUCTURES
1960	1637.1	655.5	981.6
1970	2543.6	1075.5	1473.1
1980	3677.4	1709.2	1968.3
1991	4809.5	2227.6	2581.9
Percentage change, 1960–1991	94%	240%	163%
Annual rate	3.5%	4.0%	3.2%

Source: *Survey of Current Business,* January 1992, Table 4, p. 137, and *Statistical Abstract of the United States,* 1992, Table 861.

INFRASTRUCTURE AND ECONOMIC GROWTH

Rebuilding the Lake and Marshall Bridge in Minneapolis, Minnesota. Maintenance and development of infrastructure play an important role in economic growth.

A major source of economic growth is the accumulation of capital. When we think of capital's role in economic growth, we tend to focus on private capital—the plant, equipment, and inventory of business firms. But what about *public* capital?

Recall from our earlier discussions that *capital goods* are used to produce other goods and services over time. One form of capital is infrastructure. **Infrastructure,** also called **public capital,** refers to the roads, bridges, water treatment plants, fire stations, and so on that collectively contribute to the public good.

Infrastructure has the potential for increasing productivity and growth. Good highways and bridges reduce transportation costs and make it easier to transport goods. Readily available clean water improves health and is often essential for production.

Governments are usually responsible for putting public capital into place. Throughout the 1980s, however, there was strong pressure to reduce government spending and to increase growth

in the private sector. One of the consequences of these pressures was a significant slow-down in public infrastructure investment. Some have pointed to this slowdown as a cause of the slower economic growth in the 1980s.

In June 1990, the Federal Reserve Bank of Boston held a conference on the topic of infrastructure and growth. Professor David Aschauer of Bates College opened the conference with the following challenge:

As the decade of the 1990s begins, new challenges present themselves to the citizenry of the United States. Among the most important are concerns about the environment, economic productivity, and international competitiveness, and a rearrangement of standing strategic military relationships. Our future quality of life, economic prosperity, and security depend crucially on how we choose to meet these new challenges.

The apparent failure of the communist economic system and the associated relaxation of Cold War tensions offer the potential for a significant reallocation of the nation's resources from military to other uses. A crucial question then arises whether

these resources should be channeled to the private sector, effecting overall government expenditure reduction, or kept within the public sector, thereby inducing an alteration in the composition of government spending.

The first direction, expenditure reduction, certainly has merit to a broad class of individuals. Many would point to the fact that total federal government outlays, expressed relative to gross national product, rose from 14.8 percent in 1950 to 21.6 percent in 1980 and, in 1989, to 21.8 percent. Others would point to the persistence of federal budget deficits. To both groups, expenditure reduction would be of benefit to economic performance, either by reducing the overall scale of government activity in the economy or by allowing a reduction in interest rates and an expansion in domestic investment activity.

But the second direction, expenditure reorientation, may also have merit. It could well be the case that quality of life and economic performance would be best served by retaining the resources within the public sector and expanding expenditure in certain critical areas. One candidate area is infrastructure, the public stock of social and economic overhead capital. Indeed, it has been claimed in the popular press that "it's hard to escape America's crumbling infrastructure" and that "even though the deterioration of U.S. highways, bridges, airports, harbors, sewage systems, and other building blocks of the economy has been exhaustively documented in recent years, there has been scant progress" in addressing the postulated need to renew the public capital stock (Industry Week, May 21, 1990).

Clearly, someone was listening. Prior to taking office, President Bill Clinton held an economic summit to discuss ideas for stimulating economic growth. A major focus of the discussion was infrastructure, and it led to Clinton's call for $16 billion in public works spending in his 1993 State of the Union address.

Source: "Is There a Shortfall in Public Capital Investment?", Proceedings of a Conference sponsored by the Federal Reserve Bank of Boston, Alicia Munnell, Editor, June 1990.

Increases in Human Capital

Investment in human capital is another important source of economic growth. People in good health are more productive than people in poor health; people with skills are more productive than people without them.

Human capital can be produced in a number of ways. Individuals can invest in themselves by going to school, or college, or vocational training programs. Firms can invest in human capital through on-the-job training. The government invests in human capital with programs to improve health, to underwrite schooling, and to provide job training.

Table 35.5 shows that the level of educational attainment has risen significantly since 1940. The percentage of the population with four or more years of college has risen from under 5% in 1940 to 21.4% in 1991. In 1940 less than one person in four had completed a high school education; in 1991, nearly eight in ten had.

Increases in Productivity

Growth that cannot be explained by increases in the *quantity* of inputs can be explained only by an increase in the *productivity* of those inputs. In this case, each unit of input must be producing more output. The productivity of an input, or a factor of production, can be affected by several factors, including technological change, other advances in knowledge, and economies of scale.

TECHNOLOGICAL CHANGE   The Industrial Revolution was in part sparked by important new technological developments. The development of new techniques of spinning and weaving—the invention of the "mule" and the "spinning jenny," for example—were critical. The high-tech boom that swept the United States in the early 1980s was driven by the rapid development and dissemination of semiconductor technology.

Technological change affects productivity in two stages. First, there is an advance in knowledge, or an **invention.** But knowledge by itself does nothing unless it is used. When new knowledge is used to produce a new product or to produce an existing product more efficiently, there is **innovation.**

Technological change cannot be measured directly. Some studies have presented data on "indicators" of the rate of technical change—the number of new patents, for example—but none are very satisfactory. Still, we know that technological changes that have improved productivity are all around us. Computer technology

invention An advance in knowledge.

innovation The use of new knowledge to produce a new product or to produce an existing product more efficiently.

TABLE 35.5
Years of School Completed by People Over 25 Years Old, 1940–1991

	PERCENTAGE WITH LESS THAN FIVE YEARS OF SCHOOL	PERCENTAGE WITH FOUR YEARS OR MORE OF HIGH SCHOOL	PERCENTAGE WITH FOUR YEARS OR MORE OF COLLEGE
1940	13.7	24.5	4.6
1950	11.1	34.3	6.2
1960	8.3	41.1	7.7
1970	5.5	52.3	10.7
1980	3.6	66.5	16.2
1991	2.4	78.4	21.4

Source: *Statistical Abstract of the United States, 1990,* Table 215, and *Statistical Abstract of the United States, 1992,* Table 219.

has revolutionized the office, hybrid seeds have dramatically increased the productivity of land, and more efficient and powerful aircraft have made air travel routine and relatively inexpensive.

OTHER ADVANCES IN KNOWLEDGE   Over and above invention and innovation, advances in other kinds of knowledge can also improve productivity. One important category of knowledge is what we might call "managerial knowledge." For example, because of the very high cost of capital during the early 1980s, firms learned to manage their inventories much better. Many were able to keep production lines and distribution lines flowing with a much lower stock of inventories. Inventories are part of a firm's capital stock, and trimming them reduces costs and raises productivity. This is an example of a *capital-saving* innovation; many of the advances that we are used to thinking about, such as the introduction of robotics, are *labor-saving.*

In addition to managerial knowledge, improved personnel management techniques, accounting procedures, data management, and the like can also make production more efficient, reduce costs, and increase measured productivity.

ECONOMIES OF SCALE   *External economies of scale* are cost savings that result from increases in the size of industries. The economies that accompany growth in size may arise from a variety of causes. For example, as firms in a growing industry build plants at new locations, they may have lower transport costs. There may also be some economies of scale associated with R&D (research and development) spending and job-training programs.

OTHER INFLUENCES ON PRODUCTIVITY   In addition to technological change, other advances in knowledge, and economies of scale, other forces may affect productivity. During the 1970s and 1980s, for example, many firms were required by the government to reduce the air and water pollution they were producing. These requirements diverted capital and labor from the production of measured output and thus *reduced* measured productivity. Similarly, in recent years requirements imposed by the Occupational Safety and Health Act (OSHA) have required firms to protect workers better from accidental injuries and potential health problems. This also diverts resources from measured output.

It is important to understand that negative effects such as these are more a problem of *measurement* than of truly declining productivity. The EPA (Environmental Protection Agency) regulates air and water quality because clean air and water presumably have a value to society. Thus, the resources diverted to produce that value are not wasted. A perfect measure of output produced that is of value to society would include environmental quality and good health.

The list of factors that can affect productivity could go on and on. Weather can have an enormous impact on agricultural productivity. In 1986, for example, a severe drought across the southeastern United States reduced total agricultural output by over 15% with losses estimated near $5 billion. A drought in the Midwest in the summer of 1988 had similar effects. Labor disputes that are long and costly also reduce measured productivity.

Having presented the major factors that influence productivity, we now turn to the growth record for the United States and to an estimate of how these factors have combined to produce a record of steady growth that has lasted well over 100 years.

GROWTH AND PRODUCTIVITY IN THE U.S. ECONOMY

Modern economic growth in the United States began in the middle of the nineteenth century. After the Civil War, the railroads spread out across the country and the economy took off. Table 35.6 shows the rate of growth of real output in the United States since 1871.

The conventional wisdom is that over the long haul, real output in the United States has been growing at about 3.0% annually. Between 1871 and 1909, the growth rate was very healthy, ranging from 4.0% to 5.5% per year. Because of the dislocations of the Great Depression, growth was slower during the next two decades, but the 1950s and 1960s saw renewed growth and vigor in the economy. Although the 1970s contained some good years and some bad, during the decade output rose by an average of 2.8% per year, a credible performance. Between 1980 and 1992, the rate of growth fell to 2.2 percent, a below-average performance.

Table 35.7 summarizes the growth experience of the U.S. economy since 1950. Gross domestic product in nominal terms, or current dollars, increased about twenty-fold between 1950 and 1992, but much of that increase was the result of price increases. Real output more than tripled, growing at 3.0% per year during the 42 years. During the same period, population increased by 1.3% per year. Thus, real GDP per capita grew at a rate of 1.7% per year (3.0% − 1.3%).

Table 35.8 on the next page shows growth rates of real GDP since 1961 for the United States and several other countries. Growth has been slowing everywhere. Virtually all the countries in the table experienced less growth during the 1970s than during the 1960s and continued to grow even more slowly during the 1980s.

Sources of Growth in the U.S. Economy Since 1929

For many years, Edward Denison, of the Brookings Institution in Washington, has been studying the growth process in the United States and sorting out the relative importance of the various causal factors. Table 35.9 on the next page presents the results of his most recently published major work.

Denison estimates that about half of U.S. growth in output over the entire period from 1929 to 1982 has come from increases in factors of production and the other half from increases in productivity. Growth in the labor force accounted for about 20% of overall growth, while growth in capital stock (both human and physical) accounted for 33 percent. Of the capital stock growth figure, human capital (that is, education and training) accounted for 19% of the total, and physical capital accounted for 14 percent. Growth of knowledge was the single most important factor contributing to increases in the productivity of inputs.

TABLE 35.6
Growth of Real GDP in the United States, 1871–1992

	AVERAGE GROWTH RATE PER YEAR
1871–1889	5.5
1889–1909	4.0
1909–1929	2.9
1929–1950	2.7
1950–1960	3.2
1960–1970	3.8
1970–1980	2.8
1980–1992	2.2
1950–1992	3.0

Source: *Historical Statistics of the United States: Colonial Times to 1970.* Tables F47-70, F98-124; *Survey of Current Business,* March 1993.

TABLE 35.7
Economic Growth in the United States, 1950–1992

	GDP (BILLIONS OF DOLLARS)	REAL GDP (BILLIONS OF 1987 DOLLARS)	REAL GDP PER CAPITA (1987 DOLLARS)
1950	288.3	1425.1	9395
1992	5950.7	4922.6	19,272
Annual rate of change	7.5%	3.0%	1.7%

Source: Survey of Current Business, March 1993.

TABLE 35.8
Annual Growth Rates of Real GDP for Selected Countries, 1961–1991 (percentage)

AREA AND COUNTRY	1961–65 ANNUAL AVERAGE	1966–70 ANNUAL AVERAGE	1971–75 ANNUAL AVERAGE	1976–80 ANNUAL AVERAGE	1981—85 ANNUAL AVERAGE	1986	1987	1988	1989	1990	1991	1986–91 ANNUAL AVERAGE
OECD countries*	5.3	4.6	3.1	3.4	2.4	2.8	3.2	4.4	3.3	2.4	0.8	2.8
United States	4.6	3.0	2.4	3.2	2.6	2.9	3.1	3.9	2.5	0.8	–1.2	2.0
Canada	5.3	4.6	5.2	4.0	2.9	3.3	4.2	5.0	2.3	–0.5	–1.7	2.1
Japan	12.4	11.0	4.5	4.6	3.8	2.6	4.1	6.2	4.7	5.2	4.4	4.5
European Community†	4.9	4.6	2.9	3.2	1.4	2.8	2.7	4.1	3.4	2.9	1.5	2.9
France	5.9	5.4	3.5	3.1	1.5	2.5	2.3	4.5	4.1	2.2	1.2	2.8
Germany‡	4.7	4.2	2.2	3.3	1.1	2.2	1.3	3.6	3.3	4.8	3.7	3.1
Italy	4.8	6.6	2.8	4.8	1.4	2.9	3.1	4.1	2.9	2.2	1.4	2.8
United Kingdom	3.2	2.5	2.1	1.9	2.0	4.1	4.8	4.4	2.1	0.5	–2.2	2.3
Former USSR	4.8	5.0	3.0	1.8	1.7	4.1	1.3	2.1	1.5	–3.7	–13.0	–1.5
China	–.2	8.3	5.5	6.2	10.0	7.7	10.2	11.3	3.6	4.8	NA	NA

*OECD (Organization for Economic Cooperation and Development) includes Australia, Austria, Belgium, Denmark, Finland, France, Germany, Greece, Iceland, Ireland, Italy, Luxembourg, Netherlands, New Zealand, Norway, Portugal, Spain, Sweden, Switzerland, Turkey, and United Kingdom, not shown separately.

†Includes Belgium, Denmark, Greece, Ireland, Luxembourg, Netherlands, Portugal, and Spain, not shown separately.

‡Formerly West Germany

NA = not available

Source: *Economic Report of the President, 1991,* Table B-110, and *Economic Report of the President, 1993,* Table B-108.

The relative importance of these causes of growth varied considerably over the years. Between 1929 and 1948, for example, physical capital played a much smaller role than it did in other periods. But each of the separate periods included times that were, for one reason or another, atypical. The period between 1929 and 1948 included the dislocations and uncertainties of the Great Depression and World War II. From 1948 to 1973, the economy enjoyed a period of unusual stability and expansion.

TABLE 35.9
Sources of Growth in the United States, 1929–1982

	PERCENT OF GROWTH ATTRIBUTABLE TO EACH SOURCE			
	1929–1982	1929–1948	1948–1973	1973–1979
Increases in inputs	53	49	45	94
Labor	20	26	14	47
Capital	14	3	16	29
Education (human capital)	19	20	15	18
Increases in productivity	47	51	55	6
Advances in knowledge	31	30	39	8
Other factors*	16	21	16	-2
Total	100	100	100	100
Annual growth rate in actual real national income	2.8	2.4	3.6	2.6

*Note: Economies of scale, weather, pollution abatement, worker safety and health, crime, labor disputes, and so forth.
Source: Edward Denison, *Trends in American Economic Growth, 1929–1982* (Washington: Brookings Institution, 1985).

The Productivity "Problem": 1973–1992

The years since 1973 have deserved much of the special attention they have received. During the early years of the Reagan administration, the "productivity problem" was much discussed. Some economics textbooks published in the early 1980s had entire chapters discussing the decline in productivity that seemed to be taking place during the late 1970s. In January of 1981, the Congressional Budget Office published a report entitled "The Productivity Problem: Alternatives for Action."

What exactly was this productivity problem? While the overall growth rate in the United States remained at 2.5% between 1973 and 1979—not far off the long-run average for the United States—*measured output per employed worker* dropped precipitously in the same period. Figure 35.2 chronicles the decline from a growth rate of 2.9% in the 1960—1965 period to 1.0% or less in each of the next three five-year periods. Since 1980, the productivity growth rate has been around 1.5 percent.

Many explanations were offered for the productivity decline of the late 1970s. Some economists pointed to the low rate of saving in the United States compared to other parts of the world. Others blamed increased environmental and government regulation of U.S. businesses. Still others argued that the country was not spending as much on research and development as it should have been. Finally, some suggested, high energy costs in the 1970s led to investment designed to save energy rather than to enhance productivity. (We discuss exactly how each of these factors influence growth later in this chapter.)

Many of these factors seem to have turned around during the 1980s. Private investment in plant and equipment increased from a long-run level of under 8% of GDP to nearly 10 percent during the decade. Energy prices fell dramatically. The Reagan administration reduced the amount of government regulation substantially. R&D spending rose to its highest percentage of GDP since 1970. Figure 35.2 shows that from 1980 to 1985 productivity growth resumed but then dropped again during the second half of the decade.

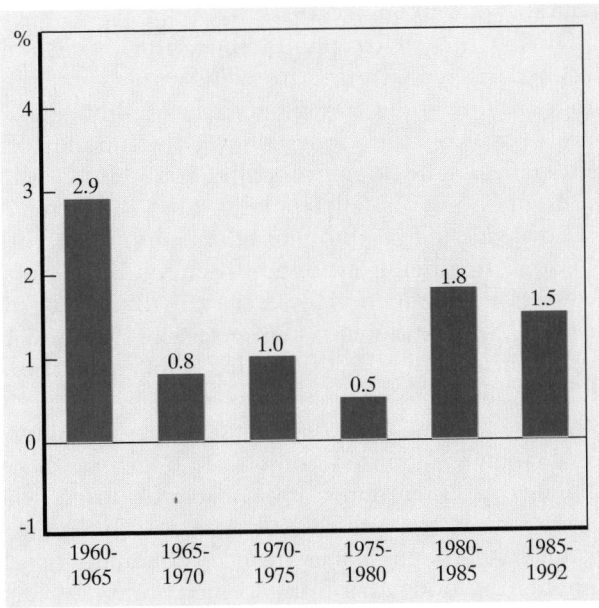

FIGURE 35.2
Labor Productivity Growth Rates in the United States, 1960–1992

Source: *Economic Report of the President, 1993,* Table B-11.

Between the recession of 1990–1991 and 1993, productivity rose sharply. GDP grew for eight consecutive quarters beginning in the spring of 1991, but total employment hardly grew at all during that time. Many economists believe that U.S. firms became "lean and mean," keeping payrolls down and pushing productivity up, during this period. Over the next few years it will be interesting to see whether this trend continues. It certainly seems, however, that productivity is not now the problem it appeared to be at the beginning of the 1980s.

ECONOMIC GROWTH AND PUBLIC POLICY

The decline in productivity that caused so much concern during the late 1970s and early 1980s led to a protracted national discussion about the role of government in stimulating economic growth. This debate was spurred in part by increasing concern in the United States regarding Japanese competition. The enormous success of the Japanese in world markets and their extraordinary postwar annual rates of growth have led more and more people to look to the Far East for economic instruction.

It is clear that the Japanese government plays a more active role in managing the economic affairs of Japan than the U.S. government does in the United States. The Japanese Ministry of Trade and Industry (MITI), for example, plays a significant role in allocating capital across sectors. The national rate of saving is twice as high in Japan as it is in the United States, and investment is a much higher fraction of GDP in Japan than it is in the United States.

Several strategies for increasing the rate of growth in the United States have been suggested, and some have even been enacted into law. These strategies include policies aimed toward improving the quality of education, increasing the saving rate, increasing research and development, and reducing regulation as well as pursuing an industrial policy.

POLICIES TO IMPROVE THE QUALITY OF EDUCATION The Denison study, discussed earlier, shows that the contribution of education and training (human capital production) to growth in the United States has remained relatively constant at about 20% since 1929.

During the 1970s, public education came under siege. Teachers' salaries declined sharply in real terms, while property tax limitations and cuts in federal programs forced the curtailment of school budgets. In the last few years, battles have been waged in Congress over the amount of federal dollars set aside for scholarships and loans to college students. Whatever the policies of the moment, however, all federal, state, and local expenditures on education acknowledge the need to build the nation's stock of human capital.

Soon after being elected, President Bush pronounced himself to be the "education president." However, very little happened to change the character of the U.S. educational system between 1988 and 1992. In fact, state and local budget crises in the 1990s have left public education in dire financial straits.

POLICIES TO INCREASE THE SAVING RATE The amount of capital accumulation in an economy is ultimately constrained by its rate of saving. The more saving in an economy, the more funds are available for investment. Many people have argued that the tax system and the social security system in the United States are biased against saving. Some public finance economists favor shifting to a system of consumption taxation rather than income taxation to reduce the tax burden on saving.

Others claim that the social security system, by providing guaranteed retirement incomes, reduces the incentive for people to save. Private pension plans make deposits to workers' accounts, the balances of which are invested in the stock market and bond market and are made available to firms for capital investment. Social security benefits, on the other hand, are paid out of current tax receipts, and no such accumulations are available for investment. Thus, the argument goes, if social security substitutes for private saving, the national saving rate is reduced. Evidence on the extent to which taxes and social security reduce the saving rate has not been clear to date.

POLICIES TO INCREASE RESEARCH AND DEVELOPMENT As Table 35.9 shows, increases in knowledge accounted for 31% of total growth in the United States between 1929 and 1982. Although not shown in the table, during the years of high R&D expenditures, 1953 to 1973, the figure reached 40 percent. Research also shows that the rate of return on investment in R&D is quite high. Estimates place the rate of return at around 30 percent.[2]

It can be argued that new knowledge is like a public good. While the United States has a patent system to protect the gains of R&D for inventors and innovators, many of the benefits flow to imitators and others, including the public. This logic has been used to justify public subsidization of R&D spending.

REDUCED REGULATIONS One of the cornerstones of the Reagan and Bush administrations was a commitment to reducing government regulation, which, many believe, stands in the way of U.S. industry.

For this reason, the position of the last two Republican presidential administrations has been antiregulation, with an emphasis on reducing government controls. Critics of these policies argue that many of the regulations on the books serve perfectly legitimate economic purposes. For example, environmental regulations, if properly administered, improve efficiency. Judicious use of antitrust laws can also improve the allocation of resources and stimulate investment and production.

Denison estimated that regulation of occupational health and safety, and of the environment, reduced the annual growth rate between 1973 and 1979 by 0.13%, from 2.74% to 2.61% per year. The question is: Has the value of the improved environment and increased safety been worth it?

INDUSTRIAL POLICY In the last few years, a number of economists have called for increased government involvement in the allocation of capital across manufacturing sectors, a practice known as **industrial policy.** Those who favor industrial policy argue that because governments of other countries are "targeting" industries for special subsidies and rapid investment, the United States should follow suit to avoid losing out in international competition. The Japanese Ministry of Trade and Industry, for example, picked the automobile industry very early on and decided to expand its role in world markets. The strategy succeeded very well—at the expense of the U.S. auto industry.

Critics of industrial policy argue that having the government involved in the allocation of capital would be disastrous. Investment always involves risk, they believe, and the best people to judge the extent and appropriateness of that risk are those making the investments and those actually involved in the industry.

industrial policy Government involvement in the allocation of capital across manufacturing sectors.

---

[2]See M. Nadiri, "Contributions and Determinants of Research and Development Expenditures in the U.S. Manufacturing Industries," in George M. von Furstenberg, ed., *Capital Efficiency and Growth* (Cambridge, Mass.: Ballinger Press, 1980).

GROWTH POLICY—A LONG-RUN PROPOSITION When President Ford and Congress passed the dramatic tax cuts of 1975 in an effort to stimulate the economy and end the deep recession, the results were observable within a few months. Fiscal and monetary policies designed to counteract the cyclical up-and-down swings in the economy can produce measurable results in a short period of time.

However, the effects of policies designed to increase the rate of growth may not have observable effects for many years—they are by definition designed to mold the long-run growth path of the economy. For example, a policy that succeeded in raising the rate of growth by one percentage point, say from 2.5% to 3.5%, would be viewed by all as a tremendous success. Yet it would be almost a decade before such a policy would raise GDP by 10 percent.

The fact that pro-growth policies can be costly in the short run and do not produce measurable results for a long time often pushes them far down on politicians' lists of priorities. Some economists who opposed the Tax Reform Act of 1986, for example, argued that the elements of the tax code that had been favorable to capital investment and growth were cut for precisely these reasons. Defenders of the Tax Reform Act claim that it is indeed possible to oversubsidize investment and that the pre-1986 tax code had been doing just that.

But whether pro-growth policies work or not in the long run, are they worth pursuing? Not everyone agrees that the top priority in a developed economy should be continued growth. To close the chapter, we now turn to this debate.

THE PROS AND CONS OF GROWTH

As we said at the beginning of this chapter, there are those who believe that growth should be the primary objective of any society and those who believe that the costs of growth are too great. It is worth reviewing the arguments on both sides.

The Pro-Growth Argument

Advocates of growth argue that growth *is* progress. Resources in a market economy are used to produce what people want; if you produce something that people do not want, you are out of business. Even in a centrally planned economy, resources are targeted to fulfill needs and wants. If a society is able to produce those things more efficiently and at less cost, how can that be bad?

By applying new technologies and better production methods, resources are freed to produce new and better products. Certainly, for Colleen and Bill, accumulation of capital—a house, a water system, and so forth—and advancing knowledge were necessary to improve life on a formerly uninhabited island. In a modern industrial society, as well, capital accumulation and new technology improve the quality of life.

One way to think about the benefits of growth is to compare two periods of time, say 1950 and 1990. In 1990, real GDP per capita was more than twice what it was in 1950. This means that incomes have grown twice as fast as prices so that we can buy that much more. (As we pursue this comparison, remember that no one is telling anyone what to buy, and most people can spend much more now than they could then.)

While it is true that the things available in both time periods are not exactly the same, growth has given us *more* choice, not less. Consider transportation. In the 1950s, the interstate highway system (social capital) had not been built. Driving from Chicago to New York took several days. We had automobiles, but the highway system did not compare to what we have today. And even more significant advances have been made in air travel. Flying between the two cities was possible, but more costly, less comfortable, and slower in 1950 than it is today. In 1994, it is cheaper to get from New York to Chicago than it was in the 1950s, and it takes a fraction of the time.

Do these changes improve the quality of life? Yes, because they give us more freedom. We can travel more frequently. I can see my mother more often. I spend less time getting where I want to go so I can spend more time there. People are able to get to more places for less money.

What about consumer durables—dishwashers, microwave ovens, compact disc players, power lawn mowers, and so forth? Do they really enhance the quality of life? If they do not, why do we buy them? Few such things were around in the 1950s. In 1950, about 3% of all homes had dishwashers; today the figure is close to 50 percent. In 1950, less than 2% of all homes had air conditioners; today the figure is over 60 percent.

What makes a dishwasher worthwhile? It saves the most valuable commodity of all: *time*. Many consumer durables have no intrinsic value—that is, they don't provide satisfaction directly. They do free us from tasks and chores that are not fun, however—no one really likes to wash clothes or dishes, for example. If a product allows us to perform these tasks more easily and quickly, it gives us more time for other things.

And think of the improvement in the *quality* of those things that do yield satisfaction directly. Record players in the 1950s reproduced sound very imperfectly; high fidelity was just being developed, and stereo was in the future. Today you can get a compact disc player for your car. Small "boxes" available at discount stores for under $30 reproduce sound far better than the best machines available in the early 1950s. And the range of tapes and compact discs available is extraordinary.

Growth also makes it possible to improve conditions for the less fortunate in society. The basic logic is simple: When there is more to go around, the sacrifice required to help the needy is smaller. With higher incomes, we can better afford the sacrifices needed to help the poor. Growth also produces jobs. When population growth is not accompanied by growth in output, unemployment and poverty increase.

It is easy for those in advanced societies to be complacent about growth, or even critical of it, but leaders of developing countries understand its benefits well. When 75% of a country's population is poor, redistributing existing incomes does not do much. The only hope for improvement in the long run is economic growth.

The Anti-Growth Argument

Those who argue against economic growth generally make four major points:

1. Any measure of output measures only the value of those things that are exchanged in the market. Many things that affect the quality of life are not traded in the market, and those things generally lose value when growth occurs.

2. For growth to occur, industry must cause consumers to develop new tastes and preferences. Therefore, we have no real need for many of the things we now consume. Wants are created in order to be satisfied, and consumers have become the servants, rather than the masters, of the economy.

3. The world has a finite quantity of resources, and rapid growth is consuming them at a rate that cannot continue. Because the available resources impose limits to growth, we should begin now to plan for the future, when growth will be impossible.

4. Growth requires that income be distributed unfairly.

Each of these points deserves some elaboration.

GROWTH HAS NEGATIVE EFFECTS ON THE QUALITY OF LIFE Perhaps the most dramatic "unmeasurable" changes that affect the quality of life occur in the early stages of growth when societies become industrialized. It is true that more is produced: Agricultural productivity is higher, more manufactured goods are available, and so forth. But most people are crowded into cities, and their lives change drastically.

Before industrialization, most people in the Western World lived in small towns in the country. Most were poor, and they worked long hours to produce enough food to survive. After industrialization and urbanization in eighteenth-century England, men, women, and children worked long hours at routine jobs in hot, crowded factories. They were paid low wages and had very little control over their lives.

Even today, growth continues to change the quality of life in ways that are observable but that are not taken into account when we calculate growth rates. U.S. agriculture, for example, is becoming more and more productive every year. As productivity goes up, food prices drop, and fewer and fewer resources are needed in the agricultural sector. States such as those in New England that once had thriving farms have found their climates and soils simply not good enough to compete any more. In 1959, 56,000 farms covered 9.3 million acres in the six New England states; in 1987, 25,000 farms covered 4.2 million acres. The agricultural sector had been cut in half.

During the early 1970s, small family farmers all over the United States found that making a living was becoming nearly impossible. The villain? Growth and progress. The cost? The decline of a lifestyle that many people want to maintain and that many others think of as an important part of America.

There are other consequences of growth that are not counted in the growth calculation. Perhaps the most significant is environmental damage. As the industrial engine is fed, waste is produced. Often both the feeding and the waste cause massive environmental damage. A dramatic example is the surface, or strip, mining of coal that has ravaged many parts of the United States. Another is the uncontrolled harvesting of U.S. forests. Modern growth requires paper and wood products, and large areas of timber in many states have been cleared and never replanted.

The disposal of industrial wastes has not begun to keep pace with industrial growth. It is now clear that growing and prosperous chemical companies have for decades been dumping hazardous, often carcinogenic, waste products into the nation's soil and water. It is costing billions to clean them up. Those costs were never taken into account when the market was allocating resources to the growing chemical industry.

Growth-related problems are by no means confined to the United States. Japan, for example, paid little attention to the environment during the early years of its rapid economic growth. Many of the results were disastrous. The best known of these results were the horrifying birth defects following the dumping of industrial mercury into the waters of Minamata Bay. In addition to birth defects, thousands of cases of "Minamata disease" in adults have been documented, and hundreds have died.

GROWTH ENCOURAGES THE CREATION OF ARTIFICIAL NEEDS The nature of preferences has been debated within the economics profession for many years. The orthodox view, which lies at the heart of modern welfare economics, is that preferences exist among consumers and that the economy's purpose is to serve those needs. According to the notion of *consumer sovereignty,* people are free to choose, and things that people do not want will not sell. Thus, the consumer rules.

The opposite view is that preferences are formed within the economic system. In order to continue growing, firms must face a continuously expanding set of demands. To ensure that demand grows, firms create it by managing our minds and manipulating our behavior with elaborate advertising, fancy packaging, and other marketing techniques that persuade us to buy things for which we have no intrinsic need.

An extreme extension of this argument against growth challenges the fundamental principle of insatiable wants. If we were not continuously being told that we need things, this theory goes, we would do perfectly well without most of them. Big industry, in its pursuit of growth, has transformed us into mere "consumer units" whose principal function is to demand products. We have become the slaves, not the masters, of the economic system.

GROWTH MEANS THE RAPID DEPLETION OF A FINITE QUANTITY OF RESOURCES
In 1972, the Club of Rome, a group of "concerned citizens," contracted with a group at MIT to do a study entitled *The Limits to Growth*.[3] The book-length final report presented the results of computer simulations that assumed present growth rates of population, food, industrial output, and resource exhaustion. According to these data, sometime after the year 2000 the limits will be reached, and the entire world economy will come crashing down:

> Collapse occurs because of nonrenewable resource depletion. The industrial capital stock grows to a level that requires an enormous input of resources. In the very process of that growth, it depletes a large fraction of the resource reserves available. As resource prices rise and mines are depleted, more and more capital must be used for obtaining resources, leaving less to be invested for future growth. Finally, investment cannot keep up with depreciation and the industrial base collapses, taking with it the service and agricultural systems, which have become dependent on industrial inputs (such as fertilizers, pesticides, hospital laboratories, computers, and especially energy for mechanization. . . . Population finally decreases when the death rate is driven upward by the lack of food and health services.[4]

This argument is similar to one offered almost 200 years ago by Thomas Malthus, whom we mentioned earlier in this chapter. To Malthus, the limiting constraint was land and the capacity to produce food. What he left out, or at least failed to predict, however, was the tremendous rate of increase in productivity that resulted primarily from technological change. Many critics of the more modern "doomsday" models claim that they too leave out the ability of technology to counteract impending resource constraints.

In the early 1970s, many thought that the predictions of the Club of Rome had come true. It seemed as if the world were starting to run up against the limits of world energy supplies; the prices of energy products shot up, and there were serious shortages. But dramatic changes have occurred in the years since. New reserves have been found, new sources of energy have been discovered and developed, conservation measures have been tremendously successful (automobile gas mileage has been pushed up to levels that were inconceivable 15 years ago), and what was a worldwide shortage has turned into a glut. Energy prices have fallen to levels that in real terms are actually below those of the 1960s.

A variation of the depletion-of-resources argument stops short of predicting doomsday. It does point out, however, that unchecked growth in the developed world may have very undesirable distributional consequences. To fuel our growth, we are buying vast quantities of minerals and other resources from the developing countries, who have become dependent on the proceeds of those sales to buy food and other commodities on world markets. If this process continues, by the time these countries have grown to the point that they need mineral resources, their resources may be gone.

---

[3]Dennis L. Meadows, et al., *The Limits to Growth* (Washington: Potomac Associates, 1972).

[4]Meadows, *Limits*, pp. 131–132.

GROWTH REQUIRES AN UNFAIR INCOME DISTRIBUTION AND PROPAGATES IT One of the principal causes of growth is capital accumulation. Capital investment requires saving, and saving comes mostly from the rich. Certainly the rich save more than the poor, and in the developing countries most people are poor and need to use whatever income they have for survival.

Critics also claim that the real beneficiaries of growth are the rich. Choices open to the "haves" in society are greatly enhanced, but the choices open to the "have-nots" remain severely limited. If the benefits of growth trickle down to the poor, why are there more homeless today than there were 20 years ago?

SUMMARY: NO RIGHT ANSWER We have presented the arguments for and against economic growth in overly simple and categorical terms. In reality, even those who take extreme positions in this debate acknowledge that there is no "right answer." To suggest that all economic growth is bad is wrong; to suggest that economic growth should run unchecked is equally wrong. The real question for society is: How can we derive the benefits of growth and at the same time minimize its undesirable consequences?

Society must make some hard choices, and there are many trade-offs. For example, we can grow faster if we pay less attention to environmental concerns. But how much environmental damage should we accept to get how much economic growth? Many argue that we can achieve an acceptable level of economic growth *and* protect the environment at the same time. There is also a trade-off between growth and the distribution of income. More financial inequality would probably lead to more saving and ultimately to more capital and faster growth. On the other hand, using taxes and income transfers to redistribute some of the benefits of growth to the poor probably does slow the rate of growth. But it is not a question of all or nothing; society must decide how much inequality is desirable.

As long as these trade-offs exist, people will disagree. The debate in contemporary politics is largely about the costs and benefits of shifting more effort toward the goal of economic growth and away from environmental and social welfare goals.

SUMMARY

1. *Modern economic growth* is the period of rapid and sustained increase in real output per capita that began in the Western World with the Industrial Revolution.

The Growth Process: From Agriculture to Industry

2. All societies face limits imposed by the resources and technologies available to them. Economic growth expands these limits and shifts society's production possibilities frontier up and to the right.

The Sources of Economic Growth

3. If growth in output outpaces growth in population, and if the economic system is producing what people want, growth will increase the standard of living. Growth occurs either when (1) society acquires more resources, or (2) society discovers ways of using available resources more efficiently.

4. An *aggregate production function* embodies the technological relationship between inputs—the labor force and the stock of capital—and total national output.

5. A number of factors contribute to *economic growth*: (1) an increase in the supply of labor; (2) an increase in physical capital—plant and equipment; (3) an increase in human capital—education, training, and health; (4) technological change; (5) other advances in knowledge—managerial skills and so forth; and (6) economies of scale.

Growth and Productivity in the U.S. Economy

6. Modern economic growth in the United States dates to the middle of the nineteenth century. For the last 100 years, the nation's growth in real output has averaged about 3.0% per year. Between 1929 and 1982, about half of U.S. growth in output came from increases in factors of production and the other half from increases in productivity.

7. There was much concern during the late 1970s that the rate of growth in the United States was slowing. Between 1965 and 1980, measured labor productivity grew on average 1.0% or less per year. Since 1980 the growth rate has been around 1.5 percent.

Economic Growth and Public Policy

8. A number of public policies have been pursued with the aim of improving the growth of real output. These policies include efforts to improve the quality of education, to encourage saving, to stimulate research and development, and to reduce regulation. Some economists also argue for increased government involvement in the allocation of capital across manufacturing sectors, a practice known as *industrial policy*.

The Pros and Cons of Growth

9. Advocates of growth argue that growth is progress. Growth gives us more freedom—that is, more choices. It saves time, improves the standard of living, and is the only way to improve conditions for the poor. Growth creates jobs and increases income simply because there is more to go around.

10. Those who argue against growth generally make four major points. First, many things that affect the quality of life are not traded in the market, and these things generally lose value when there is growth. Second, to have growth, industry must cause consumers to develop new tastes and preferences for many things that they have no real need for. Third, the world has a finite quantity of resources, and rapid growth is eating them up at a rate that cannot continue. Fourth, growth requires that income be distributed inequitably.

REVIEW TERMS AND CONCEPTS

PROBLEM SET

1. Tables 1, 2, and 3 present some data on three hypothetical economies. Complete the tables by figuring the measured productivity of labor and the rate of output growth. What do the data tell you about the causes of economic growth? (*Hint:* How fast are L and K growing?)

2. In earlier chapters, you learned that aggregate expenditure ($C + I + G$) must be equal to aggregate output for the economy to be in equilibrium. You also saw that when consumption spending rises, $C + I + G$ increases, inventories fall, and aggregate output rises. Thus, policies that simultaneously increase consumer spending and reduce saving would lead to a higher level of GDP. In this chapter, we have argued that a higher saving rate, even with lower consumption spending, is the key to long-run GDP growth. How can both of these arguments be correct?

3. Suppose that you have just been elected to Congress and that you find yourself on the Ways and Means Committee—

TABLE 1

PERIOD	L	K	Y	Y/L	GROWTH RATE OF OUTPUT
1	1052	3065	4506		
2	1105	3095	4674		
3	1160	3126	4842		
4	1218	3157	5019		

TABLE 2

PERIOD	L	K	Y	Y/L	GROWTH RATE OF OUTPUT
1	1052	3065	4506		
2	1062	3371	4683		
3	1073	3709	4866		
4	1084	4079	5055		

TABLE 3

PERIOD	L	K	Y	Y/L	GROWTH RATE OF OUTPUT
1	1052	3065	4506		
2	1062	3095	4731		
3	1073	3126	4967		
4	1084	3157	5216		

the committee in the House that decides on tax matters. Suppose further that the committee is debating a bill that would make major changes in tax policy. First, the corporate tax would be lowered substantially in an effort to stimulate investment. The bill contains a 15% investment tax credit—firms would be able to reduce their taxes by 15% of the value of investment projects that they undertake. To keep revenues constant, the bill would impose a national sales tax that would raise the price of consumer goods and reduce consumption. What trade-offs do you see involved in this bill? What are the pros and cons? How would you vote?

4. The optimal level of pollution is never zero. From an economist's point of view, explain why this statement is true.

5. Economists generally agree that high budget deficits today will reduce the growth rate of the economy in the future. Why is this the case? Do the reasons for the high budget deficit matter? In other words, does it matter whether the deficit is caused by lower taxes, increased defense spending, job-training programs, etc.?

6. Why can growth lead to a more unequal distribution of income? Assuming this is true, how is it possible for the poor to benefit from economic growth?

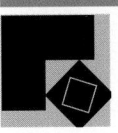

FROM BATTLESHIPS TO COMPUTER CHIPS: INDUSTRIAL POLICY IN THE UNITED STATES

■ In 1992, U.S. productivity (as measured by total output per worker) experienced its greatest growth in two decades. This was a welcome change from the 1970s and 80s, a period in which productivity fell below historic norms and the service sector of the economy grew at the expense of manufacturing (see Figure 1). This slowdown in productivity coincided with increased global competition and it wasn't long before policy makers began to look at countries like Japan for the reasons underlying their gains in trade and worker productivity. What they found was a formal network of political and economic support for key industries, a system that has become known as *industrial policy*.

To some extent, the United States has had an informal industrial policy for many years. Initiatives during the Reagan administration, for example, helped to create the most technologically advanced military industry in the world. Not all U.S. industrial policy is this open, however. Tariffs (taxes on imports) and quotas (a limit on the quantity of imports) protect specific industries from competition. Farm subsidies help expand the variety of agricultural products available to consumers and help ensure the economic survival of some small farm owners.

Not all people agree that industrial policy is a good thing, however. During the Reagan and Bush administrations, for example, the notion of an open industrial policy (at least for nonmilitary industries) was philosophically incompatible with the prevailing laissez-faire attitudes. But the issue blossomed into one of the more heated debates in the election of 1992.

During his campaign, President Clinton argued for a more aggressive approach to industrial policy,

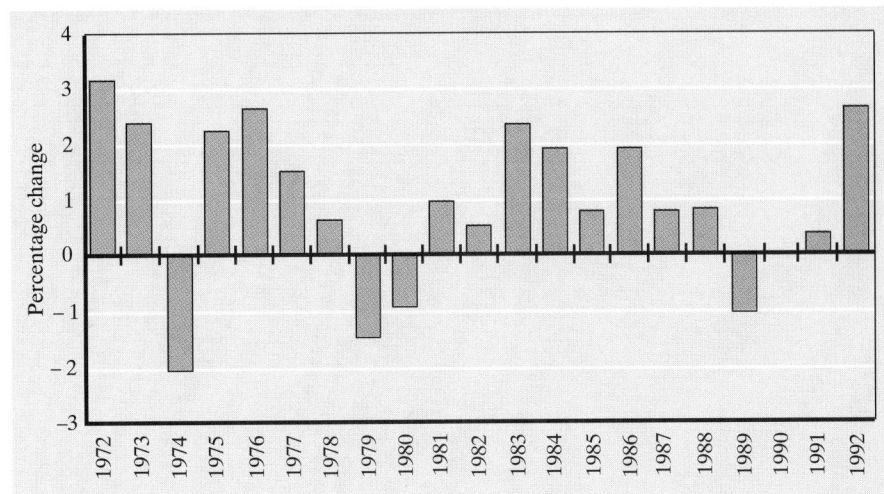

FIGURE 1

U.S. Productivity Growth: Output Per Worker, 1972–1992

Source: *International Financial Statistics*

proposing many high-tech ventures. Among these were a digital "superhighway" of optical-fiber linkages between homes, businesses, and schools; tax incentives for investment in start-up companies; technology transfers from the private to the public sector, most notably in the areas of aerospace and military operations; and a more aggressive application of trade policies to open up foreign markets.

Advocates of President Clinton's plan argued (and continue to argue) that the government must play a role in directing, restructuring, and monitoring the economy if the United States is to remain competitive in global markets. Many favor an industrial policy focus on small businesses, primarily because they believe that small and medium-sized businesses have the greatest potential for innovation and job growth.

There are three general arguments against industrial policy. First, opponents argue that industrial policy restricts trade and can lead only to

market inefficiencies and a misallocation of resources. Second, they say, industrial policy encourages risk-taking behavior at taxpayer expense. Finally, opponents argue, policy makers are simply not capable of deciding which industries will benefit most from targeted programs. For this reason, free-market forces should be allowed to decide which markets are most efficient and able to compete globally.

The debate over industrial policy is a sensitive one with no obvious solutions. The issues are as much political as they are economic. But as we move toward the year 2000, two things are clear: The forces of global competition are likely to become more intense, and those nations that can adapt and respond to the changing landscape are the most likely to succeed.

QUESTIONS FOR ANALYTICAL THINKING

1. Summarize the main arguments for and against industrial policy in a debate between a propo-

nent of supply-side economics and a Keynesian economist.

2. Suppose you were asked to advise your member of Congress on the pros and cons of industrial policy. Are there ways for government to improve the climate for small businesses in key industries without direct subsidies, tariffs, or regulations?

3. List the factors that determine economic growth. How has the relative importance of these factors changed during the past three decades? List the ways that government might influence each of these factors.

INTERNATIONAL
ECONOMICS

PART TEN

The Global Economy

Since Chapter 1, we've emphasized the fact that the U.S. economy does not operate in a vacuum. In the last decade, the role of imports and exports in the U.S. economy and the international mobility of capital have become increasingly important. As newer and faster methods of communication and transportation are developed, the economies of the world's nations become ever more intertwined.

While a large portion of our emphasis until this point has been on economic issues in the United States, the economics you have learned applies to all other countries as well. Like the United States, all countries face limited resources and must answer the three basic economic questions: what to produce, how to produce, and who gets what is produced.

In this part, we examine international economics in more detail. In the chapters that follow, you will see:

- Why countries find it profitable to trade with each other (Chapter 36).

- Both sides of the debate over protecting domestic industries from foreign competition (Chapter 36).

- What determines the level of imports and exports in an economy (Chapter 37).

- The importance of exchange rates in determining the flow of international trade (Chapter 37).

- Some of the problems facing the world's developing nations and some of the strategies these nations have undertaken to foster economic development (Chapter 38).

- How economic factors led to the disintegration of the Soviet Union in 1991, the philosophical and ideological bases of the economic system of China, and the reasons Japan's economy has grown so rapidly in recent years (Chapter 39).

International Trade, Comparative Advantage, and Protectionism

Over the last 25 years, international transactions have become increasingly important to the U.S. economy. As recently as 1970, imports represented only about 7% of U.S. gross domestic product. The figure now stands at around 11 percent. In 1992 alone, the United States imported $666.7 billion worth of goods and services. Chapter 3 presented an overview of the international sector in the United States.

The "internationalization" or "globalization" of the U.S. economy has occurred on all fronts—in the private and public sectors, in input and output markets, and in business firms and households. Once relatively uncommon, foreign products are now everywhere, from the utensils we eat with to the cars we drive. In 1970, for example, foreign-produced cars made up only a small percentage of all the cars in the United States. At that time, it was difficult to find mechanics who knew how to repair foreign cars, and replacement parts were hard to obtain. Today, the roads are full of Toyotas and Nissans from Japan, Volvos from Sweden, and BMWs from Germany, and any service station that cannot repair foreign-produced automobiles probably won't get much business. Half of all the cars and 80% of all the consumer electronics (televisions, CD players, and so forth) that U.S. consumers buy are produced abroad.

At the same time, the United States exports billions of dollars worth of agricultural goods, aircraft, and industrial machinery. Financial capital flows smoothly and swiftly across international boundaries in search of high returns. In 1991, for example, German interest rates rose and U.S. interest rates fell. Almost immediately, billions of investor dollars shifted out of interest-bearing U.S. securities and into German securities.

The inextricable connection of the U.S. economy to the economies of the rest of the world has had a profound impact on the discipline of economics and is the basis of one of its most important insights:

> All economies, regardless of their size, depend to some extent on other economies and are affected by events outside their borders.

As a means of getting you more fully acquainted with the international economy, this chapter discusses the economics of international trade. First, we describe the recent tendency of the United States to import more than it exports. Next, we explore the basic logic of trade. Why should the United States—or any other country, for that matter—engage in international trade? Finally, we address the controversial issue of protectionism. Should we provide certain industries with protection in the form of import quotas, tariffs, or subsidies?

THE INTERNATIONAL ECONOMY: TRADE SURPLUSES AND DEFICITS

Until the 1970s, the United States generally exported more than it imported. When a country exports more than it imports, it runs a **trade surplus.** When a country imports more than it exports, it runs a **trade deficit.** Before 1975, the United States generally ran a trade surplus for goods and services as a whole, as well as for merchandise. Table 36.1 shows the U.S. balance of trade for merchandise and total goods and services for selected years since 1929.

In the mid-1970s, the United States began to import more merchandise than it exported. Merchandise deficits climbed steadily after 1975, reaching over $150 billion in 1987 before dropping back somewhat after that. The overall goods-and-services deficit shows much wider variation, but it is also quite large from 1984 through 1990.

The large trade deficits that characterized the middle and late 1980s touched off serious political controversy. Foreign competition hit U.S. markets hard. Less expensive foreign goods—among them steel, textiles, and automobiles—began driving U.S. manufacturers out of business at an alarming rate, and thousands of jobs were lost in important industries. Cities such as Pittsburgh, Youngstown, and Detroit found themselves with major unemployment problems.

The natural reaction, of course, was to call for protection of U.S. industries. That is, many people wanted the President and Congress to impose taxes and import restrictions that would make foreign goods less available and more expensive, a situation that, in turn, would protect U.S. jobs. As you might guess, this argument was not new to the 1980s. For hundreds of years, industries have petitioned governments for protection, and societies have debated the pros and cons of free and open trade. For the last century and a half, the principal argument used against protection has been the theory of comparative advantage, which we first discussed in Chapter 2.

TABLE 36.1
U.S. Balance of Trade (Exports minus Imports) 1929–1992, (billions of dollars)

	MERCHANDISE	GOODS AND SERVICES
1929	−0.5	+1.1
1933	−0.3	+0.4
1945	+2.2	−0.5
1955	+2.9	+3.0
1960	+4.9	+2.4
1965	+5.0	+3.9
1970	+2.6	+1.2
1975	+8.9	+13.6
1976	−9.5	−2.3
1977	−31.1	−23.7
1978	−33.9	−26.1
1979	−27.6	−23.8
1980	−25.5	−14.7
1981	−28.0	−14.7
1982	−36.5	−20.6
1983	−67.1	−51.4
1984	−112.5	−102.7
1985	−122.2	−115.6
1986	−145.1	−132.5
1987	−159.6	−143.1
1988	−127.0	−108.0
1989	−115.7	−79.7
1990	−108.9	−68.9
1991	−73.4	−21.8
1992	−100.0	−30.4

Source: *Historical Statistics of the United States; Statistical Abstract of the United States; and Economic Report of the President,* February 1993. Updated figures used for 1992.

trade surplus, trade deficit *Trade surplus:* The situation when a country exports more than it imports. *Trade deficit:* The situation when a country imports more than it exports.

THE ECONOMIC BASIS FOR TRADE: COMPARATIVE ADVANTAGE

Corn Laws The tariffs, subsidies, and restrictions enacted by the British Parliament in the early nineteenth century to discourage imports and encourage exports of grain.

Perhaps the best-known debate on the issue of free trade took place in the British Parliament during the early years of the nineteenth century. At that time, the landed gentry—the landowners—controlled Parliament. For a number of years, imports and exports of grain had been subject to a set of tariffs, subsidies, and restrictions collectively called the **Corn Laws.** Designed to discourage imports of grain and encourage exports, the Corn Laws' purpose was to keep the price of food high. The landlords' incomes, of course, depended on the prices they got for what their land produced. The Corn Laws thus clearly worked to the advantage of those in power.

With the Industrial Revolution, a class of wealthy industrial capitalists began to emerge. The industrial sector had to pay workers at least enough to live on, and a living wage depended to a great extent on the price of food. Tariffs on grain imports and export subsidies that kept grain and food prices high increased the wages that capitalists had to pay, and these high wage payments cut into their profits. The political battle raged for years. But as time went by, the power of the landowners in the House of Lords was significantly reduced. When the conflict ended in 1848, the Corn Laws were repealed.

theory of comparative advantage Ricardo's theory that specialization and free trade will benefit all trading partners (real wages will rise), even those that may be absolutely less efficient producers.

Participating in this battle on the side of repeal was David Ricardo, a businessman, economist, member of Parliament, and one of the fathers of modern economics. Ricardo's principal work, *Principles of Political Economy and Taxation,* was published in 1817, two years before he entered Parliament. Ricardo's **theory of comparative advantage,** which he used to argue against the Corn Laws, claimed that trade enables countries to specialize in producing the products that they produce best. According to the theory:

> Specialization and free trade will benefit all trading partners (real wages will rise), even those that may be absolutely less efficient producers.

This basic argument remains at the heart of free-trade debates even today. It was invoked numerous times by Presidents Reagan and Bush as they wrestled with Congress over various pieces of protectionist legislation.

SPECIALIZATION AND TRADE: THE TWO-PERSON CASE Perhaps the easiest way to understand the theory of comparative advantage is to examine a simple two-person society. Recall Bill and Colleen, who were stranded on a deserted island in Chapter 2. Suppose that they have only two basic tasks to accomplish each week: gathering food to eat and cutting logs that will be used in constructing a house. If Colleen could cut more logs than Bill in a day and Bill could gather more berries and fruits, specialization would clearly benefit both of them.

But suppose that Bill is slow and somewhat clumsy and that Colleen is better at both cutting logs *and* gathering food. Ricardo's point is that it still pays for them to specialize. They can produce more in total by specializing than they can by sharing the work equally. (It may be helpful to review the discussion of comparative advantage in Chapter 2 before proceeding.)

Absolute Advantage versus Comparative Advantage

absolute advantage The advantage in the production of a product enjoyed by one country over another when it uses fewer resources to produce that product than the other country does.

A country is said to enjoy an **absolute advantage** over another country in the production of a product if it uses fewer resources to produce that product than the other country does. For example, suppose that country A and country B produce wheat, but that A's climate is more suited to wheat and its labor is more productive. Country A will therefore produce more wheat per acre than country B and use less labor in growing it and bringing it to market. Country A thus enjoys an absolute advantage over country B in the production of wheat.

A country enjoys a **comparative advantage** in the production of a good if that good can be produced at lower cost *in terms of other goods*. Suppose that countries C and D both produce wheat and corn and that C enjoys an absolute advantage in the production of both—that is, C's climate is better than D's, and fewer of C's resources are needed to produce a given quantity of both wheat and corn. Now C and D must each choose between planting land with wheat or corn. To produce more wheat, either country must transfer land from corn production; to produce more corn, either country must transfer land from wheat production. Thus, the cost of wheat in each country can be measured in bushels of corn, and the cost of corn can be measured in bushels of wheat.

Suppose that in country C, a bushel of wheat has an opportunity cost of two bushels of corn—that is, to produce an additional bushel of wheat, C must give up two bushels of corn. At the same time, suppose that producing a bushel of wheat in country D requires the sacrifice of only one bushel of corn. Even though C has an *absolute* advantage in the production of both products, D enjoys a *comparative* advantage in the production of wheat because the *opportunity cost* of producing wheat is lower in D. Under these circumstances, Ricardo claims, D can benefit from trade if it specializes in the production of wheat.

GAINS FROM MUTUAL ABSOLUTE ADVANTAGE   To illustrate Ricardo's logic in more detail, let's start with a very simple case. Suppose that Australia and New Zealand each have a fixed amount of land and are isolated from the rest of the world. Suppose further that there are only two goods—wheat, used to produce bread, and cotton, used to produce clothing. This kind of two-country/two-good world does not exist, of course, but its operations can be generalized to many countries and many goods.

Before we proceed, we have to make some assumptions about the preferences of the people living in New Zealand and those living in Australia. If the citizens of both countries go around naked, there is no need to produce cotton at all; all the land can be used to produce wheat. For the sake of simplicity, however, let us assume that people in both countries have similar preferences with respect to food and clothing: The populations of both countries use both cotton and wheat. We will also assume that preferences for food and clothing are such that both countries consume equal amounts of wheat and cotton.

Finally, we shall assume that each country has only 100 acres of land for planting and that land yields are those given in Table 36.2. Notice that New Zealand can produce three times the wheat that Australia can on one acre of land, and that Australia can produce three times the cotton that New Zealand can in the same space. New Zealand thus has an absolute advantage in the production of wheat, and Australia has an absolute advantage in the production of cotton. In cases like this, we say that the two countries have *mutual absolute advantage*.

If there is no trade and each country divides its land to obtain equal units of cotton and wheat production, each country produces 150 bushels of wheat and 150 bales of cotton. New Zealand puts 75 acres into cotton but only 25 acres into wheat, while Australia does the reverse. (See Table 36.3 on the next page.)

comparative advantage The advantage in the production of a product enjoyed by one country over another when that product can be produced at lower cost in terms of other goods than it could be in the other country.

	NEW ZEALAND	AUSTRALIA
Wheat	6 bushels	2 bushels
Cotton	2 bales	6 bales

TABLE 36.2
Yield per Acre of Wheat and Cotton

	NEW ZEALAND	AUSTRALIA
Wheat	25 acres × 6 bu/acre 150 bushels	75 acres × 2 bu/acre 150 bushels
Cotton	75 acres × 2 bales/acre 150 bales	25 acres × 6 bales/acre 150 bales

We can organize the same information in a somewhat different way if we construct separate production possibilities frontiers for each country. In Figure 36.1, which presents the positions of the two countries before trade, each country is constrained by its own resources and productivity. If Australia put all its land into cotton, it would produce 600 bales of cotton (100 acres × 6 bales/acre) and no wheat; if it put all its land into wheat, it would produce 200 bushels of wheat (100 acres × 2 bu/acre) and no cotton. The opposite is true for New Zealand. As you recall from Chapter 2, a country's production possibilities frontier represents all combinations of goods that can be produced, given the country's resources and state of technology. Each country must pick a point along its own production possibilities curve.

Because both countries have an absolute advantage in the production of one product, it is reasonable to expect that specialization and trade will benefit both countries. Clearly, Australia should produce cotton and New Zealand should produce wheat. Transferring all land to wheat production in New Zealand yields a total of 600 bushels; transferring all land to cotton production in Australia yields 600 bales. An agreement to trade 300 bushels of wheat for 300 bales of cotton would double both wheat and cotton consumption in both countries. (Remember, before trade both countries produced 150 bushels of wheat and 150 bales of cotton. After trade, each country will have 300 bushels

FIGURE 36.1
Production Possibility Frontiers for Australia and New Zealand before Trade
Without trade, countries are constrained by their own resources and productivity.

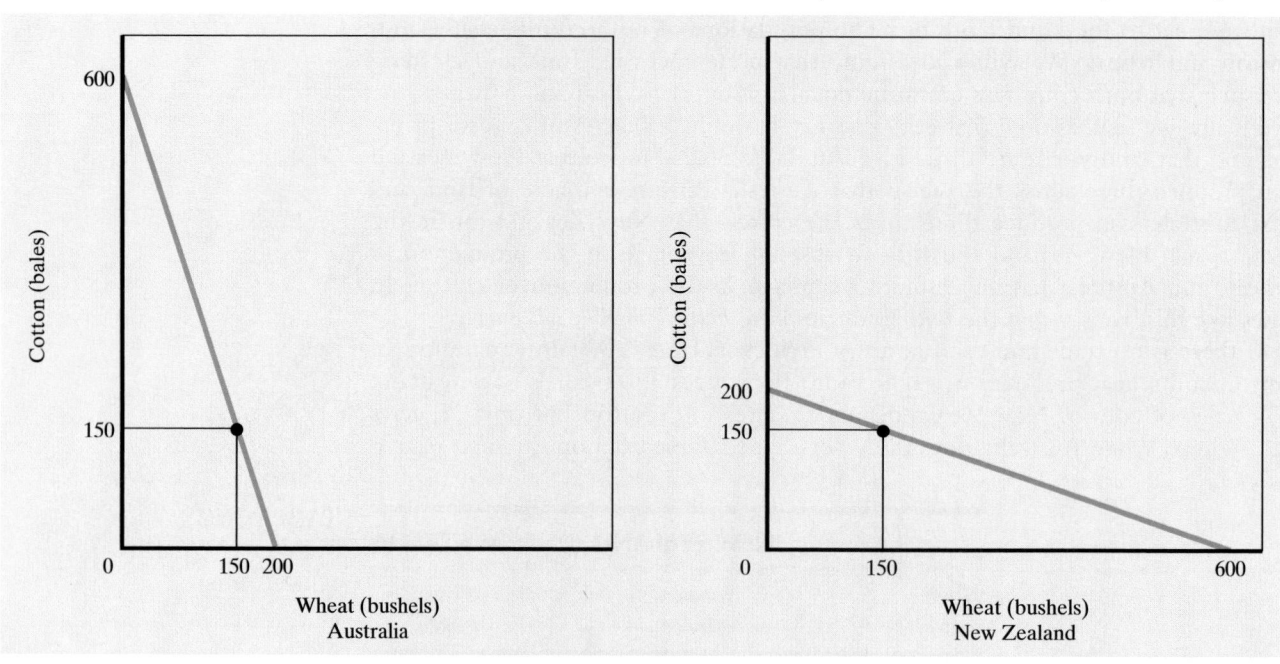

| | PRODUCTION | | | CONSUMPTION | |
	New Zealand	Australia		New Zealand	Australia
Wheat	100 acres × 6 bu/acre 600 bu	0 acres 0	Wheat	300 bu	300 bu
Cotton	0 acres 0	100 acres × 6 bales/acre 600 bales	Cotton	300 bales	300 bales

of wheat and 300 bales of cotton to consume. Final production and trade fig-ures are given in Table 36.4 and Figure 36.2.) Thus,

> Trade enables both countries to move out beyond their previous resource and productivity constraints.

The advantages of specialization and trade seem obvious when one country is technologically superior at producing one product and another country is technolog-ically superior at producing another product. Now, however, let us turn to the case in which one country has an absolute advantage in the production of *both* goods.

GAINS FROM COMPARATIVE ADVANTAGE   Table 36.5 on the next page contains different land yield figures for New Zealand and Australia. In this new case, New Zealand has a considerable absolute advantage in the production of both cotton and wheat, with one acre of land yielding six times as much wheat and twice as much cotton as one acre in Australia. Ricardo would argue that *special-ization and trade are still mutually beneficial.*

Assume again that preferences for food and clothing imply consumption of equal units of cotton and wheat in both countries. With no trade, New Zealand would divide its 100 available acres evenly, or 50/50, between the two crops. The result would be 300 bales of cotton and 300 bushels of wheat. Australia would divide its land

TABLE 36.4
Consumption and Production of Wheat and Cotton After Specialization

FIGURE 36.2
Expanded Possibilities After Trade

Trade enables both countries to move out beyond their own resource constraints—beyond their individual production pos-sibility frontiers.

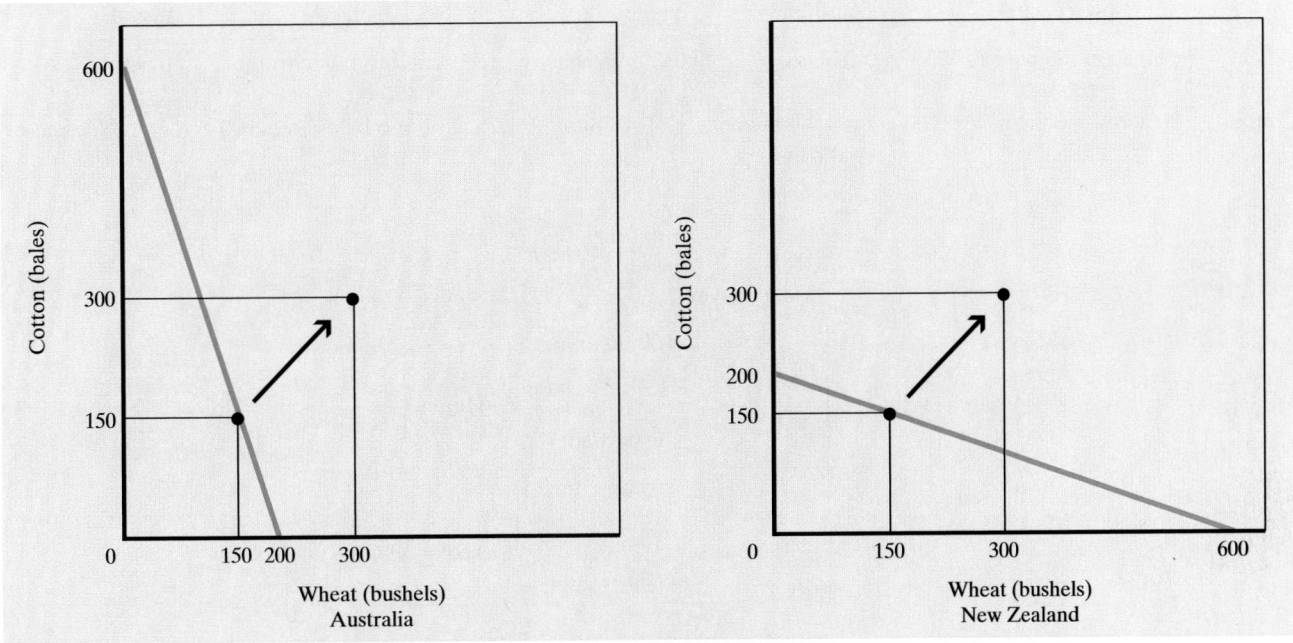

TABLE 36.5
Yield per Acre of Wheat and
Cotton

TABLE 36.5
Yield per Acre of Wheat and
Cotton

	NEW ZEALAND	AUSTRALIA
Wheat	6 bushels	1 bushels
Cotton	6 bales	3 bales

75/25. Table 36.6 shows that final production in Australia would be 75 bales of cotton and 75 bushels of wheat. (Remember, we are assuming that in each country, people consume equal amounts of cotton and wheat.) Once again, before any trade takes place each country is constrained by its own domestic production possibilities curve.

Now imagine that we are at a meeting of trade representatives of both countries. As a special adviser, David Ricardo is asked to demonstrate that trade can benefit both countries. The professor divides his demonstration into three stages, which you can follow in Table 36.7.

In stage 1, Australia transfers all its land into cotton production. When it does, it will have no wheat at all and 300 bales of cotton. New Zealand cannot completely specialize in wheat because it will not be able to get enough cotton from Australia. This is because we are assuming that each country wants to consume equal amounts of cotton and wheat. Thus, in stage 2 New Zealand transfers 25

TABLE 36.6
Total Production of Wheat
and Cotton—Assuming No
Trade

	NEW ZEALAND	AUSTRALIA
Wheat	50 acres × 6 bu/acre 300 bushels	75 acres × 1 bu/acre 75 bushels
Cotton	50 acres × 6 bales/acre 300 bales	25 acres × 3 bales/acre 75 bales

TABLE 36.7
Realizing a Gain from Trade When One Country Has a Double Absolute Advantage

	STAGE 1			STAGE 2	
	New Zealand	Australia		New Zealand	Australia
Wheat	50 acres × 6 bu/acre 300 bu	0 acres 0	Wheat	75 acres × 6 bu/acre 450 bu	0 acres 0
Cotton	50 acres × 6 bales/acre 300 bales	100 acres × 3 bales/acre 300 bales	Cotton	25 acres × 6 bales/acre 150 bales	100 acres × 3 bales/acre 300 bales

STAGE 3

	New Zealand	Australia
Wheat	100 bu (trade) → 350 bu (after trade)	100 bu
Cotton	200 bales (trade) ← 350 bales (after trade)	100 bales

acres out of cotton and into wheat. Now New Zealand has 25 acres in cotton that produce 150 bales and 75 acres in wheat that produce 450 bushels.

Finally, the two countries trade. We assume that New Zealand ships 100 bushels of wheat to Australia in exchange for 200 bales of cotton. After the trade, New Zealand has 350 bales of cotton and 350 bushels of wheat; Australia has 100 bales of cotton and 100 bushels of wheat. Both countries are better off than they were before the trade (review Table 36.6), and both have moved beyond their own production possibilities frontiers.

WHY DOES RICARDO'S PLAN WORK? To understand why Ricardo's scheme works, let us return to the definition of comparative advantage.

The real cost of producing cotton is the wheat that must be sacrificed in order to produce it. *When we think of cost this way, it is less costly to produce cotton in Australia than to produce it in New Zealand, even though an acre of land produces more cotton in New Zealand.* Consider the "cost" of three bales of cotton in the two countries. In terms of opportunity cost, three bales of cotton in New Zealand cost three bushels of wheat; in Australia, however, three bales of cotton cost only one bushel of wheat. Because three bales are produced by one acre of Australian land, to get three bales an Australian must transfer one acre of land from wheat to cotton production. And because an acre of land produces a bushel of wheat, losing one acre to cotton implies the loss of one bushel of wheat. Thus, *Australia has a comparative advantage in cotton production* because its opportunity cost, in terms of wheat, is lower than New Zealand's. This situation is illustrated in Figure 36.3.

Conversely, New Zealand has a comparative advantage in wheat production. A unit of wheat in New Zealand costs one unit of cotton; a unit of wheat in Australia costs three units of cotton.

> When countries specialize in producing those goods in which they have a comparative advantage, they maximize their combined output and allocate their resources more efficiently.

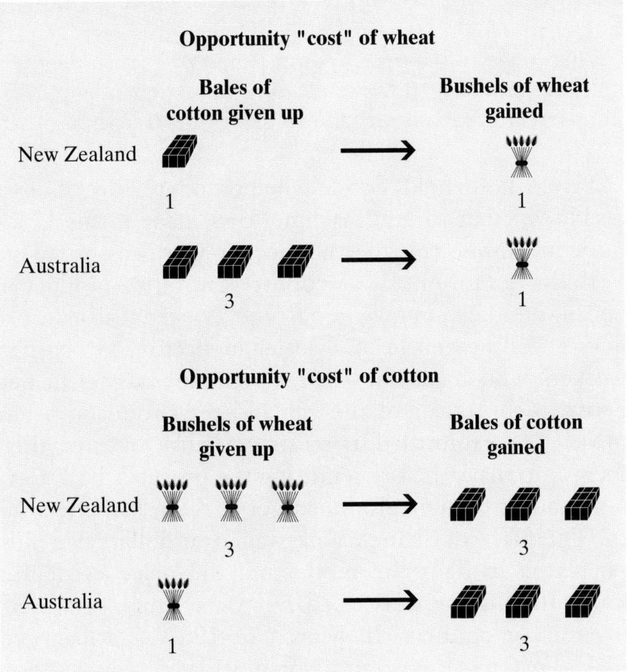

FIGURE 36.3
Comparative Advantage Means Lower Opportunity Cost

The real cost of cotton is the wheat that must be sacrificed to obtain it. The cost of three bales of cotton in New Zealand is three bushels of wheat (one half acre of land must be transferred from wheat to cotton—refer to Table 36.5). But the cost of three bales of cotton in Australia is only one bushel of wheat (one acre of land must be transferred). Thus, Australia has a comparative advantage over New Zealand in the production of cotton.

Terms of Trade

terms of trade The ratio at which a country can trade domestic products for imported products.

Ricardo might suggest a number of options open to the trading partners. The one we just examined benefited both partners; in percentage terms, Australia made out slightly better. Other deals might have been more advantageous to New Zealand.

The ratio at which a country can trade domestic products for imported products is called the **terms of trade.** The terms of the trade determine how the gains from trade are distributed among the trading partners. In the case we just considered, the agreed-upon terms of trade were one bushel of wheat for two bales of cotton. Such terms of trade benefit New Zealand, which can now get two bales of cotton for each bushel of wheat. If it were to transfer its own land from wheat to cotton, it would get only one. The same terms of trade benefit Australia, which can now get one bushel of wheat for two bales of cotton. A direct transfer of its own land would force it to give up three bales of cotton for one bushel of wheat.

If the terms of trade changed to three bales of cotton for every bushel of wheat, only New Zealand would benefit. In fact, at those terms of trade *all* the gains from trade would flow to New Zealand. Such terms do not benefit Australia at all because the opportunity cost of producing wheat domestically is *exactly the same* as the trade cost: One bushel of wheat costs three bales of cotton. If the terms of trade went the other way—one bale of cotton for each bushel of wheat—only Australia would benefit. New Zealand gains nothing, because it can already substitute cotton for wheat at that ratio. To get a bushel of wheat domestically, however, Australia must give up three bales of cotton, and one-for-one terms of trade would make wheat much less costly for Australia.

Clearly, both parties must have something to gain for trade to take place. In this case, you can see that both Australia and New Zealand will gain when the terms of trade are set between 1:1 and 3:1, cotton to wheat.

Exchange Rates

The examples we have used thus far have shown that trade can result in gains to both parties. We have not yet discussed, however, how trade actually comes about.

> When trade is free (that is, unimpeded by government-instituted barriers), patterns of trade and trade flows result from the independent decisions of thousands of importers and exporters and millions of private households and firms.

Private households decide whether to buy Toyotas or Chevrolets, and private firms decide whether to buy machine tools made in the United States or machine tools made in Taiwan, raw steel produced in Germany or raw steel produced in Pittsburgh.

Before a citizen of one country can buy a product made in, or sold by, someone in another country, a currency swap must take place. Consider Shane, who buys a Volkswagen from a dealer in Boston. He pays in dollars, but the German workers who made the car receive their salaries in deutsche marks. Somewhere between the buyer of the car and the producer, a currency exchange must be made. The regional distributor probably takes payment in dollars and converts them into marks before remitting the proceeds back to Germany.

To buy a foreign-produced good, then, I in effect have to buy foreign currency. The price of Shane's Volkswagen in dollars depends on both the price of the car stated in deutsche marks and the price of deutsche marks. You probably know the ins and outs of currency exchange very well if you have ever traveled in another country. In March of 1991, a dollar exchanged for 5.23 French francs, making each franc worth $0.191. Now suppose that you are in France, and you see a nice bottle of Bordeaux wine for 120 francs. How can you figure out whether you want to buy it? You know what dollars will buy you in the United States, so you have to convert the price into dollars. Since each franc will cost you $0.191, 120 francs is worth 120 × 0.191, or $22.92.

The relative attractiveness of foreign goods to U.S. buyers, and of U.S. goods to foreign buyers, depends in part on **exchange rates,** the ratio at which two currencies are traded for each other. If the rate at which dollars could be converted into francs suddenly jumped to 10 francs for every dollar, that same bottle of wine would cost only $12.

Thus, to understand the patterns of trade that result from the actions of thousands of independent buyers and sellers—households and firms—we must know something about the factors that determine exchange rates. Exchange rate determination is very complicated. Here, however, we can demonstrate two things:

exchange rate The ratio at which two currencies are traded for each other. The price of one currency in terms of another.

> First, for any pair of countries, there is a range of exchange rates that can lead automatically to both countries realizing the gains from specialization and comparative advantage. Second, within that range, the exchange rate will determine which country gains the most from trade. In short, exchange rates determine the terms of trade.

TRADE AND EXCHANGE RATES IN A TWO–COUNTRY/TWO–GOOD WORLD Consider first a simple two-country/two-good model. Suppose that both the United States and Germany produce only two goods—rolled steel and raw timber. Table 36.8 gives the current prices of both goods as domestic buyers see them. In Germany timber is priced at three deutsche marks (DM) per foot, and steel is priced at four DM per meter. In the United States, timber costs $1 per foot and steel costs $2 per meter.

Now suppose that U.S. and German buyers have the option of buying at home or importing to meet their needs. The options they ultimately choose will depend on the exchange rate. For the time being, we will ignore transportation costs between countries and assume that German and U.S. products are of equal quality.

Let us start with the assumption that the exchange rate is $1 = 1 DM. From the standpoint of U.S. buyers, neither German steel nor German timber is competitive at this exchange rate. A dollar buys a foot of timber in the United States, but if converted into a mark, it will buy only one third of a foot. The price of German timber to an American is $3 because it will take $3 to buy the necessary three DM. Similarly, $2 buys a meter of rolled steel in the United States, but the same $2 buys only half a meter of German steel. The price of German steel to an American is $4, twice the price of domestically produced steel.

At this exchange rate, however, Germans find that U.S.-produced steel and timber are both less expensive than steel and timber produced in Germany. Timber at home costs three DM, but three DM buys $3, which buys three times as much timber in the United States. Similarly, steel costs four DM at home, but four DM buys $4, which buys twice as much U.S.-made steel. Thus, at an exchange rate of $1 = 1 DM, Germany will import steel and timber and the United States will import nothing.

But now suppose that the exchange rate is 1 DM = $0.25. We could thus say that the "price" of a DM is $0.25. This means that a dollar buys four DM. At this exchange rate, the Germans buy timber and steel at home and the Americans import both goods. At this exchange rate, Americans must pay a dollar for a foot of U.S. timber, but the same amount of timber can be had in Germany for the equivalent of $0.75. (Since one DM costs $0.25, three DM can be purchased for $0.75.) Similarly, steel that costs $2 per meter in the United States costs an American half as much in Germany, because $2 buys eight DM, which buys two

TABLE 36.8
Domestic Prices of Timber (per foot) and Rolled Steel (per meter) in the United States and Germany

	UNITED STATES	GERMANY
Timber	$1	3 DM
Rolled steel	$2	4 DM

meters of German steel. At the same time, Germans are not interested in importing, because both goods are cheaper when purchased from a German producer. In this case, the United States imports both goods and Germany imports nothing.

So far, we can see that at exchange rates of $1 = 1 DM and $1 = 4 DM we get trade flowing in only one direction. Let us now try an exchange rate of $1 = 2 DM, or 1 DM = $0.50. First, notice that Germans will buy timber in the United States. German timber costs three DM per foot, but three DM buys $1.50, which is enough to buy one and one half feet of U.S. timber. Buyers in the United States will find German timber too expensive, but Germany will import timber from the United States. At this same exchange rate, however, both German and U.S. buyers will be indifferent between German and U.S. steel. To U.S. buyers, domestically produced steel costs $2. Since $2 buys four DM, a meter of imported German steel also costs $2. German buyers also find that steel costs four DM, whether domestically produced or imported. Thus, there is likely to be no trade in steel.

But what happens if the exchange rate rises so that $1 buys 2.1 DM instead of just two? While U.S. timber is still cheaper to both Germans and Americans, German steel begins to look good to U.S. buyers. Steel produced in the United States costs $2 per meter, but $2 buys 4.2 DM, which buys more than a meter of steel in Germany. Thus, when the exchange rate rises above $1 = 2 DM, trade begins to flow in both directions: Germany will import timber and the United States will import steel.

If you examine Table 36.9 carefully, you will see that in fact trade flows in both directions as long as the exchange rate settles between $1 = 2 DM and $1 = 3 DM. Stated the other way around, trade will flow in both directions if the price of a DM is between $0.33 and $0.50.

EXCHANGE RATES AND COMPARATIVE ADVANTAGE   Let us continue our example. If the foreign exchange market drives the exchange rate to anywhere between two and three DM per dollar, the countries will automatically adjust and comparative advantage will be realized. At these exchange rates, U.S. buyers begin buying all their steel in Germany. The U.S. steel industry finds itself in trouble. Plants close, and U.S. workers begin to lobby for tariff protection against German steel. At the same time, the U.S. timber industry does well, fueled by strong export demand from Germany. Thus, the timber-producing sector expands. Resources, including capital and labor, are attracted into timber production.

The opposite occurs in Germany. The German timber industry suffers losses as export demand dries up and Germans turn to cheaper U.S. imports. In Germany, lumber companies turn to the government and ask for protection from cheap U.S.

TABLE 36.9

Trade Flows Determined by Exchange Rates

EXCHANGE RATE	PRICE OF DM	RESULT
$1 = 1 DM	$ 1.00	Germany imports timber and steel.
$1 = 2 DM	$.50	Germany imports timber.
$1 = 2.1 DM	$.48	Germany imports timber; United States imports steel.
$1 = 2.9 DM	$.34	Germany imports timber; United States imports steel.
$1 = 3 DM	$.33	United States imports steel.
$1 = 4 DM	$.25	United States imports timber and steel.

timber. But steel producers in Germany are happy. Not only are they supplying 100% of the domestically demanded steel, but they are selling to U.S. buyers as well. Thus, the steel industry expands, and the timber industry contracts. Resources, including labor, flow into steel.

With this expansion-and-contraction scenario in mind, let us look again at our original definition of comparative advantage. If we assume that prices reflect resource use and that resources can be transferred from sector to sector, we can calculate the opportunity cost of steel/timber in both countries. In the United States, the production of a meter of rolled steel consumes twice the resources that the production of a foot of timber consumes. Assuming that resources can be transferred, the opportunity cost of a meter of steel is two feet of timber. (Refer again to Table 36.8.) In Germany, however, a meter of steel uses resources costing four DM, while a unit of timber costs three DM. Thus, to produce a meter of steel means the sacrifice of only four thirds, or one and one third, feet of timber. Because the opportunity cost of a meter of steel (in terms of timber) is lower in Germany, we say that Germany has a comparative advantage in steel production.

Conversely, consider the opportunity cost of timber in the two countries. Increasing timber production in the United States requires the sacrifice of half a meter of steel for every foot of timber—producing a meter of steel uses $2 worth of resources, while producing a foot of timber requires only $1 worth of resources. But each foot of timber production in Germany requires the sacrifice of three fourths of a meter of steel. Because the opportunity cost of timber is lower in the United States, the United States has a comparative advantage in the production of timber.

In short:

> If exchange rates end up in the right ranges, the free market will drive each country to shift resources into those sectors in which it enjoys a comparative advantage. Only those products in which a country has a comparative advantage will be competitive in world markets.

THE SOURCES OF COMPARATIVE ADVANTAGE

You have now seen that specialization and trade can benefit all trading partners, even those that may be inefficient producers in an absolute sense. If markets are competitive, and if foreign exchange markets are linked to goods-and-services exchange, countries will specialize in producing those products in which they have a comparative advantage.

So far, however, we have said nothing about the sources of comparative advantage. What determines whether a country has a comparative advantage in heavy manufacturing or in agriculture? What explains the actual trade flows observed around the world? Various theories and empirical work on international trade have provided a number of partial answers to these questions. Most economists look to **factor endowments**—that is, to the quantity and quality of labor, land, and natural resources—as the principal sources of comparative advantage. Factor endowments seem to explain a significant portion of actual world trade patterns.

The Heckscher-Ohlin Theorem

Eli Heckscher and Bertil Ohlin, two Swedish economists who wrote in the first half of this century, expanded and elaborated on Ricardo's theory of comparative advantage. The **Heckscher-Ohlin theorem** ties the theory of compara-

factor endowments The quantity and quality of labor, land, and natural resources of a country.

Heckscher-Ohlin theorem A theory that explains the existence of a country's comparative advantage by its factor endowments: A country has a comparative advantage in the production of a product if that country is relatively well endowed with inputs used intensively in the production of that product.

tive advantage to factor endowments. It assumes that products can be produced using differing proportions of inputs and that inputs are mobile between sectors in each economy, but that factors are not mobile *between* economies. According to the Heckscher-Ohlin theorem:

A country has a comparative advantage in the production of a product if that country is relatively well endowed with inputs used intensively in the production of that product.

This idea is fairly simple. A country with a lot of good fertile land is likely to have a comparative advantage in agriculture. A country with a large amount of accumulated capital is likely to have a comparative advantage in heavy manufacturing. A country with a lot of human capital is likely to have a comparative advantage in highly technical goods.

After an extensive study, Edward Leamer of UCLA has concluded that a relatively short list of factors accounts for a surprisingly large portion of world trade patterns. Natural resources, knowledge capital, physical capital, land, and skilled and unskilled labor, Leamer believes, explain "a large amount of the variability of net exports across countries."[1]

Other Explanations for Observed Trade Flows

Comparative advantage is not the only reason that countries trade, of course. It does not explain why many countries both import and export the same kinds of goods. The United States, for example, both exports and imports automobiles.

Another explanation for international trade is that just as industries within a country differentiate their products in order to capture a domestic market, so too do they differentiate their products to please the wide variety of tastes that exists worldwide. The Japanese automobile industry, for example, began producing small, fuel-efficient cars long before U.S. automobile makers did. In doing so, they developed expertise in creating products that attracted a devoted following and that elicited considerable brand loyalty. BMWs, made only in Germany, and Volvos, made only in Sweden, also have their champions in many countries. Just as product differentiation is a natural response to diverse preferences within an economy, it is also a natural response to diverse preferences across economies.

This idea is not inconsistent with the theory of comparative advantage. If the Japanese have developed skills and knowledge that gave them an edge in the production of fuel-efficient cars, that knowledge can be thought of as a very specific kind of capital not currently available to other producers. The Volvo company invested in a form of intangible capital that we call *goodwill*. That goodwill, which may come from establishing a reputation for safety and quality over the years, is one source of the comparative advantage that keeps Volvos selling on the international market. Some economists distinguish between gains from *acquired comparative advantages* and those acquired from *natural comparative advantages*.

Yet another explanation for international trade holds that some economies of scale may be available when producing for a world market that would not be available when producing only for a more limited domestic market. But because the evidence suggests that economies of scale are exhausted at relatively small size in most industries, it seems unlikely that they constitute a valid explanation of world trade patterns.

---

[1]Edward E. Leamer, *Sources of International Comparative Advantage: Theory and Evidence* (Cambridge, Mass: MIT Press, 1984), p. 187.

TRADE BARRIERS: TARIFFS, SUBSIDIES, AND QUOTAS

Trade barriers—also called *obstacles to trade*—take many forms, the three most common of which are tariffs, subsidies, and quotas. All of these are forms of **protection** through which some sector of the economy is shielded from foreign competition.

A **tariff** is a tax on imports. The average tariff on imports into the United States is now about 5%, although certain protected items have much higher tariffs. For example, the tariff rate on concentrated orange juice is a flat $0.35 per gallon. On rubber footwear, the tariff ranges from 20% to 48%, and on canned tuna it is 35 percent.

Export **subsidies**—government payments made to domestic firms to encourage exports—can also act as a barrier to trade. One of the provisions of the Corn Laws that stimulated Ricardo's musings in the nineteenth century was an export subsidy that was automatically paid to farmers by the British government when the price of grain fell below a specified level. The subsidy served to keep domestic prices high, but it flooded the world market with cheap subsidized grain. Foreign farmers who were not subsidized were driven out of the international marketplace by the artificially low prices.

Farm subsidies remain very much a part of the international trade landscape today. Many countries, especially those in Europe, continue to appease their farmers by heavily subsidizing exports of agricultural products. In fact, the political power of the farm lobby in many countries has had an important effect on recent international trade negotiations aimed at reducing trade barriers.

Closely related to subsidies is the practice of **dumping.** Dumping takes place when a firm or an industry sells products on the world market at prices *below* the cost of production. In recent years, many have accused Japan of dumping in the U.S. market. The charge has been levied against several specific Japanese industries, including automobiles, consumer electronics, and silicon computer chips.

Generally, a company dumps when it wants to dominate a world market. After the lower prices of the dumped goods have succeeded in driving out all the competition, the dumping company can exploit its position by raising the price of its product. Such practices, if committed by a U.S. firm in an attempt to monopolize a domestic market, are in violation of the Sherman Antitrust Act of 1890, which prohibits predatory pricing.

The current U.S. tariff laws contain several provisions aimed at counteracting the effects of dumping. The 1974 Trade Act contains a clause that qualifies an industry for protection if it has been "injured" by foreign competition. Building on that legislation, more recent trade bills, including the Comprehensive Trade Act of 1988, contain clauses that permit the President to impose trade sanctions when investigations reveal dumping by foreign companies or countries. These sanctions have not always been effective, however, as the Global Perspective box titled "Laptop Computer Screens: The Demise of a Tariff" points out.

A **quota** is a limit on the quantity of imports. Quotas can be mandatory or voluntary, and they may be legislated or negotiated with foreign governments. The best-known voluntary quota, or "voluntary restraint," was negotiated with the Japanese government in 1981. Japan agreed to reduce the number of automobiles it exported to the United States by 7.7%, from the 1980 level of 1.82 million units to 1.68 million units. In 1985, when President Reagan decided not to ask Japan to continue its restraints, auto imports jumped to 2.3 million units, nearly 20% of the U.S. market. Quotas currently apply to products as diverse as mushrooms, heavy motorcycles, and color television sets.

protection The practice of shielding a sector of the economy from foreign competition.

tariff A tax on imports.

subsidies Government payments made to domestic firms to encourage exports.

dumping Takes place when a firm or industry sells products on the world market at prices below the cost of production.

quota A limit on the quantity of imports.

The United States has traditionally been a high-tariff nation, with average tariffs of over 50% for much of its history. The highest tariffs were in effect during the Great Depression following enactment of the **Smoot-Hawley tariff,** which pushed the average tariff rate to 60% in 1930. The Smoot-Hawley tariff set off an international trade war when the United States' trading partners retaliated with tariffs of their own. Many economists point to the decline in trade that followed as one of the causes of the worldwide depression of the 1930s.[2]

In 1947 the United States, along with 22 other nations, agreed to reduce barriers to trade. It also established an organization to promote liberalization of foreign trade. This **General Agreement on Tariffs and Trade (GATT),** first considered an interim arrangement, continues in effect today and has been quite effective. The most recent round of world trade talks sponsored by the GATT, the "Uruguay Round," began in Uruguay in 1986 and continued until it collapsed without an agreement in December 1990 in a dispute over farm subsidies.

Every president who has held office since the General Agreement was signed has argued for free-trade policies, yet each one used his powers to protect one sector or another. Eisenhower and Kennedy restricted Japanese exports of textiles; Johnson restricted meat imports; Nixon restrained imports of steel and tightened restrictions on textiles; Carter protected steel, textiles, and footwear; Reagan restricted imports of sugar and automobiles.

Despite these cases, however, the general movement in the United States has been away from tariffs and quotas and toward freer trade. The Reciprocal Trade Agreements Act of 1934 authorized the President to negotiate trade agreements on behalf of the United States. As part of trade negotiations, the President can confer *most-favored-nation status* on individual trading partners. Exports from countries with most-favored-nation status are taxed at the lowest negotiated tariff rates. In addition, in recent years several successful rounds of tariff-reduction negotiations have reduced trade barriers to their lowest levels ever.

ECONOMIC INTEGRATION **Economic integration** occurs when two or more nations join to form a free-trade zone. In 1992, the European Community (EC, or the Common Market) began the process of forming the largest free-trade zone in the world. Under the terms of the EC agreement, tariff barriers and other impediments to trade will be removed over a 10-year period, and capital and labor will be freely mobile within the bloc. In a sense, the economic relationship among the nations of the EC (the United Kingdom, Belgium, France, Germany, Italy, the Netherlands, Luxembourg, Denmark, Greece, Ireland, Spain, Switzerland, and Portugal) will be very similar to the economic relationship among the 50 United States. Many economists feel that the advantages of free trade within the bloc, a reunited Germany, and the ability to work as a bloc will make the EC (and especially Germany) the most powerful player in the international marketplace in the coming decades.

The United States is not a part of the EC. However, in 1988 the United States (under President Reagan) and Canada (under Prime Minister Mulroney) signed the **U.S.-Canadian Free-Trade Agreement,** which will remove all barriers to trade, including tariffs and quotas, between the two countries by 1998.

In addition, during the last days of the Bush administration, the United States, Mexico, and Canada signed the **North American Free-Trade Agreement (NAFTA),** in which the three countries agreed to establish all of North America as a free-trade zone. The North American free-trade area will include 360 million people and a total output of over $7 trillion—a larger output than that of the

Smoot-Hawley tariff The U.S. tariff law of the 1930s, which set the highest tariffs in U.S. history (60 percent). It set off an international trade war and caused the decline in trade that is often considered a cause of the worldwide depression of the 1930s.

General Agreement on Tariffs and Trade (GATT) An international agreement signed by the United States and 22 other countries in 1947 to promote the liberalization of foreign trade.

economic integration Occurs when two or more nations join to form a free-trade zone.

U.S.-Canadian Free-Trade Agreement An agreement in which the United States and Canada agreed to eliminate all barriers to trade between the two countries by 1998.

North American Free-Trade Agreement (NAFTA) An agreement signed by the United States, Mexico, and Canada in which the three countries agreed to establish all of North America as a free-trade zone.

---

[2]See especially Charles Kindleberger, *The World in Depression 1929–1939* (London: Allen Lane, 1973).

LAPTOP COMPUTER SCREENS: THE DEMISE OF A TARIFF

In July 1991, the U.S. government imposed a 62.67% tariff on imports of active-matrix liquid crystal display screens (also referred to as "flat-panel displays" and primarily used for laptop computers) from Japan. The Commerce Department and the International Trade Commission agreed that Japanese producers were selling their screens in the U.S. market at a price below cost and that this "dumping" threatened the survival of domestic laptop screen producers. The tariff was meant to protect the infant U.S. industry until it could compete head-on with the Japanese.

Unfortunately for U.S. producers of laptop computers and for consumers who purchase them, the tariff had an unintended (though predictable) effect on the industry. Because U.S. laptop screens were generally recognized to be of lower quality than their Japanese counterparts, imposition of the tariff left U.S. computer manufacturers with three options: (1) They could use the screens available from U.S. producers and watch sales of their final product decline in the face of *higher quality* competition from abroad; (2) They could pay the tariff for the higher quality screens and watch sales of their final product decline in the face of *lower priced* competition from

abroad; or (3) They could do what was the most profitable for them to do—move their production facilities abroad in order to avoid the tariff completely. This is exactly what both Apple and IBM announced that they would do. In the end, not only were the laptop industry and its consumers hurt by the imposition of the tariff (due to higher costs of production and to higher laptop computer prices), but the U.S. screen industry was hurt as well (due to its loss of buyers for its product) by a policy specifically designed to help it.

All parties involved with the tariff discovered that the costs of imposing it far outweighed any gains it provided. In fact, of the three active U.S. screen producers who originally requested the tariff, only one remains—Guardian Industries Corporation. As the following excerpt from the *Wall Street Journal* notes, it was Guardian itself that led the way in petitioning for removal of the tariff in early 1993:

> The Commerce Department said it plans to revoke anti-dumping duties on imports of certain Japanese-made display screens commonly used in laptop computers.
>
> The decision follows a campaign by major computer makers to get the tariffs lifted. Companies that buy display screens, including Apple Computer Inc., International Business Machines Corp., Rockwell

In 1991, some members of the U.S. computer industry lobbied for an imposition of tariffs on imported laptop computer screens. Two years later, after the U.S. computer industry had been seriously damaged by the tariff, the tariff was lifted.

International Corp. and Sun Microsystems Inc., supported a lifting of the duties.

> The department, citing "changed circumstances," made its decision after the sole remaining U.S. maker of the screens recently asked the Commerce Department to eliminate the tariff. It said the tariff should be lifted next month. . . .
>
> In its decision to lift the tariffs, the Commerce Department said that it couldn't identify any U.S. makers of active-matrix displays other than Guardian.*

*Source: Asra Q. Nomani, "U.S. Cuts Duties on Some Japanese Computer Screens," *Wall Street Journal*, January 21, 1993.

European Community. The agreement will eliminate all tariffs over a 10–15 year period and remove restrictions on most investments.

During the presidential campaign of 1992, NAFTA was a hot topic of debate. Both Bill Clinton and George Bush supported the agreement; Ross Perot opposed it. Not surprisingly, industrial labor unions that might be affected by increased imports from Mexico (like those in the automobile industry) opposed the agreement, while industries whose exports to Mexico might increase as a result of the agreement (for example, the machine tool industry) supported it. Another concern raised by many was that Mexican companies were not subject to the same environmental regulations as U.S. firms and that U.S. firms might move to Mexico for this reason. The Clinton administration vowed to make a number of minor changes to the Agreement in 1993 and to submit it to Congress for approval.

FREE TRADE OR PROTECTION?

As we pointed out earlier in this chapter, one of the great economic debates of all time revolves around the free-trade versus protection controversy. The arguments in favor of each are summarized briefly in the following discussion.

The Case for Free Trade

In one sense, the theory of comparative advantage *is* the case for free trade. Trade has potential benefits for all nations. A good is not imported unless its net price to buyers is below that of the domestically produced alternative. When the Germans in our earlier example found U.S. timber less expensive than their own, they bought it, yet they continued to pay the same price for homemade steel. Americans bought less-expensive German steel, but they continued to buy domestic timber at the same lower price. Under these conditions, *both Americans and Germans ended up paying less and consuming more.*

At the same time, resources, including labor, move out of steel production and into timber production in the United States. In Germany, resources, including labor, move out of timber production and into steel production. Thus, the resources in both countries are more efficiently used. Tariffs, subsidies, and quotas, which interfere with the free movement of goods and services around the world, reduce or eliminate the gains of comparative advantage.

We can use supply and demand curves to illustrate this point. Suppose that Figure 36.4 shows domestic supply and demand for textiles. In the absence of

FIGURE 36.4

The Gains from Trade and Losses from the Imposition of a Tariff

A tariff of t increases the market price facing consumers from P_w to $P_w + t$. The government collects revenues equal to the grey shaded area. The loss of efficiency has two components. First, consumers must pay a higher price for goods that could be produced at lower cost. Second, marginal producers are drawn into textiles and away from other goods, resulting in inefficient domestic production.

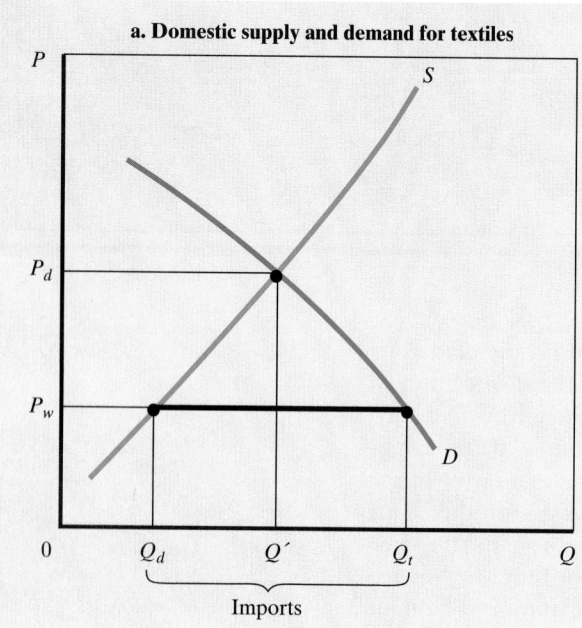

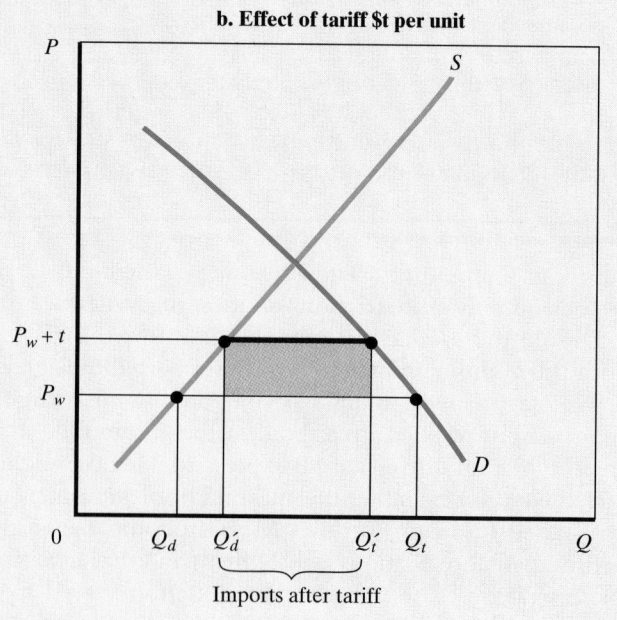

trade, the market clears at price of P_d. At equilibrium, Q' units of textiles are produced and consumed.

Assume now that textiles are available at a world price of P_w. P_w is the price in dollars that Americans must pay for textiles from foreign sources. If we assume that an unlimited amount of textiles is available at P_w and that there is no difference in quality between domestic and foreign textiles, no domestic producer will be able to charge more than P_w. In the absence of trade barriers, the world price sets the price in the United States. As the price in the United States falls from P_d to P_w, the quantity demanded by consumers increases from Q' to Q_t, but the quantity supplied by domestic producers drops from Q' to Q_d. The difference between Q_d and Q_t ($Q_t - Q_d$) is the quantity of textiles imported.

The argument for free trade holds that each country should specialize in producing the goods and services in which it enjoys a comparative advantage. Clearly, if foreign producers can produce textiles at a much lower price than domestic producers, they have a comparative advantage. As the world price of textiles falls to P_w, domestic (U.S.) supply drops and resources are transferred to other sectors. These other sectors, which may be export industries or domestic industries, are not shown in Figure 36.4a. It is clear, however, that the allocation of resources is more efficient at price P_w. Why should the United States use domestic resources to produce what foreign producers can produce at a lower cost? U.S. resources should move into the production of the things it produces best.

Now consider what happens to the domestic price of textiles when a trade barrier is imposed. Figure 36.4b shows the effect of a set tariff, t, imposed on each unit of imported textiles. The tariff raises the domestic price of textiles to $P_w + t$. The result is that some of the gains from trade are lost. First, consumers are forced to pay a higher price for the same good; the quantity of textiles demanded drops from Q_t under free trade to Q_t' because some consumers simply are not willing to pay the higher price.

At the same time, the higher price of textiles draws some marginal domestic producers who could not make a profit at P_w into textile production. As the price rises to $P_w + t$, the quantity supplied by producers rises from Q_d to Q_d'. The overall result is a decrease in imports.

Finally, the imposition of the tariff means that the government collects revenue equal to the shaded gray area in Figure 36.4b. This shaded area is simply equal to the tariff rate per unit, t, times the number of units that are imported after the tariff is in place ($Q_t' - Q_d'$).

What is the final result of the tariff? The answer should be clear. Domestic producers that were receiving revenues of only P_w per unit before the tariff was imposed now receive a higher price and earn higher profits. But these higher profits are achieved at a loss of allocative efficiency. All of this leads us to conclude that:

> Trade barriers prevent a nation from reaping the benefits of specialization, push it to adopt relatively inefficient production techniques, and force consumers to pay higher prices for protected products than they would otherwise pay.

The Case for Protection

Arguments can also be made in favor of tariffs and quotas, of course. Over the course of U.S. history, these arguments have been made so many times by so many industries before so many congressional committees that it almost seems as if all pleas for protection share the same themes. The most frequently heard of these pleas are described below.

PROTECTION SAVES JOBS   The main argument for protection is that foreign competition costs Americans their jobs. When we buy Toyotas, U.S. cars go unsold. This leads to layoffs in the domestic auto industry. When we buy Japanese or German steel, steel workers in Pittsburgh lose their jobs. When we buy shoes or textiles from Korea or Taiwan, the millworkers in Maine and Massachusetts, as well as in South Carolina and Georgia, lose their jobs.

It is true that when we buy goods from foreign producers, domestic producers in the U.S. economy do suffer. But there is no reason to believe that the workers laid off in the contracting sectors will not be ultimately reemployed in other expanding sectors. Foreign competition in textiles, for example, has clearly meant the loss of U.S. jobs in that industry. Many thousands of textile workers in New England lost their jobs as the textile mills there closed down over the last 35 years. But with the tremendous expansion of high-tech industries, the unemployment rate in Massachusetts fell to one of the lowest in the country in the mid-1980s, and New Hampshire, Vermont, and Maine also boomed.

By the 1990s, New England had suffered another severe downturn, due partly to the fact that high-technology hardware manufacturing had moved abroad. But in 1993 it became clear that small- to medium-sized companies in such newly developing areas as biotechnology and software were beginning to pick up steam just as hardware manufacturing had done a decade earlier. Over time the United States lost its comparative advantage in textiles to countries with larger unskilled labor pools, but other new industries have grown up in which the United States does have a comparative advantage.

The adjustment process is far from costless, however. The knowledge that some other industry, perhaps in some other part of the country, may be expanding is of little comfort to the person whose skills become obsolete or whose pension benefits are lost when his or her company abruptly closes a plant or goes bankrupt. The social and personal problems brought about by industry-specific unemployment, obsolete skills, and bankruptcy as a result of foreign competition are significant.

These problems can be addressed in two ways. We can ban imports and give up the gains from free trade, acknowledging that we are willing to pay premium prices to save domestic jobs in industries that can produce more efficiently abroad. Or we can aid the victims of free trade in a constructive way, helping to retrain them for jobs with a future. In some instances, programs to relocate people in expanding regions may be in order. Some programs deal directly with the transition without forgoing the gains from trade.

SOME COUNTRIES ENGAGE IN UNFAIR TRADE PRACTICES   Attempts by U.S. firms to monopolize an industry are illegal under the Sherman and Clayton Acts. If a strong company decides to drive the competition out of the market by setting prices below cost, it would be aggressively prosecuted by the Antitrust Division of the Justice Department. But, the argument goes, if we won't allow a U.S. firm to monopolize an industry or a market, can we stand by and let a German firm or a Japanese firm do so in the name of free trade? This is a legitimate argument and one that has gained significant favor in recent years. How should we respond when a large international company or a country behaves strategically against a domestic firm or industry? Free trade may be the best solution when everybody plays by the rules, but sometimes we have to fight back.

CHEAP FOREIGN LABOR MAKES COMPETITION UNFAIR   Let us say that a particular country gained its "comparative advantage" in textiles by paying its workers low wages. How can U.S. automobile companies compete with companies that pay wages that are less than a quarter of what U.S. companies pay?

First, we need to remember that wages in a competitive economy reflect productivity. Workers in the United States earn higher wages because they are more productive. The United States has more capital per worker, and its workers are better trained. Second, trade flows not according to *absolute* advantage but according to *comparative* advantage: All countries benefit, even if one country can produce everything more cheaply.

PROTECTION SAFEGUARDS NATIONAL SECURITY   Beyond simply saving jobs, certain sectors of the economy may appeal for protection for other reasons. The steel industry has argued for years with some success that it is vital to national defense. In the event of a war, the United States would not want to depend on foreign countries for products as vital as steel. Even if we acknowledge another country's comparative advantage, we may want to protect our own resources.

No industry has ever asked for protection without invoking the national defense argument. The testimony on behalf of the scissors and shears industry argued that "in the event of a national emergency and imports cutoff, the United States would be without a source of scissors and shears, basic tools for many industries and trades essential to our national defense." (See the Issues and Applications box titled "The Never-Ending Plea for Protection.") The question, then, lies not in the merit of the argument but in just how seriously it can be taken if *every* industry uses it.

PROTECTION DISCOURAGES DEPENDENCY   Closely related to the national defense argument is the claim that countries, particularly small or developing countries, may come to rely too heavily on one or more trading partners for many items. If Lilliput comes to rely on a major power for food or energy or some important raw material in which the large nation has a comparative advantage, it may be difficult for the smaller nation to remain politically neutral. Some critics of free trade argue that the superpowers have consciously engaged in trade with smaller countries to create these kinds of dependencies.

Therefore, the argument goes, small independent countries should consciously avoid trading relationships that might lead to political dependence. This may involve developing domestic industries in areas where a country has a comparative disadvantage. To do so would mean protecting that industry from international competition.

PROTECTION SAFEGUARDS INFANT INDUSTRIES   Young industries in a given country may have a difficult time competing with established industries in other countries. And in a dynamic world, a protected **infant industry** might mature into a strong one worldwide because of an acquired, but real, comparative advantage. If such an industry is undercut and driven out of world markets at the beginning of its life, that comparative advantage might never develop.

infant industry A young industry which may need temporary protection from competition from the established industries of other countries in order to develop an acquired comparative advantage.

It is interesting to note that young industries are usually not the ones asking for protection. For example, the high-tech industries that seem to have a real comparative advantage in the United States today have by and large resisted asking for help. Most action in Washington has been on behalf of old, declining industries that are losing their comparative advantage.

PROTECTION PROVIDES PROTECTION DURING TEMPORARY CURRENCY OVERVALUATIONS   In 1983 and 1984, many people argued that the dollar was artificially strong—that is, that it bought more yen, DM, and francs than it should have. An overvalued dollar makes U.S. goods look undesirable to foreigners, who have to pay more to get dollars, and makes foreign goods look cheap to Americans.

Scissors: Essential to national defense?

Trade Expansion Act of 1962: Statement of B. C. Deuschle in Hearings before the Eighty-Seventh Congress, Second Session; Committee on Ways and Means, House of Representatives

MR. KEOGH (presiding). You are recognized, Mr. Deuschle.

MR. DEUSCHLE. Thank you, Mr. Chairman.

Mr. Chairman and members of the Committee on Ways and Means, my name is B. C. Deuschle.

I am vice president of the Acme Shear Co., located in Bridgeport, Connecticut. I appear before this committee as president of the Shears, Scissors & Manicure Implement Manufacturers Association, the only national trade association of domestic manufacturers of scissors and shears. . . .

During the past fifteen years representatives of our association have appeared before this committee and other Congressional committees, the Committee for Reciprocity Information and the Tariff Commission, to present our views on the impact of imported scissors and shears on our domestic industry.

We have never requested or suggested that a complete embargo be placed on the import of scissors and shears. All that we have asked

for and desire is a fair competitive opportunity, not an advantage. . . .

The workers in the domestic scissor and shear industry do not want to become wards of the State; they want to use their skills, which have taken years to develop. These workers are not interested in retraining; over many years they have developed a skill they are proud of and want to continue the work they are happy doing.

If the scissors and shears imported during 1961 had been manufactured in the United States, it would have provided over 2 million man-hours of factory work, or full-time employment for over 1,000 American employees.

Domestic manufacturers of scissors and shears have modernized and automated their operations in an effort to meet foreign competition. But foreign manufacturers also have modern equipment and with their lower wage rates are underselling domestic firms in the U.S. market at today's rate of duty.

H.R. 9900 would give the President unrestricted authority to reduce duties and thereby further reduce the cost of imported scissors and shears in our market. Under the provisions of this bill, scissors and shears would be buried in a category with many other items and the duty cut 50 percent.

This would mean a reduction of at least

20 cents per pair at the retail level for scissors and shears now being retailed at $1 to $1.29 per pair. . . . manufacturers would be forced to close their doors and discharge their employees. The United States would then become wholly dependent on imported scissors and shears.

We cannot understand how it could be in the national interest to permit such a loss. We would lose the skills of the employees and management of the industry as well as the capital investment in production equipment. In the event of a national emergency and imports cut off, the United States would be without a source of scissors and shears, basic tools for many industries and trades essential to our defense.

The scissor and shear industry is one of the oldest in the world. The skill was brought to the United States from Germany at a time when the United States needed new industry and a scissor and shear industry in particular.

Scissors and shears of all sizes and types are used in every school, retail establishment, office, factory, hospital, and home in the United States. Scissors cannot be classified as a luxury, gimmick, or novelty.

Scissors are used to separate us from our mothers at birth; to cut our toenails; to trim the leather in our shoes; to cut and trim the materials used in every piece of clothing that we wear.

They are used to cut our fingernails, to trim our mustaches, the hair in our ears and nose, and to cut the hair on our heads—even down to the end of the road when our best suit or dress is cut down the back so that the undertaker can dress us for the last ride. Scissors are truly used from birth to death. They are essential to our health, education, and general welfare.

I ask you gentlemen, is this an industry that should be permitted to become extinct in this country?. . .

MR. KNOX. Then, in your opinion, and in many other people's opinion, the industry, itself, would be unable to operate in competition if the duty was cut by 50 percent?

MR. DEUSCHLE. Yes, sir. . . .

When such a situation arises, whether artificially or normally but *temporarily,* protection might be required to help certain industries make it through the tough times. It is extremely difficult, however, to decide just what the "proper" exchange rate should be.

AN ECONOMIC CONSENSUS

You now know something about how international trade fits into the structure of the economy.

Critical to our study of international economics is the important debate between free-traders and protectionists. On one side is the theory of comparative advantage, formalized by David Ricardo in the early part of the nineteenth century. According to this view, all countries benefit from specialization and trade. The gains from trade are real, and they can be large; free international trade raises real incomes and improves the standard of living.

On the other side of the debate are the protectionists, who point to the loss of jobs and argue for the protection of workers from foreign competition. But although foreign competition can cause job loss in specific sectors, it is unlikely to cause net job loss in an economy, and workers will over time be absorbed into expanding sectors.

> Foreign trade and full employment can be pursued simultaneously. Although economists disagree about many things, the vast majority of them favor free trade.

SUMMARY

1. All economies, even large economies like that of the United States, depend to some extent on other economies and are affected by events outside their borders.

The International Economy: Trade Surpluses and Deficits

2. Beginning in the early 1970s, the volume of international trade increased sharply as a percentage of GDP in the United States. In 1992 U.S. imports were around 11% of U.S. GDP. In 1992 U.S. imports of goods and services exceeded U.S. exports by (a trade deficit of) $30.4 billion.

The Economic Basis for Trade: Comparative Advantage

3. The *theory of comparative advantage,* dating to the writings of David Ricardo in the nineteenth century, holds that specialization and free trade will benefit all trading partners, even those that may be absolutely less efficient producers.

4. A country enjoys an *absolute advantage* over another country in the production of a product if it uses fewer resources to produce that product than the other country does. A country has a *comparative advantage* in the production of a product if that product can be produced at a lower cost in terms of other goods.

5. Trade enables countries to move out beyond their previous resource and productivity constraints. When countries specialize in producing those goods in which they have a comparative advantage, they maximize their combined output and allocate their resources more efficiently.

6. When trade is free, patterns of trade and trade flows result from the independent decisions of thousands of importers and exporters and millions of private households and firms.

7. The relative attractiveness of foreign goods to U.S. buyers and of U.S. goods to foreign buyers depends in part on *exchange rates.*

8. For any pair of countries, there is a range of exchange rates that will lead automatically to both countries realizing the gains from specialization and comparative advantage. Within that range, the exchange rate will determine which country gains the most from trade. This leads us to conclude that exchange rates determine the terms of trade.

9. If exchange rates end up in the right range (that is, in a range that facilitates the flow of goods between nations), the free market will drive each country to shift resources into those sectors in which it enjoys a comparative advantage. Only those products in which a country has a comparative advantage will be competitive in world markets.

The Sources of Comparative Advantage

10. The *Heckscher-Ohlin theorem* looks to relative *factor endowments* to explain comparative advantage and trade flows. According to the theorem, a country has a comparative advantage in the production of a product if that country is relatively well endowed with the inputs that are used intensively in the production of that product.

11. A relatively short list of inputs—natural resources, knowledge capital, physical capital, land, and skilled and unskilled labor—explains a surprisingly large portion of world trade patterns. But the simple version of the theory of comparative advantage cannot explain why many countries import and export the same goods.

12. Some theories argue that comparative advantage can be acquired. Just as industries within a country differentiate their products in order to capture a domestic market, so too do they differentiate their products to please the wide variety of tastes that exists worldwide. This theory is not inconsistent with the theory of comparative advantage.

Trade Barriers: Tariffs, Subsidies, and Quotas

13. Trade barriers take many forms, the three most common of which are *tariffs, subsidies,* and *quotas.* All of these are forms of *protection* through which some sector of the economy is shielded from foreign competition.

14. Although the United States has historically been a high-tariff nation, the general movement is now away from tariffs and quotas. *The General Agreement on Tariffs and Trade (GATT),* signed by the United States and 22 other countries in 1947, continues in effect today; its purpose is to reduce barriers to world trade and keep them down. Also important are the *U.S.-Canadian Free Trade Agreement,* signed in 1988, and the *North American Free-Trade Agreement,* signed by the United States, Mexico, and Canada in the last days of the Bush administration.

Free Trade or Protection?

15. In one sense, the theory of comparative advantage is the case for free trade. Trade barriers prevent a nation from reaping the benefits of specialization, push it to adopt relatively inefficient production techniques, and force consumers to pay higher prices for protected products than they would otherwise pay.

16. The case for protection rests on a number of propositions, one of which is that foreign competition results in a loss of domestic jobs. But there is no reason to believe that the workers laid off in the contracting sectors will not be ultimately reemployed in other expanding sectors. This adjustment process is far from costless, however.

17. Other arguments for protection hold that cheap foreign labor makes competition unfair; that some countries engage in unfair trade practices; that it protects the national security and discourages dependency; and that it protects *infant industries.* Despite these arguments, however, most economists favor free trade.

REVIEW TERMS AND CONCEPTS

PROBLEM SET

1. The following table gives 1990 figures for yield per acre in Illinois and Kansas:

	WHEAT	SOYBEANS
Illinois	48	39
Kansas	40	24

Source: U.S. Dept. of Agriculture, *Crop Production*, 1992.

a. If we assume that farmers in Illinois and Kansas use the same amount of labor, capital, and fertilizer, which state has an absolute advantage in wheat production? Soybean production?

b. If we transfer land out of wheat into soybeans, how many bushels of wheat do we give up in Illinois per additional bushel of soybeans produced? In Kansas?

c. Which state has a comparative advantage in wheat production? In soybean production?

The following table gives the distribution of land planted for each state in millions of acres in 1990:

	TOTAL ACRES UNDER TILL	WHEAT	SOYBEANS
Illinois	22.9	1.9 (8.3%)	9.1 (39.7%)
Kansas	20.7	11.8 (57.0%)	1.9 (9.2%)

Are these data consistent with your answer to part c? Explain.

2. The United States imported $26.5 billion worth of "food feeds and beverages" in 1991 and exported $36.1 billion worth.

a. Name some of the imported items that you are aware of in this category. Also name some of the exported items.

b. The United States is said to have a comparative advantage in the production of agricultural goods. How would you go about testing this proposition? What data would you need?

c. Are the numbers above consistent with the theory of comparative advantage? Suppose you had a more detailed breakdown of which items the United States imports and which it exports. What would you look for?

d. What other theories of international trade might explain why the same goods are imported and exported?

3. You can think of the United States as a set of 50 separate economies with no trade barriers. In such an open environment, each state specializes in the products that it produces best.

a. What product or products does your state specialize in?

b. Can you identify the source of the comparative advantage that lies behind the production of one or more of these products (a natural resource, plentiful cheap labor, a skilled labor force, etc.)?

c. Do you think that the theory of comparative advantage and the Heckscher-Ohlin theorem help to explain why your state specializes in the way that it does?

4. Export subsidies have been proposed to prop up food prices and help struggling family farmers. Would you favor such subsidies?

5. Germany and France produce white and red wines. Current domestic prices for each are given in the following table:

	GERMANY	FRANCE
White wine	5 DM	10 francs
Red wine	10 DM	15 francs

Suppose that the exchange rate is 1 deutsche mark = 1 franc.

a. If the price ratios within each country reflect resource use, which country has a comparative advantage in the production of red wine? White wine?

b. Assume that there are no other trading partners and that the only motive for holding foreign currency is to buy foreign goods. Will the current exchange rate lead to trade flows in both directions between the two countries?

c. What adjustments might you expect in the exchange rate? Be specific.

d. What would you predict about trade flows between Germany and France in the long run?

6. The European Community (EC) is scheduled to remove all trade barriers within its member countries in the next 10 years. Its goal is to become one "common market" with one uniform currency. Explain the likely benefits and costs to the EC's member countries. Should the United States be concerned about the new common market? Why or why not?

37 Open-Economy Macroeconomics: The Balance of Payments and Exchange Rates

When we began our discussion of macroeconomics, we pointed out that the economies of the world have become increasingly interdependent over the last two decades. No economy operates in a vacuum, and economic events in one country can have repercussions on the economies of other countries.

International trade is a major part of today's world economy. U.S. imports now account for over 11% of U.S. GDP, and billions of dollars flow through the international capital market each day. In Chapter 36 we explored the main reasons for the existence of international exchange. Countries trade with each other to obtain goods and services they cannot produce themselves or because other nations can produce goods and services at a lower cost than they can. You can see the various connections between the domestic economy and the rest of the world in Figure 21.2. Foreign countries supply goods and services, labor, and capital to the United States, and the United States supplies goods and services, labor, and capital to the rest of the world.

From a macroeconomic point of view, the main difference between an international transaction and a domestic transaction concerns currency exchange:

When people in different countries buy from and sell to each other, an exchange of currencies must also take place.

French wine exporters, for example, cannot spend U.S. dollars in France—they need French francs. Nor can a U.S. wheat exporter use French francs to buy a tractor or to pay the rent on her warehouse. Somehow, international exchange must be managed in a way that allows each partner in the transaction to wind up with his or her own currency.

As you know from Chapter 36, the direction of trade between two countries depends on **exchange rates**—that is, the price of one country's currency in terms of the other country's currency. If the German deutsche mark were very expensive, for example (thus making the dollar cheap), both Germans and Americans would buy from U.S. producers. If the deutsche mark were very cheap (thus making the U.S. dollar expensive), however, both Germans and Americans would buy from German producers. Within a certain range of exchange rates, trade flows in both directions, each country specializes in producing the goods in which it enjoys a comparative advantage, and trade is mutually beneficial.

Because exchange rates play such a major role in determining the flow of international trade, the way they are determined is very important. Since the turn of the century, the world monetary system has been changed on several occasions by international agreements and events. In the early part of the century, nearly all currencies were backed by gold. Their values were fixed in terms of a specific number of ounces of gold, which in turn determined their values (i.e., exchange rates) in international trading.

In 1944, with the international monetary system in chaos as the end of World War II drew near, a large group of experts unofficially representing 44 countries met in **Bretton Woods,** New Hampshire, and drew up a number of agreements. One of these agreements established a system of essentially fixed exchange rates under which each country agreed to intervene in the foreign exchange market when necessary to maintain the agreed-upon value of its currency.

In 1971, most countries, including the United States, gave up trying to fix exchange rates formally and began allowing them to be determined essentially by supply and demand. For example, without government intervention in the marketplace, the price of British pounds in dollars is determined by the interaction of those who want to exchange dollars for pounds (those who "demand" pounds) and those who want to exchange pounds for dollars (those who "supply" pounds). If the quantity of pounds demanded exceeds the quantity of pounds supplied, the price of pounds will rise, just as the price of peanuts or paper clips would rise under similar circumstances. (A more detailed discussion of the various monetary systems that have been in place since 1900 is found in the appendix to this chapter.)

In this chapter, we explore what has come to be called "open-economy macroeconomics" in more detail. First, we discuss the *balance of payments*—that is, the record of a nation's transactions with the rest of the world. We then go on to consider how the analysis we presented in Chapters 24 through 33 changes when we allow for the international exchange of goods, services, and capital.

exchange rate The price of one country's currency in terms of another country's currency; the ratio at which two currencies are traded for each other.

Bretton Woods The site in New Hampshire where a group of experts from 44 countries met in 1944 and agreed on an international monetary system of fixed exchange rates.

THE BALANCE OF PAYMENTS

We sometimes find it convenient to lump all foreign currencies—Swiss francs, Japanese yen, Brazilian cruzeiros, and so forth—together under the heading *foreign exchange.* Specifically, **foreign exchange** is simply all currencies other than the domestic currency of a given country (in the case of the United States, the U.S. dollar). The United States' demand for foreign exchange arises because its citizens want to buy things whose prices are quoted in other currencies, such as Australian wines, vacations in France, and bonds or stocks issued by Sony Corporation of

foreign exchange All currencies other than the domestic currency of a given country.

Japan. Whenever U.S. citizens make these purchases, Australians, French, and Japanese gain U.S. dollars, which, from their point of view, are foreign exchange.

But where does the *supply* of foreign exchange come from? The answer is simple: The United States (actually, U.S. citizens or firms) earns foreign exchange whenever it sells products, services, or assets to another country. Just as France earns foreign exchange when U.S. tourists go to visit the Eiffel Tower, the United States earns foreign exchange (in this case, French francs) when French tourists come to the United States to visit the Statue of Liberty. Similarly, Saudi Arabian purchases of stock in General Motors or Colombian purchases of real estate in Miami increase the U.S. supply of foreign exchange.

The record of a country's transactions in goods, services, and assets with the rest of the world is known as its **balance of payments.** The balance of payments is also the record of a country's sources (supply) and uses (demand) of foreign exchange.

Balance-of-payments accounting is quite straightforward if you remember the following simple rule:[1]

> Any transaction that brings in foreign exchange for a country is a credit (positive) item in that country's balance of payments; any transaction that causes a country to lose foreign exchange is a debit (negative) item.

Also keep in mind that the balance of payments is a record of all the ways a country earns foreign exchange and all the uses to which that foreign exchange is put.[2]

The Current Account

The balance of payments is typically divided up into two major accounts, the *current account* and the *capital account,* and a number of subaccounts. These are shown in Table 37.1, which provides data on the U.S. balance of payments for 1992. The balance of payments is subdivided in this manner because different kinds of transactions have different motivations, or causes, and imply different things for the functioning of the U.S. economy.

Consider first the current account. The first item in this account is U.S. trade in *merchandise.* This category includes exports of computer chips, potato chips, and Sting records and imports of Scotch whiskey, Japanese calculators, and Mexican oil. U.S. merchandise exports *earn* foreign exchange for the United States and are thus a credit (+) item on the balance of payments. U.S. merchandise imports *use up* foreign exchange (we must surrender some of our holdings of foreign currencies to purchase foreign-produced goods and services) and are thus debit (−) items. The difference between a country's merchandise exports and its merchandise imports is its merchandise trade balance, more commonly called the **balance of trade.** If exports of goods are less than imports, as was the case in 1992 in the United States, a country is said to run a **trade deficit.** In this case, the balance of trade is negative.

The second item in the current account concerns *services.* Like most other countries, the United States buys services from and sells services to other countries. For example, a U.S. firm shipping wheat to England might purchase insurance from a British insurance company. A Dutch flower grower may fly her flowers to the

balance of payments The record of a country's transactions in goods, services, and assets with the rest of the world; also the record of a country's sources (supply) and uses (demand) of foreign exchange.

balance of trade A country's merchandise exports minus its merchandise imports. Also called the *merchandise trade balance.*

trade deficit Occurs when a country's exports of goods are less than its imports of goods in a given period.

---

[1]Bear in mind the distinction between the balance of payments and a balance sheet. A *balance sheet* for a firm or a country measures that entity's stock of assets and liabilities at a moment in time. The *balance of payments,* by contrast, measures *flows,* usually over a period of a month, a quarter, or a year. Despite its name, the balance of payments is *not* a balance sheet.

[2]As we shall see later, one of these uses is to add to existing stocks of foreign exchange. Thus, total uses of foreign exchange completely account for every unit of foreign exchange that is earned.

CURRENT ACCOUNT

Merchandise exports	439.3
Merchandise imports	−535.5
(1) Balance of trade	**−96.2**
Exports of services	178.5
Imports of services	−123.4
(2) Net export of services	**55.1**
Income received on investments	109.2
Income payments on investments	−99.1
(3) Net investment income	**10.1**
(4) Net transfer payments and other	**−31.4**
(5) Balance on current account (1 + 2 + 3 + 4)	**−62.4**

CAPITAL ACCOUNT

(6) Change in private U.S. assets abroad (increase is −)	**−47.8**
(7) Change in foreign private assets in the United States	**80.1**
(8) Change in U.S. government assets abroad (increase is −)	**2.9**
(9) Change in foreign government assets in the United States	**40.3**
(10) Balance on capital account (6 + 7 + 8 + 9)	**75.5**
(11) Statistical discrepancy	**−13.1**
(12) Balance of Payments (5 + 10 + 11)	0

Source: U.S. Department of Commerce, *Survey of Current Business,* March 1993.

TABLE 37.1

United States Balance of Payments, 1992

All transactions that bring foreign exchange into the United States are credited (+) to the balance of payments; all transactions that cause the United States to lose foreign exchange are debited (−) to the balance of payments.

United States aboard an American airliner. In the first case, the United States is importing services and therefore using up foreign exchange; in the second, it is selling services to foreigners and earning foreign exchange. In 1992, the United States exported $55.1 billion more in services than it imported.

The third item in the current account concerns *investment income.* U.S. citizens hold foreign assets (stocks, bonds, and real assets like buildings and factories). Dividends, interest, rent, and profits paid to U.S. asset holders are a source of foreign exchange. Conversely, when foreigners earn dividends, interest, and profits on assets held in the United States, foreign exchange is used up. In 1992, income received on investments held outside the United States exceeded income paid to foreigners by $10.1 billion.

The fourth item in Table 37.1 is *net transfer payments and other.* Transfer payments from the United States to foreigners are another use of foreign exchange. Some of these transfer payments are from private U.S. citizens and some are from the U.S. government. You may send a gift to your aunt in Spain or the government may send a social security check to a retiree living in Italy. Conversely, some foreigners make transfer payments to the United States. "Net" refers to the difference between payments from the United States to foreigners and payments from foreigners to the United States. If we add the balance of trade, net export of services, net investment income, and net transfer payments and other,[3] we get the **balance on current account.**

balance on current account The balance of trade plus net exports of services, plus net investment income, plus the category "net transfer payments and other."

---

[3]"Other" includes interest paid by the U.S. government to foreigners. Contrary to the treatment of private interest payments, government interest payments are not counted as imports of services. (This treatment is similar to that for government interest payments to domestic citizens, as discussed in Chapter 22.) These payments are a use of funds, however, so they must be included in computing the balance on current account.

The balance on current account is important because it shows how much a nation has spent on foreign goods, services, and transfers relative to how much it has earned from other countries. When the balance is negative, which it was for the United States in 1992, a nation has spent more on foreign products (plus investment income and transfers paid) than it has earned through the sales of its goods and services to the rest of the world (plus investment income and transfers received). If a nation has spent more on foreign goods and services than it has earned, its net asset position vis-à-vis the rest of the world must decrease. By "net" we mean a nation's assets abroad minus its liabilities to the rest of the world. A country's liabilities to the rest of the world are assets of foreigners. (A Japanese-owned building in Manhattan, for example, is a foreign liability of the United States and an asset of Japan.) A nation settles its accounts with the rest of the world through its capital account.

The Capital Account

The second major account in a nation's balance of payments, the capital account, records the nation's capital inflows and outflows.

Governments and citizens around the world exchange physical assets (such as office buildings) and paper assets (such as stocks and bonds) across international boundaries. When a U.S. citizen buys a Canadian bond or a U.S. firm purchases an office tower in France, for example, foreign exchange is used up. Domestic banks also make loans to foreign countries. For instance, several New York banks made huge loans to developing countries during the 1970s. When a U.S. bank makes a loan to the Mexican National Oil Company or to a steel company in Korea, the bank receives an IOU in exchange. Thus a loan made to Mexico (or any other country) is a *use* of foreign exchange also. If U.S. citizens and banks increase their holdings of private assets abroad, the figure recorded in the capital account is negative (a debit). In 1992, U.S. citizens increased their private holdings abroad by $47.8 billion. (See item 6 in Table 37.1.)

On the other hand, foreign purchases of domestic assets *earn* foreign exchange for a country. When a Japanese company bought Rockefeller Center in New York in 1990, for example, the transaction earned foreign exchange for the United States. Thus, when foreign citizens increase their holdings of private assets, the transactions are recorded in the capital account as positive figures (credits). As item 7 in Table 37.1 shows, foreign private investment in the United States increased by $80.1 billion in 1992.

Finally, governments hold foreign assets as well. Specifically, central banks, like the Federal Reserve in the United States and the Bundesbank in Germany, keep assets on hand that can be used to settle international obligations. An increase in the U.S. Federal Reserve Bank's holdings of German marks is considered an increase in U.S. government assets abroad (item 8 in Table 37.1). In 1992, the U.S. government reduced its holdings of foreign assets by $2.9 billion, and foreign governments increased their holdings of U.S. assets by $40.3 billion. The sum of items 6 through 9 in Table 37.1 is the **balance on capital account.**

The Statistical Discrepancy

Every use of foreign exchange must have a source. That is, every bit of foreign exchange that a country uses to buy foreign goods, services, or assets must come from somewhere. Thus,

> The overall sum of all the entries in the balance of payments must be zero.

balance on capital account In the United States, the sum of the following (measured in a given period): the change in private U.S. assets abroad, the change in foreign private assets in the United States, the change in U.S. government assets abroad, and the change in foreign government assets in the United States.

This implies that if the current account is in *deficit,* there must be a *surplus* in the capital account. Similarly, if the current account is in surplus, the capital account must be in deficit.

To be more specific: Ignoring investment income and transfers, a country runs a current account deficit if it imports more than it exports. Where does the foreign exchange come from to pay for these imports? It must come from the sale of assets (or borrowing). When a country sells more of its assets than it buys abroad, it runs a capital account surplus. In essence, such a country is borrowing foreign exchange from abroad.

As you can see from Table 37.1, the $62.4 billion current account deficit in 1992 was offset by a surplus on the capital account of $75.5 billion. The difference between the balance on current account and the balance on capital account is listed as a *statistical discrepancy.* In 1992 it was −$13.1 billion. The statistical discrepancy is an error of measurement. If there were no errors in compiling the data, the statistical discrepancy would be zero.

The United States as a Debtor Nation

When a Japanese bank buys a Treasury note, the note is an asset to the Japanese bank but a liability (debt) to the U.S. government. When a U.S. bank makes a loan to Poland, the loan is an asset to the bank but a liability to Poland, which is in debt to the U.S. bank. Thus,

> When foreign assets in the United States increase, the United States is increasing its debt to the rest of the world. Conversely, when the United States acquires assets abroad, it is in essence loaning money, and foreign debts to the United States increase.

Until the mid-1980s, the United States had invested heavily in foreign countries. U.S. multinational companies bought foreign firms and plants, and U.S. banks loaned money to foreign companies and governments. All the while, U.S. exports were competing well in world markets. The United States ran balance-of-trade surpluses year after year. In essence, the United States bought foreign assets and foreigners bought U.S. goods and services. A current account surplus balanced a capital account deficit, and the United States was a net creditor nation.

This situation turned around completely during the 1980s when the United States started importing much more than it was exporting. At the same time, the United States began borrowing from abroad. That is, foreigners began buying up U.S. assets. Funds from Japan, the Netherlands, England, and Hong Kong began to flood into U.S. asset markets. Foreign investors bought buildings, houses, Treasury bills, stock, and bonds. As a result, the United States ran current account deficits and capital account surpluses in the second half of the 1980s and the early 1990s.

The consequence is that the United States is currently the largest debtor nation in the world. Foreign private citizens owned about $2.5 trillion worth of U.S. assets by the end of 1991, while private U.S. holdings of foreign assets totaled about $2.1 trillion that year.

EQUILIBRIUM OUTPUT (INCOME) IN AN OPEN ECONOMY

Everything that we have said so far has been descriptive. It is now time to turn to analysis. Just how are all these trade and capital flows determined, and what impacts do they have on the economies of the countries involved? To simplify our discussion in this part of the chapter, we will assume that exchange rates are fixed. We will relax this assumption a little later.

The International Sector and Planned Aggregate Expenditure

Our earlier descriptions of the multiplier took into account the consumption behavior of households (C), the planned investment behavior of firms (I), and the spending of the government (G). We defined the sum of these three components as planned aggregate expenditure (AE). Equilibrium is achieved when planned aggregate expenditure is equal to the total amount of product available to be purchased—that is, to aggregate output (income) (Y):

$$AE \equiv C + I + G,$$

or at equilibrium,

$$Y = C + I + G.$$

To analyze the international sector, we must include the goods and services a country exports to the rest of the world, as well as those that it imports from abroad. If we call our exports of goods and services EX, it should be clear that EX is properly considered to be a component of total output and income. A U.S. razor blade that is sold to a buyer in Mexico is as much a part of U.S. production as a similar blade that is sold in Pittsburgh. Exports simply represent demand for domestic products not by domestic households and firms and the government but by the rest of the world.

But what about imports? Remember that imports are *not a part of domestic output (Y)*. The reason is quite simple. By definition, imports are not produced by the country that is importing them. Remember also that when we look at the total consumption spending of households, the total investment spending of firms, and the total spending of the government, imports are included. Therefore, to calculate domestic output correctly, we must subtract the parts of consumption, investment, and government spending that constitute imports. Hence the definition of planned aggregate expenditure becomes:

> Planned aggregate expenditure in an open economy:
> $$AE \equiv C + I + G + EX - IM.$$

Note that if we look at the last two terms ($EX - IM$) together, we have the country's **net exports of goods and services.**

net exports of goods and services (EX-IM) The difference between a country's total exports and total imports.

DETERMINING IMPORT AND EXPORT LEVELS We must now ask: What determines the level of exports and imports in a country? For present purposes, we will simply assume that imports are a function of income (Y). The rationale is simple: When U.S. income is higher, U.S. citizens buy more of everything, including U.S. cars and peanut butter, Japanese TV sets, and Korean steel and videocassette recorders. Thus, when income rises, imports tend to go up. Algebraically, we can write

$$IM = mY,$$

where Y is income and m is some positive number.[4] Recall from Chapter 24 that the marginal propensity to consume (MPC) measures the change in consumption that results from a $1 change in income, or $\Delta C/\Delta Y$. Similarly, the **marginal propensity to import,** which we will abbreviate as MPM or m, is the change in imports caused by a $1 change in income, or $\Delta IM/\Delta Y$. If $m = 0.2$, or 20%, and income is $1000, then imports, IM, are equal to $0.2 \times \$1000 = \$200$. If income rises by $100 to $1100, then the change in imports will be equal to $m \times$ (the change in income) $= 0.2 \times \$100 = \$20$.

marginal propensity to import (MPM) The change in imports caused by a $1 change in income.

Regarding exports, first note that one country's exports are other countries' imports. If a country's income (Y) affects its imports, as we have assumed, then

---

[4]We usually assume that $0 < m < 1.0$. Otherwise, a $1 increase in income generates an increase in imports of more than $1, which does not make sense.

the amount of goods and services that other countries import from the United States (U.S. exports) depends on the incomes of those countries. If foreign incomes go up, other countries' imports, and thus U.S. exports, should increase. For our purposes here, we will assume that exports (*EX*) are given. For now, we are simply assuming that U.S. exports are not affected, even indirectly, by the state of the U.S. economy. (We relax this assumption later in the chapter.)

SOLVING FOR EQUILIBRIUM With all this in mind, we can now solve for equilibrium income. This procedure is illustrated in Figure 37.1. Starting from the blue line (the consumption function) in Figure 37.1a, we gradually build up the components of planned aggregate expenditure. Assuming for simplicity's sake that planned investment, government purchases, and exports are all constant and do not depend on income, we move easily from the blue line to the brown line by simply adding the fixed amounts of *I*, *G*, and *EX* to consumption at every level of income. In this example, we take $I + G + EX$ to equal 80.

$C + I + G + EX$, however, includes spending on imports, which are not part of domestic production. To correct this problem, we must subtract the amount that is imported at each level of income. In Figure 37.1b, we assume that $m = .25$. That is, 25% of total income is spent on goods and services produced in foreign countries. Imports are a constant fraction of total income, and therefore at higher levels of income a larger amount is spent on foreign goods and services. For example, at $Y = 200$, $IM = .25Y$, or 50. Similarly, at $Y = 400$, $IM = .25Y$, or 100.

Remember that the *AE* function in Figure 37.1 must be planned aggregate expenditure on *domestically* produced goods and services. As income rises, some of the additional income is saved and the rest is spent. But not all of that added spending is on domestically produced goods and services. In fact, as income rises, some is saved and some is spent on imports. The brown dashed line in Figure 37.1b shows imports subtracted out of the *AE* function.

FIGURE 37.1
Determining Equilibrium Output in an Open Economy

In panel a, planned investment spending (*I*), government spending (*G*), and total exports (*EX*) are added to consumption (*C*) to arrive at planned aggregate expenditure. But $C + I + G + EX$ includes spending on imports because imports are part of planned aggregate expenditure. In panel b, the amount that is imported at every level of income is subtracted from planned aggregate expenditure. Equilibrium output occurs at Y* = 200, the point at which planned domestic aggregate expenditure crosses the 45° line.

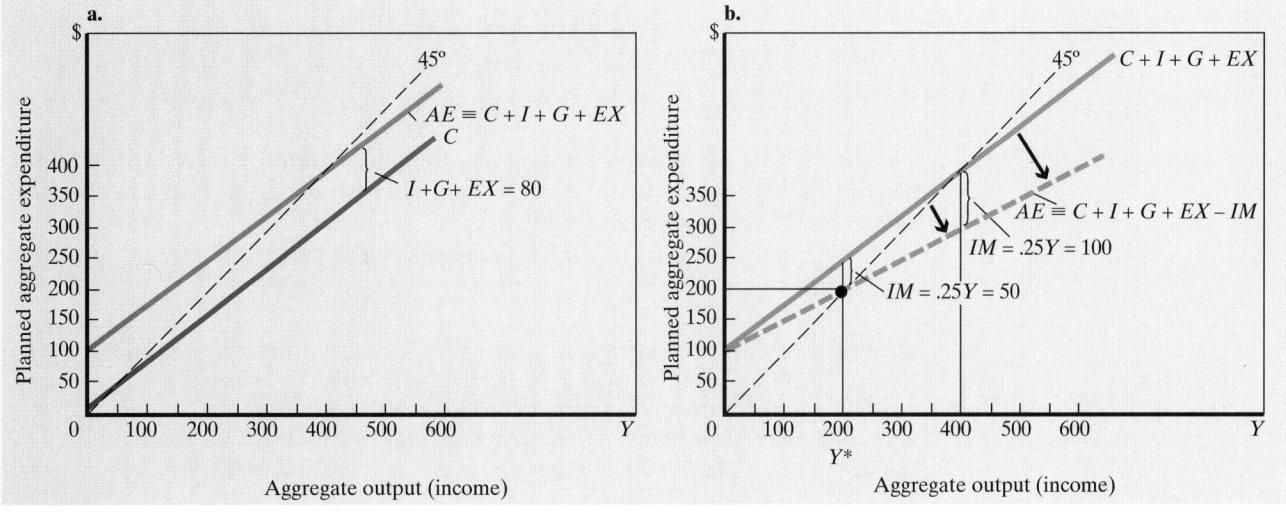

As before, equilibrium is reached when planned aggregate expenditure on domestic output is equal to aggregate domestic output (income). This is true at only one level of aggregate output, $Y^* = 200$, in Figure 37.1b. If Y were below Y^*, planned expenditure would exceed output, inventories would be lower than planned, and output would rise. At levels above Y^*, output would exceed planned expenditure, inventories would be larger than planned, and output would fall.

THE OPEN-ECONOMY MULTIPLIER   All of this has implications for the size of the multiplier. Recall the multiplier story, which we first introduced in Chapter 24, and consider a sustained rise in government purchases (G). Initially, the increase in G will cause planned aggregate expenditure to be greater than aggregate output. Domestic firms will find their inventories to be lower than planned and thus will increase their output. But added output means more income. More workers are hired and profits are higher. Some of the added income is saved, and some is spent. The added consumption spending leads to a second round of inventories being lower than planned and rising output. Thus, equilibrium output rises by a multiple of the initial increase in government purchases. This is the multiplier.

In Chapters 24 and 25, we showed that the simple multiplier is equal to $1/(1 - MPC)$, or ($1/MPS$). That is, a sustained increase in government purchases equal to ΔG will lead to an increase in aggregate output (income) of $\Delta Y = \Delta G[1/(1 - MPC)]$. For example, if the MPC were .75 and government purchases rose by $10 billion, equilibrium income would rise by $4 \times$ $10 billion, or $40 billion. The multiplier is $[1/(1 - .75)] = [1/.25] = 4.0$.

In an open economy, however, some of the increase in income brought about by the increase in G is spent on imports rather than on domestically produced goods and services. The part of income that is spent on imports does not increase domestic income (Y) because imports are produced by foreigners. Thus, to compute the multiplier we need to know how much of the increased income is used to increase domestic consumption. (We are assuming here that all imports are consumption goods. In practice, some imports are investment goods and some are goods purchased by the government.) In other words, we need to know the marginal propensity to consume *domestic* goods. Domestic consumption is $C - IM$. So the marginal propensity to consume domestic goods is the marginal propensity to consume all goods (the MPC) minus the marginal propensity to import (the MPM). The marginal propensity to consume domestic goods is thus ($MPC - MPM$). Consequently, the open-economy multiplier is 1 divided by 1 minus the marginal propensity to consume domestic goods:

$$\text{Open-Economy Multiplier} \quad \frac{1}{1 - (MPC - MPM)}.$$

If the MPC is .75 and the MPM is .25, then the multiplier is $1/.5$, or 2.0. Note that this multiplier is smaller than the multiplier in which imports are not taken into account, which is $1/.25$, or 4.0.

The major message of the open-economy multiplier model can be put quite succinctly:

The effect of a sustained increase in government spending (or investment) on income—that is, the multiplier—is smaller in an open economy than in a closed economy. The reason is simply that when government spending (or investment) increases and income and consumption rise, some of the extra consumption spending that results is on foreign products and not on domestically produced goods and services.

The Determinants of Imports and Exports

When U.S. citizens buy U.S. cars, they generate income for the U.S. firm that sold the cars and thus increase U.S. output. When U.S. citizens buy Japanese cars, however, they generate income for a Japanese firm and have no effect on U.S. output.

But buying a Japanese car does provide a stimulus for the Japanese economy. This, in turn, leads to an increase in Japanese income and therefore to an increase in Japanese spending on imports, which include exports from the United States. In this section, we discuss the determinants of imports and exports.

THE DETERMINANTS OF IMPORTS   For the sake of simplicity, we have thus far assumed that the amount of spending on imports depends only on income. In reality, however, the amount of spending on imports depends on factors other than income. In fact, the same factors that affect the consumption behavior of households and the investment behavior of firms are likely to affect the demand for imports because some imported goods are consumption goods and some are investment goods.

Anything that increases consumption spending, for example, is likely to increase the demand for imports. When U.S. citizens want to buy more cars or spaghetti, some of their extra purchases will be U.S. made and some will be made in Japan or Italy. We saw in Chapters 24 and 32 that such factors as the after-tax real wage, after-tax nonlabor income, and interest rates also affect consumption spending. These factors thus affect spending on imports. Higher interest rates, for example, should discourage consumption of both domestically produced goods and foreign-produced goods.

There is one additional consideration in determining spending on imports: the *relative prices* of domestically produced and foreign-produced goods. If the prices of foreign goods are low relative to the prices of domestic goods, people will consume more foreign goods relative to domestic goods. Thus, when Japanese cars are cheap relative to U.S. cars, consumption of Japanese cars should be high. When U.S. cars are relatively inexpensive compared with Japanese cars, consumption of Japanese cars should be lower.

THE DETERMINANTS OF EXPORTS   Now let us relax our assumption that exports are fixed. The demand for U.S. exports by other countries is identical to their demand for imports from the United States. Germany imports goods, some of which are U.S. produced. So do France, Spain, and so on. Total expenditure on imports in Germany is a function of the factors we have just discussed, except that the variables are German variables rather than U.S. variables. This is true, of course, for all other countries as well. The demand for U.S. exports thus depends on economic activity in the rest of the world—rest-of-the-world real wages, wealth, nonlabor income, interest rates, and so on—as well as on the prices of U.S. goods relative to the price of rest-of-the-world goods.

If economic activity abroad is high and foreign GDP's are booming, U.S. exports tend to increase. U.S. exports also tend to increase when U.S. prices are low relative to those in the rest of the world as people abroad substitute away from their domestic goods to the cheaper U.S. goods.

THE TRADE FEEDBACK EFFECT   We can now combine what we know about the demand for imports and the demand for exports to discuss the **trade feedback effect.** Suppose, for example, that the United States finds its exports increasing, perhaps because the British suddenly decide they prefer U.S. hot dogs to British sausages. If U.S. exports to England rise by $100 million, will net U.S. exports (exports minus imports) increase by $100 million as well?

trade feedback effect The tendency for an increase in the economic activity of one country to lead to a worldwide increase in economic activity.

FIGURE 37.2

The Trade Feedback Effect

An increase in U.S. income (Y_{US}) causes an increase in U.S. imports from the rest of the world (IM_{US}). But U.S. imports are ROW (rest of the world) exports (EX_{ROW}). When the rest of the world's export sales increase, income abroad (Y_{ROW}) goes up. Higher foreign income, in turn, leads the rest of the world to demand more imports (IM_{ROW}). Some of the imports of the rest of the world are exports of the United States (EX_{US}). Thus, an increase in U.S. income leads, through the trade feedback effect, to an increase in U.S. exports, which further increases U.S. income.

$$\uparrow Y_{US} \rightarrow (\uparrow IM_{US} \equiv \uparrow EX_{ROW}) \rightarrow \uparrow Y_{ROW} \rightarrow (\uparrow IM_{ROW} \equiv \uparrow EX_{US})$$

The answer is no. When U.S. exports increase, U.S. income rises, just as it would if consumption, investment, or government purchases were higher. This increase in U.S. income, in turn, increases U.S. demand for imports, so that some of the "extra" $100 million in export revenues goes to pay for additional purchases from abroad. Assume, for example, that a $1.00 increase in exports increases GDP by $1.40, and a $1.00 increase in income raises import spending by $0.15. In such a case, a $100 million increase in exports will raise imports by $21 million (or 1.4 × .15). On balance, then, the $100 million in extra export revenues increases U.S. net exports by only $79 million, because $21 million of the $100 million is taken up by additional spending on imports.

There is however, still more to the story. Because U.S. imports are somebody else's exports, the extra import demand from the United States raises the exports of the rest of the world. When other countries' exports to the United States go up, their output and incomes also rise, which in turn leads to an increase in the demand for imports from the rest of the world. Some of the extra imports demanded by the rest of the world come from the United States, so U.S. exports increase. The increase in U.S. exports stimulates U.S. economic activity even more, which leads to a further increase in the U.S. demand for imports, and so on. The various steps in this process are depicted in Figure 37.2, which shows that:

> An increase in U.S. economic activity leads to a worldwide increase in economic activity, which then "feeds back" to the United States. U.S. imports stimulate other countries' exports, which stimulate those countries' imports, which stimulate U.S. exports, and so on. In short, imports affect exports, and vice versa. This is the trade feedback effect.

IMPORT AND EXPORT PRICES We have talked about the price of imports, but we have not yet discussed the factors that influence import prices. The consideration of import prices is complicated by the fact that more than one currency is involved. When we talk about "the price of imports," do we mean the price in dollars, in francs, or in yen? And because the exports of one country are the imports of another, the same question holds for the price of exports. When France exports wine to the United States, for example, French wine growers are interested in the price of wine in terms of francs, because francs are what they use for transactions in France. U.S. consumers, on the other hand, are interested in the price of wine in terms of dollars, because dollars are what they use for transactions in the United States. The link between the two prices is, of course, the dollar/franc exchange rate.

Suppose France is experiencing an inflation and the price of wine in French francs rises from 20 francs per bottle to 30 francs per bottle. France's export price for wine (in terms of francs) will in general go up by the same amount.[5] If the dollar/franc exchange rate remains unchanged at, say, $0.20 per franc, then France's export price for wine in terms of dollars will also rise, from $4 per bottle to $6 per bottle. Because France's exports to the United States are by definition U.S. imports

---

[5]France's wine exporters could raise the export price but keep it less than the domestic price (to try to stay competitive with the rest of the world), but we ignore this possibility here.

$$\uparrow P_G \rightarrow (\uparrow P_G^{EX} \equiv \uparrow P_F^{IM}) \rightarrow \uparrow P_F \rightarrow (\uparrow P_F^{EX} \equiv \uparrow P_G^{IM})$$

FIGURE 37.3
The Price Feedback Effect
An increase in the German price level (P_G) implies an increase in the price of German exports to France (P_G^{EX}). But because German exports to France are identical to French imports from Germany, an export price increase shows up as an increase in the price of French imports (P_F^{IM}). In turn, France's domestic prices (P_F) rise when import prices rise. This means that the prices of French exports (P_F^{EX}) go up, which causes German import prices (P_G^{IM}) to rise. But we know that an increase in German import prices tends to push up German domestic prices. An increase in the German price level thus feeds back on itself through interaction with the rest of the world.

from France, an increase in the dollar prices of French exports to the United States means an increase in the prices of U.S. imports from France. Therefore, when France's export prices rise with no change in the dollar/franc exchange rate, U.S. import prices rise. This holds for any country. The point is clear:

Export prices of other countries affect U.S. import prices.

A country's export prices tend to move fairly closely with the general price level in that country. If France is experiencing a general increase in prices, it is quite likely that this change will be reflected in price increases of all domestically produced goods, both exportable and nonexportable. Therefore,

The general rate of inflation abroad is likely to affect U.S. import prices. If the inflation rate abroad is high, U.S. import prices are likely to rise.

THE PRICE FEEDBACK EFFECT We have just seen that when a country experiences an increase in domestic prices, the prices of its exports will increase. But it is also true that when the prices of a country's *imports* increase, the prices of domestic goods may increase in response. There are at least two mechanisms by which this can occur.

First, an increase in the prices of imported inputs will shift a country's aggregate supply curve to the left. In Chapter 29 we discussed the macroeconomy's response to a cost shock. Recall that a leftward shift in the aggregate supply curve due to a cost increase causes aggregate output to fall and prices to rise (stagflation).

Second, if import prices rise relative to domestic prices, households will tend to substitute domestically produced goods and services for imports. This is equivalent to a rightward shift of the aggregate demand curve. If the domestic economy is operating on the upward-sloping part of the aggregate supply curve, the overall domestic price level will rise in response to an increase in aggregate demand. Perfectly competitive firms will see market-determined prices rise, and imperfectly competitive firms will experience an increase in the demand for their products. Studies have shown, for example, that the price of automobiles produced in the United States moves very closely with the price of cars imported from Japan and Europe.

But this is not the end of the story. Suppose that a particular country—say, Germany—experiences an increase in its domestic price level. This will increase the price of its exports to France (and to all other countries as well). In turn, the increase in the price of French imports from Germany will lead to an increase in domestic prices in France if the French economy is operating on the steep part of the *AS* curve. But France also exports to Germany. Thus, the increase in French prices causes an increase in the price of French exports to Germany, making the inflation in Germany even worse.

This process is called the **price feedback effect,** and it is summarized in Figure 37.3. The price feedback effect shows that inflation is "exportable." An increase in the price level in one country can drive up prices in other countries; this, in turn, increases the price level in the first country. Through export and import prices, a domestic price increase can "feed back" on itself.

price feedback effect The process by which a domestic price increase in one country can "feed back" on itself through export and import prices. An increase in the price level in one country can drive up prices in other countries; this, in turn, increases the price level in the first country.

THE OPEN ECONOMY WITH FLEXIBLE EXCHANGE RATES

floating, or market-determined, exchange rates Exchange rates that are determined by the unregulated forces of supply and demand.

To a large extent, the fixed exchange rates set by the Bretton Woods agreements served as the centerpiece of international monetary arrangements until 1971. Then, in 1971 the United States and most other countries decided to abandon the fixed exchange rate system in favor of **floating,** or **market-determined, exchange rates.** While governments still intervene periodically to ensure that exchange rate movements are "orderly," exchange rates today are largely determined by the unregulated forces of supply and demand.

Understanding how an economy interacts with the rest of the world when exchange rates are not fixed is not as simple as it is when we assume fixed exchange rates. Exchange rates determine the price of imported goods relative to domestic goods and can have significant effects on the level of imports and exports. For example, consider a 20% drop in the value of the dollar against the deutsche mark. This means that dollars buy fewer marks and that marks buy more dollars. Both Germans, who now get more dollars for marks, and U.S. citizens, who get fewer marks for dollars, find that U.S. goods and services are more attractive. Thus, exchange rate movements can and do have important impacts on imports, exports, and the movement of capital between countries.

The Market for Foreign Exchange

What determines exchange rates under a floating rate system? To explore this issue, we will assume for now that there are just two countries, the United States and Great Britain. It is easier to understand a world with only two countries, and most of the points we will make can be generalized to a world with many trading partners.

THE SUPPLY OF AND DEMAND FOR POUNDS Governments, private citizens, banks, and corporations exchange pounds for dollars and dollars for pounds every day. In our two-country case, those who *demand* pounds are holders of dollars seeking to exchange them for pounds. Those who *supply* pounds are holders of pounds seeking to exchange them for dollars. It is important not to confuse the supply of dollars (or pounds) on the foreign exchange market with the U.S. (or British) money supply. The latter is the sum of all the money currently in circulation. The supply of dollars on the foreign exchange market is the number of dollars that holders seek to exchange for pounds in a given time period. The demand for, and supply of, dollars on foreign exchange markets determines *exchange* rates; the demand for money balances and the total domestic money supply determine the *interest* rate.

The most common reason for exchanging dollars for pounds is to buy something produced in Great Britain. U.S. importers who purchase Jaguar automobiles or Scotch whiskey must pay with pounds. U.S. citizens traveling in Great Britain who want to ride the train, stay in a hotel, or eat at a restaurant must acquire pounds for dollars in order to do so. If a U.S. corporation builds a plant in Great Britain, it must pay for that plant in pounds.

At the same time, some people may want to buy British stocks or bonds. Implicitly, when a U.S. citizen buys a bond issued by the British government or by a British corporation, he or she is making a loan, but the transaction requires a currency exchange. The British bond seller must ultimately be paid in pounds.

On the supply side of the market, the situation is reversed. Here we find people—usually British citizens—holding pounds with which they want to buy dollars. Again, the most common reason is to buy things produced in the United States. If a British importer decides to import golf carts made in Georgia, the producer must be paid in

THE DEMAND FOR POUNDS (SUPPLY OF DOLLARS)

1. Firms, households, or governments that import British goods into the United States
2. U.S. citizens traveling in Great Britain
3. Holders of dollars who want to buy British stocks, bonds, or other financial instruments
4. U.S. companies that want to invest in Great Britain
5. Speculators who anticipate a decline in the value of the dollar relative to the pound

THE SUPPLY OF POUNDS (DEMAND FOR DOLLARS)

1. Firms, households, or governments that import U.S. goods into Great Britain
2. British citizens traveling in the United States
3. Holders of pounds who want to buy stocks, bonds, or other financial instruments in the United States
4. British companies that want to invest in the United States
5. Speculators who anticipate a rise in the value of the dollar relative to the pound

TABLE 37.2
Some Private Buyers and Sellers in International Exchange Markets: United States and Great Britain

dollars. Similarly, British tourists visiting New York may ride in cabs, eat in restaurants, and tour Ellis Island. Doing these things requires dollars. When a British firm builds an office complex in Los Angeles, it must pay the contractor in dollars.

In addition to buyers and sellers who exchange money to engage in transactions, some people and institutions hold currency balances for speculative reasons. If I think that the U.S. dollar is going to decline in value relative to the pound, I may want to hold some of my wealth in the form of pounds. Table 37.2 summarizes some of the major categories of private foreign exchange demanders and suppliers in the two-country case of the United States and Great Britain.

Figure 37.4 shows the demand curve for pounds in the foreign exchange market. When the price of pounds (the exchange rate) is lower, it takes fewer dollars to buy British goods and services, to build a plant in Liverpool, to travel to London, and so forth. Lower net prices (in dollars) should increase the demand for British-made products and encourage investment and travel in

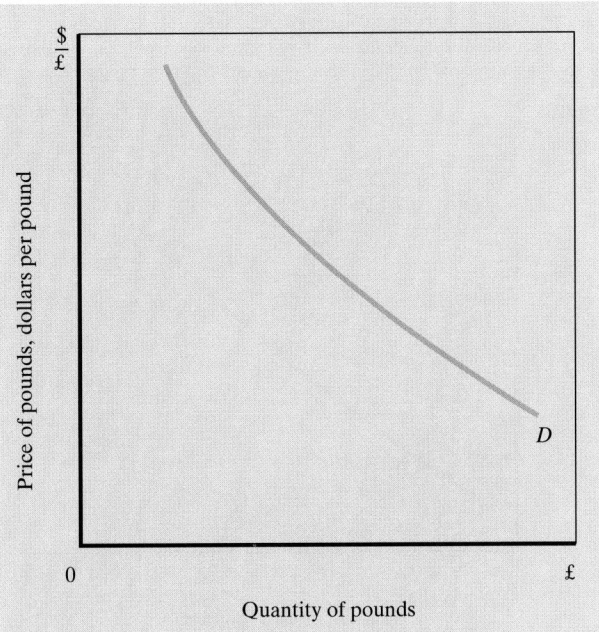

FIGURE 37.4
The Demand for Pounds in the Foreign Exchange Market

When the price of pounds falls, British-made goods and services appear less expensive to U.S. buyers. If British prices are constant, U.S. buyers will buy more British goods and services, and the quantity of pounds demanded will rise.

Great Britain. If prices (in pounds) in Britain do not change, an increase in the quantity of British goods and services demanded by foreigners will increase the quantity of pounds demanded. Thus, the demand-for-pounds curve in the foreign exchange market has a negative slope.

Figure 37.5 shows a supply curve for pounds in the foreign exchange market. At a higher exchange rate, each pound buys more dollars, in which case the price of U.S.-produced goods and services is lower to the British. The British are thus more apt to buy U.S.-made goods when the price of pounds is high (the value of the dollar is low). An increase in British demand for U.S. goods and services is likely to increase the quantity of pounds supplied. Thus, the curve representing the supply of pounds in the foreign exchange market has a positive slope.[6]

THE EQUILIBRIUM EXCHANGE RATE   When exchange rates are allowed to float, they are determined the same way that other prices are determined:

> The equilibrium exchange rate occurs at the point at which the quantity demanded of a foreign currency equals the quantity of that currency supplied.

This is illustrated in Figure 37.6.

An excess demand for pounds (quantity demanded in excess of quantity supplied) will cause the price of pounds to rise—that is, the pound will **appreciate** with respect to the dollar. An excess supply of pounds will cause the price of pounds to fall—that is, the pound will **depreciate** with respect to the dollar.

appreciation of a currency The rise in value of one currency relative to another.

depreciation of a currency The fall in value of one currency relative to another.

---

[6]While Figure 37.5 shows the supply-of-pounds curve in the foreign exchange market with a positive slope, under certain circumstances the curve may bend back. Suppose, for example, that the price of a pound rises from $1.50 to $2.00. Consider a British importer who buys 10 Chevrolets each month at $15,000 each, including transportation costs. When a pound exchanges for $1.50, he will supply 100,000 pounds per month to the foreign exchange market—100,000 pounds brings $150,000, enough to buy 10 cars. Now suppose that the cheaper dollar causes him to buy 12 cars. Twelve cars will cost a total of $180,000, but at $2.00 = 1 pound, he will spend only 90,000 pounds per month. Thus, the supply of pounds on the market actually falls when the price of pounds rises. The reason for this seeming paradox is simple. The number of pounds a British importer needs to buy U.S. goods depends on both the quantity of goods he buys and the price of those goods in pounds. If demand for imports is inelastic so that the percentage decrease in price resulting from the depreciated currency is greater than the percentage increase in the quantity of imports demanded, importers will spend fewer pounds and the quantity of pounds supplied in the foreign exchange market will fall. The supply of pounds will slope upward as long as the demand for U.S. imports is elastic.

FIGURE 37.5
The Supply of Pounds in the Foreign Exchange Market

When the price of pounds rises, the British can obtain more dollars for each pound. This means that U.S.-made goods and services appear less expensive to British buyers. Thus, the quantity of pounds supplied is likely to rise with the exchange rate.

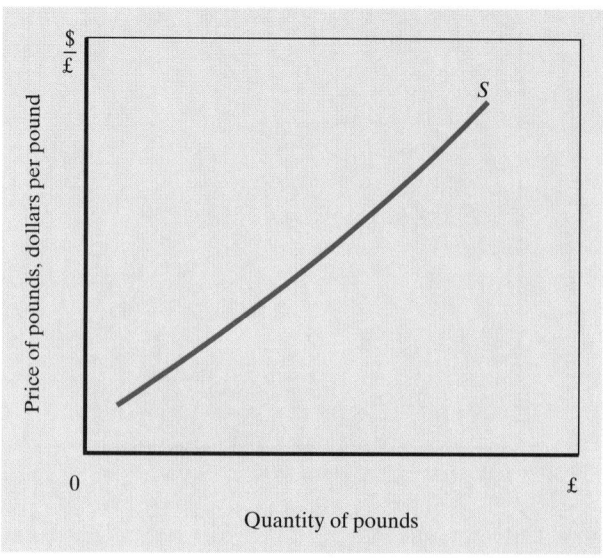

Quantity of pounds

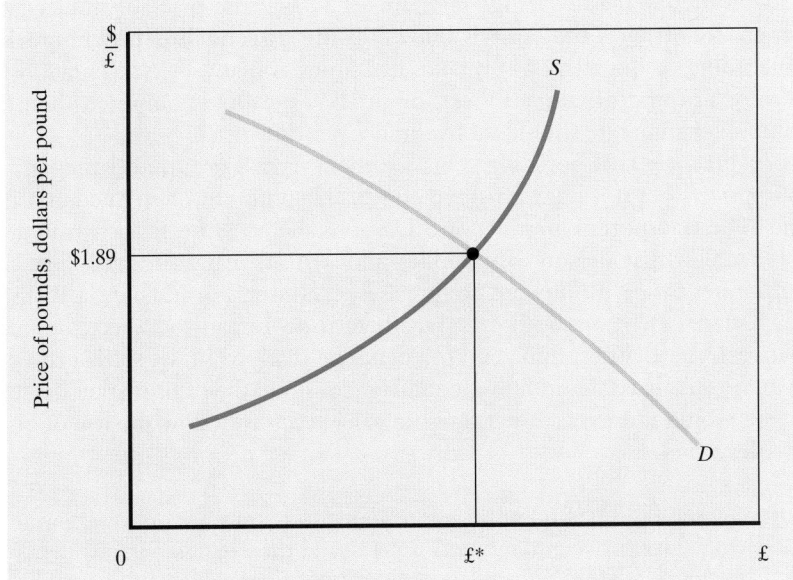

FIGURE 37.6
The Equilibrium Exchange Rate

When exchange rates are allowed to float, they are determined by the forces of supply and demand. An excess demand for pounds will cause the pound to appreciate against the dollar. An excess supply of pounds will lead to a depreciating pound.

Factors That Affect Exchange Rates

We now have enough information to discuss the factors likely to influence exchange rates. Anything that changes the behavior of the people listed in Table 37.2 can cause demand and supply curves to shift and the exchange rate to adjust accordingly.

PURCHASING POWER PARITY: THE LAW OF ONE PRICE   If the costs of transporting goods between two countries are small, we would expect the price of the same good in both countries to be roughly the same. The price of basketballs should be roughly the same in Canada and the United States, for example.

It is not hard to see why this is so. Suppose that the price of basketballs is cheaper in Canada. In this case, it will pay for someone to buy balls in Canada at a low price and sell them in the United States at a higher price. This decreases the supply and pushes up the price in Canada and increases the supply and pushes down the price in the United States. This process should continue as long as the price differential, and therefore the profit opportunity, persists. For a good with trivial transportation costs, therefore, we would expect this **law of one price** to hold. The price of a good should be the same regardless of where we buy it.

If the law of one price held for all goods, and if each country consumed the same market basket of goods, the exchange rate between the two currencies would be determined simply by the relative price levels in the two countries. If the price of a basketball were $10.00 in the United States and $12.00 in Canada, then the U.S.-Canada exchange rate would have to be $1.00 U.S. per $1.20 Canadian. If the rate were instead one-to-one, it would pay people to buy the balls in the United States and sell them in Canada. This would increase the demand for U.S. dollars in Canada, thereby driving up their price in terms of Canadian dollars to one U.S. dollar per 1.2 Canadian dollars, at which point no one could make a profit shipping basketballs across international lines, and the process would cease.[7]

law of one price If the costs of transportation are small, the price of the same good in different countries should be roughly the same.

---

[7]Of course, if the rate were $1.00 U.S. to $2.00 Canadian, then it would pay people to buy basketballs in Canada (at $12.00 Canadian, or $6.00 U.S.) and sell them in the United States. This would weaken demand for the U.S. dollar, and its price would fall from $2.00 Canadian until it reached $1.20 Canadian.

purchasing-power-parity theory
A theory of international exchange that holds that exchange rates are set so that the price of similar goods in different countries is the same.

The theory that exchange rates are set so that the price of similar goods in different countries is the same is known as the **purchasing-power-parity theory.** According to this theory, if it takes five times as many French francs as U.S. dollars to buy a pound of salt, a TV set, or an IBM personal computer, then the equilibrium exchange rate should be five francs per dollar.

In practice, transportation costs for many goods are quite large, and the law of one price does not hold for these goods. (Haircuts are often cited as a good example. The transportation costs for a U.S. resident to get a French haircut are indeed large unless that person is an airline pilot.) Also, many products that are potential substitutes for each other are not precisely identical. For instance, a Rolls Royce and a Mercedes Benz are both cars, but there is no reason to expect the exchange rate between the British pound and the deutsche mark to be set so that the prices of the two are equalized. In addition, countries consume different market baskets of goods, so we would not expect the aggregate price levels to follow the law of one price.

Nevertheless,

> A high rate of inflation in one country relative to another puts pressure on the exchange rate between the two countries, and there is a general tendency for the currencies of relative high-inflation countries to depreciate.

Figure 37.7 shows the adjustments that are likely to take place following an increase in the U.S. price level relative to the price level in Great Britain. This change in relative prices will affect citizens of both countries. Higher prices in the United States make imports relatively less expensive. Thus, U.S. citizens are likely to increase their spending on imports from Britain, shifting the demand for pounds to the right, from D to D'. At the same time, the British see U.S. goods getting more expensive and reduce their demand for exports from the United States. Consequently, the supply of pounds shifts to the left, from S to S'. The result is an increase in the price of pounds. Before the change in relative prices, one pound sold for $1.89; after the change, one pound costs $2.25. The pound appreciates and the dollar is worth less.

FIGURE 37.7
Exchange Rates Respond to Changes in Relative Prices

This figure shows the effects of an increase in the U.S. price level relative to the price level in Great Britain. The higher price level in the United States makes imports relatively less expensive. Thus, U.S. citizens are likely to increase their spending on imports from Britain, shifting the demand for pounds to the right, from D to D'. At the same time, the British see U.S. goods getting more expensive and reduce their demand for exports from the United States. Thus, the supply of pounds shifts to the left, from S to S'. The result is an increase in the price of pounds. The pound appreciates and the dollar is worth less.

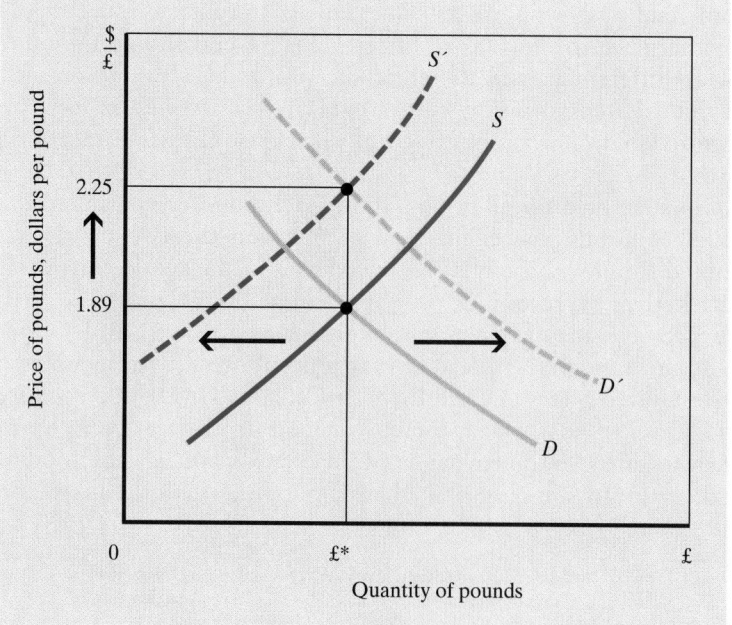

RELATIVE INTEREST RATES   Another important factor that influences a country's exchange rate is the level of its interest rate relative to other countries' interest rates. If the interest rate is 7% in the United States and 9% in Germany, people with money to lend have an obvious incentive to buy German securities rather than U.S. securities. Although it is sometimes difficult for individuals in one country to buy securities in another country, it is quite easy for international banks and investment companies to do so. If the interest rate is lower in the United States than in Germany, there will be a movement of funds out of U.S. securities into German securities as banks and firms move their funds to the higher-yielding securities.

How does a U.S. bank buy German securities? It takes its dollars, buys German deutsche marks, and then uses the marks to buy the German securities. The bank's purchase of marks drives up the price of marks in the foreign exchange market. In other words, there is an increased demand for marks, which increases the price of the mark (and decreases the price of the dollar). Thus, a high interest rate in Germany relative to the interest rate in the United States tends to depreciate the dollar.

Figure 37.8 shows the effect of rising interest rates in the United States on the pound-dollar exchange rate. Higher interest rates in the United States attract British investors. To buy U.S. securities, the British need dollars. Thus, the supply of pounds (the demand for dollars) shifts to the right, from S to S'. The same relative interest rates affect the portfolio choices of U.S. banks, firms, and households. With higher interest rates at home, there is less incentive for U.S. residents to buy British securities. Thus, the demand for pounds drops at the same time as the supply increases and the demand curve shifts to the left, from D to D'. The net result is a depreciating pound and an appreciating dollar. The price of pounds falls from $1.89 to $1.25.

During the early 1980s, the Federal Reserve pursued a tight money policy to fight the inflation that began in the late 1970s. At the same time, Congress and the President were pursuing a loose fiscal policy. The result was very high interest rates, particularly in 1981. These high interest rates attracted a great deal of foreign capital, particularly from Japan. The Japanese have had a very high saving rate for many years, and interest rates in Japan are very low. In order to buy U.S. stocks and

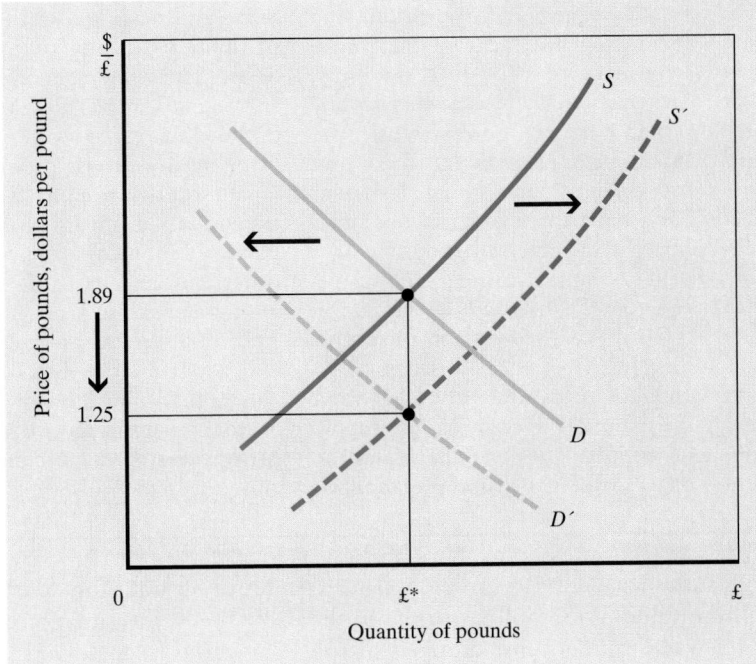

Quantity of pounds

FIGURE 37.8
Exchange Rates Respond to Changes in Relative Interest Rates

If U.S. interest rates rise relative to British interest rates, British citizens holding pounds may be attracted into the U.S. securities market. To buy bonds in the United States, British buyers must exchange pounds for dollars. Thus, the supply of pounds shifts to the right, from S to S'. But U.S. citizens are less likely to be interested in British securities, because interest rates are higher at home. Thus, the demand for pounds also shifts to the left, from D to D'. The result is a depreciated pound and a stronger dollar.

THE DOLLAR AND THE YEN IN 1993

Although the Tokyo Stock Market dropped dramatically in 1993 as Japan experienced a recession, the value of the yen still increased against the value of the U.S. dollar that year.

One of the most important economic events of the last few years was the sharp drop in the value of the dollar against the Japanese yen (¥) in late 1992 and early 1993. On April 22, 1993, the exchange rate closed on international markets at 110.71 yen—an all-time low. A year earlier, the dollar had been worth 135 yen; 10 years earlier, it had been worth 238 yen. What was behind this decrease, and what effect is it likely to have on the economies of the United States and Japan?

First, the decline was expected to have a significant impact on the U.S. balance of trade with Japan. Neither Japan nor the United States has experienced much inflation during the past decade, and certainly inflation rates in both nations were very low in 1992 and 1993. Thus, the decline of the dollar clearly made goods and services produced in the United States less expensive to the Japanese and made goods and services produced in Japan more expensive to U.S. buyers. Thus, U.S. citizens were expected to buy fewer Japanese goods, while the Japanese were expected to buy more American goods. This was good news for U.S. exporters, who hoped that increased exports would help sustain the nation's slow recovery from the 1990-1991 recession.

Why has the yen appreciated so sharply? Most economists point to changes in capital flows between the countries. Recall that the supply of yen (demand for dollars) and the demand for yen (supply of dollars) on foreign exchange markets is driven by both the demand for foreign-produced goods and the demand for stocks, bonds, and other investment opportunities. During the early 1980s the combination of a high saving rate and low interest rates in Japan and high interest rates in the United States produced a great demand for dollars that drove the dollar to more than 250 yen. This high exchange rate made Japanese goods seem inexpensive to Americans and made U.S. goods appear expensive to the Japanese. The result was a high trade deficit with Japan balanced by a large capital account surplus.

In 1993, however, interest rates in the United States were about the same as interest rates in Japan, whose economy was in recession and whose stock market had dropped dramatically. Having lost money and income at home, Japanese citizens were selling off some of their assets in the United States and sending a smaller portion of their net saving to the United States. Thus, the demand for dollars for capital-account transactions declined sharply.

None of this was pleasing to the Japanese government. Because an expensive yen means that Japanese goods are more expensive to Americans, experts predicted a drop in exports to the United States. In April of 1993, as the dollar continued to drop, the Bank of Japan "intervened" by buying up dollars on foreign exchange markets in an attempt to stop the decline and stabilize the yen.

bonds, the Japanese had to buy dollars. This drove up both the demand for dollars and the value of the dollar sharply. In the early 1990s, this situation reversed itself, as the value of the dollar dropped sharply against the Japanese yen. For the complete story, see the Global Perspective box titled "The Dollar and the Yen in 1993."

The Effects of Exchange Rates on the Economy

We are now ready to discuss some of the implications of floating exchange rates. Recall that when exchange rates are fixed, households spend some of their incomes on imports and the multiplier is smaller than it would otherwise be. Imports are a "leakage" from the circular flow, very much like taxes and saving are. Exports, on the other hand, are like investment and government purchases; they represent spending on U.S.-produced goods and services ("injections" into the circular flow) and can stimulate output.

The world is far more complicated when exchange rates are allowed to float. First, the level of imports and exports depends on exchange rates as well as on income and other factors. Thus, when events cause exchange rates to adjust, the level of imports and exports will change. Changes in exports and imports can, in turn, affect the level of real GDP and the price level. To complicate matters further, exchange rates themselves also adjust to changes in the economy. For example, suppose the government decides to stimulate the economy with an expansionary monetary policy. This will affect interest rates, which may in turn affect exchange rates.

EXCHANGE RATE EFFECTS ON IMPORTS, EXPORTS, AND REAL GDP As we already know, when a country's currency depreciates (falls in value), its import prices rise and its export prices (in foreign currencies) fall. When the U.S. dollar is cheap, U.S. products are more competitive with products produced in the rest of the world, and foreign-made goods look expensive to U.S. citizens.

A depreciation of a country's currency, then, can serve as a stimulus to the economy. Suppose, for example, that the U.S. dollar falls in value, as it did sharply between 1985 and 1988. If foreign buyers increase their spending on U.S. goods, and domestic buyers substitute U.S.-made goods for imports, aggregate expenditure on domestic output will rise, inventories will fall, and real GDP (Y) will increase. Thus,

> A depreciation of a country's currency is likely to increase its GDP.[8]

EXCHANGE RATES AND THE BALANCE OF TRADE: THE J CURVE Because a depreciating currency tends to increase exports and decrease imports, you might think that it will also reduce a country's trade deficit. In fact, the effect of a depreciation on the balance of trade is ambiguous.

Many economists believe that a depreciation is likely to worsen the balance of trade for the first few quarters (perhaps three to six) after the initial depreciation. After that time, the balance of trade may improve. This effect is graphed in Figure 37.9 on the next page. The curve in this figure resembles the letter J, and the movement in the balance of trade that it describes is sometimes called the **J-curve effect.** The main point of the J shape is that the balance of trade gets worse before it gets better following a currency depreciation.

J-curve effect Following a currency depreciation, a country's balance of trade may get worse before it gets better. The graph showing this effect is shaped like the letter J, hence the name "J-curve effect."

---

[8]For this reason, some countries are tempted at times to intervene in foreign exchange markets, depreciate their currencies, and thus stimulate their economies. If all countries attempt to lower the value of their currencies simultaneously, there will be no gain in income for any of them. Although the exchange rate system at the time was different, such a situation actually occurred during the early years of the Great Depression. So-called beggar-thy-neighbor policies of competitive devaluations were practiced by many countries in a desperate attempt to maintain export sales and employment.

FIGURE 37.9

The Effect of a Depreciation on the Balance of Trade (the J Curve)

Initially, a depreciation of a country's currency may worsen its balance of trade. The negative effect on the price of imports may initially dominate the positive effects of an increase in exports and a decrease in imports.

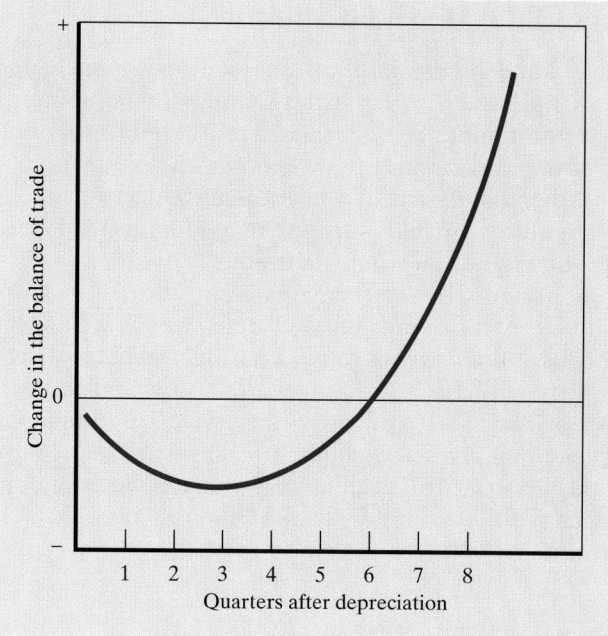

How does the J curve come about? Recall that the balance of trade is equal to export revenue minus import costs, including exports and imports of services:

$$\text{Balance of trade} = \text{Dollar price of exports} \times \text{Exports} \\ - \text{Dollar price of imports} \times \text{Imports}.$$

A currency depreciation affects at least three of the items on the right-hand side of this equation. First, the quantity of exports increases, and the quantity of imports decreases, both of which have a *positive* effect on the balance of trade (lowering the trade deficit or raising the trade surplus). Second, the dollar price of exports is not likely to change very much, at least not initially. The dollar price of exports changes when the U.S. price level changes, but the initial effect of a depreciation on the domestic price level is not likely to be large. Third, the dollar price of imports increases. Imports into the United States are more expensive, because one dollar buys fewer French francs and German deutsche marks than before. Thus, an increase in the dollar price of imports has a *negative* effect on the balance of trade.

An example may help to clarify this last point. The dollar price of a Japanese car that costs 2,000,000 yen rises from $10,000 to $15,000 when the exchange rate moves from 200 yen per dollar to 133 yen per dollar. Thus, after the currency depreciation, the United States ends up spending more (in dollars) for the Japanese car than it did before. Of course, the United States will end up buying fewer Japanese cars than it did before. But does the number of cars drop enough so that the quantity effect is bigger than the price effect, or vice versa? In other words, does the value of imports increase or decrease?

Clearly, the net effect of a depreciation on the balance of trade could go either way. The depreciation stimulates exports and cuts back imports, but it also increases the dollar price of imports. It seems generally to be the case that the negative effect dominates initially. The impact of a depreciation on the price of imports is generally felt quickly, while it takes some time for export and import quantities to respond to price changes. In the short run, the value of imports increases more than the value of exports, so the balance of trade worsens. The initial effect is thus likely to be negative; but after exports and imports have had time to respond, the net effect turns positive. The more elastic the demand for exports and imports, the larger the eventual improvement in the balance of trade.

Between 1985 and 1988, the value of the dollar dropped nearly 50% on average against heavily traded currencies. The balance-of-trade deficit grew in 1986 and 1987, but by 1988 things seemed to be improving. In 1988 there was a large increase in the real volume of U.S. exports, which finally led to an improvement in the U.S. balance of trade.

EXCHANGE RATES AND PRICES The depreciation of a country's currency tends to increase its price level. There are two reasons for this. First, when a country's currency is less expensive, its products are more competitive on world markets, so exports rise. In addition, domestic buyers tend to substitute domestic products for the now-more-expensive imports. This means that planned aggregate expenditure on domestically produced goods and services rises, and the aggregate demand curve shifts to the right. The result is a higher price level, higher output, or both. If the economy is close to capacity, the result is likely to be higher prices. In the spring of 1988, exports took a big jump upward, and many people began to fear inflation, as the economy was operating near full employment.

Second, a depreciation makes imported inputs more expensive. If costs increase, the aggregate supply curve shifts to the left. If aggregate demand remains unchanged, the result is an increase in the price level.

MONETARY POLICY WITH FLEXIBLE EXCHANGE RATES Let us now put everything we have learned in this chapter together and consider what happens when monetary policy is used first to stimulate the economy and then to contract the economy.

Suppose that the economy is below full employment and the Fed decides to expand the money supply. The volume of reserves in the system is expanded, perhaps through open-market purchases of U.S. government securities by the Fed. This results in a decrease in the interest rate. The lower interest rate stimulates planned investment spending and consumption spending.

This added spending causes inventories to be lower than planned and aggregate output (income)(Y) to rise. But there are two additional important effects. First, the lower interest rate has an impact in the foreign exchange market. A lower interest rate means a lower demand for U.S. securities by foreigners, and thus the demand for dollars drops off. In addition, U.S. investment managers will be more likely to buy foreign securities (which are now paying relatively higher interest rates), so the supply of dollars rises. These events push down the value of the dollar.

A cheaper dollar is a good thing if the goal of the monetary expansion is to stimulate the domestic economy, because a cheaper dollar means more U.S. exports and fewer imports. If consumers substitute U.S.-made goods for imports, both the added exports and the decrease in imports mean more spending on domestic products, so the multiplier actually increases.

Now suppose that inflation is a problem and that the Fed wants to slow it down with tight money. Here again, floating exchange rates help. Tight monetary policy works through a higher interest rate. A higher interest rate lowers investment and consumption spending, reducing aggregate expenditure, reducing output, and lowering the price level. The higher interest rate also attracts foreign buyers into U.S. financial markets, driving up the value of the dollar. This, in turn, increases the price of U.S. exports and reduces the price of imports. The reduction in the price of imports also helps fight the inflation.

FISCAL POLICY WITH FLEXIBLE EXCHANGE RATES The openness of the economy and flexible exchange rates do not always work to the advantage of policy makers. Consider, for example, a policy of cutting taxes to stimulate the economy. Suppose Congress enacts a major tax cut designed to raise output. Spending by households rises, but not all of this added spending is on domestic products. Some of this spending leaks out of the U.S. economy, and the multiplier is reduced.

As income (Y) rises, so too does the demand for money (M^d)—not the demand for dollars in the foreign exchange market, but the amount of money that people desire to hold for transactions. Unless the Fed is fully accommodating, the interest rate will rise. A higher interest rate tends to attract foreign demand for U.S. securities. This, in turn, tends to drive the price of the dollar up, which further blunts the effectiveness of the tax cut. If the value of the dollar rises, U.S. exports are less competitive in world markets, and the quantity of exports will decline. Similarly, a strong dollar makes imported goods look cheaper, and U.S. citizens spend more on foreign goods and less on U.S. goods.

All this leaves us with yet another caveat to add to the simple multiplier story of Chapters 24 and 25. Without a fully accommodating Fed, three factors work to reduce the multiplier: (1) A higher interest rate from the increase in money demand may crowd out private investment and consumption; (2) some of the increase in income from the expansion will be spent on imports; and (3) a higher interest rate may cause the dollar to appreciate, discouraging exports and further encouraging imports.

AN INTERDEPENDENT WORLD ECONOMY

The increasing interdependence of countries in the world economy has made the problems facing policy makers more difficult. We used to be able to think of the United States as a relatively self-sufficient region. Twenty-five years ago, economic events outside U.S. borders had relatively little effect on its economy. This is no longer true. If the events of the past two decades have taught us anything, it is that the United States is a part of a global economy and that the performance of the U.S. economy is heavily dependent on events outside its borders.

This chapter and the previous one have provided only the bare bones of open-market macroeconomics. If you continue your study of economics, as we hope you will, more will be added to the basic story we have presented.

The next two chapters keep us in the international arena. Chapter 38 deals with the problems of developing countries, and Chapter 39 explores special features of the economies of Japan, China, and the former republics of the Soviet Union.

SUMMARY

1. The main difference between an international transaction and a domestic transaction concerns currency exchange: When people in different countries buy from and sell to each other, an exchange of currencies must also take place.

2. The *exchange rate* is the price of one country's currency in terms of another country's currency.

The Balance of Payments

3. *Foreign exchange* is simply all currencies other than the domestic currency of a given country. The record of a nation's transactions in goods, services, and assets with the rest of the world is known as its *balance of payments*. The balance of payments is also the record of a country's sources (supply) and uses (demand) of foreign exchange.

Equilibrium Output (Income) in an Open Economy

4. In an open economy, some income is spent on foreign-produced goods rather than domestically produced goods. Thus, to measure planned aggregate expenditure in an open

economy, we must add total exports but subtract total imports: $AE \equiv C + I + G + EX - IM$. The open economy is in equilibrium when aggregate output (income) (Y) equals planned aggregate expenditure (AE).

5. In an open economy, the multiplier equals $1/1 - (MPC - MPM)$, where MPC is the marginal propensity to consume and MPM is the marginal propensity to import. The *marginal propensity to import* is the change in imports caused by a $1 change in income.

6. In addition to income, other factors that affect the level of imports are the after-tax real wage rate, after-tax nonlabor income, interest rates, and the relative prices of domestically produced and foreign-produced goods.

7. An increase in U.S. economic activity leads to a worldwide increase, which then "feeds back" to the United States. U.S. imports stimulate other countries' exports, which stimulate those countries' imports, which stimulate U.S. exports, and so on. This is the *trade feedback effect.*

8. Export prices of other countries affect U.S. import prices. The general rate of inflation abroad is therefore likely to affect U.S. import prices. If the inflation rate abroad is high, U.S. import prices are likely to rise.

9. Because one country's exports are another country's imports, an increase in export prices in turn increases other countries' import prices. An increase in other countries' import prices in turn leads to an increase in their domestic prices and thus their export prices. In short, export prices affect import prices, and vice versa. This *price feedback effect* shows that inflation is "exportable"; an increase in the price level in one country can drive up prices in other countries, thus making inflation in the first country worse.

The Open Economy With Flexible Exchange Rates

10. The equilibrium exchange rate occurs when the quantity demanded of a foreign currency in the foreign exchange market equals the quantity of that currency supplied in the foreign exchange market.

11. *Depreciation of a currency* occurs when a nation's currency falls in value relative to another country's currency.

12. According to the *law of one price,* if the costs of transportation are small, the price of the same good in different countries should be roughly the same. The theory that exchange rates are set so that the price of similar goods in different countries is the same is known as *purchasing-power-parity theory.* In practice, transportation costs are significant for many goods, and the law of one price does not hold for these goods.

13. A high rate of inflation in one country relative to another puts pressure on the exchange rate between the two countries. There is a general tendency for the currencies of relatively high-inflation countries to depreciate.

14. A depreciation of the dollar tends to increase U.S. GDP by making U.S. exports cheaper (and hence more competitive abroad) and by making U.S. imports more expensive (and thus encouraging consumers to switch to domestically produced goods and services).

15. The effect of a depreciation of a nation's currency on its balance of payments is unclear. In the short run, a currency depreciation may actually increase the balance-of-payments deficit, because it raises the price of imports. Although this price increase causes a decrease in the quantity of imports demanded, the impact of a depreciation on the price of imports is generally felt quickly, while it takes some time for export and import quantities to respond to price changes. The initial effect is thus likely to be negative; but after exports and imports have had time to respond, the net effect turns positive. The tendency for the balance-of-payments deficit to widen and then to decrease as the result of a currency depreciation is known as the *J-curve effect.*

16. The depreciation of a country's currency tends to raise its price level for two reasons. First, a currency depreciation increases planned aggregate expenditure, which shifts the aggregate demand curve to the right. If the economy is close to capacity, the result is likely to be higher prices. Second, a depreciation makes imported inputs more expensive. If costs increase, the aggregate supply curve shifts to the left. If aggregate demand remains unchanged, the result is an increase in the price level.

REVIEW TERMS AND CONCEPTS

PROBLEM SET

1. List the balance-of-payments account under which each of the following transactions would be classified and explain whether the item represents a credit or debit entry in the U.S. balance of payments.

    a. You go on vacation to Mexico and spend $300 there on a hotel room, food, transportation, and so forth.

    b. You bring back an Oriental carpet that you bought on a trip to the Middle East. The carpet is worth $10,000, but you do not declare it at customs, and no official record of the transaction exists.

    c. You buy a new Toyota (made in Japan) for $12,000.

    d. You send your cousin in Canada a birthday present worth $50.

    e. Volkswagen Inc. of Germany buys a factory in the United States for $100 million.

    f. Toyota of Japan buys 10% of all the shares in General Motors.

    g. You loan your uncle in Canada $5000.

    h. Your uncle pays you $500 in interest on the money you previously loaned him. He also repays $1000 of the principal.

2. Suppose that the following situation prevailed on the foreign exchange market in 1993 with floating exchange rates:

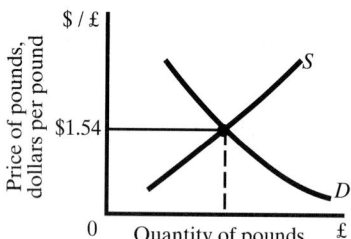

    a. Name three phenomena that might shift the demand curve to the right.

    b. Which, if any, of these three might cause a simultaneous shift of the supply curve to the left?

    c. What effects might the three phenomena have on the balance of payments? On the balance of trade?

3. During 1981 and 1982, the President and the Congress were pursuing a very expansionary fiscal policy. In 1980 and 1981, the Federal Reserve was pursuing a very restrictive monetary policy in an attempt to rid the economy of inflation. Ultimately, the economy went into a deep recession, but before it did interest rates went to record levels with the prime rate topping out at over 21 percent.

    a. Explain how this policy mix led to very high interest rates.

    b. Show graphically the effect of the high interest rates on the foreign exchange market. What do you think would happen to the value of the dollar?

    c. What impact was such a series of events likely to have on the trade deficit in countries like Japan? Explain your answer.

4. The exchange rate between the U.S. dollar and the Japanese yen is floating freely—neither government intervenes at all in the market for either currency. Suppose that because of a large trade deficit with Japan, the United States decides to impose quotas on certain Japanese products imported into the United States and, as a result, the value of these imports falls.

    a. The decrease in spending on Japanese products increases spending on U.S.-made goods. Why? What effect will this have on U.S. output and employment? On Japanese output and employment?

    b. What happens to U.S. imports from Japan when U.S. output (or income) rises? If the quotas initially reduce imports from Japan by $25 billion, why is the final reduction in imports likely to be less than $25 billion? Explain in terms of the trade feedback effect.

    c. Suppose that the quotas do succeed in reducing imports from Japan by $15 billion. What will happen to the demand for yen? Why?

    d. What will happen to the dollar-yen exchange rate, and why? (*Hint:* There is an excess supply of yen, or an excess demand for dollars.) What effects will the change in the value of each currency have on employment and output in the United States? What about the balance of payments? (You can ignore complications such as the J curve.)

    e. Considering the macroeconomic effects of a quota on Japanese imports, could a quota actually reduce employment and output in the United States, or have no effect at all? Explain.

5. What effect will each of the following events have on the balance of payments and the exchange rate if the exchange rate is fixed? If it is floating?

    a. The U.S. government cuts taxes, and income rises.

    b. The U.S. inflation rate increases, and prices in the United States rise faster than those in the countries with which the United States trades.

    c. The United States adopts an expansionary monetary policy. Interest rates fall (and are now lower than those in other countries), and income rises.

    d. Textile companies' "Buy American" campaign is successful, and U.S. consumers switch from purchasing imported products to those made in the United States.

6. You are given the following model, which describes the economy of Hypothetica.

    (1) Consumption function: $C = 100 + .8 \, Y^d$
    (2) Planned investment: $I = 38$
    (3) Government spending: $G = 75$
    (4) Exports: $EX = 25$
    (5) Imports: $IM = .05 \, Y^d$
    (6) Disposable income: $Y^d \equiv Y - T$
    (7) Taxes: $T = 40$
    (8) Planned aggregate expenditure:
        $AE \equiv C + I + G + (EX - IM)$
    (9) Definition of equilibrium income: $Y = AE$.

    a. What is equilibrium income in Hypothetica? What is the government deficit? What is the current account balance?

b. If government spending is increased to $G = 80$, what happens to equilibrium income? Explain, using the government spending multiplier. What happens to imports? Now suppose that the amount of imports is limited to $IM = 40$ by a quota on imports. If government spending is again increased from 75 to 80, what happens to equilibrium income? Explain why the same increase in G has a bigger effect on income in the second case. What is it about the presence of imports that changes the value of the multiplier?

c. If exports are fixed at $EX = 25$, what must income be in order to ensure a current account balance of zero? (*Hint:* Imports depend on income, so what must income be in order for imports to be equal to exports?) By how much must we cut government spending in order to balance the current account? (*Hint:* Use your answer to the first part of this question to determine how much of a decrease in income is needed. Then use the multiplier to calculate the decrease in G needed to reduce income by that amount.)

7. The table below shows that over the course of a decade, the U.S. dollar has appreciated slightly against the British pound; the price of pounds in 1993 was down just $0.02 against its 1983 level. In the same time period, the dollar fell dramatically against the yen; the price of yen more than doubled between 1983 and 1993. Explain why this might be so.

	MAY 1983	APRIL 1993
Pound sterling	$1.56	$1.54
Yen	.0042	.0090

APPENDIX TO CHAPTER 37
WORLD MONETARY SYSTEMS SINCE 1900

Since the beginning of the twentieth century, the world has operated under a number of different monetary systems. This appendix provides a brief history of each and a description of how they worked.

THE GOLD STANDARD

The gold standard was the major system of exchange rate determination before 1914. All currencies were priced in terms of gold—that is, an ounce of gold was worth so much in each currency. When all currencies exchanged at fixed ratios to gold, exchange rates could be determined easily. For instance, one ounce of gold was worth $20 U.S.; that same ounce of gold exchanged for four British pounds. Since $20 and £4 were each worth one ounce of gold, the exchange rate between dollars and pounds was $20/£4, or $5 to £1.

For the gold standard to be effective, however, it had to be backed up by the country's willingness to buy and sell gold at the determined price. As long as countries maintain their currencies at a fixed value in terms of gold *and* as long as each is willing to buy and sell gold, exchange rates are fixed. If at the given exchange rate the number of U.S. citizens who want to buy things produced in Great Britain is equal to the number of British citizens who want to buy things produced in the United States, the currencies of the two countries will simply be exchanged. But what if U.S. citizens suddenly decide they want to drink imported Scotch instead of domestic bourbon? If the British do not in turn have an increased desire for U.S. goods, they would still accept U.S. dollars because they could be redeemed in gold. This gold could then be immediately turned into pounds.

As long as a country's overall balance of payments remained in balance, no gold would enter or leave the country, and the economy would be in equilibrium. If U.S. citizens bought more from the British than the British bought from the United States, however, the U.S. balance of payments would be in deficit, and the U.S. stock of gold would begin to fall. Conversely, Britain would start to accumulate gold because it would be exporting more than it spent on imports.

But under the gold standard, gold was an important determinant of the money supply.[1] An inflow of gold into a country caused that country's money supply to expand, and an outflow of gold caused that country's money supply to contract. If gold were flowing from the United States to Great Britain, the British money supply would expand and the U.S. money supply would contract.

Now recall from earlier chapters the impacts of a change in the money supply. An expanded money supply in Britain will lower British interest rates and stimulate aggregate demand. As a result, aggregate output (income) and the price level in Britain will increase. Higher British prices will discourage U.S. citizens from buying British goods. At the same time, British citizens will have more income and will face relatively lower import prices, causing them to import more from the States.

On the other side of the Atlantic, U.S. citizens will face a contracting domestic money supply. This will cause

---

[1] In the days when currencies were tied to gold, changes in the amount of gold influenced the supply of money in two ways. A change in the quantity of gold coins in circulation had a direct effect on the supply of money; indirectly, gold served as a backing for paper currency. A decrease in the central bank's gold holdings meant a decline in the amount of paper money that could be supported.

higher interest rates, declining aggregate demand, lower prices, and falling output (income). This, in turn, will lower demand in the United States for British goods. Thus, changes in relative prices and incomes that resulted from the inflow and outflow of gold would automatically bring trade back into balance.

Problems with the Gold Standard

Two major problems were associated with the gold standard. First, the gold standard implied that a country had little control over its money supply. The reason, as we have just seen, is that the money stock increased when the overall balance of payments was in surplus (gold inflow) and decreased when the overall balance was in deficit (gold outflow). A country that was experiencing a balance-of-payments deficit could correct the problem only by the painful process of allowing its money supply to contract. This brought on a slump in economic activity, a slump that would eventually restore balance-of-payments equilibrium, but only after reductions in income and employment. Countries could (and often did) act to protect their gold reserves, and this prevented the adjustment mechanism from correcting the deficit.

Making the money supply depend on the amount of gold available had another disadvantage as well. When major new gold fields were discovered (as in California in 1849 or South Africa in 1886), the world's supply of gold (and therefore of money) increased. The price level rose and income increased. When no new gold was discovered, the supply of money remained unchanged and prices and income tended to fall.

When President Reagan took office in 1981, he established a commission to consider returning the nation to the gold standard. The final commission report recommended against such a move. An important part of the reasoning behind this was that the gold standard puts enormous economic power in the hands of gold-producing nations.

FIXED EXCHANGE RATES AND THE BRETTON WOODS SYSTEM

As World War II drew to a close, a group of economists from the United States and Europe met to formulate a new set of rules for exchange rate determination that they hoped would avoid the difficulties of the gold standard. The rules they designed became known as the **Bretton Woods system,** after the town in New Hampshire where the delegates met.[2] The Bretton Woods system was based on two (not necessarily compatible) premises. First, countries were to maintain fixed exchange rates with each other. Instead of pegging their currencies directly to gold, however, currencies were fixed in terms of the U.S. dollar, which was fixed in value at $35 per ounce of gold. The British pound, for instance, was fixed at roughly $2.40, which meant that an ounce of gold was worth approximately 14.6 pounds. As we shall see, the pure system of fixed exchange rates would work in a manner very similar to the pre-1914 gold standard.

The second aspect of the Bretton Woods system, however, added a new wrinkle to the operation of the international economy. Countries experiencing a "fundamental disequilibrium" in their balance of payments were allowed to change their exchange rates. (The term "fundamental disequilibrium" was necessarily vague, but it came to be interpreted as a large and persistent balance-of-payments deficit.) Thus, exchange rates were not really fixed under the Bretton Woods system; they were, as someone once remarked, only "fixed until further notice."

The point of allowing countries with serious balance-of-payments problems to alter the value of their currency was to avoid the harsh recessions that the operation of the gold standard would have produced under these circumstances. But the experience of the European economies in the years between World War I and World War II suggested that it might not be a good idea to give countries complete freedom to change their exchange rates whenever they wished.

During the Great Depression, many countries undertook so-called competitive devaluations in order to protect domestic output and employment. That is, countries would try to encourage exports—a source of output growth and employment—by attempting to set as low an exchange rate as possible, thereby making their exports competitive with foreign-produced goods. Unfortunately, such policies had a built-in flaw. A devaluation of the pound against the French franc may help encourage British exports to France, but if those additional British exports cut into French output and employment, France is likely to respond by devaluing the franc against the pound, which, of course, undoes the effects of the pound's initial devaluation.

To solve this problem of exchange rate rivalry, the Bretton Woods agreement created the International Monetary Fund (IMF). Its job was to assist countries experiencing temporary balance-of-payments problems.[3] It was also supposed to certify that a "fundamental disequilibrium" existed before a country was allowed to change its exchange rate. You can think of the IMF as an international economic traffic cop whose job is to ensure that all countries are playing the game according to the agreed-upon rules and to provide emergency assistance where needed.

"Pure" Fixed Exchange Rates

Under a pure fixed exchange rate system, governments set a particular *fixed* rate at which their currencies will exchange for each other and then commit themselves to

---

[2]The key architect of the system was John Maynard Keynes, whose contributions to economics were discussed in detail in Chapters 21 through 28.

[3]The idea was that the IMF would make short-term loans to a country with a balance-of-payments deficit. The loans would enable the country to correct the balance-of-payments problem gradually, without bringing on a deep recession, running out of foreign exchange reserves, or devaluing the currency.

maintaining that rate. Thus, a true fixed exchange rate system is like the gold standard in that exchange rates are supposed to stay the same forever.[4] Because currencies are no longer backed by gold, however, they have no fixed, or standard, value relative to each other. There is therefore no automatic mechanism to keep exchange rates aligned with each other, as was the case with the gold standard.

The result is that under a pure fixed exchange rate system, governments must at times intervene in the foreign exchange market to keep currencies aligned at their established values. Economists define government intervention in the foreign exchange market as the buying or selling of foreign exchange for the purpose of manipulating the exchange rate. What kind of intervention is likely to occur under a fixed exchange rate system, and how does it work?

We can see how intervention works by looking at Figure 37A.1. Initially, the market for Italian lira is in equilibrium. At the fixed exchange rate of $0.02 per lira, the supply of lira is exactly equal to the demand for lira. No government intervention is necessary to maintain the exchange rate at this level. Now suppose that Italian wines are found to be contaminated with antifreeze, and U.S. citizens decide to switch to California wines. This substitution away from the Italian product shifts the U.S. demand curve for lira to the left: The United States demands fewer lira at every exchange rate (cost of a lira) because it is purchasing less from Italy than it did before.

If the price of lira were set by a completely unfettered market, the shift in the demand curve would lead to a fall in the price of lira, just the way the price of wheat would fall if there was an excess supply of wheat. Remember, though, that the Italian and U.S. governments have committed themselves to maintaining the rate at $0.02 per lira. To do this, either the U.S. government or Italian government (or both) must buy up the excess supply of lira to keep the price of the lira from falling. In essence, the fixed exchange rate policy commits governments to making up any difference between the supply of a currency and the demand so as to keep the price of the currency (exchange rate) at the desired level. The government promises to act as the supplier (or demander) of last resort, who will ensure that the amount of foreign exchange demanded by the private sector will be equal to the supply at the fixed price.

Problems with the Bretton Woods System

As it developed after the end of World War II, the system of more-or-less fixed exchange rates had some important flaws that ultimately led to its abandonment in 1971.

First, there was a basic asymmetry built into the rules of international finance. Countries experiencing large and persistent balance-of-payments deficits—what the Bretton

---

4Of course, "forever" is a very long time. Some countries in Central America have maintained fixed exchange rates with the U.S. dollar for almost 30 years, which is practically forever in the world of international finance.

FIGURE 37A.1
Government Intervention in the Foreign Exchange Market

If the price of lira was set by a completely unfettered market, the price of a lira would be .020 when demand is D and .015 when demand is D'. If the government has committed itself to keeping the value of a lira at .020, it must buy up the excess supply of lira ($Q^s - Q^d$).

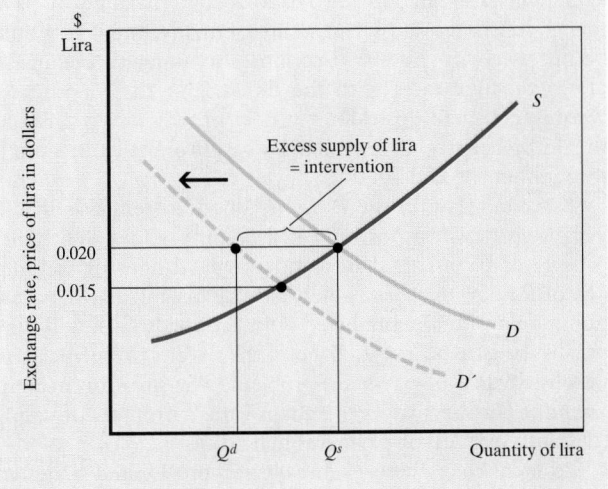

Woods agreements termed "fundamental disequilibria"—were obliged to devalue their currencies and/or take measures to cut their deficits by contracting their economies. Both of these alternatives were unpleasant, because devaluation meant rising prices and contraction meant rising unemployment. But a country with a balance-of-payments deficit had no choice. By definition, it was losing its stock of foreign currencies. When its stock of foreign currencies became exhausted, it had to change its exchange rate, because further intervention (selling off some of its foreign exchange reserves) became impossible.

Countries experiencing balance-of-payments surpluses were in a different position. By definition, they were gaining foreign exchange reserves. Although these countries were supposed to stimulate their economies and/or revalue their currencies to restore balance to their balance of payments, they were not obliged to do so. They could easily maintain their fixed exchange rate by buying up any excess supply of foreign exchange with their own currency, of which they had plentiful supply.

In practice, this meant that some countries—especially Germany and Japan—tended to run large and chronic balance-of-payments surpluses and were under no compulsion to take steps to correct the problem. The U.S. economy, stimulated by expenditures on the Vietnam War, experienced a large and prolonged balance-of-payments deficit (capital outflow) in the 1960s, which was the counterpart of these surpluses. The United States was, however, in a unique position under the Bretton Woods system. The value of gold was fixed in terms of the U.S. dollar at $35 per ounce of gold. Other countries fixed their exchange rates in terms of U.S. dollars (and therefore only indirectly in terms of gold). This meant that the United States could never accomplish anything by devaluing its currency in terms of gold. If the dollar was devalued from $35 to $40 per ounce of gold, the yen, pegged at 200 yen per dollar, would move in parallel with the dollar (from 7000 yen per ounce of gold to 8000 yen per ounce), with the dollar-yen exchange rate unaffected. To correct its balance-of-payments deficits vis-à-vis Japan and Germany, then, it would be necessary for those two countries to adjust their currencies' exchange rates with the dollar. But these countries were reluctant to do so for a variety of reasons. As a result, the U.S. balance of payments was chronically in deficit throughout the late 1960s.

A second flaw in the Bretton Woods system was that it permitted devaluations only if a country had a "chronic" balance-of-payments deficit and was in danger of running out of foreign exchange reserves. This meant that devaluations could often be predicted quite far in advance, and they usually had to be rather large if they were to correct any serious balance-of-payments problem. The situation made it tempting for speculators to "attack" the currencies of countries with balance-of-payments deficits.

Problems like these eventually led the United States to abandon the Bretton Woods rules in 1971. Essentially, the U.S. government refused to continue pegging the value of the dollar in terms of gold. This meant that the prices of all currencies were free to find their own levels.

The alternative to fixed exchange rates is a system that allows exchange rates to move freely or flexibly in response to market forces. Two types of flexible exchange rate systems are usually distinguished. In a *freely floating system,* governments do not intervene at all in the foreign exchange market.[5] They do not buy or sell currencies with the aim of manipulating the rates. In a *managed floating system,* governments intervene if markets are becoming "disorderly"—that is, if they are fluctuating more than a government feels is desirable. Governments may also intervene if they think a currency is increasing or decreasing too much in value, even though the day-to-day fluctuations may be small.

Since the demise of the Bretton Woods system in 1971, the world's exchange rate system is probably best described as a managed floating one. One of the important features of this system has been times of large fluctuations in exchange rates. For example, the yen-dollar rate went from 347 in 1971 to 210 in 1978 to 125 in 1988. These are very large changes, changes that have important effects on the international economy, some of which we have covered in this text.

---

[5]However, governments may from time to time buy or sell foreign exchange for their own needs (rather than to influence the exchange rate). For example, the U.S. government might need British pounds to buy land for a U.S. embassy building in London. For our purposes, we ignore this behavior since it is not "intervention" in the strict sense of the word.

1. The gold standard was the major system of exchange rate determination before 1914. All currencies were priced in terms of gold. Difficulties with the gold standard led to the *Bretton Woods* agreement following World War II. Under this system, countries maintained fixed exchange rates with each other and fixed the value of their currencies in terms of the U.S. dollar. Countries experiencing a "fundamental dis-equilibrium" in their balance of payments were permitted to change their exchange rates.

2. The Bretton Woods system was abandoned in 1971. Since then, the world's exchange rate system has been one of managed floating rates. Under this system, governments intervene if foreign exchange markets are fluctuating more than the government thinks desirable.

PROBLEM SET

1. The currency of Atlantis is the wimp. In 1994, Atlantis developed a balance-of-payments deficit with the United States as a result of an unanticipated decrease in exports; U.S. citizens simply cut back on the purchase of Atlantean goods. Assume that Atlantis is operating under a system of fixed exchange rates.

   a. How does the drop in exports affect the market for wimps? Identify the deficit graphically.

   b. How must the government of Atlantis act (in the short run) to maintain the value of the wimp?

   c. If originally Atlantis was operating at full employment (potential GDP), what impact will these events have on its economy? Explain your answer.

   d. The chief economist of Atlantis suggests expansionary monetary policy to restore full employment; the secretary of commerce suggests a tax cut (expansionary fiscal policy). Given the fixed exchange-rate system, describe the effects of these two policy options on Atlantis's balance of payments.

   e. How would your answers to a, b, and c change if the two countries operated under a floating-rate system?

38 Economic Growth in Developing Nations

Our primary focus in this text has been on economic issues facing the United States. Rent control in New York City, the Clinton tax proposals in 1993, antitrust action against AT&T, and the savings-and-loan crisis are familiar to Americans. But the economics we have been studying also applies to other countries: Parisians may face rent-control programs, the Major government in the United Kingdom may repeal the hated "head tax" (a fixed tax levied on every person regardless of circumstance), and Japan may decide to fight its recent recession with public works spending. We can analyze these and other issues in Britain, France, and Japan with some confidence because these countries have so much in common with the United States. In spite of differences in languages and cultures, all these countries have modern industrialized economies that rely heavily on markets to allocate resources. But what about the economic problems facing Somalia or Haiti? Can we apply the same economic principles that we have been studying to these less-developed countries (sometimes called LDCs)?

The answer is yes. All economic analysis deals with the basic problem of making choices under conditions of scarcity, and the problem of satisfying their citizens' wants and needs is certainly as real for Somalia and Haiti as it is for France, England, and the United States. The universality of scarcity is what makes economic analysis relevant to all nations, regardless of their level of material well-being or ruling political ideology.

The basic tools of supply and demand, theories about consumers and firms, and theories about the structure of markets all contribute to an understanding of the economic problems confronting the world's developing nations. However, these nations often face economic problems quite different from those faced by richer, more developed countries. In the developing nations, the economist may have to worry about chronic food shortages, explosive population growth, and hyperinflations that reach triple, and even quadruple, digits. The United States and other industrialized economies rarely encounter such difficulties.

The instruments of economic management also vary from nation to nation. The United States has well-developed financial market institutions and a strong central bank (the Federal Reserve) through which the government can control the macroeconomy to some extent. But even limited intervention is impossible in some of the developing countries. In the United States, tax laws can be changed to stimulate saving, to encourage particular kinds of investments, or to redistribute income. In most developing countries, there are neither meaningful personal income taxes nor effective tax policies.

But even though economic problems and the policy instruments available to tackle them vary across nations, economic thinking about these problems can be transferred quite easily from one setting to another. In this chapter we turn to a discussion of several of the economic problems specific to developing nations in an attempt to capture some of the insights that economic analysis can offer.

LIFE IN THE DEVELOPING NATIONS: POPULATION AND POVERTY

In 1993 the population of the world reached over 5.5 billion people. Most of the world's more than 200 nations belong to the developing world, in which about three fourths of the world's population lives.

In the early 1960s, the nations of the world could be assigned rather easily to categories: The *developed countries* included most of Europe, North America, Japan, Australia, and New Zealand; the *developing countries* included the rest of the world. The developing nations were often referred to as the "Third World" to distinguish them from the Western industrialized nations (the "First World") and the former Socialist bloc of Eastern European nations (the "Second World").

In the 1990s, however, the world does not divide into three neat parts as easily as it once did. Rapid economic progress has brought some developing nations closer to developed economies. Countries such as Argentina and Korea, while still considered to be "developing," are often referred to as middle-income, or newly industrialized, countries. Meanwhile, other countries, such as much of sub-Saharan Africa and some of South Asia, have stagnated and fallen so far behind the economic advances of the rest of the world that a new designation, the "Fourth World," has been coined to describe them. It is not clear yet where the republics of the former Soviet Union and other formerly communist countries of Eastern Europe will end up. Production has fallen sharply in many of them. For example, between 1989 and 1992 industrial production fell 47.3% in Albania, 46% in Bulgaria, and 44% in the former East Germany. One estimate puts current per capita GDP in Russia at around $1,200, and some of the new republics now have more in common with developing countries than with developed countries.

While the countries of the developing world exhibit considerable diversity, both in their standards of living and in their particular experiences of growth, marked differences continue to separate them from the developed nations. To begin with, the developed countries have a higher average level of material well-being. By material well-being, we mean the amounts of food, clothing, shelter, and other commodities consumed by the average person. Comparisons of gross national product (GNP) per capita—that is, of the value of goods and services produced per person in an economy—are often used as a crude index of the level of material well-being across nations. As you can see from Table 38.1, GNP per capita in the industrial market economies significantly exceeds that of both the low- and middle-income developing economies.

Other characteristics of economic development include improvements in basic health and education. The degree of political and economic freedom enjoyed by individual citizens might also be part of a comprehensive definition of what it means to be a developed nation. Some of these criteria are easier to quantify than others; Table 38.1 presents data for different types of economies according to some of the more easily measured indexes of development. As you can see, the industrial market economies enjoy higher standards of living according to whatever indicator of development is chosen.

Behind these statistics lies the reality of the very difficult life facing the people of the developing world. For most, meager incomes provide only the basic necessities of life. Most meals are the same, consisting of the food staple—typically rice, wheat, or corn—of the region. Shelter is primitive. Many people share a small room, usually with an earthen floor and no sanitary facilities. The great majority of the population lives in rural areas where agricultural work is hard and extremely time-consuming. Productivity (output produced per worker) is low because household plots are small and only the crudest of farm implements are available. Low productivity means that farm output per person is at levels barely sufficient to feed a farmer's own family, with nothing left over to sell to others. School-age children may receive some formal education, but illiteracy remains chronic for young and old alike. Infant mortality runs seven times higher than in the United States. Although parasitic infections are common and debilitating, there is only one physician per 5,000 people. In addition, as the Global Perspective box titled

TABLE 38.1
Indicators of Economic Development

COUNTRY GROUP	GNP PER CAPITA, 1990 (DOLLARS)	LIFE EXPECTANCY, 1990 (YEARS)	INFANT MORTALITY, 1990 (DEATHS BEFORE AGE ONE PER 1,000 BIRTHS)	SECONDARY-SCHOOL ENROLLMENT, 1989 (NUMBER ENROLLED AS PERCENTAGE OF POPULATION AGED 12–17)	PERCENTAGE OF LABOR FORCE IN URBAN AREAS, 1990
Low-income (e.g., China, Ethiopia, Haiti, India)	350	62	69	38	38
Lower middle-income (e.g., Guatemala, Mexico, Philippines, Thailand)	1,530	65	51	54	52
Upper middle-income (e.g., Korea, Portugal, Venezuela)	3,410	68	45	56	71
Industrial market economies (e.g., Japan, Germany, New Zealand, United States)	19,590	77	8	95	77

Note: GDP data not reported.

Source: World Bank, *World Development Report,* 1992. Note that all numbers refer to weighted averages for each country group, where the weights equal the populations of each nation in a specific country group.

"The Challenges of Development in Sub-Saharan Africa" points out, many developing nations are engaged in civil and external warfare.

Life in the developing nations is a continual struggle against the circumstances of poverty, and prospects for dramatic improvements in living standards for most people are dim. However, as with all generalizations, there are important exceptions. Some nations are better off than others, and in any given nation, an elite group always lives in considerable luxury. Just as in any advanced economy, income is distributed in a fashion that allows a small percentage of households to consume a disproportionately large share of national income. Income distribution in developing countries is often so skewed that the richest households of very poor nations surpass the living standards of many high-income families in the advanced economies. Table 38.2 presents some data on the distribution of income in some developing countries.

Clearly, poverty—not affluence—dominates the developing world. Recent studies suggest that 40% of the population of the developing nations have annual incomes insufficient to provide for adequate nutrition.

> While the developed nations account for only about one quarter of the world's population, they are estimated to consume three quarters of the world's output. This leaves the developing countries with about three fourths of the world's people, but only one fourth of the world's income. The simple result is that most of our planet's population is poor.

In the United States, the poorest one fifth of the population receives just under 5% of total income, while the richest one fifth of the population receives about 40% of the income. But the inequality in the world distribution of income, is much greater. When we look at the population of the world, the poorest one fifth of the population earns about 0.5% of the total world income and the richest one fifth earn 79% of world income.

ECONOMIC DEVELOPMENT: SOURCES AND STRATEGIES

Economists have been trying to understand the process of economic growth and development since the days of Adam Smith and David Ricardo in the eighteenth and nineteenth centuries, but the study of development economics as it applies to the developing nations has a much shorter history. The geopolitical struggles that followed World War II brought increased attention to the developing nations and their economic problems. During this period, the central question of the new field of development economics was simply: Why are some nations poor and others rich? If economists could understand the barriers to economic growth that prevent

TABLE 38.2
Income Distribution in Some Developing Countries

UNITED STATES		SRI LANKA	BOTSWANA	BRAZIL	PAKISTAN	INDONESIA
$21,790	Per Capita GNP 1990	470	2040	2680	380	570
4.7	Bottom 20%	4.8	2.5	2.4	7.8	8.8
11.0	Second 20%	8.5	6.5	5.7	11.2	12.4
17.4	Third 20%	12.1	11.8	10.7	15.0	16.0
25.0	Fourth 20%	18.4	20.2	18.6	20.6	21.5
41.9	Top 20%	56.1	59.0	62.6	45.6	41.3
25.0	Top 10%	43.0	42.8	46.2	31.3	26.5

Source: World Bank, *World Development Report, 1992* Table 30.

THE CHALLENGES OF DEVELOPMENT IN SUB-SAHARAN AFRICA

The following extract is taken from a speech given in late 1991 by Lawrence H. Summers, vice president and chief economist at the World Bank. Professor Summers was later appointed under secretary of the Treasury for international affairs by President Clinton.

Why in the face of so much development progress have 36 countries with a combined population of over half a billion people actually regressed? Any analysis of the right way forward for Nigeria and these other nations must start by answering this question. Broadly speaking, the 1991 World Development Report provides two explanations for development failure. First, national development failures are the fault of national policies—they cannot be blamed on a hostile inter-

A Somali mother gives her starving daughter a drink from a plastic water container outside an international aid agency's feeding center. The prolonged civil wars in Somalia have been just one cause of that developing nation's problems.

national environment or on any kind of physical limits to growth. Second, national policies have failed when governments thwarted progress, supplanting markets rather than supporting them.

There is one simple but often neglected lesson that comes from any consideration of development failures. War stops development. Almost all of the 36 countries that have lost ground over the last 25 years have been involved in a substantial military conflict. Nowhere has war been more costly than in Africa, claiming 7 million victims directly in the last 30 years and millions more deaths indirectly by making the provision of food and basic social services difficult or impossible. The Middle East is often thought of as the world's tinderbox; yet relative to population, Africans have three times as high a war fatality rate. Today, after the Cold War, the threat of hot war in Africa persists: Sub-Saharan African governments spend four times as much on the military as on health and as much on the military as on education. It comes as no surprise that spending on both health and education far exceeds spending on the military in East Asia.

nations from developing and the prerequisites that would help them to develop, then they could prescribe suitable strategies for achieving economic advancement.

The Sources of Economic Development

While a general theory of economic development applicable to all nations has not emerged and probably never will, some basic factors that limit a poor nation's economic growth have been suggested. These include insufficient capital formation, a shortage of human resources, a lack of social overhead capital, and the constraints imposed by dependency on the already developed nations.

CAPITAL FORMATION One explanation for low levels of output in developing nations is the absence of sufficient quantities of necessary inputs. Developing nations have diverse resource endowments—Zaire, for instance, is abundant in natural resources, while Bangladesh is resource poor. Almost all developing nations have a scarcity of physical capital relative to other resources, especially labor. The small stock of physical capital, including factories, machinery, farm equipment, and other types of productive capital, constrains labor's productivity and holds back national output.

But citing capital shortages as the cause of low productivity does not really explain much. To get to the heart of the matter, we need to know why capital is in such short supply in developing countries. Many explanations have been offered. One, the **vicious-circle-of-poverty hypothesis,** suggests that a poor nation must consume most of its income just to maintain its already low standard of living. Just like a poor family, a poor nation finds that the opportunity cost of forgoing current consumption (that is, saving instead of consuming) is too high. Consuming most of national income implies limited saving, and this, in turn, implies low levels of investment. Without investment, the capital stock does not grow, income remains low, and the vicious circle is complete. Poverty becomes self-perpetuating.

The difficulty with the vicious-circle argument is that if it were true, no nation could ever develop. For example, Japanese GDP per capita at the turn of the century was well below that of many of today's developing nations. If the vicious-circle explanation were completely correct, Japan could never have grown into the industrial power it is today. The vicious-circle argument fails to recognize that every nation has some surplus above consumption needs that is available for investment. Often this surplus is most visible in the conspicuous-consumption habits of the nation's richest families. In short,

> Poverty alone cannot explain capital shortages, nor is poverty necessarily self-perpetuating.

In a developing economy, scarcity of capital may have more to do with a lack of incentives for citizens to save and invest productively than with any absolute scarcity of income available for capital accumulation. The inherent riskiness and uncertainty that surround a developing nation's economy and its political system tend to reduce incentives to invest in any activity, especially those that require long periods of time to yield a return. Many of the rich in developing countries take their savings and invest them in Europe or in the United States rather than risk holding them in what is often an unstable political climate. Savings transferred to the United States do not lead to physical capital growth in the developing countries. In addition, a range of government policies including price ceilings, import controls, and even outright appropriation of private property tend to discourage investment activity.

Whatever the causes of capital shortages, it is clear that the absence of productive capital prevents income from rising in any economy. The availability of capital is a necessary, but not a *sufficient,* condition for economic growth. The Third World landscape is littered with idle factories and abandoned machinery. Clearly, other ingredients are required to achieve economic progress.

HUMAN RESOURCES Capital is not the only factor of production required to produce output. Labor is an equally important input. But the quantity of available labor rarely constrains a developing economy. In most developing nations, rapid population growth for several decades has resulted in rapidly expanding labor supplies. The *quality* of available labor, however, may pose a serious constraint on the growth of income. Or, to put it another way, the shortage of *human capital*—the stock of knowledge and skill embodied in the work force—may act as a barrier to economic growth.

Human capital may be developed in a number of ways. Because malnutrition and the lack of basic health care can substantially reduce labor productivity, programs to improve nutrition and health represent one kind of human capital investment that can lead to increased productivity and higher incomes. The more familiar forms of

vicious-circle-of-poverty hypothesis Suggests that poverty is self-perpetuating because poor nations are unable to save and invest enough to accumulate the capital stock that would help them grow.

human capital investment, including formal education and on-the-job training, may also play an important role. Basic literacy, as well as specialized training in farm management, for example, can yield high returns to both the individual worker and the economy. Education has grown to become the largest category of government expenditure in many developing nations, in part because of the belief that human resources are the ultimate determinant of economic advance.

Unfortunately, those lucky enough to get an education often leave developing countries because they can do better financially in the developed world. Just as financial capital seeks the highest and safest return, so does human capital. Thousands of students from developing countries, many of whom were supported by their governments, graduate every year from U.S. colleges and universities as engineers, doctors, scientists, economists, and the like. After graduation, these people face a difficult choice: to remain in the United States and earn a high salary or to return home and accept a job at a much lower salary. Many people choose to remain in the United States. This **brain drain** siphons off many of the most talented minds from developing countries.

brain drain The tendency for talented people from developing countries to become educated in a developed country and remain there after graduation.

Another frequently cited barrier to economic development is the apparent shortage of entrepreneurial activity in developing nations. Innovative entrepreneurs who are willing to take risks are an essential human resource in any economy. In a developing nation, new techniques of production rarely need to be invented, since they can usually be adapted from the technology already developed by the technologically advanced nations. But entrepreneurs who are willing and able to organize and carry out economic activity appear to be in short supply in many of the developing countries. Family and political ties often seem to be more important than ability when it comes to securing positions of authority. Whatever the explanation:

> Development cannot proceed without human resources capable of initiating and managing economic activity.

SOCIAL OVERHEAD CAPITAL   Anyone who has spent time in a developing nation knows how difficult it can be to send a letter, make a local phone call, or travel within the country itself. Add to this list of obstacles problems with water supplies, frequent electrical power outages—in the few areas where electricity is available at all—and often ineffective mosquito and pest control, and you soon realize how deficient even the simplest, most basic government-provided goods and services can be.

In any economy, Third World or otherwise, the government has considerable opportunity and responsibility for involvement where conditions encourage natural monopoly (as in the utilities industries) and where public goods (such as health care and education) must be provided. In a developing economy, the government must place particular emphasis on creating a basic infrastructure—roads, power generation, irrigation systems. There are often good reasons why such projects, referred to as **social overhead capital,** cannot successfully be undertaken by the private sector. Many of these projects operate with economies of scale, which means that they can be efficient only if they are very large. In that case, they may be simply too large for any private company, or even a group of such companies, to carry out.

social overhead capital Basic infrastructure projects such as roads, power generation, and irrigation systems.

Second, many socially useful projects cannot be undertaken by the private sector because there is no way for private agents to capture enough of the returns to make such projects profitable. This so-called *free-rider problem* is common in the economics of the developed world. Consider as an example national defense. Since everyone in a country benefits from national defense, whether they have paid for it or not, anyone who attempted to go into the private business of providing national defense would quickly go broke. Why should I buy any national defense at all if your purchase of defense will also protect me? Why should you buy any if my purchase will also protect you?

> The governments of developing countries can do important and useful things to encourage development, but many of their efforts must be concentrated in areas that the private sector would never touch. If government action in these realms is not forthcoming, economic development may be curtailed by a lack of social overhead capital.

DEPENDENCY THEORIES   Some economists take an entirely different approach to understanding why some nations are rich and others poor. Some find the explanation within the developing nations themselves. In advanced industrial economies, these economists explain, the early merchant classes were responsible for breaking down traditional feudalism and replacing it with a market economy oriented toward growth and development. In many developing nations, however, the class that could foster capitalism has not followed the same path, perhaps out of fear of a socialist takeover. In the view of some analysts, potential capitalists have not transformed traditional societies but have instead acted to maintain the status quo and have thus retarded economic advancement.

Another position, **dependency theory,** holds that the poverty of the Third World is due to the "dependence" of the developing world on nations that are already developed. (A dependent country is one whose economy is dependent on the development and expansion of another country's economy.) During the colonial period, European powers dominated much of the political and economic life of what is today the developing world. Colonial powers sometimes directly destroyed local industries, either by prohibiting certain economic activities or by flooding the colony's markets with manufactured goods from the parent country. Furthermore, by not developing basic physical infrastructure or local human capital, and by draining mineral wealth from the colonies, colonialism created countries that had become helpless and economically dependent by the time they achieved political independence.

Some economists contend that economic dependency is maintained today, even though colonialism is long past, through the structure of international trade relations. Developed economies provide important markets for the exports of developing nations and often are their only sources of critical inputs. Industrialized economies also influence world interest rates, capital flows, and exchange rates. Through their economic power, it is argued, industrialized nations often determine to their own advantage—and the disadvantage of others—the relative prices and conditions under which the international exchange of goods takes place.

Dependency theorists argue that the unequal relationship between rich and poor nations in world markets works to the detriment of the developing world. This view has led many Third World leaders to call for a *new international economic order.* Such an arrangement would require agreements between developed and developing nations that would increase the gains that accrue to the developing world from international exchange. Plans for such a set of agreements have been widely discussed in the developing world. But because of divisions among the developing nations and a lack of cooperation from most developed countries there has been virtually no progress in reaching any sort of accord.

dependency theory The theory that the poverty of the Third World is due to the "dependence" of the developing world on nations that are already developed; it suggests that even after the end of colonialism, this dependence is maintained because developed countries are able to use their economic power to determine their own advantage—and the disadvantage of others—the relative prices and conditions under which the international exchange of goods takes place.

Strategies for Economic Development

Just as no single theory appears to explain lack of economic advancement, so too is it unlikely that one development strategy will succeed in all nations. In fact, many alternative development strategies for the Third World have been proposed over the past 30 or 40 years. Although these strategies have been very different, they all share the recognition that a developing economy faces certain basic trade-offs. An insufficient amount of both human and physical resources dictates that choices must be made. Some of the basic trade-offs that underlie any development strategy include those between agriculture and industry, exports and import substitution, and central planning and free markets.

AGRICULTURE OR INDUSTRY? Most Third World countries began to gain political independence just after World War II. The tradition of promoting industrialization as the solution to the problems of the developing world dates from this time. The early five-year development plans of India called for promoting manufacturing; the current government in Ethiopia (an extremely poor country) has similar intentions.

Industry has several apparent attractions over agriculture. First, if it is true that capital shortages constrain economic growth, then the building of factories is an obvious step toward increasing a nation's stock of capital. Second, and perhaps most important, one of the primary characteristics of more developed economies is their structural transition away from agriculture and toward manufacturing and modern services. As Table 38.3 shows, agriculture's share in GDP declines substantially as per capita incomes increase. The share of services increases correspondingly, especially in the early phases of economic development.

Many economies have pursued industry at the expense of agriculture. In many countries, however, industrialization has been either unsuccessful or disappointing—that is, it has not brought the benefits that were expected. Experience suggests that simply trying to replicate the structure of developed economies does not in itself guarantee, or even promote, successful development.

Since the early 1970s, the agricultural sector has received considerably more attention. Agricultural strategies have had numerous benefits. Although some agricultural projects (such as the building of major dams and irrigation networks) are very capital intensive, many others (such as services to help teach better farming techniques and small-scale fertilizer programs) have low capital and import requirements. Programs like these can affect large numbers of households, and because their benefits are directed at rural areas, they are most likely to help a country's poorest families.

TABLE 38.3
The Structure of Production in Developed and Developing Economies, 1990

| COUNTRY GROUP | SHARE OF GROSS DOMESTIC PRODUCT (PERCENTAGE) | | | |
| | | INDUSTRY | | |
	AGRICULTURE	MANUFACTURING ONLY	OTHER INDUSTRY	SERVICES
Low-income	31	27	9	35
Lower middle-income	12	25	11	50
Upper middle-income	9	25	15	51
Industrial market economies*	3	23	12	62

*Note: Figures are for 1988.
Source: World Bank, *World Development Report*, 1990, Table 3.

Experience over the last three decades suggests that some balance between these approaches leads to the best outcome—that is, it is important and effective to pay attention to both industry and agriculture. The Chinese have referred to this dual approach to development as "walking on two legs."

EXPORTS OR IMPORT SUBSTITUTION? As developing nations expand their industrial activities, they must decide what type of trade strategy to pursue. The choice usually boils down to one of two major alternatives: import substitution or export promotion.

Import substitution is an industrial trade strategy that favors developing local industries that can manufacture goods to replace imports. For example, if fertilizer is currently imported, import substitution calls for establishment of a domestic fertilizer industry to produce replacements for fertilizer imports. This strategy gained prominence throughout South America in the 1950s. At that time, most developing nations exported agricultural and mineral products, goods that faced uncertain and often unstable international markets. Furthermore, the *terms of trade* for these nations—the ratio of export to import prices—seemed to be on a long-run decline.[1] A decline in a country's terms of trade means that its imports of manufactured goods become relatively expensive in the domestic market, while its exports—mostly primary goods such as rubber and wheat and oil—become relatively inexpensive in the world market.

> **import substitution** An industrial trade strategy that favors developing local industries that can manufacture goods to replace imports.

Under these conditions, the call for import-substitution policies was understandable. Special government actions, including tariff and quota protection and subsidized imports of machinery, were set up to encourage new domestic industries. Multinational corporations were also invited into many countries to begin domestic operations.

Most economists believe that import-substitution strategies have failed almost everywhere they have been tried. With domestic industries sheltered from international competition by high tariffs (often as high as 200%), major economic inefficiencies were created. For example, Peru has a population of just over 20 million, only a tiny fraction of whom could ever afford to buy an automobile. Yet at one time the country had five or six different automobile manufacturers, each of which produced only a few thousand cars per year. Since there are substantial economies of scale in automobile production, the cost per car was much higher than it needed to be, and valuable resources that could have been devoted to another, much more productive, activity were squandered producing cars.

Furthermore, policies designed to promote import substitution often encouraged capital-intensive production methods, which limited the creation of jobs and hurt export activities. Obviously, a country like Peru could not export automobiles, since it could produce them only at a cost far greater than their price on the world market. Worse still, import-substitution policies encouraged the use of expensive domestic products, such as tractors and fertilizer, instead of lower-cost imports. These policies thus served to tax the very sectors that might have successfully competed in world markets. To the extent that the Peruvian sugar industry had to rely on domestically produced, high-cost fertilizer, for example, its ability to compete in international markets was reduced, because its production costs were artificially raised.

---

[1]It now appears that the terms of trade for Third World countries as a group were not actually on a long-run decline. Of course, the prices of commodities have changed, with some doing very well and others doing quite poorly. During the 1950s, however, many policy makers believed that the purchasing power of developing-country exports was in a permanent slump.

export promotion A trade policy designed to encourage exports.

As an alternative to import substitution, some nations have pursued strategies of export promotion. **Export promotion** is simply the policy of encouraging exports. As an industrial market economy, Japan is a striking example to the developing world of the economic success that exports can provide. With an average annual per capita real GDP growth rate of roughly 6% per year since 1960, Japan's achievements are in part based on industrial production oriented toward foreign consumers.

Several countries in the developing world have attempted to emulate Japan's success. Starting around 1970, Hong Kong, Singapore, Korea, and Taiwan (sometimes called the "four little dragons" between the two big dragons, China and Japan) all began to pursue export promotion of manufactured goods. Today their growth rates have surpassed even Japan's. Other nations, including Brazil, Colombia, and Turkey, have also had some success at pursuing a more outward-looking trade policy.

Government support of export promotion has often taken the form of maintaining an exchange rate that is favorable enough to permit exports to compete with products manufactured in developed economies. For example, many people believe that the Japanese kept the value of the yen artificially low during the 1970s. Because "cheap" yen means inexpensive Japanese goods in the United States, sales of Japanese goods (especially automobiles) increased dramatically. Governments also have provided subsidies to export industries.

During 1992 and 1993, Japan slipped into recession and the yen became very expensive during the spring of 1993. Overall, Japan's performance since 1990 has not been as strong as its pre-1990 performance. But its recent troubles do not diminish the incredible performance of the Japanese economic machine between 1960 and 1990.

While export promotion generally succeeded during the 1970s and 1980s, protectionism in the industrial market economies may limit the gains that developing nations can expect in the years ahead. If the industrialized nations can set increasing limits on their imports of manufactured products from the developing nations, one of the more successful economic development strategies will be substantially weakened.

CENTRAL PLANNING OR THE MARKET? As part of its strategy for achieving economic development, a nation must decide how its economy will be directed. Its basic choices lie between a market-oriented economic system and a centrally planned one.

In the 1950s and into the 1960s, development strategies that called for national planning commanded wide support. The rapid economic growth of the Soviet Union, a centrally planned economy, provided a historical example of the speed with which a less developed agrarian nation could be transformed into a modern industrial power. (The often appalling costs of this strategy—namely severe discipline, gross violation of human rights, and environmental damage—were less widely known.) In addition, the underdevelopment of many commodity and asset markets in the Third World led many experts to believe that market forces could not direct an economy reliably and that major government intervention was therefore necessary. Even the United States, with its commitment to free enterprise in the marketplace, supported early central planning efforts in many developing nations.

Today, planning takes many forms in the developing nations. In some settings, central planning has replaced market-based outcomes with direct, administratively determined controls over such economic variables as prices, output, and employment. In other situations, national planning amounts to little more than the formulation of general five- or ten-year goals that serve as rough blueprints for a nation's economic future.

The economic appeal of planning lies theoretically in its ability to channel savings into productive investment and to coordinate economic activities that private actors in the economy might not otherwise undertake. The reality of central planning, however, is that it is technically difficult, highly politicized, and a nightmare to administer. Given the scarcity of human resources and the unstable political environment in many developing nations, planning itself, let alone the execution of the plan, becomes a formidable task.

The failure of many central planning efforts has brought increasing calls for less government intervention and more market orientation in developing economies. The elimination of price controls, privatization of state-run enterprises, and reductions in import restraints are examples of market-oriented reforms that are frequently recommended by such international agencies as the **International Monetary Fund,** whose primary goals are to stabilize international exchange rates and to lend money to countries that have problems financing their international transactions, and the **World Bank,** which lends money to individual countries for projects that promote economic development.

Members' contributions to both organizations are determined by the size of their economies. Only 20% of the World Bank's funding comes from contributions; the other 80% comes from retained earnings and investments in capital markets. Throughout the developing world, a recognition of the value of market forces in determining the allocation of scarce resources appears to be increasing. Nonetheless, government still has a major role to play. In the decades ahead, the governments of developing nations will need to determine those situations where planning is superior to the market and those where the market is superior to planning.

International Monetary Fund An international agency whose primary goals are to stabilize international exchange rates and to lend money to countries that have problems financing their international transactions.

World Bank An international agency that lends money to individual countries for projects that promote economic development.

Growth versus Development

Until now, we have used the words "growth" and "development" as if they meant essentially the same thing. But this may not always be the case. One can easily imagine instances in which a country has achieved higher levels of income (growth) with little or no benefit accruing to most of its citizens (development). Thus, one central question in evaluating alternative strategies for achieving economic development is whether economic growth necessarily brings about economic development.

In the past, most development strategies were aimed at increasing the growth rate of income per capita. Many still are, based on the theory that benefits of economic growth will "trickle down" to all members of society. If this theory is correct, then growth should promote development.

By the early 1970s, however, the relationship between growth and development was being questioned more and more. A major study by the World Bank in 1974 concluded that

> it is now clear that more than a decade of rapid growth in underdeveloped countries has been of little or no benefit to perhaps a third of their population. . . . Paradoxically, while growth policies have succeeded beyond the expectations of the first development decade, the very idea of aggregate growth as a social objective has increasingly been called into question.

The World Bank study indicated that increases in GDP per capita did not guarantee significant improvements in such development indicators as nutrition, health, and education. Although GDP per capita did indeed rise, its benefits trickled down to only a small minority of the population. This realization prompted a call for new development strategies that would directly address the problems of poverty. Such new strategies favored agriculture over industry, called for domestic redistribution of income and wealth (especially land), and encouraged programs to satisfy such basic needs as food and shelter.

In the late 1970s and early 1980s, the international macroeconomic crises of high oil prices, worldwide recession, and Third World debt forced attention away from programs designed to eliminate poverty directly. Nonetheless, the lesson remains:

> Economic growth does not guarantee economic development. Concerted efforts may be required to transform growing output capacity into economic benefits that reach most of a nation's people.

ISSUES IN ECONOMIC DEVELOPMENT

Every developing nation has a cultural, political, and economic history all its own and therefore confronts a unique set of problems. Still, it is possible to discuss common economic issues that each nation must face in its own particular way. These issues include rapid population growth, food shortages, agricultural output and pricing policies, and the Third World debt problem.

Population Growth

The populations of the developing nations are estimated to be growing at a rate of about 1.7% per year. (Compare this with a population growth rate of only 0.6% per year in the industrial market economies.) If the Third World's population growth rate remains at 1.7%, it will take only 41 years for the population of the Third World to double from its 1990 level of 4.1 billion to over 8 billion by the year 2031. It will take the industrialized nations 116 years to double their populations. What is so immediately alarming about these numbers is that given the developing nations' current economic problems, it is hard to imagine how they can possibly absorb so many more people in such a relatively short period.

Concern over world population growth is not new. The Reverend Thomas Malthus (who would one day become England's first professor of political economy) expressed his fears about the population increases he observed 200 years ago. Malthus believed that populations grow geometrically (that is, at a constant growth rate: thus the absolute size of the increase each year gets larger and larger), but that food supplies grow much more slowly because of the diminishing marginal productivity of land.[2] These two phenomena led Malthus to predict the increasing impoverishment of the world's people unless population growth could be slowed.

Malthus's fears for Europe and America proved unfounded, because he neither anticipated the technological changes that revolutionized agricultural productivity nor the eventual decrease in population growth rates in Europe and North America. But Malthus's prediction may have been right, only premature. Do the circumstances in the developing world now fit his predictions? While some contemporary observers believe that the Malthusian view is correct and that the earth's population will eventually grow to a level that the world's resources will be unable to support, others argue that technological change and demographic transitions (to slower population growth rates) will permit further increases in global welfare.

---

[2]The law of diminishing marginal productivity says that with a fixed amount of some resource (land), additions of more and more of a variable resource (labor) will produce smaller and smaller gains in output.

THE CONSEQUENCES OF RAPID POPULATION GROWTH Surprisingly, we know far less about the economic consequences of rapid population growth than you might expect. Conventional wisdom warns of dire economic consequences from the Third World's "population explosion," but these predictions are difficult to substantiate with the available evidence. The rapid economic growth of the United States, for example, was accompanied by relatively rapid population growth by historical standards. Nor has any slowing of population growth been necessary for the economic progress achieved by many of the newly industrialized countries. Nonetheless, population expansion in many of today's poorest nations is of a magnitude unprecedented in world history, as Figure 38.1 clearly shows. From the year 1 A.D. until the mid-1600s, populations grew slowly, at rates of only about 0.04% per year. Since then, and especially since 1950, rates have skyrocketed. Today, populations are growing at rates of 1.5% to 4.0% per year throughout the developing world.

Because growth rates like these have never occurred before the twentieth century, no one knows what impact they will have on future economic development. But a basic economic concern is that such rapid population growth may limit investment and thus restrain increases in labor productivity and income. Rapid population growth changes the age composition of a population, generating many dependent children relative to the number of productive working adults. Such a situation may diminish saving rates, and hence investment, as the immediate consumption needs of the young take priority over saving for the future.

Even if low saving rates are not a necessary consequence of rapid population growth, as some authorities contend, other economic problems remain. The ability to improve human capital through a broad range of programs, from infant nutrition to formal secondary education, may be severely limited if the population explosion continues. Such programs are most often the responsibility of the state, and governments that are already weak cannot be expected to improve their services under the burden of population pressures that rapidly increase demands for all kinds of public goods and services.

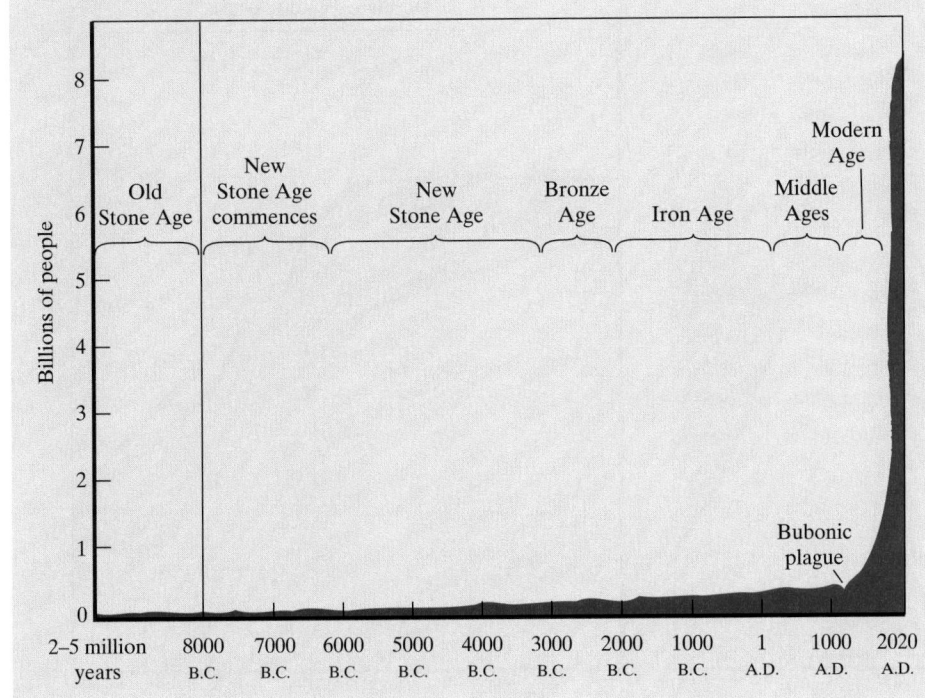

FIGURE 38.1

The Growth of World Population, Projected to 2020 A.D.

For thousands of years, population grew slowly. From 1 A.D. until the mid-1600s, population grew at about .04% per year. Since the Industrial Revolution, population growth has occurred at an unprecedented rate.

For example, Kenya's population growth rate—3.5%—is one of the highest in the world. It is likely that its 1991 population of over 24 million people will grow by about 10 million in the next decade. This is a daunting prospect, and it is hard to imagine how in so little time Kenya will be able to provide its population with the physical and human capital needed to maintain, let alone improve, already low standards of living.

CAUSES OF RAPID POPULATION GROWTH Population growth is determined by the relationship between births and deaths—that is, between **fertility rates** and **mortality rates.** The **natural rate of population increase** is defined as the difference between the birth rate and the death rate. If the birth rate is 4%, for example, and the death rate is 3%, the population is growing at a rate of 1% per year.

Historically, low rates of population growth were maintained because of high mortality rates despite high levels of fertility. That is, families had many children, but average life expectancies were low, and many children (and adults) died young. In Europe and North America, improvements in nutrition, in public health programs (especially those concerned with drinking water and sanitation services), and in medical practices have led to a drop in the mortality rate and hence to more rapid population growth. Eventually fertility rates also fell, returning population growth to a low and stable rate, as you can see in Figure 38.2.

Public health programs and improved nutrition over the past 30 years have brought about precipitous declines in mortality rates in the developing nations also. But fertility rates have not declined as quickly, and the result has been high rates of population growth. Reduced population growth depends to some extent on decreased birth rates, but attempts to lower fertility rates must take account of how different cultures feel and behave with regard to fertility.

fertility rate The birth rate. Equal to (the number of births per year divided by the average population) × 100.

mortality rate The death rate. Equal to (the number of deaths per year divided by the average population) × 100.

natural rate of population increase The difference between the birth rate and the death rate. It does not take migration into account.

FIGURE 38.2
The Natural Rate of Population Increase, 1775–1990

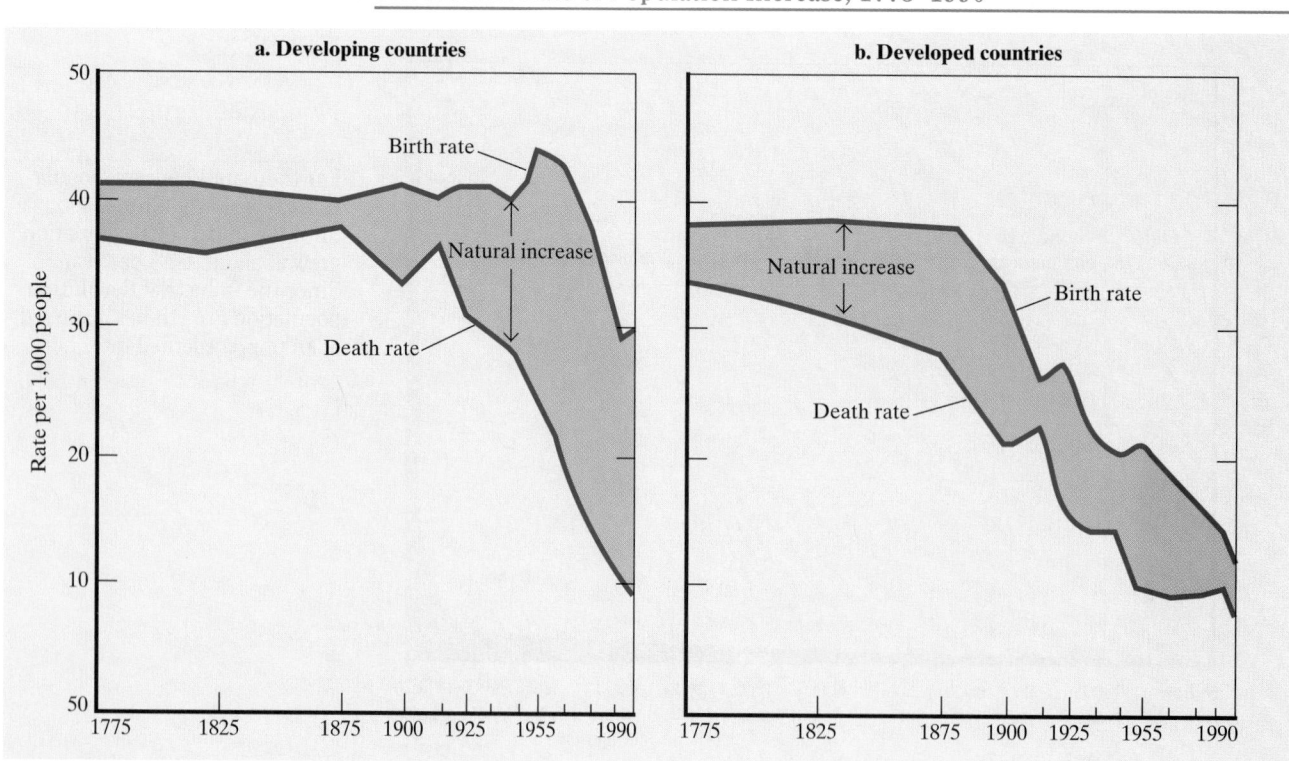

942 PART TEN: THE GLOBAL ECONOMY

Family planning and modern forms of birth control are important mechanisms for decreasing fertility, but by themselves such programs have had rather limited success in most countries where they have been tried. If family planning strategies are to be successful, they must make sense to the people who are supposed to benefit from them. The planners of such strategies must therefore understand why families in developing nations have so many children.

To a great extent, in developing countries people want large families because they believe they need them. Economists have attempted to understand fertility patterns in the developing countries by focusing on the determinants of the demand for children. In agrarian societies, children are important sources of farm labor, and they may thus make significant contributions to household income. In societies without public old-age support social security programs, children may also provide a vital source of income for parents who are too old to support themselves. With the high value of children enhanced by high rates of infant mortality, it is no wonder that families try to have many children to ensure that a sufficient number will survive into adulthood.

Cultural and religious values also affect the number of children families want to have, but the economic incentives to have large families are extremely powerful. Only when the relationship between the costs and benefits of having children changes will fertility rates decline. Expanding the opportunities for women in an economy increases the opportunity costs of child rearing (by giving women a more highly valued alternative to raising children) and often leads to lower birth rates. Government incentives for smaller families, such as subsidized education for families with fewer than three children, can have a similar effect. In general, rising incomes appear to decrease fertility rates, indicating that economic development itself reduces population growth rates.

Economic theories of population growth suggest that fertility decisions made by poor families should not be viewed as uninformed and uncontrolled. An individual family may find that having many children is a rational strategy for economic survival given the conditions in which it finds itself. This does not mean, however, that having many children is a net benefit to society as a whole. When a family decides to have a large number of children, it imposes costs on the rest of society; the children must be educated, their health provided for, and so forth. In other words, what makes sense for an individual household may create negative effects for the nation as a whole. Thus,

> Any nation that wants to slow its rate of population growth will probably find it necessary to have in place economic incentives for fewer children as well as family planning programs.

Food Shortages: Acts of Nature or Human Mistakes?

Television footage and newspaper photos portraying victims of the famine in Somalia burned indelible images of starving people into the minds of most Americans. No other event in recent memory so forcefully dramatized the ongoing food crisis in many of the developing nations. The famines that have struck various parts of Africa and Asia in the past ten years represent the most acute form of the chronic food shortage confronting the developing nations.

Pictures of the parched Somalian countryside might lead a casual observer to conclude that famines are ultimately acts of nature. After all, if the rains do not come or the locusts do, human beings can do little but sit and wait. But this simplistic view of food shortages fails to recognize the extent to which contemporary food crises are the result of human behavior. Even such natural events as severe flooding can often be traced to the overharvesting of firewood, which denudes the landscape, increases soil erosion, and exacerbates spring floods.

Human behavior is indeed a very strong factor in the inadequate distribution of available food to those who need it. India now grows enough grains to feed its vast population, for example, but malnutrition remains widespread because many people cannot afford to feed themselves. Other parts of the distribution problem involve failures to stockpile adequate food reserves in years of good harvests and transportation and communication barriers that prevent supplies from reaching those in need. World and domestic politics also heavily influence where, how, and whether food is available. During the Ethiopian famine in 1988, for example, the Ethiopian government blocked relief agencies from delivering food and medical supplies to the famine area because a civil war was being waged there. Similar events occurred when the United Nations attempted to aid Somalia in 1992. This led to U.S. military intervention in 1992 and 1993.

While food shortages are recognized chronic problems, developing nations often pursue farm policies that actually discourage agricultural production. Agricultural production in sub-Saharan Africa today is lower than it was 20 years ago. Economists believe that misguided agricultural policies are responsible for much of this decline.

Agricultural Output and Pricing Policies

Few governments in either industrialized or developing nations have permitted market forces alone to determine agricultural prices. In the United States and much of Europe, farm subsidies often encourage production that results in food surpluses rather than shortages. Some developing nations follow similar policies, maintaining high farm prices both to increase agricultural production and to maintain farm incomes. However, many developing nations follow a different route, offering farmers low prices for their output.

produce-marketing boards The channels through which the governments of some developing countries buy domestic farm output and then sell it to urban residents at government-controlled prices.

In order to appreciate the motives behind different pricing policies, you need to understand several things about the structure of agricultural markets in many developing nations. Often the government is the primary purchaser of both basic foodstuffs and export crops. Through **produce-marketing boards,** the governments of some developing countries buy farm output and sell it to urban residents at government-controlled prices. By setting the prices they pay to farmers at low levels, the government can afford to sell basic foodstuffs to urban consumers at low prices. Governments often find this an attractive course of action because the direct political influence of the relatively small urban population typically far outweighs the influence of the majority who live in the countryside. Because most city dwellers spend about half their incomes on food, low consumer prices bolster the real incomes of the urban residents and help keep them content. Urban food riots have been common in developing nations over the years, and whether a government is allowed to exist may hinge on its food-pricing strategy.

While we can easily appreciate the political motives behind food pricing, policies that set artificially low prices have significant pitfalls. Farmers react to these prices—often set so low that farmers cannot cover their production costs—by reducing the amount of output they produce. In the city, meanwhile, excess demand for food at the artificially low ceiling prices imposed by the government may promote the emergence of black markets.

Many developing economies that have followed low agricultural pricing policies have experienced exactly these results. Until recently, for example, Mexico kept corn prices low in order to hold down the price of tortillas, the staple in the diet of much of Mexico's urban population. As a result, corn production fell as farmers switched to crops whose prices the government did not control. Domestic corn shortages became widespread, and corn had to be imported to sustain urban demand.

AGRICULTURAL OUTPUT: THE SUPPLY SIDE   In 1992, a single U.S. farmer could provide enough food to feed 75 people. In most developing economies, a single farmer can provide barely enough food to feed his or her own family. While differences in agricultural pricing policies account for a part of this gap, other factors are also at work. Traditionally, low agricultural productivity in the developing world was blamed on the ignorance and laziness of peasant farmers. Today's more enlightened view traces the problem to a shortage of inputs, including land, fertilizer, irrigation, machinery, new seed varieties, and agricultural extension services (which provide credit and technical advice to farmers).

Modern agricultural science has created a so-called **Green Revolution** (not to be confused with the "environmental revolution") based on new, high-yield varieties of wheat, rice, and other crops. Using new, faster-growing varieties instead of the single-crop plants they have relied upon for centuries, some farmers can now grow three crops of rice a year. In Mexico, under ideal conditions, "miracle" wheat has produced 105 bushels of grain per acre, compared with traditional varieties that yield only 11.5 bushels per acre.

Green Revolution The agricultural breakthroughs of modern science, such as the development of new, high-yield crop varieties.

If the Green Revolution suggests that science can, in principle, solve world food shortages, the often disappointing history of developing countries' experiments with scientific agriculture offers a less optimistic outlook. Economic factors have greatly limited the adoption of Green Revolution techniques in developing countries. New seeds are expensive, and their cultivation requires the presence of many complementary inputs, including fertilizers and irrigation. With poorly developed rural credit markets, farmers often face interest rates so high that new technologies, regardless of their promise of higher crop yields, are out of reach or ultimately unprofitable. Although the reluctance of peasant farmers to adopt new agricultural techniques has often been blamed on superstition or lack of education, such decisions typically reflect a rational choice. Given the costs and benefits of new inputs and the inherent riskiness of any new method of cultivation, it is not surprising that it has been difficult to get farmers in the developing nations to accept the advances of the Green Revolution.

Peasant farmers in developing nations are also constrained by the amount of land they have to work. In some countries, high population density in the rural areas requires highly labor-intensive cultivation. In other countries, poor distribution of land decreases agricultural output. Throughout Latin America, for example, it is estimated that less than 2% of all landowners control almost 75% of the land under cultivation. Improved crop yields often follow land reforms that redistribute holdings, because owner households are often more productive than tenant farmers. Land reform has had positive effects on output in countries with economic systems as diverse as those of Korea and the People's Republic of China.

In sum:

Although acts of nature will always threaten agricultural production, human actions, especially policies designed to support the agricultural sector, can have a major impact on reducing the food problems of the developing world.

THIRD WORLD DEBT

In the 1970s, development experts worried about many crises facing the developing world, but the debt crisis was not among them. Within a decade, this situation changed dramatically. The financial plight of nations such as Brazil, Mexico, and the Philippines has become front-page news. What alarmed those familiar with the debt situation was not only its potential impact on the developing nations, but a belief that it threatened the economic welfare of the developed nations as well.

Between 1970 and 1984, developing nations borrowed so much money from other nations that their combined debt increased by 1000%, to almost $700 billion. Three nations alone—Brazil, Mexico, and Venezuela—had outstanding loans to three major U.S. banks (Citibank, Chase-Manhattan, and Manufacturer's Hanover) that were more than double the net worth of those financial institutions. As recession took hold in the economically advanced countries during the early 1980s, growth in the exports of the debtor countries slowed, and many found they could no longer pay back the money they owed. The prospect of loan defaults by Third World nations threatened the entire international financial system and transformed the debt crisis into a global problem.

The Evolution of the Debt Crisis

International financial crises, including threatened and actual defaults on foreign obligations, have a long history that extends well back into the nineteenth century. But the roots of the current debt crisis go back only as far as the early 1970s. A simple analysis of the supply and demand for credit explains much of the present situation.

With domestic capital scarce and increased saving obtainable only with great difficulty, developing nations often wish to secure foreign capital. Obviously, outright grants in the form of foreign aid from friendly governments are the most desirable form of such assistance, because they do not require any repayment. But the amount of money achieved through such aid is usually small, and it has decreased over time. Thus, developing nations have come to rely on loans from abroad. The lower the price of capital and the greater the expected return, the more the developing nations will wish to borrow. Meanwhile, suppliers of capital are willing to lend to developing nations if the interest rate they can charge for loans is high enough to offset the relatively greater risks of lending overseas.

The debt crisis began soon after the first OPEC oil price increase in 1973. Many OPEC members suddenly found themselves awash in dollars, money they literally could not spend fast enough to keep up with the funds flowing into their coffers.[3] Rather than spending these "petrodollars," many OPEC countries ended up with large cash reserves. These vast sums had to end up somewhere, and they naturally found their way into the international banking system. Banks were of course eager to recycle these funds by lending them to countries that wanted to borrow. Because funds were in such abundant supply, they were often available at interest rates that were extremely low, or even negative after allowing for inflation.

---

[3]Many OPEC countries embarked on vast and ambitious development plans, building new cities, roads, universities, and so on. Even so, their small populations and underdeveloped economies simply could not absorb the funds they received from their oil exports.

Banks in the developed nations also noted the rapid growth in many developing economies and concluded that profitable investments were available and that Third World growth prospects were encouraging. Meanwhile, oil price hikes increased the demand for foreign capital in non-OPEC developing countries. Nations such as Brazil found that their oil import bills had suddenly soared as a result of the OPEC price increase. With no corresponding increases in export revenues to pay for the extra imports, borrowing from abroad became even more attractive. Together, all these forces propelled Third World borrowing to new heights.

A second oil price shock occurred in 1979, and soon the international financial situation changed abruptly. Advanced economies, especially the United States, responded to escalating inflation with a tight monetary policy. Interest rates rose sharply, thus increasing the interest payments on Third World loans, most of which had variable interest rate provisions. As obligations to Western banks increased, the developing nations' ability to pay fell. With the recession in the industrial market economies, demand for Third World exports declined. Export volumes and prices dropped, and growing protectionism in the United States and Europe worsened the situation for developing-country borrowers.

Unable to find the export earnings needed to pay back their foreign obligations, developing nations could meet their payments in two ways: by decreasing imports or by borrowing even more from abroad. Different countries adopted different approaches. Decreasing imports threatened economic growth at home, because imports of oil and machinery are vital to the functioning of most developing countries' economies.

Unfortunately, the only alternative to decreasing imports—borrowing more from abroad—at best only forestalls inevitable adjustments. The worsening debt crisis was revealed by growing **debt service ratios,** which measure the amount of debt service—repayment of loan principal plus interest payments—as a percentage of export revenues. In some extreme cases, these ratios approached 100%, meaning that all of a debtor nation's export revenues would be required just to satisfy debt repayment, with little, if any, foreign exchange left over to pay for imports.

As the situation continued to deteriorate, another option appeared: Debtor nations might simply repudiate their debts outright and default on their outstanding loans. When *default* (nonpayment) occurs with domestic loans, some collateral is usually available to cover all or part of the remaining debt. For loans to another country, however, such collateral is virtually impossible to secure. Given their extensive involvement with Third World borrowers, Western banks did not want to set in motion a pattern of international default. Nor did borrowers want to default. Leaders of the developing nations recognized that to default might result in the denial of access to developed-country banking facilities and to markets in the industrial countries. Such results would pose major obstacles to further development efforts.

Various countries rescheduled their debt as an interim solution. Under a **debt rescheduling** agreement, banks and borrowers negotiate a new schedule for the repayment of existing debt, often with some of the debt written off and with repayment periods extended. In return, borrowing countries are expected to sign an agreement with the International Monetary Fund to revamp their economic policies to provide incentives for higher export earnings and lower imports. This kind of agreement is often referred to as a **stabilization program,** and it usually requires painful austerity measures such as currency devaluations, a reduction in government expenditures, and an increase in tax revenues.

debt service ratio The repayment amount of loan principal plus interest payments as a percentage of export revenues.

debt rescheduling An agreement between banks and borrowers through which a new schedule of repayments of the debt is negotiated; often some of the debt is written off and the repayment period is extended.

stabilization program An agreement between a borrower country and the International Monetary Fund in which the country agrees to revamp its economic policies to provide incentives for higher export earnings and lower imports.

After the Debt Crisis: An Epilogue

By the end of the 1980s, the debt crisis was not over but it had lessened somewhat, largely as a result of macroeconomic events that led to reduced interest rates. The international economy has revived somewhat, helping some nations to increase their export earnings. Other nations have benefited from new domestic policies. Still other countries, including Panama, and many African nations, however, continue to face debt burdens that are unmanageable in the short run.

One of the major economic lessons of the last ten years is that proper management of foreign capital in developing countries is essential. Much foreign borrowing was wasted on projects that had little chance of generating the returns necessary to pay back their initial costs. In other cases, domestic policies that used debt as a substitute for adjusting to new economic circumstances proved to be harmful in the long run. And, overall, much of the optimism about the prospects of the developing economies was inappropriate. Whatever else we may have learned from these mistakes, the debt crisis underscored the growing interdependence of all economies—rich and poor, large and small.

SUMMARY

1. The economic problems facing the developing countries are often quite different from those confronting industrialized nations. The policy options available to governments may also differ. Nonetheless, the tools of economic analysis are as useful in understanding the economies of less developed countries as in understanding the U.S. economy.

Life in the Developing Nations: Population and Poverty

2. The central reality of life in the developing countries is poverty. Although there is considerable diversity across the Third World, most of the people in most developing countries are extremely poor by U.S. standards.

Economic Development: Sources and Strategies

3. Almost all developing nations have a scarcity of physical capital relative to other resources, especially labor. The *vicious-circle-of-poverty hypothesis* argues that poor countries cannot escape from poverty because they cannot afford to postpone consumption (that is, to save) in order to make investments. In its crude form, the hypothesis is wrong inasmuch as some prosperous countries were at one time poorer than many developing countries are today. However, it is often difficult to mobilize savings efficiently in many developing nations.

4. Human capital—the stock of education and skills embodied in the work force—plays a vital role in economic development.

5. Developing countries are often burdened by inadequate *social overhead capital,* ranging from poor public health and sanitation facilities to inadequate roads, telephones, and court systems. Such social overhead capital is often expensive to provide, and many governments are simply not in a position to undertake many useful projects because they are too costly.

6. *Dependency theory* argues that the reason for the poverty of the Third World is the relationship between the advanced industrial nations and the developing countries, a relationship designed by the former to work to their own advantage at the expense of the latter.

7. Because developed economies are characterized by a large share of output and employment in the industrial sector, many developing countries seem to believe that development and industrialization are synonymous. In many cases, developing countries have pursued industry at the expense of agriculture, with mixed results. Recent evidence suggests that some balance between industry and agriculture leads to the best outcome.

8. *Import substitution* policies, a trade strategy that favors developing local industries that can manufacture goods to replace imports, were once very common in the developing nations. In general, such policies have not succeeded as well as those promoting open, export-oriented economies.

9. The failure of many central planning efforts has brought increasing calls for less government intervention and more market orientation in developing economies.

10. Economic growth does not guarantee economic development. Concerted efforts may be required to transform growing output capacity (economic growth) into economic benefits that reach most of a nation's people (economic development).

Issues in Economic Development

11. Rapid population growth is characteristic of many developing countries. Large families can be economically rational for parents who need support in their old age, or because children offer an important source of labor. But just because parents find it in their interests to have large families, this does not mean that having many children is a net benefit to society as whole. Rapid population growth can put a strain on already overburdened public services, such as education and health.

12. Food shortages in developing countries are not simply the result of bad weather. Public policies that depress the prices of agricultural goods, thereby lowering farmers' incentives to produce, are common throughout the developing nations, and human behavior is very much behind the inadequate distribution of available food to those who need it. While acts of nature will always threaten agricultural production, human actions, especially policies designed to support the agricultural sector, can have a major impact on reducing the food problems of the developing world.

Third World Debt

13. Since 1970 the debts of the developing countries have grown tenfold. As recession took hold in the advanced countries during the early 1980s, growth in the exports of the debtor countries slowed, and many found they could no longer pay back money they owed. The prospect of loan defaults by Third World nations threatened the entire international financial system and transformed the debt crisis into a global problem.

REVIEW TERMS AND CONCEPTS

brain drain   934
debt rescheduling   947
debt service ratio   947
dependency theory   935
export promotion   938
fertility rate   942

Green Revolution   945
import substitution   937
International Monetary Fund   939
mortality rate   942
natural rate of population
    increase   942

produce-marketing boards   944
social overhead capital   934
stabilization program   947
vicious-circle-of-poverty
    hypothesis   933
World Bank   939

PROBLEM SET

1. The GDP of any country can be divided into two kinds of goods: capital goods and consumption goods. The proportion of national output devoted to capital goods determines, to some extent, the nation's growth rate.
   a. Explain how capital accumulation leads to economic growth.
   b. Briefly describe how a market economy determines how much investment will be undertaken each period.
   c. "Consumption versus investment is a more painful conflict to resolve for developing countries." Comment.
   d. If you were the benevolent dictator of a less-developed country, what plans would you implement to increase per capita GDP?

2. "The main reason developing countries are poor is that they don't have enough capital. If we give them machinery, or build factories for them, we can greatly improve their situation." Comment.

3. "Poor countries are trapped in a vicious circle of poverty. In order for output to grow, they must accumulate capital. In order to accumulate capital, they must save (consume less than they produce). But because they are poor, they have little or no extra output available for savings—it must all go to feed and clothe the present generation. Thus they are doomed to stay poor forever." Comment on each step in this argument.

4. Explain the meaning of the term "human capital" and assess its relevance in economic development.

5. If children are an "investment in the future," why do some developing nations offer incentives to households that limit the size of their families? Why are these incentives often ignored?

6. If you were in charge of economic policy for a developing country and wanted to promote rapid economic growth, would you choose to favor industry over agriculture? What about exports versus import substitution? In each case, briefly explain your reasoning. How do you explain the fact that many countries chose industry and a protectionist import-substitution policy?

7. "All we need to do is to promote rapid growth of per capita incomes in the developing nations and the poverty problems will take care of themselves." Comment.

8. "Famines are acts of God, resulting from bad weather or other natural disasters. There is nothing we can do about them except to send food relief after they occur." Explain why this position is inaccurate. Concentrate on agricultural pricing policies and distributional issues.

39

Alternative Systems, the Collapse of Communism, and the Road to Economic Reform

For 40 years, between the end of World War II and the mid-1980s, a powerful rivalry existed between the Soviet Union and the United States. This "cold war" pitted the two superpowers against each other in a bitter struggle for influence and fueled the nuclear arms race. Indeed, at one time the mutual distrust between the United States and the Soviet Union was so strong that the concept of "mutual assured destruction" became a dominant theme in international relations.

But the world began to change in the mid-1980s as the political and economic structures of the Soviet Union and the Eastern European communist countries started to crumble. In 1989, relatively peaceful revolutions took place in rapid succession in Poland, Hungary, and Czechoslovakia. A bloody revolution in Romania toppled Nicolae Ceausescu, who had ruled with an iron fist for 24 years. The Berlin Wall, which had separated the two halves of Germany since 1961, was knocked down and the country reunited. Then, in August 1991, after a failed coup attempt by hard-line communists, the Soviet Union itself began to come apart. By the end of 1991, the Soviet Union had dissolved into 15 independent states, the largest of which is the Russian Republic. Ten of these 15 republics formed Commonwealth Independent States (CIS) in December 1991. The Cold War was over.

Why do we reflect on historical political rivalries in an economics text? There are two reasons. First, the 40-year struggle between the United States and the Soviet Union was fundamentally a struggle between two economic systems: market-based capitalism (the U.S. system) and centrally planned socialism (the Soviet system). Second, the Cold War ended so abruptly in the late 1980s because the Soviet and Eastern European economies virtually collapsed during that period. In a sense, one could say that 1991 was the year that the market triumphed.

But what now? The independent states of the former Soviet Union and the other former communist economies of Eastern Europe are struggling to make the transition from centrally planned socialism to some form of market-based capitalism. In some countries, such as Serbia and Bosnia-Herzegovina, economic reforms have taken a back seat to bitter and violent ethnic and political rivalries that have been simmering for decades. In other countries, like Poland and Russia, the biggest issue continues to be economic transformation.

The success or failure of this transition from centrally planned socialism to market-based capitalism will determine the course of history, yet it has no historical precedent. Although many countries have made the transition from a market-based system to a centrally planned system, the opposite has never occurred. Undoubtedly, the process has been and will continue to be painful. Between 1989 and 1992, industrial production fell more than 40% in countries like the former East Germany, Albania, Poland, and Romania. In Russia, production decreased about 30 percent. In all these nations, fairly prosperous people suddenly found themselves with annual real incomes closer to those of people in developing countries. For many people, the issue became survival: how to get enough food and fuel to get through the winter.

In this chapter, we focus on the ongoing debate over economic reform. What can be done to make the transition from socialism to capitalism successful? In what sequence should changes be made? How quickly can market institutions be established? How much help from the United States and the rest of the world will be required? These questions and others like them are already dogging President Clinton, who was elected in part on his promise to spend more time than his predecessor on domestic issues.

To understand the transformation process, it is necessary to begin with some history. From what are these countries making a transition? Our chapter starts with a discussion of alternative economic systems, the vision of communism, and a brief description of the economic structure of the former Soviet Union. We then turn to the current debate over the transition process, focusing on the experiences of Poland and Russia. We end the chapter by examining a different kind of economic transformation that has been ongoing for some time in China and discussing the performance of the Japanese economy after World War II.

POLITICAL SYSTEMS AND ECONOMIC SYSTEMS: SOCIALISM, CAPITALISM, AND COMMUNISM

Every society has both a political system and an economic system. Unfortunately, the political and economic dimensions of a society are often confused.

The terms "democracy" and "dictatorship" refer to *political* systems. A *democracy* is a system of government in which ultimate power rests with the people, who make governmental decisions either directly through voting or indirectly through representatives. A *dictatorship* is a political system in which ultimate power is concentrated either in a small elite or a single person.

socialist economy An economy in which most capital is owned by the government rather than by private citizens. Also called social ownership.

capitalist economy An economy in which most capital is privately owned.

communism An economic system in which the people control the means of production (capital and land) directly, without the intervention of a government or state.

Historically, two major alternative *economic* systems have existed: socialism and capitalism. A **socialist economy** is one in which most capital—factories, equipment, buildings, railroads, and so forth—is owned by the government rather than by private citizens. *Social ownership* is another term that is often used to describe this kind of system. A **capitalist economy** is one in which most capital is privately owned. Beyond these systems is a purely theoretical economic system called *communism*.

Communism is an economic system in which the people control the means of production (land and capital) directly, without the intervention of a government or state. In the world envisioned by communists, the state would wither away and society would plan the economy in much the same way that a collective would. In fact, although some countries still consider themselves communist—including China, North Korea, Cuba, and Tanzania—economic planning is done by the government in all of them. Thus,

> In terms of comparing economies today, the real distinction is between centrally planned socialism and capitalism, not between capitalism and communism.

No pure socialist economies and no pure capitalist economies exist. Even the Soviet Union, which was basically socialist, had a large private sector. Fully one fourth of agricultural output in what was the USSR was legally produced on private plots and sold, and in a large "second economy" private citizens provided goods and services to each other, sometimes in violation of the law. Conversely, the strongly capitalistic United States supports many government enterprises, including the postal system. In the United States, governments employ about 15% of the total U.S. labor force. Nonetheless, public ownership is the exception in the United States and private ownership was the exception in the Soviet Union.

Whether particular kinds of political systems tend to be associated with particular kinds of economic systems is hotly debated. The United States and Japan are examples of countries with essentially capitalist economic systems and essentially democratic political institutions. China and North Korea have basically socialist economies with political power highly concentrated in a single political party. These observations do not imply that all capitalist countries have democratic political institutions, however, or that all socialist countries are subject to totalitarian party rule.

Many countries—Indonesia and Taiwan, for example—have basically capitalist economies without democratic political systems. Many other countries that are much closer to the socialist end of the economic spectrum also maintain strong democratic traditions. The people of France, for instance, elected the socialist government of François Mitterrand in 1981, and that government promptly nationalized several major industries. Great Britain and Sweden are other examples of democratic countries that support certain strong socialist institutions.

But do certain kinds of economic systems lead to repressive governments? Austrian economist Friedrich Hayek argues that the answer is yes:

> Economic reforms and government coercion are the road to serfdom. . . . Personal and economic freedoms are inseparable. Once you start down the road to government regulation and planning of the economy, the freedom to speak minds and select political leaders will be jeopardized.[1]

The recent events in Eastern Europe and Russia seem to support Hayek's thesis. There, economic and political reforms are proceeding side by side, and the evidence is mounting that the heart of both the market system *and* democracy is individual freedom.

[1]Friedrich Hayek, *The Road to Serfdom* (Chicago: University of Chicago Press, 1944).

Nonetheless, some counter Hayek's argument by claiming that social reform and active government involvement in the economy are the only ways to prevent the rise of a totalitarian state. They argue that free and unregulated markets lead to inequality and the accumulation of economic power. Accumulated economic power, in turn, leads to political power that is inevitably used in the interests of the wealthy few, not in the interests of all.

Central Planning versus the Market

In addition to the degree to which capital is owned by private citizens rather than the government, economic systems also differ significantly in the extent to which economic decisions are made through central planning rather than through a market system. In some socialist economies, the allocation of resources, the mix of output, and the distribution of output are determined centrally according to a plan. The former Soviet Union, for example, generated one-year and five-year plans laying out specific production targets in virtually every sector of the economy. In market economies, decisions are made independently by buyers and sellers responding to market signals. Producers produce only what they expect to sell. Labor is attracted into and out of various occupations by wages that are determined by the forces of supply and demand.

Just as there are no pure capitalist and no pure socialist economies, there are no pure market economies and no pure planned economies. Even in the former Soviet Union markets existed and determined, to a large extent, the allocation of resources. Production targets in the United States are set by many agencies, including the Pentagon.

Generally, socialist economies favor central planning over market allocation, while capitalist economies rely to a much greater extent on the market. Nonetheless, some variety exists. Yugoslavia, for example, was a socialist country that made extensive use of the market. While ownership of capital and land rested with the government, individual firms determined their own output levels and prices and made their own investment plans. Yugoslavian firms borrowed from banks to finance investments and paid interest on their loans. This type of system, which combines government ownership with market allocation, is often referred to as a **market–socialist economy**.

market–socialist economy An economy that combines government ownership with market allocation.

THE ECONOMIC THEORIES OF KARL MARX

The conflict between economic systems has taken place on two levels. On one hand, there are alternative economic *theories* that lead to dramatically different conclusions about the relative merits of market-capitalist and planned socialist systems. On the other hand, the actual *performance* of these differently organized economies must be considered.

The events of the early 1990s in Eastern Europe provide strong evidence that central planning has come up a big loser on the basis of performance. Why, then, should we spend time studying the theoretical underpinnings of communism and socialism? There are at least three reasons. First, for over 70 years in the Soviet Union, and for over 40 years in most parts of Eastern Europe and China, socialist ideology was dominant. Until very recently, about one third of the world's population lived in countries whose economies were based on socialist and communist philosophies. Second, even though the economies of the republics of the former

Soviet Union and the economies of Eastern Europe are moving rapidly toward a market-based system, a number of other countries remain firmly committed to the ideas of centrally planned socialism. Finally, to understand the capitalist system, one must understand the criticisms that have been leveled against it.

Marxian Economics: An Overview

Perhaps no single modern thinker has had a greater impact on the world in the twentieth century than Karl Marx, whose work is the basis of the communist ideology. Stated simply, Marxian economic analysis concludes that the capitalist system is morally wrong and doomed to ultimate failure.

The most common misconception about Marx's work is that it contains a blueprint for the operation of a socialist or communist economy. In fact, Marx did not write much about socialism; he wrote about capitalism. Published mostly after his death in 1883, his major work, the three-volume *Das Kapital*, is an extensive analysis of how capitalist economies function and how they are likely to develop over time. *The Communist Manifesto* (written with Friedrich Engels and published in 1848) and his other writings contain only a rough sketch of the socialist and communist societies that Marx predicted would ultimately replace capitalism.

Marx's economic theories lie at the root of his interpretation of history. In examining his work, let us begin with what might be called "Marxian microeconomics" and then turn to the macroeconomic conclusions that emerge from it.

The Labor Theory of Value

labor theory of value Marx's theory that the value of a commodity depends exclusively upon the amount of labor required to produce it. Commodities are the physical embodiment of the labor that produced them, and capital is the physical embodiment of the past labor used to produce it.

The centerpiece of Marx's economic theories is the **labor theory of value**. Marx argued that the value of a commodity depends exclusively upon the amount of labor required to produce it. Commodities are thus the physical embodiment of the labor that produced them:

> A commodity has value, because it is a crystallization of social labor. The greatness of its value, of its relative value, depends upon the greater or less amount of that social substance contained in it. . . .The relative values of commodities are, therefore, determined by the respective quantities or amounts of labor, worked up, realized, fixed in them.[2]

The labor theory of value, of course, also had to address the nature and uses of capital. As you know, goods can be produced with a variety of combinations of capital and labor. Are goods produced with a lot of capital and little labor worth less than those produced with a lot of labor and little capital? The answer is no. Capital, according to Marx, is the physical embodiment of the *past labor* that was used to produce it. When used in production, capital contributes value by passing that past labor through to the final product. A machine that took 100 hours to build contributes 100 hours of value to final products over its lifetime. The value of a commodity is thus the sum of the values contributed by present labor and past labor (capital).

The Nature of Profit: The Marxian View

means of production Marx's term for land and capital.

If, as Marx believed, commodity values depend only on labor's contribution, where does profit come in? The answer is simple. Capitalists own the **means of production**, Marx's term for land and capital. They hire individual workers who have no way to make a living except by selling their labor power. Capitalists make a profit by paying workers a daily wage that is less than the value that workers contribute to final products in a day.

---

[2]Karl Marx, *Wages, Price and Profit* (Beijing: Foreign Languages Press, 1975), pp. 34–35.

The wage rate is the **value of labor power**, and it is determined in the same way as the value of any other commodity. That is, the value of labor power depends on the amount of labor required to "produce" it. To produce and sustain labor power requires food, clothing, shelter, basic education, medical care, and so forth. The value of labor power, then, is determined by the amount of labor it takes to produce those things necessary to sustain a worker and his or her family. In essence, Marx was proposing a *subsistence theory of wages*: Capitalists will pay a wage that is just enough for laborers to live on.

Let's suppose that it takes four hours to produce everything necessary to sustain a worker for a day. Marx would argue in this case that a day's wage paid by capitalists will be the equivalent of four hours' worth of value. If a worker is employed for 12 hours, the capitalist ends up with a final product containing 12 hours of value but needs to give only four hours' worth of value–or wages–to the worker. The difference (eight hours), which Marx called **surplus value**, is profit.

Profit is thus value created by workers but "expropriated" by capitalists. Capitalists are able to expropriate surplus value because they own the means of production and control access to them. Profit is not a reward for any productive activity; it is extracted solely by virtue of ownership. Marx referred to the ratio of surplus value to the value of labor power as the **rate of exploitation**.

value of labor power The wage rate, dependent on the amount of clothing, shelter, basic education, medical care, and so on required to produce and sustain labor power.

surplus value The profit a capitalist earns by paying workers less than the value of what they produce.

rate of exploitation The ratio of surplus value to the value of labor power.

The Nature of Profit: The Neoclassical View

The bulk of this text has presented mainstream, or neoclassical, economic theory, with its deep roots in nineteenth-century philosophy. At this point we should reflect briefly on the nature of profit in that model, because it is so different from the Marxian notion of surplus value.

Neoclassical economics views both capital and labor as productive factors of production. If you have one worker digging a hole and you want a bigger hole faster, you can accomplish your goal by hiring a second worker *or* by giving the first worker a better shovel. Add labor and you get more product; add capital and you also get more product. According to neoclassical theory, every factor of production in a competitive market economy ends up being paid in accordance with the market value of its product. Profit-maximizing firms hire labor and capital as long as both contribute more to the final value of a product than they cost.

In sum:

> Neoclassical theory views profit as the legitimate return to capital. Marx, however, saw profit as value created by labor and unjustly expropriated by nonproductive capitalists who are able to exploit labor by virtue of their ownership of the means of production.

Marx's Predictions

The labor theory of value led Marx to conclude that capitalism was doomed. The essence of his argument was that the rate of profit has a natural tendency to fall over time. With the rate of profits falling, capitalists increase the rate of exploitation, pushing workers deeper and deeper into misery. At the same time, the ups and downs of business cycles become more and more extreme. Ultimately, Marx believed, workers would rise up and overthrow the repressive capitalist system.

Marx came to the surprising conclusion that the falling rate of profit results from the accumulation of capital. He had observed that over time processes of production tend to become more capital intensive. As technology changes and capitalists become wealthy, new machines are introduced and factories grow larger. Marx saw this process of capital accumulation as a natural result of capitalists' search for more and more profit.

But the process of capital accumulation contains a trap. Remember that, in Marxian theory, capital is the embodiment of past labor that is simply passed through into the value of final commodities. If a capitalist buys a machine produced with 100 hours of labor, 100 hours of value must be paid to acquire it. The machine, in turn, ultimately adds 100 hours' worth of value to final product, but *only 100 hours and nothing more*. In other words, there is no profit or surplus value in past labor. Surplus value comes only from paying *present* labor less than the amount of value that it produces.

If the ratio of past labor to present labor embodied in a product rises, profit as a percentage of product value must fall. Suppose that past labor contributes one fourth of a product's value, and present labor contributes three fourths. Further, suppose that the rate of exploitation is one third: Of the value created by present workers, one third goes to capitalists and two thirds is paid to workers as wages. Profit, or surplus value, is thus 25% of the value of product (one third of three quarters). But if past labor accounted for half of final product value instead of only one quarter, the same rate of exploitation would produce a profit equal to only one sixth of product value (one third of one half). Thus, capital accumulation actually causes the rate of profit to fall.

To counteract this falling rate of profit, Marx argued, capitalists are forced to increase the rate of exploitation. One way to increase the rate of exploitation is to lengthen the working day. If a worker puts in 14 hours instead of 12, but still receives the same daily wage, profits will rise. Wages, of course, can be cut only to subsistence levels.

Another way to counteract the falling rate of profit is to seek higher profits abroad. The establishment of colonies opens up new investment opportunities from which surplus value can be extracted. Thus, capitalist countries not only exploit their own workers but also ultimately become imperialists, exploiting workers around the world.

Marx's Theory of History

Marx's theory that capitalism would ultimately collapse under its own weight was part of a longer view of history. Capitalism had emerged naturally from a previous stage (*feudalism*) which had emerged from an even earlier stage (*ancient slavery*), and so forth. In the economic evolutionary process, Marx believed, capitalism would come to be replaced by socialism, which ultimately would be replaced by communism.

At each stage of economic evolution, Marx said, a set of rules called the *social relations of production* defines the economic system. Contradictions and conflicts inevitably arise at each stage, and these problems are ultimately resolved in the establishment of a new set of social relations. The conflicts in capitalism include alienation, increasing exploitation, misery (or, as Marx called it, "emiserization"), and deeper and deeper business cycles.

It is clear that Marx was eager for the demise of capitalism. He advocated strong and powerful labor unions for two reasons. First, unions would push wages above subsistence and transfer some surplus value back to workers. Second, unions were a way of raising the consciousness of workers about their condition. Only through class consciousness, Marx believed, would workers be empowered to throw off the shackles of capitalism.

At the heart of Marx's ideas is the argument that private ownership and profit are unfair and unethical. Even if it could be demonstrated that the incentives provided by the institution of private property result in faster economic growth or improved living standards, anyone who accepts Marx's interpretation has to reject capitalism on moral grounds, on ideological grounds, or on both.

FROM THEORY TO PERFORMANCE   Does theory give us any reason to prefer a private ownership/market system to a centrally planned socialist system? Some believe that it does. If you accept Marx's basic premises, you need go no further. To Marxists, the actual performance of the economy is not as important as the basic morality (or immorality) of the system by which it operates. If you agree with Hayek that central planning inevitably leads to repression, however, then you will agree that the market is better even though it may not lead to efficient or equitable results.

Neither mainstream economic theory nor socialist theory establishes beyond doubt that markets work better than economic planning or that socialism is better than capitalism. Without a compelling theoretical argument on one side or the other, we must turn to an evaluation of the actual performance of a number of systems.

ALTERNATIVE ECONOMIC SYSTEMS: THE RISE AND FALL OF COMMUNISM IN RUSSIA AND EASTERN EUROPE

The Eastern European nations' transitions to market systems were in large measure the result of the economic failures of centrally planned socialism, which had ultimately failed to "deliver the goods." To understand the failure of the Eastern European socialist economies and the difficult process of transition that lies ahead for them, students of economics must be aware of these countries' economic histories. In this section, we briefly describe the Soviet system as it existed for nearly 75 years and the changes taking place today. Although the transformation process is well underway, it will be some time before the process of dismantling the old system is complete.

The History of the Soviet Union

Marx believed that socialist revolution would occur in advanced capitalist states where a repressive industrial society would push workers to unite and rise up against their industrialist masters. The Russian nation in 1913 had experienced the beginnings of modern economic growth, but it could hardly have been called an advanced capitalist system. Table 39.1 shows that its relative position in terms of per capita income had improved in the half century prior to 1913, but that it still lagged far behind the other industrial countries of the world.

When the Bolsheviks took power after the October Revolution in 1917, they found themselves without the advanced industrial base that Marx had envisioned and with no real blueprint for running a socialist or communist state. Marx's writings provided only the broadest guidelines. Undaunted, the new government immediately abolished private land ownership and ordered that the land be distributed to those who worked on it. It also established worker control of industry and nationalized the banks. Sweeping nationalization of industry began in June 1918. Money, private trade, and wage differentials were abolished. All decisions were made centrally.

The headlong rush into uncharted waters was too much too soon, and between 1921 and 1928 Soviet leaders retreated from their initial hard line back toward a

TABLE 39.1
Per Capita Income (Rubles)

	1861	1913
Russia	71	119
U.K.	323	580
France	150	303
Germany	175	374
U.S.	450	1,033
Netherlands	—	366
Norway	166	659
Sweden	112	340
Italy	183	261
Spain	—	199
Austria-Hungary	—	190

Source: Paul Gregory and Robert Stuart, *Soviet Economic Structure and Performance*, 2nd ed. (New York: Harper & Row, 1981), p. 20.

New Economic Policy The Soviet economic policy in effect between 1921 and 1928; characterized by decentralization and a retreat to a market orientation.

five-year plans Plans developed in the Soviet Union that provided general guidelines and directions for the next five years.

market orientation. The **New Economic Policy** of the period was characterized by decentralization. Most smaller industrial enterprises were denationalized, although the peasants remained in control of agriculture. State control of production was replaced by market links between consumers and industry and between industry and agriculture.

The relative merits and demerits of these two periods, 1917—1921 and 1921–1928, were debated at length among the Soviet leadership. Finally, in 1928, the Soviet Union settled on an economic structure that lasted into the 1980s: comprehensive central planning and collectivization of agriculture. In 1928, under the leadership of Joseph Stalin, the first of many **five-year plans** was approved. The plan emphasized rapid industrialization and the production of industrial capital; in fact, the plan called for a doubling of the fixed capital stock of the Soviet Union in five years. Consumer goods were to be produced only when all other needs of the new industrial structure had been met.

The industrialization program depended on a steady flow of food and agricultural raw materials from the countryside, and that did not come easily. As a result, Stalin was forced to rely more and more on coercion. In 1929 the land holdings of the peasants were organized into collective farms that were obligated to deliver state-ordered quotas of farm products. Repression was severe, and millions of peasants perished.[3]

No serious debate about economic matters took place in the Soviet Union until after Stalin's death in 1953. In 1965 official reforms were introduced by the government of Alexei Kosygin. More recently, Mikhail Gorbachev announced a series of reforms in 1986 and more dramatic reforms in 1987, but the structure of the economy was not changed fundamentally on either of these occasions.

Since 1991, Boris Yeltsin has been president of the Russian Republic and the champion of reform. Yeltsin has deregulated most prices, begun the privatization process, and attempted to stabilize the macroeconomy. By mid-1993, however, little change in economic conditions had occurred and the evidence was mounting that reform would take much longer than previously estimated. Hard-liners in the Russian Parliament attempted to reduce Yeltsin's power in 1993, but a national referendum confirmed the Russian people's support both for Yeltsin and for economic reform.

THE HISTORICAL COMPONENTS OF THE SOVIET ECONOMY   Until the dramatic changes that began to take place at the start of the 1990s, the Soviet economy was a centrally planned socialist economy. Virtually all of its productive assets, including most land and capital, were publicly owned. There was no formal private business sector, no market for capital goods, and virtually no income from property. Outside of money made from private farm plots, the only incomes to households were wages and transfer payments from the government. State-owned enterprises might earn "socialist profits," but the profits accrued to the state, which used them for a variety of purposes.

Although the state controlled supply in Soviet output markets, leaving demand essentially unmanaged, the opposite was true in the labor market. The state took the supply of labor and the distribution of skills as fixed in the short run. Just as consumers were essentially free to choose among outputs in the marketplace, workers were essentially free to choose their occupations and their places of work. Wages were set to clear the labor market and to attract workers into undesirable occupations and regions of the country.

[3]George Orwell's novel *Animal Farm* is a parable of this period in Soviet history.

In the long run, the government could influence the supply of labor and skills. Educational planners and economic planners maintained a close relationship to ensure that the system was producing workers with the right skills. Graduates of secondary and vocational schools and discharged military personnel were placed in local enterprises or were directed to jobs by local authorities. Trainees did not seem to be forced to accept any particular assigned job, although college graduates were obligated to work where the state assigned them for three years.

ECONOMIC PERFORMANCE   The Stalinist/Soviet strategy to achieve high rates of growth worked for many years. The highest rates of growth in Soviet GNP were during the 1950s. Official Soviet statistics put the real growth rate during that decade at over 10%, an extraordinary rate at which real output would double every seven years. Even the CIA's more conservative estimates, shown in Table 39.2, estimated the Soviet growth rate at 5.7%, nearly 80% above the U.S. average for the decade.

In 1957, the Soviet Union's GNP stood at about 39% of the United States' GNP. A year later, Soviet GNP had jumped to nearly 44% of U.S. GNP. The rate at which the Soviet Union was catching up was so remarkable that it prompted Soviet Premier Nikita Khrushchev to promise, "We will bury you!" If the Soviet growth rate estimates had been correct, and if both countries had continued to grow at the same rates that they did during the 1950s, Soviet GNP would indeed have surpassed U.S. GNP by 1970.

The primary force behind Soviet growth was capital accumulation. During the 1950s, the capital stock of the USSR grew at 9.5% annually; in the United States, the corresponding figure was only 3.6 percent. Through 1975 Soviet capital stocks grew at twice the rate of capital accumulation in the United States. But these growth rates did not continue, and during the late 1970s they slowed down. Between 1975 and 1985, even the slowly growing U.S. economy outperformed the Soviet Union. In 1975, per capita GNP in the Soviet Union stood at 48.2% of per capita GNP in the United States. In 1985 the figure was 48.1 percent.

TABLE 39.2
Economic Growth and Investment in the Soviet Union and the United States, 1950–1990

ANNUAL AVERAGE RATE OF GROWTH

	USSR NET MATERIAL PRODUCT (USSR, OFFICIAL FIGURES)	USSR REAL GNP (CIA)	USA REAL GNP	USSR CAPITAL STOCK	USA CAPITAL STOCK
1950–1960	10.3	5.7	3.2	9.5	3.6
1960–1970	7.1	5.1	4.0	8.0	4.0
1970–1975	5.7	3.7	2.6	7.9	4.0
1975–1980	4.3	2.7	3.7	6.8	3.9
1980–1984	—	2.6	2.7	6.3*	3.6
1984–1987	—	1.8	2.4	NA	NA
1988–1990	—	0.0	2.4	NA	NA

Note:*1980–1983. NA = not available. GDP data not available.

Sources: Abram Bergson, "Gorbachev calls for Intensive Growth," *Challenge*, Nov/Dec., 1985. For the United States, *Statistical Abstract of the United States, 1986, Historical Statistics of the United States*, and *Economic Report of the President, 1990*.

Part of the reason for the slowdown was the sluggishness of Soviet agriculture. Despite the fact that Russia once served as the "breadbasket of Europe," the Soviet Union became unable to meet its own basic food needs. The grain harvest, perhaps the key indicator of agricultural productivity, fell. According to one estimate, the average annual harvest for the years 1979–1990 was 15% below the average annual harvest for the years 1973–1978. Agricultural imports during the later period amounted to nearly 20% of total domestic production.

The lackluster performance of the Soviet economy in recent decades spurred a series of economic reforms. The first, and until 1987 the most significant, was the package announced in 1965 by Premier Alexei Kosygin. The Kosygin plan reduced the controls placed on enterprise managers by the central system and encouraged them to respond spontaneously to changing conditions as reflected in profits, sales, and worker performance. The number of targets was reduced significantly, and more emphasis was placed on enterprise profits. A system of investment finance was established, and enterprises assumed a larger role in investment planning. Enterprise managers were also given more freedom to control an expanded incentive bonus system for workers.

The period from 1966 to 1978 saw a gradual reemergence of earlier policies. Strict controls were placed on the size and distribution of enterprise incentive funds. Managerial bonuses were tied to the fulfillment of targets, and the number of targets was expanded. By the late 1970s, the Soviet system was very much as it had been in the early 1960s, with output, prices, and investment centrally planned and administered.

Then, in July of 1979, the Soviet Union announced another "sweeping" set of reforms. But observers agree that these changes did nothing but reinforce the traditional features of the system and increase the rigidity of the central planning system.

GORBACHEV AND *PERESTROIKA*   In March 1985, Mikhail Gorbachev became general secretary of the Soviet Communist Party and almost immediately began to press for reforms that had an enormous impact on the world. In 1990, Gorbachev won the Nobel Peace Prize for ending the Cold War and was named "Man of the Decade" by *Time* magazine. Yet despite his enormous popularity around the world and his political successes, one prize continued to elude Gorbachev: improved economic performance in the Soviet Union.

Gorbachev's reforms fell into two broad categories: *glasnost* ("openness") and *perestroika* ("restructuring"). *Glasnost* led to the almost completely open discussion of virtually every aspect of political and economic reform in the Soviet Union. It also led to a new set of political institutions, including an end to the power monopoly of the Communist Party[4] and more free elections. *Glasnost* was relatively easy to achieve, but the establishment of new economic structures—the key element of Gorbachev's *perestroika*—proved much more difficult.

The initial goal of *perestroika* was to increase workers' responsibilities and discipline by attacking corruption and alcoholism. In these arenas, Gorbachev

---

[4]For many years, membership in and loyalty to the Communist Party were the ticket to the good life in the Soviet Union. Under the *nomenklatura* party patronage system, Communist Party leaders received power and privilege in exchange for loyalty to the party. In addition to determining the staffing of government and industrial posts (a practice that led to a good deal of favoritism and nepotism), party members also enjoyed the right to shop at special state-run stores. These stores stocked luxury items that were not available to the general public. Travel privileges, admissions to the best colleges and universities, larger apartments, and bigger cars also went to members of the *nomenklatura*. In 1990, the Central Committee of the Soviet Communist Party approved a proposal by President Gorbachev calling for an end to the party's constitutional guarantee of power and thus an end to the *nomenklatura*. After the failed August 1991 coup, the Communist Party was completely dismantled.

met with some success. Numerous bureau chiefs were replaced, alcoholism was reduced through strict law enforcement, absenteeism declined, and productivity increased. Then, in 1986, the focus of reform shifted to the performance of agriculture. In that year, Gorbachev announced a major restructuring of the agricultural sector that gave local farm units and the peasantry significant new freedoms. Local farm units, for example, were allowed to use the market to dispose of any surplus over five-year plan levels. Payments to state and collective farm workers were tied to productivity and profits, and local directors were given much more authority over management and investment decisions.

But the best was yet to come. In June of 1987, Gorbachev announced yet another series of reforms. The package included some surprising changes. First, price subsidies were to be drastically reduced or eliminated, even on such staple items as meat, bread, dairy products, and housing. Second, all limits on what workers could earn were to be removed, and salaries were to be tied directly to performance. Third, the decision-making authority of the farms and enterprises was to be greatly expanded. Central plans were to contain far less detail than in previous years. At the same time, Gorbachev called for sharp increases in small-scale family farming and for a "competitive atmosphere" among enterprises to ensure that goods were sold to consumers at the lowest possible prices that would still cover costs of production.

Perhaps the most radical of the 1987 reforms, however, was that job security, a sacred tenet of the Soviet system, would be reduced. For the first time, enterprises could actually fire lazy workers, and unproductive enterprises could be shut down.

ECONOMIC CRISIS AND COLLAPSE   Although many of Gorbachev's ideas seemed promising, the situation in the Soviet Union deteriorated sharply after 1987. The attempted transition from central planning to a partly free-market system caused major problems. Growth of output slowed to a crawl in 1989 and 1990, and in 1991 the economic system collapsed. Industrial production dropped sharply, food shortages grew worse, inflation became a serious problem, and external debt increased rapidly.

Gorbachev ran out of time in August of 1991 as the struggle between the hard-liners and the radical reformers came to a head. The hard-liners took Gorbachev prisoner and assumed control of the government. The coup lasted only three days. People took to the streets of Moscow and resisted the tanks, the Soviet army refused to obey orders, and the hard-liners were out.

But the end was near for both Gorbachev and the Soviet Union. In December of 1991, the Soviet Union was dissolved, 10 of the former Soviet republics formed the Commonwealth of Independent States (CIS), and Boris Yeltsin became president of the Russian Republic, as Gorbachev became part of history. From the beginning, Yeltsin showed himself to be a reformer committed to converting the Russian economy rapidly into a market system while maintaining hard-won political freedoms for the people. His reform plan called for deregulating prices, privatizing public enterprises, and stabilizing the macroeconomy.

By 1993, the commitment to reform in most parts of Eastern Europe and Russia was strong. In April of 1993, President Yeltsin, feeling pressure from an increasingly intransigent Congress of People's Deputies, asked for a Russian national referendum on the reforms that he had proposed. The Russian people responded by giving Yeltsin and his reforms a strong vote of confidence.

The Transition to a Market Economy

The reforms underway in the Russian Republic and in the other formerly communist countries of Eastern Europe have taken shape very slowly and amid a great deal of debate about how best to proceed. It is important to remember that there is absolutely no historical precedent to provide lessons. Despite this lack of precedent, however, there is substantial agreement among economists about what needs to be done. Specifically:

> Economists generally agree on six basic requirements for a successful transition from socialism to a market-based system: (1) macroeconomic stabilization; (2) deregulation of prices and liberalization of trade; (3) privatization of state-owned enterprises and development of new private industry; (4) the establishment of market-supporting institutions, such as property and contract laws, accounting systems, and so forth; (5) a social safety net to deal with unemployment and poverty; and (6) external assistance.

We discuss each of these components in the sections that follow. While we focus on the experience of the Russian Republic, keep in mind that these principles apply to all economies in transition.

MACROECONOMIC STABILIZATION   Virtually every one of the countries in transition has had a problem with inflation, but nowhere has it been worse than in Russia. As economic conditions worsened, the government found itself with serious budget problems. As revenue flows slowed and expenditure commitments increased, large budget deficits resulted. At the same time, each of the new republics established its own central bank. Each central bank began issuing "ruble credits" to keep important enterprises afloat and to pay the government's bills. The issuance of these credits, which were generally accepted as a means of payment throughout the country, led to a dramatic expansion of the money supply.

Almost from the beginning, the expanded money supply meant that too much money was chasing too few goods. This situation was made worse by government-controlled prices set substantially below market-clearing levels. The combination of monetary expansion and price control was deadly. Government-run shops that sold goods at controlled prices were empty. People waited in line for days and often became violent when their efforts to buy goods at low official prices were thwarted. At the same time, suppliers found that they could charge much higher prices for their products on the black market—which grew bigger by the day, further exacerbating the shortage of goods at government shops. Over time, the ruble became worth less and less as black market prices continued to rise ever more rapidly. As a result, Russia found itself with near hyperinflation in 1992.

To achieve a properly functioning market system, prices must be stabilized. To do so, the government must find a way to move toward a balanced budget and to bring the supply of money under control.

DEREGULATION OF PRICES AND LIBERALIZATION OF TRADE   To move successfully from central planning to a market system, individual prices must be deregulated. A system of freely moving prices forms the backbone of a market system. When people want more of a good than is currently being produced, its price will rise. This higher price increases producers' profits and provides an incentive for existing firms to expand production and for new firms to enter the industry. Conversely, if an industry is producing a good for which there is no market or a good that people no longer want in the same quantity, the result will be excess supply and the price of that good will fall. This reduces profits or creates losses, providing an incentive for some existing firms to cut back on production and for others to go out of business. In short, an unregulated price mechanism ensures an efficient allocation of resources across industries. Until prices are deregulated, this mechanism cannot function.

Trade barriers must also be removed. To achieve a successful transition, reform-minded countries must be able to import capital, technology, and ideas from abroad. In addition, it makes no sense to continue to subsidize industries that cannot be competitive on world markets. If it is cheaper to buy steel from an efficient West German steel mill than to produce it in a subsidized antiquated Russian mill, the Russian mill should be modernized or shut down. Ultimately, as the theory of comparative advantage suggests, liberalized trade will push each country to produce those products that it produces best.

Deregulating prices and eliminating subsidies can bring serious political problems. Many products in Russia and the rest of the socialist world were priced below market-clearing levels for equity reasons. Housing, food, and clothing were considered by many to be entitlements. Making them more expensive, at least relative to their prices in previous times, is not likely to be popular. In addition, forcing inefficient firms to operate without subsidies will lead many to go out of business, and jobs will be lost. So while price deregulation and trade liberalization are necessary, they are very difficult politically.

PRIVATIZATION   One problem with a system of central ownership is a lack of accountability. Under a system of private ownership, owners reap the rewards of their successes and suffer the consequences of their failures. Private ownership provides a strong incentive for efficient operation, innovation, and hard work that is lacking when ownership is centralized and profits are distributed to the people.

The classic story used to illustrate this point is called the **tragedy of commons**. Suppose that an agricultural community has 10,000 acres of grazing land. If the land were held in common so that all farmers had unlimited rights to graze their animals, each farmer would have an incentive to overgraze. He or she would reap the full benefits from grazing additional calves while the costs of grazing the calves would be borne collectively. The system provides no incentive to manage the land efficiently. Similarly, if the efficiency and benefits of my hard work and managerial skills accrue to others or to the state, what incentive do I have to work hard or to be efficient?

tragedy of commons The idea that collective ownership may not provide the proper private incentives for efficiency because individuals do not bear the full costs of their own decisions but do enjoy the full benefits.

One solution to the tragedy of commons attempted in eighteenth-century Britain was to divide up the land into private holdings. Today, many economists argue, the solution to the incentive problem encountered in state-owned enterprises is to privatize them and let the owners compete.

In addition to increasing accountability, privatization means creating a climate in which new enterprises can flourish. If there is market demand for a product not currently being produced, individual entrepreneurs should be free to set up a business and make a profit. During the last months of the Soviet Union's existence, private enterprises such as taxi services, car repair services, restaurants, and even hotels began to spring up all over the country.

Like deregulation of prices, privatization is difficult politically. Privatization means that many protected enterprises will go out of business because they cannot compete at world prices. Going out of business means a loss of jobs, at least temporarily.

MARKET-SUPPORTING INSTITUTIONS In 1991 and 1992, U.S. firms raced to Eastern Europe in search of markets and investment opportunities and immediately became aware of a major obstacle. The institutions that make the market function relatively smoothly in the United States do not exist in Eastern Europe.

For example, the capital market, which channels private saving into productive capital investment in developed capitalist economies, is made up of hundreds of different institutions. The banking system, venture capital funds, the stock market, the bond market, the commodity exchanges, brokerage houses, investment banks, and the like have all developed in the United States over a period of hundreds of years, and they will not simply be replicated overnight in the formerly communist world. (For more details on the struggles of the emerging banking system in Poland, see the Global Perspective box titled "Private Banking Comes to Poland.")

Many market-supporting institutions are so basic that Americans take them for granted. The institution of private property, for example, is a set of rights that must be protected by laws that the government must be willing to enforce. Suppose that the French hotel chain Novotel decides to build a new hotel in Moscow. Novotel must first acquire land. Then it will construct a building based on the expectation of renting rooms to customers. These investments are made with the expectation that the owner has a right to use them and a right to the profits that they produce. For such investments to be undertaken, these rights must be guaranteed by a set of property laws. This is equally true for large business firms and for Russian entrepreneurs who want to start their own enterprises.

Similarly, the law must provide for the enforcement of contracts. In the United States, a huge body of law determines what happens to you if you decide to break a formal promise made in good faith. Businesses exist on promises to produce and promises to pay. Without recourse to the law when a contract is breached, contracts will not be entered into, goods will not be manufactured, and services will not be provided.

Another seemingly simple matter that turns out to be quite complex is the establishment of a set of accounting principles. In the United States, the rules of the accounting game are embodied in a set of Generally Accepted Accounting Principles (GAAP) that carry the force of law. Companies are required to keep track of their receipts, expenditures, and liabilities so that their performance can be observed and evaluated by shareholders, taxing authorities, and others who have an interest in the company. If you have ever taken a course in accounting, you know how detailed these rules have become. Imagine trying to do business in a country operating under hundreds of different sets of rules and you can imagine what was happening in Russia.

Another institution worthy of mention is insurance. Whenever a venture undertakes a high-risk activity, it buys insurance to protect itself. Several years ago, Amnesty International (a non-profit organization that works to protect civil liberties around the world), sponsored a worldwide concert tour with a number of well-known rock bands and performers. The most difficult part of organizing the tour was obtaining insurance for the artists and their equipment when they played in the then-communist countries of Eastern Europe.

SOCIAL SAFETY NET In a centrally planned socialist economy, the labor market does not function freely. Everyone who wants a job is guaranteed one somewhere. The number of jobs is determined by a central plan to match the number of workers. Thus, in centrally planned economies, there is essentially no such thing as unemployment. This, it has been argued, is one of the great advantages of a planned system. In addition, a central planning system provides basic housing,

PRIVATE BANKING COMES TO POLAND

As we saw in the text, a country must develop a number of market-supporting institutions to achieve a successful transition from socialism to a market-based economic system. One critical set of such institutions is the capital market, whose purpose is to move private saving into productive investment and to allocate private capital efficiently across various industries without central direction. The first capital market institution to develop in most countries is the private bank. The following excerpt describes the emerging private banking system in Eastern Europe.

WARSAW—More than three years after dismantling Communism, Poland is struggling to get a grip on that most basic of capitalist tools, the banking system.

For decades banks here, as in other Communist countries, played little economic role other than to channel the money allocated by central planners to state-owned industries. In an economic culture that revolved around manufacturing, banking was a low-paid backwater.

But now banks and bankers are being called on to play a critical part in the transformation to a market economy by financing the growth and modernization of business and the expansion of trade, and they are having trouble keeping up with the needs of an increasingly vibrant economy.

"The banking system has existed in other countries for a century or more," said Hanna Gronkiewicz Waltz, president of the Polish central bank. "In three years we've done a lot, but we're still in the beginning.". . .

Beginning this year, the Poles are preparing to sell their state banking system of nine commercial banks to private investors—. . .

There is a budding private system, as well. Dozens of privately financed banks have sprung up, but nearly all of them are extremely small, have little financial backing, and are limited in the amounts they can lend. . . .

Banks remain saddled with antiquated record-keeping and telephone systems that are being modernized very slowly because of the high cost. Branch systems and deposit taking are extremely limited, so the banks remain largely reliant on the central bank for funds to lend to customers.

And bankers have little experience in assessing creditworthiness. Small- and medium-sized businesses are the source of most Polish economic growth, but many owners have little to offer banks in the way of collateral or experience. . . .

Many of the problems facing Poland plague other, formerly Communist European nations, as well. Banks in Hungary, for example, were badly squeezed last year when new and tougher bankruptcy laws forced many enterprises and their lenders to recognize their bad debts as such.

For decades, Polish banks' primary responsibility was the transfer of money from the central planners to state-owned industries. Now, banks like the Bank of Regional Cooperation in Cracow (pictured here) have become an important part of the transition to a market economy.

Source: Richard W. Stevenson, "Poles Forge Private Bank System," *New York Times*, February 23, 1990.

---

food, and clothing at very affordable levels for all. With no unemployment and necessities available at very low prices, there is no need for unemployment insurance, welfare, or other social programs.

Transition to a free labor market and liberalization of prices means that some workers will end up unemployed and everyone will pay higher prices for necessities. Indeed, during the early phases of the transition process, unemployment will be high. Inefficient state-owned enterprises will go out of business; some sectors will contract while others expand. As more and more people experience unemployment, popular support for reform is likely to drop unless some sort of social safety net is erected to ease the transition. This social safety net might include unemployment insurance, aid for the poor, and food and housing assistance. The experiences of the developed world have shown that such programs are expensive.

EXTERNAL ASSISTANCE   Very few believe that the transition to a market system can be achieved without outside support and some outside financing. Knowledge of and experience with capitalist institutions that exist in the United States, Western Europe, and Japan are of vital interest to the Eastern European nations. The basic skills of accounting, management, and enterprise development can be taught to Eastern Europe, and many argue that it is in everyone's best interest to do so. Many also argue that the world's biggest nightmare is an economically weak or desperate Russia armed with nuclear weapons giving up on reform or falling into the hands of a dictator.

There is little agreement about the extent of *financial* support that should be given, however. The United States has pushed for a worldwide effort to provide billions of dollars in aid. This aid, many argue, will help Russia stabilize its macroeconomy and buy desperately needed goods from abroad. However, critics in both the United States and other potential donor countries argue that pouring money into Russia now is like pouring it into a black hole. No matter how much money we donate, they say, it will have little impact on the ultimate success or failure of the reforms.

Shock Therapy or Gradualism?

Although economists generally agree on what the former socialist economies need to do, much debate exists about the sequence and timing of specific reforms.

shock therapy The approach to transition from socialism to market capitalism that advocates rapid deregulation of prices, liberalization of trade, and privatization.

The popular press describes the debate as one between those who believe in "shock therapy" (sometimes called the "Big Bang" approach) and those who prefer a more gradual approach. Advocates of **shock therapy** believe that the economies in transition should proceed immediately on all fronts. That is, they should stop printing money, deregulate prices and liberalize trade, privatize, develop market institutions, build a social safety net, and acquire external aid—all as quickly as possible. The pain will be severe, the argument goes, but in the end it will be forgotten as the transition raises living standards. Advocates of a *gradualist* approach believe the best course of action is to build up market institutions first, gradually decontrol prices, and privatize only the most efficient government enterprises first.

Those who favor moving quickly point to the apparent success of Poland, which moved quite rapidly through the first phases of reform (see the Global Perspective box titled "What's Next for Eastern Europe and the Russian Republic?" in Chapter 2). Russia's experience during the first two years of its transition have demonstrated that, at least in that country, change must be to some extent gradual. In theory, stabilization and price liberalization can be achieved instantaneously. But to enjoy the benefits of liberalization, a good deal of privatization must have taken place—and that will take more time. As one analyst has said, privatization means "selling assets with no value to people with no money." Some estimates suggest that as many as half of Russian state-owned enterprises are incapable of making a profit at world prices. Simply cutting them loose would create chaos. In a sense, Russia has no choice but to move slowly.

ALTERNATIVE ECONOMIC SYSTEMS: THE PEOPLE'S REPUBLIC OF CHINA AND JAPAN

Continuing around the globe eastward from the Russian Republic lies China, the world's most populous country. With 1.15 billion people, mainland China accounts for one out of every five people in the world.

China in 1994 remains a country in which political dissent is not tolerated and the economic system remains communist but in which private enterprise is permitted and even encouraged. This seemingly incongruous system is performing, at least for now, as well as any economy in the world. China, like Russia, is an enormously important power in the world, and understanding its history and the nature of its economic institutions is an essential part of understanding economics.

The People's Republic of China

Compared to the United States, the People's Republic of China is very large and very poor. Per capita income in China is about one twentieth of per capita income in the United States. The history of the People's Republic, established after the communist victory in the revolution of 1949, has been marked by wild gyrations of policy and some extraordinary economic experiments.

SOCIALIZATION UNDER MAO ZEDONG   Soon after gaining power, the Chinese Communists, under the leadership of Chairman Mao Zedong, became involved in the Korean War and found themselves heavily dependent on the Soviet Union. Not surprisingly, then, the early structure of the Chinese economic system was built on the Soviet-Stalinist model. China's first five-year plan, from 1953 to 1957, focused on developing capital-intensive heavy industries. Agriculture was collectivized, household farming was eliminated, and compulsory output quotas were put in place.

In 1958 China departed sharply from the Soviet model and launched a new economic strategy called the **Great Leap Foward**. The focus of production shifted from large-scale, capital-intensive industry to small-scale, labor-intensive industry scattered across the countryside. In addition, material incentives were reduced and replaced by the motivating power of revolutionary ideology and inspiration. Although initially successful, the strategy ultimately failed. In the early 1960s, output fell below 1958 levels. Between 1961 and 1965, material incentives were restored and a period of relative calm followed.

During the late 1960s and 1970s, economic development in China suffered a heavy blow from the **Great Proletarian Cultural Revolution** which began in 1966. For almost a decade, the rule was ideological purity. The faithful—which included almost everyone—denounced those who favored material incentives and reform, and scientists, engineers, managers, and scholars whose views were out of favor were sent to the countryside to work in the fields. The universities were essentially closed down. Untrained revolutionary *cadres* (small groups of leaders) replaced trained specialists in almost all jobs, and the economy suffered terribly. Most estimates place per capita income and consumption in the late 1970s at levels only slightly above the levels of 1956–1957.[5]

THE REFORMS OF DENG XIAOPING   When Chairman Mao died in September of 1976, the Cultural Revolution formally ended. In the meantime, China watched as its once poor neighbors—Japan, South Korea, Taiwan, and Singapore—enjoyed extraordinary growth and prosperity.

In December of 1978, the Chinese Central Committee, under the leadership of Deng Xiaoping, announced sweeping reforms. These early reforms focused on agriculture, and they signaled the beginning of profound changes in the Chinese economy that would continue over the next ten years.

Great Leap Forward The economic strategy in the People's Republic of China which began in 1958 when it departed from the Soviet model and shifted from large-scale, capital-intensive industry to small-scale, labor-intensive industry scattered across the countryside. Material incentives were reduced and replaced by the motivating power of revolutionary ideology and inspiration.

Great Proletarian Cultural Revolution (1966–1976) A period of ideological purity in the People's Republic of China: Material incentives and reforms were denounced and highly trained specialists were sent to work in the fields. The effect of the Cultural Revolution on the Chinese economy was catastrophic.

[5]See Nicholas Lardy, "Agricultural Reform," *Journal of International Affairs*, Winter 1986.

Prior to 1978, each agricultural commune had distributed the harvest equally among its members. Incentives were purely collective, with everything done for the glory of the revolution. Because the cadres often overstated harvests, the state raised local delivery quotas, leaving the peasants with barely enough to go around. The new system begun under Deng Xiaoping gave individual families, through a 15-year family contract, formal rights to the land that they worked. Families were also given the rights to dispose of any surpluses and to hire out part of the family labor force to enterprises outside the family plot. Deng gave the Chinese peasants permission to enrich themselves, and they did.

The results were extraordinary. Output of grain and other basic necessities, such as cotton, increased substantially. More importantly, rural industry grew dramatically, employing over 20% of the rural labor force by 1985. From 1978 through 1983, wheat production increased at an annual rate of 8.6%, rice at 4.3%, and cotton at 16.4 percent. From 1981 to 1984, the growth rate of all agricultural output reached 11.0% annually. In 1984 China actually became an exporter of food, despite a population of over one billion. Peasant income more than doubled in less than a decade, and private consumption and housing construction increased sharply.[6]

Similar reforms were implemented in Chinese industry on an experimental basis in 1978. Initially, enterprises were able to retain 15% to 25% of any profits over and above those specified by the plan. By 1984, Chinese enterprises across the country were retaining over 85% of increased profits. As with agricultural reform, the goals of industrial reform were to increase the role of the producing unit, to increase individual incentives, and to reduce the role of the state and the central planners.

The most significant element of all these reforms, however, was the movement by the Chinese government to support the expansion of enterprise rights. In the spirit of the Soviet New Economic Policy of the 1920s, the Chinese are actively encouraging small private trade and manufacturing. Today there is an increasingly important Chinese private sector competing with state stores in style, service, quality, and even price. By 1986, 480,000 "new economic associations" were employing 4.2 million people.[7] China is also now encouraging foreign investment. Initially only joint ventures with the government were permitted, but now foreigners retain 100% ownership in several projects.

CHINA AFTER TIANANMEN SQUARE   Despite the economic advances that China has made in the last decades, there is a great deal of political unrest in the country. In May of 1989, thousands of university students openly challenged the authority of the government by occupying Tiananmen Square in Beijing. Many went on hunger strikes to protest China's lack of democracy. The "democracy movement" was crushed on June 3, 1989, when the government cleared the square with troops and tanks as the world watched in horror.

The events of 1989 turned the tide of world opinion against the Chinese and at least temporarily slowed the movement toward economic reform. A number of joint ventures were canceled, and the amount of direct aid flowing into China was reduced. But even before Tiananmen Square, Chinese economic reforms were beginning to encounter difficulty.

---

[6]"China: Economic Performance in 1985, A Report to the Subcommittee on Economic Resources, Competitiveness and Security of the Joint Economic Committee." The Central Intelligence Agency, Washington, D.C.: March 17, 1986 (mimeo), p. 2.

[7]*Beijing Review*, no. 25, June 23, 1986.

CHINA: FREE ENTERPRISE IN A COMMUNIST COUNTRY

The following excerpt from a January 1993 *New York Times* article summarizes quite nicely what seems to be happening in a rapidly changing China:

QIAOTOU, China,—For a glimpse into China's economic revolution, it is useful to stroll down the main street of this humble little town. . . [which] has propelled itself over the last dozen years into the button capital of the world.

Each year, the privately run factories of Qiaotou produce about 12 billion buttons. . . . This button boom, amounting to two buttons annually per inhabitant on earth, has transformed rice paddies into factory districts, and peasants into tycoons.

One of them is Zhan Yusheng, a 27-year-old who began making buttons in his home 10 years ago. Today he owns a button factory with 100 employees, and last year he had sales of nearly $200,000.

"Now we need to upgrade our quality and produce more high-quality buttons," said Chen Jianlin, Qiaotou's Communist Party secretary. "Then we can expand on the international market.". . . Mr. Chen sees his mission primarily as promoting private enterprise.

"My most important job is building up the economy," Mr. Chen said as he sipped tea at the conference table in his

Each year, the privately-run factories of Qiaotou, China produce about 12 billion buttons, primarily of the inexpensive variety found on discount-priced clothing.

office. "People here say: 'If you push the economy along, you're a good leader. Otherwise, you're not.'"

While his salary is only $20 a month, about a third as much as the 20,000 migrant workers employed in Qiaotou's factories,. . . the party covers most of his expenses, supplies him with a house, a chauffered Audi, a phone with international direct dialing, a beeper, and a Mastercard.

"A lot of people here now carry credit cards when they travel," Mr. Chen said, beaming as he passed around his Mastercard for inspection. "Credit cards are very convenient and you don't have to carry so much cash."

Source: Nicholas D. Kristof, "Free Enterprise Encouraged," *New York Times*, January 18, 1993.

In 1988, China experienced serious inflation for the first time. By late 1988, prices were rising in historically unprecedented amounts, nearly 30% per year. In September, the government began implementing an austerity program that included strict price controls, reduced state investment, and reduced imports. The rate of inflation had dropped by 1989, but output of goods and services in China fell in 1989 and grew only slightly in 1990.

The years 1991–1993 saw a dramatic turnaround for China. While the current communist government has retained power and maintained a hard line on the political front, economic freedoms have been extended into every sphere. Private enterprise continues to be encouraged (see the Global Perspective box titled "China: Free Enterprise in a Communist Country"). A stock market has been established and stock prices have boomed dramatically. Everyone in China, it seems, wants a piece of the action. In October of 1992, First Boston Corporation, Merrill Lynch and Co., and Salomon Brothers offered five million shares in and raised more than $75 million for the JinBei Vehicle Manufacturing Company in the city of Shenyang. Hundreds of billions of dollars in foreign investment are now flowing into China from the United States, Japan, Singapore, Taiwan, and Korea.

Recent estimates put China's growth rate at more than 10% per year and climbing. There has been a real estate boom in Shanghai, where a middle-class home is now more expensive than a comparable house in the United States. There are stories of a kind of "capitalist mania" breaking out in a number of locations. The Global Perspective box mentioned above discusses a remarkably different attitude toward free enterprise than was the case in the Soviet Union.

Is this the beginning of a different kind of peaceful transition from socialism to the market? Many are convinced that it is and that China will be successful. But, as with the economies of Eastern Europe and Russia, much uncertainty remains.

Japan

No discussion of alternative economic systems would be complete without a few words on Japan. No country in history has accomplished what the Japanese economy has during the post–World War II period. Japan's economic progress over the last several decades is, with good reason, called the "Japanese economic miracle."

Since 1950 per capita GNP in Japan has grown from less than 20% of U.S. GNP to over 70 percent. Between 1951 and 1973, real GNP in Japan grew at an average annual rate of over 10%—in just over two decades, a seven-and-a-half-fold increase. Since the mid-1970s, economic growth in Japan has slowed, but the Japanese economy has still significantly outperformed the U.S. economy. Table 39.3 presents real growth rates for several economies, including Japan and the United States, between 1961 and 1990.

What led to the Japanese "miracle"? Was it simply a matter of culture? Japan is a very disciplined society with a strong work ethic and a long tradition of cooperation. But although cultural differences may be part of the story, there is far more to it than that.

Structurally, Japan's is essentially a free-market capitalist economy. No industrialized country in the world has a smaller public sector, and none has a more "probusiness" government. To a very large extent, the private decisions of households and firms produced the miracle.

---

[8]This discussion owes much to an excellent paper by Hugh Patrick and Henry Rosovsky, "Japan's Economic Performance: An Overview" in *Asia's New Giant*, Hugh Patrick and Henry Rosovsky, eds. (The Brookings Institution, 1976).

TABLE 39.3
Growth Rates of Real GNP (Percent), 1961–1990

	UNITED STATES	JAPAN	CANADA	FRANCE	WEST GERMANY	ITALY	GREAT BRITAIN
1961–1965	4.6	12.4	5.3	5.9	4.7	4.8	3.2
1966–1970	3.0	11.0	4.6	5.4	4.2	6.6	2.5
1971–1975	2.2	4.3	5.2	4.0	2.1	2.4	2.1
1976–1980	3.4	5.0	3.7	3.6	3.4	3.8	1.7
1981–1987	2.7	3.2	2.9	1.6	1.5	1.9	2.2
1988	4.4	5.7	5.0	3.4	3.6	3.9	4.2
1989	3.0	4.8	2.9	3.4	4.3	3.3	2.3
1990	1.0	6.1	1.1	2.5	4.2	2.6	1.6

Source: *Economic Report of the President,* 1988 and 1990.

To explain Japan's success more specifically, analysts point to four major factors: (1) very high rates of saving and investment, (2) a highly trained labor force, (3) rapid absorption and effective utilization of technology, much of it imported, and (4) a pro-growth government policy.[8] Of these, perhaps the single most important cause of Japan's growth has been its incredible rate of investment. Between 1951 and 1973, the capital stock of Japan grew by more than 9% per year, and for a substantial period of time investment approached 40% of GNP. Between 1960 and 1980, the capital stock in the United States increased at about 4% per year, while gross investment fluctuated between 15% and 17% per year. Virtually all of Japan's investment was financed with domestic saving. Japan's rate of saving by households has been the highest in the world.

Until recent years, rates of return on new investment in Japan were high. But today Japan faces a new problem. Its high rates of investment have virtually exhausted the investment opportunities in the nation and pushed rates of return on saving to very low levels. The saving rate has remained high, however, and this has led many Japanese citizens to look abroad for a place to put their savings. A significant part of those savings flowed to the United States during the 1980s. Real interest rates are much higher in the United States than in Japan, and a considerable number of new U.S. government bonds are now being sold to the Japanese. The Japanese are also investing billions of dollars in U.S. common stocks and real estate.

The second factor contributing to Japan's economic success is the quality of the Japanese labor force. As early as 1950, Japan had an education level comparable to that of the United States, despite a much lower level of economic development. Most Japanese workers were employed in jobs that demanded extremely low productivity relative to the education and training of those holding them. As the country's capital stock grew, workers moved easily into higher-productivity jobs. In other growing countries, low labor skills have slowed the adoption of modern, capital-intensive production techniques.

Japan also consciously adopted the most advanced industrial technologies in the world. Much of the knowledge necessary to do this was available in technical journals or obtainable in American graduate schools, and some came embodied in machinery and equipment imported into Japan. The Japanese were extremely effective at improving upon and commercializing what they imported. By importing technology, Japan did not have to develop it on its own; and, until recently, Japan devoted a smaller portion of its GNP to research and development than did the United States.

The role of government in the Japanese economy is certainly different from the role of government in the United States. There is disagreement among economists about the importance of government as an instrument of growth in Japan. It is clear that the main source of growth has been the private sector but that the government has played a supportive role. For example, after World War II, the Japanese government, through the **Ministry of Trade and Industry (MITI)**, used tariffs and quotas to protect and subsidize a number of key industries, including coal, steel, electric power, and shipbuilding. During the 1960s, chemicals and machinery were added to the list. In the mid-1980s, the government and the private sector launched a partnership designed to develop and market the next generation of computers. MITI also helps some sectors of the economy plan orderly reductions in capacity. In short, the Japanese government is actively involved in the allocation process and has much to say about which industries will grow and which will not.

A number of economists have suggested that the United States adopt an "industrial policy" similar to Japan's. Others disagree, arguing that private capital markets do a much better job than any government agency of deciding which industries will grow and which will not.

Ministry of Trade and Industry (MITI) The agency of the Japanese government responsible for industrial policy, it uses tariffs and subsidies to protect and subsidize key industries and helps some sectors plan orderly reductions in capacity.

JAPAN IN THE 1990S The enormous success of the Japanese economy led to seemingly unbounded optimism at the end of the 1980s. Spurred by the profitability of Japanese firms, the market prices of Japanese stocks raced to unprecedented levels. At the same time, Japanese land values boomed. At one point, land in Tokyo was trading for as much as $6000 per square foot. At that price, a small 100 by 100 foot plot of land (less than a quarter of an acre) was worth $60 million!

Then, in 1992, the bottom fell out of the Japanese stock market and land prices began to fall. For the first time in the history of modern Japan, confidence in the future was shaken. During 1992 and 1993, Japan slipped into a recession and real GDP fell. People in Japan began referring to the 1980s as the period of the "bubble economy."

Despite these setbacks, Japan remains an enormous economic power and a vital U.S. trading partner. As the economy becomes even more globalized in the coming years, it will be essential to understand more fully the successes and failures of Japanese industrial policy.

CONCLUSION

This chapter has introduced very briefly the structure, history, and performance of several different economic systems. It has also discussed the enormous problems of transforming a socialist economy into a market-based economy. So brief a description and analysis, we acknowledge, must be somewhat frustrating. After all, many volumes have been written on these topics. But a study of basic economics without such a "tour," however hasty, would be incomplete.

Studying alternative economic systems is a fitting way to conclude an introduction to economics. One of the themes running through this book has been the role of government in a market economy. We have tried to present a balanced description of how economies function, both in theory and in the real world. Throughout, we have focused on the potential benefits and problems associated with public-sector involvement. Eastern Europe, Russia, China, and Japan present very different perspectives on the interaction between the private and public sectors.

Concluding with this chapter is also, we hope, an enticement to further study. This is an exciting time in the world's economic history. Never before have systems changed so dramatically in such a short time. Many believe that the reforms in China, Eastern Europe, and Russia have brought the world much closer together and that the time is ripe for a significant reduction in world political tensions. Others believe that the problems of transition are so difficult that the whole process will disintegrate into chaos. Only time will tell.

SUMMARY

Political Systems and Economic Systems: Socialism, Capitalism, and Communism

1. A *socialist economy* is one in which most capital is owned by the government rather than by private citizens. A *capitalist economy* is one in which most capital is privately owned. *Communism* is a theoretical economic system in which the people directly control the means of production (capital and land) without the intervention of a government or state.

2. Economies differ in the extent to which decisions are made through central planning rather than through a market system. Generally, socialist economies favor central planning over market allocation, and capitalist economies rely to a much greater extent on the market. Nonetheless, there are markets in all societies, and planning takes place in all economies.

The Economic Theories of Karl Marx

3. According to Marxian thought, private ownership and profit are both unfair and unethical. Profit is value that is created by labor but expropriated by nonproductive capitalists, who are able to exploit labor by virtue of their ownership of the means of production (land and capital).

4. Marx predicted that falling rates of profit, increasing exploitation, and deeper business cycles would eventually cause capitalism to collapse.

5. Neoclassical economics sees profit as a return to a productive factor—capital—just as wages are the return to another productive factor—labor.

Alternative Economic Systems: The Rise and Fall of Communism in Russia and Eastern Europe

6. When the Bolsheviks took power in Russia after the October Revolution in 1917, they found themselves without the advanced industrial base that Marx had envisioned and with no real blueprint for running a socialist or communist state. Marx had written mainly about capitalism, not socialism.

7. In 1928, the Soviet Union settled into comprehensive central planning and collectivization of agriculture, an economic structure that lasted into the 1980s. Virtually all productive assets, including most land and capital, were publicly owned. There was no formal private business sector, no market for capital goods, and no income from property.

8. The Soviet Union grew rapidly through the mid-1970s. During the late 1950s, the Soviet Union's economy was growing much faster than that of the United States. The key to early Soviet success was rapid planned capital accumulation. The late 1970s saw things begin to deteriorate. Dramatic reforms were finally introduced by Mikhail Gorbachev after his rise to power in 1985. Nonetheless, the Soviet economy collapsed in 1991. The Soviet Union was dissolved, and the new president of the Russian Republic, Boris Yeltsin, was left to start the difficult task of transition to a market system.

9. Economists generally agree on six requirements for a successful transition from socialism to a market-based system: (1) macroeconomic stabilization, (2) deregulation of prices and liberalization of trade, (3) privatization, (4) the establishment of market-supporting institutions, (5) a social safety net, and (6) external assistance.

10. Much debate exists about the sequence and timing of specific reforms. The idea of *shock therapy* is to proceed immediately on all six fronts, including rapid deregulation of prices and privatization. The gradualist approach is to build up market institutions first, gradually decontrol prices, and privatize only the most efficient government enterprises first.

Alternative Economic Systems: The People's Republic of China and Japan

11. China, the largest country in the world, became communist following the revolution of 1949. In its early years under Chairman Mao Zedong, China organized under the Soviet model of central planning and rapid capital accumulation in heavy industry. In 1958, China departed sharply from the Soviet model, shifting instead to emphasis on small-scale, labor-intensive industry scattered around the countryside.

12. In 1978 Deng Xiaoping instituted sweeping reforms in the organization of the Chinese economy, particularly in agriculture. These reforms moved China away from central planning toward a system driven by market incentives.

13. China in 1994 remains a country in which political dissent is not tolerated and the economic system remains communist, but in which private enterprise is permitted and even encouraged. In the last two years the country has enjoyed rapid growth and substantial outside investment.

14. No country in history has accomplished what the Japanese economy has during the post-war period. Analysts point to four major factors to explain Japan's success: (1) a very high rate of saving and investment, (2) a highly trained labor force, (3) rapid absorption and effective utilization of technology, much of it imported, and (4) a pro-growth government policy. Despite some setbacks in the 1990s, Japan remains an important economic power.

REVIEW TERMS AND CONCEPTS

capitalist economy   952
communism   952
five-year plans   958
Great Leap Forward   967
Great Proletarian Cultural
    Revolution   967

labor theory of value   954
market-socialist economy   953
means of production   954
Ministry of Trade and Industry
    (MITI)   971
New Economic Policy   958

rate of exploitation   955
shock therapy   966
socialist economy   952
surplus value   955
tragedy of commons   963
value of labor power   955

PROBLEM SET

1. "The difference between the United States and the Soviet Union is that we have a capitalist economic system and they had a totalitarian government." Explain how this comparison confuses the economic and political aspects of the two societies. What words describe the former economic system of the Soviet Union?

2. What is the "tragedy of commons"? Suppose that all workers in a factory are paid the same wage and have no chance of being fired. Use the logic of the "tragedy of commons" to predict the result. How would you expect workers to behave?

3. In 1993, Boris Yeltsin was locked into a battle with political rivals in the Russian Congress of People's Deputies. What specific reforms is Yeltsin trying to move forward? What objections do his opponents raise to the reforms? Should the Russian Republic move rapidly or slowly?

4. You are assigned the task of debating the strengths of a socialist economy (regardless of your own viewpoint). Outline the points that you would make in the debate. Be sure to define socialism carefully in your presentation.

5. Explain why Karl Marx thought profit was unjustified. Be sure to specifically define the labor theory of value. Contrast the Marxian view with the neoclassical view of profit.

6. Do you agree or disagree with each of the following statements? Explain your answers.

   a. Over time, the Chinese have shifted from a decentralized approach to economic development to a more centrally planned system. Since the events of 1989 in Tiananmen Square, there has been a severe crackdown on private businesses.

   b. Both Japan and the Soviet Union grew rapidly during the 1950s and 1960s. Growth in the Soviet Union was based on rapid accumulation of capital forced by the central plan under Stalin and Khrushchev. In Japan, the growth was not due to capital accumulation.

   c. Although economists generally agree that transition from socialism to a market-based system must proceed rapidly, there is little agreement about what must be done to make the transition successful.

7. The distribution of income in a capitalist economy is likely to be more unequal than it is in a socialist economy. Why is this so? Is there a tension between the goal of limiting inequality and the goal of motivating risk taking and hard work? Explain your answer in detail.

8. "There is no doubt that a centrally planned socialist system has the potential to grow faster than a market-oriented capitalist system." Do you agree or disagree? What are some of the trade-offs facing socialist planners who set target growth rates?

9. In the 1990s the world witnessed the rapid decline of several Eastern European governments (East Germany, Poland, and Romania, to name just a few). Poland immediately began moving its socialist economy toward a capitalist economy. Some of the effects of this transition have been increased unemployment and price inflation. Can you explain why? (*Hint*: Focus on differences between socialist and capitalist systems regarding the determination of prices and production levels.)

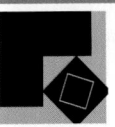

CASE STUDY
THE EUROPEAN COMMUNITY AND THE COMMON AGRICULTURAL POLICY

Since 1990, the number of free-trade agreements has grown rapidly in all regions of the world, particularly in developing countries. The largest and best-known attempt at economic integration to date is the European Community (EC). The EC was initially an agreement between six countries to coordinate their coal and steel industries. Eventually, the agreement expanded to allow the free movement of goods, services, capital, and people within the EC. In 1993, the EC consisted of 13 nations but was negotiating the liberalization of trade with the European Free Trade Association and considering the applications of Austria, Turkey, and a number of Eastern European nations for membership.

The EC must operate within the world trading system and within the framework set by the General Agreement on Tariffs and Trade (GATT). One source of friction between the EC and other GATT members, particularly the United States, has been trade in agricultural products. In 1962, the EC adopted the Common Agricultural Policy (CAP), which created a price-support system for agriculture. At the time, the EC was not self-sufficient in food production. So, rather than setting import quotas, the EC adopted a variable levy on imports equal to the difference between the import price and the domestic target price. Today, however, EC farmers produce 25% more than EC citizens consume, and these surpluses are purchased by the countries' governments and either stored or sold below cost on the world market. In 1991, these operations cost the average EC citizen $400 a year in higher taxes and food prices. That same year, transfer payments (direct and indirect) to agriculture totaled over $140 billion and almost 50% of farmers' income came

from transfer payments (see Figure 1).

The impetus for reform created by the rising cost of maintaining the subsidies was reinforced by changes in the international arena in the 1990s. Agriculture was a significant part of the Uruguay Round of GATT negotiations on trade liberalization as a number of nations, including the United States, pressured the EC for a reduction in both trade barriers and subsidized exports. In response to this pressure, the EC announced reforms in the CAP that would reduce the level of CAP prices (which were more than double the world market price for wheat in 1992). As target prices approach world prices by 1997, the value of subsidized exports (although not necessarily the volume) should fall. The cost to the EC will not fall immediately, as farmers will be compensated by direct payments in return for taking at least 15% of their land out of production. In addition, the distribution of payments (which in 1992 favored large farmers, who received 80% of the payments) should not change much. However, these reforms should allow the completion of the Uruguay Round of GATT negotiations because they meet many, although not all, of the demands of nations that export large volumes of agricultural products.

QUESTIONS FOR ANALYTICAL THINKING

1. Austria is one of several nations that subsidize farmers to graze their cattle in highland fields, rather than in lower-cost valleys, to maintain a picturesque countryside that lures tourists. Austria is seeking to join the EC. How often do you think policies that are created to secure a domestic goal also influence international trade?

Country	Total (billions of $)	$ per capita		
		Taxpayers	Consumers	Total
Austria	4.1	143	381	524
EC	142.0	168	241	409
Sweden	3.6	100	316	416
Norway	4.2	493	494	987
U.S.	81.0	200	1,189	318
Australia	1.2	41	29	70
Japan	63.2	16	494	510

FIGURE 1
Transfer Payments to Agriculture, 1991
Source: OECD.

2. In 1992, the United States was ready to impose a 300% tariff on some European wine in retaliation for France's oilseed subsidies. To what extent is a country justified in using economic sanctions to force changes in another country's domestic economic policies?

3. The EC subsidizes primarily cereals, oilseeds, beef, and dairy products. Much of what it does not consume is exported at subsidized prices, often below world prices. In West Africa, herdsmen are finding that they can no longer sell their cattle (the primary source of income for many villages) because subsidized European beef is exported to the region. Ironically, foreign aid is being used to build a slaughterhouse to help modernize the cattle industry in the region. Discuss.

4. Some of the nations in Eastern Europe that are in transition from socialist to market economies have expressed an interest in joining the EC. All expect the nations of the EC to be a primary market and source

of investment; they already are a significant source of economic aid. However, the comparative advantage of many of these countries lies in agriculture (and steel), and the CAP prevents exports of these products from entering the EC. What sort of policy reforms might be implemented that could leave the structure of CAP in place but be more consistent with the EC policy of contributing to economic development and stability in the region?

5. Why would an organization created to foster free trade create a system of price controls and quotas? What makes agriculture different from industry?

6. In May 1993, the EC agreed to limit the amount of land devoted to oilseed production. This had been a major stumbling block to progress in the GATT talks; the United States had threatened to impose retaliatory duties on $1 billion of EC exports. Why would these nations allow negotiations on one group of products to endanger trade liberalization in general? What is the advantage to negotiating multilateral agreements (that is, agreements among many nations) on broad product groups, rather than bilateral agreements (agreements between two nations) on limited lists of products?

Case Study Sources

PART 1 The Ivory Market
"The Elephant as a Natural Resource," *Wildlife Conservation*, March/April 1993. • "The Elephant Wars," *Wildlife Conservation*, March/April 1993. • "The War to Save the Tsavo Reserve," *Newsweek*, April 12, 1993. • "Why No Rhino?" *Economist*, March 6, 1993. • "Wild about Africa," *Economist*, April 24, 1993.

PART 2 The Broiler Industry—Almost Perfectly Competitive
Bierbuske, J. C., "Poultry Stock Perspective—Industry Report," A. G. Edwards & Sons, Inc., December 28, 1992. • "Broilers: Differentiating a Commodity," in *Industry Studies*, ed. Larry Deutsch. Englewood Cliffs, N.J.: Prentice Hall, 1993, pp. 3–32.

PART 3 The Cable TV Industry
"Boob Tubes No More," *Business Week*, June 7, 1993. • "Cable-TV Firms' Higher-Priced 'Tiers' Bring Cries of Outrage from Consumers," *Wall Street Journal*, January 15, 1992. • "FCC Angers Cable Firms, Aids Networks," *Wall Street Journal*, April 2, 1993. • "FCC Widens Price Controls for Cable TV," *Wall Street Journal*, June 14, 1991. • "50,000 Channels and Nothing to Watch," *Business Week*, March 22, 1993. • "A Satellite TV System Is Quickly Moving Asia into the Global Village," *Wall Street Journal*, May 10, 1993. • "Telephone Service Seems on the Brink of Huge Innovations," *Wall Street Journal*, February 10, 1993.

PART 4 Rebuilding America's Cities with Enterprise Zones
"Ad for New Jersey Store Irks New York Officials," *New York Times*, November 26, 1992. • "Aid Bargaining Is Now Centered on Enterprise Zones for Cities," *Congressional Quarterly*, June 6, 1992. • "Battle Zones," *National Journal*, June 6, 1992. • "Clinton Proposes New Zone Plan," *Congressional Quarterly*, May 8, 1993. • "Enterprise Zone Alchemy: 90s-Style Urban Renewal," *Congressional Quarterly*, August 8, 1992. • "Recasting Enterprise Zones: Federal Action Could Give a Shot of Adrenaline to What's Already Happening at the State Level," *Nation's Business*, February 1993.

PART 5 The Underground Economy
"America's Homes Hide an Underground Economy," *Washington Post*, February 14, 1993. • "'Cash' Economy Costs Billions in Lost Taxes," *Chicago Tribune*, February 21, 1993. • Feige, Edgar L., "Defining and Estimating Underground and Informal Economies: The New Institutional Economic Approach," *World Development*, 19, no. 7 (1990). • Gutmann, Peter M., "Statistical Illusions, Mistaken Policies," *Challenge*, 22 (November, December 1979). • "Notes from the Underground Economy," Business Week, February 15, 1993. • "The Underground Economy in the United States," Occasional Paper No. 2, U.S. Department of Labor, September 1992.

PART 6 Commodity Money on the Island of Yap
"The Economic Organisation of a POW Camp," *Economica*, November 1945, pp. 189–201. • "Fixed Assets, Or: Why a Loan in Yap Is Hard to Roll Over," *Wall Street Journal*, March 29, 1984. • "Ration Coupons as Money," *New York Times*, February 16, 1992.

PART 7 An Economy In Crisis: The Brazilian Experience
"Comparative Advantage," *Economist*, January 25, 1992. • Latin American Economy & Business, *Quarterly Update*, November 1992. • "A Survey of Brazil: Drunk Not Sick," *Economist*, December 7, 1991. • "Time to Get Moving," *Economist*, April 17, 1993.

PART 8 Does Social Security Discourage Saving?
"Demographers Track Down the Cause of Clinton's Behavior: He's a Boomer," *Wall Street Journal*, May 28, 1993. • "From New Deal to Raw Deal," *Business Week*, April 5, 1993. • "Privatize Social Security," *Wall Street Journal*, May 21, 1993. • "Social Security's Structural Weaknesses," *American Enterprise*, March/April 1993.

PART 9 From Battleships to Computer Chips: Industrial Policy in the United States
"The Calls for an Industrial Policy Grow Louder," *New York Times*, July 19, 1992. • "Chipping Away at Industrial Policy," *Regulation*, Fall 1992. • "The Hidden Dangers of Industrial Policy," *Wall Street Journal*, March 1, 1993. • "Industrial Policy a Sloppy Slogan," *New York Times*, February 12, 1992. • "Industrial Policy Takes Off," *Wall Street Journal*, May 4, 1993. • Kuttner, Robert, "Facing Up to Industrial Policy," *New York Times Magazine*, April 19, 1992. • "Lessons for a High-Tech President," *New York Times*, January 24, 1993. • "Reasons to Smile Again: Clinton Industrial Policy," *New York Times*, March 8, 1993. • "Return of Industrial Policy Hailed," *Washington Times*, February 24, 1993.

PART 10 The European Community and the Common Agricultural Policy
"Better Barter," *Economist*, May 22, 1993. • "The CAP and the GATT" and "EC Farm Policy: Getting Better," *Economist*, May 23, 1992. • "France Gives Lift to World Trade Talks by Dropping Opposition to Oilseed Pact," *Wall Street Journal*, June 9, 1993. • "Spudsidies," Economist, April 10, 1993. • "They Reap as They Sow" and "Don't Wait until the Cows Come Home," *Economist*, December 12, 1992.

Glossary of Economic Terms

ability-to-pay principle A theory of taxation which holds that citizens should bear tax burdens in line with their ability to pay taxes.

absolute advantage The advantage in the production of a product enjoyed by one country over another when it uses fewer resources to produce that product than the other country does.

accelerator effect The tendency for investment to increase when aggregate output increases and decrease when aggregate output decreases, thus accelerating the growth or decline of output.

actual investment The actual amount of investment that takes place; it includes items such as unplanned changes in inventories.

adjustment costs The costs that a firm incurs when it changes its production level—for example, the administration costs of laying off employees or the training costs of hiring new workers.

adverse selection Can occur when a buyer or seller enters into an exchange with another party who has more information.

aggregate behavior The behavior of all households and firms taken together.

aggregate demand The total demand for goods and services in an economy.

aggregate demand (AD) curve A curve that shows the negative relationship between aggregate output (income) and the price level. Each point on the AD curve is a point at which both the goods market and the money market are in equilibrium.

aggregate income The total income received by all factors of production in a given period.

aggregate output (income) (Y) A combined term used to remind you of the exact equality between aggregate output and aggregate income.

aggregate output The total quantity of goods and services produced (or supplied) in an economy in a given period.

aggregate production function The mathematical representation of the technological relationship between inputs and national output, or gross domestic product.

aggregate supply The total supply of goods and services in an economy.

aggregate supply (AS) curve A graph that shows the relationship between the aggregate quantity of output supplied by all firms in an economy and the overall price level.

American Federation of Labor (AFL) Founded in 1881, the AFL was successfully led by Samuel Gompers from 1886 until 1924. A practical, nonideological union, the AFL existed as a "confederation" of individual craft unions representing skilled workers, each with an independent organization and an exclusive jurisdiction. Now merged with the CIO, the AFL maintains a preeminent position among unions today.

animal spirits of entrepreneurs A phrase coined by Keynes to describe the feelings of investors.

Antitrust Division (of the Department of Justice) One of two federal agencies empowered to act against those in violation of antitrust laws. It initiates action against those who violate antitrust laws and decides which cases to prosecute and against whom to bring criminal charges.

appreciation of a currency The rise in value of one currency relative to another.

automatic destabilizers Revenue and expenditure items in the federal budget that automatically change with the economy in such a way as to destabilize GDP.

automatic stabilizers Revenue and expenditure items in the federal budget that automatically change with the state of the economy in such a way as to stabilize GDP.

autonomous variable A variable that is taken as a given.

average fixed cost (AFC) Total fixed cost divided by the number of units of output; a per unit measure of fixed costs.

average product (AP) The average amount produced by each unit of a variable factor.

average propensity to consume (APC) The proportion of income households spend on consumption. Determined by dividing consumption (C) by income (Y).

average total cost (ATC) Total cost divided by the number of units of output.

average variable cost (AVC) Total variable cost divided by the number of units of output.

average-cost pricing Setting price to cover average cost per unit including a fair return.

Averch-Johnson effect The tendency for regulated monopolies to build more capital than they need. Usually occurs when allowed rates of return are set by a regulatory agency at some percent of fixed capital stocks.

balance of payments The record of a country's transactions in goods, services, and assets with the rest of the world; also the record of a country's sources (supply) and uses (demand) of foreign exchange.

balance of trade A country's merchandise exports minus its merchandise imports. Also called the merchandise trade balance.

balance on capital account In the United States, the sum of the following (measured in a given period): the change in private U.S. assets abroad, the change in foreign private assets in the United States, the change in U.S. government assets abroad, and the change in foreign government assets in the United States.

balance on current account The balance of trade plus net exports of services, plus net investment income, plus the category "net transfer payments and other."

balanced-budget multiplier The ratio of change in the equilibrium level of output to a change in government spending where the change in government spending is balanced by a change in taxes so as not to create any deficit. The balanced-budget multiplier is equal to one: The change in Y resulting from the change in G and the equal change in T is exactly the same size as the initial change in G or T itself.

barrier to entry Something that prevents new firms from entering and competing in an industry.

barter The direct exchange of goods and services for other goods and services.

benefits-received principle A theory of fairness which holds that taxpayers should contribute to government (in the form of taxes) in proportion to the benefits that they receive from public expenditures.

black market A market in which illegal trading takes place at market-determined prices.

brain drain The tendency for talented people from developing countries to become educated in a developed country and remain there after graduation.

breaking even The situation in which a firm is earning exactly a normal profit rate.

Bretton Woods The site in New Hampshire where a group of experts from 44 countries met in 1944 and agreed on an international monetary system of fixed exchange rates.

budget constraint The limits imposed on household choices by income, wealth, and product prices.

budget deficit The difference between what a government spends and what it collects in taxes in a given period: G - T.

business cycle The cycle of short-term ups and downs in the economy.

capital Those goods produced by the economic system that are used as inputs in the production of future goods and services.

capital gain An increase in the value of an asset over the price initially paid for it.

capital income Income earned on savings that have been put to use through financial capital markets.

capital market The input, or resource, market in which households supply their savings, for interest or for claims to future profits, to firms that demand funds in order to buy capital goods.

capital stock The current market value of a firm's plant, equipment, inventories, and intangible assets.

capital-intensive technology A technique of production that uses a large amount of capital relative to labor.

capitalist economy An economy in which most capital is privately owned.

cartel A group of firms that gets together and makes joint price and output decisions in order to maximize joint profits.

Cartesian coordinate system A common method of graphing two variables that makes use of two perpendicular lines against which the variables are plotted.

Celler-Kefauver Act (1950) Extended the government's authority to ban mergers and prevented firms from acquiring the physical stock of competitors.

ceteris paribus Literally, "all else equal." Used to analyze the relationship between two variables while the values of other variables are held unchanged.

change in business inventories The amount by which firms' inventories change during a period. Inventories are the goods that firms produce now but intend to sell later.

change in inventory Production minus sales.

choice set, or opportunity set The set of options that is defined and limited by a budget constraint.

circular flow A diagram showing the income received and payments made by each sector of the economy.

Clayton Act Passed by Congress in 1914 to strengthen the Sherman Act and clarify the "rule of reason," the act outlawed specific monopolistic behaviors such as tying contracts, price discrimination, and unlimited mergers.

Coase theorem Under certain conditions, when externalities are present, private parties can arrive at the efficient solution without government involvement.

collective bargaining The process by which union leaders bargain with management as the representatives of all union employees.

collusion The act of working with other producers in an effort to limit competition and increase joint profits.

command economy An economy in which a central authority or agency draws up a plan that establishes what will be produced and when, sets production goals, and makes rules for distribution.

commodity monies Items used as money that also have intrinsic value in some other use.

communism An economic system in which the people control the means of production (capital and land) directly, without the intervention of a government or state.

comparative advantage The advantage in the production of a product enjoyed by one country over another when that product can be produced at lower cost in terms of other goods than it could be in the other country.

compensating differentials Differences in wages that result from differences in working conditions. Risky jobs usually pay higher wages; highly desirable jobs usually pay lower wages.

compensation of employees Includes wages, salaries, and various supplements—employer contri-butions to social insurance and pension funds, for example—paid to households by firms and the government.

complementary and substitutable inputs Factors of production that can be used together to enhance each other are complementary inputs. Factors of production that can be used in place of each other are substitutable inputs.

complements, complementary goods Goods that "go together"; a decrease in the price of one results in an increase in demand for the other, and vice versa.

Congress of Industrial Organizations (CIO) Founded by John L. Lewis, president of the United Mine Workers, after the AFL rejected his plan to organize the steel, rubber, automobile, and chemical industries in 1935, the CIO was the first union to organize semiskilled laborers in the mass production industries. After 20 years of independence, it merged with the AFL in 1955.

consent decrees Formal agreements on remedies between all the parties to an antitrust case that must be approved by the courts. Consent decrees can be signed before, during, or after a trial.

constant returns to scale An increase in scale of production has no effect on average costs per unit produced.

constant-cost industry An industry that shows no economies or diseconomies of scale as the industry grows. Such industries have flat, or horizontal, long-run supply curves.

constrained supply of labor The amount a household actually works in a given period at the current wage rate.

consumer goods Goods produced for present consumption.

consumer price index (CPI) A price index computed each month by the Bureau of Labor Statistics using a bundle that is meant to represent the "market basket" purchased monthly by the typical urban consumer.

consumer sovereignty The idea that consumers ultimately dictate what will be produced (or not produced) by choosing what to purchase (and what not to purchase).

consumer surplus The difference between the maximum amount a person is willing to pay for a good and its current market price.

consumption function The relationship between consumption and income.

contraction, recession, or slump The period in the business cycle from a peak down to a trough, during which output and employment fall.

contractionary fiscal policy A decrease in government spending or an increase in net taxes aimed at decreasing aggregate output (income) (Y).

contractionary monetary policy A decrease in the money supply aimed at decreasing aggregate output (income) (Y).

Corn Laws The tariffs, subsidies, and restrictions enacted by the British Parliament in the early nineteenth century to discourage imports and encourage exports of grain.

corporate bonds Promissory notes issued by corporations when they borrow money.

corporate income taxes Taxes levied on the net incomes of corporations. (Profits from proprietorships and partnerships are taxed as ordinary personal income of the owners.)

corporate profits The income of corporate businesses.

corporation A form of business organization resting on a legal charter that establishes the corporation as an entity separate from its owners. Owners hold shares and are liable for the firm's debts only up to the limit of their investment, or share in the firm.

cost shock, or supply shock A change in costs that shifts the aggregate supply (AS) curve.

cost-benefit analysis The formal technique by which the benefits of a public project are weighed against its costs.

cost-of-living adjustments (COLAs) Contract provisions that tie wages to changes in the cost of living. The greater the inflation rate, the more wages are raised.

cost-push, or supply-side, inflation Inflation caused by an increase in costs.

Cournot model A model of a two-firm industry (duopoly) in which a series of output-adjustment decisions leads to a final level of output that is between that which would prevail if the market were organized competitively and that which would be set by a monopoly.

cross-price elasticity of demand A measure of the response in the quantity of one good demanded to a change in the price of another good.

crowding-out effect The tendency for increases in government spending to cause reductions in private investment spending.

currency debasement The decrease in the value of money that occurs when its supply is increased rapidly.

current dollars The current prices that one pays for goods and services.

cyclical deficit The deficit that occurs because of a downturn in the business cycle.

cyclical unemployment The increase in unemployment that occurs during recessions and depressions.

debt rescheduling An agreement between banks and borrowers through which a new schedule of repayments of the debt is negotiated; often some of the debt is written off and the repayment period is extended.

debt service ratio The repayment amount of loan principal plus interest payments as a percentage of export revenues.

decreasing returns to scale, or diseconomies of scale An increase in a firm's scale of production leads to higher average costs per unit produced.

decreasing-cost industry An industry that realizes external economies—that is, an industry in which average costs decrease as the industry grows. The long-run supply curve for such an industry has a negative slope.

deficit response index (DRI) The amount by which the deficit changes with a one dollar change in GDP.

deflation A decrease in the overall price level.

demand curve A graph illustrating how much of a given product a household would be willing to buy at different prices.

demand determined price The price of a good that is in fixed supply; it is determined exclusively by what firms and households are willing to pay for the good.

demand schedule A table showing how much of a given product households would be willing to buy at different prices.

demand-pull inflation Inflation that is initiated by an increase in aggregate demand.

dependency theory The theory that the poverty of the Third World is due to the "dependence" of the developing world on nations that are already developed; it suggests that even after the end of colonialism, this dependence is maintained because developed countries are able to use their economic power to determine their own advantage—and the disadvantage of others—the relative prices and conditions under which the international exchange of goods takes place.

depreciation The decline in the economic value of an asset over time.

depreciation of a currency The fall in value of one currency relative to another.

depression A prolonged and deep recession. The precise definitions of "prolonged" and "deep" are debatable.

derived demand The demand for resources (inputs) that is dependent on the demand for the outputs those resources can be used to produce.

descriptive economics The compilation of data that describe phenomena and facts.

desired, or optimal, level of inventories The level of inventory at which the extra cost (in lost sales) from lowering inventories by a small amount is just equal to the extra gain (in interest revenue and decreased storage costs).

desired, or planned, investment Those additions to capital stock and inventory that are planned by firms.

diamond/water paradox A paradox stating (1) that the things with the greatest value in use frequently have little or no value in exchange and (2) that the things with the greatest value in exchange frequently have little or no value in use.

discount rate Interest rate that banks pay to the Fed to borrow from it.

discouraged-worker effect The decline in the measured unemployment rate that results when people who want to work but cannot find jobs grow discouraged and stop looking, thus dropping out of the ranks of the unemployed and the labor force.

disposable, or after-tax, income (Y_d) Total income minus net taxes: $Y - T$. The amount that households have to spend or save.

dividends The portion of a corporation's profits that the firm pays out each period to shareholders. Also called "distributed profits."

dominant strategy In game theory, a strategy that is best no matter what the opposition does.

double coincidence of wants The condition necessary for successful barter: Both parties to an exchange must want what the other has.

drop-in-the-bucket problem A problem intrinsic to public goods: The good or service is usually so costly that its provision generally does not depend on whether or not any single person pays.

dumping Takes place when a firm or industry sells products on the world market at prices below the cost of production.

durable goods Goods that last a relatively long time, such as cars and household appliances.

easy monetary policy Fed policies designed to expand the money supply in an effort to stimulate the economy.

economic costs The full costs of production including (1) a normal rate of return on investment, and (2) the opportunity cost of each factor of production.

economic growth An increase in the total output of an economy. It occurs when a society acquires new resources or when it learns to produce more using existing resources.

economic income The amount of money a household can spend during a given time period without increasing or decreasing its net assets. Wages, salaries, dividends, interest income, transfer payments, rents, and so forth are sources of economic income.

economic integration Occurs when two or more nations join to form a free-trade zone.

economic problem Given scarce resources, how exactly do large, complex societies go about answering the three basic economic questions?

economic profits, or excess profits Profits over and above the normal rate of return on investment; anything greater than the normal opportunity cost of capital.

economic theory A statement or set of related statements about cause and effect, action and reaction, in economic life.

economics The study of how individuals and societies choose to use the scarce resources that nature and previous generations have provided.

efficiency The condition in which the economy is producing what people want at least possible cost.

efficiency wage theory An explanation for unemployment that holds that the productivity of workers increases with the wage rate. If this is so, firms may have an incentive to pay wages above the market clearing rate.

efficient market A market in which profit opportunities are eliminated almost instantaneously.

elastic demand Elastic demand describes a demand relationship in which the percentage change in quantity demanded is larger in absolute value than the percentage change in price.

elasticity of labor supply A measure of the response of labor supplied to a change in the price of labor. Can be positive or negative.

elasticity of supply A measure of the response of quantity of a good supplied to a change in price of that good. Likely to be positive in output markets.

empirical economics The collection and use of data to test economic theories.

employed Any person 16 years old or older (1) who works for pay, either for someone else or in his or her own business for one or more hours per week, (2) who works without pay for 15 or more hours per week in a family enterprise, or (3) who has a job but has been temporarily absent, with or without pay.

entrepreneur A person who organizes, manages, and assumes the risks of a firm, taking a new idea or a new product and turning it into a successful business.

equilibrium Occurs when there is no tendency for change. The condition that exists when quantity supplied and quantity demanded are equal. In the macroeconomic goods market, equilibrium occurs when planned aggregate expenditure is equal to aggregate output.

equilibrium price level The point at which the aggregate demand and aggregate supply curves intersect.

equity Fairness.

excess burden The amount by which the burden of a tax exceeds the total revenue collected. Also called "dead weight losses."

excess demand The condition that exists when quantity demanded exceeds quantity supplied at the current price.

excess labor, excess capital Labor and capital that are not needed to pro-duce the firm's current level of output.

excess reserves The difference between a bank's actual reserves and its required reserves.

excess supply The condition that exists when quantity supplied exceeds quantity demanded at the current price.

exchange rate The price of one country's currency in terms of another country's currency; the ratio at which two currencies are traded for each other.

excise taxes Taxes on specific commodities.

expansion, or boom The period in the business cycle from a trough up to a peak, during which output and employment rise.

expansionary fiscal policy An increase in government spending or a reduction in net taxes aimed at increasing aggregate output (income) (Y).

expansionary monetary policy An increase in the money supply aimed at increasing aggregate output (income) (Y).

expected rate of return The annual rate of return that a firm expects to obtain through a capital investment.

expenditure approach, income approach Two methods of computing GDP. The expenditure approach measures the amount spent on all final goods during a given period. The income approach measures the income—wages, rents, interest, and profits—received by all factors of production in producing final goods.

explicit contracts Employment contracts that stipulate workers' wages, usually for a period of one to three years.

export promotion A trade policy designed to encourage exports.

external economies and diseconomies When industry growth results in a decrease of long-run average costs, there are external economies; when industry growth results in an increase of long-run average costs, there are external diseconomies.

externality A cost or benefit resulting from some activity or transaction that is imposed or bestowed upon parties outside the activity or transaction. Sometimes called spillovers or neighborhood effects.

factor endowments The quantity and quality of labor, land, and natural resources of a country.

factor substitution effect The tendency of firms to substitute away from a factor whose price has risen and toward a factor whose price has fallen.

factors of production The inputs into the production process. Land, labor, and capital are the three key factors of production.

fallacy of composition The belief that what is true for a part is necessarily true for the whole.

favored customers Those who receive special treatment from dealers during shortages.

featherbedding The common union practice of preserving jobs even when it is inefficient to do so.

G-3

Federal Open Market Committee (FOMC)
A group composed of the seven members of the Fed's Board of Governors, the president of the New York Federal Reserve Bank, and four of the other 11 district bank presidents on a rotating basis; it sets goals regarding the money supply and interest rates and directs the operation of the Open Market Desk in New York.

Federal Reserve System (the Fed) The central bank of the United States.

Federal Trade Commission (FTC) A federal regulatory group created by Congress in 1914 to investigate the structure and behavior of firms engaging in interstate commerce, to determine what constitutes unlawful "unfair" behavior, and to issue cease-and-desist orders to those found in violation of antitrust law.

federal budget The budget of the federal government.

federal debt The total amount owed by the federal government to the public; the total of all accumulated federal deficits minus surpluses over time, or the total amount of U.S. government obligations (bills, notes, and bonds) outstanding.

federal deficit The difference between what the government spends and what it receives in tax revenue (G – T).

fertility rate The birth rate. Equal to (the number of births per year divided by the average population) × 100.

fiat, or token, money Items designated as money that are intrinsically worthless.

filtering The process whereby the newest and best housing goes to the wealthy, whose former housing passes down to those of middle income, whose former housing passes down to those of low income. Thus housing "filters" down the income-distribution ladder.

final goods and services Newly produced goods that are not resold to someone else.

financial capital market The complex set of institutions in which suppliers of capital (households that save) and the demand for capital (business firms wanting to invest) interact.

financial intermediaries Banks and other institutions that act as a link between those who have money to lend and those who want to borrow money.

fine tuning The phrase coined by Walter Heller to refer to the government's role in regulating inflation and unemployment.

firm An organization that transforms resources (inputs) into products (outputs). Firms are the primary producing units in a market economy.

fiscal drag The negative effect on the economy that occurs when average tax rates increase because taxpayers have moved into higher income brackets during an expansion.

fiscal policy The spending and taxing policies used by the government to influence the economy.

five-year plans Plans developed in the Soviet Union that provided general guidelines and directions for the next five years.

fixed cost Any cost that a firm bears in the short run that does not depend on its level of output. These costs are incurred even if the firm is producing nothing. There are no fixed costs in the long run.

floating, or market-determined, exchange rates Exchange rates that are determined by the unregulated forces of supply and demand.

food stamps Vouchers that have a face value greater than their cost and that can be used to purchase food at grocery stores.

foreign exchange All currencies other than the domestic currency of a given country.

free entry The condition that exists when there are no barriers to prevent new firms from competing for profits in a profitable industry.

free exit The condition that exists when firms can simply stop producing their product and leave a market. Firms incur no additional costs by exiting the industry; hence the term "free exit."

free-rider problem A problem intrinsic to public goods: Because people can enjoy the benefits of public goods whether they pay for them or not, they are usually unwilling to pay for them.

frictional unemployment The portion of unemployment that is due to the normal working of the labor market; used to denote short-run job/skill matching problems.

full-employment budget What the federal budget would be if the economy were producing at a full-employment level of output.

game theory Analyzes oligopolistic behavior as a complex series of strategic moves and reactive countermoves among rival firms. In game theory, firms are assumed to anticipate rival reactions.

GDP deflator An overall measure of prices in the economy. Equal to the ratio of nominal GDP to real GDP multiplied by 100.

General Agreement on Tariffs and Trade (GATT) An international agreement signed by the United States and 22 other countries in 1947 to promote the liberalization of foreign trade.

general equilibrium The condition that exists when all markets in an economy are in simultaneous equilibrium.

ghetto premium Evidence suggests that during the 1960s and 1970s, housing in sections of U.S. cities inhabited predominantly by African-Americans was more expensive than comparable housing in white neighborhoods. The price difference came to be called a ghetto premium.

Gini coefficient A commonly used measure of inequality of income derived from a Lorenz Curve. It can range from zero to a maximum of one.

goods market The market in which goods and services are exchanged and in which the equilibrium level of aggregate output is determined.

government failure Occurs when the government becomes the tool of the rent seeker and the allocation of resources is made even less efficient by the intervention of government.

government franchise A monopoly by virtue of government directive.

government interest payments Cash payments made by the government to those who own government bonds.

government purchases of goods and services (G) Expenditures by federal, state, and local governments for final goods and labor.

government spending multiplier The ratio of the change in the equilibrium level of output to a change in government spending.

government transfer payments Cash payments made by the government directly to households for which no current services are received. They include social security benefits, unemployment compensation, and welfare payments.

Gramm-Rudman-Hollings Bill Passed by the U.S. Congress and signed by President Reagan in 1986, this law set out to reduce the federal deficit by $36 billion per year, with a deficit of zero slated for 1991. The law has not succeeded in its goal, and the deficit remains very high.

graph A two-dimensional representation of a set of numbers, or data.

Great Depression The period of severe economic contraction and high unemployment that began in 1929 and continued throughout the 1930s.

Great Leap Forward The economic strategy in the People's Republic of China which began in 1958 when it departed from the Soviet model and shifted from large-scale, capital-intensive industry to small-scale, labor-intensive industry scattered across the countryside. Material incentives were reduced and replaced by the motivating power of revolutionary ideology and inspiration.

Great Proletarian Cultural Revolution (1966–1976) A period of ideological purity in the People's Republic of China: Material incentives and reforms were denounced and highly trained specialists were sent to work in the fields. The effect of the Cultural Revolution on the Chinese economy was catastrophic.

Green Revolution The agricultural breakthroughs of modern science, such as the development of new, high-yield crop varieties.

gross domestic product (GDP) The total market value of all final goods and services produced within a given period by factors of production located within a country.

gross investment The total value of all newly produced capital goods (plant, equipment, housing, and inventory) produced in a given period.

gross national product (GNP) The total market value of all final goods and services produced within a given period by factors of production owned by a country's citizens, regardless of where the output is produced.

gross private investment (I) Total investment—that is, the purchase of new housing, plants, equipment, and inventory—by the private (or nongovernment) sector.

Hart-Scott-Rodino Act The 1980 antitrust legislation that extended the antitrust laws to proprietorships and partnerships and requires that all proposed mergers be reported to the Department of Justice.

Heckscher-Ohlin theorem A theory that explains the existence of a country's comparative advantage by its factor endowments: A country has a comparative advantage in the production of a product if that country is relatively well endowed with inputs used intensively in the production of that product.

Herfindahl-Hirschman Index (HHI) A mathematical calculation that uses market share figures to determine whether or not a proposed merger will be challenged by the government.

homogeneous products Undifferentiated outputs: products that are identical to, or indistinguishable from, one another.

households The consuming units in an economy.

human capital A form of intangible capital that includes the skills and other knowledge that workers have or acquire through education and training and which yields valuable services to a firm over time.

hyperinflation A period of very rapid increases in the overall price level.

identity Something that must be true at all times.

imperfect competition An industry in which single firms have some control over price and competition. Imperfectly competitive industries give rise to an inefficient allocation of resources.

imperfect information The absence of full knowledge regarding product characteristics, available prices, and so forth.

imperfectly competitive industry An industry in which single firms have some control over the price of their output.

implementation lag The time that it takes to put the desired policy into effect once economists and policy makers recognize that the economy is in a slump or a boom.

import substitution An industrial trade strategy that favors developing local industries that can manufacture goods to replace imports.

impossibility theorem A proposition demonstrated by Kenneth Arrow which shows that no system of aggregating individual preferences into social decisions will always yield consistent, nonarbitrary results.

income The sum of all a household's wages, salaries, profits, interest payments, rents, and other forms of earnings in a given period of time. It is a flow measure.

income effect of higher wages When wages rise, people are better off. If leisure is a normal good, they may decide to consume more of it and to work less.

income elasticity of demand Measures the responsiveness of demand with respect to changes in income.

incomes policies Direct attempts by the government to control prices and wages.

increasing returns to scale, or economies of scale An increase in scale of production leads to lower average costs per unit produced.

increasing-cost industry An industry that encounters external diseconomies—that is, an industry in which average costs increase as the industry grows. The long-run supply curve for such an industry has a positive slope.

indifference curve A set of points, each point representing a combination of goods X and Y, all of which yield the same total utility.

indirect taxes Taxes like sales taxes, customs duties, and license fees.

inductive reasoning The process of observing regular patterns from raw data and drawing generalizations from them.

Industrial Revolution The period in England during the late eighteenth and early nineteenth centuries in which new manufacturing technologies and improved transportation gave rise to the modern factory system and a massive movement of the population from the countryside to the cities.

industrial policy Government involvement in the allocation of capital across manufacturing sectors.

industry All the firms that produce a similar product. The boundaries of a "product" can be drawn very widely—"agricultural products"—less widely—"dairy products"—or very narrowly—"cheese." The term industry can be used interchangeably with the term market.

inelastic demand Demand that responds somewhat, but not a great deal, to changes in price. Inelastic demand always has a numerical value between zero and minus one.

infant industry A young industry which may need temporary protection from competition from the established industries of other countries in order to develop an acquired comparative advantage.

inferior goods Goods for which income elasticity is negative. Demand for inferior goods rises when income decreases and decreases when income rises.

inflation An increase in the overall price level.

inflation rate The percentage change in the price level.

injunction A court order forbidding the continuation of behavior that leads to damages.

innovation The use of new knowledge to produce a new product or to produce an existing product more efficiently.

input, or resource, markets The markets in which the resources used to produce products are exchanged.

inputs The goods and services that firms purchase and turn into output.

intangible capital Nonmaterial things that contribute to the output of future goods and services.

interest rate The annual interest payment on a loan expressed as a percentage of the loan. Equal to the amount of interest received per year divided by the amount of the loan.

interest sensitivity or insensitivity of planned investment The responsiveness of planned investment spending to changes in the interest rate. Interest sensitivity means that planned investment spending changes a great deal in response to changes in the interest rate; interest insensitivity means little or no change in planned investment as a result of changes in the interest rate.

interest The fee that a borrower pays to a lender for the use of his or her funds. Almost always expressed as an annual rate.

intermediate goods Goods that are produced by one firm for use in further processing by another firm.

International Monetary Fund An international agency whose primary goals are to stabilize international exchange rates and to lend money to countries that have problems financing their international transactions.

international sector From any one country's perspective, the economies of the rest of the world.

Interstate Commerce Commission (ICC) A federal regulatory group created by Congress in 1887 to oversee and correct abuses in the railroad industry.

invention An advance in knowledge.

inventory investment Occurs when a firm produces more output than it sells within a given period.

investment New capital additions to a firm's capital stock. Although capital is measured at a given point in time (a stock), investment is measured over a period of time (a flow). The flow of investment increases the stock of capital.

IS curve A curve illustrating the negative relationship between the equilibrium values of aggregate output (income) (Y) and the interest rate in the goods market.

isocost line A graph that shows all the combinations of capital and labor available for a given total cost.

isoquant A graph that shows all the combinations of capital and labor that can be used to produce a given amount of output.

J-curve effect Following a currency depreciation, a country's balance of trade may get worse before it gets better. The graph showing this effect is shaped like the letter J, hence the name "J-curve effect."

job search The process of gathering information about job availability and job characteristics.

kinked demand curve model A model of oligopoly in which the demand curve facing each individual firm has a "kink" in it. The kink follows from the assumption that competitive firms will follow suit if a single firm cuts price but will not follow suit if a single firm raises price.

Knights of Labor One of the earliest successful labor organizations in the United States, it recruited both skilled and unskilled laborers. Founded in 1869, the power of the Knights declined after the Chicago Haymarket bombing in 1886.

labor demand curve A graph that illustrates the amount of labor that firms want to employ at the particular wage rate.

labor force The number of people employed plus the number of unemployed.

labor market The input, or resource, market in which households supply work for wages to firms that demand labor.

labor market discrimination Occurs when one group of workers receives inferior treatment from employers because of some characteristic irrelevant to job performance.

labor-force participation rate The ratio of the labor force to the total population 16 years old or older.

labor supply curve A diagram that shows the quantity of labor supplied as a function of the wage rate. Its shape depends on how households react to changes in the wage rate.

labor theory of value Marx's theory that the value of a commodity depends exclusively upon the amount of labor required to produce it. Commodities are the physical embodiment of the labor that produced them, and capital is the physical embodiment of the past labor used to produce it.

labor-intensive technology Technology that relies heavily on human labor rather than capital.

Laffer Curve The graph, named after Arthur Laffer, with the tax rate measured on the vertical axis and tax revenue measured on the horizontal axis. The Laffer Curve shows that there is some tax rate beyond which the supply response is large enough to lead to a decrease in tax revenue for further increases in the tax rate.

laissez-faire economy Literally from the French: "allow [them] to do." An economy in which individual people and firms pursue their own self-interests without any central direction or regulation.

land market The input, or resource, market in which households supply land or other real property in exchange for rent.

land use planning A regulatory system, generally overseen by local zoning boards, that stipulates what kinds of industries, businesses, and housing may locate in an area, and under what conditions.

law of demand The negative relationship between price and quantity demanded: As price rises, quantity demanded decreases, and as price falls, quantity demanded increases.

law of diminishing marginal utility The more of any one good consumed in a given period, the less satisfaction (utility) generated by consuming each additional (marginal) unit of the same good.

law of diminishing returns When additional units of a variable input are added to fixed inputs after a certain point, the marginal product of the variable input declines.

law of one price If the costs of transportation are small, the price of the same good in different countries should be roughly the same.

law of supply The positive relationship between price and quantity of a good supplied: An increase in market price will lead to an increase in quantity supplied, and a decrease in market price will lead to a decrease in quantity supplied.

legal tender Money that a government has required to be accepted in settlement of debts.

lender of last resort One of the functions of the Fed: It provides funds to troubled banks that cannot find any other sources of funds.

liability rules Laws that require A to compensate B for damages imposed.

life-cycle theory of consumption A theory of household consumption: Households make lifetime consumption decisions based on their expectations of lifetime income.

liquidity property of money The property of money that makes it a good medium of exchange as well as a store of value: It is portable and readily accepted and thus easily exchanged for goods.

LM curve A curve illustrating the positive relationship between the equilibrium values of aggregate output (income) (*Y*) and the interest rate in the money market.

logrolling Occurs when congressional representatives trade votes, agreeing to help each other get certain pieces of legislation passed.

long run That period of time for which there are no fixed factors of production. Firms can increase or decrease scale of operation, and new firms can enter and existing firms can exit the industry.

long-run average cost curve (LRAC) A graph that shows the different scales on which a firm can choose to operate in the long run.

long-run competitive equilibrium When P = SRMC = SRAC = LRAC and economic profits are zero.

long-run industry supply curve (LRIS) A graph that traces out price and total output over time as an industry expands.

Lorenz Curve A widely used graph of the distribution of income, with cumulative percentage of families plotted along the horizontal axis and cumulative percentage of income plotted along the vertical axis.

Lucas supply function The supply function, originated by Robert Lucas, that embodies the idea that output (*Y*) depends on the difference between the actual price level and the expected price level.

luxury goods Goods for which income elasticity is positive and greater than one.

M1, or transactions money Money that can be directly used for transactions.

M2, or broad money M1 plus savings accounts, money market accounts, and other near monies.

macroeconomics The branch of economics that deals with the economy as a whole. Macroeconomics focuses on the determinants of total national income, deals with aggregates such as aggregate consumption and investment, and looks at the overall level of prices rather than individual prices.

marginal cost (MC) The increase in total cost that results from producing one more unit of output.

marginal damage cost (MDC) The additional harm done by increasing the level of an externality-producing activity by one unit. If producing product X pollutes the water in a river, MDC is the additional cost imposed by the added pollution that results from increasing output by one unit of X per period.

marginal efficiency of investment (MEI) A curve that shows the total amount of investment that would be undertaken in an economy in a given period of time at every possible interest rate.

marginal factor cost (MFC) The additional cost of using one more unit of a given factor of production.

marginal private cost (MPC) The amount that a consumer pays to consume an additional unit of a particular good.

marginal product (MP) The additional output that can be produced by adding one more unit of a specific input ceteris paribus.

marginal product of labor (MP$_L$) The additional output produced by one additional unit of labor.

marginal productivity theory of income distribution At equilibrium, all factors of production end up receiving rewards determined by their productivity as measured by marginal revenue product.

marginal propensity to cosume (MPS) That fraction of a change in income that is consumed, or spent.

marginal propensity to import (MPM) The change in imports caused by a $1 change in income.

marginal propensity to save (MPS) That fraction of a change in income that is saved.

marginal rate of substitution (MRS) The rate at which a person is willing to substitute Y for X; it is the number of units of Y a person is willing to give up in exchange for a unit of X. More formally, it is the ratio of the marginal utility derived from consuming good X to the marginal utility derived from consuming good Y.

marginal rate of technical substitution The rate at which a firm can substitute capital for labor and hold output constant.

marginal rate of transformation (MRT) The value of the slope of the production possibilities frontier. The number of units of one kind of good you can get by giving up one unit of another kind of good.

marginal revenue (MR) The additional revenue that a firm takes in when it increases output by one additional unit. In perfect competition, P = MR.

marginal revenue product (MRP) The additional revenue a firm earns by employing one additional unit of input, ceteris paribus.

marginal revenue product of labor (MRP$_L$) The additional revenue that a firm will take in by hiring an additional unit of labor, ceteris paribus. For perfectly competitive firms, marginal revenue product of labor is equal to the marginal physical product of labor times the price of output.

marginal social cost (MSC) The total cost to society of producing an additional unit of a good or service. MSC is equal to the sum of the marginal costs of producing the product and the correctly measured damage costs involved in the process of production.

marginal utility The additional satisfaction gained by the consumption or use of one more unit of something.

market An institution through which buyers and sellers interact and engage in exchange.

market demand The sum of all the quantities of a good or service demanded per period by all the households buying in the market for that good or service.

market failure Occurs when resources are misallocated, or allocated inefficiently. The result is waste or lost value.

market organization The way an industry is structured. Structure is defined by how many firms there are in an industry, whether products are differentiated or are virtually the same, whether or not firms in the industry can control prices or wages, and whether or not competing firms can enter and leave the industry freely.

market power An imperfectly competitive firm's ability to raise price without losing all demand for its product.

market supply The sum of all that is supplied each period by all producers of a single product. market The institution through which buyers and sellers interact and engage in exchange.

market-socialist economy An economy that combines government ownership with market allocation.

maximin strategy In game theory, a strategy chosen to maximize the minimum gain that can be earned.

means of production Marx's term for land and capital.

Medicare and Medicaid In-kind government transfer programs that provide health and hospitalization benefits: Medicare to the aged and their survivors and to certain of the disabled, regardless of income, and Medicaid to people with low incomes.

medium of exchange, or means of payment What sellers generally accept and buyers generally use to pay for goods and services.

microeconomics The branch of economics that deals with the functioning of individual industries and the behavior of individual decision-making units—business firms and households.

midpoint formula A more precise way of calculating percentages using the value halfway between P1 and P2 for the base in calculating the percentage change in price, and the value halfway between Q1 and Q2 as the base for calculating the percentage change in quantity demanded.

minimum wage The lowest wage that firms are permitted to pay workers.

minimum wage laws Laws that set a floor for wage rates—that is, a minimum hourly rate for any kind of labor.

Ministry of Trade and Industry (MITI) The agency of the Japanese government responsible for industrial policy; it uses tariffs and subsidies to protect and subsidize key industries and helps some sectors plan orderly reductions in capacity.

model A formal statement of a theory. Usually a mathematical statement of a relationship between two or more variables.

modern economic growth The period of rapid and sustained increase in real output per capita that began in the Western World with the Industrial Revolution.

monetary policy The behavior of the Federal Reserve regarding the money supply.

money income The measure of income used by the Census Bureau. Because it excludes noncash transfer payments and capital gains income, it is less inclusive than "economic income."

money market The market in which financial instruments are exchanged and in which the equilibrium level of the interest rate is determined.

money multiplier The multiple by which deposits can increase for every dollar increase in reserves; equal to one divided by the required reserve ratio.

monocentric models Models of residential location that assume central employment. As people move farther from the center, their costs of commuting increase. Equilibrium in the housing market exists only where land prices just offset the lower transport costs closer to the center.

monopolistic competition A common form of industry (market) structure in the United States, characterized by a large number of firms, none of which can influence market price by virtue of size alone. Some degree of market power is achieved by firms producing differentiated products. New firms can enter and established firms can exit such an industry with ease.

monopoly An industry structure (or market organization) in which there is only one large firm that produces a product for which there are no close substitutes. Monopolists can set prices but are subject to market discipline. For a monopoly to continue to exist, something must prevent potential competitors from entering the industry and competing for profits.

monopsony A market in which there is only one buyer for a good or service.

moral hazard Arises when one party to a contract passes the cost of his or her behavior on to the other party to the contract.

moral suasion The pressure exerted by the Fed on member banks to discourage them from borrowing heavily from the Fed.

mortality rate The death rate. Equal to (the number of deaths per year divided by the average population) × 100.

movement along a demand curve What happens when a change in price causes quantity demanded to change.

multiplier The ratio of the change in the equilibrium level of output to a change in some autonomous variable. For purposes of this chapter, the autonomous variable is planned investment.

Nash equilibrium In game theory, the result of all players playing their best strategy given what their competitors are doing.

National Labor Relations Board (NLRB) A watchdog board established by the Wagner Act in 1935 whose duties include ensuring that all workers are guaranteed the right to join unions and that firm managers participate fairly in collective bargaining if so requested by a majority of their employees.

national debt The total amount of outstanding government securities held by the public.

national income and product accounts Data collected and published by the government describing the various components of national income and output in the economy.

natural monopoly An industry that realizes such large economies of scale in producing its product that single-firm production of that good or service is most efficient.

natural rate of population increase The difference between the birth rate and the death rate. It does not take migration into account.

natural rate of unemployment The unemployment that occurs as a normal part of the functioning of the economy. Sometimes taken as the sum of frictional unemployment and structural unemployment.

near monies Close substitutes for transactions money, such as savings accounts and money market accounts.

negative demand shock Something that causes a shift in consumption or investment schedules or that leads to a decrease in U.S. exports.

net exports (EX − IM) The difference between exports (sales to foreigners of U.S.-produced goods and services) and imports (U.S. purchases of goods and services from abroad). The figure can be positive or negative.

net factor payments to the rest of the world Payments of factor income to the rest of the world minus the receipt of factor income from the rest of the world.

net income The profits of a firm.

net interest The interest paid by business.

net investment Gross investment minus depreciation.

net taxes (T) Taxes paid by firms and households to the government minus transfer payments made to households by the government.

New Economic Policy The Soviet economic policy in effect between 1921 and 1928; characterized by decentralization and a retreat to a market orientation.

nominal GDP Gross domestic product measured in current dollars.

nominal wage rate The wage rate in current dollars.

nondurable goods Goods that are used up fairly quickly, such as food and clothing.

nonexcludable A characteristic of most public goods: Once a good is produced, no one can be excluded from enjoying its benefits.

nonlabor, or nonwage, income Any income that is received from sources other than working—inheritances, interest, dividends, transfer payments, and so on.

nonresidential investment Expenditures by firms for machines, tools, plants, and so on.

nonrival in consumption A characteristic of public goods: One person's enjoyment of the benefits of a public good does not interfere with another's consumption of it.

nonsynchronization of income and spending The mismatch between the timing of money inflow to the household and the timing of money outflow for household expenses.

normal goods Goods for which demand goes up when income is higher and for which demand goes down when income is lower.

normal rate of profit, or normal rate of return A rate of profit that is just sufficient to keep owners and investors satisfied; for relatively risk-free firms it should be nearly the same as the interest rate on risk-free government bonds.

normative economics An approach to economics that analyzes outcomes of economic behavior, evaluates them as good or bad, and may prescribe preferred courses of action.

North American Free-Trade Agreement (NAFTA) An agreement signed by the United States, Mexico, and Canada in which the three countries agreed to establish all of North America as a free-trade zone.

not in the labor force The subset of unemployed people who are not looking for work, either because they do not want a job or because they have given up looking.

occupational segregation The concentration of men and women in certain occupations. Women are concentrated in administrative support positions, men in executive, administrative, and management positions.

Ockham's razor The principle that irrelevant detail should be cut away.

Okun's Law The theory, put forth by Arthur Okun, that the unemployment rate decreases about one percentage point for every 3% increase in GDP. Later research and data have shown that the relationship between output and unemployment is not as stable as Okun's "law" predicts.

oligopoly A form of industry (market) structure characterized by a few firms, each large enough to influence market price. Products may be homogeneous or differentiated. The behavior of any one firm in an oligopoly depends to a great extent on the behavior of others. In general, entry of new firms into an oligopolistic industry is difficult but possible.

on-the-job training The principal form of human capital investment financed primarily by firms.

Open Market Desk The office in the New York Federal Reserve Bank from which government securities are bought and sold by the Fed.

open market operations The purchase and sale by the Fed of government securities in the open market; a tool used to expand or contract the amount of reserves in the system and thus the money supply.

operating profit (or loss) or net operating revenue Total revenue minus total variable cost (TR − TVC). Also called net operating revenue.

opportunity cost That which we forgo, or give up, when we make a choice or a decision.

optimal level of provision for a public good The level at which resources are drawn from the production of other goods and services only to the extent that people want the public good and are willing to pay for it. At this level, society's willingness to pay per unit is equal to the marginal cost of producing the good.

optimal method of production The production method that minimizes cost.

optimal scale of plant The scale of plant that minimizes cost.

origin On a Cartesian coordinate system, the point at which the horizontal and vertical axes intersec.

outputs Usable products.

Pareto efficiency, or Pareto optimality A condition in which no change is possible that will make some members of society better off without making some other members of society worse off.

partial equilibrium analysis The process of examining the equilibrium conditions in individual markets and for households and firms separately.

partnership A form of business organization in which there is more than one proprietor. The owners are responsible jointly and separately for the firm's obligations.

patent A barrier to entry that grants exclusive use of the patented product or process to the inventor.

per capita GDP or GNP A country's GDP or GNP divided by its population.

per se rule A rule enunciated by the courts declaring a particular action or outcome to be a per se (intrinsic) violation of antitrust law, whether the result is reasonable or not.

perfect competition An industry structure (or market organization) in which there are many firms, each small relative to the industry, producing virtually identical products and in which no firm is large enough to have any control over prices. In perfectly competitive industries, new competitors can freely enter and exit the market.

perfect knowledge The assumption that households possess a knowledge of the qualities and prices of everything available in the market and that firms have all available information regarding input prices and qualities.

perfect substitutes Identical products.

perfectly contestable market A market in which entry and exit are costless.

perfectly elastic demand Demand in which quantity demanded drops to zero at the slightest increase in price.

perfectly inelastic demand Demand in which quantity demanded does not respond at all to a change in price.

permanent income The average level of one's expected future income stream.

personal consumption expenditures (C) A major component of GDP: expenditures by consumers on goods and services.

personal income The total income of households. Equals (national income) minus (retained corporate profits) minus (social insurance payments) plus (interest income received by households) plus (transfer payments to households). The income received by households after paying social insurance taxes but before paying personal income taxes.

personal saving The amount of disposable income that is left after total personal spending in a given period.

personal saving rate The percentage of personal disposable income that is saved. If the personal saving rate is low, households are spending a large amount relative to their incomes; if it is high, households are spending cautiously.

Phillips Curve A graph showing the relationship between the inflation rate and the unemployment rate.

physical, or tangible, capital Material things used as inputs in the production of future goods and services. The major categories of physical capital are nonresidential structures, durable equipment, residential structures, and inventories.

planned aggregate expenditure (AE) The total amount the economy plans to spend in a given period. Equal to consumption plus planned investment: AE ≡ C + I.

plant-and-equipment investment Purchases by firms of additional machines, factories, or buildings within a given period.

policy mix The combination of monetary and fiscal policies in use at a given time.

political business cycle A business cycle generated by policy makers for the purpose of maximizing their chances of being reelected.

positive economics An approach to economics that seeks to understand behavior and the operation of systems without making judgments. It describes what exists and how it works.

post hoc, ergo propter hoc Literally, "after this (in time), therefore because of this." A common error made in thinking about causation: If Event A happens before Event B happens, it cannot be inferred that A caused B.

potential output, or potential GDP The level of aggregate output that can be sustained in the long run without inflation.

poverty line The officially established income level that distinguishes the poor from the non-poor. It is set at three times the cost of the Department of Agriculture's minimum food budget.

preference map A consumer's set of indifference curves.

present value (PV), or present discounted value The present discounted value of R dollars to be paid t years in the future is the amount you need to pay today, at current interest rates, to insure that you end up with R dollars t years from now. It is the current market value of receiving R dollars in t years.

price The amount that a product sells for per unit. It reflects what society is willing to pay.

price ceiling A maximum price that sellers may charge for a good, usually set by government.

price discrimination Occurs when a firm charges different buyers different prices for the same product. Such strategies are illegal if they drive out competition.

price elasticity of demand The ratio of the percentage change in quantity demanded to the percentage change in price.

price feedback effect The process by which a domestic price increase in one country can "feed back" on itself through export and import prices. An increase in the price level in one country can drive up prices in other countries; this, in turn, increases the price level in the first country.

price index A measurement showing how the average price of a bundle of goods changes over time.

price leadership A form of oligopoly in which one dominant firm sets prices and all the smaller firms in the industry follow its pricing policy.

price rationing The process by which the market system allocates goods and services to consumers when quantity demanded exceeds quantity supplied.

price surprise The actual price level minus the expected price level.

principle of neutrality All else equal, taxes that are neutral with respect to economic decisions (that is, taxes that do not distort economic decisions) are generally preferable to taxes that distort economic decisions. Taxes that are not neutral impose excess burdens.

principle of second best The fact that a tax distorts an economic decision does not always imply that such a tax imposes an excess burden. If previously existing distortions exist, such a tax may actually improve efficiency.

private goods Products produced by firms for sale to individual households.

private sector Includes all independently owned profit-making firms, nonprofit organizations, and households; all the decision-making units in the economy that are not part of the government.

privatization The transfer of government business to the private sector.

produce-marketing boards The channels through which the governments of some developing countries buy domestic farm output and then sell it to urban residents at government-controlled prices.

producer price indexes Measures of prices that producers receive for products at all stages in the production process.

producers Those people or groups of people, whether private or public, who transform resources into usable products, or output.

product differentiation A strategy that firms use to achieve market power. Accomplished by producing products that have distinct positive identities in the minds of consumers.

product, or output, markets The markets in which goods and services are exchanged.

production function or (total product (TP) function) A mathematical or numerical expression of a relationship between inputs and outputs. It shows units of total product as a function of units of inputs.

production possibility frontier (ppf) A graph that shows all the combinations of goods and services that can be produced if all of society's resources are used efficiently.

production The process by which inputs are combined, transformed, and turned into outputs.

production technology The relationship between inputs and outputs.

productivity, or labor productivity Output per worker hour; the amount of output produced by an average worker in one hour.

productivity of an input The amount of output produced per unit of the input.

profit The difference between total revenues and total costs.

progressive tax A tax whose burden, expressed as a percentage of income, increases as income increases.

promissory notes Promises to pay that are signed by a borrower and given to a lender.

property income Income from the ownership of real property and financial holdings. It takes the form of profits, interest, dividends, and rents.

proportional tax A tax whose burden is the same proportion of income for all households.

proprietors' income The income of unincorporated businesses.

proprietorship A form of business organization in which a person simply sets up to provide goods or services at a profit. In a proprietorship, the proprietor, or owner, is the firm. The assets and liabilities of the firm are the owner's assets and liabilities.

protection The practice of shielding a sector of the economy from foreign competition.

public assistance, or welfare Government transfer programs that provide cash benefits to (1) families with dependent children whose incomes and assets fall below a very low level and (2) the very poor regardless of whether or not they have children.

public choice theory An economic theory that proceeds on the assumption that the public officials who set economic policies and regulate the players act in their own self-interest, just as firms do.

public debt The privately held (non-government-owned) debt of the U.S. government.

public goods (social or collective goods) Goods or services that bestow collective benefits on members of society. Such goods are both nonrival in consumption and their benefits are nonexcludable.

public sector Includes all agencies at all levels of government—federal, state, and local.

public, or social, goods Goods and services whose benefits are social, or collective.

purchasing-power-parity theory A theory of international exchange that holds that exchange rates are set so that the price of similar goods in different countries is the same.

pure monopoly An industry with a single firm that produces a product for which there are no close substitutes and in which significant barriers to entry prevent other firms from entering the industry to compete for profits.

pure rent The return to any factor of production that is in fixed supply.

quantity demanded The amount (number of units) of a product that a household would buy in a given period if it could buy all it wanted at the current market price.

quantity supplied The amount of a particular product that a firm would be willing and able to offer for sale at a particular price during a given time period.

quantity theory of money The theory based on the identity $M \cdot V \equiv P \cdot Y$ and the assumption that the velocity of money (V) is constant (or virtually constant).

queuing A nonprice rationing mechanism that uses waiting in line as a means of distributing goods and services.

quota A limit on the quantity of imports.

racial covenants Provisions spelled out in property deeds that prohibit sale of that property to members of specific racial or ethnic groups.

rate of exploitation The ratio of surplus value to the value of labor power.

ration coupons Tickets or coupons that entitle individual persons to purchase a certain amount of a given product per month.

rational-expectations hypothesis The hypothesis that people know the "true model" of the economy and that they use this model to form their expectations of the future.

Rawlsian justice A theory of distributional justice that concludes that the social contract emerging from the "original position" would call for an income distribution that would maximize the well-being of the worst-off member of society.

real GDP Gross domestic product measured in the prices of a fixed, or base, year.

real interest rate The difference between the interest rate on a loan and the inflation rate.

real wage rate The nominal wage rate adjusted for changes in the price level over time.

real wealth, or real balance, effect The change in consumption brought about by a change in real wealth that results from a change in the price level.

recession Roughly, a period in which real GDP declines for at least two con-secutive quarters. Marked by falling output and rising unemployment.

recognition lag The time it takes for policy makers to recognize the existence of a boom or slump.

regressive tax A tax whose burden, expressed as a percentage of income, falls as income increases.

relative-wage explanation of unemployment An explanation for sticky wages (and therefore unemployment): If workers are concerned about their wages relative to other workers in other firms and industries, they may be unwilling to accept a wage cut unless they know that all other workers are receiving similar cuts.

rent-seeking behavior Actions taken by households or firms to preserve extranormal profits.

rental income The income received by property owners in the form of rent.

required reserve ratio The percentage of its total deposits that a bank must keep as reserves at the Federal Reserve.

reserves The deposits that a bank has at the Federal Reserve bank plus its cash on hand.

residential investment Expenditures by households and firms on new houses and apart-

resources or inputs Anything provided by nature or previous generations that can be used directly or indirectly to satisfy human wants.

response lag The time that it takes for the economy to adjust to the new conditions after a new policy is implemented; the lag that occurs because of the operation of the economy itself.

retained earnings The profits that a corporation keeps, usually for the purchase of capital assets. Also called "undistributed profits."

revenue, or total revenue Receipts from the sale of a product. $P \times q$.

rule of reason The criterion introduced by the Supreme Court in 1911 to determine whether a particular action was illegal ("unreasonable") or legal ("reasonable") within the terms of the Sherman Act.

run on a bank Occurs when many of those who have claims on a bank (deposits) present them at the same time.

saving (S) The part of its income that a household does not consume in a given period. To be distinguished from savings, which is the current stock of accumulated saving.

services The things we buy that do not involve the production of physical things, such as legal and medical services and education.

share of stock Financial instruments that give to the holder a share in the ownership of a firm and therefore the right to share in the profits of the firm.

Sherman Act Passed by Congress in 1890, the act declared every contract or conspiracy to restrain trade among states or nations illegal and declared any attempt at monopoly, successful or not, a misdemeanor. Interpretation of which specific behaviors were illegal fell to the courts.

shift of a demand curve The change that takes place in a demand curve when a new relationship between quantity demanded of a good and the price of that good is brought about by a change in the original conditions.

shock therapy The approach to transition from socialism to market capitalism that advocates rapid deregulation of prices, liberalization of trade, and privatization.

short run The period of time for which two conditions hold: The firm is operating under a fixed scale (fixed factor) of production and firms can neither enter nor exit an industry.

short-run industry supply curve The sum of marginal cost curves (above AVC) of all the firms in an industry.

shut-down point The lowest point on the average variable cost curve. When price falls below the minimum point on AVC, total revenue is insufficient to cover variable costs and the firm will shut down and bear losses equal to fixed costs.

slope A measurement that indicates whether the relationship between variables is positive or negative and how much of a response there is in Y (the variable on the vertical axis) when X (the variable on the horizontal axis) changes.

Smoot-Hawley tariff The U.S. tariff law of the 1930s, which set the highest tariffs in U.S. history (60 percent). It set off an international trade war and caused the decline in trade that is often considered a cause of the worldwide depression of the 1930s.

social capital, or infrastructure Capital that provides services to the public. Most social capital takes the form of public works (roads and bridges) and public services (police and fire protection).

social choice The problem of deciding what society wants. The process of adding up individual preferences to make a choice for society as a whole.

social, or implicit, contracts Unspoken agreements between workers and firms that firms will not cut wages.

social insurance, or payroll, taxes Taxes levied at a flat rate on wages and salaries. Proceeds support various government-administrated social-benefit programs. The largest of these is the social security system, which issues various cash and health benefits to retirees, the disabled, and survivors of workers who paid into the system; another program is the unemployment compensation system.

social overhead capital Basic infrastructure projects such as roads, power generation, and irrigation systems.

social security system The federal system of social insurance programs. It includes three separate programs that are financed through separate trust funds: the Old Age and Survivors Insurance program (OASI), the disability Insurance program (DI), and the Health Insurance program (HI).

socialist economy An economy in which most capital is owned by the government rather than by private citizens. Also called social ownership.

sources side/uses side The impact of a tax may be felt on one or the other or on both sides of the income equation. A tax may cause net income to fall (damage on the sources side), or it may cause prices of goods and services to rise so that income buys less (damage on the uses side).

speculation motive One reason for holding bonds instead of money: Because the market value of interest-bearing bonds is inversely related to the interest rate, investors may wish to hold bonds when interest rates are high with the hope of selling them when interest rates fall.

spreading overhead The process of dividing total fixed costs by more units of output. Average fixed cost declines as q rises.

stability A condition in which output is steady or growing, with low inflation and full employment of resources.

stabilization policy A term used to describe both monetary and fiscal policy, the goals of which are to smooth out fluctuations in output and employment and to keep prices as stable as possible.

stabilization program An agreement between a borrower country and the International Monetary Fund in which the country agrees to revamp its economic policies to provide incentives for higher export earnings and lower imports.

stagflation Occurs when the overall price level rises rapidly (inflation) during periods of recession or high and persistent unemployment (stagnation).

sticky prices Prices that do not always adjust rapidly to maintain equality between quantity supplied and quantity demanded.

sticky wages The downward rigidity of wages as an explanation for the existence of unemployment.

store of value An asset that can be used to transport purchasing power from one period of time to another.

structural deficit The deficit that remains at full employment.

structural unemployment The portion of unemployment that is due to changes in the structure of the economy that result in a significant loss of jobs in certain industries.

subsidies (1) Government payments made to domestic firms to encourage exports. (2) Payments made by the government for which it receives no goods or services in return.

substitutes Goods that can serve as replacements for one another; when the price of one increases, demand for the other goes up.

substitution effect of higher wages Consuming an additional hour of leisure means sacrificing the wages that would be earned by working. Thus, when the wage rate rises leisure becomes a more expensive commodity, and households may "buy" less of it. This means working more.

sunk costs Costs that cannot be avoided, regardless of what is done in the future, because they have already been incurred. Another name for fixed costs in the short run because firms have no choice but to pay them.

supply curve A graph illustrating how much of a product a firm will supply at different prices.

supply schedule A table showing how much of a product firms will supply at different prices.

supply-side policies Government policies that focus on aggregate supply and increasing production rather than stimulating aggregate demand.

surplus value The profit a capitalist earns by paying workers less than the value of what they produce.

sustained inflation An increase in the overall price level that continues over a significant period of time.

tacit collusion Collusion occurs when price- and quantity-fixing agreements among producers are explicit. Tacit collusion occurs when such agreements are implicit.

tariff A tax on imports.

tax base The measure or value upon which a tax is levied.

tax incidence The ultimate distribution of tax's burden.

tax multiplier The ratio of change in the equilibrium level of output to a change in taxes.

tax rate structure The percentage of a tax base that must be paid in taxes—25% of income, for example.

tax shifting Occurs when households can alter their behavior and do something to avoid paying a tax.

technological change The introduction of new methods of production or new products intended to increase the productivity of existing inputs or to raise marginal products.

terms of trade The ratio at which a country can trade domestic products for imported products.

theory of comparative advantage Ricardo's theory that specialization and free trade will benefit all trading parties, even those that may be absolutely less efficient producers.

three basic questions The questions that all societies must answer: (1) What will be produced? (2) How will it be produced? (3) Who will get what is produced?

tight monetary policy Fed policies designed to contract the money supply in an effort to restrain the economy.

time lags Delays in the economy's response to stabilization policies.

times series graph A graph illustrating how a variable changes over time.

total costs Fixed costs plus variable costs.

total fixed costs (TFC), or overhead The total of all costs that do not change with output, even if output is zero.

total revenue (TR) The total amount that a firm takes in from the sale of its product: The price per unit times the quantity of output the firm decides to produce ($P \times q$).

total utility The total amount of satisfaction obtained from consumption of a good or service.

total variable cost (TVC) The total of all costs that depend on, or vary with, output in the short run.

total variable cost curve A graph that shows the relationship between total variable cost and the level of a firm's output.

trade deficit Occurs when a country's exports of goods are less than its imports of goods in a given period.

trade feedback effect The tendency for an increase in the economic activity of one country to lead to a worldwide increase in economic activity.

trade surplus The situation when a country exports more than it imports.

tragedy of commons The idea that collective ownership may not provide the proper private incentives for efficiency because individuals do not bear the full costs of their own decisions but do enjoy the full benefits.

transaction motive The main reason that people hold money–to buy things.

transfer payments Cash payments made by the government to people who do not supply goods, services, or labor in exchange for these payments. They include social security benefits, veterans' benefits, and welfare payments.

Treasury bonds, notes, and bills Promissory notes issued by the federal government when it borrows money.

trust An arrangement in which shareholders of independent firms agree to give up control of their stock in exchange for trust certificates that entitle them to a share of the common profits. A group of trustees then operates the combined firm as a monopoly, controlling output and setting price.

U.S.-Canadian Free-Trade Agreement An agreement in which the United States and Canada agreed to eliminate all barriers to trade between the two countries by 1998.

unconstrained supply of labor The amount a household would like to work within a given period at the current wage rate if it could find the work.

underground economy The part of the economy in which transactions take place and in which income is generated that is unreported and therefore not counted in GDP.

unemployed A person 16 years old or older who is not working, is available for work, and has made specific efforts to find work during the previous four weeks.

unemployment compensation A state government transfer program that pays cash benefits for a certain period of time to laid-off workers who have worked for a specified period of time for a covered employer.

unemployment rate The ratio of the number of people unemployed to the total number of people in the labor force. The percentage of the labor force that is unemployed.

unit of account A standard unit that provides a consistent way of quoting prices.

unitary elasticity A demand relationship in which the percentage change in quantity of a product demanded is the same as the percentage change in price (a demand elasticity of −1).

urban decline The deterioration of the private and social capital stock of a city that results from the lack of investment by both private and public sectors.

urban renewal Government programs designed to confront and correct the problems of urban decay.

utilitarian justice The idea that "a dollar in the hand of a rich person buys less than a dollar in the hand of a poor person." If the marginal utility of income declines with income, transferring income from the rich to the poor will increase total utility.

utility The basis of choice. The satisfaction, or reward, a product yields relative to its alternatives.

utility possibilities frontier A graphical representation of a two-person world that shows all points at which A's utility can be increased only if B's utility is decreased. That is, it represents all Pareto efficient points at which A can be made better off only by making B worse off.

value added The difference between the value of goods as they leave a stage of production and the cost of the goods as they entered that stage.

value of labor power The wage rate, dependent on the amount of clothing, shelter, basic education, medical care, and so on required to produce and sustain labor power.

variable A measure that can change from time to time or from observation to observation.

variable cost Any cost that a firm bears that depends on the level of production chosen.

velocity of money The number of times a dollar bill changes hands, on average, during the course of a year; the ratio of nominal GDP to the stock of money.

vicious-circle-of-poverty hypothesis Suggests that poverty is self-perpetuating because poor nations are unable to save and invest enough to accumulate the capital stock that would help them grow.

voting paradox A simple demonstration of how majority-rule voting can lead to seemingly contradictory and inconsistent results. A commonly cited illustration of the kind of inconsistency described in the impossibility theorem.

wealth, or net worth The total value of what a household owns minus what it owes. It is a stock measure.

Wheeler-Lea Act (1938) Extended the language of the Federal Trade Commission Act to include "deceptive" as well as "unfair" methods of competition.

Willis-Graham Act (1921) Declared the telephone industry a natural monopoly and exempted telephone mergers from review.

World Bank An international agency that lends money to individual countries for projects that promote economic development.

X axis On a Cartesian coordinate system, the horizontal line against which a variable is plotted.

Y axis On a Cartesian coordinate system, the vertical line against which a variable is plotted.

Y-intercept The point at which a graph intersects the Y axis.

yellow-dog contracts Contracts in which workers agree not to join unions.

zoning The designation of certain areas for industry, commerce, and housing. Often these categories are broken down into subcategories that specify the number of families allowed within a single residential building, how much land a residence must have around it, and so on.

Index

I-8

National Labor Relations Act, 498
National Labor Relations Board (NLRB),
    creation of, 498
*National Longitudinal Survey of Labor Force
    Behavior,* 14
Natural monopoly, 336-40
    characteristics of, 338
    definition of, 336
    regulation of, 338, 340, 388-90
Natural rate of population increase, 942
Natural rate of unemployment, 579, 757
Near monies, 651
Negative demand shock, definition of, 768
Negative wealth, 788
Negotiable order of withdrawal (NOW)
    accounts, 651
Neighborhood effects. *See* Externalities
Neoclassical view, profit, 955
Net exports, 557-58, 634
    of goods and services, 904
Net factor payments to rest of world, in gross
    domestic product (GDP), 561
Net income, of corporation, 55
Net interest, definition of, 558
Net investment, 557
Net national product (NNP), definition of, 562
Net taxes, 621
Net worth
    calculation of, 656
    definition of, 82
Neumann, John von, 298, 364
New classical macroeconomics, 836-41
    development of, 836-37
    Lucas supply function, 839-40
    rational-expectations hypothesis, 837-38,
        840-42
New Deal, union legislation, 497-98
New Economic Policy, 958
Newton, Sir Isaac, 18
Noerr-Pennington Doctrine, 382
Nominal gross domestic product, 563-64, 584
Nominal wage rate, 791
Nondurable goods, 555
Nonexcludable, public goods, 410
Nonlabor income, 792
    definition of, 792, 814
    dividends as, 815
    and fiscal policy, 814
Nonresidential investment, 556
Nonrival in consumption, public goods, 410, 412
Nonsynchronization of income and spending,
    677
Normal goods, 82, 129
Normal rate of profit, 175-76
Normal rate of return. *See* Normal rate of profit
Normative economics, definition of, 12
Norris-LaGuardia Act, 497
North American Free-Trade Agreement
    (NAFTA), 10, 69, 888-89

O
Ockham's razor, meaning of, 15
Official poverty line, 437
Ohlin, Bertil, 885
Oil
    oil embargo and price, 108, 110, 117
    oil import fee, 115-17
Okun, Arthur, 822
Okun's Law, 822
Old Age and Survivors Insurance program, 444

Oligopoly, 59, 356-68
    characteristics of, 59
    collusion model, 357-58, 360
    as concentrated industry, 357
    and contestable markets, 366-67
    Cournot model, 363-64
    definition of, 59, 356
    and economic performance, 367
    entry barriers, 367
    game theory, 364-65
    and imperfect competition, 307
    industry examples of, 357
    kinked demand curve model, 362-63
    price-leadership model, 360-62
    product differentiation, 367
On-the-job training, 483
Open economy
    equilibrium output, 902-10
    exchange rates, 910-20
    open-economy multiplier, 906
Open Market Desk, 660, 670
Open market operations, 668-71
    control of money supply, 668, 670
    workings of, 669-70
Operating profit (or loss)
    definition of, 222
    graphic representation of, 223
Opportunity costs
    and comparative advantage, 881
    definition of, 32
    and economic costs, 176
    example of, 32-33
    increasing of, 39-41
    meaning of, 5-6
Opportunity set, 142-43
    definition of, 142
Optimal level of inventories, 805
Optimal method of production, 178
Optimal scale of plant, 233
Organization of Petroleum Exporting Countries
    (OPEC)
    as cartel, 358, 360
    and debt crisis, 946-47
    oil embargo and price, 9, 108, 110, 117
Output
    aggregate. *See* Aggregate output (income)
    definition of, 31
    distribution of, 47
    efficient distribution among households, 302
    efficient mix of, 303-5
    and monopolistic competition, 352-55
    and unemployment, 822-23, 824
Output effects
    of factor price increases and decreases, 253
    on input demand curve, 253
    of price change, 252-53
    size, determinants of, 264
Output per worker, 822
Output (product) markets, 76
    characteristics of supply and demand in, 100
    definition of, 76
    demand in, 78-88
    relationship to input markets, 264-66, 291, 292
    supply and demand in, 100
    supply in, 88-94

P
Paradox of thrift, 673
Pareto efficiency, 298-300
    definition of, 299

example of, 300
Pareto, Vilfredo, 299
Parital equilibrium analysis, 292
Partnership, 54
    characteristics of, 54
Patents, 319-21
    as barrier to entry, 319-20
    effects on profits, 320
Payroll taxes, 68, 463-67
    federal revenues from, 463
    and labor supply curve, 464
    payees of, 464-66
Peoples' Republic of China, 967-70
    Beijing, use of land laws, effect of, 511
    economic reforms, 967-68
    five-year plans, 967
    Great Leap Forward, 967
    Great Proletarian Cultural Revolution, 967
    post-Tiananmen Square conditions, 968-70
P/E ratio, stocks, 820
Per capita gross domestic product, 566, 567, 822
    for selected countries, 566
Perestroika, 960-61
Perfect competition, 56-57, 172-73
    compared to monopoly, 329-32
    definition of, 56, 172
    efficiency of, 300-305
    example of, 57
    free entry and free exit in, 173
    products of, 172
    versus real markets, 305-6
Perfectly contestable markets, definition of, 366
Perfectly elastic demand, 120
Perfectly inelastic demand, 119-20
Perfect price discrimination, 385
Permanent income, 789
Perot, H. Ross, 10
Per se rule, 376
Persian Gulf War, 9, 91, 583
Personal consumption expenditures, definition of,
    555
Personal income, 562-63
    calculation from national income, 562
    definition of, 562
    disposable personal income, 563
Personal saving, 563
Personal saving rate, 563
Petrodollars, 946
Phillips, A.W., 751
Phillips curve, 751-55, 837
    and aggregate supply/aggregate demand
        analysis, 752-54
    and expectations, 754-55
    historical view, 751-52
    and import prices, 754
    long-run, natural rate of unemployment,
        756, 757
Planned aggregate expenditure, 622, 661-62
    definition of, 661
    and international trade, 633-34
Planned investment, 661
Plant-and-equipment investment, 800
Poland, private banking system, 965
Policy mix, 706-8
    definition of, 706
    effects of, 708
    and interest rates, 707
Political business cycle, 776-80
    Bush defeat as example, 778-80
    definition of, 778

Photo Credits

Unemployment Rate, 1970 I–1992 IV

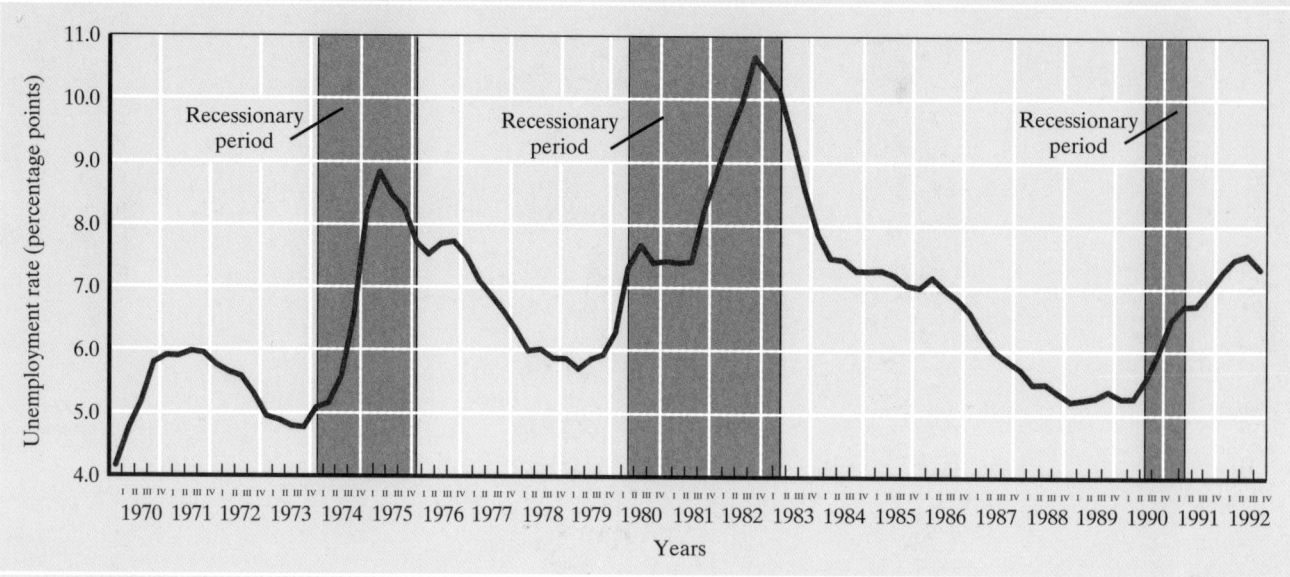

Percentage Change in the GDP Deflator (four-quarter average), 1970 I–1992 IV

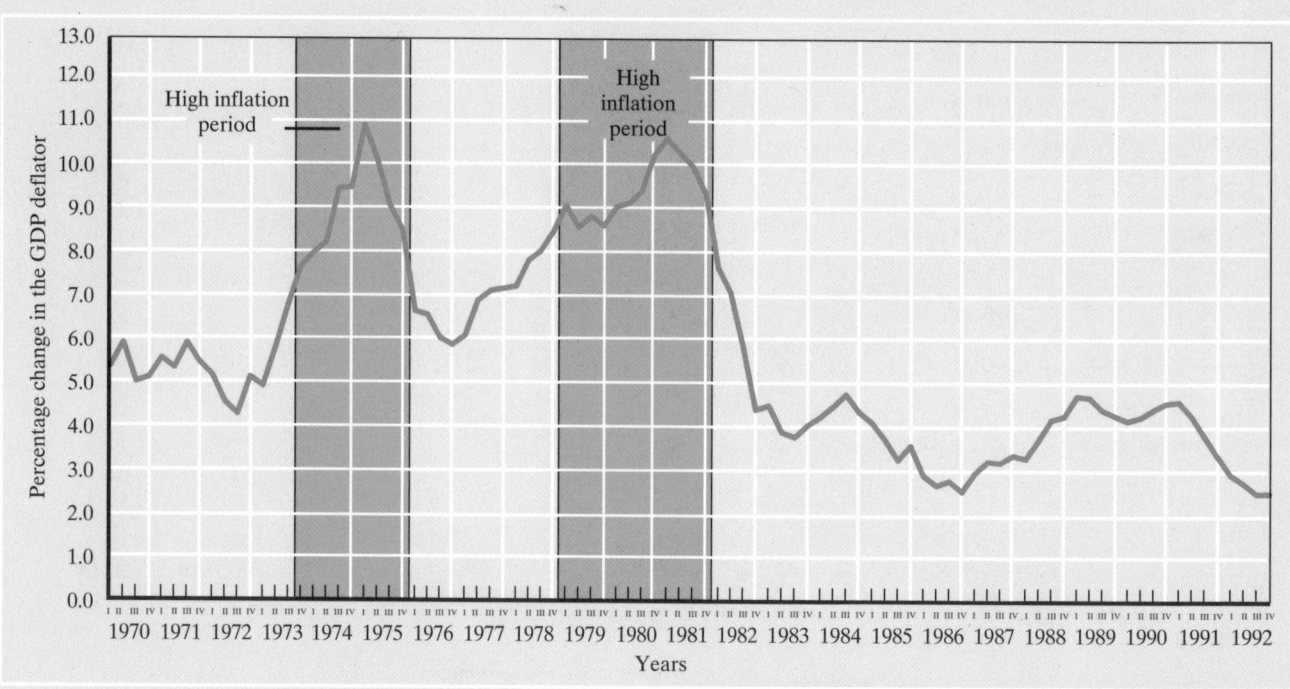